WHO'S WHO
IN
BASEBALL
History

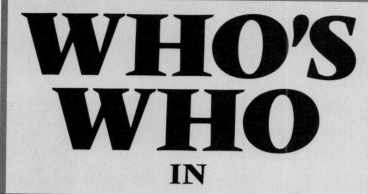

WHO'S WHO IN BASEBALL History

LLOYD JOHNSON & BRENDA WARD

BARNES & NOBLE BOOKS

NEW YORK

This edition published by
Barnes and Noble Inc.,
by arrangement with Brompton Books
Corporation

Produced by Brompton Books Corporation
15 Sherwood Place
Greenwich, CT 06830

ISBN 1-56619-469-5

Printed in USA

Page 2: top: The first Hall of Famers in
Cooperstown, 1939. Front row (l to r) –
Eddie Collins, Babe Ruth, Connie Mack and
Cy Young. Back row (l to r) – Honus
Wagner, Grover Alexander, Tris Speaker,
Nap Lajoie, George Sisler and Walter
Johnson. (National Baseball Library,
Cooperstown, NY).
Page 2, Bottom left: Joe DiMaggio signs
autographs. (The Bettmann Archive);
Bottom middle: Ernie Banks hits a home run.
(Chicago Sun Times); *Bottom right:* Kirby
Puckett at bat. (Allsport/Otto Greule, Jr.)

Right: The crowd at Boston Grand Pavilion,
c 1890. (National Baseball Library,
Cooperstown, NY)

Preface

It is our pleasure to bring you these brief biographies of 3,000 baseball players, coaches, managers, executives, umpires and a few others who have made a mark in the history of the national pastime. We have included in this book everyone in the Hall of Fame, almost every batter with 500 or more hits, almost every pitcher with 50 or more wins or saves, players notable for other reasons, all league presidents and commissioners, selected Negro Leaguers and team owners, and managers who managed at least one season.

Dozens of sources were consulted in the preparation of this book. The major league statistics in this volume came from *Total Baseball*, and Negro Leagues statistics from *The Baseball Encyclopedia*. Career statistics for players and managers in the National Association (NA) have been combined with those of the American and National Leagues, since the NA was the first professional league. Other sources consulted include: *The Ballplayers*; *Biographical Dictionary of American Sports: Baseball*; *The Great All-Time Baseball Record Book*; *19th Century Stars*; *The Book of Baseball Records*; Preston Orem's *Baseball, 1882-1891*; *The Encyclopedia of Minor League Baseball*; *The Negro Baseball Leagues: A Photographic History*; *The World Series* by Neft and Cohen, most of Fred Lieb's books and many other biographies and histories of individuals, leagues and teams. The files of the National Baseball Library at the National Baseball Hall of Fame and Museum in Cooperstown, New York, were consulted, as were newspapers and other periodicals at the Kansas City Public Library, Kansas City, Missouri, and the Johnson County Library, Johnson County, Kansas. The authors wish to thank the many experts consulted.

The following major league baseball clubs supplied media guides and other information: Atlanta, Houston, Los Angeles, Montreal, New York, Philadelphia, Pittsburgh, San Diego and San Francisco of the National League; and Baltimore, Boston, California, Chicago, Cleveland, Kansas City, Milwaukee, New York, Seattle, Texas and Toronto of the American League.

All-Star outfielder and power hitter Barry Bonds joined the Giants in 1993 after having helped the Pirates take three division titles. (Allsport/Otto Greule, Jr.)

The following abbreviations were used:

Pos – Position	OF – Outfield	HRs – Home Runs	W-L – Won-Lost
P – Pitcher	DH – Designated Hitter	BB – Base(s) on Balls	WS – World Series
C – Catcher	ShOs – Shutouts	Pct – Percentage	n – National Association
1B – First Base	ERA – Earned Run Average	NA – Not available	UA or U – Union Association
2B – Second Base	SOs – Strikeouts	inc. – Incomplete	PL or P – Players' League
3B – Third Base	RBI – Run(s) Batted In	AA – American Association	FL or F – Federal League
SS – Shortstop	BA – Batting Average	AL or A – American League	PCL – Pacific Coast League
		NL or N – National League	
		AS – All-Star	

The following abbreviations were used for cities:

AC – Atlantic City	Cin – Cincinnati	Flo – Florida	Lou – Louisville	Nwk – Newark	StL – St Louis
Alt – Altoona	Cle – Cleveland	Har – Hartford	Mad – Madison	Oak – Oakland	StP – St Paul
Atl – Atlanta	Col – Columbus	Hbg – Harrisburg	Mem – Memphis	OK – Oklahoma	Syr – Syracuse
Bal – Baltimore	(Negro Leagues	Hom – Homestead	Mid – Middletown	Phi – Philadelphia	Tex – Texas
Bir – Birmingham	or AA)	Hou – Houston	Mil – Milwaukee	Pit – Pittsburgh	Tol – Toledo
Bos – Boston	Col – Colorado	Ind – Indianapolis	Min – Minnesota	Pro – Providence	Tor – Toronto
Brk – Brooklyn	(National League)	Jac – Jacksonville	Mon – Montreal	Ric – Richmond	Tro – Troy
Buf – Buffalo	Day – Dayton	Keo – Keokuk	Mro – Monroe	Roc – Rochester	Was – Washington
Cal – California	Det – Detroit	KC – Kansas City	Nas – Nashville	Rok – Rockford	WB – West Baden
Chi – Chicago	Eliz – Elizabeth	LA – Los Angeles	NH – New Haven	SD – San Diego	Wil – Wilmington
			NO – New Orleans	SF – San Francisco	WL – West Lick
			NY – New York	Sea – Seattle	Wor – Worcester

National Association teams and Negro League teams have their nicknames listed along with the cities. In playing career lines, a team appears only once, even if the player played with the team more than once. The less-than-nine-inning no-hitters have been included in the no-hit totals.

Special thanks go to Mike Buster, Kirk Buster, Patrick Rock, Bill Deane and Bill Carle. Barbara Thrasher of Brompton Books has been our diligent, patient and competent editor, and we are very grateful to her. Thanks also to David Eldred, who designed the book, and Sara Dunphy, who did the picture research.

Hank Aaron
Aaron, Henry Louis
B: Feb 5, 1934
Hall of Fame 1982

Pos: OF	BA: .305
Hits: 3,771	HRs: 755
RBI: 2,297	BBs: 1,402

Hank Aaron broke Babe Ruth's long-standing record of most home runs hit during a career. Aaron's quest for the home run record overshadowed a brilliant career as a clean-up hitter behind slugger Eddie Mathews. Hammerin' Hank holds other major league career records, including most total bases, most extra-base hits, and most runs batted in. Aaron is second in runs scored, games played, and at-bats. He holds a lifetime slugging average of .555.

Though coming to the Braves' system from the Negro Leagues as a second baseman, Aaron starred in the outfield, where he won a Gold Glove in 1958. His defensive play earned him a rank of sixth in putouts and chances among outfielders. Aaron played in 24 All-Star Games and two World Series. He won the National League MVP Award in 1957. In 1956 and 1963, Aaron was honored as Major League Player of the Year by *The Sporting News*.
Playing Career: *1954-1976; Mil N, Atl N, Mil A*

Don Aase
Aase, Donald William
B: Sep 8, 1954

Pos: P	ERA: 3.80
W-L: 66-60	SOs: 641
ShOs: 5	Saves: 82

An erratic starter who became a reliever, Aase posted 82 saves during his career. Elbow surgery in 1982 limited his outings, but a banner season four years later earned him an appearance in the 1986 All-Star Game. That year he posted 34 saves with the Orioles – setting a club record.
Playing Career: *1977-1982, 1984-1990; Bos A, Cal A, Bal A, NY N, LA N*

Ed Abbaticchio
Abbaticchio, Edward James
B: Apr 15, 1877   D: Jan 6, 1957

Pos: 2B, SS	BA: .254
Hits: 772	HRs: 11
RBI: 324	BBs: 289

In the 1908 pennant race, Pittsburgh, who finished one game behind the winning Chicago Cubs, lost an apparent victory when Abbaticchio's late-inning grand slam home run was ruled foul by the umpire. A woman struck by the ball later sued for damages, saying she had been in fair territory.
Playing Career: *1897-1898, 1903-1905, 1907-1910; Phi N, Bos N, Pit N*

Glenn Abbott
Abbott, William Glenn
B: Feb 16, 1951

Pos: P	ERA: 4.39
W-L: 62-83	SOs: 484
ShOs: 5	No-hitters: 1

One of the original Mariners claimed from the Athletics in the expansion draft, Abbott remained in Seattle longer than any of the other draftees. His claim to fame was pitching in Charlie Finley's four-pitcher no-hitter with Vida Blue, Paul Lindblad and Rollie Fingers, on the last day of the 1975 season.
Playing Career: *1973-1984; Oak A, Sea A, Det A*

Ted Abernathy
Abernathy, Theodore Wade
B: Mar 6, 1933

Pos: P	ERA: 3.46
W-L: 63-69	SOs: 765
ShOs: 2	Saves: 148

A relief pitcher during the 1960s who threw underhanded, Abernathy would have fit well in the early days of baseball when several submarine pitchers played. After a late start in the majors due to injuries and control problems, he was twice honored as National League Fireman of the Year, in 1965 and 1967.
Playing Career: *1955-1957, 1960, 1963-1972; Was A, Cle A, Chi N, Atl N, Cin N, StL N, KC A*

Jim Acker
Acker, James Justin
B: Sep 24, 1958

Pos: P	ERA: 3.92
W-L: 33-49	SOs: 471
ShOs: 0	Saves: 30

Acker tried to resuscitate his struggling career with the Mariners. His best season ended with a 7-2 record with 10 saves for the Blue Jays in 1985. In seven appearances in two League Championship Series, Acker has a 0.73 ERA for 12 innings of work.
Playing Career: *1983-1992; Tor A, Atl N, Sea A*

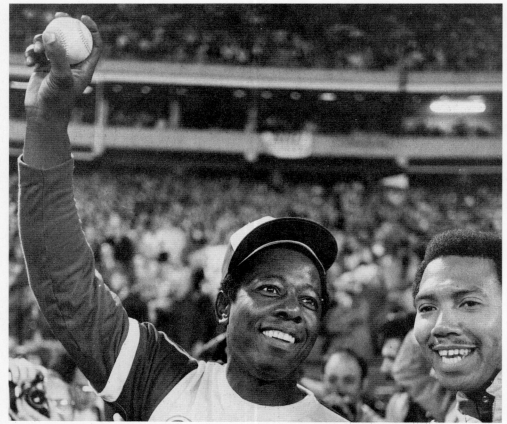

Hank Aaron holds up the ball that broke Babe Ruth's HR record, April 8, 1974.

Jerry Adair
Adair, Kenneth Jerry
B: Dec 17, 1936   D: May 31, 1987

Pos: 2B   BA: .254
Hits: 1,022   HRs: 57
RBI: 366   BBs: 208

Tough Jerry Adair once took a throw in the mouth requiring 11 stitches during the first game of a doubleheader, then played the second contest. An outstanding fielder, he set AL records for consecutive errorless games and for most errorless chances handled – both marks set during the 1964 and 1965 seasons.
Playing Career: *1958-1970; Bal A, Chi A, Bos A, KC A*

Ace Adams.

Ace Adams
Adams, Ace Townsend
B: Mar 2, 1912

Pos: P   ERA: 3.47
W-L: 41-33   SOs: 171
ShOs: 0   Saves: 49

Appropriately named by his parents, Ace Adams led the NL in games 1942-1944, and in saves 1944-1945. He held the league record for appearances. Adams's career came to an abrupt stop when he jumped to the outlaw Mexican League and was subsequently suspended for five years.
Playing Career: *1941-1946; NY N*

Babe Adams
Adams, Charles Benjamin
B: May 18, 1882   D: Jul 27, 1968

Pos: P   ERA: 2.76
W-L: 194-140   SOs: 1,036
ShOs: 47   Saves: 15

As an 18-year-old, Adams beat the Detroit Tigers three times in the 1909 World Series, including a six-hit shutout in the seventh and deciding game. Adams combined a good fastball with an intimidating curve and amazing control (430 bases on balls in 2,995 innings) to pitch for 19 years in the big leagues. Adams performed solidly in both the dead ball era and the lively ball era. In 1920 he walked only 18 batters in 263 innings.

Charles "Babe" Adams.

Adams completed 206 of his 355 starts as he led the NL in shutouts in 1911 and 1920.

Adams returned to the minors in 1917, where he regained his stuff, then spent nine more years at the major league level. Adams left the Pirates in 1926. After playing two more seasons in the minors he became a sportswriter, traveling overseas during World War II and the Korean Conflict.
Playing Career: *1906-1907, 1909-1916, 1918-1926; StL N, Pit N*

Bobby Adams
Adams, Robert Henry
B: Dec 14, 1921

Pos: 2B, 3B   BA: .269
Hits: 1,082   HRs: 37
RBI: 303   BBs: 414

In his 14-year career, Adams was a handy man to have around the diamond. He once rapped six consecutive pinch hits. Adams's brother Dick played briefly with the Athletics, and his sons played parts of five seasons with three teams.
Playing Career: *1946-1959; Cin N, Chi A, Bal A, Chi N*

Sparky Adams
Adams, Earl John
B: Aug 26, 1894   D: Feb 24, 1989

Pos: 2B, 3B   BA: .286
Hits: 1,588   HRs: 9
RBI: 394   BBs: 453

An infield veteran of 1,424 games, Sparky was a leadoff hitter and scored more than 90 runs six times in his career. Adams played in two World Series for the St. Louis Cardinals. The Redbirds traded him with Paul Derringer to Cincinnati in 1933, bringing Leo Durocher to the Gas House Gang and baseball immortality. Adams played with some of baseball's all-time greats during his National League stops in Chicago, Pittsburgh, Cincinnati and St. Louis.
Playing Career: *1922-1934; Chi N, Pit N, StL N, Cin N*

Joe Adcock
Adcock, Joseph Wilbur
B: Oct 30, 1927

Pos: 1B   BA: .277
Hits: 1,832   HRs: 336
RBIs: 1,122   BBs: 594
Managerial Record
Won: 75   Lost: 87   Pct: .463

Adcock was a powerfully built slugger who was the first to hit a ball into the center field bleachers of the old Polo Grounds in New York, 505 feet from home plate. Adcock batted behind Eddie Mathews and Hank Aaron in Milwaukee, forming a trio that became the National League's most feared lineup during the 1950s.

In 1960 Adcock played in both All-Star Games. His bat slowing, Adcock left the Braves in 1963 for the Cleveland Indians and Los Angeles Angels. After his playing career he managed Cleveland in the American League and Seattle in the Pacific Coast League before retiring to raise thoroughbred horses in Louisiana.

Adcock holds the major league record for total bases in one game, earned when he rapped four homers and a double against the Dodgers. His home run the previous day makes him tied for the National League record of five homers in two days.
Playing Career: *1950-1966; Cin N, Mil N, Cle A, LA A, Cal A*
Managerial Career: *1967; Cle A*

Joe Adcock.

Bob Addy
Addy, Robert Edward
B: Feb 1845   D: Apr 9, 1910

Pos: 2B, 3B, OF   BA: .276
Hits: 339   HRs: 1
RBI: 105 (inc.)   BB: 20
Managerial Record
Won: 8   Lost: 23   Pct: .258

The vision of a runner sliding in a cloud of dust at home plate should make fans think of Bob Addy – he invented the slide. Whether the slide was invented accidentally or evolved from natural running movements, Addy was the first player credited with using it in the 19th century.
Playing Career: *1871, 1873-1877; Rok Forest Citys n, Phi White Stockings n, Bos Red Stockings n, Har Dark Blues n, Chi N, Cin N*
Managerial Career: *1875, 1877; Phi White Stockings n, Cin N*

Tommie Agee
Agee, Tommie Lee
B: Aug 9, 1924

Pos: OF	BA: .255
Hits: 999	HRs: 130
RBI: 433	BBs: 342

Agee was American League Rookie of the Year in 1966. Playing for the New York Mets in 1969, he made two of the most sensational World Series catches ever. The two Game Three snatches stunned the Baltimore squad and led the Mets to the World Series Championship in a tremendous upset. Agee won two Gold Gloves and appeared in two All-Star Games.
Playing Career: *1962-1973; Cle A, Chi A, NY N, Hou N, StL N*

Juan Agosto
Agosto y Gonzalez, Juan Roberto
B: Feb 23, 1958

Pos: P	ERA: 3.99
W-L: 40-33	SOs: 304
ShOs: 0	Saves: 29

Juan Agosto led the NL in games with 82 for the Astros as a middle reliever in 1990. In 1988 he had a magic touch when he went 10-2 with a 2.26 ERA.
Playing Career: *1981-1992; Chi A, Min A, Hou N, StL N, Sea A*

Rick Aguilera
Aguilera, Richard Warren
B: Dec 31, 1961

Pos: P	ERA: 3.27
W-L: 55-49	SOs: 641
ShOs: 0	Saves: 156

"Aggie" flourished with a move from the Big Apple to Minnesota. Out from under the glare of New York sportswriters, Aguilera became the stopper from the bullpen that the Mets had hoped for when they switched him to relief. Aguilera's 0.59 ERA in eight Championship Series games makes him one of the best clutch performers in postseason play, and a World Series hero for the Twins. Aguilera is one of the top firemen in the game today, saving 115 games in 1990-92.
Playing Career: *1985-; NY N, Min A*

Hank Aguirre
Aguirre, Henry John
B: Jan 31, 1932

Pos: P	ERA: 3.25
W-L: 75-72	SOs: 856
ShOs: 9	Saves: 33

The story goes that Aguirre was a three-for-eight hitter – three hits in eight seasons. On the mound, however, he was a tough right-hander who led the American League in ERA in 1962. His 16-7 record earned him an All-Star appearance that year.
Playing Career: *1955-1970; Cle A, Det A, LA N, Chi N*

Eddie Ainsmith
Ainsmith, Edward Wilbur
B: Feb 4, 1892   D: Sep 6, 1981

Pos: C	BA: .232
Hits: 707	HRs: 22
RBI: 317	BBs: 263

Despite an anemic bat, Ainsmith caught for 15 years and played more than 1,000 games. He played on the Giants' pennant winner in 1924. In a one-sided game versus the Athletics, Ainsmith stole second, third and home, the only catcher ever to achieve the feat.
Playing Career: *1910-1924; Was A, Det A, StL N, Brk N, NY N*

Jack Aker.

Jack Aker
Aker, Jack Delane (Chief)
B: Jul 13, 1940

Pos: P	ERA: 3.28
W-L: 47-45	SOs: 404
ShOs: 0	Saves: 123

One tough Indian, Aker threw his sidearm sinkerball for 123 major league saves. His accomplishment of 32 saves in 1966 was the major league record until 1970. Aker was the player representative when his Athletics feuded with Charlie Finley, and he found himself drafted by the expansion Seattle club, let go by the A's vengeful owner. He proceeded from team to team, carrying the tag of union man, before becoming a successful minor league manager and pitching coach.
Playing Career: *1964-1974; KC A, Oak A, Sea A, NY A, Chi N, Atl N, NY N*

Vic Aldridge
Aldridge, Victor Eddington
B: Oct 25, 1893   D: Apr 17, 1973

Pos: P	ERA: 3.76
W-L: 97-80	SOs: 526
ShOs: 8	Saves: 6

The highlight of Aldridge's career was winning Games Two and Five for the Pirates in the 1925 World Series, before being knocked out in the first inning of the deciding Game Seven. The Pirates rallied to win the game 9-7. The Bucs were in postseason play again in 1927, but the big right-hander performed poorly in the World Series and was traded to the Giants for Burleigh Grimes. Aldridge finished his career with New York, pitching there for only one year.
Playing Career: *1917-1918, 1922-1928; Chi N, Pit N, NY N*

Doyle Alexander
Alexander, Doyle Lafayette
B: Sep 4, 1950

Pos: P	ERA: 3.76
W-L: 194-174	SOs: 1,528
ShOs: 18	Saves: 3

Journeyman is an apt term for Alexander, one of only four pitchers who have recorded victories over all major league teams – 26 at the time. In 1985 and 1987 he figured spectacularly in the AL pennant race. In 1984 he led the AL in winning percentage (.739, 17-6). For the Blue Jays in 1985, he won 17 games, including the division clincher on the next-to-last day of the season. Two years later, Alexander salvaged his career by winning nine straight games, including two over the rival Blue Jays, during the final days of the season to give the Detroit Tigers the divisional flag. Despite almost 200 wins, Alexander pitched in only one All-Star Game.
Playing Career: *1971-1989; LA N, Bal A, NY A, Tex A, Atl N, SF N, Tor A, Det A*

Doyle Alexander.

Grover Cleveland Alexander.

Grover Alexander
Alexander, Grover Cleveland (Pete)
B: Jan 26, 1887   D: Nov 4, 1950
Hall of Fame 1938

Pos: P	ERA: 2.56
W-L: 373-208	SOs: 2,199
ShOs: 90	Saves: 31

With the bases loaded in the bottom of the seventh inning in the seventh game of the 1926 World Series, ''Ol' Pete'' stepped on the stage of baseball immortality by retiring the Yankees' Tony Lazzeri. Alexander gave St. Louis its first World Championship.

Despite doing a lot of his pitching in tiny Baker Bowl with its cozy 254-foot right field fence, Alexander won 30 or more games three consecutive years. He hurled an NL record 16 shutouts in 1916. He is tied with Christy Mathewson for the NL record of 373 wins and holds the NL record for shutouts. His fast, no windup motion enabled him to routinely pitch games in less than 90 minutes.

In his first season, Alexander won 28 games – a record for a rookie. He was traded to the Cubs in 1918, then served in the army during World War I, earning sergeant's stripes, but causing him later to suffer hearing loss and epileptic seizures. It was after the war that Alexander was picked up by St. Louis. He continued to pitch in semipro baseball until well past the age of 50.
Playing Career: *1911-1930; Phi N, Chi N, StL N*

Bernie Allen
Allen, Bernard Keith
B: Apr 16, 1939

Pos: 2B	BA: .239
Hits: 815	HRs: 73
RBI: 351	BBs: 370

After a rookie year when he hit 12 homers, accumulated 64 RBI and batted .269, a great future was predicted for Allen, a former Purdue University quarterback. Instead of an impact player, he became known as a defensive specialist for the remainder of his career.
Playing Career: *1962-1973; Min A, Was A, NY A, Mon N*

Dick Allen
Allen, Richard Anthony (Richie)
B: Mar 8, 1942

Pos: 3B, 1B, DH, OF	BA: .292
Hits: 1,848	HRs: 351
RBI: 1,119	BBs: 894

Allen was a controversial player who infuriated managers by being different. He wore a batting helmet while playing in the field, skipped spring training, grew long sideburns and a goatee, abandoned his team a week before the end of the season.

After winning the NL Rookie of the Year Award and fueling the Phillies' drive to the 1964 pennant, Allen found himself consistently in hot water with management. He was traded frequently and built a reputation of being unmanageable. Allen's three best seasons were with the Chicago White Sox, where he won an MVP Award in 1972 and led the AL in home runs in 1972 with 37, and in 1974 with 32.

Dick Allen.

Allen left the game at the end of the 1977 season. Raising horses in retirement, he became the darling of the movement to do away with the proliferation of artificial turf in baseball parks by stating, ''If horses can't eat it, I won't play on it.''
Playing Career: *1963-1977; Phi N, StL N, LA N, Chi A, Oak A*

Ethan Allen
Allen, Ethan Nathan
B: Jan 1, 1904   D: Sep 15, 1993

Pos: OF	BA: .300
Hits: 1,325	HRs: 47
RBI: 501	BBs: 223

Coming directly from college to the major leagues, Allen lasted 13 years as a hard-hitting, savvy outfielder. He hit .330 and led the NL in doubles with 42 in 1934. After his playing career he served as a hitting coach and was later the film director for the National League.

Allen was the inventor of 'All-Star Baseball' one of the most popular baseball board games ever. He also published a popular instructional baseball book.
Playing Career: *1926-1938; Cin N, NY N, StL N, Phi N, Chi N, StL A*

Johnny Allen
Allen, John Thomas
B: Sep 30, 1905   D: Mar 29, 1959

Pos: P	ERA: 3.75
W-L: 142-75	SOs: 1,070
ShOs: 17	Saves: 18

A terrible temper and an explosive fastball were Johnny Allen's trademarks. After a spectacular 17-4 rookie season with the Yankees, Allen took his sore arm and sore head to Cleveland where he won 20 games in 1936, made the All-Star team in 1938, and had winning streaks of 15 games in 1937 and 12 in 1938. As a late season acquisition in 1941, he went 3-0 with a 2.51 ERA for the pennant-winning Dodgers. Allen finished with a .609 won-lost percentage in 13 years of pitching wizardry.
Playing Career: *1932-1944; NY A, Cle A, StL A, Brk N, NY N*

Neil Allen
Allen, Neil Patrick
B: Jan 24, 1958

Pos: P	ERA: 3.88
W-L: 58-70	SOs: 611
ShOs: 6	Saves: 75

Traded to the St. Louis Cardinals for Keith Hernandez, Allen faced the pressure of replacing a local hero by tossing a shutout in his first start. Unfortunately, inconsistency became the rule rather than the exception for the talented right-hander. Allen was switched to relief and his career languished in the bullpen.
Playing Career: *1979-1989; NY N, StL N, NY A, Chi A, Cle A*

Newt Allen
Allen, Newton Henry
B: May 19, 1901   D: Jun 11, 1988

Pos: 2B, SS, 3B	BA: .298
Hits: 963	HRs: 20
RBI: NA	BBs: NA

Managerial Record
Won: 12   Lost: 7   Pct: .632

A Negro Leagues player with the Kansas City Monarchs, the switch-hitting Allen was a line drive hitter and a skillful bunter. Allen twice led the Monarchs in hits, doubles and stolen bases. He paired with shortstops Dobie Moore and Jesse Williams to form potent double play combinations, leading the Monarchs into the Negro World Series in 1924, 1925, 1937 and 1942. In 1948 Allen and former teammate Bullet Rogan brought Little League Baseball to Kansas City kids.
Playing Career: *1922-1932, 1935-1944; KC Monarchs, StL Stars, Det Wolves*
Managerial Career: *1941; KC Monarchs*

Gene Alley
Alley, Leonard Eugene
B: Jul 10, 1940

Pos: SS	BA: .254
Hits: 999	HRs: 55
RBI: 342	BBs: 300

In 1966 Alley teamed with second baseman Bill Mazeroski for a major league record 215 double plays. Alley won Gold Gloves in 1966 and 1967 and appeared in the 1967 and 1968 All-Star Games. He was in postseason play with the Pirates 1970-72, and in the World Series in 1971.
Playing Career: *1963-1973; Pit N*

Bob Allison
Allison, William Robert
B: Jul 11, 1934

Pos: OF	BA: .255
Hits: 1,281	HRs: 256
RBI: 796	BBs: 795

A powerful athlete who played football better than baseball in college, Allison became a feared power hitter for the Washington Senators and Minnesota Twins during the 1960s. In 1959 he hit 30 home runs, was in the All-Star Game, and was named AL Rookie of the Year. He and roommate Harmon Killebrew smashed grand slam home runs in the same inning for a major league first. In 1963 Allison hit three consecutive home runs in a game.
Playing Career: *1958-1970; Was A, Min A*

Doug Allison
Allison, Douglas L.
B: Jul 1845   D: Dec 19, 1916

Pos: C, OF, SS	BA: .269
Hits: 379	HRs: 2
RBI: 92 (inc.)	BBs: 23

A five-year veteran of the National Association, Allison was widely respected as a top flight catcher. He started his professional career with the Forest City club of Cleveland who battled the Cincinnati Red Stockings during their historic first season.
Playing Career: *1869-1873; Was Olympics n, Tro Haymakers n, Brk Eckfords n, Eliz Resolutes n, NY Mutuals n, Har Dark Blues n, Har N, Pro N, Bal AA*

Bill Almon
Almon, William Francis
B: Nov 21, 1952

Pos: SS, 3B, OF, 2B, 1B	BA: .254
Hits: 846	HRs: 36
RBI: 296	BBs: 250

Almon was named College Player of the Year by *The Sporting News*, and was the first player chosen in the June 1974 draft, signing with the Padres for $100,000. He became the starting shortstop for San Diego in 1977, but unfortunately lost the job the following year to a young phenomenon named Ozzie Smith. He spent the rest of his 15-year career playing many positions for many teams.
Playing Career: *1974-1988; SD N, Mon N, NY N, Chi A, Oak A, Pit N, Phi N*

Roberto Alomar.

Roberto Alomar
Alomar y Velasquez, Roberto
B: Feb 5, 1968

Pos: 2B	BA: .297
Hits: 1,054	HRs: 56
RBI: 395	BBs: 372

The son of Sandy Alomar, Roberto is one of the brightest young talents in the game today. Many 1992 World Series observers felt that Alomar was the Blue Jays' most dependable player. He has 247 stolen bases and has scored 548 runs in only six years. Alomar has been chosen for his league's All-Star team for the past four straight years, and has played in the World Series for the past two.
Playing Career: *1988-; SD N, Tor A*

Sandy Alomar
Alomar y Conde, Santos
B: Oct 19, 1943

Pos: 2B, SS, 3B	BA: .245
Hits: 1,168	HRs: 13
RBI: 282	BBs: 301

An infielder with exceptional range, Alomar played 648 consecutive games for the California Angels from 1969 to 1973. During his career, he played every position except pitcher and catcher. Alomar's influence on the game reaches beyond his own career. Alomar taught his sons, Roberto and Sandy, Jr., fundamental skills that make them among the best players in the big leagues today.
Playing Career: *1964-1978; Mil N, Atl N, NY N, Chi A, Cal A, NY A, Tex A*

Sandy Alomar, Jr.
Alomar, Santos y Velasquez
B: Jun 18, 1966

Pos: C, DH	BA: .263
Hits: 306	HRs: 18
RBI: 137	BBs: 60

Sandy Alomar, Jr., was AL Rookie of the Year in 1990, the year his career blossomed after a slow beginning in the minor leagues. He has been hindered by injuries, but is still considered the hope of the Indians.
Playing Career: *1988-; SD N, Cle A*

Felipe Alou
Alou, Felipe Rojas
B: May 12, 1935

Pos: OF, 1B	BA: .286
Hits: 2,101	HRs: 206
RBIs: 852	BBs: 423

Managerial Record
Won: 164   Lost: 123   Pct: .571

The long-time Latin American manager burst on to the National League scene to lead the underdog Montreal Expos to a surprising second-place finish in 1992. One of his most surprising moves was to bring up his nephew Moises Alou and install him as the three-hole hitter.

Felipe Alou's managerial debut capped a long successful career in baseball. The oldest of three brothers who played in the major leagues, he joined the San Francisco Giants in 1958. All three eventually played for the Giants, and they made up the entire outfield for one game in 1963. Felipe Alou was traded to the Braves where he starred in both Milwaukee and Atlanta. Twice leading the NL in at-bats and hits, Alou also scored 122 runs in 1966. He was chosen for three NL All-Star teams and played in the 1962 World Series. He stayed in baseball, managing in the Latin American leagues and holding a variety of jobs until becoming manager of the Expos in 1992.
Playing Career: *1958-1974; SF N, Mil N, Atl N, Oak A, NY A, Mon N, Mil A*
Managerial Career: *1992-; Mon N*

The Alou brothers (l-r) Jesus, Matty, and Felipe, as Giants in 1963.

Jesus Alou

Alou, Jesus Maria Rojas
B: Mar 24, 1942

Pos: OF	BA: .280
Hits: 1,216	HRs: 32
RBI: 377	BBs: 138

Jesus Alou joined his siblings in San Francisco late in 1963. The next season, Felipe was traded and Jesus replaced him as the Giants' right fielder. Jesus, the biggest but slowest of the three brothers, hit .300 or more four times. A contact hitter, he lacked brother Felipe's power and brother Matty's speed, but he persevered, and played for the World Champion Oakland A's as a designated hitter in 1973 and 1974.
Playing Career: *1963-1979; SF N, Hou N, Oak A, NY N*

Matty Alou

Alou, Mateo Rojas
B: Dec 22, 1938

Pos: OF	BA: .307
Hits: 1,777	HRs: 31
RBI: 427	BBs: 311

A very good hitter, Matty Alou ripped an NL high 231 hits, including another NL high 41 doubles, in 1969, but did not win the batting title. He lacked power but struck out only 377 times in 5,789 at-bats.

Matty, the middle of the three Alou brothers, came to the majors in 1960, playing for the San Francisco Giants. He was part of the historic 1963 season when all three siblings were Giants, then was traded to Pittsburgh in 1966 where he had his greatest years. Stroking 986 hits in five years for a lofty .327 mark, Matty became a feared two-hole hitter. He won a batting title with the Pirates with a .342 mark, beginning a four-year streak of .331 or better. An injury ended his career abruptly in 1974 while he was with the San Diego Padres.
Playing Career: *1960-1974; SF N, Pit N, StL N, Oak A, NY A, SD N*

Walter Alston

Alston, Walter Emmons (Smokey)
B: Dec 1, 1911   D: Oct 1, 1984
Hall of Fame 1983

Managerial Record
Won: 2,040   Lost: 1,613   Pct: .558

Despite striking out in his only major league at-bat and making an error in his only major league game appearance, Walter Alston was inducted into the Hall of Fame in 1983. He was one of the most successful managers in the history of the game.

Alston was a good hitter in the minor leagues; he won four batting titles while in the St. Louis Cardinals' farm system. More importantly, Branch Rickey spotted Alston's leadership potential and installed him as a playing manager. When Rickey went to Brooklyn he took Alston with him to manage the Dodgers' top farm teams at St. Paul and Montreal, where he won pennants.

Taking over the Dodgers in 1954, Alston stayed for the next 23 years. He won pennants in 1955, 1956, 1959, 1963, 1965, 1966 and 1974. The transition from small Ebbets Field to the leviathan 92,000-seat Coliseum, did not hamper Alston's winning style. He was named Manager of the Year by *The Sporting News* in 1955, 1959 and 1963.
Managerial Career: *1954-1976; Brk N, LA N*

George Altman

Altman, George Lee
B: Mar 20, 1933

Pos: OF	BA: .269
Hits: 832	HRs: 101
RBI: 403	BBs: 268

Altman was a left-handed power hitter. In his best year, 1961, he rapped 27 home runs, led the NL in triples and hit a home run in the All-Star Game. From 1968 to 1975, Altman played in Japan, compiling a .309 average and 205 home runs.
Playing Career: *1959-1967; Chi N, StL N, NY N*

Walter Alston (r) with (l to r) Clem Labine, Carl Erskine, Billy Loes and Don Newcombe.

Joe Altobelli
Altobelli, Joseph Salvatore
B: May 26, 1932

Pos: 1B, OF   BA: .210
Hits: 54   HRs: 5
RBI: 28   BBs: 23
Managerial Record
Won: 437   Lost: 407   Pct: .518

Joe Altobelli was the manager of the 1983 World Champion Orioles who bested the Phillies in five games. Coming to Baltimore, he had the unenviable task of replacing winning manager Earl Weaver. But Altobelli's relaxed style was a direct contrast to Weaver's nervous habits and frequent rages, and the team responded well. Altobelli won the Manager of the Year Award three times in the minor leagues, and was honored as Manager of the Year with the Giants in 1978.
Playing Career: *1955, 1957, 1961; Cle A, Min A*
Managerial Career: *1977-1979, 1983-1985, 1991; SF N, Bal A, Chi N*

Nick Altrock
Altrock, Nicholas
B: Sep 15, 1876   D: Jan 20, 1965

Pos: P   ERA: 2.67
W-L: 83-75   SOs: 425
ShOs: 16   Saves: 7

A loose-jointed, florid-faced pitcher, Altrock became famous for his baseball clown act after his playing days ended. His performances, first with Germany Schaefer then with Al Schacht, entertained millions of fans during the frenetic 1920s and the lean years of the Depression. Altrock also turned in many fine performances as a pitcher, including a 20-victory season and one World Series triumph for the "Hitless Wonder" White Sox in 1906. A sore arm curtailed a promising career.
Playing Career: *1898, 1902-1909, 1912-1915, 1918-1919, 1924; Lou N, Bos A, Chi A, Was A*

Max Alvis
Alvis, Roy Maxwell
B: Feb 2, 1938

Pos: 3B   BA: .247
Hits: 895   HRs: 111
RBI: 373   BBs: 262

A serious bout with spinal meningitis disrupted a fine start of a career for Alvis. His high marks, a .274 average and 22 home runs, were posted in his rookie year with Cleveland. Staging a remarkable comeback, Alvis made the AL All-Star team in 1965 and 1967, whacking 21 homers each of those seasons.
Playing Career: *1962-1970; Cle A, Mil A*

Joey Amalfitano
Amalfitano, John Joseph
B: Jan 23, 1934

Pos: 2B   BA: .264
Hits: 418   HRs: 9
RBI: 123   BBs: 185
Managerial Record
Won: 66   Lost: 116   Pct: .363

A bonus-baby turned bench jockey who was ejected from a major league game before he ever played in one, Amalfitano learned baseball from Leo Durocher. Light hitting Amalfitano never played regularly, but he learned enough from Durocher to get a stint as manager for the Chicago Cubs.
Playing Career: *1954-1955, 1960-1967; NY N, SF N, Hou N, Chi N*
Managerial Career: *1979-1981; Chi N*

Ruben Amaro
Amaro y Mora, Ruben
B: Jan 6, 1936

Pos: SS   BA: .234
Hits: 505   HRs: 8
RBI: 156   BBs: 227

A versatile shortstop with wide range and a good glove, Amaro played in the majors for 11 years. He won a Gold Glove in 1964 with the Phillies. Amaro's father, Ruben Sr., was a long-time star in the Latin American leagues.
Playing Career: *1958, 1960-1969; StL N, Phi N, NY A, Cal A*

Leon "Red" Ames.

Red Ames
Ames, Leon Kessling
B: Aug 2, 1882   D: Oct 8, 1936

Pos: P   ERA: 2.45
W-L: 183-167   SOs: 1,702
ShOs: 27   No-hitters: 2

Red Ames tossed a five-inning no-hitter in his 1903 major league debut and a ten-inning no-hitter on opening day 1909, losing in the 13th inning. A solid starter for McGraw's Giants, he pitched on four New York pennant winners. He teamed first with Mathewson and McGinnity, then with Mathewson and Marquard to give the New Yorkers an unbeatable starting rotation. Ames's best season was 1905 when he went 22-8. He left the Giants in 1913 to hurl for the Reds, for whom he lost a league-leading 23 games in 1914. Transformed to a relief pitcher, Ames saved 33 games in his career, leading the NL

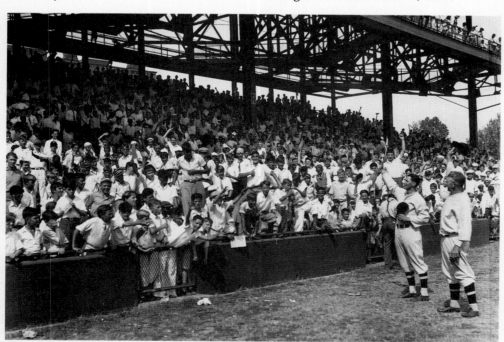

Nick Altrock (r) and Al Schacht entertain the crowd in Washington in 1932.

in 1914 with six saves and in 1916 with eight.
Playing Career: *1903-1919; NY N, Cin N, StL N, Phi N*

Sandy Amoros
Amoros, Edmundo
B: Jan 30, 1930

Pos: OF	BA: .255
Hits: 334	HRs: 43
RBI: 180	BBs: 211

In seven years with the Dodgers, Amoros was never more than a part-time player, but he is remembered for one great play. In Game Seven of the 1955 World Series he sped to the corner where he snagged Yogi Berra's line drive to preserve Johnny Podres's 2-0 shutout over the mighty Bronx Bombers.
Playing Career: *1952-1960; Brk N, LA N*

Larry Andersen
Andersen, Larry Eugene
B: May 6, 1953

Pos: P	ERA: 3.10
W-L: 39-37	SOs: 731
ShOs: 0	Saves: 49

Known as a prankster and a bon vivant, Andersen spent 10 years in the minors before settling in with Seattle. His question to the press, "Why do we drive on the parkway and park in the driveway?" made national headlines. He appeared in two World Series games for the Phillies in 1983.
Playing Career: *1975-; Cle A, Sea A, Phi N, Hou N, Bos A, SD N*

Allan Anderson
Anderson, Allan Lee
B: Jan 7, 1964

Pos: P	ERA: 4.11
W-L: 49-54	SOs: 339
ShOs: 3	Saves: 1

Anderson led the AL in ERA in 1988 despite pitching in the batter-friendly Metrodome. After a promising beginning with the Twins, he fell on hard times and was sent back to the minors in 1991. The Yankees picked him up as a free agent but kept him in the minors in 1992.
Playing Career: *1986-1991; Min A*

Brady Anderson
Anderson, Brady Kevin
B: Jan 18, 1964

Pos: OF	BA: .244
Hits: 553	HRs: 44
RBI: 234	BBs: 315

Brady Anderson blossomed in 1992 as a center fielder and leadoff man for the Orioles in the new Camden Yards. He scored 100 runs in 1992, nearly half his total up to that time of 239. He had joined the Orioles in the trade that took Mike Boddicker to the Red Sox.
Playing Career: *1988-; Bos A, Bal A*

John Anderson
Anderson, John Joseph (Terrible Swede)
B: Dec 14, 1873   D: Jul 23, 1949

Pos: OF, 1B	BA: .290
Hits: 1,841	HRs: 48
RBI: 870	BBs: 310

Stealing second base with the bases loaded was called a "John Anderson" during the first decade of the 20th century. Anderson's baserunning capers overshadowed his heavy hitting – he had 22 triples and a .494 slugging average to lead the NL in 1898 – in a 14-year career. The Norwegian slugger hit .330 for the original Milwaukee Brewers, charter members of the AL in 1901.
Playing Career: *1894-1899, 1901-1908; Brk N, Was N, Mil A, StL A, NY A, Was A, Chi A*

Sparky Anderson
Anderson, George Lee
B: Feb 22, 1934

Pos: 2B	BA: .218
Hits: 104	HRs: 0
RBI: 34	BBs: 42
Managerial Record	
Won: 2,081 Lost: 1,688 Pct: .552	

Sparky Anderson changed the way baseball people look at the pennant race because of his 35-5 start as manager of the Detroit Tigers in 1984. Before that season, a manager tried to stay close, then get hot in August and September to win the pennant. Sparky won the pennant in April and May.

Only marginally talented as a player, Anderson played in the minor leagues for 10 seasons. An International League Most Valuable Player Award with Montreal in 1958 gave Anderson a chance in the majors. He played only one year for the Phillies, who could not afford to keep the savvy but weak-hitting second baseman on the roster.

Anderson's teams have won five pennants and seven division titles. His .571 World Series won-lost percentage is third on the all-time list.
Playing Career: *1959; Phi N*
Managerial Career: *1970-; Cin N, Det A*

Ed Andrews
Andrews, George Edward
B: Apr 5, 1859   D: Aug 12, 1934

Pos: OF	BA: .257
Hits: 830	HRs: 12
RBI: 278	BBs: 194

A star for the Phillies before they became the hitting terrors of the NL, in 1887 Andrews batted .325 and scored 110 runs while stealing a league-high 56 bases. Andrews stole at least 205 bases during his career; the records are incomplete, lacking statistics for at least two years.
Playing Career: *1884-1891; Phi N, Ind N, Brk P, Cin AA*

Mike Andrews
Andrews, Michael Jay
B: Jul 9, 1943

Pos: 2B	BA: .258
Hits: 803	HRs: 66
RBI: 316	BBs: 458

Andrews made two errors in the 1973 World Series. When the A's owner tried to put him on the disabled list because of the errors, enraged fans contacted the commissioner, who reinstated Andrews. A's Manager Dick Williams resigned after the Series.
Playing Career: *1966-1973; Bos A, Chi A, Oak A*

Sparky Anderson and Johnny Bench celebrate their 1975 World Series victory.

Joaquin Andujar.

Joaquin Andujar
Andujar, Joaquin
B: Dec 21, 1952

Pos: P   ERA: 3.58
W-L: 127-118   SOs: 1,032
ShOs: 19   Saves: 9

Self-styled "One Tough Dominican," Andujar led the NL in victories in 1984 and was chosen for the All-Star team in 1977, 1979, 1984 and 1985. He was a workhorse for the Cardinals and a major factor in two Red Bird pennants during the 1980s. His back-to-back 20-game seasons (1984-1985) were the first in the NL since his former Astro teammate Joe Niekro accomplished it in 1979-1980.

An unfortunate incident in the 1985 World Series led to Andujar's banishment from the Cardinals. Andujar had won 21 games that year, but had not been pitching well since early September. He was brought into Game Seven with his team trailing 9-0. The volatile Andujar charged the umpire while working with the second batter and was booted out of the game, succeeding his manager, Whitey Herzog, who had been given the thumb on the previous pitch. The Cardinals lost the Series; Andujar was traded to Oakland that winter, where he labored for two seasons before finishing his career with Houston.
Playing Career: *1976-1988; Hou N, StL N, Oak A*

Cap Anson
Anson, Adrian Constantine
B: Apr 11, 1852   D: Apr 14, 1922
Hall of Fame 1939

Pos: 1B   BA: .332
Hits: 3,415   HRs: 98
RBI: 1,981   BBs: 952
Managerial Record
Won: 1,296   Lost: 947   Pct: .578

The best player of the 19th century, Cap Anson was the first to achieve 3,000 hits and the first manager to win 1,000 games. The winner of three batting titles (although one is disputed), he hit more than .300 for 24 seasons and scored 1,996 runs.

As a manager, Anson won five pennants. He was a stern taskmaster, but he also insisted that White Stockings players be allowed to travel to a warm southern location before the season to prepare for the year. The practice was soon copied by other teams and persists today as spring training.

In 1875 Anson was one of several well-known players who jumped contracts and went to the White Stockings. In order to legitimize the new contracts, team owner and star pitcher William Hulbert and Albert Spalding founded the National League of Professional Base Ball Clubs. Anson's refusal to join the Players' League during the great strike of 1890 probably saved the NL.
Playing Career: *1871-1897; Rok Forest Citys n, Phi Athletics n, Chi N*
Managerial Career: *1875, 1879-1898; Phi Athletics n, Chi N, NY N*

Cap Anson.

Johnny Antonelli
Antonelli, John August
B: Apr 12, 1930

Pos: P   ERA: 3.34
W-L: 126-110   SOs: 1,162
ShOs: 26   Saves: 21

Handsome Johnny Antonelli was one of the first bonus babies during the late 1940s. He signed with the Boston Braves for $65,000, but had limited success there. After a stint with Uncle Sam, Antonelli was traded to the Giants, where he hushed critics by posting a 21-7 record and leading New York to the pennant and the World Series in 1954. He led the league in winning percentage, ERA and shutouts that year. He was chosen for the All-Star team in 1954, and 1956-1959.
Playing Career: *1948-1950, 1953-1961; Bos N, Mil N, NY N, SF N, Cle A*

Luis Aparicio.

Luis Aparicio
Aparicio y Montiel, Luis Ernesto
B: Apr 29, 1934
Hall of Fame 1984

Pos: SS   BA: .262
Hits: 2,677   HRs: 83
RBI: 791   BBs: 736

The first player since Ty Cobb to record 50 or more stolen bases in three consecutive seasons, Aparicio reinstituted the stolen base as an offensive weapon. At shortstop he displayed superlative fielding, winning nine Gold Glove Awards.

He began his career by replacing his father at shortstop for the Maracaibo Gavilanes. Aparacio then worked his way through the minors before breaking in with the White Sox in 1956, when he was named AL Rookie of the Year. In 1959 he led the Sox to their first pennant since the ill-fated flag in 1919.

Aparicio led the AL in stolen bases nine consecutive years. He tied a major league record by leading AL shortstops in fielding for eight consecutive years, broke the record for assists by pacing AL shortstops six straight years, and holds the record for most games played at shortstop, 2,581. He was selected for the All-Star team 10 times.
Playing Career: *1956-1973; Chi A, Bal A, Bos A*

Pete Appleton
Appleton, Peter William
B: May 20, 1904   D: Jan 18, 1974

Pos: P   ERA: 4.30
W-L: 57-66   SOs: 420
ShOs: 6   Saves: 26

Peter Appleton worked in organized baseball for more than 30 years, but he played as Peter Jablonowski from 1927 to 1933. He graduated from college as an accomplished musician, but chose baseball as his career. Appleton managed in the minors during the 1940s and 1950s.
Playing Career: *1927-1928, 1930-1933, 1936-1942, 1945; Cin N, Cle A, Bos A, NY A, Was A, Chi A, StL A*

Luke Appling
Appling, Lucius Benjamin
B: Apr 2, 1907   D: Jan 3, 1991
Hall of Fame 1964

Pos: SS   BA: .310
Hits: 2,749   HRs: 43
RBI: 1,116   BBs: 1,302
Managerial Record
Won: 10 Lost: 30   Pct: .250

"Old Aches and Pains" was once refused free tickets for his friends by a penurious White Sox front office. He put out his own cash for the tickets, but during his first at-bat fouled off 14 pitches into the stands. Fans kept the balls; the price of the tickets had been recouped.

Appling was a consistent starter who once held the AL record for games played at shortstop. It was his bat, however, that brought him to the majors from Atlanta in the Southern Association for the startling Depression-era sum of $20,000. Appling did not disappoint Windy City fans. He won two AL batting titles, hitting .388 in 1936 as a high mark, and passed the .300 mark 16 times. Appling was so skilled as a batsman that he still hit .301 at 42 years of age. After retirement as a player, he stayed in baseball as a coach and manager.
Playing Career: *1930-1943, 1945-1950; Chi A*
Managerial Career: *1967; KC A*

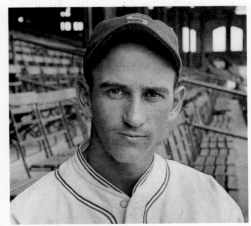
Luke Appling.

Jimmy Archer
Archer, James Peter
B: May 13, 1883   D: Mar 29, 1958

Pos: C   BA: .250
Hits: 660   HRs: 16
RBI: 296   BBs: 124

Jimmy Archer was the first catcher to throw effectively from a squat. Archer replaced Johnny Kling in 1909 when the star receiver held out, and his strong arm made Kling expendable in 1911. He appeared in two World Series.
Playing Career: *1904, 1907, 1909-1918; Pit N, Det A, Chi N, Brk N, Cin N*

Tony Armas
Armas y Machado, Antonio Rafael
B: Jul 2, 1953

Pos: OF, DH   BA: .252
Hits: 1,302   HRs: 251
RBI: 815   BBs: 260

Tony Armas was one of the top power hitters in the early 1980s, and the great hope for Boston, who hoped he would replace Fred Lynn's bat. From 1980 to 1985 Armas hit more home runs than any other player in the American League. In the strike-shortened 1981 season, Armas led the AL in home runs and was selected for the All-Star team. His best year was 1984 when he hit .268 with a league-leading 43 home runs and 123 RBI and played in the All-Star Game.
Playing Career: *1976-1989; Pit N, Oak A, Bos A, Cal A*

Bill Armour
Armour, William R.
B: Sep 3, 1869   D: Dec 2, 1922

Managerial Record
Won: 382   Lost: 347   Pct: .524

While managing Detroit, Bill Armour was credited with finding Ty Cobb and buying him for $500. He later owned a portion of the Toledo American Association club, scouted for the Cardinals, and was business manager for the minor league Milwaukee Brewers and Kansas City Blues.
Managerial Career: *1902-1906; Det A*

Morrie Arnovich
Arnovich, Morris
B: Nov 16, 1910   D: Jul 20, 1959

Pos: OF   BA: .287
Hits: 577   HRs: 22
RBI: 261   BBs: 185

Morrie Arnovich was a stocky line drive hitter who batted .324 and made the All-Star team in 1939 while playing with Philadelphia. Following his playing career, Arnovich became a manager, leading teams in the Western Association, Southeastern and Three-I Leagues.
Playing Career: *1936-1941, 1946; Phi N, Cin N, NY N*

Luis Arroyo
Arroyo, Luis Enrique
B: Feb 18, 1927

Pos: P   ERA: 3.86
W-L: 42-32   SOs: 336
ShOs: 1   Saves: 44

Little Looie made Whitey Ford a 25-game winner in 1961 by saving many of his victories. Both Ford and Arroyo blossomed under Ralph Houk that year; Arroyo won 15 and saved 29. Unfortunately his screwball baffled AL hitters for only one season. Arm trouble the following spring ended his dominance.
Playing Career: *1955-1957, 1959-1963; StL N, Pit N, Cin N, NY A*

Richie Ashburn.

Richie Ashburn
Ashburn, Don Richard
B: Mar 19, 1927

Pos: OF   BA: .308
Hits: 2,574   HRs: 29
RBI: 586   BBs: 1,198

Richie Ashburn got lost among the roster of power-hitting center fielders in the 1950s. He did not have Mays's grace, Mantle's power, or Snider's consistency, but he deserves to be in the Hall of Fame as surely as they do. Ashburn averaged 50 more putouts per year than Mays, the Gold Glove winner. His arm won the 1950 pennant for the Whiz Kids, when he gunned down Cal Abrams at the plate to preserve a tie in the season's final game. The Phillies won the game and the flag in the tenth.

Ashburn led the NL in steals and hit safely in 23 straight games as a Phillies rookie in 1948. The hitting streak was the rookie record until 1987. Ashburn led the league in hitting in 1955 and 1958. He batted over .300 in nine of 15 seasons. Three times he led the NL in hits; four times in bases on balls. His career on-base percentage is almost .400. Ashburn retired to become a top broadcaster for the Phillies.
Playing Career: *1948-1962; Phi N, Chi N, NY N*

Alan Ashby
Ashby, Alan Dean
B: Jul 8, 1951

Pos: C	BA: .245
Hits: 1,010	HRs: 90
RBI: 513	BBs: 461

Ashby gave the Astros 10 solid years of catching before a bad back, his refusal to be traded, and rookie Craig Biggio sent him into retirement. Ashby was disabled five times, mainly by Joe Niekro's knuckleball. He tied the NL record for most no-hitters caught, receiving for Ken Forsch, Nolan Ryan and Mike Scott. Ashby also hit home runs from both sides of the plate in one game. He led the NL catchers in fielding in 1987.
Playing Career: *1973-1989; Cle A, Tor A, Hou N*

Emmett Ashford
Ashford, Emmett Littleton
B: Nov 23, 1914   D: Mar 1, 1980

The first black umpire in organized baseball, Ashford integrated both the minor leagues and the AL. His 1966 entrance into the big leagues marked a victory for civil rights advocates. Ashford's umpiring career began in 1951 with the Southwest International League. He later became the first black umpire in the Pacific Coast League. Ashford's AL stint lasted through the 1970 season. He was known for his flamboyant style.
Umpiring Career: *1966-1970; AL (1 WS, 1 AS)*

Bob Aspromonte
Aspromonte, Robert Thomas
B: Jun 19, 1938

Pos: 3B	BA: .252
Hits: 1,103	HRs: 60
RBI: 457	BBs: 333

Bob Aspromonte set an NL record by playing 57 consecutive errorless games at third base in 1962. For a time he also held the record for fewest errors in a season; he had only 11 in 1964. Aspromonte was the last original Colt .45 to leave the franchise.
Playing Career: *1956, 1960-1971; Brk N, LA N, Hou N, Atl N, NY N*

Ken Aspromonte
Aspromonte, Kenneth Joseph
B: Sep 22, 1931

Pos: 2B	BA: .249
Hits: 369	HRs: 19
RBI: 124	BBs: 179
Managerial Record	
Won: 220 Lost: 260 Pct: .458	

After leading the Pacific Coast League in hitting in 1957, Aspromonte compiled a rather lackluster major league career. He was later a coach and manager, developing George Hendrick as a batter while skipper of the Indians.
Playing Career: *1957-1963; Bos A, Was A, Cle A, LA A, Mil N, Chi N*
Managerial Career: *1972-1974; Cle A*

Al Atkinson
Atkinson, Albert Wright
B: Mar 9, 1861   D: Jun 17, 1952

Pos: P	ERA: 3.96
W-L: 51-51	SOs: 247
ShOs: 3	No-hitters: 2

Al Atkinson tossed two no-hitters, 1884 and 1886, for the American Association Philadelphia Athletics, yet neither was a shutout. The winner of 51 games in four years, Atkinson's promising major league career was cut short, apparently by drinking.
Playing Career: *1884-1887; Phi AA, Chi-Pit U, Bal U*

Jerry Augustine
Augustine, Gerald Lee
B: Jul 24, 1952

Pos: P	ERA: 4.23
W-L: 55-59	SOs: 348
ShOs: 6	Saves: 11

Jerry Augustine labored for the Brewers as a starter, then as a reliever during the lean years in Milwaukee. He was the team's rookie of the year in 1976. Favoring hot weather, Augustine tossed a 1-0 shutout August 24, 1976, and a second one a year later.
Playing Career: *1975-1984; Mil A*

Eldon Auker
Auker, Eldon LeRoy
B: Sep 21, 1910

Pos: P	ERA: 4.42
W-L: 130-101	SOs: 594
ShOs: 14	No-hitters: 1

Eldon Auker threw the submarine style pitch that has fallen out of favor these days. He was forced to adapt the underhand technique because of a shoulder injury suffered while playing football at Kansas State University, where he also starred in baseball and basketball. Auker pitched in two World Series for the Tigers, led the AL in winning percentage in 1935, and pitched the first night game in St. Louis in 1940. Auker was a good hitting pitcher, with six lifetime home runs.
Playing Career: *1933-1942; Det A, Bos A, StL A*

Jimmy Austin
Austin, James Philip
B: Dec 8, 1879   D: Mar 6, 1965

Pos: 3B	BA: .246
Hits: 1,328	HRs: 13
RBI: 390	BBs: 592
Managerial Record	
Won: 31 Lost: 44 Pct: .413	

Jimmy Austin was the rookie whose manager – knowing Nap Lajoie's tendency to break third basemen's legs with sharp hits down the line – ordered him to play deep as Lajoie dropped seven bunts on the last day of the season in his quest for the 1910 batting title.

Notwithstanding such a debut, Austin played 12 years, leading AL third sackers at various times in total chances, putouts, assists, and fielding average. He stole 244 bases. Austin later served as manager, then coach for the Browns and the White Sox.
Playing Career: *1909-1923, 1925-1926, 1929; NY A, StL A*
Managerial Career: *1913, 1918, 1923; StL A*

Earl Averill
Averill, Howard Earl
B: May 21, 1902   D: Aug 16, 1983
Hall of Fame 1975

Pos: OF	BA: .318
Hits: 2,020	HRs: 238
RBI: 1,165	BBs: 775

Earl Averill hit a home run on his first major league at-bat and never looked back. After three sensational seasons with San Francisco in the Pacific Coast League, Averill was purchased by the Indians in 1929 for $50,000. He proved worth every penny. Cleveland did not win pennants during the 1930s, but the Indians generated enough income and enthusiasm for the city to build mammoth Municipal Stadium in 1932, in the depths of the Depression.

Averill felt he should have been in the Hall of Fame much earlier than 1975. "I guess stats alone aren't enough," he said. In addition to

Earl Averill.

impressive offensive figures, Averill was a better than average outfielder, leading all outfielders in putouts twice. Respected by his peers, Averill was the only outfielder chosen for all first six All-Star teams.

Averill's most famous play was a line drive off the foot of NL hurler Dizzy Dean which broke his toe, and contributed to the end of Ol' Diz's career.
Playing Career: *1929-1941; Cle A, Det A, Bos N*

Bobby Avila
Avila y Gonzalez, Roberto Francisco
B: Apr 2, 1924

Pos: 2B	BA: .281
Hits: 1,296	HRs: 80
RBI: 465	BBs: 562

Bobby Avila was the first Mexican citizen to become a big star in the major leagues. He was already a Mexican League star when purchased by the Indians for $17,500 in 1949. By the time Avila won the AL batting title with a .341 mark in 1954, he was a national hero south of the border. Soccer training enabled Avila to become a skilled and daring baserunner and bunter. He was especially adept at kicking the ball out of fielders' gloves.

Indians manager Al Lopez said of him, "Avila has a fine swing, a sharp eye, a good spirit of competition . . . and a world of confidence in himself." The stylish Avila was traded three times late in his career and returned to Mexico in 1960, where he later became the president of the Mexican League.
Playing Career: *1949-1959; Cle A, Bal A, Bos A, Mil N*

Doc Ayers
Ayers, Yancy Wyatt
B: May 20, 1890   D: May 26, 1968

Pos: P	ERA: 2.84
W-L: 66-79	SOs: 622
ShOs: 17	Saves: 14

Doc Ayers studied medicine and spread germs with his spitball. His best season, a 14-9 year, was with the Senators. Ayers was one of the hurlers who were allowed to continue their trick pitches after the spitball and others were banned prior to the 1920 season.
Playing Career: *1913-1921; Was A, Det A*

Joe Azcue
Azcue y Lopez, Jose Joaquin
B: Aug 18, 1939

Pos: C	BA: .252
Hits: 712	HRs: 50
RBI: 304	BBs: 207

Joe Azcue hit into major league baseball's first unassisted triple play in 41 years when he lined a shot to shortstop Ron Hansen in 1968. Azcue's next claim to fame was hitting .280 in 1968, when he made the All-Star team. Azcue caught two no-hitters.
Playing Career: *1960, 1962-1970, 1972; Cin N, KC A, Cle A, Bos A, Cal A, Mil A*

Bobby Avila, second baseman for the Cleveland Indians, in a 1952 photo.

Wally Backman
Backman, Walter Wayne
B: Sep 22, 1959

Pos: 2B	BA: .275
Hits: 893	HRs: 10
RBI: 240	BBs: 371

Backman was in the right place at the right time; he played for the Tidewater team managed by Davey Johnson in 1983. The successful skipper liked the fiesty infielder and when Johnson went to the Mets, he sent for Backman. The second baseman starred in a platoon system, hitting .320 for the 1986 World Champion Mets. He scored five runs in the NLCS to lead the Mets past the Astros, including the final run in the Game Six 14-inning thriller.
Playing Career: *1980-; NY N, Min A, Pit N, Phi N, Sea A*

Jim Bagby
Bagby, James Charles Jacob, Jr.
B: Sep 8, 1916   D: Sep 2, 1988

Pos: P	ERA: 3.96
W-L: 97-96	SOs: 431
ShOs: 13	Saves: 9

The son of big league pitcher "Sarge" Bagby, Jim Jr. made the AL All-Star team in 1942 and 1943. After a stint in the Merchant Marine for part of the 1944 season, he returned to the majors, but his pitching prowess did not. He won only eight more games before he retired.
Playing Career: *1938-1947; Bos A, Cle A, Pit N*

Jim Bagby
Bagby, James Charles Jacob, Sr. (Sarge)
B: Oct 5, 1889   D: Jul 28, 1954

Pos: P	ERA: 3.10
W-L: 127-88	SOs: 450
ShOs: 16	Saves: 29

Jim Bagby was the ace of the World Champion 1920 Cleveland Indians' staff. He won 31 games, leading the AL in winning percentage, games, complete games and innings pitched. Bagby also won a game in the World Series. In that Game Five win, he became the

Jim Bagby Jr. and Sr.

first pitcher to hit a home run in the World Series. Indians catcher Elmer Smith contributed the first Series grand slam, and Tribe second baseman Bill Wambsganss made the unassisted triple play.

Bagby was never the same after that year. The strain of almost 1,500 innings in his first five years caught up with him in 1921, and he lasted only two more years at the major league level.
Playing Career: *1912, 1916-1923; Cin N, Cle A, Pit N*

Stan Bahnsen
Bahnsen, Stanley Raymond
B: Dec 15, 1944

Pos: P	ERA: 3.61
W-L: 146-149	SOs: 1,359
ShOs: 16	Saves: 20

Bahnsen tossed a seven-inning perfect game for Syracuse in 1967, his second no-hitter in the International League. He broke into the AL the following year with the Yankees, posting 17 wins and earning Rookie of the Year honors. Bahnsen lost a no-hitter in 1973 with two out in the ninth inning. Following control and ERA problems, he started a second career as a middle reliever. His bullpen help aided the Expos in their 1981 playoff bid.
Playing Career: *1966, 1968-1982; NY A, Chi A, Oak A, Mon N, Cal A, Phi N*

Bob Bailey
Bailey, Robert Sherwood
B: Oct 13, 1942

Pos: 3B	BA: .257
Hits: 1,564	HRs: 189
RBI: 773	BBs: 852

Expos Manager Gene Mauch said, "Bailey means wood, Bailey doesn't mean leather." Despite this reputation Bailey led NL third basemen in fielding in 1971 with a .960 mark.

Bailey was a bonus baby, signing with the Pirates in 1961 for $175,000. *The Sporting News* named him Minor League Player of the Year in 1962. Bailey was the regular third baseman with the Pirates for the next four years.
Playing Career: *1962-1978; Pit N, LA N, Mon N, Cin N, Bos A*

Ed Bailey
Bailey, Lonas Edgar
B: Apr 15, 1931

Pos: C	BA: .256
Hits: 915	HRs: 155
RBI: 540	BBs: 545

A heavy-hitting platoon catcher who made the All-Star team five times, Bailey also appeared in the 1961 World Series with the Giants. As a pinch hitter, he stroked two grand slam home runs. When the Reds had a record 221 home runs in 1956, 28 of those were Bailey's.
Playing Career: *1953-1966; Cin N, SF N, Mil N, Chi N, Cal A*

Bob Bailor
Bailor, Robert Michael
B: Jul 10, 1951

Pos: OF, SS, 2B, DH	BA: .264
Hits: 775	HRs: 9
RBI: 222	BBs: 187

The number one expansion draft pick for the Toronto Blue Jays organization in 1976, Bailor hit .310 for the Jays in 1977. He spent four seasons as a starter, then injuries cut short his promising career. Bailor helped Los Angeles to the division title in 1985.
Playing Career: *1975-1985; Bal A, Tor A, NY N, LA N*

Harold Baines
Baines, Harold Douglas
B: Mar 15, 1959

Pos: OF, DH	BA: .288
Hits: 2,060	HRs: 261
RBI: 1,144	BBs: 704

White Sox owner Bill Veeck scouted 12-year-old Baines as a Little Leaguer in Easton, Maryland. Six years later, the Sox made Baines their number one draft pick. His potential Hall of Fame career included a 10-year stop at Comiskey Park. Baines was chosen for five All-Star teams. He became the first White Sox batter to hit 20 or more homers for six consecutive years.

Harold Baines.

Languishing in Texas, Baines improved when he was traded to the pennant-contending A's in 1990. He hit .375 in the 1990 ALCS. In the 1992 ALCS he hit .440.
Playing Career: *1980-; Chi A, Tex A, Oak A, Bal A*

Doug Bair
Bair, Charles Douglas
B: Aug 22, 1949

Pos: P	ERA: 3.63
W-L: 55-43	SOs: 689
ShOs: 0	Saves: 81

Doug Bair played on three pennant-winning teams and appeared in two World Series. More valuable in a solid bullpen than when featured as the main stopper, most of Bair's saves came early in his career with the Reds. When he was swapped to the Cardinals he played second banana to Bruce Sutter. Bair's best season was 1978 when he won seven, saved 28 and posted an ERA of 1.97.
Playing Career: *1976-1990; Pit N, Oak A, Cin N, StL N, Det A, Phi N, Tor A*

Del Baker
Baker, Delmar David
B: May 3, 1892   D: Sep 11, 1973

Pos: C	BA: .209
Hits: 63	HRs: 0
RBI: 22	BBs: 32
Managerial Record	
Won: 394 Lost: 341 Pct: .536	

Baker guided the Tigers through the topsy-turvy AL pennant race of 1940 when as many as five different teams led the league at one time or another. The Tigers lost in the Series four games to three.

After 22 years in professional baseball as a catcher, with three years at the major league level, Baker started his second career in 1927, managing in the minors.
Playing Career: *1914-1916; Det A*
Managerial Career: *1933, 1938-1942; Det A*

Dusty Baker
Baker, Johnnie B., Jr.
B: Jun 15, 1949

Pos: OF	BA: .278
Hits: 1,981	HRs: 242
RBI: 1,013	BBs: 762
Managerial Record:	
Won: 103 Lost: 59 Pct: .636	

A Gold Glove outfielder in 1981, Baker made the All-Star team in 1981 and 1982, and helped his teams get to three World Series. The talented batsman hit .321 in his first full season. The next season he scored 101 runs and drove in 99 runs. His career highlight came in the 1977 NLCS, when he drove in eight runs in four games to fuel the Dodger triumph.
Playing Career: *1968-1986; Atl N, LA N, SF N, Oak A*
Managerial Career: *1993-; SF N*

Floyd Baker
Baker, Floyd Wilson
B: Oct 10, 1916

Pos: 3B	BA: .251
Hits: 573	HRs: 1
RBI: 196	BBs: 382

After an unimpressive beginning epitomized by his two strikeouts as a pinch hitter in the 1944 World Series, Baker developed into one of the best fielders in the AL. His .317 batting mark for the 1950 White Sox was the high point of his career.
Playing Career: *1943-1955; StL A, Chi A, Was A, Bos A, Phi N*

Home Run Baker
Baker, John Franklin
B: Mar 13, 1886   D: Jun 28, 1963
Hall of Fame 1955

Pos: 3B	BA: .307
Hits: 1,838	HRs: 96
RBI: 1,013	BBs: 473

The Maryland farm boy hit game-winning home runs off Giants aces Rube Marquard and Christy Mathewson on successive days in the 1911 World Series. John Franklin Baker was known thereafter as "Home Run." He led or tied for the home run lead four consecutive years, 1911-1914.

A left-handed hitter, Baker held the hot corner position in Connie Mack's fabled $100,000 infield. After four World Series in five years, when he also led the AL in RBI in 1912-1913, Baker sat out the 1915 season in a contract dispute with the Athletics. He was traded to the Yankees where he furnished power to the lineup preceding the famed Murderers' Row. After two more World Series with the Yanks he retired to manage in the Eastern Shore League. One of his prized finds was Jimmie Foxx. Only the Hall of Fame induction ceremonies and guest appearances

John Franklin "Home Run" Baker.

at Old Timers Games kept him from his farm in Trappe, Maryland.
Playing Career: *1908-1914, 1916-1919, 1921-1922; Phi A, NY A*

Steve Balboni
Balboni, Stephen Charles (Bye-Bye)
B: Jan 16, 1957

Pos: 1B, DH	BA: .229
Hits: 714	HRs: 181
RBI: 495	BBs: 273

"Bye Bye" Balboni hit more than 200 minor league home runs, yet his major league highlights are a blooper single that won Game Three of the 1985 ALCS and a line drive single that rallied the Royals in the sixth game of that year's World Series. Balboni averaged .320 for the Series.
Playing Career: *1981-1990, 1993; NY A, KC A, Sea A, Tex A*

Jack Baldschun
Baldschun, Jack Edward
B: Oct 16, 1936

Pos: P	ERA: 3.70
W-L: 48-41	SOs: 555
ShOs: 0	Saves: 60

The "Phutile Phillies" of the early 1960s had Jack Baldschun as their relief ace. From 1962 to 1964 he was good for 50 saves and 29 wins. His ERA marks were 2.96, 2.30 and 3.12 in those years. On April 14, 1962, Baldschun posted wins in relief for both ends of a doubleheader.
Playing Career: *1961-1967, 1969-1970; Phi N, Cin N, SD N*

Mark Baldwin
Baldwin, Marcus Elmore (Fido)
B: Oct 29, 1863   D: Nov 10, 1929

Pos: P	ERA: 3.36
W-L: 154-165	SOs: 1,354
ShOs: 14	Saves: 4

A top pitcher in the Players' League, Baldwin's 32 wins in 1890 tied for the league lead. He also led that season in games, complete games, innings pitched and strikeouts. Baldwin was a workhorse, tossing 296 complete games in 328 starts over a seven-year period. He fanned 368 batters in 1889. Nicknamed for his bulldog-like tenacity Baldwin won 20 games or more for four straight years.
Playing Career: *1887-1893; Chi N, Col AA, Chi P, Pit N, NY N*

Neal Ball
Ball, Cornelius
B: Apr 22, 1881   D: Oct 15, 1957

Pos: SS, 2B, 3B	BA: .251
Hits: 404	HRs: 4
RBI: 151	BBs: 99

On July 19, 1909, Neal Ball took a line drive, stepped on second to double off a Red Sox runner and tagged a runner coming from first

base for the first unassisted triple play in major league history. In the same inning, he hit an inside-the-park home run.
Playing Career: *1907-1913; NY A, Cle A, Bos A*

George Bamberger
Bamberger, George Irvin
B: Aug 1, 1925

Pos: P	ERA: 9.42
W-L: 0-0	SOs: 3
ShOs: 0	Saves: 1
Managerial Record	
Won: 458 Lost: 478 Pct: .489	

One of the top pitching coaches of all time, Bamberger's 1971 Orioles staff boasted four 20-game winners. As a pitcher he made only token appearances in the majors, but won 213 minor league games in 18 years. Bamberger was named Manager of the Year for bringing the Brewers to third place in 1978. Heart trouble caused him to step down, but the Mets and the Brewers lured him from retirement.
Playing Career: *1951-1952, 1959; NY N, Bal A*
Managerial Career: *1978-1980, 1982-1983, 1985-1986; Mil A, NY N*

Dave Bancroft
Bancroft, David James (Beauty)
B: Apr 20, 1891   D: Oct 9, 1972
Hall of Fame 1971

Pos: SS	BA: .279
Hits: 2,004	HRs: 32
RBI: 591	BBs: 827
Managerial Record	
Won: 238 Lost: 336 Pct: .415	

From the first moment he stepped into Philadelphia's Baker Bowl in 1915, Bancroft was a major league shortstop. He replaced popular Mickey Doolan and led the hapless Phils to the pennant. After two subsequent second-

Dave Bancroft.

place finishes he was sold to the Giants. In New York, Bancroft was a big star, anchoring the pennant-winning Giants' infield and supplying punch at the plate. Bancroft went 6-for-6 in a game in 1920 and hit for the cycle in 1921. In 1921 and 1922 he led NL shortstops in putouts, assists and double plays.

As a favor to Braves President Christy Mathewson, John McGraw traded the 32-year-old Bancroft to Boston. McGraw said, "I'm giving you the best shortstop in the league." Bancroft became the manager of the Braves and led by example, hitting .319 and .311 in 1925 and 1926. He played in four World Series.
Playing Career: *1915-1930; Phi N, NY N, Bos N, Brk N*
Managerial Career: *1924-1927; Bos N*

Frank Bancroft
Bancroft, Frank Carter
B: May 9, 1846   D: Mar 30, 1921

Managerial Record
Won: 375   Lost: 333   Pct: .530

Baseball pioneer Frank Bancroft helped establish the general manager position to run the business side of a team. After managing the Cincinnati Reds, he served as the club's business manager for many years. Bancroft's adventures as a field manager included being an early exploiter of the lefty-righty advantage with pitchers; taking a team of stars to Cuba in 1879; and managing the 1884 Providence Grays, who captured the NL flag on the strength of Old Hoss Radbourn's 60-win season.
Managerial Career: *1880-1885, 1887, 1889, 1902; Wor N, Det N, Cle N, Pro N, Phi AA, Ind N, Cin N*

Sal Bando
Bando, Salvatore Leonard
B: Feb 13, 1944

Pos: 3B	BA: .254
Hits: 1,790	HRs: 242
RBI: 1,039	BBs: 1,031

Sal Bando is remembered for steady play and solid hitting with the Oakland A's in the midst of Charlie Finley's circus atmosphere. His performance contributed to the A's victories in three straight World Series. He appeared in four All-Star Games.

Bando was the leader of the Finley brigade on and off the field. He scored the winning run in the 1972 World Series, hit two home runs in Game Two of the ALCS in 1973, and hit two more in the ALCS the following year.

Off the field, his observation that manager Al Dark couldn't manage a meat market reached owner Finley's ears, prompting the subsequent dismissal of Dark. Bando organized the wearing of black armbands in the 1973 World Series to demonstrate support for Mike Andrews, the second baseman Finley publicly criticized and placed on the disabled list following two errors in Game Two.
Playing Career: *1966-1981; KC A, Oak A, Mil A*

Alan Bannister
Bannister, Alan
B: Sep 3, 1951

Pos: OF, 2B, SS, 3B	BA: .270
Hits: 811	HRs: 19
RBI: 288	BBs: 292

Highly touted in college, Bannister was the Phillies' first-round draft pick in 1973. Versatile, he played every position except pitcher and catcher, but the only year he played 100 games at the same position, he led AL shortstops in errors.
Playing Career: *1974-1985; Phi N, Chi A, Cle A, Hou N, Tex A*

Floyd Bannister
Bannister, Floyd Franklin
B: Jun 10, 1955

Pos: P	ERA: 4.06
W-L: 134-143	SOs: 1,723
ShOs: 16	No-hitters: 0

In 1982 Bannister became the top free agent available by virtue of his AL-high 209 strikeouts, 12 wins, 3.43 ERA and an All-Star Game appearance. The White Sox won the battle for his services. After a disappointing beginning, Bannister settled down to a record of 13-1 with a 2.23 ERA after the All-Star break. He led Chicago to a division title. Bannister played in Japan but returned after one year.
Playing Career: *1977-1989, 1991-1992; Hou N, Sea A, Chi A, KC A, Cal A, Tex A*

Red Barber
Barber, Walter
B: Feb 17, 1908   D: Oct 22, 1992

Red Barber was baseball's top broadcaster for more than three decades. His work delighted fans and led to increased attendance for his teams. When Cincinnati's Larry MacPhail left the Reds to run the Brooklyn franchise, he took Barber with him to announce Dodger games. Barber's soft Southern drawl and his colorful phrases, ''tearin' up the pea patch,'' ''the bases are FOB – full of Brooklyns,'' and ''sitting in the Cat Bird seat'' contributed to the tremendous popularity of postwar baseball in the New York area. Barber was the broadcaster for the first televised game in 1939. He won the J. G. Taylor Spink Award for an outstanding career in baseball broadcasting. Barber's final announcing days were spent with the Yankees, who foolishly dismissed him for referring to empty seats in Yankee Stadium. In retirement, the beloved redhead gave a popular weekly baseball report on National Public Radio until his death.

Ernie Banks.

Ernie Banks
Banks, Ernest
B: Jan 31, 1931
Hall of Fame 1977

Pos: SS, 1B	BA: .274
Hits: 2,583	HRs: 512
RBI: 1,636	BBs: 763

''Let's play two,'' was the motto of the greatest home run hitter ever to play shortstop. Named MVP in 1958 and 1959, Banks challenged the concept that a player had to be on a winning team to earn awards. Following service in the army and a season with the Kansas City Monarchs in the Negro Leagues, Banks exploded on the major league scene. In 10 games for the Chicago Cubs in 1953, he hit two home runs and drove in six for a .314 batting average and a .571 slugging average.

After switching to a lighter bat in 1955 – starting the practice that exists today – he clubbed 44 homers, including an NL record five grand slams. Banks led the league in home runs in 1958 and 1960, led in RBI in 1958 and 1959, won a Gold Glove in 1960 and was selected to the All-Star team 11 times. Following his retirement in 1971, the Cubs hoisted a pinstriped pennant with number 14 atop the left field foul pole at Wrigley Field. He was the first Cubs player to have his number retired.
Playing Career: *1953-1971; Chi N*

Red Barber, one of baseball's first and most popular broadcasters.

Steve Barber
Barber, Stephen David
B: Feb 22, 1939

Pos: P	ERA: 3.36
W-L: 121-106	SOs: 1,309
ShOs: 21	No-hitters: 1

Steve Barber became famous as the weekday soldier and weekend pitcher in 1962 while fulfilling his military requirements with Uncle Sam. This schedule resulted in victories in his first two starts, but the experiment was ground to a halt by booming AL bats.

Barber was a flamethrower who had bouts with wildness. He became Baltimore's first modern 20-game winner in 1963 and was chosen for the All-Star squad that year and again in 1966.
Playing Career: *1960-1974; Bal A, NY A, Sea A, Chi N, Atl N, Cal A, SF N*

Jesse Barfield
Barfield, Jesse Lee
B: Oct 29, 1959

Pos: OF	BA: .256
Hits:1,219	HRs: 241
RBI: 716	BBs: 551

With one of the best arms ever to play the game, Jesse Barfield led AL outfielders in assists 1985-1987, and won Gold Gloves in 1986 and 1987. He was the first Blue Jays player to pinch-hit a grand slam, and the first to hit 20 home runs and steal 20 bases in the same season. Barfield began to concentrate on power in 1986 when he scored 107 runs, drove in 108, smashed a league-leading 40 home runs, hit 35 doubles, and was named to the All-Star team.
Playing Career: *1981-1992; Tor A, NY A*

Len Barker
Barker, Leonard Harold
B: Jul 27, 1955

Pos: P	ERA: 4.34
W-L: 74-76	SOs: 975
ShOs: 7	No-hitters: 1

Hard-throwing Barker tossed a perfect game in 1981, the first since Catfish Hunter's feat in 1968. With his 96-mph fastball, Barker led the AL in strikeouts twice, and was selected for the All-Star team in 1981.
Playing Career: *1976-1985, 1987; Tex A, Cle A, Atl N, Mil A*

Al Barlick
Barlick, Al
B: Apr 2, 1915
Hall of Fame 1989

Umpire Al Barlick earned the respect of peers and players alike with his basso profundo calls, clear and decisive hand signals, knowledge of the rules, proficiency calling balls and strikes, knack of anticipating and handling rough situations, and unceasing hustle. He was a professional umpire for five

Umpire Al Barlick.

decades, and at age 25, one of the youngest to reach the majors, where he worked 27 full seasons.

Barlick was a World War II Coast Guard veteran who did not take any guff. He once delayed a game forcing the ground crew to rechalk the coaching box. Another time he forfeited a game in Philadelphia when unruly fans pelted him with a tomato and hit fellow umpire Lee Ballanfant with a bottle. Barlick once called Andy Pafko's catch a trapped ball and while Pafko argued rookie Rocky Nelson circled the bases with a 220-foot home run.
Umpiring Career: *1940-1943, 1946-1955, 1958-1970; NL (7 WS, 7 AS)*

E. S. Barnard
Barnard, Ernest Sargent (Barny)
B: Jul 17, 1874   D: Mar 27, 1931

Barnard's three-year term as AL president was the culmination of a long baseball career. After graduating from Otterbein Academy and College, he coached the baseball and football teams there for the next three years. He then moved to Ohio where he worked for the *Columbus Dispatch*, becoming sports editor in 1900.

Barnard got into the new AL when Indians owner Charles Somers hired him as traveling secretary. He rose through the ranks to

AL President E.S. Barnard.

become business manager, introducing uniform numbers in 1911. When James Dunn bought the Indians in 1916 he fired Barnard, but brought him back in time to win the 1920 World Championship. Upon Dunn's death in 1922 Barnard assumed the presidency of the club. He played an increasingly important role in league politics, especially as mediator between AL president Ban Johnson and new Commissioner Landis. When the AL owners ousted Johnson in 1927, they turned to Barnard, who quietly upgraded the efficiency of the AL office and left the spotlight to the commissioner.

Jesse Barnes
Barnes, Jesse Lawrence
B: Aug 26, 1892   D: Sep 9, 1961

Pos: P	ERA: 3.22
W-L: 153-150	SOs: 653
ShOs: 26	No-hitters: 1

When John McGraw salvaged Jesse Barnes off the scrap pile known as the Boston Braves, Barnes's his career took off. He had come up with the Braves, then served in World War I. With the Giants, he won 25 games in 1919, leading the NL. He won 20 again the next year. When the Giants acquired pitching help for Barnes they won two pennants. Traded back to Boston, Barnes led the NL in shutouts in 1924.
Playing Career: *1915-1927; Bos N, NY N, Brk N*

Ross Barnes
Barnes, Roscoe Charles
B: May 8, 1850   D: Feb 5, 1915

Pos: 2B	BA: .358
Hits: 857	HRs: 7
RBI: 250 (inc.)	BBs: 114

Barnes was baseball's top slugger until a debilitating illness robbed him of his strength in 1877. He led the league in numerous offensive categories for several years, winning the very first NL batting title in 1876. His offensive weapon, the fair-foul hit, was achieved by slamming the pitch downward with the bat, adding a side spin which would cause the ball to hit in fair territory but immediately shoot foul. Meanwhile, Barnes circled the bases. Records show he scored 697 runs.
Playing Career: *1871-1877, 1879, 1881; Bos Red Stockings n, Chi N, Cin N, Bos N*

Virgil Barnes
Barnes, Virgil Jennings
B: Mar 5, 1897   D: Jul 24, 1958

Pos: P	ERA: 3.66
W-L: 61-59	SOs: 275
ShOs: 7	Saves: 11

After his brother Jesse Barnes left the Giants, Virgil became a star, pitching in the 1923 and 1924 Series. A serious injury forced his early retirement.
Playing Career: *1919-1920, 1922-1928; NY N, Bos N*

Clyde Barnhart
Barnhart, Clyde Lee
B: Dec 29, 1895   D: Jan 21, 1980

Pos: OF, 3B	BA: .295
Hits: 788	HRs: 27
RBI: 436	BBs: 265

Barnhart was a Pirate regular for seven seasons. The third baseman when Pie Traynor joined the team, Barnhart was moved into the outfield to keep his bat in the lineup. He hit more than .318 four times, driving in 114 runs in 1925 for the pennant-winning Pirates.
Playing Career: *1920-1928; Pit N*

Clyde Barnhart.

Bill Barnie
Barnie, William Harrison (Bald Billy)
B: Jan 26, 1853   D: Jul 15, 1900

Pos: C, OF, SS	BA: .169
Hits: 54	HRs: 0
RBI: NA	BBs: 3
Managerial Record	
Won: 632 Lost: 810 Pct: .438	

Bald Billy was working in a brokerage house when he began his baseball career in 1871 as a catcher. Barnie was responsible for keeping the Baltimore franchise together in its early years. He was managing Hartford in the Eastern League when he died in midseason of asthmatic bronchitis.
Playing Career: *1874-1875, 1883, 1886; Har Dark Blues n, Keo Westerns n, NY Mutuals n, Bal AA*
Managerial Career: *1883-1894, 1897-1898; Bal AA, Was N, Lou N, Brk N*

Jim Barr
Barr, James Leland
B: Feb 10, 1948

Pos: P	ERA: 3.56
W-L: 101-112	SOs: 741
ShOs: 20	Saves: 12

Jim Barr holds the record for retiring consecutive batters – 41. He signed a pro contract off the championship University of Southern California squad, then appeared in the NLCS in his first season. His amazing streak in 1972 assured him a starting role.
Playing Career: *1971-1983; SF N, Cal A*

Ed Barrow, innovative business manager of the New York Yankees from 1921 to 1945.

Jimmy Barrett
Barrett, James Erigena
B: Mar 28, 1875   D: Oct 24, 1921

Pos: OF	BA: .291
Hits: 962	HRs: 16
RBI: 255	BBs: 440

Barrett had an exceptional arm, leading AL outfielders in assists three of the first four years of the new league. He led the AL in walks twice and hit over the .300 mark four times. Barrett led the league in on-base average in 1904. He scored 580 runs.
Playing Career: *1899-1908; Cin N, Det A, Bos A*

Marty Barrett
Barrett, Martin Glenn
B: Jun 23, 1958

Pos: 2B, SS, DH	BA: .278
Hits: 938	HRs: 18
RBI: 314	BBs: 304

Barrett ripped 161 doubles in seven seasons with the Red Sox. He hit .303 in 1984, scored 94 runs in 1986 and played in three ALCS. In 1986 Barrett hit .367 in the ALCS and .433 in the World Series. A serious injury forced his release by the Padres in 1991.
Playing Career: *1982-1991; Bos A, SD N*

Red Barrett
Barrett, Charles Henry
B: Feb 14, 1915   D: Jul 28, 1990

Pos: P	ERA: 3.53
W-L: 69-69	SOs: 333
ShOs: 11	Saves: 7

On August 10, 1944, Red Barrett completed a game using only 58 pitches. Barrett's finest season was 1945, when he led the NL in wins (23) complete games (24) and innings pitched, 284. He appeared in the 1948 World Series.
Playing Career: *1937-1940, 1943-1949; Cin N, Bos N, StL N*

Ed Barrow
Barrow, Edward Grant
B: May 10, 1868   D: Dec 15, 1958
Hall of Fame 1953

Managerial Record	
Won: 310 Lost: 320 Pct: .492	

During his 24-year tenure as the Yankees' top executive, Ed Barrow created the mightiest empire baseball has ever known. An accomplished manager who led the 1918 Boston Red Sox to a pennant, he ended his field career in 1920 to become business manager of the Yankees. His trades and scouting systems resulted in 14 pennants and 10 World Championships between 1921 and 1945.

Barrow was responsible for converting Babe Ruth from a pitcher to an outfielder. He discovered Honus Wagner, pioneered night baseball, sanctioned the only woman to pitch in organized baseball (Lizzie Arlington, Eastern League, 1897) was the first to paint distances on outfield fences, and the first to put large numbers on players' uniforms.
Managerial Career: *1903-1904, 1918-1920; Det A, Bos A*

Jack Barry
Barry, John Joseph
B: Apr 26, 1887   D: Apr 23, 1961

Pos: SS	BA: .243
Hits: 1,009	HRs: 10
RBI: 429	BBs: 396
Managerial Record	
Won: 90 Lost: 62 Pct: .592	

Barry was the shortstop for Connie Mack's $100,000 infield. Signed off the Holy Cross campus, he helped the Athletics win four flags in five years. Barry was a vital cog in the A's machine despite his low batting average. Many historians feel that Cobb's spiking of Barry in the heat of the 1909 pennant race won the flag for the Tigers by depriving the A's of a key player.

Barry led AL shortstops in double plays in 1912. Three years later, Mack sold Barry and

teammate Eddie Collins to prevent them from jumping to the Federal League. Barry played in the World Series with the Red Sox in 1915, and became their manager in 1917. After military service in 1918, he played only 31 games in 1919, and was traded back to the Athletics. Barry chose to retire rather than report to the last-place A's. He returned to his alma mater where he coached for many years.
Playing Career: *1908-1917, 1919; Phi A, Bos A*
Managerial Career: *1917; Bos A*

Shad Barry
Barry, John C.
B: Oct 27, 1878   D: Nov 27, 1936

Pos: OF	BA: .267
Hits: 1,072	HRs: 10
RBI: 390	BBs: 279

During World War I Shad Barry was in charge of baseball programs for the American Expeditionary Forces. In the major leagues, he played every position but pitcher and catcher. Barry's best year was 1904, when he hit .304, splitting the season between two teams.
Playing Career: *1899-1908; Was N, Bos N, Phi N, Chi N, StL N, NY N*

Dick Bartell
Bartell, Richard William (Rowdy Richard)
B: Nov 22, 1907

Pos: SS	BA: .284
Hits: 2,165	HRs: 79
RBI: 710	BBs: 748

A pepperpot who usually batted first or second in the order, Bartell hit over .300 six times in his career. He scored 1,130 runs. In 1933 Rowdy Richard tied a record with four doubles in one game. At the top of his game

in 1936, he hit .298 for the Giants and led all shortstops in assists, double plays, and total chances per game. Teammate Carl Hubbell was the MVP with 26 victories, but Bartell played every day and may have had more overall value.

In the 1936 World Series Bartell hammered Yankee pitchers at a .381 clip in a losing cause. The Giants won the NL pennant again in 1937, as he hit .306 and again led in total chances per game. In 1940 Bartell was traded to Detroit where he hit only .233, but the Tigers won more than they had without him and rose all the way from fifth place to first.
Playing Career: *1927-1943, 1946; Pit N, Phi N, NY N, Chi N, Det A*

Kevin Bass
Bass, Kevin Charles
B: May 12, 1959

Pos: OF	BA: .270
Hits: 1,173	HRs: 107
RBI: 544	BBs: 305

Bass is a power-hitting, good-fielding, high-average outfielder. In 1986 he put it all together with 20 homers, a .311 batting average, 33 doubles and 83 runs scored. He made the All-Star team that year. In the 1986 NLCS Bass hit .292.
Playing Career: *1982-; Mil A, Hou N, SF N, NY N*

Charley Bassett
Bassett, Charles Edwin
B: Feb 9, 1863   D: May 28, 1942

Pos: 2B, 3B, SS	BA: .231
Hits: 806	HRs: 15
RBI: 396	BBs: 239

Bassett led the NL second basemen in fielding three of five years, 1887-1891. He did not

jump to the Players' League, opting to stay in New York during that tumultuous season. Bassett broke in with the Providence pennant-winners in 1884.
Playing Career: *1884-1892; Pro N, KC N, Ind N, NY N, Lou N*

Johnny Bassler
Bassler, John Landis
B: Jun 3, 1895   D: Jun 29, 1979

Pos: C	BA: .304
Hits: 704	HRs: 1
RBI: 318	BBs: 437

One of the few players who chose to play in the Pacific Coast League instead of the big leagues, Bassler was an excellent catcher and a sure .300 hitter. A valued performer when he did go to the majors, he finished sixth, seventh, and fifth in AL MVP voting.
Playing Career: *1913-1914, 1921-1927; Cle A, Det A*

John Bateman
Bateman, John Alvin
B: Jul 21, 1942

Pos: C	BA: .230
Hits: 765	HRs: 81
RBI: 375	BBs: 172

John Bateman hit the last home run at Connie Mack Stadium on September 29, 1970. His best year was 1966 when he hit 17 taters, driving in 70 runs. After leaving the major leagues he played for Eddie Feignor's King and his Court traveling softball team.
Playing Career: *1963-1972; Hou N, Mon N, Phi N*

Johnny Bates
Bates, John William
B: Aug 21, 1882   D: Feb 10, 1949

Pos: OF	BA: .277
Hits: 1,088	HRs: 25
RBI: 417	BBs: 504

Bates was a journeyman outfielder, but he played more than 100 games in seven of his first eight years in the major leagues. He scored 565 runs and stole 187 bases in his career. In Bates's best season he hit .305 for the 1910 Phillies.
Playing Career: *1906-1914; Bos N, Phi N, Cin N, Bal F*

Earl Battey
Battey, Earl Jesse
B: Jan 5, 1935

Pos: C	BA: .270
Hits: 969	HRs: 104
RBI: 449	BBs: 421

Despite numerous injuries, Battey was a Gold Glove, All-Star catcher who played 805 of the Twins' 970 games from 1961 to 1966. He had a chronic bad knee, several dislocated fingers and a goiter problem. Twice Battey had cheekbones broken by pitched balls; he

Dick Bartell (l) and Glenn Wright hoist the flag to open the 1933 season.

Earl Battey (r).

wore a special helmet after 1962. In the 1965 World Series, he ran into a neck-high crossbar while chasing a foul pop. Battey finished the Series even though he could not speak.
Playing Career: *1955-1967; Chi A, Was A, Min A*

Hank Bauer
Bauer, Henry Albert
B: Jul 31, 1922

Pos: OF	BA: .277
Hits: 1,424	HRs: 164
RBI: 703	BBs: 521
Managerial Record	
Won: 594 Lost: 544 Pct: .522	

A former Marine commander, Bauer was the Yankee leader on and off the field, keeping players in line by snarling, "Don't mess with my money." At his best when the games counted most, Bauer played in nine World Series in 10 years. In 53 World Series games he stroked 46 hits, scored 21 times and drove in 24 runs. His Series batting averages included .429 in 1955 and .323 in 1958. As the leadoff man, Bauer hit safely in 17 straight Fall Classic games.

During his career, Bauer hit 18 leadoff home runs and scored 833 times. He started three All-Star Games, 1952-1954, and led the AL in triples in 1957. Bauer was traded to the A's in the deal that brought Roger Maris to the Yankees. After his playing career, Bauer piloted the Orioles to a pennant and a four-game sweep in the World Series, making him one of only three managers who have never lost a game in the Fall Classic.
Playing Career: *1948-1961; NY A, KC A*
Managerial Career: *1961-1962, 1964-1969; KC A, Bal A, Oak A*

Frank Baumann
Baumann, Frank Matt
B: Jul 1, 1933

Pos: P	ERA: 4.11
W-L: 45-38	SOs: 384
ShOs: 7	Saves: 13

Baumann led the AL in ERA with a 2.67 mark in 1960 when he compiled a record of 13-6 and saved three. Traded from Boston, where he was never used much due to his high ERA, Baumann found that the big ballpark in Chicago helped him.
Playing Career: *1955-1965; Bos A, Chi A, Chi N*

Frankie Baumholtz
Baumholtz, Frank Conrad
B: Oct 7, 1918

Pos: OF	BA: .290
Hits: 1,010	HRs: 25
RBI: 272	BBs: 258

Baumholtz played pro baseball and basketball. His first pro year he hit .283 with 32 doubles, scored 96 runs and made 18 assists. He was fifth in Rookie of the Year voting. Baumholtz hit over .300 twice with the Cubs.
Playing Career: *1947-1949, 1951-1957; Cin N, Chi N, Phi N*

Harry Bay
Bay, Harry Elbert
B: Jan 17, 1878   D: Mar 20, 1952

Pos: OF	BA: .277
Hits: 730	HRs: 5
RBI: 141	BBs: 195

One of the fastest people of all time, Bay's foot speed was captured by early filmmakers trying to prove that both a runner's feet leave the ground at the same time. He led the AL twice in stolen bases and hit .301 in 1905.
Playing Career: *1901-1908; Cin N, Cle A*

Don Baylor
Baylor, Don Edward
B: Jun 28, 1949

Pos: DH, OF	BA: .260
Hits: 2,135	HRs: 338
RBI: 1,276	BBs: 806
Managerial Record	
Won: 67 Lost: 95 Pct: .414	

Don Baylor served many teams with hard hitting on the field and leadership in the clubhouse. He played for seven division winners and three pennant champions. Baylor became the 1979 MVP when he decorated his .296 batting average with 36 home runs and a league-high 139 RBI.

Playing as designated hitter in nearly half of his more than 2,300 games, Baylor hit more than 300 homers and drove in nearly 1,300 runs. Baylor also had an admirable reputation as a team leader and a steadying influence in the clubhouse. While such things are not subject to statistical evaluaton, most of the teams he hit for were winners. Baylor was chosen to be the manager of the expansion Colorado Rockies.
Playing Career: *1970-1988; Bal A, Oak A, Cal A, NY A, Bos A, Min A*
Managerial Career: *1993-; Col N*

Don Baylor, seen here with the California Angels in 1982.

Gene Bearden
Bearden, Henry Eugene
B: Sep 5, 1920

Pos: P	ERA: 3.96
W-L: 45-38	SOs: 259
ShOs: 7	Saves: 1

As a 20-game winning rookie with Cleveland, Bearden won the 1948 playoff game over the Red Sox. He also won a game in the World Series. The neophyte and his nasty knuckleball led the AL in ERA with a 2.43 mark that year.
Playing Career: *1947-1953; Cle A, Was A, Det A, StL A, Chi A*

Ginger Beaumont
Beaumont, Clarence Howeth
B: Jul 23, 1876   D: Apr 10, 1956

Pos: OF	BA: .311
Hits: 1,760	HRs: 38
RBI: 617	BBs: 425

Beaumont was the batting champ and outfielder on the 1902 Pirate team that led the NL by 27½ games when they won the pennant. He batted over .320 in six of twelve seasons. Blazing fast, Beaumont was generally the leadoff hitter. He made six infield hits and scored each time on July 22, 1899. Beaumont led the NL in hits four times and in runs scored once, with 137 in 1903. He scored 100 or more runs four consecutive years.
Playing Career: *1899-1910; Pit N, Bos N, Chi N*

Walter Beck
Beck, Walter William (Boom-Boom)
B: Oct 16, 1904   D: May 7, 1987

Pos: P	ERA: 4.30
W-L: 38-69	SOs: 352
ShOs: 3	Saves: 6

Boom-Boom got his nickname from the sound of baseballs coming off the bats of his opponents. Infuriated at being pulled from a game once, Beck threw the ball against the upper deck. The snoozing right fielder, Hack Wilson, heard the ricochet, chased down the ball and fired it to second.
Playing Career: *1924, 1927-1928, 1933-1934, 1939-1945; StL A, Brk N, Phi N, Det A, Cin N, Pit N*

Beals Becker
Becker, David Beals
B: Jul 5, 1886   D: Aug 16, 1943

Pos: OF	BA: .276
Hits: 763	HRs: 45
RBI: 292	BBs: 241

Beals Becker played in tiny Baker Bowl where the fans' negative comments could clearly be heard. He played much better on the road. In Becker's best season he hit .316 with 9 home runs, 13 triples and 24 doubles.
Playing Career: *1908-1915; Pit N, Bos N, NY N, Cin N, Phi N*

Glenn Beckert
Beckert, Glenn Alfred
B: Oct 12, 1940

Pos: 2B	BA: .283
Hits: 1,473	HRs: 22
RBI: 360	BBs: 260

Glenn Beckert was a fixture at second base for the Cubs for nine years, where he combined with shortstop Don Kessinger to give the team great stability up the middle. Beckert and third baseman Ron Santo won Gold Glove Awards in 1968; Kessinger got one in 1969. A four time All-Star performer, Beckert could also hit, once posting a .342 average. In 1968 he led the NL in runs scored with 98. In 5,208 career at-bats, he struck out only 243 times.
Playing Career: *1965-1975; Chi N, SD N*

"Old Eagle Eye" Jake Beckley.

Jake Beckley
Beckley, Jacob Peter (Old Eagle Eye)
B: Aug 4, 1867   D: Jun 25, 1918
Hall of Fame 1971

Pos: 1B	BA: .308
Hits: 2,931	HRs: 88
RBI: 1,575	BBs: 616

Jake Beckley played more games at first base than any other major league player. Sporting a handlebar mustache, he epitomized the turn-of-the-century power hitter. He batted more than .300 13 times, and hit three home runs in one game in 1897 (a feat not accomplished again until 1922). Beckley's 246 triples – twice he hit three in a game – rank him fourth on the all-time list.

When ballplayers revolted against management in 1890 and formed the short-lived Players' League, Beckley was one of the many stars who jumped with them. "I'm only in this game for the money," he said candidly. But Beckley played with verve. Sometimes he turned the bat around and bunted with the handle. His favorite stunt was to hide the ball under first base, then pull it out and shock the runner who had just seen him barehanded.
Playing Career: *1888-1907; Pit N, Pit P, NY N, Cin N, StL N*

John Beckwith
Beckwith, John
B: 1922   D: 1956

Pos: SS, C	BA: .366
Hits : 637	HRs: 104
RBI: NA	BBs: NA

John Beckwith was only 19 when he hit the first ball ever batted over the left field fence at Redland Field, Cincinnati. A right-handed pull hitter, he went on to rank as one of the great long-ball sluggers in the Negro Leagues, clouting 72 and 54 home runs in two consecutive seasons against all competition.
Playing Career: *1919-1938; Chi Giants, Chi Am Giants, Bal Black Sox, Hom Grays, Har Giants, AC Bach Giants, NY Lincoln Giants, NY Black Yankees, Nwk Browns, Brk Royal Giants.*

Steve Bedrosian
Bedrosian, Stephen Wayne
B: Dec 6, 1957

Pos: P	ERA: 3.31
W-L: 75-75	SOs: 856
ShOs: 0	Saves: 184

Combining a 96-mph fastball with a hard slider, Bedrosian is one of the most effective relief pitchers. In a 1987 game against the Cardinals, he faced a situation with the bases loaded in the ninth inning, nobody out, the winning run on third, and the top of the lineup coming to the plate. Bedrosian shut down the most explosive, speediest leadoff trio in baseball. Bedrosian won the Cy Young Award that year on the strength of 40 saves, a 2.83 ERA, and a 5-3 record.

Atlanta's failed experiment with Bedrosian as a starter led them to trade him to the Phillies, where he established himself as one of the premier stoppers in the game. In 1988 he

Steve Bedrosian.

saved 28 of the Phillies' 65 wins, even though he missed the first month of the season due to pneumonia. Bedrosian pitched in the 1987 All-Star Game and saved three games in the 1989 NLCS for the Giants. Arm trouble forced him to sit out the 1992 season.
Playing Career: *1981-1991, 1993-; Atl N, Phi N, SF N, Min A*

Fred Beebe
Beebe, Frederick Leonard
B: Dec 31, 1880   D: Oct 30, 1957

Pos: P	ERA: 2.86
W-L: 62-83	SOs: 634
ShOs: 9	Saves: 4

Fred Beebe was the toughest pitcher to hit against in the 1908 NL. He compiled a record of 5-13 with a league-low .193 opponents' batting average for the dreadful Cardinals, who scored only 371 runs for the entire season.
Playing Career: *1906-1911, 1916; Chi N, StL N, Cin N, Phi N, Cle A*

Joe Beggs
Beggs, Joseph Stanley
B: Nov 4, 1910   D: Jul 19, 1983

Pos: P	ERA: 2.96
W-L: 48-35	SOs: 178
ShOs: 4	Saves: 29

Joe Beggs played on the greatest minor league team in baseball history, the 1937 Newark Bears. He went 21-4 for Newark, but did not pitch well for the Yankees, who shipped him off to the Reds. Beggs helped them win the pennant, and led the league in saves.
Playing Career: *1938, 1940-1944, 1946-1948; NY A, Cin N, NY N*

Mark Belanger
Belanger, Mark Henry
B: Jun 8, 1944

Pos: SS, 2B	BA: .228
Hits: 1,316	HRs: 20
RBI: 389	BBs: 576

Mark Belanger only made the All-Star team once, but he was the glue that held together a great infield for a Baltimore team that won six division crowns and four pennants. He played in 43 postseason games, and holds several ALCS fielding records. Belanger even hit the first home run in ALCS history! He made up for his normally anemic bat with his fielding prowess, winning eight Gold Glove Awards. Seldom fancy – he rarely nabbed a ball one-handed or made a sidearmed throw – Belanger navigated the infield with sure-handed ease and grace.

Granted free agency after 1981, Belanger signed with the Dodgers for his final season. A longtime player representative with Baltimore, he became a special assistant with the Players' Association after retiring from the field.
Playing Career: *1965-1982; Bal A, LA N*

Bo Belinsky
Belinsky, Robert
B: Dec 7, 1936

Pos: P	ERA: 4.10
W-L: 28-51	SOs: 476
ShOs: 4	No-hitters: 1

Belinsky's autobiography, written at the ripe old age of 25, was called *Pitching and Wooing* and concentrated more on the latter than the former. Playing for the expansion Los Angeles Angels suited him, as did the starlet population in the area.
Playing Career: *1962-1967, 1969-1970; LA A, Phi N, Hou N, Pit N, Cin N*

Roy "Beau" Bell.

Beau Bell
Bell, Roy Chester
B: Aug 20, 1907   D: Sep 14, 1977

Pos: OF, 1B, 3B	BA: .297
Hits: 806	HRs: 46
RBI: 509	BBs: 272

A good hitter, Bell led the AL in hits with 218 and doubles with 51, and was selected for the 1937 All-Star Game. He hit .340 or more in 1936 and 1937, collecting 430 hits in two seasons. Alcoholism kept him from being a star.
Playing Career: *1935-1941; StL A, Det A, Cle A*

Mark Belanger, Baltimore Orioles shortstop from 1965 to 1981.

James "Cool Papa" Bell (sliding), one of the Negro Leagues' finest players.

Buddy Bell

Bell, David Gus
B: Aug 27, 1951

Pos: 3B   BA: .279
Hits: 2,514   HRs: 201
RBI: 1,106   BBs: 836

Buddy Bell and his dad Gus formed one of the most power-laden father-son duos in baseball history. The combo amassed 407 home runs, 4,337 hits, 2,016 runs scored and 2,048 RBI. Buddy was raised at the ballpark. He had hitting in his genes but learned to be an outstanding fielder, winning six Gold Glove Awards, 1979-1984.

He led AL third basemen five times in total chances, three times in putouts and assists, and twice in double plays and fielding percentage. Bell was selected for the All-Star team five times, but never played on a division-winning team. Bell was the regular third baseman for 16 consecutive years, playing 116 or more games each season.

Playing Career: *1972-1989; Cle A, Tex A, Cin N, Hou N*

Buddy Bell (l) with son David in 1974.

Cool Papa Bell

Bell, James
B: May 17, 1903   D: Mar 7, 1991
Hall of Fame 1974

Pos: OF, P   BA: .337
Hits: 1,241   HRs: 63
RBI: NA   BB: NA

Combining speed, daring and batting skill, Cool Papa ranked in the top echelon of players in the Negro Leagues. Contemporaries rated him the fastest man on the basepaths, especially from first to third. Bell had power and speed, twice reaching double figures in home runs and leading the league in stolen bases.

The switch-hitting center fielder broke in with the St. Louis Stars as a left-handed pitcher. He got his nickname while warming up before a rowdy crowd in Chicago. His calm demeanor despite the ruckus caused American Giants owner Rube Foster to remark, "Look at that guy, he's so cool warming up before this big crowd." Bell always felt he should have continued as a pitcher. He had an unhittable knuckler, but it was also uncatchable. "Only my sister could ever catch it," he said.

Playing Career: *1922-1946; StL Stars, Det Wolves, KC Monarchs, Pit Crawfords, Chi Am Giants, Hom Grays*

Gary Bell

Bell, Gary (Ding Dong)
B: Nov 17, 1936

Pos: P   ERA: 3.68
W-L: 121-117   SOs: 1,378
ShOs: 9   Saves: 51

Gary Bell was the roomate Jim Bouton made famous in *Ball Four*. Bell spent much of his career shifting from starting to relief, working for seven Indians managers in nine years. He posted wins in double figures seven times and saves in double figures twice. Bell was selected for the All-Star Game in 1960, one of his worst years. Selected twice more, he did not play due to injuries, but he pitched in the 1967 World Series.

Playing Career: *1958-1969; Cle A, Bos A, Sea A, Chi A*

George Bell

Bell y Mathey, Jorge Antonio
B: Oct 21, 1959

Pos: OF   BA: .278
Hits: 1,702   HRs: 265
RBI: 1,002   BBs: 331

Talented and productive George Bell once hit three home runs on Opening Day, the only batter ever to do so. He, Jesse Barfield and Lloyd Mosby formed the 1980s' best outfield. Bell was the AL MVP in 1987 when he had a .308 batting average, 47 home runs, 134 RBI, 111 runs scored, and a .605 slugging average. He has played on three AL All-Star teams, and made two postseason appearances for the Toronto Blue Jays, hitting .321 in the 1985 ALCS.

Playing Career: *1981, 1983-; Tor A, Chi N, Chi A*

Gus Bell

Bell, David Russell
B: Nov 15, 1928

Pos: OF   BA: .281
Hits: 1,823   HRs: 206
RBI: 942   BBs: 470

Drafted as one of the original Mets, Bell punched the first base hit in Mets history, a single on April 11, 1962. Selected for the All-Star squad four times, Bell figured in the 1957 ballot-stuffing incident in Cincinnati which caused the commissioner to remove Reds outfielders Bell and Wally Post from the team. All-Star skipper Walter Alston chose Bell for the team anyway, and he responded by slapping a double, driving in two runs. He is the father of Buddy Bell, who played the major leagues for 18 years.

Playing Career: *1950-1964; Pit N, Cin N, NY N, Mil N*

Jay Bell
Bell, Jay Stuart
B: Dec 1, 1965

Pos: SS	BA: .267
Hits: 814	HRs: 48
RBI: 290	BBs: 299

Bell is one of the strongest-hitting shortstops in the NL. He homered in his first big league at-bat. When Bell became a regular with the Pirates, batting second in the lineup, the Bucs won three straight division titles.
Playing Career: *1986-; Cle A, Pit N*

Les Bell
Bell, Lester Rowland
B: Dec 14, 1901 D: Dec 26, 1985

Pos: 3B	BA: .290
Hits: 938	HRs: 66
RBI: 509	BBs: 276

An early product of the Cardinal farm system, Bell helped the Red Birds win the 1926 championship. He hit .325 that year with 17 home runs, 14 triples and 100 RBI. Bell later socked three homers and a triple in one game for the Braves.
Playing Career: *1923-1931; StL N, Bos N, Chi N*

Steve Bellan
Bellan, Estaban Enrique
B: 1850 D: Aug 8, 1932

Pos: SS, 3B, OF	BA: .248
Hits: 69	HRs: 0
RBI: 42 (inc.)	BBs: 11

The Cuban learned baseball in the U.S., then played in the National Association. When Bellan returned to Cuba he started pro leagues there, becoming known as the Father of Cuban baseball. He was the first to hit three homers in a game in Cuba.
Playing Career: *1871-1873; Tro Haymakers n, NY Mutuals n*

Harry Bemis
Bemis, Harry Parker
B: Feb 1, 1874 D: May 23, 1947

Pos: C	BA: .255
Hits: 569	HRs: 5
RBI: 234	BBs: 79

Cleveland's platoon catcher in the new AL, Bemis hit .312 in his rookie year. He followed that performance by leading AL catchers in fielding average in 1903. As a left-handed hitting receiver he played about 90 games per year.
Playing Career: *1902-1910; Cle A*

Johnny Bench
Bench, Johnny Lee
B: Dec 7, 1947
Hall of Fame 1989

Pos: C	BA: .267
Hits: 2,048	HRs: 389
RBI: 1,376	BBs: 891

Bench may have been the greatest catcher ever; he had power, a rocket arm, and technique behind the plate that redefined the position. Prior to Bench all catchers were taught to shift their feet for outside pitches. Bench had such body control that he merely shifted his weight without moving his feet.

Labeled "can't miss" from the beginning in Binger, Oklahoma, the Cherokee's powerful throwing arm accounted for 102 assists in his rookie year. Hardly anyone ran on him again. The first NL catcher to win the Rookie of the Year Award, Bench also won 10 consecutive Gold Glove Awards, was selected to the All-Star team 14 times, led the NL in home runs twice and in RBI three times, and played on six division-winning teams. He batted fourth or fifth in the famed "Big Red Machine" lineup. In the 1976 World Series against the Yankees, Bench outhit rival catcher Thurman Munson .533 to .529 and was declared the Series MVP.
Playing Career: *1967-1983; Cin N*

Chief Bender.

Chief Bender
Bender, Charles Albert
B: May 5, 1884 D: May 22, 1954
Hall of Fame 1953

Pos: P	ERA: 2.46
W-L: 210-127	SOs: 1,711
ShOs: 41	No-hitters: 1

Albert, as Connie Mack called his Chippewa hurler, was the best money pitcher in baseball. Bender led the AL in winning percentage three times and finished with a career mark of .625. He has a 6-4 World Series record with nine complete games in ten starts. An all-round performer, Bender played several games in the outfield and pinch hit 29 times. He saved 34 games, leading the AL twice. For three consecutive years his ERA was under 2.00.

Raised on a reservation, Bender was sent to a religious school in Philadelphia at the age of eight. He attended Carlisle Indian School, where he played sports. Soon he caught the eye of the Philadelphia Athletics, where he was the mainstay on a great team. After his big league career was over, Bender managed and pitched for Richmond where he went 29-2 in 1919 for a .935 percentage, one of the greatest minor league seasons in history.
Playing Career: *1903-1917, 1925; Phi A, Bal F, Phi N, Chi A*

Bruce Benedict
Benedict, Bruce Edwin
B: Aug 18, 1955

Pos: C	BA: .242
Hits: 696	HRs: 18
RBI: 260	BBs: 328

Benedict was chosen for the All-Star team twice and helped Atlanta to the division title once, despite playing regularly only five years. The Braves searched for a better bat during most of Benedict's career, but they couldn't find a better glove or arm.
Playing Career: *1978-1989; Atl N*

Johnny Bench drove the "Big Red Machine" as catcher and heavy hitter.

Ray Benge
Benge, Raymond Adelphia
B: Apr 22, 1902

Pos: P	ERA: 4.52
W-L: 101-130	SOs: 655
ShOs: 12	Saves: 19

Pitching in cozy Baker Bowl, Benge won 57 games in five years as a starter and a reliever. He once struck out 13 batters to tie a Phillies record. Benge lost only 130 games pitching for some of the most hapless teams in baseball.
Playing Career: *1925-1926, 1928-1936, 1938; Cle A, Phi N, Brk N, Bos N, Cin N*

Juan Beniquez (sliding).

Juan Beniquez
Beniquez y Torres, Juan Jose
B: May 13, 1950

Pos: OF	BA: .274
Hits: 1,274	HRs: 79
RBI: 476	BBs: 349

Beniquez began as a shortstop, made six errors in two days – a major league record – then was transformed into a Gold Glove outfielder for the Rangers. The Puerto Rican also hit more than .300 four consecutive years.
Playing Career: *1971-1972, 1974-1988; Bos A, Tex A, NY A, Sea A, Cal A, Bal A, KC A, Tor A*

Charlie Bennett
Bennett, Charles Wesley
B: Nov 21, 1854   D: Feb 24, 1927

Pos: C	BA: .256
Hits: 978	HRs: 56
RBI: 438	BBs: 478

Bennett was a popular catcher who lost his legs in a railroad accident in 1894. Grieving

Al Benton in his last year as pitcher for the Cleveland Indians, in 1950.

Detroit team officials renamed their field Charlie Bennett Park; it was on the site where Tiger Stadium stands today. Bennett, in his wheelchair, was a fixture at turn-of-the-century baseball games.

The prototype of 19th-century catchers, Bennett had led the league many times in putouts and assists. He led NL catchers in fielding percentage seven times, including four years in a row. Bennett played for the Detroit Wolverine franchise the entire time of its existence, the highlight being the 1887 pennant and World Series.

The train accident occurred in Wellsville, Kansas, when Bennett was returning from a hunting expedition. The former catcher later ran a dry goods store which was heavily patronized by members of the sporting class.
Playing Career: *1878, 1880-1893; Mil N, Wor N, Det N, Bos N*

Gene Benson
Benson, Gene
B: Oct 4, 1913

Pos: OF	BA: .294
Hits: 547	HRs: 14
RBI: NA	BB: NA

Gene Benson was Jackie Robinson's last roommate in the Negro Leagues. Benson, a longtime center fielder and proponent of the basket catch, was asked by the Negro League veterans to counsel Robinson on how to act like a professional ballplayer.
Playing Career: *1934-1947; AC Bach Giants, Phi Stars, Pit Crawfords*

Jack Bentley
Bentley, Jack Needles
B: Mar 8, 1895   D: Oct 24, 1969

Pos: P, 1B	ERA: 4.01
W-L: 46-33	SOs: 259
ShOs: 4	Saves: 9

Touted as the new Babe Ruth, Bentley was the leading hitter and part-time hurler for the Baltimore Orioles of the International League. McGraw purchased him in 1923, but he never developed at either position. His career batting average was .291.
Playing Career: *1913-1916, 1923-1927; Was A, NY N*

Al Benton
Benton, John Alton
B: Mar 18, 1911   D: Apr 14, 1968

Pos: P	ERA: 3.66
W-L: 98-88	SOs: 697
ShOs: 10	Saves: 66

Al Benton pitched in the big leagues for 14 seasons spread over 19 years, and has the dubious distinction of giving up home runs to both Babe Ruth and Mickey Mantle. Benton was selected for three All-Star teams. He led the AL in saves with 17 in 1940, yet did not appear in the World Series that year. He did pitch in the 1945 Series. Benton's best year was 1941 when he went 15-6 with seven saves and a 2.97 ERA.
Playing Career: *1934-1935, 1938-1942, 1945-1950, 1952; Phi A, Det A, Cle A, Bos A*

Larry Benton
Benton, Lawrence James
B: Nov 20, 1897   D: Apr 3, 1953

Pos: P	ERA: 4.03
W-L: 127-128	SOs: 670
ShOs: 13	Saves: 22

Larry Benton was traded twice for Hugh McQuillan, who was considered the primary compensation both times. Benton led the NL in winning percentage in 1927 and again in 1928, when he also led with 25 victories and 28 complete games.
Playing Career: *1923-1935; Bos N, NY N, Cin N*

Rube Benton
Benton, John Clebon
B: Jun 27, 1887   D: Dec 12, 1937

Pos: P	ERA: 3.09
W-L: 156-144	SOs: 950
ShOs: 24	Saves: 21

Benton was a premier starting pitcher from 1912 to 1925. He pitched in the 1917 World Series with a 1-1 record and an ERA of 0.00. Benton had a 1.88 ERA when Uncle Sam called him to serve in World War I. When he returned he became the fourth starter, then a spot starter for the NL champs in 1921. He was sold to the Reds in 1922 despite having not played all season. He put in three more decent years with the Reds before retiring in 1925.
Playing Career: *1910-1921, 1923-1925; Cin N, NY N*

Joe Benz
Benz, Joseph Louis
B: Jan 21, 1886   D: Apr 22, 1957

Pos: P	ERA: 2.42
W-L: 76-75	SOs: 538
ShOs: 17	No-hitters: 1

Using a spitter and a knuckleball, Benz served the White Sox as a spot starter and a reliever. In eight years, he never had an ERA over 2.90, posting a 2.48 or less four times. In his no-hitter the Indians scored on him due to three errors.
Playing Career: *1911-1919; Chi A*

Johnny Berardino
Berardino, John
B: May 1, 1917

Pos: 2B, SS, 3B	BA: .249
Hits: 755	HRs: 36
RBI: 387	BBs: 384

Berardino left a major league career to star as Dr. Hardy on the long-running soap opera "General Hospital." He hit well early in his baseball career, knocking 16 home runs in 1940, driving in 89 runs in 1941. Berardino played in the 1948 World Series, in his first year with Cleveland.
Playing Career: *1939-1942, 1946-1952; StL A, Cle A, Pit N*

Juan Berenguer
Berenguer, Juan Bautista
B: Nov 30, 1954

Pos: P	ERA: 3.90
W-L: 67-62	SOs: 975
ShOs: 2	Saves: 32

Berenguer was the ultimate reliever: long-haired and mean-looking, with a hot fastball and a propensity to throw inside. Nicknamed "Pancho Villa" by his teammates, Berenguer's 8-1 record helped the Twins win the 1987 AL pennant.
Playing Career: *1978-1992; NY N, KC A, Tor A, Det A, SF N, Min A, Atl N*

Moe Berg
Berg, Morris
B: Mar 2, 1902   D: May 29, 1972

Pos: C	BA: .243
Hits: 441	HRs: 6
RBI: 206	BBs: 78

"Spoke twelve languages and couldn't hit in any of them," was the popular assessment of Berg's batting. As a spy for U.S. Army Intelligence, Berg took photos when he accompanied an All-Star team to Japan in 1934, and he later worked in atomic espionage. Berg declined the Congressional Medal of Honor.

Even before Berg's espionage activities were known, Casey Stengel called him "the strangest man ever to play baseball." Why he spent his talent as a third-string catcher, warming up relief pitchers, is beyond most historians. He said, "I'd rather be a ballplayer than a justice on the U.S. Supreme Court."

In 1928 Berg swatted 16 doubles. The next year, the only season he played regularly, he compiled a .287 batting average – his highest.
Playing Career: *1923, 1926-1939; Brk N, Chi A, Cle A, Was A, Bos A*

Bill Bergen
Bergen William Aloysius
B: Jun 13, 1878   D: Dec 19, 1943

Pos: C	BA: .170
Hits: 516	HRs: 2
RBI: 193	BBs: 88

Bill Bergen was the worst hitter ever to play regularly in the majors; his career average hovers 42 points below that of any other batter with 2,500 at-bats. In the lineup for his arm, Bergen's 202 assists in 1909 make the ninth-best season record in baseball history.
Playing Career: *1901-1911; Cin N, Brk N*

Moe Berg, "the strangest man ever to play baseball" (Casey Stengel).

Wally Berger
Berger, Walter Antone
B: Oct 10, 1905   D: Nov 30, 1988

Pos: OF   BA: .300
Hits: 1,550   HRs: 242
RBI: 898   BBs: 435

Wally Berger hit 38 home runs and had 119 RBI in his first major league season. In 1933 he hit a dramatic grand slam on the final day of the season, raising the Braves to fourth place and the upper division for the first time in 12 years. Berger led the NL in 1935 with 34 homers and 130 RBI. A shoulder injury limited his activity after 1936, but he played in the World Series in 1937 and 1939. He was selected for the All-Star team four times.
Playing Career: *1930-1940; Bos N, NY N, Cin N, Phi N*

Dave Bergman
Bergman, David Bruce
B: Jun 6, 1953

Pos: 1B, OF, DH   BA: .258
Hits: 690   HRs: 54
RBI: 289   BBs: 380

Bergman was a platoon player in a power position. He won two minor league batting crowns in the Yankee farm system, but the best he did on the major league level was .294 for the Tigers in 1988. Bergman was traded twice in the same day, March 24, 1984.
Playing Career: *1975, 1977-1992; NY A, Hou N, SF N, Det A*

Tony Bernazard
Bernazard y Garcia, Antonio
B: Aug 24, 1956

Pos: 2B   BA: .262
Hits: 968   HRs: 75
RBI: 391   BBs: 428

Using computer analysis, the White Sox decided in 1983 that the Mariners' second baseman, Julio Cruz, would perform better in

Tony Bernazard.

The colorful Yogi Berra salutes the crowd on "Yogi Berra Day" at Yankee Stadium in 1959.

Comiskey Park than Bernazard. The Mariners were skeptical, but agreed to swap players anyway. Cruz and the Sox won the pennant; Bernazard and the Mariners finished last.
Playing Career: *1979-1987, 1991; Mon N, Chi A, Sea A, Cle A, Oak A, Det A*

Bill Bernhard
Bernhard, William Henry (Strawberry Bill)
B: Mar 16, 1871   D: Mar 30, 1949

Pos: P   ERA: 3.04
W-L: 116-82   SOs: 545
ShOs: 14   Saves: 3

Bernhard did not break into the majors until he was 28, but he became the most effective pitcher outside of Cy Young in the AL from 1901 to 1904. Bernhard won 72 and lost 34 games, posting ERAs of 2.20, 2.15 and 2.12 in the last three years.
Playing Career: *1899-1907; Phi N, Cle A*

Dale Berra
Berra, Dale Anthony
B: Dec 13, 1956

Pos: SS, 3B   BA: .236
Hits: 603   HRs: 49
RBI: 278   BBs: 210

Fans at Three River Stadium teased Yogi Berra's son by cooing, "Heeeeyy, Boo-Boo, Wheeeere's Yogi?" As a regular for the Pirates, Berra was the hardest-hitting short-stop in the NL, but after a .222 season he was traded to his dad in New York.
Playing Career: *1977-1987; Pit N, NY A, Hou N*

Yogi Berra
Berra, Lawrence Peter
B: May 12, 1925
Hall of Fame 1972

Pos: C   BA: .258
Hits: 2,150   HRs: 358
RBI: 1,430   BBs: 704
Managerial Record
Won: 484   Lost: 444   Pct: .522

As a player and as a manager, Yogi was a winner. Yogi holds Series records for games, at-bats, hits and doubles, and is second in runs scored and batted in, third in home runs and walks. Bill James made a comparative study that touts Berra as the best catcher ever to play the game.

He won three MVP Awards, but ironically, not for 1950, his best season. That year he hit .322, scored 116 runs, drove in 124, blasted 28 home runs and 30 doubles, and struck out only 12 times. He was on the All-Star team for 15 consecutive years. The Yankees won 14 pennants from 1947 to 1963 and another with Yogi managing in 1964. He also won a pennant as skipper of the Mets. Colorful on and off the field, Yogisms are frequently quoted.
Playing Career: *1946-1963, 1965; NY A, NY N*
Managerial Career: *1964, 1972-1975, 1984-1985; NY A, NY N*

Charlie Berry
Berry, Charles Francis
B: Oct 18, 1902   D: Sep 6, 1972

Pos: C	BA: .267
Hits: 539	HRs: 23
RBI: 256	BBs: 160

After a professional football career in the 1920s, Berry played baseball in the major leagues until he was shipped to the minors. He then became an AL umpire.
Playing Career: *1925, 1928-1936, 1938; Phi A, Bos A, Chi A*
Umpiring Career: *1942-1962; AL*

Ken Berry
Berry, Allen Kent
B: May 10, 1941

Pos: OF	BA: .255
Hits: 1,053	HRs: 58
RBI: 343	BBs: 298

Berry was an exceptional fielder who led the league in fielding percentage three times. He captured two Gold Glove Awards, and he made the AL All-Star Team in 1967. He once fielded 510 chances in a row without an error.
Playing Career: *1962-1975; Chi A, Cal A, Mil A, Cle A*

Bob Bescher
Bescher, Robert Henry
B: Feb 25, 1884   D: Nov 29, 1942

Pos: OF	BA: .258
Hits: 1,171	HRs: 28
RBI: 345	BBs: 619

Very fast and having a good eye, Bescher was an ideal leadoff hitter. He stole 427 bases, scoring 749 runs, most of them in an eight-year period. He led the NL in runs scored in 1912 and walks in 1913. He pilfered the stolen base title from 1909 to 1912. His top mark of 81 stolen bases was the modern NL record until Maury Wills broke it in 1962 when he swiped 104. It was unfortunate that Bescher seldom played for a winning team.
Playing Career: *1908-1918; Cin N, NY N, StL N, Cle A*

Huck Betts
Betts, Walter Martin
B: Feb 18, 1897   D: Jun 13, 1987

Pos: P	ERA: 3.93
W-L: 61-68	SOs: 323
ShOs: 8	Saves: 16

Betts, who loved huckleberries, had two different shots at the big leagues. The first time he was a relief pitcher. The second time Betts was a winning starter for the Braves, who were struggling to break into the first division.
Playing Career: *1920-1925, 1932-1935; Phi N, Bos N*

Jim Bibby.

Jim Bibby
Bibby, James Blair
B: Oct 29, 1944

Pos: P	ERA: 3.76
W-L: 111-101	SOs: 1,079
ShOs: 19	No-hitters: 1

Bibby was a college basketball star, whose brother Henry played in the NBA. Bibby led the NL in winning percentage in 1980, the year he was selected to the All-Star team. He once retired 27 consecutive batters in a game after surrendering a leadoff single.
Playing Career: *1972-1981, 1983-1984; StL N, Tex A, Cle A, Pit N*

Louis Bierbauer
Bierbauer, Louis W.
B: Sep 23, 1865   D: Jan 31, 1926

Pos: 2B	BA: .267
Hits: 1,521	HRs: 33
RBI: 706 (inc.)	BBs: 268

The Allegheny base ball club of Pittsburgh signed Bierbauer to a contract in 1891, in violation of the agreement that settled the Players' League, since all players were supposed to return to their 1889 clubs. When Bierbauer signed and played in Pittsburgh, his former team, the Philadelphia Athletics, charged them with open piracy and began to call the club "Pirates." Bierbauer hit .300 or more three times, reaching his peak in 1890 with a .306 mark.
Playing Career: *1886-1898; Phi AA, Brk P, Pit N, StL N*

Bob Bescher (l) shakes hands with Ty Cobb.

Carson Bigbee
Bigbee, Carson Lee
B: Mar 31, 1895   D: Oct 17, 1964

Pos: OF   BA: .287
Hits: 1,205   HRs: 17
RBI: 324   BBs: 344

Bigbee was the regular right fielder for the Pirates for seven years. When the ball got livelier, so did Bigbee's average; he hit .323 in 1921 and .350 in 1922. He hit .333 in the 1925 World Series for the champion Pirates.
Playing Career: *1916-1926; Pit N*

Larry Biittner
Biittner, Lawrence David
B: Jul 27, 1945

Pos: OF, 1B   BA: .273
Hits: 861   HRs: 29
RBI: 354   BBs: 236

Biittner was a successful pinch hitter, ranking 10th on the all-time list when he retired. He batted over .300 twice. His most productive season was 1977, when he hit .298 with 12 home runs and 28 doubles. He even pitched once, but posted a 54.00 ERA.
Playing Career: *1970-1983; Was A, Tex A, Mon N, Chi N, Cin N*

Jack Billingham
Billingham, John Eugene
B: Feb 21, 1943

Pos: P   ERA: 3.83
W-L: 145-113   SOs: 1,141
ShOs: 27   Saves: 15

Billingham has credentials as the best money pitcher of all time. He was 2-0 in three World Series, with a 0.36 ERA, the best in history. He was a top hurler, yet never won 20 games in a season. He was chosen for an All-Star team, but never got into the game.

Billingham was trained as a relief pitcher in the Dodger system. Traded to the Astros, he went into the starting rotation where he found his calling, winning 10 or more games for the next 10 years. Billingham led the NL in shutouts with 7 in 1973. The Reds won four division titles in five years as Billingham twice captured 19 games. He gave up Hank Aaron's 714th home run in his first start of 1974.
Playing Career: *1968-1980; LA N, Hou N, Cin N, Det A, Bos A*

Doug Bird
Bird, James Douglas
B: Mar 5, 1950

Pos: P   ERA: 3.99
W-L: 73-60   SOs: 680
ShOs: 3   Saves: 60

Bird was the closer for the Royals prior to their acquisition of Dan Quisenberry. After three successful years in the bullpen, Bird became a starter with mixed results. In all he pitched in six games during three ALCS, winning one and losing one with a 2.35 ERA.
Playing Career: *1973-1983; KC A, Phi N, NY A, Chi N, Bos A*

Joe Birmingham
Birmingham, Joseph Leo
B: Aug 6, 1884   D: Apr 24, 1946

Pos: OF   BA: .254
Hits: 667   HRs: 6
RBI: 265   BBs: 129
Managerial Record
Won: 170   Lost: 191   Pct: .471

Birmingham attended Cornell University before joining the Cleveland team, then called the Naps. He stole 108 bases during his career, and scored the only run in Addie Joss's perfect game. Birmingham's best year was 1911 when he hit .304.
Playing Career: *1906-1914; Cle A*
Managerial Career: *1912-1915; Cle A*

Max Bishop.

Max Bishop
Bishop, Max Frederick
B: Sep 5, 1899   D: Feb 24, 1962

Pos: 2B   BA: .271
Hits: 1,216   HRs: 41
RBI: 379   BBs: 1,153

Averaging a walk in every five at-bats, Max Bishop drew nearly .86 bases on balls per

Jack Billingham throwing for the Reds in 1974.

game for his career. His .423 on-base average is 13th on the all-time list. Bishop led off for Connie Mack's Athletics and scored 966 runs in 12 seasons.

Bishop arrived in the majors late in his career because he had been playing for the Baltimore Orioles when they were the greatest minor league dynasty ever, winners of seven straight pennants. Once Bishop got to the big leagues, he made the most of it. Leading the AL in walks with 128 in 1929, he drew an average of 107 over a 10-year period, scoring an average of 89.5 runs annually over the same period. He played in three World Series and led the league in fielding three times. After his major league career he coached baseball at the U.S. Naval Academy.
Playing Career: *1924-1935; Phi A, Bos A*

Del Bissonette
Bissonette, Adelphia Louis
B: Sep 6, 1899   D: Jun 9, 1972

Pos: 1B	BA: .305
Hits: 699	HRs: 66
RBI: 391	BBs: 233
Managerial Record	
Won: 25 Lost: 36 Pct: .410	

Bissonette's career was injury-plagued but power-packed. A Brooklyn limerick went: "The Dodgers have Del Bissonette. No meal has he ever missed yet. The question that rises is one that surprises: Who paid for all Del Bissonette?" He drove in 381 runs in four years.
Playing Career: *1928-1931, 1933; Brk N*
Managerial Career: *1945; Bos N*

Bud Black
Black, Harry Ralston
B: Jun 30, 1957

Pos: P	ERA: 3.74
W-L: 113-112	SOs: 977
ShOs: 12	Saves: 11

The Houdini of baseball, Bud Black brought his career back from the dead. After a stellar season in 1984 when he went 17-12, Black floundered and was traded. Finding new life as a starter in 1988, Black is now a solid fourth or fifth man in a pitching rotation.
Playing Career: *1981-; Sea A, KC A, Cle A, Tor A, SF N*

Joe Black
Black, Joseph
B: Feb 8, 1924

Pos: P	ERA: 3.91
W-L: 30-12	SOs: 222
ShOs: 0	Saves: 25

Coming from the Negro Leagues, Joe Black was Rookie of the Year in 1952 when he went 15-4, with 15 saves for the Dodgers. He started and won the first game of the 1952 World Series. Black posted a .714 career won-lost percentage.
Playing Career: *1952-1957; Brk N, Cin N, Was A*

Lena Blackburne
Blackburne, Russell Aubrey
B: Oct 23, 1886   D: Feb 29, 1968

Pos: SS, 3B, 1B	BA: .214
Hits: 387	HRs: 4
RBI: 139	BBs: 162
Managerial Record	
Won: 99 Lost: 133 Pct: .427	

The "baseball mud" company that supplies the substance used to rub up baseballs before games was founded by Blackburne. His inheritance of two million dollars from a Philadelphian uncle in 1911 made Blackburne the first player to be worth more than $1 million.
Playing Career: *1910, 1912, 1914-1915, 1918-1919, 1927, 1929; Chi A, Cin N, Bos N, Phi N*
Managerial Career: *1928-1929; Chi A*

Ewell Blackwell

Ewell Blackwell
Blackwell, Ewell (The Whip)
B: Oct 23, 1922

Pos: P	ERA: 3.30
W-L: 82-78	SOs: 839
ShOs: 16	No-hitters: 2

In his era, Ewell Blackwell was the meanest, most difficult right-handed pitcher that a right-handed batter could face. He came within two outs of tossing back-to-back no-hitters. The 6'6" stringbean hurler threw a side-winding pitch that appeared to come from third base. Hitters batted only .235 off Blackwell during his entire career. In 1950 they hit an NL low .210 off the right-hander.

Blackwell's best year was 1947 when he won 22, completed 23 games, and struck out 197, all NL highs. He was selected for the NL All-Star team six consecutive years, and he pitched in the 1952 World Series. Arm problems sometimes slowed the snap in the "Whip" notably during the 1948 and 1949 seasons, and again in 1952. But after his retirement in 1955, batters hoped that there would never be another pitcher like him.
Playing Career: *1942, 1946-1953, 1955; Cin N, NY A, KC A*

Ray Blades
Blades, Francis Raymond
B: Aug 6, 1896   D: May 18, 1979

Pos: OF	BA: .301
Hits: 726	HRs: 50
RBI: 340	BBs: 331
Managerial Record	
Won: 107 Lost: 85 Pct: .557	

Blades played on four Cardinal pennant-winning teams from 1926 to 1931. He was a high-average hitter albeit in a limited role. Blades managed the Cardinals to 92 wins in 1939, but was fired when the club started slowly in 1940.
Playing Career: *1922-1928, 1930-1932; StL N*
Managerial Career: *1939-1940, 1948; StL N, Brk N*

George Blaeholder
Blaeholder, George Franklin
B: Jan 26, 1904   D: Dec 29, 1947

Pos: P	ERA: 4.54
W-L: 104-125	SOs: 572
ShOs: 13	Saves: 12

Reputed to be the inventor of the "slider," Blaeholder could have used some hitting as he spent most of his career as a workhorse starter for the hapless Browns. He led the AL in shutouts with four in 1929, and went 15-19 in 1933.
Playing Career: *1925, 1927-1936; StL A, Phi A, Cle A*

Paul Blair
Blair, Paul L.
B: Feb 1, 1944

Pos: OF	BA: .239
Hits: 1,513	HRs: 67
RBI: 620	BBs: 449

Blair was well on his way to a Hall of Fame career when felled by a pitch from Ken Tatum. He never again hit 20 home runs or scored 80 runs in a season. Even so, Blair was an excellent center fielder who won eight Gold Glove Awards. He led the AL in triples in 1967. Nine times he swatted more than 20 doubles. He stole 171 bases in a career that included two All-Star Games. Blair also appeared in eight LCS and six World Series.
Playing Career: *1964-1980; Bal A, NY A, Cin N*

Paul Blair.

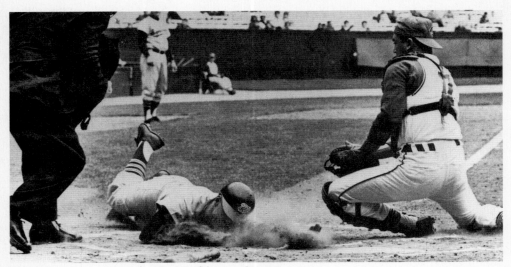

Don Blasingame scores for the Washington Senators.

Sheriff Blake
Blake, John Frederick
B: Sep 17, 1899   D: Oct 31, 1982

Pos: P	ERA: 4.13
W-L: 87-102	SOs: 621
ShOs: 11	Saves: 8

The law enforcer for the Cubs' pitching staff during the 1920s was Sheriff Blake. Of his 87 career wins, he won 81 from 1924 to 1930, and led the NL in shutouts with four in 1928. Blake was the losing pitcher in the famous 10-run inning during the 1929 Fall Classic.
Playing Career: *1920, 1924-1931, 1937; Pit N, Chi N, Phi N, StL A, StL N*

Ted Blankenship
Blankenship, Theodore
B: May 10, 1901   D: Jan 14, 1945

Pos: P	ERA: 4.32
W-L: 77-79	SOs: 378
ShOs: 8	Saves : 4

Ted Blankenship's best year was 1925 when he went 17-8 with a 3.03 ERA, and battled the Cubs in a 2-2, 18-inning tie during the World Series. He was an ace starter for the White Sox during the 1920s, when the team was struggling to overcome the 1919 Black Sox scandal.
Playing Career: *1922-1930; Chi A*

Cy Blanton
Blanton, Darrell Elijah
B: Jul 6, 1908   D: Sep 13, 1945

Pos: P	ERA: 3.55
W-L: 68-71	SOs: 611
ShOs: 14	Saves: 4

A minor league strikeout champion, Cy Blanton burst on to the NL scene with an 18-13 record, leading the league in shutouts with four, and in ERA at 2.58. That year batters hit only .229 off the neophyte hurler. He was selected for the All-Star team twice.
Playing Career: *1934-1942; Pit N, Phi N*

Don Blasingame
Blasingame, Don Lee
B: Mar 16, 1932

Pos: 2B	BA: .258
Hits: 1,366	HRs: 21
RBI: 308	BBs: 552

Blasingame hit into fewer double plays, one in every 123 at-bats, than any other player in history except Don Buford. Four times Blasingame broke up no-hitters, twice in August 1963. The hustling infielder made the 1958 NL All-Star team after having scored 108 runs the year before. He followed his All-Star year with an even better season, and he played in the 1961 World Series. Blasingame finished his playing career in Japan.
Playing Career: *1955-1966; StL N, SF N, Cin N, Was A, KC A*

Steve Blass
Blass, Stephen Robert
B: Apr 18, 1942

Pos: P	ERA: 3.63
W-L: 103-76	SOs: 896
ShOs: 16	Saves: 2

On the roller coaster of major league baseball, Blass went from star pitcher to emotionally devastated has-been to top media broadcaster. The star of the 1971 World Series, Blass pitched two complete game victories. He was even better the next year, going 19-8 with a 2.49 ERA and an All-Star Game performance. Seriously affected by Roberto Clemente's death, Blass performed poorly for the following two seasons and he retired to the broadcasting booth.
Playing Career: *1964, 1966-1974; Pit N*

Curt Blefary
Blefary, Curtis Leroy
B: Jul 5, 1943

Pos: OF, 1B, C	BA: .237
Hits: 699	HRs: 112
RBI: 382	BBs: 456

Curt Blefary was the 1965 AL Rookie of the Year when he hit 22 home runs and had 70 RBI. Fielding problems led to several switches in position, which he blamed for a decline offensively. He caught Tom Phoebus's no-hitter.
Playing Career: *1965-1972; Bal A, Hou N, NY A, Oak A, SD N*

Jimmy Bloodworth
Bloodworth, James Henry
B: Jul 26, 1917

Pos: 2B, 3B	BA: .248
Hits: 874	HRs: 62
RBI: 453	BBs: 200

An infielder with consistent if moderate skills, Bloodworth played major league baseball for 11 seasons stretched over 15 years. Afterwards, he took his consistency to the minors where he managed in the Three-I, Tri-State and South Atlantic leagues.
Playing Career: *1937, 1939-1943, 1946-1947, 1949-1951; Was A, Det A, Pit N, Cin N, Phi N*

Lu Blue
Blue, Luzerne Atwell
B: Mar 5, 1897   D: Jul 28, 1958

Pos: 1B	BA: .287
Hits: 1,696	HRs: 44
RBI: 692	BBs: 1,092

Blue was a good switch hitter who drew walks, enabling him to get on base. He compiled a .402 lifetime on-base average, and scored 1,151 runs. He also stole 185 bases and swatted 319 doubles. In his rookie year, Blue hit .308, scored 103 runs and fielded well enough to move Harry Heilmann off first base into the outfield. Blue stayed at first despite his lack of height, and his less than cordial relations with Tiger manager Ty Cobb. Blue hit .300 or more five times.
Playing Career: *1921-1933; Det A, StL A, Chi A, Brk N*

Vida Blue
Blue, Vida Rochelle
B: Jul 28, 1949

Pos: P	ERA: 3.36
W-L: 209-161	SOs: 2,175
ShOs: 37	No-hitters: 2

In the midst of Vida Blue's contract dispute with the A's, President Richard Nixon called Blue "the best pitcher in baseball." Called up in 1970 at age 21, Blue tossed a no-hitter against the division champion Twins. In 1971 he had 17 wins before the All-Star break. Blue finished the season with a 24-8 record, 301 strikeouts, and league-leading figures of a 1.82 ERA, 8 shutouts, and opponents' batting average of .189. He won the Cy Young and MVP Awards that year.

The following spring, Blue held out for more money, getting the attention of the president, the commissioner and baseball fans. It was at this time that Blue developed the drug problem that would dog him the rest

Bert Blyleven (in hat), October 5, 1979.

Vida Blue pitching for the San Francisco Giants in 1981.

of his career. Blue rebounded to win 109 games in the next six years, but he was never again the dominating pitcher he had been in 1971. Selected for six All-Star teams, Blue pitched in five LCS and three World Series.
Playing Career: *1969-1983, 1985-1986; Oak A, SF N, KC A*

Ossie Bluege
Bluege, Oswald Louis
B: Oct 24, 1900   D: Oct 14, 1985

Pos: SS, 3B	BA: .272
Hits: 1,751	HRs: 43
RBI: 848	BBs: 724
Managerial Record	
Won: 375 Lost: 394 Pct: .488	

Bluege played in three World Series and the 1935 All-Star Game. Never drawing more than $10,000 a year, Bluege worked the off-season as an accountant. Owner Calvin Griffith ordered him to quit, fearing that the detailed work would ruin his batting eye – but Griffith did not raise Bluege's salary! Managing the Senators, Bluege finished second in 1943 and 1945.
Playing Career: *1922-1939; Was A*
Managerial Career: *1943-1947; Was A*

Bert Blyleven
Blyleven, Rik Aalbert
B: Apr 6, 1951

Pos: P	ERA: 3.31
W-L: 287-250	SOs: 3,701
ShOs: 60	No-hitters: 1

The big Dutchman was named AL Rookie of the Year in 1970. AL managers voted Blyle-

ven's curveball the best in the league, but batters could have told them that. His 3,701 strikeouts rank him third behind Nolan Ryan and Steve Carlton on the all-time list.

Blyleven won 20 games in a season just once, in 1973, but he led the AL in shutouts three times and is ninth on the all-time shutout roster. He also led the AL in innings pitched in 1985 and 1986, and in strikeouts in 1986. He was selected for the All-Star squad twice. Blyleven battled injuries in his attempts to hang on and win 300 games, but he seems like a shoo-in for the Hall of Fame. In his prime, he could beat any team on any day.
Playing Career: *1970-1990, 1992; Min A, Tex A, Pit N, Cle A, Cal A*

Bruce Bochte
Bochte, Bruce Anton
B: Nov 12, 1950

Pos: 1B, OF, DH	BA: .282
Hits: 1,478	HRs: 100
RBI: 658	BBs: 653

Bochte retired abruptly at the end of the 1982 season, explaining, ''I was the Mariners' player rep for three years and became aware of a cold, impersonal attitude on the part of management, and wanted no part of that.'' Bochte's best year was 1979 when he hit .316, slammed 38 doubles and 16 home runs, and compiled 100 RBI. He was selected for the All-Star team that year. In 1984 the A's lured him back for three more productive years.
Playing Career: *1974-1982, 1984-1986; Cal A, Cle A, Sea A, Oak A*

Mike Boddicker
Boddicker, Michael James
B: Aug 23, 1957

Pos: P	ERA: 3.80
W-L: 134-116	SOs: 1,330
ShOs: 16	Saves: 3

Boddicker invented the fosh ball, a cross between the knuckler and a palm ball, while with the Orioles. As a rookie in 1983 he went 16-6 with a 2.77 ERA and threw five shutouts. In the ALCS that year he threw a shutout, striking out a record 14 batters. Boddicker also tossed a three-hit, complete game victory in the World Series. He was named AL Rookie Pitcher of the Year. The next year Boddicker led the AL in wins and ERA. In 1992 he was switched to the bullpen.
Playing Career: *1980-; Bal A, Bos A, KC A, Mil A*

Ping Bodie
Bodie, Frank Stephan
B: Oct 8, 1887   D: Dec 17, 1961

Pos: OF	BA: .275
Hits: 1,011	HRs: 43
RBI: 516	BBs: 312

Ping Bodie, born Francesco Stephano Pezzollo, chose his nickname because it approximated the sound of the ball coming off his bat. Said columnist Bugs Baer of Ping's base stealing, "There was larceny in his heart, but his feet were honest."
Playing Career: *1911-1914, 1917-1921; Chi A, Phi A, NY A*

Joe Boehling
Boehling, John Joseph
B: Mar 20, 1891   D: Sep 8, 1941

Pos: P	ERA: 2.97
W-L: 55-50	SOs: 386
ShOs: 9	Saves: 5

Boehling went 17-7 with a 2.14 ERA in his rookie year, and was the catalyst in the Senators' surprise second-place finish in 1913. He dropped out of baseball for several years but returned to a long minor league career.
Playing Career: *1912-1917, 1920; Was A, Cle A*

Wade Boggs
Boggs, Wade Anthony
B: Jun 15, 1958

Pos: 3B, DH	BA: .335
Hits: 2,267	HRs: 87
RBI: 746	BBs: 1,078

George Brett and Wade Boggs will be remembered as the best hitters of the 1980s. As a rookie in 1982, Boggs batted .349. That turned out to be an "off" year. He topped .350 in five of the next six years, winning five batting titles. A terrific leadoff batter despite an apparent lack of speed, Boggs scored 1,150 runs, and possesses a .428 on-base average. Boggs was named AL All-Star third base-

Wade Boggs.

man for eight consecutive years. He hit .438 in the 1990 ALCS. Boggs had a hidden .400 season, from June 13, 1985 through June 8, 1986, when he hit exactly .400.

A bit of an odd duck, Boggs has superstitions involving the number seven. He warms up at 7:17, does seven wind sprints and takes seven warmup swings. Boggs also believes that eating red meat slows reactions and clogs the arteries, so he eats chicken. The poultry diet was also used by a 19th-century pitcher named Charles Pabor, who was widely known as the "Chicken Man."
Playing Career: *1982-; Bos A, NY A*

Bobby Bolin
Bolin, Bobby Donald
B: Jan 29, 1939

Pos: P	ERA: 3.40
W-L: 88-75	SOs: 1,175
ShOs: 10	Saves: 50

Bobby Bolin put together a .540 won-lost percentage over 13 years. A sidearming right-hander, he pitched in the World Series in 1962. Bolin posted a 1.99 ERA with a 10-5 record in 1968. He won the first game in Brewer history.
Playing Career: *1961-1973; SF N, Mil A, Bos A*

Frank Bolling
Bolling, Frank Elmore
B: Nov 16, 1931

Pos: 2B	BA: .254
Hits: 1,415	HRs: 106
RBI: 556	BBs: 462

Frank Bolling played every inning of every game in his major league career at second base. He led the league in fielding four times, winning a Gold Glove Award in 1958. Bolling was named to the NL All-Star team twice. Bolling's older brother Milt played seven years of major league ball, and their uncle Jack Bolling played briefly for the Phillies and Dodgers.
Playing Career: *1954, 1956-1966; Det A, Mil N, Atl N*

Tommy Bond
Bond, Thomas Henry
B: Apr 2, 1856   D: Jan 24, 1941

Pos: P	ERA: 2.25 (inc.)
W-L: 234-115	SOs: 860 (inc.)
ShOs: 35	No-hitters: 0
Managerial Record	
Won: 2 Lost: 4 Pct: .333	

Tommy Bond is the only major league pitcher since 1876 to win 40 or more games three years in a row. Accused of ruining catchers with his cannonball delivery, Bond played right field in 1875 while learning the curveball from teammate Candy Cummings. The next year Bond had mastered the pitch and returned to the box to hurl 45 of Hartford's first 47 games. At that point he was suspended for the rest of the season for publicly accusing the team captain of throwing games.

He moved to Boston where he had three 40-game seasons, leading the Red Stockings to two pennants and one second-place finish. Bond's reign as the superior NL hurler came abruptly to an end due to lack of a crack catcher. He managed at Worcester, and later tried a comeback with Boston in the Union Association. In retirement he worked with young pitchers, including John Clarkson and Tim Keefe.
Playing Career: *1874-1882, 1884; Brk Atlantics n, Har Dark Blues n, Har N, Bos N, Wor N, Bos U, Ind AA*
Managerial Career: *1882; Wor N*

Barry Bonds
Bonds, Barry
B: Jul 24, 1964

Pos: OF	BA: .283
Hits: 1,165	HRs: 222
RBI: 679	BBs: 737

Barry Bonds signed a free-agent contract with the Giants that is reported to be worth more than $40 million, or roughly half the value of the poorer franchises in baseball. Bonds is the

Barry Bonds.

ultimate franchise player. After his Pittsburgh sidekick Bobby Bonilla signed a lucrative agreement with the Mets, Bonds was left to almost single-handedly bring the division title to the Pirates, their third straight with Bonds batting in the power position.

The son of a top major leaguer, Bobby Bonds, Barry has developed much faster into a much better player than any scout imagined. In 1992 he slugged .624, a rarefied mark reached only once in the NL since 1981. Bonds has played in two All-Star Games and three NLCS. He is patient at the plate – a rare ability for one so young. His walks outnumber his strikeouts; in 1992 he walked 127 times and fanned only 69 times.

Playing Career: *1986-; Pit N, SF N*

Bobby Bonds
Bonds, Bobby Lee
B: Mar 15, 1946

Pos: OF	BA: .268
Hits: 1,886	HRs: 332
RBI: 1,024	BBs: 914

With great power and speed, Bobby Bonds was touted as the next Willie Mays. In 1969 Bonds hit 32 home runs and stole 45 bases to become only the fourth person in the "30-30"

club. In following years he did it again, five times in all, and in both leagues. Bonds swiped 461 bases and scored 1,258 runs in his career. He hit 35 leadoff home runs, 11 in one season, both records at the time. He was an All-Star three times, and won three Gold Glove Awards. He also struck out 1,757 times, placing him sixth on the all-time list.

After seven seasons with the Giants, Bonds became a nomad, spending the next seven years with seven teams, all of them looking for his instant offense. In 1979, at age 33, he hit 25 home runs and stole 34 bases for the Indians. His son Barry has hit 222 dingers to give the Bondses the lead in the father-son home run derby.

Playing Career: *1968-1981; SF N, NY A, Cal A, Chi A, Tex A, Cle A, StL N, Chi N*

Bill Bonham
Bonham, William Gordon
B: Oct 1, 1948

Pos: P	ERA: 4.00
W-L: 75-83	SOs: 985
ShOs: 4	Saves: 11

A hard thrower, Bill Bonham sometimes had control problems, and was plagued by poor team support. When he was traded to the

Reds his won-lost record improved to 22-13 over three years. He alternated between starting and relieving during his career.

Playing Career: *1971-1980; Chi N, Cin N*

Tiny Bonham
Bonham, Ernest Edward
B: Aug 16, 1913   D: Sep 15, 1949

Pos: P	ERA: 3.06
W-L: 103-72	SOs: 478
ShOs: 21	Saves: 9

Bonham was a high-quality pitcher beseiged by chronic back problems. Using control and a forkball, he recorded a league-leading 21-5 record in 1942. Bonham was selected for All-Star duty twice, and he pitched in three World Series.

Playing Career: *1940-1949; NY A, Pit N*

Bobby Bonilla
Bonilla, Roberto Martin Antonio, Jr.
B: Feb 23, 1963

Pos: OF	BA: .277
Hits: 1,173	HRs: 169
RBI: 683	BBs: 535

Bonilla was originally signed by the Pirates, who lost him to the White Sox when they failed to protect him in the minor league draft. Pirates General Manager Syd Thrift reacquired Bonilla, who showed his gratitude by hitting .300. Named to the All-Star squad four consecutive years, Bonilla averaged 101 RBI, 24 home runs, 99 runs scored and 38 doubles during that time. Bonilla then signed a lucrative free-agent contract with the Mets.

Playing Career: *1986-; Chi A, Pit N, NY N*

Bobby Bonds, a member of the "30-30" club, with the San Francisco Giants in 1973.

Bobby Bonilla.

Barry Bonnell
Bonnell, Robert Barry
B: Oct 27, 1953

Pos: OF   BA: .272
Hits: 833   HRs: 56
RBI: 355   BBs: 229

Bonnell was a platoon outfielder who hit for average, but seldom displayed power. His best season was 1983 when he hit .318. Unfortunately for him, he was trying to break into the Blue Jays outfield–the best hitting and throwing threesome of the 1980s.
Playing Career: *1977-1986; Atl N, Tor A, Sea A*

Zeke Bonura
Bonura, Zeke
B: Sep 20, 1908

Pos: 1B   BA: .307
Hits: 1,099   HRs: 119
RBI: 704   BBs: 404

Despite leading AL first basemen in fielding percentage three times, Bonura was criticized for his lack of mobility around the bag. Paid to hit home runs, he pounded 27 in spacious Comiskey Park, where he broke in hitting .302 and slugging .545 with 110 RBI in 1934.
Playing Career: *1934-1940; Chi A, Was A, NY N, Chi N*

Bob Boone
Boone, Robert Raymond
B: Nov 19, 1947

Pos: C   BA: .254
Hits: 1,810   HRs: 105
RBI: 817   BBs: 646

Bob Boone caught more games than any other receiver in the history of baseball at his retirement. As a defensive catcher he was one of the best, leading the league in assists in 1973 and 1974. His 89 assists in 1973 was the most for a rookie since Johnny Bench had 108. With the Angels 1982-1988, Boone tossed out 45 percent of would-be base stealers. AL runners had never seen such an arm.

Boone played on six division-winning teams and on one World Championship team, the 1980 Phillies. He was selected for the All-Star team four times. The son of Ray Boone, Bob seemed to improve with age and responsibility. He has a .311 lifetime average in postseason games, including .400 for the Phillies in the 1977 NLCS and .455 for the Angels in the 1986 ALCS. He swatted .412 in the 1980 World Series.
Playing Career: *1972-1990; Phi N, Cal A, KC A*

Ray Boone.

Ray Boone
Boone, Raymond Otis
B: Jul 27, 1923

Pos: SS, 3B, 1B   BA: .275
Hits: 1,260   HRs: 151
RBI: 737   BBs: 608

Ray Boone was hitting .355 in the Texas League in late 1948 when the Indians' shortstop, Lou Boudreau, was injured. Boone was called up in time to earn a World Series share. Traded to Detroit where he moved to third base, Boone concentrated on his hitting. His average shot up 40 points, his homers doubled, and his RBI total doubled, leading the league with 116 in 1955. He was selected to the All-Star team in 1954 and 1956.
Playing Career: *1948-1960; Cle A, Det A, Chi A, KC A, Mil N, Bos A*

Pedro Borbon
Borbon y Rodriguez, Pedro
B: Dec 2, 1946

Pos: P   ERA: 3.52
W-L: 69-39   SOs: 409
ShOs: 0   Saves: 80

Borbon was one of the role players who fit into the Big Red Machine of the 1970s, making it almost invincible. He was the top reliever, but not the only good one. Borbon's best years were 1972-1977, when the Reds won four division titles in six years.
Playing Career: *1969-1980; Cal A, Cin N, SF N, StL N*

Defensive weapon Bob Boone in his crouch while with the Phillies.

Frenchy Bordagaray
Bordagaray, Stanley George
B: Jan 3, 1910

Pos: OF, 2B, 3B	BA: .283
Hits: 745	HRs: 14
RBI: 270	BBs: 173

Frenchy showed up at spring training in 1935 with a mustache, and baseball has never been the same. When Bordagaray was once fined for spitting at an umpire he exclaimed, "That's more than I expectorated." He played in two World Series.
Playing Career: *1934-1939, 1941-1945; Chi A, Brk N, StL N, Cin N, NY A*

Steve Boros
Boros, Stephen
B: Sep 3, 1936

Pos: 3B	BA: .245
Hits: 308	HRs: 26
RBI: 149	BBs: 181

Managerial Record
Won: 168   Lost: 200   Pct: .457

Boros signed a $25,000 bonus contract with the Tigers off the University of Michigan campus. After a promising rookie year, Boros broke his collarbone and his play never quite recovered. He stayed in baseball as a coach and manager.
Playing Career: *1957-1958, 1961-1965; Det A, Chi N, Cin N*
Managerial Career: *1983-1986; Oak A, SD N*

Hank Borowy
Borowy, Henry Ludwig
B: May 12, 1916

Pos: P	ERA: 3.50
W-L: 108-82	SOs: 690
ShOs: 17	Saves: 7

A wartime starter for the Yankees, Borowy posted a 15-4 record his rookie year. In a surprise move, the Yanks traded him to the Cubs in mid-1945, and he went 11-2, becoming the ace of the staff. Borowy has a 3-2 record in six games in three World Series – in 1942 and 1943 with the Yankees and in 1945 with the Cubs.
Playing Career: *1942-1951; NY A, Chi N, Phi N, Pit N, Det A*

Dick Bosman
Bosman, Richard Allen
B: Feb 17, 1944

Pos: P	ERA: 3.67
W-L: 82-85	SOs: 757
ShOs: 10	No-hitters: 1

Bosman tossed a no-hitter, and he almost had a perfect game, but lost it on his own error. Spending most of his career with the Senators/Rangers organization, Bosman won the league ERA title in 1969. His 11-4 season helped the Oakland A's to a division title in 1975.
Playing Career: *1966-1976; Was A, Tex A, Cle A, Oak A*

Lyman Bostock
Bostock, Lyman Wesley, Jr.
B: Nov 22, 1950   D: Sep 23, 1978

Pos: OF	BA: .311
Hits: 624	HRs: 23
RBI: 250	BBs: 171

Lyman Bostock was killed in a tragic accident just as his career was blossoming. In 1977 he was runner-up to teammate Rod Carew for the batting title with a .336 average, 104 runs scored, 36 doubles, 12 triples, 14 home runs, and 90 RBI.
Playing Career: *1975-1978; Min A, Cal A*

Daryl Boston
Boston, Daryl Lamont
B: Jan 4, 1963

Pos: OF	BA: .251
Hits: 641	HRs: 79
RBI: 264	BBs: 231

The New York Mets counted heavily on Boston, but he was inexplicably inconsistent, twice hitting over .270 and three times under .230. He ripped three singles in his debut with the White Sox after having hit .312 in the minor league American Association.
Playing Career: *1984-; Chi A, NY N, Col N*

Dave Boswell
Boswell, David Wilson
B: Jan 20, 1945

Pos: P	ERA: 3.52
W-L: 68-56	SOs: 882
ShOs: 6	No-hitters: 0

When Boswell fanned 204 batters in 1967, he made the Twins the first team ever to have three pitchers with 200 or more K's. Two years later he had a fistfight with manager Billy Martin, and won only four more games the rest of his career.
Playing Career: *1964-1971; Min A, Det A, Bal A*

Ken Boswell
Boswell, Kenneth George
B: Feb 23, 1946

Pos: 2B	BA: .248
Hits: 625	HRs: 31
RBI: 244	BBs: 246

After making three errors on Opening Day for the 1969 Mets, Boswell went to work on his fielding. The following year he led all major league second basemen in fielding and had 85 consecutive errorless games. Boswell played in two World Series.
Playing Career: *1967-1977; NY N, Hou N*

Jim Bottomley
Bottomley, James Leroy (Sunny Jim)
B: Apr 23, 1900   D: Dec 11, 1959
Hall of Fame 1974

Pos: 1B	BA: .310
Hits: 2,313	HRs: 219
RBI: 1,422	BBs: 664

Managerial Record
Won: 21   Lost: 56   Pct: .273

Sunny Jim, named for his happy disposition, drove in 12 runs in a 1924 game on two homers, a double, and three singles, for the highest RBI total by one player in a game. Detractors say this alone got him into the Hall of Fame, but he hit over .300 eight times, and batted in 100 or more runs six years in a row. He helped the Cards win four pennants.

The NL MVP in 1928, Bottomley led the league in RBI and triples and tied the lead for homers with Hack Wilson. In 1931 Bottomley lost in the closest batting race ever: teammate Chick Hafey won with a .3489 mark, Bill Terry finished second at .3486, and Bottomley batted .3482. The Cardinals traded him to the Reds but he eventually returned to Sportsman's Park, where he played for the Browns. He hit .295 for them in 1936.
Playing Career: *1922-1937; StL N, Cin N, StL A*
Managerial Career: *1937; StL A*

"Sunny Jim" Bottomley (2nd from r) with (l-r) Hafey, Frisch, and Harper.

Lou Boudreau.

Lou Boudreau
Boudreau, Louis
B: Jul 17, 1917
Hall of Fame 1970

Pos: SS	BA: .295
Hits: 1,779	HRs: 68
RBI: 789	BBs: 796

Managerial Record
Won: 1,162   Lost: 1,224   Pct: .487

In 1948 Indians owner Bill Veeck tried to trade Boudreau to the Browns. Irate Tribe fans petitioned to keep Boudreau and trade Veeck. Boudreau started the season determined to prove his owner wrong. He had a superb year, hitting .355, with 18 home runs and 106 RBI. Player-manager Boudreau pinch hit winning runs, inspired teammates to career years, and led the Indians in a four-way pennant race. In the one-game playoff, Boudreau sprung a surprise rookie starter on the Sox, but won it himself with four hits, including two home runs. The Indians won the World Series, and Boudreau was chosen MVP by more than 100 votes.

Selected for eight All-Star teams, Boudreau led the AL in doubles three times, and he won the 1944 batting title. He also led AL shortstops in fielding eight times in nine years, but after 1948 everything Boudreau did was anticlimatic.
Playing Career: *1938-1952; Cle A, Bos A*
Managerial Career: *1942-1950, 1952-1957, 1960; Cle A, Bos A, KC A, Chi N*

Jim Bouton
Bouton, James Alan (Bulldog)
B: Mar 8, 1939

Pos: P	ERA: 3.57
W-L: 62-63	SOs: 720
ShOs: 11	Saves: 6

Jim Bouton wrote *Ball Four*, the best-selling baseball book of all time. A close-up of locker room mentality and the professional athlete off the field, *Ball Four* touched off rounds of denials and animosity from players and officials. It rubbed management the wrong way just at the time the Players' Union was beginning to make demands. It also got Bouton a job as a sportscaster. He used his notoriety to take another shot at baseball, and actually returned to pitch five games for the Braves in 1978, eight years after his retirement from the Astros.

On the field Bouton won 21 games and was selected for the All-Star team in 1963. He pitched in two World Series. Known for working so hard on the mound that he knocked his cap off with each pitch, Bouton will always be remembered as the enigmatic, wise-cracking, vulnerable bullpen pitcher for the Seattle Pilots.
Playing Career: *1962-1970, 1978; NY A, Sea A, Hou N, Atl N*

Seattle Pilots pitcher Jim Bouton in 1969.

Larry Bowa.

Larry Bowa
Bowa, Lawrence Robert
B: Dec 6, 1945

Pos: SS	BA: .260
Hits: 2,191	HRs: 15
RBI: 525	BBs: 474

Managerial Record
Won: 81   Lost: 127   Pct: .389

Larry Bowa was a throwback to players of olden days. He took his position seriously and got as much as he could out of his talent, leading league shortstops in fielding six times, winning two Gold Gloves and making the NL All-Star team five times. When he retired, Bowa had played more games at shortstop than any other NL player. He holds the NL record for fewest errors in a season of 150 games or more. He also holds the major league record for highest career fielding average, .980.

At first Bowa was a powerless switch hitter, but with hard work he became a solid .267 to .290 swatter. He led the NL in triples with 13 in 1972. His best season was 1975 when he hit .305. He smashed 31 doubles two years later. The Phillies won four division titles in six years with Bowa at shortstop, and the Cubs won another when they traded for Bowa.
Playing Career: *1970-1985; Phi N, Chi N, NY N*
Managerial Career: *1987-1988; SD N*

Frank Bowerman
Bowerman, Frank Eugene
B: Dec 5, 1868   D: Nov 30, 1948

Pos: C	BA: .251
Hits: 852	HRs: 13
RBI: 392	BBs: 129

Managerial Record
Won: 23   Lost: 54   Pct: .299

Bowerman played 10 of his 15 years with John McGraw and the old Orioles and Giants. He was a good, smart second-string catcher. His

team made it to the 1905 World Series, but Bowerman never got in to play.
Playing Career: *1895-1909; Bal N, Pit N, NY N, Bos N*
Managerial Career: *1909; Bos N*

Joe Bowman
Bowman, Joseph Emil
B: Jun 17, 1910   D: Nov 22, 1990

Pos: P	ERA: 4.40
W-L: 77-96	SOs: 502
ShOs: 5	Saves: 11

When Kansas City A's owner Charlie Finley was booted out of Muncipal Stadium, he stored the club's records at Bowman's house. Bowman's career went up and down between the minors and the majors; returned to the big leagues during the war years.
Playing Career: *1932, 1934-1941, 1944-1945; Phi A, NY N, Phi N, Pit N, Bos A, Cin N*

Bob Boyd
Boyd, Robert Richard (The Rope)
B: Oct 1, 1926

Pos: 1B, OF	BA: .293
Hits: 567	HRs: 19
RBI: 175	BBs: 167

A Negro Leagues slugger who was past his prime by the time he got to the major leagues, Boyd still hit over .300 four times. In the Negro Leagues Boyd hit .362 for four seasons with the Memphis Red Sox and led the league in triples one year and doubles the next.
Playing Career: *1951, 1953-1954, 1956-1961; Chi A, Bal A, KC A, Mil N*

Oil Can Boyd
Boyd, Dennis Ray
B: Oct 6, 1959

Pos: P	ERA: 4.04
W-L: 78-77	SOs: 799
ShOs: 10	No-hitters: 0

Boyd used every ounce of his 155-pound frame to throw his fastball. His best year was 1986, when he went 16-10 and pushed the Red Sox over the top. He appeared in the ALCS and the World Series. His father was a player in the Negro Leagues.
Playing Career: *1982-1991; Bos A, Mon N, Tex A*

Clete Boyer
Boyer, Cletis Leroy
B: Feb 9, 1937

Pos: 3B	BA: .242
Hits: 1,396	HRs: 162
RBI: 654	BBs: 470

Clete Boyer was the best-fielding third baseman in the AL during his eight years as a Yankee, but he was not awarded a Gold Glove until he moved to the NL away from the shadow of Brooks Robinson. In 1962, his best year, Boyer hit .272 with 18 home runs and 85 runs scored, and hit .318 in the World

Series. Boyer and his brother Ken, who was playing for the opposing team (the Cardinals), both hit home runs in Game Seven of the 1964 Fall Classic.
Playing Career: *1955-1957, 1959-1971; KC A, NY A, Atl N*

Ken Boyer
Boyer, Kenton Lloyd
B: May 20, 1931   D: Sep 7, 1982

Pos: 3B	BA: .287
Hits: 2,143	HRs: 282
RBI: 1,141	BBs: 713
Managerial Record	
Won: 166 Lost: 190 Pct: .466	

The best of six ballplaying brothers, Ken Boyer won Gold Gloves, led NL third basemen in fielding, and led the league in home runs. Boyer was everything one could want in a third baseman; the only reason he is not in the Hall of Fame is that several of the best hot corner men ever to play had careers that overlapped his.

Boyer won the MVP Award in 1964 as he led the NL in RBI. He was selected to the NL All-Star team seven times. Five times Boyer led NL third basemen in double plays. He won six Gold Gloves, and even played center field in 1957, leading NL outfielders in fielding. His kid brother, Clete, may have been a better fielder, but lacked Ken's big bat. Ken hit over .300 five times and slugged 20 or more home runs eight times.
Playing Career: *1955-1969; StL N, NY N, Chi A, LA N*
Managerial Career: *1978-1980; StL N*

Jack Boyle
Boyle, John Anthony
B: Mar 22, 1866   D: Jan 7, 1913

Pos: C, 1B	BA: .253
Hits: 1,067	HRs: 24
RBI: 523	BBs: 328

Boyle was a catcher on the St. Louis Browns team that won four pennants in a row. He led league catchers in fielding, 1887-1888. Boyle played 11 years as a regular, hitting .300 in 1894 when the entire NL batted .309.
Playing Career: *1886-1898; Cin AA, StL AA, Chi P, NY N, Phi N*

Bill Bradley
Bradley, William Joseph
B: Feb 13, 1878   D: Mar 11, 1954

Pos: 3B	BA: .271
Hits: 1,472	HRs: 33
RBI: 552	BBs: 280
Managerial Record	
Won: 97 Lost: 98 Pct: .497	

Cleveland's first big star when the Indians were called the Blues, Bradley hit safely in 29 straight games, still a team record. His hitting declined after a serious illness in 1905, but his fielding remained tops. On the last out of Addie Joss's perfect game, the batter hit a scorcher to the hot corner. Bradley was able to field it but threw low. First baseman Stovall made a great pickup.
Playing Career: *1899-1910, 1914-1915; Chi N, Cle A, Brk F, KC F*
Managerial Career: *1905, 1914; Cle A, Brk F*

Teammates greet Ken Boyer after his game-winning grand slam in the 1964 WS.

George Bradley
Bradley, George Washington (Grin)
B: Jul 13, 1852   D: Oct 2, 1931

Pos: P, 1B, 3B	ERA: 2.50 (inc.)
W-L: 171-125	SOs: 611 (inc.)
ShOs: 32	No-hitters: 1

George Washington Bradley pitched the first no-hitter in NL history in 1876. That year he pitched all 64 St. Louis games, leading them to a second-place finish with 45 wins. His 16 shutouts set a major league record that stood for 40 years. In Chicago, Bradley was less effective with a better team. He spent the rest of his career playing field positions.
Playing Career: *1875-1877, 1879-1884, 1886, 1888; StL Brown Stockings n, StL N, Chi N, Tro N, Pro N, Det N, Cle N, Phi AA, Cin U, Bal AA*

Phil Bradley
Bradley, Philip Poole
B: Mar 11, 1959

Pos: OF, DH	BA: .286
Hits: 1,058	HRs: 78
RBI: 376	BBs: 432

An All-Big Eight quarterback at the University of Missouri, Bradley chose baseball over football, and became one of the Mariners' early stars. Selected for the AL All-Star team in 1985, Bradley hit .300 or more three times and scored 100 runs twice.
Playing Career: *1983-1990; Sea A, Phi N, Bal A, Chi A*

Bobby Bragan
Bragan, Robert Randall
B: Oct 30, 1917

Pos: SS, C	BA: .240
Hits: 456	HRs: 15
RBI: 172	BBs: 110
Managerial Record	
Won: 443 Lost: 478 Pct: .481	

One of the most colorful performers in baseball, Bragan started as a shortstop, then became a catcher with the 1947 Dodgers, joining the team the same time as Jackie Robinson. Bragan was a lively minor and major league manager, wrangling with umpires and creating headlines every day. He also later served as president of the Texas League and the National Association of Professional Baseball Leagues.
Playing Career: *1940-1944, 1947-1948; Phi N, Brk N*
Managerial Career: *1956-1958, 1963-1966; Pit N, Cle A, Mil N, Atl N*

Dave Brain
Brain, David Leonard
B: Jan 24, 1879   D: May 25, 1959

Pos: SS, 2B, 3B, OF	BA: .252
Hits: 641	HRs: 27
RBI: 303	BBs: 134

Dave Brain is the most obscure home run champ. He led the NL with 10 taters in 1907. Playing regularly, but as a utility person for five years, 1903-1907, Brain had some power, socking 52 triples. He was reputed to be a clumsy fielder.
Playing Career: *1901, 1903-1908; Chi A, StL N, Pit N, Bos N, Cin N, NY N*

Ralph Branca.

Ralph Branca
Branca, Ralph Theodore Joseph
B: Jan 6, 1926

Pos: P	ERA: 3.79
W-L: 88-68	SOs: 829
ShOs: 12	Saves: 19

Branca pitched the famous ball that Bobby Thomson hit for a home run to win the 1951 playoff game for the Giants. When reporters questioned him Branca said, "All I thought was: why me? Why me?" He changed his number 13 uniform, but it did not improve his luck. Suffering a pelvic injury in the off-season, Branca won only 12 more games in his last four seasons. Branca won 21 games in 1947, and pitched in the World Series. He was chosen for three NL All-Star teams.
Playing Career: *1944-1954, 1956; Brk N, Det A, NY A*

Safe! Phil Bradley scores for the Phillies in 1988.

Ed Brandt
Brandt, Edward Arthur
B: Feb 17, 1905   D: Nov 1, 1944

Pos: P	ERA: 3.86
W-L: 121-146	SOs: 877
ShOs: 18	Saves: 17

Ed Brandt's claim to fame in the major leagues was that he threw a forkball. He began his major league career by losing 21 for the Braves, but he improved with them, winning 18 twice and 16 twice before falling to 5-19 with the 1935 Braves, one of baseball's all-time worst teams.
Playing Career: *1928-1938; Bos N, Pit N*

Jackie Brandt
Brandt, John George
B: Apr 28, 1934

Pos: OF	BA: .262
Hits: 1,020	HRs: 112
RBI: 485	BBs: 351

After splitting an outstanding rookie season between the Cardinals and Giants, Brandt served Uncle Sam, then joined the Giants in San Francisco. Chosen for the AL All-Star team in 1961, Brandt had solid skills but never really blossomed.
Playing Career: *1956, 1958-1967; StL N, NY N, SF N, Bal A, Phi N, Hou N*

Kitty Bransfield
Bransfield, William Edward
B: Jan 7, 1875   D: May 1, 1947

Pos: 1B	BA: .270
Hits: 1,352	HRs: 14
RBI: 634	BBs: 221

Bransfield was the starting first baseman for the three-time pennant-winning Pittsburgh Pirates, from 1901 through 1904. He fielded well, leading NL first sackers in fielding average in 1909. Bransfield played eight games in the 1903 World Series, smacking two triples. He hit over .300 twice. His best year was 1901 before the foul strike came in. That year he hit .295 with 16 triples, scored 92 runs and drove in 91.
Playing Career: *1898, 1901-1911; Bos N, Pit N, Phi N, Chi N*

Steve Braun
Braun, Stephen Russell
B: May 8, 1948

Pos: OF, 3B, 2B, SS	BA: .271
Hits: 989	HRs: 52
RBI: 388	BBs: 579

Braun was a top pinch hitter after having been a regular outfielder with the Twins for six years. His best season was 1975, when he hit .302, but he stood out in the 1982 World Series when he belted opposing pitching at a .500 clip for the Cardinals. He played three more seasons with them before retiring.
Playing Career: *1971-1985; Min A, Sea A, KC A, Tor A, StL N*

Garland Braxton
Braxton, Edgar Garland
B: Jun 10, 1900   D: Feb 26, 1966

Pos: P	ERA: 4.13
W-L: 50-53	SOs: 411
ShOs: 2	Saves: 32

Braxton led the AL in games with 58, and in saves with 13, in 1927. The next year he became a starter and led the AL with a 2.51 ERA. After that he split time between roles. He became a scratch golfer in retirement, winning several senior titles.
Playing Career: *1921-1922, 1925-1931, 1933; Bos N, NY A, Was A, Chi A, StL A*

Alpha Brazle
Brazle Alpha Eugene
B: Oct 19, 1913   D: Oct 24, 1973

Pos: P	ERA: 3.31
W-L: 97-64	SOs: 554
ShOs: 9	Saves: 60

Brazle was another pitcher who flourished as a starter and as a reliever. Sidearm throwing Brazle won games in double figures five consecutive years as a starter, then turned to the bullpen where he led the NL in saves twice. He pitched in two World Series, winning two games against the Yankees in 1943.
Playing Career: *1943, 1946-1954; StL N*

Sid Bream
Bream, Sidney Eugene
B: Aug 3, 1960

Pos: 1B	BA: .262
Hits: 798	HRs: 90
RBI: 448	BBs: 344

Scoring the winning run from second on a short single in Game Seven of the 1992 NLCS, Bream gave the Braves their second NL pennant in a row. He set an NL record for first basemen with 166 assists in 1986, his first full season.
Playing Career: *1983-; LA N, Pit N, Atl N*

Harry Brecheen
Brecheen, Harry David (The Cat)
B: Oct 14, 1914

Pos: P	ERA: 2.92
W-L: 132-92	SOs: 901
ShOs: 25	Saves: 18

Brecheen was one of the finest left-handers in baseball. Outstanding in World Series play, he sported a 4-1 record with a 0.83 ERA, a mark that is the second lowest in Series history. When Enos Slaughter raced around third to score the winning run in the 1946 Fall Classic, Brecheen was the pitcher of record. It was his third triumph, making him the first pitcher since Stan Coveleski in 1920 to win three games in one Series.

In 1948 Brecheen won 20 and had the best winning percentage and ERA, 2.34, in the league. Named "the Cat" because of his ability to pounce on bunts and field his posi-

Harry Brecheen.

tion, Brecheen spent 11 years with the Cardinals then pitched his final season with the Browns. He joined the Orioles as a coach, and is credited with turning Bob Turley into a fine hurler. He was still around when the "Baby Birds" matured into Steve Barber, Jim Palmer, Dave McNally and Wally Bunker, all 20-game winners.
Playing Career: *1940-1953; StL N, StL A*

Ted Breitenstein
Breitenstein, Theodore P.
B: Jun 1, 1869   D: May 3, 1935

Pos: P	ERA: 4.04
W-L: 160-170	SOs: 889
ShOs: 12	No-hitters: 2

Ted Breitenstein was the best left-handed pitcher in baseball during the mid-1890s when he won 127 games in six years. He pitched a no-hitter in his first start. In 1893 Breitenstein was involved with 20 one-run games, winning only eight of them. His career picked up when he was sold to the contending Reds. After 1901 Breitenstein went to the Southern Association where he amassed a 157-89 record, then became an umpire.
Playing Career: *1891-1901; StL AA, StL N, Cin N*

Bob Brenly
Brenly, Robert Earl
B: Feb 25, 1954

Pos: C	BA: .247
Hits: 647	HRs: 91
RBI: 333	BBs: 317

In a 1986 game, Brenly made four errors at third base in one inning. Following that he hit a solo home run and swatted a two-run single. With two out in the bottom of the ninth, he smacked another tater to win the contest. In one game Brenly found the essence of baseball.
Playing Career: *1981-1989; SF N, Tor A*

Bressler was a player with two careers, both performed with distinction. As a pitcher he broke in with a 10-4 record for the contending AL champion Athletics, but crashed along with the team to a 4-17 mark. Another under par year resulted in his being shipped off to the Reds.

There Bressler bought a first base mitt and began to work out at that position. He hit .307 in 1921, his first full year away from the mound. In the mid-1920s he strung together seasons of .347, .348, and .357 batting averages as the Reds competed for pennants.
Playing Career: *1914-1932; Phi A, Cin N, Brk N, Phi N, StL N*

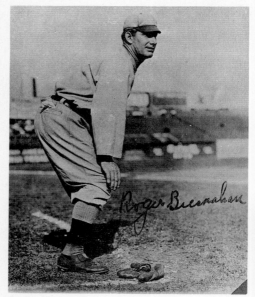

Roger Bresnahan.

Roger Bresnahan
Bresnahan, Roger Philip
B: Jun 11, 1879   D: Dec 4, 1944
Hall of Fame 1945

Pos: C	BA: .280
Hits: 1,253	HRs: 26-32
RBI: 530	BBs: 714

Managerial Record
Won: 328   Lost: 432   Pct: .432

An innovative backstop and a Hall of Famer, Roger Bresnahan was the first catcher to wear shinguards openly. He also invented a pneumatic batting helmet, and became the first manager to work for a female club owner, the Cardinals' Helene Britton Robison, who later fired him.

John McGraw brought Bresnahan with him from Baltimore when he jumped to the AL. He caught Mathewson and McGinnity, both 30-game winners, leading to the 1904 and 1905 pennants. During the 1905 World Series Bresnahan caught four shutouts and batted .313. Bresnahan was fast and a good baserunner, frequently batting first or second in the lineup. He led the NL in walks once. A fine athlete, he could have played any position, and in fact started his career as a pitcher for the Washington Nationals.
Playing Career: *1897, 1900-1915; Was N, Chi N, Bal A, NY N, StL N, Chi N*
Managerial Career: *1909-1912, 1915; StL N, Chi N*

Rube Bressler
Bressler, Raymond Bloom
B: Oct 23, 1894   D: Nov 7, 1966

Pos: P	ERA: 3.40
W-L: 26-32	SOs: 229
ShOs: 3	Saves: 2

Pos: OF, 1B	BA: .301
Hits: 1,170	HRs: 32
RBI: 586	BBs: 449

Rube Bressler.

Eddie Bressoud
Bressoud, Edward Francis
B: May 2, 1932

Pos: SS	BA: .252
Hits: 925	HRs: 94
RBI: 365	BBs: 359

Bressoud played in the World Series with the Cardinals in 1967, his last year in the major leagues. A utility shortstop, his best years were in Boston where he adapted his swing to Fenway Park and hit 40 doubles twice, as well as 20 home runs.
Playing Career: *1956-1967; NYG N, SF N, Bos A, NYM N, StL N*

George Brett
Brett, George Howard
B: May 15, 1953

Pos: 3B, 1B, DH	BA: .305
Hits: 3,154	HRs: 317
RBI: 1,595	BBs: 1,096

Always an outstanding hitter, George Brett was absolutely ferocious the year he batted .390, the highest average since Ted Williams's .406 mark. On September 4, 1980, Brett's average stood at an incredible .404. He was AL MVP that year.

George Brett.

His ferocity was evident again the day he zinged a Goose Gossage fastball into the upper deck at Yankee Stadium, only to be robbed of the home run when umpires agreed with Yanks Manager Billy Martin that Brett's bat had excessive pine tar on it. Brett charged toward the umpires like a raging bull. Martin won the battle but lost the war; the home run was eventually reinstated, giving the Royals the victory when the game was resumed three weeks later.

A disciple of hitting guru Charley Lau, Brett won three batting titles. He led the AL in hits, triples and slugging three times, and in doubles once. A 12-time All-Star, he won a Gold Glove in 1985. Brett carried the Royals to seven division titles, two pennants and one World Championship. His .373 career World Series batting average is the fourth best of all time.
Playing Career: *1973-1993; KC A*

Ken Brett
Brett, Kenneth Alven
B: Sep 18, 1948

Pos: P	ERA: 3.93
W-L: 83-85	SOs: 807
ShOs: 9	Saves: 11

Ken Brett played his entire career at the wrong position. Considered a better hitter than his younger brother George, Ken nonetheless pursued pitching. He pitched in the World Series at age 19. He later hit home runs in four consecutive starts.
Playing Career: *1967, 1969-1981; Bos A, Mil A, Phi N, Pit N, NY A, Chi A, Cal A, Min A, LA N, KC A*

Chet Brewer
Brewer, Chester Arthur
B: Jan 14, 1907   D: Mar 26, 1990

Pos: P	ERA: NA
W-L: 89-63 (inc.)	SOs: 552 (inc.)
ShOs: 14 (inc.)	Saves: 3 (inc.)

Brewer pitched in the Negro Leagues, then managed a West Coast version of the Monarchs, called the KC Royals. He was the manager who conducted Jackie Robinson's big league tryout.
Playing Career: *1925-1937, 1941, 1946-1948; KC Monarchs, Was Pilots, NY Cubans, Phi Stars, Chi Am Giants, Cle Buckeyes*

Jim Brewer
Brewer, James Thomas
B: Nov 14, 1937   D: Nov 16, 1987

Pos: P	ERA: 3.07
W-L: 69-65	SOs: 810
ShOs: 1	Saves: 132

Best known for having been sucker-punched by Billy Martin in a confrontation on the mound in 1962, Brewer's jaw was broken and his career put in serious jeopardy. On a tip from Warren Spahn, Brewer added a screwball to his repertoire and turned his career around, becoming one of the top relievers in the game. He saved 117 games in six years, 1968-1973. Brewer pitched in the 1973 All-Star Game, and in three World Series for the Dodgers.
Playing Career: *1960-1976; Chi N, LA N, Cal A*

Tom Brewer
Brewer, Thomas Austin
B: Sep 3, 1931

Pos: P	ERA: 4.00
W-L: 91-82	SOs: 733
ShOs: 13	Saves: 3

Tom Brewer is only known today as a relatively obscure starting pitcher who toiled for the Red Sox for eight years. He was their most effective starter in the mid-1950s. Brewer's best season was 1956, when he went 19-9 and was chosen to pitch in the All-Star Game.
Playing Career: *1954-1961; Bos A*

Rocky Bridges
Bridges, Everett Lamar
B: Aug 7, 1927

Pos: 3B, 2B, SS	BA: .247
Hits: 562	HRs: 16
RBI: 187	BBs: 205

Unable to hit well enough to be a full-time player, Rocky Bridges went to the minors where he became a quotable skipper. He said "There are three things the average man thinks he can do better than anybody else: build a fire, run a hotel, and manage a baseball team."
Playing Career: *1951-1961; Brk N, Cin N, Was A, Det A, StL N, LA A*

Tommy Bridges
Bridges, Thomas Jefferson Davis
B: Dec 28, 1906   D: Apr 19, 1968

Pos: P	ERA: 3.57
W-L: 194-132	SOs: 1,674
ShOs: 33	Saves: 10

In his first major league appearance, Bridges faced Babe Ruth and Lou Gehrig with runners on base. Ruth grounded out and Gehrig fanned; Bridges was off to a good start. He won 20 games three years in a row, leading the league in victories with 23 in 1936. He led AL hurlers in strikeouts in 1935 and 1936. Bridges had control problems early in his career, walking more than 100 batters in each of his first six full seasons, but he was acknowledged as having the best curveball in the big leagues in his era.
He barely missed a perfect game in 1932 when with two out, pinch hitter Dave Harris singled. Bridges posted a 4-1 record in four World Series with the Tigers. The one all Tiger fans know about is Game Six in the 1935 Series when Bridges gave up a leadoff triple to Stan Hack, then slammed the door with a strikeout, a grounder, and a fly-out to make the Tigers World Champions.
Playing Career: *1930-1946; Det A*

Tommy Bridges.

Al Bridwell
Bridwell, Albert Henry
B: Jan 4, 1884   D: Jan 23, 1969

Pos: SS	BA: .255
Hits: 1,064	HRs: 2
RBI: 348	BBs: 559

Bridwell was famous for hitting the single that started the chain of events referred to as the "Merkle Boner." Bridwell's batting was inconsistent, his average moved from .218 to .285 and .294, and back to .236. He led NL shortstops in fielding in 1907.
Playing Career: *1905-1915; Cin N, Bos N, NY N, Chi N, StL F*

Johnny Briggs
Briggs, John Edward
B: Mar 10, 1944

Pos: OF	BA: .253
Hits: 1,041	HRs: 139
RBI: 507	BBs: 663

Briggs was a bonus baby who was rushed into the big leagues. He always had a world of potential which only began to be realized when he switched leagues and played with the Brewers in their early years. Briggs hit 21 home runs twice for Milwaukee.
Playing Career: *1964-1975; Phi N, Mil A, Min A*

Nellie Briles
Briles, Nelson Kelley
B: Aug 5, 1943

Pos: P	ERA: 3.43
W-L: 129-112	SOs: 1,163
ShOs: 17	Saves: 22

Briles was in the Cardinals' bullpen when ace Bob Gibson suffered a broken leg. The Red Birds called on Briles to fill in. He went 14-5 with a 2.43 ERA and hurled a complete game victory in the 1967 World Series. His 19-11 record the next season helped propel the Cards back into the Series. Briles was traded to the Pirates in 1971 and helped them to post-season play in 1971 and 1972. He pitched a two-hit shutout in the 1971 World Series.
Playing Career: *1965-1978; StL N, Pit N, KC A, Tex A, Bal A*

Ed Brinkman
Brinkman, Edwin Albert
B: Dec 8, 1941

Pos: SS	BA: .224
Hits: 1,355	HRs: 60
RBI: 461	BBs: 444

An original member of the Washington Senators, Brinkman played for them for 10 years before he was traded to the Tigers. The shortstop was a poor hitter until Manager Ted Williams adjusted his batting stance and swing. Brinkman's average jumped 80 points and stayed in the .265 range.
Playing Career: *1961-1975; Was A, Det A, StL N, Tex A, NY A*

Dave Bristol
Bristol, James David
B: Jun 23, 1933

Managerial Record
Won: 657   Lost: 764   Pct: .462

Dave Bristol led the Reds to a third-place finish in 1969. Manager Sparky Anderson replaced him and then made the blockbuster trade with the Astros that set up the Reds' dynasty. Bristol later piloted several teams that competed successfully.
Managerial Career: *1966-1972, 1976-1977, 1979-1980; Cin N, Mil A, Atl N, SF N*

Greg Brock
Brock, Gregory Allen
B: Jun 14, 1957

Pos: 1B, DH	BA: .248
Hits: 794	HRs: 110
RBI: 462	BBs: 434

The Dodgers demanded that Brock play first base like Steve Garvey and hit home runs like Duke Snider; a task impossible to achieve. He hit 71 home runs in four years then was traded to Milwaukee where he cut down on his swing, sacrificing power for average.
Playing Career: *1982-1991; LA N, Mil A*

Lou Brock
Brock, Louis Clark
B: Jun 18, 1939
Hall of Fame 1985

Pos: OF	BA: .293
Hits: 3,023	HRs: 149
RBI: 900	BBs: 761

Brock was not only the catalyst for the Cardinals' offense in the 1960s and 1970s, he was one of the best leadoff men ever to play baseball. Arriving in St. Louis in a controversial trade – Brock for Ernie Broglio – in mid-1964, Brock hit 85 points higher than his previous best and sparked the Cardinals to a thrilling, come-from-behind NL pennant.

Oddly, fans considered Brock a power hitter and he was not particularly known for his base stealing prowess. His opponents over the next 15 years wished they had less knowledge of that ability. He led the NL in thefts eight of nine years 1966-1974. He stole more bases after the age of 30 than any other player in baseball history, ending with 938 thefts. While his home run power diminished from a high of 21 in 1967, his runs scored number increased. Twice he led the NL, totaling 1,610 runs scored in his career. Brock set the modern single-season stolen base record with 118 in 1974, a mark later surpassed.
Playing Career: *1961-1979; Chi N, StL N*

Steve Brodie
Brodie, Walter Scott
B: Sep 11, 1868   D: Oct 30, 1935

Pos: OF	BA: .303
Hits: 1,726	HRs: 25
RBI: 900	BBs: 420

Steve Brodie played center field and was a catalyst for the famed Baltimore Orioles of 1894-1896. He batted .361, .366, .348, .297, .306, and .309 for Baltimore. The gap in Brodie's major league career occurred when he spent the 1900 season in the AL with the White Stockings. At the time, the AL was an independent minor league. He stole 289 bases during his career.
Playing Career: *1890-1899, 1901-1902; Bos N, StL N, Bal N, Pit N, Bal A, NY N*

Ernie Broglio
Broglio, Ernest Gilbert
B: Aug 27, 1935

Pos: P	ERA: 3.74
W-L: 77-74	SOs: 849
ShOs: 18	Saves: 2

Broglio had the misfortune of being traded for a player who proved to be a superstar. The trade overshadowed a fine career start for Broglio, who won a league-leading 21 games in 1960 and 18 in 1963. He won only seven games for Cubs the rest of his career.
Playing Career: *1959-1966; StL N, Chi N*

Jack Brohamer (r), after a 1980 home run.

Jack Brohamer
Brohamer, John Anthony
B: Feb 26, 1950

Pos: 2B, 3B, DH	BA: .245
Hits: 613	HRs: 30
RBI: 227	BBs: 222

Brohamer started and ended his career in Cleveland. In between he was a utility infielder who started two triple plays. His best season statistically was 1974, but Brohamer played 136 games, the most in his career, and was named to the All-Rookie team in 1972.
Playing Career: *1972-1980; Cle A, Chi A, Bos A*

Tom Brookens
Brookens, Thomas Dale
B: Aug 10, 1953

Pos: 3B	BA: .246
Hits: 950	HRs: 71
RBI: 431	BBs: 281

Brookens must have been Sparky Anderson's type of player. He was an average fielder, twice leading the AL in errors. He was short on power and struggled to hit .250, yet was a semi-regular for a Tiger team that won two division titles and one World Series.
Playing Career: *1979-1990; Det A, NY A, Cle A*

Hubie Brooks
Brooks, Hubert
B: Sep 24, 1956

Pos: 3B, SS, OF	BA: .270
Hits: 1,594	HRs: 148
RBI: 810	BBs: 385

Though Brooks has struggled recently, he was a line drive hitting energizer for the Mets and Expos. He batted .340 in 1986, and drove in 100 runs the previous year. When Brooks came to the Mets' lineup as a 23-year-old, he appeared to be the answer to their perennial third base dilemma. Brooks hit .309 and .307 his first two seasons. With stability at third the Mets built the team that won it all in 1986, but by then, Brooks was gone.
Playing Career: *1980-; NY N, Mon N, LA N, Cal A, KC A*

The Cards' stealing sensation Lou Brock in action versus the Pirates in 1978.

Jim Brosnan
Brosnan, James Patrick
B: Oct 24, 1929

Pos: P	ERA: 3.54
W-L: 55-47	SOs: 507
ShOs: 2	Saves: 67

Brosnan, more than anyone in the 1950s, dispelled the myth of the dumb jock by publishing two well-received books. He was not bad on the mound either. When the Reds acquired him and Bill Henry as closers they became pennant contenders. Cincinnati won the NL flag in 1961, and Brosnan pitched six innings in three games in the 1961 World Series. He pitched eight straight seasons with an ERA under 3.80.
Playing Career: *1954-1963; Chi N, StL N, Cin N, Chi A*

Dan Brouthers
Brouthers, Dennis Joseph
B: May 8, 1858   D: Aug 2, 1932
Hall of Fame 1945

Pos: 1B	BA: .342
Hits: 2,296	HRs: 106
RBI: 1,057	BBs: 840

One of baseball's mightiest sluggers, Brouthers played in an era of 500-foot fences and constant rule changes. In various seasons of his career a base on balls was awarded after three, seven, then four balls; walks counted as base hits; it took four strikes instead of three to make an out. When Brouthers came to the big leagues pitchers hurled underhanded from 45 feet, then they were moved back to 50, then they started throwing overhanded, and finally they were moved back to 60'6". In 1890 almost all of the good players went on strike against the major leagues and formed their own, the Players' League.

Through all the changes, one constant was that Brouthers could be counted on to hit .300 or more and score 100 runs. He won five batting titles and seven slugging titles. He scored 1,523 runs, slugged 460 doubles and 205 triples, and stole 235 bases while striking out only 238 times.
Playing Career: *1879-1896, 1904; Tro N, Buf N, Det N, Bos N, Bos P, Bos AA, Brk N, Bal N, Lou N, Phi N, NY N*

Dan Brouthers.

Bobby Brown (r) in his first year as AL president, with league VP Bob Fishel.

Bobby Brown
Brown, Robert William (Doctor)
B: Nov 25, 1924

Pos: 3B	BA: .279
Hits: 452	HRs: 22
RBI: 237	BBs: 214

Brown studied medicine at Tulane University while he played baseball for the New York Yankees. After signing for a substantial bonus in 1946, he had a star-studded year and won advancement to the parent club. Platooned at third base, he played against right-handers. In four World Series (1947, 1949-1951), he batted .439 and made eight extra-base hits among his 17 total hits. Brown was then drafted and missed the entire 1953 season. After appearing in 28 games in 1954, he retired to his medical internship.

From 1958 to 1984 Brown was a cardiologist in Ft. Worth, Texas. Then he was offered the presidency of the American League, "an offer too tempting to turn down." At the 1992 winter meetings he was called upon to use his medical skills as he attempted to revive Florida Marlins president Carl Barger. Brown has served the AL admirably since 1984.
Playing Career: *1946-1952, 1954; NY A*

Buster Brown
Brown, Charles Edward
B: Aug 31, 1881   D: Feb 9, 1914

Pos: P	ERA: 3.20
W-L: 51-103	SOs: 501
ShOs: 10	Saves: 4

Brown was saddled with poor teams, and plagued by wildness. Despite posting good ERAs, Brown never had a winning season. In 1908, the former Ames College star kept his ERA to 2.67 but went 9-23. He lost 103 games in his nine-year career.
Playing Career: *1905-1913; StL N, Phi N, Bos N*

Clint Brown
Brown, Clinton Harold
B: Jul 8, 1903   D: Dec 31, 1955

Pos: P	ERA: 4.26
W-L: 89-93	SOs: 410
ShOs: 7	Saves: 64

Brown was a relief ace who set a major league record for appearances in 1939 with the White Sox. He was a junkball pitcher who used underhand, sidearm and three-quarter-arm positions. Brown led the AL in shutouts in 1930, and in saves in 1937.
Playing Career: *1928-1942; Cle A, Chi A*

Gates Brown
Brown, William James
B: May 2, 1939

Pos: OF	BA: .257
Hits: 582	HRs: 84
RBI: 322	BBs: 242

Gates hit a monstrous .370 in 1968 as a pinch hitter and part-time player. The Tigers won the pennant with Brown's big bat. He was one of the most dangerous pinch hitters, knocking 107 hits in 414 at-bats, including 16 home runs.
Playing Career: *1963-1975; Det A*

Hal Brown
Brown, Hector Harold (Skinny)
B: Dec 11, 1924

Pos: P	ERA: 3.81
W-L: 85-92	SOs: 710
ShOs: 13	Saves: 11

Skinny, who was somewhat chubby, was a reliever who spent most of his career in the AL. He had fine control despite depending on a knuckleball. For the Orioles in 1960, Brown tossed 36 consecutive scoreless innings.
Playing Career: *1951-1964; Chi A, Bos A, Bal A, NY A, Hou N*

Larry Brown
Brown, Larry Leslie
B: Mar 1, 1940

Pos: SS, 2B, SS	BA: .233
Hits: 803	HRs: 47
RBI: 254	BBs: 317

Brown was a good fielding second baseman for the Indians in a pitcher's era. He was always a .230 hitter but he had some power until he was in an on-field collision in 1966 in which he suffered fractures of the skull, nose and cheekbone.
Playing Career: *1963-1974; Cle A, Oak A, Bal A, Tex A*

Lloyd Brown.

Lloyd Brown
Brown, Lloyd Andrew (Gimpy)
B: Dec 25, 1904   D: Jan 14, 1974

Pos: P	ERA: 4.20
W-L: 91-105	SOs: 510
ShOs: 10	Saves: 21

Brown won 46 games from 1930 to 1932, after which he went 33-53. Chiefly remembered as the pitcher who gave up the most home runs to Lou Gehrig, Brown pitched and managed for 30 years and later scouted for the Phillies and Senators.
Playing Career: *1925, 1928-1937, 1940; Brk N, Was A, StL A, Bos A, Cle A, Phi N*

Mace Brown
Brown, Mace Stanley
B: May 21, 1909

Pos: P	ERA: 3.47
W-L: 76-57	SOs: 435
ShOs: 3	Saves: 48

Brown won 15 games in relief and made a league-leading 51 appearances in 1938, but is remembered for one pitch he threw to Gabby Hartnett – the famous Homer in the Gloamin' that essentially won the pennant for the Cubs. Brown appeared in the NL All-Star Game that year. In 1942 Brown led the AL in relief wins, with nine.
Playing Career: *1935-1943, 1946; Pit N, Brk N, Bos A*

Ollie Brown
Brown, Ollie Lee (Downtown)
B: Feb 11, 1944

Pos: OF	BA: .265
Hits: 964	HRs: 102
RBI: 454	BBs: 314

Brown earned his nickname by hitting 40 home runs in the Pacific Coast League in 1964, presumably in the direction of the business district. Chosen in the expansion draft by the Padres, he hit 20 taters in 1969 and 23 the next year. His younger brother, Oscar, played for Atlanta for five years.
Playing Career: *1965-1977; SF N, SD N, Oak A, Mil A, Hou N, Phi N*

Ray Brown
Brown, Raymond
B: Feb 23, 1908   D: Deceased

Pos: P	ERA: NA
W-L: 109-34	SOs: 312 (inc.)
ShOs: 18	No-hitters: 1

A six-time Negro League All-Star, Brown had a career winning percentage of .762. He tossed a 7-inning perfect game. In the 1944 Negro World Series he threw a one-hitter. He played for Cum Posey's Homestead Grays – with whom he appeared in five Negro World Series – and later played in the Mexican and Canadian Provincial Leagues.
Playing Career: *1932-1945; Det Wolves, Hom Grays, Was Grays*

Mordecai "Three-Finger" Brown.

Three-Finger Brown
Brown, Mordecai Peter Centennial (Miner)
B: Oct 19, 1876   D: Feb 14, 1948
Hall of Fame 1949

Pos: P	ERA: 2.06
W-L: 239-130	SOs: 1,375
ShOs: 57	Saves: 48
Managerial Record	
Won: 50 Lost: 63 Pct: .442	

Brown, who lost his index finger and part of his middle finger in a farm accident, threw a terribly effective pitch resembling a cross between the modern split-finger fastball and a knuckler. He had an ERA under 2.00 six times, with an off-year of 2.17. He won 20 or more six straight years. Brown would have led the NL four straight years in saves had they been counted. He went 5-4 in four World Series, including three shutouts.

Brown's biggest win was the 1908 makeup game for the Cubs-Giants match suspended earlier due to the Merkle Boner. The makeup game was played in New York where Brown and other Cubs received death threats before taking the field. When Cubs starter Jack Pfeister got into trouble in the very first inning, manager Frank Chance called on Brown, who had already won 28 in 43 appearances. He took the mound amid hisses, catcalls, and a police guard, but shut down the Giants, 4-2, for his 29th win.
Playing Career: *1903-1916; StL N, Chi N, StL F, Brk F, Chi F, Chi N*
Managerial Career: *1914; StL F*

Tom Brown
Brown, Thomas Tarlton
B: Sep 21, 1860   D: Oct 25, 1927

Pos: OF   BA: .265
Hits: 1,952   HRs: 64
RBI: 529   BBs: 748
Managerial Record
Won: 64   Lost: 72   Pct: .471

Tom Brown was one of the best but least-known ballplayers of the 19th century. He accompanied Spalding on the around-the-world tour in 1888-1889. Brown scored 1,521 runs, hit 138 triples, and stole 627 bases during his 17-year career. Brown led the 1891 American Association in hits with 189, runs with 177, triples with 21, and stolen bases with 106, while playing only 137 games. He hit .321 that year.
Playing Career: *1882-1898; Bal AA, Col AA, Pit AA, Pit N, Ind N, Bos N, Bos P, Bos AA, Lou N, StL N, Was N*
Managerial Career: *1897-1898; Was N*

Willard Brown
Brown, Willard Jesse
B: Jun 26, 1911

Pos: SS, OF   BA: .355
Hits: 635   HRs: 62
RBI: NA   BBs: NA
(Negro Leagues only)

Batting star Brown led the Negro Leagues in home runs seven times, in hitting twice, doubles six times, and hits four times. Inexplicably floundering in 27 games with the Browns in 1947, he was still the first black player to hit a home run in the AL.
Playing Career: *1935-1943, 1946-1949; KC Monarchs, StL A*

George Browne
Browne, George Edward
B: Jan 12, 1876   D: Dec 9, 1920

Pos: OF   BA: .273
Hits: 1,176   HRs: 18
RBI: 303   BBs: 259

Between stints in the City of Brotherly Love, Browne batted leadoff for John McGraw's Giants, and led the NL in runs scored with 99 in 1904. He had 105 the previous year and hit .313 to boot. Browne stole 20 or more bases five straight years.
Playing Career: *1901-1912; Phi N, NY N, Bos N, Chi N, Was A, Chi A, Brk N*

Pete Browning
Browning, Louis Rogers (The Gladiator)
B: Jun 17, 1861   D: Sep 10, 1905

Pos: OF   BA: .341
Hits: 1,646   HRs: 44
RBI: 353   BBs: 466

Pete Browning was the original Louisville Slugger for whom the bat is named, but his teammates called him "the Gladiator" because when he played ball he really made

Pete Browning.

war. Browning recorded the 11th-highest batting average of all time and captured four batting titles, although one is disputed. He took the American Association crown in 1882 and 1885, but lost the 1886 title to his teammate Guy Hecker, who was a pitcher.

Browning jumped to the Players' League in 1890 where he led his peers with a .391 mark. Ironically, his greatest achievement occurred off the field. Early in 1884 Browning broke his favorite bat. He was approached by a young apprentice cabinetmaker and ardent fan. Bud Hillerich offered to make another bat, tailored to Browning's specifications. After that, many ballplayers began to order bats from Hillerich.
Playing Career: *1882-1894; Lou AA, Cle P, Pit N, Cin N, StL N, Brk N*

Tom Brunansky
Brunansky, Thomas Andrew
B: Aug 20, 1960

Pos: OF, DH   BA: .246
Hits: 1,495   HRs: 261
RBI: 885   BBs: 746

While never leading the league, Brunansky hit 20 or more homers for eight consecutive years in the big leagues, followed by annual totals of 16, 16 and 15. Just as consistent with doubles, Brunansky hit more than 20 two-baggers for 11 years, and twice hit more than 30. He made the All-Rookie team in 1982 and was selected for the AL All-Star team in 1986. He hit .412 with a 1.000 slugging percentage in the 1987 ALCS, helping the Twins become World Champions.
Playing Career: *1981- ; Cal A, Min A, StL N, Bos A, Mil A*

George Brunet
Brunet, George Stuart
B: Jun 8, 1935   D: Oct 25, 1991

Pos: P   ERA: 3.62
W-L: 69-93   SOs: 921
ShOs: 15   Saves: 4

Brunet pitched for 32 seasons in organized baseball. He holds the all-time minor league strikeout record with 3,175, and he also won 244 games. At the major league level he pitched 16 years, three times winning in double figures.
Playing Career: *1956-1971; KC A, Mil N, Hou N, Bal A, LA A, Cal A, Sea A, Was A, Pit N, StL N*

John T. Brush
Brush, John Tomlinson
B: Jun 15, 1845   D: Nov 26, 1912

John T. Brush was the clothing store magnate who profoundly influenced baseball as owner and operator of three NL clubs. Unhappy with the financial arrangements in the 1903 World Series, Brush refused to let his team play in the 1904 Series. He wrote the rules and regulations for the World Series which are still being used today.

Brush organized the original franchise in Indianapolis, becoming president in 1887. The next year he pushed through the salary limitation rule, which helped spark the revolt that led to the Players' League. When the NL dropped his Indianapolis club he invested in the New York Giants, then he was awarded the Cincinnati franchise in the reorganized 12-team NL. He sold the Reds and bought the Giants in 1902. Brush was a supporter of Andrew Freedman's "Syndicate Ball" concept in which all NL teams would be owned by a trust and good players would be sent to the best drawing cities. This idea was defeated at the 1902 NL winter meeting.

John T. Brush.

Billy Bruton
Bruton, William Haron
B: Dec 22, 1925

Pos: OF	BA: .273
Hits: 1,651	HRs: 94
RBI: 545	BBs: 482

Bruton was the fleet-footed center fielder who was the leadoff hitter for the powerhouse Braves teams of the 1950s. He led the NL in stolen bases his first three years, totaling 207 in his career. He led the NL in runs with 112 and in triples with 13 in 1960. A knee injury cost him an opportunity to play in the 1957 World Series, but he hit .412 in the 1958 Series, including a home run in Game Two. Showing more power, he hit home runs into double figures from 1960 to 1962.
Playing Career: *1953-1964; Mil N, Det A*

Ron Bryant
Bryant, Ronald Raymond
B: Nov 12, 1947

Pos: P	ERA: 4.02
W-L: 57-56	SOs: 509
ShOs: 6	Saves: 1

Bryant seemingly reached his potential when he won an NL-leading 24 games in 1973, with a .667 winning percentage. The following spring he injured himself in a diving accident. His back and career never recovered. The Giants traded him to St. Louis after a 3-15 season in 1974.
Playing Career: *1967, 1969-1975; SF N, StL N*

Steve Brye
Brye, Stephen Robert
B: Feb 4, 1949

Pos: OF	BA: .258
Hits: 515	HRs: 30
RBI: 193	BBs: 144

Brye misjudged George Brett's fly ball on his last at-bat of the 1976 season, allowing Brett to edge out his teammate Hal McRae for the AL batting title by .001. In his only season as a regular Brye led AL outfielders in fielding with a .997 mark. He played for the Twins for seven of his nine seasons.
Playing Career: *1970-1978; Min A, Mil A, Pit N*

Al Buckenberger
Buckenberger, Albert C.
B: Jan 31, 1861   D: Jul 1, 1917

Managerial Record
Won: 490   Lost: 541   Pct: .475

Buckenberger was a kindhearted leader who wanted his players to be sober gentlemen at a time when such conduct was not the rule. His highest major league finish was second, with the Pirates in 1893. The following year he was replaced by Connie Mack.
Managerial Career: *1889-1890, 1892-1895, 1902-1904; Col AA, Pit N, StL N, Bos N*

Bill Buckner
Buckner, William Joseph
B: Dec 14, 1949

Pos: 1B, OF, DH	BA: .289
Hits: 2,715	HRs: 174
RBI: 1,208	BBs: 450

Bill Buckner was the scapegoat in one of the most controversial rallies in World Series history. In the sixth game of the 1986 Series Buckner's Red Sox had just gone ahead 5-3 in the top of the 10th. The first two Mets made outs, then three straight singles left runners on first and third with one run in. A new pitcher threw a wild pitch; the tying run scored. The next batter, Mookie Wilson, slapped a grounder to first. The ball went through Buckner's war-torn legs and the Mets stayed alive to win in seven games.

Buckner had a full career: a batting title in 1980; two World Series, 1974 and 1986; 1,077 runs scored; 183 stolen bases; 498 doubles; and 2,517 games – all this despite chronic ankle problems. He even had his first five-hit game in 1986. Buckner came off the Arizona State campus, signed a sizable bonus, and hit more than .300 in his three minor league seasons. He was named to the All-Rookie team in 1971.
Playing Career: *1969-1990; LA N, Chi N, Bos A, Cal A, KC A*

Bill Buckner rejoined the Red Sox in 1990, his last season of major league play.

Steve Buechele
Buechele, Steven Bernard
B: Sep 26, 1961

Pos: 3B	BA: .248
Hits: 941	HRs: 122
RBI: 486	BBs: 354

Buechele became third baseman for the Rangers when Buddy Bell was traded to the Reds. Expected to swing a home run bat, Buechele hit taters into double figures in his first four full seasons. He was acquired by Pittsburgh, where he hit .304 in the 1991 NLCS.
Playing Career: *1985-; Tex A, Pit N, Chi N*

Charlie Buffinton.

Charlie Buffinton
Buffinton, Charles G.
B: Jun 14, 1861   D: Sep 23, 1907

Pos: P	ERA: 2.96
W-L: 233-152	SOs: 1,700
ShOs: 30	Saves: 3
Managerial Record	
Won: 61 Lost: 54 Pct: .530	

In 1884 Buffinton won 47 games, compiled a 2.16 ERA, completed more than 60 starts, pitched 587 innings, walked 76, struck out 417 and pitched 8 shutouts. He also played 13 games in the outfield and 11 at first base, batting .267. He was 22 years old when the season started. Developing arm trouble in 1886, Buffinton was released by the Red Stockings. The Phillies picked him up, and he responded by winning 76 games in the next three years.

One of the best hitting pitchers of his day, Buffinton amassed 543 hits, including 7 home runs, with a lifetime mark of .245. As a pitcher, he had a great overhand curve. Some historians say that he invented that pitch, but there is no proof of it. He once pitched back-to-back one-hitters, on August 6 and 9, 1887.
Playing Career: *1882-1892; Bos N, Phi N, Phi P, Bos AA, Bal N*
Managerial Career: *1890; Phi P*

Don Buford
Buford, Donald Alvin
B: Feb 2, 1937

Pos: OF	BA: .264
Hits: 1,203	HRs: 93
RBI: 418	BBs: 672

Buford hit leadoff and was the catalyst for three pennant-winning Orioles teams. Scoring 99 runs all three seasons, Buford was also the most difficult man to double up in baseball history, hitting into only 33 double plays in 4,553 at-bats.
Playing Career: *1963-1972; Chi A, Bal A*

Bob Buhl
Buhl, Robert Ray
B: Aug 12, 1928

Pos: P	ERA: 3.55
W-L: 166-132	SOs: 1,268
ShOs: 20	Saves: 6

Bob Buhl was the worst hitter of all time. Going 0-for-70 in 1962, he finished with a lifetime average of .089; luckily he was a pitcher. Although Buhl took a back seat to Warren Spahn and Lew Burdette, he had a strong record that helped the Braves compete for the pennant year after year. Famed as a Dodger-killer, he beat them eight times in 1956 alone. Buhl led the NL in shutouts with four in 1959 and was selected for the 1960 NL All-Star Game.
Playing Career: *1953-1967; Mil N, Chi N, Phi N*

Morgan Bulkeley.

Morgan Bulkeley
Bulkeley, Morgan
B: Dec 26, 1837   D: Nov 6, 1922
Hall of Fame 1937

Financier and Connecticut politician Morgan Bulkeley was chosen as the first president of the NL in 1876 in an attempt to unify East and West teams. He was president of the Hartford team in the National Association at the time of his election. Bulkeley was a founder of the U.S. Bank of Hartford and was also the president of the Aetna Life Insurance Company for more than 40 years. Serving as mayor of Hartford for two terms, Bulkeley went on to become governor of Connecticut and then a U.S. Senator. He was the president of the Hartford Dark Blues baseball club in 1874-1875. When William Hulbert approached team leaders about secession from the National Association, he wanted a figurehead to lead them. Bulkeley was the perfect man for the league presidency during its maiden year, but when he failed to appear at the 1877 winter meetings, club owners elected William Hulbert to take his place.

Al Bumbry
Bumbry, Alonza Benjamin
B: Apr 21, 1947

Pos: OF	BA: .281
Hits: 1,422	HRs: 54
RBI: 402	BBs: 471

One of the few major league players who went to the Vietnam War, Bumbry won a Bronze Star for meritorious service. Back in the civilian world Bumbry was a leadoff man for the Orioles, a team that won four division titles and two pennants between 1973 and 1983. Bumbry was the first Oriole to collect 200 hits. He also holds the team record for stolen bases with 254. He was selected to the AL All-Star team in 1980, the year he scored 118 runs.
Playing Career: *1972-1985; Bal A, SD N*

Wally Bunker
Bunker, Wallace Edward
B: Jan 25, 1945

Pos: P	ERA: 3.51
W-L: 60-52	SOs: 569
ShOs: 5	Saves: 5

Young Wally Bunker won 19 games at age 19, leading the AL in winning percentage. He shut out the mighty Dodgers on six hits in Game Three of the 1966 World Series. Arm trouble plagued him throughout his career, and finally gave up in 1971.
Playing Career: *1963-1971; Bal A, KC A*

Jim Bunning
Bunning, James Paul David
B: Oct 23, 1931

Pos: P	ERA: 3.27
W-L: 224-184	SOs: 2,855
ShOs: 40	No-hitters: 2

Bunning, the father of nine children, tossed a perfect game on Father's Day at Shea Stadium in 1964. He has career statistics that deserve careful consideration for the Hall of Fame. Bunning won 100 games in both leagues, and pitched a no-hitter in both. He won 20 games once and 19 four times. A menacing pitcher who threw sidearm, he was particularly effective with right-handed batters. He led the AL twice in strikeouts and the NL once, garnering 1,000 K's in each league. When Bunning retired, he had the

The Phillies' big Jim Bunning shows his trademark sidearm throw.

second most strikeouts in baseball history. He managed for five years, then turned to politics.

With a degree in economics, Bunning went into Republican party politics in his home state of Kentucky when he left baseball. He lost a bid to become governor, but later won a seat in the U.S. House of Representatives.
Playing Career: *1955-1971; Det A, Phi N, Pit N, LA N*

Lew Burdette
Burdette, Selva Lewis (Nitro)
B: Nov 22, 1926

Pos: P	ERA: 3.66
W-L: 203-144	SOs: 1,074
ShOs: 33	No-hitters: 1

Fans still talk about ''Nitro'' Lew, the former Yankees farm hand going for his third World Series win over the Yanks in 1957. Burdette shut them out, 2-0, to become only the seventh pitcher in history to post three complete game victories in the Fall Classic. His ERA was 0.67 for the Series.

Burdette bounced around quite a bit, and he was 27 before he became the number two starter behind Warren Spahn. Lew was 30 when he became a very good pitcher, winning 19 and leading the NL in ERA. He won

60 games and saved 31 from 1958 through 1960, and led the NL in strikeouts 1959-1961. He used a fastball, a curve and a wet curve that, curiously, broke like a spitter.

Spahn and Burdette gave the Braves 443 victories between them. The duo made the franchise an instant pennant contender. Burdette went back to Nitro, West Virginia, when his fastball flamed out.
Playing Career: *1950-1967; NY A, Bos N, Mil N, StL N, Chi N, Phi N, Cal A*

Jack Burdock
Burdock, John Joseph
B: Apr 1852   D: Nov 28, 1931

Pos: 2B, 3B	BA: .250
Hits: 1,229	HRs: 19
RBI: 438	BBs: 142
Managerial Record	
Won: 30 Lost: 24 Pct: .556	

Burdock was an intense 19th-century player well-known for encouraging teammates to excel. His best year was 1883, when he hit .330 and led Boston to a surprising upset in the NL pennant race. He led NL second basemen in fielding five times.
Playing Career: *1872-1888, 1891; Brk Atlantics n, NY Mutuals n, Har Dark Blues n, Har N, Bos N, Brk AA*
Managerial Career: *1883; Bos N*

Smoky Burgess
Burgess, Forrest Harrill
B: Feb 6, 1927   D: Sep 15, 1991

Pos: C	BA: .295
Hits: 1,318	HRs: 126
RBI: 673	BBs: 477

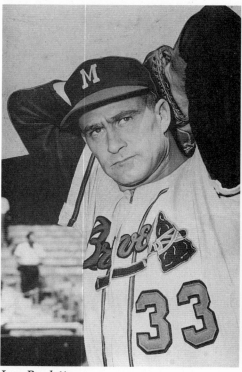

Lew Burdette.

Forrest ''Smoky'' Burgess.

Burgess's reputation for pinch hitting overshadowed a top-notch catching career. He led NL receivers in fielding three different years, 1953, 1960-1961. After hitting 50 home runs at Nashville in 1948, he came up with the Cubs the next year. Burgess was selected for the NL All-Star team four times. In 1954 Burgess hit .368 in 108 games for the Phillies. His .333 batting average in the 1960 World Series helped the Pirates win it all. Pinch hitting, Burgess had 507 at-bats and 145 hits, making him second on the all-time list.
Playing Career: *1949, 1951-1967; Chi N, Phi N, Cin N, Pit N, Chi A*

Tom Burgmeier
Burgmeier, Thomas Henry
B: Aug 2, 1943

Pos: P	ERA: 3.23
W-L: 79-55	SOs: 584
ShOs: 0	Saves: 102

Burgmeier was a consistent and durable reliever until tendinitis in his shoulder ended his career at age 40. The savvy, good-fielding Burgmeier had 102 lifetime saves. Signed by the Astros, he debuted instead with the Angels and went to the Royals in the 1968 expansion draft. In 1971 he was 9-7 with 17 saves and a 1.74 ERA. He had a career-high 24 saves for Boston in 1980, when he was chosen for the AL All-Star squad.
Playing Career: *1968-1984; Cal A, KC A, Min A, Bos A, Oak A*

Eddie Burke
Burke, Edward D.
B: Oct 6, 1866   D: Nov 26, 1907

Pos: OF	BA: .279
Hits: 979	HRs: 30
RBI: 413	BBs: 317

Eddie Burke batted leadoff and hit .389 for the Giants who pulled a surprising upset of the Orioles in the 1894 Temple Cup Series. In three of four years, 1893-1896, he scored 120 or more runs. Burke stole 291 bases, 54 in 1894 alone.
Playing Career: *1890-1897; Phi N, Pit N, Mil AA, Cin N, NY N*

Jimmy Burke
Burke, James Timothy (Sunset Jimmy)
B: Oct 12, 1874   D: Mar 26, 1942

Pos: 3B	BA: .244
Hits: 475	HRs: 1
RBI: 187	BBs: 112
Managerial Record	
Won: 206 Lost: 236 Pct: .466	

Released by Charles Comiskey in 1901, Burke was picked up by the Pirates. Sunset Jimmy had the good fortune to play on one of the greatest teams of all time, the Pirates of 1901-1902.
Playing Career: *1898-1899, 1901-1905; Cle N, StL N, Mil A, Chi A, Pit N, StL N*
Managerial Career: *1905, 1918-1920; StL N, StL A*

Tim Burke
Burke, Timothy Philip
B: Feb 19, 1959

Pos: P	ERA: 2.72
W-L: 49-33	SOs: 444
ShOs: 0	Saves: 102

Burke set an NL rookie record with a league-leading 78 appearances in 1985 when he was the set-up man for Jeff Reardon. Burke won his first eight major league decisions, and finished 9-4 with eight saves. After Reardon was traded, Burke became the leader of Montreal's bullpen-by-committee, going 7-0 with 18 saves and a 1.19 ERA and walking only 19 hitters in 91 innings in 1987. In 1989 Burke saved 28, was 9-3, and was chosen for the All-Star team.
Playing Career: *1985-1992; Mon N, NY N, NY A*

Jesse Burkett
Burkett, Jesse Cail
B: Dec 4, 1868   D: May 27, 1953
Hall of Fame 1946

Pos: OF, P	BA: .339
Hits: 2,853	HRs: 75
RBI: 952	BBs: 1,029

Young Jesse Burkett got to the majors during the Players' League rebellion. He started as a pitcher, but found that he was better at hitting. He swatted .309 in his rookie year, but compiled a pitching record of 3-10. He was sold to the Cleveland Spiders. Error-prone as an outfielder, Burkett made up for his blunders by scoring 119 runs and stealing 36 bases in his first full season.

Jesse Burkett.

It was hitting that put Burkett into the Hall of Fame. He was a line drive hitter, batting .400 or more three times. He led the NL in batting and in hits three times, stole 389 bases and scored 1,720 runs. When he jumped to the AL his hitting suffered and Burkett left the big leagues for the minors. He bought the Worcester Eastern League club in 1906 and served as owner, manager and outfielder until 1913. He also coached at Holy Cross and later worked for John McGraw.
Playing Career: *1890-1905; NY N, Cle N, StL N, StL A, Bos A*

Rick Burleson
Burleson, Richard Paul
B: Apr 29, 1951

Pos: SS	BA: .273
Hits: 1,401	HRs: 50
RBI: 449	BBs: 420

Burleson was a four-time All-Star who provided the Red Sox with solid play at shortstop and in the leadoff position. He set the major league record for double plays involving shortstops with 147 in 1980. His tremendous arm suffered a rotator cuff injury in 1982 and he retore it in 1984, missing the entire '85 season. After a year off, he was voted AL Comeback Player of the Year when he hit .284 in 93 games for the Angels.
Playing Career: *1974-1984, 1986-1987; Bos A, Cal A, Bal A*

Johnny Burnett
Burnett, John Henderson
B: Nov 1, 1904   D: Aug 13, 1959

Pos: 2B, SS, 3B, OF	BA: .284
Hits: 521	HRs: 9
RBI: 213	BBs: 163

Johnny Burnett once got nine hits in an 18-inning game, a major league record. Combined with the two hits he got the day before, Burnett had a second record, 11 hits in two consecutive games. He played regularly only two years, batting .300 and .297.
Playing Career: *1927-1935; Cle A, StL A*

George Burns
Burns, George Henry (Tioga George)
B: Jan 31, 1893   D: Jan 7, 1978

Pos: 1B	BA: .307
Hits: 2,018	HRs: 72
RBI: 951	BBs: 363

Burns was named "Tioga George" to distinguish him from another George Burns who played in the NL at the same time he played in the AL. Burns astonished observers in 1923 by making an unassisted triple play against the Indians, who had traded him two years earlier.

Hitting was his forte. Burns scored the winning run in the 1920 World Series for the Indians, and hit .361 for them in 1921. In the mid-1920s he strung together four straight years of .310, .336, .358 and .319 batting marks. He knocked in 114 runs in 1926. Burns

led the AL twice in hits, in 1918 and 1926, with 178 and 216, respectively. In the latter year, he smacked 64 doubles, then a major league record, and was named AL MVP.
Playing Career: *1914-1929; Det A, Phi A, Cle A, Bos A, NY A*

George Burns

Burns, George Joseph
B: Nov 24, 1889   D: Aug 15, 1966

Pos: OF	BA: .287
Hits: 2,077	HRs: 41
RBI: 611	BBs: 872

The NL George Burns batted leadoff and played the sunfield at the Polo Grounds with a special long-billed cap that had sunglasses attached. Very fast, Burns stole 383 bases and scored 1,188 runs, besides setting a league record by playing 459 consecutive games. He led the NL in at-bats and stolen bases twice, and in runs scored and walks five times. He appeared in three World Series, batting .333 in the 1921 Series and leading the Giants with 11 hits, including four in Game Three.

After the 1921 season Manager McGraw reluctantly traded Burns to the Reds for third baseman Heinie Groh. Burns hit well for the Reds, but declined at the plate and was released in 1924. The Phillies picked him up and he responded by hitting .292. He then managed minor league clubs in the International, New York-Pennsylvania, Blue Ridge, Eastern, and Texas Leagues. He was a playing manager, never failing to hit at least .295.
Playing Career: *1911-1925; NY N, Cin N, Phi N*

George Joseph Burns.

Tom Burns

Burns, Thomas Everett
B: Mar 30, 1857   D: Mar 19, 1902

Pos: SS, 3B	BA: .264
Hits: 1,299	HRs: 40
RBI: 571	BBs: 270
Managerial Record	
Won: 185 Lost: 168 Pct: .524	

Tommy Burns played third base in the "Stonewall" infield of the White Stockings who won five pennants in six years. He started at shortstop 1880-1885, then he and Ned Williamson switched positions. Fred Pfeffer at second and Cap Anson at first rounded out the greatest infield of the 1880s. The group was known for outwitting opposing baserunners with their trick plays, and like a stone wall, nothing could get through them.

Burns and Anson were the only White Stockings regulars who did not jump to the Players' League in 1890. Burns stayed with the team manager and became known as Anson's right-hand man. Burns once slammed a major league record three extra-base hits in one inning on September 6, 1883, tying the following single-inning records: eight total bases, three hits, three runs, three times facing a pitcher and two doubles, all in that glorious inning.
Playing Career: *1880-1892; Chi N, Pit N*
Managerial Career: *1892, 1898-1899; Pit N, Chi N*

Tom Burns

Burns, Thomas P. (Oyster)
B: Sep 6, 1864   D: Nov 11, 1928

Pos: OF	BA: .300
Hits: 1,395	HRs: 65
RBI: 675	BBs: 464

Burns has been given a colorful moniker, but the story surrounding it smells fishy – there is no documentation of his selling shellfish in the off-season, or being called "Oyster" by teammates. A popular Dodger outfielder and utility man, Burns led the NL with 123 RBI and finished second in home runs with 13, with the 1890 pennant winners.
Playing Career: *1884-1885, 1887-1895; Wil U, Bal AA, Brk AA, Brk N, NY N*

Ray Burris

Burris, Bertram Ray
B: Aug 22, 1950

Pos: P	ERA: 4.17
W-L: 108-134	SOs: 1,065
ShOs: 10	Saves: 4

After two years in the Cubs' bullpen, Burris became their ace starter in 1975, going 15-10 for a mediocre team. After spending time on the disabled list in 1979 and 1980, he recovered to help the Expos win the division title in 1981, and logged a win in the second game of the NLCS.
Playing Career: *1973-1987; Chi N, NY A, NY N, Mon N, Oak A, Mil A, StL N*

Jeff Burroughs.

Jeff Burroughs

Burroughs, Jeffrey Alan
B: Mar 7, 1951

Pos: OF	BA: .261
Hits: 1,443	HRs: 240
RBI: 882	BBs: 831

At age 23 Burroughs was a budding superstar. He was an All-Star who led the AL in RBI with 118 in 1974, winning the MVP Award. Three years later he smashed 41 home runs with the Braves and drove in 114 runs. The next year NL hurlers feared the young slugger so much that he walked a league-leading 117 times for a league-high .436 on-base percentage, and was selected again for the All-Star team.

Suddenly, Burroughs was hit by a power outage. After 1978 he never hit 20 home runs in a season, and even his doubles count dropped below 20. Used as a designated hitter and a pinch hitter for the last four years of his career, he appeared in the ALCS with Toronto in 1985.
Playing Career: *1970-1985; Was A, Tex A, Atl N, Sea A, Oak A, Tor A*

Jim Busby

Busby, James Franklin
B: Jan 8, 1927

Pos: OF	BA: .262
Hits: 1,113	HRs: 48
RBI: 438	BBs: 310

Busby was a good outfielder who led the league twice in putouts and once in fielding percentage. Batting a career-high .312 for the Senators in 1953, he also knocked 28 doubles and drove in 82 runs. After his playing days, Busby coached in the big leagues.
Playing Career: *1950-1962; Chi A, Was A, Cle A, Bal A, Bos A, Hou N*

Steve Busby
Busby, Steve
B: Sep 29, 1949

Pos: P	ERA: 3.72
W-L: 70-54	SOs: 659
ShOs: 7	No-hitters: 2

One of the brightest prospects in baseball history, Busby threw two no-hitters in his first three years, when a rotator cuff injury hampered his promising career. He played on two All-Star teams and was the first great Royals star, setting a team record for wins with 22 in 1974. AL Rookie Pitcher of the Year in 1973, Busby was the only pitcher to throw no-hitters in his first two full seasons. In the second no-hitter he retired the last 24 batters he faced. Combining those with the nine he retired in his next start, Busby set an AL record of putting down 33 consecutive batters. He is now a top sportscaster.
Playing Career: *1972-1976, 1978-1980; KC A*

Gussie Busch (r) with Manager Keane.

Gussie Busch
Busch, Augustus Adolphus
B: Mar 28, 1899   D: Sep 29, 1989

When the St. Louis Cardinals planned to move to Milwaukee in 1953, Busch bought the team for $3.75 million in order to keep it at home. He spent $7 million more to buy new players, redevelop the farm system, and to buy and refurbish old Sportsman's Park. Later he spearheaded a drive to construct Busch Memorial Stadium in downtown St. Louis. It was the last major sports complex to be built with private money. Busch's efforts produced pennant-winners in 1964, 1967, 1968, 1982, 1985 and 1987 and World Champions in 1964, 1967 and 1982.

Busch was personally involved in Cardinal

(l-r) Donie Bush with Sox President Bill Veeck and Cubs owner William Wrigley, Jr., 1931.

operations and his hands-on approach may have cost his team the services of pitchers Steve Carlton and Jerry Reuss. In the midst of campus riots, the Vietnam War, player unionization and President Nixon's request for a national freeze in wages, Busch told the Phillies owner about his trouble with Carlton who wanted a $500 raise. The Phillies owner had a trouble spot of his own with Rick Wise. "Let's swap," said Busch. It was the last unencumbered deal in baseball.

Donie Bush
Bush, Owen Joseph
B: Oct 8, 1887   D: Mar 28, 1972

Pos: SS	BA: .250
Hits: 1,804	HRs: 9
RBI: 436	BBs: 1,158
Managerial Record	
Won: 497 Lost: 539 Pct: .480	

Donie Bush grasped the essentials of a good leadoff batter. He got on base at least 3,000 times in 1,946 games, scoring 1,280 of those times. Bush led the AL in bases on balls five times.

As a manager Bush led the 1927 Pirates into the slaughterhouse called Yankee Stadium. His primary mistake was letting the Pirates watch the Yankees' batting practice. Following his major league managing career he went to the minors where his longtime association with Indianapolis led to the stadium there being named for him. Bush Stadium was used in the filming of *Eight Men Out* because it more closely resembled 1919 Comiskey Park than 1989 Comiskey Park. Bush spent more than 65 years in baseball at all capacities – player, manager, scout, owner, coach – but most of all he was a fan of baseball.
Playing Career: *1908-1923; Det A, Was A*
Managerial Career: *1923, 1927-1933; Was A, Pit N, Chi A, Cin N*

Guy Bush
Bush, Guy Terrell
B: Aug 23, 1901   D: Jul 2, 1985

Pos: P	ERA: 3.86
W-L: 176-136	SOs: 850
ShOs: 16	Saves: 34

Bush was one of the winningest Cubs pitchers, posting a record of 152-101. He frequently did double duty as a starter and a reliever. He led the NL in either relief wins or saves in four different seasons (1925, 1926, 1929 and 1935), and started at least 15 times in each of those years. In 1929 he led the league in games with 50, won 18 and saved eight for

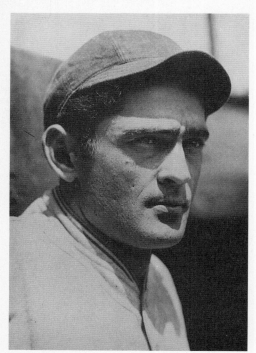

Guy Bush.

the pennant-winning Cubs. Bush contributed 19 wins to the 1932 NL champs, and had his only 20-win season the following year.

He was traded to the Pirates in 1935. On May 25, Bush relieved against the Braves in a game at Forbes Field and gave up the last two home runs of Babe Ruth's career.
Playing Career: *1923-1938, 1945; Chi N, Pit N, Bos N, StL N, Cin N*

Joe Bush
Bush, Leslie Ambrose (Bullet Joe)
B: Nov 27, 1892   D: Nov 1, 1974

Pos: P	ERA: 3.51
W-L: 194-183	SOs: 1,319
ShOs: 35	No-hitters: 1

The *Saturday Evening Post* ran a series of articles by Joe Bush about his baseball career. In one article he explained how he threw his forkball. He may have been the first major league pitcher to throw that elusive precursor to the split-finger fastball.

When Bullet Joe was only 20, Connie Mack was forced to insert him into the Athletics' starting rotation. Bush responded with a 14-6 season, helping the A's win the 1913 pennant. He added a five-hit victory in the World Series. The young Bush stuck with Mack through two pennant-winning years and three last-place finishes. Then he was traded. He was an instant shot in the arm for ailing pitching staffs; both the Red Sox and New York won pennants immediately after acquiring Bush. He also played on the 1927 NL Champion Pirates before returning to Mr. Mack and his A's. He was a good hitter, batting .253 while slugging .345.
Playing Career: *1912-1928; Phi A, Bos A, NY A, StL A, Was A, Pit N, NY N*

Randy Bush
Bush, Robert Randall
B: Oct 5, 1958

Pos: DH, OF, 1B	BA: .252
Hits: 763	HRs: 96
RBI: 344	BBs: 413

Randy Bush serves the Twins as a left-handed designated hitter. He has hit home runs in the double figures six times despite never having batted more than 395 times. He once pinch-hit two consecutive home runs to tie the AL record. He played in the 1987 and 1991 World Series.
Playing Career: *1982-; Min A*

Max Butcher
Butcher, Albert Maxwell
B: Sep 21, 1910   D: Sep 15, 1957

Pos: P	ERA: 3.73
W-L: 95-106	SOs: 485
ShOs: 15	Saves: 9

In the middle of the 1939 season, Butcher stood 2-13 with the Phillies when he was traded for the Pirates' popular first baseman Gus Suhr. The deal made fans mad, but two years later Suhr was out of baseball and Butcher was the ace of the Pittsburgh staff.
Playing Career: *1936-1945; Brk N, Phi N, Pit N*

Leslie A. "Bullet Joe" Bush.

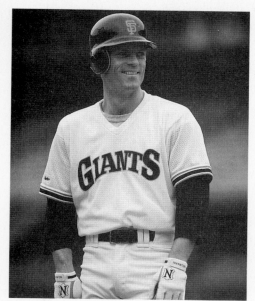

Brett Butler.

Brett Butler

Butler, Brett Morgan
B: Jun 15, 1957

Pos: OF   BA: .289
Hits: 1,958   HRs: 45
RBI: 481   BBs: 943

When baseball analyst Bill James announced that Butler was not only the best center fielder in baseball, he was one of the best leadoff men ever, fans began to notice him. Butler draws walks, steals bases and scores runs. He averaged 103 runs per season 1984-1991. Butler has led both the AL and NL in triples as well as in fielding.

Butler is the ideal leadoff person. A left-handed batter who is an adept drag bunter, he is a skilled base stealer, with a 67 percent success rate in more than 600 attempts. He has been selected for the All-Star team only once, yet has appeared in two LCS and one World Series. His 1989 postseason play is indicative of his abilities; he had eight hits, five walks, two stolen bases and seven runs scored despite hitting only .242.
Playing Career: *1981-; Atl N, Cle A, SF N, LA N*

John Buzhardt

Buzhardt, John William
B: Aug 17, 1936

Pos: P   ERA: 3.66
W-L: 71-96   SOs: 678
ShOs: 15   Saves: 7

Buzhardt mercifully ended a Phillies' 23-game losing streak by beating the Braves 7-4 in the second game of a doubleheader. He had a blazing fastball which was most effective in 1965 when he went 13-6. Buzhardt had several years of ERA's under 3.00, but toiled mainly for second-division teams.
Playing Career: *1958-1967; Chi N, Phi N, Chi A, Bal A, Hou N*

Bill Byrd

Byrd, Bill
B: Jul 15, 1907   D: Jan 3, 1991

Pos: P   ERA: NA
W-L: 115-72 (inc.)   SOs: 579 (inc.)
ShOs: 8 (inc.)   Saves: 7 (inc.)

Byrd was a big man with a wicked spitball which opposing batters claimed he really did not need. Playing in the Negro Leagues, he led in won-lost percentage with an .818 mark in 1942, in ERA with a 2.85 in 1943, in strikeouts with 57 in 1943, and in wins in 1948. He was an All-Star from 1936 to 1946.
Playing Career: *1933-1939, 1941-1950; Nash Elite Giants, Cle Red Sox, Was Elite Giants, Bal Elite Giants*

Sammy Byrd

Byrd, Samuel Dewey (Babe Ruth's Legs)
B: Oct 15, 1907   D: May 11, 1981

Pos: OF   BA: .274
Hits: 465   HRs: 38
RBI: 220   BBs: 198

The well-known late-inning substitute for Babe Ruth played parts of eight seasons and appeared in the 1932 World Series. One of his nicknames was "Babe Ruth's Legs." In his best season, 1932, Byrd hit .297. He played his last two seasons with the Reds.
Playing Career: *1929-1936; NY A, Cin N*

Bobby Byrne

Byrne, Robert Matthew
B: Dec 31, 1884   D: Dec 31, 1964

Pos: 3B   BA: .254
Hits: 1,225   HRs: 10
RBI: 329   BBs: 456

One reason the Pirates took the 1909 pennant was that they had Bobby Byrne on their team. Byrne led the NL in hits and doubles in 1910 as well as scoring 101 runs. He led NL third basemen in fielding twice. He stole 176 bases during his career.
Playing Career: *1907-1917; StL N, Pit N, Phi N, Chi A*

Tommy Byrne

Byrne, Thomas Joseph
B: Dec 31, 1919

Pos: P   ERA: 4.11
W-L: 85-69   SOs: 766
ShOs: 12   Saves: 12

Byrne was a good-hitting pitcher whom Manager Joe McCarthy tried to convince to move to first base. On the mound he was wild but effective, winning 15 or more games three times. He was chosen for the 1950 All-Star team, and appeared in four World Series.
Playing Career: *1943, 1946-1957; NY A, StL A, Chi A, Was A*

Sammy Byrd, also known as "Babe Ruth's Legs," played for the Yankees from 1929 to 1934.

Enos Cabell
Cabell, Enos Milton
B: Oct 8, 1949

Pos: 1B, 3B, SS, OF	BA: .277
Hits: 1,647	HRs: 60
RBI: 596	BBs: 259

Signed by Baltimore, Cabell had a tough time breaking into the majors because the Orioles already had Brooks Robinson at third base. Cabell's career did not take off until he did – moving to Houston and becoming a regular player for the Astros. The speedy base thief stole a career-high 42 sacks in 1977.
Playing Career: *1972-1986; Bal A, Hou N, SF N, Det A, LA N*

Leon Cadore
Cadore, Leon Joseph
B: Nov 20, 1890   D: Mar 16, 1958

Pos: P	ERA: 3.14
W-L: 68-72	SOs: 445
ShOs: 10	Saves: 3

Cadore had his most memorable season in 1920; he won a career-high 15 contests, and pitched in all 26 innings of the longest game ever played in major league history. The marathon ended in a 1-1.
Playing Career: *1915-1924; Brk N, Chi A, NY N*

Ivan Calderon
Calderon y Perez, Ivan
B: Mar 19, 1962

Pos: OF	BA: .272
Hits: 901	HRs: 104
RBI: 444	BBs: 306

Calderon has been plagued with injuries his entire big league career. Some thought he would surely be Rookie of the Year in 1985, but an August hand injury foiled his chances. Traded to the White Sox, Calderon hit 28 home runs in 1987 but a ribcage pull and shoulder surgery cut short his 1988 season. He rebounded with a .300 season for the Expos and an NL All-Star appearance in 1991.
Playing Career: *1984-; Sea A, Chi A, Mon N, Bos A*

Mike Caldwell.

Mike Caldwell
Caldwell, Ralph Michael
B: Jan 22, 1949

Pos: P	ERA: 3.81
W-L: 137-130	SOs: 939
ShOs: 23	Saves: 18

Caldwell's unshaven, unkempt appearance belied a savvy hurler who was at his best in important games. His best seasons were with the Brewers, where he was hailed as Comeback Player of the Year in 1978 after rebounding from elbow surgery. Caldwell compiled a record of 22-9 that year with a 2.36 ERA, and he threw 23 complete games to lead the AL. He pitched in the 1982 ALCS and in the World Series, beating the Cardinals twice.
Playing Career: *1971-1984; SD N, SF N, Cin N, Mil A*

Ray Caldwell
Caldwell, Raymond Benjamin (Slim)
B: Apr 26, 1888   D: Aug 17, 1967

Pos: P	ERA: 3.21
W-L: 133-120	SOs: 1,005
ShOs: 20	Saves: 9

Caldwell should have been called "Sparks." Struck by lightning in a Yankees game against the Athletics, he pulled himself together to finish the game and beat the A's 2-1. Caldwell was a veteran spitball thrower who was allowed to continue using the pitch after it was banned. He used it most effectively in 1920 when his 20 victories augmented the Indians' staff of Bagby and Coveleski to take pennant and win the World Series.
Playing Career: *1910-1921; NY A, Bos A, Cle A*

Nixey Callahan
Callahan, James Joseph
B: Mar 18, 1874   D: Oct 4, 1934

Pos: P, OF	ERA: 3.39
W-L: 99-73	SOs: 445
ShOs: 11	No-hitters: 1
Managerial Record	
Won: 394 Lost: 458 Pct: .462	

A versatile player with leadership abilities, Callahan did tours of duty in the outfield and infield as well as on the pitcher's mound. The player/manager had two 20-win seasons, 1898 and 1899, and was the top pitcher for the White Sox, the 1901 AL flag bearers. He was one of the best base stealers of all pitchers, with 186 thefts.
Playing Career: *1894, 1897-1905, 1911-1913; Phi N, Chi N, Chi A*
Managerial Career: *1903-1904, 1912-1914, 1916-1917; Chi A, Pit N*

Johnny Callison
Callison, John Wesley
B: Mar 12, 1939

Pos: OF	BA: .264
Hits: 1,757	HRs: 226
RBI: 840	BBs: 650

A good all-around player, Oklahoma-born Callison was an All-Star three times, and was second in the MVP voting in 1964. That year he hit a dramatic three-run home run in the bottom of the ninth to defeat the AL All-Star squad and draw his NL teammates even with the AL with 17 All-Star Games apiece. It was important to NL history because the Senior

Johnny Callison.

Dolph Camilli shakes hands with Mayor Fiorello LaGuardia of New York before the 1941 WS.

Rick Camp
Camp, Rick Lamar
B: Jun 10, 1953

Pos: P	ERA: 3.37
W-L: 56-49	SOs: 407
ShOs: 0	Saves: 57

Camp surprised himself and everyone else when he hit a home run in the 16th inning of a July 4, 1985 game, tying the score. Despite his efforts at the plate Camp lost the game in the 19th. His best season was 1981 when he had 17 saves and a 1.78 ERA.
Playing Career: *1976-1978, 1980-1985; Atl N*

Roy Campanella
Campanella, Roy (Campy)
B: Nov 19, 1921   D: Jun 26, 1993
Hall of Fame 1969

Pos: C	BA: .276
Hits: 1,161	HRs: 242
RBI: 856	BBs: 533

One of baseball's most beloved players, Roy Campanella was confined to a wheelchair after an automobile accident, but nothing put a damper on his spirit. In retirement, Campanella became a traveling symbol of baseball's greatness, touring the country and providing inspiration for fans of all ages.

As a player Campy was a superb catcher, and a batter who hit both for average and with power. The roly-poly receiver was quick and agile behind the plate and possessed a rifle arm which he used to gun down potential base stealers. He was an expert handler of pitchers and a natural leader of the Brooklyn Dodgers from 1948 to 1957. He hit 242 home runs in 10 years of major league competition. He pushed and pulled the Dodgers to five pennants in 1949, 1952, 1953, 1955 and 1956. Campanella was an All-Star eight times and was named MVP three times. He started his career in the Negro Leagues at age 15.
Playing Career: *1937-1942, 1944-1945, 1948-1957; Bal Elite Giants, Brk N*

Circuit had trailed since the All-Star Game began in 1933.

Though Callison batted over .300 only once, he had 100 or more RBI twice, and scored in three figures twice (107 in 1962 and 101 in 1964). His best season was 1964 when the Phillies made their famous nose dive, losing 10 straight games near the end of the season. They had been a cinch for first place.
Playing Career: *1958-1973; Chi A, Phi N, Chi N, NY A*

Ernie Camacho
Camacho, Ernest Carlos
B: Feb 1, 1955

Pos: P	ERA: 4.21
W-L: 10-20	SOs: 159
ShOs: 0	Saves: 45

Macho Camacho was the main man for Indians manager Pat Corrales. He saved 23 games in 1984, was on the disabled list most of 1985, but was back in 1986 with 20 saves. He once complained that he got headaches on the mound because he never blinked while pitching.
Playing Career: *1980-1990; Oak A, Pit N, Cle A, Hou N, SF N, StL N*

Dolph Camilli
Camilli, Adolph Louis
B: Apr 23, 1907

Pos: 1B	BA: .277
Hits: 1,482	HRs: 239
RBI: 950	BBs: 947

The likeable, hard-hitting Italian was one of the most popular Dodgers ever. A top NL player in the 1930s, Camilli was the first man Larry MacPhail recruited when he began renovating the dilapidated Dodgers in 1938. MacPhail's move paid off; Camilli was a big bat, and the team's calm port in the rough seas of Leo Durocher's managing style. A former boxer, Camilli could squelch clubhouse rhubarbs with a quiet word and a meaningful look.

At the plate, he was equally menacing. For eight consecutive seasons Camilli hit at least 23 home runs. In 1941 he led the league in home runs with 34, and in RBI with 120. Camilli was NL MVP that year as he and the Dodgers charged through the pennant race to the World Series. Camilli was named to the All-Star squad twice.
Playing Career: *1933-1943, 1945; Chi N, Phi N, Brk N, Bos A*

Howie Camnitz
Camnitz, Samuel Howard
B: Aug 22, 1881   D: Mar 2, 1960

Pos: P	ERA: 2.75
W-L: 133-106	SOs: 915
ShOs: 19	No-hitters: 1

Solid pitching was the commodity Camnitz sold; he became the sixth Buccaneer pitcher to win 100 games. Camnitz won 20 games or more three times. In 1909 he tied Christy Mathewson for the NL lead in winning percentage, .806, with a 25-6 record and a 1.63 ERA. He pitched in the World Series that year. Traded to the Phillies in 1913, the pull of Pittsburgh was so great for Camnitz that he played in only nine games for Philadelphia before he returned to the Steel City with the Federal League.
Playing Career: *1904, 1906-1915; Pit N, Phi N, Pit F*

Roy Campanella.

Bert Campaneris
Campaneris y Blanco, Dagoberto (Campy)
B: Mar 9, 1942

Pos: SS	BA: .259
Hits: 2,249	HRs: 79
RBI: 646	BBs: 618

Campaneris took off with a home run on the very first pitch thrown to him in a major league game, and he never looked back. The speedster stole 649 bases and scored 1,181 runs. He is credited with inspiring the great Oakland teams of the 1970s with his competitive spirit. Chosen for six All-Star Games, Campaneris also played in the ALCS six times, and in three World Series.

When the A's were still in Kansas City, Campaneris was the center of a Charlie Finley publicity stunt, playing every position in a nine inning game. He had pitched before – in a Florida State League game where he threw left-handed and right-handed in the same inning. In response, officials instituted the Campaneris rule that states a pitcher must declare with which hand he will pitch before the batter takes the first pitch.
Playing Career: *1964-1981, 1983; KC A, Oak A, Tex A, Cal A, NY A*

Bill Campbell
Campbell, William Richard
B: Aug 9, 1948

Pos: P	ERA: 3.55
W-L: 83-68	SOs: 864
ShOs: 1	Saves: 126

Campbell provided a lot of relief for the Twins and the Red Sox before his elbow gave out. In 1976 he posted 20 saves and led the Twins with 17 wins. The same year his .773 winning percentage topped the league, as did his 78 appearances. In Boston, Campbell led the league with 31 saves. He was named Fireman of the Year by *The Sporting News* two years in a row. Campbell played in one ALCS and World Series, and he was an All-Star in 1977.
Playing Career: *1973-1987; Min A, Bos A, Chi N, Phi N, StL N, Det A, Mon N*

Bruce Campbell
Campbell, Bruce Douglas
B: Oct 20, 1909

Pos: OF	BA: .290
Hits: 1,382	HRs: 106
RBI: 766	BBs: 548

The solid-hitting outfielder was struck by spinal meningitis in the middle of his career. Making a remarkable comeback in 1936, Campbell hit .372 in 76 games.
Playing Career: *1930-1942; Chi A, StL A, Cle A, Det A, Was A*

John Candelaria
Candelaria, John Robert (The Candy Man)
B: Nov 6, 1953

Pos: P	ERA: 3.33
W-L: 177-122	SOs: 1,673
ShOs: 13	No-hitters: 1

Known for his control, Candelaria might have had one of the greatest pitching careers ever if not for the many injuries he suffered. In addition to 177 wins, he saved 29 games. Throughout the late 1970s, Pittsburgh depended on Candelaria. He helped the Pirates win the division in his rookie year and set a record, striking out 14 in Game Three of the 1975 NLCS. He was the first Pirate to pitch a no-hitter at home.

In 1977 he led the league in ERA with a 2.34 mark and in winning percentage, .800, on his record of 20-5. He was selected for the All-Star Game that year. In the 1979 Fall Classic he gave the Bucs the victory in Game Six. When the Pirates unloaded their high salaried players in 1985, the Candy Man was sold to California. Overcoming chronic back problems, Candelaria was named AL Comeback Player of the Year in 1986.
Playing Career: *1975-; Pit N, Cal A, NY N, NY A, Mon N*

Tom Candiotti
Candiotti, Thomas Caesar (Candy)
B: Aug 31, 1957

Pos: P	ERA: 3.41
W-L: 103-103	SOs: 1,185
ShOs: 10	No-hitters: 0

Persistent Candiotti toiled in the Milwaukee farm system for six years, enduring two failed tryouts at the big league level. Then he picked up a knuckleball. Cleveland signed him in 1986 and the payback was a package of 16 victories, a 3.57 ERA, and a league-leading 17 complete games.
Playing Career: *1983-1984, 1986-; Mil A, Cle A, LA N*

Chris Cannizzaro
Cannizzaro, Christopher John
B: May 3, 1938

Pos: C	BA: .235
Hits: 458	HRs: 18
RBI: 169	BBs: 241

Staying in the majors on a wing and a prayer, Cannizzaro played 13 years as a third-string catcher. He was one of the first expansion picks for the Mets, and also played for the expansion Padres, where he hit a career-high .311. He was an All-Star in 1969.
Playing Career: *1960-1965, 1968-1974; StL N, NY N, Pit N, SD N, Chi N, LA N*

"The Candy Man," John Candelaria was the first Pirate to pitch a no-hitter at home.

LEFT: Hammerin' Hank Aaron holds several major league career records, including most home runs. (Photo by Malcolm Emmons)
BELOW: Hall of Fame catcher Johnny Bench helped Cincinnati's Big Red Machine win four pennants and two World Championships. (Photo by Chance Brockway)
ABOVE: Barry Bonds signed with the Giants in 1993 for a record-breaking sum. (Photo by Otto Greule, Jr./Allsport)

OPPOSITE: Three-time All-Star Ralph Branca won 21 games for Brooklyn in 1947, then pitched in the World Series. (UPI/Bettmann Newsphotos)

LEFT ABOVE: In 1980 the Royals' George Brett hit .390, the highest mark in 39 years. A clutch hitter in the postseason, he averaged .373 in two World Series. (National Baseball Library, Cooperstown, NY)

LEFT: Despite chronic ankle problems, durable and talented Bill Buckner played for 22 years, scoring 1,077 runs and batting in 1,208. (Photo by Damian Strohmeyer/Allsport)

ABOVE: A skilled base stealer and drag bunter, center fielder Brett Butler is the ideal leadoff man. (Photo by Otto Greule, Jr./Allsport)

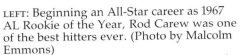

LEFT: Beginning an All-Star career as 1967 AL Rookie of the Year, Rod Carew was one of the best hitters ever. (Photo by Malcolm Emmons)

BELOW LEFT: A control artist with a 95-mph fastball, Roger Clemens has won three Cy Young Awards and four ERA crowns. (Photo by Scott Halleran/Allsport)

BELOW: During Steve Carlton's illustrious 24-year career he struck out 4,136 batters – second on the all-time list – and won 329 games. (Photo by Chance Brockway)

OPPOSITE ABOVE: The Pirates' Hall of Fame outfielder Roberto Clemente won 12 Gold Glove Awards and four batting titles during his career. (Photo by Malcolm Emmons)

OPPOSITE BELOW: Gold Glove outfielder Andre Dawson has had 36 multiple home run games. (Photo by Rick Stewart/Allsport)

ABOVE: Dizzy Dean won 30 games in 1934, then two in the World Series for the Cardinals. (Brompton Photo Library)

BELOW: Larry Doby was chosen for the All-Star team seven years in a row, 1949-1955. (Brompton Photo Library)

RIGHT: At 38, Darrell Evans became the oldest player ever to hit 40 home runs. (Photo by Janis Rettaliata/Allsport)

BELOW RIGHT: In 1965 Don Drysdale won 23 games while leading the Dodgers in batting. (Photo by Malcolm Emmons)

BELOW FAR RIGHT: Hall of Famer Joe DiMaggio played in 13 All-Star Games and 10 World Series. (Brompton Photo Library)

OPPOSITE: With 212 hits in 1986, Toronto's Tony Fernandez set a 20th-century record for most hits by a shortstop. (Photo by Otto Greule, Jr./Allsport)

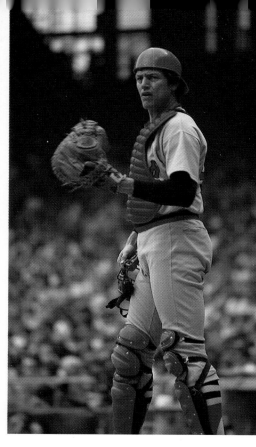

LEFT: Cecil Fielder blasted 51 homers for the Tigers in 1990. (Photo by Brian Masck/Allsport)

ABOVE: Carlton Fisk's 12th-inning homer won Game Six of the 1975 World Series. (Photo by Nancy Hogue)

BELOW LEFT: Gold Glove outfielder Curt Flood's landmark antitrust lawsuit against baseball in 1970 paved the way for change. (Photo by Chance Brockway)

BELOW: Hall of Famer Whitey Ford holds virtually all of the World Series career pitching records. (Brompton Photo Library)

WHITEY FORD Pitcher

YANKEES

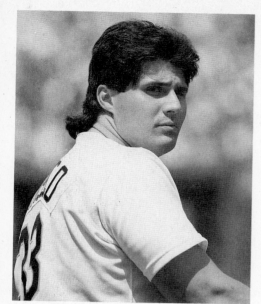

Jose Canseco.

Jose Canseco
Canseco, Jose
B: Jul 2, 1964

Pos: OF	BA: .266
Hits: 1,033	HRs: 245
RBI: 780	BBs: 449

Jose Canseco is one of the biggest crowd draws in baseball today. Legions of Spanish-speaking fans pack the right field bleachers in every AL city when Canseco comes to town. He has extraordinary reflexes, a quick bat and strong wrists. Canseco can generate power as few of today's players can.

The exceedingly popular Canseco was 1986 Rookie of the Year, edging out Wally Joyner on the strength of his 33 home runs. Two years later Canseco hit a league-leading 42 home runs and stole 40 bases. He also led the league with 124 RBI and won the AL MVP Award – and this time there was no close second. In the 1988 ALCS Canseco hit three home runs. One of them dented a television camera more than 400 feet from home plate. Jose's twin brother, Ozzie, played with the Cardinals.
Playing Career: *1985-; Oak A, Tex A*

Ben Cantwell
Cantwell, Benjamin Caldwell
B: Apr 13, 1902   D: Dec 4, 1962

Pos: P	ERA: 3.91
W-L: 76-108	SOs: 348
ShOs: 6	Saves: 21

Cantwell had two good years with the Braves: 1932 when he led NL relievers with a 12-8 record, and 1933 when he led the league in winning percentage with a .667 mark. Two years later he struggled through 25 losses with the 1935 Braves, one of the worst teams of all time.
Playing Career: *1927-1937; NY N, Bos N, Brk N*

Harry Caray
Caray, Harry
B: Mar 1, 1920

Charismatic and unabashedly biased towards his home team, Harry Caray has led the cheers of baseball fans from the broadcast booth for more than four decades. Starting with the Cardinals in 1945, Caray has worked for the A's, the White Sox and the Cubs. His antics – broadcasting games from the center field bleachers with a cooler of beer, using a fishing net to scoop foul balls off the backstop – his raucus singing, and his famous home run call – "It might be . . . It could be . . . It is!" – have endeared him to fans throughout the Midwest.

Bernie Carbo
Carbo, Bernard
B: Aug 5, 1947

Pos: OF	BA: .264
Hits: 722	HRs: 96
RBI: 358	BBs: 538

It was Carbo who set up Carlton Fisk's dramatic extra-inning home run in Game Six of the 1975 World Series with a pinch-hit homer of his own to tie the score in the eighth. Carbo was Rookie of the Year in 1970.
Playing Career: *1969-1980; Cin N, StL N, Bos A, Mil A, Cle A, Pit N*

Jose Cardenal
Cardenal, Jose Rosario Domec
B: Oct 7, 1943

Pos: OF	BA: .275
Hits: 1,913	HRs: 138
RBI: 775	BBs: 608

Cardenal was known for his superstitions: refusing to sleep in an upper berth, and going through a ritual of warmup exercises. The moody Cuban immigrant continued to migrate in the States, playing for nine teams in 18 seasons of major league ball. In Cleveland, Cardenal tied a major league record for outfielders in 1968 when he made two unassisted double plays. He had a good year with the Cardinals in 1970, hitting .293 with 32 doubles, and batting in 74 runs. The next year he landed in Milwaukee, the year after that in Chicago. Cardenal stayed with the Cubs for six years.

Feeling at home at last, Cardenal led the Cubs in hitting with a .303 mark in 1973. He also topped the club with 33 doubles and 19 stolen bases, and the Windy City's baseball writers named him Chicago Player of the Year. Cardenal played for three more teams before he retired, ending with the excitement of the 1980 World Series with the Royals.
Playing Career: *1963-1980; SF N, Cal A, Cle A, StL N, Mil A, Chi N, Phi N, NY N, KC A*

Jose Cardenal crosses the plate after hitting a homer in 1965.

Hall of Famer Rod Carew with the California Angels in 1980.

Leo Cardenas
Cardenas y Alfonso, Leonardo Lazaro (Chico)
B: Dec 17, 1938

Pos: SS	BA: .257
Hits: 1,725	HRs: 118
RBI: 689	BBs: 522

Cardenas was the ideal shortstop; a snazzy fielder and a power hitter. He won a Gold Glove Award in 1965, led the NL in fielding and putouts twice and in double plays once. Cardenas even had a 20 home run season in Cincinnati in 1966, setting a record for Reds shortstops. His bat was evident again in 1969 when he hit .280 for the Twins and led AL shortstops in three defensive categories. He was an All-Star five times.
Playing Career: *1960-1975; Cin N, Min A, Cal A, Cle A, Tex A*

Don Cardwell
Cardwell, Donald Eugene
B: Dec 7, 1935

Pos: P	ERA: 3.92
W-L: 102-138	SOs: 1,211
ShOs: 17	No-hitters: 1

A fine Cubs pitcher with endurance, Cardwell led the NL with 38 starts in 1961. Overcoming serious arm trouble in 1964, the big right-hander rebounded with a 13-10 record for Pittsburgh in 1965 despite six one-run losses. Cardwell helped the Mets get to the 1969 World Series.
Playing Career: *1957-1970; Phi N, Chi N, Pit N, NY N, Atl N*

Rod Carew
Carew, Rodney Cline
B: Oct 1, 1945
Hall of Fame 1991

Pos: 2B, 1B	BA: .328
Hits: 3,053	HRs: 92
RBI: 1,015	BBs: 1,018

Known as one of the best hitters in baseball history, Carew was also a great all-around player. Twins manager Frank Quilici said "There's nobody alive, nobody, who could turn a single into a double, a double into a triple the way Rod could. He may have been the most complete player of his time." Part of that well-rounded ability was Carew's base stealing. His career total of 353 included seven steals of home in 1969 – one shy of Ty Cobb's 1912 mark of eight.

Rookie of the Year in 1967, Carew collected seven batting titles, an MVP Award, and 18 All-Star Game bids. He hit .300 or more for 15 consecutive seasons, and scored 1,424 runs. Calvin Griffith, who switched Carew to first base in order to lengthen his career, placed the keystone sacker in the same class with Rogers Hornsby and Charlie Gehringer. Carew played in four ALCS, but sadly, never got to the World Series.
Playing Career: *1967-1985; Min A, Cal A*

Andy Carey
Carey, Andrew Arthur
B: Oct 18, 1931

Pos: 3B	BA: .260
Hits: 741	HRs: 64
RBI: 350	BBs: 268

A big eater, but not a big bat, Carey was the reason the Yankees stopped letting players sign for meals. His best year was 1954 when he hit .302. In 1955 he figured in four double plays in one game, tying the major league record for third basemen.
Playing Career: *1952-1962; NY A, KC A, Chi A, LA N*

Max Carey
Carey, Max George
B: Jan 11, 1890   D: May 30, 1976
Hall of Fame 1961

Pos: OF	BA: .285
Hits: 2,665	HRs: 69
RBI: 800	BBs: 1,040
Managerial Record	
Won: 146 Lost: 161 Pct: .476	

Carey was the best-fielding NL center fielder of his era, and a great base stealer. He led the NL in putouts and total chances nine times and in assists four times. His lifetime total of 339 assists ranks him in the top 10 for major league outfielders. Carey's amazing speed and range in the outfield allowed him to lead in most fielding chances per game seven times. He holds the NL outfielders' record for double plays with 86.

His speed was equally useful running bases. Carey was NL leader in stolen bases 10 times with a lifetime total of 738. His success rate in steals ranks second only to Davey Lopes. Playing leadoff, Carey scored an incredible 42% of the time he reached base, netting 1,545 runs. After his playing days, Carey was a scout and a manager, first in the big leagues, then in the minors.
Playing Career: *1910-1929; Pit N, Brk N*
Managerial Career: *1932-1933; Brk N*

Max Carey.

Tom Carey
Carey, Thomas John
B: 1849   D: Feb 13, 1899

Pos: 2B, SS   BA: .270
Hits: 646   HRs: 6
RBI: 194   BBs: 15
Managerial Record
Won: 27   Lost: 21   Pct: .563

Born J. J. Norton, Tom Carey was one of the top players in the old National Association. With a .334 batting average, he scored 76 runs in 56 games for the Lord Baltimores of 1873, the second of his two years there.
Playing Career: *1871-1879; Ft. Wayne Kekiongas n, Bal Lord Baltimores n, NY Mutuals n, Har Dark Blues n, Har N, Pro N, Cle N*
Managerial Career: *1873-1874; Bal Lord Baltimores n, NY Mutuals n*

Tex Carleton
Carleton, James Otto
B: Aug 19, 1906   D: Jan 11, 1977

Pos: P   ERA: 3.91
W-L: 100-76   SOs: 808
ShOs: 16   No-hitters: 1

Tex was one of the "country boys" during the 1930s that made fans think baseball was dominated by rural elements, when actually it has always had a preponderance of players from the city. Carleton was good for at least 10 victories a year; he played in three World Series.
Playing Career: *1932-1938, 1940; StL N, Chi N, Brk N*

Hal Carlson
Carlson, Harold Gust
B: May 17, 1892   D: May 28, 1930

Pos: P   ERA: 3.97
W-L: 114-120   SOs: 590
ShOs: 17   Saves: 19

A good pitcher who was also a respectable batter – he once supplied a pinch-hit home run – Carlson won 17 games in 1926 and pitched in two World Series games in 1929 for the Cubs. He died of a stomach hemorrhage in the midst of his 14th season.
Playing Career: *1917-1930; Pit N, Phi N, Chi N*

Steve Carlton
Carlton, Steven Norman (Lefty)
B: Dec 22, 1944

Pos: P   ERA: 3.22
W-L: 329-244   SOs: 4,136
ShOs: 55   Saves: 2

Cardinals fans still groan at the mention of Steve Carlton's name. In a tiff over a pay-raise, owner Gussie Busch sent the great left-hander packing to Philadelphia, where the pitcher continued his glorious career in the wrong red hat. Carlton won more games than all but one other left-handed pitcher – Warren Spahn – and he ranks second only to Nolan Ryan on the all-time strikeout list. The winner of four Cy Young Awards, Carlton led the NL in wins four times, in ERA once and in strikeouts five times. He was on the All-Star team 10 times, and led his teams to five NLCS and four World Series.

An enigmatic personality, Carlton stopped talking to the press altogether in 1978, and was silent for eight years until leaving Philadelphia in 1986. No one could believe his career was over – least of all Carlton. He made four heart-rending attempts to revive it before finally retiring in 1988.
Playing Career: *1965-1988; StL N, Phi N, SF N, Chi A, Cle A, Min A*

Don Carman
Carman, Donald Wayne
B: Aug 14, 1959

Pos: P   ERA: 4.04
W-L: 53-54   SOs: 598
ShOs: 3   Saves: 11

Carman came to the big leagues as a reliever, earning a save in his debut, but was sent back to the minors to learn to be a starter. His career never took off as the Phillies projected, and a broken thumb in 1987 slowed him down.
Playing Career: *1983-1992; Phi N, Cin N, Tex A*

Hick Carpenter
Carpenter, Warren William (Old Hickory)
B: Aug 16, 1855   D: Apr 18, 1937

Pos: 3B   BA: .259
Hits: 1, 201   HRs: 18
RBI: 204   BBs: 111

The term "hot corner" in reference to third base was inspired by Carpenter's smooth handling of sharply hit balls there. Cincinnati sportswriter O. P. Caylor bestowed the label after watching Carpenter play. Old Hickory played more than 1,000 games as a left-handed third baseman. He once led the AA in fielding with an .835 third base mark.
Playing Career: *1879-1889, 1892; Syr N, Cin N, Wor N, Cin AA, StL N*

Chico Carrasquel
Carrasquel y Colon, Alfonso
B: Jan 23, 1926

Pos: SS   BA: .258
Hits: 1,199   HRs: 55
RBI: 474   BBs: 491

Carrasquel was a skillful shortstop who once accepted 297 chances without an error. He was picked for four All-Star Games. A weight problem slowed his sparkling play and he retired to his native Venezuela to become a baseball broadcaster.
Playing Career: *1950-1959; Chi A, Cle A, KC A, Bal A*

Four-time Cy Young Award winner Steve Carlton.

Bill Carrigan
Carrigan, William Francis
B: Oct 22, 1883   D: Jul 8, 1969

Pos: C   BA: .257
Hits: 506   HRs: 6
RBI: 235   BBs: 206
Managerial Record
Won: 489   Lost: 500   Pct: .494

Carrigan had been used as a platoon catcher before he took over the leadership of the Red Sox as player-manager in 1913. Boston finished second under his command the following year. In 1915 and 1916, Carrigan had Babe Ruth in his pitching rotation, and the Red Sox won the World Series both years. Another managing stint a decade later, during the lively ball era, was not successful.
Playing Career: *1906, 1908-1916; Bos A*
Managerial Career: *1913-1916, 1927-1929; Bos A*

Clay Carroll
Carroll, Clay Palmer
B: May 2, 1941

Pos: P   ERA: 2.94
W-L: 96-73   SOs: 681
ShOs: 0   Saves: 143

Carroll was a solid, dependable reliever, best known for his contribution to the success of Cincinnati's Big Red Machine of the 1970s. In the 1970 World Series, Carroll appeared in four games without allowing a run, and he had the Reds' only win. It was the same story in 1975, but with a different ending. Carroll won Game Seven for the Reds, making them World Champions.

A product of the Braves' farm system, Carroll was traded to Cincinnati in 1968. He relied on his fastball, but used a variety of breaking pitches to break the hearts of opposing batters. He appeared in 50 games in each of his eight seasons in Cincinnati. In 1972 he was named Fireman of the Year by *The Sporting News*. Not to be confused with Tom Carroll, a spot starter for the Reds in 1974-1975, Clay Carroll was selected for the All-Star team twice, and played in four NLCS. He recorded 88 relief wins and 143 saves during his career.
Playing Career: *1964-1978; Mil N, Atl N, Cin N, Chi A, StL N, Pit N*

Cliff Carroll
Carroll, Samuel Clifford
B: Oct 18, 1859   D: Jun 12, 1923

Pos: OF   BA: .251
Hits: 995   HRs: 31
RBI: 347   BBs: 361

Despite his being a first baseman and catcher in the minor leagues, Carroll played all his big league games as an outfielder. He led NL left fielders in putouts three times. After a hiatus, Carroll returned to baseball and had his best year.
Playing Career: *1882-1888, 1890-1893; Pro N, Was N, Pit N, Chi N, StL N, Bos N*

Ownie Carroll
Carroll, Owen Thomas
B: Nov 11, 1902   D: Jun 8, 1975

Pos: P   ERA: 4.43
W-L: 65-90   SOs: 311
ShOs: 2   Saves: 5

Detroit signed Carroll after his outstanding career at Holy Cross College, posting a record of 50-2 over three seasons. He led the Tigers' staff with 16 wins in 1928, but suffered through a succession of lower division teams and never realized his potential.
Playing Career: *1925, 1927-1934; Det A, NY A, Cin N, Brk N*

Kid Carsey
Carsey, Wilfred
B: Oct 22, 1870   D: Mar 29, 1960

Pos: P   ERA: 4.95
W-L: 116-138   SOs: 484
ShOs: 4   Saves: 3

It is amazing that Philadelphia accepted Kid Carsey after his disastrous rookie year with Washington, starting 53 games and losing 37 of them. But he had some good years with the Phillies, including 1895 when his record was 24-16.
Playing Career: *1891-1899, 1901; Was AA, Phi N, StL N, Cle N, Was N, Brk N*

Gary Carter
Carter, Gary Edmund
B: Apr 8, 1954

Pos: C, OF, 1B   BA: .262
Hits: 2,092   HRs: 324
RBI: 1,225   BBs: 848

Once Johnny Bench had retired, the path was clear for Gary Carter to become the premier catcher of his era. Known for durability, defensive technique and clutch hitting, Carter also got a reputation for being a chatterbox and a publicity hound. In any case, he

Relief pitcher Clay Carroll (c) with Bernie Carbo and Johnny Bench, October 3, 1970.

Catcher Gary Carter also played outfield.

was a key member of the talent-laden Montreal Expos of the late 1970s who were always expected to be in postseason play, but made it only once, in 1981.

Carter was named Rookie of the Year by *The Sporting News* in 1975 after breaking in as an outfielder. Coached by Norm Sherry, Carter became a catcher full-time in 1977. He led the NL in most chances six times, in putouts five times, in assists four times, and in double plays three times. Carter won three Gold Glove Awards, and set a record for fewest passed balls in 150 or more games with just one. He finally played in the World Series with the Mets in 1986. He returned to Montreal for his last season.

Playing Career: *1974-1992; Mon N, NY N, SF N, LA N*

Joe Carter
Carter, Joseph Chris
B: Mar 7, 1960

Pos: OF, 1B	BA: .262
Hits: 1,523	HRs: 275
RBI: 994	BBs: 349

Drafted by the Cubs out of Wichita State University, Carter played only briefly for them before being swapped in the seven-man deal for Rick Sutcliffe in 1984. Carter's first good year in Cleveland was 1986, when he pounded out a .302 average with 29 home runs and drove in 121, the most in the majors that year. Overcoming constant shifting between first base and the outfield, Carter continued hitting home runs in 1987 when he cooked 30 taters. He also stole 30 bases that year. He has averaged close to 31 HRs and 110 RBI each year from 1986 to 1992.

Carter's recognition as the most prolific power hitter in baseball came with his arrival in Toronto in 1991. He led the Blue Jays to three division titles and a World Championship in 1992, making the AL All-Star team all three years. In the sixth and final game of the 1993 World Series, his ninth-inning homer made Toronto two-time champs.

Playing Career: *1983- ; Chi N, Cle A, SD N, Tor A*

Alexander Cartwright
Cartwright, Alexander
B: Apr 17, 1820   D: Jul 13, 1853
Hall of Fame 1938

Cartwright is largely responsible for developing baseball as we know it today, and for spreading it around the world like a bat-toting Johnny Appleseed. A bank teller from New York City, Cartwright was the chief designer of a set of rules for the game, and he organized the first team to play by those rules, the Knickerbocker Base Ball Club. Three Knickerbocker innovations made the game more challenging for adult play: the length between bases was increased to 90 feet; fair and foul territories were defined, reducing the number of defensive players needed; and the practice of "soaking" – putting out baserunners by throwing the ball at them – was forbidden.

Alexander Cartwright.

In 1849 Cartwright sojourned to California to look for gold, and along the way he stopped to teach people how to play baseball. Struck with dysentery and finding his property overrun by gold seekers in California, Cartwright moved west again, to Hawaii's healthful climate. He introduced baseball there in 1852, and subsequently in Japan.

Rico Carty
Carty, Ricardo Adolfo Jacobo
B: Sep 1, 1939

Pos: OF, DH	BA: .279
Hits: 1,677	HRs: 204
RBI: 890	BBs: 642

As a lad in the Dominican Republic, naive Carty signed professional contracts with 10 different baseball teams. When the mess was finally straightened up, it was determined that Carty belonged to the Milwaukee Braves. He hit .330 in his first major league season, but lost the Rookie of the Year Award to Richie Allen and the batting title to Roberto Clemente.

Carty overcame serious health problems – tuberculosis, seven shoulder dislocations, a broken knee – to compile a respectable record over a 15-season career. He hit .342 in 1969, and .366 in 1970, the highest major league batting average since Ted Williams hit .388 in 1957. He led the NL in batting average in that year and was a write-in candidate who made the All-Star team. Carty played in one league championship series.

Playing Career: *1963-1967, 1969-1970, 1972-1979; Mil N, Tex A, Chi N, Oak A, Cle A, Tor A*

Joe Carter lays down a bunt for the Indians in 1989.

Bob Caruthers
Caruthers, Robert Lee (Parisian Bob)
B: Jan 5, 1864   D: Aug 5, 1911

Pos: P	ERA: 2.83
W-L: 218-99	SOs: 900
ShOs: 25	Saves: 3

Managerial Record
Won: 16   Lost: 32   Pct: .333

After the 1885 season, Caruthers vacationed in France where he negotiated his salary for the upcoming year via telegraph lines. Failing to show up for spring training, he wired from Paris, "Will report soon." The salary battle was settled when "Parisian Bob" accepted the huge sum of $3,200.

Caruthers ranks among the all-time best pitchers in winning percentage, with a .692 mark. In 1885 and again in 1889 he won 40 games while leading his teams to pennants. Known as a thinking pitcher, he observed batters' weaknesses and preyed upon them. Caruthers had plenty of opportunity to observe from the other side of the plate, too. He became a solid hitter and had one great year with a bat. In 1887 he played 61 games in the field in addition to his 39 pitching starts. He recovered from malaria enough to hit .357 with eight home runs and 59 stolen bases.
Playing Career: *1884-1893; StL AA, Brk AA, Brk N, StL N*
Managerial Career: *1892; StL N*

Paul Casanova
Casanova y Ortiz, Paulino
B: Dec 21, 1941

Pos: C	BA: .225
Hits: 627	HRs: 50
RBI: 252	BBs: 101

Enthusiastic and fun-loving, Casanova made a good beginning as *The Sporting News"* AL rookie catcher in 1966. The next year he made the All-Star team. He had a strong, accurate arm and led AL catchers in double plays three times as the Senators' backstop. His hitting faded after two years.
Playing Career: *1965-1974; Was A, Atl N*

George Case
Case, George Washington
B: Nov 11, 1915   D: Jan 23, 1989

Pos: OF	BA: .282
Hits: 1,415	HRs: 21
RBI: 377	BBs: 425

Despite a career riddled with injuries, Case swiped 349 bases and scored 785 runs in 11 years. He led the major leagues in stolen bases for five consecutive seasons, 1939-1943, and again in 1945. His 61 thefts in 1943 constituted the highest major league single-season total in the four decades spanning 1921-1961. The same year, Case led the AL in runs scored and he was the starting right fielder in the first All-Star Game played at night. After his playing career, Case coached in the Mariners' farm system.
Playing Career: *1937-1947; Was A, Cle A*

Doc Casey
Casey, James Patrick
B: Mar 15, 1870   D: Dec 31, 1936

Pos: 3B	BA: .258
Hits: 1,122	HRs: 9
RBI: 354	BBs: 270

Doc Casey was a catcher with the Pawtucket team in the New England League when future Hall of Famer Nap Lajoie saw him play. Lajoie had been dubious about playing professional baseball until he saw the 5'6" Casey in action. Casey switched to third base in the majors. He played on the Brooklyn pennant winner in 1899.
Playing Career: *1898-1907; Was N, Brk N, Det A, Chi N*

Hugh Casey
Casey, Hugh Thomas
B: Oct 14, 1913   D: Jul 3, 1951

Pos: P	ERA: 3.45
W-L: 75-42	SOs: 349
ShOs: 3	Saves: 55

Hugh Casey was the pitching half of the battery that allowed Tommy Henrich to get on base and start a game-winning rally against the Dodgers in Game Four of the 1941 World Series. Casey, a heavy drinking loner, pitched in another World Series, totaling 16 innings of work and an ERA of 1.72 in the Fall Classic. Of the 343 games Casey pitched, he relieved in 287, leading the NL in saves twice and in relief wins three times.
Playing Career: *1935, 1939-1942, 1946-1949; Chi N, Brk N, Pit N, NY A*

Dave Cash
Cash, David
B: Jun 11, 1948

Pos: 2B	BA: .283
Hits: 1,571	HRs: 21
RBI: 426	BBs: 424

Cash finally became a regular second baseman in the sixth year of his career. He led NL second basemen in double plays three years in a row, in assists in 1974, putouts in 1975 and fielding average in 1976. Offensively, Cash led the league in hits in 1975. In 1976 he led in triples and struck out only 13 times in more than 600 at-bats. He made the All-Star team three times in a row, and played in four NLCS and one World Series.
Playing Career: *1969-1980; Pit N, Phi N, Mon N, SD N*

George Case was an early AL speed demon with Washington and Cleveland.

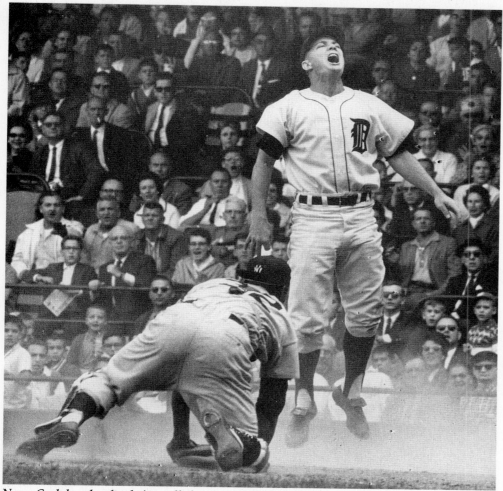

Norm Cash howls after being called out at home in 1961.

Norm Cash
Cash, Norman Dalton (Stormin' Norman)
B: Nov 10, 1934   D: Oct 12, 1986

Pos: 1B	BA: .271
Hits: 1,820	HRs: 377
RBI: 1,103	BBs: 1,043

Cash had an outstanding season in 1961, yet it was completely overshadowed by the Maris-Mantle home run battle. Cash batted .361, slugged .662, got 193 hits, pounded 41 home runs, drove in 132 and scored 119 runs, winning the batting title. After Cash retired from baseball, he admitted using a corked bat in 1961.

In the field, Cash was one of the best first basemen in baseball. He led the AL in putouts in 1961, in fielding average in 1964 and 1967, and in assists in 1966 and 1967. With a bat, Cash was a slugger. He hit 30 home runs or more five times and 20 or more 11 times, including nine consecutive seasons (1961-1969). Cash and roommate Al Kaline combined for 647 home runs as teammates, ranking them fourth on the all-time list. An All-Star four times, Cash played in one ALCS and two World Series, batting .385 in the 1968 Series for the Champion Tigers.
Playing Career: *1958-1974; Chi A, Det A*

George Caster
Caster, George Jasper
B: Aug 4, 1907   D: Dec 18, 1955

Pos: P	ERA: 4.54
W-L: 76-100	SOs: 595
ShOs: 6	Saves: 39

For once, a man's career improved when he went to the St. Louis Browns. Caster became an effective reliever with his knuckleball, leading the AL in saves in 1944, the year the Browns won their only pennant.
Playing Career: *1934-1935, 1937-1946; Phi A, StL A, Det A*

Bill Castro
Castro y Checo, William Radhames
B: Dec 13, 1953

Pos: P	ERA: 3.33
W-L: 31-26	SOs: 203
ShOs: 0	Saves: 45

For six years Castro was an important member of the Brewers' bullpen. He led the staff with a 2.52 ERA in 1975. Castro was known for getting batters to hit into double plays.
Playing Career: *1974-1983; Mil A, NY A, KC A*

Danny Cater
Cater, Danny Anderson
B: Feb 25, 1940

Pos: 1B, 3B, OF	BA: .276
Hits: 1,229	HRs: 66
RBI: 519	BBs: 254

Cater's teammates called him one of baseball's great worriers; he would refigure and quote his statistics after each at-bat. The Texas native was low-key by nature and he blamed that and his lazy-looking batting swing for his being traded five times.
Playing Career: *1964-1975; Phi N, Chi A, Oak A, NY A, Bos A, StL N*

Bill Caudill
Caudill, William Holland
B: Jul 13, 1956

Pos: P	ERA: 3.68
W-L: 35-52	SOs: 620
ShOs: 0	Saves: 106

Caudill was nicknamed "The Inspector" when he investigated teammates' bats, looking for missing hits. The Pink Panther theme would accompany him from the bullpen to the mound. During a hopelessly one-sided game, Caudill emerged from the dugout with one side of his beard shaved off. Between antics, he was also a very good pitcher, setting team records for saves in Seattle. In 1984 he saved 36 for Oakland and was selected for the All-Star team.
Playing Career: *1979-1987; Chi N, Sea A, Oak A, Tor A*

Wayne Causey
Causey, James Wayne
B: Dec 26, 1936

Pos: SS, 2B, 3B	BA: .252
Hits: 819	HRs: 35
RBI: 285	BBs: 390

A $50,000 bonus baby for the Orioles, Causey was a hard-working, consistent infielder who kept getting beaten out of regular jobs by hot-shot rookies. Finally a regular with the A's, Causey led the team in hitting twice and became team captain.
Playing Career: *1955-1957, 1961-1968; Bal A, KC A, Chi A, Cal A, Atl N*

Phil Cavarretta
Cavarretta, Philip Joseph
B: Jul 19, 1916

Pos: 1B	BA: .293
Hits: 1,977	HRs: 95
RBI: 920	BBs: 820
Managerial Record	
Won: 169 Lost: 213 Pct: .442	

Cavarretta was only 18 years old when he became the Cubs' regular first baseman, a position he retained for 20 seasons. A pitcher as a youngster, Cavarretta signed a pro contract before he was out of high school. In the Cubs' minor league system, he played outfield, and

Phil Cavarretta.

Cesar Cedeno
Cedeno y Encarnacion, Cesar
B: Feb 25, 1951

Pos: OF, 1B	BA: .285
Hits: 2,087	HRs: 199
RBI: 976	BBs: 664

Cedeno made the mistake of hitting .320 his first two seasons in the majors. He was touted as the next Willie Mays, and seen as a cross between Mickey Mantle and Jackie Robinson. Nobody could live up to the potential of young Cesar Cedeno, but the comparisons were inevitable given his playing abilities. Cedeno led the NL in doubles twice, stole 50 bases or more six times, and won five Gold Glove Awards. He was an All-Star four times, and played in four NLCS and two World Series.

Cedeno's career bounced between bright and dismal. He made a number of comebacks of sorts, most notably when he joined the contending Cardinals in 1985. His late-inning heroics won several important games in the pennant stretch, including a 1-0 extra-inning victory over the Mets.
Playing Career: *1970-1986; Hou N, Cin N, StL N, LA N*

Orlando Cepeda
**Cepeda y Penne, Orlando Manuel
(The Baby Bull)**
B: Sep 17, 1937

Pos: 1B	BA: .297
Hits: 2,351	HRs: 379
RBI: 1,365	BBs: 588

Cepeda was called The Baby Bull because he played like his father Perucha, The Bull. Perucha Cepeda was considered the greatest player ever from Puerto Rico, an island which has produced many outstanding ballplayers, including Roberto Clemente. The Baby Bull made his mark in the major leagues. He was named Rookie of the Year for hitting .312 with 25 home runs and 38 doubles, a league-leading figure. He also batted in 96 runs. No sophomore jinx for Cepeda, he improved his numbers to 27 home runs, 105 RBI and a .317 average in his second season.

Cepeda led the NL in homers and RBI in 1961 with 46 and 146 respectively, and he topped the league in RBI again in 1967, the year he won MVP honors. Cepeda was on the All-Star team seven times.
Playing Career: *1958-1974; SF N, StL N, Atl N, Oak A, Bos A, KC A*

hit for the cycle in his professional debut in the Central League in 1934. He skipped to the majors that year.

Overcoming two broken ankle injuries – the same one twice – Cavarretta hit his stride in the 1940s. In 1944 he had 197 hits to tie Stan Musial for the NL lead. Cavarretta was an All-Star that year, and he set a record in the game by reaching base five times. His .355 average in 1945 won the batting title and helped the Cubs win the pennant. Cavarretta was MVP that year, and he hit .423 in the World Series. As player/manager in 1951, he led the NL in pinch hits.
Playing Career: *1934-1955; Chi N, Chi A*
Managerial Career: *1951-1953; Chi N*

Ollie Caylor
Caylor, Oliver Perry (O.P.)
B: Dec 14, 1849   D: Oct 19, 1897

Managerial Record
Won: 163   Lost: 182   Pct: .472

Caylor was baseball editor of the *Cincinnati Enquirer* for 20 years. In 1877 he organized a curveball exhibition in which Bobby Mathews tossed the ball inside one post and outside the other. Professors from the nearby Univeristy of Cincinnati declared it an optical illusion – the controversy about whether a ball can curve has raged ever since. In 1880 he arranged for the Cincinnati Reds to play a series against J.G. Taylor-Spink's St. Louis Browns. It was that series of contests that led to the formation of the American Association. Caylor was later part owner of the New York Metropolitans but was barred from the 1887 meeting of the American Association officials because he was also a sportswriter!
Managerial Career: *1885-1887; Cin AA, NY AA*

Cesar Cedeno sprints to first for the Houston Astros in 1981.

Rick Cerone
Cerone, Richard Aldo
B: May 19, 1954

Pos: C	BA: .241
Hits: 877	HRs: 54
RBI: 402	BBs: 282

When Yankees owner George Steinbrenner chewed out his team before a crucial playoff game in 1981, Cerone gained the respect of his teammates by standing up to him. Cerone was a solid catcher, whose pitchers consistently posted lower ERAs with him than with rival Yankee catcher Butch Wynegar.
Playing Career: *1975-1992; Cle A, Tor A, NY A, Atl N, Mil A, Bos A, NY N, Mon N*

John Cerutti
Cerutti, John Joseph
B: Apr 28, 1960

Pos: P	ERA: 3.94
W-L: 49-43	SOs: 398
ShOs: 2	Saves: 4

John Cerutti, who holds a degree in economics from Amherst College, told the Blue Jays if he did not make the big leagues in five years he would become a player agent. He came up soon afterward. In his best season he went 11-4 with an ERA of 4.40.
Playing Career: *1985-1991; Tor A, Det A*

Bob Cerv
Cerv, Robert Henry
B: May 5, 1926

Pos: OF	BA: .276
Hits: 624	HRs: 105
RBI: 374	BBs: 212

Big Bob Cerv made Roger Maris's life bearable in 1961 by sharing a house with him and Mickey Mantle. Those three Midwesterners tore the cover off the ball. Cerv was an All-Star in 1958. Sitting in the Yankees' dugout one day, he was approached by Manager Casey Stengel who said, "Nobody knows this, but one of us has been traded to Kansas City." Cerv looked around; he was the only player there.
Playing Career: *1951-1962; NY A, KC A, LA A, Hou N*

Ron Cey
Cey, Ronald Charles (Penguin)
B: Feb 15, 1948

Pos: 3B	BA: .261
Hits: 1,868	HRs: 316
RBI: 1,139	BBs: 1,012

Nicknamed for his running style, Cey nonetheless made good use of those short, stocky legs. He was the Dodgers' regular at the hot corner for 10 seasons, and an All-Star 1974-1979. Cey put together a streak of 11 seasons with 20 or more home runs that was interrupted by the players' strike of 1981 and a broken arm the same year. Amazingly, he was back in uniform in time for the World

Ron Cey.

Series, only to be the victim of a beaning by a Goose Gossage fastball. Despite that he was named co-MVP of the Series.

Traded to Chicago, Cey helped the Cubs win the 1984 Eastern Division title with 25 home runs and 97 RBI. Altogether he was in postseason play five times, continuing to the World Series four times.
Playing Career: *1971-1987; LA N, Chi N, Oak A*

Henry Chadwick
Chadwick, Henry
B: Oct 5, 1824   D: Apr 20, 1908
Hall of Fame 1938

Henry Chadwick was one of the game's pioneers, although he never played professionally. As an early baseball enthusiast, he

Henry Chadwick.

decided to make baseball "a national sport for Americans" just as cricket was for the English. Chadwick convinced the New York newspapers to cover baseball games, offering to write the reports himself. He devised the box score, authored the first rule book, wrote numerous manuals on how to play the game, and edited the early baseball information guides.

Chadwick was also one of the organizers of the National Association of Base Ball Players in 1858. Perhaps more than anyone else, he helped popularize the game in its infancy. Baseball historian Lee Allen said, "Chadwick was an influence for good at a time when the game badly needed such a person. For years he kept pounding away in print on such subjects as the desirability of temperance and the need for fair treament of umpires, and he lived to see improvements in those and other areas."

Dave Chalk
Chalk, David Lee
B: Aug 30, 1950

Pos: SS, 3B	BA: .252
Hits: 733	HRs: 15
RBI: 243	BBs: 295

Chalk played in the All-Star Game as a rookie in 1974 despite having led AL shortstops with 29 errors. He overcame that beginning to develop into a very good fielder. He was elected again in 1975 but did not play. In 1977 Chalk hit .277 with 69 RBI, but could not generate enough power to stick in the majors.
Playing Career: *1973-1981; Cal A, Tex A, Oak A, KC A*

Ice Box Chamberlin
Chamberlin, Elton P.
B: Nov 5, 1867   D: Sep 22, 1929

Pos: P	ERA: 3.57
W-L: 157-120	SOs: 1,133
ShOs: 15	No-hitters: 1

Chamberlin was one of three 19th-century pitchers to throw in a major league game both left-handed and right-handed. He was way ahead of Kansas City in an 1886 game, so tossed the last two innings southpaw. Chamberlin won 30 games once and 20 or more twice for a .567 lifetime record.
Playing Career: *1886-1896; Lou AA, StL AA, Col AA, Phi AA, Cin N, Cle N*

Chris Chambliss
Chambliss, Carroll Christopher
B: Dec 26, 1948

Pos: 1B	BA: .279
Hits: 2,109	HRs: 185
RBI: 972	BBs: 632

Chambliss made Yankee Stadium explode with his dramatic ninth-inning home run in Game Five of the 1976 ALCS, giving the Yankees their first pennant in 12 years. He tied or broke five records for hits and RBI on his .524 average during the series.

Drafted twice in high school and a third time in college, Chambliss signed with Cleveland in 1970 and hit .342 to lead the minor league American Association that year. In his second season of professional ball, Chambliss was AL Rookie of the Year, hitting .275 and playing solid defense at first base. He led his team in batting the next two years. Traded to New York, Chambliss was a calm, focused player on a turbulent, frenetic team. He played well, averaging 92 RBI from 1976 to 1978, and he won a Gold Glove Award in 1978. Chambliss performed well in the NL too, hitting 20 homers in 1982 and 1983 for the Braves. He led the league in pinch hits in 1986.

Playing Career: *1971-1986, 1988; Cle A, NY A, Atl N*

Dean Chance
Chance, Wilmer Dean
B: Jun 1, 1941

Pos: P	ERA: 2.92
W-L: 128-115	SOs: 1,534
ShOs: 33	No-hitters: 2

Chance made batters nervous: he was a tad wild, and once he had the signal from his catcher, he delivered the pitch without looking at home plate. Leading the AL in wins and ERA in 1964, Chance was honored with the Cy Young Award. After mediocre performances in 1965 and 1966, Chance put together a very good year in 1967, compiling a record of 20-14 with a 2.73 ERA. He was named Comeback Player of the Year. An All-Star in 1964 and 1967, Chance once pitched a five-inning perfect game. He had 23 saves.

Playing Career: *1961-1971; Cal A, Min A, Cle A, NY N, Det A*

Frank Chance
Chance, Frank Leroy
B: Sep 9, 1877   D: Sep 15, 1924
Hall of Fame 1946

Pos: 1B	BA: .276
Hits: 1,271	HRs: 20
RBI: 596	BBs: 554
Managerial Record	
Won: 946 Lost: 648 Pct: .593	

Albert B. "Happy" Chandler (r), baseball's second commissioner, in 1945.

Frank Chance was the first baseman in the double play combination (with Joe Tinker and Johnny Evers) immortalized in Franklin Adams's poem "Baseball's Sad Lexicon." Bound by verse for all time, their names repeated in the refrain "Tinker to Evers to Chance," the trio was inducted into the Hall of Fame together in 1946.

It was Chance who became player-manager of the Cubs in 1905 and led them to pennants in 1906, 1907, 1908 and 1910. Aggressive and opinionated, he never backed down from an argument, and he did not allow players to slack off in performance. Chance sometimes used his fists to get his ideas across and to enforce discipline. In seven seasons he won 100 games or more four times, never finishing below third place. The Cubs won a major league record 116 games in 1906, but lost the World Series to the White Sox. Later managing stints were not as successful, probably due to Chance's poor health.

Playing Career: *1898-1914; Chi N, NY A*
Managerial Career: *1905-1914, 1923; Chi N, NY A, Bos A*

Happy Chandler
Chandler, Albert B.
B: Jul 14, 1898   D: Jun 15, 1991
Hall of Fame 1982

A former Governor of Kentucky and U.S. Senator, Chandler succeeded Judge Kenesaw Mountain Landis as the second commissioner of baseball. Chandler led baseball through six turbulent years which included the debut of Jackie Robinson, the raiding of the majors by the Mexican League and Federal charges against baseball in regard to violations of the antitrust laws. Known as a "players' commissioner" because of his broad concern for all phases of the game, his lack of sentiment for the owners got him voted out of office in 1951. Chandler's accomplishments included putting the players' pension fund on a sound basis, averting threats to the reserve clause and helping to integrate baseball. He said, "I felt that if black men could fight on the beaches of Okinawa and Iwo Jima, they certainly shouldn't come home to be told they couldn't play the great American game."

Spud Chandler
Chandler, Spurgeon Ferdinand
B: Sep 12, 1907   D: Jan 9, 1990

Pos: P	ERA: 2.84
W-L: 109-43	SOs: 614
ShOs: 26	Saves: 6

Chandler set the record for career winning percentage for pitchers with 100 or more games. When he retired in 1947, his mark was an amazing .717. A baseball and football player at the University of Georgia, Chandler opted for a professional baseball career. He suffered with arm problems and did not get to the big leagues until age 30. Once he did arrive, Chandler was a whirlwind.

In 1943 he led the league in wins and ERA,

Frank Chance with the other members of the famed trio, Joe Tinker and Johnny Evers.

in complete games, shutouts and winning percentage, and was honored as MVP. Chandler pitched and won two games for the Yankees in the Fall Classic, including the game that clinched the World Championship for his team. In 1946 Chandler returned from military duty to post a record of 20-8. He led the AL in ERA for the second time in 1947. Chandler played in four World Series and was an All-Star four times.
Playing Career: *1937-1947; NY A*

Spud Chandler.

Ben Chapman
Chapman, William Benjamin
B: Dec 25, 1908

Pos: OF	BA: .302
Hits: 1,958	HRs: 90
RBI: 977	BBs: 824
Managerial Record	
Won: 196 Lost: 276 Pct: .415	

Temperamental Ben Chapman was a high-spirited baserunner who also had a good throwing arm. He led the league in stolen bases 1931-1933, and led AL outfielders in assists in 1933 and 1935. Chapman accrued 287 stolen bases and 1,144 runs scored during his career. As a player-manager in the minor leagues in 1942, Chapman punched an umpire and was suspended for a year. He returned to the big leagues in 1944 as a pitcher, going 5-3 with a 3.40 ERA!
Playing Career: *1930-1941, 1944-1946; NY A, Was A, Bos A, Cle A, Chi A, Brk N, Phi N*
Managerial Career: *1945-1948; Phi N*

John Chapman
Chapman, John Curtis
(Death to Flying Things)
B: May 8, 1843   D: Jun 10, 1916

Pos: OF	BA: .248
Hits: 124	HRs: 0
RBI: 5 (inc.)	BBs: 7
Managerial Record	
Won: 353 Lost: 504 Pct: .412	

In an era when fielding ability was more respected than hitting, Chapman became famous for his long running catches, and was dubbed "Death to Flying Things." He was on the Brooklyn Atlantics team that broke the historic Cincinnati Red Stockings' two-season winning streak in 1871. Chapman, whose baseball career started in 1860, became a highly respected manager after his playing days were over.
Playing Career: *1874-1876; Brk Atlantics n, StL Brown Stockings n, Lou N*
Managerial Career: *1876-1879, 1882-1885, 1889-1892; Lou N, Mil N, Wor N, Det N, Buf N, Lou AA*

Ray Chapman
Chapman, Raymond Johnson
B: Jan 15, 1891   D: Aug 17, 1920

Pos: SS	BA: .278
Hits: 1,053	HRs: 18
RBI: 364	BBs: 452

Popular, talented Ray Chapman had a flourishing career when he died in his ninth major league season. Batting against Carl Mays on August 16, 1920, Chapman was crowding the plate, as he usually did. The pitch from Mays struck him in the temple, knocking him out. Chapman died in the hospital 12 hours later, never having regained consciousness. The mourning Indians wore black armbands on their uniforms the rest of the season, and Manager Tris Speaker drove them to win the club's first World Championship. Trick pitches subsequently were banned.

Chapman was an expert base stealer with 233 career thefts. He led the Indians in stolen bases four times, swiping 52 in 1917 alone, a club record that stood until 1980. In 1918 Chapman led the league in runs scored and walks. At the time of his death, Chapman was hitting .303 with 97 runs scored.
Playing Career: *1912-1920; Cle A*

Sam Chapman
Chapman, Samuel Blake
B: Apr 11, 1916

Pos: OF	BA: .266
Hits: 1,329	HRs: 180
RBI: 773	BBs: 562

Another college football player who chose baseball as a career, Chapman was fast, had a good throwing arm and could hit with power. He hit 20 or more home runs five times, and led AL outfielders in putouts four times, assists once and errors twice.
Playing Career: *1938-1941, 1945-1951; Phi A, Cle A*

Ed Charles
Charles, Edwin Douglas (Glider)
B: Apr 29, 1933

Pos: 3B	BA: .263
Hits: 917	HRs: 86
RBI: 421	BBs: 372

Published poet Ed Charles was nicknamed "Glider" for his smooth, graceful running and fielding. Stuck in the Milwaukee farm system for eight years, Charles finally was traded to Kansas City and became a regular.
Playing Career: *1962-1969; KC A, NY N*

Oscar Charleston
Charleston, Oscar
B: Oct 14, 1896   D: Oct 5, 1954
Hall of Fame 1976

Pos: OF, 1B	BA: .350 (inc.)
Hits: 1,069 (inc.)	HRs: 151 (inc.)
RBI: NA	BBs: NA
Managerial Record (inc.)	
Won: 230 Lost: 186 Pct: .553	

Perhaps the greatest of all Negro League players, Charleston hit with great power and

Ray Chapman tips his hat to the camera in this 1916 publicity photo.

Oscar Charleston.

First baseman Hal Chase in 1919, at spring training with the NY Giants.

consistency, and was an intimidating baserunner. He batted .366 in the Negro National League in 1920 and followed that with .434 in 1921. Charleston batted .318 with 11 home runs in 53 barnstorming games against white major leaguers.

Growing up in Indianapolis, Charleston saw a lot of baseball while serving the ABC's as batboy. After military service at age 15, Charleston played for several Negro League teams, became a player-manager in the late 1920s, and was active as a manager until his death in 1954. When Branch Rickey decided to break white baseball's color line, he asked Charleston to scout the Negro Leagues. Among Charleston's recommendations for players to integrate baseball were Jackie Robinson and Roy Campanella.

Playing Career: *1915-1941; Ind ABCs, NY Lincoln Giants, Chi Am Giants, Det Stars, StL Giants, Harrisburg Giants, Phi Hilldales, Hom Grays, Pit Crawfords, Tol Crawfords*
Managerial Career: *1932-1938, 1940-1954; Pit Crawfords, Tol Crawfords, Phi Stars, Brk Brown Dodgers, Ind Clowns*

Hal Chase
Chase, Harold Homer
B: Feb 13, 1883   D: May 18, 1947

Pos: 1B	BA: .291
Hits: 2,158	HRs: 57
RBI: 941	BBs: 276

Managerial Record
Won: 86   Lost: 80   Pct: .518

Chase was a talented player who abused his position in baseball by repeatedly throwing games to make money betting against his own team. At various times he was suspended, reinstated, accused, tried and finally banned from baseball, in part for his involvement in the notorious Black Sox affair.

Chase did have talent. Contemporary observers believed him to be the best fielding first baseman ever. He led AL first basemen in putouts and assists in 1911, but also topped them in errors. In fact, he holds the AL career record for first baseman errors with 285. Chase led the FL in home runs in 1915, and the NL in batting average in 1916, one of the four times he hit more than .300. During his career Chase stole 363 bases.
Playing Career: *1905-1919; NY A, Chi A, Buf F, Cin N, NY N*
Managerial Career: *1910-1911; NY A*

Larry Cheney
Cheney, Laurence Russell
B: May 2, 1886   D: Jan 6, 1969

Pos: P	ERA: 2.70
W-L: 116-100	SOs: 926
ShOs: 20	Saves: 19

Cheney had a traumatic late season debut in 1911 when he deflected a Zack Wheat line drive with his pitching hand, breaking his thumb and nose. No longer able to grip the ball tightly, Cheney developed a knuckleball and won 26 games as a rookie in 1912. Adding a spitball, he became an effective pitcher, leading the NL in saves and appearances in 1913 while compiling a 17-14 record. In 1914 he led the league in games, starts and bases on balls.
Playing Career: *1911-1919; Chi N, Brk N, Bos N, Phi N*

Jack Chesbro
Chesbro, John Dwight
B: Jun 5, 1874   D: Nov 6, 1931
Hall of Fame 1946

Pos: P	ERA: 2.68
W-L: 199-132	SOs: 1,265
ShOs: 35	Saves: 5

Ed Walsh and Jack Chesbro were the greatest spitball pitchers of all time. Chesbro added the pitch to his repertoire in 1902 and it helped him lead the league in wins that year and again in 1904. Playing for the New York Highlanders – later known as the Yankees – Chesbro had a stellar season in 1904. He won 41 games, completed his first 30 starts, and pitched 454 innings in 55 games. He won 20 games or more five times.

After Chesbro retired from the major leagues he played semipro ball, traveling around New England to take on milltown teams. He coached baseball at Amherst College and had a stint as coach with the Senators.
Playing Career: *1899-1909; Pit N, NY A, Bos A*

Jack Chesbro.

Cupid Childs
Childs, Clarence Algernon
B: Aug 8, 1867   D: Nov 8, 1912

Pos: 2B	BA: .306
Hits: 1,720	HRs: 20
RBI: 654	BBs: 991

An ideal leadoff hitter and excellent baserunner, Childs accumulated 269 stolen bases and scored 1,214 runs during his career. A lifetime .306 hitter, Childs hit .345 in the 1890 major league American Association, and pounded a league-high 33 doubles. He led the league in runs scored with 136 in 1892. In 1893 Childs walked 120 times while striking out only 12 times. He hit his stride during the years with the Cleveland Spiders, batting .300 or more for five out of eight seasons.

His nickname came from his innocent face and the youthful age at which he broke in with the 1888 Phillies. The Phils were a hard-drinking rowdy bunch, even though Harry Wright was their manager.
Playing Career: *1888, 1890-1901; Phi N, Syr AA, Cle N, StL N, Chi N*

Bob Chipman
Chipman, Robert Howard
B: Oct 11, 1918   D: Nov 8, 1973

Pos: P	ERA: 3.72
W-L: 51-46	SOs: 322
ShOs: 7	Saves: 14

Managers alternated Chipman between middle relief and spot starts over his major league career. Chapman's first year with the Cubs, 1944, was his best, when he compiled a 12-10 season. He pitched in one World Series with the Cubs, in 1945.
Playing Career: *1941-1952; Brk N, Chi N, Bos N*

Larry Christenson
Christenson, Larry Richard
B: Nov 10, 1953

Pos: P	ERA: 3.79
W-L: 83-71	SOs: 781
ShOs: 6	Saves: 4

Christenson was the Phillies' first pick in the June 1972 draft. Beginning with his 1973 major league debut victory, Christenson improved steadily, overcoming three elbow surgeries and a broken collarbone. He pitched in three NLCS and one World Series.
Playing Career: *1973-1983; Phi N*

Marc Christman
Christman, Marquette Joseph
B: Oct 21, 1913   D: Oct 9, 1976

Pos: 3B, SS	BA: .253
Hits: 781	HRs: 19
RBI: 348	BBs: 219

Christman was an ardent Cardinals fan who ended up playing most of his career across town with the Browns. A consistent fielder, Christman led AL third basemen with a .972 fielding average in 1944. His 83 RBI that season marked a career high. He played in one World Series.
Playing Career: *1938-1939, 1943-1949; Det A, StL A, Was A*

Russ Christopher
Christopher, Russell Ormand
B: Sep 12, 1917   D: Dec 5, 1954

Pos: P	ERA: 3.37
W-L: 54-64	SOs: 424
ShOs: 3	Saves: 35

Christopher pitched for seven major league seasons, in a relief role the last two. He won games in double digits three times, the best season being 1944 when he posted 14 victories. The next year he was elected to the AL All-Star team. In 1948 his league-leading 17 saves helped the Indians win the World Series.
Playing Career: *1942-1948; Phi A, Cle A*

Eddie Cicotte.

Eddie Cicotte
Cicotte, Edward Victor
B: Jun 19, 1884   D: May 5, 1969

Pos: P	ERA: 2.37
W-L: 208-149	SOs: 1,374
ShOs: 36	No-hitters: 1

Another of the players banned from baseball for involvement in the 1919 Black Sox scandal, Cicotte was an excellent pitcher who succumbed to the temptation of a $10,000 bribe. He had a gallery of artful pitches and pinpoint control; he walked few batters. Cicotte led the league in ERA in 1917, and in wins in 1917 and 1919. He was also a good-fielding pitcher.

A clause in Cicotte's 1919 contract specified a bonus if he had 30 victories. Some claim that Charlie Comiskey kept Cicotte out of games after he had won 29. The records show that Cicotte tossed only 18 innings after September 5 that year. Explaining his acceptance of the Black Sox bribe, Cicotte said he planned to buy a farm for his family's financial security, that he "did it for the wife and kiddies." Losing his baseball job, Cicotte toiled for Ford in Detroit many years before he retired.
Playing Career: *1905, 1908-1920; Det A, Bos A, Chi A*

Gino Cimoli
Cimoli, Gino Nicholas
B: Dec 18, 1929

Pos: OF	BA: .265
Hits: 808	HRs: 44
RBI: 321	BBs: 221

Cimoli was a valuable man to have on the bench, especially for the Pirates. When Bob Skinner got injured during the 1960 World Series, Cimoli pinch-hit a single that sparked the Game Seven rally culminating in Mazeroski's dramatic Series-winning home run.
Playing Career: *1956-1965; Brk N, LA N, StL N, Pit N, Mil N, KC A, Bal A, Cal A*

Bill Cissell
Cissell, Chalmer William
B: Jan 3, 1904   D: Mar 15, 1949

Pos: 2B, SS	BA: .267
Hits: 990	HRs: 29
RBI: 423	BBs: 212

Charles Comiskey wanted Cissell on his team badly enough to pay $123,000 for his contract in 1928. Cissell struggled in Chicago, sensitive to the pressure of the deal. He later said "The ballyhoo I got when Portland sold me for that sum was the greatest burden any player ever carried to the majors."
Playing Career: *1928-1934, 1937-1938; Chi A, Cle A, Bos A, Phi A, NY N*

Bill Cissell.

Jim Clancy
Clancy, James
B: Dec 18, 1955

Pos: P	ERA: 4.23
W-L: 140-167	SOs: 1,422
ShOs: 11	Saves: 10

An original Blue Jay, Clancy was picked in the 1976 expansion draft, and was the only Toronto player who remained on the team for each of their first 12 seasons. In the early 1980s he combined with Dave Stieb as the backbone of the Jays' starting rotation. Clancy's best year was 1982 when he won 16 games, had an ERA of 3.71 and was selected for the All-Star team. He was three outs from a perfect game that year, but ended up with a one-hit shutout.
Playing Career: *1977-1991; Tor A, Hou N, Atl N*

John Clapp
Clapp, John Edgar
B: Jul 17, 1851   D: Dec 18, 1904

Pos: C, SS, 2B, OF	BA: .285
Hits: 718	HRs: 7
RBI: 218	BBs: 113
Managerial Record	
Won: 174 Lost: 237	Pct: .423

As a youngster Clapp wrote to Harry Wright asking what a ballplayer must do in order to turn pro. Wright's run-on answer has become a baseball classic. He wrote, "What kind of pitching having you caught, how fast was it, what other positions do you play, can you play third, can you catch a swift pitcher like Spalding up close and behind, can you bat swift pitching with confidence, are you prepared to come at your own risk to show what you can do?" He could, he was, he did.
Playing Career: *1872-1881, 1883; Mid Mansfields n, Phi Athletics n, StL N, Ind N, Buf N, Cin N, Cle N, NY N*
Managerial Career: *1872, 1878-1881, 1883; Mid Mansfields n, Ind N, Buf N, Cin N, Cle N, NY N*

Jack Clark
Clark, Jack Anthony
B: Nov 10, 1955

Pos: OF, 1B, DH	BA: .267
Hits: 1,826	HRs: 340
RBI: 1,180	BBs: 1,262

Clark was one of the most formidable sluggers in baseball, and also one of the most injury prone – "Jack the Ripper" was an appropriate nickname for more than one reason. A good outfielder, leading the league in assists in 1981, Clark was transferred to first base to reduce the risk of injury.

An inspiring clutch hitter, Clark led the NL in game-winning RBI with 18 in 1980, and tied for the NL lead in 1982 with 21. With the Cardinals in 1985, Clark was the hero of the NLCS when he lifted a ninth-inning three-run homer over the wall in Game Six. He missed almost all of the 1986 season due to

Jack Clark warms up his big bat for the San Francisco Giants in 1978.

injuries, but he was back with a vengeance in 1987. That year Clark led the NL in slugging average (.597), walks (136), and home run percentage (35 of his 120 hits were homers). He had 106 RBI and scored 93 runs that year. An ankle injury ended his season on September 9, probably costing the Cardinals the World Championship.
Playing Career: *1975-1992; SF N, StL N, NY A, SD N, Bos A, Mon N*

Watty Clark
Clark, William Watson
B: May 16, 1902   D: Mar 4, 1972

Pos: P	ERA: 3.66
W-L: 111-97	SOs: 643
ShOs: 14	Saves: 16

Clark started his career in Cleveland, but had his best years in Brooklyn. For the Dodgers, Clark won games in double digits for five years, 1928-1932, but also lost a league-high 19 contests in 1929. He won 20 games in 1932.
Playing Career: *1924, 1927-1937; Cle A, Brk N, NY N*

Will Clark
Clark, William Nuschler (Will the Thrill)
B: Mar 13, 1964

Pos: 1B, DH	BA: .299
Hits: 1,278	HRs: 176
RBI: 713	BBs: 506

A member of the 1984 Olympic baseball team, Clark entered professional baseball in the following year when he was drafted second in the nation. Will started providing thrills right away. He hit home runs in his first minor league at-bat and his first major league at-bat, the latter off Nolan Ryan. No sophomore jinx for Clark; in 1987 he put together a string of nine games in which he drove in runs, tying a club record with the likes of Orlando Cepeda, Willie Mays and Willie McCovey. Clark's 35 home runs, 91 RBI and .308 batting average took the Giants to the NL West title.

There were more landmarks in 1988. Clark led the NL in RBI with 109, and in walks with 100. He was elected to the All-Star team in 1988-1992. Clark, Brett Butler, Kevin Mitchell and Robby Thompson combined for the hot-

test top four of any lineup in 1989. Clark was MVP of the 1989 NLCS, hitting .650 with two home runs.
Playing Career: *1986- ; SF N*

Bill Clarke
Clarke, William Jones (Boileryard)
B: Oct 18, 1868   D: Jul 29, 1959

Pos: C, 1B   BA: .256
Hits: 858   HRs: 21
RBI: 431   BBs: 176

Also known as "Noisy Bill" and "Old Reliable," Clarke shared catching duties with Wilbert Robinson on the 1894-1896 Baltimore teams that won three consecutive pennants. He switched to first base with the new AL Senators, and ended his career with the Giants. Clarke was later the baseball coach at Princeton.
Playing Career: *1893-1905; Bal N, Bos N, Was A, NY N*

Fred Clarke
Clarke, Fred Clifford
B: Oct 3, 1872   D: Aug 14, 1960
Hall of Fame 1945

Pos: OF   BA: .312
Hits: 2,675   HRs: 67
RBI: 1,015   BBs: 874
Managerial Record
Won: 1,602   Lost: 1,181   Pct: .576

By the time Clarke retired he ranked among all-time leaders in batting average, hits, runs scored (1,621), triples (220) and stolen bases (506). In addition, he was Pittsburgh's winningest manager, and held a number of club records. Clarke was a fierce competitor and a daring baserunner, often compared to Ty Cobb.

Discovered by Louisville Colonels owner Barney Dreyfuss, Clarke was 5-for-5 in his first game, still a major league record. He quickly established himself as a star player, and at age 25, became manager in 1897. He hit .406 that year. When Dreyfuss decided to merge his Louisville and Pittsburgh teams, Clarke was one of 14 players who went to the Pirates. Clarke's managerial ability, his big bat and his star lineup led to four NL pennants and two World Series. In 1909 the Pirates won 110 games and took the World Championship in seven games.
Playing Career: *1894-1911, 1913-1915; Lou N, Pit N*
Managerial Career: *1897-1915; Lou N, Pit N*

Horace Clarke
Clarke, Horace Meredith (Hoss)
B: Jun 2, 1940

Pos: 2B, SS, 3B   BA: .256
Hits: 1,230   HRs: 27
RBI: 304   BBs: 365

Clarke became the regular keystone sacker for the Yankees in 1967, and played 143 games or more for the next seven years. He led the league's second basemen with a .990 fielding average in 1967, in assists for six consecutive years (1967-1972), and in putouts 1968-1971. A switch hitter, Clarke led the AL in at-bats twice. He stole 151 bases. In 1970 he broke up three no-hitters, all in the ninth inning.
Playing Career: *1965-1974; NY A, SD N*

Jay Clarke
Clarke, Jay Justin
B: Dec 15, 1882   D: Jun 15, 1949

Pos: C   BA: .254
Hits: 390   HRs: 6
RBI: 127   BBs: 138

With the Corsicana, Texas League team, Clarke hit eight home runs in one historic game played at Ennis, Texas, in 1902. In the majors, the Canadian was a top defensive catcher who suffered from arm problems. He had one great day in baseball, and is a member of the Canadian Baseball Hall of Fame.
Playing Career: *1905-1911, 1919-1920; Cle A, Det A, StL A, Phi N, Pit N*

John Clarkson.

John Clarkson
Clarkson, John Gibson
B: Jul 1, 1861   D: Feb 4, 1909
Hall of Fame 1963

Pos: P   ERA: 2.81
W-L: 328-178   SOs: 1,978
ShOs: 37   No-hitters: 1

Clarkson and teammate Mike "King" Kelly were sold to the Boston Nationals in 1888 for $10,000 apiece. Never before had a player been sold to another team like cattle. A new era in baseball dawned with Clarkson at the apex.

Clarkson was a record-setting hurler who led the way to glory for many of his teams. In 1885, 1887 and 1889, Clarkson topped the league in wins, appearances, starts, complete games, innings and strikeouts. He led in shutouts in 1885 and 1889, and in ERA in 1889. He posted 53 victories in 1885, and 49 in 1889. Clarkson played on four pennant-winning teams. He once pitched a lemon instead of a baseball to prove to the umpire that it was too dark to continue the game.
Playing Career: *1882, 1884-1894; Wor N, Chi N, Bos N, Cle N*

Manager Fred Clarke (in bowler hat) speaks with members of his Pittsburgh Pirates team.

Mark Clear
Clear, Mark Alan
B: May 27, 1956

Pos: P	ERA: 3.83
W-L: 71-49	SOs: 798
ShOs: 0	Saves: 83

Clear had an amazing curveball that was almost impossible to hit, but it was not usually in the strike zone. A good, but never overpowering reliever, Clear was the ace of the Red Sox bullpen in 1982. He won 14 and saved 14 that year. He was selected for the All-Star Game twice, 1979 and 1982.
Playing Career: *1979-1988; Cal A, Bos A, Mil A*

Roger Clemens
Clemens, Roger (Rocket)
B: Aug 4, 1962

Pos: P	ERA: 2.94
W-L: 163-86	SOs: 2,033
ShOs: 35	No-hitters: 0

Clemens is the premier pitcher in baseball today, rivaled only by Nolan Ryan, whom he idolized as a youngster. Clemens has led the AL in wins, ERA, strikeouts and shutouts several times using his 95-mph fastball and outstanding control. Drafted by the Red Sox out of college, Clemens tore through their farm system, littering the ballparks with strikeout victims. He began the 1984 season with the AAA Pawtucket club but was promoted to the big leagues in May, finishing the season 9-4.

Shoulder problems in 1985 required surgery in August. Everyone watched nervously in 1986. Not to worry; Clemens won his first three starts and never looked back. He broke the major league record for strikeouts in a game with a 20-K victory that year, tying an AL record for consecutive strikeouts in the same game. Clemens finished the year with a 24-4 record and a 2.48 ERA. He won the Cy Young and MVP Awards, and pitched in the ALCS and World Series. The Cy Young Award was his again in 1987 and 1991.
Playing Career: *1984- ; Bos A*

Roberto Clemente
Clemente y Walker, Roberto
B: Aug 18, 1934 D: Dec 31, 1972
Hall of Fame 1973

Pos: OF	BA: .317
Hits: 3,000	HRs: 240
RBI: 1,305	BBs: 621

Indisputably one of the best ballplayers ever, Clemente played his entire career in Pittsburgh, outside the illumination of media coverage that stars received in New York or Los Angeles. Overcoming a chronic bad back, an arm injury, and a bout of malaria, the Puerto Rican played more than 100 games in each of his 18 major league seasons. Ranked among the all-time leaders in batting average and hits – he won four batting titles – Clemente also scored 1,416 runs, and hit 440

Roberto Clemente (r) got his start in the Caribbean winter leagues.

doubles and 166 triples. His strong throwing arm was legendary, and he frequently made dramatic leaping or diving catches. He led the NL in assists five times, won 12 consecutive Gold Glove Awards, 1961-1972, was NL MVP in 1966, and was elected to the All-Star team 12 times.

The Pirates had lost 100 games for three straight years when Clemente joined the club. He led them to three NLCS and two World Series. Clemente's greatest performance was in the 1971 Fall Classic, when he hit .414 and played with reckless abandon to help the Bucs win the World Championship. A hero in death as in life, Clemente boarded a plane carrying relief supplies to earthquake victims in Nicaragua; it crashed in the Atlantic Ocean. On the bluffs of Pittsburgh overlooking Three Rivers Stadium the bereaved city put its simple message in lights: "Adios, Amigo."
Playing Career: *1955-1972; Pit N*

Jack Clements
Clements, John J.
B: Jul 24, 1864 D: May 23, 1941

Pos: C	BA: .286
Hits: 1,226	HRs: 77
RBI: 673	BBs: 339

Managerial Record
Won: 13 Lost: 6 Pct: .684

Clements was a rarity – a left-handed catcher. He caught 1,157 games, 105 of them in 1892. If a baserunner broke for second when Clements was behind the plate, he would fire away, batter or no. Wary right-handed hitters quickly learned to duck.
Playing Career: *1884-1900; Phi U, Phi N, StL N, Cle N, Bos N*
Managerial Career: *1890; Phi N*

Donn Clendenon
Clendenon, Donn Alvin
B: Jul 15, 1935

Pos: 1B	BA: .274
Hits: 1,273	HRs: 159
RBI: 682	BBs: 379

Big Donn Clendenon hit three home runs in the 1969 World Series, powering the Amazing Mets to the World Championship. He was named MVP for the Series. Clendenon, now an attorney in Sioux Falls, South Dakota, was originally drafted by the Cleveland Browns football team and the Harlem Globetrotters basketball team as well as the Pirates. Choosing baseball, Clendenon hit .302 in his rookie season. In 1966 he batted .299, hit 28 home runs and had 98 RBI.
Playing Career: *1961-1972; Pit N, Mon N, NY N, StL N*

Reggie Cleveland
Cleveland, Reginald Leslie
B: May 23, 1948

Pos: P	ERA: 4.02
W-L: 105-106	SOs: 930
ShOs: 12	Saves: 25

Among the many talented Canadian baseball players, Cleveland is the only Saskatchewan native to star in the major leagues. NL Rookie of the Year in 1971, Cleveland won at least 10 games for seven consecutive seasons. He was later used in relief.
Playing Career: *1969-1981; StL N, Bos A, Tex A, Mil A*

Tex Clevenger
Clevenger, Truman Eugene
B: Jul 9, 1932

Pos: P	ERA: 4.18
W-L: 36-37	SOs: 361
ShOs: 2	Saves: 30

Clevenger was called up to Beantown after a 16-2 season in the minors in 1953. The workhorse led the AL with 55 appearances in 1958 with the Senators and had a record of 9-9. He was drafted by California for the 1961 expansion season.
Playing Career: *1954, 1956-1962; Bos A, Was A, Cal A, NY A*

Harlond Clift.

Harlond Clift
Clift, Harlond Benton
B: Aug 12, 1912   D: Apr 27, 1992

Pos: 3B	BA: .272
Hits: 1,558	HRs: 178
RBI: 829	BBs: 1,070

Clift was one of the most consistent slugging third basemen of his time, but he went un-

noticed, playing for the lowly St. Louis Browns. He led AL third basemen in homers 1936-1939. In nine seasons, Clift averaged 19 home runs, 31 doubles and 104 walks, hit .300 twice and slugged .500 three times. In 1937 Clift set records with 50 double plays and 405 assists. He ranks near the top of the all-time list in total chances and double plays for third basemen. Ironically, Clift was traded the year before the Browns won their only pennant in 1944.
Playing Career: *1934-1945; StL A, Was A*

Gene Clines
Clines, Eugene Anthony
B: Oct 6, 1946

Pos: OF	BA: .277
Hits: 645	HRs: 5
RBI: 187	BBs: 169

In his debut season with the Pirates, Clines hit .405 in 31 games. His good defensive skills made him a useful fourth outfielder for the Bucs. In 1971 Clines hit .308, and in 107 games in 1972 compiled a .334 mark. He appeared in three NLCS and one World Series. Clines became a coach in 1979.
Playing Career: *1970-1979; Pit N, NY N, Tex A, Chi N*

Billy Clingman
Clingman, William Frederick
B: Nov 21, 1869   D: May 14, 1958

Pos: 2B, 3B	BA: .246
Hits: 697	HRs: 8
RBI: 301	BBs: 303

Clingman entered major league baseball in the historic Players' League of 1890. He was thought to be the fastest infielder with the most accurate arm of the 1890s. Clingman led

the NL in assists once and fielding average twice.
Playing Career: *1890-1891, 1895-1901, 1903; Cin P, Cin-Mil AA, Pit N, Lou N, Chi N, Was A, Cle A*

Lu Clinton
Clinton, Luciean Louis
B: Oct 13, 1937

Pos: OF	BA: .247
Hits: 532	HRs: 65
RBI: 269	BBs: 188

Strong defensive and offensive skills made Clinton a Red Sox regular in the early 1960s. He had 52 extra-base hits in 1962 and again in 1963 when he also lifted 22 home runs and drove in 77. Traded frequently the next four seasons, his hitting dropped off.
Playing Career: *1960-1967; Bos A, Cal A, KC A, Cle A, NY A*

Tony Cloninger
Clonginer, Tony Lee
B: Aug 13, 1940

Pos: P	ERA: 4.07
W-L: 113-97	SOs: 1,120
ShOs: 13	Saves: 6

Cloninger is the only NL player ever to hit two grand slam home runs in one game, on July 3, 1966. He also pitched and won the game. A $100,000 bonus baby, Cloninger peaked in 1965 when he compiled a 24-11 record with the Braves. He cooled off in 1967 when a shoulder injury and an eye problem caused his record to fall to 4-7. In Cincinnati he won nine games as the Reds won the pennant in 1970.
Playing Career: *1961-1972; Mil N, Cin N, StL N*

Pitcher Tony Cloninger is greeted by Felipe Alou after smacking a home run in 1966.

Andy Coakley
Coakley, Andrew James
B: Nov 20, 1882   D: Sep 27, 1963

Pos: P	ERA: 2.36
W-L: 60-59	SOs: 428
ShOs: 11	Saves: 3

Coakley is the answer to the trivia question: "Who was the only non-Hall of Fame pitcher to start a game in the 1905 World Series?" A college player from Holy Cross before joining the big leagues, Coakley was Lou Gehrig's coach at Columbia after he retired.
Playing Career: *1902-1909, 1911; Phi A, Cin N, Chi N, NY A*

Gil Coan
Coan, Gilbert Fitzgerald
B: May 18, 1922

Pos: OF	BA: .254
Hits: 731	HRs: 39
RBI: 278	BBs: 232

At Griffith Stadium, rookie Coan competed with AL stolen-base champ George Case in a footrace. "It was a darn good promotion and pulled a lot of people into the ballpark, including General Eisenhower," Case said. Coan had two .302 seasons in a row.
Playing Career: *1946-1956; Was A, Bal A, Chi A, NY N*

Ty Cobb
Cobb, Tyrus Raymond (The Georgia Peach)
B: Dec 18, 1886   D: Jul 17, 1961
Hall of Fame 1936

Pos: OF	BA: .367
Hits: 4,191	HRs: 118
RBI: 1,961	BBs: 1,249
Managerial Record	
Won: 479 Lost: 444 Pct: .519	

The old joke about a talking dog has the skeptical talent agent querying "Who was the greatest baseball player ever?" The dog barks "Ruth!" The agent throws him out in disgust, mumbling about hoaxes. Out on the sidewalk, the dog tells his master, "Maybe I should have said Cobb."

Cobb's career batting average is the highest of any major league baseball player. He amassed 2,246 runs, 891 stolen bases, 724 doubles and 295 triples on the way to 12 batting titles and one Triple Crown. He was MVP in 1911. Also an excellent baserunner and fielder, he held an incredible 90 major league records at the time of his retirement. Cobb played in three World Series with the Tigers. Notorious for his nasty style of play and his bullying disposition, Cobb was nonetheless the very first man inducted into the Hall of Fame.
Playing Career: *1905-1928; Det A, Phi A*
Managerial Career: *1921-1926; Det A*

Mickey Cochrane
Cochrane, Gordon Stanley (Black Mike)
B: Apr 6, 1903   D: Jun 28, 1962
Hall of Fame 1947

Pos: C	BA: .320
Hits: 1,652	HRs: 119
RBI: 832	BBs: 857
Managerial Record	
Won: 379 Lost: 278 Pct: .577	

A fierce competitor, Cochrane was nicknamed "Black Mike" because he was always dirty – a result of his intense style of play. Teammate Doc Cramer said of Cochrane's temperament: "Lose a 1-0 game and you didn't want to get into the clubhouse with either Grove or Cochrane. You'd be ducking stools and gloves and bats and whatever else would fly."

Cochrane hit .330 his rookie year and led AL catchers in fielding that year and the three following. Six times he led receivers in putouts and twice in double plays and assists. Cochrane batted .357 in 1930, but 1932 was perhaps his best season. That year he hit 23 home runs, had 112 RBI and scored 118 of his 1,041 career runs. Cochrane hit for the cycle in 1932 and 1933. He was MVP twice and an All-Star twice, and played in five World Series, managing the Bengals to two.
Playing Career: *1925-1937; Phi A, Det A*
Managerial Career: *1934-1938; Det A*

Never a sweetheart, Ty Cobb steps out of character for a publicity photo titled, "Georgia Peach Teaches Peaches How to Bat."

made up for the down times with some grand up times. Colavito hit 20 or more home runs for the Indians for 11 consecutive seasons. He hit .303 with 41 taters in 1958 when he also had 113 RBI. Leading the AL in home runs in 1959 actually caused him to be traded. Stunned fans learned that Cleveland General Manager Frank Lane, seeking a better average and less power, had a bizarre clause in Colavito's contract that would have actually paid him for hitting fewer than 40 home runs.

Some consider the demoralizing loss of the outfielder with the big bat and strong arm responsible for the decades of lackluster baseball that ensued in Cleveland. Colavito had his greatest year in Detroit in 1961, batting .290 with 45 home runs and 140 RBI. He was an All-Star six times. In his final season, Colavito became the last position player to get a win as a pitcher.
Playing Career: *1955-1968; Cle A, Det A, KC A, Chi A, LA N, NY A*

Nate Colbert
Colbert, Nathan
B: Apr 9, 1946

Pos: 1B	BA: .243
Hits: 833	HRs: 173
RBI: 520	BBs: 383

Young Colbert was at Sportsman's Park the day Stan Musial hit five home runs, never dreaming he would tie Musial's record in a doubleheader in 1972. The hottest batter in the Padres' early days, Colbert hit 163 home runs in six seasons in San Diego.
Playing Career: *1966, 1968-1976; Hou N, SD N, Det A, Mon N, Oak A*

Jim Colborn
Colborn, James William
B: May 22, 1946

Pos: P	ERA: 3.80
W-L: 83-88	SOs: 688
ShOs: 8	No-hitters: 1

A baseball and basketball star in college, Colborn found the going tougher in the major leagues. He was selected to pitch in the All-Star Game in 1973, the year he became the first Brewer to post 20 victories in a season. He later won 18 for the Royals.
Playing Career: *1969-1978; Chi N, Mil A, KC A, Sea A*

Gordy Coleman
Coleman, Gordon Calvin
B: Jul 5, 1934

Pos: 1B	BA: .273
Hits: 650	HRs: 98
RBI: 387	BBs: 177

Coleman won the Triple Crown and was 1959 MVP in the Southern Association, but he had only two good years in the majors. As the Reds' first baseman, Coleman hit 26 then 28 homers in 1961 and 1962, helping the Reds win the NL pennant in 1961.
Playing Career: *1959-1967; Cle A, Cin N*

Mickey Cochrane (l) and Lefty Grove with souvenirs in Japan.

Dick Coffman
Coffman, Samuel Richard
B: Dec 18, 1906   D: Mar 24, 1972

Pos: P	ERA: 4.65
W-L: 72-95	SOs: 372
ShOs: 9	Saves: 38

Coffman beat Lefty Grove 1-0 to break the southpaw's 16-game winning streak, causing Grove to go on a legendary pout. Coffman was one of the first to log more than 300 games as a reliever, although he began his career as a starter with the Senators and Browns. He pitched in two World Series.
Playing Career: *1927-1940, 1945; Was A, StL A, NY N, Bos N, Phi N*

Rocky Colavito
Colavito, Rocco Domenico
B: Aug 10, 1933

Pos: OF	BA: .266
Hits: 1,730	HRs: 374
RBI: 1,159	BBs: 951

"Don't Knock the Rock!" said a Cleveland sportswriter when detractors berated the beloved Colavito. Prone to slumps, the all-time favorite ballplayer at Municipal Stadium

Rocky Colavito.

Jerry Coleman
Coleman, Gerald Francis
B: Sep 14, 1924

Pos: 2B, SS	BA: .263
Hits: 558	HRs: 16
RBI: 217	BBs: 235

Managerial Record
Won: 73   Lost: 89   Pct: .451

Coleman was a promising talent who led AL keystone sackers in fielding his rookie year and was an All-Star as a sophomore, but a 1951 injury put a crimp in his playing style. As a top sports announcer, Coleman was dubbed "Master of the Malaprop" due to statements such as "He slides into second with a standup double."
Playing Career: *1949-1957; NY A*
Managerial Career: *1980; SD N*

Joe Coleman
Coleman, Joseph Howard
B: Feb 3, 1947

Pos: P	ERA: 3.69
W-L: 142-135	SOs: 1,728
ShOs: 18	Saves: 7

Despite a minor league record of 9-32, Coleman became a 20-game winner in the majors. He was the first player chosen by the Senators in the 1965 free-agent draft, but his best seasons were played in Detroit. In Motor City Coleman had 21 victories in 1971, 19 in 1972, and 23 in 1973. He pitched in the 1972 ALCS, setting a record with 14 strikeouts. Coleman, whose father was also a major league player, finished his career in relief.
Playing Career: *1965-1979; Was A, Det A, Chi N, Oak A, Tor A, SF N, Pit N*

Joe Coleman
Coleman, Joseph Patrick
B: Jul 30, 1922

Pos: P	ERA: 4.38
W-L: 52-76	SOs: 444
ShOs: 11	Saves: 6

The father of Joseph Howard Coleman, Joseph Patrick won games in double digits three times. He was discovered by Brother Gilbert, the Baltimore cleric who had brought Babe Ruth to the attention of Orioles owner Jack Dunn. Coleman was an All-Star in 1948.
Playing Career: *1942, 1946-51, 1953-55; Phi A, Bal A, Det A*

Vince Coleman
Coleman, Vincent
B: Sep 22, 1960

Pos: OF	BA: .266
Hits: 1,175	HRs: 20
RBI: 280	BBs: 401

Vince Coleman was the unanimous pick as NL Rookie of the Year in 1985, when his 110 stolen bases and 107 runs scored led the Cardinals to the pennant. But a freak accident with the automatic tarpaulin machine just

Vince Coleman.

prior to Game Four of the 1985 NLCS sidelined him for the remainder of postseason play, seriously damaging the Cardinals' chances in the World Series, which they lost to the Royals in seven games.

Coleman forces NL pitchers and catchers to fear the stolen base as an offensive weapon. He is the only player in history to steal 100 or more bases in his first three seasons. In only nine seasons with the Cardinals and Mets, Coleman has scored 712 runs and stolen 648 bases. A college football player, Coleman tried out for the Washington Redskins as a punter, but he chose baseball. Coleman faced suspension from baseball in 1993, when he was involved in a post-game firecracker throwing incident in which a young girl was injured.
Playing Career: *1985- ; StL N, NY N*

Darnell Coles
Coles, Darnell
B: Jun 2, 1962

Pos: 3B, OF, SS	BA: .248
Hits: 641	HRs: 67
RBI: 335	BBs: 211

Coles was the third baseman in the incredible all-20 home run infield of the 1986 Tigers. He turned down a scholarship at UCLA to play pro ball, but perhaps he could have used the seasoning. Somewhat of a defensive liability, Coles has struggled to find a position. He hit .312 for the Reds in 1992.
Playing Career: *1983- ; Sea A, Det A, Pit N, SF N, Cin N, Tor A*

Dave Collins
Collins, David Scott
B: Oct 20, 1952

Pos: OF	BA: .273
Hits: 1,322	HRs: 32
RBI: 370	BBs: 454

Collins has done a good job in all the roles he has filled, but he has been used as a regular player only once, by the Reds in 1980. He stole 79 bases that year. Collins developed into a fair leadoff hitter, and batted .300 twice while with the Reds. With Toronto in 1984, he batted .308 and led the AL with 15 triples. He returned to the Reds in the late 1980s.
Playing Career: *1975-1990; Cal A, Sea A, Cin N, NY A, Tor A, Oak A, Det A, StL N*

Eddie Collins
Collins, Edward Trowbridge, Sr.
B: May 2, 1887   D: Mar 25, 1951
Hall of Fame 1939

Pos: 2B	BA: .333
Hits: 3,311	HRs: 47
RBI: 1,299	BBs: 1,503

Managerial Record
Won: 174   Lost: 160   Pct: .521

One of the best all-around ballplayers ever, Collins was also one of the most enduring, playing 25 seasons in the major leagues. He never won a batting title because his career coincided with Ty Cobb's, but Collins set a number of records and led the AL in several categories. His statistics are awesome and include 1,818 runs scored, 437 doubles, 187 triples and 743 stolen bases. Collins ranks among the all-time greats in batting average and hits; he led the AL in stolen bases four times and in runs scored three years in a row.

The premier infielder on the great Athletics teams of 1909-1914, Collins was instrumental in the capture of four flags in those six years. After retiring from the playing field, he stayed in baseball as a manager and administrator. Collins had a brief but stunning scouting career – he made one trip to California, returning with prospects Bobby Doerr and Ted Williams.
Playing Career: *1906-1930; Phi A, Chi A*
Managerial Career: *1924-1926; Chi A*

Jimmy Collins
Collins, James Joseph
B: Jan 16, 1870   D: Mar 6, 1943
Hall of Fame 1945

Pos: 3B	BA: .294
Hits: 1,997	HRs: 65
RBI: 983	BBs: 426

Managerial Record
Won: 455   Lost: 376   Pct: .548

Considered baseball's premier third baseman until Pie Traynor came along in the 1920s, Collins set numerous records for the hot corner position. He was the best there was at fielding bunts. He accepted 601 chances at third in 1899, still a league record. He led NL third sackers in putouts five times, assists

Eddie Collins with the Chicago White Sox, with whom he played from 1915 to 1926.

Jimmy Collins.

four times and double plays twice. Collins ranks second on the all-time list for putouts at third base.

An extraordinary hitter and baserunner, Collins hit .300 or more five times. He led the league in home runs in 1898, when he also had more than 100 RBI for the second year in a row, and scored more than 100 runs for the third of four times. He scored 1,055 runs during his career.
Playing Career: *1895-1908; Bos N, Lou N, Bos A, Phi A*
Managerial Career: *1901-1906; Bos A*

Joe Collins
Collins, Joseph Edward
B: Dec 3, 1922   D: Aug 30, 1989

Pos: 1B, OF	BA: .256
Hits: 596	HRs: 86
RBI: 329	BBs: 338

Collins had success as a power hitter in post-season play, although he did not hit for average. Playing in seven Fall Classics in eight years, he hit four home runs, one each in 1951 and 1953, two in 1955. He was usually platooned with Johnny Mize.
Playing Career: *1948-1957; NY A*

Phil Collins
Collins, Philip Eugene (Fidgety Phil)
B: Aug 27, 1901   D: Aug 14, 1948

Pos: P	ERA: 4.66
W-L: 80-85	SOs: 423
ShOs: 4	Saves: 24

It is said that Phil was fidgety on the mound in Philadelphia's small Baker Bowl because the team in the field behind him finished last in the league in fielding five of the six years Collins was there. Somehow he still had three winning seasons. In 1933 he led the league in relief saves and losses.
Playing Career: *1923, 1929-1935; Chi N, Phi N, StL N*

Rip Collins
Collins, Harry Warren
B: Feb 26, 1896   D: May 27, 1968

Pos: P	ERA: 3.99
W-L: 108-82	SOs: 569
ShOs: 16	Saves: 5

The erstwhile Collins was thought to play major league baseball only to support his true vocations – hunting, fishing, drinking and partying. He won 14 games three times and pitched in one World Series.
Playing Career: *1920-1931; NY A, Bos A, Det A, StL A*

Ripper Collins
Collins, James Anthony
B: Mar 30, 1904   D: Apr 15, 1970

Pos: 1B, OF	BA: .276
Hits: 1,121	HRs: 135
RBI: 659	BBs: 356

The banty rooster of the Cardinals' Gas House Gang, Collins was a slugger who was all the more dangerous because of his deceptive size. At 5'9" and 165 pounds, he led the NL with a .615 slugging average and 35 homers in 1934. Collins played in three World Series, batting .367 in the Cardinals' winning cause in 1934, and was an All-Star three times. Hailing from the coal mining area of Pennsylvania, home of so many good baseball players, Collins spent 30 years in the major leagues as a player, coach and manager. He later worked as a sportscaster.
Playing Career: *1931-1938, 1941; StL N, Chi N, Pit N*

Shano Collins
Collins, John Francis
B: Dec 4, 1885   D: Sep 10, 1955

Pos: OF, 1B	BA: .264
Hits: 1,687	HRs: 22
RBI: 705	BBs: 331
Managerial Record	
Won: 73 Lost: 134 Pct: .353	

Shano played on the 1919 Black Sox, but neither he nor the other Collins, Eddie, had a part in the notorious fix. Known as a versatile and cooperative team player, Collins was shifted from first base to right field where he became one of the AL's top defensive outfielders. He filled in at first in 1915 and again in 1920 when teammate Chick Gandil sat out the entire season. He played in one World Series.
Playing Career: *1910-1925; Chi A, Bos A*
Managerial Career: *1931-1932; Bos A*

Earle Combs.

Charlie Comiskey.

Dave Concepcion.

Earle Combs
Combs, Earle Bryan
(The Kentucky Colonel)
B: May 14, 1899   D: Jul 21, 1976
Hall of Fame 1970

Pos: OF	BA: .325
Hits: 1,866	HRs: 58
RBI: 629	BBs: 620

Until Rickey Henderson came along, Earle Combs was considered the 20th century's greatest leadoff hitter. He scored almost half the time he reached base, 1,186 times during his career. The king of triples, Combs knocked three in one game in 1927, led the league in three-base hits three times, and amassed 154 during his career. Playing among stars, Combs was frequently overshadowed. But he hit over .300 nine times, and in 1927 led the AL in hits with 231.

Patrolling the cavernous center field at Yankee Stadium, Combs led AL center fielders in putouts in 1927. In 1934 he was chasing a fly ball in center field at Sportsman's Park in St. Louis when he crashed into the wall, fracturing his skull. Combs recovered but his playing did not. He became a coach in 1935.
Playing Career: *1924-1935; NY A*

Charlie Comiskey
Comiskey, Charles Albert
B: Aug 15, 1859   D: Oct 26, 1931
Hall of Fame 1939

Pos: 1B	BA: .264
Hits: 1,531	HRs: 29
RBI: 467	BBs: 197

Managerial Record
Won: 840   Lost: 541   Pct: .608

Player, manager, owner, league founder, baseball promoter and controversial figure, Comiskey left more than a ballpark in Chicago. His baseball legacy included purchasing a Western League team and relocating it in Chicago to play in the new AL in 1900. Comiskey christened the team "White Stockings." Years later his image was seriously tarnished when details of his petty, greed-driven management methods were made public. Many lay the blame for the Black Sox scandal of 1919 squarely on his shoulders.

As a player Comiskey pioneered the move of the first baseman off the bag to be more active as a fielder. He scored 994 runs and stole 378 bases. As a manager he led the Browns to four pennants in a row during the years 1885-1888, and was the victor in the only winner-take-all World Series ever played, in 1886.
Playing Career: *1882-1894; StL AA, Chi P, Cin N*
Managerial Career: *1883-1894: StL AA, Chi P, Cin N*

Adam Comorosky
Comorosky, Adam Anthony
B: Dec 9, 1905   D: Mar 2, 1951

Pos: OF	BA: .285
Hits: 795	HRs: 28
RBI: 417	BBs: 214

Comorosky had one great season, 1930. The rest of his career he spent perpetually fighting for a job. He led the NL in triples with 23 in 1930, the year he hit .313 with 112 runs, 47 doubles, and 119 RBI. He played on the 1927 NL champ Pirate team.
Playing Career: *1926-1935; Pit N, Cin N*

Dave Concepcion
Concepcion y Benitez, David Ismael
B: Jun 17, 1948

Pos: SS	BA: .267
Hits: 2,326	HRs: 101
RBI: 950	BBs: 736

Venezuela-born Concepcion would have a shot at the Hall of Fame but for the fact that the Big Red Machine has already supplied five. Johnny Bench and Joe Morgan have already been enshrined; Tony Perez, Pete Rose and Sparky Anderson are waiting. On lesser teams Concepcion would have been a top offensive threat; for the Reds he batted eighth, in front of the pitcher. He scored 993 runs and stole 321 bases.

Working his entire career for the Reds, Concepcion made the All-Star squad nine times. He won five Gold Glove Awards and played on five division-winning teams, four of them capturing the pennant. He hit .266 in 20 World Series games.
Playing Career: *1970-1988; Cin N*

David Cone
Cone, David Brian
B: Jan 2, 1963

Pos: P	ERA: 3.14
W-L: 95-65	SOs: 1,418
ShOs: 16	Saves: 1

After achieving fame and fortune in New York and Toronto, Cone signed with his hometown Kansas City team for the 1993 season. Several years earlier, he had left the Royals in one of the strangest, unexplained trades in baseball history. Kansas City sent Cone to the Mets for second-string catcher Ed Hearn, who reported a rotator cuff injury one month into the season. Cone, meanwhile went 20-3 in New York and faced his former AL colleagues in the All-Star Game.

In subsequent years, Cone developed his own Shea Stadium cheering section called "Coneheads." Wearing pointed hats fashioned after the costumes of "Saturday Night Live" characters, they kept track of his prodigious number of strikeouts. He has averaged 228 in the last five years.
Playing Career: *1986-; KC A, NY N, Tor A*

Tony Conigliaro
Conigliaro, Anthony Richard
B: Jan 7, 1945   D: Feb 24, 1990

Pos: OF
Hits: 849
RBI: 516

BA: .264
HRs: 166
BBs: 287

Conigliaro was the youngest player ever to reach 100 home runs. He was a powerful star still in development when he was struck in the face with a Jack Hamilton fastball in 1967. The Red Sox gamely fought on to win the AL pennant that year, but their hearts were broken. Conigliaro was never the same.
Playing Career: *1964-1967, 1969-1971, 1975; Bos A, Cal A*

Jocko Conlan
Conlan, John Bertrand
B: Dec 6, 1899   D: Apr 16, 1989
Hall of Fame 1974

Pos: OF
Hits: 96
RBI: 31

BA: .263
HRs: 0
BBs: 33

A weak-hitting outfielder began a Hall of Fame umpiring career by happenstance. When Red Ormsby, who was umpiring a 1935 game between the White Sox and St. Louis, was overcome by the heat, Conlan was asked to fill in. The following year he launched his new career. A polka-dot tie, balloon chest protector and quick grin became Conlan's trademarks. He won the respect of

Umpire Jocko Conlan.

players and managers alike with his hustle, accuracy and fairness. Jackie Robinson was at bat in a 1955 game when Conlan was behind the plate. Suffering from arthritis and unable to bend to the proper position, Conlan made a bad call. He left the field and removed himself from the game rather than perform at less than his best.
Playing Career: *1934-1935; Chi A*
Umpiring Career: *1941-1964; NL (5 WS, 6 AS)*

Gene Conley
Conley, Donald Eugene
B: Nov 10, 1930

Pos: P
W-L: 91-96
ShOs: 13

ERA: 3.82
SOs: 888
Saves: 9

Conley was the first white athlete to be a highly rated pro in both baseball and basketball. Dave Debusschere followed in Conley's footsteps and made it to the basketball Hall of Fame. Conley spent winters with the Celtics and summers with the Braves and later, the Red Sox. At 6'8" he was difficult to hit against. He made three All-Star squads and hurled in the 1957 World Series.
Playing Career: *1952, 1954-1963; Bos N, Mil N, Phi N, Bos A*

Sarge Connally
Connally, George Walter
B: Aug 31, 1898   D: Jan 27, 1978

Pos: P
W-L: 49-60
ShOs: 2

ERA: 4.30
SOs: 345
Saves: 31

Connally saw service in World War I, hence his nickname. As a spot starter he won 10 games in 1927, but lost 13 in 1924. He was fairly successful as a reliever, but only once had an ERA under 4.00.
Playing Career: *1921, 1923-1929, 1931-1934; Chi A, Cle A*

Tommy Connolly
Connolly, Thomas
B: Dec 31, 1870   D: Apr 28, 1961
Hall of Fame 1953

Englishman Tom Connolly began an association with America's new game, baseball, around the turn of the century. Starting as an umpire in the NL in 1898, he switched to the AL in 1901 when Ban Johnson hired him upon Connie Mack's recommendation. Connolly officiated at major league games for 34 seasons. Quiet and unobtrusive, he was a strict disciplinarian; yet he once went 10 consecutive years without ejecting a player! The last player he thumbed was Babe Ruth, and the incident marked the last time Ruth was ever tossed out of a game. Incensed by taunts from the stands in 1922, Ruth charged toward the fans. The little umpire blocked the Babe's path, saying, "You should be ashamed of yourself." Connolly served many years as the supervisor of AL umpires.
Umpiring Career: *1898-1931; NL, AL (8 WS)*

Hurler David Cone threw for the New York Mets from 1987 to 1992.

Roger Connor.

Roger Connor

Connor, Roger

B: Jul 1, 1857   D: Jan 4, 1931
Hall of Fame 1976

Pos: 1B	BA: .317
Hits: 2,467	HRs: 136
RBI: 1,125	BBs: 1,002

Managerial Record
Won: 8   Lost: 37   Pct: .178

Connor was the first NL player to hit a grand slam home run. A pure slugger, he was the career leader in four-base hits among 19th-century players. He rapped 233 triples, ranking him fifth on the all-time list. He hit 441 doubles and scored 1,620 runs. Coming to New York when the league shifted the Troy franchise, Connor bloomed in the Big Apple. In his first game he hit such a magnificent shot that the delirous patrons passed the hat to buy him a $500 gold watch.

Connor was the key player on Jim Mutrie's "We are the People" Giants who won back-to-back pennants in 1888-1889. He hit three homers in a game versus Indianapolis in 1888. Two years later Connor led his peers in the Players' League with 14 round-trippers. At age 38 he went 6-for-6 off Jouett Meekin in 1894. He continued to play minor league baseball in the Connecticut and New England Leagues as owner and manager.
Playing Career: *1880-1897; Tro N, NY N, NY P, Phi N, StL N*
Managerial Career: *1896; StL N*

Wid Conroy

Conroy, William Edward

B: Apr 5, 1877   D: Dec 6, 1959

Pos: 3B, 2B, SS, OF	BA: .248
Hits: 1,256	HRs: 22
RBI: 452	BBs: 345

Conroy was a good glove man who replaced shortstop Honus Wagner on the Paterson team in the Atlantic League, then later played short for the great Pirates team of 1902. He found himself playing third base in the AL the next few seasons.
Playing Career: *1901-1911; Mil A, Pit N, NY A, Was A*

Duff Cooley

Cooley, Duff Gordan

B: Mar 14, 1873   D: Aug 9, 1937

Pos: OF	BA: .294
Hits: 1,576	HRs: 25
RBI: 557	BBs: 365

Referred to as "Sir Richard" for his aristocratic manner, Cooley batted high in the lineup, scoring 847 runs and stealing 224 bases during his career. Afterwards, he bought and operated the Topeka and Salt Lake City teams for many years.
Playing Career: *1893-1905; StL N, Phi N, Pit N, Bos N, Det A*

Jack Coombs

Coombs, John Wesley

B: Nov 18, 1882   D: Apr 15, 1957

Pos: P	ERA: 2.78
W-L: 158-110	SOs: 1,052
ShOs: 35	Saves: 8

Managerial Record
Won: 18   Lost: 44   Pct: .290

Coombs is the only pitcher to reach the .300 mark at the plate and win three games in one World Series. He batted .385 and tossed three complete game victories in the 1910 Fall Classic. Signed off the campus of Colby College in Maine, Coombs immediately pitched the 24-inning tie game which set the AL record that still stands for most innings pitched. His 13 shutouts in 1913 is also an AL record.

Coombs never lost a game in World Series play, adding a victory in 1911 and another in 1916 with the Dodgers to the three in 1910. After his major league career, Coombs spent years at Duke University where he won championships and sent players to the

A's pitcher Jack Coombs won 31 games in 1910, then three in the WS.

majors, especially to his mentor and former manager, Connie Mack.
Playing Career: *1906-1918, 1920; Phi A, Brk N, Det A*
Managerial Career: *1919; Phi N*

Johnny Cooney
Cooney, John Walter
B: Mar 18, 1901   D: Jul 8, 1986

Pos: OF	BA: .286
Hits: 965	HRs: 2
RBI: 219	BBs: 208

Managerial Record
Won: 20   Lost: 25   Pct: .444

Johnny Cooney had two careers – first as a pitcher, then as an outfielder. He posted 34 pitching victories out of 76 starts, tossing 44 complete games for the Braves. He pitched seven shutouts and made six saves. A sore arm curtailed his mound duties, forcing him to the minors where he won a batting title. After a hitch with the Dodgers, Cooney returned to the Braves where he hit over .300 in 1940-1941. His outfield play was compared favorably with Joe DiMaggio's.
Playing Career: *1921-1930, 1935-1944; Bos N, Brk N, NY A*
Managerial Career: *1949; Bos N*

Andy Cooper
Cooper, Andy
B: Mar 4, 1896   D: Jun 10, 1941

Pos: P	ERA: NA
W-L: 118-57	SOs: 476
ShOs: 15	Saves: 30

Managerial Record (inc.)
Won: 80   Lost: 37   Pct: .684

The Waco southpaw won more games in the Negro Leagues than all but two other hurlers, Willie Foster and Satchel Paige. He finished his career with one season for the Detroit Stars, when his 15-6 record helped them to the playoffs. As a manager he captured four pennants.
Playing Career: *1920-1930; Det Stars, KC Monarchs*
Managerial Career: *1935-1941; KC Monarchs*

Cecil Cooper
Cooper, Cecil Celester
B: Dec 20, 1949

Pos: 1B, DH	BA: .298
Hits: 2,192	HRs: 241
RBI: 1,125	BBs: 448

The Red Sox traded Cooper, a left-handed high-average hitter for a right-handed power hitter, George Scott. Both clubs were happy with the deal. Cooper pounded out seven .300 seasons in a row, topping .350 once, but never winning a batting title. He did lead the AL in doubles and RBI twice. Altogether he hit 415 doubles and scored 1,012 runs. Cooper also won two Gold Gloves, 1979-1980. He was selected for the All-Star team five times, and played in the 1982 ALCS.
Playing Career: *1971-1987; Bos A, Mil A*

Stellar backstop Walker Cooper with the Cardinals in the early 1940s.

Mort Cooper
Cooper, Morton Cecil
B: Mar 2, 1913   D: Nov 17, 1958

Pos: P	ERA: 2.97
W-L: 128-75	SOs: 193
ShOs: 33	No-hitters: 0

His greatest day in baseball came on the saddest day of his life. Cooper won Game Two over the Yankees in the 1943 World Series the day his father passed away. Cooper was the best pitcher in the NL during the war years, and he started the 1942 and 1943 All-Star Games. He won 65 games during the Cardinals' pennant three-peat of 1942-1944. Mort and catcher Walker Cooper formed the most popular sibling battery ever. They played together eight years.
Playing Career: *1938-1947, 1949; StL N, Bos N, NY N, Chi N*

Walker Cooper
Cooper, William Walker
B: Jan 8, 1915   D: Apr 11, 1991

Pos: C	BA: .285
Hits: 1,341	HRs: 173
RBI: 812	BBs: 309

Cooper was the best catcher in the NL during most of his career, which began and ended with the Cardinals. He was selected NL All-Star receiver from 1942 to 1948, there being no game in 1945. Cooper swung a big bat. He did not hit as many home runs as Campanella, but neither did he play in a small park for a slugging team in the media limelight. Cooper shone when he went to the Giants, who paid $175,000 for him while he was still in the Navy. The 1947 Giants rocked the Polo Grounds with an NL record 221 home runs. Cooper contributed 35 of those.

Cooper later toiled for the Braves and taught a young receiver named Del Crandall to block pitches and shift his feet. Walker was able to stay in baseball so long because clubs appreciated the way he taught and influenced their young catchers.
Playing Career: *1940-1957; StL N, NY N, Cin N, Bos N, Mil N, Pit N, Chi N*

Wilbur Cooper
Cooper, Arley Wilbur
B: Feb 24, 1892   D: Aug 7, 1973

Pos: P   ERA: 2.89
W-L: 216-178   SOs: 1,252
ShOs: 36   Saves: 14

Cooper was a workhorse. In the early 1920s he won 20 games or more four times, completed 20 games or more eight times, and started at least 20 games for 12 consecutive years. He holds the club record in Pittsburgh for most wins by a left-hander, with 202. Inexplicably, when the Pirates got close to the NL pennant they traded him. Cooper led the NL once in shutouts and once in saves. In 1916 he turned in a 1.87 ERA.
Playing Career: *1912-1926; Pit N, Chi N, Det A*

Doug Corbett
Corbett, Douglas Mitchell
B: Nov 4, 1952

Pos: P   ERA: 3.32
W-L: 24-30   SOs: 343
ShOs: 0   Saves: 66

Corbett started his major league career with an 8-6 record and a 1.98 ERA with 23 saves. He never again topped those rookie marks. Insiders say he was too soft. He sometimes yelled, "Look out!" when a pitch sailed. He won Game Four of the 1986 ALCS.
Playing Career: *1980-1987; Min A, Cal A, Bal A*

Larry Corcoran
Corcoran, Lawrence J.
B: Aug 10, 1859   D: Oct 14, 1891

Pos: P   ERA: 2.36
W-L: 177-89   SOs: 1,103
ShOs: 22   No-hitters: 3

Corcoran was a meteoric flash across the sky of baseball history. Once he found a catcher who could hold him, Corcoran became a big star for the White Stockings. He won 43 games as a rookie, winning 170 games in five years, and compiling a .663 won-lost percentage. He won 30 or more games three times 1881-1884, putting him in the ranks of Kid Nichols, Tim Keefe, John Clarkson, Cy Young and Tony Mullane.

In 1885 Corcoran's arm began to show signs of strain in the shoulder. He pitched some innings left-handed to relieve the pressure. When his arm failed to come around, the White Stockings released him. The two games Corcoran won for the Giants that season were his last victories. After a couple

Larry Corcoran.

years alternating between the majors and minors, Corcoran fell ill in the spring of 1891 and died of Bright's disease that autumn. He had all the characteristics of a star player except durability.
Playing Career: *1880-1887; Chi N, NY N, Was N, Ind N*

Tommy Corcoran
Corcoran, Thomas William
B: Jan 4, 1869   D: Jun 25, 1960

Pos: SS   BA: .256
Hits: 2,251   HRs: 34
RBI: 1,135   BBs: 382

Corcoran played through the transition of baseball from the old barehanded days to the days of modern equipment. With the Reds he teamed with Miller Huggins, the inventor of the delayed double steal, contributing to his career total of 387 steals. In his best season, 1894, he batted .300, scored 123 runs, slashed 20 triples and 21 doubles, and drove in 92 runs. A top fielder, Corcoran set the major league record for assists with 14 in a nine-inning game and led his league four times in fielding percentage.
Playing Career: *1890-1907; Pit P, Phi AA, Brk N, Cin N, NY N*

Pop Corkhill
Corkhill, John Stewart
B: Apr 11, 1858   D: Apr 4, 1921

Pos: OF   BA: .254
Hits: 1,120   HRs: 30
RBI: 268   BBs: 174

Corkhill was a top defensive player before outfielders were expected to be sluggers,

leading the AA four times in fielding percentage. His Reds team captured the first AA pennant, and he later played on two Dodgers teams that won flags, 1889-1890.
Playing Career: *1883-1892; Cin AA, Brk AA, Brk N, Phi AA, Cin N, Pit N*

Pat Corrales
Corrales, Patrick
B: Mar 20, 1941

Pos: C   BA: .216
Hits: 166   HRs: 4
RBI: 54   BBs: 75
Managerial Record
Won: 572   Lost: 634   Pct: .474

Corrales had the reputation of being able to turn around struggling franchises. He would rebuild the entire system – coaches, scouts, and minor league instructors. As a result several teams he developed flourished after he left them.
Playing Career: *1964-1966, 1968-1973; Phi N, StL N, Cin N, SD N*
Managerial Career: *1978-1980, 1982-1987; Tex A, Phi N, Cle A*

Pete Coscarart
Coscarart, Peter Joseph
B: Jun 16, 1913

Pos: 2B, SS, 3B   BA: .243
Hits: 728   HRs: 28
RBI: 269   BBs: 295

Coscarart had a fine rookie season at second base for the Dodgers, hitting .277 with 22 doubles. That was his best year; his power declined and the Dodgers secured Hall of Famer Billy Herman to replace him in 1941. Coscarart played a backup role in the World Series that year.
Playing Career: *1938-1946; Brk N, Pit N*

Chuck Cottier
Cottier, Charles Keith
B: Jan 18, 1936

Pos: 2B   BA: .253
Hits: 348   HRs: 19
RBI: 127   BBs: 137
Managerial Record
Won: 98   Lost: 119   Pct: .452

"Good field, no hit" was the tag applied to Cottier as a player. Managing the Mariners during the lean years, he once threw all the bats and balls onto the playing field and sailed first base into the outfield in protest of an umpire's call.
Playing Career: *1959-1965, 1968-1969; Mil N, Det A, Was A, Cal A*
Managerial Career: *1984-1986; Sea A*

Bill Coughlin
Coughlin, William Paul
B: Jul 12, 1878   D: May 7, 1943

Pos: 3B   BA: .253
Hits: 976   HRs: 15
RBI: 380   BBs: 203

Coughlin spent his best days in the early AL. As third baseman for the Tigers he played in the 1907 and 1908 World Series. He had the misfortune of playing when batting was at its nadir, but he hit around the league average.
Playing Career: *1899, 1901-1908; Was N, Was A, Det A*

Clint Courtney
Courtney, Clinton Dawson (Scrap Iron)
B: Mar 16, 1927   D: Jun 16, 1975

Pos: C	BA: .268
Hits: 750	HRs: 38
RBI: 313	BBs: 265

"Scrap Iron" had a tendency to get into fights despite being only 5'8" tall and wearing glasses. He was involved in a lulu with Billy Martin of the Yankees in 1953; even the fans leapt onto the playing field. The incident resulted in AL record fines of $850.

Courtney, the first catcher to wear spectacles, was acquired by the Browns on the recommendation of Rogers Hornsby. He rewarded Hornsby with a .286 average and 50 RBI, winning the AL Rookie of the Year nod in 1952. His production increased as his playing time decreased; platooning augmented his career. Courtney was involved in the biggest trade to that date. The Orioles shipped him and four no-names to the White Sox for two players. Courtney later managed Richmond in the International League.
Playing Career: *1951-1961; NY A, StL A, Bal A, Chi A, Was A, Bal A, KC A*

Harry Coveleski
Coveleski, Harry Frank (Harry, the Giant Killer)
B: Apr 23, 1886   D: Aug 4, 1950

Pos: P	ERA: 2.39
W-L: 81-55	SOs: 511
ShOs: 13	Saves: 9

Coveleski beat the 1908 Giants three times in September – after the Merkle boner – costing John McGraw the NL pennant. Stuck with his appellation, Coveleski fled to the AL where he starred with the Tigers, winning 65 games in three years. His brother Stanley is in the Baseball Hall of Fame.
Playing Career: *1907-1910, 1914-1918; Phi N, Cin N, Det A*

Stan Coveleski
Coveleski, Stanley Anthony
B: Jul 13, 1889   D: Mar 20, 1984
Hall of Fame 1969

Pos: P	ERA: 2.89
W-L: 215-142	SOs: 981
ShOs: 38	Saves: 21

One of the greatest control pitchers ever, Coveleski walked a scant 802 batters in 3,082 innings. He learned control by throwing rocks during lunch breaks at school and at the coal mines where he worked as a youngster. He always claimed that the spitball made him a big league pitcher, but his three-hit shutout debut for Connie Mack's Athletics in 1912 was sans spitter.

Coveleski controlled Babe Ruth and Ty Cobb by jamming them with fastballs on the inside when they were looking for the spitter out and away. Several times he retired the side on three pitches. His three five-hit victories over the Dodgers in the 1920 World Series brought the World Championship to the Indians. Coveleski won 20 games five times, including four seasons in a row, 1918-1921. When he was traded to the Senators he pitched them to their second straight flag with a 20-5 record and a 2.84 ERA in 1925, both AL high marks. His elder brother Harry pitched in the majors for nine years.
Playing Career: *1912, 1916-1928; Phi A, Cle A, Was A, NY A*

Clint Courtney is out at home plate in a squeeze attempt during a 1955 game.

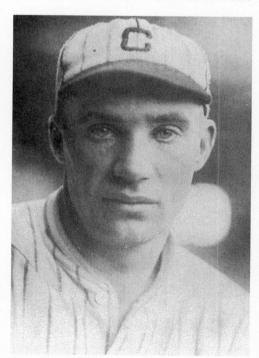
Stan Coveleski.

Wes Covington
Covington, John Wesley
B: Mar 27, 1932

Pos: OF	BA: .279
Hits: 832	HRs: 131
RBI: 499	BBs: 247

Extremely successful as a platoon outfielder, Covington made two brilliant catches in the 1957 World Series. He hit 21 and 24 home runs for the 1957-1958 pennant-winning Braves despite getting only 328 and 294 at-bats. Covington posted a lifetime .466 slugging average.
Playing Career: *1956-1966; Mil N, Chi A, KC A, Phi N, Chi N, LA N*

Al Cowens
Cowens, Alfred Edward
B: Oct 25, 1951

Pos: OF	BA: .270
Hits: 1,494	HRs: 108
RBI: 717	BBs: 389

Cowens was recently chosen as the right-fielder on the 25th Anniversary All-Time Royals Team. His best season was 1977, when he hit .312 with 23 homers and 112 RBI. With Cowens in right, the Royals won three straight AL Western division titles (1976-1978).
Playing Career: *1974-1986; KC A, Cal A, Det A, Sea A*

Billy Cox
Cox, William Richard
B: Aug 29, 1919   D: Mar 30, 1978

Pos: 3B	BA: .262
Hits: 974	HRs: 66
RBI: 351	BBs: 298

Cox returned from World War II to find himself one of the top shortstops in the NL. The Dodgers acquired him in 1948 and he became a legendary fielder at third base and one of the storied ''Boys of Summer'' who took the team to so many pennants in the 1950s. Cox led NL third basemen in fielding in 1950, but he consistently tried for impossible plays and made errors. He hit .302 in 15 World Series games over three different trips.
Playing Career: *1941, 1946-1955; Pit N, Brk N, Bal A*

Bobby Cox
Cox, Robert Joe
B: May 21, 1941

Pos: 3B, 2B	BA: .225
Hits: 141	HRs: 9
RBI: 58	BBs: 75
Managerial Record	
Won: 957 Lost: 862 Pct: .526	

One of the most astute talent judges in baseball, Cox put together the two top teams of the early 1990s, the Blue Jays and Braves. Ironically, the teams met in the 1992 World Series, with the Birds prevailing over the Tribe.

Cox played for seven years in the Dodgers' farm system before going into the Braves' and Yankees' systems. When bad knees forced his retirement as a player, he managed the Yankees' farmhands. He then guided the Braves and moved on to the Blue Jays in 1982. Cox was named Manager of the Year when he led the Jays to the 1985 pennant. He was lured back to Atlanta in 1986, where he won two pennants in a row, 1991-1992, as a bench manager after having served as general manager, 1986-1989. Some said that the advantage Bobby Cox had as general manager was Bobby Cox as field manager.
Playing Career: *1968-1969; NY A*
Managerial Career: *1978-1985, 1990-; Atl N, Tor A*

Casey Cox
Cox, Joseph Casey
B: Jul 3, 1941

Pos: P	ERA: 3.70
W-L: 39-42	SOs: 297
ShOs: 0	Saves: 20

Ted Williams said Cox was the best right-handed reliever in the AL, but unfortunately he toiled in the obscurity of a second-division team. Even being with the Senators did not help. In two years as a stopper he recorded only 14 saves. As a starter he turned in a dismal 8-12 record.
Playing Career: *1966-1973; Was A, Tex A, NY A*

Danny Cox
Cox, Danny Bradford
B: Sep 21, 1959

Pos: P	ERA: 3.34
W-L: 72-71	SOs: 671
ShOs: 5	Saves: 5

A team leader on the Cardinals' pennant-winning clubs of 1985 and 1987, Cox, as the only big guy on the Red Birds, was always first onto the field to back up his teammates in a fight. Arm trouble caused him to miss three years but he made a comeback in 1991.
Playing Career: *1983-1988, 1991-; StL N, Phi N, Pit N, Tor A*

Harry Craft
Craft, Harry Francis
B: Apr 19, 1915

Pos: OF	BA: .253
Hits: 533	HRs: 44
RBI: 267	BBs: 110
Managerial Record	
Won: 360 Lost: 485 Pct: .426	

A disputed home run Craft hit in the Polo Grounds hastened the use of foul pole screens in major league ballparks. A good glove man in the outfield, Craft played in two World Series with the Reds in 1939-1940. After his playing days he managed for years in the minors and majors.
Playing Career: *1937-1942; Cin N*
Managerial Career: *1957-1959, 1961-1964; KC A, Chi N, Hou N*

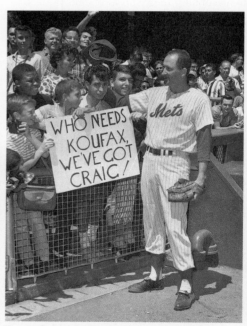

Roger Craig during his 5-22 1963 season.

Roger Craig
Craig, Roger Lee
B: Feb 17, 1930

Pos: P	ERA: 3.82
W-L: 74-98	SOs: 803
ShOs: 7	Saves: 19
Managerial Record	
Won: 738 Lost: 737 Pct: .500	

Craig went from the highly successful Dodgers organization to the worst team in modern baseball, the early Mets. As the ace of the staff, he won 10 then 5, but lost 24 then

Manager Bobby Cox.

22 in the club's first two dismal years. Playing with six major league teams, Craig learned a lot of baseball from his managers, especially Walt Alston and Casey Stengel.

A successful pitching coach, Craig consistently gets more out of pitchers than was thought possible. He was the pitching coach for the Tigers when they burst out of the gate with a 35-5 record in 1984. Craig guided the San Francisco Giants to two division titles and one pennant.
Playing Career: *1955-1966; Brk N, LA N, NY N, StL N, Cin N, Phi N*
Managerial Career: *1978-1979, 1985-1992; SD N, SF N*

Doc Cramer
Cramer, Roger Maxwell
B: Jul 22, 1905   D: Sep 9, 1990

Pos: OF	BA: .296
Hits: 2,705	HRs: 37
RBI: 842	BBs: 571

Cramer was a competitor. Playing for the 1929 Blue Ridge League, he was locked into a batting race with Joe Vosmik. Cramer pitched the final game of the season against Vosmik and walked him all four at-bats, winning the championship himself with a .404 average.

Cramer joined the A's in time for their 1929 pennant campaign, and helped them win that one and the two following. He played on

Doc Cramer.

the 1945 Tigers World Championship team. Cramer scored 1,357 runs during his career. He was elected to the All-Star team six times, though he played in only three. Batting over .300 seven of nine years, 1932-1940, Cramer peaked with .336 and .332 averages in 1932 and 1935. He went 6-for-6 twice, the only AL hitter to do so. Cramer was nicknamed Doc because he gained rudimentary medical knowledge by observing a local physician.
Playing Career: *1929-1948; Phi A, Bos A, Was A, Det A*

Del Crandall
Crandall, Delmar Wesley
B: Mar 5, 1930

Pos: C	BA: .254
Hits: 1,276	HRs: 179
RBI: 657	BBs: 424
Managerial Record	
Won: 364 Lost: 469 Pct: .437	

Crandall replaced Walker Cooper as the Braves' regular catcher in 1953, and remained the team's pillar of strength for the next 10 years. He appeared in eight All-Star Games and won four Gold Glove Awards. Crandall homered in the 1957 and 1958 World Series. He managed in the minors – leading Albuquerque to an amazing 94-38 record in 1982 – then in the majors before joining the White Sox broadcast team.
Playing Career: *1949-1950, 1953-1966; Bos N, Mil N, SF N, Pit N, Cle A*
Managerial Career: *1972-1975, 1983-1984; Mil A, Sea A*

Doc Crandall
Crandall, James Otis
B: Oct 8, 1887   D: Aug 17, 1951

Pos: P	ERA: 2.92
W-L: 102-62	SOs: 606
ShOs: 10	Saves: 19

Crandall was the first to be a relief specialist, filling that role for John McGraw from 1910 to 1913. Crandall was also an excellent batter with a .285 lifetime average. He had an ERA of 1.69 in three World Series for the New York Giants.
Playing Career: *1908-1916, 1918; NY N, StL F, StL A, Bos N*

Cannonball Crane
Crane, Edward Nicholas
B: May 1862   D: Sep 19, 1896

Pos: P	ERA: 3.99
W-L: 72-96	SOs: 720
ShOs: 6	No-hitters: 1

A fastball pitcher, as his nickname implies, Crane was plagued by inconsistency. He led the AA with a 2.45 ERA in 1891, but two years later posted a 6.89 mark. He played in four different major leagues in a seven-year period. He committed suicide by drinking carbolic acid.
Playing Career: *1884, 1886, 1888-1893; Bos U, Was N, NY N, NY P, Cin AA, Cin N, Brk N*

Sam Crane
Crane, Samuel Newhall
B: Jan 2, 1854   D: Jun 26, 1925

Pos: 2B	BA: .203
Hits: 276	HRs: 4
RBI: 45	BBs: 60
Managerial Record	
Won: 73 Lost: 79 Pct: .480	

An old-time ballplayer who was the dean of New York City newspaper writers from 1900 to 1925, Crane had a special rapport with Giants manager John McGraw, who included him in many of his escapades in Cuba and south Texas during spring training.
Playing Career: *1880, 1883-1887, 1890; Buf N, NY AA, Cin U, Det N, StL N, Was N, NY N, Pit N*
Managerial Career: *1880, 1884; Buf N, Cin U*

Gavvy Cravath
Cravath, Clifford Carlton (Cactus)
B: Mar 23, 1881   D: May 23, 1963

Pos: OF	BA: .287
Hits: 1,134	HRs: 119
RBI: 719	BBs: 561
Managerial Record	
Won: 91 Lost: 137 Pct: .399	

Cravath was the leading slugger in the NL during the second decade of the 20th century. He came to the big leagues from Minneapolis after leading that club to American Association pennants in 1910 and 1911. The short right field fence at Philadelphia's Baker Bowl was the perfect site for Cravath's home runs; he led the NL in round-trippers five times.

As the premier dead-ball era slugger, Cravath set NL marks for the next generation of sluggers to break. Along the way, he developed a prickly personality, and picked up a nickname to match. After his playing career, he was a Justice of the Peace.
Playing Career: *1908-1909, 1912-1920; Bos A, Chi A, Was A, Phi N*
Managerial Career: *1919-1920; Phi N*

Playing manager Gavvy Cravath (l), 1919.

Bill Craver
Craver, William H.
B: Jun 1844   D: Jun 17, 1901

Pos: 2B, SS, C	BA: .292
Hits: 458	HRs: 2
RBI: 128 (inc.)	BBs: 25

Managerial Record
Won: 70   Lost: 66   Pct: .515

Craver was a notorious and openly crooked ballplayer. A Syracuse newspaper once detailed the accusations against him, and the subsequent beatings he suffered at the hands of his teammates. In 1877 Craver was suspended for life for throwing games.
Playing Career: *1871-1877; Tro Haymakers n, Bal Lord Baltimores n, Phi White Stockings n, Phi Athletics n, Phi Centennials n, NY N, Lou N*
Managerial Career: *1871-1872, 1874-1875; Tro Haymakers n, Bal Lord Baltimores n, Phi White Stockings n, Phi Centennials n*

Sam Crawford
Crawford, Samuel Earl (Wahoo Sam)
B: Apr 18, 1880   D: Jun 15, 1968
Hall of Fame 1957

Pos: OF	BA: .309
Hits: 2,964	HRs: 97
RBI: 1,525	BBs: 760

Ty Cobb campaigned to get Crawford elected to the Hall of Fame. Crawford ranks first on the all-time triples list with 312. He scored 1,393 runs and stole 366 bases. In World Series play, Crawford hit .243 in 17 games.
Crawford and Cobb held out before the 1914 season; asking for a four-year contract and $20,000, respectively. They got what they wanted. Crawford received a four-year

Sam Crawford.

agreement at age 34, unheard of in those days. He was released at the end of the contract period. Playing in the Pacific Coast League, Crawford led the league with 239 hits. He always said that if he had known what a big deal 3,000 hits would be, he would have stayed in the majors to get his.
Playing Career: *1889-1917; Cin N, Det A*

Willie Crawford
Crawford, Willie Murphy
B: Sep 7, 1946

Pos: OF	BA: .268
Hits: 921	HRs: 86
RBI: 419	BBs: 431

Crawford played 12 of his 14 seasons with the Dodgers, who kept waiting for him to realize his vast potential. He was signed out of a local high school for $100,000 and hit .500 in the 1965 World Series at the age of 19.
Playing Career: *1964-1977; LA N, StL N, Hou N, Oak A*

Birdie Cree
Cree, William Franklin
B: Oct 22, 1882   D: Nov 8, 1942

Pos: OF	BA: .292
Hits: 761	HRs: 11
RBI: 332	BBs: 269

Cree played left field at Hilltopper Park with the Yankees when they were called the Highlanders. A top defensive outfielder, he batted .348 and .332 in 1911 and 1912. He eventually left baseball and became a banker in Pennsylvania.
Playing Career: *1908-1915; NY A*

Jim Creighton
Creighton, James
B: Apr 15, 1841   D: Oct 18, 1862

Creighton was probably baseball's first professional player (predating individual player statistics), a pitcher recruited and paid by boosters of the Excelsior Club in Brooklyn, New York. The Excelsiors took him on their first road trip in 1860, when they played in Buffalo, Rochester and Albany. Creighton once played an entire season without being put out. He was also the first pitcher to put wrist spin on the ball. He died from internal hemorrhage when an organ ruptured as he smashed a home run.
Playing Career: *1860-1862; Brk Niagaras, Brk Stars, Brk Excelsiors*

Lou Criger
Criger, Louis
B: Feb 3, 1872   D: May 14, 1934

Pos: C	BA: .221
Hits: 709	HRs: 11
RBI: 342	BBs: 309

After a successful NL career as a part-time catcher, Criger became Cy Young's special receiver. He caught Young with the Spiders, Cardinals and Pilgrims – later known as the

Red Sox – before finally parting ways with him in 1909.
Playing Career: *1896-1910, 1912; Cle N, StL N, Bos A, StL A, NY A*

Hugh Critz
Critz, Hugh Melville
B: Sep 17, 1900   D: Jan 10, 1980

Pos: 2B, SS	BA: .268
Hits: 1,591	HRs: 38
RBI: 531	BBs: 289

Critz has lifetime statistics remarkably similar to those of perennial Hall of Fame candidate Phil Rizzuto. Critz topped second basemen in fielding five times and led in double plays three. He had decent power, hitting more than 20 doubles and 10 or more triples in four seasons.
Playing Career: *1924-1935; Cin N, NY N*

Warren Cromartie
Cromartie, Warren Livingston
B: Sep 29, 1953

Pos: OF, 1B	BA: .281
Hits: 1,104	HRs: 61
RBI: 391	BBs: 325

A top prospect in the late 1970s, when Cromartie failed to achieve his goals he left the country. Returning from eight years of Japanese baseball, he hit .313 for the Royals. He wrote a book, *Slugging it out in Japan*.
Playing Career: *1974, 1976-1983, 1991; Mon N, KC A*

Joe Cronin
Cronin, Joseph Edward
B: Oct 12, 1906   D: Sep 7, 1984
Hall of Fame 1956

Pos: SS	BA: .301
Hits: 2,285	HRs: 170
RBI: 1,424	BBs: 1,059

Managerial Record
Won: 1,236   Lost: 1,055   Pct: .540

Ballplayer, manager, AL president, mover and shaker, Joe Cronin served baseball and it, in turn, rewarded him well. Starting with the 1927 Pirates, Cronin was an offensive shortstop in the same vein as Honus Wagner. He drove in 100 or more runs eight times, scored 1,233 runs and slugged 515 doubles. As a boy manager he won a pennant for the Senators in 1933. Then as a bench manager he led the Red Sox to the 1946 pennant and the exciting seven-game World Series with the Cardinals.
Senators owner Clark Griffith introduced Cronin to his niece, who was working in Griffith's office. They fell in love and married. Uncle Griffith's wedding present was to sell his new nephew to the Red Sox for $225,000, the most ever paid for a ballplayer up to 1935. Griffith always said he hated to do it, but that was a lot of money.
Playing Career: *1926-1945; Pit N, Was A, Bos A*
Managerial Career: *1933-1947; Was A, Bos A*

New 26-year-old manager Joe Cronin with his team in 1933 at the Senators' training camp in Biloxi, Mississippi.

Jack Crooks
Crooks, John Charles
B: Nov 9, 1866   D: Jan 29, 1918

Pos: 2B, 3B, OF	BA: .240
Hits: 668	HRs: 21
RBI: 251	BBs: 610

Managerial Record
Won: 27   Lost: 33   Pct: .450

Crooks was the first minor league player to hit four home runs in one game. He later led the NL twice in bases on balls and twice in fielding. He had an extremely high on-base percentage, .385 lifetime.
Playing Career: *1889-1893, 1895-1896, 1898; Col AA, StL N, Was N, Lou N*
Managerial Career: *1892; StL N*

Frank Crosetti
Crosetti, Frank Peter Joseph (Cro)
B: Oct 4, 1910

Pos: SS	BA: .245
Hits: 1,541	HRs: 98
RBI: 649	BBs: 792

Legend has it that the Yankees sent Crosetti and Tony Lazzeri to San Francisco to pick up a new teammate, a fellow West Coast Italian, Joe DiMaggio. The three notoriously quiet players rode in silence until they got to Kansas. DiMaggio cleared his throat. Crosetti asked, "Did you say something?" Lazzeri replied, "No, he didn't." The trip to New York continued in peace.

Crosetti is said to have cashed more World Series checks than any other person in baseball history. He played in seven Series with the Yankees and coached in 15 more, 1947-1964. He hit a home run off Dizzy Dean in the 1938 Fall Classic. Crosetti was an All-Star in 1936 and 1939. He scored 1,006 runs and stole 113 bases, leading the AL with 27 in 1938. His ability to steal signs came in handy again when he coached third base for the Yankees and in the 1970 ALCS for the Twins.
Playing Career: *1932-1948; NY A*

Powel Crosley
Crosley, Powel Jr.
B: Sep 18, 1886   D: Mar 28, 1961

Crosley was an inventor and manufacturer of automobiles, refrigerators and radios, who purchased the Cincinnati Reds in 1934 at the

Frank Crosetti at bat in the 1938 WS.

request of General Manager Larry MacPhail. Having the NL's worst franchise, the two experimented fearlessly. They brought night baseball to the big leagues; hired Red Barber to broadcast every game over the radio; tried indoor professional baseball during the winter; issued media guides.

Most importantly, Crosley and MacPhail brought in good players. The Reds won the pennant in 1939, and again in 1940 despite the suicide of the team's catcher, Willard Hershberger. When the Reds whipped the Tigers in the 1940 World Series, the hapless club Crosley had bought for $450,000 was suddenly worth a couple of million dollars. Crosley had stepped up to rescue the club when no one else would. Grateful Cincinnati fans called their ballpark Crosley Field, an honor retained until the stadium was abandoned in 1970, when the Reds moved into their new stadium.

Lave Cross
Cross, Lafayette Napoleon
B: May 12, 1866   D: Sep 6, 1927

Pos: 3B	BA: .292
Hits: 2,644	HRs: 47
RBI: 1,345	BBs: 464

Managerial Record
Won: 8   Lost: 30   Pct: .211

In the middle of a long, productive playing career, Cross became the manager of the forgettable Cleveland Spiders of 1899. Cross was too good a player for the arachnids so the team owners moved him back to the Cardinals. The bowlegged infielder had played for Philadelphia in four different leagues. He stole 301 bases and scored 1,333 runs.
Playing Career: *1887-1907; Lou AA, Phi AA, Phi P, Phi N, StL N, Cle N, Brk N, Phi A, Was A*
Managerial Career: *1899; Cle N*

Monte Cross
Cross, Montford Montgomery
B: Aug 31, 1869   D: Jun 21, 1934

Pos: SS
BA: .234
Hits: 1,364
HRs: 31
RBI: 621
BBs: 616

Monte Cross jumped to the AL to fill the shortstop hole in Connie Mack's infield. In the 1905 World Series, Cross batted a dismal .176, but it ranked him fourth highest on the team which was shut out four times.
Playing Career: *1892, 1894-1907; Bal N, Pit N, StL N, Phi N, Phi A*

Alvin "General" Crowder.

General Crowder
Crowder, Alvin Floyd
B: Jan 11, 1899   D: Apr 3, 1972

Pos: P
ERA: 4.12
W-L: 167-115
SOs: 799
ShOs: 16
Saves: 22

Crowder was called "General" after General Enoch Crowder, the initiator of the 1917 military draft. One of the top AL hurlers of his era, Crowder pitched in the very first All-Star Game, which the AL won 4-2. The General led AL pitchers with 26 and 24 wins in 1932 and 1933. He averaged 20 wins for six years, 1928-1933, and pitched in three consecutive World Series, 1933-1935.
Playing Career: *1926-1936; Was A, StL A, Det A*

Walt Cruise
Cruise, Walton Edwin
B: May 6, 1890   D: Jan 9, 1975

Pos: OF
BA: .277
Hits: 644
HRs: 30
RBI: 272
BBs: 238

Cruise was a journeyman ballplayer who batted .295 in his only full season, 1917 with the Cardinals. He was married at home plate in Cincinnati between games of a doubleheader. Cruise did not play the nightcap.
Playing Career: *1914, 1916-1924; StL N, Bos N*

Jose Cruz
Cruz y Dilan, Jose
B: Aug 8, 1947

Pos: OF
BA: .284
Hits: 2,251
HRs: 165
RBI: 1,077
BBs: 898

Jose Cruz got 2,000 hits, scored 1,000 runs, accumulated 1,000 RBI, and stole 300 bases in virtual anonymity. He was confused with a number of other players named Cruz – Hector, Julio, Todd, and Victor – and he played for many years in Houston. Playing in the Astrodome cut down on his statistics, and the Houston press covered spring football instead of baseball.

Cruz hit over .300 five times, including three consecutive seasons. The third year he passed the .300 mark, he was finally named to the All-Star team. He hit .400 in the 1980 NLCS. During his career, Cruz ripped 391 doubles. He never had 100 RBI, but three times drove in 90 or more runs. He leads the Astros' all-time list in games, at-bats, hits, triples and RBI. Few players have appeared in more major league games without going to the World Series than Cruz.
Playing Career: *1970-1988; StL N, Hou N, NY A*

Julio Cruz
Cruz, Julio Louis
B: Dec 2, 1954

Pos: 2B
BA: .237
Hits: 916
HRs: 23
RBI: 276
BBs: 478

Julio Cruz figured in a famous trade when the White Sox and Mariners swapped second basemen as a result of data analysis supplied by a computer. In numbers, the two looked comparable, but Cruz proved to be a catalyst in Chicago. Seattle faded.
Playing Career: *1977-1986; Sea A, Chi A*

Jose Cruz whacks one for the Houston Astros in 1980.

Tony Cuccinello
Cuccinello, Anthony Francis
B: Nov 8, 1907

Pos: 2B   BA: .280
Hits: 1,729   HRs: 94
RBI: 884   BBs: 579

Tony Cuccinello was too old to draft for World War II, so he played in the AL and finished second in 1945 to Snuffy Sturnweiss with a .308 average. Four months later Cuccinello was let go by the White Sox, who expected the younger players to be returning from the War.

Cuccinello batted .312 and .315 in his first two years in the big leagues. He was too good to be in Cincinnati, then the Siberia of baseball. The Dodgers traded Babe Herman and Ernie Lombardi to get Cuccinello and Joe Stripp. Cuccinello turned out to be a crowd favorite in Brooklyn, though he hardly fit the Daffy Dodger profile. Cuccinello later coached under Al Lopez with the White Sox.
Playing Career: *1930-1940, 1942-1945; Cin N, Brk N, Bos N, NY N, Chi A*

Tony Cuccinello.

Mike Cuellar.

Mike Cuellar
Cuellar y Santana, Miguel Angel
B: May 8, 1937

Pos: P   ERA: 3.14
W-L: 185-130   SOs: 822
ShOs: 36   Saves: 11

Cuellar was the master of the Cuban Forkball, also known as the "dry spitter" or palm ball. He signed with the Havana Sugar Kings of the International League at age 20, and was pitching in the major leagues two years later. Cuellar then spent several years in the minors before returning to the big leagues. Winning 139 games in seven years, he pitched the Orioles to three pennants, two additional division titles and a World Championship.

Cuellar shared a Cy Young Award with Denny McLain in 1969, and led the AL in winning percentage twice, recording a .587 mark for his career. He was on four All-Star Game rosters, and compiled a 2-2 record in both ALCS and World Series play. He hit a home run in the 1970 ALCS. Extremely superstitious, Cuellar sat only on the lucky end of the bench, would not allow anyone to touch his glove, would warm up only with Elrod Hendricks, did not touch the top step of the dugout, and took care never to step on the foul line.
Playing Career: *1959, 1964-1977; Cin N, StL N, Hou N, Bal A, Cal A*

Roy Cullenbine
Cullenbine, Roy Joseph
B: Oct 18, 1913   D: May 28, 1991

Pos: OF   BA: .276
Hits: 1,072   HRs: 110
RBI: 599   BBs: 852

Cullenbine started and ended his career with the Tigers, playing with them in the 1945 World Series. He hit only .227, but drew eight walks and scored five runs. He made two All-Star squads, 1941 and 1944.
Playing Career: *1938-1947; Det A, Brk N, StL A, Was A, NY A, Cle A*

Ray Culp
Culp, Raymond Leonard
B: Aug 6, 1941

Pos: P   ERA: 3.58
W-L: 122-101   SOs: 1,411
ShOs: 22   Saves: 1

Culp was a bonus baby in 1959 and NL Rookie Pitcher of the Year in 1963. He made the All-Star squad twice, once as a rookie with a 14-11 record and a 2.97 ERA, and again in 1969 with the Red Sox and his new palm ball. He won 17 games in both 1969 and 1970.
Playing Career: *1963-1973; Phi N, Chi N, Bos A*

George Culver
Culver, George Raymond
B: Jul 8, 1943

Pos: P   ERA: 3.62
W-L: 48-49   SOs: 451
ShOs: 2   No-hitters: 1

Culver operated as both a starter and reliever, tossing a no-hitter in 1968 and accumulating 23 saves during his career. He became a minor league manager, then a major league pitching coach, after retirement from the mound.
Playing Career: *1966-1974; Cle A, Cin N, StL N, Hou N, LA N, Phi N*

Candy Cummings
Cummings, Candy
B: Oct 18, 1848   D: May 16, 1924
Hall of Fame 1939

Pos: P   ERA: 2.58 (inc.)
W-L: 145-94   SOs: 111 (inc.)
ShOs: 19   No-hitters: 0

Cummings claimed he invented the curveball. He said the idea came from throwing clam shells on a New England beach. Working on the pitch for years, Cummings noticed that the "curve" worked better into the wind. Cummings once broke his wrist throwing the pitch. He was a hot commodity, playing with four National Association clubs in four years, always winning at least 28 games. Of small stature, 5'9", 120 pounds, Cummings relied on skill and subtlety rather than heat to get batters out.

Cummings's claim to curveball glory came from a 1908 article, "How I pitched the First Curve." The story was supported by Henry Chadwick, the highly respected sportswriter. Fred Goldsmith always claimed to be the pitch's originator, having given the first public demonstration of the curveball on Aug 16, 1870.
Playing Career: *1872-1877; NY Mutuals n, Bal Lord Baltimores n, Phi White Stockings n, Har Dark Blues n, Har N, Cin N*

Bert Cunningham
Cunningham, Ellsworth Elmer
B: Nov 25, 1865   D: May 14, 1952

Pos: P	ERA: 4.22
W-L: 142-167	SOs: 718
ShOs: 4	Saves: 2

Cunningham had two careers: one pitching 50 feet from home plate, and another from 60 feet 6 inches. He entered major league baseball during the rough-and-tumble days of the 1887 season when batters got four strikes to an out and bases on balls counted as base hits. After an 11-14 season, Cunningham returned to the minors. When he came back to the big leagues, the pitcher had farther to throw. But Cunningham became a top pitcher for Louisville in 1898 with 28 wins.
Playing Career: *1887-1891, 1895-1901; Brk AA, Bal AA, Phi P, Buf P, Lou N, Chi N*
Umpiring Career: *1901; NL*

Joe Cunningham
Cunningham, Joseph Robert
B: Aug 27, 1931

Pos: OF	BA: .291
Hits: 980	HRs: 64
RBI: 436	BBs: 599

Joe Cunningham had a tremendous on-base percentage before that statistic was tracked. He posted a .406 on-base average for his career. Cunningham posted .440 or more for three years in a row. In 1959 he batted .345 and was selected for the All-Star team.
Playing Career: *1954, 1956-1966; StL N, Chi A, Was A*

George Cuppy
Cuppy, George Joseph
B: Jul 3, 1869   D: Jul 27, 1922

Pos: P	ERA: 3.49
W-L: 162-98	SOs: 504
ShOs: 9	Saves: 5

Born George Maceo Koppe, Cuppy was the ace of the Cleveland Spiders' staff that included Cy Young. With that formidable one-two punch the Spiders played in three postseason Series, winning the 1895 Temple Cup.
   Cuppy won 28 games his rookie season and won 24, 26, and 25 games in 1894-1896. When the pitching rubber was moved back to 60'6", Cuppy's ERA ballooned from 2.51 in 1892 to 4.47 in 1893.
Playing Career: *1892-1901; Cle N, StL N, Bos N, Bos A*

John Curtis
Curtis, John Duffield
B: Mar 9, 1948

Pos: P	ERA: 3.96
W-L: 89-97	SOs: 825
ShOs: 14	Saves: 11

A lefty perpetually in search of a team, Curtis resolved the search for a left-handed pitcher for several clubs. A college star at Clemsen,

John Curtis laughs after a 1972 win.

he went 11-8 and 13-13 for the Red Sox.
Playing Career: *1970-1984; Bos A, StL N, SF N, SD N, Cal A*

Ned Cuthbert
Cuthbert, Edgar Edward
B: Jun 20, 1845   D: Feb 6, 1905

Pos: 1B	BA: .253
Hits: 540	HRs: 7
RBI: 136 (inc.)	BBs: 67
Managerial Record	
Won: 37 Lost: 43 Pct: .463	

Cuthbert was a mainstay of the Athletics in the original National Association. As a manager of the Browns in the AA's first season, he should receive credit for the development of young Charles Comiskey as first baseman and team leader.
Playing Career: *1871-1877, 1882-1884; Phi Athletics n, Phi White Stockings n, Chi White Stockings n, StL Brown Stockings n, StL N, Cin N, StL AA, Bal U*
Managerial Career: *1882; StL AA*

George Cutshaw
Cutshaw, George William
B: Jul 27, 1887   D: Aug 22, 1973

Pos: 2B	BA: .265
Hits: 1,487	HRs: 25
RBI: 653	BBs: 300

The Society for American Baseball Research voted Cutshaw the top defensive second baseman of the 1910-1920 era. He led in putouts five times, assists four, double plays twice and fielding three times. He also stole 271 bases, and fanned only 10 times in 1920.
Playing Career: *1912-1923; Brk N, Pit N, Det A*

Kiki Cuyler
Cuyler, Hazen Shirley
B: Aug 30, 1899   D: Feb 11, 1950
Hall of Fame 1968

Pos: OF	BA: .321
Hits: 2,299	HRs: 127
RBI: 1,065	BBs: 676

Cuyler was an underrated ballplayer, sharing the spotlight with Rogers Hornsby, Hack Wilson and Joe McCarthy. He was acquired by the Pirates, who wanted Cuyler to replace Max Carey, who had been traded to the Dodgers. An effective base thief, Cuyler stole 328 during his careeer. He was also a free swinger, hard hitter and good baserunner, scoring 1,305 times. Cuyler had become a favorite in Pittsburgh by 1925, when he doubled with the bases loaded off Walter Johnson to win Game Seven of the World Series.
   Pirates fans were mystified when Cuyler was first benched, then traded to the Cubs. He had led the league in triples with 26 in 1925, but had fallen into disfavor with the management. With the Cubs, Cuyler batted behind Hack Wilson. In 1930, when Wilson hit 56 home runs and drove in 190, Cuyler scored 155 runs and drove home 134 as he slugged .547. Cuyler played in two World Series for the Cubs and was named to the 1934 NL All-Star team.
Playing Career: *1921-1938; Pit N, Chi N, Cin N, Brk N*

Cubs center fielder Kiki Cuyler in 1932.

Bill Dahlen, player-manager of the Brooklyn Nationals (1910-11).

John D'Acquisto
D'Acquisto, John Francis
B: Dec 24, 1951

Pos: P	ERA: 4.56
W-L: 34-51	SOs: 600
ShOs: 2	Saves: 15

Named Rookie Pitcher of the Year in 1974, D'Acquisto required elbow surgery after his first season. He pitched his first four seasons in San Francisco, then played for five teams his next six years. A change from starter to reliever saved his career; D'Acquisto came up with 10 saves and a 2.13 ERA for the Padres, and his opponents batted .185 against him in 1978.
Playing Career: *1973-1982; SF N, SD N, Mon N, Cal A, Oak A*

Bill Dahlen
Dahlen, William Frederick
B: Jan 5, 1870   D: Dec 5, 1950

Pos: SS, 3B	BA: .272
Hits: 2,460	HRs: 84
RBI: 1,233	BBs: 1,064
Managerial Record	
Won: 251 Lost: 355 Pct: .414	

Bill Dahlen is the ever-eligible, never-elected Hall of Fame candidate. With more hits and more runs scored than many Hall of Famers, Dahlen should be a shoo-in if he had not suffered from playing on teams with bigger stars.

Dahlen, also known as "Bad Bill," was notorious for his tremendous temper. Highstrung and stubborn, he got into fights with managers and umpires. He was put out of many games, and once even put off the train by White Stockings manager Cap Anson. Dahlen frequently drew walks and was adept at getting hit by pitches. He was not a slugger, but he did lead the NL in RBI in 1904, his first year with the Giants. He scored 1,590 runs and stole 547 bases during his 21-year career, while playing for four pennant winners, two in Brooklyn and two in New York. He played in the 1905 World Series.
Playing Career: *1891-1911; Chi N, Brk N, NY N, Bos N*
Managerial Career: *1910-1913; Brk N*

Babe Dahlgren belts a homer the day he replaced Lou Gehrig, May 3, 1939.

Babe Dahlgren
Dahlgren, Ellsworth Tenney
B: Jun 15, 1912

Pos: 1B   BA: .261
Hits: 1,056   HRs: 82
RBI: 569   BBs: 390

"Alright, Lou, Babe will play first base today." With those immortal words, Manager Joe McCarthy made Dahlgren the man who replaced Gehrig at first base after his string of 2,130 consecutive games. Dahlgren hit a home run that day. He had waited two years to replace Gehrig. Two years later, they traded him. Dahlgren made the 1943 All-Star team. When the stars came back from the war, Dahlgren retired.
Playing Career: *1935-1946; Bos A, NY A, Bos N, Chi N, StL A, Brk N, Phi N, Pit N*

Ed Daily
Daily, Edward M.
B: Sep 7, 1862   D: Oct 21, 1891

Pos: P   ERA: 3.39
W-L: 66-70   SOs: 407
ShOs: 6   Saves: 1

Daily tossed 440 innings in his rookie year but never again approached that level of achievement. He went 26-23 that season. Daily played through the turbulent time of the Players' League before his early demise.
Playing Career: *1885-1891; Phi N, Was N, Col AA, Brk AA, NY N, Lou AA*

One Arm Daily
Daily, Hugh Ignatius
B: 1857   D: Deceased

Pos: P   ERA: 2.74
W-L: 73-87   SOs: 846
ShOs: 9   No-hitters: 1

Rising to the challenge of having only one hand, Daily became a good pitcher. He struck out 469 and won 28 games in 1884, including back-to-back one-hitters and a no-hitter. He played for eight teams in six years, then disappeared after 1887.
Playing Career: *1882-1887; Buf N, Cle N, Chi U, Pit U, Was U, StL N, Was N, Cle AA*

Bruce Dal Canton
Dal Canton, John Bruce
B: Jun 15, 1942

Pos: P   ERA: 3.68
W-L: 51-49   SOs: 485
ShOs: 2   Saves: 19

Dal Canton was teaching high school when the Pirates decided to take a second look at prospects they had passed over earlier. Dal Canton made the big leagues in his second year of professional ball. With a 9-4 record, the big right-hander helped the Pirates to the 1970 division title.
Playing Career: *1967-1977; Pit N, KC A, Atl N, Chi A*

Bud Daley
Daley, Leavitt Leo
B: Oct 7, 1932

Pos: P   ERA: 4.03
W-L: 60-64   SOs: 549
ShOs: 3   Saves: 10

Daley had been a natural right-hander but switched sides as a result of polio he contracted as a youngster. Though he spent most of his career as a reliever, he won 16 games and made All-Star appearances as a starter in 1959 and 1960. He pitched in the 1961 and 1962 World Series.
Playing Career: *1955-1964; Cle A, KC A, NY A*

Abner Dalrymple
Dalrymple, Abner Frank
B: Sep 9, 1857   D: Jan 25, 1939

Pos: OF   BA: .288
Hits: 1,202   HRs: 43
RBI: 298   BBs: 204

Dalrymple was a starter on the great White Stockings teams of the 1880s that won five pennants. He was one of four White Stockings who hit 20 or more homers in 1884, a freak season during which the team played on a diamond with a 195-foot fence in right field. The same season, he and teammate Cap Anson hit four doubles apiece in the same game. Dalrymple generally batted leadoff, but he led the NL in home runs in 1885. He scored 813 runs in 12 years.
Playing Career: *1878-1888, 1891; Mil N, Chi N, Pit N, Mil AA*

Clay Dalrymple
Dalrymple, Clayton Errol
B: Dec 3, 1936

Pos: C   BA: .233
Hits: 710   HRs: 55
RBI: 327   BBs: 387

Known for his strong arm, Dalrymple led the league in assists three times, but he got his job by hitting .272 in his rookie year. He pinch hit twice in the 1969 World Series for the Orioles, getting hits both times for a 1.000 average.
Playing Career: *1960-1971; Phi N, Bal A*

Tom Daly
Daly, Thomas Peter
B: Feb 7, 1866   D: Oct 29, 1938

Pos: 2B, C   BA: .278
Hits: 1,582   HRs: 49
RBI: 811   BBs: 687

Daly was the lone catcher on the White Stockings squad that made the 1888-1889 World Tour. He scored 1,022 runs and stole 385 bases during his career. Daly later scouted for the Indians and Yankees.
Playing Career: *1887-1896, 1898-1903; Chi N, Was N, Brk N, Chi A, Cin N*

Yankee pitcher Bud Daley in 1964.

Ray Dandridge (r) with Cuban League teammates, including Willie Mays (3rd from r).

Ray Dandridge
Dandridge, Ray
B: Aug 31, 1913
Hall of Fame 1987

Pos: 3B, SS	BA: .332
Hits: 283	HRs: 5
RBI: NA	BBs: NA

Dandridge was a terrific third baseman – perhaps the best who never played in the white major leagues. A contact hitter, Dandridge concentrated on hitting the ball where it was pitched. He hit .347 against white big league pitching in barnstorming exhibitions. His best mark in the Negro National League was .370 in 1944. He hit .545 in three East-West All-Star Games.

Much of Dandridge's career was spent in the Mexican and Cuban Leagues. He spurned an offer from Cleveland in 1948. Signed by the Giants in 1950, Dandridge was Willie Mays's roommate in Triple-A Minneapolis in 1951. They were at the cinema together when the word came from New York to send Willie up. Dandridge played seven seasons of minor league ball but never played in the majors.
Playing Career: *1933-1945; Det Stars, Nash Elite Giants, Nwk Dodgers, Nwk Eagles, NY Cubans*

Dave Danforth
Danforth, David Charles
B: Mar 7, 1890   D: Sep 19, 1970

Pos: P	ERA: 3.88
W-L: 71-66	SOs: 484
ShOs: 2	Saves: 23

A slender southpaw discovered by Connie Mack, Danforth was terrifically fast and a strikeout champion in the minor leagues. Back and forth between the minors and majors, he had a good record, 11-6, in 1917, and pitched in the World Series.
Playing Career: *1911-1912, 1916-1919, 1922-1925; Phi A, Chi A, StL A*

Kal Daniels
Daniels, Kalvoski
B: Aug 20, 1963

Pos: OF, 1B	BA: .286
Hits: 666	HRs: 104
RBI: 360	BBs: 365

Hitting .320 and .334 in his first two seasons, Daniels looked like the second coming of Willie Mays, but turned out to be a reincarnation of Tony Oliva. Before age 30, Daniels had undergone five knee operations that brought his career up short.
Playing Career: *1986-1992; Cin N, LA N, Chi N*

Giants shortstop 1950-1956, Al Dark.

Harry Danning
Danning, Harry (Harry the Horse)
B: Sep 6, 1911

Pos: C	BA: .285
Hits: 847	HRs: 57
RBI: 397	BBs: 187

Danning earned his nickname for his durability, often playing with injuries. He played in the 1936-1937 World Series and was selected for five straight All-Star Games, 1938-1942. He retired after military service.
Playing Career: *1933-1942; NY N*

Al Dark
Dark, Alvin Ralph (Blackie)
B: Jan 7, 1922

Pos: SS	BA: .289
Hits: 2,089	HRs: 126
RBI: 757	BBs: 430
Managerial Record	
Won: 994 Lost: 954 Pct: .510	

Al Dark, Rookie of the Year in 1948, was honored by fans in 1969 when they named him the top shortstop in Giants history. It was Dark who started the ninth-inning rally which led to Bobby Thomson's famous home run and the Giants' pennant of 1951.

Dark had been a football star at Louisiana State University. He made up for the late start in baseball by batting over .300 four times and leading the NL in doubles in 1951. He played in the 1948, 1951 and 1954 World Series, batting over .400 in the latter two, and was the NL All-Star shortstop twice. As a manager, he captured two division titles, and pennants for the Giants and the A's.
Playing Career: *1946, 1948-1960; Bos N, NY N, StL N, Chi N, Phi N, Mil N*
Managerial Career: *1961-1964, 1966-1971, 1974-1975, 1977; SF N, KC A, Cle A, Oak A, SD N*

Ron Darling
Darling, Ronald Maurice
B: Aug 19, 1960

Pos: P	ERA: 3.71
W-L: 122-98	SOs: 1,413
ShOs: 13	No-hitters: 0

Darling, who as a college hurler lost an 11-inning no-hitter in the 12th to Frank Viola in the NCAA playoffs, is now one of the top pitchers in major league baseball. Darling has a .568 won-lost percentage and a reputation for working hard. He has won 15 games or more four times, pacing his teams to division titles in 1986, 1988 and 1992. Darling won Game Four in the 1986 Fall Classic for the Mets. He was selected for the All-Star team in 1985 when his season record was 16-6 with a 2.90 ERA.

Darling's pickoff move is good for a right-hander. He once hit home runs in two consecutive starts. A native of Hawaii, Darling has found a home in Oakland, closer to the Islands than New York.
Playing Career: *1983- ; NY N, Mon N, Oak A*

Bobby Darwin
Darwin, Arthur Bobby Lee
B: Feb 16, 1943

Pos: P, OF	BA: .251
Hits: 559	HRs: 83
RBI: 328	BBs: 160

Signed as a pitcher, Darwin struck out 202 batters in 153 innings his first year in pro ball. That got him a cup of coffee with the big club, but it was years before he was a regular player. Switching to the outfield in 1971, Darwin averaged 22 home runs a year for the Twins during the next three years, also leading the league in strikeouts those seasons.
Playing Career: *1962, 1969, 1971-1977; LA A, LA N, Min A, Mil A, Bos A, Chi N*

Danny Darwin
Darwin, Daniel Wayne
B: Oct 25, 1955

Pos: P	ERA: 3.47
W-L: 138-135	SOs: 1,561
ShOs: 9	Saves: 32

Darwin broke into the majors with a 94-mph fastball, which he used to post a 13-4 record with eight saves in 1980. A fight with fans outside Comiskey Park resulted in a broken knuckle, diminishing his effectiveness. Traded to Houston, Darwin regained some of his lost ability. He posted back-to-back 11-4 seasons in 1989-1990, winning the NL ERA title with a 2.21 mark in 1990. He was then signed by the Red Sox as a free agent.
Playing Career: *1978-; Tex A, Mil A, Hou N, Bos A*

Jake Daubert
Daubert, Jacob Ellsworth
B: Apr 17, 1884   D: Oct 9, 1924

Pos: 1B	BA: .303
Hits: 2,326	HRs: 56
RBI: 722	BBs: 623

Daubert was the best all-round NL first baseman of his day. He won back-to-back batting titles in 1913 and 1914, and his steady play in the field made him a favorite in Brooklyn. The left-hander reached or exceeded the .300 mark 10 times during his career. Daubert twice led the league in triples and had 165 altogether. He also had a league-high 392 sacrifices, four in one 1914 game.

Daubert left the Pennsylvania coal mines to become a model of consistency, fielding above .988 for 15 straight years. He was mobile enough to average more than 10 chances per game, making 1,199 double plays. His fielding and hitting helped the Reds capture the NL pennant and World Championship in 1919. Daubert benefited from the change to the lively ball. In 1922, at age 38, he had 205 hits for a .336 average, scored 114 runs, and hit 12 home runs. Late in the 1924 season he became ill, and a month later died from complications after an appendectomy.
Playing Career: *1910-1924; Brk N, Cin N*

Rich Dauer
Dauer, Richard Fremont
B: Jul 27, 1952

Pos: 2B	BA: .257
Hits: 984	HRs: 43
RBI: 372	BBs: 297

The Orioles handed Dauer the Bobby Grich job at second base. He was adroit with the glove – once going 86 games without an error – and led the league in fielding in 1981. But he never hit up to expectations; .284 in 1980 was his best. He played in the 1979 World Series.
Playing Career: *1976-1985; Bal A*

Darren Daulton
Daulton, Darren Arthur
B: Jan 3, 1962

Pos: C	BA: .237
Hits: 623	HRs: 99
RBI: 414	BBs: 458

Daulton reached the greatness predicted for him in the 1992 season. When the Phillies first traded away Bo Diaz and Ozzie Virgil to make room for the Darren Daulton/John Russell catching platoon, injuries limited Daulton's playing time. A home-plate collision with Mike Heath ended his 1986 season in June. But Daulton emerged from these problems in 1992 with 27 home runs and a league-leading 109 RBI. He slugged .524 and was chosen for the All-Star team.
Playing Career: *1983, 1985-; Phi N*

Hooks Dauss
Dauss, George August
B: Sep 22, 1889   D: Jul 27, 1963

Pos: P	ERA: 3.30
W-L: 222-182	SOs: 1,201
ShOs: 22	Saves: 40

Hooks Dauss.

Dauss was the Tigers' all-time winningest pitcher. He won 10 or more games for 14 years in a row. Amazingly, he also lost 11 or more in 12 of those years. A stocky right-hander nicknamed for his sharp-breaking curves, Dauss is one of the least known of the Tigers' stars. He is one of six players with 15 or more years of service with Detroit. Dauss spent most of his time bogged down with the team in the second division.

Five times Hooks posted ERAs under 3.00; three times he won 20 or more games, with a

Jake Daubert receives a trophy gold bat in Brooklyn.

high of 24 in 1915. He had 10 winning seasons and a winning percentage considerably better than his team's. Although Dauss led the league in hit batsmen three times and is tenth on the lifetime list, many thought that he was too soft on the hitters.
Playing Career: *1912-1926; Det A*

Vic Davalillo
Davalillo y Romero, Victor Jose
B: Jul 31, 1936

Pos: OF	BA: .279
Hits: 1,122	HRs: 36
RBI: 329	BBs: 212

Davalillo started as a pitcher who was so good a hitter that he was switched to the outfield. With the Indians, he won a Gold Glove in 1964 and made an All-Star Game appearance the following season. After a sojourn in the Mexican League, Davalillo began a second career as a clutch pinch hitter. He played on five division-winning teams and in four World Series, collecting 95 pinch hits during his career.
Playing Career: *1963-1974, 1977-1980; Cle A, Cal A, StL N, Pit N, Oak A, LA N*

Jim Davenport.

Jim Davenport
Davenport, James Houston
B: Aug 17, 1933

Pos: 3B	BA: .258
Hits: 1,142	HRs: 77
RBI: 456	BBs: 382
Managerial Record	
Won: 56 Lost: 88 Pct: .389	

Davenport served the Giants organization as player, coach and manager. Compared to Billy Cox by manager Bill Rigney, Davenport was a solid fielder with home run pop in his bat. He hit 50 homers in his first five years. Davenport won a Gold Glove in 1962, the same year he was chosen for the All-Star team. He led NL third basemen in fielding three straight years.
Playing Career: *1958-1970; SF N*
Managerial Career: *1985; SF N*

Bob Davids
Davids, L. Robert
B: Mar 19, 1926

Davids, a baseball writer and historian, founded the Society for American Baseball Research (SABR) on August 10, 1971, in Cooperstown, New York. He and 15 other baseball scholars met at the Hall of Fame's National Baseball Library to organize a forum for statistical and historical research into all aspects of the national pastime. SABR's greatest accomplishments include: presenting convincing evidence to the Veteran's Committee of the Hall of Fame that resulted in the induction of certain 19th-century players; research and compilation of minor leagues data; and the improvement and expansion of the statistical analysis of baseball.

Alvin Davis
Davis, Alvin Glenn
B: Sep 9, 1960

Pos: 1B, DH	BA: .280
Hits: 1,189	HRs: 160
RBI: 683	BBs: 685

AL Rookie of the Year in 1984, Davis was the first young Mariners star and holds a raft of single-season team records, including RBI, walks and grand slams. Lately he has suffered a power outage and has gone to Japan to recapture his swing and glory.
Playing Career: *1984-1992; Sea A, Cal A*

Chili Davis
Davis, Charles Theodore
B: Jan 17, 1960

Pos: OF, DH	BA: .267
Hits: 1,677	HRs: 244
RBI: 930	BBs: 778

Chili Davis is an excellent role player. He has power and speed, and a whopping .444 life-time batting average against Dwight Gooden. Usually batting down in the lineup, sixth or seventh, Davis is a switch hitter who has connected from both sides in the same game seven times. Davis played in the 1984 and 1986 All-Star Games. In the 1991 World Series he aided the Twins' Championship cause with a two-run homer in Game Two.
Playing Career: *1981-; SF N, Cal A, Min A*

Curt Davis
Davis, Curtis Benton
B: Sep 7, 1903   D: Oct 13, 1965

Pos: P	ERA: 3.42
W-L: 158-131	SOs: 684
ShOs: 24	Saves: 33

The Cubs traded Davis, two other players and $185,000 for Dizzy Dean in 1938. As a rookie, Davis led the NL in games pitched. He was consistent, winning in double figures 11 of 12 seasons. Davis also worked in relief, saving seven contests and winning 22 in 1939. He was voted onto the 1936 and 1939 NL All-Star squads, and he started Game One of the 1941 World Series for the Dodgers.
Playing Career: *1934-1946; Phi N, Chi N, StL N, Brk N*

Dixie Davis
Davis, Frank Talmadge
B: Oct 12, 1890   D: Feb 4, 1944

Pos: P	ERA: 3.97
W-L: 75-71	SOs: 460
ShOs: 10	Saves: 2

After several cups of coffee in the big leagues, Davis won his first major league game at age 30. In 1921 he pitched a 19-inning game, winning 8-6. In the 16th inning he hit an inside-the-park home run, only to be called out for missing first base.
Playing Career: *1912, 1915, 1918, 1920-1926; Cin N, Chi A, Phi N, StL A*

Chili Davis gets back to first in an attempted pick-off play in 1984.

Eric Davis comes home after hitting a grand slam against the Pirates in 1986.

Eric Davis
Davis, Eric Keith
B: May 29, 1962

Pos: OF	BA: .262
Hits: 935	HRs: 202
RBI: 632	BBs: 516

Eric Davis is a superstar who has been held back by injuries. His record has a long, sad list of problems, including herniated disk in the neck, sprained left shoulder, left wrist fracture, wrist and shoulder surgery – and that is just 1992! When Davis is in good health, he is hard to beat. He hit three grand slams in one month, he had 11 two-homer games and two three-homer contests. He homered in his first World Series at-bat.

Davis received the Gold Glove Award three years in a row, 1987-1989, and he has blazing speed on the basepaths. He once pilfered 33 on consecutive attempts, and has the highest lifetime stolen base percentage of anyone who has more than 300 attempts, an 86.9 percent mark, for 301 steals in 346 attempts. Reunited in Los Angeles with his boyhood chum Darryl Strawberry, Davis hoped to recover the magic that surrounded him in Cincinnati, but found himself traded to Detroit instead.
Playing Career: *1984-; Cin N, LA N, Det A*

George Davis
Davis, George Stacey
B: Aug 23, 1870   D: Oct 17, 1940

Pos: SS	BA: .295
Hits: 2,660	HRs: 73
RBI: 1,437	BBs: 870
Managerial Record	
Won: 107 Lost: 139 Pct: .435	

Davis has the statistics to be in the Hall of Fame, but he is not. He played 20 seasons, scored 1,539 runs and stole 616 bases, yet few know about him. Dealt to the Giants in a sensational trade for Buck Ewing, Davis did not disappoint his new team. He posted a nine-year total of 1,423 hits, averaging .332 with 93 runs and 91 RBI.

While the AL and NL were stealing each other's players and ignoring each other's contracts, Davis jumped to the AL White Sox in 1902, then back to the NL Giants. When the resolution decreed all players should return to their original teams, Davis engaged celebrated attorney John Montgomery Ward to sue the AL, putting the tenuous peace in danger and incurring the wrath of major league owners. He won the right to continue with the White Sox and was a star in their 1906 World Series upset victory.
Playing Career: *1890-1909; Cle N, NY N, Chi A*
Managerial Career: *1895, 1900-1901; NY N*

Glenn Davis
Davis, Glenn Earle
B: Mar 28, 1961

Pos: 1B, DH	BA: .259
Hits: 965	HRs: 190
RBI: 603	BBs: 370

Davis was a power hitter in the Astrodome; general managers lick their lips thinking what he could do in a normal ballpark. The Orioles traded for him in 1991 when he was recovering from a ribcage muscle pull. With the Astros, Davis ripped three homers in the same game twice. An NL All-Star two times, Davis has a lifetime .467 slugging percentage.
Playing Career: *1984-; Hou N, Bal A*

Harry Davis
Davis, Harry H. (Jasper)
B: Jul 19, 1873   D: Aug 11, 1947

Pos: 1B	BA: .277
Hits: 1,839	HRs: 74
RBI: 951	BBs: 525
Managerial Record	
Won: 54 Lost: 71 Pct: .432	

Davis was part of Connie Mack's original Athletics franchise, and later, an element in the $100,000 infield. The top slugger in the AL from 1904 to 1907, Davis led the league in home runs each season. Davis also scored 998 runs, stole 285 bases, and was an excellent sign stealer. He stayed with Mack as a coach until 1927, leaving him only in 1912 to manage the Indians. He was elected Philadelphia city councilman while still with the Athletics.
Playing Career: *1895-1899, 1901-1917; NY N, Pit N, Lou N, Was N, Phi A, Cle A*
Managerial Career: *1912; Cle A*

Harry Davis.

Jody Davis
Davis, Jody Richard
B: Nov 12, 1956

Pos: C	BA: .245
Hits: 877	HRs: 127
RBI: 490	BBs: 333

Known for his ability to hit in the clutch, especially against the Cardinals, Davis was an outstanding defensive catcher. He has two All-Star appearances and a Gold Glove to show for it. He starred in the 1984 NLCS as he hit .389 with two homers and six RBI.
Playing Career: *1981-1990; Chi N, Atl N*

Mark Davis
Davis, Mark William
B: Oct 19, 1960

Pos: P	ERA: 4.08
W-L: 51-83	SOs: 978
ShOs: 2	Saves: 96

The 1989 NL Cy Young Award winner, Davis signed a $13 million contract that became an albatross around his neck. In Kansas City, Davis was branded ineffective because he seemed unable to throw strikes. The NL is apparently the best place for Davis; NL batters swing at his sharp breaking slider, but AL hitters wait on it. Davis made two All-Star teams, in 1988 and 1989.
Playing Career: *1980-1981, 1983-; Phi N, SF N, SD N, KC A, Atl N*

Mike Davis
Davis, Michael Dwayne
B: Jun 11, 1959

Pos: OF, 1B, DH	BA: .259
Hits: 778	HRs: 91
RBI: 371	BBs: 236

Unknown except to the Bay Area press, Davis held down right field for the A's for five years. His moment of glory came in the 1988 World Series. As a pinch hitter with two out in the ninth, Davis drew a walk, stole second and scored on Kirk Gibson's home run to win Game One.
Playing Career: *1980-1989; Oak A, LA N*

Ron Davis
Davis, Ronald Gene
B: Aug 6, 1955

Pos: P	ERA: 4.05
W-L: 47-53	SOs: 597
ShOs: 0	Saves: 130

Davis strung together three consecutive seasons with ERAs under 3.00 as a set-up man for Yankee teammate Goose Gossage. In a 1981 contest, he fanned eight consecutive Oakland batters. Out on his own as the stopper, the 6' 4" Davis recorded 116 saves in four years for the Twins, 1982-1985.
Playing Career: *1978-1988; NY A, Min A, Chi N, LA N, SF N*

Spud Davis
Davis, Virgil Lawrence
B: Dec 20, 1904   D: Aug 14, 1984

Pos: C	BA: .308
Hits: 1,312	HRs: 77
RBI: 647	BBs: 386
Managerial Record	
Won: 1 Lost: 2 Pct: .333	

One of the finest NL hitters of the 1930s and 1940s, Davis topped the .300 mark 10 times in his career, seven times in a row, 1930-1936. He hit .342 and .349 for the Phillies in 1930 and 1933. Perennially outvoted in favor of catchers Gabby Hartnett, Al Lopez, and Ernie Lombardi, Davis was never selected for the All-Star Game, but he batted 1.000 in the 1934 World Series for the victorious St. Louis Cardinals.
Playing Career: *1928-1941, 1944-1945; StL N, Phi N, Cin N, Pit N*
Managerial Career: *1946; Pit N*

Storm Davis
Davis, George Earl
B: Dec 26, 1961

Pos: P	ERA: 4.04
W-L: 111-92	SOs: 1,010
ShOs: 5	Saves: 11

Storm has had a tempestuous career. He was a highly regarded rookie with 35 wins by the age of 22, but every so often he loses his fastball. After a 3-8 year in 1987, he rebounded to lead the A's to pennants in 1988 and 1989 with a total of 35 wins those two years. He pitched in the 1983 and 1988 ALCS, won a game in the 1983 World Series, but lost two starts in the 1988 Fall Classic.
Playing Career: *1982-; Bal A, SD N, Oak A, KC A, Det A*

Tommy Davis
Davis, Herman Thomas
B: Mar 21, 1939

Pos: OF	BA: .294
Hits: 2,121	HRs: 153
RBI: 1,052	BBs: 381

When Davis drove in 153 runs in 1962, it was the most in the NL since Joe Medwick knocked home 154 in 1937. Nobody has topped either mark since. Jackie Robinson convinced Davis to sign with the Dodgers, and he was off to a brilliant career. He won two batting titles, 1962-1963, and collected 230 hits in 1962, a mark bested only once since then, by Matty Alou with 231 in 1969.

Davis hit .400 in the Dodgers' four-game sweep of the Yankees in the 1963 World Series. A broken ankle in 1965 sidelined a great hitting career. Davis became a hired bat and drifted to the AL, where he became a designated hitter for the A's and Orioles. He batted in three ALCS, hitting .295 in 12 games. Becoming a pinch hitter, Davis ended his career with the highest pinch-hitting average on record, .320, with 63 hits in 197 at-bats.
Playing Career: *1959-1976; LA N, NY N, Chi A, Sea A, Hou N, Chi N, Oak A, Bal A, Cal A, KC A*

Willie Davis
Davis, William Henry
B: Apr 15, 1940

Pos: OF	BA: .279
Hits: 2,561	HRs: 182
RBI: 1,053	BBs: 418

The Dodgers had the services of Willie Davis for 14 years. He had speed, accumulating 398 stolen bases and scoring 1,217 runs, and he had good defensive skills, winning three Gold Glove Awards. Davis was an All-Star twice. Traded several times, Davis spent two seasons in Japan, then returned to help the Angels win their first divison title. He hit .500 in the ALCS that year.
Playing Career: *1960-1976, 1979; LA N, Mon N, Tex A, StL N, SD N, Cal A*

Tommy Davis, outfielder for the Seattle Pilots in 1969.

Andre Dawson.

Andre Dawson
Dawson, Andre Fernando (Hawk)
B: Jul 10, 1954

Pos: OF	BA: .281
Hits: 2,630	HRs: 412
RBI: 1,492	BBs: 569

Dawson has statistics which are greater than those of many players who are in the Hall of Fame. He did something that no other player has ever done: signed a blank contract with the Cubs. Dawson decided that he wanted to play on the grass in Wrigley Field. He signed with them in March 1987, and let the Cubs fill in the amount at their leisure. He hit 49 home runs and drove home 139 runners. He was NL MVP, Player of the Year, had a three-homer game, hit for the cycle and even doubled off Saberhagen in the All-Star Game.

Dawson has eight Gold Gloves and has made eight All-Star Game appearances. He has 473 doubles, 1,303 runs, 312 stolen bases, and a lifetime .484 slugging average. The author of six grand slams and 36 multiple home run games, Dawson twice hit three in a game. Bad knees and Father Time have failed to stop Dawson's onslaught against baseball's record book.
Playing Career: *1976-; Mon N, Chi N, Bos A*

John Day
Day, John B.
B: Sep 23, 1847   D: Jan 25, 1925

Managerial Record
Won: 29   Lost: 35   Pct: .453

Day was one of the most influential 19th-century baseball team owners. He served on the 1890 NL War Committee which was charged with defeating the Players' League movement. Day brought politically connected Andrew Freedman into baseball as part owner of the Giants. Through Day, Freedman was able to express his central theme of "Syndicate Baseball" that involved setting up a trust to govern the sport. Day also lured John McGraw back into the NL to combat the new AL. McGraw and his Giants dominated New York City until 1920 when Babe Ruth arrived to wear Yankee pinstripes.
Managerial Career: *1899; NY N*

Leon Day
Day, Leon
B: Oct 30, 1916

Pos: P	ERA: NA
W-L: 63-26 (inc.)	SOs: 256 (inc.)
ShOs: 9 (inc.)	No-hitters: 1

Hall of Famer Monte Irvin said of Day, "If we had one game to win, we wanted Leon to pitch." Day established himself as one of the best pitchers in the Negro Leagues with his good curveball and excellent control. Competing with athletes the calibre of Satchel Paige, Day was repeatedly chosen for the East-West Game, the allstar event of the Negro Leagues. In 1937 he compiled a hurling record of 13-0 while batting .320. Fanning 18 in a nine-inning game in 1942, Day set a league record.

In 1942 and 1943 he was named to the Pittsburgh Courier's All-American Team for the Negro Leagues. Despite a hiatus of more than two years for military duty, Day returned in 1946 to pitch a no-hitter on Opening Day. He spent 1947 and 1948 playing in the Mexican League, then returned to Newark. In 1950 Day signed with Winnipeg in the Canadian League, and was promoted to Toronto in the the International League in 1951, 18 seasons after his pro career began.
Playing Career: *1934-1949; Brk Eagles, Nwk Eagles*

Leon Day.

Ken Dayley
Dayley, Kenneth Grant
B: Feb 25, 1959

Pos: P	ERA: 3.64
W-L: 33-45	SOs: 406
ShOs: 0	Saves: 41

Dayley is a slender southpaw with an odd motion that aids his effectiveness. Despite a high number of wild pitches, 62, Dayley comes through in the big games. He has four saves and an ERA of 0.00 in NLCS action.
Playing Career: *1982-1991, 1993-; Atl N, StL N, Tor A*

Charlie Deal
Deal, Charles Albert
B: Oct 30, 1891   D: Sep 16, 1979

Pos: 3B	BA: .257
Hits: 752	HRs: 11
RBI: 318	BBs: 135

Deal filled in for injured Red Smith during the Braves' 1914 pennant drive, nearly doubling his $2,500 salary with the World Series winner's $2,200 share. Jumping to the Federal League, Deal later became an outstanding third sacker for the Cubs, leading the NL in fielding for three seasons.
Playing Career: *1912-1921; Det A, Bos N, StL F, StL A, Chi N*

Dizzy Dean
Dean, Jay Hanna
B: Jan 16, 1911   D: Jul 17, 1974
Hall of Fame 1953

Pos: P	ERA: 3.04
W-L: 150-83	SOs: 1,155
ShOs: 26	Saves: 30

Dizzy and his brother Paul became household names when they won four games in the 1934 World Series – the first Fall Classic to be nationally broadcast. Dizzy, comic foil to the intensity of the Depression on the Great Plains, once built a fire in front of the dugout in 110-degree heat and wrapped himself in an Indian blanket. He was conked on the noggin breaking up a double play in the Series and headlines proclaimed, "X-RAYS OF DEAN'S HEAD SHOW NOTHING."

Dean brought the Gas House Gang to victory 30, 28, then 24 times from 1934 to 1936. He led the NL in strikeouts 1932-1935. His meteoric career came crashing down with an Earl Averill line drive which broke Dean's toe. With the Cardinals in a pennant race, Dean continued to pitch, compensating for his toe injury with an altered delivery which strained his arm. He was never the same.

After retirement from baseball, Dean became a popular broadcaster. Once Dean told the Browns that he could do better than their pitchers. They challenged him; he tossed four innings without giving up a run, and got a hit in his only AL at-bat. As Diz always said, "It ain't braggin' if you can do it."
Playing Career: *1930, 1932-1941, 1947; StL N, Chi N, StL A*

Paul Dean
Dean, Paul Dee (Daffy)
B: Aug 14, 1913   D: Mar 17, 1981

Pos: P	ERA: 3.75
W-L: 50-34	SOs: 387
ShOs: 8	No-hitters: 1

Dizzy Dean always claimed that his brother Paul was the better pitcher, he just never had a manager smart enough to understand it. Paul was a strikeout pitcher, winning 19 games in 1934 and 1935 for the Cardinals, and logging two World Series wins in 1934. A sore arm ended his career at age 30.
Playing Career: *1934-1941, 1943; StL N, NY N, StL A*

Doug DeCinces
DeCinces, Douglas Vernon
B: Aug 29, 1950

Pos: 3B, DH	BA: .259
Hits: 1,505	HRs: 237
RBI: 879	BBs: 618

A home run hitting third baseman for the Orioles, DeCinces was supposed to make fans forget about the fielding gap left when Brooks Robinson retired. A bad back curtailed DeCinces's performance and rendered him vulnerable. The Orioles traded him when Cal Ripkin, Jr. came up as a third baseman.

With the Angels, DeCinces discovered his home run bat. California won two division titles while he hit .316 and .286 in the 1982 and 1986 ALCS. His best year was his first with the Angels, 1982, when he hit .301 with 30

Doug DeCinces upends the Pirates' Phil Garner at second base during the 1979 WS.

homers, 94 runs scored, and 97 RBI. In 1987 DeCinces moved his act to Japan.
Playing Career: *1973-1987; Bal A, Cal A, StL N*

Harry Decker
Decker, Earl Harry
B: Sep 3, 1854   D: Deceased

Pos: C, OF, 3B, 2B, 1B	BA: .242
Hits: 138	HRs: 5
RBI: 49 (inc.)	BBs: 41

Decker is credited with the development of the modern catcher's glove. He made a wire form and tied pieces of leather around it, then stuffed it with padding. Spalding Sporting Goods modified the mitt.
Playing Career: *1884, 1886, 1889-1890; Ind AA, KC U, Det N, Was N, Phi N, Pit N*

Ivan DeJesus
DeJesus y Alvarez, Ivan
B: Jan 9, 1953

Pos: SS	BA: .254
Hits: 1,167	HRs: 21
RBI: 324	BBs: 466

DeJesus was involved in one of baseball's most lopsided trades. When Dallas Green was fired as manager of the Phillies, he be-

Dizzy Dean (r) with his brother Paul, who pitched together for the Cards, 1934-1937.

Shortstop Ivan DeJesus in action for the Phillies in 1982.

came the general manager of the Cubs. Green immediately contacted his former team about trading shortstops, Ivan DeJesus for Larry Bowa. Since the Phillies would get a power hitter – DeJesus looked like a power hitter in Wrigley Field – while the Cubs would not, Green contended, Philadelphia should toss in a second baseman from their farm system, a guy named Ryne Sandberg. The Phillies agreed and have been subjected to ridicule ever since.

With the Phillies, DeJesus led the NL in runs with 104 in 1978. He stole 194 bases, including a high of 41 in 1978. Bowa made fewer errors, but had considerably less range. The Phillies won the pennant in 1983 with DeJesus at shortstop.
Playing Career: *1974-1988; LA N, Chi N, Phi N, StL N, NY A, SF N, Det A*

Ed Delahanty
Delahanty, Edward James (Big Ed)
B: Oct 30, 1867   D: Jul 2, 1903
Hall of Fame 1945

Pos: OF	BA: .346
Hits: 2,597	HRs: 101
RBI: 1,464	BBs: 741

Delahanty's death in a plunge over Niagara Falls was the subject of a book by Mike Sowell, and remains a mystery to fans and police. Delahanty's family believed that Big Ed was murdered by agents of the AL. He reportedly had a telegram from John McGraw telling him to report to the Giants. His defection from the AL in 1903 would have jeopardized the recently concluded baseball peace.

Delahanty was one of the hardest-hitting outfielders in baseball history. He hit 185 triples and 522 doubles, five times leading his league. He also collected 1,599 runs and 455 stolen bases. He batted over .400 three times; no one ever exceeded that accomplishment. Five times he led the league in slugging. He has a lifetime .412 on-base percentage, once achieving a fantastic .500 in 1895.
Playing Career: *1888-1903; Phi N, Cle P, Was A*

Jim Delahanty
Delahanty, James Christopher
B: Jun 20, 1879   D: Oct 17, 1953

Pos: 3B, 2B, OF, 1B	BA: .283
Hits: 1,159	HRs: 18
RBI: 489	BBs: 378

One of the five Delahanty brothers who played major league baseball, Jim's career was second best to Big Ed's. Jim Delahanty hit .339 with the 1911 Tigers, ripping 30 doubles and 14 triples as he drove in 94 runs. He hit .317 with the Senators in 1908.
Playing Career: *1901-1902, 1904-1912, 1914-1915; Chi N, NY N, Bos N, Cin N, StL A, Was A, Det A, Brk F*

Jose DeLeon
DeLeon y Chestaro, Jose
B: Dec 20, 1960

Pos: P	ERA: 3.66
W-L: 78-113	SOs: 1,464
ShOs: 7	Saves: 4

DeLeon once faced 33 batters in 11 innings, allowing just two hits. In his very next outing

he retired the first 15 batters. When DeLeon is in top form, he is very, very good, but when he is bad, as the poem goes, he is horrid. In 1985 he suffered through a 2-19 season. Rebounding with the Cardinals, DeLeon won 16 games and led the NL in strikeouts with 201 in 1989.
Playing Career: *1983-; Pit N, Chi A, StL N, Phi N*

Ike Delock
Delock, Ivan Martin
B: Nov 11, 1929

Pos: P	ERA: 4.03
W-L: 84-75	SOs: 672
ShOs: 6	Saves: 31

Delock was a good reliever who was used less frequently out of the bullpen as the Red Sox decided to make a starter of him. Delock's record as a starting pitcher was 50-60. A knee injury in 1962 led to his retirement.
Playing Career: *1952-1963; Bos A, Bal A*

Jim Delsing
Delsing, James Henry
B: Nov 13, 1925

Pos: OF	BA: .255
Hits: 627	HRs: 40
RBI: 286	BBs: 299

Delsing was the pinch runner for Eddie Gaedel, the midget who batted in a 1951 Browns game as a promotional stunt. A good minor league hitter, Delsing's best major league season was 1953 with the Tigers when he hit .288 and scored 77 runs.
Playing Career: *1948-1956, 1960; Chi A, NY A, StL A, Det A, KC A*

Joe DeMaestri
DeMaestri, Joseph Paul
B: Dec 9, 1928

Pos: SS	BA: .236
Hits: 813	HRs: 49
RBI: 281	BBs: 168

DeMaestri came to the Yankees with Roger Maris in 1960. DeMaestri was switched from a regular to a utility player, but he played on two pennant winners and in the 1960 World Series. He went 6-for-6 in 1955. He led the AL in fielding 1958-1959, making the All-Star team in 1957.
Playing Career: *1951-1961; Chi A, StL A, Phi A, KC A, NY A*

Albert Demaree
Demaree, Albert Wentworth
B: Sep 8, 1884   D: Apr 30, 1962

Pos: P	ERA: 2.77
W-L: 80-72	SOs: 514
ShOs: 14	Saves: 9

Demaree became a sports cartoonist for *The Sporting News* after his big league career was finished. He pitched on two pennant-winning teams, the 1913 Giants and 1915 Phillies.

On September 20, 1916, he pitched and won both ends of a doubleheader.
Playing Career: *1912-1919; NY N, Phi N, Chi N, Bos N*

Frank Demaree
Demaree, Joseph Franklin
B: Jun 10, 1910   D: Aug 30, 1958

Pos: OF	BA: .289
Hits: 1,241	HRs: 72
RBI: 591	BBs: 359

Born Joseph Franklin Dimaria, Demaree came up with the Cubs in 1932, swatting a three-run homer in the fourth game of the World Series that year. He hit only .272 the next year and was sent back to the Pacific Coast League in 1934, where he won the Triple Crown, hitting .383 with 45 homers and 190 RBI. Demaree was back in the majors in 1935, hitting .300 or more for the next three seasons. He was an All-Star 1936-1937. Altogether he played in three World Series.
Playing Career: *1932-1933, 1935-1944; Chi N, NY N, Bos N, StL N, StL A*

Don Demeter
Demeter, Donald Lee
B: Jun 25, 1935

Pos: OF	BA: .265
Hits: 912	HRs: 163
RBI: 563	BBs: 180

Demeter was the owner of a 1.000 fielding average for two consecutive seasons during which he put together a string of 266 errorless games. He also averaged 21 homers per year from 1961 to 1965, one season hitting .307 with 29 homers and 107 RBI.
Playing Career: *1956, 1958-1967; Brk N, LA N, Phi N, Det A, Bos A, Cle A*

Rick Dempsey celebrates after the Orioles beat the Phillies in the 1983 WS.

Gene DeMontreville
DeMontreville, Eugene Napoleon
B: Mar 26, 1874   D: Feb 18, 1935

Pos: SS, 2B	BA: .303
Hits: 1,096	HRs: 17
RBI: 497	BBs: 174

The French-Canadian DeMontreville was a good hitter and base thief with 228 steals during his career, but a fielder he was not. Besides leading the league in errors his first two seasons, DeMontreville fielded below .891 in three of his first four years. DeMontreville's name was so striking that author James Thurber remembered it when he wrote "You Could Look It Up," a short story featuring ballplayer Pearl DuMonville.
Playing Career: *1894-1904; Pit N, Was N, Bal N, Chi N, Brk N, Was A, StL A*

Bingo DeMoss
DeMoss, Elwood
B: Sep 5, 1889   D: Jan 26, 1965

Pos: 2B	BA: .242 (inc.)
Hits: 398 (inc.)	HRs: 4 (inc.)
RBI: NA	BBs: NA
Managerial Record (inc.)	
Won: 105 Lost: 100 Pct: .512	

DeMoss was a winning second sacker for many years for the American Giants in the Negro National League. He was the team captain and acting manager when Rube Foster was away. A Topeka, Kansas native, DeMoss could turn double plays so quickly and smoothly, it looked as if he never touched the ball. With great range and quick on his feet for his height (6'2"), he was the best second baseman of his day. He batted .300 in the 1925 Nego World Series.
Playing Career: *1910, 1913-1921, 1923-1929; OK Giants, KC Giants, WL Plutos, Chi Am Giants, StL Giants, WB Sprudels, Ind ABCs, Det Stars*
Managerial Career: *1926-1929; Ind ABCs, Det Stars*

Rick Dempsey
Dempsey, John Rikard
B: Sep 13, 1949

Pos: C	BA: .233
Hits: 1,093	HRs: 96
RBI: 471	BBs: 592

Dempsey was at his best when the game was on the line. He batted .385 in the 1983 World Series, winning Game Two with a two-run double, and pounding a home run and a double in Game Five. Dempsey was selected Series MVP. In the 1988 NLCS he hit .400 for the Dodgers, and appeared in another World Series that year. Stuck behind Thurman Munson in the Yankees' farm system, Dempsey's big break came with a massive 10-player trade that sent him to Baltimore with Rudy May, Tippy Martinez and Scott McGregor for Ken Holtzman, Doyle Alexander, Grant Jack-

Don Demeter is welcomed home after a three-run homer in spring training.

son and Elrod Hendricks. Settling in as a regular catcher, Dempsey led AL receivers in fielding twice, and in assists once. He retired from playing in spring training, 1993.
Playing Career: *1969-1992; Min A, NY A, Bal A, Cle A, LA N, Mil A*

Jerry Denny
Denny, Jeremiah Dennis
B: Mar 16, 1859   D: Aug 16, 1927

Pos: 3B, SS, 2B	BA: .260
Hits: 1,286	HRs: 74
RBI: 512	BBs: 173

Denny snared batted balls equally well with either hand, seldom using a glove. He is the all-time leader in putouts and total chances per game for third basemen with 1,000 or more games. Denny went 6-for-6 once and hit the first home run in postseason championship play in 1884 with Providence.
Playing Career: *1881-1891, 1893-1894; Pro N, StL N, Ind N, NY N, Cle N, Phi N, Lou N*

John Denny
Denny, John Allen
B: Nov 8, 1952

Pos: P	ERA: 3.58
W-L: 123-108	SOs: 1,146
ShOs: 18	No-hitters: 0

With the Cardinals in 1976, Denny led the league in ERA with 2.52. In 1983 he went 19-6 for the Phillies, made the All-Star team, and captured the Cy Young Award.
Playing Career: *1974-1986; StL N, Cle A, Phi N, Cin N*

Bucky Dent
Dent, Russell Earl
B: Nov 25, 1951

Pos: SS	BA: .247
Hits: 1,114	HRs: 40
RBI: 423	BBs: 328
Managerial Record	
Won: 36 Lost: 53 Pct: .404	

Primarily a glove man, Dent hit the most important home run of New York's Steinbrenner Era. It was a three-run shot over the Green Monster in Fenway Park to turn around the 1978 Eastern Division playoffs in favor of the Yankees. Dent batted .349 in 12 games in two World Series, led the AL three times in fielding, and made the All-Star squad three times. Managing in the minors, Dent won the Governor's Cup in the 1987 International League.
Playing Career: *1973-1984; Chi A, NY A, Tex A, KC A*
Managerial Career: *1989-1990; NY A*

Bob Dernier
Dernier, Robert Eugene
B: Jan 5, 1957

Pos: OF	BA: .255
Hits: 634	HRs: 23
RBI: 152	BBs: 222

Paul Derringer winds up for the Reds, for whom he produced 20-win seasons four times.

Bob Dernier was a much anticipated prospect. He had batted .636 with five stolen bases in 20 games during two September stints in the majors. NL pitchers and injuries cut him down to size. Batting high in the lineup, he scored 374 runs and stole 218 bases.
Playing Career: *1980-1989; Phi N, Chi N*

The Yankees' Bucky Dent in 1981.

Paul Derringer
Derringer, Samuel Paul ('Oom Paul)
B: Oct 17, 1906   D: Nov 17, 1987

Pos: P	ERA: 3.46
W-L: 223-212	SOs: 1,507
ShOs: 32	Saves: 29

Derringer won 40 games at Rochester in the International League and led them to pennants in 1929 and 1930. He went 18-8, leading the NL with a .692 percentage as a rookie, but he was not the Cardinals' prize prospect. The Red Birds kept Dizzy Dean and sent Derringer to Cincinnati for Leo Durocher, who would plug a major hole at shortstop for the Gas House Gang.

Upon Derringer's square shoulders the Reds rebuilt their franchise. He won 22 games in 1935, and 20 or more games each year from 1938 to 1940. Derringer was the victor in 10 1-0 games during his career. An All-Star seven times, Derringer played in four World Series.
Playing Career: *1931-1945; StL N, Cin N, Chi N*

Art Devlin
Devlin, Arthur McArthur
B: Oct 16, 1879   D: Sep 18, 1948

Pos: 3B	BA: .269
Hits: 1,185	HRs: 10
RBI: 504	BBs: 576

When the Giants acquired Devlin from Newark, mentor McGraw guaranteed them the pennant in 1904. Devlin was a star. He fielded with the best, ranking 15th on the all-time list in chances per game. In 1908 Devlin was the top fielding third baseman, leading in putouts. He never hit more than two homers in any year, but connected with the bases loaded on his first major league at-bat.
Playing Career: *1904-1913; NY N, Bos N*

Jim Devlin
Devlin, James Alexander
B: 1849   D: Oct 10, 1883

Pos: P, 1B, OF, 3B, SS	ERA: 1.89 (inc.)
W-L: 72-60	SOs: 263
ShOs: 9	No-hitters: 0

In 1877 Devlin was one of the brightest stars in baseball. He won 30 contests or more two years in a row, finishing 127 of 129 starts and leading the NL in games, innings pitched and complete games. But Devlin was banned from baseball for fixing games.
Playing Career: *1873-1877; Phi White Stockings n, Chi White Stockings n, Lou N*

Charlie Dexter
Dexter, Charles Dana
B: Jun 15, 1876   D: Jun 9, 1934

Pos: C, OF, 3B	BA: .261
Hits: 749	HRs: 16
RBI: 346	BBs: 198

Dexter was a multipurpose player toiling for one of the worst clubs in the 12-team NL. He hit .314 in 1898, his personal best. Dexter was picked up by the Cubs after being cut by the league when it dropped Louisville and three other clubs in 1900.
Playing Career: *1896-1903; Lou N, Chi N, Bos N*

Bo Diaz
Diaz y Seijas, Baudilio Jose
B: Mar 23, 1953   D: Nov 23, 1990

Pos: C	BA: .255
Hits: 834	HRs: 87
RBI: 452	BBs: 188

Diaz had his best year in 1981 when he hit .313, resulting in an All-Star Game appearance and a trade to the Phillies. In the 1983 World Series, Diaz hit .333. He had an up-and-down career, but made a comeback with the Reds in the late 1980s.
Playing Career: *1977-1989; Bos A, Cle A, Phi N, Cin N*

Rob Dibble
Dibble, Robert Keith
B: Jan 24, 1964

Pos: P	ERA: 2.74
W-L: 26-23	SOs: 619
ShOs: 0	Saves: 88

With a near-100-mph fastball, Dibble is the premier relief pitcher in the NL. One of

Cincinnati's "Nasty Boys," as the Reds' bullpen was dubbed, Dibble was alternated with Randy Myers and Norm Charlton to shut out the A's in each 1990 World Series game.
Playing Career: *1988-; Cin N*

Lew Dickerson
Dickerson, Lewis Pessano (Buttercup)
B: Oct 11, 1858   D: Jul 23, 1920

Pos: OF	BA: .284
Hits: 500	HRs: 4
RBI: 127	BBs: 47

Dickerson starred in several minor leagues in upstate New York. He joined three of his Worcester teammates on the first blacklist in 1881 for dissipation. Dickerson led the NL in triples in 1879 with 14.
Playing Career: *1878-1885; Cin N, Tro N, Wor N, Pit AA, StL U, Bal AA, Lou AA, Buf N*

Bill Dickey
Dickey, William Malcolm
B: Jun 6, 1907   D: Nov 12, 1993
Hall of Fame 1954

Pos: C	BA: .313
Hits: 1,969	HRs: 202
RBI: 1,209	BBs: 678
Managerial Record	
Won: 57 Lost: 48 Pct: .543	

Dickey's peers and his fans considered him the greatest catcher in baseball. He caught 100 games or more for 13 consecutive years, and

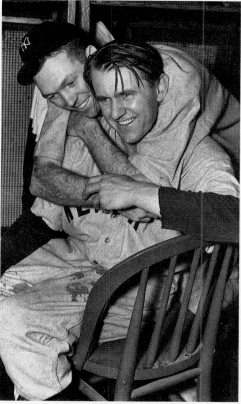
Bill Dickey (l) and Lefty Gomez, 1937.

he carried a big stick. Dickey's .362 batting average in 1936 was a record for catchers. Elected to the All-Star squad 11 times, he also played in eight World Series. In the Fall Classic Dickey was always great in the clutch. He hit five home runs and drove in 24. His ninth-inning single won the Game One in 1939, and his two-run homer gave the Yankees the victory in Game Five in 1943.

As a defensive catcher his skills were so good that the Yankees brought him back to teach their ingenue, Yogi Berra. Berra explained to the press, "Bill Dickey is learnin' me all his experience." Dickey did that job just as he did his own: quietly and efficiently.
Playing Career: *1928-1943, 1946; NY A*
Managerial Career: *1946; NY A*

Pitcher Murry Dickson, 1953.

Murry Dickson
Dickson, Murry Monroe
B: Aug 21, 1916   D: Sep 21, 1989

Pos: P	ERA: 3.66
W-L: 172-181	SOs: 1,281
ShOs: 27	Saves: 23

Dickson's major league career was disrupted twice; he went back to the minors to work on the sixth pitch in his repetoire, then he was drafted for service in World War II. While on furlough, he pitched in the 1943 World Series.

Finally becoming a regular starter at age 29, Dickson's first year back was a success. He led the NL with a .716 won-lost percentage with a record of 15-6, and he went 0-1, but batted .400 in the 1946 World Series for the champion Cardinals. Dickson was then shipped to the hapless Pirates where he won 20 games, but followed that performance by leading the NL in losses for three seasons in a row. Dickson was chosen for the All-Star team once, and he appeared in the 1958 World Series for the Yankees.
Playing Career: *1939-1940, 1942-1943, 1946-1959; StL N, Pit N, Phi N, KC A, NY A*

Larry Dierker
Dierker, Lawrence Edward
B: Sep 22, 1946

Pos: P   ERA: 3.30
W-L: 139-123   SOs: 1,493
ShOs: 25   No-hitters: 1

Larry Dierker was the Houston franchise. Vigorously pursued by 17 other major league clubs, Dierker's signing in 1964 gave the expansion Astros their first quality player. He made his NL debut at age 18. Careful to protect the club's position, manager Harry Walker once responded to locker room rough-housing, "Lighten up, if Dierker gets hurt we're all out of a job."

Dierker flirted with no-hitters, four times taking one into the ninth inning before he finally completed one against the Expos. He recorded 20 victories in 1969, the year he led the Astros' staff to a new major league strikeout record. Three Houston pitchers fanned 200 or more batters that year, as the staff totaled 1,221 K's. An arm injury in 1973 cost Dierker that season and limited his arsenal, which, in the early days, included a fastball, curve, screwball, slider and change-up.
Playing Career: *1964-1977; Hou N, StL N*

Bill Dietrich
Dietrich, William John
B: Mar 29, 1910   D: Jun 20, 1978

Pos: P   ERA: 4.48
W-L: 108-128   SOs: 660
ShOs: 18   No-hitters: 1

Connie Mack released Dietrich because he refused to wear his eyeglasses. Dietrich once had a no-hitter going, but thought he had lost it when it seemed an error was called a hit. He did not realize the no-hitter stood until he was mobbed by his teammates at the end of the game.
Playing Career: *1933-1948; Phi A, Was A, Chi A*

Martin Dihigo
Dihigo, Martin
B: May 25, 1905   D: May 20, 1971
Hall of Fame 1977

Pos: P, 1B, 2B, OF, 3B   BA: .316 (inc.)
Hits: 453 (inc.)   HRs: 64 (inc.)
RBI: NA   BBs: NA

Martin Dihigo, whose Spanish surname means "son of somebody," certainly inherited the right genes from someone. He was one of the most versatile athletes in the history of baseball. In a career that lasted from 1923 to 1945, Dihigo starred as a pitcher, as a hitter, as an outfielder, and occasionally as an infielder.

As a pitcher, counting several seasons in Mexico, Venezuela, and the Dominican Republic, Dihigo was 256-136. He batted over .400 three times in Cuba and in the U.S. He led the Eastern Colored League in homers in 1926 and the Negro American League in batting with a .386 mark in 1929. Reportedly, his

Martin Dihigo.

longest home run came in Pittsburgh in 1936, a 500-foot shot that landed on a hospital roof.
Playing Career: *1923-1931, 1935-1936, 1945; Cuban Stars, Hom Grays, Phi Hilldales, Bal Black Sox, NY Cubans*

Miguel Dilone
Dilone y Reyes, Miguel Angel
B: Nov 1, 1954

Pos: OF   BA: .265
Hits: 530   HRs: 6
RBI: 129   BBs: 142

Dilone was a free-swinging, swift, base-stealing leadoff man. He had a couple of great years, batting .341 with 61 stolen bases in 1980, and pulling off 27 steals in 29 attempts in 1984. He played only 800 games in 12 years, yet stole 267 bases.
Playing Career: *1974-1985; Pit N, Oak A, Chi N, Cle A, Chi A, Mon N, SD N*

Dom DiMaggio
DiMaggio, Dominic Paul
(The Little Professor)
B: Feb 12, 1917

Pos: OF   BA: .298
Hits: 1,680   HRs: 87
RBI: 618   BBs: 750

The Red Sox always claimed that they had the DiMaggio they wanted. Nobody believed them, but popular Dom made the AL All-Star team in seven of nine seasons. He also averaged 104 runs per season for a total of 1,046. Batting leadoff, DiMaggio hit safely in 34 consecutive games in 1949, 27 in 1951. He led the AL twice in runs scored and at-bats. DiMaggio shared the outfield with brother Joe in three All-Star Games and drove him home with a single in 1941.
Playing Career: *1940-1942, 1946-1953; Bos A*

Joe DiMaggio
DiMaggio, Joseph Paul
(The Yankee Clipper)
B: Nov 25, 1914
Hall of Fame 1955

Pos: OF   BA: .325
Hits: 2,214   HRs: 361
RBI: 1,537   BBs: 790

Marilyn Monroe said to DiMaggio after returning from her USO tour of Korea, "Oh Joe, you've never heard such cheering." DiMaggio replied quietly, "Yes, Marilyn, I have." DiMaggio's 12 full seasons were interrupted by military duty, and he missed half the 1949 season with a painful bone spur in his heel. Nonetheless, Joltin' Joe amassed awesome numbers. He scored 1,390 runs while smacking 389 doubles, 131 triples, and striking out only 369 times. He covered center field in Yankee Stadium with such grace that he made even difficult plays look easy.

DiMaggio played on the All-Star team each year of his career, and nearly accomplished that with the World Series as well, missing only 1940, 1946 and 1948. He holds the sixth all-time highest slugging average, .579. DiMaggio has a .271 batting average in 51 World Series games, hitting eight homers and scoring 27 runs, while driving in 30.
Playing Career: *1936-1942, 1946-1951; NY A*

Vince DiMaggio
DiMaggio, Vincent Paul
B: Sep 6, 1912   D: Oct 3, 1986

Pos: OF   BA: .249
Hits: 959   HRs: 125
RBI: 584   BBs: 412

Vince was the eldest of the three DiMaggio brothers who played in the major leagues. He was a minor league home run king, but was prone to strike out in the majors, leading the NL in whiffs six times. DiMaggio played in the 1942 and 1943 All-Star Games.
Playing Career: *1937-1946; Bos N, Cin N, Pit N, Phi N, NY N*

Bill Dinneen
Dinneen, William Henry (Big Bill)
B: Apr 5, 1876   D: Jan 13, 1955

Pos: P   ERA: 3.01
W-L: 170-177   SOs: 1,127
ShOs: 24   No-hitters: 1

Rejected after a tryout by the hometown Syracuse Stars of the Eastern League, Dinneen took his skills to league rival Toronto, where prejudice against the Irish would not prevent him from pitching.

Named after labor agitator Big Bill Haywood, Dinneen wasted little time breaking into the major leagues following a 21-win season in Canada. A star from the beginning, he jumped from the Boston NL Braves to the crosstown AL Red Sox. He compiled three straight 20-win seasons, and also worked in relief, leading the AL in 1903 and 1907 in saves. Dinneen won three games in the 1903

A young Joe DiMaggio signs autographs for fans at Yankee Stadium.

World Series. Retiring in 1909, Dinneen appeared 10 days later as an umpire in the AL, a job he held for the next 29 years.
Playing Career: *1898-1909; Was N, Bos N, Bos A, StL A*

Frank DiPino
DiPino, Frank Michael
B: Oct 22, 1956

Pos: P	ERA: 3.83
W-L: 35-38	SOs: 515
ShOs: 0	Saves: 56

DiPino went 9-0 with a 2.45 ERA for the 1989 Cardinals. He spent his minor league career with the Brewers but only two of his 684 major league innings were pitched in the AL. Elbow surgery slowed his progress, causing him to miss the 1991 season.
Playing Career: *1981-1990, 1992-; Mil A, Hou N, Chi N, StL N, KC A*

Art Ditmar
Ditmar, Arthur John
B: Apr 3, 1929

Pos: P	ERA: 3.98
W-L: 72-77	SOs: 552
ShOs: 5	Saves: 14

When Bill Mazeroski pounded Ralph Terry for that famous game-winning home run in the 1960 World Series, radio broadcasters mistakenly reported that Ditmar was the pitcher. When Anheuser-Busch used tape of the famous radio call in a national ad campaign, Ditmar sued them for damaging his reputation, and won. Ditmar posted 28 victories for the Yankees in the years 1959-1960, but the Pirates knocked him out of two games in the 1960 Series.
Playing Career: *1954-1962; Phi A, KC A, NY A*

Bill Doak
Doak, William Leopold
B: Jan, 28 1891   D: Nov 26, 1954

Pos: P	ERA: 2.98
W-L: 170-157	SOs: 1,014
ShOs: 34	Saves: 16

Doak was a top pitcher, twice leading the NL in ERA with a 1.72 mark in 1914 and a 2.59 mark in 1921. He won 20 games in 1920. That year he made a suggestion to Rawlings Sporting Goods Company about improving baseball gloves. Doak suggested that a web be sewn between the forefinger and thumb of the glove, making it a catching device.

When Doak broke into the majors, gloves were flat or "pancake" style. Their main

Cardinals hurler Bill Doak, 1921.

function was to protect the players' hands. Doak's idea led to the creation of a pocket in the glove, extending fielders' range two or three more inches. When the new style gloves hit the ballparks, fielding averages went up. The Bill Doak Glove was the most popular model ever produced; from 1921 to 1942 it sold like hotcakes. Bill Doak received a bonus and occasionally, a free glove.
Playing Career: *1912-1924, 1927-1929; Cin N, StL N, Brk N*

Chuck Dobson
Dobson, Charles Thomas
B: Jan 10, 1944

Pos: P	ERA: 3.78
W-L: 74-69	SOs: 758
ShOs: 11	No-hitters: 0

Dobson was a starter on the A's just before their glory years, leading the AL in shutouts in 1970. The Kansas City native played his first major league ball game in his hometown. Tormented by an injured rotator cuff, he missed parts of 1966, and all of 1972.
Playing Career: *1966-1971, 1973-1975; KC A, Oak A, Cal A*

Joe Dobson
Dobson, Joseph Gordon (Burrhead)
B: Jan 20, 1917

Pos: P	ERA: 3.62
W-L: 137-103	SOs: 992
ShOs: 22	Saves: 18

Dobson grew up in dustbowl era Oklahoma. Overcoming an accident as a teenager – he blew off his thumb and index finger playing with dynamite caps – Dobson became a major league pitcher at age 22. Consistent on the mound, he reached double figures in wins eight times, peaking at 18 in 1947. Dobson pitched 100 innings or more 12 times, and hurled more than 200 innings four times. He won Game Five of the 1946 World Series, and was an All-Star in 1948.
Playing Career: *1939-1943, 1946-1954; Cle A, Bos A, Chi A*

Pat Dobson
Dobson, Patrick Edward
B: Feb 12, 1942

Pos: P	ERA: 3.54
W-L: 122-129	SOs: 1,301
ShOs: 14	Saves: 19

A $35,000 bonus baby with the Tigers, Dobson was one of the Orioles' quartet who won 20 games apiece in 1971. The next year he was 16-18 with a 2.65 ERA, and was selected to the All-Star squad. Baltimore traded him and Davey Johnson to the Braves for Earl Williams. Then Dobson was swapped to the Yankees, where he regained some of his lost smoke and had his best year since 1971, going 19-15 in 1974. A dismal 3-12 season in 1977 ended his career.
Playing Career: *1967-1977; Det A, SD N, Bal A, Atl N, NY A, Cle A*

Larry Doby.

Larry Doby
Doby, Lawrence Eugene
B: Dec 13, 1924

Pos: OF, 2B   BA: .283
Hits: 1,515   HRs: 253
RBI: 969   BBs: 871
Managerial Record
Won: 37   Lost: 50   Pct: .425

Replacing Willie Wells at second base, Doby teamed with Monte Irvin and Leon Day to capture the 1946 Black World Series for the Newark Eagles. Signed to an AL contract four months after Jackie Robinson broke the color line in baseball, Doby had the satisfaction of playing on championship teams both in the Negro Leagues and in the AL. Doby was chosen for the All-Star team for seven years in a row. He led the AL in homers twice, knocked in 100 runs or more five times, and scored 90 runs or more six times. Doby was the leader of the 1954 Indians team that set the AL record with 111 wins and interrupted the Yankees' string of pennants that otherwise stretched from 1949 to 1959. Doby was the second African-American to manage in the AL.
Playing Career: *1947-1959; Cle A, Chi A, Det A*
Managerial Career: *1978; Chi A*

Bobby Doerr
Doerr, Robert Pershing
B: Apr 7, 1918
Hall of Fame 1986

Pos: 2B   BA: .288
Hits: 2,042   HRs: 223
RBI:1,247   BBs: 809

As a young hitter, Doerr resisted rookie Ted Williams's advice on batting in 1939. Williams responded "It's alright with me if you want to be a lousy .280/.290 hitter your whole life." Doerr decided to pay attention after all; he hit .318 that season.

He made the All-Star team nine times between 1941 and 1951, taking time out for military service in 1945. Ironically, 1949 – the year Doerr was not selected – was one of his better years, with a .309 average, 109 RBI, 91 runs scored, 30 doubles slashed, and 18 home runs pounded. A versatile hitter and second baseman, Doerr led the AL in slugging with a .528 mark in 1944, and he led the league four times in fielding average. In the 1946 World Series, Doerr carried the Red Sox, batting .406 with one home run and three RBI. He scored more than 1,000 runs during his career.
Playing Career: *1937-1944, 1946-1951; Bos A*

Bobby Doerr.

Ed Doheny
Doheny, Edward R.
B: Nov 24, 1874   D: Dec 29, 1916

Pos: P   ERA: 3.75
W-L: 75-83   SOs: 567
ShOs: 6   Saves: 2

Doheny had a boatload of talent, but no control. His prime years were with the Pirates, when he recorded 16-4 and 16-8 seasons. A serious illness prevented Doheny from appearing in the 1903 World Series. Teammate Deacon Phillippe pitched five complete games in the eight-game Series.
Playing Career: *1895-1903; NY N, Pit N*

Cozy Dolan
Dolan, Patrick Henry
B: Dec 3, 1872   D: Mar 29, 1907

Pos: P, OF   BA: .269
Hits: 858   HRs: 10
RBI: 316   BBs: 229

Dolan had an inauspicious beginning as a pitcher, then returned to the minors to learn another position. He came back as an outfielder, hitting .284 in his best season. Dolan died of typhoid fever during spring training in 1907.
Playing Career: *1892, 1895-1896, 1900-1906; Was N, Bos N, Chi N, Brk N, Chi A, Cin N*

Jiggs Donahue
Donahue, John Augustus
B: Jul 13, 1879   D: Jul 19, 1913

Pos: 1B   BA: .255
Hits: 730   HRs: 5
RBI: 327   BBs: 215

Donahue was the beneficiary of spitball-throwing White Sox pitchers; he recorded a major league record 1,846 putouts and 1,998 total chances at first base in 1907. He led the Hitless Wonder White Sox with a .333 average in their surprising 1906 World Series.
Playing Career: *1900-1902, 1904-1909; Pit N, Mil A, StL A, Chi A, Was A*

Red Donahue
Donahue, Francis Rostell
B: Jan 23, 1873   D: Aug 25, 1913

Pos: P   ERA: 3.61
W-L: 167-175   SOs: 788
ShOs: 25   No-hitters: 1

The last Phillie to pitch a no-hitter in Philadelphia was Red Donahue. He tossed a 5-0 gem at Baker Bowl on July 8, 1898. The compactly built, crafty right hander was three times a 20-game winner, even though he was a notorious warm weather pitcher. Teams sometimes held him out of play until the summer heated up.

Donahue pitched for the famed King Kelly at Allentown in the early 1890s. Reminiscing to an incredulous reporter, Donahue said he was the treasurer for the club because he was the only one sober enough to keep track of the payroll and attendant debts. Most of his teammates were in debt for several days' pay; Kelly himself was two months in arrears to the club.
Playing Career: *1893-1906; NY N, StL N, Phi N, StL A, Cle A, Det A*

Atley Donald
Donald, Richard Atley
B: Aug 19, 1910

Pos: P   ERA: 3.52
W-L: 65-33   SOs: 369
ShOs: 5   Saves: 1

Donald was a star hurler with the 1938 Newark Bears, the best minor league team

ever. Eye and elbow injuries limited his appearances with the Yankees, but not his performance. Donald's lifetime record is 65-33 with a .663 percentage.
Playing Career: *1938-1945; NY A*

Mike Donlin
Donlin, Michael Joseph (Turkey Mike)
B: May 30, 1878   D: Sep 24, 1933

Pos: OF	BA: .334
Hits: 1,286	HRs: 51
RBI: 543	BBs: 312

Flamboyant Turkey Mike strutted across the field before the game, and strutted back when the game was over. Playing his best for John McGraw, Donlin had adventures Huck Finn would envy. Donlin served time in jail for assault; sat out the entire 1907 season to get more money; left baseball altogether in 1909; married Broadway actress Mabel Hite; and went on tour with a vaudeville act. Hite's untimely death brought Donlin back to baseball in 1911.

Donlin had some great years. He batted .340 in 1901, .351 in 1903, .356 in 1905, and .334 in 1908. He was 6-for-6 in a 1901 game, smashing two triples, two doubles, and two singles. He was one of the greatest natural hitters the game ever produced, but few managers understood the Donlin flare for the dramatic. McGraw was empathetic, and even acted in a few of Donlin's Hollywood films.
Playing Career: *1899-1906, 1908, 1911-1912, 1914; StL N, Bal A, Cin N, NY N, Bos N, Pit N*

Pete Donohue
Donohue, Peter Joseph
B: Nov 5, 1900   D: Feb 23, 1988

Pos: P	ERA: 3.87
W-L: 134-118	SOs: 571
ShOs: 16	Saves: 12

When the Reds won the 1919 World Series, they envisioned a sequence of NL triumphs that would resemble those of the 1869 Red Stockings. The Reds of the 1920s counted heavily on a pitching rotation of Eppa Rixey, Dolf Luque, Carl Mays and Donohue, who won 20 games three times between 1922 and 1926. He also tossed 220 or more innings five times. Donohue was the man who perfected the change-up pitch.
Playing Career: *1921-1932; Cin N, NY N, Cle A, Bos A*

Bill Donovan
Donovan, William Edward (Wild Bill)
B: Oct 13, 1876   D: Dec 9, 1923

Pos: P	ERA: 2.69
W-L: 186-139	SOs: 1,552
ShOs: 35	Saves: 6
Managerial Record	
Won: 245 Lost: 301 Pct: .449	

Although he walked a lot of batters, Wild Bill was a winning pitcher. Some historians consider him the best hitter and baserunner among pitchers in his time period. Donovan was the hurler who threw more than 240 pitches during the famous four-hour, 17-

"Wild Bill" Donovan (r).

inning, 9-9 tie that gave the Tigers the 1907 pennant. His record was 25-4 that season.

Donovan won 25 games twice, leading the NL in 1901, and he achieved a .572 lifetime winning percentage. After a poor 1911 season he returned to the minors to begin a new career as a manager. He returned to the majors as pilot of the Highlanders, the team that would later be called the Yankees. Donovan was killed in a train wreck while traveling to baseball's winter meetings. In the berth above Donovan was his business manager, George Weiss, who escaped unharmed.
Playing Career: *1898-1912, 1915-1916, 1918; Was N, Brk N, Det A, NY A*
Managerial Career: *1915-1917, 1921; NY A, Phi N*

Dick Donovan
Donovan, Richard Edward
B: Dec 7, 1927

Pos: P	ERA: 3.67
W-L: 122-99	SOs: 880
ShOs: 25	Saves: 5

Donovan did not win a game until he was 27 years old and playing for his third major league team. That year he posted 15 victories for the White Sox, and was selected for the All-Star team, an honor he would have two more times. Picked in the expansion draft by the new Washington Senators in 1961, Donovan fooled his former team and the rest of the AL when he led the league in ERA with a 2.40 mark. He won 20 games the next year.
Playing Career: *1950-1952, 1954-1965; Bos N, Det A, Chi A, Was A, Cle A*

"Turkey Mike" Donlin (l) with Dan Frohman in 1919.

Patsy Donovan
Donovan, Patrick Joseph
B: Mar 16, 1865   D: Dec 25, 1953

Pos: OF   BA: .300
Hits: 2,246   HRs: 16
RBI: 736   BBs: 453
Managerial Record
Won: 684   Lost: 879   Pct: .438

Donovan was another of the ballplayers who started a long and illustrious career in 1890 when there were three major leagues operating. A handsome Irishman, Donovan was a leader on the field as well as in the dugout. He scored 1,318 runs, and stole 518 bases, but he played on only one pennant winner, the NL Dodgers in 1890. When Donovan managed, his teams finished in the first division twice; the 1901 St. Louis Cardinals and 1910 Boston Red Sox.
Playing Career: *1890-1907; Bos N, Brk N, Lou AA, Was AA, Was N, Pit N, StL N, Was A*
Managerial Career: *1897, 1899, 1901-1904, 1906-1908, 1910-1911; Pit N, StL N, Was A, Brk N, Bos A*

Red Dooin
Dooin, Charles Sebastian
B: Jun 12, 1879   D: May 12, 1952

Pos: C   BA: .240
Hits: 961   HRs: 10
RBI: 344   BBs: 155
Managerial Record
Won: 392   Lost: 370   Pct: .514

Dooin, a fine defensive catcher, reportedly wore papier-maché shinguards under his stockings prior to Roger Bresnahan inventing the type worn outside the uniform in 1907. Dooin led NL catchers in assists in 1908, the same year he reported that a bribe had been offered him to throw a series of games. Named manager in 1910, Dooin spent his later years in baseball developing young talent such as Grover Cleveland Alexander.
Playing Career: *1902-1916; Phi N, Cin N, NY N*
Managerial Career: *1910-1914; Phi N*

Mickey Doolan
Doolan, Michael Joseph (Doc)
B: May 7, 1880   D: Nov 1, 1951

Pos: SS   BA: .230
Hits: 1,376   HRs: 15
RBI: 554   BBs: 370

Doolan was named Michael J. Doolittle at birth, but he actually did quite a lot. A solid fielder, Doolan led the league three times in fielding percentage. He played for the Phillies during some lean years, and had been traded by the time they won a pennant in 1915 with Dave Bancroft at shortstop. Off the field, Doolan served as vice-president of the Players' Fraternity, founded in 1912 by David Fultz. After his baseball career, Doolan became a dentist.
Playing Career: *1905-1916, 1918; Phi N, Bal F, Chi F, Chi N, NY N, Brk N*

Bill Doran turns a double play in 1984.

Bill Doran
Doran, William Donald
B: May 28, 1958

Pos: 2B, SS, 3B   BA: .266
Hits: 1,366   HRs: 84
RBI: 497   BBs: 709

A collegiate All-American at Miami University in Ohio, Doran is one of the best multipurpose fielders in baseball. He was acquired by the Brewers to shore up the infield for their contending team.
Playing Career: *1982-; Hou N, Cin N, Mil A*

Mike Dorgan
Dorgan, Michael Cornelius
B: Oct 2, 1853   D: Apr 26, 1909

Pos: C, 1B, OF   BA: .274
Hits: 802   HRs: 5
RBI: 207   BBs: 118
Managerial Record
Won: 67   Lost: 70   Pct: .489

Dorgan played on the legendary independent Syracuse Stars teams of 1876, 1878 and 1879. His marriage in 1879 broke up the jolly team of bachelors and was the social event of the year in Syracuse.
Playing Career: *1877, 1879-1881, 1883-1887, 1890; StL N, Syr N, Pro N, Wor N, Det N, NY N, Syr AA*
Managerial Career: *1879-1881; Syr N, Pro N, Wor N*

Harry Dorish
Dorish, Harry
B: July 13, 1921

Pos: P   ERA: 3.38
W-L: 45-43   SOs: 332
ShOs: 2   Saves: 44

One of the first relievers to specialize in closing out the game, Dorish did not get recognition because his clubs never won any pennants. Dorish led the league in saves in 1952. The next year he went 10-6 with 18 saves, his best record.
Playing Career: *1947-1956; Bos A, StL A, Chi A, Bal A, Bos A*

Richard Dotson
Dotson, Richard Elliott
B: Jan 10, 1959

Pos: P   ERA: 4.23
W-L: 111-113   SOs: 973
ShOs: 11   No-hitters: 0

Dotson was traded as an 18-year-old in the deal that brought Brian Downing to the Angels. Dotson became a starter three years later for the White Sox. In 1983 he won 22 games and led the AL in winning percentage. He was an All-Star in 1984.
Playing Career: *1979-1990; Chi A, NY A, KC A*

Patrick Dougherty
Dougherty, Patrick Henry
B: Oct 27, 1876   D: Apr 30, 1940

Pos: OF   BA: .284
Hits: 1,294   HRs: 17
RBI: 413   BBs: 378

Dougherty played on two World Series championship teams in his first five years in the AL. A real scrapper, he was waived after fighting Highlander manager Clark Griffith. Dougherty stole 261 bases, leading the AL with 47 in 1908.
Playing Career: *1902-1911; Bos A, NY A, Chi A*

Phil Douglas
Douglas, Phillip Brooks (Shufflin' Phil)
B: Jun 17, 1890   D: Aug 1, 1952

Pos: P   ERA: 2.80
W-L: 93-93   SOs: 1,626
ShOs: 20   Saves: 8

Douglas was an extraordinary pitcher when sober, recording ERAs under 3.00 six of nine years. He defeated the Yankees twice in the 1921 World Series. Giants manager John McGraw went so far as to hire a companion to keep Douglas from drinking, but the pressure of life pushed the hurler over the edge. In an effort to retaliate against McGraw, Douglas offered to throw a series of games. His hastily-conceived plan was discovered and he was banned from baseball for life.
Playing Career: *1912, 1914-1915, 1917-1922; Chi A, Cin N, Brk N, Chi N, NY N*

Klondike Douglass
Douglass, William Bingham
B: May 10, 1872   D: Dec 13, 1953

Pos: C, SS, 1B, 3B, OF   BA: .274
Hits: 766   HRs: 10
RBI: 275   BBs: 227

Playing as a utility man for Chris Von der Ahe's Browns, Douglass was a big crowd draw in 1897 when he hit .329. He won himself a starting position with the Phillies the next year, and stayed with them the remaining seven years of his career.
Playing Career: *1896-1904; StL N, Phi N*

Taylor Douthit
Douthit, Taylor Lee
B: Apr 22, 1901   D: May 28, 1986

Pos: OF   BA: .291
Hits: 1,201   HRs: 29
RBI: 396   BBs: 443

One of the early products of the Cardinal farm system, Douthit had a great year in 1926. Batting leadoff, he hit .308, scored 96 runs, and played in the World Series. Douthit was a very good fielder, leading NL outfielders in putouts three times. Lacking power, he hit for average, reaching .336, .303 and .331 in the years 1929-1931. Douthit played in 13 World Series games in three different years, 1926, 1928 and 1930.
Playing Career: *1923-1933; StL N, Cin N*

Taylor Douthit at the plate for St. Louis in the 1926 WS.

Giants pitcher "Shufflin' Phil" Douglas was banned from baseball in 1922.

Tommy Dowd
**Dowd, Thomas Jefferson
(Buttermilk Tommy)**
B: Apr 20, 1869   D: Jul 2, 1933

Pos: OF, 2B, 3B   BA: .217
Hits: 1,492   HRs: 23
RBI: 501   BBs: 369
Managerial Record
Won: 31   Lost: 60   Pct: .341

Dowd was one of the Browns' managers the season they had a quintet of them – 1896. He played more than 100 games in each of his 10 years in the majors, spending the majority of his career toiling for the Browns. The Holy Cross graduate scored 903 runs and stole 366 bases during his career.
Playing Career: *1891-1899, 1901; Bos AA, Was AA, Was N, StL N, Phi N, Cle N, Bos A*
Managerial Career: *1896-1897; StL N*

Al Downing
Downing, Alphonso Erwin
B: Jun 28, 1941

Pos: P   ERA: 3.22
W-L: 123-107   SOs: 1,639
ShOs: 24   Saves: 3

Downing was a super prospect for the Yankees whose claim to fame turned out to be giving up Hank Aaron's 715th home run. Downing's fearsome fastball and sharp-breaking curve led the AL in strikeouts in 1964. The year before, opposing batters had

hit only .184 against him. Arm trouble forced him to forego the heat he used to throw and become a more versatile pitcher. Downing captured 20 victories in 1971. He pitched in three World Series.
Playing Career: *1961-1977; NY A, Oak A, Mil A, LA N*

Brian Downing
Downing, Brian Jay
B: Oct 9, 1950

Pos: OF, DH, C	BA: .267
Hits: 2,099	HRs: 275
RBI: 1,073	BBs: 1,197

Downing was constantly confused with Brian Dowling – the football player upon whom Garry Trudeau based the character "BD" in the comic strip "Doonesbury" – because both came to prominence in sports at the same time. Downing's batting eye enabled him to walk more than he struck out, a rarity in today's game. He scored 1,188 runs, going over 100 in 1987. Twice he fielded 1.000 as an outfielder. He batted .326 and was named an All-Star in 1979, and he played in three ALCS.
Playing Career: *1973-1992; Chi A, Cal A, Tex A, Min A*

Denny Doyle
Doyle, Robert Dennis
B: Jan 17, 1944

Pos: 2B	BA: .250
Hits: 823	HRs: 16
RBI: 237	BBs: 205

Doyle and his brothers run a baseball training school in Florida. The highlight of his professional playing career came in the 1975 World Series for the Red Sox. In Game Five Doyle tripled and scored to give the Sox a temporary lead in the Series.
Playing Career: *1970-1977; Phi N, Cal A, Bos A*

Dirty Jack Doyle
Doyle, John Joseph
B: Oct 25, 1869   D: Dec 31, 1958

Pos: 1B	BA: .299
Hits: 1,808	HRs: 25
RBI: 924	BBs: 437

Managerial Record
Won: 40   Lost: 40   Pct: .500

Dirty Jack was a hustler who developed a reputation for doing anything to win the ball game. He starred in the Temple Cup Series, playing on three winning teams and twice hitting over .500 for the Series. Doyle scored 977 runs, smacked 316 doubles and stole 516 bases in an up-and-down career.
Playing Career: *1889-1905; Col AA, Cle N, NY N, Bal N, Was N, Chi N, Was A, Brk N, Phi N, NY A*
Managerial Career: *1895, 1898; NY N, Was N*

Larry Doyle
Doyle, Lawrence Joseph (Laughing Larry)
B: July 31, 1886   D: Mar 1, 1974

Pos: 2B	BA: .290
Hits: 1,887	HRs: 74
RBI: 793	BBs: 625

"It's great to be young and a Giant," were the flamboyant words of Larry Doyle. The hard-nosed second baseman was a McGraw type of player. After making a crucial ninth-inning error in his first major league game, Doyle expected to be lambasted by McGraw when he met him that evening. Instead McGraw praised his efforts and encouraged him to do better the next time. Doyle hit .300 or more four of the next five seasons. He won a batting title in 1915, while also leading the NL in hits and doubles. He swatted 299 doubles and 123 triples in his career. Doyle also scored 960 runs and stole 297 bases, pilfering home 17 times. He left the Giants in 1916 and returned in 1918, missing the year of their 26-game winning streak.
Playing Career: *1907-1920; NY N, Chi N*

Doug Drabek
Drabek, Douglas Dean
B: Jul 25, 1962

Pos: P	ERA: 3.21
W-L: 108-88	SOs: 1,053
ShOs: 18	No-hitters: 0

Destined for greatness as a youngster in the Yankees' farm system, Drabek had a 7-8 rookie year and New York traded him.

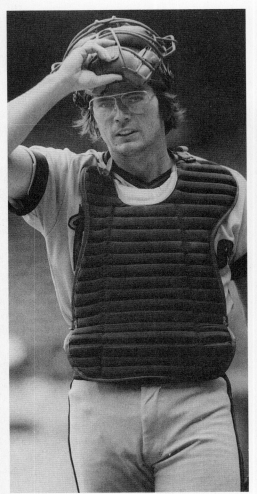

The Angels' Brian Downing in 1979.

"Laughing Larry" Doyle takes a swing for the New York Giants.

Drabek began to fulfill his destiny in 1990 when he won 22 and captured the NL Cy Young Award.
Playing Career: *1986-; NY A, Pit N, Hou N*

Moe Drabowsky
Drabowsky, Myron Walter
B: Jul 21, 1935

Pos: P	ERA: 3.71
W-L: 88-105	SOs: 1,162
ShOs: 6	Saves: 55

Drabowsky was a wild man. He used the bullpen phone to order pizza during a game. He called the opposing bullpen and disguising his voice, ordered two pitchers to get up and throw. He hit four batters in one inning, adding to his total of 10 during the 1957 season. In Game One of the 1966 World Series Drabowsky gave a memorable performance in relief, striking out 11 and winning the game to aid the Orioles' four-game sweep.
Playing Career: *1956-1972; Chi N, Mil N, Cin N, KCA A, Bal A, KCR A, StL N, Chi A*

Dick Drago
Drago, Richard Anthony
B: Jun 25, 1945

Pos: P	ERA: 3.62
W-L: 108-117	SOs: 987
ShOs: 10	Saves: 58

Drago was the ace of the 1971 Royals' staff, winning 17 games with four shutouts and a 2.98 ERA. After six years of starting, he became a stopper. The Sox won the pennant with Drago in the bullpen in 1975; he contributed 15 saves. He saved two more in the ALCS, but lost a game in the World Series. It was Drago's three scoreless innings in Game Six, however, that enabled the Sox to hang on and win it on Carlton Fisk's homer.
Playing Career: *1969-1981; KC A, Bos A, Cal A, Bal A, Sea A*

Dave Dravecky
Dravecky, David Francis
B: Feb 14, 1956

Pos: P	ERA: 3.13
W-L: 64-57	SOs: 558
ShOs: 9	Saves: 10

In a dramatic 1989 comeback from cancer in his throwing arm, Dravecky made two starts, winning both of them. Unfortunately, the cancer eventually necessitated amputation of the arm. Dravecky had pitched in the 1984 World Series and 1983 All-Star Game.
Playing Career: *1982-1989; SD N, SF N*

Chuck Dressen
Dressen, Charles Walter
B: Sep 20, 1898   D: Aug 10, 1966

Pos: 3B, SS	BA: .272
Hits: 603	HRs: 11
RBI: 221	BBs: 219
Managerial Record	
Won: 1,008 Lost: 973 Pct: .509	

Chuck Dressen had an up-and-down managerial career. When he asked the Dodgers for a multi-year contract in 1953 after winning two straight pennants, it was denied and he was fired. His successor Walter Alston, signed a record 24 one-year pacts in a row. Dressen's management style was characterized by a favorite challenge to the team: "Hold them, boys. I'll think of something."

A former quarterback for the Decatur Stanleys, Dressen was an inveterate gambler, and was adept at picking racetrack winners. He always tried to wear number seven. When Joe Medwick joined the Dodgers, he asked for seven. Dressen gave it to him, then appeared on the coaching lines wearing number 77. He always thought of something.
Playing Career: *1925-1931, 1933; Cin N, NY N*
Managerial Career: *1934-1937, 1951-1953, 1955-1957, 1960-1961, 1963-1966; Cin N, Brk N, Was A, Mil N, Det A*

Barney Dreyfuss
Dreyfuss, Barney
B: Feb 23, 1865   D: Feb 5, 1932

An influential team owner and policy maker, Dreyfuss first became interested in baseball in Paducah, Kentucky, where he organized a semipro team. Later moving to Louisville, Dreyfuss purchased part of the NL team called the Colonels. Buying out his partners for $50,000 in 1899, he merged the Colonels with the Pittsburgh Pirates in 1900. The Pirates were an immediate powerhouse in the NL, winning three pennants in a row.

Barney Dreyfuss.

In 1902 Dreyfuss worked hard to forge a peaceful agreement between leagues with regard to recruiting players and honoring contracts. In 1903 the Boston Pilgrims Club challenged the Pirates to a series of championship games. Due to injury and illness, Dreyfuss had only one pitcher, but agreed to play the games to avoid upsetting the delicate balance of power achieved only the year before. The Pirates lost the championship contest, but the games became an institution known as the World Series.

Dan Driessen
Driessen, Daniel
B: Jul 29, 1951

Pos: 1B	BA: .267
Hits: 1,464	HRs: 153
RBI: 763	BBs: 761

Driessen had big shoes to fill when the Reds traded Tony Perez to make room for him at first base in 1977. He responded by hitting .300 and driving in 91 runs. Driessen subsequently led the NL in fielding three times and playing on another division-winning team in 1979. He finished his career with the NL champion Cardinals, playing in the NLCS and World Series in place of injured Jack Clark.
Playing Career: *1973-1987; Cin N, Mon N, SF N, Hou N, StL N*

Walt Dropo
Dropo, Walter (Moose)
B: Jan 30, 1923

Pos: 1B	BA: .270
Hits: 1,113	HRs: 152
RBI: 704	BBs: 328

The big, slow-footed slugger was AL Rookie of the Year in 1950. Dropo led the league in RBI that year with 144, smashing 34 homers and scoring 101 runs, all careers highs. He was chosen for the All-Star squad. In 1952 Dropo rapped 12 straight hits.
Playing Career: *1949-1961; Bos A, Det A, Chi A, Cin N, Bal A*

Don Drysdale
Drysdale, Donald Scott
B: Jul 23, 1936   D: Jul 3, 1993
Hall of Fame 1984

Pos: P	ERA: 2.95
W-L: 209-166	SOs: 2,486
ShOs: 49	Saves: 6

Drysdale had a long and colorful career as a pitcher. As an established Dodger star, he held out in tandem with Sandy Koufax after the 1965 season, when the pair hired an agent to represent them in dealing with Walter O'Malley and his attorneys. The holdout represented a turning point in player-owner relations. Satisfied enough with their deal to return to the playing field, the two masters of the mound led the Dodgers to the NL pennant in 1966.

Drysdale was one of the best hitting

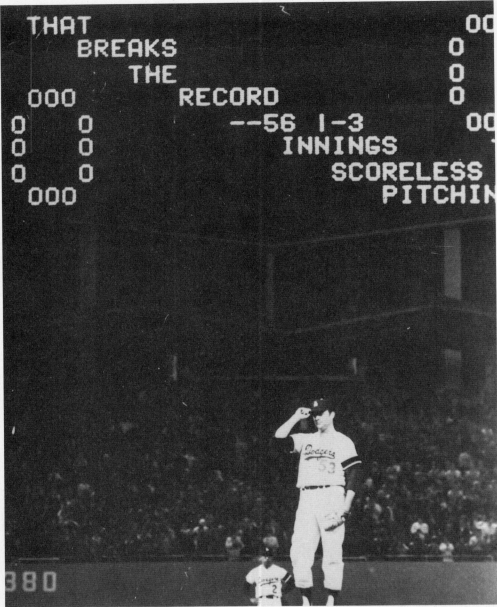

Don Drysdale breaks the record for consecutive scoreless innings pitched, 1968.

pitchers of his era. In 1965 his .300 batting average led the Dodgers, and he also hit seven home runs. Drysdale worked like a Clydesdale, hurling more than 200 innings for 12 consecutive years. He was the NL Cy Young Award winner in 1962 when he posted 25 wins. He led the NL in strikeouts three times, and in 1968 Drysdale tossed 58.2 consecutive scoreless innings. He was selected for the All-Star team eight times. Drysdale was later a broadcaster for the Dodgers.
Playing Career: *1956-1969; Brk N, LA N*

Jean Dubuc
Dubuc, Jean Joseph Octave
B: Sep 15, 1888   D: Aug 28, 1958

Pos: P	ERA: 3.04
W-L: 86-76	SOs: 438
ShOs: 12	Saves: 13

Dubuc allegedly overheard – but did not report – Hal Chase and Heinie Zimmerman discussing throwing games in 1918. Dubuc almost certainly had nothing to do with throwing games, but he was banned from baseball for life in 1920.
Playing Career: *1908-1909, 1912-1916, 1918-1919; Cin N, Det A, Bos A, NY N*

Frank Duffy
Duffy, Frank Thomas
B: Oct 14, 1946

Pos: SS	BA: .232
Hits: 619	HRs: 26
RBI: 240	BBs: 171

Duffy was the starting shortstop for the Indians 1972-1977, playing almost 1,000 games in his career. While never hitting better than .265, he led the AL shortstops in fielding twice, 1973 and 1976. He appeared in one NLCS game for the Giants.
Playing Career: *1970-1979; Cin N, SF N, Cle A, Bos A*

Hugh Duffy
Duffy, Hugh
B: Nov 26, 1866   D: Oct 19, 1954
Hall of Fame 1945

Pos: OF	BA: .324
Hits: 2,283	HRs: 105
RBI: 1,299	BBs: 662
Managerial Record	
Won: 535 Lost: 671 Pct: .444	

Duffy recorded the highest batting average ever in 1894 when he hit a resounding .440. The entire league hit .309 that year – the second that the pitching distance was lengthened to 60'6" – but Duffy was better than everyone. He won the Triple Crown, leading the league in batting average, home runs (18), and RBI (145) as well as hits (236), doubles (50) and slugging percentage (.679).

Having been rejected by the White Stockings for being too small, the 5'7" Duffy signed with arch-rival Boston. There he teamed with future Hall of Famers Tommy McCarthy, Jimmy Collins, and Kid Nichols to make the Beaneaters the best team of the decade. Duffy and McCarthy perfected hit-and-run plays and double steals, and came to be called the "Heavenly Twins." Duffy scored 1,551 runs and stole 583 bases. He was later coach emeritus for the Red Sox.
Playing Career: *1888-1901, 1904-1906; Chi N, Chi P, Bos AA, Bos N, Mil A, Phi N*
Managerial Career: *1901, 1904-1906, 1910-1911, 1921-1922; Mil A, Phi N, Chi A, Bos A*

Hugh Duffy.

Joe Dugan
Dugan, Joseph Anthony (Jumping Joe)
B: May 12, 1897   D: Jul 7, 1982

Pos: 3B	BA: .280
Hits: 1,515	HRs: 42
RBI: 571	BBs: 250

Dugan was Babe Ruth's favorite buddy and a pallbearer at his funeral, where he commented, "Geez, it's hot. I'd like a beer." Waite Hoyt replied, "So would the Babe." Dugan's acquisition by the Yankees on July 23, 1922 spread alarm and despondency through AL teams, who accused the pinstripes of "buying the pennant." The hoopla resulted in the establishment of the June 15 trading deadline. Dugan played in five World Series in seven years.
Playing Career: *1917-1929, 1931; Phi A, Bos A, NY A, Bos N, Det A*

Bill Duggleby
Duggleby, William James
B: Mar 16, 1874   D: Aug 30, 1944

Pos: P	ERA: 3.19
W-L: 92-102	SOs: 452
ShOs: 17	Saves: 4

Duggleby hit a grand slam home run in his first major league at-bat and was the winning pitcher as well. He jumped from the Phillies to the new AL, then was ordered back to the Phillies as part of the peace settlement between leagues.
Playing Career: *1898, 1901-1907; Phi N, Phi A, Pit N*

Dave Duncan
Duncan, David Edwin
B: Sep 26, 1945

Pos: C	BA: .214
Hits: 617	HRs: 109
RBI: 341	BBs: 252

Duncan is the top pitching coach in the game today. He currently works for Tony LaRussa and the pennant-winning A's. As a player he appeared in two ALCS and the 1972 World Series for the Oakland A's, batting .500 in the 1971 ALCS. He was chosen for the 1971 All-Star team.
Playing Career: *1964, 1967-1976; KC A, Oak A, Cle A, Bal A*

Frank Duncan
Duncan, Frank
B: Feb 14, 1901   D: Dec 4, 1973

Pos: C	BA: .246 (inc.)
Hits: 546 (inc.)	HRs: 13 (inc.)
RBI: NA	BB: NA

Managerial Record (inc.)
Won: 61   Lost: 79   Pct: .436

Duncan spent 20 years with the Kansas City Monarchs, playing in the first two Negro World Series, 1924-1925. As player-manager he guided the Monarchs to victory in the 1942 Series in a huge upset over the Homestead Grays. Satchel Paige was Duncan's battery-mate and the winning pitcher in all four contests. The Monarchs boasted seven major league calibre pitchers to counter the Grays' dynamic Hall of Fame tandem, Josh Gibson and Buck Leonard.
Playing Career: *1921-1932, 1935-1945; Chi Am Giants, KC Monarchs, NY Harlem Stars, Hom Grays, Pit Crawfords, NY Cubans*
Managerial Career: *1942-1945; KC Monarchs*

Pat Duncan
Duncan, Louis Baird
B: Oct 6, 1893   D: Jul 17, 1960

Pos: OF	BA: .307
Hits: 827	HRs: 23
RBI: 374	BBs: 184

Duncan was one of the unsung heroes who whipped the White Sox in the 1919 World Series. The Reds and some of the White Sox players claimed Cincinnati won the Series legitimately, despite the game-fixing scandal. Duncan led the team with eight RBI in eight games.
Playing Career: *1915, 1919-1924; Pit N, Cin N*

Fred Dunlap
Dunlap, Frederick C. (Sure Shot)
B: May 21, 1859   D: Dec 1, 1902

Pos: 2B	BA: .291
Hits: 1,159	HRs: 41
RBI: 366 (inc.)	BBs: 283

Managerial Record
Won: 145   Lost: 102   Pct: .587

Dunlap was reported to be the highest paid player of the 19th century. He made between $8,000 and $16,000 one year; the figures quoted vary. During his career, Dunlap scored 759 runs, including 160 in 101 games for the 1884 St. Louis Union Association team. Dunlap also managed that year, as the team posted a 66-16 record for an .805 won-lost percentage. For his part, Dunlap batted .412 and led the ill-fated UA in runs, hits, home runs, on-base percentage, slugging average, and fielding average for second baseman. It was a legendary year. Although he never again approached league domination, Dunlap was highly sought after. He played on the great 1887 Detroit Wolverine team that decimated the Browns in a 15-game 19th-century World Series.
Playing Career: *1880-1891; Cle N, StL U, StL N, Det N, Pit N, NY P, Was AA*
Managerial Career: *1882, 1884-1885, 1889; Cle N, StL U, StL N, Pit N*

Pittsburgh's Fred Dunlap, 1888.

Jack Dunn, Orioles owner, 1918.

Jack Dunn
Dunn, John Joseph
B: Oct 6, 1872   D: Oct 22, 1928

Pos: P	ERA: 4.11
W-L: 64-59	SOs: 171
ShOs: 3	Saves: 3

Pos: 2B, SS, OF, 3B	BA: .245
Hits: 397	HRs: 1
RBI: 164	BBs: 83

Dunn was the owner of the International League Baltimore Orioles who first signed Babe Ruth, then sold him to the Red Sox. He also signed stars such as Lefty Grove, Rube Parnham, George Earnshaw, Max Bishop, Jack Bentley, and George Puccinelli. These IL Orioles swept seven pennants in a row. Grove won 100 games for Dunn before he went to the majors.

Dunn's skirmish with the Federal League caused him to lose Ruth and embittered him. He nearly lost his franchise, transferring it to Richmond, Virginia. Upon Baltimore's return to the International League he was forced to pay a re-entry fee.
Playing Career: *1897-1904; Brk N, Phi N, Bal A, NY N*

Shawon Dunston
Dunston, Shawon Donnell
B: Mar 21, 1963

Pos: SS   BA: .259
Hits: 867   HRs: 73
RBI: 344   BBs: 137

Dunston was a first-round draft pick by the Cubs. He made the big league club at age 22, and some feel that he was pressured into the job too soon. He has hit consistently around .260, and has one of the strongest arms of all the shortstops in baseball. Due to injury he had only 10 at-bats in 1993.
Playing Career: *1985-; Chi N*

Ryne Duren
Duren, Rinold George
B: Feb 22, 1929

Pos: P   ERA: 3.83
W-L: 27-44   SOs: 630
ShOs: 1   Saves: 57

A totally unnerving sight from the batter's box was Duren on his hands and knees feeling around on the pitcher's mound for his contact lens. Earlier, Duren had worn thick, dark eyeglasses and typically sent his first 98-mph pitch over the batter's head. Duren was the most intimidating AL relief pitcher in 1958 and 1959. He posted a 2.03 ERA in five World Series Games for the Yankees.
Playing Career: *1954, 1957-1965; Bal A, KC A, NY A, LA A, Phi N, Cin N, Was A*

Leon Durham
Durham, Leon (Bull)
B: Jul 31, 1957

Pos: 1B   BA: .277
Hits: 992   HRs: 147
RBI: 530   BBs: 444

Durham was traded from the Cardinals to Chicago in the Bruce Sutter deal. He repaid the Cubs with 96 RBI, leading them to a division title in 1984. Average in statistics, but exceptional in heart, Durham is playing in the minors as he works to make a comeback.
Playing Career: *1980-1989; StL N, Chi N, Cin N*

Leo Durocher
Durocher, Leo Ernest (The Lip)
B: Jul 27, 1905   D: Oct 7, 1991

Pos: SS   BA: .247
Hits: 1,320   HRs: 24
RBI: 567   BBs: 377
Managerial Record
Won: 2,008   Lost: 1,709   Pct: .540

His contemporaries said, "Leo was never at a loss for words, and what words they were!" Involved in controversy throughout his career, the foul-mouthed man known as "The Lip" argued with everybody. He was ejected, fined, suspended, and fired many times. In 1941 the Dodgers were on a train headed home after winning the pennant on

Leo Durocher at an Old-timers Game.

the road. The players became excited and agitated as they got into Brooklyn, and Durocher convinced the train engineer to skip one stop and hurry on to their station. Unfortunately, the bypassed stop was where team owner Larry MacPhail and his friends were waiting to board the train to congratulate the players. Durocher was fired – but re-hired in time for the World Series.

The Flatbush faithful were shocked when Durocher jumped to the hated Giants in mid-season 1948. With Durocher at the helm, the Giants won two pennants in 1951 and 1954. He made a comeback in the late 1960s and almost won the NL flag with the Cubs.
Playing Career: *1925, 1928-1941, 1943, 1945; NY A, Cin N, StL N, Brk N*
Managerial Career: *1939-1946, 1948-1955, 1966-1973; Brk N, NY N, Hou N, Chi N*

Frank Dwyer
Dwyer, John Francis
B: Mar 25, 1868   D: Feb 4, 1943

Pos: P   ERA: 3.85
W-L: 176-152   SOs: 563
ShOs: 12   Saves: 6
Managerial Record
Won: 52   Lost: 83   Pct: .385

After playing for six teams in five years, Dwyer spent the next seven years with the Reds as the ace of their staff. He won 18 games or more seven times. Dwyer was the starting pitcher in at least 28 games for nine consecutive years, finishing 230 of 272 starts over that period.
Playing Career: *1888-1899; Chi N, Chi P, Cin AA, Mil AA, StL N, Cin N*
Managerial Career: *1902; Det A*

Jim Dwyer
Dwyer, James Edward
B: Jun 3, 1950

Pos: OF, DH   BA: .260
Hits: 719   HRs: 77
RBI: 349   BBs: 402

Dwyer was a minor league batting champion who became a pinch hitter in the majors. In his first World Series appearance he homered off John Denny in 1983. In 1987 Dwyer hit 15 homers in only 241 at-bats.
Playing Career: *1973-1990; StL N, Mon N, NY N, Bos A, Bal A, Min A*

Eddie Dyer
Dyer, Edwin Hawley
B: Oct 11, 1900   D: Apr 20, 1964

Pos: P   ERA: 4.75
W-L: 15-15   SOs: 63
ShOs: 2   Saves: 3
Managerial Record
Won: 446   Lost: 325   Pct: .578

Pitcher Dyer was used frequently as a pinch hitter, but struggled on the mound. He did post a win in the 1926 World Series. After leaving St. Louis, Dyer managed nine minor league champion teams before taking over the Cardinals' minor league operations in 1943. When Billy Southworth left the big club to manage the Braves, Dyer replaced him. He won the 1946 pennant with the Cards, then guided the Red Birds to the Series win over the Red Sox.
Playing Career: *1922-1927; StL N*
Managerial Career: *1946-1950; StL N*

Jimmy Dygert
Dygert, James Henry
B: Jul 5, 1884   D: Feb 8, 1936

Pos: P   ERA: 2.65
W-L: 57-49   SOs: 583
ShOs: 16   No-hitters: 1

Dygert was the Athletics' starting pitcher in the 1909 17-inning 9-9 tie game that gave the pennant to the Tigers. The little spitballer won a career-high 21 that season. When he lost control of the slippery elm pitch he left the big leagues.
Playing Career: *1905-1910; Phi A*

Jimmy Dykes
Dykes, James Joseph
B: Nov 10, 1896   D: Jun 15, 1976

Pos: 3B, 2B, SS, 1B, OF   BA: .280
Hits: 2,256   HRs: 109
RBI: 1,071   BBs: 954
Managerial Record
Won: 1,406   Lost: 1,541   Pct: .477

Dykes was trained to replace Connie Mack as manager of the Athletics. Yet when the time came for the changeover, no one, least of all Dykes, was prepared for the A's without Mack. Fans were curious at first, but reality set in quickly. The last-place Tigers drew

Jimmy Dykes.

almost twice as many fans as the 1952 fourth-place A's. Dykes left after 1953. In all his 21 years of managing, Dykes's teams finished in the first division only eight times. In August, 1960, when the Indians and Tigers were lower in the standings than their owners thought they should be, the two teams swapped managers. It was the only trade of managers in the history of the game.
Playing Career: *1918-1939; Phi A, Chi A*
Managerial Career: *1934-1946, 1951-1954, 1958-1961; Phi A, Bal A, Cin N, Cle A, Det A*

Lenny Dykstra
Dykstra, Leonard Kyle
B: Feb 10, 1963

Pos: OF	BA: .288
Hits: 1,112	HRs: 71
RBI: 349	BBs: 513

Dykstra's first major league hit was a home run. He was part of a center field trio, with Mookie Wilson and Kevin Mitchell, who fueled the 1986 Mets' championship season. Dykstra led off Game Three of the Series with a home run, the 14th person to start a Fall Classic game with a round trip. An ideal lead-off hitter, Dykstra led the NL in hits and batted .325 in 1990, his first year as a Phillie. He scored 143 runs with 129 walks as the Phillies won the 1993 pennant.
Playing Career: *1985-; NY N, Phi N*

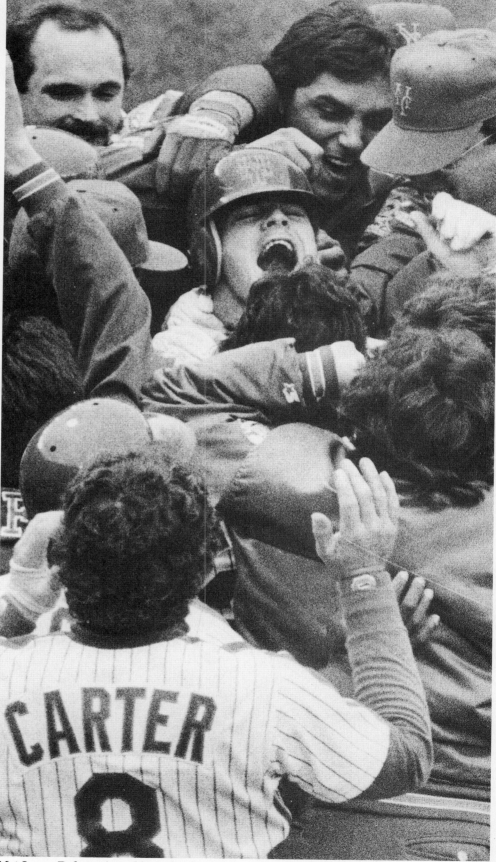

Met Lenny Dykstra is mobbed after his homer that won Game Three of the 1986 NLCS.

Jake Early
Early, Jacob Willard
B: May 19, 1915   D: May 31, 1985

Pos: C   BA: .241
Hits: 532   HRs: 32
RBI: 264   BBs: 280

Alternating with Rick Ferrell to catch the Senators' four knuckleballers, Early was a part-time player except in 1943, when he also caught the entire All-Star Game. He was a chatterbox behind the plate, mocking play-by-play broadcasts to distract hitters.
Playing Career: *1939-1943, 1946-1949; Was A, StL A*

George Earnshaw
Earnshaw, George Livingston (Moose)
B: Feb 15, 1900   D: Dec 1, 1976

Pos: P   ERA: 4.38
W-L: 127-93   SOs: 1,005
ShOs: 18   Saves: 12

The big right-hander from Swarthmore College pitched a shutout in Game Five of the 1930 World Series. Manager Connie Mack

George Earnshaw.

played a hunch and started the big guy in Game Six, two days later. Earnshaw won, 7-1. He posted 24 victories in l929, 86 in the years 1929-1932. Earnshaw was a fastball and curveball pitcher whose major league career was delayed by an extended stint with the minor league Baltimore Orioles.
Playing Career: *1928-1936; Phi A, Chi A, Brk N, StL N*

Mike Easler
Easler, Michael Anthony
B: Nov 29, 1950

Pos: OF, DH   BA: .293
Hits: 1,078   HRs: 118
RBI: 522   BBs: 321

A bat for hire, Easler always hit but rarely fielded. He was traded three times in the minor leagues before finally winning a full-time job with the Pirates in 1980. There he hit .338 with 21 homers and 74 RBI in 393 at-bats. He batted in the 1981 All-Star Game.
Playing Career: *1973-1987; Hou N, Cal A, Pit N, Bos A, NY A, Phi N*

Luke Easter
Easter, Lucious
B: Aug 4, 1914   D: Mar 28, 1979

Pos: 1B, OF   BA: .274
Hits: 472   HRs: 93
RBI: 340   BBs: 174

Easter played ball with the Homestead Grays in the Negro Leagues before signing with Cleveland. He hit 28 home runs as a rookie, including a 477-foot shot which is considered the longest ever hit at Cleveland's Municipal Stadium. Easter compiled a .481 lifetime slugging average. After leaving the Indians, he continued playing ball in Buffalo, where he is credited with revitalizing interest in the sport in that former NL city. His real age was not known until his death. Easter was actually 34 during his rookie season.
Playing Career: *1949-1954; Cle A*

Rawly Eastwick
Eastwick, Rawlins Jackson
B: Oct 24, 1950

Pos: P   ERA: 3.30
W-L: 28-27   SOs: 295
ShOs: 0   Saves: 68

Eastwick never lost in 10 postseason games, going 4-0 with two saves. He was a rookie sensation in 1975, tying for the NL lead with 22 saves and a 2.60 ERA. The next year he led the NL with 26 saves, earning him the Fireman of the Year Award.
Playing Career: *1974-1981; Cin N, StL N, NY A, Phi N, KC A, Chi N*

Charlie Ebbets
Ebbets, Charles Hercules
B: Oct 29, 1859   D: Apr 18, 1925

Managerial Record
Won: 38   Lost: 68   Pct: .358

Charlie Ebbets (r) with Judge Landis.

Charlie Ebbets joined the Dodgers organization as a bookkeeper in 1883, gradually bought shares in the club, then become president in 1898. His monument was the Brooklyn ballpark, which was financed in 1912 by selling half of the club to the McKeever brothers, who were Brooklyn contractors. When the park was opened the next year, Ebbets quizzed the local sportswriters about the name. They suggested Ebbets Field. His Dodgers flew pennant flags there in 1916 and 1920.

Ebbets is sometimes credited with inventing the rain check and with suggesting that teams with the worst records should draft first. He had a deserved reputation for honesty and was popular in Brooklyn. At the turn of the century, Ebbets was widely quoted when he said, "Baseball is in its infancy."
Managerial Career: *1898; Brk N*

Dennis Eckersley
Eckersley, Dennis Lee
B: Oct 3, 1954

Pos: P   ERA: 3.45
W-L: 183-149   SOs: 2,198
ShOs: 20   No-hitters: 1
                         Saves: 275

Eckersley is the best relief pitcher in the game today. His control is legendary; he walked only 55 batters in the six years from 1987 to 1992. Eckersley broke into the AL with the Indians in 1975 as a cocky 20-year-old with

Dennis Eckersley celebrates his no-hitter.

shoulder-length hair and an explosive fast-ball. He fanned 200 batters in 1976, and no-hit the Angels 1-0 on May 30, 1977. He compiled a 20-8 record with a 2.99 ERA with the Red Sox in 1978. Then his fastball deserted him.

Eckersley became the stopper out of the bullpen, and he is simply the best there ever was at the position. In 1988 he led the AL with 45 saves, capturing 236 saves from 1987 to 1992. In 1992 he was better than ever, saving 51 contests and racking up a 7-1 record with a 1.91 ERA. He won both the Cy Young and the MVP Awards. Selected for the All-Star Game six times, Eckersley has also pitched in five LCS and three World Series.
Playing Career: *1975-; Cle A, Bos A, Chi N, Oak A*

Spike Eckert
Eckert, William Dole
B: Jan 20, 1909

Eckert was a retired Air Force general, then a supply officer who specialized in negotiating defense contracts before he was elected commissioner of baseball in 1965. When he became baseball's leader, he knew nothing about baseball's inner workings and had not attended a game in 10 years. Eckert was quiet, bright, honest and willing, but he was in the wrong place at the wrong time. Lee McPhail was appointed to advise him, but Eckert became a symbol of executive futility, incurring the public's ire by refusing to cancel games after the assassinations of Robert Kennedy and Martin Luther King. He earned the owners' disdain by refusing to deal forcefully with player unionization. Having no confidence in Eckert's ability to handle the situation, the owners voted him out in early 1969, though he still had three years left on his contract.

Hank Edwards
Edwards, Henry Albert
B: Jan 29, 1919   D: Jun 22, 1988

Pos: OF	BA: .280
Hits: 613	HRs: 51
RBI: 276	BBs: 208

Edwards hit .301 and led the AL with 16 triples in 1946, his only full season. He hit 15 homers the next year, but a series of injuries–including dislocating a shoulder landing on a fence while making a leaping catch–ended his days as a regular player.
Playing Career: *1941-1943, 1946-1953; Cle A, Chi N, Brk N, Cin N, Chi A, StL A*

Johnny Edwards
Edwards, John Alban
B: Jun 10, 1938

Pos: C	BA: .242
Hits: 1,106	HRs: 81
RBI: 524	BBs: 465

Edwards was one of the best defensive catchers in baseball. He turned the young Astros pitchers into a fearsome staff. In 1969 the Houston rotation struck out 1,221 batters, and Edwards recorded 1,135 putouts and 1,221 total chances, all major league records. Edwards was a strong-armed, take-charge receiver from Ohio State University. He won two Gold Gloves and was chosen for three All-Star teams. As a rookie playing in the 1961 World Series he hit .364 for the Reds.
Playing Career: *1961-1974; Cin N, StL N, Hou N*

Dick Egan
Egan, Richard Joseph
B: Jun 23, 1884   D: Jul 7, 1947

Pos: 2B	BA: .249
Hits: 767	HRs: 4
RBI: 292	BBs: 291

Egan hit over .250 only once in four years as the Reds' regular second baseman, but he stole 141 bases. Teammate Bob Bescher led the NL each year in stolen bases, and the two often teamed on double steals. Egan led NL second basemen in fielding in 1912.
Playing Career: *1908-1916; Cin N, Brk N, Bos N*

Howard Ehmke
Ehmke, Howard Jonathan
B: Apr 24, 1894   D: Mar 17, 1959

Pos: P	ERA: 3.75
W-L: 166-166	SOs: 1,030
ShOs: 20	No-hitters: 1

Ehmke was the surprise starter in the 1929 World Series opener. The stunned Cubs struck out a record 13 times as Athletics pitchers Lefty Grove, George Earnshaw and Rube Walberg watched from the bench. Foxy manager Connie Mack had scouted the right-handed hitting Cubs and thought the submarine hurling of Ehmke would give them trouble. He was right. Earlier, Ehmke was a star pitcher; in 1923 he won 20 games and tossed a no-hitter.
Playing Career: *1915-1917, 1919-1930; Buf F, Det A, Bos A, Phi A*

Red Ehret
Ehret, Philip Sydney
B: Aug 31, 1868   D: Jul 28, 1940

Pos: P	ERA: 4.02
W-L: 139-167	SOs: 848
ShOs: 14	Saves: 4

Ehret was a top pitcher on the famous Louisville team that went from last place in the AA in 1889 to the pennant in 1890. Ehret's record went from 10-29 to 25-14. He lost 167 games pitching for poor teams in the 1890s.
Playing Career: *1888-1898; KC AA, Lou AA, Pit N, StL N, Cin N, Lou N*

Commissioner William "Spike" Eckert (c) with Ford Frick (r) and Lee McPhail, 1965.

Mark Eichhorn.

Mark Eichhorn
Eichhorn, Mark Anthony
B: Nov 21, 1960

Pos: P	ERA: 2.99
W-L: 41-36	SOs: 581
ShOS: 0	Saves: 31

Eichhorn, with his distinctive sidearm, underhand delivery, is a terror to right-handed batters. In specialty relief, he has managed to appear in an average of 62 games per year since becoming a bullpen staple in 1986, the year he went 14-6 with a 1.72 ERA. He led AL pitchers in games with 89 in 1987.
Playing Career: *1982, 1986-; Tor A, Atl N, Cal A*

Jim Eisenreich
Eisenreich, James Michael
B: Apr 18, 1959

Pos: OF, 1B, DH	BA: .283
Hits: 709	HR: 32
RBI: 291	BBs: 176

Eisenreich struggled in Minnesota for several years before he was properly diagnosed with Tourette's Syndrome. He retired in 1984, but made a dramatic comeback, aided by new drug therapy. His courage and persistence are an inspiration for other ballplayers. He hit .318 for the pennant-winning Phillies in 1993.
Playing Career: *1982-1984, 1987-; Min A, KC A, Phi N*

Kid Elberfeld
Elberfeld, Norman Arthur
(The Tabasco Kid)
B: Apr 13, 1875   D: Jan 13, 1944

Pos: SS	BA: .271
Hits: 1,237	HRs: 10
RBI: 535	BBs: 427
Managerial Record	
Won: 27 Lost: 71 Pct: .276	

The Tabasco Kid played a fiery brand of baseball, challenging baserunners to slash him out of their way. He used whiskey as a disinfectant, pouring it over the spike wounds on his legs, which were badly scarred. Elberfeld broke in with the Tigers as a shortstop and batted .308 in 1901, his first full season. Popular in New York, he was the Highlanders' regular shortstop from 1903 to 1909, except for the 1908 season, when he managed.
Playing Career: *1898-1899, 1901-1911, 1914; Phi N, Cin N, Det A, NY A, Was A, Brk N*
Managerial Career: *1908; NY A*

Lee Elia
Elia, Lee Constantine
B: Jul 16, 1937

Pos: SS	BA: .203
Hits: 43	HRs: 3
RBI: 25	BBs: 15
Managerial Record	
Won: 238 Lost: 300 Pct: .442	

Elia, who managed the Cubs before lights were installed at Wrigley Field, had a theory about the employment status of Cubs fans in the bleachers. Elia felt they were all unemployed degenerates – who else could attend afternoon baseball games?
Playing Career: *1966, 1968; Chi A, Chi N*
Managerial Career: *1982-1983, 1987-1988; Chi N, Phi N*

Lee Elia.

Hod Eller
Eller, Horace Owen
B: Jul 5, 1894   D: Jul 18, 1961

Pos: P	ERA: 2.62
W-L: 61-40	SOs: 381
ShOs: 10	No-hitters: 1

Eller produced two complete game victories in the 1919 World Series for the Reds, and fanned six straight batters in Game Five. That year he went 19-9 with a 2.39 ERA, his best ever. Arm troubles ended his effectiveness in 1921.
Playing Career: *1917-1921; Cin N*

Bob Elliott
Elliott, Robert Irving
B: Nov 26, 1916   D: May 4, 1966

Pos: 3B	BA: .289
Hits: 2,061	HRs: 170
RBI: 1,195	BBs: 967
Managerial Record	
Won: 58 Lost: 96 Pct: .377	

Braves players called Elliott "Mr. Team." He was his manager's dream: hard working, conscientious and very good. The 1947 NL MVP, Elliott batted .317, hit 22 homers and 35 doubles, drove in 113, scored 93 runs, and led the league's third basemen in fielding. A seven-time All-Star because of his big bat, Elliott averaged 20 homers and 29 doubles from 1947 to 1951. He was a top fielder as well, frequently leading the league in assists, putouts and double plays.

When the Braves made it to the World Series against the Indians in 1948, Elliott hit .333 with two home runs and five RBI.
Playing Career: *1939-1953; Pit N, Bos N, NY N, StL A, Chi A*
Managerial Career: *1960; KC A*

Jumbo Elliott
Elliott, James Thomas
B: Oct 22, 1900   D: Jan 7, 1970

Pos: P	ERA: 4.24
W-L: 163-74	SOs: 453
ShOs: 8	Saves: 12

At 6'3" and 240 pounds, Elliott was the biggest man in the majors until Jumbo Brown came along. Elliott tied for the NL lead with 19 wins and a 4.27 ERA while pitching for the sixth-place Phillies in 1931, his best season.
Playing Career: *1923, 1925, 1927-1934; StL A, Brk N, Phi N, Bos N*

Dock Ellis
Ellis, Dock Phillip
B: Mar 11, 1945

Pos: P	ERA: 3.45
W-L: 138-119	SOs: 1,136
ShOs: 14	No-hitters: 1

Ellis was the most controversial character in one of baseball's most chaotic eras. He antagonized the Pirates' front office by dressing wildly and hanging around the clubhouse

Phillies pitcher Dick Ellsworth, in 1967.

Bob Elliott crosses the plate after hitting a three-run homer during the 1948 WS.

with curlers in his Afro hairstyle. He threw a no-hitter while tripping on acid. Later, Ellis tied Dizzy Dean's record by hitting the first three batters he faced, claiming it was an attempt to rouse his teammates from lethargy. He won 19 games in 1971, and appeared in the All-Star Game and the NLCS.
Playing Career: *1968-1979; Pit N, NY A, Oak A, Tex A, NY N*

John Ellis
Ellis, John Charles
B: Aug 21, 1948

Pos: C, 1B, DH	BA: .262
Hits: 699	HRs: 69
RBI: 391	BBs: 190

Ellis was a part-time player whose lack of fielding made him a designated hitter. He hit .270 and .285 for the Indians, then had a .419 average for the Rangers in May 1976, when he suffered a broken leg, dislocated ankle, and torn ligaments sliding into second.
Playing Career: *1969-1981; NY A, Cle A, Tex A*

Sammy Ellis
Ellis, Samuel Joseph
B: Feb 11, 1941

Pos: P	ERA: 4.15
W-L: 63-58	SOs: 677
ShOs: 3	Saves: 18

Armed with a blazing fastball and fluttering knuckleball, Ellis won a career-high 22 games in 1965, but always claimed he was more valuable to Cincinnati the previous year when he went 10-3 with 14 saves and a 2.57 ERA. Since finishing his playing career in 1969, Ellis has served the Yankees and Cubs as pitching coach.
Playing Career: *1962, 1964-1969; Cin N, Cal A, Chi A*

Dick Ellsworth
Ellsworth, Richard Clark
B: Mar 22, 1940

Pos: P	ERA: 3.72
W-L: 115-137	SOs: 1,140
ShOs: 9	Saves: 5

Coming from the fertile crescent of pitchers, Fresno High School, California, Ellsworth joined fellow graduates Tom Seaver and Jim Maloney in the big leagues. Ellsworth won 22 games in 1962 with a 2.11 ERA. He was an All-Star selection the following year.
Playing Career: *1958, 1960-1971; Chi N, Phi N, Bos A, Cle A, Mil A*

Don Elston
Elston, Donald Ray
B: Apr 6, 1929

Pos: P	ERA: 3.69
W-L: 49-54	SOs: 519
ShOs: 0	Saves: 63

After a brief interlude with the Dodgers, Elston returned to the Cubs, where he switched to relief and became one of the NL's best firemen. In 1958 he set a club record with a league-leading 69 appearances. Elston was picked for the 1959 NL All-Star team.
Playing Career: *1953, 1957-1964; Chi N, Brk N*

Bones Ely
William Frederick
B: Jun 7, 1863   D: Jan 10, 1952

Pos: SS	BA: .258
Hits: 1,331	HRs: 24
RBI: 586	BBs: 257

Ely left the major leagues in 1902 to become a playing manager in the minors. He had been the Pirates' shortstop from 1896 to 1901, when he was dismissed from the team for allegedly trying to persuade players to jump to the new American League.
Playing Career: *1884, 1886, 1890-1891, 1893-1901; Buf N, Lou AA, Syr AA, Brk N, StL N, Pit N, Phi A, Was A*

Cubs third baseman/shortstop Woody English with his new wife in 1930.

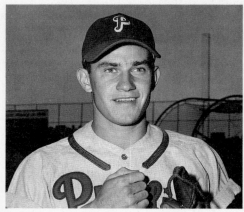

Rookie of the Year Del Ennis, 1946.

Joe Engel
Engel, Joseph William
B: Mar 12, 1893   D: Jun 12, 1969

Pos: P	ERA: 3.38
W-L: 17-23	SOs: 151
ShOs: 2	Saves: 4

The greatest promoter in minor league baseball history, Engel was the owner of the Southern Association Chattanooga Lookouts after his playing career. He staged elephant hunts. He hired Jackie Mitchell, a female ballplayer, to pitch in an exhibition game, where she struck out Babe Ruth and Lou Gehrig. Engel gave away bizarre and valuable gifts to pack people into his baseball park, and he was highly successful.
Playing Career: *1912-1915, 1917, 1919-1920; Was A, Cin N, Cle A*

Clyde Engle
Engle, Arthur Clyde
B: Mar 19, 1884   D: Dec 26, 1939

Pos: OF, 1B	BA: .262
Hits: 431	HRs: 31
RBI: 181	BBs: 120

Engle, a utility player, pinch-hit for the Red Sox in the 10th inning of Game Eight of the 1912 World Series. The Giants' center fielder muffed Engle's fly ball, and Tris Speaker singled him in to tie the score. The Red Sox won the Series on Larry Gardner's sacrifice fly.
Playing Career: *1909-1916; NY A, Bos A, Buf F, Cle A*

Woody English
English, Elwood George
B: Mar 2, 1907

Pos: SS, 3B	BA: .286
Hits: 1,356	HRs: 32
RBI: 422	BBs: 571

English was the three-hole hitter who was a principle contributor in 1930 to Hack Wilson's 190-RBI season. A singles hitter, English left loads of runners on base for Wilson. English batted a career-best .335 that year and was among NL leaders in runs scored, triples and walks. He hit .319 the next season while leading NL shortstops in putouts. He led NL third basemen in fielding with a .973 mark in 1933 and played in the All-Star Game that year.
Playing Career: *1927-1938; Chi N, Brk N*

Del Ennis
Ennis, Delmer
B: Jun 8, 1925

Pos: OF	BA: .284
Hits: 2,063	HRs: 288
RBI: 1,284	BBs: 597

The first Rookie of the Year Award went to Ennis in 1946, when he hit .313. He played on the All-Star Game that year and in two others. Ennis knocked in more than 100 runs seven times, leading the NL with 126 RBI in 1950. He was a power hitter, exceeding 30 home runs twice, and hitting three in one game on July 23, 1955. He broke up no-hitters three times in his career. In 1983, the Phillies'

100th anniversary year, Ennis was chosen for the "Centennial Team."
Playing Career: *1946-1959; Phi N, StL N, Cin N, Chi A*

Mike Epstein
Epstein, Michael Peter
B: Apr 4, 1943

Pos: 1B	BA: .244
Hits: 695	HRs: 130
RBI: 380	BBs: 448

Epstein was a power hitter who was Minor League Player of the Year in 1966 with Rochester. A top prospect stuck behind Boog Powell, Epstein had his best years with the Senators. In 1970 he smacked 30 homers with 85 RBI.
Playing Career: *1966-1974; Bal A, Was A, Oak A, Tex A, Cal A*

Carl Erskine
Erskine, Carl Daniel (Oisk)
B: Dec 13, 1926

Pos: P	ERA: 4.00
W-L: 122-78	SOs: 981
ShOs: 14	No-hitters: 2

Erskine combined with Don Newcombe to lead the pitching staff of the powerful Dodgers teams of the 1950s. He won 61 percent of his decisions, all with the Dodgers. Although only 2-2 in World Series play, Erskine broke Howard Ehmke's strikeout record when he fanned 14 Yankees in Game Three of the 1953 World Series. His record lasted until another Dodger, Sandy Koufax, fanned 15 Yankees in Game One of the 1963 Series. Erskine tossed no-hitters on June 19, 1952, and on May 12, 1956.

The 5'10" right-hander injured his shoulder during his rookie season and pitched in pain most of his career. He won 20 games only once, in 1953, leading the NL in won-lost percentage with a .769 mark. He was a straight fastball pitcher with a curve and change-up in his repertoire. Just before the Dodgers deserted Brooklyn, Erskine's arm problems worsened and he became a bullpen pitcher, retiring after two seasons in Los Angeles.
Playing Career: *1948-1959; Brk N, LA N*

Nick Esasky
Esasky, Nicholas A.
B: Feb 24, 1960

Pos: 1B, 3B, OF	BA: .250
Hits: 677	HRs: 122
RBI: 427	BBs: 314

Esasky replaced Johnny Bench at third base for the Reds in 1983, and made the Topps all-rookie team. After six years in Cincinnati, Esasky found a home in Boston, where he batted .277 with 30 homers and 108 RBI in 1989. He signed a free agent contract with the Braves but became ill.
Playing Career: *1983-1990; Cin N, Bos A, Atl N*

Duke Esper
Esper, Charles H.
B: Jul 28, 1868   D: Aug 31, 1910

Pos: P	ERA: 4.40
W-L: 101-100	SOs: 456
ShOs: 4	Saves: 5

Esper's career rode a seesaw. He was 20-15 with the Phillies in 1891, then lost 28 games with the pathetic Senators in 1893. The next year he found himself in the starting rotation for the legendary Orioles. He tossed a shutout in the 1895 Temple Cup Series, and the following year had a 14-5 record for a .737 winning percentage.
Playing Career: *1890-1898; Phi AA, Pit N, Phi N, Was N, Bal N, StL N*

Chuck Essegian
Essegian, Charles Abraham
B: Aug 9, 1931

Pos: OF	BA: .255
Hits: 260	HRs: 47
RBI: 150	BBs: 97

Essegian, a member of Stanford's 1952 Rose Bowl team, pinch-hit two home runs for the Dodgers in the 1959 World Series. He batted .667, and slugged 1.667. His sixth-inning pinch homer tied Game Two, and he had another pinch-hit round-tripper in the final game as the Dodgers took their first World Championship in Los Angeles.
Playing Career: *1958-1963; Phi N, StL N, LA N, Bal A, KC A, Cle A*

Bobby Estalella
Estalella y Ventoza, Roberto
B: Apr 25, 1911   D: Jan 6, 1991

Pos: OF	BA: .282
Hits: 620	HRs: 44
RBI: 308	BBs: 350

The Cuban-born Estalella was a regular during World War II because he was exempted from the draft. He batted .298 and .299 for the Athletics in 1944 and 1945. After jumping to the Mexican League, he was suspended from 1946 to 1948.
Playing Career: *1935-1936, 1939, 1941-1945, 1949; Was A, StL A, Phi A*

Dude Esterbrook
Esterbrook, Thomas John
B: Jun 9, 1857   D: Apr 30, 1901

Pos: 1B, OF, C, 3B	BA: .261
Hits: 741	HRs: 6
RBI: 203 (inc.)	BBs: 70
Managerial Record	
Won: 2 Lost: 8 Pct: .200	

Fashionably dressed, and sporting a trendy Van Dyke beard, Esterbrook was a favorite in New York. He played there six seasons, including the 1883-1884 seasons, when the players took Native American names in a silly public relations campaign.
Playing Career: *1880, 1882-1891; Buf N, Cle N, NY AA, NY N, Ind N, Lou AA, Brk N*
Managerial Career: *1889; Lou AA*

Andy Etchebarren
Etchebarren, Andrew Auguste
B: Jun 20, 1943

Pos: C	BA: .235
Hits: 615	HRs: 49
RBI: 309	BBs: 246

Etchebarren made the All-Star squad twice while hitting less than .222. He caught for six division-winning teams, including the 1966 Orioles who swept the highly favored Dodgers in the World Series. His best season was 1971, when he hit .270 and made another World Series appearance.
Playing Career: *1962, 1965-1978; Bal A, Cal A, Mil A*

Nick Etten
Etten, Nicholas Raymond Thomas
B: Sep 19, 1913   D: Oct 18, 1990

Pos: 1B	BA: .277
Hits: 921	HRs: 89
RBI: 526	BBs: 480

When Etten was traded to New York in 1943 after two seasons with the dismal Phillies, he exclaimed, "Imagine a man in that environment hearing that he had been sold to the Yankees!" Etten led the AL with 22 homers and 97 walks in 1944, and with 111 RBI in 1945.
Playing Career: *1938-1939, 1941-1947; Phi A, Phi N, NY A*

Bill Evans
Evans, William G.
B: Feb 10, 1884   D: Jan 23, 1956
Hall of Fame 1973

One of the foremost umpires in AL history, Evans developed a dignified style and a reputation for fairness and integrity. In Game Two of the 1909 World Series, the Pirates' Dots Miller hit a low line drive along the right field foul line toward some temporary bleachers that obstructed the views of Evans and Bill Klem, the other umpire. Neither saw the ball land. The arbiters marched to the outfield and Evans questioned the fans. He decided the ball had landed fair then bounced into the crowd. Miller, who had circled the bases, was

Umpire Bill Evans.

sent back to second with a ground rule double.

From 1920 to 1927 Evans wrote a syndicated column, "Billy Evans Says." He also authored a book, *Umpiring From the Inside.* After his 22-year umpiring career, Evans became the first general manager for the Indians. He was later director of the farm system for Boston and president of the Southern Association.
Umpiring Career: *1906-1927; AL (6 WS)*

Darrell Evans
Evans, Darrell Wayne
B: May 26, 1947

Pos: 3B, 1B	BA: .248
Hits: 2,223	HRs: 414
RBI: 1,354	BBs: 1,605

Evans became the oldest player in history to reach the 40-home run mark when he clobbered 40 in 1985, giving him the home run title. He hit more four-baggers than any other player past the age of 40, and he was the only player to hit 40 homers in each league. In 1973 and 1974 he led the NL in walks with 124 and 126. He is ranked eighth in walks on the all-time list.

Evans credits Ted Williams's book for teaching him to hit, and Eddie Mathews with teaching him to pull the ball. Batting third in front of Hank Aaron, Evans was one of the trio of 1973 Braves to wallop 40 or more homers – Aaron hit 40, Evans 41, and Davey Johnson 43. On June 15, 1983, Evans hit three homers in a game. After that season, he signed with the Tigers, who earned dividends immediately when he hit a three-run tater on Opening Day 1984. Detroit went on to a 35-5 start as they coasted to the AL pennant and World Series Championship.
Playing Career: *1969-1989; Atl N, SF N, Det A*

Dwight Evans.

Dwight Evans
Evans, Dwight Michael (Dewey)
B: Nov 3, 1951

Pos: OF	BA: .272
Hits: 2,446	HRs: 385
RBI: 1,384	BBs: 1,391

Only Carl Yastrzemski has played more games for the Red Sox than Dwight Evans. Originally breaking into the majors as a rocket-armed outfielder, Evans gradually became one of the AL's better hitters, averaging 19 home runs and 30 doubles each season from 1978 through 1989. He led the AL in homers with 22 in the strike-shortened 1981 season. He also developed into a terror on the bases, four times topping the .400 mark in on-base percentage. He drew more walks than anyone else in the AL three times, and ranks 20th on the all-time bases on balls list.

In the 11th inning of Game Six of the 1975 World Series, Evans made a lunging catch that robbed Joe Morgan of a Series-ending home run. The out started the inning-ending double play that set the stage for Carlton Fisk's famous "moon shot" home run in the 12th. The next year Evans won the first of eight Gold Glove Awards. Among outfielders, only Willie Mays, Roberto Clemente and Al Kaline have more.
Playing Career: *1972-1991; Bos A, Bal A*

Joe Evans
Evans, Joseph Patton (Doc)
B: May 15, 1895   D: Aug 9, 1953

Pos: OF, 3B	BA: .259
Hits: 529	HRs: 3
RBI: 209	BBs: 211

Evans hit .308 in the 1920 World Series for the Indians, slashing three hits in Game Six. He had been converted from third base to the outfield that year, alternating with left fielder Charlie Jamieson. Evans became a physician after leaving baseball.
Playing Career: *1915-1925; Cle A, Was A, StL A*

Steve Evans
Evans, Louis Richard
B: Feb 17, 1885   D: Dec 28, 1943

Pos: OF	BA: .285
Hits: 963	HRs: 32
RBI: 466	BBs: 359

Evans had a reputation as a comedian, once appearing in the outfield with a parasol to shade himself from the sun. His best season was 1914 with the Tip Tops of the Federal League, when he batted .348, hit 41 doubles and drove in 96.
Playing Career: *1908-1915; NY N, StL N, Brk F, Bal F*

Hoot Evers
Evers, Walter Arthur
B: Feb 8, 1921   D: Jan 25, 1991

Pos: OF	BA: .272
Hits: 1,055	HRs: 98
RBI: 565	BBs: 415

Hoot Evers never attained the stardom predicted for him. Delayed four years by World War II, he got his first major league hit at age 25. Evers hit over .300 three straight years, making the All-Star Game twice and leading the AL in triples in 1950.
Playing Career: *1941, 1946-1956; Det A, Bos A, NY N, Bal A, Cle A*

Johnny Evers
Evers, John Joseph (Trojan; The Crab)
B: Jul 21, 1881   D: Mar 28, 1947
Hall of Fame 1939

Pos: 2B	BA: .270
Hits: 1,658	HRs: 12
RBI: 538	BBs: 778
Managerial Record	
Won: 180 Lost: 192 Pct: .484	

The middle of Franklin Pierce Adams's immortal refrain, "Tinkers to Evers to Chance," Evers was also the middle of the Cubs' infield that led the team to four pennants in five years. An all-around good player, he was also the brains of the outfit, and carried a tattered copy of the playing rules in his back pocket.

In 1908 Evers's knowledge of the rules gave the Cubs a pennant. In a September 3 game at the Polo Grounds, Al Bridwell singled in

Manager Johnny Evers (3rd from r) and his team greet the King of England in 1924.

Mike McCormick from third with two out in the bottom of the ninth to give the Giants an apparent victory. The runner at first base, Giants rookie Fred Merkle, did not touch second, but as was the custom of the day, headed for the clubhouse. Evers called for the ball and touched the keystone bag for the force-out. Umpire Hank O'Day called Merkle out and declared the game a tie. When the two teams ended the season tied for the NL pennant, a rematch was scheduled for the September 3 game; the Cubs won.

Playing Career: *1902-1917, 1922, 1929; Chi N, Bos N, Phi N, Chi A*
Managerial Career: *1913, 1921, 1924; Chi N, Chi A*

Bob Ewing
Ewing, George Lemuel
B: Apr 24, 1873   D: Jun 20, 1947

Pos: P	ERA: 2.49
W-L: 125-118	SOs: 998
ShOs: 19	Saves: 4

Ewing was a workhorse for the Reds during the century's first decade, compiling 200 or more innings for eight consecutive seasons, and topping 300 innings three times. Ewing threw his spitball for a 20-11 record in 1905. His 1907 ERA was 1.73.

Playing Career: *1902-1912; Cin N, Phi N, StL N*

Buck Ewing
Ewing, William
B: Oct 17, 1859   D: Oct 20, 1906
Hall of Fame 1946

Pos: C, 1B, OF, 3B	BA: .303
Hits: 1,625	HRs: 70
RBI: 738 (inc.)	BBs: 392
Managerial Record	
Won: 489 Lost: 395 Pct: .553	

Until Mickey Cochrane, Bill Dickey and Gabby Hartnett came along, Ewing was the catcher on everyone's dream team. One of the best all-around players of the 19th century, Ewing's stolen base total was 354 despite the fact that steals have not yet been counted for the first six years he played. In 1988 he stole a career-high 53 bases. He was NL home run champ in 1883, and he topped the league with 20 triples in 1884. He scored 1,129 runs during his career.

Ewing was good at throwing out baserunners; he led NL catchers in assists three times in the 1880s, and in double plays twice. In addition to catching, he was frequently stationed in the outfield or at first base. Ewing also pitched 47 innings. His brother John pitched for New York in the 1890 Players' League when Buck was the catcher and manager. The next year John and Buck combined for a 21-8 record, leading the NL with a .724 winning percentage and a 2.27 ERA.

Playing Career: *1880-1897; Tro N, NY N, NY P, Cle N, Cin N*
Managerial Career: *1890, 1895-1900; NY P, Cin N, NY N*

Nineteenth-century catcher Buck Ewing set the standard for play at that position.

Red Faber

Faber, Urban Charles
B: Sep 6, 1888   D: Sep 25, 1976
Hall of Fame 1964

Pos: P	ERA: 3.15
W-L: 254-213	SOs: 1,471
ShOs: 30	Saves: 28

Purchased by the White Sox for $3,500 in 1913, Faber was loaned to the Giants for a postseason world tour before he ever pitched an inning of major league ball for his own club. Faber won four games against his future teammates during the world tour. In the 1917 World Series, the Iowa farm boy won three games. Service in the U.S. Navy caused Faber to miss most of the 1918 season, but he returned to help win the pennant in 1919. At the time of the Black Sox scandal, Faber was on the bench with recurring arm trouble.

From 1914 through 1923, Faber had 10 consecutive winning seasons. His best years were 1921 and 1922, when he won 25 and 21 games and led the league in ERA and complete games both years. In the 4,087 innings Faber pitched, he allowed only 110 home runs, and hit only 104 batters. A solid hitter himself, Faber was also a good base stealer. After his playing days, Faber was a White Sox pitching coach, then worked for the Cook County Highway Department well into his eighties.
Playing Career: *1914-1933; Chi A*

Roy Face

Face, Elroy Leon
B: Feb 20, 1928

Pos: P	ERA: 3.48
W-L: 104-95	SOs: 877
ShOs: 0	Saves: 193

Many knowledgeable fans consider Face the best relief pitcher in history. He compiled a record of 18-1 in 1959, winning 17 in a row. He was absolutely cool under pressure, even when the bases were loaded with runners. Face was at his best in the 1960 World Series when he saved the Pirates' first three victories, each stifling the Yankees' record-setting slugging.

Shy but gutsy, the 5'8" right-hander was twice drafted by Branch Rickey, first for the Dodgers, then in 1952, for the Pirates. Face recorded 96 career relief wins, and holds the major league mark for most relief wins in a season (18). He owns the NL career record for most games pitched for one club (802), for Pittsburgh. Face led the NL three times in saves and twice in number of game appearances.
Playing Career: *1953, 1955-1969; Pit N, Det A, Mon N*

Ferris Fain

Fain, Ferris Roy
B: May 29, 1921

Pos: 1B	BA: .290
Hits: 1,139	HRs: 48
RBI: 570	BBs: 904

Ferris Fain won two batting crowns, hitting .344 in 1951 and .327 in 1952, and had one other .300 year. His ability to get on base was exceptional. Fain walked 100 times in five seasons, and was in the AL top five every season he was healthy, yet only once did he strike out more than 37 times in a season. Fain's lifetime .425 on-base average is the eighth highest of all time.

Considered the AL's best-fielding first baseman until Vic Power entered the scene, Fain had great range and regularly fielded bunts on the third base line. He holds the major league record for double plays in a season with 194 in 1949. Fain set the AL record for double plays in a nine-inning game with six on September 1, 1947. He led the league four times in assists and twice each in total chances per game and double plays. Fain ranks third among all first basemen in assists per game.
Playing Career: *1947-1955; Phi A, Chi A, Det A, Cle A*

Ron Fairly

Fairly, Ronald Ray
B: Jul 12, 1938

Pos: 1B, OF	BA: .266
Hits: 1,913	HRs: 215
RBI: 1,044	BBs: 1,052

Urban "Red" Faber (l) with Charlie Root.

Roy Face had won 10 straight in relief when this photo was taken on June 17, 1959.

Ferris Fain is greeted at home by Athletics teammates after belting a grand slam.

One of the few players who have played 1,000 games or more at two positions, Fairly guarded first base and patrolled the outfield.

Fairly took over first base for the Dodgers in 1962 and led NL first basemen in fielding in 1963. He surrendered the position to Gold Glover Wes Parker in 1966. Traded to the expansion Expos in 1969, Fairly escaped the vastness of Dodger Stadium and his batting average and power rebounded.

An All-Star in 1973 and 1977, he batted over .300 twice, in 1961 and 1975. He whacked 307 doubles in a career that spanned 21 seasons. A consistent hitter with at least 10 home runs 14 times, Fairly also walked often enough to post on-base averages over .400 four times. As a designated hitter for the 1977 expansion Blue Jays, he hit 19 homers, his personal best.
Playing Career: *1958-1978; LA N, Mon N, StL N, Oak A, Tor A, Cal A*

Pete Falcone
Falcone, Peter
B: Oct 1, 1953

Pos: P	ERA: 4.07
W-L: 70-90	SOs: 865
ShOs: 7	Saves: 7

The southpaw went 12-11 his rookie season, but lost the Rookie Pitcher of the Year Award to teammate John Montefusco. The Giants kept Montefusco and shipped Falcone to the Cardinals in 1976, where he won 12 games with a 3.23 ERA.
Playing Career: *1975-1984; SF N, StL N, NY N, Atl N*

Bibb Falk
Falk, Bibb August
B: Jan 27, 1899   D: Jun 8, 1989

Pos: OF	BA: .314
Hits: 1,463	HRs: 69
RBI: 785	BBs: 412
Managerial Record	
Won: 1 Lost: 0 Pct: 1.000	

A long-time University of Texas baseball coach, Falk was a versatile athlete, an All-Conference tackle in football and undefeated in three years of varsity pitching. He gave the White Sox nine strong seasons, averaging .314 at the plate and three times topping 90 RBI. From 1940 to 1967 – with time out for World War II – Falk coached baseball at his alma mater. His 468-176 record resulted in 20 Southwest Conference titles and two national championships.
Playing Career: *1920-1931; Chi A, Cle A*
Managerial Career: *1933; Cle A*

Cy Falkenberg
Falkenberg, Frederick Peter
B: Dec 17, 1880   D: Apr 14, 1961

Pos: P	ERA: 2.68
W-L: 131-123	SOs: 1,164
ShOs: 27	Saves: 7

Contemporaries claimed Falkenberg was seven feet tall, but he was actually 6'5". He was a minor league strikeout champion in 1904 and 1916. Falkenberg won 23 games for the Indians in 1913, and was intensely recruited by the Federal League the next year. Jumping to the new league with a lucrative contract, he drove Indianapolis to the pennant with 25 wins, 49 games, 43 starts, 9 shutouts, 377 innings, and 236 strikeouts, all league-leading marks.
Playing Career: *1903, 1905-1911, 1913-1915, 1917; Pit N, Was A, Cle A, Ind F, Nwk F, Brk F, Phi A*

Ed Farmer
Farmer, Edward Joseph
B: Oct 18, 1949

Pos: P	ERA: 4.30
W-L: 30-43	SOs: 395
ShOs: 0	Saves: 75

A well-traveled reliever and spot starter, Farmer reached the apex of his career in 1980 with 30 saves and an All-Star Game appearance as a member of the White Sox. The big right-hander was used exclusively as a stopper in 1980 and 1981.
Playing Career: *1971-1974, 1977-1983; Cle A, Det A, Phi N, Bal A, Mil A, Tex A, Chi A, Oak A*

Steve Farr
Farr, Steven Michael
B: Dec 12, 1956

Pos: P	ERA: 3.18
W-L: 46-44	SOs: 644
ShOs: 1	Saves: 128

After languishing for eight seasons in the minors and being cut by the Indians, Farr capitalized on a tryout with the Royals in 1985. Relying on a baffling slider and sharp curveball, he became the team stopper. In 1988 Farr saved 20 games and led the staff with a 2.50 ERA. Surprising everyone, Kansas City signed NL Cy Young Award winner Mark Davis to a four-year $13 million contract, reducing Farr's role to setup. He went to the Yankees in November 1990 as a free agent, saving 53 games over the next two seasons.
Playing Career: *1984- ; Cle A, KC A, NY A*

Duke Farrell
Farrell, Charles Andrew
B: Aug 31, 1866   D: Feb 15, 1925

Pos: C, 3B, OF, 1B	BA: .275
Hits: 1,563	HRs: 51
RBI: 912	BBs: 477

Farrell was a versatile switch hitter discovered by Cap Anson while barnstorming in New England. Farrell played for championship teams six times. He was the last home run and RBI leader of the American Association, in 1891. In 1894 he caught for the Temple Cup winners. He played with Hanlon's pennant-winning Superbas – later called the Dodgers – in 1899 and 1900. Pinch-hitting in the last years of his career, he retired to scout for the Braves.
Playing Career: *1888-1905; Chi N, Chi P, Bos AA, Pit N, Was N, NY N, Brk N*

John Farrell
Farrell, John A. (Moose)
B: Jul 5, 1857   D: Feb 10, 1914

Pos: 2B	BA: .243
Hits: 877	HRs: 22
RBI: 241 (inc.)	BBs: 197
Managerial Record	
Won: 24 Lost: 27 Pct: .471	

One of the legendary Syracuse Stars of the late 1870s, Farrell was a solid infielder who later held down second for the Grays, who played in the first World Series of the 19th century in 1884. He hit .444 in a three-game sweep.
Playing Career: *1879-1889; Syr N, Pro N, Was N, Bal AA*
Managerial Career: *1881; Pro N*

Turk Farrell
Farrell, Richard Joseph
B: Apr 8, 1934   D: Jun 10, 1977

Pos: P   ERA: 3.45
W-L: 106-111   SOs: 1,177
ShOs: 5   Saves: 83

Farrell made his debut as a Phillies starter in 1956, then relieved in his next 258 appearances. The Colt 45s drafted Farrell and returned him to the starting rotation. Realizing their mistake, the Phillies reacquired Farrell, but sent him to the bullpen again. He did quite well despite spending most of his career with second-division teams. An NL All-Star four times, in the 1958 contest Farrell struck out four of the seven batters he faced, including Ted Williams.
Playing Career: *1956-1969; Phi N, LA N, Hou N*

Bob Feller
Feller, Robert William Andrew
B: Nov 3, 1918
Hall of Fame 1962

Pos: P   ERA: 3.25
W-L: 266-162   SOs: 2,581
ShOs: 46   No-hitters: 3

Shoeless Joe Jackson had good reason to mistake Iowa for heaven in the movie *Field of Dreams* – the Hawkeye State gave us Bob Feller. Unlike many prodigies, Feller fulfilled his potential; he may have been the best pitcher ever. With his legendary fastball and dangerous curve, Feller was the strikeout king of his era.

Feller's accomplishments began at an early age. When he was 17, he whiffed eight Cardinals in three innings in a major league exhibition game. In his AL debut Feller fanned 15, then set a major league record with 18 strikeouts at age 19. Feller had 24 wins in 1939 at age 20, 27 the following season at age 21. After missing nearly four seasons to military

Bob "Rapid Robert" Feller.

duty – he was decorated eight times – Feller continued his assault on AL batters. During his career Feller led the league in ERA once and in strikeouts seven times. He was an All-Star eight times, but pitched in only one World Series. His retirement years have been spent promoting baseball.
Playing Career: *1936-1941, 1945-1956; Cle A*

Oscar "Happy" Felsch.

Happy Felsch
Felsch, Oscar Emil
B: Aug 22, 1891   D: Aug 17, 1964

Pos: OF   BA: .293
Hits: 825   HRs: 38
RBI: 446   BBs: 207

A superb center fielder with exceptional range and a rifle arm, Felsch still shares the records for double plays by an outfielder in a season (15), and assists in a game (4). Fun-loving Felsch gravitated to the rowdier members of the team, who turned out to be the ringleaders of the Black Sox conspiracy. Felsch got in over his head. The gamblers controlled him through threats, forcing him to throw games in 1919 and 1920, when he was banned from baseball for life.
Playing Career: *1915-1920; Chi A*

Frank Fennelly
Fennelly, Francis John
B: Feb 18, 1860   D: Aug 4, 1920

Pos: SS   BA: .257
Hits: 781   HRs: 34
RBI: 132 (inc.)   BBs: 378

Fennelly played for the Reds during the 1880s, when Cincinnati was a hotbed of rabid fans. On Sundays 12,000-14,000 fans would gather at the ballpark. They voted Fennelly "thinnest," but he hit a big fat .311 in 1884, his best season.
Playing Career: *1884-1890; Was AA, Cin AA, Phi AA, Brk AA*

Alex Ferguson
Ferguson, James Alexander
B: Feb 16, 1897   D: Apr 26, 1976

Pos: P   ERA: 4.91
W-L: 61-85   SOs: 386
ShOs: 2   Saves: 10

A late acquisition by the 1925 Senators, Ferguson was 1-1 in the World Series that year. A forkball specialist, he had his best season for the 1924 Red Sox, when he won 14. Saddled with losing teams, he lost 58 percent of his career decisions.
Playing Career: *1918, 1921-1929; NY A, Bos A, Was A, Phi N, Brk N*

Bob Ferguson.

Bob Ferguson
Ferguson, Robert V.
(Death to Flying Things)
B: Jan 31, 1845   D: May 3, 1894

Pos: 3B   BA: .265
Hits: 918   HRs: 1
RBI: 294   BBs: 126
Managerial Record
Won: 299   Lost: 373   Pct: .445

Ferguson was one of the most outstanding and influential ballplayers of the 19th century. He drove in the tying run, then scored the winning run that ended the famous Cincinnati Red Stockings' two-year winning streak. A leader, Ferguson managed every team he played for from 1871 through 1884. His nickname came from his ability to snag line drives.

Ferguson had an unimpeachable character at a time when many baseball players had questionable morals and were often the pawns of gamblers. In 1872 he was elected president of the first pro league, the National Association of Professional Baseball Players.

Ferguson umpired throughout his career. Fair and honest when calm, Ferguson could also become angry; he once broke a player's arm with a bat to finish an argument.
Playing Career: *1871-1884; NY Mutuals n, Brk Atlantics n, Har Dark Blues n, Har N, Chi N, Tro N, Phi N, Pit AA*
Managerial Career: *1871-1884, 1886-1887; NY Mutuals n, Brk Atlantics n, Har Dark Blues n, Har N, Chi N, Tro N, Phi N, Pit AA, NY AA*
Umpiring Career: *1872-1873, 1875, 1886-1889, 1891; NA, AA*

Charlie Ferguson
Ferguson, Charles J.
B: Apr 17, 1863   D: Apr 29, 1888

Pos: P	ERA: 2.67
W-L: 99	SOs: 728
ShOs: 13	Saves: 4

Ferguson was on his way to becoming one of the greatest players of the 19th century when typhoid fever struck him down. He won more than 60 percent of the games he pitched, and batted .337 in his last season.
Playing Career: *1884-1887; Phi N*

Joe Ferguson
Ferguson, Joseph Vance
B: Sep 19, 1946

Pos: C	BA: .240
Hits: 719	HRs: 122
RBI: 445	BBs: 562

Ferguson became the Dodgers' regular catcher in 1973 and set a major league catching record, committing only three errors, and leading the league in fielding average and double plays. Ferguson slugged .450 in two World Series for the Dodgers, 1974 and 1978.
Playing Career: *1970-1983; LA N, StL N, Hou N, Cal A*

Chico Fernandez
Fernandez y Perez, Humberto
B: Mar 2, 1932

Pos: SS	BA: .240
Hits: 666	HRs: 40
RBI: 259	BBs: 213

A promising talent with the Dodgers, but stuck behind Pee Wee Reese, Fernandez was finally traded to the Phillies for five players. He hit a career-high .262 for them in 1957. The Tigers played him regularly and he surprised them with 20 home runs in 1962.
Playing Career: *1956-1963; Brk N, Phi N, Det A, NY N*

Sid Fernandez
Fernandez, Charles Sidney
B: Oct 12, 1962

Pos: P	ERA: 3.15
W-L: 98-79	SOs: 1,458
ShOs: 9	Saves: 1

Fernandez broke in with the Dodgers as a strikeout pitcher who sometimes had trouble with control. Today he is one of baseball's top left-handers, and he has a wicked pickoff move to first. Fernandez has an outstanding ratio of hits to innings pitched. He has appeared in two All-Star Games, and in two postseason series with the Mets. Fernandez struck out 16 Braves in a game in 1989, the year he went 14-5. The number 50 on his uniform commemorates his home state of Hawaii.
Playing Career: *1983- ; LA N, NY N*

Tony Fernandez
Fernandez y Castro, Octavio Antonio
B: Aug 6, 1962

Pos: SS	BA: .285
Hits: 1,612	HRs: 53
RBI: 543	BBs: 454

To the Blue Jays, Tony Fernandez represented the best of all possible worlds – a shortstop who could hit. He led them to the division title in his sophomore year. A great defensive player, Fernandez led AL shortstops in fielding percentage in 1986 and 1989, and has received four Gold Glove Awards. At the plate, Fernandez led the AL in triples in 1990 and has hit more than 250 doubles in nine years. He has scored 740 runs, and stolen 202 bases. In 1986 Fernandez set a major league record for most hits by a shortstop in this century, collecting 213. He batted .333 and .350 in the 1985 and 1989 ALCS.
  With one week to go in the 1987 season, Fernandez suffered an elbow injury. The Blue Jays folded without his leadership, and the Tigers took the division title. Fernandez has been elected to the All-Star team four times. Hailing from San Pedro de Macoris, the Dominican Republic's warehouse of middle infielders, Fernandez is active in Little League Baseball in his hometown.
Playing Career: *1983- ; Tor A, SD N, NY N*

Rick Ferrell
Ferrell, Richard Benjamin
B: Oct 12, 1905
Hall of Fame 1984

Pos: C	BA: .281
Hits: 1,692	HRs: 28
RBI: 734	BBs: 931

Rick Ferrell was the AL catcher in the first All-Star Game; he caught all nine innings. The North Carolina farm boy, who saved pennies to buy his first catcher's mitt for $1.50, went on to become one of the most durable receivers in baseball. Ferrell's 1,805 games caught was an AL record until Carlton Fisk surpassed it in 1988.
  A fine defensive catcher with a strong arm, Ferrell was considered one of the best handlers of pitchers, at one time catching for a quartet of knuckleballers on the 1945 Senators' staff. He was a good hitter who topped .300 four times, although he had little home run power. Ferrell struck out only 277 times in his career. From 1934 to 1938, Ferrell and his brother Wes formed one of the more successful sibling batteries in baseball history. They were so in tune with each other's thoughts that Rick could catch a whole game without giving Wes signs.
Playing Career: *1929-1945, 1947; StL A, Bos A, Was A*

Wes Ferrell
Ferrell, Wesley Cheek
B: Feb 2, 1908   D: Dec 9, 1976

Pos: P	ERA: 4.04
W-L: 193-128	SOs: 985
ShOs: 17	No-hitters: 1

Cheek was his middle name and never was a boy more aptly named. A tremendous pitcher and very good hitter, Ferrell had a

Manager Bucky Harris shakes hands with Wes Ferrell (r) as Rick Ferrell looks on.

world-class temper. He was once fined for refusing to leave a game in 1932. Four years later he was fined and suspended for leaving a game without permission. Later, as a minor league manager, Ferrell was handed a lengthy suspension for belting the umpire and removing his team from the field.

Ferrell batted .280 with 38 home runs during his 15-year career, and won 20 games or more pitching in each of his first four full seasons. He had a league-high 25 wins for the Red Sox in 1935. The next season he won 20 again. A member of the first AL All-Star team, Ferrell had a career .601 won-lost percentage with 13 saves. He led AL pitchers four times in complete games, and three times in innings pitched. Arm trouble cooled his blazing fastball and prevented him from attaining Hall of Fame status.
Playing Career: *1927-1941; Cle A, Bos A, Was A, NY A, Brk N, Bos N*

Tom Ferrick
Ferrick, Thomas Jerome
B: Jan 6, 1915

Pos: P	ERA: 3.47
W-L: 40-40	SOs: 245
ShOs: 1	Saves: 56

Joining the Yankees in June 1950, Ferrick was the man Casey Stengel turned to when he lost faith in bullpen ace Joe Page. On the way to the pennant, Ferrick won eight games and saved nine in just 30 appearances. Ferrick is now a scout for the Royals.
Playing Career: *1941-1942, 1946-1952; Phi A, Cle A, StL A, Was A, NY A*

Hobe Ferris
Ferris, Albert Sayles
B: Dec 7, 1877   D: Mar 18, 1938

Pos: 2B, 3B	BA: .239
Hits: 1,146	HRs: 39
RBI: 550	BBs: 161

The hero of the very first World Series was Hobe Ferris. He batted in all three Red Sox runs in their shutout final victory over the Pirates. Ferris played 130 or more games in each of the nine years he played in the major leagues. He finished his career with two seasons as the Browns' third baseman.
Playing Career: *1901-1909; Bos A, StL A*

Boo Ferriss
Ferriss, David Meadow
B: Dec 5, 1921

Pos: P	ERA: 3.64
W-L: 65-30	SOs: 296
ShOs: 12	Saves: 8

The 1945 rookie sensation, Ferriss compiled a record of 21-10, and defeated all seven opponent clubs the first time around the league. The next year he went 25-6, leading the Red Sox to the 1946 pennant, and won Game Three of the World Series. His career was cut short by asthma and arm trouble.
Playing Career: *1945-1950; Bos A*

Mark Fidrych
Fidrych, Mark Steven (The Bird)
B: Aug 14, 1954

Pos: P	ERA: 3.10
W-L: 29-19	SOs: 170
ShOs: 5	No-hitters: 0

The slender, gawky, 6'3" right-hander with flowing blond curls was the talk of baseball in 1976. Fidrych built a reputation as an eccentric personality, carefully molding the mound to his specifications and talking to the ball while he pitched. His performance earned him Rookie of the Year honors, based on a 19-9 record with 24 complete games and a league-leading 2.34 ERA. He started the All-Star Game that year, but arm trouble limited him to just 10 wins after that first sensational season.
Playing Career: *1976-1980; Det A*

Cecil Fielder
Fielder, Cecil Grant
B: Sep 21, 1963

Pos: 1B, DH	BA: .259
Hits: 743	HRs: 191
RBI: 590	BBs: 377

Scouts predicted that Fielder would blossom into one of the most feared hitters in baseball, but what an unlikely success story! Originally signed by the Royals, Fielder was traded to Toronto before he reached the big leagues. In a brief trial with the Blue Jays he batted .311 in 1985 and appeared in the ALCS, then was relegated to a part-time role. He hit .269 with 14 dingers in 1987. A year later, the big first baseman/DH left the big leagues for Japan, where he could bang out home runs to his heart's desire. After unqualified success with the Hanshin Tigers, Fielder returned to a skeptical AL in 1990 and signed a contract with the Detroit Tigers.

Critics say of Fielder, "All he does is hit home runs." But he has lofty company in that endeavor. Fielder led the majors in RBI for the third consecutive season in 1992; the last player to do so was Babe Ruth. Fielder hit 51 homers in 1990, the most in the majors since George Foster lifted 52 in 1977.
Playing Career: *1985-1988, 1990- ; Tor A, Det A*

Ed Figueroa
Figueroa y Padilla, Eduardo
B: Oct 14, 1948

Pos: P	ERA: 3.51
W-L: 80-67	SOs: 571
ShOs: 12	Saves: 1

Figueroa won 55 games for the pennant-winning Yankees teams of 1976-1978. In 1978 he became the first Puerto Rican to win 20 games in the major leagues, turning in a 20-9 record with a 2.99 ERA. Figueroa required elbow surgery in 1979, and lost his effectiveness afterwards.
Playing Career: *1974-1981; Cal A, NY A, Tex A, Oak A*

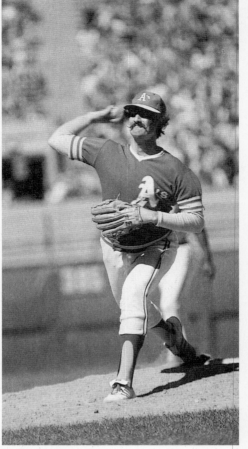

Rollie Fingers.

Rollie Fingers
Fingers, Roland Glen
B: Aug 25, 1946
Hall of Fame 1992

Pos: P	ERA: 2.90
W-L: 114-118	SOs: 1,299
ShOs: 2	Saves: 341

Renowned for his World Series performances with Oakland in the early 1970s, Fingers is also fondly remembered for his handlebar moustache. The lanky right-hander used impeccable control and an ability to compete under pressure to build a career spanning 17 seasons. Always at his best in postseason play, Fingers compiled a 5-4 record with nine saves. In Game Seven of the 1972 World Series against the Reds, he worked out of a bases-loaded, one-out jam in the eighth inning to preserve the 3-2 victory and give Oakland its first championship.

In 1981 Fingers led the AL with 28 saves and a 1.04 ERA, and guided the Brewers to their first postseason appearance. During his career, Fingers figured in 55 percent of the victories posted by his teams. He won both the MVP Award and the Cy Young Award. He missed the entire 1983 season due to a sore arm, but came back in 1984 to post a 1.96 ERA with 23 saves.
Playing Career: *1968-1982, 1984-1985; Oak A, SD N, Mil A*

KC Athletics owner Charlie O. Finley takes a ride on the team mascot, 1965.

Charlie Finley
Finley, Charles O.
B: Feb 22, 1918

An innovative yet controversial baseball personality, Finley owned the Athletics from 1960 to 1981. He quickly displayed a knack for finding talent by signing Ed Charles and Jose Tartabull. Finley's penchant for being involved in feuds with his players and managers was also soon made apparent. In 1962 he ordered Manny Jimenez, who was leading the AL with a .350 average, to start hitting home runs. Manager Hank Bauer stood up for Jimenez and was fired after the season. In 1967 Finley fined and suspended pitcher Lew Krausse for rowdyism, and publicly berated his players over an airplane incident. A near mutiny followed. Finley fired manager Alvin Dark, then released the A's best hitter, Ken Harrelson, who had publicly said that Finley was "a menace to baseball." An innovative promoter, Finley staged numerous spectacles, installed a petting zoo, and built a picnic area around a movable right field fence called the "pennant porch." He tried using yellow baseballs at night. Finley built the last team to win three straight World Series; the players were galvanized around dislike for his methods.

Chuck Finley
Finley, Charles Edward
B: Nov 26, 1962

Pos: P	ERA: 3.40
W-L: 89-76	SOs: 1,026
ShOs: 8	No-hitters: 0

Finley is one of the best pitchers in baseball despite having an inexplicable 1992 7-12 season. In 1989 he harnessed his strikeout potential to go 16-9 with a 2.57 ERA. Finley followed with two straight 18-win seasons.
Playing Career: 1986- ; Cal A

Lou Finney
Finney, Louis Klopsche
B: Aug 13, 1910   D: Apr 22, 1966

Pos: OF, 1B	BA: .287
Hits: 1,329	HRs: 31
RBI: 494	BBs: 329

Finney was scheduled to replace Al Simmons when Connie Mack sold Al to the White Sox. Finney hit well, three times over .300, but was not a slugger like Simmons. Traded to the Red Sox, he filled in for Jimmie Foxx at first base and pinch hit, leading the league with 13 pinch hits in 1939. After managing in the low minors, he and his brother Hal, a reserve catcher with the Pirates, ran a feed store in Alabama.
Playing Career: 1931, 1933-1942, 1944-1947; Phi A, Bos A, StL A, Phi N

Bill Fischer
Fischer, William Charles
B: Oct 11, 1930

Pos: P	ERA: 4.34
W-L: 45-58	SOs: 313
ShOs: 2	Saves: 13

In 1962 Fischer broke one of baseball's earliest established records when he pitched 84⅓ consecutive innings without giving up a walk, surpassing Christy Mathewson's mark of 68, set in 1913. Fischer later became a pitching coach for the Reds and Red Sox.
Playing Career: 1956-1964; Chi A, Det A, Was A, KC A, Min A

Eddie Fisher
Fisher, Eddie Gene
B: Jul 16, 1936

Pos: P	ERA: 3.41
W-L: 85-70	SOs: 812
ShOs: 2	Saves: 81

While in the White Sox bullpen with Hoyt Wilhelm, Fisher experimented with the flutter pitch under the watchful eye of the master. In 1965 the two combined for a record 53 saves. That year Fisher led AL pitchers with 82 relief appearances and 15 relief wins; he also saved 24. Fisher pitched two shutout innings in the 1965 All-Star Game. Splitting the 1966 season between Chicago and Baltimore, Fisher again led the AL with 67 appearances.
Playing Career: 1959-1973; SF N, Chi A, Bal A, Cle A, StL N

Eddie Fisher in 1973 game action.

Jack Fisher
Fisher, John Howard
B: Mar 4, 1939

Pos: P	ERA: 4.06
W-L: 86-139	SOs: 1,017
ShOs: 9	Saves: 9

A starter with a .500 won-lost percentage, Fisher went to the Mets in 1964 and watched his average go down the drain. There was no helping the club that met defeat in 417 out of 647 games, 1964-1967. Fisher accumulated 73 losses in four years.
Playing Career: 1959-1969; Bal A, SF N, NY N, Chi A, Cin N

Ray Fisher
Fisher, Raymund Lyle
B: Oct 4, 1887   D: Nov 3, 1982

Pos: P	ERA: 2.82
W-L: 100-94	SOs: 680
ShOs: 19	Saves: 7

Fisher's big year was 1915, when he was 18-11 with a 2.11 ERA. He was banned from baseball in 1920 because of a petty dispute between Commissioner Landis and others. Fisher became the baseball coach at the University of Michigan.
Playing Career: *1910-1917, 1919-1920; NY A, Cin N*

Carlton Fisk
Fisk, Carlton Ernest (Pudge)
B: Dec 26, 1947

Pos: C, DH, 1B	BA: .269
Hits: 2,356	HRs: 376
RBI: 1,330	BBs: 849

Growing from a fledgling receiver to a fearsome slugger, Fisk was voted Rookie of the Year and chosen for seven All-Star Games. He also won a Gold Glove in 1972. Boston fans will never forget Fisk's 1975 season. That year Fisk injured his knee in spring training and did not play until June, but he hit .331 in

Carlton Fisk.

79 games to help the Red Sox win the pennant. In Game Six of the 1975 World Series, Fisk drilled a Pat Darcy pitch off the left field foul pole for a 12th-inning, game-winning home run in what many fans consider the most dramatic game in recent history.

Fisk shocked Red Sox fans in 1981 by signing with the White Sox. Boston's front office failed to postmark his new contract in time, making Fisk a free agent. Changing Sox, Fisk flip-flopped his uniform number from 27 to 72. In Chicago, Fisk defied Father Time. He hit more home runs than any catcher, and in 1993 he surpassed Bob Boone's record of games caught by two.
Playing Career: *1969, 1971-1993; Bos A, Chi A*

Ed Fitzgerald
Fitzgerald, Edward Raymond
B: May 21, 1924

Pos: C	BA: .260
Hits: 542	HRs: 19
RBI: 217	BBs: 185

Fitzgerald's career was distinguished by two unusual plays on the field. In a 1953 game, the catcher turned a rare unassisted double play. In 1959 he became the first major leaguer to hit into a triple play on Opening Day.
Playing Career: *1948-1959; Pit N, Was A, Cle A*

Al Fitzmorris
Fitzmorris, Alan James
B: Mar 21, 1946

Pos: P	ERA: 3.6
W-L: 77-59	SOs: 458
ShOs: 11	Saves: 7

A switch hitter who began his career as an outfielder, Fitzmorris was the first Royal to get hits from both sides of the plate in one game. Fitzmorris, picked up in the expansion draft, won 44 games, 1974-1976, and helped the Royals win their first division title in 1976.
Playing Career: *1969-1978; KC A, Cle A, Cal A*

Freddie Fitzsimmons
Fitzsimmons, Frederick Landis (Fat Freddie)
B: Jul 26, 1901   D: Nov 18, 1979

Pos: P	ERA: 3.51
W-L: 217-146	SOs: 870
ShOs: 29	Saves: 13
Managerial Record	
Won: 105 Lost: 181 Pct: .367	

After a long successful pitching career, Fitzsimmons managed teams in two professional sports – baseball and football. Playing for the Giants, he used a knuckle curve to compile a 19-7 record and lead the NL with a .731 winning percentage in 1930. Fitzsimmons won 170 games in 12½ seasons for the Giants and pitched in the 1933 and 1936 World Series, but he did not become famous until he pitched in Brooklyn.

Freddie Fitzsimmons.

Fitzsimmons was the favorite Sunday pitcher for Da Bums. He was at the top of the league with a 16-2 record and a winning percentage of .889 in 1940, setting a club record. The next year he went 6-1, winning crucial games late in the season during the pennant drive. On September 11, 1941, Fitzsimmons pitched the opener of a set of important games against the Cardinals, the Dodgers' main rival. Fitzsimmons, who had turned 40 the previous July, held off the Cards for an 11-inning, 10 hit, 6-4 victory. It was his finest hour.
Playing Career: *1925-1943; NY N, Brk N*
Managerial Career: *1943-1945; Phi N*

Max Flack
Flack, Max John
B: Feb 5, 1890   D: Jul 31, 1975

Pos: OF	BA: .278
Hits: 1,461	HRs: 35
RBI: 301	BBs: 474

Flack was a superior outfielder with a good batting eye. He walked almost twice as often as he struck out. Flack had a .974 fielding average when he retired, the best ever for right fielders. Breaking in with the Federal League Chicago Whales, Flack played 1,411 games, scoring 783 runs and stealing 200 bases. He led NL outfielders in fielding in 1916 and 1921. Between games of a 1922 doubleheader, Flack was traded to St. Louis. He scored 82 runs for the Cardinals the next year.
Playing Career: *1914-1925; Chi F, Chi N, StL N*

Ira Flagstead leaps for a catch in 1921.

Ira Flagstead
Flagstead, Ira James
B: Sep 22, 1893   D: Mar 13, 1940

Pos: OF   BA: .290
Hits: 1,201   HRs: 40
RBI: 450   BBs: 465

Flagstead was a good fielder who batted over .300 five times and was part of Detroit's all-.300-hitting outfield. Flagstead holds the AL record for the most double plays started by an outfielder in a game, with three on April 19, 1926.
Playing Career: *1917, 1919-1930; Det A, Bos A, Was A, Pit N*

Patsy Flaherty
Flaherty, Patrick Joseph
B: Jun 29, 1876   D: Jan 23, 1968

Pos: P, OF   ERA: 3.10
W-L: 67-84   SOs: 271
ShOs: 7   Saves: 2

Part of the historic merger of the Louisville and Pittsburgh teams in 1900, Flaherty had an up-and-down career. With the 1904 Pirates he was 19-9. Flaherty was sometimes used as a pinch hitter or in the outfield. He hit .287 in his last season.
Playing Career: *1899-1900, 1903-1905, 1907-1908, 1910-1911; Lou N, Pit N, Chi A, Bos N, Phi N*

Mike Flanagan
Flanagan, Michael Kendall
B: Dec 16, 1951

Pos: P   ERA: 3.90
W-L: 167-143   SOs: 1,491
ShOs: 19   Saves: 4

Flanagan was the left-handed counterpart to Jim Palmer with the Orioles. From 1977 to 1987, no AL pitcher started more games than did Flanagan. His 1979 Cy Young season included 23 wins and five shutouts, both league-leading totals. Finishing sixth in the MVP voting that year, Flanagan was honored by the American Legion and Babe Ruth Baseball as Graduate of the Year. After he suffered several injuries, the Blue Jays took a chance on him; Flanagan was 3-2 with a 2.37 ERA in 1987.
Playing Career: *1975-1992; Bal A, Tor A*

Tim Flannery
Flannery, Timothy Earl
B: Sep 29, 1957

Pos: 2B, 3B, SS   BA: .255
Hits: 631   HRs: 9
RBI: 209   BBs: 277

Flannery hit the grounder that eluded Cubs first baseman Leon Durham to start the Padres' winning rally in the deciding game of the 1984 NLCS. Flannery batted .280 as San Diego's second baseman the next two seasons, but lost his job to Joey Cora, then to Roberto Alomar.
Playing Career: *1979-1989; SD N*

Art Fletcher
Fletcher, Arthur
B: Jan 5, 1885   D: Feb 6, 1950

Pos: SS   BA: .277
Hits: 1,534   HRs: 32
RBI: 675   BBs: 203
Managerial Record
Won: 237   Lost: 383   Pct: .382

Legendary manager John McGraw discovered Fletcher in Dallas during spring training. Fletcher was berating the Giants! Such brass impressed McGraw enough to purchase him on the spot. Fletcher played shortstop for over a decade, providing the Giants with brilliant fielding, dependable hitting, and leadership on the field. Known as a replica of the belligerent McGraw during the

Art Fletcher.

game, off the field Fletcher was a church-going family man.

Fletcher managed four second-division Phillies teams. Later, when Yankee manager Miller Huggins died suddenly in 1929, Fletcher stepped in as interim skipper, but he would refuse all other offers to manage. In 1927 Fletcher had become third base coach for the Yankees, a post he retained until 1945. Much of the Yankees' success was due to Fletcher's ability to read and steal opponents' signs. He frequently signaled which pitch was coming.
Playing Career: *1909-1920, 1922; NY N, Phi N*
Managerial Career: *1923-1926, 1929; Phi N, NY A*

Elbie Fletcher
Fletcher, Elburt Preston
B: Mar 18, 1916

Pos: 1B   BA: .271
Hits: 1,323   HRs: 79
RBI: 616   BBs: 851

After half a decade of career ups-and-downs, Elbie Fletcher learned how to draw walks and get on base. He did it better than anyone else in the NL during the years 1939-1941, with on-base averages of .418, .421, and .417. Fletcher was selected for the 1943 All-Star Game. The next year he paced the Bainbridge, Maryland, Naval Training Station team – which included baseball veterans Dick Bartell and Buddy Blattner – in hitting.
Playing Career: *1934-1935, 1937-1943, 1946-1947, 1949; Bos N, Pit N*

Scott Fletcher
Fletcher, Scott Brian
B: Jul 30, 1958

Pos: SS, 2B, DH   BA: .264
Hits: 1,292   HRs: 30
RBI: 482   BBs: 479

Fletcher is a utility player whose services have been purchased by the White Sox twice, 1983-1985 and 1989-1991. He hit .300 with the Rangers in 1986 and put together a 19-game hitting streak.
Playing Career: *1981- ; Chi N, Chi A, Tex A, Mil A, Bos A*

Elmer Flick
Flick, Elmer Harrison
B: Jan 11, 1876   D: Jan 9, 1971
Hall of Fame 1963

Pos: OF   BA: .313
Hits: 1,755   HRs: 48
RBI: 756   BBs: 597

Following the 1907 season, Detroit manager Hughie Jennings offered Ty Cobb to Cleveland for Elmer Flick. Cobb had just won his first batting title, while Flick had hit only .302, but Cobb was hated by his teammates and his reputation had already spread. Cleveland declined the offer.

Largely unknown by modern fans, Flick

was one of the great all-around ballplayers at the turn of the century. He narrowly missed the NL batting title in 1900 – .378 to Honus Wagner's .381 – and posted a .441 on-base average. After compiling a .344 batting mark in four years in the NL, Flick jumped to the AL and ended up in Cleveland, where he batted over .300 four times during his first six seasons. Flick led the league in triples three times, stolen bases twice, and runs scored once, scoring 948 times and swiping 330 bases altogether. For the last three seasons of his career, Flick was tormented by a mysterious stomach ailment and played only 99 games.
Playing Career: *1898-1910; Phi N, Cle A*

Silver Flint
Flint, Frank Sylvester
B: Aug 3, 1855   D: Jan 14, 1892

Pos: C   BA: .239
Hits: 682   HRs: 21
RBI: 219   BBs: 53
Managerial Record
Won: 5   Lost: 12   Pct: .294

In order to demonstrate the ferocity of the style of play in 19th-century baseball, congressional aides once asked senators and representatives to look at a photograph of Silver Flint's hands. His gnarled, misshapen fingers were a testament to the roughness of the national pastime in the old days. In the days before catcher's mitts and protective equipment, Flint used to prepare for the season by laying his hands on top of a bucket of sand and getting his teammates to beat his palms with baseball bats.
Playing Career: *1875, 1878-1889; StL Reds n, Ind N, Chi N*
Managerial Career: *1879; Chi N*

Frank "Silver" Flint.

Curt Flood.

Curt Flood
Flood, Curtis Charles
B: Jan 18, 1938

Pos: OF   BA: .293
Hits: 1,861   HRs: 85
RBI: 636   BBs: 444

On January 16, 1970, Curt Flood filed a lawsuit against Major League Baseball. The Cardinals had traded him and three others to the Phillies the previous October. Flood refused to report to Philadelphia, which had a bad team and a worse stadium, not to mention hostile fans. He asked Commissioner Bowie Kuhn to declare him a free agent, but Kuhn denied the request, so Flood filed a suit stating that baseball had violated the nation's antitrust laws. Flood lost his case in the Supreme Court but paved the way for change.
    Flood had a marvelous career. He was named to the All-Star squad three times and played in three World Series. He batted over .300 six times in 12 years. In 1963 Flood accumulated 112 of the 851 runs scored during his career. He led the NL in hits with 211 in 1964. Flood earned seven consecutive Gold Glove Awards. Knowing his career would be in jeopardy if he filed the landmark lawsuit, he proceeded, hoping that future generations of players would not have to endure what he had.
Playing Career: *1956-1969, 1971; Cin N, StL N, Was A*

Doug Flynn
Flynn, Robert Douglas
B: Apr 18, 1951

Pos: 2B   BA: .238
Hits: 918   HRs: 7
RBI: 284   BBs: 142

Flynn was good with his glove. The second sacker played a reserve role on two pennant-winning Reds teams. When Flynn was traded to the Mets he became a regular and won a Gold Glove Award in 1980. His best year was 1976, when he hit .283.
Playing Career: *1975-1985; Cin N, NY N, Tex A, Mon N, Det A*

Lee Fohl
Fohl, Leo Alexander
B: Nov 28, 1870   D: Oct 30, 1965

Managerial Record
Won: 713   Lost: 792   Pct: .474

Fohl, who played only five games at the major league level (1902-1903), was the manager of a couple of near-miss teams. His Indians finished second to the Red Sox by two and a half games in 1918. In 1922 Fohl's Browns came within one game of winning the pennant.
Managerial Career: *1915-1919, 1921-1926; Cle A, StL A, Bos A*

Tom Foley
Foley, Thomas Michael
B: Sep 9, 1959

Pos: SS, 2B, 3B   BA: .245
Hits: 627   HRs: 29
RBI: 246   BBs: 217

In high school Foley played baseball and football, but with a twist. Being ambidextrous, he was a right-handed shortstop and a left-handed quarterback. Foley has become a valuable left-handed hitting utility player in the major leagues.
Playing Career: *1983- ; Cin N, Phi N, Mon N, Pit N*

Tim Foli
Foli, Timothy John
B: Dec 6, 1950

Pos: SS   BA: .251
Hits: 1,515   HRs: 25
RBI: 501   BBs: 265

Foli struck out only 399 times in 6,047 at-bats. He led shortstops of both leagues in fielding percentage – the NL in 1980, and the AL two years later. Foli paced NL shortstops twice in double plays and total chances, and once in putouts. He became the first Expo ever to hit for the cycle on April 21, 1976. Not a strong hitter, Foli turned into a tiger in the postseason. He batted .333 with six RBI in 10 ALCS and World Series games for the 1979 World Champion Pirates.
Playing Career: *1970-1985; NY N, Mon N, SF N, Pit N, Cal A, NY A*

Dee Fondy
Fondy, Dee Virgil
B: Oct 13, 1924

Pos: 1B, OF   BA: .286
Hits: 1,000   HRs: 69
RBI: 373   BBs: 203

A Dodger farm hand stuck behind Gil Hodges, Fondy led the Texas League in hits in 1948. Three years later he batted .376 in the Pacific Coast League. When Fondy finally got to the big leagues, he found Wrigley Field suited him; three times he batted over .300.
Playing Career: *1951-1958; Chi N, Pit N, Cin N*

Shortstop Tom Foley completes a throw to first for a double play, 1985.

1927 comedy starring Joe E. Brown. Fonseca later used film to detect flaws in his players' techniques when he was manager of the White Sox.

Versatile in the field and spectacular at the plate, Fonseca played only two full seasons as a regular, batting .369 and .312. He played every position except catcher, even pitching when he was the manager of the White Sox in 1932. His career was hampered by injuries. He suffered a broken leg in 1928, but came back to win the 1929 AL batting title. A broken arm in 1930 was followed by a damaged knee that ended his career.
Playing Career: *1921-1925, 1927-1933; Cin N, Phi N, Cle A, Chi A*
Managerial Career: *1932-1934; Chi A*

Davy Force
Force, David W.
B: Jul 27, 1849   D: Jun 21, 1918

Pos: SS	BA: .249
Hits: 1,060	HRs: 1
RBI: 209	BBs: 156

Davy Force was involved in a celebrated case over the "revolving" issue. He signed two contracts in 1874, one to return to the White Stockings, then another more lucrative one with the Athletics. The National Association Judicial Committee upheld the earlier contract with the White Stockings. Then just before the 1875 season, the Judicial Committee reversed its decision, claiming that Force had signed before the official date for a valid contract. White Stockings President William Hulbert vowed to get even with the National Association. One year later he formed the National League, displacing the Association in major league ball.

Force reputedly invented the bunt; at least he was an early proponent of it. Never a big hitter in the NL, he had posted an NA average of .326. Force was considered the best shortstop of his era, excepting George Wright. After his last season with the Nationals in Washington, Force was player-manager and sometimes umpire in the minor leagues.
Playing Career: *1871-1886; Was Olympics n, Tro Haymakers n, Bal Lord Baltimores n, Chi White Stockings n, Phi Athletics n, Phi N, NY N, StL N, Buf N, Was N*

Lew Fonseca.

Lew Fonseca
Fonseca, Lewis Albert
B: Jan 21, 1899   D: Nov 26, 1989

Pos: OF, 2B, 1B, 3B	BA: .316
Hits: 1,075	HRs: 31
RBI: 485	BBs: 186
Managerial Record	
Won: 120 Lost: 196 Pct: .380	

Fonseca pioneered the use of film for instructional and promotional purposes in baseball. He appeared in several movies commissioned by Major League Baseball during the 1930s and 1940s. Fonseca became interested in cameras while acting in *Slide, Kelly, Slide*, a

Dan Ford
Ford, Darnell Glenn
B: May 19, 1952

Pos: OF	BA: .270
Hits: 1,123	HRs: 121
RBI: 566	BBs: 303

Ford became a regular for the Twins in 1974. After several seasons he was traded to California, where he had career highs of .290, 21 homers, 101 RBI, and 100 runs scored in 1979. Ford homered in Games One and Two of the Angels' first ALCS, and batted .294 in the World Series.
Playing Career: *1975-1985; Min A, Cal A, Bal A*

Hod Ford
Ford, Horace Hills
B: Jul 23, 1897   D: Jan 29, 1977

Pos: SS, 2B	BA: .263
Hits: 1,269	HRs: 16
RBI: 494	BBs: 351

A Tufts University graduate, Ford was a smooth fielder who led the league twice in fielding percentage. He set the record for double plays by a shortstop with 128 in 1928. The Reds turned 194 double plays that year, a record that stood for 30 years.
Playing Career: *1919-1932; Bos N, Cin N, StL N*

Russ Ford
Ford, Russell William
B: Apr 25, 1883   D: Jan 24, 1960

Pos: P	ERA: 2.59
W-L: 99-71	SOs: 710
ShOs: 15	Saves: 9

After Ford accidentally discovered that a scuffed baseball could be made to break sharply, he began using emery paper to doctor the ball, then disguised his pitches as spitballs, which were legal at the time. Ford was 26-6 as a rookie with the Highlanders in 1910. The next year he compiled a 22-11 record. Jumping to the Federal League in 1914, he led its pitchers with a .769 winning percentage based on a 21-6 record, and with saves, turning in six.
Playing Career: *1909-1915; NY A, Buf F*

Whitey Ford
Ford, Edward Charles (Slick)
B: Oct 21, 1926
Hall of Fame 1974

Pos: P	ERA: 2.75
W-L: 236-106	SOs: 1,956
ShOs: 45	Saves: 10

Ford was called ''The Chairman of the Board'' with good reason; the fearless hurler was the ace of the Yankees' pitching staff for more than a decade. The Yankees counted on Ford's mastery of the mental aspects of pitching and his pinpoint control. Batters faced his repertoire of change-ups, curves and fastballs, and risked being picked off third base – if they made it that far.

Ford posted ERAs under 3.00 in 11 of 16 seasons. His .690 winning percentage ranks third on the all-time list and first among modern pitchers with 200 or more wins. He allowed an average of only 10.94 baserunners per nine innings and posted eight 1-0 victories. At his best under pressure, Ford started 22 World Series games, with a 10-8 record. He holds virtually all of the World Series career pitching records, including a streak of 33 scoreless innings. Ford was selected for the All-Star team eight times. He led the AL numerous times in wins, winning percentage, innings pitched, shutouts and ERA.
Playing Career: *1950, 1953-1967; NY A*

Frank Foreman
Foreman, Francis Isaiah
B: May 1, 1863   D: Nov 19, 1957

Pos: P	ERA: 3.97
W-L: 96-93	SOs: 586
ShOs: 7	Saves: 4

Foreman played for Baltimore in three different leagues, winning 23 games in 1889 for the AA team. His 15 minutes of fame derived from his discovery of future Hall of Fame left-hander Eddie Plank, who was pitching at Gettysburg College.
Playing Career: *1884-1885, 1889-1893, 1895-1896, 1901-1902; Chi-Pit U, KC U, Bal AA, Cin N, Was AA, Was N, Bal N, NY N, Bos A, Bal A*

Mike Fornieles
Fornieles y Torres, Jose Miguel
B: Jan 18, 1932

Pos: P	ERA: 3.96
W-L: 63-64	SOs: 576
ShOs: 4	Saves: 55

Cuban-born Fornieles alternated between starting and relieving throughout his career. In 1960 he went 10-5 and led the league with 14 saves and an AL-record 70 appearances. The next year he posted 15 saves and made the All-Star team.
Playing Career: *1952-1963; Was A, Chi A, Bal A, Bos A, Min A*

Bob Forsch after his 1978 no-hitter.

Bob Forsch
Forsch, Robert Herbert
B: Jan 13, 1950

Pos: P	ERA: 3.76
W-L: 168-136	SOs: 1,133
ShOs: 19	No-hitters: 2

Only Hall of Famers Bob Gibson and Jesse Haines pitched more years or won more games for the Cardinals than Forsch, who gave them 163 victories. He led the Red Birds'

''The Chairman of the Board,'' Whitey Ford.

staff in wins six times. Converted from a third baseman, Forsch threw two no-hitters in the minors, then he and his brother Ken became the first pair of siblings to toss no-hitters in the major leagues. He went 3-4 in postseason play with the Cardinals after leading them to three pennants.

A power pitcher early in his career, Forsch came to rely on pinpoint control, a change-up, and a sinker with an occasional fastball. Helping himself in the field and at the plate, Forsch was a smooth fielder and an excellent bunter who also had home run power. He won the Silver Slugger Award in 1980 and 1987, symbolic of the best hitter at his position.
Playing Career: *1974-1989; StL N, Hou N*

Ken Forsch
Forsch, Kenneth Roth
B: Sep 8, 1946

Pos: P	ERA: 3.37
W-L: 114-113	SOs: 1,047
ShOs: 18	No-hitters: 1

The Forsch brothers – Ken and Bob – are the only siblings to hurl no-hitters in the major leagues. Ken supplemented his fastball with a fluttering forkball during a 16-year career which was split between starting and relieving. Forsch saved 51 games from 1973 to 1978. In 1976 he was named to the NL All-Star team as a reliever; he saved 19 games that year. In 1981 he was named to the AL All-Star team as a starter. He was 11-7 that season.
Playing Career: *1970-1984, 1986; Hou N, Cal A*

Terry Forster
Forster, Terry Jay
B: Jan 14, 1952

Pos: P	ERA: 3.23
W-L: 54-65	SOs: 791
ShOs: 0	Saves: 127

A pitching phenom at 18, Forster was pitching in the majors by age 19. From 1971 to 1973 he hurled an incredible 138⅓ innings without surrendering a home run. Forster was the AL Fireman of the Year in 1974, with a league-high 24 saves. That September his fastball was clocked at 94.9 mph. Toward the end of his career Forster struggled with a weight problem, but not at the plate, where he was a lifetime .397 hitter.
Playing Career: *1971-1986; Chi A, Pit N, LA N, Atl N, Cal A*

Ray Fosse
Fosse, Raymond Earl
B: Apr 4, 1947

Pos: C	BA: .256
Hits: 758	HRs: 61
RBI: 324	BBs: 203

Pete Rose scored the winning run in the 12th inning of the 1970 All-Star Game by creaming Fosse at home plate. The catcher played with a fractured shoulder until another injury ended that season. He never showed power again. Fosse played in two World Series.
Playing Career: *1967-1977, 1979; Cle A, Oak A, Sea A, Mil A*

Eddie Foster
Foster, Edward Cunningham
B: Feb 13, 1887   D: Jan 15, 1937

Pos: 3B, 2B, SS	BA: .264
Hits: 1,490	HRs: 6
RBI: 446	BBs: 528

Foster was widely regarded as the premier hit-and-run man of his day. His best year was 1912, when he batted .285 with 34 doubles and scored 98 runs. He stole 27 bases that season, 195 in his career. Foster was known for his clutch hitting, once depriving Hall of Famer Eddie Plank of a no-hitter. Plank had gone 8 ⅔ innings without allowing a hit. He walked a batter, then Foster doubled the runner home to end Plank's bid.
Playing Career: *1910, 1912-1923; NY A, Was A, Bos A, StL A*

George Foster.

George Foster
Foster, George Arthur
B: Dec 1, 1948

Pos: OF	BA: .274
Hits: 1,925	HRs: 348
RBI: 1,239	BBs: 666

In 1977 Foster pounded 52 home runs, becoming only the fifth NL player to reach that milestone in one season. Originally signed by the Giants, Foster soon became an important cog in the Big Red Machine of the 1970s. For seven years, starting in 1975, Foster averaged 32 homers and 107 RBI for Cincinnati. He led the league in RBI for three consecutive years, 1976-1978. In 1977 he was NL MVP with a .320 average, 149 RBI, 124 runs scored, and 52 taters. In 11 seasons with the Reds Foster hit .326 in 13 games in three World Series, and he appeared in five All-Star Games. Then he was traded.

The Mets' new owners, Nelson Doubleday and Fred Wilpon, signed Foster to a five-year pact, the first $2 million-per-year contract. Without the supporting cast that he had in Cincinnati, Foster's act suffered. He felt compelled to hit a home run on every at-bat.
Playing Career: *1969-1986; SF N, Cin N, NY N, Chi A*

Hall of Famer Rube Foster.

Rube Foster
Foster, Andrew
B: Sep 17, 1879   D: Dec 9, 1930
Hall of Fame 1981

Pos: P, OF	ERA: NA
W-L: 14-14 (inc.)	SOs: 82 (inc.)
ShOs: 3 (inc.)	Saves: NA
Managerial Record	
Won: 278 Lost: 161 Pct: .633	

Foster overcame childhood illness, parental objection, and racial prejudice to become an outstanding pitcher, a shrewd manager, and one of the dominant executives of black baseball. In 1902, when Foster went to New York to play with the Cuban X-Giants he looked up John McGraw, whom he had met in Hot Springs two years earlier. Foster taught Christy Mathewson how to throw the screwball. Leaving New York for Chicago, Foster developed the Leland/American Giants into the team with the best record ever, 123-6 in 1910. After frustrating dealings with East Coast booking agents, Foster founded the Negro National League in order to cut out the middleman, who had been taking 50 percent or more of the gate. The league operated in the Midwest from 1920 through 1931, with Foster serving as president until 1926. The Eastern Colored League was organized in 1923 and a Negro World Series between the two leagues was staged from 1924 through 1927.
Playing Career: *1902-1918; Chi Union Giants, Cuban X-Giants, Phi Giants, Chi Leland Giants, Chi Am Giants*
Managerial Career: *1910-1925; Chi Am Giants*

Rube Foster
Foster, George
B: Jan 5, 1888   D: Mar 1, 1976

Pos: P	ERA: 2.35
W-L: 58-34	SOs: 297
ShOs: 15	No-hitters: 1

In a short but eventful career, Foster made it to two World Series, both won by his team. He won two games in the 1915 Series, and batted .500. Taught to throw a fastball by Red Sox teammate Smokey Joe Wood, Foster no-hit the Yankees on June 21, 1916.
Playing Career: *1913-1917; Bos A*

Willie Foster.

Willie Foster
Foster, William Hendrick
B: Jun 12, 1904   D: Sep 16, 1978

Pos: P   ERA: NA
W-L: 137-62   SOs: 734
ShOs: 34   Saves: 12

The younger half brother of Andrew "Rube" Foster, Willie was a lean left-hander. When Willie wanted to be a baseball player, Rube wanted him to get an education; when Rube later changed his mind and wanted Willie to pitch, he hesitated. The two finally reached common ground, and during the mid-1920s, Willie achieved stardom and helped carry the American Giants to two consecutive Negro League World Championships.

Foster had some of his best games against the Kansas City Monarchs, at one time shutting them out twice in one day to win the Negro National League Championship. Against major league All-Stars he was devastating, with his left-handed sidearm delivery. In face-to-face combat against Satchel Paige, Foster held the edge in 21 games. As incredible as it may seem, he won more than 80 games – counting exhibition contests – in two seasons, 1926-1927. Foster also fulfilled brother Rube's dream; he graduated from Alcorn University.
Playing Career: *1923-1937; Mem Red Sox, Chi Am Giants, Bir Black Barons, Hom Grays, KC Monarchs, Pit Crawfords*

Bob Fothergill
Fothergill, Robert Roy (Fats)
B: Aug 16, 1897   D: Mar 20, 1938

Pos: OF   BA: .325
Hits: 1,064   HRs: 36
RBI: 582   BBs: 202

Fothergill was an outstanding hitter who was also well-known for his girth. Charitably listed at 230 pounds, the 5'10" outfielder was the object of Leo Durocher's complaint that it was illegal to have two men in the batter's box. During a fasting program, Fothergill allegedly bit an umpire after a called third strike. There were several accounts of his shattering outfield fences in pursuit of fly balls. In 1927 he batted .359 with 114 RBI; his average never fell below .300.
Playing Career: *1922-1933; Det A, Chi A, Bos A*

Jake Fournier
Fournier, John Frank
B: Sep 29, 1892   D: Sep 5, 1973

Pos: 1B, OF   BA: .313
Hits: 1,631   HRs: 136
RBI: 859   BBs: 587

A slugger with a hole in his glove, Fournier moved from the Class D Western Canada League in 1911 to the White Sox in 1912. Sox manager Clarence Rowland benched Fournier despite his league-leading slugging average of .491 in 1915. He returned to the minors to learn to hit better, recognizing that his fielding was hopeless. With the lively ball, Fournier stepped forward, hitting .343 for the Cardinals in 1921, and .351, .334 then .350 for the Dodgers, 1923-1925.
Playing Career: *1912-1918, 1920-1927; Chi A, NY A, StL N, Brk N, Bos N*

Dave Foutz
Foutz, David Luther (Scissors)
B: Sep 7, 1856   D: Mar 5, 1897

Pos: P   ERA: 2.84
W-L: 147-66   SOs: 790
ShOs: 16   Saves: 4
Managerial Record
Won: 264   Lost: 257   Pct: .507

A double-duty pitcher, Foutz recorded the second-highest lifetime won-lost percentage in history, .690, and batted .277 with 32 home runs and 263 stolen bases. Browns owner Chris Von der Ahe acquired Foutz by purchasing the entire Bay City, Michigan franchise. Paired with Parisian Bob Caruthers, Foutz pitched the Browns to AA pennants 1885-1887. Foutz won 41 games in 1886 with a .719 percentage and a 2.11 ERA, all league-leading statistics. The next year he won only 25 games, but hit .357 in 65 games as an outfielder and first baseman. On Independence Day Foutz hit a homer in the morning game and went 5-for-6 in the afternoon with two homers and nine RBI. The Browns sold Caruthers and Foutz to Brooklyn in 1888 for $13,500. With the hard-hitting Foutz at first

Dave Foutz.

base, the Dodgers won the 1889 AA flag, switched to the NL, and won another pennant in 1890. In 1893 Foutz became a playing manager.
Playing Career: *1884-1896; StL AA, Brk AA, Brk N*
Managerial Career: *1893-1896; Brk N*

Art Fowler
Fowler, John Arthur
B: Jul 3, 1922

Pos: P   ERA: 4.03
W-L: 54-51   SOs: 539
ShOs: 4   Saves: 32

After Fowler's major league career, manager Billy Martin used the 48-year-old as a player-coach for Denver in 1970. He saved 15 games and won 9, with a 1.59 ERA. Fowler accompanied Martin to several major league teams, where he served as pitching coach.
Playing Career: *1954-1957, 1959, 1961-1964; Cin N, LA N, LA A*

Bud Fowler
Fowler, John W.
B: Mar 16, 1858   D: Feb 26, 1913

Born John W. Jackson in upstate New York in 1858, and raised in Cooperstown, Fowler first achieved recognition as a 20-year-old pitcher for a Chelsea, Massachusetts team. In April 1878, Fowler defeated the National League's Boston club in an exhibition game. Later that season, he hurled three games for the Lynn Live Oaks of the International Association, and another for Worcester in the New England League. Fowler played for 17 teams in nine leagues, seldom batting less than .300

Versatile pitcher/second baseman Bud Fowler (c) with the Keokuk club.

for a season. In 1886 he led the Western League in triples.

Fowler was a good player, very versatile, a fast runner, and a slick fielder at second base. People came to see him play since he usually was the only black player on a white team. Fowler was not docile when threatened and had several confrontations with other players and managers during his career. "He is one of the best general players in the country," reported *Sporting Life* in 1885, "and if he had a white face he would be playing with the best of them."

Dick Fowler
Fowler, Richard John
B: Mar 30, 1921   D: May 22, 1972

Pos: P	ERA: 4.11
W-L: 66-79	SOs: 382
ShOs: 11	No-hitters: 1

The best pitcher on the dreadful Athletics teams of the late 1940s, Fowler twice won 15 games with his sharp fastball and biting curve. Fresh out of the Canadian Army, he tossed a no-hitter versus the Browns on September 9, 1945.
Playing Career: *1941-1942, 1945-1952; Phi A*

Charlie Fox
Fox, Charles Francis
B: Oct 7, 1921

Managerial Record
Won: 377   Lost: 371   Pct: .504

Fox caught only three games for the Giants in 1942, but he hit .429. He then began managing in their farm system at the Class-D level and worked his way up to the majors. Fox led the Giants to the 1971 Western Division championship and was voted Manager of the Year. He later served as both general manager and interim manager of the Expos and interim manager of the Cubs.
Managerial Career: *1970-1974, 1976, 1983; SF N, Mon N, Chi N*

Nellie Fox
Fox, Jacob Nelson
B: Dec 25, 1927   D: Dec 1, 1975

Pos: 2B	BA: .288
Hits: 2,663	HRs: 35
RBI: 790	BBs: 719

The top AL second basemen for more than a decade, Fox got off to an inauspicious start. Traded to the White Sox after an unimpressive 1948 rookie season, Fox played 798 consecutive games at the keystone sack. Teaming first with Chico Carrasquel and then with Luis Aparicio, he gave Chicago a tough double play combination. Fox led the league in fielding average six times.

Originally a poor batter, he worked hard to become a .300 hitter, reaching the mark six times. He made the All-Star team 12 times. Fox scored 1,279 runs and smashed 355 doubles as he led the AL in hits four times. More importantly, he rarely struck out; he had the fewest strikeouts in the AL 11 times, whiffing only 216 times in 9,232 career at-bats. In 1959, when the White Sox won their first pennant in 40 years, Fox was named AL MVP. After he left baseball, the White Sox retired his uniform number.
Playing Career: *1947-1965; Phi A, Chi A, Hou N*

Pete Fox
Fox, Ervin
B: Mar 8, 1909   D: Jul 5, 1966

Pos: OF	BA: .298
Hits: 1,678	HRs: 65
RBI: 694	BBs: 392

Fox was a mainstay of the hard-hitting Detroit teams of the mid-1930s. First signed as a pitcher, Fox led the Texas League in hitting within three seasons after switching to the outfield. Promoted to the Tigers, he became a steady fielder with a good arm, leading the AL outfield with a .994 fielding average in 1938. Fox hit over .300 five times. He had six doubles in the 1934 World Series, and was the top batter in the 1935 Fall Classic, slashing 10 hits in 26 at-bats for a .385 average, helping his Tigers defeat the Cubs four games to two.
Playing Career: *1933-1945; Det A, Bos A*

Terry Fox
Fox, Terrence Edward
B: Jul 31, 1935

Pos: P	ERA: 2.99
W-L: 29-19	SOs: 185
ShOs: 0	Saves: 59

A solid reliever with a 29-19 record, Fox won 60 percent of his games. In 1961 he posted a 1.41 ERA in 39 games for Detroit, winning five and saving 12, but surrendered Roger Maris's 58th homer. The next year he recorded a 1.71 ERA with 16 saves.
Playing Career: *1960-1966; Mil N, Det A, Phi N*

Jimmie Foxx
Foxx, James Emory (Double X, The Beast)
B: Oct 22, 1907   D: Jul 21, 1967
Hall of Fame 1951

Pos: 1B	BA: .325
Hits: 2,646	HRs: 534
RBI: 1,921	BBs: 1,452

Foxx was one of the greatest power hitters in baseball history. Lefty Gomez said that The Beast was not scouted but trapped. Foxx broke in as a catcher, but moved to first base when Mickey Cochrane emerged as the receiver for Connie Mack's 1920s Athletics. Before long, Foxx was being called "the right-handed Babe Ruth." He drove in over 100 runs a season 13 times. He won the Triple Crown in 1933, hitting .356 with 48 homers and 163 RBI. His best RBI season was 1938 when he drove in 175. That year he would have captured his second Triple Crown, but Hank Greenberg hit 58 homers. Foxx was the home run champ four times despite competition from Babe Ruth, Lou Gehrig, Joe DiMaggio and Greenberg. Posting a lifetime .609 slugging average, Foxx scored 1,751 runs, and hit .344 in three World Series with the A's. He was selected for the AL All-Star squad nine straight years, 1933-1941.
Playing Career: *1925-1942, 1944-1945; Phi A, Bos A, Chi N, Phi N*

Paul Foytack
Foytack, Paul Eugene
B: Nov 16, 1930

Pos: P	ERA: 4.14
W-L: 86-87	SOs: 827
ShOs: 7	Saves: 7

Sometimes beset by control problems, Foytack became a mainstay of the Tigers' staff during the 1950s. Playing for the Angels on July 31, 1963, Foytack set a record by giving up four consecutive home runs – to Woodie Held, Pedro Ramos, Tito Francona and Larry Brown – in one inning.
Playing Career: *1953, 1955-1964; Det A, LA A*

John Franco
Franco, John Anthony
B: Sep 17, 1960

Pos: P	ERA: 2.62
W-L: 62-47	SOs: 517
ShOs: 0	Saves: 236

Local boy Franco returned to New York to anchor the Mets' bullpen. Having graduated from the same high school as Mets President Fred Wilpon – not to mention Sandy Koufax and the Aspromonte brothers – Franco has a hometown stake in his success. He has led the NL in saves twice, with 39 in 1988 and 33 in 1990. He posted ERAs under 2.00 twice, in 1988 and 1992.
Playing Career: *1984-; Cin N, NY N*

Julio Franco
Franco, Julio Cesar
B: Aug 23, 1958

Pos: 2B, SS, DH	BA: .300
Hits: 1,784	HRs: 100
RBI: 763	BBs: 561

The first Texas Ranger to win a batting title, Franco was crowned in 1991 when he hit .341. He was also the fifth AL player since 1945 to

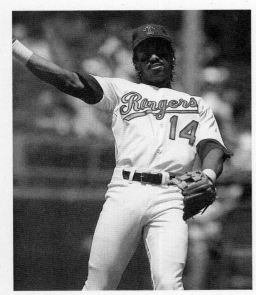

Julio Franco.

have 100 runs, 200 hits and 30 stolen bases. After his great 1991 season Franco sat out most of 1992 following knee surgery.

Franco was once the star of the Phillies' farm system. Playing regularly for the first time in Cleveland, he averaged 175 hits over six years. Franco's hitting was not timely, however, and he made a lot of errors. He was traded to Texas for Pete O'Brien, Jerry Browne and Oddibe McDowell before the 1989 season. There Franco emerged as a team leader and mentor to Rafael Palmeiro and Ruben Sierra. Franco hit .316 with 92 RBI and 21 stolen bases in 1989. He has been chosen for the All-Star team three times.
Playing Career: *1982- ; Phi N, Cle A, Tex A*

Tito Francona
Francona, John Patsy
B: Nov 4, 1933

Pos: OF, 1B	BA: .272
Hits: 1,395	HRs: 125
RBI: 656	BBs: 544

Francona hit .363 in 1959, but did not win the batting crown because he was a platoon player. Frequently used as a left-handed pinch hitter, Francona journeyed through baseball as a "supersub." In 1960 he led the AL with 36 doubles. He was elected to the 1961 All-Star team. Francona led the AL with 15 pinch hits in 1970. His son Terry played major league baseball for 10 years.
Playing Career: *1956-1970; Bal A, Chi A, Det A, Cle A, StL N, Phi N, Atl N, Oak A, Mil A*

Fred Frankhouse
Frankhouse, Frederick Meloy
B: Apr 9, 1904   D: Aug 17, 1989

Pos: P	ERA: 3.92
W-L: 106-97	SOs: 622
ShOs: 10	No-hitters: 1

In 1937 Frankhouse outdueled Carl Hubbell to break his record 24-game winning streak. Frankhouse won 17 games in his only All-Star year, 1934. He recorded 12 saves and made 216 starts in 402 appearances.
Playing Career: *1927-1939; StL N, Bos N, Brk N*

Herman Franks
Franks, Herman Louis
B: Jan 4, 1914

Pos: C	BA: .199
Hits: 80	HRs: 3
RBI: 43	BBs: 57
Managerial Record	
Won: 605 Lost: 521 Pct: .537	

A graduate of the University of Utah, Franks was the backup catcher behind Mickey Owen in the Dodgers' chain of receivers. He made one appearance in the 1941 World Series. Franks later scouted for the Giants, then became manager of their Salt Lake City club in 1961. From 1965 to 1968 he managed the Giants to four straight second-place finishes. After a successful business career, he formed

Cubs Manager Herman Franks, 1979.

a group that tried to buy the Yankees in 1972. Franks came out of retirement to manage the Cubs.
Playing Career: *1939-1941, 1947-1949; StL N, Brk N, Phi A, NY N*
Managerial Career: *1965-1968, 1977-1979; SF N, Chi N*

Chick Fraser
Fraser, Charles Carrolton
B: Mar 17, 1871   D: May 8, 1940

Pos: P	ERA: 3.68
W-L: 175-212	SOs: 1,098
ShOs: 22	No-hitters: 1

Fraser is 30th on the all-time loss list with 212, but he pitched for some truly terrible teams, losing 20 games or more five times. He jumped to the new AL in 1901, but succumbed to threats of legal action and went back to the NL Phillies. Fraser tossed a no-hitter in 1903. He later became a coach with masterful control of the fungo bat. Fraser was the brother-in-law of Hall of Famer Fred Clarke; they married sisters. Clarke signed Fraser as a scout.
Playing Career: *1896-1909; Lou N, Cle N, Phi N, Phi A, Bos N, Cin N, Chi N*

George Frazier
Frazier, George Allen
B: Oct 13, 1954

Pos: P	ERA: 4.20
W-L: 35-43	SOs: 449
ShOs: 0	Saves: 29

In 1981 Frazier matched the World Series record for most losses, with three. He tied with Lefty Williams, who was throwing games for gamblers in 1919. Frazier also pitched in the 1987 Fall Classic. His best year was the strike-shortened 1981 season when he saved three with a 1.63 ERA.
Playing Career: *1978-1987; StL N, NY A, Cle A, Chi N, Min A*

Andrew Freedman
Freedman, Andrew
B: Sep 1, 1860 D: Dec 4, 1915

One of the most despicable people in baseball history, Freedman owned the New York Giants from 1895 to 1902. Easily provoked and inclined to be arbitrary to the point of tyranny, Freedman was a Tammany Hall politician who kept the AL out of New York by building a street through any piece of property where the new league wanted to build a ballpark.

In a move that outraged observers, Freedman tried to introduce Syndicate Baseball to fellow team owners. He felt that baseball would be more lucrative if all of the players' contracts were held in common, and the best players were shifted to the better-drawing cities. He convinced four other owners to sign a secret agreement forming the National League Baseball Trust. Remaining club owners turned to Albert Spalding to lead the tumultous 1902 league meeting that defeated "Freedmanism." The Giants floundered during Freedman's regime and attendance dwindled. He lost several lawsuits and eventually sold the club when it failed to produce the anticipated revenue.

Bill Freehan
Freehan, William Ashley
B: Nov 29, 1941

Pos: C	BA: .262
Hits: 1,591	HRs: 200
RBI: 758	BBs: 626

Freehan was the catalyst in the 1968 World Series. The Cardinals led three games to one against the Tigers, and in Game Five the Red Birds were ahead 3-2. Lou Brock came steaming around third with the fourth run to put the Cardinals' championship on ice. Freehan took a throw from outfielder Willie Horton and tagged Brock, who could not get through the catcher to score. It was the moment that ignited the Tigers. They scored three runs in the seventh to win the game, pounded the Cardinals 13-1 in Game Six, then beat Bob Gibson in Game Seven to win their first World Series Championship since 1945.

A University of Michigan baseball and football star, Freehan signed with the Tigers for a $100,000 bonus in 1961. Two years later he became the regular catcher and held the position for 14 seasons. He evolved into the AL's best receiver, and was selected for the All-Star Game 11 times. Freehan earned five Gold Glove Awards, and wrote *Behind the Mask*, a diary of the 1969 season.
Playing Career: *1961, 1963-1976; Det A*

Buck Freeman
Freeman, John Frank
B: Oct 30, 1871 D: Jun 25, 1949

Pos: OF, 1B	BA: .294
Hits: 1,238	HRs: 82
RBI: 713	BBs: 272

The home run record Babe Ruth broke in 1919 had been set by Buck Freeman. Originally a pitcher like Ruth, Freeman returned to the minors to learn how to hit. In his first full NL season, he hit 25 home runs. Freeman jumped to the new AL in 1901 and was the power hitter on the pennant-winning Red Sox teams of 1903 and 1904. He led the AL in homers in 1903. Freeman and Sam Crawford are the only two sluggers to lead both the NL and AL in homers.
Playing Career: *1891, 1898-1907; Was AA, Was N, Bos N, Bos A*

Gene Freese
Freese, Eugene Lewis
B: Jan 8, 1934

Pos: 3B	BA: .254
Hits: 877	HRs: 115
RBI: 432	BBs: 243

Freese ranks among the all-time leaders with nine pinch-hit home runs, including two consecutive blasts in April 1959. Gene and his brother George played together with the 1955 Pirates, and battled each other for the third base job.
Playing Career: *1955-1966; Pit N, StL N, Phi N, Chi A, Cin N, Hou N*

Jim Fregosi
Fregosi, James Louis
B: Apr 4, 1942

Pos: SS	BA: .265
Hits: 1,726	HRs: 151
RBI: 706	BBs: 715
Managerial Record	
Won: 527 Lost: 540 Pct: .494	

Fregosi was the power-hitting shortstop for the Angels during the 1960s. Known as a cheerleader, Fregosi was tabbed early as a future manager. In New York, however, Fregosi was known as the disappointing player the Mets received in the Nolan Ryan trade.

Fregosi hit for the cycle twice, on July 28, 1964, and again on May 20, 1968. His best year was 1970, when he had career highs of 22 homers, 82 RBI, and 95 runs while hitting .278. He never regained his earlier form after going to the Mets. He then began his managerial career with the Angels in 1978. The next year he guided them to the division title, and the Phils to the pennant in 1993.
Playing Career: *1961-1978; LA A, Cal A, NY N, Tex A, Pit N*
Managerial Career: *1978-1981, 1986-1988, 1991- ; Cal A, Chi A, Phi N*

The Detroit Tigers' All-Star, Gold Glove catcher, Bill Freehan.

Cubs pitcher Larry French, 1935.

Larry French
French, Lawrence Herbert
B: Nov 1, 1907   D: Feb 9, 1987

Pos: P	ERA: 3.44
W-L: 197-171	SOs: 1,187
ShOs: 40	Saves: 17

In the 1930s French pitched 2,481 innings, more than anyone but Carl Hubbell. The rugged left-hander started 20 or more games and finished 10 or more for 11 consecutive seasons. He led the NL in shutouts 1935-1936. During the Cubs' famous 21-game winning streak in September 1935, French claimed five triumphs. In 1942 he was 15-4 with a 1.83 ERA. After 14 seasons of major league baseball, French joined the Navy, retiring in 1969 with the rank of captain.
Playing Career: *1929-1942; Pit N, Chi N, Brk N*

Benny Frey
Frey, Benjamin Rudolph
B: Apr 6, 1906   D: Nov 1, 1937

Pos: P	ERA: 4.50
W-L: 57-82	SOs: 179
ShOs: 7	Saves: 7

Frey was a sidearm relief pitcher with the Reds, who first retired, then committed suicide when he was asked to go back to the minors. Frey's actions had a profound affect on catcher Willard Hershberger, his companion in the bullpen who took his own life in the 1940s.
Playing Career: *1929-1936; Cin N, StL N*

Jim Frey
Frey, James Gottfried
B: May 26, 1931

Managerial Record
Won: 323   Lost: 287   Pct: .530

Frey piloted the Royals to the pennant in his first year as a major league manager, but was fired before the end of the next season. A minor league batting champ in 1960, he began his managerial career in the Orioles' farm system in 1964. Frey coached for the Orioles before taking the Kansas City job. He was instrumental in two recent Cubs division titles, as manager in 1984, then as part of the front office staff in 1989.
Managerial Career: *1980-1981; 1984-1986; KC A, Chi N*

Lonnie Frey
Frey, Linus Reinhard
B: Aug 23, 1910

Pos: 2B, SS, OF	BA: .269
Hits: 1,482	HRs: 61
RBI: 549	BBs: 752

Frey played in three All-Star Games. He has lifetime statistics comparable to those of middle infielders Phil Rizzuto, Dick Bartell, Billy Rogell, Billy Jurges and Eddie Joost. Frey was a smart infielder who led NL second basemen in fielding and double plays twice, as well as leading the league in stolen bases with 22 in 1940. He played in three World Series, 1939, 1940 and 1947.
Playing Career: *1933-1943, 1946-1948; Brk N, Chi N, Cin N, NY A, NY N*

Barney Friberg
Friberg, Bernard Albert
B: Aug 18, 1899   D: Dec 8, 1958

Pos: 2B, OF, SS, 3B, 1B	BA: .281
Hits: 1,170	HRs: 38
RBI: 471	BBs: 471

Born Gustaf Bernhard Friberg, Barney Friberg was playing in the majors by age 19. His best season was 1923, when he hit at a .318 pace with 91 runs, 88 RBI, 27 doubles, and 12 home runs for the Cubs. The Phillies tried to make a pitcher of him during the 1930s.
Playing Career: *1919-1920, 1922-1933; Chi N, Phi N, Bos A*

Ford Frick
Frick, Ford Christopher
B: Dec 19, 1894   D: Apr 8, 1978
Hall of Fame 1970

During the trying months after Jackie Robinson's debut with the Dodgers in 1947, Ford Frick served baseball as NL president. His unswerving allegience to fair play and integration guided baseball through racial discrimination incidents and proposed strikes. Devoted to the national pastime in a variety of roles, the DePauw graduate was originally a sportswriter. His emcee performance at the first New York Baseball Writers' Dinner in 1924 brought him to prominence. Frick also worked as a broadcaster before becoming the director of the NL Service Bureau in 1934. Nine months later he was elected league president, a position he held for 17 years. He combined forces with Kenesaw Mountain Landis, Stephen Clark and Alexander Cleland in obtaining support for the establishment of the Hall of Fame. In 1951 he replaced Happy Chandler as commissioner, serving baseball for another 14 years.

Bob Friend
Friend, Robert Bartmess
B: Nov 24, 1930

Pos: P	ERA: 3.58
W-L: 197-230	SOs: 1,734
ShOs: 36	Saves: 11

After 15 seasons with the Pirates, Friend played for both the Yankees and the Mets in his final season. A member of the celebrated Baby Buc brigade in 1952, Friend was part of the pitching rotation of General Manager Branch Rickey's youthful team. In 1955 Friend led the NL with an ERA of 2.83. Three years later he tied with Warren Spahn to top the league with 22 wins. Friend pitched in three All-Star Games and one World Series.
Playing Career: *1951-1966; Pit N, NY A, NY N*

NL President Ford Frick with his wife (r) at the Dodgers-Giants opener in 1937.

Pirates hurler Bob Friend, 1955.

Frank Frisch
Frisch, Frank Francis (The Fordham Flash)
B: Sep 9, 1898   D: Mar 12, 1973
Hall of Fame 1947

Pos: 2B	BA: .316
Hits: 2,880	HRs: 105
RBI: 1,244	BBs: 708

Managerial Record
Won: 1,138   Lost: 1,078   Pct: .514

Frisch was one of the most spectacular players in baseball history. He stole 419 bases, scored 1,532 runs, hit 138 triples, and struck out only 272 times. Frisch hit .294 in eight World Series. He went from Fordham University directly to the Giants without playing in the minors. A natural athlete with great speed and dexterity, Frisch was personally tutored by Manager John McGraw, who named Frisch captain in his second season with the Giants. He was instrumental in four consecutive Giants pennant-winning seasons, and batted .363 in those four World Series, 1921-1924.

Then came the trade. Frisch went to the Cardinals in exchange for Rogers Hornsby, the six-time NL batting champ and manager of the World Champion Red Birds. No player, with the exception of Jackie Robinson in 1947, ever started a season with more pressure than Frisch had in 1927. He batted .337, leading the NL in stolen bases and fielding percentage, and by midseason, he had Cardinals fans saying, "You know, Hornsby was an SOB. I never liked him." The rest of Frisch's career was anticlimactic, but extremely eventful. He was the manager of the Gas House Gang, a radio broadcaster, then leader of the Baseball Hall of Fame Veterans Committee.
Playing Career: *1919-1937; NY N, StL N*
Managerial Career: *1933-1938, 1940-1946, 1949-1951; StL N, Pit N, Chi N*

Danny Frisella
Frisella, Daniel Vincent
B: Mar 4, 1946   D: Jan 1, 1977

Pos: P	ERA: 3.32
W-L: 34-40	SOs: 471
ShOs: 0	Saves: 57

A forkball pitcher, Frisella had one of the shortest single-season stints in baseball history when he pitched just four innings for the 1969 Mets. He was coming off a strong 1976 season when he was killed in a New Year's Day dunebuggy accident.
Playing Career: *1967-1976; NY N, Atl N, SD N, Mil A*

Art Fromme
Fromme, Arthur Henry
B: Sep 3, 1883   D: Aug 24, 1956

Pos: P	ERA: 2.90
W-L: 80-90	SOs: 638
ShOs: 14	Saves: 4

Early in 1913 Fromme, four other players and $20,000 left the Reds and went to the Giants. Although he went 20-11 over two years, McGraw did not use him in the 1913 World Series or the 1913-14 Around the World tour. Fromme had won 19 games with a 1.90 ERA in 1909 for the Reds.
Playing Career: *1906-1915; StL N, Cin N, NY N*

Woodie Fryman
Fryman, Woodrow Thompson
B: Apr 15, 1940

Pos: P	ERA: 3.77
W-L: 141-155	SOs: 1,587
ShOs: 27	Saves: 58

Fryman was a Kentucky tobacco farmer who signed his first pro contract at age 25, then spent 18 years as a spot starter and reliever. After only 12 minor league games, Fryman started the 1966 season with the Pirates and hurled three consecutive shutouts. He tossed four one-hitters. Fryman was elected to two All-Star teams, in 1968 and 1976. He also appeared with his teams in the ALCS in 1972 and NL division playoffs in 1981.
Playing Career: *1966-1983; Pit N, Phi N, Det A, Mon N, Cin N*

Tito Fuentes
Fuentes y Peat, Rigoberto
B: Jan 4, 1944

Pos: 2B	BA: .268
Hits: 1,491	HRs: 45
RBI: 438	BBs: 298

Fuentes hit .313 and slugged .563 for the Giants in the 1971 NLCS. The nimble Cuban was a flamboyant fielder, setting an NL record by committing only six errors in 1973. He led the NL in fielding percentage, but did not win a Gold Glove. He led NL second basemen in errors the previous two seasons. A productive switch hitter, Fuentes drove in 78 runs for the Giants in 1973, and scored 83 times for the Tigers in 1977, when he batted a career-high .309.
Playing Career: *1965-1967, 1969-1978; SF N, SD N, Det A, Oak A*

Shorty Fuller
Fuller, William Benjamin
B: Oct 10, 1867   D: Apr 11, 1904

Pos: SS	BA: .236
Hits: 867	HRs: 6
RBI: 310	BBs: 444

Fuller started almost every game for the kamikaze 1891 Browns, yet escaped his teammates' fate of being described in the newspapers as drunken reprobates. During his career Fuller scored 652 runs and stole 260 bases.
Playing Career: *1888-1896; Was N, StL AA, NY N*

"The Fordham Flash," Frank Frisch, with the St. Louis Cardinals.

Hugh S. Fullerton
Fullerton, Hugh S.
B: Sep 10, 1873   D: Sep 15, 1965

By the first decade of the 20th century, Fullerton had become one of the best-known baseball writers in the country. He was part of the Chicago crop of sportswriters that included Ring Lardner, Sy Sanborn and Charles Dryden. Fullerton and other sportswriters grew outraged by the attitude of teams toward the press. During the 1907 and 1908 World Series, the Tigers' front office seated sportswriters on the roof of old Bennent Field, where the temperature dropped into the thirties during the October games. Fullerton and Joseph Jackson, from the *Detroit Free Press*, founded the Base Ball Writers Association of America in 1908 as a means to improve working conditions. One of the first to write stories on the inner workings of baseball, Fullerton was instrumental in exposing the Black Sox scandal in 1919. Fullerton was awarded the J. G. Taylor Spink Award in 1964 for his contributions to the game.

Chick Fullis
Fullis, Charles Philip
B: Feb 27, 1904   D: Mar 28, 1946

Pos: OF   BA: .295
Hits: 548   HRs: 12
RBI: 167   BBs: 132

Fullis batted .400 for the Gas House Gang in the 1934 World Series. In his only season as a regular, he whacked 200 hits for a .309 average, and led the NL in at-bats and putouts for the 1933 Phillies. He retired early due to eye trouble.
Playing Career: *1928-1934, 1936; NY N, Phi N, StL N*

Chick Fulmer
Fulmer, Charles John
B: Feb 12, 1851   D: Feb 15, 1940

Pos: SS, 2B, OF, 3B   BA: .261
Hits: 637   HRs: 8
RBI: 110 (inc.)   BBs: 42

At age 14, Fulmer enlisted as a drummer-boy in the Army during the Civil War, but did not participate in the fighting. An outstanding glove man, Fulmer claimed he made an unassisted triple play in 1873 while with the Philadelphia White Stockings.
Playing Career: *1871-1876, 1879-1880, 1882-1884; Rok Forest Citys n, NY Mutuals n, Phi White Stockings n, Lou N, Buf N, Cin AA, StL AA*

Carl Furillo
Furillo, Carl Anthony (The Reading Rifle)
B: Mar 8, 1922   D: Jan 21, 1989

Pos: OF   BA: .299
Hits: 1,910   HRs: 192
RBI: 1,058   BBs: 514

Furillo was one of the Boys of Summer made famous by author Roger Kahn, who described the outfielder as "The Hard Hat Who Sued Baseball." Furillo filed suit against the Dodgers in 1960 for releasing him while he was disabled. He was awarded $21,000 in settlement. Furillo, who never got another job in baseball after the lawsuit, believed he had been blacklisted.

In 1949 Furillo batted .322 with 18 homers, 10 triples, 95 runs scored, and 106 RBI. He followed that season with almost exactly the same numbers in 1950: a .305 batting average with 18 homers, 30 doubles, 99 runs, and 106 RBI. Furillo had a gun for an arm, and could play the tricky, 40-foot right field wall in Ebbets Field better than any of his contemporaries. He once threw out Reds pitcher Mel Queen at first base on a 300-foot hit into the right field gap. Furillo won the NL batting title in 1953, when he hit .344. That year he hit a game-tying, ninth-inning home run in the World Series.
Playing Career: *1946-1960; Brk N, LA N*

Dodgers outfielder Carl Furillo.

Eddie Gaedel

Gaedel, Edward
B: Jun 8, 1925   D: Jun 18, 1961

Pos: PH	BA: .000
Hits: 0	HRs: 0
RBI: 0	BBs: 1

One of the more bizarre publicity stunts pulled by St. Louis Browns owner Bill Veeck centered around Gaedel. An actor who was 3'7" tall, Gaedel was hired to appear in an August 18, 1951 game at Sportsman's Park. Pinch hitting for Frank Saucier, and instructed not to swing, Gaedel was walked on four pitches. The crowd gave him a standing ovation as he left the field for pinch runner Jim Delsing. The incident illustrates the lighter side of baseball that has all but disappeared in the dollar-driven game of today.
Playing Career: *1951; StL A*

Gary Gaetti.

Gary Gaetti

Gaetti, Gary Joseph
B: Aug 19, 1958

Pos: 3B	BA: .252
Hits: 1,604	HRs: 245
RBI: 922	BBs: 433

Gaetti hit a home run off Charlie Hough in his first big league at-bat. In 1982 he replaced former co-Rookie of the Year John Castino at the hot corner for the Twins. An outstanding defensive player, Gaetti has led the league several times in putouts, assists and double plays. His offense finally caught up with his defense in 1986, when he hit .287 with 34 home runs and 108 RBI. Gaetti followed that performance with 31 round-trippers and 109 RBI in 1987.

In the 1987 ALCS Gaetti became the first player ever to hit two home runs in his first two at-bats of postseason play. He was named ALCS MVP, won his second straight Gold Glove, and set a club record for third basemen with a .973 fielding average. Gaetti was the center of publicity in the 1989 All-Star Game when he displayed a religious slogan on his batting gloves to the TV cameras during the pre-game introductions.
Playing Career: *1981-; Min A, Cal A, KC A*

Greg Gagne

Gagne, Gregory Christopher
B: Nov 12, 1961

Pos: SS	BA: .253
Hits: 995	HRs: 79
RBI: 392	BBs: 221

Gagne won Minnesota's shortstop job in 1985. Though Gagne led AL shortstops with 26 errors in 1987, he also set a club record for shortstops with 47 errorless games in a row. Gagne's bat figured prominently in postseason play that year; he hit two solo homers in the ALCS and one in the World Series. He also singled in the winning run in Game Seven of the World Series. In 1993 the Royals acquired Gagne to fill a big gap at shortstop.
Playing Career: *1983-; Min A, KC A*

Augie Galan

Galan, August John
B: May 25, 1912

Pos: OF	BA: .287
Hits: 1,706	HRs: 100
RBI: 830	BBs: 979

Galan was one of the top center fielders in the NL during the 1940s. He scored 1,004 runs, leading the NL with 133 in 1935. He stole 123 bases, leading the league twice. Galan was injury-prone, but managed to put together a good career. He was the first everyday major leaguer to play an entire season without hitting into a double play.

After batting .304 for the Cubs in 1939, the switch hitter broke his right knee in 1940. The Cubs gave up on Galan and his injuries, dealing him to the Dodgers in 1941. Two years later, he was back in the starting lineup, hit-

Augie Galan.

ting over .300 each season from 1944 through 1947 before age slowed him down. From 1945 to the end of his career, Galan batted left-handed exclusively. He played in three All-Star Games, ripping a home run in the 1936 contest. Galan also made it to three World Series, in 1935, 1938 and 1941, but was never on the winning side.
Playing Career: *1934-1949; Chi N, Brk N, Cin N, NY N, Phi A*

Andres Galarraga

Galarraga, Andrew (Big Cat)
B: Jun 18, 1961

Pos: 1B	BA: .279
Hits: 1,083	HRs: 138
RBI: 570	BBs: 259

Galarraga moved to Colorado for a new lease on life with the 1993 expansion Rockies. Originally signed by the Expos, and possessing a world of talent, he has been prone to slumps. Capable of awesome power, Galarraga has sacrificed some distance for batting average, passing the .300 mark in both 1987 and 1988, and winning the NL title in 1993. Nicknamed for his quickness at first base, Galarraga won Gold Gloves in 1989-1990.
Playing Career: *1985- ; Mon N, StL N, Col N*

Rich Gale

Gale, Richard Blackwell
B: Jan 19, 1954

Pos: P	ERA: 4.53
W-L: 55-56	SOs: 518
ShOs: 5	Saves: 2

Gale, one of baseball's tallest hurlers, was Rookie Pitcher of the Year in 1978, when he went 14-8 with a 3.09 ERA. That turned out to be his best season, but in 1980 he was 13-9, with a 3.91 ERA, helping the Royals win the pennant.
Playing Career: *1978-1984; KC A, SF N, Cin N, Bos A*

Denny Galehouse
Galehouse, Dennis Ward
B: Dec 7, 1911

Pos: P	ERA: 3.98
W-L: 109-118	SOs: 851
ShOs: 17	Saves: 13

During the summer of 1944, Galehouse had two jobs–working weekdays in an Akron, Ohio, factory, and pitching on Sundays at Sportsman's Park in St. Louis. The Browns needed every one of his nine victories to win the pennant.
Playing Career: *1934-1944, 1946-1947; Cle A, Bos A, StL A*

Bert Gallia
Gallia, Melvin Allys
B: Oct 14, 1891   D: Mar 19, 1976

Pos: P	ERA: 3.14
W-L: 65-68	SOs: 550
ShOs: 7	Saves: 10

After winning 26 for Kansas City in the minor league American Association, Gallia was acquired by the Senators. The Texan won 17 games in back-to-back seasons, 1915-1916. The Browns gave up Burt Shotton and Doc Lavan plus $15,000 for Gallia in 1917.
Playing Career: *1912-1920; Was A, StL A, Phi N*

Chick Galloway
Galloway, Clarence Edward
B: Aug 4, 1896   D: Nov 7, 1969

Pos: SS	BA: .264
Hits: 946	HRs: 17
RBI: 407	BBs: 274

Galloway played shortstop regularly for the Athletics until an errant batting practice pitch fractured his skull. His top season was 1922, when he hit .324. After his playing days, he returned to his alma mater, Presbyterian College, to coach baseball.
Playing Career: *1919-1928; Phi A, Det A*

Pud Galvin
Galvin, James Francis
B: Dec 25, 1856   D: Mar 7, 1902
Hall of Fame 1965

Pos: P	ERA: 2.87
W-L: 360-308	SOs: 1,799
ShOs: 57	No-hitters: 2

Managerial Record
Won: 7   Lost: 17   Pct: .292

The 300-pound Galvin was the best pitcher, pound for pound, in the 1880s. He was a workhorse. One year he pitched 656 innings, the next year 636. He had one 593-inning season and six more topping 400 innings. Galvin had two seasons with 46 wins, one with 37, and seven years with 20 to 29 victories.

With the 1877 Allegheny independent baseball club, Galvin pitched a 1-0 shutout and won his own game with a home run, the first pitcher ever to do so, at any level.

James Francis "Pud" Galvin.

Throwing from 50 feet with an underhand delivery, Galvin had the greatest pickoff move of his day, once nailing three baserunners in the same inning. He defeated Hoss Radbourn in 1884, stopping an 18-game winning streak. On July 21, 1892, Galvin faced Tim Keefe for the last time; both were 300-game winners. The next such contest would take place in 1986. Galvin is second to Cy Young with 310 losses, 5,941 innings pitched, and 639 complete games.
Playing Career: *1875, 1879-1892; StL Reds n, Buf N, Pit AA, Pit N, Pit P, StL N*
Managerial Career: *1885; Buf N*

Oscar Gamble
Gamble, Oscar Charles
B: Dec 20, 1949

Pos: OF, DH	BA: .265
Hits: 1,195	HRs: 200
RBI: 666	BBs: 610

Gamble, the Cubs' brightest prospect, shone the most when he went to New York, where he played in three postseason series. In 1976 he helped the Yankees win their first pennant in 12 years by belting 17 home runs and driving in 57 in 340 at-bats. Gamble's wife, Juanita, did some belting of her own, singing the national anthem at Yankee Stadium that season. Gamble returned to the AL after a lucrative free-agent contract with the Padres.
Playing Career: *1969-1985; Chi N, Phi N, Cle A, NY A, Chi A, SD N, Tex A*

Chick Gandil
Gandil, Arnold
B: Jan 19, 1887   D: Dec 13, 1970

Pos: 1B	BA: .277
Hits: 1,176	HRs: 11
RBI: 557	BBs: 273

Gandil rejoined the White Sox in 1917, having been a rookie with them in 1910. He was a malcontent who later would be considered the ringleader of the 1919 Black Sox scandal. A smooth fielder, Gandil led AL first sackers in fielding four times, but his life off the field was not nearly so graceful. At age 17, he ran away from home to play ball in towns along the Arizona-Mexico border. He also boxed for $150 a night. Just where he met Sport Sullivan, a gambler and bookie, is not known.

Sullivan had rich and powerful friends, and his relationships with ballplayers like Gandil were crucial to a World Series fixing scheme he wanted to arrange. Gandil's involvement with Sullivan, Abe Attell and Billy Maharg led directly to one of the saddest episodes in baseball history. In the 1919 World Series, Gandil batted only .233 and committed an error. He sat out the 1920 season over a salary dispute, then was banned from baseball for life by Commissioner Landis in 1921.
Playing Career: *1910, 1912-1919; Chi A, Was A, Cle N*

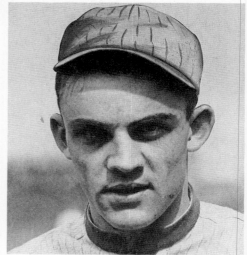

Arnold "Chick" Gandil.

Ron Gant
Gant, Ronald
B: Mar 2, 1965

Pos: OF, 2B, 3B	BA: .262
Hits: 836	HRs: 147
RBI: 480	BBs: 300

Off to a poor start as an infielder, Gant changed to the outfield and became a home run hitter, ripping 32 in both 1990 and 1991. Gant had become the Braves' starting second baseman at the age of 23 in 1988, and he enjoyed a solid year at the plate, finishing with 19 homers and 60 RBI.
Playing Career: *1987-; Atl N*

Jim Gantner
Gantner, James Elmer
B: Jan 5, 1953

Pos: 2B, DH	BA: .274
Hits: 1,696	HRs: 47
RBI: 568	BBs: 383

Gantner, Robin Yount and Paul Molitor played together in more games than any other trio in baseball history. Gantner became the Brewers' starting second baseman in 1981 and has led the AL in total chances at the position three times. His best year was 1983, when he hit .282 with career highs of 11 homers, 74 RBI and 85 runs scored. He was the Brewers' MVP the following year. A serious knee injury in 1989 decreased his mobility around the bag, forcing him to DH more.
Playing Career: *1976-1992; Mil A*

Charlie Ganzel
Ganzel, Charles William
B: Jun 18, 1862   D: Apr 7, 1914

Pos: C, OF, 1B, 2B	BA: .259
Hits: 774	HRs: 10
RBI: 412 (inc.)	BBs: 161

As a reserve catcher Ganzel spent five years of his career playing with Count Getzien. Together they formed the popular "Pretzel Battery." He played in two postseason championship series, 1887 and 1892.
Playing Career: *1884-1897; StP U, Phi N, Det N, Bos N*

John Ganzel
Ganzel, John Henry
B: Apr 7, 1874   D: Jan 14, 1959

Pos: 1B	BA: .251
Hits: 682	HRs: 18
RBI: 336	BBs: 136
Managerial Record	
Won: 90 Lost: 99 Pct: .476	

Ganzel was a top-fielding first baseman who led his league three times in fielding percentage. In 1905 he acquired the Grand Rapids Western League club, then bought his release from the Yankees for $3,000 so he could play there. Ganzel led the NL in triples with 16 in 1907. He was one of five brothers to play pro ball; one, Charlie, caught for 14 years in the major leagues.
Playing Career: *1898, 1900-1901, 1903-1904, 1907-1908; Pit N, Chi N, NY N, NY A, Cin N*
Managerial Career: *1908, 1915; Cin N, Brk F*

Joe Garagiola
Garagiola, Joseph Henry
B: Feb 12, 1926

Pos: C	BA: .257
Hits: 481	HRs: 42
RBI: 255	BBs: 267

Highly sought after as a prospect, Garagiola was chosen over his neighbor Yogi Berra when the Cardinals were looking for catch-

Joe Garagiola (c) celebrates the Cardinals' World Series victory in 1946.

ers. Garagiola hit .316 in the Red Birds' 1946 World Series victory over the Red Sox. A shoulder separation in 1950 made Garagiola realize that he would be wise to have another career. He wrote a book of colorful anecdotes *Baseball is a Funny Game*.

Garagiola's broadcasting career began in 1955 with the Cardinals. In 1961 he started appearing on NBC's "Major League Baseball," where he continued through 1988. In 1965 Garagiola replaced Mel Allen on Yankee broadcasts, then in 1969 became host of NBC's daily "Today Show," remaining until 1973.
Playing Career: *1946-1954; StL N, Pit N, Chi N, NY N*

Gene Garber
Garber, Henry Eugene
B: Nov 13, 1947

Pos: P	ERA: 3.34
W-L: 96-113	SOs: 940
ShOs: 0	Saves: 218

Garber's corkscrew motion was one of the strangest sights in baseball. The sidearmer was inconsistent – Garber pitched 10 seasons with ERAs under 3.00 and eight with ERAs over 4.00 – but became one of baseball's all-time leaders in saves, games pitched, and relief wins. Garber pitched in three NLCS.

The crafty pitcher relied mainly on a change-up to save 20 games or more five times. He led the NL in games pitched with 71 in 1975. Garber established Braves team records for career saves (131), and single season saves (30). He also holds Braves and Phillies records for most relief losses in a season. In 1982 Garber set Braves club records with 56

appearances and 30 saves as the team went to the playoffs. The bullpen won the Rolaids' Awards as the outstanding relief corps.
Playing Career: *1969-1970, 1972-1988; Pit N, KC A, Phi N, Atl N*

Damaso Garcia
Garcia y Sanchez, Damaso Domingo
B: Feb 7, 1957

Pos: 2B	BA: .283
Hits: 1,108	HRs: 36
RBI: 323	BBs: 130

A strong-hitting second baseman, Garcia was also a good base stealer. After swiping 203 bases, his career was suddenly cut short by a serious knee injury in 1987. He sometimes acted impetuously; once he demanded to bat leadoff after two years of .300 hitting farther down in the lineup. Another time Garcia burned his uniform in the clubhouse after a particularly poor performance.
Playing Career: *1978-1986, 1988-1989; NY A, Tor A, Atl N, Mon N*

Dave Garcia
Garcia, David
B: Sep 15, 1920

Managerial Record	
Won: 307 Lost: 310 Pct: .498	

Garcia was a minor league infielder for 20 years, never playing in the majors. After managing in the minors and coaching for the Padres, Indians and Angels, he became California's manager in July 1977. In four full seasons, he finished as high as fifth only once.
Managerial Career: *1977-1982; Cal A, Cle A*

Mike Garcia.

Mike Garcia
Garcia, Edward Miguel (The Big Bear)
B: Nov 17, 1923   D: Jan 13, 1986

Pos: P | ERA: 3.27
W-L: 142-97 | SOs: 1,117
ShOs: 27 | Saves: 23

Part of the great Indians pitching staff that included Bob Feller, Early Wynn and Bob Lemon, Garcia won 79 games in the years 1951-1954. He was chosen for three All-Star teams. Garcia led the AL in shutouts and ERA twice. In 1954 only 28 percent of the batters he faced reached base, the best percentage in the AL. After a back injury in 1958, he was released by Cleveland. Garcia pitched in relief for the White Sox and Senators before retiring.
Playing Career: *1948-1961; Cle A, Chi A, Was A*

Danny Gardella
Gardella, Daniel Lewis
B: Feb 26, 1920

Pos: 1B, OF | BA: .267
Hits: 145 | HRs: 24
RBI: 85 | BBs: 267

The wartime Giants did not appreciate the services of Gardella, who hit 18 homers for them in 1945. Offered an unacceptable contract in 1946, he jumped to the Mexican League. Commissioner Happy Chandler suspended Gardella for five years, so the infielder sued baseball, claiming he had been bound only by the controversial reserve clause, not a contract. The antitrust case against baseball, Gardella v. Chandler, was dismissed at the district court level in 1948, but was reversed on appeal in 1949. Fearful of this significant threat to the reserve clause, baseball officials settled with Gardella out of court for $29,000 and lifted his suspension. The case was the only successful challenge to baseball's reserve clause.
Playing Career: *1944-1945, 1950; NY N, StL N*

Billy Gardner
Gardner, William Frederick
B: Jul 19, 1927

Pos: 2B, SS, 3B | BA: .237
Hits: 841 | HRs: 41
RBI: 261 | BBs: 246
Managerial Record
Won: 330   Lost: 417   Pct: .442

Gardner was the Orioles' second baseman from 1956 to 1959, and led the AL in doubles (36), and fielding average in 1957. He was in the Twins' debut Opening Day lineup, but was traded to the 1961 Yankees. Gardner pinch-hit in the 1961 World Series. Ticketed to be the Royals' third-base coach in 1987, Gardner instead became the team's manager when terminally ill Dick Howser resigned during spring training.
Playing Career: *1954-1963; NY N, Bal A, Was A, Min A, NY A, Bos A*
Managerial Career: *1981-1985, 1987; Min A, KC A*

Billy Gardner.

Larry Gardner
Gardner, William Lawrence
B: May 13, 1886   D: Mar 11, 1976

Pos: 3B | BA: .289
Hits: 1,931 | HRs: 27
RBI: 929 | BBs: 654

The 1912 World Series was the only one ended by an out by the winning team. Gardner knocked in the winning run with a sacrifice fly in the eighth game. A steady third baseman and an above-average hitter, Gardner batted over .300 five times, including for teams that won pennants in 1912, 1916 and 1920. He hit 129 triples, 301 doubles, and scored 866 runs during his career.

Gardner was a regular third baseman from 1912 through 1922, leading the league in fielding in 1920. After a year with the last-place Athletics, Gardner joined former teammate Tris Speaker in Cleveland. He had his two best years for Speaker, batting .310 and .319, driving in 118 and 129, and slugging .414 and .437 in 1920 and 1921. He played in the World Series in 1920. Gardner later coached baseball at the University of Vermont, his alma mater, where he became athletic director.
Playing Career: *1908-1924; Bos A, Phi A, Cle A*

Wayne Garland
Garland, Marcus Wayne
B: Oct 26, 1950

Pos: P | ERA: 3.89
W-L: 55-66 | SOs: 450
ShOs: 7 | Saves: 6

Whenever the evils of free agency and long-term contracts are discussed, Garland's name pops up. After a great year – 1976, when he was 20-7 – he signed a five-year contract with the Indians. He lost 19 the next season, then had rotator cuff surgery in 1978.
Playing Career: *1973-1981; Bal A, Cle A*

Mike Garman
Garman, Michael Douglas
B: Sep 16, 1949

Pos: P | ERA: 3.63
W-L: 22-27 | SOs: 213
ShOs: 0 | Saves: 42

Boston's number-one pick in the June 1967 draft, Garman began as a middle reliever and graduated to the stopper role. He saved a dozen games for the 1977 NL champion Dodgers, and another one in the NLCS. Garman's postseason ERA was 0.00.
Playing Career: *1969, 1971-1978; Bos A, StL N, Chi N, LA N, Mon N*

Deb Garms
Garms, Debs C.
B: Jun 26, 1908   D: Dec 16, 1984

Pos: OF | BA: .293
Hits: 910 | HRs: 18
RBI: 328 | BBs: 288

Garms won the NL batting championship with a .355 average in 1940. He had earlier broken Johnny Vander Meer's consecutive hitless string of 21⅓ innings. At age 37, Garms was cut by the Cardinals after hitting .336 in 74 games in 1945.
Playing Career: *1932-1935, 1937-1941, 1943-1945; StL A, Bos N, Pit N, StL N*

Phil Garner
Garner, Philip Mason
B: Apr 30, 1949

Pos: 2B, 3B | BA: .260
Hits: 1,594 | HRs: 109
RBI: 738 | BBs: 564
Managerial Record
Won: 161   Lost: 163   Pct: .498

Garner established himself as the A's second baseman under manager Chuck Tanner. When Tanner moved to Pittsburgh, he promptly traded for Garner, who repaid him by batting .500 with a .667 slugging average in the 1979 World Series. The previous year Garner tied a major league record by pounding grand slam home runs in two consecutive games. He helped the Astros to a division title in 1986.

Playing Career: *1973-1988; Oak A, Pit N, Hou N, LA N, SF N*
Managerial Career: *1992- ; Mil A*

Ralph Garr
Garr, Ralph Allen
B: Dec 12, 1945

Pos: OF	BA: .306
Hits: 1,562	HRs: 75
RBI: 408	BBs: 246

A Grambling football star, Garr was slow reaching the big leagues because of the Braves' talent-laden outfield. He won two batting titles in the International League, 1969-1970. Once he got to Atlanta, Garr got 200 hits or more for three of four years, once leading the NL with a .353 average. He led the league in triples, 1974-1975.

Garr put together four monster years before he was traded to the White Sox, where he still hit .300, but was no longer the speedster he had been. During arbitration hearings after the 1974 season, Garr was granted a 108 percent salary increase. Fan fallout from such a large increase caused resentment. Among baseball insiders, Garr was known as much for his squeaky voice, Hank Aaron imitations, and nonstop comic monologues as for his bat. He later became a hitting and baserunning instructor.

Playing Career: *1968-1980; Atl N, Chi A, Cal A*

Scott Garrelts
Garrelts, Scott William
B: Oct 30, 1961

Pos: P	ERA: 3.29
W-L: 69-53	SOs: 703
ShOs: 4	Saves: 48

The hard-throwing Garrelts was Roger Craig's best reclamation project. By adding a split-finger fastball, Garrelts came out of the bullpen to post a 14-7 record with a league-leading 2.28 ERA as the Giants won the division title in 1989.

Playing Career: *1982-1991; SF N*

Wayne Garrett
Garrett, Ronald Wayne
B: Dec 3, 1947

Pos: 3B	BA: .239
Hits: 786	HRs: 61
RBI: 340	BBs: 561

The Amazin' Mets benefited from rookie Garrett's play at the hot corner in their first pennant-winning season. He hit .385 in the 1969 NLCS. The next time they won the flag was Garrett's best year; he batted .256 with 16 homers, 20 doubles and 76 runs scored in 1973.

Playing Career: *1969-1978; NY N, Mon N, StL N*

Ned Garver
Garver, Ned Franklin
B: Dec 25, 1925

Pos: P	ERA: 3.73
W-L: 129-157	SOs: 881
ShOs: 18	Saves: 12

When Garver won 20 games for the 1951 Browns he became the second pitcher in baseball history to reach that plateau for a team that lost 100. Garver also batted .305 that year. He was the highest paid player in Browns' history when he signed a $25,000 contract in 1952.

Playing Career: *1948-1961; StL A, Det A, KC A, LA A*

Steve Garvey
Garvey, Steven Patrick (Iron Man)
B: Dec 22, 1948

Pos: 1B	BA: .294
Hits: 2,599	HRs: 272
RBI: 1,308	BBs: 479

Called "Iron Man" for his durability at first base, Garvey played 1,207 consecutive games to set the NL record. He was part of the great Dodgers infield quartet – with Ron Cey, Davey Lopes and Bill Russell – that played together for eight years. Elected to the All-Star

Ralph Garr smacks one for Atlanta in 1971.

Steve "Iron Man" Garvey.

team as a write-in candidate in 1974, Garvey ended up being voted MVP of the game. He played in nine more All-Star Games and in five World Series. The winner of the 1974 NL MVP Award and four Gold Gloves, he retired with a .996 fielding average.

A tremendous local favorite, Garvey had a junior high school named after him while he was still an active player. Considered a role model on and off the field, fans were shocked when the first indication of trouble came. There was a locker room fight with Don Sutton. Then came rumors, paternity suits and divorce. Garvey's wife Cyndy, who wrote about their marriage in a best-selling book, is now a well-known radio talk show host.
Playing Career: *1969-1987; LA N, SD N*

Ned Garvin
Garvin, Virgil Lee
B: Jan 1, 1874   D: Jun 16, 1908

Pos: P	ERA: 2.72
W-L: 57-97	SOs: 612
ShOs: 13	Saves: 4

Garvin pitched a 13-hit shutout in 1899 with the Cubs. He won the complete game 3-0 over the Braves. Usually a victim of extremely bad luck, in 1904 Garvin compiled a record of 5-15 with an ERA of 1.68! He lost almost 100 games, yet sported an ERA under 3.00.
Playing Career: *1896, 1899-1904; Phi N, Chi N, Mil A, Chi A, Brk N, NY A*

Cito Gaston
Gaston, Clarence Edwin
B: Mar 17, 1944

Pos: 1B	BA: .256
Hits: 799	HRs: 91
RBI: 387	BBs: 185
Managerial Record	
Won: 426 Lost: 315 Pct: .575	

Hired by Bobby Cox as batting instructor for the Blue Jays in 1982, Cito Gaston found himself – as Toronto manager – facing Cox as

Manager Cito Gaston (l).

opposing manager in the 1992 World Series. Gaston whipped his former boss four games to two.

The Padres had taken Gaston from the Braves in the 1968 expansion draft. In his best season as an infielder, he hit .318 with 29 homers and 93 RBI, and appeared in the 1970 All-Star Game. He returned to Atlanta in 1975 and roomed with all-time home run champ Hank Aaron. Aaron urged him to take the Blue Jays job in 1982. After being released by the Braves, Gaston played in the abortive AAA Inter-American League. He then went to Mexico for two more years. Named Toronto's manager in mid-1989, Gaston drove the club to the division title. In fact he has won four division titles in five years.
Playing Career: *1967, 1969-1978; Atl N, SD N, Pit N*
Managerial Career: *1989- ; Tor A*

Milt Gaston
Gaston, Nathaniel Milton
B: Jan 27, 1896

Pos: P	ERA: 4.55
W-L: 97-164	SOs: 615
ShOs: 10	Saves: 8

Gaston and his moving forkball were acquired by the Browns along with Joe Bush, in exchange for Urban Shocker. Going 38-49 in three years, he was shipped off to the Senators. He stayed in the majors for 10 years despite a won-lost record of 97-164.
Playing Career: *1924-1934; NY A, StL A, Was A, Bos A, Chi A*

Hank Gastright
Gastright, Henry Carl
B: Mar 29, 1865   D: Oct 9, 1937

Pos: P	ERA: 4.20
W-L: 72-63	SOs: 514
ShOs: 6	Saves: 2

Young Gastright was so much a competitor that he once refused to leave the mound after his manager changed pitchers. When the skipper allowed him to stay, the opposing team protested the game. Gastright was finally removed, but the 1890 game was later forfeited because the home team ran out of baseballs.
Playing Career: *1889-1894, 1896; Col AA, Was N, Pit N, Bos N, Brk N, Cin N*

Rich Gedman
Gedman, Richard Leo
B: Sep 26, 1959

Pos: C	BA: .252
Hits: 795	HRs: 88
RBI: 382	BBs: 236

From AL Rookie of the Year in 1981, Gedman quickly became one of baseball's top catchers. Using a wide-open batting stance that became his trademark, Gedman hit .295 and drove in 80 runs in 1985, his best season. The number of base stealers he threw out that year approached 50 percent. As he struggled

with injuries, Gedman's offensive production decreased. In 1988 and 1989, he was used in a platoon situation with Rick Cerone.
Playing Career: *1980-1992; Bos A, Hou N, StL N*

Lou Gehrig
Gehrig, Henry Louis (The Iron Horse)
B: Jun 19, 1903   D: Jun 2, 1941
Hall of Fame 1939

Pos: 1B	BA: .340
Hits: 2,721	HRs: 493
RBI: 1,990	BBs: 1,508

Depression-era hero Lou Gehrig embodied the American work ethic: quietly effective, enduring and potent. His incredible career statistics include a .632 slugging average – placing him third on the all-time list – 1,888 runs scored, 535 doubles and 162 triples. Gehrig hit .361 in seven World Series, belting 10 home runs. These accomplishments paled in comparison, however, to The Streak.

The Iron Horse played 2,130 consecutive games. He played with colds, fevers, excruciating lumbago. In 1934, the year he won the Triple Crown, Gehrig fractured a toe. He was knocked unconscious by a wild pitch, but he was at his position the next day and collected four hits. When Gehrig finally took himself out of the lineup, he was very ill with amyotrophic lateral sclerosis. On July 4, 1939, he stood before 61,000 fans at Yankee Stadium denying that his illness was a bad break, saying instead that he considered himself "the luckiest man on the face of the earth."
Playing Career: *1923-1937; NY A*

Lou Gehrig with his mother (center).

Charlie Gehringer
Gehringer, Charles Leonard
B: May 11, 1903 D: Jan 21, 1993
Hall of Fame 1949

Pos: 2B	BA: .320
Hits: 2,839	HRs: 184
RBI: 1,427	BBs: 1,185

The press called Gehringer "the Mechanical Man," but his fans remember him as the smoothest fielder they ever saw. He led AL second basemen in assists seven times, and topped the list nine times in fielding average. A left-handed hitter, Gehringer slapped hits to all fields, chalking up 146 triples and 574 doubles (he is 11th on the all-time doubles list) and stealing 182 bases, leading to 1,774 runs scored.

Gehringer batted more than .300 in 13 of his 16 full seasons, and led the AL with a .371 mark in 1937 to earn MVP honors. He drove in more than 100 runs seven times. Gehringer was even tougher in World Series play. His home run in the fifth game in the 1934 Series beat Dizzy Dean and the Gas House Gang. A year later he singled in the ninth against the Cubs and scored the winning run that gave Detroit the championship.
Playing Career: *1924-1942; Det A*

Gary Geiger
Geiger, Gary Merle
B: Apr 4, 1937

Pos: OF	BA: .246
Hits: 633	HRs: 77
RBI: 283	BBs: 341

Charlie Gehringer.

A part-time performer, Geiger reached his peak in 1959-1963, when he averaged 14 home runs, 15 doubles and 59 runs scored with a .254 batting mark. Various ailments and injuries, including a collapsed lung and fractured skull, prevented Geiger from achieving greatness.
Playing Career: *1958-1970; Cle A, Bos A, Atl N, Hou N*

Charley Gelbert
Gelbert, Charles Magnus
B: Jan 26, 1906 D: Jan 13, 1967

Pos: SS, 3B	BA: .267
Hits: 766	HRs: 17
RBI: 350	BBs: 290

Gelbert saw action in two World Series with the Cardinals. He set the record for shortstops in the 1931 seven-game Series with 42 chances, 29 assists, 6 double plays and a 1.000 fielding average. Gelbert was sent down in 1933 to make room for Leo Durocher.
Playing Career: *1929-1932, 1935-1937, 1939-1940; StL N, Cin N, Det A, Was A, Bos A*

Joe Genewich
Genewich, Joseph Edward
B: Jan 15, 1897 D: Dec 21, 1985

Pos: P	ERA: 4.29
W-L: 73-92	SOs: 316
ShOs: 7	Saves: 12

Going directly to the major leagues from the sandlot, Genewich won 13 games in his rookie year with the Braves. He later caught the eye of John McGraw, who traded four players for him in midseason 1928. Genewich was 11-4 the rest of the year.
Playing Career: *1922-1930; Bos N, NY N*

Jim Gentile
Gentile, James Edward (Diamond Jim)
B: Jun 3, 1934

Pos: 1B	BA: .260
Hits: 759	HRs: 179
RBI: 549	BBs: 475

When he finally got to the big leagues for real in 1960 after eight years in the minors, Gentile had a spectacular season. He batted .302 with 46 home runs – five of them grand slams – and drove in a club record 141 runs on only 147 hits in 1961.
Playing Career: *1957-1958, 1960-1966; Brk N, LA N, Bal A, KC A, Hou N, Cle A*

Wally Gerber
Gerber, Walter
B: Aug 18, 1891 D: Jun 19, 1951

Pos: SS	BA: .257
Hits: 1,309	HRs: 7
RBI: 476	BBs: 465

Error-prone at the beginning of his career, Gerber led AL shortstops in miscues in 1919 and 1920. But he learned his position well and later led the league in double plays four

"The Iron Horse" is honored at Yankee Stadium on "Lou Gehrig Day," July 4, 1939.

times. He was the center of the Browns' infield for nine seasons. Developing a reputation as parsimonious, Gerber was as sure-handed with money as with hot grounders. He invested his earnings wisely and was a source of financial assistance for former teammates during the Depression.
Playing Career: *1914-1915, 1917-1929; Pit N, StL A, Bos A*

Joe Gerhardt
Gerhardt, John Joseph
B: Feb 14, 1855   D: Mar 11, 1922

Pos: 2B, SS, OF, 1B, 3B   BA: .227
Hits: 939   HRs: 7
RBI: 235 (inc.)   BBs: 162
Managerial Record
Won: 72   Lost: 61   Pct: .541

One of the most competitive players of the 19th century, Gerhardt played barehanded, and he had tremendous range. In fact, his range factor numbers are among the highest ever recorded, explaining how a .227 hitter could stay in the majors for 15 years.
Playing Career: *1873-1879, 1881, 1883-1887, 1890-1891; Was Nationals n, Bal Lord Baltimores n, NY Mutuals n, Lou N, Cin N, Det N, Lou AA, NY N, NY AA, Brk AA, StL AA*
Managerial Career: *1883, 1890; Lou AA, StL AA*

Dick Gernert
Gernert, Richard Edward
B: Sep 28, 1928

Pos: 1B   BA: .254
Hits: 632   HRs: 103
RBI: 402   BBs: 363

An off-season school teacher, Genert was a power hitter out of Temple University. He swatted 19 homers in his rookie season and 21 as a sophomore, 20 in 1958. He pinch-hit four times without success for the Reds in the 1961 World Series.
Playing Career: *1952-1962; Bos A, Chi N, Det A, Cin N, Hou N*

Cesar Geronimo
Geronimo y Zorrilla, Cesar Francisco
B: Mar 11, 1948

Pos: OF   BA: .258
Hits: 977   HRs: 51
RBI: 392   BBs: 354

Originally signed by the Yankees, Geronimo was the outstanding defensive center fielder on five Reds divisional championship teams. They were World Series victors in 1975 and 1976. Geronimo came to the Reds from the Astros in the Joe Morgan deal.
Playing Career: *1969-1983; Hou N, Cin N, KC A*

Doc Gessler
Gessler, Harry Homer
B: Dec 23, 1880   D: Dec 26, 1924

Pos: OF   BA: .281
Hits: 831   HRs: 14
RBI: 363   BBs: 333
Managerial Record
Won: 3   Lost: 8   Pct: .273

Gessler was known as one of the strongest men in baseball, but he never parlayed his strength into extra-base power. Instead he hit for average as was the custom in his era. Gessler pinch-hit twice in the 1906 World Series. He later became a physician.
Playing Career: *1903-1906, 1908-1911; Det A, Brk N, Chi N, Bos A, Was A*
Managerial Career: *1914; Pit F*

Charlie Getzien
Getzien, Charles H. (Pretzels)
B: Feb 14, 1864   D: Jun 19, 1932

Pos: P   ERA: 3.46
W-L: 145-139   SOs: 1,070
ShOs: 11   No-hitters: 1

The ace of the 1887 World Series, Getzien led his Detroit Wolverine team against the defending World Champion St. Louis Browns. He was 4-2 in the 15-game Series. A top hurler of the late 1880s, Getzien won 30

games in 1886, 29 in 1887. Capitalizing on the German names of pitcher Getzien and catcher Charlie Ganzel, teammates named them the Pretzel Battery.
Playing Career: *1884-1892; Det N, Ind N, Bos N, Cle N, StL N*

Bart Giamatti
Giamatti, A. Bartlett
B: Apr 4, 1938   D: Sep 1, 1989

Proof that the national pastime transcends class, cultural background and career, Giamatti was a lifelong baseball enthusiast and Red Sox fan who just also happened to be a PhD Renaissance scholar on the faculty of Princeton, then Yale University. He served as president of Yale for eight years and was frequently seen on campus in his Red Sox baseball cap. Giamatti wrote books and articles on Renaissance literature, as well as a number of baseball essays.

Named president of the NL in December 1986, his first major hurdle was a 30-day suspension of Pete Rose in 1988 for shoving umpire Dave Pallone. Giamatti also chastised the Reds' radio announcers for inciting the crowd. After succeeding Peter Ueberroth as commissioner of baseball in April 1989, he was faced with another Pete Rose problem – gambling. This time the commissioner suspended the immensely popular Rose for life. A week later, Giamatti died of a massive heart attack.

Joe Gibbon
Gibbon, Joseph Charles
B: Apr 10, 1935

Pos: P   ERA: 3.52
W-L: 61-65   SOs: 743
ShOs: 4   Saves: 32

Gibbon was an All-American basketball player at the University of Mississippi. Big and fast, he followed his 9.00 ERA in the 1960 Fall Classic for the World Champion Pirates with a 13-10 record and a 3.32 ERA in 1961.
Playing Career: *1960-1972; Pit N, SF N, Cin N, Hou N*

Bob Gibson
Gibson, Robert
B: Nov 9, 1935
Hall of Fame 1981

Pos: P   ERA: 2.91
W-L: 251-174   SOs: 3,117
ShOs: 56   No-hitters: 1

In an era when power pitching was the status quo, fire-breathing, flame-throwing Bob Gibson was the dominant right-hander. Overpoweringly intimidating on the mound, Gibson put every ounce of strength he could muster into his pitches – a dangerous fastball and a trademark slider. Gibson, who had a reputation as a headhunter, insisted he hardly ever threw at batters, but went on to explain, "When I did, I hit them."
In 1968 he registered a 1.12 ERA, the lowest in NL history; hurled 13 shutouts, second

A. Bartlett Giamatti, NL president from 1986 to 1989, then baseball commissioner.

Bob Gibson.

most in league annals; compiled a won-lost record of 22-9; and fanned a record 35 batters in the World Series. Seventeen of those strikeouts came in one World Series game when he shut out the Tigers and 31-game winner Denny McLain. Gibson was a fierce competitor, winning two Cy Young Awards and one MVP Award during his career. In three Fall Classics Gibson's record was 7-2 with a 1.89 ERA, and 92 strikeouts in 81 innings of work.
Playing Career: *1959-1975; StL N*

George Gibson
Gibson, George C. (Moon)
B: *Jul 22, 1880*   D: *Jan 25, 1967*

Pos: C	BA: .236
Hits: 893	HRs: 15
RBI: 345	BBs: 286

Managerial Record
Won: 413   Lost: 344   Pct: .546

The first catcher to appear in 150 games in a season, Gibson accomplished the feat in 1909. The Pirates won 110 games that year, the second most in NL history. Gibson did not hit much, but led the league's receivers in fielding three times, and was elected to the Canadian Baseball Hall of Fame.

In the 1909 World Series victory over the Tigers, Gibson threw out five Bengal base-stealers. The Pirates outstole the Tigers, 18 to 6; Gibson even swiped two bases himself. Gibson, an easygoing guy, found it difficult to enforce discipline on the Pirates and Cubs teams he managed. His most successful managerial endeavors were with the Pirates, who finished second three times – in 1921, 1932 and 1933 – under his direction.
Playing Career: *1905-1918; Pit N, NY N*
Managerial Career: *1920-1922, 1925, 1932-1934; Pit N, Chi N*

Josh Gibson
Gibson, Josh
B: *Dec 21, 1911*   D: *Jan 20, 1947*
Hall of Fame 1972

Pos: C	BA: .362
Hits: 607	HRs: 146
RBI: NA	BBs: NA

A tremendous gate attraction during the 1930s and 1940s, Josh Gibson was known for his home run power. In Negro League and semipro games he was credited with 75 homers in 1931, and 69 in 1934. His batting average topped .400 at least twice. Combining with Buck Leonard in a Ruth-Gehrig style tandem, Gibson led the Grays to nine straight pennants, 1937-1945.

Teammates referred to the receiver as "Boxer" early in his career because they said he caught foul pops as though he were wearing boxing gloves. Gibson mastered his craft with work, handling every type of pitch from the spitter to the shineball. He was 35 years old when Jackie Robinson signed up to play for the Dodgers in 1946. Reportedly Gibson was bitter at having been passed over. There was a good chance he would have been signed by a major league team in 1947, but he died in January of that year. Doctors attributed Gibson's death to brain hemorrhage; popular opinion was that he died of a broken heart.
Playing Career: *1930-1946; Hom Grays, Pit Crawfords*

George Gibson.

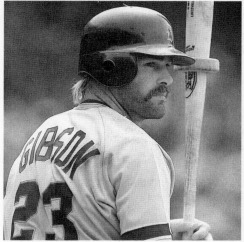

Kirk Gibson.

Kirk Gibson
Gibson, Kirk Harold
B: *May 28, 1957*

Pos: OF	BA: .268
Hits: 1,403	HRs: 223
RBI: 763	BBs: 643

One of the greatest moments in World Series history came in Game One, 1988, with two out in the bottom of the ninth. The Dodgers trailed 4-3, but they had a runner on base. Gibson had been held out of the game because of a painful leg injury, but came in to pinch-hit. Wincing on every swing, he fouled off four pitches before blasting a slider into the right field stands. The stands exploded as Gibson limped around the bases for the game-winning run. It was his only World Series at-bat.

An All-Star football and baseball player at Michigan State University, Gibson signed with the Tigers and was hailed by Manager Sparky Anderson as the "next Mickey Mantle." The two sluggers have at least one thing in common, both hit tape-measure shots of almost 600 feet into the lumber yard outside Tiger Stadium. Gibson has endured numerous injuries. After his 1988 MVP year he played only 71 games in 1989.
Playing Career: *1979-; Det A, LA N, KC A, Pit N*

Billy Gilbert
Gilbert, William Oliver
B: *Jun 21, 1876*   D: *Aug 8, 1927*

Pos: 2B	BA: .247
Hits: 695	HRs: 5
RBI: 237	BBs: 270

Gilbert starred at second base for John McGraw's greatest team, the 1904-1905 Giants. The keystone sacker hit .235 in the 1905 Series, when every game ended in a shutout. He had jumped leagues with McGraw, who brought several Orioles with him to the Giants.
Playing Career: *1901-1906, 1908-1909; Mil A, Bal A, NY N, StL N*

Wally Gilbert
Gilbert, Walter John
B: Dec 19, 1901   D: Sep 7, 1958

Pos: 3B	BA: .269
Hits: 624	HRs: 7
RBI: 214	BBs: 162

A member of the "Daffy Dodgers" for four years, Gilbert was the regular third baseman and hit .304 in 1929 and .294 the next season. He was traded with Babe Herman and Ernie Lombardi to the Reds in 1932. Cincinnati released him when he batted .214.
Playing Career: *1928-1932; Brk N, Cin N*

Warren Giles
Giles, Warren Crandall
B: May 28, 1896   D: Feb 7, 1979
Hall of Fame 1979

Warren Giles was elected president of the Moline club in the Three-I League in 1919, beginning a 50-year career in baseball that took him all the way to the presidency of the NL. He headed the Reds' organization from 1937 to 1951, capturing pennants in 1939-1940, and becoming club president in 1948.

In 1951, during the owners' voting for a new commissioner, Giles and Ford Frick were stalemated through 17 ballots until Giles withdrew his name. The following year, he was elected president of the NL. During his 18-year tenure he presided over historic franchise shifts, including the Dodgers' and Giants' move to the West Coast and the Boston Braves' relocation to Milwaukee and later to Atlanta. New NL franchises were added: the Mets in New York, the Colt 45s in Houston, the Padres in San Diego, and the Expos in Montreal.

Pete Gillespie
Gillespie, Peter Patrick
B: Nov 30, 1851   D: May 5, 1910

Pos: OF	BA: .276
Hits: 809	HRs: 10
RBI: 351	BBs: 106

Gillespie was bred in the ballplayer-rich coal country of Pennsylvania. He headed east to play with the Lynn Live Oaks and the Holyokes, then accompanied the Troy team to New York when the franchise moved. He batted .314 that first year in the Big Apple, 1883.
Playing Career: *1880-1887; Tro N, NY N*

Junior Gilliam
Gilliam, James William
B: Oct 17, 1928   D: Oct 8, 1978

Pos: 2B, 3B	BA: .265
Hits: 1,889	HRs: 65
RBI: 558	BBs: 1,036

Called Junior by his Baltimore Elite Giant teammates in the old Negro Leagues, Gilliam and shortstop Pee Wee Butts formed one of the slickest double play combos in 1940s Negro Leagues. Gilliam made the Negro League East All-Star team three straight years, 1948-1950. Then he signed with the Dodgers.

Gilliam was so hot at second base that the Dodgers moved Jackie Robinson to third in 1953. Gilliam set an NL rookie record with 100 walks. He led the NL with 17 triples, scored 125 runs, and was named Rookie of the Year. He swatted switch-hit homers in the 1953 World Series. Three times Gilliam finished second to Willie Mays in stolen bases, post-ing 203 for his career. He scored at least 100 runs in each of his first four seasons, totaling 1,163. He was selected for two All-Star teams, hitting a homer in the second 1959 contest. The Dodgers retired his number following his sudden death just prior to the 1978 World Series.
Playing Career: *1953-1966; Brk N, LA N*

Dave Giusti
Giusti, David John
B: Nov 27, 1939

Pos: P	ERA: 3.60
W-L: 100-93	SOs: 1,103
ShOs: 9	Saves: 145

Kent Tekulve and Dave Giusti were the best relief pitchers in Pirates history. A lacrosse player from Syracuse, Giusti learned a palmball when he switched from starting to stopping in 1970. He was named NL Fireman of the Year in 1971 when his 30 saves led the league. That year Giusti became the first NL reliever to appear in every game of a four-game NLCS; he recorded three saves. It was also his first of six seasons with double-digit save totals.
Playing Career: *1962, 1964-1977; Hou N, StL N, Pit N, Oak A, Chi N*

Dan Gladden
Gladden, Clinton Daniel
B: Jul 7, 1957

Pos: OF	BA: .270
Hits: 1,215	HRs: 74
RBI: 446	BBs: 337

Gladden smacked a grand slam off Bob Forsch in Game One of the 1987 World Series that set the tone for the Twins' first World Championship. In the tenth inning of the 1991 World Series finale, he scored the Twins' winning run. His big league career started in San Francisco late in 1984. Hot as a pistol, Gladden batted .351 with 31 stolen bases in 86 games. Topps and *Baseball Digest* both named him to their all-rookie teams that year. Gladden is also a good base stealer; he had 222 by the end of the 1993 season.
Playing Career: *1983-; SF N, Min A, Det A*

Fred Gladding
Gladding, Fred Earl
B: Jun 28, 1936

Pos: P	ERA: 3.13
W-L: 48-34	SOs: 394
ShOs: 0	Saves: 109

Gladding appeared in 450 games, but he started only one. An inconsistent performer, twice he spun ERAs under 2.00, but four times he went over 4.00. Gladding spearheaded the Astros' 1969 drive toward the pennant that fell just short, and is chronicled so hilariously in Jim Bouton's book *Ball Four*. Gladding led the NL in saves with 29 that year. He also managed only one hit in 63 career at-bats.
Playing Career: *1961-1973; Det A, Hou N*

NL President Warren Giles awards Hank Aaron a silver bat, 1956.

ABOVE: A 10-time All-Star, Steve Garvey batted .319 in five World Series. (Photo by Nancy Hogue)

BELOW: Yankee legend Lou Gehrig played in 2,130 consecutive games. (Brompton Photo Library)

ABOVE RIGHT: In 1968 Bob Gibson fanned a record 35 batters in the World Series. (Photo by Malcolm Emmons)

RIGHT: Fireman Goose Gossage ranks high on the all-time lists for saves and relief wins. (Photo by Nancy Hogue)

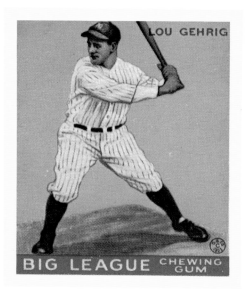

LOU GEHRIG

BIG LEAGUE CHEWING GUM

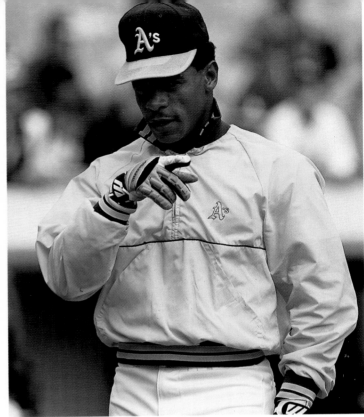

ABOVE LEFT: Ken Griffey, Jr. (Photo by Otto Greule, Jr./Allsport)
ABOVE: Rickey Henderson. (Photo by Otto Greule, Jr./Allsport)
LEFT: In 1988 Orel Hershiser pitched 59 consecutive scoreless innings. (Photo by Scott Halleran/Allsport)
BELOW: Dodger great Gil Hodges. (Brompton Photo Library)
OPPOSITE: Ken Griffey, Sr. played in Seattle with his son. (Photo by Stephen Dunn/Allsport)

GIL HODGES
Dodgers

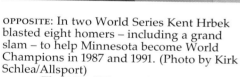

OPPOSITE: In two World Series Kent Hrbek blasted eight homers – including a grand slam – to help Minnesota become World Champions in 1987 and 1991. (Photo by Kirk Schlea/Allsport)

ABOVE: The 6'7", 255-pound Frank Howard began his 16-year career as 1960 NL Rookie of the Year. Known as "Capital Punishment," he rapped 136 homers, 1968-1970. (Photo by Malcolm Emmons)

ABOVE RIGHT: Hall of Fame hurler Catfish Hunter helped the A's to three World Championships, 1972-1974. Author of a perfect game, Hunter also helped boost the Yankees to victory. (Photo by Chance Brockway)

RIGHT: After seven years in the Negro Leagues, Monte Irvin made his big league debut with the Giants in 1949. His NL-leading 121 RBI and 24 homers in 1951 led the Giants to the pennant. Hall of Famer Irvin batted .394 in two World Series. (Brompton Photo Library)

FAR RIGHT: Playing professional baseball and football at the same time, Bo Jackson belted 22 or more homers in each of his first four seasons as a regular. (Photo by Jim Commentucci/Allsport)

OPPOSITE: Reggie Jackson blasted three home runs on three pitches for the Yankees in the 1977 World Series finale. Mr. October slugged a record .755 in 27 Fall Classic games. Winner of four home run crowns, Jackson was inducted into the Hall of Fame in 1993. (Photo by Malcolm Emmons)
ABOVE: Hall of Fame slugger Harmon Killebrew delivered eight 40-homer seasons. (Photo by Malcolm Emmons)
RIGHT: Ferguson Jenkins won the Cy Young Award in 1971 when he won an NL-leading 24 games with 263 strikeouts. The All-Star hurler strung together six consecutive 20-win seasons for the Cubs. (Photo by Malcolm Emmons)
FAR RIGHT: In a five-year span, 1962-1966, Dodger Sandy Koufax pitched four no-hitters and won five ERA titles, three Cy Young Awards and one MVP Award. In four World Series he compiled a 0.95 ERA. (Photo by Malcolm Emmons)

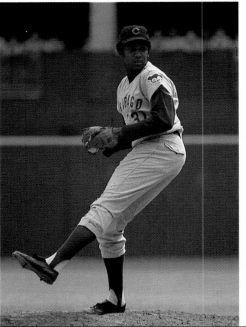

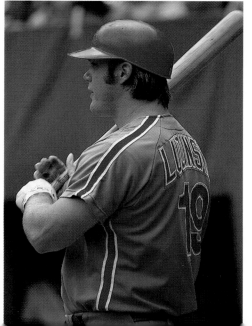

ABOVE: Dodger skipper Tommy Lasorda is doused with beer in the clubhouse celebration following the team's 1985 division title win. The first NL manager to win pennants his first two seasons, Lasorda has led his teams to four pennants and two World Championships. (Reuters/Bettmann Newsphotos)

FAR LEFT: Three-time All-Star Mickey Lolich posted three wins for Detroit in the 1968 Fall Classic, giving up only five runs with a 1.67 ERA, and smacking his only major league home run. Durable Lolich pitched more than 200 innings a season for 12 straight years, four times exceeding 300 innings. (Photo by Malcolm Emmons)

LEFT: Power-hitting outfielder and DH Greg Luzinski logged career highs with Philadelphia in 1977, batting .309 with 39 homers and 130 RBI. In five LCS the Bull blasted five round-trippers. (Photo by Nancy Hogue)

Jack Glasscock.

Jack Glasscock
Glasscock, John Wesley (Pebbly Jack)
B: Jul 22, 1859   D: Feb 24, 1947

Pos: SS   BA: .290
Hits: 2,040   HRs: 27
RBI: 779   BBs: 439
Managerial Record
Won: 35   Lost: 35   Pct: .500

Glasscock was among the greatest 19th-century shortstops. He was called "Pebbly Jack" for his habit of picking up and tossing away pebbles. He played barehanded until very late in his career, leading NL shortstops in fielding six times. He may have been the first to use a signal to inform his catcher which infielder would cover second on a steal, and was one of the first shortstops to back up throws to the second baseman.

While managing Indianapolis in 1889, he discovered 18-year-old future Hall of Famer Amos Rusie. The next year Glasscock went to the Giants when most of the NL talent defected to the Players' League. He led the NL in batting with a .336 average in 1890, including a six-hit game in September. He scored 1,163 runs and stole 334 bases during his career. After each season he went back to Wheeling, West Virginia, and worked as a carpenter.
Playing Career: *1879-1895; Cle N, Cin U, StL N, Ind N, NY N, Pit N, Lou N, Was N*
Managerial Career: *1889, 1892; Ind N, StL N*

Tom Glavine
Glavine, Thomas
B: Mar 25, 1966

Pos: P   ERA: 3.53
W-L: 95-66   SOs: 764
ShOs: 12   No-hitters: 0

Glavine may be the best pitcher in today's NL. He won 20 games in 1992 following his 1991 Cy Young Award-winning year, when he captured 20 victories with a 2.55 ERA. Glavine started the 1991 and 1992 All-Star Games, the first NL pitcher to start two consecutive years since Robin Roberts in 1953-1955.
Playing Career: *1987-; Atl N*

Bill Gleason
Gleason, William G. (Brother Bill)
B: Nov 12, 1858   D: Jul 21, 1932

Pos: SS   BA: .267
Hits: 907   HRs: 7
RBI: 66 (inc.)   BBs: 179

St. Louis native Gleason spent his entire eight-year major league career in the American Association. A proponent of aggressive coaching, Gleason was known to collide with opposing fielders in order to help his baserunners.
Playing Career: *1882-1889; StL AA, Phi AA, Lou AA*

Kid Gleason
Gleason, William J.
B: Oct 26, 1866   D: Jan 2, 1933

Pos: P   ERA: 3.79
W-L: 134-131   SOs: 744
ShOs: 11   Saves: 6

Pos: 2B   BA: .261
Hits: 1,944   HRs: 15
RBI: 823   BBs: 500
Managerial Record
Won: 392   Lost: 364   Pct: .519

Sadly, Gleason is best known today as the betrayed and heartbroken manager of the infamous Black Sox, but he was a star player in the 19th century. He began as a pitcher with the Phillies, blossoming in 1890 with a 38-17 record. Three more times Gleason won 20 games or more. When the mound distance

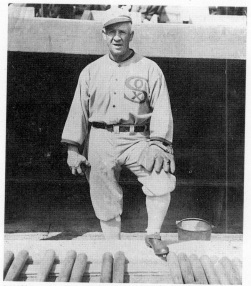

William J. "Kid" Gleason.

was increased to 60'6" in 1893, he lost stamina but not effectiveness, going 15-5 for the 1894 pennant-winning Orioles.

Gleason was team captain and second baseman with the Giants, then jumped to the new American League in 1901, but returned to the NL with the Phillies in 1903. In all, he played 20 full seasons in the majors, scoring 1,020 runs and stealing 328 bases. He became a coach and later manager of the White Sox.
Playing Career: *1888-1908, 1912; Phi N, StL N, Bal N, NY N, Det A, Chi A*
Managerial Career: *1919-1923; Chi A*

Fred Goldsmith
Goldsmith, Fred Ernest
B: May 15, 1856   D: Mar 28, 1939

Pos: P   ERA: 2.73
W-L: 112-68   SOs: 433
ShOs: 16   Saves: 1

Just after he had learned that Candy Cummings had been elected to the Hall of Fame as the inventor of the curveball, Goldsmith was found dead with a yellowed newspaper article claiming he, not Cummings, had developed the pitch.

Goldsmith was certainly one of the earliest practitioners of the pitch, having reportedly attended a pitching clinic with Cummings, Will White, Harry McCormick and catcher Deacon White at Watertown, New York in 1875. All four hurlers became curveball pitchers. Goldsmith won 20 or more games for four consecutive years, winning 62 percent overall.
Playing Career: *1875, 1879-1884; NH Elm Citys n, Tro N, Chi N, Bal AA*

Dave Goltz
Goltz, David Allan
B: Jun 23, 1949

Pos: P   ERA: 3.69
W-L: 113-109   SOs: 1,106
ShOs: 13   Saves: 8

A scout for the Twins discovered Goltz pitching in his parents' backyard. He became the first native Minnesotan signed by the Twins to make their major league roster. Goltz, a Vietnam veteran, never had a losing season. He won 20 in 1977.
Playing Career: *1972-1983; Min A, LA N, Cal A*

Lefty Gomez
Gomez, Vernon Louis (El Goofy)
B: Nov 26, 1908   D: Feb 17, 1989
Hall of Fame 1972

Pos: P   ERA: 3.34
W-L: 189-102   SOs: 1,468
ShOs: 28   Saves: 9

"Goofy" Gomez was one of the best left-handed pitchers of the 1930s. He won 20 games or more four times, including 26 in 1934. He led the AL in strikeouts three times, with a top mark of 194 in 1938. In five World Series, he posted six wins without a loss. He was chosen for seven All-Star Games in a row. In 1937 he led the league in wins, ERA and shutouts, then posted two WS wins.

Gomez pitched for the powerful Yankees teams of the 1930s. He gave his team strong performances and they gave him baseball's most consistent support with their bats and gloves. Gomez knew he was lucky to pitch at Yankee Stadium, where "Death Valley" in the left field power alley swallowed up long drives from right-handed hitters. He took his pitching seriously, but he had the ability to laugh at himself. Commenting on the secret of his success, Gomez said, "clean living and a fast outfield – I'm the guy who made Joe DiMaggio famous."
Playing Career: *1930-1943; NY A, Was A*

Preston Gomez
Gomez y Martinez, Pedro
B: Apr 20, 1923

Managerial Record
Won: 346   Lost: 529   Pct: .395

After appearing in eight games for the Senators in 1944 at age 21 – and slapping two hits in his total seven at-bats – Gomez never returned to the majors as a player. He endured a long managerial apprenticeship in the minors before he was named Padres manager in 1969.
Managerial Career: *1969-1972, 1974-1975, 1980; SD N, Hou N, Chi N*

Ruben Gomez
Gomez y Colon, Ruben
B: Jul 13, 1927

Pos: P	ERA: 4.09
W-L: 76-86	SOs: 677
ShOs: 15	Saves: 5

Puerto Rican Ruben Gomez was the enforcer for Giants manager Leo Durocher. He was fast and good, but sometimes wild. Gomez was involved in the celebrated beanball incidents with Carl Furillo, Joe Adcock and Frank Robinson.
Playing Career: *1953-1960, 1962, 1967; NY N, SF N, Phi N, Cle A, Min A*

Juan Gonzalez
Gonzalez y Vazquez, Juan Alberto
B: Oct 16, 1969

Pos: OF	BA: .274
Hits: 497	HRs: 121
RBI: 348	BBs: 122

Gonzalez broke into the big leagues at age 19, and has improved steadily every year. In 1992 he hit 43 homers, making him one of the youngest players ever to lead the major leagues in that category. On June 7, 1992, he whacked three homers.
Playing Career: *1989-; Tex A*

Mike Gonzalez
Gonzalez y Cordero, Miguel Angel
B: Sep 24, 1890   D: Feb 19, 1977

Pos: C	BA: .253
Hits: 717	HRs: 13
RBI: 263	BBs: 231

Managerial Record
Won: 9   Lost: 13   Pct: .409

Gonzalez originated the saying "Good field, No hit," in a telegram to describe a prospect. Had the phrase been common while Gonzalez was playing, it might have been applied to him. The first Latino and the first Cuban to play regularly in the major leagues, Gonzalez enjoyed a long association with the Cardinals as player, manager and scout. His only World Series appearance was with the Cubs.
Playing Career: *1912, 1914-1921, 1924-1929, 1931-1932; Bos N, Cin N, StL N, NY N, Chi N*
Managerial Career: *1938, 1940; StL N*

Tony Gonzalez
Gonzalez y Gonzalez, Andres Antonio
B: Aug 28, 1936

Pos: OF	BA: .286
Hits: 1,485	HRs: 103
RBI: 615	BBs: 467

The first regular center fielder – and only the third outfielder – ever to field 1.000, Gonzalez reached the apex in 1962. Two years later he spearheaded the famous Phillies pennant drive that made the last week of the season dramatic. In 1967 Gonzalez hit a career-high .339, and once again led the league's outfielders in fielding. He hit a homer off Tom Seaver in Game One of the 1969 NLCS.
Playing Career: *1960-1971; Cin N, Phi N, SD N, Atl N, Cal A*

Johnny Gooch
Gooch, John Beverley
B: Nov 9, 1897   D: Mar 15, 1975

Pos: C	BA: .280
Hits: 662	HRs: 7
RBI: 293	BBs: 206

Gooch was a switch hitter and slick-fielding catcher for Pittsburgh, 1922-1927. He was part of the Pirates' youth movement which made them contenders in the 1920s. Gooch hit .329 as a rookie while he platooned at catcher, as was the custom in those days.
Playing Career: *1921-1930, 1933; Pit N, Brk N, Cin N, Bos A*

Wilbur Good
Good, Wilbur David
B: Sep 28, 1885   D: Dec 30, 1963

Pos: OF	BA: .258
Hits: 609	HRs: 9
RBI: 187	BBs: 190

A minor league hitting legend, Good was an extra outfielder in the majors. He whacked the first pinch-hit homer in Cubs history, and still holds their team record as the only Bearcub to steal second, third and home in the same inning.
Playing Career: *1905, 1908-1916, 1918; NY A, Cle A, Bos N, Chi N, Phi N, Chi A*

Dwight Gooden
Gooden, Dwight Eugene (Doc)
B: Nov 16, 1964

Pos: P	ERA: 3.04
W-L: 154-81	SOs: 1,835
ShOs: 23	Saves: 1

Gooden broke into the majors with a 17-9 record, a 2.60 ERA, and 276 strikeouts to win the NL Rookie of the Year Award at age 20, the youngest player ever to win it. He posted 744 whiffs in his first three seasons, inspiring fans to nickname him "Dr. K," after the symbol scorekeepers use to denote a strikeout. The Doctor's followers began displaying "K" banners in Shea Stadium, draping one over the grandstand after each whiff.

The Giants' Mike Gonzalez, 1921.

Mets hurler Dwight Gooden, 1986.

Gooden surpassed Herb Score's rookie strikeout record in early September of 1984. With a 2.04 ERA, he has an 0-1 record in two NLCS with the Mets. He is also a good hitting pitcher; he smashed 21 hits in 1985, and in 1990 drove in four runs in a single game. Gooden's .655 won-lost percentage is twelfth best on the all-time list.
Playing Career: *1984-; NY N*

Billy Goodman.

Billy Goodman
Goodman, William Dale
B: Mar 22, 1926   D: Oct 1, 1984

Pos: 3B, 2B, 1B, OF, SS   BA: .300
Hits: 1,691   HRs: 19
RBI: 591   BBs: 669

Goodman was a strong hitter who lacked a position. Tested at first base in 1949, Goodman led the league in fielding, but his hitting faded. He won the AL batting title with a .354 mark the next year as a utility player. He was a .300 hitter who hit 20 or more doubles for nine consecutive years.

The All-Star Game roster held his name twice, in 1949 and 1953. He was later traded to the Orioles, where he backed up George Kell at third base, giving the White Sox the idea that Goodman could play the hot corner and hit. They traded for him in 1958. In Chicago Goodman proved to be a valuable reserve in the drive to the 1959 pennant. But in the regular season he hit .231 as the third baseman.
Playing Career: *1947-1962; Bos A, Bal A, Chi A, Hou N*

Ival Goodman
Goodman, Ival Richard (Goody)
B: Jul 23, 1908   D: Nov 25, 1984

Pos: OF   BA: .381
Hits: 1,104   HRs: 95
RBI: 525   BBs: 382

A member of the Cincinnati Reds Hall of Fame, Goodman led the NL in triples his first two seasons, and also set a Reds home run mark of 30 in 1938. He played in two All-Star Games and two World Series, batting .295.
Playing Career: *1935-1944; Cin N, Chi N*

Power-hitting second baseman Joe Gordon takes a big swing for the Yanks.

Joe Gordon
Gordon, Joseph Lowell (Flash)
B: Feb 18, 1915   D: Apr 14, 1978

Pos: 2B   BA: .268
Hits: 1,530   HRs: 253
RBI: 975   BBs: 759
Managerial Record
Won: 305   Lost: 308   Pct: .498

Flash Gordon ranged over the Yankee infield, making plays that other second basemen only dreamed about. He led AL second sackers in assists four times. In his first six years with the Yankees, they went to the World Series five times. Gordon seldom hit for average, but he had power. In 1942 he batted .322 and was named AL MVP.

Traded to Cleveland after he returned from World War II, Gordon combined with Lou Boudreau to form what many still consider the best double play combination ever. In 1948 Gordon had his greatest season, batting .280 with 32 homers and 124 RBI, and the Indians won the World Championship. Gordon became Cleveland's manager in 1958 and later figured in the only known trade of managers when the Indians swapped him for Tigers pilot Jimmy Dykes.
Playing Career: *1938-1943, 1946-1950; NY A, Cle A*
Managerial Career: *1958-1961, 1969; Cle A, Det A, KC A*

Sid Gordon
Gordon, Sidney
B: Aug 13, 1917   D: Jun 17, 1975

Pos: OF   BA: .283
Hits: 1,415   HRs: 202
RBI: 805   BBs: 731

Being a local boy, Gordon became a Giants favorite. In 1948 he peaked with 30 homers, 107 RBI, and a .299 batting average. He held out the next spring but finally settled for $2,500 less than he had asked. Following the 1949 season Gordon was sent to the Braves in a multi-player deal. After the trade, Giants owner Horace Stoneham sent Gordon a personal check for $2,500 to show his esteem for the outfielder.
Playing Career: *1941-1943, 1946-1955; NY N, Bos N, Mil N, Pit N*

George Gore
Gore, George F.
B: May 3, 1857   D: Sep 16, 1933

Pos: OF	BA: .301
Hits: 1,612	HRs: 46
RBI: 526	BBs: 717

Managerial Record
Won: 6   Lost: 9   Pct: .400

Gore is one of three players in baseball history who scored more runs, 1,327, than games played, 1,310. Signed by Cap Anson after playing in an exhibition against the White Stockings, Gore was a catalyst for the famous team. When the White Stockings lost the famous winner-take-all postseason championship series with the St. Louis Browns, Anson blamed the team's failure on Gore. He was sent to the Gothams – later called the Giants – and played in two more championship series, hitting .455 in 1888 and .333 in 1889.

Gore's records include a 6-for-6 game, five consecutive extra-base hits in one game, and seven stolen bases in a game. His .360 NL-leading batting mark in 1880 was 115 points above the league average. NL players marveled at Gore in 1886 when he drew 102 bases on balls – at that time it took seven balls for a walk.
Playing Career: *1879-1892; Chi N, NY N, StL N*
Managerial Career: *1892; StL N*

Tom Gorman
Gorman, Thomas Aloysius
B: Jan 4, 1925

Pos: P	ERA: 3.77
W-L: 36-36	SOs: 321
ShOs: 2	Saves: 42

Gorman pitched for the Yankees in the 1952 and 1953 World Series, going 0-0 with a 2.45 ERA. In 1955 he was traded to the Athletics with Ewell Blackwell for $50,000. Gorman saved 18 games in 1955, but was not so successful as a starter.
Playing Career: *1952-1959; NY A, KC A*

Goose Goslin
Goslin, Leon Allen
B: Oct 16, 1900   D: May 15, 1971
Hall of Fame 1968

Pos: OF	BA: .316
Hits: 2,735	HRs: 248
RBI: 1,609	BBs: 949

When Goose met Clark Griffith during the off-season, he reminded the Senators' owner that no Washington team had ever won a pennant without a Goslin in the outfield. The Senators acquired the Goose and captured the 1924, 1925 and 1933 AL flags. Goslin batted .300 or more in each of his first seven full years as a Senator. In 1924 he led the AL in RBI with 129, hit .344 and knocked 12 homers. The Senators won their first pennant and only World Series, as Goslin at one point set a record with six consecutive hits.

Washington Senators star Leon "Goose" Goslin helped his team win three pennants.

The next year the Senators won their second pennant, as Goslin led the AL in triples while hitting .334 with 18 home runs and 113 RBI. He hit .354 and .334 the next two seasons, then was best in the AL in 1928 with a .379 mark in the closest batting race in league history. Goslin singled in his last at-bat of the season to edge out Heinie Manush by .001. Goslin played in five World Series during his career, scored 1,483 runs and hit 500 doubles.
Playing Career: *1921-1938; Was A, StL A, Det A*

Goose Gossage
Gossage, Richard Michael
B: Jul 5, 1951

Pos: P	ERA: 2.98
W-L: 121-107	SOs: 1,473
ShOs: 0	Saves: 309

Gossage was one of the most consistent relief pitchers ever; he ranks fourth on the all-time saves list with 309, and third in relief victories with 112. He led the league in saves in 1975 with 26, earning him the first of nine All-Star Game selections. The next year the White Sox switched him to the starting rotation, but Gossage went 9-17 and never started another game. He reached a career-high 33 saves in 1980.

Gossage was nearly un-hittable during the strike-shortened 1981 season, allowing just 22 hits in 47 innings to go with 48 strikeouts, 20 saves and an ERA of 0.77. He saved all three Yankees wins over Milwaukee during the divisional playoffs, and both wins over the Dodgers in the World Series. In 1983 Gossage gave up the disputed "Pine Tar" home run to George Brett.
Playing Career: *1972-; Chi A, Pit N, NY A, SD N, Chi N, SF N, Tex A, Oak A*

Jim Gott
Gott, James William
B: Aug 3, 1959

Pos: P	ERA: 3.73
W-L: 49-67	SOs: 789
ShOs: 3	Saves: 86

Gott is a pitcher with impressive stuff, steadily improving with age. His ERA has been under 3.00 since 1988. Specializing in middle relief, Gott learned the split-finger fastball from Roger Craig in 1985.
Playing Career: *1982-; Tor A, SF N, Pit N, LA N*

Hank Gowdy
Gowdy, Henry Morgan
B: Aug 24, 1889   D: Aug 1, 1966

Pos: C	BA: .270
Hits: 738	HRs: 21
RBI: 322	BBs: 311

Managerial Record
Won: 3   Lost: 1   Pct: .750

Patriotic Gowdy enlisted for military duty in both World War I and World War II. When he was not fighting World Wars, he battled World Series pitching, hitting at a .310 clip in 14 games in three Fall Classics. Gowdy compiled a .545 batting average and a 1.273 slug-

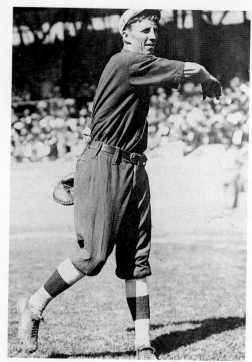

Hank Gowdy.

ging percentage in the 1914 Series sweep of the Athletics by the "Miracle" Braves. He caught no-hitters by George Davis and Tom Hughes.
Playing Career: *1910-1917, 1919-1925, 1929-1930; NY N, Bos N*
Managerial Career: *1946; Cin N*

Mark Grace
Grace, Mark Eugene
B: Jun 28, 1964

Pos: 1B	BA: .304
Hits: 1,033	HRs: 60
RBI: 453	BBs: 412

Grace is one of the steadiest players in baseball today. NL Rookie of the Year in 1988, Grace hit .296 with seven homers and 57 RBI in 486 at-bats. Since then he's batted over .300 in four of the last five years. He hit .647 in the 1989 NLCS.
Playing Career: *1988-; Chi N*

Mike Grady
Grady, Michael William
B: Dec 23, 1869   D: Dec 3, 1943

Pos: C, 1B, OF, 3B, SS	BA: .294
Hits: 881	HRs: 35
RBI: 459	BBs: 311

Grady once committed three errors on one play. At third base he booted a ground ball, then overthrew first. When the batter advanced all the way to third, Grady dropped the throw from the first baseman, then launched the ball over the catcher's head as the runner headed home.
Playing Career: *1894-1901, 1904-1906; Phi N, StL N, NY N, Was A*

Alex Grammas
Grammas, Alexander Peter
B: Apr 3, 1926

Pos: SS	BA: .247
Hits: 512	HRs: 12
RBI: 163	BBs: 206
Managerial Record	
Won: 137 Lost: 191 Pct: .418	

Baseball has had the services of Grammas for almost 50 years. He was the Cardinals' everyday shortstop in the mid-1950s, then coached for the Pirates, Reds, Braves and Tigers. He is now the third base coach for Sparky Anderson in Detroit.
Playing Career: *1954-1963; StL N, Cin N, Chi N*
Managerial Career: *1969, 1976-1977; Pit N, Mil A*

Jack Graney
Graney, John Gladstone
B: Jun 10, 1886   D: Apr 20, 1978

Pos: OF	BA: .250
Hits: 1,178	HRs: 18
RBI: 420	BBs: 713

The first ballplayer to make the transition from field to broadcast booth was Graney. He was also the first 20th-century player to appear with a number on his uniform. In 1911 the Indians experimented with numbers on players' sleeves; Graney was the leadoff batter. He was past his prime by the time he got into the 1920 World Series. But he had led the AL in doubles in 1916, and in walks in 1917 and 1919.
Playing Career: *1908, 1910-1922; Cle A*

Jack Graney.

Wayne Granger
Granger, Wayne Allan
B: Mar 15, 1944

Pos: P	ERA: 3.14
W-L: 35-35	SOs: 303
ShOs: 0	Saves: 108

Two pennants in the first three years got Granger's major league career off to a great start. In 1969 he set an NL record with 90 appearances. That year he saved 27 while compiling a 9-6 record and a 2.79 ERA, winning the first of two consecutive Fireman of the Year Awards. Granger's 35 saves in 1970 set another NL mark. In the World Series that year, pitcher Dave McNally hit a grand slam off Granger, who never really performed well again.
Playing Career: *1968-1976; StL N, Cin N, Min A, NY A, Chi A, Hou N, Mon N*

Charlie Grant
Grant, Charles (Chief Tokahoma)
B: Unknown   D: Jul 1932

Most historians consider Grant to be the best of early black players. John McGraw tried to pass him as a Cherokee, but AL rival Charles Comiskey caught the deception. Grant was the second baseman for the black championship teams of 1903 and 1904, in Chicago.
Playing Career: *1896-1910; Adrian Page Fence Giants, Chi Columbia Giants, NY Cuban X-Giants, Phi Giants, NY Black Sox*

Eddie Grant
Grant, Edward Leslie
B: May 21, 1883   D: Oct 5, 1918

Pos: 3B	BA: .249
Hits: 844	HRs: 5
RBI: 277	BBs: 233

Trying out for Cleveland in 1905, Grant got three hits his first game, but was hitless the next day against Cy Young and was sent to the minors. After his big league career, Grant practiced law in New York City. In World War I, he led a mission in the Argonne Forest offensive to rescue the "Lost Battalion" trapped behind German lines. Met with machine gun fire, Grant became the only major league player killed in the war. A monument was placed at the Polo Grounds in his memory.
Playing Career: *1905, 1907-1915; Cle A, Phi N, Cin N, NY N*

Mudcat Grant
Grant, James Timothy
B: Aug 13, 1935

Pos: P	ERA: 3.63
W-L: 145-119	SOs: 1,267
ShOs: 18	Saves: 53

Colorful Mudcat Grant pitched 14 years in the big leagues, won two games in the 1965 World Series, worked as a radio broadcaster, and sang in a group called "Mudcat and the Kittens." In 1965 he won 21 games, leading

the AL in wins, winning percentage and shutouts, but drew nary a vote for the Cy Young Award – Sandy Koufax was the unanimous choice. The incident helped motivate the AL and NL to make separate awards.
Playing Career: *1958-1971; Cle A, Min A, LA N, Mon N, StL N, Oak A, Pit N*

George Grantham
Grantham, George Farley
B: May 20, 1900   D: Mar 16, 1954

Pos: 2B, 1B, 3B	BA: .302
Hits: 1,508	HRs: 105
RBI: 712	BBs: 717

Grantham's controversial trade to Pittsburgh helped the Pirates ascend into pennant heaven. In a 1924 postseason deal, the Bucs sent Rabbit Maranville, Charlie Grimm and Wilbur Cooper to the Cubs for Grantham, Vic Aldridge and Al Niehaus. Many Pittsburgh fans criticized trading three popular players for defensively inconsistent Grantham, a 31-year-old pitcher and a little-known first baseman, but the trade paid off for the Bucs.

Grantham switched from second to first base, and batted a career-high .326 as Pittsburgh won the 1925 NL pennant and World Series over the Senators. The Cubs finished last that year. Two years later Grantham moved back to second and led the Pirates to another World Series. He hit .364 in a losing effort; the Yankees were victorious. Grantham developed power after 1927, slugging .533 and .534 in the next two years. He batted over .300 eight straight years while alternating between first and second base.
Playing Career: *1922-1934; Chi N, Pit N, Cin N, NY N*

George Grantham.

Pete Gray
Gray, Peter Wyshner
B: Mar 6, 1915

Pos: OF	BA: .218
Hits: 51	HRs: 0
RBI: 13	BBs: 13

A one-armed player who played wartime ball, Gray patrolled the outfield, caught fly balls, then tucked his thinly padded glove under his stump and rolled the ball across his chest to throw. He played for the 1945 Browns, the AL defending champs.
Playing Career: *1945; StL A*

Sam Gray
Gray, Samuel David
B: Oct 15, 1897   D: Apr 16, 1953

Pos: P	ERA: 4.20
W-L: 112-115	SOs: 735
ShOs: 16	Saves: 22

A tremendously talented hurler who returned to the minors after 10 years in the majors, Gray went 20-12 for the Browns in 1928. But he suffered a series of misfortunes, including the death of his wife, that kept him from building an outstanding record.
Playing Career: *1924-1933; Phi A, StL A*

Ted Gray
Gray, Ted Glenn
B: Dec 31, 1924

Pos: P	ERA: 4.37
W-L: 59-74	SOs: 687
ShOs: 7	Saves: 4

Signed off the Detroit sandlots, Gray was a pitching star in World War II military baseball. In the majors, the forkballer was hindered by chronic blisters, holding his ERA below 4.00 only once in nine seasons.
Playing Career: *1946, 1948-1955; Det A, Chi A, Cle A, NY A, Bal A*

Dallas Green
Green, George Dallas
B: Aug 4, 1934

Pos: P	ERA: 4.26
W-L: 20-22	SOs: 268
ShOs: 2	Saves: 4
Managerial Record	
Won: 272 Lost: 273 Pct: .499	

Green found his niche as manager and general manager after a less than spectacular pitching career. The Phillies won the 1980 World Series with Green as skipper. He rebuilt the Cubs' farm system, and was instrumental in their 1984 and 1989 divisional championships. In 1989 he worked with Yankees General Manager Syd Thrift to rebuild the Bombers, but was fired by owner George Steinbrenner before the season ended.
Playing Career: *1960-1967; Phi N, Was A, NY N*
Managerial Career: *1979-1981, 1989, 1993-; Phi N, NY A, NY N*

Yankee Manager Dallas Green, 1989.

Danny Green
Green, Edward
B: Nov 6, 1876   D: Nov 9, 1914

Pos: OF	BA: .293
Hits: 1,021	HRs: 29
RBI: 422	BBs: 315

One of the original members of the AL, Green tried his hand at coaching as well as playing. He had players rollerskating instead of jogging for conditioning in the spring. After his big league career, Green returned to the minors, where he died from a beaning.
Playing Career: *1898-1905; Chi N, Chi A*

Dick Green
Green, Richard Larry
B: Apr 21, 1941

Pos: 2B	BA: .240
Hits: 960	HRs: 80
RBI: 422	BBs: 345

Bert Campaneris and Green were slick double play partners on the A's powerhouse teams of 1972-1974. The light-hitting second sacker turned six double plays in the 1974 Fall Classic, including one to end Game Four.
Playing Career: *1963-1974; KC A, Oak A*

Lenny Green
Green, Leonard Charles
B: Jan 6, 1933

Pos: OF	BA: .267
Hits: 788	HRs: 47
RBI: 253	BBs: 368

In 1961 Green put together a 24-game hitting streak which remained a Twins record until Ken Landreaux broke it in 1980. Green scored 97 runs in 1962 for the Twins. Twice in his career, he was traded to a club that his team opposed in its very next game.
Playing Career: *1957-1968; Bal A, Was A, Min A, LA A, Bos A, Det A*

Tigers slugger and Hall of Famer "Hammerin' Hank" Greenberg.

Hank Greenberg
Greenberg, Henry Benjamin
B: Jan 1, 1911   D: Sep 4, 1986
Hall of Fame 1956

Pos: 1B, OF	BA: .313
Hits: 1,628	HRs: 331
RBI: 1,276	BBs: 852

The New York Giants had been searching for a Jewish baseball star for 20 years when they found Greenberg at a local high school. John McGraw ended up rejecting Greenberg because he was too clumsy around first base. Greenberg turned down an offer from the Yankees and signed with the Tigers, becoming one of baseball's greatest players and heir to the slugging throne of Babe Ruth and Jimmie Foxx. Greenberg's career slugging average, .605, ranks him fifth on the all-time list.

Despite losing more than four seasons to military duty and another to a broken wrist, Greenberg put up awesome numbers. He was the AL MVP in 1935 and 1940, and led the league in homers and RBI four times. He was also chosen for the All-Star squad 1937-1940. In 1937 he drove in 183 runs, one shy of the AL record. The next year he bashed 58 home runs, and had 11 multi-homer games, a record. Greenberg hit a famous grand slam on the final day of the 1945 season to capture the pennant for Detroit.
Playing Career: *1930, 1933-1941, 1945-1947; Det A, Pit N*

Gus Greenlee
Greenlee, William Augustus (Big Red)
B: 1897   D: Jul 7, 1952

Greenlee built the Pittsburgh Crawfords into the finest team in the history of Black baseball. Oscar Charleston managed the team that included Cool Papa Bell, Judy Johnson, Josh Gibson, Satchel Paige and Smoky Joe Williams. Greenlee resurrected organized Black baseball by establishing the Negro National Association that became known as the Negro National League. He served as president for the first five years. In 1932 he built Greenlee Field for the Crawfords, and he staged boxing matches and other promotions in addition to baseball.

The next year, he initiated the East-West All-Star Game that was held in Comiskey Park and became the annual showcase for Black baseball. When many of the Crawfords' stars went to the Dominican Republic to play for General Trujillo, Greenlee disbanded the team and razed Greenlee Field. He later worked with Branch Rickey to establish a rival Black league during the 1940s.

Mike Greenwell
Greenwell, Michael Lewis
B: Jul 18, 1963

Pos: OF	BA: .307
Hits: 1,082	HRs: 97
RBI: 561	BBs: 366

The Red Sox heir to Ted Williams, Carl Yastrzemski and Jim Rice in left field, Greenwell has strung together six straight years of batting .300 or more. His first three major league hits were home runs. In 1988 Greenwell won the left field job from Rice by hitting .325 with 22 homers, 119 RBI, and only 38 strikeouts. He has not yet shown the power of his predecessors, but raps solid line drives. Greenwell appears to have made a full recovery from arthroscopic knee and major elbow surgeries in 1992.
Playing Career: *1985-; Bos A*

Vean Gregg
Gregg, Sylveanus Augustus
B: Apr 13, 1885   D: Jul 29, 1964

Pos: P	ERA: 2.70
W-L: 91-63	SOs: 720
ShOs: 14	Saves: 12

Gregg had a great 1910 season in the Pacific Coast League, winning 32 and throwing 14 shutouts. The next year, his AL rookie season, Gregg won 23 games and led the league with a .767 winning percentage and a 1.81 ERA. He had two more 20-win years.
Playing Career: *1911-1916, 1918, 1925; Cle A, Bos A, Phi A, Was A*

Bobby Grich
Grich, Robert Anthony
B: Jan 15, 1949

Pos: 2B	BA: .266
Hits: 1,833	HRs: 224
RBI: 864	BBs: 1,087

Grich was a power-hitting infielder who starred as the AL's best all-around second baseman for 15 seasons, earning All-Star squad recognition six times over 11 years. Grich came up with the Orioles as a 23-year-old rookie shortstop, but moved to second base where he won the first of four consecutive Gold Glove Awards. He reached double figures in home runs and stolen bases each year from 1973 to 1976, while hitting near .260. Grich became a free agent after the 1976 season.

The Angels signed Grich, but he spent most of the 1977 season on the DL. Developing power as he aged, Grich whacked 30 homers in 1979 and tied for the lead in the AL with 22 round-trippers in the strike-shortened 1981 season. He also led the league with a .543 slugging percentage while batting a career-high .304 that year. In the field, Grich regained his fielding record with a .997 percentage, committing only two errors all season.
Playing Career: *1970-1986; Bal A, Cal A*

Second baseman Bobby Grich, 1982.

Ken Griffey, Jr.
Griffey, George Kenneth, Jr.
B: Nov 21, 1969

Pos: OF	BA: .303
Hits: 832	HRs: 132
RBI: 453	BBs: 316

Ken Griffey, Jr. is probably the best player in baseball today. He has unbelievable offensive and defensive skills, honed by his father, former major league player Ken Griffey, Sr. The father-son combination roamed the Mariners' outfield together in 1990 and 1991. The Mariners' number one choice in the 1987 draft, Griffey, Jr. began his professional baseball career at age 17. He has been the star in every league in which he has played. Griffey, Jr. was injured in his rookie season, but has hit more than 20 home runs and batted over .300 in every year since.

Griffey, Jr. homered in eight straight games in 1993, tying the major league record. A superb defensive outfielder, he has won four straight Gold Gloves.
Playing Career: *1989-; Sea A*

Ken Griffey
Griffey, George Kenneth, Sr.
B: Apr 10, 1950

Pos: OF	BA: .297
Hits: 2,077	HRs: 147
RBI: 824	BBs: 694

Ken Griffey, Sr. was an unsung hero with the Big Red Machine in Cincinnati, 1975-1981. He hit .307 in his first nine years with the Reds, challenging for the NL batting title in 1976 and 1977, with .336 and .317 respectively. Griffey scored 1,100 runs with 198 stolen bases in his 19-year career. The right fielder played in three NLCS, batting .313 in nine games. Griffey also appeared in 11 World Series games as the Reds defeated Boston and New York.

Griffey's career went into a nosedive after he went to the Yankees in 1981. Platooned at first base and in the outfield, and hampered by injuries, Griffey struggled in the Big Apple. A move to Atlanta rejuvenated his career. In 1988 he returned to Cincinnati, reunited with the Reds and Pete Rose. Two years later, he and Ken Griffey, Jr. made baseball history as the first father and son to play major league baseball at the same time, and on the same team.
Playing Career: *1973-1991; Cin N, NY A, Atl N, Sea A*

Alfredo Griffin
Griffin, Alfredo Claudino
B: Oct 6, 1957

Pos: SS, 2B	BA: .249
Hits: 1,688	HRs: 24
RBI: 527	BBs: 338

There were two winners of the 1979 AL Rookie of the Year Award, John Castino and Alfredo Griffin. The starting shortstop in Toronto for six years, Griffin accumulated 392 consecutive games. In 1980 he led the AL in triples with 15, and in 1984 he made the All-Star team. He developed into an offensive player in Oakland, then was traded to Los Angeles in a 1988 move that helped both teams so much that they met that year in the World Series.
Playing Career: *1976-; Cle A, Tor A, Oak A, LA N*

Doug Griffin
Griffin, Douglas Lee
B: Jun 4, 1947

Pos: 2B	BA: .245
Hits: 524	HRs: 7
RBI: 165	BBs: 158

Griffin was becoming a solid-hitting middle infielder when he was beaned by a Nolan Ryan fastball on April 30, 1974. The 1972 Gold Glove second baseman was never the same at the plate. Ironically, the Angels had traded him in 1970 for Tony Conigliaro, another beaning victim.
Playing Career: *1970-1977; Cal A, Bos A*

Mike Griffin
Griffin, Michael Joseph
B: Mar 20, 1865   D: Apr 10, 1908

Pos: OF	BA: .297
Hits: 1,759	HRs: 42
RBI: 625	BBs: 809
Managerial Record	
Won: 1 Lost: 3 Pct: .250	

Many historians consider Griffin the best center fielder of the 19th century. He led the NL six times in fielding percentage. Fleet of foot, in 1887 he stole 94 bases to set a rookie record that stood almost 100 years; Vince Coleman stole 110 in 1985. Griffin pilfered 473 bags during his career. In 1889 he led the AA in runs scored with 152. He scored 1,405 runs altogether, topping 100 in 10 of 12 years.
Playing Career: *1887-1898; Bal AA, Phi P, Brk N*
Managerial Career: *1898; Brk N*

Tom Griffin
Griffin, Thomas James
B: Feb 22, 1948

Pos: P	ERA: 4.07
W-L: 77-94	SOs: 1,054
ShOs: 10	Saves: 5

One-third of the trio of Houston starters who each struck out 200 or more in a season, Griffin broke in with a record of 11-10 and 200 whiffs in 1969. He also won the NL Rookie Pitcher of the Year Award. Griffin was a good-hitting pitcher, with 10 homers in 405 at-bats.
Playing Career: *1969-1982; Hou N, SD N, Cal A, SF N, Pit N*

Cal Griffith
Griffith, Calvin Robertson
B: Dec 11, 1911

Cal Griffith was the nephew and adopted son of Washington Senators owner Clark Griffith. The younger Griffith started his baseball career as team secretary of the Chattanooga

Ken Griffey Sr. and Jr. – both Seattle Mariners in 1990 – with Dave Winfield (l).

Cal Griffith.

Lookouts in 1935; he was made president two years later. While playing semi-pro ball, Griffith managed concessions for the Senators. He gradually assumed more of the baseball operations and became president when Clark Griffith died in 1955.

Griffith moved the team to Minneapolis in the 1961 expansion and changed the team's name to the Twins. He fashioned a hard-hitting squad that won the 1965 AL pennant. Griffith's Twins always competed and finished high in the standings. With the advent of free agency, Griffith became a dinosaur–the last of the owners whose only business was baseball. He sold off his expensive stars and brought up a bunch of talented kids. The kids finished last in 1981 and 1982, but with the help of General Manager Andy MacPhail, won World Championships in 1987 and 1991.

Senators President Clark Griffith, 1940.

Clark Griffith
Griffith, Clark Calvin (The Old Fox)
B: Nov 20, 1869   D: Oct 27, 1955
Hall of Fame 1946

Pos: P	ERA: 3.31
W-L: 237-146	SOs: 955
ShOs: 22	Saves: 6
Managerial Record	
Won: 1,491 Lost: 1,367 Pct: .522	

Clark Griffith was the man who kept baseball going during World War II. His friendships with Postmaster General James A. Farley and President Franklin D. Roosevelt were responsible for the famous "Green Light" letter from the President, urging that baseball continue as a morale booster during the war. Griffith began his baseball career as a pitcher, winning 20 or more games six straight years in the NL. Jumping to the AL in 1901, Griffith pitched and managed the White Sox to the first flag in the new league's history. He took over the fledgling New York Highlanders – later called the Yankees – in 1903. Griffith managed the Reds for three years, then was asked to rescue the failing Washington fran-

chise in 1912. Mortgaging his ranch, Griffith bought 10 percent of the club; he took over as president of the Senators in 1920. Although the team won a World Championship in 1924 and pennants in 1925 and 1933, Griffith was always financially strapped. In 1934 he was forced to sell his manager-shortstop and son-in-law Joe Cronin, for $225,000.
Playing Career: *1891, 1893-1907, 1909, 1912-1914; StL AA, Bos AA, Chi N, Chi A, NY A, Cin N, Was A*
Managerial Career: *1901-1920; Chi A, NY A, Cin N, Was A*

Tommy Griffith
Griffith, Thomas Herman
B: Oct 26, 1889   D: Apr 13, 1967

Pos: OF	BA: .280
Hits: 1,383	HRs: 52
RBI: 619	BBs: 351

The year after Griffith was traded to the Dodgers they won the NL flag and played in the 1920 World Series. Griffith was a swift right fielder with one of the best arms in the NL. He was consistently in double figures for assists, topping 20 three times. His best sea-

Burleigh Grimes.

son was 1921, when he hit .312 with 12 homers and 71 RBIs.
Playing Career: *1913-1925; Bos N, Cin N, Brk N, Chi N*

Bob Grim
Grim, Robert Anton
B: Mar 8, 1930

Pos: P	ERA: 3.61
W-L: 61-41	SOs: 443
ShOs: 4	Saves: 37

When Grim won 20 games in 1954, he was the first Yankee rookie to do so since Russell Ford in 1910. His blazing fastball and sharp slider damaged his arm, forcing him into the bullpen. Grim saved Game One of the 1955 World Series and led the AL with 19 saves in 1957.
Playing Career: *1954-1960, 1962; NY A, KC A, Cle A, Cin N, StL N*

John Grim
Grim, John Helm
B: Aug 9, 1867   D: Jul 28, 1961

Pos: C	BA: .267
Hits: 705	HRs: 16
RBI: 296	BBs: 85

The Louisville clubs of 1892-1894 excelled in fighting and carousing, but not baseball. Grim caught half their games, as was the practice for catchers of that era, then transferred to Brooklyn, where he was also a platoon catcher.
Playing Career: *1888, 1890-1899; Phi N, Roc AA, Mil AA, Lou N, Brk N*

Burleigh Grimes
Grimes, Burleigh Arland
(Ol' Stubblebeard)
B: Aug 9, 1893   D: Dec 6, 1985
Hall of Fame 1964

Pos: P	ERA: 3.53
W-L: 270-212	SOs: 1,512
ShOs: 35	Saves: 18
Managerial Record	
Won: 131 Lost: 171 Pct: .434	

Burleigh Grimes threw the last legal spitball in 1934. A workhorse who led the NL in innings pitched three times, Grimes topped 300 innings in five different seasons. Three times he pitched 30 or more complete games. His greatest years were with the Dodgers, where he won 20 games or more four times between 1918 and 1926.

Grimes never shaved on game day, adding to his ominous appearance on the mound. He won 25 games in 1928, and began an odyssey of being released, traded and sold – eight times from 1927 to 1934. No other Hall of Famer was moved as much as Grimes. After his playing career, Grimes took over the bedraggled Dodgers from a frustrated Casey Stengel, but did not get along with new owner Larry MacPhail.
Playing Career: *1916-1934; Pit N, Brk N, NY N, Bos N, StL N, Chi N, NY A*
Managerial Career: *1937-1938; Brk N*

The Cubs' playing manager, Charlie Grimm.

Charlie Grimm
Grimm, Charles John (Jolly Cholly)
B: Aug 28, 1898　D: Nov 15, 1983

Pos: 1B	BA: .290
Hits: 2,299	HRs: 79
RBI: 1,078	BBs: 578

Managerial Record
Won: 1,287　Lost: 1,067　Pct: .547

In a fairy tale career, Grimm batted .364 in two World Series as a Cubs player and won three pennants as their manager. Grimm frolicked through 20 seasons as a player, then became a manager known for tolerance who could coax career-years from mediocre players. The most skillful first baseman of his era, Grimm won nine fielding titles. In Pittsburgh, he connected with fellow free spirits Rabbit Maranville and Cotton Tierney. Grimm and Maranville were traded to the Cubs in 1925, and continued their fun-loving ways in Chicago.

In 1932 Grimm became manager of a Cubs team that had responded badly to Rogers Hornsby's stern discipline. They captured pennants in 1932 and 1935. After stints as a broadcaster, coach and minor league manager, Grimm was back at the helm in Wrigley Field. In 1945 his Cubs won another pennant, the last one to date. After Grimm's death, his widow scattered his ashes over Wrigley Field.

Playing Career: *1916, 1918-1936; Phi A, StL N, Pit N, Chi N*
Managerial Career: *1932-1938, 1944-1949, 1952-1956, 1960; Chi N, Bos N, Mil N*

Ross Grimsley
Grimsley, Ross Albert II
B: Jan 7, 1950

Pos: P	ERA: 3.81
W-L: 124-99	SOs: 750
ShOs: 15	Saves: 3

Grimsley compiled a 2-1 record on only seven innings of work in the 1972 World Series. He was a starter for the powerful Big Red Machine from 1971 to 1973. Grimsley's refusal to conform to the Reds' short-hair policy got him traded to the Orioles. In 1978 Grimsley signed with the Expos as a free agent, played in the All-Star Game, and posted 20 victories.
Playing Career: *1971-1980, 1982; Cin N, Bal A, Mon N, Cle A*

Marv Grissom
Grissom, Marvin Edward
B: Mar 31, 1918

Pos: P	ERA: 3.41
W-L: 47-45	SOs: 459
ShOs: 3	Saves: 58

Grissom won Game One of the 1954 World Series, relieving Don Liddle, who faced only one batter. Grissom's best year was 1954 when he won 10, saved 19 and appeared in the All-Star Game. His brother Lee pitched for the Reds in the 1930s.
Playing Career: *1946, 1949, 1952-1959; NY N, Det A, Chi A, Bos A, SF N, StL N*

Dick Groat.

Dick Groat
Groat, Richard Morrow
B: Nov 4, 1930

Pos: SS	BA: .286
Hits: 2,138	HRs: 39
RBI: 707	BBs: 490

Groat never played minor league ball; he was one of the Baby Bucs of Branch Rickey's 1952 experiment with the Pirates. Groat stayed long enough to win the 1960 NL batting title and field shortstop while the Pirates trekked to a fantastic World Series triumph over the Yankees.

Groat was an All-American basketball player at Duke University. He played professional basketball with the Fort Wayne Pistons, 1952-1953. Bringing his basketball moves to the shortstop position, Groat combined with Bill Mazeroski to form the NL's best double play tandem. Groat was the complete ballplayer, batting over .300 four times, and always landing near the top in putouts, assists and double plays. With Groat at short, the Cardinals won the World Championship in 1964.
Playing Career: *1952, 1955-1967; Pit N, StL N, Phi N, SF N*

Heinie Groh
Groh, Henry Knight
B: Sep 18, 1889　D: Aug 22, 1968

Pos: 3B	BA: .292
Hits: 1,774	HRs: 26
RBI: 566	BBs: 696

Managerial Record
Won: 7　Lost: 3　Pct: .700

The unique "bottle bat," with a non-tapered barrel, became Groh's trademark. He used it while playing in five World Series for three different NL teams. Groh was the ultimate winning ballplayer. Known for his offense, he also led NL third basemen in fielding five times. He frequently drew walks, twice leading the NL in on-base percentage.

John McGraw always regretted giving up Groh to Cincinnati, where the third baseman starred. After a bitterly contested holdout in 1921, he finally renewed with the Reds in June on the stipulation that he would be traded. Groh was immediately swapped to New York but Commissioner Landis nixed the deal. In December 1921, the Giants reacquired him and the fiery Groh helped them win three straight pennants. His older brother Lew played two games with the A's in 1919 as a 36-year-old rookie.
Playing Career: *1912-1927; NY N, Cin N, Pit N*
Managerial Career: *1918; Cin N*

Heinie Groh.

Steve Gromek
Gromek, Stephen Joseph
B: Jan 15, 1920

Pos: P   ERA: 3.41
W-L: 123-108   SOs: 904
ShOs: 17   Saves: 23

Gromek started, finished and won Game Four of the 1948 World Series. The following day's newspaper photo of Gromek hugging black teammate Larry Doby – who had homered – was a poignant and effective statement on race relations in the second year of integrated baseball. Gromek launched his career as an infielder, but made the big leagues as a hurler. He made the AL All-Star team in 1945 when he went 19-9. He later won 18 games for his hometown Detroit Tigers.
Playing Career: *1941-1957; Cle A, Det A*

Bob Groom
Groom, Robert
B: Sep 12, 1884   D: Feb 19, 1948

Pos: P   ERA: 3.10
W-L: 119-150   SOs: 1,159
ShOs: 22   No-hitters: 1

Groom had the dubious distinction of a 19-game losing streak until members of the Society for American Baseball Research discovered a victory in the midst of the legendary streak. A good pitcher who had a tendency to be wild, Groom won 24 games with a 2.62 ERA in 1912. Jumping to the Federal League in 1914, he lost 20, but returned to the AL and no-hit the White Sox in the second game of a doubleheader.
Playing Career: *1909-1918; Was A, StL F, StL A, Cle A*

Greg Gross
Gross, Gregory Eugene
B: Aug 1, 1952

Pos: OF   BA: .287
Hits: 1,073   HRs: 7
RBI: 308   BBs: 523

Gross hit .314 for the Astros in 1974, winning NL Rookie of the Year honors. Amazingly, he never played full-time again. A contact hitter who struck out only 250 times in 3,745 at-bats, Gross was one of the best pinch hitters of his era.
Playing Career: *1973-1989; Hou N, Chi N, Phi N*

Kevin Gross
Gross, Kevin Frank
B: Jun 8, 1961

Pos: P   ERA: 3.92
W-L: 111-127   SOs: 1,399
ShOs: 14   No-hitters: 1

Plagued by back trouble most of his career, Gross was also suspended in 1987 when he was caught using sandpaper to scuff balls. Despite that, he made the All-Star team in 1988. Gross won only eight games in 1992, but one was a no-hitter and two others were shutouts.
Playing Career: *1983-; Phi N, Mon N, LA N*

Wayne Gross
Gross, Wayne Dale
B: Jan 14, 1952

Pos: 3B, 1B, DH, OF   BA: .233
Hits: 727   HRs: 121
RBI: 396   BBs: 482

A home run hitter in Oakland's gigantic ballpark, Gross twice bashed 22 homers, in 1977 and 1984. He represented the A's in the All-Star Game as a rookie in 1977. Practically unknown, Gross was a fine player who regularly held down first or third in Oakland.
Playing Career: *1976-1986; Oak A, Bal A*

Jerry Grote
Grote, Gerald Wayne
B: Oct 6, 1942

Pos: C   BA: .252
Hits: 1,092   HRs: 39
RBI: 404   BBs: 399

Lou Brock once said that Jerry Grote was the toughest catcher in the NL to steal against. Grote was behind the plate on his birthday when the Mets won their first pennant in 1969. He caught every inning of the 1969 and 1973 NLCS and World Series.
Playing Career: *1963-1964, 1966-1978, 1981; Hou N, NY N, LA N, KC A*

Johnny Groth
Groth, John Thomas
B: Jul 23, 1926

Pos: OF   BA: .279
Hits: 1,064   HRs: 60
RBI: 486   BBs: 419

Heralded as a rookie phenom in 1949 after a sensational minor league season, Groth had two solid years, but hit only 23 home runs for the Tigers. The sure-handed outfielder spent most of his career as a part-time player.
Playing Career: *1946-1960; Det A, StL A, Chi A, Was A, KC A*

Lefty Grove
Grove, Robert Moses
B: Mar 6, 1900   D: May 22, 1975
Hall of Fame 1947

Pos: P   ERA: 3.06
W-L: 300-141   SOs: 2,266
ShOs: 35   Saves: 55

Stalled with Baltimore in the International League, Grove posted more than 100 victories before he ever got to the majors. Connie Mack paid a record $106,000 for Grove, who left baseball revered as the greatest left-

Pitcher Kevin Gross is congratulated at the mound by Manager John Felske, 1986.

Robert Moses "Lefty" Grove.

hander ever to play the game. Grove led the AL in strikeouts seven consecutive years, and in wins four times, including 1931 when he posted 31. He was the undisputed ERA champ, leading nine times. Grove was an All-Star six times.

In 1931 Grove had tied the AL record with 16 consecutive wins and was going for the record-setting 17th against the last-place Browns. An A's outfielder substituting for Al Simmons – who was away with a sick relative – made an error that allowed the Browns to score a run. Incredibly, the A's failed to score and the lowly Browns shut them out. Grove went on a monumental rampage. He never forgave Simmons, whom he claimed would not have made the error, and would have knocked in at least one run! Grove tested the saintly patience of Connie Mack, but handed the placid patriarch three pennants.
Playing Career: *1925-1941; Phi A, Bos A*

Orval Grove
Grove, Orval Leroy
B: Aug 29, 1919   D: Apr 20, 1992

Pos: P	ERA: 3.78
W-L: 63-73	SOs: 374
ShOs: 11	Saves: 4

The White Sox invited Grove to camp in 1943 with a $1 contract because he missed most of the 1942 season after knee surgery. He won his first nine decisions, setting a Sox record. Grove was a top pitcher during the war, making the All-Star team in 1944.
Playing Career: *1940-1949; Chi A*

Johnny Grubb
Grubb, John Raymond
B: Aug 4, 1948

Pos: OF	BA: .278
Hits: 1,153	HRs: 99
RBI: 475	BBs: 566

A strong, but frequently injured hitter, Grubb was an early star for the expansion Padres, setting a club record with 36 doubles. He was an important bat in the Tigers' 1984 championship line-up, swatting an 11th-inning double in Game Two of the ALCS that year.
Playing Career: *1972-1987; SD N, Cle A, Tex A, Det A*

Kelly Gruber
Gruber, Kelly Wayne
B: Feb 26, 1962

Pos: 3B	BA: .259
Hits: 818	HRs: 117
RBI: 443	BBs: 197

A Texas All-American high school football player, Gruber was first drafted by the Indians, then acquired by Toronto when Cleveland failed to protect him. Gruber emerged in 1988 as a key player in the Blue Jays' infield, hitting .278 with 16 home runs and 81 RBI. In 1990 he had two homers in one game four times. He played in three ALCS, one World Series and two All-Star Games. Traded to the Angels, Gruber opened the 1993 season on the disabled list.
Playing Career: *1984-1993; Tor A, Cal A*

Cecilio Guante
Guante y Magallane, Cecilio
B: Feb 1, 1960

Pos: P	ERA: 3.48
W-L: 29-34	SOs: 503
ShOs: 0	Saves: 35

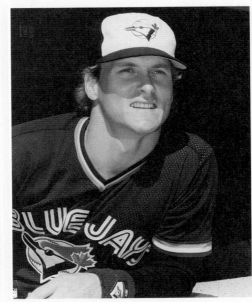

Kelly Gruber.

Guante was known as hard-throwing, but injury-prone. The Pirates wanted to groom him to replace Kent Tekulve as the stopper, but Guante's inconsistency prevented them. The Dominican started only one game, but made 363 relief appearances.
Playing Career: *1982-1990; Pit N, NY A, Tex A, Cle A*

Mark Gubicza
Gubicza, Mark Steven
B: Aug 14, 1962

Pos: P	ERA: 3.81
W-L: 109-100	SOs: 1,071
ShOs: 13	Saves: 2

Strong-armed Gubicza can fire 93-mph fastballs and 90-mph sliders. He won 20 games in 1988 and appeared in the All-Star Game. Gubicza suffered injuries three seasons in a row, then struggled in 1993 to make the staff where he was once ace.
Playing Career: *1984-; KC A*

Pedro Guerrero
Guerrero, Pedro
B: Jun 29, 1956

Pos: OF, 1B, 3B	BA: .300
Hits: 1,618	HRs: 215
RBI: 898	BBs: 609

Guerrero was a man on a mission to find a position. Luckily, his struggle did not affect his performance at the plate. Guerrero batted in five runs in the final game of the 1981 World Series, sharing MVP honors with two teammates. In 1982 and 1983 he drove in 100 and 103 runs and whacked 32 round-trippers both years. An All-Star pick five times, he led the NL in slugging in 1985, the year he blasted 15 home runs in June to tie a major league record. In 1989 Guerrero drove in 117 runs despite having only 17 homers.
Playing Career: *1978-1992; LA N, StL N*

Ron Guidry
Guidry, Ronald Ames
(Gator, Louisiana Lightning)
B: Aug 28, 1950

Pos: P	ERA: 3.29
W-L: 170-91	SOs: 1,778
ShOs: 26	Saves: 4

Guidry had a nearly perfect season in 1978. He was 25-3 with a 1.74 ERA and easily won the Cy Young Award. Finishing second to Jim Rice in AL MVP voting, Guidry set club records in strikeouts and consecutive wins at the start of a season. On June 17, he struck out 18 batters. He started the AL East playoff game against Boston on October 2, and won 5-4 in what he termed "the most tension-packed game I ever played in." Guidry was named Player of the Year, Man of the Year, and Associated Press Male Athlete of the Year. His nine shutouts tied Babe Ruth's AL record for left-handed shutouts.

A comparatively small fellow, Guidry was not given a shot as a regular starter until he

Ron Guidry.

was 26. He made up for lost time by being extra tough in big games. Guidry was 2-1 in three ALCS and 3-1 in three World Series. An outstanding all-around athlete, Guidry won five straight Gold Glove Awards, and was used briefly in the outfield twice.
Playing Career: *1975-1988; NY A*

Ozzie Guillen
Guillen y Barrios, Oswaldo Jose
B: Jan 20, 1964

Pos: SS	BA: .267
Hits: 1,149	HRs: 14
RBI: 388	BBs: 134

The White Sox drew criticism for trading LaMarr Hoyt to the Padres in 1984 to get Ozzie Guillen. It turned out to be one of the greatest swaps the Sox ever made. The Venezuelan is the best shortstop in the AL and easily won the 1985 Rookie of the Year Award. Guillen suffered a serious injury, two torn ligaments, in April 1992, but returned to his familiar starting shortstop role in 1993 as though he had never missed a season.
Playing Career: *1985-; Chi A*

Don Gullett
Gullett, Donald Edward
B: Jan 6, 1951

Pos: P	ERA: 3.11
W-L: 109-50	SOs: 921
ShOs: 14	Saves: 11

One of the earliest and costliest free agents, Gullett was hailed by Reds manager Sparky Anderson as a surefire Hall of Famer. The 19-year-old rookie flamethrower joined the Big Red Machine in 1970, and fanned six Mets in a row, tying a relief record. Hall of Famer Willie Stargell exclaimed, "Gullett throws nothing but wall-to-wall heat." Once he became a starter in 1971, Gullett posted very good won-lost percentages, going 16-6 in 1971, 18-8 in 1973, 15-4 in 1975, 11-3 in 1976, and 14-4 in 1977. The 1971 and 1975 marks were league highs.

Gullett won more than 68 percent of his de-cisions. He never made an appearance in the All-Star Game, though *The Sporting News* named him to their postseason all-star squad. When Gullett signed a lucrative free-agent contract with the Yankees, he went 14-4, then 0-2 in postseason play for the World Champions. The next season he had a rotator cuff problem that turned out to be a career-ending injury.
Playing Career: *1970-1978; Cin N, NY A*

Bill Gullickson
Gullickson, William Lee
B: Feb 20, 1959

Pos: P	ERA: 3.84
W-L: 158-131	SOs: 1,214
ShOs: 11	No-hitters: 0

Gullickson was named NL Rookie Pitcher of the Year in 1979, and finished second to hurler Steve Howe in NL Rookie of the Year voting. After pitching in Japan for two years, Gullickson came home to Sparky Anderson and the Tigers. He led the AL in wins with 20 in 1991, and is a 20-win candidate every year with the Bengals behind him. Consistency is Gullickson's hallmark; he won at least 10 games in 11 of his last 12 seasons.
Playing Career: *1979-1987, 1990-; Mon N, Cin N, NY A, Hou N, Det A*

Ad Gumbert
Gumbert, Addison Courtney
B: Oct 10, 1868   D: Apr 23, 1925

Pos: P	ERA: 4.27
W-L: 123-102	SOs: 546
ShOs: 7	Saves: 1

Gumbert pitched for pennant-contending teams every season of his career. He was usually the number two or three hurler in the rotation, but he was a welcome addition. Gumbert's 1890 Boston club won the flag in the one-season Players' League.
Playing Career: *1888-1896; Chi N, Bos P, Pit N, Brk N, Phi N*

Ace starter Don Gullett winds up for the Big Red Machine in 1976.

Harry Gumbert (above) horses around with Paul Dean at the Giants' training camp, 1941.

Harry Gumbert
Gumbert, Harry Edward
B: Nov 5, 1909

Pos: P	ERA: 3.68
W-L: 143-113	SOs: 709
ShOs: 13	Saves: 48

Gumbert was a solid starter with the best pitching staff in the NL during the 1930s. Backing up Carl Hubbell and Hal Schumaker, Gumbert hurled 200 or more innings for the Giants from 1937 to 1940. He appeared in three World Series, pitching in a total of six games, allowing 12 hits and five walks for an astronomical ERA of 27.00. After serving in the military in 1945, Gumbert returned as a reliever. He led the NL in games and saves in 1948.
Playing Career: *1935-1944, 1946-1950; NY N, StL N, Cin N, Pit N*

Randy Gumpert
Gumpert, Randall Pennington
B: Jan 23, 1918

Pos: P	ERA: 4.17
W-L: 51-59	SOs: 352
ShOs: 6	Saves: 7

As a teenager, Gumpert threw batting practice for the A's at Shibe Park two years before signing with them in 1936 for $300 a month. He lasted only three years before retooling in the minors as a good spot starter. He was 11-3 with a 2.31 ERA in 1946 for the Yankees.
Playing Career: *1936-1938, 1946-1952; Phi A, NY A, Chi A, Bos A, Was A*

Larry Gura
Gura, Lawrence Cyril
B: Nov 26, 1947

Pos: P	ERA: 3.76
W-L: 126-97	SOs: 801
ShOs: 14	Saves: 14

The Royals' Pitcher of the Year in 1978 with a 16-4 record and a 2.72 ERA, Gura was the bulwark of four Royals division-winning teams. He won 18 twice and was 2-2 in postseason play. An All-American at Arizona State, Gura pitched the club to the National Championship by beating the University of Tulsa twice in the College World Series. Gura saw limited action with both the Cubs and Yankees before flourishing with the Royals.
Playing Career: *1970-1985; Chi N, NY A, KC A*

Frankie Gustine
Gustine, Frank William
B: Feb 20, 1920   D: Apr 1, 1991

Pos: 2B, 3B, SS	BA: .265
Hits: 1,214	HRs: 38
RBI: 480	BBs: 369

Personally scouted and signed by Pirates manager Pie Traynor as a 16-year-old prospect, Gustine was 19 when he entered the big leagues. Shifted between three infield positions, Gustine was an All-Star at second base in 1946 and at third base in 1947-1948.
Playing Career: *1939-1950; Pit N, Chi N, StL A*

Don Gutteridge
Gutteridge, Donald Joseph
B: Jun 19, 1912

Pos: 3B, 2B, SS	BA: .256
Hits: 1,075	HRs: 39
RBI: 391	BBs: 309
Managerial Record	
Won: 109 Lost: 172 Pct: .388	

It was the second day of Gutteridge's major league career, not the first, that was memorable. The rookie got six hits, including an inside-the-park homer, and stole home twice in a doubleheader at Ebbets Field. He played for both the Cardinals and Browns, and was the second sacker on the pennant-winning 1944 Browns. On June 30 that year, he took part in five double plays in one game, setting a record for AL second basemen.
Playing Career: *1936-1940, 1942-1948; StL N, StL A, Bos A, Pit N*
Managerial Career: *1969-1970; Chi A*

Tony Gwynn
Gwynn, Anthony Keith
B: May 9, 1960

Pos: OF	BA: .329
Hits: 2,039	HRs: 66
RBI: 650	BBs: 542

Gwynn is a four-time NL batting champ, leading the league in hits four times. He swatted 213 for a .351 average in 1984, 211 for .329 in 1986, 218 for .370 in 1987, and 203 for .336 in 1989. Gwynn is also good at scoring runs and stealing bases; he has accumulated 912 tallies and 263 steals in 12 years. A nine-time All-Star and winner of the outfielders' Gold Glove five times, Gwynn is probably the finest pure hitter in the NL today.

A multi-sport athlete at San Diego State University, Gwynn was named All-Conference in two sports. He still holds the SDSU all-time assists record, and was drafted by the San Diego Clippers of the NBA. Gwynn's .370 batting average in 1987 was the highest in the NL since Stan Musial hit .376 in 1948. Gwynn set numerous Padres records that season. His ringing two-run double in the seventh inning of Game Five of the 1984 NLCS gave the Padres their first NL pennant. Gwynn's brother Chris plays for the Royals.
Playing Career: *1982-; SD N*

Outfielder George William "Mule" Haas.

Bert Haas
Haas, Berthold John
B: Feb 8, 1914

Pos: 1B, 3B, OF	BA: .264
Hits: 644	HRs: 22
RBI: 263	BBs: 204

An All-Star at age 33 in 1947 when he hit .286 for the Reds, Haas once pinch-hit four days in a row, collecting a single and three doubles. One of the gaps in his major league career was the result of military service in Italy during World War II.
Playing Career: *1937-1938, 1942-1943, 1946-1949, 1951; Brk N, Cin N, Phi N, NY N, Chi A*

Moose Haas
Haas, Bryan Edmund
B: Apr 22, 1956

Pos: P	ERA: 4.01
W-L: 100-83	SOs: 853
ShOs: 8	Saves: 2

Depending on control rather than heat, Haas won 54 percent of his games. He had records of 13-3 in 1983, and 7-2 in 1986, when arm trouble ended his season early. With the Brewers in 1978, Haas set a club record, since broken, by striking out 14 in an April 12 game.
Playing Career: *1976-1987; Mil A, Oak A*

Mule Haas
Haas, George William
B: Oct 15, 1903   D: Jun 30, 1974

Pos: OF	BA: .292
Hits: 1,257	HRs: 43
RBI: 496	BBs: 433

Haas hit the fly ball that Hack Wilson lost in the sun, leading to the famous 10-run inning in Game Three of the 1929 World Series. While Wilson searched for the ball, Haas circled the bases with an inside-the-park home run. Imitating Tris Speaker, Haas played center field in close to second base and ran back for long fly balls. Early in his career, he batted second in the lineup, scoring 115 runs in 1929.
Playing Career: *1925, 1928-1938; Pit N, Phi A, Chi A*

Stan Hack.

Stan Hack
Hack, Stanley Camfield
B: Dec 6, 1909   D: Dec 15, 1979

Pos: 3B   BA: .301
Hits: 2,193   HRs: 57
RBI: 642   BBs: 1,092
Managerial Record
Won: 199   Lost: 272   Pct: .423

In his 16 seasons with the Cubs, Hack helped the team win four pennants, and he batted .348 in World Series play. A good all-around player, Hack was chosen for the All-Star team four times. He led the NL in hits twice, 1940-1941, stolen bases twice, 1938-1939, and in fielding percentage twice, 1942 and 1945. He scored 1,239 runs in his 16-year-career.

Hack's most famous hit came in the sixth game of the 1935 World Series against the Tigers. The Cubs were down three games to two, and the score was tied 3-3 in Game Six. Hack led off the ninth inning by smacking a Tommy Bridges curveball over the center fielder's head for a triple. All the Cubs needed was a sacrifice fly to gain the lead. But Billy Jurges struck out, Larry French bounced out, and when Augie Galan finally hit the fly, it was too late. A half inning later the Tigers won the game and the Series.
Playing Career: *1932-1947; Chi N*
Managerial Career: *1954-1956, 1958; Chi N, StL N*

Warren Hacker
Hacker, Warren Louis
B: Nov 21, 1924

Pos: P   ERA: 4.21
W-L: 62-89   SOs: 557
ShOs: 6   Saves: 17

The right-handed knuckleball and sinkerball hurler came within two outs of a no-hitter on May 21, 1955. Hacker was pushed into baseball by his father who did not want the boy to follow him into the coal mines. His best year was 1952, with a 15-9 record and a 2.58 ERA.
Playing Career: *1948-1958, 1961; Chi N, Cin N, Phi N, Chi A*

Harvey Haddix
Haddix, Harvey (The Kitten)
B: Sep 18, 1925

Pos: P   ERA: 3.63
W-L: 136-113   SOs: 1,575
ShOs: 20   No-hitters: 1

Haddix retired 36 consecutive Braves batters on May 6, 1959, pitching 12 perfect innings, but the Pirates could not score. In the 13th, Milwaukee's leadoff hitter reached first on an error, then was sacrificed to second. Haddix intentionally walked Hank Aaron to get to Joe Adcock, who blasted a home run. Adcock passed Aaron on the basepaths, making the final score 1-0, but both the no-hitter and the game were lost. Lew Burdette pitched the 13-inning shutout for the Braves.

Haddix had a brilliant 20-9 rookie season with the Cardinals, leading the NL with six shutouts. There he was nicknamed "The Kitten" for his resemblance to Harry "The Cat" Brecheen. Like his namesake Haddix was a top fielder, winning three Gold Gloves. He appeared in three All-Star Games, and starred in the 1960 World Series for the Pirates. Haddix finished as an effective reliever for the Orioles, saving 21 games. He also served as pitching coach for the Mets, Reds, Red Sox, Indians and Pirates.
Playing Career: *1952-1965; StL N, Phi N, Cin N, Pit N, Bal A*

Bump Hadley
Hadley, Irving Darius
B: Jul 5, 1904   D: Feb 15, 1963

Pos: P   ERA: 4.25
W-L: 161-165   SOs: 1,318
ShOs: 14   Saves: 25

A hard-working and durable pitcher, Hadley simply had bad luck. He lost 20 games with the Browns twice, 1932-1933. The previous year he led the AL in appearances with 55 and opponents' batting average with .218, but finished only 11-10 with eight saves. When Hadley retired he was third on the all-time walks list with 1,442. Turning his career around with the Yankees, Hadley was 46-26 from 1936 to 1939, but fractured Mickey Cochrane's skull with a pitch in 1937, ending the catcher's career.
Playing Career: *1926-1941; Was A, Chi A, StL A, NY A, NY N, Phi A*

Mickey Haefner
Haefner, Milton Arnold
B: Oct 9, 1912

Pos: P   ERA: 3.50
W-L: 78-91   SOs: 508
ShOs: 13   Saves: 13

Haefner was one of the Senators' four 1940s knuckleball pitchers who made receiver Rick

Harvey Haddix pitched for the Pirates for five seasons, from 1959 to 1963.

Ferrell famous – and exhausted. Coming to the major leagues at age 30 as a wartime replacement, Haefner pitched an average of 200 innings or more from 1943 to 1947.
Playing Career: *1943-1950; Was A, Chi A, Bos N*

Chick Hafey
Hafey, Charles James
B: Feb 12, 1903   D: Jul 2, 1973
Hall of Fame 1971

Pos: OF	BA: .317
Hits: 1,466	HRs: 164
RBI: 833	BBs: 372

Complaining about his Cardinals contract got Hafey deported to the Siberia of the 1930s' NL – Cincinnati. Hafey hit for a good average with fair power; he was fast; he could field; and he had the best throwing arm of any NL outfielder of his era. A regular with the Cardinals by 1926, Hafey was beaned several times that season, affecting his eyesight. He was advised to wear glasses, a rarity among players of his day. He actually used three different pairs, depending on the state of his fluctuating vision and his sinusitis.

In 1932 Hafey won the closest batting race in NL history, beating Bill Terry by an eyelash, .0003. When he asked for a raise to $17,000 after winning the batting title, St. Louis traded him to Cincinnati. Hafey had several good seasons with the Reds before retiring. He played in the 1933 All-Star Game.
Playing Career: *1924-1935, 1937; StL N, Cin N*

Charles James "Chick" Hafey.

Cardinals hurler Jesse Haines, 1930.

Jesse Haines
Haines, Jesse Joseph (Pop)
B: Jul 22, 1893   D: Aug 5, 1978
Hall of Fame 1970

Pos: P	ERA: 3.64
W-L: 210-158	SOs: 981
ShOs: 24	No-hitters: 1

Until Bob Gibson came along, Jesse Haines had won more games than any Cardinals pitcher, 210. Haines did not join the team until he was 26 years old but he stayed until he was 45, earning the nickname "Pop." He posted 20 or more victories three times, and pitched a no-hitter in 1924. During his career with the Redbirds they won five pennants and three World Championships. Haines also had 10 saves, and was 3-1, with a 1.67 ERA in four World Series.

In 1926 he compiled a record of 13-4, the Cardinals won the pennant, and Haines shut out the Yankees in the World Series. It was the last time the Yankees were blanked in the Fall Classic for 16 years. In Game Seven of the 1926 World Series Haines was leading 3-2 but developed a blister from throwing a knuckler. Grover Cleveland Alexander came in from the bullpen and fanned Tony Lazzeri with the bases loaded. The Cardinals retained their lead and won the championship.
Playing Career: *1918, 1920-1937; Cin N, StL N*

Odell Hale
Hale, Arvel Odell (Bad News)
B: Aug 10, 1908   D: Jun 9, 1980

Pos: 2B, 3B	BA: .289
Hits: 1,071	HRs: 73
RBI: 573	BBs: 353

Hale was named "Bad News" by Cotton States League players when he wore out that league's pitchers. Always a good RBI man, twice he drove in 101 runs while hitting more than .300. Hale started a triple play in 1935, when he deflected a line drive off his head.
Playing Career: *1931, 1933-1941; Cle A, Bos A, NY N*

Sammy Hale
Hale, Samuel Douglas
B: Sep 10, 1896   D: Sep 6, 1974

Pos: 3B	BA: .302
Hits: 880	HRs: 30
RBI: 392	BBs: 130

The A's bought Hale from Portland for $75,000, a colossal sum in 1923. He played for the powerhouse Athletics throughout the 1929 pennant-winning season, but did not appear in the World Series. As a rookie in 1920, Hale led the AL with 17 pinch hits in 52 at-bats.
Playing Career: *1920-1921, 1923-1930; Det A, Phi A, StL A*

Dick Hall
Hall, Richard Wallace
B: Sep 27, 1930

Pos: P	ERA: 3.32
W-L: 93-75	SOs: 741
ShOs: 3	Saves: 68

The 6'6" Hall, an All-American collegiate athlete, played outfield for the Pirates after signing as a bonus baby. Failing to hit, he switched to pitching, where he struggled as a starter, but flourished as a reliever. He pitched in two postseason series.
Playing Career: *1955-1957, 1959-1971; Pit N, KC A, Bal A, Phi N*

Jimmie Hall scores for the Twins, 1965.

Jimmie Hall
Hall, Jimmie Randolph
B: Mar 7, 1938

Pos: OF	BA: .254
Hits: 724	HRs: 121
RBI: 391	BBs: 287

Hall swatted 33 homers in his rookie season. He was the center fielder for the powerful Twins, whose outfield boasted Bob Allison, Harmon Killebrew and Tony Oliva. Hall averaged 25 homers per year, 1963-1966, and made the All-Star squad twice.
Playing Career: *1963-1970; Min A, Cal A, Cle A, NY A, Chi N, Atl N*

Mel Hall
Hall, Melvin, Jr.
B: Sep 16, 1960

Pos: OF	BA: .277
Hits: 1,168	HRs: 134
RBI: 615	BBs: 266

Playing in the big leagues at age 21, Hall was forecast as a big star. He struggled at the plate, but regained his home run stroke when he went to the Yankees. Hall's best seasons were 1991-1992, when he totaled 34 homers, 58 doubles, 161 RBI, and had a .282 batting average.
Playing Career: *1981-1992; Chi N, Cle A, NY A*

Sea Lion Hall
Hall, Charles Louis
B: Jul 27, 1885   D: Dec 6, 1943

Pos: P	ERA: 3.09
W-L: 54-47	SOs: 427
ShOs: 3	Saves: 12

A minor league legend who became a major league starter and reliever, Hall won 54 percent of his minor league contests, capturing 284 victories, then won 53 percent of his big league games. He led the AL with six relief wins for Boston in both 1910 and 1911.
Playing Career: *1906-1907, 1909-1913, 1916, 1918; Cin N, Bos A, StL N, Det A*

Tom Hall
Hall, Tom Edward
B: Nov 23, 1947

Pos: P	ERA: 3.27
W-L: 52-33	SOs: 797
ShOs: 3	Saves: 32

Little known outside Cincinnati, Hall was 10-1 with 8 saves for the 1972 NL pennant-winning Reds. He always played for winners, hurling in five LCS for three different teams in two leagues. Hall also went 1-1 with a 0.00 ERA in the 1972 World Series.
Playing Career: *1968-1977; Min A, Cin N, NY N, KC A*

Wild Bill Hallahan
Hallahan, William Anthony
B: Aug 4, 1902   D: Jul 8, 1981

Pos: P	ERA: 4.03
W-L: 102-94	SOs: 856
ShOs: 14	Saves: 8

Hallahan was not called Wild Bill because of his temperament. His tremendous fastball had trouble finding the plate. He led the NL in walks in 1930, 1931 and 1933. The ace of the Cardinals' staff in the early 1930s, Hallahan also led the NL in strikeouts, 1930-1931. The NL starting pitcher in the premier All-Star Game in 1933, Hallahan also pitched in four World Series for the Red Birds, compiling a record of 3-1 with two shutouts and a 1.36 ERA.
Playing Career: *1925-1926, 1929-1938; StL N, Cin N, Phi N*

Tom Haller
Haller, Thomas Frank
B: Jun 23, 1937

Pos: C	BA: .257
Hits: 1,011	HRs: 134
RBI: 504	BBs: 477

On July 14, 1972, Tom Haller was the Tigers' catcher while his brother Bill umpired behind the plate. Tom Haller caught 98 or more games for nine straight years, and once caught all 23 innings of a Mets-Giants marathon. In the Giants' pennant-winning 1962 season, Haller slugged 18 homers as a platoon catcher. He hit 27 home runs in 1966. After serving the Giants as a coach, Haller was vice president of baseball operations through the 1986 season.
Playing Career: *1961-1972; SF N, LA N, Det A*

Bill Hallman
Hallman, William Wilson
B: Mar 31, 1867   D: Sep 11, 1920

Pos: 2B	BA: .272
Hits: 1,634	HRs: 20
RBI: 769	BBs: 425
Managerial Record	
Won: 13 Lost: 36 Pct: .265	

Hallman played for three Philadelphia teams, but none of them was the AL Athletics. Playing every position, he was primarily a second baseman. A surprisingly good hitter, Hallman also batted .300 or higher for four straight seasons in the mid-1890s.
Playing Career: *1888-1898, 1901-1903; Phi N, Phi P, Phi AA, StL N, Brk N, Cle A*
Managerial Career: *1897; StL N*

Billy Hamilton
Hamilton, William Robert
B: Feb 16, 1866   D: Dec 16, 1940
Hall of Fame 1961

Pos: OF	BA: .344
Hits: 2,158	HRs: 40
RBI: 736	BBs: 1,187

The greatest leadoff man ever, Hamilton scored more runs (1,690) than games played (1,591) and stole 912 bases with his patented head-first slides. Hamilton also holds the all-time record for runs scored in a single season, with 196 in 1894; he led the league in that category four times. Undeniably speedy, Hamilton had several other factors in his favor. He was an exceptional hitter, leading the NL twice, with a .340 mark in 1891 and .380 in 1893. His career average ranks eighth best of all time. Hamilton walked frequently, topping the NL in bases on balls five times. Additionally, throughout most of his career Hamilton was followed in the batting order by other

The Cardinals' erratic but powerful pitcher Wild Bill Hallahan, 1935.

Billy Hamilton.

outstanding hitters. In 1894 he played center field for the Phillies and hit .404, while left fielder Ed Delahanty hit .400 and right fielder Sam Thompson hit .404. Substitute outfielder Tuck Turner hit .416 in 80 games.
Playing Career: *1888-1901; KC AA, Phi N, Bos N*

Dave Hamilton
Hamilton, David Edward
B: Dec 13, 1947

Pos: P   ERA: 3.85
W-L: 39-41   SOs: 434
ShOs: 1   Saves: 31

Hamilton was the fifth starter on the A's teams that won three consecutive World Series, 1972-1974, the last club to do so. He went 19-14 over those years. Becoming a relief pitcher when he left the A's, Hamilton saved 10 games for the White Sox in 1976.
Playing Career: *1972-1980; Oak A, Chi A, StL N, Pit N*

Earl Hamilton
Hamilton, Earl Andrew
B: Jul 19, 1891   D: Nov 17, 1968

Pos: P   ERA: 3.16
W-L: 116-147   SOs: 790
ShOs: 16   No-hitters: 1

In 1920 Hamilton of the Pirates and Rube Benton of the Giants tossed 16 shutout innings before the New Yorkers won in the 17th. The Browns' leading winner, 1912-1914, Hamilton was sold to the Tigers in 1916, who released him 22 days later, when he was reclaimed by the Browns.
Playing Career: *1911-1924; StL A, Det A, Pit N, Phi N*

Steve Hamilton
Hamilton, Steve Absher
B: Nov 30, 1935

Pos: P   ERA: 3.05
W-L: 40-31   SOs: 531
ShOs: 1   Saves: 42

Late in his career Hamilton developed an arc pitch. Similar to Rip Sewell's "eephus ball," it was dubbed the "Folly Floater" by Hamilton. The hero of the sixth game of the 1964 World Series, the 6'7" hurler played professional basketball with the Lakers.
Playing Career: *1961-1972; Cle A, Was A, NY A, Chi A, SF N, Chi N*

Luke Hamlin
Hamlin, Luke Daniel (Hot Potato)
B: Jul 3, 1904   D: Feb 18, 1978

Pos: P   ERA: 3.77
W-L: 73-76   SOs: 563
ShOs: 12   Saves: 9

Hamlin got his nickname because he juggled the ball while getting ready to pitch. Many Dodger fans thought the name was given to him by manager Leo Durocher, who grew increasingly frustrated with his inability to hold leads. Hamlin won 20 for the Dodgers in 1939.
Playing Career: *1933-1934, 1937-1942, 1944; Det A, Brk N, Pit N, Phi A*

Atlee Hammaker
Hammaker, Charlton Atlee
B: Jan 24, 1958

Pos: P   ERA: 3.61
W-L: 59-67   SOs: 611
ShOs: 6   Saves: 5

Hammaker was headed for stardom in 1983 when he made the NL All-Star team. He fanned 14 Astros in September of that year, and ended the season leading the NL with a 2.25 ERA. Shoulder and elbow problems required surgery and hampered his career.
Playing Career: *1981-1985, 1987-1991; KC A, SF N, SD N*

Granny Hamner
Hamner, Granville Wilbur
B: Apr 26, 1927   D: Sep 12, 1993

Pos: SS   BA: .262
Hits: 1,529   HRs: 104
RBI: 708   BBs: 351

Hamner was one of the "Whiz Kids" who delivered a pennant to Phillies fans in 1950, their first since 1915. Hamner hit .429 in the four-game World Series loss to the Yankees. He was selected for the All-Star Game three times, once as a shortstop, once as a utility man, and once as the second baseman. When his career as an infielder ended he stayed in the game by learning to throw the knuckle-

Seventeen-year-old Granny Hamner signs with Herb Pennock's Phillies in 1944.

ball, pitching relief for the Phillies and Athletics.
Playing Career: *1944-1959, 1962; Phi N, Cle A, KC A*

Lee Handley
Handley, Lee Elmer
B: Jul 13, 1913   D: Apr 8, 1970

Pos: 3B, 2B	BA: .269
Hits: 902	HRs: 15
RBI: 297	BBs: 267

Handley broke in at second base for the Pirates in 1937, hitting .250. He got his batting average up and led the NL in steals, with 17 in 1939. After World War II, Handley moved to third base for the Pirates.
Playing Career: *1936-1941, 1944-1947; Cin N, Pit N, Phi N*

Bill Hands
Hands, William Alfred
B: May 6, 1940

Pos: P	ERA: 3.35
W-L: 111-110	SOs: 1,128
ShOs: 17	Saves: 14

When the Cubs made a dramatic run for the 1969 NL flag, Hands was the ace of their staff, not to mention the undisputed chess champion in the locker room. He won 20 games with a 2.49 ERA that year. Back ailments and muscle spasms in his pitching arm hurt his career after he left the Cubs in 1973. Switched to middle relief, Hands had his finest performance with a one-hit outing versus the Expos on August 3, 1972.
Playing Career: *1965-1975; SF N, Chi N, Min A, Tex A*

Ned Hanlon.

Fred Haney
Haney, Fred Girard
B: Apr 25, 1898   D: Nov 9, 1977

Pos: 3B	BA: .275
Hits: 544	HRs: 8
RBI: 228	BBs: 282
Managerial Record	
Won: 629 Lost: 757 Pct: .454	

A lifetime baseball man, Haney was a player, coach, manager, broadcaster and general manager during his career. Haney's Pirates finished in last place three times, but he won two straight pennants in Milwaukee and was fired after finishing in second place in 1959. He later broadcast NBC-TV's "Game of the Week," and served as general manager for the Los Angeles Angels.
Playing Career: *1922-1927, 1929; Det A, Bos A, Chi N, StL N*
Managerial Career: *1939-1941, 1953-1959; StL A, Pit N, Mil N*

Ned Hanlon
Hanlon, Edward Hugh
B: Aug 22, 1857   D: Apr 14, 1937

Pos: OF	BA: .260
Hits: 1,317	HRs: 30
RBI: 438	BBs: 471
Managerial Record	
Won: 1,315 Lost: 1,164 Pct: .530	

During the last few years of his major league career, Hanlon was a playing manager. The outfielder stole 279 bases during his career and was the center fielder for the celebrated 1887 championship Detroit Wolverines. As a skipper, Hanlon won five pennants in seven years with the Baltimore and Brooklyn clubs. The team he took over in Baltimore was mired in the cellar, and became reputedly the nastiest, most ornery bunch that ever stepped onto the playing field.

The Orioles reportedly banked foul lines so bunts would stay fair, grabbed runners' belts as they rounded third base, hid extra balls in the outfield grass, flashed mirrors in opponents' faces, faked being hit by pitches, and used the Baltimore Chop – buried cement in front of home plate, then batted balls sharply downward to get a bounce high enough to beat out. The notorious Orioles won three pennants in a row, then most of the team followed Hanlon to Brooklyn, where they won two more.
Playing Career: *1880-1892; Cle N, Det N, Pit N, Pit P, Bal N*
Managerial Career: *1889-1907; Pit N, Pit P, Bal N, Brk N, Cin N*

Ron Hansen
Hansen, Ronald Lavern
B: Apr 5, 1938

Pos: SS	BA: .234
Hits: 1,007	HRs: 106
RBI: 501	BBs: 551

An All-Star and Rookie of the Year in 1960, Hansen was uncommonly tall for a short-

stop, but was a top fielder. He led AL shortstops in double plays in 1961. On August 29, 1965, he tied an AL record with 18 chances in a single game. Then came the play. Hansen turned an unassisted triple play on July 30, 1968 – the first in the major leagues in 41 years. Hansen's 1962 season was disrupted when he spent six months in the Marines during the Cuban Missile Crisis.
Playing Career: *1958-1972; Bal A, Chi A, Was A, NY A, KC A*

Mel Harder.

Mel Harder
Harder, Melvin Leroy
B: Oct 15, 1909

Pos: P	ERA: 3.80
W-L: 223-186	SOs: 1,160
ShOs: 25	Saves: 23
Managerial Record	
Won: 3 Lost: 3 Pct: .500	

Only Bob Feller won more games for the Indians than Harder, who posted more than 20 victories in 1934 and 1935. He pitched the opening game in Cleveland's Municipal Park before 82,000 fans. Harder was at his best in the annual All-Star Game. He pitched in four contests, and was the only pitcher to work 10 or more innings without allowing an earned run. Though overshadowed by Carl Hubbell, Harder won the 1934 All-Star Game, finishing with five shutout innings. He had saves in the 1935 and 1937 contests.

After retiring from the mound, Harder coached the Indians' hurlers from 1949 through 1963, the glory years of their magnificent pitching staffs. He was credited with helping Feller, Early Wynn, Mike Garcia, Herb Score and Bob Lemon, whom he developed from a poor-hitting infielder to a Hall of Fame pitcher. Disciples said "he had a camera in his head" because of his uncanny ability to spot pitching flaws.
Playing Career: *1928-1947; Cle A*
Managerial Career: *1961-1962; Cle A*

Carroll Hardy
Hardy, Carroll William
B: May 18, 1933

Pos: OF	BA: .225
Hits: 251	HRs: 17
RBI: 113	BBs: 120

Hardy was the only player to ever pinch-hit for Ted Williams. The Splinter had fouled a pitch off his foot in 1960, and Hardy finished the at-bat. Hitting was not his strong suit, but Hardy was a good athlete; he had been a defensive back with the San Francisco 49ers in 1955.
Playing Career: *1958-1964, 1967; Cle A, Bos A, Hou N, Min A*

Steve Hargan
Hargan, Steven Lowell
B: Sep 8, 1942

Pos: P	ERA: 3.92
W-L: 87-107	SOs: 891
ShOs: 17	Saves: 4

There are mountain ranges that have fewer peaks and valleys than Hargan's career. An All-Star who led the AL with six shutouts, Hargan struggled after elbow surgery, bounced back with a record of 11-3 and a 2.90 ERA, had three bad seasons, spent a year in the minors, then returned to the majors and posted a 12-9 record.
Playing Career: *1965-1972, 1974-1977; Cle A, Tex A, Tor A, Atl N*

Bubbles Hargrave
Hargrave, Eugene Franklin
B: Jul 15, 1892   D: Feb 23, 1969

Pos: C	BA: .310
Hits: 786	HRs: 29
RBI: 376	BBs: 217

Being a catcher, Hargrave seldom played in more than 100 games, a fact that figured in the 1926 NL batting race. He hit a league-high .353 while batting only 326 times, but exceeded the minimum number of games required to win. His brother Pinky also played major league ball.
Playing Career: *1913-1915, 1921-1928, 1930; Chi N, Cin N, NY A*

Mike Hargrove
Hargrove, Dudley Michael
B: Oct 26, 1949

Pos: 1B	BA: .290
Hits: 1,614	HRs: 80
RBI: 686	BBs: 965
Managerial Record	
Won: 184 Lost: 225 Pct: .450	

Called "The Human Rain Delay" because of his batting ritual, Hargrove would take exactly three deliberate practice swings, step into the box, meticulously dig in his left foot, adjust his helmet, arrange his uniform, tug his belt, look toward the mound. Much to the consternation of pitchers, he followed this ritual before each pitch! Hargrove was the AL

Rookie of the Year in 1974. He hit over .300 in six of 12 seasons before turning to managing.
Playing Career: *1974-1985; Tex A, SD N, Cle A*
Managerial Career: *1991-; Cle A*

Dick Harley
Harley, Richard Joseph
B: Sep 25, 1872   D: Apr 3, 1952

Pos: OF	BA: .262
Hits: 755	HRs: 10
RBI: 236	BBs: 223

The 1899 Cleveland Spiders were the worst team in baseball history, and Harley was in their outfield. He led NL outfielders in errors that year. Harley was later a respected baseball coach at the University of Pittsburgh, Pennsylvania State, and Villanova.
Playing Career: *1897-1903; StL N, Cle N, Cin N, Det A, Chi N*

Bob Harmon
Harmon, Robert Green
B: Oct 15, 1887   D: Nov 27, 1961

Pos: P	ERA: 3.33
W-L: 107-133	SOs: 634
ShOs: 15	Saves: 11

The Cardinals purchased Harmon after he pitched a no-hitter in the Texas League early in 1909. He hurled a 16-inning victory over the Phillies that year. Two years later, Harmon won 23 games.
Playing Career: *1909-1916, 1918; StL N, Pit N*

Brian Harper
Harper, Brian David
B: Oct 16, 1959

Pos: C, OF, DH, 1B, 3B	BA: .297
Hits: 858	HRs: 59
RBI: 396	BBs: 124

Extremely difficult to strike out, Harper fanned only 269 times in 2,893 at-bats. Lacking a position, he was 7 for 26 as a pinch hitter for the 1985 Cardinals. Harper finally found a home behind the plate for the Twins, and has hit around .300 since joining the club.
Playing Career: *1979, 1981-; Cal A, Pit N, StL N, Det A, Oak A, Min A*

George Harper
Harper, George Washington
B: Jun 24, 1892   D: Aug 18, 1978

Pos: OF	BA: .303
Hits: 1,030	HRs: 91
RBI: 528	BBs: 389

Harper hit three home runs in the first game of a 1928 doubleheader. He hit over .340 twice and batted .331 in 1927. Harper appeared in the 1928 World Series for the Cardinals, and was still a playing manager in the minors at the age of 44.
Playing Career: *1916-1918, 1922-1929; Det A, Cin N, Phi N, NY N, StL N, Bos N*

Mike Hargrove comes in with a homer while the Indians' mascot celebrates.

Harry Harper
Harper, Harry Clayton
B: Apr 24, 1895   D: Apr 23, 1963

Pos: P	ERA: 2.87
W-L: 57-76	SOs: 623
ShOs: 12	Saves: 5

A spot starter for the up-and-down Senators early in the 20th century, Harper's best record was 14-10 with a 2.45 ERA in 1916. His worst was 6-21 in 1919. Harper left the majors in 1923, and later made a fortune as a New Jersey industrialist.
Playing Career: *1913-1921, 1923; Was A, Bos A, NY A, Brk N*

Jack Harper
Harper, Charles William
B: Apr 2, 1878   D: Sep 30, 1950

Pos: P	ERA: 3.55
W-L: 80-64	SOs: 466
ShOs: 10	Saves: 1

The hope of the hapless Cleveland Spiders of 1899, Harper ended the team's 24-game losing streak in his major league debut. He won 23 games twice, in 1901 and 1903. His career ended in controversy late in 1906, after he struck his manager with a pitch during practice.
Playing Career: *1899-1906; Cle N, StL N, StL A, Cin N, Chi N*

Tommy Harper
Harper, Tommy
B: Oct 14, 1940

Pos: OF, 3B, DH	BA: .257
Hits: 1,609	HRs: 146
RBI: 567	BBs: 753

Harper was the essence of speed combined with power before Bobby Bonds and Jose Canseco redefined the concept. A highly touted outfielder in 1965, he hit 18 home runs and led the NL with 126 runs scored. Harper pilfered 73 bases in 1969, the highest AL total since Ty Cobb's 96 in 1915. In 1970 – the year Harper was elected to the All-Star team – he hit 31 home runs and stole 38 bases, adding to his career totals of 972 runs scored and 408 stolen bases.
Playing Career: *1962-1976; Cin N, Cle A, Sea A, Mil A, Bos A, Cal A, Oak A, Bal A*

Toby Harrah
Harrah, Colbert Dale
B: Oct 26, 1948

Pos: SS, 3B, 2B	BA: .264
Hits: 1,954	HRs: 195
RBI: 919	BBs: 1,153
Managerial Record	
Won: 32 Lost: 44 Pct: .421	

Most managers can only dream of having power-hitting infielders like Harrah. He began his major league career with the reborn Senators and moved with them to Texas in 1972. Despite playing for second-division

Toby Harrah, with Cleveland in 1982.

clubs most of the time, Harrah accumulated very good statistics. He scored 1,115 runs, stole 238 bases, and made the All-Star team four times. In 1975 he hit .293 with 93 RBI and 98 walks. The next year Harrah led AL shortstops in errors, but also in putouts and total chances per game.

In 1977 came Harrah's best offensive year. He moved to third when the Rangers signed Bert Campaneris to play short. Harrah led the AL with 109 walks and hit 17 home runs, both career highs, and stole 27 bases. He and Bump Wills hit back-to-back inside-the-park home runs at Yankee Stadium, only the second time that ever occurred. In 1985 Harrah finished third in the AL with a .437 on-base average, behind Wade Boggs and George Brett.
Playing Career: *1969, 1971-1986; Was A, Tex A, Cle A, NY A*
Managerial Career: *1992; Tex A*

Bud Harrelson
Harrelson, Derrel McKinley
B: Jun 6, 1944

Pos: SS	BA: .236
Hits: 1,120	HRs: 7
RBI: 267	BBs: 633
Managerial Record	
Won: 145 Lost: 129 Pct: .529	

Harrelson was a Mets favorite, coming up at age 21 in 1965. He played in two NLCS and two World Series for them. Fans showed their allegiance when burly Pete Rose slid hard into Harrelson trying to break up a double play in the 1973 NLCS. The crowd booed, hissed and threw vegetables at the Reds star. They prevented Rose from taking his outfield position until Willie Mays intervened, asking the fans to let play resume.

Harrelson stole home on September 16, 1966, costing the Giants a key game in a pennant race they lost by one and a half games. He stole home again to beat the Pirates, who finished two games out of first place. Har-

Mets shortstop Bud Harrelson.

relson's best year was 1970, when he reached career highs in five offensive categories and tied the NL shortstop record of 54 consecutive errorless games. He won a Gold Glove Award in 1971. Late in his career, he was picked up by the Phillies for the 1978 pennant drive stretch.
Playing Career: *1965-1980; NY N, Phi N, Tex A*
Managerial Career: *1990-1991; NY N*

Ken Harrelson
Harrelson, Kenneth Smith (Hawk)
B: Sep 4, 1941

Pos: 1B, OF	BA: .239
Hits: 703	HRs: 131
RBI: 421	BBs: 382

Wearing long blond hair, Nehru jackets, love beads and bellbottomed trousers without socks, Harrelson was baseball's Bad Boy. When he was quoted as saying A's owner Charlie Finley was "a menace to baseball," Finley stunned the A's by releasing Harrelson, their best home run hitter. The Red Sox picked him up as a free agent, paid him a $73,000 bonus, and won the 1967 pennant with his help. The next year, he hit 35 homers and led the AL with 109 RBI.
Playing Career: *1963-1971; KC A, Was A, Bos A, Cle A*

Will Harridge
Harridge, William
B: Oct 16, 1883   D: Apr 9, 1971
Hall of Fame 1972

Harridge served the AL for nearly 60 years. As a Wabash Railroad ticket agent, he handled travel arrangements for AL umpires and teams. Ban Johnson hired him as a secretary in 1911. Harridge became league secretary in 1927, and four years later he succeeded Ernest Barnard as AL president, a post he held from 1931 to 1959. The league achieved new heights during Harridge's tenure, but he preferred to stay in the background, quietly enforcing league rules and maintaining decorum.

In the middle of the heated 1931 pennant race, Harridge suspended Yankees catcher Bill Dickey for a month for slugging another player. Harridge opposed night baseball until he saw that it made the game more available to families. He hated gimmicks and showboating, and was not amused when Bill Veeck used a midget as a pinch hitter. After retiring as league president in 1958, Harridge served as chairman of the AL board of directors until his death in 1971.

Bucky Harris
Harris, Stanley Raymond
(The Boy Wonder)
B: Nov 8, 1896   D: Nov 8, 1977
Hall of Fame 1975

Pos: SS	BA: .274
Hits: 1,297	HRs: 9
RBI: 506	BBs: 472
Managerial Record	
Won: 2,157 Lost: 2,218 Pct: .493	

Harris hit .333 with two home runs in the 1924 World Series to lead the Senators to victory over the Giants. He had become their skipper at age 27 and was their leader on the field and off. Though the Senators repeated as pennant winners in 1925, they lost the World Series to the Pirates. In 1929 Harris moved to Detroit as player-manager, then began a career as a manager-for-hire.

All told, Harris piloted teams for 29 years, serving multiple stints with the Senators, Tigers, Red Sox, Phillies, and Yankees. After winning the pennant with the Yankees in 1947, Harris lost a three-way race to Boston and Cleveland in 1948, and was replaced by Casey Stengel. Only Connie Mack lost more games than Bucky Harris; only Mack and John McGraw won more.
Playing Career: *1919-1929, 1931; Was A, Det A*
Managerial Career: *1924-1943, 1947-1948, 1950-1956; Was A, Det A, Bos A, Phi N, NY A*

Greg Harris
Harris, Greg Allen
B: Nov 2, 1955

Pos: P	ERA: 3.56
W-L: 69-82	SOs: 1,046
ShOs: 0	Saves: 52

The ambidextrous Harris has always threatened to pitch left-handed in the majors. He started 98 games, completing only four, but has spent most of his career in the bullpen. Harris was hit hard in the 1984 NLCS with the Padres and 1990 ALCS with the Boston Red Sox.
Playing Career: *1981-; NY N, Cin N, Mon N, SD N, Tex A, Phi N, Bos A*

Joe Harris
Harris, Joseph
B: May 30, 1891   D: Dec 10, 1959

Pos: 1B, OF	BA: .317
Hits: 963	HRs: 47
RBI: 517	BBs: 413

A strong hitter, Harris batted over .300 every single season except his last. In 1923 he hit .335 and belted 13 homers, 11 triples, and 28 doubles. Two years later he compiled a World Series average of .440, with three homers.
Playing Career: *1914, 1917, 1919, 1922-1928; NY A, Cle A, Bos A, Was A, Pit N, Brk N*

Lum Harris
Harris, Chalmer Luman
B: Jan 17, 1915

Pos: P	ERA: 4.16
W-L: 35-63	SOs: 232
ShOs: 4	Saves: 3
Managerial Record	
Won: 466 Lost: 488 Pct: .488	

Taking over as manager of the Braves in 1968, Harris constructed a batting order that protected Hank Aaron in the lineup and encouraged him to try to break Babe Ruth's career home run record. The Braves won their division championship in 1969, but were swept by the Mets in the NLCS. As a pitcher, Harris had a good fastball and a fair knuckler, but pitched for struggling Athletics clubs, losing 63 games.
Playing Career: *1941-1944, 1946-1947; Phi A, Was A*
Managerial Career: *1961, 1964-1965, 1968-1972; Bal A, Hou N, Atl N*

Mickey Harris
Harris, Maurice Charles
B: Jan 30, 1917   D: Apr 15, 1971

Pos: P	ERA: 4.18
W-L: 59-71	SOs: 1,097
ShOs: 2	Saves: 21

The Red Sox relished Harris's 17-9 record in 1946 when they won the pennant. Earning World Series starts, he was knocked out of Games Two and Six. Switched to relief after arm trouble, Harris appeared in 53 games and saved 15 for the 1950 Senators; both were AL leading marks.
Playing Career: *1940-1941, 1946-1952; Bos A, Was A*

Slim Harriss
Harriss, William Jennings Bryan
B: Dec 11, 1896   D: Sep 19, 1963

Pos: P	ERA: 4.25
W-L: 95-135	SOs: 644
ShOs: 6	Saves: 16

Harriss once retired 27 batters in a row after giving up singles to the first two men he faced. Pitching for the A's during their dull years, his only winning season was 1925,

Lum Harris (r) and Bob Swift start a snowman at spring training in Wilmington, DE.

when he was 19-12 with a 3.50 ERA. Harriss led the AL in losses in 1922 and 1927, on his way to losing 135.
Playing Career: *1920-1928; Phi A, Bos A*

Jack Harshman
Harshman, John Elvin
B: Jul 12, 1927

Pos: P	ERA: 3.50
W-L: 69-65	SOs: 741
ShOs: 12	Saves: 7

First base was Harshman's position before he became one of the best-hitting pitchers. He hit 21 home runs in the majors, and had belted 47 homers with 141 RBI in the Southern Association. Harshman set the White Sox' single game strikeout record when he whiffed 16 in 1954.
Playing Career: *1948, 1950, 1952, 1954-1960; NY N, Chi A, Bal A, Bos A, Cle A*

Jack Harshman.

Bill Hart
Hart, William Franklin
B: Jul 19, 1865   D: Sep 19, 1936

Pos: P	ERA: 4.65
W-L: 66-120	SOs: 431
ShOs: 5	Saves: 3

Hart had a lot of heart; he pitched professionally for 25 years, winning more than 250 games in the minor leagues, but losing 120 in the majors. He lost 29 games in 1896, more than anyone else in the NL. After he retired from the mound, Hart became an umpire.
Playing Career: *1886-1887, 1892, 1895-1898, 1901; Phi AA, Brk N, Pit N, StL N, Cle A*
Umpiring Career: *1901, 1914-1915; AL, NL (1 WS)*

Jim Ray Hart
Hart, James Ray
B: Oct 30, 1941

Pos: 3B, OF	BA: .278
Hits: 1,052	HRs: 170
RBI: 578	BBs: 380

A power hitter who ripped 31 homers in his rookie season, Hart blasted 20 or more round-trippers four more times. Bob Gibson welcomed him to the NL with a pitch in the back that broke his shoulder blade in 1963. When Hart returned he was beaned by Curt Simmons and missed the rest of the 1963 season. A shoulder injury in 1969 slowed him, something that NL hurlers had not been able to do. In 1970 he hit for the cycle and tied a record with six RBI in one inning.
Playing Career: *1963-1974; SF N, NY A*

Fred Hartman
Hartman, Frederick Orrin
B: Apr 25, 1868   D: Nov 11, 1938

Pos: 3B	BA: .278
Hits: 622	HRs: 10
RBI: 332	BBs: 118

A hard-hitting third baseman, Hartman did not stick with any club very long despite hitting over .300 in three of six major league seasons. His less than .900 fielding average may have been the problem. He was on the White Sox team that won the first AL pennant.
Playing Career: *1894, 1897-1899, 1901-1902; Pit N, StL N, NY N, Chi A*

Gabby Hartnett
Hartnett, Charles Leo
B: Dec 20, 1900   D: Dec 20, 1972
Hall of Fame 1955

Pos: C	BA: .297
Hits: 1,912	HRs: 236
RBI: 1,179	BBs: 703
Managerial Record	
Won: 203 Lost: 176 Pct: .536	

On September 28, 1938, Hartnett stepped up to the plate as twilight enveloped Wrigley Field. It was the bottom of the ninth, score tied, two out. The Cubs needed a victory against the Pirates, but it looked as though the game was about to be called a tie due to darkness. Hartnett smacked the 0-2 pitch into the bleachers for his famous "homer in the gloamin'." The Cubs went on to capture the pennant.

Hartnett's nickname was hung on him when, as a rookie in 1922, he said virtually nothing. An excellent defensive receiver with a powerful arm, and a take-charge handler of pitchers, he caught 1,790 games. Hartnett led NL catchers in fielding six times and was an All-Star six times. In the 1934 All-Star Game, he caught Carl Hubbell when the slender southpaw fanned Ruth, Gehrig, Foxx, Simmons and Cronin in succession. Hartnett played in four World Series with the Cubs. The NL MVP in 1935, Hartnett was widely considered the best catcher in the league until Johnny Bench came along.
Playing Career: *1922-1941; Chi N, NY N*
Managerial Career: *1938-1940; Chi N*

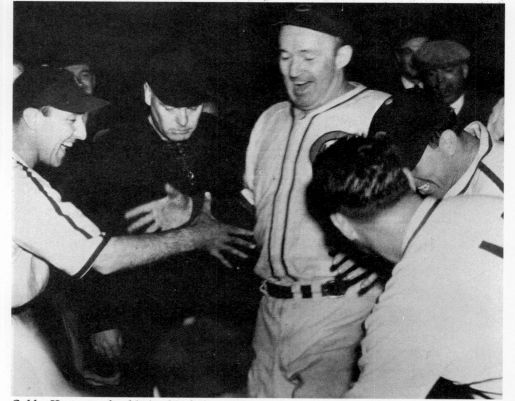

Gabby Hartnett after hitting his famous "Homer in the Gloamin'," 1938.

Topsy Hartsel
Hartsel, Tully Frederick
B: Jun 26, 1874   D: Oct 14, 1944

Pos: OF	BA: .276
Hits: 1,335	HRs: 30
RBI: 341	BBs: 837

The diminutive Hartsel was an ideal leadoff man. He used his 5'5" stature to draw walks, five times leading the league. Once on base he was a threat – he stole 247 bases and scored 826 runs. Hartsel led the AL in runs scored with 109 in 1902 and topped the league twice in on-base percentage. He had three other seasons with an on-base percentage of more than .400. Hartsel also led the AL with 47 steals in 1902. He played on four pennant-winning Philadelphia teams.
Playing Career: *1898-1911; Lou N, Cin N, Chi N, Phi A*

Clint Hartung
Hartung, Clint (Floppy, The Hondo Hurricane)
B: Aug 10, 1922

Pos: P, OF	BA: .238
Hits: 90	HRs: 14
RBI: 43	BBs: 25

The Giants' answer to Babe Ruth was Clint Hartung. He was such a good athlete that it did not matter where he played; as a result he ended up mastering no position. Hartung went 29-29 in 511 innings with a 5.02 ERA as a pitcher, but was burned out by age 30.
Playing Career: *1947-1952; NY N*

Roy Hartzell
Hartzell, Roy Allen
B: Jul 6, 1881   D: Nov 6, 1961

Pos: OF, 3B, 2B, SS	BA: .252
Hits: 1,146	HRs: 12
RBI: 397	BBs: 455

One of the few Yankees sluggers who did not hit home runs, Hartzell had 91 RBI in 1911, more than any of his teammates. The left-handed hitter shifted among second base, third base, shortstop and the outfield.
Playing Career: *1906-1916; StL A, NY A*

Bryan Harvey
Harvey, Bryan Stanley
B: Jun 2, 1963

Pos: P	ERA: 2.34
W-L: 17-25	SOs: 438
ShOs: 0	Saves: 171

One of the premier relief pitchers in baseball today, Harvey suffered a fairly serious injury in 1992. Consequently, the Angels did not protect him during the expansion draft and he was snapped up by the new Florida Marlins, saving 45 in 1993. Specializing in relief from the beginning of his big league career, Harvey was the Rookie Pitcher of the Year in 1988 with 17 saves and a 2.13 ERA.
Playing Career: *1987-; Cal A, Flo N*

Bryan Harvey with the expansion Florida Marlins in 1993.

Buddy Hassett
Hassett, John Aloysius
B: Sep 5, 1911

Pos: 1B, OF	BA: .292
Hits: 1,026	HRs: 12
RBI: 343	BBs: 209

A steady-hitting first baseman in the Yankees' farm system, Hassett was stuck behind Lou Gehrig in his prime. Hassett was traded, but when Gehrig retired the Yankees got him back. Hassett hit .333 with two RBI in the 1942 World Series.
Playing Career: *1936-1942; Brk N, Bos N, NY A*

Ron Hassey
Hassey, Ronald William
B: Feb 27, 1953

Pos: C	BA: .266
Hits: 914	HRs: 71
RBI: 438	BBs: 385

Hassey was a well-traveled receiver who was traded between the Yankees and the White Sox four times in three seasons. In 1980 his .318 batting average led all catchers. The next year he caught Len Barker's perfect game. Hassey played on three A's division-winning teams.
Playing Career: *1978-1991; Cle A, Chi N, NY A, Chi A, Oak A, Mon N*

Andy Hassler
Hassler, Andrew Earl
B: Oct 18, 1951

Pos: P	ERA: 3.83
W-L: 44-71	SOs: 630
ShOs: 5	Saves: 29

Working as a starter and a reliever during his 14-year career, Hassler tossed a pair of one-hitters: one with the 1974 Angels, and the other with the 1977 Royals. He pitched for three division-winning teams and appeared in two ALCS.
Playing Career: *1971, 1973-1985; Cal A, KC A, Bos A, NY N, Pit N, StL N*

Billy Hatcher
Hatcher, William Augustus
B: Oct 4, 1960

Pos: OF	BA: .266
Hits: 1,072	HRs: 51
RBI: 368	BBs: 249

Suspended for 10 days in 1987 for using a corked bat, Hatcher claimed he borrowed the stick from pitcher Dave Smith. In the 1986 ALCS, Hatcher hit a dramatic, 14th-inning home run for the Astros to tie Game Six. But the Mets won it in 16 innings. Hatcher batted .750 for the Reds in the 1990 World Series.
Playing Career: *1984-; Chi N, Hou N, Pit N, Cin N, Bos A*

Mickey Hatcher
Hatcher, Michael Vaughn
B: Mar 15, 1955

Pos: OF, 3B, 1B, DH	BA: .280
Hits: 946	HRs: 38
RBI: 375	BBs: 164

After hitting only one home run all year, Hatcher homered in the first inning of Games One and Five of the 1988 World Series, helping his Dodgers defeat Oakland in five games. He would have been Series MVP, but for Orel Hershiser, who won two with a 1.00 ERA. A jokester, Hatcher once wore a batting helmet with a propeller on it.
Playing Career: *1979-1990; LA N, Min A*

Grady Hatton
Hatton, Grady Edgebert
B: Oct 7, 1922

Pos: 3B, 2B	BA: .254
Hits: 1,068	HRs: 91
RBI: 533	BBs: 646

Managerial Record
Won: 164   Lost: 221   Pct: .426

A good teacher who developed young talent into major league players, Hatton won two pennants in three years with the Oklahoma City 89ers. But Hatton was not a strong tactician; in the majors, his Astros finished 8th, 9th and 10th.
Playing Career: *1946-1956, 1960; Cin N, Bos A, StL N, Bal A, Chi N*
Managerial Career: *1966-1968; Hou N*

Andy Hawkins
Hawkins, Melton Andrew
B: Jan 21, 1960

Pos: P	ERA: 4.22
W-L: 84-91	SOs: 706
ShOs: 10	No-hitters: 1

Hawkins won the Padres' only World Series victory when he allowed just one earned run in 5.1 innings of relief in Game Two of the 1984 Fall Classic. The next year he won his first 11 decisions. Soon after, his career was hampered by circulation and shoulder problems. He lost a no-hit game in 1990.
Playing Career: *1982-1991; SD N, NY A, Oak A*

Pink Hawley
Hawley, Emerson P.
B: Dec 5, 1872   D: Sep 19, 1938

Pos: P	ERA: 3.96
W-L: 167-179	SOs: 868
ShOs: 10	Saves: 3

Hawley was a knuckleballer who tossed 444 innings for Connie Mack's Pirates in the midst of the 1895 pennant race. Hawley went 31-22 that year, as a midseason injury to Frank Killen forced Mack to use Hawley every day. Pink averaged 301 innings for 10 years.
Playing Career: *1892-1901; StL N, Pit N, Cin N, NY N, Mil A*

Frankie Hayes
Hayes, Frank Witman
B: Oct 13, 1914   D: Jun 22, 1955

Pos: C	BA: .259
Hits: 1,164	HRs: 119
RBI: 628	BBs: 564

Durable Hayes caught every game for the 1944 Athletics – still the AL record. He holds the major league record for consecutive games caught, 312. In 1945 Hayes made 29 double plays, the second highest total ever. He was elected to the All-Star roster five times.
Playing Career: *1933-1934, 1936-1947; Phi A, StL A, Cle A, Chi A, Bos A*

Jackie Hayes
Hayes, Minter Carney
B: Jul 19, 1906   D: Feb 9, 1983

Pos: 2B, SS, 3B	BA: .265
Hits: 1,069	HRs: 20
RBI: 493	BBs: 309

Hayes was a far-ranging glove man who combined with shortstop Luke Appling to form a slick double play combination for the White Sox, 1932-1937. They turned 115 double plays in 1937, leading the AL. Hayes hit 196 doubles in his career. He batted .312 in 1936 and .328 in 1938.
Playing Career: *1927-1940; Was A, Chi A*

Von Hayes
Hayes, Von Francis
B: Aug 31, 1958

Pos: OF, 1B	BA: .267
Hits: 1,402	HRs: 143
RBI: 696	BBs: 712

In 1982 Hayes hit .250 with 14 homers and 82 RBI, and stole 32 bases. The figures impressed the Phillies enough to send five players to the Indians in exchange for Hayes. While he never lived up to the "five-for-one" label applied by Pete Rose, Hayes was a solid outfielder and an adequate first baseman. In 1986 he scored 107 runs and hit 46 doubles, both NL leading totals. He also batted .305 and drove in 98. Hayes stole 253 bases, including 48 in 1984.
Playing Career: *1981-1992; Cle A, Phi N, Cal A*

Joe Haynes
Haynes, Joseph Walton
B: Sep 21, 1917   D: Jan 6, 1967

Pos: P	ERA: 4.01
W-L: 76-82	SOs: 475
ShOs: 5	Saves: 21

Haynes was married to Thelma Griffith, adopted daughter of Clark Griffith. He later became a Senators coach, general manager, and vice president, moving with the franchise to Minnesota. His best season as a ballplayer was 1947, when he led the AL with a 2.42 ERA.
Playing Career: *1939-1952; Was A, Chi A*

Ray Hayworth
Hayworth, Raymond Hall
B: Jan 29, 1904

Pos: C	BA: .265
Hits: 546	HRs: 5
RBI: 238	BBs: 198

A backup catcher for all his career except 1933, when he was a starter, Hayworth was Mickey Cochrane's substitute when Detroit won pennants in 1934 and 1935. Hayworth

Von Hayes scores against the Mets on a passed ball in 1984.

Brooklyn catcher Ray Hayworth, 1939.

appeared in one 1934 World Series game. In 1936 he led AL catchers with a .988 fielding average.
Playing Career: *1926, 1929-1939, 1942, 1944-1945; Det A, Brk N, NY N, StL A*

Egyptian Healy
Healy, John J.
B: Oct 27, 1866   D: Mar 16, 1899

Pos: P	ERA: 3.84
W-L: 79-136	SOs: 822
ShOs: 9	No-hitters: 0

Nicknamed Egyptian because he hailed from Cairo, Illinois, the 6' 2" right-hander was also known as "Long John." His best year was 1890 when he won 22 for the Black Pirates of Toledo in the AA.
Playing Career: *1885-1892; StL N, Ind N, Was N, Chi N, Tol AA, Bal AA, Bal N, Lou N*

Jim Hearn
Hearn, James Tolbert
B: Apr 11, 1921

Pos: P	ERA: 3.81
W-L: 109-89	SOs: 669
ShOs: 10	Saves: 8

In 1951 Hearn was 17-9 as the third starter on the Giants' staff, behind aces Sal Maglie and Larry Jansen. The big three fueled the pennant drive for New York. Hearn was an effective sinkerball pitcher.
Playing Career: *1947-1959; StL N, NY N, Phi N*

Jeff Heath
Heath, John Geoffrey
B: Apr 1, 1915   D: Dec 9, 1975

Pos: OF	BA: .293
Hits: 1,447	HRs: 194
RBI: 887	BBs: 593

In Bob Feller's 1940 Opening Day no-hitter, Heath scored the game's only run. Heath led the AL in triples twice. He hit 184 home runs and drove in 848 from 1938 to 1948. In 1947 with the Browns he hit a career-high 27 homers with 87 RBI. Acquired by the 1948 Braves, Heath belted 20 round-trippers with a .319 average to help the club win its first pennant since 1914. In the final week of the season he broke his leg sliding and missed the World Series.
Playing Career: *1936-1949; Cle A, Was A, StL A, Bos N*

Mike Heath
Heath, Michael Thomas
B: Feb 5, 1955

Pos: C	BA: .252
Hits: 932	HRs: 78
RBI: 419	BBs: 252

The Yankees converted Heath to a catcher after he played shortstop for three years in the minors. He played in two ALCS and one World Series. Heath's most productive year was 1987 when he hit 16 doubles and 8 homers and slugged .430 in only 270 at-bats.
Playing Career: *1978-1991; NY A, Oak A, StL N, Det A, Atl N*

Cliff Heathcote
Heathcote, Clifton Earl
B: Jan 24, 1898   D: Jan 19, 1939

Pos: OF	BA: .275
Hits: 1,222	HRs: 42
RBI: 448	BBs: 367

When the Cardinals' Cliff Heathcote and the Cubs' Max Flack were traded between games of a doubleheader in 1922, they became the first players ever to play for two different teams on the same day. Later that season, in the famous 26-23 Cubs' victory over the Phillies, Heathcote tied a major league record by reaching base seven times in a nine-inning game.
Playing Career: *1918-1932; StL N, Chi N, Cin N, Phi N*

Neal Heaton
Heaton, Neal
B: Mar 3, 1960

Pos: P	ERA: 4.37
W-L: 80-96	SOs: 699
ShOs: 6	Saves: 10

Left-handed Heaton was equally reliable as a starter or a reliever. Teams sought him as the player who could fill in where there were gaps in the pitching rotation. Heaton pitched for the Pirates as they won their division championship in 1990 and 1991.
Playing Career: *1982-; Cle A, Min A, Mon N, Pit N, KC A, Mil A, NY A*

Richie Hebner
Hebner, Richard Joseph
B: Nov 26, 1947

Pos: 3B	BA: .276
Hits: 1,694	HRs: 203
RBI: 890	BBs: 687

During the off-season Hebner stayed in shape by digging graves. Signing with the Pirates for a $40,000 bonus, he made the big leagues at the age of 20 despite losing playing time to military reserve duty. He led NL rookies with a .301 average in 1969. Hebner was a solid six-hole hitter, and fueled eight division-winning teams. He holds the record for the most times on the losing side in the

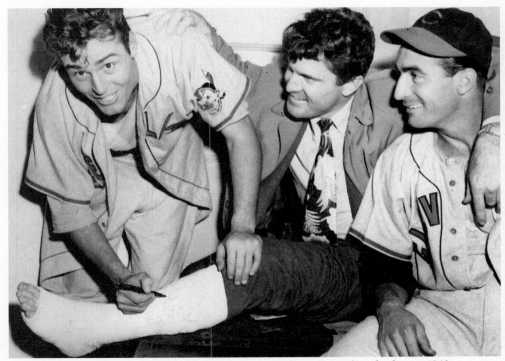

Jeff Heath has his cast signed by Gene Bearden as Johnny Berardino looks on, 1948.

LCS (seven) and the most appearances in the NLCS (eight).
Playing Career: *1968-1985; Pit N, Phi N, NY N, Det A, Pit N, Chi N*

Guy Hecker
Hecker, Guy Jackson
B: Apr 3, 1856   D: Dec 3, 1938

Pos: P	ERA: 2.92
W-L: 175-146	SOs: 1,099
ShOs: 15	No-hitters: 1

Pos: 1B, OF	BA: .283
Hits: 810	HRs: 19
RBI: 103 (inc.)	BBs: 141

Managerial Record
Won: 23   Lost: 113   Pct: .169

The only pitcher to ever win a major league batting title, Hecker once allowed four hits in a complete-game victory he pitched while registering six hits himself. He also scored a record seven runs. In 1884 he led the old American Association with a 52-20 record and a 1.80 ERA. Two years later he led the league in batting with a .342 mark. Hecker stole 48 bases in 1887. In the years 1883 to 1886, Hecker averaged 34 wins and 23 losses.
Playing Career: *1882-1890; Lou AA, Pit N*
Managerial Career: *1890; Pit N*

Don Heffner
Heffner, Donald Henry
B: Feb 8, 1911   D: Aug 1, 1989

Pos: 2B	BA: .241
Hits: 610	HRs: 6
RBI: 248	BBs: 270

Managerial Record
Won: 37   Lost: 46   Pct: .446

While a 19-year-old minor leaguer, Heffner pitched an exhibition game for an all-star team of major league players against the Negro League Baltimore Black Sox. Heffner beat them 1-0. He played on the Yankees' pennant-winning teams of 1936 and 1937.
Playing Career: *1934-1944; NY A, StL A, Phi A, Det A*
Managerial Career: *1966; Cin N*

Jim Hegan
Hegan, James Edward
B: Aug 3, 1920   D: Jun 17, 1984

Pos: C	BA: .228
Hits: 1,087	HRs: 92
RBI: 525	BBs: 456

The top AL defensive catcher in the post-World War II period, Hegan holds a record that may never be broken. He handled 18 20-game winners for the Indians between 1946 and 1957. It was not coincidental that the glory years of Cleveland pitching took place during the tenure of Hegan and pitching coach Mel Harder. Three of Hegan's hurlers, Bob Feller, Bob Lemon, and Early Wynn, are in the Hall of Fame. Feller and Wynn said Hegan was the best receiver ever. He was chosen for the All-Star team five times.
Playing Career: *1941-1942, 1946-1960; Cle A, Det A, Phi N, SF N, Chi N*

Emmett Heidrick
Heidrick, John Emmett
B: Jul 29, 1876   D: Jan 20, 1916

Pos: OF	BA: .300
Hits: 914	HRs: 16
RBI: 342	BBs: 146

Frank and Stanley Robison owned both the Cleveland Spiders and the St. Louis Perfectos, so when Heidrick said he was unhappy in Cleveland, they moved him to St. Louis. Heidrick hit .339 in 1901 as part of the Cardinals' all-.300 outfield.
Playing Career: *1898-1904, 1908; Cle N, StL N, StL A*

Louis Heilbroner
Heilbroner, Louis Wilbur
B: Jul 4, 1861   D: Dec 21, 1933

Managerial Record
Won: 23   Lost: 25   Pct: .479

Heilbroner published *The Baseball Blue Book* out of Ft. Wayne, Indiana, starting in 1909. It served as the information guide to the National Association of Professional Baseball Leagues, the governing body of the minors. He also served the Central League as president, 1912-1914.
Managerial Career: *1900; StL N*

Harry Heilmann
Heilmann, Harry Edwin (Slug)
B: Aug 3, 1894   D: Jul 9, 1951
Hall of Fame 1952

Pos: OF, 1B	BA: .342
Hits: 2,660	HRs: 183
RBI: 1,551	BBs: 856

A good hitter to start with, Heilmann became a great hitter under the tutelage of Ty Cobb. The introduction of the lively ball in 1920 also helped him. Line drives that fielders had previously reached began whizzing by their gloves before they could react. Heilmann was like a hitting machine. At the plate he rivaled Rogers Hornsby as the greatest right-handed hitter of the time. He led the AL in hitting four times, although he had little home run power. Heilmann hit 542 doubles and 151 triples. He also scored 1,291 runs. For much of his career Heilmann batted behind Cobb, driving him in many times, leading to Cobb's all-time record for runs scored. Slow and awkward in the outfield, Heilmann was moved to first base. He led AL first basemen in errors for two years, so back to the outfield

Cleveland's Jim Hegan steals second during the first game of the 1948 WS.

Harry Heilmann.

he went. He was a low-key, articulate man, who liked telling stories of his playing days. After retiring, he put those talents to work as a popular play-by-play radio broadcaster for the Tigers.
Playing Career: *1914, 1916-1930, 1932; Det A, Cin N*

Fred Heimach
Heimach, Frederick Amos
B: Jan 27, 1901   D: Jun 1, 1973

Pos: P	ERA: 4.46
W-L: 62-69	SOs: 334
ShOs: 5	Saves: 7

Heimach's fielding skills made him a useful fifth infielder, and his .236 lifetime batting average included 52 pinch-hit appearances in which he hit .385. When a broken ankle finished his career in 1933, Heimach had run up a string of errorless games that started in 1926, covering 171 chances.
Playing Career: *1920-1926, 1928-1933; Phi A, Bos A, NY A, Brk N*

Ken Heintzelman
Heintzelman, Kenneth Alphonse
B: Oct 14, 1915

Pos: P	ERA: 3.93
W-L: 77-98	SOs: 564
ShOs: 19	Saves: 7

After nearly 15 years of pro ball, Heintzelman was suddenly a successful pitcher in 1949 when he was 17-10 with a 3.02 ERA. Leading the NL with five shutouts, Heintzelman also had a nine-game winning streak. He pitched well in his only World Series start.
Playing Career: *1937-1942, 1946-1952; Pit N, Phi N*

Woodie Held
Held, Woodson George
B: Mar 25, 1932

Pos: SS, OF	BA: .240
Hits: 963	HRs: 179
RBI: 559	BBs: 509

A home run-hitting infielder in the Yankees' organization, Held was switched to the outfield by the A's, then back to shortstop by the Indians. In 1957 he hit 20 homers. On July 31, 1963, Held belted a home run, followed by Pedro Ramos with another, then Tito Francona and Larry Brown also stroked homers to set the AL record for consecutive home runs by a team. Held was known for his tantrums after striking out, something that he did with regularity.
Playing Career: *1954, 1957-1969; NY A, KC A, Cle A, Was A, Bal A, Cal A, Chi A*

Tommy Helms
Helms, Tommy Vann
B: May 5, 1941

Pos: 3B, 2B	BA: .269
Hits: 1,342	HRs: 34
RBI: 477	BBs: 231
Managerial Record	
Won: 26 Lost: 36 Pct: .419	

The NL Rookie of the Year in 1966, Helms was part of the exciting young Reds team that featured Pete Rose, Tony Perez and Johnny Bench. Helms was the first Cincinnati player to hit a home run at Riverfront Stadium. After switching to second base, he won Gold Glove

Awards in 1970 and 1971. Helms was a Reds coach, and later, manager, replacing Pete Rose in 1989.
Playing Career: *1964-1977; Cin N, Hou N, Pit N, Bos A*
Managerial Career: *1988-1989; Cin N*

George Hemming
Hemming, George Earl
B: Dec 15, 1868   D: Jun 3, 1930

Pos: P	ERA: 4.55
W-L: 91-82	SOs: 362
ShOs: 7	Saves: 6

In 1894 Hemming arrived in Baltimore to save the Orioles, who had powerful batting but no pitching. He went 4-0, but lost in his only Temple Cup start. He won 20 games the next year, then went 15-6 in the Orioles' third straight pennant-winning year.
Playing Career: *1890-1897; Cle P, Brk P, Brk N, Cin N, Lou N, Bal N*

Charlie Hemphill
Hemphill, Charles Judson
B: Apr 20, 1876   D: Jun 22, 1953

Pos: OF	BA: .271
Hits: 1,230	HRs: 22
RBI: 421	BBs: 435

A speedy fielder and good base stealer, Hemphill batted cleanup and patrolled right field in the last game the Cleveland Spiders ever played. Hemphill's best season was 1902, when he hit .308 and slugged .418. He scored 90 runs in 1906 and stole 42 bases with

Tommy Helms brings in a homer as former teammate Johnny Bench watches, 1972.

the Highlanders in 1908. When Hal Chase became ill, Hemphill stepped in to manage the Highlanders, then became a playing-manager for the Atlanta Crackers of the Southern Association.
Playing Career: *1899, 1901-1904, 1906-1911; StL N, Cle N, Bos A, Cle A, StL A, NY A*

Rollie Hemsley
Hemsley, Ralston Burdett
B: Jun 24, 1907   D: Jul 31, 1972

Pos: C	BA: .262
Hits: 1,321	HRs: 31
RBI: 555	BBs: 357

A five-time All-Star, Hemsley fought alcoholism early in his career. Playing for the 1931-1932 Cubs who patronized Al Capone's establishments, Hemsley got an appearance in the 1932 World Series and a longterm hangover. With the help of Alcoholics Anonymous he recovered and became a valuable backup receiver. Hemsley caught Bob Feller's 1940 Opening Day no-hitter. He played on two Yankees flag winners, and was named Minor League Manager of the Year in 1950 and 1963.
Playing Career: *1928-1944, 1946-1947; Pit N, Chi N, Cin N, StL A, Cle A, NY A, Phi N*

Solly Hemus
Hemus, Solomon Joseph
B: Apr 17, 1923

Pos: SS, 2B	BA: .273
Hits: 736	HRs: 51
RBI: 263	BBs: 456
Managerial Record	
Won: 190 Lost: 192 Pct: .497	

Hemus was the last major league manager who was also a regular player. The Cardinals announced his appointment while on tour in Japan in 1959. In 1952 Hemus had scored 105 runs to tie teammate Stan Musial for the NL lead. The next year he scored 110. Hemus had a lifetime slugging average of .411 – high for a middle infielder. After the Cardinals let him go in 1962, he went on to coach with the Mets and Indians.
Playing Career: *1949-1959; StL N, Phi N*
Managerial Career: *1959-1961; StL N*

Dave Henderson
Henderson, David Lee
B: Jul 21, 1958

Pos: OF, DH	BA: .259
Hits: 1,275	HRs: 192
RBI: 677	BBs: 449

In the top of the ninth inning of Game Five of the 1986 ALCS, Henderson hit a dramatic two-out, two-run homer for the Red Sox. The Angels had been within one strike of their first AL pennant and World Series appearance. But the game went into extra innings and Henderson won it on a sacrifice fly in the 11th inning. Traded to San Francisco the next year, he helped the Giants win the division title, then signed as a free agent with Oakland that winter. He played on three more division-winning teams to make five in a row, 1986-1990.
Playing Career: *1981-; Sea A, Bos A, SF N, Oak A*

Ken Henderson
Henderson, Kenneth Joseph
B: Jun 15, 1946

Pos: OF	BA: .257
Hits: 1,168	HRs: 122
RBI: 576	BBs: 589

Debuting at age 18 with the Giants, Henderson was touted as Willie Mays's successor. After four years of distinctly unMays-like playing, Henderson was traded to the White Sox. He hit 20 homers for Chicago in 1974, his personal best.
Playing Career: *1965-1980; SF N, Chi A, Atl N, Tex A, NY N, Cin N, Chi N*

Rickey Henderson
Henderson, Rickey Henley
B: Dec 25, 1957

Pos: OF	BA: .291
Hits: 2,139	HRs: 220
RBI: 784	BBs: 1,406

While Billy Martin managed the A's, he showed rookie Henderson a crouching batting stance and taught him to be intense on the field. Becoming the most potent leadoff

Rickey Henderson.

man of all time, Henderson has scored 1,586 runs, averaging more than 100 per season, and leading the league five times. He scored an incredible 146 runs in 143 games in 1985, the first man to average more than one run per game since Jimmie Foxx in 1939.

Henderson has a lifetime on-base average of .406. He has led the AL in walks three times. A power hitter as well, he has hit more than 50 leadoff home runs. Henderson demolished the single-season stolen base record in 1982, when he swiped 130 for the A's. He has led the AL in stolen bases 11 times, topping 100 three times, for a total of 1,095 at the end of the 1993 season. Henderson was honored with a Gold Glove Award in 1981, and has appeared in 11 All-Star contests, five ALCS and three World Series.
Playing Career: *1979-; Oak A, NY A, Tor A*

Steve Henderson
Henderson, Steven Curtis
B: Nov 18, 1952

Pos: OF, DH	BA: .280
Hits: 976	HRs: 68
RBI: 428	BBs: 386

Henderson lost the 1977 Rookie of the Year Award to Andre Dawson by one vote. The next year he hit with more power but his average fell 31 points. After working on his batting stroke, Henderson hit a career-high .306 in 1979.
Playing Career: *1977-1988; NY N, Chi N, Sea A, Oak A, Hou N*

Bob Hendley
Hendley, Charles Robert
B: Apr 30, 1939

Pos: P	ERA: 3.97
W-L: 48-52	SOs: 522
ShOs: 6	Saves: 12

On September 9, 1965, Cubs pitcher Bob Hendley one-hit the Dodgers, but the opposing pitcher, Sandy Koufax, tossed a perfect game

Solly Hemus slides into third as a wild throw goes by Giant Billy Gardner, 1954.

to win 1-0. It was the fewest hits ever allowed in a game. Five days later the two hurlers met again; Hendley beat Koufax, 2-1.
Playing Career: *1961-1967; Mil N, SF N, Chi N, NY N*

George Hendrick
Hendrick, George Andrew (Silent George)
B: Oct 18, 1949

Pos: OF	BA: .278
Hits: 1,980	HRs: 267
RBI: 1,111	BBs: 567

Hendrick hit for both average and power. He batted over .300 four times and averaged 20 home runs a year from 1972 to 1983. He hit three homers in a game in 1973, and twice drove in seven runs in one game. Hendrick's best season was 1980 when he blasted 25 round-trippers, knocked in 109 runs, batted .302 and slugged .498. Selected for four All-Star squads, Hendrick played in the World Series on the winning side twice, with the 1972 A's and the 1982 Cardinals. He hit .321 in the Red Birds' victory over the Brewers in the 1982 Fall Classic.

Hendrick was a shy but personable fellow, who quit speaking to the press early in his career. He was well-liked by teammates and the St. Louis fans. The beginning of his baseball career was odd; Hendrick did not play any sports at Fremont High, a school well-known for athletics, yet was signed by the Oakland A's on the strength of his sandlot performance.
Playing Career: *1971-1988; Oak A, Cle A, SD N, StL N, Pit N, Cal A*

Harvey Hendrick
Hendrick, Harvey
B: Nov 9, 1897   D: Oct 29, 1941

Pos: 1B, OF	BA: .308
Hits: 896	HRs: 48
RBI: 413	BBs: 239

Vanderbilt alumnus Hendrick hit .300 but could not stick with a team. His poor defensive work relegated him to second-division clubs after his 1923 rookie season with the pennant-winning Yankees. He hit .354 in 1929 with 14 homers and 82 RBI.
Playing Career: *1923-1925, 1927-1934; NY A, Cle A, Brk N, Cin N, StL N, Chi N, Phi N*

Ellie Hendricks
Hendricks, Elrod Jerome
B: Dec 22, 1940

Pos: C	BA: .220
Hits: 415	HRs: 62
RBI: 230	BBs: 229

Hendricks played in five ALCS and four World Series. In Game One of the 1970 World Series, he tagged Bernie Carbo with an empty glove, but the umpire's view was blocked, and Carbo was called out. Hendricks later coached for the Orioles.
Playing Career: *1968-1979; Bal A, Chi N, NY A*

George Hendrick slides as Phil Garner takes the throw too late in a 1977 game.

Jack Hendricks
Hendricks, John Charles
B: Apr 9, 1875   D: May 13, 1943

Pos: OF	BA: .207
Hits: 30	HRs: 0
RBI: 4	BBs: 15
Managerial Record	
Won: 520 Lost: 528 Pct: .496	

After playing in the big leagues for only two seasons, Hendricks enjoyed a long career managing in the minors and majors from 1906 to 1929. Hendricks won three straight pennants with Denver in the Western League, 1910-1912.
Playing Career: *1902-1903; NY N, Chi N, Was A*
Managerial Career: *1918, 1924-1929; StL N, Cin N*

Claude Hendrix
Hendrix, Claude Raymond
B: Apr 13, 1889   D: Mar 22, 1944

Pos: P	ERA: 2.65
W-L: 143-116	SOs: 1,092
ShOs: 27	No-hitters: 1

The short-lived Federal League had some good pitchers, and Hendrix was the best. He won 29 and posted a league-leading 1.69 ERA in 1914. He also batted .322 that season and was a lifetime .241 hitter with 13 home runs and 97 RBI. After the demise of the Federal League, Hendrix went to the Cubs, where he won 20 games and led the league in winning percentage in 1918. His career ended when the Cubs released him for having allegedly bet against his teammates.
Playing Career: *1911-1920; Pit N, Chi F, Chi N*

Claude Hendrix.

Tom Henke
Henke, Thomas Anthony
B: Dec 21, 1957

Pos: P	ERA: 2.67
W-L: 37-35	SOs: 774
ShOs: 0	Saves: 260

The Blue Jays selected Henke as compensation when the Rangers signed Toronto DH Cliff Johnson as a free agent. Henke had pitched spectacularly at Syracuse in the International League, surrendering only five runs in more than 50 innings. When Syracuse fans thought it was time to bring in the fireman, they would wave handkerchiefs in the air, and chant "Henke, Henke." The big right-hander was called up by the Blue Jays on July 8, 1985.

In his first month, Henke recorded eight saves. Prior to 1985, the most saves a Toronto

reliever had in an entire season was 11. Henke is an overpowering pitcher. Once he brought his 95-mph fastball under control and added a baffling forkball, he became nearly unbeatable. He set the Blue Jays' saves record with 34, and he posted a 1.92 ERA in 1989, but he has appeared in only one All-Star Game. In 1993 he returned to the Rangers.
Playing Career: *1982-; Tex A, Tor A*

Butch Henline
Henline, Walter John
B: Dec 20, 1894   D: Oct 9, 1957

Pos: C	BA: .291
Hits: 611	HRs: 40
RBI: 268	BBs: 92

When the Phillies traded away .300 hitter Irish Meusel for Henline and two other Giants in 1921, Philadelphia fans went berserk. Henline quelled the storm by ably filling the catching position for the next five years. He led NL receivers in fielding in 1922, and batted a career-high .324 in 1923.
Playing Career: *1921-1931; NY N, Phi N, Brk N, Chi A*
Umpiring Career: *1945-1948; NL*

Mike Henneman
Henneman, Michael Alan
B: Dec 11, 1961

Pos: P	ERA: 3.00
W-L: 56-30	SOs: 429
ShOs: 0	Saves: 128

Henneman came from Oklahoma State University's successful baseball program, where he was All-Conference and tossed a no-hitter. Replacing injured Willie Hernandez in 1988, Henneman has blossomed into one of the AL's best stoppers, leading the league in relief wins in 1989 and 1991.
Playing Career: *1987-; Det A*

Tommy Henrich
Henrich, Thomas David (Ol' Reliable)
B: Feb 20, 1913

Pos: OF	BA: .282
Hits: 1,297	HRs: 183
RBI: 795	BBs: 712

Fans said Henrich, Charley Keller and Joe DiMaggio composed the best outfield ever. Henrich played right field for eight championship Yankees teams. He was at bat when Mickey Owen dropped the third strike in Game Four of the 1941 Series. Henrich ran to first, igniting the game-winning rally. He also got the game-winning hits in three games of the 1947 Series. Henrich's home run beat Boston on the final day of the season in 1949. He was selected for the All-Star team five times.
Playing Career: *1937-1942, 1946-1950; NY A*

Bill Henry
Henry, William Rodman
B: Oct 15, 1927

Pos: P	ERA: 3.26
W-L: 46-50	SOs: 621
ShOs: 2	Saves: 90

Working as a starter, stopper and middle reliever, Henry enjoyed a 16-year career. As a closer, he saved 70 games from 1959 to 1963. He pitched the Reds to the NL pennant in 1961. He led the NL with 59 appearances in 1959.
Playing Career: *1952-1955, 1958-1969; Bos A, Chi N, Cin N, SF N, Pit N, Hou N*

Ron Herbel
Herbel, Ronald Samuel
B: Jan 16, 1938

Pos: P	ERA: 3.82
W-L: 42-37	SOs: 447
ShOs: 3	Saves: 16

If there is any justification in the concept of the designated hitter, Herbel's type of batting is it. He got six hits in 206 at-bats for an average of .029. Herbel was a fine starter, going 12-9 in 1965; then plagued by arm problems, he switched to long relief.
Playing Career: *1963-1971; SF N, SD N, NY N, Atl N*

Ray Herbert
Herbert, Raymond Ernest
B: Dec 15, 1929

Pos: P	ERA: 4.01
W-L: 104-107	SOs: 864
ShOs: 13	Saves: 15

Several Kansas City A's team pitching records – innings, earned runs, and losses – are held by Herbert. After a mediocre start, Herbert suddenly became a star in 1962 at age 32, when he won 20 games for the White Sox. The next year he led the AL in shutouts with seven.
Playing Career: *1950-1951, 1953-1955, 1958-1966; Det A, KC A, Chi A, Phi N*

Babe Herman
Herman, Floyd Caves
B: Jun 26, 1903   D: Nov 27, 1987

Pos: OF	BA: .324
Hits: 1,818	HRs: 181
RBI: 997	BBs: 520

Prone to gaffes on the field, Herman was treated as a comedy of errors by the press. He once gave credence to their jibes in the so-called triple play incident. With runners on first and third, Herman hit a long fly ball. He and the runner on first ran like mad, while the man on third decided the ball would be caught and stayed put. The first base runner got to third just before Herman, who landed amongst them and the third baseman, knocking them asunder. The third baseman received the ball from the outfield and tagged all three runners, exclaiming "One of you has to be out!" Herman was a great hitter nonetheless. He batted .393 in 1930 with 416 total bases, 241 hits, and 143 runs scored – still Dodgers records. In 1935 he hit the first night-game home run in big league history. Only he and Bob Meusel have hit for the cycle three times. Herman hit 399 doubles in his career.
Playing Career: *1926-1937, 1945; Brk N, Cin N, Chi N, Pit N, Det A*

Tom Henke sets a major league record with 24 consecutive saves, August 1991.

Billy Herman.

Gene Hermanski
Hermanski, Eugene Victor
B: May 11, 1920

Pos: OF	BA: .272
Hits: 533	HRs: 46
RBI: 259	BBs: 289

Hermanski played in two World Series for the Dodgers, 1947 and 1949, but his best season was sandwiched between them. In 1948 he hit .290 with 15 home runs. On August 5 that year he hit three homers in one game.
Playing Career: *1943, 1946-1953; Brk N, Chi N, Pit N*

Keith Hernandez
Hernandez, Keith
B: Oct 20, 1953

Pos: 1B	BA: .298
Hits: 2,156	HRs: 161
RBI: 1,063	BBs: 1,056

Hernandez was likely the best-fielding first baseman of all time. The winner of 11 Gold Glove Awards, he holds the record for career assists by a first baseman. He frequently fielded bunts on the third base side, often forcing the baserunner at third on a sacrifice bunt. Hernandez was also a consistent .300 hitter with doubles power – he belted 424 of them. Leading the NL in batting with a .344 average in 1979, Hernandez was voted co-MVP with World Series hero Willie Stargell.

Hernandez led two teams to World Championships. In 1982 he hit .299 and drove in 94 runs, and the Cardinals defeated the Brewers in the Fall Classic. Then he anchored the best team since the 1961 Yankees, the 1986 Mets. Trying to overcome his reputation for abusing drugs, Hernandez was the team's most intense player. A great clutch hitter with a keen eye, he led the NL in walks and posted a .414 on-base percentage. When scorekeepers were tracking the game-winning RBI statistic, Hernandez set the season and lifetime records, with 24 in 1985 and 129 during his career.
Playing Career: *1974-1990; StL N, NY N, Cle A*

Ramon Hernandez
Hernandez y Gonzalez, Ramon
B: Aug 31, 1940

Pos: P	ERA: 3.03
W-L: 23-15	SOs: 255
ShOs: 0	Saves: 46

After spending nearly 10 years in the minors, Hernandez picked up a sidearm screwball which served him and the Pirates well. He teamed with Dave Giusti to give Pittsburgh the best bullpen in the NL, 1971-1975, when they won four division titles in five years.
Playing Career: *1967-1968, 1971-1977; Atl N, Chi N, Pit N, Bos A*

Billy Herman
Herman, William Jennings Bryan
B: Jul 7, 1909   D: Sep 5, 1992
Hall of Fame 1975

Pos: 2B	BA: .304
Hits: 2,345	HRs: 47
RBI: 839	BBs: 737
Managerial Record	
Won: 189 Lost: 274 Pct: .408	

Early in the 1941 season, Herman was purchased by Brooklyn. "I just bought a pennant," Dodger owner Larry MacPhail crowed. He was right. Herman and shortstop Pee Wee Reese meshed beautifully, and the Dodgers won their first flag in 21 years.

Herman was a great hit-and-run man and a clever second baseman who played on four pennant-winning teams. He hit over .300 eight times, and scored at least 100 runs five times on his way to 1,163 career tallies. Succeeding Rogers Hornsby at the keystone sack for the Cubs in 1932, Herman helped them win the flag. In 1935 he led the NL with 227 hits and 57 doubles, and reached career highs with a .341 average and 113 runs scored. His 18 triples in 1939 led the NL. He set an NL record by handling over 900 chances at second for five straight years. Herman was an All-Star 10 times, batting .433.
Playing Career: *1931-1943, 1946-1947; Chi N, Brk N, Bos N, Pit N*
Managerial Career: *1947, 1964-1966; Pit N, Bos A*

Keith Hernandez on deck for the St. Louis Cardinals in 1980.

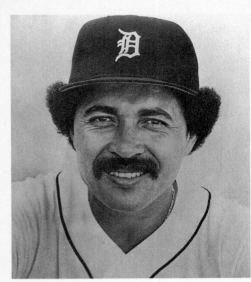

Willie Hernandez.

Willie Hernandez
Hernandez y Villanueva, Guillermo
B: Nov 14, 1954

Pos: P	ERA: 3.38
W-L: 70-63	SOs: 788
ShOs: 0	Saves: 147

Willie call-me-Guillermo Hernandez was the best pitcher in baseball during the 1984 season. His record of 9-3 with a 1.92 ERA, 32 saves in 33 chances, and his league-leading 80 appearances earned him both the MVP and Cy Young Awards. In 1985 he became the first Detroit pitcher to post back-to-back 30-save seasons, but losing a career-high 10 games Hernandez fell into disfavor with fickle Tigers fans.

Originally signed by the Phillies, Hernandez was drafted out of the minors by the Cubs, for whom he won 26 and saved 20 in six years. He reached his peak as the Tigers' stopper, but was hampered in 1985 by a number of annoying injuries that sapped his effectiveness. When he missed over 40 games on the disabled list in 1987, the Tigers replaced him with Mike Henneman.
Playing Career: *1977-1989; Chi N, Phi N, Det A*

Larry Herndon
Herndon, Larry Darnell
B: Nov 3, 1953

Pos: OF	BA: .273
Hits: 1,334	HRs: 107
RBI: 550	BBs: 353

The Sporting News named Herndon NL Rookie Player of the Year in 1976, when he batted .288 in 337 at-bats. In 1982 he hit three homers in one game. He was an important addition to the Tigers teams who won division championships in 1984 and 1987. Herndon batted over .300 both those years, and hit .333 in the 1984 World Series.
Playing Career: *1974, 1976-1988; StL N, SF N, Det A*

Tommy Herr
Herr, Thomas Mitchell
B: Apr 4, 1956

Pos: 2B	BA: .275
Hits: 1,262	HRs: 22
RBI: 493	BBs: 532

Herr guarded the keystone sack in one of the top infields of all time – with Keith Hernandez, Ozzie Smith and Ken Oberkfell. Smith and Herr led the NL in double plays three times. He made only six errors at second base in 1984, nine in 1986, and seven in 1987. The baseball world was stunned in 1985 when he batted in 110 runs with only eight homers. Herr appeared in five All-Star Games and three World Series.
Playing Career: *1979-1991; StL N, Min A, Phi N, NY N, SF N*

Ed Herrmann
Herrmann, Edward Martin
B: Aug 27, 1946

Pos: C	BA: .240
Hits: 654	HRs: 80
RBI: 320	BBs: 260

A backup catcher for most of his career, Herrmann still averaged more than 100 games per season, 1969-1974. He had the difficult task of blocking the knuckleballs of Wilbur Wood, resulting in his leading the AL in passed balls four times.
Playing Career: *1967, 1969-1978; Chi A, NY A, Cal A, Hou N, Mon N*

Garry Herrmann
Herrmann, August
B: May 3, 1859   D: Apr 25, 1931

Herrmann was the president of the Cincinnati Reds and the most influential member of the National Commission, which governed baseball from 1903 to 1919. He was instrumental in re-establishing the World Series, and in getting baseball through the lawsuits surrounding the short-lived Federal League. Herrmann's unique position developed because he held a position in the NL and he was a good friend of AL President and founder Ban Johnson.

Mike Hershberger
Hershberger, Norman Michael
B: Oct 9, 1939

Pos: OF	BA: .252
Hits: 900	HRs: 26
RBI: 344	BBs: 319

A fine outfielder who played regularly despite a low batting average, Hershberger recorded 17 assists in 1967. He lacked home run power but hit a fair number of doubles, slashing 26 in 1963, the year he batted .279 and hit three home runs.
Playing Career: *1961-1971; Chi A, KC A, Oak A, Mil A*

Orel Hershiser
Hershiser, Orel Leonard Quinton
B: Sep 16, 1958

Pos: P	ERA: 2.95
W-L: 128-96	SOs: 1,371
ShOs: 24	Saves: 5

At the end of the 1988 season, Hershiser pitched 10 scoreless innings against the Padres following five consecutive shutouts, to break Hall of Famer Don Drysdale's 58 scoreless innings record by one. The more fatigued Hershiser got when pitching, the more effective his sinkerball became. He tossed eight shutout innings in the NLCS opener against the Mets, bringing the number of scoreless innings to 67. He saved Game Four and finished off the Mets with a shutout in Game Seven.

In the World Series, Hershiser won Game Two against the A's with a three-hit shutout, hitting two doubles and a single himself. He

Garry Herrmann (r) with Benjamin Shibe.

won the finale on another complete game victory. The first NL player to be named MVP of both the NLCS and the World Series, Hershiser capped his awesome season with two awards – a Gold Glove and the Cy Young. Such exertion took its toll. After an anticlimactic 1989 season, the hurler required reconstructive shoulder surgery and sat out most of 1990, but returned in 1991.
Playing Career: *1983-; LA N*

Buck Herzog
Herzog, Charles Lincoln
B: Jul 9, 1885   D: Sep 4, 1953

Pos: 2B, SS, 3B, OF	BA: .259
Hits: 1,370	HRs: 20
RBI: 445	BBs: 427
Managerial Record	
Won: 165 Lost: 226 Pct: .422	

John McGraw and Buck Herzog had a love-hate relationship. Both men were opinionated, quick-tempered, and extremely competitive. Herzog stole 312 bases, but never hit over .300, never scored or drove in 100 runs, and never hit more than 6 homers in 13 years. Herzog did play on five pennant-winning teams in three different stints with the Giants. He batted .400 in the 1912 World Series.
Playing Career: *1908-1920; NY N, Bos N, Cin N, Chi N*
Managerial Career: *1914-1916; Cin N*

Royals Manager Whitey Herzog, 1979.

Whitey Herzog
Herzog, Dorrel Norman Elvert
B: Nov 9, 1931

Pos: OF	BA: .257
Hits: 414	HRs: 25
RBI: 172	BBs: 241
Managerial Record	
Won: 1,281 Lost: 1,125 Pct: .532	

The Yankees signed Herzog, but an injury and Mickey Mantle kept him from playing center field at Yankee Stadium. After his playing career, Herzog worked for the Mets, building their farm system, then coached for

the Rangers. Herzog took over the Royals in mid-1975 and piloted them to a second-place finish, then to three consecutive division titles. But the Royals lost the ALCS all three times, and when they finished second in 1979, Herzog was fired.

Crossing the state to St. Louis, Herzog had tremendous success. His Cardinals were World Champions in 1982 and won pennants in 1985 and 1987. "Whiteyball" meant a lineup of speedy, slick-fielding, line drive hitters, with a muscleman to bat cleanup, and plenty of left-handed pitching. Herzog was named Manager of the Year in 1976 by UPI, and in 1982 by *The Sporting News* and UPI. He was voted Manager of the Year by the Baseball Writers Association of America in 1985.
Playing Career: *1956-1963; Was A, KC A, Bal A*
Managerial Career: *1973-1990; Tex A, Cal A, KC A, StL N*

Joe Hesketh
Hesketh, Joseph Thomas
B: Feb 15, 1959

Pos: P	ERA: 3.72
W-L: 52-42	SOs: 643
ShOs: 2	Saves: 21

Prone to putter about on the mound, Hesketh was called for a balk before ever throwing his first major league pitch. His best season in Montreal was 1985, when he was 10-5. After two years in the bullpen, Hesketh got a new lease on life as a starter in Boston, where he was 12-4 in 1991.
Playing Career: *1984-; Mon N, Atl N, Bos A*

Otto Hess
Hess, Otto C.
B: Nov 13, 1878   D: Feb 24, 1926

Pos: P	ERA: 2.98
W-L: 70-90	SOs: 580
ShOs: 18	Saves: 5

Veterans pushed 14 bunts toward Hess in his major league debut, but he won the game 7-6. Born in Switzerland, Hess served in the U.S. Army during the Spanish-American War. His best major league season was 1906, when he compiled a record of 20-17.
Playing Career: *1902, 1904-1908, 1912-1915; Cle A, Bos N*

Ed Heusser
Heusser, Edward Burlton
B: May 7, 1909   D: Mar 1, 1956

Pos: P	ERA: 3.69
W-L: 56-67	SOs: 299
ShOs: 10	Saves: 18

A switch hitter who could also throw with either arm, Heusser bounced up and down between the majors and minors before emerging as a starter during World War II. In 1944 he won 13 and led the NL with a 2.38 ERA.
Playing Career: *1935-1936, 1938, 1940, 1943-1946, 1948; StL N, Phi N, Phi A, Cin N*

Joe Heving
Heving, Joseph William
B: Sep 2, 1900   D: Apr 11, 1970

Pos: P	ERA: 3.90
W-L: 76-48	SOs: 429
ShOs: 3	Saves: 63

In 1928 Heving led the Virginia League in wins, but the circuit disbanded on June 4, so he went to the South Atlantic League, where he led in ERA. He spent the rest of his 20-year baseball career bouncing between the majors and minors. In 1944 Heving was the only grandfather playing in the majors, but still topped the AL with 63 appearances, and a career-best 1.96 ERA. He led the league three times in relief wins.
Playing Career: *1930-1931, 1933-1934, 1937-1945; NY N, Chi A, Cle A, Bos A, Bos N*

John Heydler
Heydler, John Arnold
B: Jul 10, 1869   D: Apr 18, 1956

A former printer, umpire and sportswriter, Heydler was secretary to NL President Harry Pulliam, and filled in for him when Pulliam committed suicide in 1909. Heydler later became secretary-treasurer for John K. Tener, and succeeded him as NL president in 1918. Heydler supported the selection of Judge Kenesaw Mountain Landis as commissioner of baseball in 1920, helped establish the Baseball Hall of Fame, and proposed the designated hitter rule in 1928.
Umpiring Career: *1895-1897; NL*

Jim Hickman
Hickman, James Lucius
B: May 10, 1937

Pos: OF	BA: .252
Hits: 1,002	HRs: 159
RBI: 560	BBs: 491

Drafted from the Cardinals' organization, Hickman was one of the original Mets. He was the first Metropolitan to hit for the cycle and the first to hit three home runs in a game. Hickman made the NL All-Star team in 1970 when he batted .315 with 32 homers, 102 runs scored and 115 RBI.
Playing Career: *1962-1974; NY N, LA N, Chi N, StL N*

Piano Legs Hickman
Hickman, Charles Taylor
B: May 4, 1876   D: Apr 19, 1934

Pos: 1B, OF, 2B, P	BA: .295
Hits: 1,176	HRs: 59
RBI: 614	BBs: 153

One of baseball's early sluggers, Hickman just missed the 1902 Triple Crown with a .361 average, 11 homers and 110 RBI, finishing second in all three categories. Hickman, Nap Lajoie, and Bill Bradley were the first AL players to hit three consecutive home runs. Hickman always had problems in the field. In 1900 he set the NL record for errors at third

base with 91. When he tried pitching, Hickman compiled a record of 10-8 with three shutouts and four saves.
Playing Career: *1897-1908; Bos N, NY N, Bos A, Cle A, Det A, Was A, Chi A*

Kirby Higbe
Higbe, Walter Kirby
B: Apr 8, 1915   D: May 6, 1985

Pos: P	ERA: 3.69
W-L: 118-101	SOs: 971
ShOs: 11	Saves: 24

Higbe was a wrestling and drinking buddy of Ernest Hemmingway, who admired the ballplayer's life style, and encouraged him to write. The resulting autobiography, *The High Hard One*, describes Higbe's style on and off the field. He averaged one walk every two innings, yet won 54 percent of his games. Acquired from the Phillies for three players and $100,000 in 1941, Higbe and Whitlow Wyatt each won 22 games, taking the Dodgers to the NL pennant.
Playing Career: *1937-1943, 1946-1950; Chi N, Phi N, Brk N, Pit N, NY N*

Dodger pitcher Kirby Higbe, 1942.

Pinky Higgins
Higgins, Michael Franklin
B: May 27, 1909   D: Mar 21, 1969

Pos: 3B	BA: .292
Hits: 1,941	HRs: 141
RBI: 1,075	BBs: 800
Managerial Record	
Won: 560 Lost: 556 Pct: .502	

Higgins holds the major league record for hits in consecutive at-bats, with 12. He batted .333 in the 1940 World Series and handled a record 10 chances at third base in Game Four. After playing in the 1946 Series, Higgins retired. He scored 930 runs in his 14-year career, and was an All-Star three times. A man of infinite patience, Higgins was named Manager of the Year in 1955. He was later general manager and vice president for the Red Sox.
Playing Career: *1930, 1933-1944, 1946; Phi A, Bos A, Det A*
Managerial Career: *1955-1962; Bos A*

Andy High
High, Andrew Aird
B: Nov 21, 1897   D: Feb 22, 1981

Pos: 3B, 2B	BA: .284
Hits: 1,250	HRs: 44
RBI: 482	BBs: 425

There were three left-handed High brothers who played professional baseball during the 1920s, and Andy was the best. He started with Wilbert Robinson's "Daffiness Dodgers." High was a good hitter with little power who was shifted across the infield because he could play both second and third base well. He won a fielding title at third in 1929 with the Cardinals, whom he helped win three pennants, in 1928, 1930 and 1931.
Playing Career: *1922-1934; Brk N, Bos N, StL N, Cin N*

Dick Higham
Higham, Richard
B: Jul, 1851   D: Mar 18, 1905

Pos: C, OF, 2B, 3B, 1B	BA: .309
Hits: 550	HRs: 4
RBI: 147 (inc.)	BBs: 17
Managerial Record	
Won: 29 Lost: 11 Pct: .725	

Higham was the only umpire ever banned from the major leagues for dishonesty. The English-born player learned baseball from Boss Tweed's Mutuals team. He led the NL in doubles in 1876 and 1878, and in runs scored in 1878.
Playing Career: *1871-1876, 1878, 1880; NY Mutuals n, Bal Lord Baltimores n, Chi White Stockings n, Har N, Pro N, Tro N*
Managerial Career: *1874; NY Mutuals n*
Umpiring Career: *1881-1882; NL*

Oral Hilderbrand
Hilderbrand, Oral Clyde
B: Apr 7, 1907   D: Sep 8, 1977

Pos: P	ERA: 4.35
W-L: 83-78	SOs: 527
ShOs: 9	Saves: 13

The 6'3" right-hander was a star basketball player at Butler University, but Hilderbrand chose pro baseball because he saw no future in pro basketball. His best season was 1933, when he was 16-11 with a 3.76 ERA and was selected to the All-Star squad.
Playing Career: *1931-1940; Cle A, StL A, NY A*

Carmen Hill
Hill, Carmen Proctor
B: Oct 1, 1895   D: Jan 1, 1990

Pos: P	ERA: 3.44
W-L: 49-33	SOs: 264
ShOs: 5	Saves: 8

Pitching in the final game of the 1927 World Series against the Yankees, Hill gave up the home run to Babe Ruth that is pictured on the Bambino's postage stamp. Hill and Lee

Meadows were the first two pitchers to wear eyeglasses in the 20th century.
Playing Career: *1915-1916, 1918-1919, 1922, 1926-1930; Pit N, NY N, StL N*

Pete Hill
Hill, Preston
B: 1880   D: 1951

Pos: OF, 1B	BA: .308 (inc.)
Hits: 316 (inc.)	HRs: 16 (inc.)
RBI: NA	BBs: NA
Managerial Record (inc.)	
Won: 91 Lost: 65 Pct: .583	

Three of Rube Foster's greatest teams had Hill on the roster: the 1905 Philadelphia Giants, the 1910 Leland Giants, and the 1915 American Giants. Hill was captain of the American Giants for eight years. He later managed the Detroit Stars. A formidable defensive player, Hill could cover the outfield with speed and he had a strong, accurate arm. He was hard-hitting, with a trademark line drive that he could slash to all fields.
Playing Career: *1904-1925; Phi Giants, Chi Leland Giants, Chi Am Giants, Det Stars, Mil Bears, Bal Black Sox*
Managerial Career: *1920-1921, 1924-1925; Det Stars, Bal Black Sox*

Chuck Hiller
Hiller, Charles Joseph
B: Oct 1, 1934

Pos: 2B	BA: .243
Hits: 516	HRs: 20
RBI: 152	BBs: 157

Hiller was the first NL player to hit a grand slam in the World Series, connecting against the Yankees in 1962. He had some problems in the field, leading the NL second sackers with 29 errors in 1962. As a Met, Hiller led the NL with 15 pinch hits in 1966.
Playing Career: *1961-1968; SF N, NY N, Phi N, Pit N*

John Hiller
Hiller, John Frederick
B: Apr 8, 1943

Pos: P	ERA: 2.83
W-L: 87-76	SOs: 1,036
ShOs: 6	Saves: 125

Hiller nearly died when he suffered a massive stroke in 1971. After missing the 1971 season, he made a miraculous comeback as a batting-practice pitcher in June 1972, then returned to the lineup in time to help the Tigers win the division title. Hiller won Game Four of the ALCS. He was named Comeback Player of the Year and Fireman of the Year in 1973. He also compiled a 10-5 record with a 1.44 ERA and led the AL with 65 appearances and 38 saves that year.

The next season Hiller was chosen for the All-Star team, and posted 17 victories in relief. He is the Tigers' all-time saves leader. He set the major league record for saves with 38

John Hiller pitches in 1972, making a miraculous recovery from a stroke.

in 1973 – a mark that stood until Bruce Sutter broke it in 1984. Hiller, an Ontario native, was inducted into the Canadian Baseball Hall of Fame.
Playing Career: *1965-1970, 1972-1980; Det A*

Bill Hinchman
Hinchman, William White
B: Apr 4, 1883   D: Feb 21, 1963

Pos: OF	BA: .261
Hits: 793	HRs: 20
RBI: 369	BBs: 298

Hinchman took several shots at the big leagues before succeeding at age 32 with the Pirates in 1915. He batted .307 that year and .315 the next, while leading the NL in triples. As a scout for the Pirates, Hinchman signed Arky Vaughan, Lloyd Waner and Billy Cox.
Playing Career: *1905-1909, 1915-1918, 1920; Cin N, Cle A, Pit N*

Paul Hines
Hines, Paul A.
B: Mar 1, 1852   D: Jul 10, 1935

Pos: OF	BA: .302
Hits: 2,131	HRs: 56
RBI: 751 (inc.)	BBs: 366

The very first Triple Crown was awarded to Hines in 1878 when he hit .358, a career high, with four homers and 50 RBI in 62 games for Providence. Hines batted over .300 12 times. He was also famous for his running catches in

Paul Hines.

the outfield. One such catch in 1878 was labeled an unassisted triple play for years. Researchers have since found it to be an unassisted double play within a triple play.

Boston runners on first and third took off on a short fly over the shortstop's head. Hines charged in from center field to make a spectacular shoestring catch. He ran to third base to double off one runner, then threw to second to catch the other and complete the triple play. Some players later argued that both runners had rounded third before Hines tagged the base, thereby giving him an unassisted triple play. Newspaper accounts said Hines made two putouts and an assist.
Playing Career: *1872-1891; Was Nationals n, Was Washingtons n, Chi White Stockings n, Chi N, Pro N, Was N, Ind N, Pit N, Bos N, Was AA*

Chuck Hinton
Hinton, Charles Edward
B: May 3, 1934

Pos: OF, 1B, SS, 2B	BA: .264
Hits: 1,048	HRs: 113
RBI: 443	BBs: 416

The expansion Senators got Hinton in the 1960 draft, and he bade farewell to the winning Orioles organization. In Washington, Hinton was a star, batting .310 with 17 homers and 75 RBI in 1962. He played in the 1964 All-Star Game.
Playing Career: *1961-1971; Was A, Cle A, Cal A*

Larry Hisle
Hisle, Larry Eugene
B: May 5, 1947

Pos: OF	BA: .273
Hits: 1,146	HRs: 166
RBI: 674	BBs: 462

Soft-spoken Hisle was recruited for Ohio State University by the Governor of Ohio, then signed with the Phillies before graduating. A Topps Rookie All-Star in 1969, Hisle endured a sophomore jinx, and returned to the minors. He came back with the Twins, batting .314 in 1975 and .302 in 1977 when he led the AL with 119 RBI. As a free agent, Hisle signed a $3-million contract with the Brewers in 1978, when he delivered 34 homers and 115 RBI.
Playing Career: *1968-1971, 1973-1982; Phi N, Min A, Mil A*

Billy Hitchcock
Hitchcock, William Clyde
B: Jul 31, 1916

Pos: SS, 3B, 2B, 1B	BA: .243
Hits: 547	HRs: 5
RBI: 257	BBs: 264

Managerial Record
Won: 274   Lost: 261   Pct: .512

During the 1943-1945 baseball seasons, Hitchcock was in the Army Air Force and was awarded the Bronze Star. He returned to a

career as a versatile utility infielder, playing over 100 games in a season three times. Hitchcock guided the Braves during their first years in Atlanta, and also served baseball as a coach and scout. He was president of the Southern Association from 1971 to 1980.
Playing Career: *1942, 1946-1953; Det A, Was A, StL A, Bos A, Phi A*
Managerial Career: *1960, 1962-1963, 1966-1967; Det A, Bal A, Atl N*

Myril Hoag
Hoag, Myril Oliver
B: Mar 9, 1908   D: Jul 28, 1971

Pos: OF	BA: .271
Hits: 854	HRs: 28
RBI: 401	BBs: 252

Another World War II veteran who played baseball, Hoag batted .320 in three World Series for the Yankees before the war. He hit .295 in the 1939 All-Star Game. Hoag later went to the Florida State League, where he became a pitcher and led the league in batting and ERA.
Playing Career: *1931-1932, 1934-1942, 1944-1945; NY A, StL A, Chi A, Cle A*

Don Hoak
Hoak, Donald Albert
B: Feb 5, 1928   D: Oct 9, 1969

Pos: 3B	BA: .265
Hits: 1,144	HRs: 89
RBI: 498	BBs: 523

Hoak once batted off Fidel Castro in an International League game against the Havana Sugar Kings, walking on four weird pitches. His career had other bizarre events. In 1957 Hoak won an All-Star berth when Cincinnati fans stuffed the ballot box with votes for Reds players. He forced a rule change by letting a double play ground ball hit him as he ran the basepath, giving the batter a single and only one out instead of two. Hoak was the leader of the 1960 Pirates World Championship team.
Playing Career: *1954-1964; Brk N, Chi N, Cin N, Pit N, Phi N*

Glen Hobbie
Hobbie, Glen Frederick
B: Apr 24, 1936

Pos: P	ERA: 4.20
W-L: 62-81	SOs: 682
ShOs: 11	Saves: 6

For three years, 1958-1960, Hobbie was the Cubs' top pitcher. On April 2, 1959, he tossed a one-hit, 1-0 victory against the Cardinals. Stan Musial's two-out double in the seventh inning spoiled a perfect game. A strained shoulder ended Hobbie's career.
Playing Career: *1957-1964; Chi N, StL N*

Dick Hoblitzell
Hoblitzell, Richard Carleton (Doc)
B: Oct 26, 1888   D: Nov 14, 1962

Pos: 1B	BA: .278
Hits: 1,310	HRs: 27
RBI: 619	BBs: 407

A sure-handed first baseman for the Reds, Hoblitzell had plenty of power, but did not hit many home runs. Most of the ballparks of the era had 500-foot center field fences and some still allowed patrons to park their carriages around the outfield boundaries. Home runs were rare occurrences except in certain ballparks. Hoblitzell completed a rebuilding process for the Red Sox when he joined the team in 1914. They won the 1915 and 1916 World Series from the Phillies and Dodgers.
Playing Career: *1908-1918; Cin N, Bos A*

Butch Hobson
Hobson, Clell Lavern Jr.
B: Aug 17, 1951

Pos: 3B, DH, 1B	BA: .248
Hits: 634	HRs: 98
RBI: 397	BBs: 183
Managerial Record	
Won: 153 Lost: 171 Pct: .472	

Hobson became a Red Sox regular in 1977, setting team records for third basemen with 30 home runs and 112 RBI. He had hit 85 homers in three years, but his fielding was below par – he made 43 errors in 1978. The former University of Alabama football star signed a four-year free-agent contract with the Yankees in 1982, but blew out his elbow, and was sent down to AAA Columbus, where he played from 1983 to 1985. Hobson began his managerial career with Columbia in the South Atlantic League.
Playing Career: *1975-1982; Bos A, Cal A, NY A*
Managerial Career: *1992-; Bos A*

Johnny Hodapp
Hodapp, Urban John
B: Sep 26, 1905   D: Jun 14, 1980

Pos: 2B, 3B	BA: .311
Hits: 880	HRs: 28
RBI: 429	BBs: 163

AL pitching could not stop Hodapp, but knee injuries did. He batted .300 or more four straight seasons – .354 in 1930 when he led the league in hits and doubles. In 2,826 at-bats, Hodapp struck out only 136 times and walked only 163 times.
Playing Career: *1925-1933; Cle A, Chi A, Bos A*

Gil Hodges
Hodges, Gilbert Raymond
B: Apr 4, 1924   D: Apr 2, 1972

Pos: 1B	BA: .273
Hits: 1,921	HRs: 370
RBI: 1,274	BBs: 943
Managerial Record	
Won: 660 Lost: 753 Pct: .467	

One of the top guns in the Dodgers' potent arsenal from 1948 to 1959, Hodges was on the roster of seven of their pennant-winning

Reds first baseman Dick Hoblitzell.

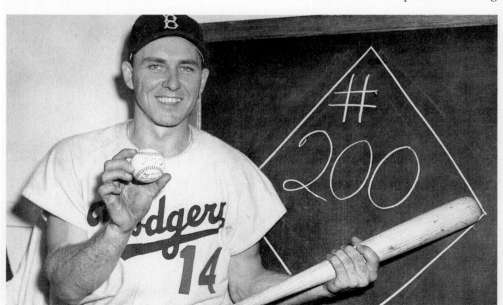
Gil Hodges holds the ball he belted for his 200th home run in 1954.

teams. He drove in 100 runs or more for seven consecutive years, making the All-Star team each time. Hodges was awarded the Gold Glove in 1957, 1958 and 1959. An even-tempered gentleman of immense physical power, Hodges relied on his inner strength to persevere through prolonged batting slumps and as manager of the dreadful Senators and pitiable Mets.

When he brought the Senators in at sixth place in 1967, it was considered a miracle, but his work with the Mets defies description. After finishing ninth in his first year, Hodges piloted the Amazing Mets to the NL pennant in 1969. The lineup of platoon and retread players was augmented by a young pitching staff of Tom Seaver, Jerry Koosman, Nolan Ryan, Gary Gentry and Tug McGraw. They defeated the favored Orioles in five games to sweep the World Series. The Mets retired Hodges's uniform number 14.
Playing Career: *1943, 1947-1963; Brk N, LA N, NY N*
Managerial Career: *1963-1971; Was A, NY N*

Billy Hoeft
Hoeft, William Frederick
B: May 17, 1932

Pos: P	ERA: 3.94
W-L: 97-101	SOs: 1,140
ShOs: 17	Saves: 33

Hoeft won 16 games for the Tigers in 1955 and 20 in 1956. He led the AL with seven shutouts in 1955, earning him a spot on the All-Star team. Hoeft then had a bullpen career, posting a 2.02 ERA in 1961. He once hit two home runs in one game.
Playing Career: *1952-1966; Det A, Bos A, Bal A, SF N, Mil N, Chi N*

Joe Hoerner
Hoerner, Joseph Walter
B: Nov 12, 1936

Pos: P	ERA: 2.99
W-L: 39-34	SOs: 412
ShOs: 0	Saves: 99

A weak heart forced Hoerner to switch to a less taxing sidearm delivery. As a red-hot reliever, he saved 60 games and posted ERAs under 2.00 for the 1966-1969 Cardinals. Hoerner was traded to the Phillies in 1970, the year he made the All-Star team.
Playing Career: *1963-1964, 1966-1977; Hou N, StL N, Phi N, Atl N, KC A, Phi N, Tex A, Cin N*

Bill Hoffer
Hoffer, William Leopold
B: Nov 8, 1870   D: July 21, 1959

Pos: P	ERA: 3.75
W-L: 91-46	SOs: 314
ShOs: 10	Saves: 3

The old National League Orioles depended on Hoffer as they won two pennants and then a Temple Cup. His winning percentage was the best in the NL in 1895 and 1896.

Glenn Hoffmann puts the tag on the Brewers' Ted Simmons in 1982.

Hoffer posted the first victory in the new AL, and celebrated at the AL 50th Anniversary bash.
Playing Career: *1895-1899, 1901; Bal N, Pit N, Cle A*

Danny Hoffman
Hoffman, Daniel John
B: Mar 2, 1880   D: Mar 14, 1922

Pos: OF	BA: .256
Hits: 761	HRs: 13
RBI: 235	BBs: 226

Port-side swinging Hoffman was snatched out of the Eastern League by Connie Mack. He was considered a top prospect when a pitch from Red Sox southpaw Jesse Tannehill hit him in the eye in 1904. Hoffman was the AL stolen base champ, with 46 in 1905 – 185 altogether.
Playing Career: *1903-1911; Phi A, NY A, StL A*

Glenn Hoffman
Hoffman, Glenn Edward
B: Jul 7, 1958

Pos: 3B, 2B, SS	BA: .242
Hits: 524	HRs: 23
RBI: 210	BBs: 136

Hoffman filled an infield hole for the Red Sox in the early 1980s. At the plate he had a disturbing tendency to follow a good season with a poor one. Hoffman spent most of the 1986 pennant-winning season on the disabled list and did not make Boston's postseason roster.
Playing Career: *1980-1987, 1989; Bos A, LA N, Cal A*

Solly Hofman
Hofman, Arthur Frederick (Circus Solly)
B: Oct 29, 1882   D: Mar 10, 1956

Pos: OF	BA: .269
Hits: 1,095	HRs: 19
RBI: 495	BBs: 421

Known for circus catches, Hofman was a star for the Cubs, who valued good defense. He played in three World Series, batting .306 in

1906 and .316 in 1908. He stole 208 bases in his career. Hofman was the sharp-eyed outfielder who spotted Merkle missing second in 1908.
Playing Career: *1903-1916; Pit N, Chi N, Brk F, Buf F, NY A*

Shanty Hogan
Hogan, James Francis
B: Mar 21, 1906   D: Apr 7, 1967

Pos: C	BA: .295
Hits: 939	HRs: 61
RBI: 474	BBs: 220

John McGraw traded Rogers Hornsby for Hogan and Jimmy Welsh. Hogan tried hard to continue the Giants' winning tradition. He hit more than .300 four of five years, and led NL receivers in fielding once, but could never bring home a pennant.
Playing Career: *1925-1937; Bos N, NY N, Was A*

Chief Hogsett
Hogsett, Elon Chester
B: Nov 2, 1903

Pos: P	ERA: 5.01
W-L: 63-87	SOs: 441
ShOs: 2	Saves: 33

The Cherokee reliever logged a 1.08 ERA in four games in two World Series for the Tigers. He won 11 games in relief to lead the AL in 1932. Hogsett left the majors in 1939 and pitched successfully for six years in AAA ball before returning for the Tigers' war effort.
Playing Career: *1929-1938, 1944; Det A, StL A, Was A*

Walter Holke
Holke, Walter Henry (Union Man)
B: Dec 25, 1892   D: Oct 12, 1954

Pos: 1B	BA: .287
Hits: 1,278	HRs: 24
RBI: 487	BBs: 191

In the 1920 Braves-Dodgers game that ended in a tie after 26 innings, Holke posted 42 putouts. A good fielder who batted over .300 twice, he was called "Union Man" for his

workmanlike attitude. Holke had been picked up in midseason by the Giants in 1916. With Buck Herzog, Art Fletcher, Heinie Zimmerman and Holke in the infield, the Giants steamrolled to an incredible 26 wins in a row. He later managed in the Three-I League for 20 years.
Playing Career: *1914, 1916-1925; NY N, Bos N, Phi N, Cin N*

Al Holland
Holland, Alfred Willis
B: Aug 16, 1952

Pos: P	ERA: 2.98
W-L: 34-30	SOs: 513
ShOs: 0	Saves: 78

"Gimme the ball!" was Holland's credo. He posted a 1.76 ERA and seven saves in his 1980 rookie year. Traded to the Phillies, he became their stopper, saving 54 games in two years, while posting a 2.26 ERA. He saved two games in 1983 postseason play.
Playing Career: *1977, 1979-1987; Pit N, SF N, Phi N, Cal A, NY A*

Bill Holland
Holland, Elvis William
B: Feb 2, 1901   D: Deceased

Pos: P	ERA: NA
W-L: 99-81 (inc.)	SOs: 576 (inc.)
ShOs: 7 (inc.)	Saves: 5 (inc.)

Holland was the top hurler for the New York Black Yankees in the 1930s. He led his league in victories three times, including 1930, when he had a 12-1 record. Holland pitched in New York for 18 seasons.
Playing Career: *1917, 1920-1934, 1936-1941; Ind ABCs, Det Stars, Chi Am Giants, NY Lincoln Giants, Brk Royal Giants, NY Black Yankees*

Bug Holliday
Holliday, James Wear
B: Feb 8, 1867   D: Feb 15, 1910

Pos: OF	BA: .316
Hits: 1, 155	HRs: 65
RBI: 617	BBs: 359

A fiesty batter, Holliday hit for the cycle on one occasion, and later scored six runs in one game in 1889, the year he hit .321 and led the AA in home runs. He later led the NL in round-trippers. Holliday stole 248 bases during his career.
Playing Career: *1889-1898; Cin AA, Cin N*
Umpiring Career: *1903; NL*

Al Hollingsworth
Hollingsworth, Albert Wayne
B: Feb 25, 1908

Pos: P	ERA: 3.99
W-L: 70-104	SOs: 608
ShOs: 7	Saves: 15

On May 28, 1938, Hollingsworth hit a grand slam home run off Lon Warneke. Hollings-

worth lost 104 games in his career, but played mainly with second-division teams. He appeared in the 1944 World Series for the Browns, and was later a good manager in the minors.
Playing Career: *1935-1940, 1942-1946; Cin N, Phi N, Brk N, Was A, StL A, Chi A*

Charlie Hollocher
Hollocher, Charles Jacob
B: Jun 11, 1896   D: Aug 14, 1940

Pos: SS	BA: .304
Hits: 894	HRs: 14
RBI: 241	BBs: 277

Hollocher led the NL with 161 hits in his 1918 rookie season. He took part in two triple plays and twice led the league in fielding average. Hollocher batted .340 in 1922, the highest mark for a shortstop since Honus Wagner. Illness forced him to retire early.
Playing Career: *1918-1924; Chi N*

Ken Holloway
Holloway, Kenneth Eugene
B: Aug 8, 1897   D: Sep 25, 1968

Pos: P	ERA: 4.40
W-L: 64-52	SOs: 293
ShOs: 4	Saves: 18

Manager Ty Cobb once fined Holloway $100 for refusing to throw a beanball at Joe Judge. A winning pitcher for Cobb in a period of escalating batting averages, Holloway dropped his ERA more than a whole run when he moved form Navin Field to League Park.
Playing Career: *1922-1930; Det A, Cle A, NY A*

Ducky Holmes
Holmes, James William
B: Jan 28, 1869   D: Aug 6, 1932

Pos: OF	BA: .282
Hits: 1,014	HRs: 17
RBI: 374	BBs: 236

When members of the press heard Holmes utter a racial slur against his team owner, Andrew Freedman, they elevated the incident to annoy proponents of Freedman's Syndicate Baseball and incite his opponents. Cantankerous Holmes got caught in the middle.
Playing Career: *1895-1899, 1901-1905; Lou N, NY N, StL N, Bal N, Det A, Was A, Chi A*

Tommy Holmes
Holmes, Thomas Francis
B: Mar 29, 1917

Pos: OF	BA: .302
Hits: 1,507	HRs: 88
RBI: 581	BBs: 480
Managerial Record	
Won: 61 Lost: 69 Pct: .469	

In 1945 Holmes hit safely in 37 consecutive games, setting the 20th-century NL record

Tommy Holmes.

that stood until Pete Rose broke it in 1978. Holmes had a great year: a .352 batting average with 28 homers, 47 doubles, 117 RBI, 125 runs scored, 15 stolen bases, and a slugging average of .577. He struck out only nine times all season, making him the only player ever to lead the league in home runs and fewest whiffs in the same season. He fanned a scant six times in 1949 and only eight times in 1950 – 122 times in his entire 11-year career.

Holmes was appointed the Braves' playing manager in mid-1951, but was fired early in the 1952 season. He went to the Dodgers as a pinch hitter, and appeared in the World Series that year. He later spent time lobbying Little League Baseball to use a rubber ball with raised seams to prevent the scores of deaths among young players who are hit with the baseball. Since Japan Little League adopted the rubber ball over a decade ago, no deaths have occurred from being hit by the ball.
Playing Career: *1942-1952; Bos N, Brk N*
Managerial Career: *1951-1952; Bos N*

Ken Holtzman
Holtzman, Kenneth Dale
B: Nov 3, 1945

Pos: P	ERA: 3.49
W-L: 174-150	SOs: 1,601
ShOs: 31	No-hitters: 2

Holtzman had it all: charisma, a fastball, and two no-hitters. Labeled the "New Koufax" as a 20-year-old rookie in 1966, Holtzman squared off against the old master on September 25 of that year. He took a no-hitter into the ninth inning but finished with a 2-1

Ken Holtzman is swarmed by fans after his no-hitter on August 19, 1969.

victory. Holtzman had a 9-0 record in 1967, when he spent most of the season in the military. In 1969 Holtzman went 17-13 for the second-place Cubs, tossed six shutouts, and pitched his first no-hitter.

Less than two years later he pitched a second no-hitter, beating the Reds 1-0. He was traded to Oakland, where he joined a staff that already included Catfish Hunter, Blue Moon Odom, and Vida Blue. Without the pressure of being the ace, Holtzman thrived, winning 77 games in four years as the A's took the division title each year. He was selected for the All-Star team in 1972 and 1973.
Playing Career: *1965-1979; Chi N, Oak A, Bal A, NY A*

Rick Honeycutt
Honeycutt, Frederick Wayne
B: Jun 29, 1952

Pos: P	ERA: 3.71
W-L: 101-139	SOs: 967
ShOs: 11	Saves: 31

Honeycutt hit .301 in his first pro season while playing first base and shortstop in addition to pitching. He was a superlative prospect stuck on a second-division team. Traded to the Rangers, he finally got everything together in 1983. Fashioning a 14-8 record, Honeycutt led the AL with a 2.42 ERA, but he was traded to the Dodgers before the end of the season. He has played on six division-winning teams in the last ten years.
Playing Career: *1977-; Sea A, Tex A, LA N, Oak A*

Harry Hooper.

Harry Hooper
Hooper, Harry Bartholomew
B: Aug 24, 1887   D: Dec 18, 1974
Hall of Fame 1971

Pos: OF	BA: .281
Hits: 2,466	HRs: 75
RBI: 817	BBs: 1,136

Playing alongside Tris Speaker and Duffy Lewis, Hooper was part of what was likely the best defensive outfield in the history of baseball. The trio played together from 1910 to 1915.

In the final game of the 1912 Series, Hooper ran back as far as he could, then leaped, speared Larry Doyle's high drive barehanded, and fell backward into the stands. Hooper's catch kept the Red Sox alive to win in the tenth. In 1915, after hitting only two home runs all season, he hit two in the final game of the World Series, the last one providing the margin of victory. After Tris Speaker moved to Cleveland, Lewis and Hooper helped the Red Sox win the 1916 title. Then Hooper and a new kid, Babe Ruth, led Boston to victory in 1918. In all, Hooper played 24 games in four World Series for Boston. Hooper was a leadoff hitter with a modest average, but he drew a lot of walks, enabling him to score 1,429 runs and steal 375 bases.
Playing Career: *1909-1925; Bos A, Chi A*

Burt Hooton
Hooton, Burt Carlton
B: Feb 17, 1950

Pos: P	ERA: 3.38
W-L: 151-136	SOs: 1,491
ShOs: 29	No-hitters: 1

At the University of Texas, Hooton was the ace of the pitching staff, going 35-3. He signed a $50,000 contract with the Cubs in 1971, and they sent him to Tacoma, where he tied a 66-year-old record with 19 strikeouts in a game. Hooton was called up that September, and was 2-0 with a 2.11 ERA. Later the Cubs grew disenchanted with Hooton and traded him to Los Angeles, where he fulfilled his early promise. Throwing the rarely seen knucklecurve, he anchored a Dodgers staff that won three NL pennants in five years.
Playing Career: *1971-1985; Chi N, LA N, Tex A*

Johnny Hopp
Hopp, John Leonard (Hippity)
B: Jul 18, 1916

Pos: OF, 1B	BA: .296
Hits: 1,262	HRs: 46
RBI: 458	BBs: 464

Hopp arrived too late to be part of the Gas House Gang, but he played with the same wild abandon as the 1930s Cardinals. In his first 100-game season as a regular, he substituted at first base for the injured Johnny Mize. Hopp batted .336 in 1944, the third consecutive year he and the Cardinals went to the World Series. He led outfielders with a

.997 fielding percentage that year. When Hopp hit .289, the Cardinals traded Mize to the Braves. Hopp played in one All-Star Game and five World Series.
Playing Career: *1939-1952; StL N, Bos N, Pit N, Brk N, NY A, Det A*

Joel Horlen
Horlen, Joel Edward
B: Aug 14, 1937

Pos: P	ERA: 3.11
W-L: 116-117	SOs: 1,065
ShOs: 18	No-hitters: 1

Jim Lonborg won the Cy Young Award in 1967, but Horlen had a great year, too. He posted a 19-7 record, leading the AL with a .731 winning percentage and a 2.06 ERA – and he tossed a no-hitter against the Tigers. He had taken a no-hitter into the ninth inning in 1963. In 1964 Horlen posted a 1.88 ERA with a 13-9 record. He pitched in both the 1972 ALCS and World Series for the A's.
Playing Career: *1961-1972; Chi A, Oak A*

Bob Horner
Horner, James Robert
B: Aug 6, 1957

Pos: 3B	BA: .277
Hits: 1,047	HRs: 218
RBI: 685	BBs: 369

As a rookie, Horner hit a home run in his first major league game. His team lost the game, but Horner won 1978 NL Rookie of Year honors. He never played in the minors, coming straight from the the campus of Arizona State University. Horner had constant weight and injury problems; he missed most of the 1984 season. He hit four homers in a losing effort in a nationally televised game.

When the Braves refused to make him a favorable offer in 1987, Horner went to Japan. The Cardinals picked him up in 1988.
Playing Career: *1978-1986, 1988; Atl N, StL N*

Rogers Hornsby
Hornsby, Rogers
B: Apr 27, 1896   D: Jan 5, 1963
Hall of Fame 1942

Pos: 2B	BA: .358
Hits: 2,930	HRs: 301
RBI: 1,584	BBs: 1,038
Managerial Record	
Won: 701 Lost: 812 Pct: .463	

Rogers Hornsby was the greatest right-handed hitter in the history of baseball. Like the greatest left-handed hitter, Ty Cobb, Hornsby was hard-headed and cantankerous. He never drank, smoked, read or watched movies because he wanted to protect his batting eye. Nicknamed "the Rajah," Hornsby had a royal disdain for the opinions and feelings of others.

The only right-handed batter to hit .400 three times, Hornsby achieved a .424 mark in 1924 to set a record for this century. He won six straight batting titles, 1920-1925, and added a seventh in 1928. Hornsby was at or near the top in multiple offensive categories for many years. Hornsby earned the Triple Crown two times and was honored as MVP twice. During his long baseball career Hornsby hit 169 triples, scored 1,579 runs, compiled a .577 slugging average, and managed the 1926 World Champion Cardinals.
Playing Career: *1915-1937; StL N, NY N, Bos N, Chi N, StL N*
Managerial Career: *1925-1928, 1930-1937, 1952-1953; StL N, NY N, Bos N, Chi N, StL A, Cin N*

Joe Hornung
Hornung, Michael Joseph (Ubbo Ubbo)
B: Jun 12, 1857   D: Oct 30, 1931

Pos: OF	BA: .257
Hits: 1,230	HRs: 31
RBI: 513	BBs: 120

When Hornung got a hit or made a good play, he exclaimed "Ubbo, Ubbo!" He played 464 consecutive games with the Bostons, helping them win the NL flag in 1883. According to the *Spalding Guide*, Hornung did not muff a fly ball during the entire 1884 season, a rare feat in those days before gloves were used.
Playing Career: *1879-1890; Buf N, Bos N, Bal AA, NY N*

Ricky Horton
Horton, Ricky Neal
B: Jul 30, 1959

Pos: P	ERA: 3.76
W-L: 32-27	SOs: 319
ShOs: 1	Saves: 15

The Cardinals were the beneficiaries of Horton's switch from starting to relieving in 1985. The crafty left-hander was great at working the corners and at holding runners on base. He was also frequently used as a pinch runner.
Playing Career: *1984-1990; StL N, Chi A, LA N*

Willie Horton.

Willie Horton
Horton, William Watterson
B: Oct 18, 1942

Pos: OF, DH	BA: .273
Hits: 1,993	HRs: 325
RBI: 1,163	BBs: 620

Horton made the dramatic throw in Game Five of the 1968 World Series that nailed Cardinals speedster Lou Brock at home plate. The play proved pivotal in that game and was the turning point of the Tigers' comeback after being down three games to one in the Series. Somebody forgot to tell Horton that

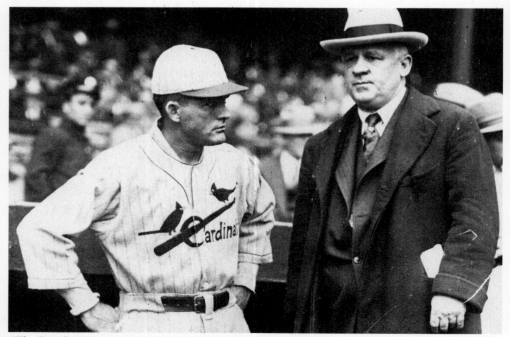
"The Rajah," Rogers Hornsby, with John McGraw in 1926.

1968 was the year of the pitcher. He slugged at a .543 clip and hit 36 home runs that year. Horton belted two home runs in a game 30 times during his career.

The four-time All-Star was remarkably consistent at the plate. He batted between .260 and .290 11 times, and slugged between .430 and .490 nine times. During an 18-year career Horton hit 284 doubles. He was the Tigers' left fielder for 10 seasons, then developed a second career as a designated hitter. In that role, he walloped 29 homers, good for 106 RBI for the Mariners in 1979.
Playing Career: *1963-1980; Det A, Tex A, Cle A, Oak A, Tor A, Sea A*

Pete Hotaling
Hotaling, Peter James (Monkey)
B: Dec 16, 1856   D: Jul 3, 1928

Pos: OF, C	BA: .267
Hits: 931	HRs: 9
RBI: 213	BBs: 224

Hotaling was typical of 19th-century players, changing teams almost every year. He even dropped back into the minors – to the Southern League – in 1886 because his friends went there to play. Hotaling was called "Monkey" for his ability to scramble after fly balls.
Playing Career: *1879-1888; Cin N, Cle N, Wor N, Bos N, Brk AA, Cle AA*

Sadie Houck
Houck, Sargent Perry
B: 1856   D: May 26, 1919

Pos: SS	BA: .250
Hits: 666	HRs: 4
RBI: 123	BBs: 48

Houck was reinstated from a blacklist in December 1882 because the NL feared that the new AA would sign all of its banned players. Houck went back to Detroit, the team that had ousted him. He later led AA shortstops in fielding with a .893 average.
Playing Career: *1879-1881, 1883-1887; Bos N, Pro N, Det N, Phi AA, Bal AA, Was N, NY AA*

Charley Hough
Hough, Charles Oliver
B: Jan 5, 1948

Pos: P	ERA: 3.70
W-L: 211-207	SOs: 2,297
ShOs: 12	Saves: 61

At age 45, knuckleballer Hough started and won the first game in Florida Marlins team history in April 1993. In a reversal of the usual scenario, Hough spent the first 10 years of his career as a reliever, then became a starter at age 34. Hough became the oldest pitcher in AL history to lead the league in starts and innings pitched when he topped those categories in 1987. He also helped the Rangers set a major league record with 73 passed balls, initiating 65 of them himself.
Playing Career: *1970-; LA N, Tex A, Chi A, Flo N*

Yankees Manager Ralph Houk (c) with Mickey Mantle (l) and Roger Maris.

Ralph Houk
Houk, Ralph George (Major)
B: Aug 9, 1919

Pos: C	BA: .272
Hits: 43	HRs: 0
RBI: 20	BBs: 12
Managerial Record	
Won: 1,619 Lost: 1,531 Pct: .514	

Combat veteran Houk won three pennants in his first three years as a manager with the Yankees. He had debuted as a catcher with the 1947 Yankees, and played in the World Series that year. But then Yogi Berra began catching full-time and Houk ended up on the bench. He played only 50 more games in seven seasons as Berra's backup. After a cameo appearance in the 1952 Series, he turned to managing.

Coaching in New York, 1958-1960, he learned the ropes and Yankees politics as he replaced Casey Stengel in 1961. Houk made Whitey Ford into a 25-game winner. He told Roger Maris and Mickey Mantle to try for Babe Ruth's home run record. The result of Houk's efforts was the best team in the last 50 years, the 1961 Yankees. Houk served the Yankees as vice president and general manager from 1964 to 1966.
Playing Career: *1947-1954; NY A*
Managerial Career: *1961-1963, 1967-1978, 1981-1984; NY A, Det A, Bos A*

Tom House
House, Thomas Ross
B: Apr 29, 1947

Pos: P	ERA: 3.79
W-L: 29-23	SOs: 261
ShOs: 0	Saves: 33

House caught Hank Aaron's 715th home run in the Braves' bullpen. As the Rangers' pitching coach, he wrote a book on baseball history and analysis. The reliever saved 11 in both 1974 and 1975 with the Braves.
Playing Career: *1971-1978; Atl N, Bos A, Sea A*

Art Houtteman
Houtteman, Arthur Joseph
B: Aug 7, 1927

Pos: P	ERA: 4.14
W-L: 87-91	SOs: 639
ShOs: 14	Saves: 20

Signed off the Detroit sandlots, Houtteman appeared with the Tigers at age 17. Later, the Army veteran overcame a fractured skull and the death of his child to continue his career. Houtteman won 15 of the Indians' 111 victories in 1954, and pitched in the World Series.
Playing Career: *1945-1950, 1952-1957; Det A, Cle A, Bal A*

Elston Howard
Howard, Elston Gene (Ellie)
B: Feb 23, 1929   D: Dec 14, 1980

Pos: C	BA: .274
Hits: 1,471	HRs: 167
RBI: 762	BBs: 373

Only two major leaguers have played in more World Series games than Howard, who appeared in 54. Coming from the Kansas City Monarchs, Howard compiled one the highest fielding percentages for a catcher in baseball history, .993. He was awarded Gold Gloves in 1963 and 1964. Howard pioneered the use of a hinged catchers mitt that led to the modern one-handed catching technique. Named to the AL All-Star team for nine consecutive years, Howard was also saluted as AL MVP in 1963 for his leadership abilities and his 28 homers and 85 RBI. A strong hitter, he topped .300 three times, with a high of .348 in 1961.
Playing Career: *1955-1968; NY A, Bos A*

Frank Howard
Howard, Frank Oliver (Hondo, Capital Punishment)
B: Aug 8, 1936

Pos: OF	BA: .273
Hits: 1,774	HRs: 382
RBI: 1,119	BBs: 782
Managerial Record	
Won: 93 Lost: 133 Pct: .412	

When 6'7", 255-pound Frank Howard came up to bat, the pitcher suddenly wanted to hide. Some of the mightiest blasts recorded in each stadium came from his bat. Howard won Rookie of the Year honors for rapping 23 homers with 77 RBI in 1960. He played in only one World Series, but it was the Dodgers' 1963 four-game sweep over the favored Yankees.

Called "Capital Punishment' when he played in Washington, Howard hit 44, 48, then 44 homers in 1968, 1969 and 1970. The 44-homer seasons put him in the AL lead in 1968 and 1970. Howard drove home 126 runs and walked 132 times in 1970. In 1968 – the Year of the Pitcher – Howard pounded 10 homers in 20 at-bats. Number 10, against Mickey Lolich, hit the roof at Tiger Stadium. The four-time All-Star is currently a batting instructor with the Yankees.
Playing Career: *1958-1973; LA N, Was A, Tex A, Det A*
Managerial Career: *1981, 1983; SD N, NY N*

Art Howe
Howe, Arthur Henry, Jr.
B: Dec 15, 1946

Pos: 3B, 1B, SS, 2B	BA: .260
Hits: 682	HRs: 43
RBI: 293	BBs: 275
Managerial Record	
Won: 392 Lost: 418 Pct: .484	

Howe finished his playing career in grand style at the World Series with the Cardinals in 1985. His best season was 1978, when he hit .293 with 33 doubles and seven homers, and compiled a .436 slugging average. After five years as a Rangers coach, Howe became the manager in Houston, where he built the Astros into formidable contenders with the wise use of younger players.
Playing Career: *1974-1982, 1984-1985; Pit N, Hou N, StL N*
Managerial Career: *1989-1993; Hou N*

Steve Howe
Howe, Steven Roy
B: Mar 10, 1958

Pos: P	ERA: 2.82
W-L: 38-37	SOs: 277
ShOs: 0	Saves: 73

The first Dodger rookie to save 17 games, Howe was named Rookie of the Year in 1980. He enjoyed four sparkling seasons, then climbed on the seesaw of drug abuse. Howe has been suspended from baseball five times, but keeps coming back.
Playing Career: *1980-1983, 1985, 1987, 1991-; LA N, Min A, Tex A, NY A*

Harry Howell
Howell, Henry Harry
B: Nov 14, 1876   D: May 22, 1956

Pos: P	ERA: 2.74
W-L: 131-146	SOs: 986
ShOs: 20	Saves: 6

After a mediocre start, Howell learned the spitball and became the workhorse of the 1904-1908 Browns, averaging 308 innings and 15 wins a season. Unfortunately, Howell was involved in pressuring the St. Louis official scorer to give an extra base hit to Nap Lajoie on the last day of the 1910 season. Popular Lajoie and the hated Ty Cobb were in a tight race for the batting title. Lajoie had eight hits against the Browns that day, but Cobb still took the title by a point. Howell was released.
Playing Career: *1898-1910; Brk N, Bal N, Bal A, NY A, StL A*

Dodger reliever Jay Howell, 1988.

Jay Howell
Howell, Jay Canfield
B: Nov 26, 1955

Pos: P	ERA: 3.22
W-L: 54-52	SOs: 644
ShOs: 0	Saves: 153

One of the hardest-throwing relief pitchers in baseball, Howell battles inconsistency. His ERA has been under 2.00 twice, and over 5.00 three times. Inexplicably, he made the All-Star team in 1987 when he was 3-4 with 16 saves and a 5.89 ERA. After a good season in 1988, Howell self-destructed in postseason play. He was 0-1 with a 27.00 ERA in the NLCS, and 0-1 with one save and a 3.38 ERA in the World Series.
Playing Career: *1980-; Cin N, NY A, Oak A, LA N, Atl N*

The Senators' heavy-hitting Frank Howard signs autographs for fans in 1971.

Ken Howell
Howell, Kenneth
B: Nov 28, 1960

Pos: P	ERA: 3.95
W-L: 38-48	SOs: 549
ShOs: 1	Saves: 31

Howell once fanned 14 consecutive batters in winter ball. A hard thrower, he averaged nearly one strikeout per inning. After being traded twice in six days, ending up with Philadelphia, Howell went 12-12 with a 3.44 ERA for the Phillies, who were in the cellar.
Playing Career: *1984-1990; LA N, Phi N*

Roy Howell
Howell, Roy Lee
B: Dec 18, 1953

Pos: 3B	BA: .261
Hits: 991	HRs: 80
RBI: 454	BBs: 318

Drafted from the Rangers in 1977, Howell became a star for the expansion Blue Jays. In September of that year, he set a team record with nine RBI in one game against the Yankees. He appeared in postseason play with the Brewers in 1981 and 1982.
Playing Career: *1974-1984; Tex A, Tor A, Mil A*

Dick Howser
Howser, Richard Dalton
B: May 14, 1936   D: Jun 17, 1987

Pos: SS	BA: .248
Hits: 617	HRs: 16
RBI: 165	BBs: 367

Managerial Record
Won: 507   Lost: 425   Pct: .544

Six months after he piloted his Royals to victory in the 1985 World Series, Howser learned that he had cancer. When he died, all of Kansas City mourned.

The feisty shortstop had signed with the Athletics for a reported $21,000 bonus and had a great rookie season. He hit .280, stole 37 bases, scored 108 runs, and was named AL Rookie of the Year by *The Sporting News.* Howser led AL shortstops in putouts – and errors – that year. In his first full season as a manager, Howser won the AL East division title for the Yankees, but was sacked when they lost the 1980 ALCS to the Royals. Kansas City grabbed him in late 1981. Howser led the Royals to the division playoffs that year and again in 1984. The 1985 World Series triumph was a fitting end to his career.
Playing Career: *1961-1968; KC A, Cle A, NY A*
Managerial Career: *1978, 1980-1986; NY A, KC A*

Dummy Hoy
Hoy, William Ellsworth
B: May 23, 1862   D: Dec 15, 1961

Pos: OF	BA: .288
Hits: 2,054	HRs: 40
RBI: 726	BBs: 1,004

Umpire hand signals were developed so that deaf outfielder Hoy could read calls of "out," "safe," "strike," and "ball." A good all-around player, he scored 1,426 runs and stole 597 bases during his career, 82 of them in his rookie year. Hoy was fast and smart. In one game he threw out three men at home plate from the outfield. He hit over .290 in nine of 14 seasons. In 1961, at the age of 99, Hoy tossed the ceremonial first pitch of the World Series between the Reds and the Yankees.
Playing Career: *1888-1899, 1901-1902; Was N, Buf P, StL AA, Cin N, Lou N, Chi A*

LaMarr Hoyt
Hoyt, Dewey LaMarr
B: Jan 1, 1955

Pos: P	ERA: 3.99
W-L: 98-68	SOs: 681
ShOs: 8	Saves: 10

Only 26 percent of all batters who faced Hoyt in 1983 reached base. He won 24 games that year, then was 1-0 in the ALCS. The White Sox lost to the Orioles, but Hoyt won the Cy Young Award. He first joined Chicago's starting rotation in 1982, winning nine consecutive decisions en route to a league-leading 19 victories. Control was his secret. Lack of self-control was his downfall. He was suspended for one year in 1987 for drug abuse, and later imprisoned for repeat violations.
Playing Career: *1979-1986; Chi A, SD N*

Waite Hoyt
Hoyt, Waite Charles (Schoolboy)
B: Sep 9, 1899   D: Aug 25, 1984
Hall of Fame 1969

Pos: P	ERA: 3.59
W-L: 237-182	SOs: 1,206
ShOs: 26	Saves: 52

"The secret of success," Hoyt once said, "is to pitch for the New York Yankees." Hoyt's baseball career included trying out for the Giants in the Polo Grounds as a schoolboy, becoming a star pitcher with baseball's greatest team, developing into a crafty relief pitcher, a radio broadcaster, and an oil painter whose works hang in the Baseball Hall of Fame. His greatest years came as a hurler for the Yankees. His 237 wins are augmented by 52 saves.

Hoyt went to seven World Series with the Yankees and A's. In the 1921 Series he pitched 27 innings without allowing an earned run – tying Christy Mathewson's World Series record – but lost the finale on an error. After being reunited with coach Babe Ruth on the 1938 Dodgers, Hoyt called it a career and became one of the most entertaining radio broadcasters in the game. Cincinnati fans

Kansas City's Dick Howser steams into home to score against the Indians, 1962.

wished for rain delays when Hoyt would spin his yarns of the good ol' days. Almost every Yankees book for 60 years used the venerable broadcaster as its source.

Playing Career: *1918-1938; NY N, Bos A, NY A, Det A, Phi A, Brk N, Pit N*

Al Hrabosky

Hrabosky, Alan Thomas (Mad Hungarian)
B: Jul 21, 1949

Pos: P	ERA: 3.11
W-L: 64-35	SOs: 548
ShOs: 0	Saves: 97

One of the most effective relievers of the 1970s, Hrabosky was named NL Fireman of the Year by *The Sporting News* in 1975. That year he compiled a record of 13-3 and 22 saves with an awesome 1.67 ERA. As a free agent in 1979, Hrabosky signed a multimillion-dollar contract with Atlanta, but posted only seven saves there. After retiring from his playing career, the Mad Hungarian became a broadcaster for the Cardinals.

Playing Career: *1970-1982; StL N, KC A, Atl N*

Kent Hrbek

Hrbek, Kent Allen
B: May 21, 1960

Pos: 1B, DH	BA: .283
Hits: 1,675	HRs: 283
RBI: 1,033	BBs: 801

Hrbek is a hometown boy who is starring for the team he followed as a youth, the Minnesota Twins. He was an instant fan favorite when he came up in 1982, and will always be remembered for hitting the first home run in the Hubert H. Humphrey Metrodome in an exhibition game against the Phillies on April 3, 1982. Hrbek made the final putout in the game that clinched the 1987 AL Western Division, then made the final putouts in the last games of the ALCS and World Series, all played at home before maniacal fans. He hit the 14th grand slam in Series history in Game Six. Not only a tremendous home run hitter, averaging 22 homers per year for 13 years, Hrbek has soft hands at first. He led AL first sackers in fielding with a .997 mark in 1990. He played in the 1982 All-Star Game, but strangely none since. Hrbek anchored the Twins' 1991 Championship team.

Playing Career: *1981-; Min A*

Cal Hubbard

Hubbard, R. Cal
B: Oct 31, 1900   D: Oct 17, 1977
Hall of Fame 1976

The only man who is a member of three national sports shrines – the Baseball Hall of Fame, Football Hall of Fame, and College Football Hall of Fame, Hubbard was an efficient and authoritative umpire who was respected both for his imposing size and for his great ability. After eight years in the minors, he reached the AL in 1936, then excelled at his job for 15 seasons before a hunting accident led to his premature retirement. Hubbard had taken up umpiring in the summers while still an NFL football player. After retiring from the playing field, he was a supervisor of umpires for the AL for another 15 years.

Umpiring Career: *1937-1951; AL (4 WS, 3 AS)*

Glenn Hubbard

Hubbard, Glenn Dee
B: Sep 25, 1957

Pos: 2B	BA: .244
Hits: 1,084	HRs: 70
RBI: 448	BBs: 539

Hubbard was known for using the smallest glove in baseball. He led NL second basemen three times in double plays and twice in assists. His best season at the plate was 1983, when he hit .263 and smacked 12 round-trippers. He was also selected for the All-Star Game that year. As he got older and learned how to position himself for specific batters, Hubbard's range expanded. He played in the 1988 World Series for the losing Athletics, but he hit well and had a stolen base. In 1989 the A's replaced him with a platoon of Tony Phillips and Mike Gallego.

Playing Career: *1978-1989; Atl N, Oak A*

Carl Hubbell

Hubbell, Carl Owen (King Carl, The Meal Ticket)
B: Jun 22, 1903   D: Nov 21, 1988
Hall of Fame 1947

Pos: P	ERA: 2.97
W-L: 253-154	SOs: 1,678
ShOs: 36	No-hitters: 1

King Carl, with his gaunt, unshaven, yet smiling face, was a tireless worker, and a hero during the Depression. Hubbell tossed so many screwballs that his left hand faced outward, instead of inward, when at rest by his side. In the 1934 All Star Game, he fanned Babe Ruth, Lou Gehrig, Jimmie Foxx, Al Simmons and Joe Cronin in succession. It gave the AL a taste of what NL batters had to put up with during the 1930s. In 1933 Hubbell had burst upon the scene as a superior pitcher with an 18-inning shutout, 46 scoreless innings, 10 shutouts, and an ERA of 1.66. He was honored as MVP that year.

In the 1933 World Series against the Senators, Hubbell tossed 20 innings without giving up an unearned run. He captured a second MVP Award in 1936 when he ended the season on a 16-game winning streak. He won 20 or more games for five straight seasons and saved 33 games. An All-Star nine times, Hubbell worked for the Giants until 1977, when a stroke relegated him to part-time scouting duties. The Giants retired his number 11.

Playing Career: *1928-1943; NY N*

Ken Hubbs

Hubbs, Kenneth Douglass
B: Dec 23, 1941   D: Feb 15, 1964

Pos: 2B	BA: .247
Hits: 310	HRs: 14
RBI: 98	BB: 74

Raw, brash Hubbs was chosen Rookie of the Year and awarded a Gold Glove in 1962. That year he set a record with 78 consecutive errorless games at the keystone sack, handling 418

Kent Hrbek.

Umpire Cal Hubbard.

The Giants' ace hurler Carl Hubbell in 1936, the year he won his second MVP Award.

The 1927 Yankees may have been the greatest team of all time, and Huggins was their manager. Both the 1927 and 1928 teams swept the World Series in four straight games. Huggins managed Babe Ruth – a formidable task. He fought the Babe, fined him, suspended him, was dangled over the rear platform of trains by him, and above all won pennants with him – six in eight years.

As a player, Huggins scored 947 runs, stole 324 bases and invented the delayed double steal. He was an exceptional fielder, frequently recording 14 or 15 chances in a game. After Huggins prodded two third-place finishes from mediocre St. Louis teams, he came to the attention of Yankees owner Jacob Ruppert. Huggins took NL techniques to the Yankees and stood the AL on its head. When the little guy died suddenly of blood poisoning in 1929, Ruth cried unashamedly at the news. Their monuments now stand side by side in Yankee Stadium's center field.
Playing Career: *1904-1916; Cin N, StL N*
Managerial Career: *1913-1929; StL N, NY A*

Jim Hughes
Hughes, James Jay
B: Jan 22, 1874   D: Jun 2, 1924

Pos: P	ERA: 3.00
W-L: 83-41	SOs: 370
ShOs: 8	No-hitters: 1

Hughes averaged 21 wins a year in the major leagues. In 1899 he led the NL in victories with 28, and in winning percentage with a .824 mark. Preferring to play near his Sacramento home, Hughes left the majors in 1903 when the Pacific Coast League formed.
Playing Career: *1898-1899, 1901-1902; Bal N, Brk N*

chances. He perished young in an attempt to pilot his new plane in a snowstorm.
Playing Career: *1961-1963; Chi N*

Willis Hudlin
Hudlin, George Willis (Ace)
B: May 23, 1906

Pos: P	ERA: 4.41
W-L: 158-156	SOs: 677
ShOs: 11	Saves: 31

One word said it all when it came to Hudlin's pitching prowess – Ace. Only Mel Harder and Bob Feller pitched more games for the Indians than Hudlin. Never quite winning 20 games in a season, he was still effective, particularly against the Yankees. He won 14 from the Bronx Bombers when they had the Murderers' Row lineup, 1927-1929. The pedagogical Hudlin served as a coach for Detroit from 1957 to 1959.
Playing Career: *1926-1940, 1944; Cle A, Was A, StL A, NY N*

Sid Hudson
Hudson, Sidney Charles
B: Jan 3, 1917

Pos: P	ERA: 4.28
W-L: 104-152	SOs: 734
ShOs: 11	Saves: 13

Hudson broke in with 17 wins his rookie season. The next two years he was selected for the All-Star team. A good-hitting pitcher, Hudson batted .308 in 1947. After playing until age 39, Hudson became a pitching coach, instructor and scout.
Playing Career: *1940-1942, 1946-1954; Was A, Bos A*

Miller Huggins
Huggins, Miller James
B: Mar 27, 1879   D: Sep 25, 1929
Hall of Fame 1964

Pos: 2B	BA: .265
Hits: 1,474	HRs: 9
RBI: 318	BBs: 1,002
Managerial Record	
Won: 1,413 Lost: 1,134	Pct: .555

Hall of Fame Manager Miller Huggins piloted the Yanks to six pennants.

Long Tom Hughes
Hughes, Thomas James
B: Nov 29, 1878   D: Feb 8, 1956

Pos: P   ERA: 3.09
W-L: 131-175   SOs: 1,368
ShOs: 25   Saves: 16

As a rookie, Hughes tossed 308 innings, completing 32 games and striking out 225. In 1903 Hughes won 20 games for the pennant-bound Boston club. Pitching in the first World Series, Hughes was the third pitcher behind Cy Young and Bill Dineen. Hughes lost Game Three, being relieved in the third inning by Young. No other Red Sox pitcher appeared in the Series.
Playing Career: *1900-1909, 1911-1913; Chi N, Bal A, Bos A, NY A, Was A*

Roy Hughes.

Roy Hughes
Hughes, Roy John (Jeep)
B: Jan 11, 1911

Pos: SS   BA: .273
Hits: 705   HRs: 5
RBI: 205   BBs: 222

Hughes broke in with the Indians, hitting .293 and .295 in his first two years. He scored 112 runs and stole 20 bases in 1936, his only year as a regular. Hughes played shortstop for the Cubs in the 1945 World Series, hitting .295 in the seven-game loss to the Tigers.
Playing Career: *1935-1940, 1944-1946; Cle A, StL A, Phi N, Chi N*

Tom Hughes
Hughes, Thomas L.
B: Jan 28, 1884   D: Nov 1, 1961

Pos: P   ERA: 2.56
W-L: 56-39   SOs: 476
ShOs: 9   No-hitters: 2

A very tough pitcher, Hughes threw two no-hitters, losing one in the 11th inning, and striking out Honus Wagner to end the game in the other. In 1915 and 1916 he won 16 games, and in the latter year he also had 5 saves and led the NL with a won-lost percentage of .842.
Playing Career: *1906-1907, 1909-1910, 1914-1918; NY A, Bos N*

Tex Hughson
Hughson, Cecil Carlton
B: Feb 9, 1916   D: Aug 6, 1993

Pos: P   ERA: 2.94
W-L: 96-54   SOs: 693
ShOs: 19   Saves: 17

A three-time All-Star with a fastball and a sharp curve, Hughson won 22 games in 1942 and 20 in 1946. He threw 200 innings or more four times, and led the AL in winning percentage in 1944. Arm problems prematurely ended the World War II veteran's career.
Playing Career: *1941-1944, 1946-1949; Bos A*

William Hulbert
Hulbert, William Ambrose (Bill)
B: Oct 23, 1832   D: Apr 10, 1882

William Hulbert was the founder of the National League. As owner of the Chicago White Stockings, Hulbert thought it might be nice to have a league with enforced rules, regular schedules, civilized behavior, and scores that were not known until the games had been played. In 1876 he called together like-minded owners and convinced them to organize. They called their new alliance the National League of Professional Base Ball Clubs. As a sop to the eastern teams, they elected Morgan Bulkeley of Hartford as league president.

In 1877, after Chicago had won the first NL pennant, Bulkeley did not show up at the league meeting. The club owners then elected Hulbert president. He acted arbitrarily at times, kicking New York and Philadelphia out of the league for failing to fulfill their schedules, banning four players for life for throwing games, and chasing St. Louis and

William Hulbert.

Cincinnati out of the league because of repeated liquor violations. At the time of his death, however, Hulbert was recognized as the "Saviour of the Game."

Rudy Hulswitt
Hulswitt, Rudolph Edward
B: Feb 23, 1877

Pos: SS, 2B, 3B   BA: .253
Hits: 564   HRs: 3
RBI: 203   BBs: 136

A good-hitting, part-time infielder for two dreadful teams in the first decade of the 20th century, Hulswitt played on clubs that finished seventh or eighth in five of six seasons. He batted .280 in 1909, and had 22 doubles in 1903.
Playing Career: *1899, 1902-1904, 1908-1910; Lou N, Phi N, Cin N, StL N*

Tom Hume
Hume, Thomas Hubert
B: Mar 29, 1953

Pos: P   ERA: 3.85
W-L: 57-71   SOs: 536
ShOs: 0   Saves: 92

Hume emerged as the winner of the relief sweepstakes in Cincinnati after Sparky Anderson and his bullpen-by-committee idea left town. In 1980 the bespectacled hurler was named co-winner of the NL Fireman of the Year Award, with a record of 9-10, 25 saves, and a 2.56 ERA. That winter, he and teammate Bill Bonham were trapped in a Las Vegas hotel fire and had to be rescued from the roof. Hume injured his knee in 1982 in a turf seam, and was never very effective again.
Playing Career: *1977-1987; Cin N, Phi N*

John Hummel
Hummel, John Edwin
B: Apr 4, 1883   D: May 18, 1959

Pos: 2B, OF   BA: .254
Hits: 991   HRs: 29
RBI: 394   BBs: 346

Hummel's career in organized baseball spanned 24 years. He managed minor league teams in Saskatoon, Binghamton, Harrisburg, Scranton and Wheeling, then finished at Springfield in 1927. Hummel was the starting second baseman for the Dodgers in 1910 and 1911, leading the NL in fielding both years.
Playing Career: *1905-1918; Brk N, NY A*

Bert Humphries
Humphries, Albert
B: Sep 26, 1880   D: Sep 21, 1945

Pos: P   ERA: 2.79
W-L: 50-43   SOs: 258
ShOs: 9   Saves: 6

The lowest ERA ever recorded in minor league history belonged to Humphries at

Tampa in the 1920 Florida State League. It was a 0.76 mark. He had one outstanding season in the majors, for the 1913 Cubs, when he led the NL with an .800 winning percentage and was 16-4 with a 2.69 ERA.
Playing Career: *1910-1915; Phi N, Cin N, Chi N*

Johnny Humphries
Humphries, John William
B: Jun 23, 1915   D: Jun 24, 1965

Pos: P	ERA: 3.78
W-L: 52-63	SOs: 317
ShOs: 9	Saves: 12

Humphries had a 20-7 record – including a no-hitter – in the 1937 Southern Association. He jumped to Cleveland in 1938, leading the AL with 45 appearances and eight relief wins as the Indians' Rookie of the Year. All four of Humphries's 1941 White Sox victories were shutouts.
Playing Career: *1938-1946; Cle A, Chi A, Phi N*

Randy Hundley
Hundley, Cecil Randolph (Hot Rod)
B: Jun 1, 1942

Pos: C	BA: .236
Hits: 813	HRs: 82
RBI: 381	BBs: 271

The greatest Cubs catcher since Gabby Hartnett, Hundley and the Cubs almost won a pennant in 1969, the third year in a row that he caught more than 150 games. He won a Gold Glove in 1967, when he committed only four errors.
Playing Career: *1964-1977; SF N, Chi N, Min A, SD N*

Ron Hunt
Hunt, Ronald Kenneth
B: Feb 23, 1941

Pos: 2B	BA: .273
Hits: 1,429	HRs: 39
RBI: 370	BBs: 555

"Some people give their bodies to science, I give mine to baseball," explained Hunt, who was a master of being hit by pitches. He retired with two major league records for Hit By Pitcher: 243 career; 50 in 1971; and a tie for three in a game. Hunt made the All-Star team in 1964 and 1966. He seldom struck out, fanning only 19 times in 1973 and again in 1974, for a total of 382 in 12 years.
Playing Career: *1963-1974; NY N, LA N, SF N, Mon N, StL N*

Billy Hunter
Hunter, Gordon William
B: Jun 4, 1928

Pos: SS	BA: .219
Hits: 410	HRs: 16
RBI: 144	BBs: 111
Managerial Record	
Won: 146 Lost: 108 Pct: .575	

Catfish Hunter (l) is kidded in the dugout by Bobby Bonds, 1975.

Hunter worked the hidden ball trick on Jimmy Piersall twice in 1953. He was an All-Star as a fancy-fielding Browns rookie who was hitting .252 at the time, but finished the season at .219. As the Orioles' third base coach, Hunter was famous for his frenetic, arm-wheeling "Go!" signal.
Playing Career: *1953-1958; StL A, Bal A, NY A, KC A, Cle A*
Managerial Career: *1977-1978; Tex A*

Catfish Hunter
Hunter, James Augustus
B: Apr 8, 1946
Hall of Fame 1987

Pos: P	ERA: 3.26
W-L: 224-166	SOs: 2,012
ShOs: 42	No-hitters: 1

Catfish Hunter was the ace of the great A's teams in the early 1970s, then he helped the Yankees win three straight pennants in the second half of the decade. In his first season, the 18-year-old right hander pitched only batting practice for the A's. In 1965 Hunter became a regular starter and went 8-8. He was named to the AL All-Star team in 1967, the year his record was 13-17 with the tenth-place A's. He pitched a perfect game in 1968 but did not have a winning season until 1970, when he was 18-14.

In 1971, 1972 and 1973 Hunter went 21-11, 21-7, and 21-5. He won the Cy Young Award in 1974 with a 25-12 mark and a league-leading 2.49 ERA. The A's won three World championships, 1972-1974, with his help. Hunter sued A's owner Charlie Finley for breach of contract and ended up winning a bigger award than the Cy Young – a five-year, $3.75 million contract with the Yankees. His best year in New York was his first, when he was 25-14. In postseason play Hunter was 4-3 in 10 ALCS games, and 5-3 in 12 World Series games.
Playing Career: *1965-1979; KC A, Oak A, NY A*

Clint Hurdle
Hurdle, Clinton Merrick
B: Jul 30, 1957

Pos: OF, 1B, C	BA: .259
Hits: 360	HRs: 32
RBI: 193	BBs: 176

The right fielder for the 1980 Royals, Hurdle hit .294 with 10 homers and 60 RBI, helping his team win the AL pennant. He hit .417 in the 1980 World Series. The former number one draft pick was laid up with a back injury most of 1981, and was never able to regain his stroke.
Playing Career: *1977-1983, 1985-1987; KC A, Cin N, NY N, StL N*

Bruce Hurst
Hurst, Bruce Vee
B: Mar 24, 1958

Pos: P	ERA: 3.86
W-L: 143-112	SOs: 1,665
ShOs: 23	Saves: 0

Hurst excelled at Fenway Park – unusual for a left-hander – winning 56 games there. Mel Parnell is the only southpaw with more victories in front of the Green Monster. Hurst

whipped the Mets twice in the 1986 World Series, and had been voted Series MVP before the Mets rallied to win Game Six. The award was presented to Ray Knight when the Mets won the final game. Hurst became baseball's most coveted free agent after the 1988 season.
Playing Career: *1980-; Bos A, SD N, Col N*

Fred Hutchinson
Hutchinson, Frederick Charles
B: Aug 12, 1919   D: Nov 12, 1964

Pos: P	ERA: 3.73
W-L: 95-71	SOs: 591
ShOs: 13	Saves: 7

Managerial Record
Won: 830   Lost: 827   Pct: .501

At age 18, Hutchinson approached his hometown Seattle Rainiers and told them that he was going to be a star and that they should sign him to sell to the majors. The Rainiers did exactly that. When Hutchinson won 25 games and batted .271 as a rookie, Seattle sold him for $35,000 and four experienced players. They won the next three Pacific Coast League pennants, 1940-1942, on the basis of that deal. Hutchinson was an aggressively relentless pitcher. Lacking overwhelming speed, he prevailed with cunning and guile.

Hutchinson's career with the Tigers was interrupted by four years in the Navy, his best season coming in 1947 when he won 18. A lifetime .263 hitter, he was used 91 times as a pinch hitter. Hutchinson hit four home runs in that role. Noted for tremendous temper tantrams, Hutchinson was given to tossing furniture about the clubhouse and smashing light bulbs after defeats. Despite this, he was extremely well-liked as a player, and as a manager he was loved and venerated by his players. His Reds fought hard and almost won the 1964 pennant as Hutchinson was dying from cancer.
Playing Career: *1939-1940, 1946-1953; Det A*
Managerial Career: *1952-1954, 1956-1964; Det A, StL N, Cin N*

Bill Hutchison
Hutchison, William Forrest
B: Dec 17, 1859   D: Mar 19, 1926

Pos: P	ERA: 3.58
W-L: 184-163	SOs: 1,236
ShOs: 21	Saves: 3

While in New Haven, Hutchison played weekend ball as a hobby, then graduated from Yale and went straight to the majors. He was a great pitcher for the White Stockings after a fitful beginning with the Kansas City Unions, the only club to make money in the 1884 Union Association. Hutchison led the NL for three straight years in wins, putting together back-to-back 42- and 44-win seasons. In his off year Hutchison won 37. From 1890 to 1892, he tossed 188 complete games in 1,791 innings of work.
Playing Career: *1884, 1889-1895, 1897; KC U, Chi N, StL N*

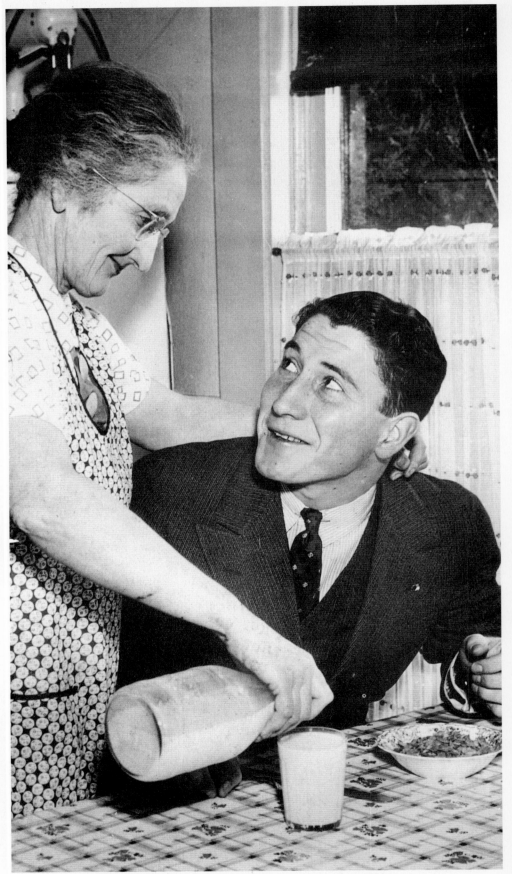

Nineteen-year-old Fred Hutchinson (seen with his mother) in late 1938.

Pete Incaviglia
Incaviglia, Peter Joseph (Inky)
B: Apr 2, 1964

Pos: OF, DH   BA: .249
Hits: 873   HRs: 170
RBI: 559   BBs: 301

One of the few players to go directly from college ball to the major leagues, Incaviglia was *Baseball America*'s College Player of the Year in 1985. The home run hitter has had some problems with defense. He is currently a backup outfielder with the Phillies.
Playing Career: *1986-; Tex A, Det A, Hou N, Phi N*

Dane Iorg
Iorg, Dane Charles
B: May 11, 1950

Pos: OF, 1B   BA: .276
Hits: 455   HRs: 14
RBI: 216   BBs: 107

Iorg hit .529 for the Cardinals in the 1982 World Series, then .500 against them in the 1985 Series. He won Game Six of the 1985 Fall Classic for the Royals with a two-run pinch-hit single in the bottom of the ninth. A clutch hitter, he batted .526 and slugged .842 in two ALCS and two World Series. Major leaguer Garth Iorg is his brother.
Playing Career: *1977-1986; Phi N, StL N, KC A, SD N*

Garth Iorg
Iorg, Garth Ray
B: Oct 12, 1954

Pos: 3B, 2B   BA: .258
Hits: 633   HRs: 20
RBI: 238   BBs: 114

One of the original Blue Jays, Iorg was drafted from the Yankees in 1976. He stayed in Toronto his entire nine-year career, often in a platoon role with third baseman Rance Mulliniks. Iorg hit .313 and slugged .469, both personal highs, for the 1985 division-winning Jays.
Playing Career: *1978, 1980-1987; Tor A*

Monte Irvin
Irvin, Monford Merrill
B: Feb 25, 1919
Hall of Fame 1973

Pos: OF   BA: .293
Hits: 731   HRs: 99
RBI: 443   BBs: 351

Monte Irvin played with the New York Giants after an outstanding career in the Negro Leagues, where he won two batting titles, hitting .396 in 1941 and .398 in 1946. Playing shortstop for the Newark Eagles in 1946 after two years of military service, Irvin combined with second baseman Larry Doby to help his team win the Negro Leagues championship, defeating Satchel Paige's Kansas City Monarchs in the postseason.

With the Giants, Irvin hit .299 in 1950, then raised his average to .312 in 1951 when he led the NL with 121 RBI, blasted 24 home runs, and was third in MVP balloting. The future Hall of Famer batted more than .400 during the pennant race as the Giants chased the Dodgers to a playoff game. In the World Series, he hit .458 and stole home against Yankee pitcher Allie Reynolds in Game One. Irvin was on the commissioner of baseball's staff during the 1980s.
Playing Career: *1949-1956; NY N, Chi N*

Arthur Irwin
Irwin, Arthur Albert
B: Feb 14, 1858   D: Jul 16, 1921

Pos: SS   BA: .241
Hits: 934   HRs: 5
RBI: 308   BBs: 309
Managerial Record
Won: 416   Lost: 427   Pct: .493

Irwin was a top 19th-century shortstop, and is in the Canadian Baseball Hall of Fame. He is credited with introducing the modern fielder's glove – though catchers and first basemen were already using gloves – which he devised to cover a sore finger. When his finger healed, he continued to use the glove, and the trend spread. In 1921 Irwin was lost at sea, in an apparently successful suicide attempt.
Playing Career: *1880-1891, 1894; Wor N, Pro N, Phi N, Was N, Bos P, Bos AA*
Managerial Career: *1889, 1891-1892, 1894-1896, 1898-1899; Was N, Bos AA, Phi N, NY N*

Charlie Irwin
Irwin, Charles Edwin
B: Feb 15, 1869   D: Sep 21, 1925

Pos: 3B   BA: .267
Hits: 981   HRs: 16
RBI: 488   BBs: 286

A sure-handed fielder and one of the fastest third basemen of his day, Irwin was always among NL defensive leaders in the 1890s. He showed a flash of power in 1894, with eight home runs for Chicago.
Playing Career: *1893-1902; Chi N, Cin N, Brk N*

Monte Irvin shows the number of hits he had in the first two games of the 1951 WS.

Frank Isbell
Isbell, William Frank
B: Aug 21, 1875   D: Jul 15, 1941

Pos: SS, 1B, 3B, 2B, OF   BA: .250
Hits: 1,056   HRs: 13
RBI: 455   BBs: 190

Isbell was a 1906 World Series hero when he hit .300 for the White Sox. Ironically, the normally weak-hitting Isbell set several Series records that still stand: most hits in two consecutive games (seven), and most doubles and extra-base hits in a game (four).
Playing Career: *1898, 1901-1909; Chi N, Chi A*

Mike Ivie
Ivie, Michael Wilson
B: Aug 8, 1952

Pos: 1B, C, 3B   BA: .269
Hits: 724   HRs: 81
RBI: 411   BBs: 214

Ivie could not find a position for the Padres, who wanted him to catch, though he preferred first base. Traded to the Giants, he hit a career-high .308 in 1978 and became a leading pinch hitter. Ivie tied a major league record with two pinch-hit grand slams that season.
Playing Career: *1971, 1974-1983; SD N, SF N, Hou N, Det A*

Ray Jablonski
Jablonski, Raymond Leo (Jabbo)
B: Dec 17, 1926   D: Nov 25, 1985

Pos: 3B   BA: .268
Hits: 687   HRs: 83
RBI: 438   BBs: 196

In the mid-1950s, the Cardinals had a group known as the Polish Falcons; Ray Jablonski, Rip Repulski and Steve Bilko. Jablonski set rookie records in 1953, with 21 homers and 112 RBI. He was named to the All-Star squad in 1954, when he hit .296.
Playing Career: *1953-1960; StL N, Cin N, NY N, SF N, KC A*

Al Jackson
Jackson, Alvin Neil
B: Dec 25, 1935

Pos: P   ERA: 3.98
W-L: 67-99   SOs: 738
ShOs: 14   Saves: 10

Jackson had the dubious distinction of being the ace of the abominable Mets pitching staffs of 1962-1965. He lost 20 games twice. Traded

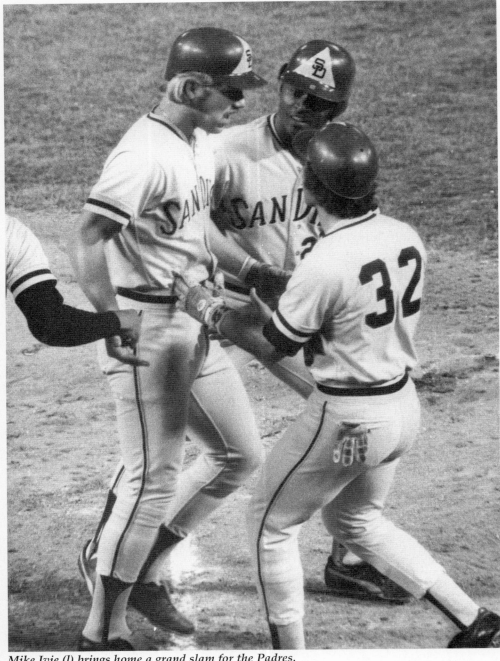
Mike Ivie (l) brings home a grand slam for the Padres.

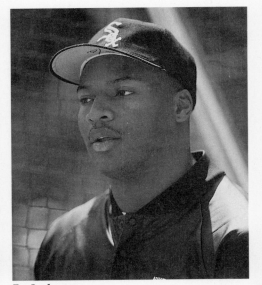
Bo Jackson.

"Shoeless Joe" Jackson (c) with Ty Cobb (l) and Sam Crawford.

to St. Louis, he went 9-4 with the 1967 World Champions, but did not appear in the World Series.
Playing Career: *1959-1969; Pit N, NY N, StL N, Cin N*

Bo Jackson
Jackson, Vincent Edward
B: Nov 30, 1962

Pos: OF, DH	BA: .247
Hits: 542	HRs: 128
RBI: 372	BBs: 180

Jackson put on a baseball uniform comparatively late in life and began belting tape-measure home runs, and making record distance throws. Under contract to professional baseball and football teams simultaneously, Jackson has always been a tremendous crowd draw. He strikes out frequently, but can be counted on when the pressure is on. In 1991 Jackson suffered a severe hip injury playing football. After surgery and rehabilitation, he won the Comeback Player of the Year Award in 1993.
Playing Career: *1986-1991, 1993-; KC A, Chi A*

Danny Jackson
Jackson, Danny Lynn
B: Jan 5, 1962

Pos: P	ERA: 3.82
W-L: 93-103	SOs: 858
ShOs: 13	Saves: 1

The Royals were down three games to one in the 1985 playoffs when Jackson came through with an eight-hit shutout. In an identical situation, he pitched a five-hit complete game in the 1985 World Series. He won 23 games for the Reds in 1988 and finished second in the Cy Young Award voting.
Playing Career: *1983-; KC A, Cin N, Chi N, Pit N, Phi N*

Grant Jackson
Jackson, Grant Dwight
B: Sep 28, 1942

Pos: P	ERA: 3.46
W-L: 86-75	SOs: 889
ShOs: 5	Saves: 79

Pitching in the World Series for three different teams during the 1970s, Jackson was as hot as a house afire. In postseason play his record was 2-0 in seven LCS games and 1-0 in six World Series games. In 1979 he was a member of the Pirates' "We are Family" team. As the number-two man in the bullpen behind stopper Kent Tekulve, Jackson posted an 8-5 record with 14 saves. He appeared in the All-Star Game in 1969.
Playing Career: *1965-1982; Phi N, Bal A, NY A, Pit N, Mon N, KC A*

Joe Jackson
Jackson, Joseph Jefferson (Shoeless Joe)
B: Jul 16, 1889   D: Dec 5, 1951

Pos: OF	BA: .356
Hits: 1,774	HRs: 54
RBI: 785	BBs: 519

"Ah hit .408, and ah hit .395, and ah still don't win the batting title. This is a mighty tough league," drawled Jackson. That .408 mark, from 1911, is the all-time rookie record. Jackson was the greatest natural hitter in his era; Babe Ruth emulated his batting stance and swing. The Southerner hit 168 triples and 307 doubles, and stole 202 bases. Traded to the White Sox in 1915, Jackson found himself on a team divided into cliques. Despite internal problems, the White Sox won the 1917 pennant and World Series.

In 1919 Jackson was led like a sheep into the World Series fix by his teammates. A simple, uneducated man from a rural background, Jackson likely never understood the ramifications of throwing the games. Grossly under-paid at $8,000, he was also an easy mark for the gamblers. Jackson batted .375 for the Series, and returned in 1920, but was banned for life that year for his involvement in the Black Sox scandal.
Playing Career: *1908, 1910-1920; Phi A, Cle A, Chi A*

Larry Jackson
Jackson, Lawrence Curtis
B: Jun 2, 1931   D: Aug 28, 1990

Pos: P	ERA: 3.40
W-L: 184-183	SOs: 1,709
ShOs: 37	Saves: 20

For a dozen years in a row, Jackson won 13 or more games. Although he had only one 20-game season, he was selected for the All-Star team four times. In 1964 he was 24-11 with a 3.14 ERA, finishing second in the Cy Young voting. A fine fielding pitcher, he led all hurlers in chances and fielding average several times. Rather than report to the expansion Expos in 1969, Jackson returned to Idaho, becoming a sportswriter and later, a state legislator.
Playing Career: *1955-1968; StL N, Chi N, Phi N*

Larry Jackson, pitching in 1967.

Randy Jackson
Jackson, Ransom Joseph
(Handsome Ransom)
B: Feb 10, 1926

Pos: 3B	BA: .261
Hits: 835	HRs: 103
RBI: 415	BBs: 281

After a luminous football career that included playing in two Cotton Bowl games, Jackson became a power hitter for the Cubs. He averaged 20 home runs, 1953-1955. The Dodgers acquired him to replace Jackie Robinson at third, but a serious knee injury in 1957 ended his career early.
Playing Career: *1950-1959; Chi N, Brk N, LA N, Cle A*

Reggie Jackson.

Reggie Jackson
Jackson, Reginald Martinez (Mr. October)
B: May 18, 1946
Hall of Fame 1993

Pos: OF, DH	BA: .262
Hits: 2,584	HRs: 563
RBI: 1,702	BBs: 1,375

The final game of the 1977 World Series – when Jackson blasted three home runs for the Yankees, each on the first ball pitched to him – will be forever etched in the memories of those who saw it. In 27 Fall Classic games, Mr. October batted .357 and slugged .755, the latter mark being the all-time best in the majors. Wherever Jackson played, his team was a winner. In the dozen seasons from 1971 to 1982, teams with Jackson on the roster won ten division crowns and five World Championships.

Jackson is sixth on the all-time home run list, and he won four home run crowns. He launched a ball against a light tower on the roof of Tiger Stadium in the 1971 All-Star Game. In 1973 Jackson led the league with 32 homers and 117 RBI, and was named AL MVP. Intelligent and articulate, Jackson carried a big stick, but did not speak softly. His arguments with club owners and managers were legendary, but in the end, he delivered what they most wanted.
Playing Career: *1967-1987; KC A, Oak A, Bal A, NY A, Cal A*

Ron Jackson
Jackson, Ronnie Damien
B: May 9, 1953

Pos: 1B, 3B, OF, DH	BA: .259
Hits: 774	HRs: 56
RBI: 342	BBs: 213

One of 13 children, Jackson learned how to do a lot of things well, and it landed him a handyman role in major league baseball. In 1979 he smashed 14 homers and 40 doubles, scoring 85 runs and batting .271. Jackson was 1-for-1 in the 1982 ALCS for a 1.000 average.
Playing Career: *1975-1984; Cal A, Min A, Det A, Bal A*

Roy Jackson
Jackson, Roy Lee
B: May 1, 1954

Pos: P	ERA: 3.77
W-L: 28-34	SOs: 351
ShOs: 0	Saves: 34

Jackson played for a trio of expansion clubs, the Mets, Blue Jays and Padres. He was Toronto's top reliever until Tom Henke came over from the Rangers. Jackson's mark of 10 single-season saves was a club record when he left in 1984.
Playing Career: *1977-1986; NY N, Tor A, SD N, Min A*

Sonny Jackson
Jackson, Roland Thomas
B: Jul 9, 1944

Pos: SS	BA: .251
Hits: 767	HRs: 7
RBI: 162	BBs: 250

The Astros thought Jackson was the cat's pajamas when he hit .292 and stole 49 bases in 1966 – his rookie season – in Houston. He combined with Joe Morgan to form a space-age double play combination. A sophomore jinx got him traded to Atlanta.
Playing Career: *1963-1974; Hou N, Atl N*

Travis Jackson
Jackson, Travis Calvin (Stonewall)
B: Nov 2, 1903   D: Jul 27, 1987
Hall of Fame 1982

Pos: SS	BA: .291
Hits: 1,768	HRs: 135
RBI: 929	BBs: 412

The shortstop of the Giants' Hall of Fame infield, Jackson combined with Bill Terry, Freddie Lindstrom and Mel Ott as key players on their pennant-contendng teams of the late 1920s and early 1930s. Jackson was the first of John McGraw's final generation of great rookies. Succeeding Dave Bancroft at shortstop in 1924, the 5'10" Arkansan was reliable

Shortstop Travis Jackson played on the NY Giants' greatest teams, from 1922 to 1936.

and had good range. He led NL shortstops in assists four times, total chances three times, and fielding average twice.

Defensively, Jackson's strongest feature was his powerful throwing arm. He was a better hitter than the dozen shortstops who were his contemporaries, and even learned to pull the ball to take advantage of the short foul lines in the Polo Grounds. His greatest achievement came in 1936, when as a 32-year-old with bad knees, he played the entire season at third base as the Giants captured the pennant. He retired after the World Series, and later managed in the minor leagues.
Playing Career: *1922-1936; NY N*

Baby Doll Jacobson
Jacobson, William Chester (Jake)
B: Aug 16, 1890   D: Jan 16, 1977

Pos: OF	BA: .311
Hits: 1,714	HRs: 84
RBI: 819	BBs: 355

The 1912 Opening Day band in Mobile played "Oh, You Beautiful Doll" after Jacobson hit a home run. The next day's paper captioned his photo, "Baby Doll." After a decade in the minors, he spent 1917 in the majors, served a year in the military, and returned to the Browns at age 28. As the lively ball era progressed, Jacobson and his slugging mates began to seriously punish AL hurlers. Starting in 1919, he strung together seven straight years of .300 averages, batting more than .350 in 1920-1921.

In St. Louis, Jacobson was flanked in center field by Ken Williams and Jack Tobin; each of them batted over .300 for seven consecutive years, except for Tobin who hit .299 in 1924. At 6'3" and 215 pounds, Jacobson was the league's biggest man, but he was a good outfielder. At one time he held 13 fielding marks; his 484 putouts in 1924 stood as a record for 24 years.
Playing Career: *1915, 1917, 1919-1927; Det A, StL A, Bos A, Cle A, Phi A*

Brook Jacoby
Jacoby, Brook Wallace
B: Nov 23, 1959

Pos: 3B, 1B	BA: .270
Hits: 1,220	HRs: 120
RBI: 545	BBs: 439

Cleveland's best trade ever was the Len Barker for Rick Behenna, Brett Butler and Brook Jacoby deal. Jacoby made the All-Star team in 1986 and 1990. He was a streaky hitter who once pounded 32 home runs, yet had only 69 RBI because 27 of the homers were solo shots.
Playing Career: *1981, 1983-1992; Atl N, Cle A, Oak A*

Bill James
James, William
B: Oct 5, 1949

Primarily responsible for the newfound interest in the statistical analysis of baseball, James combined interesting prose with his numbers and sold 100,000 copies of the *Bill James Baseball Abstract* every year for 10 years. The principle developer of sabremetrics, James applied mathematical tests to widely accepted baseball precepts and sometimes got startling results. He is now involved in a variety of enterprises, including providing information for the Bill James Fantasy League, rotisserie baseball.

Bill James
James, William Henry (Big Bill)
B: Jan 20, 1887   D: May 24, 1942

Pos: P	ERA: 3.20
W-L: 65-71	SOs: 408
ShOs: 9	Saves: 4

There were two Bill Jameses pitching at the same time in the major leagues. Big Bill, who was 6'4", compiled a record of 15-14 with a 2.85 ERA for the Browns in 1914, earning a spot on the barnstorming AL all-star squad. He pitched in the 1919 World Series.
Playing Career: *1911-1912, 1914-1919; Cle A, StL A, Det A, Bos A, Chi A*

Bill James
James, William Lawrence (Seattle Bill)
B: Mar 12, 1892   D: Mar 10, 1971

Pos: P	ERA: 2.28
W-L: 37-21	SOs: 253
ShOs: 5	Saves: 2

One of the Big Three of the 1914 Miracle Braves staff, James spun a 26-7 record with a 1.90 ERA. He also went 2-0 in the four-game World Series sweep of the highly favored Athletics. He enlisted for military duty during World War I, then returned to the West Coast.
Playing Career: *1913-1915, 1919; Bos N*

Bob James
James, Robert Harvey
B: Aug 18, 1958

Pos: P	ERA: 3.80
W-L: 24-26	SOs: 340
ShOs: 0	Saves: 73

Saving 32 games with a 2.13 ERA in 1985, James fueled the White Sox pennant drive. Unfortunately, the next season he tore a muscle in his pitching arm. Although recovered, James never regained his 92-mph fastball.
Playing Career: *1978-1979, 1982-1987; Mon N, Det A, Chi A*

Charlie Jamieson
Jamieson, Charles Devine
B: Feb 7, 1893   D: Oct 27, 1969

Pos: OF	BA: .303
Hits: 1,990	HRs: 18
RBI: 550	BBs: 748

When Jamieson replaced Jack Granney as the Indians' leadoff batter, he became only their

Charlie Jamieson.

second leadoff man from 1910 to 1931. Always hitting around .300 and sporting a .378 lifetime on-base average, Jamieson hit .333 in the 1920 World Series. Pitching the occasional game in his early days, he was 2-1 in 13 games over five years. Traded from the Philadelphia A's to Cleveland in 1919, Jamieson played outfield – from 1920 to 1931 he owned left field at League Park.

The lively ball brought Jamieson to the forefront, just as it had the same effect on other line drive hitters. He had nine full seasons with batting averages over .300, including a .359 mark in 1924. In 1923 he had a 23-game hitting streak and led the AL with 222 hits and 644 at-bats. In the field, Jamieson made spectacular diving catches and powerful, accurate throws. His 22 outfield assists led the league in 1928, the same year he started two triple plays in a 17-day span. Jamieson was a frequent MVP Award candidate, though never a winner.
Playing Career: *1915-1932; Was A, Phi A, Cle A*

Larry Jansen
Jansen, Lawrence Joseph
B: Jul 16, 1920

Pos: P	ERA: 3.58
W-L: 122-89	SOs: 842
ShOs: 17	Saves: 10

After winning more than 30 games in the Pacific Coast League in 1946, Jansen had a magnificient NL rookie year, compiling a 21-5 record and leading the league in winning percentage. Jansen led the NL with five shutouts in 1950. The next year, the right hander combined with Sal Maglie to help the Giants win the pennant. They tied for the league lead in victories, with 23 each. As coach for the Giants, he developed Juan Marichal and Gaylord Perry.
Playing Career: *1947-1954, 1956; NY N*

Pat Jarvis
Jarvis, Robert Patrick
B: Mar 18, 1941

Pos: P	ERA: 3.58
W-L: 85-73	SOs: 8
ShOs: 8	Saves: 3

Before playing baseball, Jarvis was a rodeo rider. The tough-as-nails right-hander was the number three starter for the Braves, 1967-1971, averaging 13 wins a season for five years. He started and lost the final NLCS game to the Mets in 1969.
Playing Career: *1966-1973; Atl N, Mon N*

Al Javery
Javery, Alva William
B: Jun 5, 1918   D: Sep 13, 1977

Pos: P	ERA: 3.80
W-L: 53-74	SOs: 470
ShOs: 15	Saves: 5

Javery was a wartime ace of the Braves staff before the heavy workload caught up with him in 1945. He tossed over 800 innings in three years, making the All-Star squad in 1943 and 1944. Javery's record was 39-51 for those years.
Playing Career: *1940-1946; Bos N*

Julian Javier
Javier y Liranzo, Manuel Julian
B: Aug 9, 1936

Pos: 2B	BA: .257
Hits: 1,469	HRs: 78
RBI: 506	BBs: 314

When the Cardinals brought in Javier to play second base, they plugged a gap left by Red Schoendienst's departure in 1956. The Cards even brought the Redhead back in the early 1960s to teach Javier the inside game at second. His range and speed enabled St. Louis to build the finest infield in the NL. In 1963 Javier joined teammates Ken Boyer, Dick Groat and Bill White to make up an all-Cardinal starting infield in the All-Star Game. He hit .360 in the 1967 World Series, contributing to the Cardinals' Championship by belting a three-run homer in Game Seven.
Playing Career: *1960-1972; StL N, Cin N*

Stan Javier
Javier, Stanley Julian
B: Sep 1, 1965

Pos: OF	BA: .251
Hits: 511	HRs: 13
RBI: 175	BBs: 218

The son of Cardinals star Julian Javier, Stan has not been the star he was predicted to be, but he drove in the only two runs the A's scored against Orel Hershiser in the 1988 World Series. He went 2-for-4 in both the ALCS and World Series that year.
Playing Career: *1984, 1986-; NY A, Oak A, LA N, Phi N, Cal A*

Joey Jay
Jay, Joseph Richard
B: Aug 15, 1935

Pos: P	ERA: 3.77
W-L: 99-91	SOs: 999
ShOs: 16	Saves: 7

Almost barred from Little League at age 12 because of his large size, Jay became the first Little League player to reach the majors. Jay hurled a three-hit shutout for the Braves in his debut at age 18. In 1961 Jay led the NL in wins and was 1-1 in the World Series.
Playing Career: *1953-1955, 1957-1966; Mil N, Cin N*

Hal Jeffcoat
Jeffcoat, Harold Bentley
B: Sep 6, 1924

Pos: P, OF	ERA: 4.22
W-L: 39-37	SOs: 239
ShOs: 1	Saves: 25

Jeffcoat broke in with the Cubs as an outfielder. When his light hitting forced him into a backup role by 1950, he converted to pitching. Jeffcoat became a top reliever, making 50 appearances with a 2.95 ERA in 1955, and compiling a record of 8-2 in 1956.
Playing Career: *1948-1959; Chi N, Cin N, StL N*

Greg Jefferies
Jefferies, Gregory Scott
B: Aug 1, 1967

Pos: 3B, 2B, DH, 1B	BA: .290
Hits: 830	HRs: 68
RBI: 363	BBs: 245

In each of his first three seasons in the minor leagues, Jefferies was MVP. He hit .333 in the 1988 NLCS for the Mets. A line drive hitter, he led the NL in doubles with 40 in 1990. Jefferies hit .285 with the Royals in 1992, and was traded to the Cardinals, who made him into a first baseman and hitting star.
Playing Career: *1987-; NY N, KC A, StL N*

Fats Jenkins
Jenkins, Clarence R.
B: Jan 19, 1898   D: Dec 6, 1968

Pos: OF	BA: .335 (inc.)
Hits: 616 (inc.)	HRs: 14 (inc.)
RBI: NA	BBs: NA

A good all-around athlete who also played professional basketball with the Renaissance team, Jenkins appeared in the 1933 and 1935 East-West All-Star Games of the Negro Leagues. At 37, he hit .305 and stole nine base for the 1935 Brooklyn Eagles. In his last season he batted .351.
Playing Career: *1920-1938; NY Lincoln Giants, AC Bach Giants, Hbg Giants, Pit Crawfords, NY Black Yankees, Brk Eagles, Nwk Dodgers*

Fergie Jenkins
Jenkins, Ferguson Arthur
B: Dec 13, 1943
Hall of Fame 1991

Pos: P	ERA: 3.34
W-L: 284-226	SOs: 3,192
ShOs: 49	Saves: 7

Even though Jenkins spent nine years pitching in Wrigley Field, a hitter's ballpark, he strung together six consecutive 20-win seasons – the last pitcher to do so. The Canadian set a modern Cubs record with 236 strikeouts in 1967, then raised the record each of the next three seasons to 260, 273 and 274. In the 15-inning 1967 All-Star Game, Jenkins fanned six batters in three innings. He pitched in the

Julian Javier steals second as Tony Taylor waits for the throw, 1960.

The Cubs' Ferguson Jenkins, 1967.

Tiger Manager Hughie Jennings.

All-Star Game again in 1971, the year he led the NL with a 24-13 record, 263 strikeouts, a 2.77 ERA, and 30 complete games to win the Cy Young Award. He also batted .243 and hit six home runs!

Jenkins had excellent control with a good fastball and curve, walking only 997 in 4,500 innings. In 1974, after being traded to the Rangers, he put together a 25-12 season, leading the AL in wins and complete games. He struck out 225 and walked only 45 that year. He pitched with great prowess for 19 years, but was never on a division or pennant-winning team.
Playing Career: *1965-1983; Phi N, Chi N, Tex A, Bos A*

Hughie Jennings
Jennings, Hugh Ambrose
B: Apr 2, 1869   D: Feb 1, 1928
Hall of Fame 1945

Pos: SS, 1B, 2B	BA: .312
Hits: 1,532	HRs: 17
RBI: 840	BBs: 347
Managerial Record	
Won: 1,163 Lost: 984 Pct: .542	

A Cornell Law School graduate, Jennings was a great ballplayer, and became a great manager. He took over as Detroit skipper in 1907 and won pennants in his first three years. His nickname was "Eeyah," because he used to yell that from the coaching box, claiming it was Hawaiian for "Watch out!" As shortstop and captain of the Baltimore Orioles, he led them to three straight pennants in his first three years, 1894-1896, and the Temple Cup playoffs the next year.

Jennings's speciality was getting hit with the pitch, which he accomplished 49 times in 1896, the record until Ron Hunt broke it in 1971. The infamous Orioles would take close pitches, then roll on the ground faking pain,

while raising welts by pinching themselves. Jennings had a hard head: his skull was fractured by an Amos Rusie pitch in 1897; an accidental dive into an empty swimming pool fractured it again.
Playing Career: *1891-1903, 1907-1909, 1912, 1918; Lou AA, Lou N, Bal N, Brk N, Phi N, Det A*
Managerial Career: *1907-1920; Det A*

Jackie Jensen
Jensen, Jack Eugene
B: Mar 9, 1927   D: Jul 14, 1982

Pos: OF	BA: .279
Hits: 1,463	HRs: 199
RBI: 929	BBs: 750

Jackie Jensen was a former Rose Bowl football star, whose effectiveness in baseball was negated by his refusal to fly in airplanes. He was AL MVP in 1958 when he hit 35 homers, drove in 122 and slugged .535. Jensen drove in 100 or more runs five of his seven years with the Red Sox and led the league three times. An All-Star three times, Jensen led the AL in stolen bases in 1954 and in triples in 1956, but he also hit into double plays, grounding into 185 in 11 years, once every 28 at-bats.
Playing Career: *1950-1961; NY A, Was A, Bos A*

Woody Jensen
Jensen, Forrest Docenus
B: Aug 11, 1907

Pos: OF	BA: .285
Hits: 774	HRs: 26
RBI: 235	BBs: 69

It is inevitable that a man named Forrest who played ball in the semipro Timber League would be nicknamed Woody. With the

Pirates, he hit .324 in 1935. The next year he batted 696 times as leadoff man, the most in major league history for a 154-game schedule.
Playing Career: *1931-1939; Pit N*

Sam Jethroe
Jethroe, Samuel (Jet)
B: Jan 20, 1922

Pos: OF	BA: .261
Hits: 460	HRs: 49
RBI: 181	BBs: 177

The 1950 NL Rookie of the Year, Jethroe was a seven-year veteran of the Negro Leagues. He batted .340 in six Negro League seasons, and was selected for the East-West All-Star Game four times. Jethroe won the league batting title in 1944 and 1945 with averages of .353 and .393, leading the Buckeyes to the Negro World Championship in the latter year. After pilfering 89 bases in the International League in 1949, Jethroe was brought up to the Braves, where he led the NL in stolen bases twice.
Playing Career: *1950-1952, 1954; Bos N, Pit N*

Tommy John
John, Thomas Edward
B: May 22, 1943

Pos: P	ERA: 3.34
W-L: 288-231	SOs: 2,245
ShOs: 46	Saves: 4

In 1974 John had a 13-3 record when he blew out his elbow in July. Dr. Frank Jobe transplanted a tendon from John's right forearm to his left elbow. The revolutionary operation saved the pitcher's career. After a year of rehabilitation, John successfully made the transition from a flamethrower to a soft-throwing finesse pitcher. He won the Comeback Player of the Year Award with a 10-10 record in 1976.

John posted 20 victories in three of the next

Tommy John with Tommy Lasorda, 1978.

four seasons, and made the All-Star team three straight years, 1978-1980. Control and a consistent sinker served him well during the rest of his 26-year major league career. He returned to the Yankees in 1986 and led the club in innings pitched as a 44-year-old in 1987. John often explained his unusual durability by pointing out that his pitching arm was much younger than his chronological age.
Playing Career: *1963-1974, 1976-1989; Cle A, Chi A, LA N, NY A, Cal A, Oak A*

Alex Johnson
Johnson, Alexander
B: Dec 7, 1942

Pos: OF	BA: .288
Hits: 1,331	HRs: 78
RBI: 525	BBs: 244

Caught up in the turmoil of the early 1970s when the new breed of players clashed head-on into the old guard of managers and general managers, Johnson was suspended for being a "bad influence." He retired on mental disability after intervention by the Players' Union. Johnson led the AL in batting with a .329 average in 1970, and made the All-Star squad that year. Johnson admitted that he never gave 100 percent and never hustled. He once told a reporter "I'm just paid to hit."
Playing Career: *1964-1976; Phi N, StL N, Cin N, Cal A, Cle A, Tex A, NY A, Det A*

Ban Johnson
Johnson, Byron Bancroft
B: Jan 6, 1865   D: Mar 28, 1931
Hall of Fame 1937

Ban Johnson was one of baseball's most influential figures for a quarter of a century. As president of the Western League, he changed its name to the American League in 1900 and claimed major league status in 1901. Following player raids in 1902, the existing National League recognized the new AL, which attained parity with the NL by winning the 1903 World Series.

Ban Johnson.

Johnson was more responsible for making baseball the national game than anyone in the history of the sport. Forceful, aggressive and a brilliant organizer, he raised the money which built the ballparks and established the franchises that made the AL. Johnson recruited millionaires to bankroll teams, appointed managers, negotiated trades, and apportioned players. He arranged schedules to spread travel costs equitably, interpreted rules, levied fines and suspensions, issued statistics, and even persuaded President William Howard Taft to throw out the ceremonial first pitch on Opening Day in 1910. By elevating the status of umpires, he helped eliminate the element of rowdyism, enhancing the game's reputation.

Billy Johnson
Johnson, William Russell
B: Aug 30, 1918

Pos: 3B	BA: .271
Hits: 882	HRs: 61
RBI: 487	BBs: 347

In four World Series with the Yankees, Johnson was a terror at the plate. His bases-loaded triple in the eighth inning of Game Three in 1943 won the contest. Johnson hit three triples in the 1947 Series. He was platooned at third base with Bobby Brown.
Playing Career: *1943, 1946-1953; NY A, StL N*

Bob Johnson
Johnson, Robert Wallace
B: Mar 4, 1936

Pos: SS, 2B, 3B, 1B	BA: .272
Hits: 628	HRs: 44
RBI: 230	BBs: 156

A versatile infielder who played in eight cities in eleven years, Johnson led the league in pinch hits in 1964, 1967 and 1969. He batted .348 in 1967, but his best season was 1962, when he had career highs of 12 homers, 58 runs scored, and 43 RBI.
Playing Career: *1960-1970; KC A, Was A, Bal A, NY N, Cin N, Atl N, StL N, Oak A*

Cliff Johnson
Johnson, Clifford (Heathcliff)
B: Jul 22, 1947

Pos: DH, 1B, C, OF	BA: .258
Hits: 1,016	HRs: 196
RBI: 699	BBs: 568

A powerful hitter with a career slugging average of .459, Johnson holds the major league record for pinch hit home runs with 20, including five hit during his first full season. Traded to the Yankees in 1977, Johnson walloped three home runs 15 days later, including two in the eighth inning. He hit .400 in the ALCS that year. In 1979 he broke Rich Gossage's thumb in a locker room scuffle, and was consequently traded to Cleveland.
Playing Career: *1972-1986; Hou N, NY A, Cle A, Chi N, Oak A, Tor A, Tex A*

Connie Johnson
Johnson, Clifford C.
B: Dec 27, 1922

Pos: P	ERA: 3.44
W-L: 40-39	SOs: 497
ShOs: 8	Saves: 1

Johnson pitched for the Kansas City Monarchs for two years before and two years after military service in World War II. He led the Negro Leagues in wins in 1946. Johnson still holds the Orioles' single-game strikeout record for a right-hander. In 1957 he won 14 with a 3.20 ERA.
Playing Career: *1953, 1955-1958; Chi A, Bal A*

Darrell Johnson
Johnson, Darrell Dean
B: Aug 25, 1928

Pos: C	BA: .234
Hits: 75	HRs: 2
RBI: 28	BBs: 26
Managerial Record	
Won: 472 Lost: 590 Pct: .444	

The highlight of Johnson's short career as a second-string catcher was his .500 batting average in the 1961 World Series. After success managing in the Red Sox farm system, he was named Boston's skipper in 1974. The next year they won the pennant.
Playing Career: *1952, 1957-1958, 1960-1962; StL A, Chi A, NY A, StL N, Phi N, Cin N, Bal A*
Managerial Career: *1974-1980, 1982; Bos A, Sea A, Tex A*

Davey Johnson
Johnson, David Allen
B: Jan 30, 1943

Pos: 2B, 1B, 3B	BA: .261
Hits: 1,252	HRs: 136
RBI: 609	BBs: 559
Managerial Record	
Won: 648 Lost: 482 Pct: .573	

A top ranked player who became a highly respected manager, Johnson holds the record for homers by a second baseman, and has won nearly 60 percent of his games as a skipper, finishing in first place twice and in second place four times in eight years. Johnson won Gold Glove Awards at second base 1969-1971, but was remembered as a home run hitter. He walloped 43 in 1973, one behind the NL leader, making the Braves the only team ever to boast three players who hit 40 or more home runs in the same season – Johnson, Hank Aaron and Darrell Evans.

Johnson began his managerial career in 1979, winning three championships in three minor league seasons. He combined his computer knowledge and a degree from Trinity University with his experience playing under Earl Weaver. Johnson disliked the bunt and managed according to Weaver's credo of "strong pitching and wait for a three-run homer." Johnson took over a team that had not won since 1973 but had a raft of talented

Davey Johnson, with Baltimore in 1970.

young players. He acquired veterans Keith Hernandez and Gary Carter to teach the youngsters and the result was the 1986 World Champion Mets, who won 108 games.
Playing Career: *1965-1975, 1977-1978; Bal A, Atl N, Phi N, Chi N*
Managerial Career: *1984-1990, 1993-; NY N, Cin N*

Deron Johnson
Johnson, Deron Roger
B: Jul 17, 1938   D: Apr 23, 1992

Pos: 1B, 3B, DH, OF	BA: .244
Hits: 1,447	HRs: 245
RBI: 923	BBs: 585

Once dubbed ''the next Mickey Mantle'' by the New York press, Johnson hit a lot of home runs, but struck out frequently, causing managers to use him as a reserve player. He had a monster 1965 season, rapping 32 homers, 30 doubles, and driving in 130 runs. With the Phillies in 1971, Johnson tied a major league record by hitting four home runs in consecutive at-bats, July 10-11. He hit .300 in the 1973 World Series for the A's.
Playing Career: *1960-1962, 1964-1976; NY A, KC A, Cin N, Atl N, Phi N, Oak A, Mil A, Bos A, Chi A*

Earl Johnson
Johnson, Earl Douglas
B: Apr 2, 1919

Pos: P	ERA: 4.30
W-L: 40-32	SOs: 250
ShOs: 4	Saves: 17

Johnson spent four years in the Army, earning a Silver Star, Bronze Star, and a cluster for heroism during the Battle of the Bulge. After World War II he pitched in the 1946 World Series, winning one game and compiling a 2.70 ERA.
Playing Career: *1940-1941, 1946-1951; Bos A, Det A*

Ernie Johnson
Johnson, Ernest Rudolph
B: Apr 29, 1888   D: May 1, 1952

Pos: SS, 2B, 3B	BA: .265
Hits: 697	HRs: 19
RBI: 256	BBs: 181

When Swede Risberg was banned from baseball after the Black Sox scandal, Ernie Johnson replaced him at shortstop. Johnson hit .295 that year, but errors and a 1923 salary holdout got him sold to the Yankees. He appeared in the 1923 World Series with New York.
Playing Career: *1912, 1915-1918, 1921-1925; Chi A, StL F, StL A, NY A*

Hank Johnson
Johnson, Henry Ward
B: May 21, 1906   D: Aug 20, 1982

Pos: P	ERA: 4.75
W-L: 63-56	SOs: 568
ShOs: 4	Saves: 11

A relief pitcher and spot starter, Johnson had a knack for beating Lefty Grove. In 1928 he went 4-0 against the great southpaw and fashioned a 14-9 career mark versus Grove. Johnson played on three Yankee pennant-winning teams, but never appeared in the World Series.
Playing Career: *1925-1936, 1939; NY A, Bos A, Phi A, Cin N*

Howard Johnson
Johnson, Howard Michael (Hojo)
B: Nov 29, 1960

Pos: 3B, SS, OF	BA: .253
Hits: 1,148	HRs: 211
RBI: 698	BBs: 934

Johnson hits like an outfielder, steals bases like an infielder and fields like a reserve player. Saddled with a strong but erratic arm and poor range, Johnson was platooned at third base early in his career. When he became a full-time player his offensive performance escalated. Johnson averaged 96 runs, 31 home runs and 95 RBI from 1987 to 1991.

In 1987 he and Darryl Strawberry became the first teammates to hit 30 homers and steal 30 bases, and Johnson's 36 dingers set a league record for switch hitters. He led the NL in runs scored in 1989 and in homers and RBI in 1991. Opposing managers repeatedly had Johnson's bat checked for cork, but eventually realized his power was real. He has played in two All-Star Games and two World Series.
Playing Career: *1982-; Det A, NY N*

Indian Bob Johnson
Johnson, Robert Lee
B: Nov 26, 1906   D: Jul 6, 1982

Pos: OF	BA: .296
Hits: 2,051	HRs: 288
RBI: 1,283	BBs: 1,073

Arriving two years after Connie Mack's last pennant in 1931, Johnson hit home runs and amassed RBI at a terrific rate for 13 years, but nobody noticed. He averaged 23 homers, 97 runs scored and 101 RBI from 1933 to 1944. The Cherokee slugger walloped 30 or more home runs three times, 40 doubles twice and 30 doubles six times. He hit safely in 26 straight games in 1934.

On June 16, 1934, he went six-for-six with two homers and two doubles. The next year Johnson set a major league record with six RBI in one inning on a grand slam and a double. He batted over .300 five times, and led the AL in on-base percentage with a .431

NY Met Howard Johnson after hitting a homer in 1989.

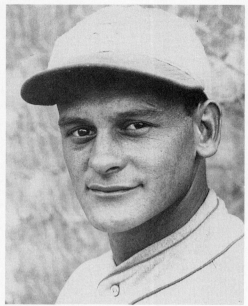

Indian Bob Johnson.

Judy Johnson.

mark in 1944. The eight-time All-Star broke up three no-hitters, once with a home run off Lefty Gomez.
Playing Career: *1933-1945; Phi A, Was A, Bos A*

Jerry Johnson
Johnson, Jerry Michael
B: Dec 3, 1943

Pos: P	ERA: 4.31
W-L: 48-51	SOs: 489
ShOs: 2	Saves: 41

Originally signed as a third baseman, Johnson switched to pitching late in life and spent much of his career travelling between the minor and major leagues. His big season was 1971, when he won 12 and saved 18 for the division champion Giants. He appeared in the NLCS that year.
Playing Career: *1968-1977; Phi N, StL N, NY N, Cle A, Hou N, SD N, Tor A*

Judy Johnson
Johnson, William Julius
B: Oct 20, 1900   D: Jun 15, 1989
Hall of Fame 1975

Pos: 3B	BA: .301 (inc.)
Hits: 789 (inc.)	HRs: 19 (inc.)
RBI: NA	BBs: NA

Considered the Negro Leagues' top third baseman of the 1920s and 1930s, Johnson was an outstanding fielder and a fine clutch hitter. He was also valued for the steadying influence he exerted on his teammates. After World War I, Johnson played semipro ball for $5 per game. The Hilldales purchased his services for $100 in 1920, and in 1921 paid him $150 a month. Johnson's club won a championship that year.
The Hilldales played in the first two Negro League World Series. In the 1924 Series, Hill-

dale lost to the Kansas City Monarchs, but Johnson led both teams batting .341 and had five doubles, a triple, and a home run. In 1925 the teams met again, but with different results. After baseball's color barrier was broken, Johnson scouted and coached for the Philadelphia Athletics. He worked for the Phillies from 1959 to 1973, recruiting such talent as Richie Allen.
Playing Career: *1919-1938; Mad Stars, Phi Hilldales, Hom Grays, Pit Crawfords*

Ken Johnson
Johnson, Kenneth Travis
B: Jun 16, 1933

Pos: P	ERA: 3.46
W-L: 91-106	SOs: 1,042
ShOs: 7	No-hitters: 1

Johnson pitched a no-hitter against the Reds on April 24, 1964, but lost 1-0 on two walks and two errors. He saw action in the 1961 World Series, then had his best season in 1965, posting 16 victories. Normally a starter, Johnson also saved nine games.
Playing Career: *1958-1970; KC A, Cin N, Hou N, Mil N, Atl N, NY A, Chi N, Mon N*

Lamar Johnson
Johnson, Lamar
B: Sep 2, 1950

Pos: 1B, DH	BA: .287
Hits: 755	HRs: 64
RBI: 381	BBs: 211

In 1977 Johnson sang "The Star Spangled Banner" before a Chicago game, then hit two homers and a double. He batted over .300 in three of his first four years with the White Sox, then hit .309 for them in 1979. Johnson also put together a 19-game hitting streak that year.
Playing Career: *1974-1982; Chi A, Tex A*

Lance Johnson
Johnson, Kenneth Lance
B: Jul 6, 1963

Pos: OF	BA: .281
Hits: 731	HRs: 4
RBI: 223	BBs: 156

Given a chance to start by the White Sox, Johnson has gradually improved from batting ninth to the second spot in the lineup. He led the AL in triples 1991-1993. Johnson has scored 333 runs, and has stolen 166 bases. He led the AL with 14 triples in 1993.
Playing Career: *1987-; StL N, Chi A*

Lou Johnson
Johnson, Louis Brown (Sweet Lou)
B: Sep 22, 1934

Pos: OF	BA: .258
Hits: 529	HRs: 48
RBI: 232	BBs: 110

A terror in postseason play for the Dodgers, Johnson smashed two homers, including the winning shot in the finale of the 1965 Fall Classic victory over the Twins. In the 1966 World Series against the Orioles, his .267 average and one run scored led the Dodgers.
Playing Career: *1960-1962, 1965-1969; Chi N, LA A, Mil N, LA N, Cle A, Cal A*

Randy Johnson
Johnson, Randall David
B: Sep 10, 1963

Pos: P	ERA: 3.78
W-L: 68-56	SOs: 1,126
ShOs: 8	No-hitters: 1

The most intimidating pitcher in baseball, Johnson is 6'10" and the tallest major leaguer ever. He hurled more than 200 innings and averaged well over 200 strikeouts, 1990-1993. He was selected for two All-Star Games. He led the AL with 308 strikeouts in 1993.
Playing Career: *1988-; Mon N, Sea A*

Roy Johnson
Johnson, Roy Cleveland
B: Feb 23, 1903   D: Sep 10, 1973

Pos: OF	BA: .296
Hits: 1,292	HRs: 58
RBI: 556	BBs: 489
Managerial Record	
Won: 0 Lost: 1 Pct: .000	

Indian Bob's brother broke in with the Tigers after a sensational career in the Pacific Coast League. His rookie year totals included a .314 batting average, 128 runs scored, an AL-leading 45 doubles, 14 triples and 20 stolen bases. A strong-armed outfielder, he twice led the league in assists, but also led in errors, and still holds the AL record with 31 outfield errors in 1929. He led the AL in triples with 19 in 1931, and played in the 1936 World Series.
Playing Career: *1929-1938; Det A, Bos A, NY A, Bos N*
Managerial Career: *1944; Chi N*

The Braves' Lou Johnson is safe at third in a 1962 game vs. the Pirates.

Si Johnson
Johnson, Silas Kenneth
B: Oct 5, 1906

Pos: P	ERA: 4.09
W-L: 101-165	SOs: 840
ShOs: 13	Saves: 15

Stuck pitching for second-division clubs, Johnson lost 165 games during his career. A workhorse for the Reds, he pitched more than 200 innings a year from 1931 to 1934. Johnson avoided two last-place finishes by serving in the Navy in 1944 and 1945.
Playing Career: *1928-1943, 1946-1947; Cin N, StL N, Phi N, Bos N*

Syl Johnson
Johnson, Sylvester
B: Dec 31, 1900   D: Feb 20, 1985

Pos: P	ERA: 4.06
W-L: 112-117	SOs: 920
ShOs: 13	Saves: 43

A fourth or fifth starter for the Cardinals during their glory years of the 1930s, Johnson pitched in three World Series, going 0-1 with a 4.50 ERA. During his injury-plagued career, batted balls broke his cheekbone, ribs, big toe, and three fingers.
Playing Career: *1922-1940; Det A, StL N, Cin N, Phi N*

Walter Johnson
Johnson, Walter Perry (The Big Train)
B: Nov 6, 1887   D: Dec 10, 1946
Hall of Fame 1936

Pos: P	ERA: 2.17
W-L: 416-279	SOs: 3,508
ShOs: 110	No-hitters: 2
Managerial Record	
Won: 529 Lost: 432 Pct: .550	

One of the five ballplayers elected for the first Hall of Fame induction ceremony, Walter Johnson is considered by many to be the greatest pitcher of all time. In 21 years with the chronically pathetic Senators, he won more than 20 games 12 times. He led the AL in wins six times, in ERA five times, and in strikeouts 12 times. In 1908, Johnson hurled three shutouts in four days, giving up 12 hits in the three games, yet he had to settle for a 14-14 record with his last-place club.

His greatest season was 1913, when he posted a 36-7 record with a 1.09 ERA. In 346 innings that year, he gave up only 230 hits, struck out 243 and walked only 38. He pitched 11 shutouts with 55 ⅔ consecutive scoreless innings, a mark which stood until 1968. Johnson even set the record for fielding that year, with no errors in 103 chances. He was voted AL MVP. Johnson finally made it to the World Series in 1924 at the age of 36. The old man was 23-7 that year and led the league in his usual categories: wins, ERA, strikeouts, and shutouts. The writers gave him another MVP Award.
Playing Career: *1907-1927; Was A*
Managerial Career: *1929-1935; Was A, Cle A*

Dick Johnston
Johnston, Richard Frederick
B: Apr 6, 1863   D: Apr 4, 1934

Pos: OF, SS	BA: .251
Hits: 751	HRs: 33
RBI: 386	BBs: 133

Johnston's eight-year major league career ended after he played for King Kelly's Killers in Cincinnati. The team drank heavily and played badly. Some of the men deliberately got arrested on Sunday nights and stayed in jail to save on hotel bills. Johnston led the NL in triples with 18 in 1888, the fourth of five years he played for the Boston Beaneaters.
Playing Career: *1884-1891; Ric AA, Bos N, Bos P, NY P, Cin AA*

Doc Johnston
Johnston, Wheeler Roger
B: Sep 9, 1887   D: Feb 17, 1961

Pos: 1B	BA: .263
Hits: 992	HRs: 14
RBI: 379	BBs: 264

Playing for Cleveland against his brother Jimmy in the 1920 World Series, Doc outhit his sibling .273 to .214. In 1919 Johnston rapped nine consecutive hits in a four-game stretch. He was a speedster, stealing 139 bases, with 26 his high mark in 1915.
Playing Career: *1909, 1912-1916, 1918-1922; Cin N, Cle A, Pit N, Phi A*

Jimmy Johnston
Johnston, James Harle
B: Dec 10, 1889   D: Feb 14, 1967

Pos: 3B, 2B, SS, OF	BA: .294
Hits: 1,493	HRs: 22
RBI: 410	BBs: 391

After stealing a record-setting 112 bases in the Pacific Coast League, Johnston pilfered 169 more in the majors. He hit .300 with the Dodgers in the 1916 World Series, then

Walter "Big Train" Johnson with a Salvation Army member.

played against his brother Doc in the 1920 Fall Classic. Jimmy batted .325, .319 and .325 in 1921-1923, scoring 325 runs in those three years and twice slashing 203 hits. After his playing days, Johnston coached the Dodgers and managed in the minors for several years.
Playing Career: *1911, 1914, 1916-1926; Chi A, Chi N, Brk N, Bos N, NY N*

Jay Johnstone (r), after a 1982 homer.

Jay Johnstone
Johnstone, John William
B: Nov 20, 1945

Pos: OF   BA: .267
Hits: 1,254   HRs: 102
RBI: 531   BBs: 429

Sophomoric witticisms and pranks contributed to Johnstone's reputation as baseball's leading flake. He was also a very good ballplayer, and was occasionally spectacular with the bat, as when he hit .778 and slugged 1.111 in the 1976 NLCS. He starred in the 1981 World Series, belting a pinch-hit, two-run homer as the Dodgers came back from a 6-3 deficit to win Game Four. After his playing career Johnstone became a broadcaster.
Playing Career: *1966-1985; Cal A, Chi A, Oak A, Phi N, NY A, SD N, LA N, Chi N*

Bob Jones
Jones, Robert Walter
B: Dec 2, 1889   D: Aug 30, 1964

Pos: 3B   BA: .265
Hits: 791   HRs: 7
RBI: 316   BBs: 208

When Ty Cobb was his manager in 1921, Jones hit .303 with 72 RBI. After his major league seasons with the Tigers, Jones returned to the Pacific Coast League, where he had starred before reaching the majors.
Playing Career: *1917-1925; Det A*

Charley Jones.

Charley Jones
Jones, Charles Wesley
B: Apr 30, 1850   D: Deceased

Pos: OF, 1B, P   BA: .298
Hits: 1,114   HRs: 56
RBI: 224 (inc.)   BBs: 237

Born Benjamin Wesley Rippay, Charley Jones was the first popular slugger in the NL, and its first blacklisted player. Jones lived it up in Cincinnati but left in anticipation of the club folding. In 1879 he signed a three-year pact with Boston. He led the NL with 9 home runs, 85 runs scored and 62 RBI that season. The next year he became the first player to hit two homers in one inning.

When the champion Boston club failed to pay his salary on time later that season, Jones sued them. The court garnished box office receipts in Cleveland. The Reds' response was to blacklist Jones – he missed two years. Then the American Association, composed of cities that had been kicked out of the NL, began play. Jones signed with the new Cincinnati club and continued his career. In 1884 he became the third man to hit three triples in one game. That year he scored 117 runs in 112 games with only 148 hits. The following year he hit a career-high .322.
Playing Career: *1875-1880, 1883-1888; Keo Westerns n, Har Dark Blues n, Cin N, Chi N, Bos N, Cin AA, NY AA, KC AA*

Cleon Jones
Jones, Cleon Joseph
B: Aug 4, 1942

Pos: OF   BA: .281
Hits: 1,196   HRs: 93
RBI: 524   BBs: 360

The 1969 World Champion Mets had some unlikely postseason heroes, including Jones. He batted .429 in the NLCS, then really stayed on his toes in Game Five of the World Series. With the Mets trailing 3-0, Jones took a pitch on the foot. The umpires did not believe him until they recovered the ball, which showed the telltale smear of shoe polish. Jones went to first and the next batter drove him in with a home run to begin the Mets' comeback.
Playing Career: *1963, 1965-1976; NY N, Chi A*

Dalton Jones
Jones, James Dalton
B: Dec 10, 1943

Pos: 2B, 3B, 1B   BA: .235
Hits: 548   HRs: 41
RBI: 237   BBs: 191

In the heat of the four-team 1967 pennant race, Jones hit a 10th-inning, game-winning home run at Tiger Stadium. He led the AL with 13 pinch hits that season. Jones once pinch hit a grand slam but passed a runner in the basepaths, making it a single.
Playing Career: *1964-1972; Bos A, Det A, Tex A*

The White Sox' Fielder Jones, 1908.

Davy Jones
Jones, David Jefferson (Kangaroo)
B: Jun 30, 1880 D: Mar 31, 1972

Pos: OF	BA: .270
Hits: 1,020	HRs: 9
RBI: 289	BBs: 478

Jones provided a classic description of ballplayers from his era when he said, "baseball attracted all sorts of people in those days. We had stupid guys, smart guys, tough guys, mild guys, crazy guys, college men, slickers from the city, and hicks from the country." Jones stole 207 bases and scored 643 runs in 1,098 games. He hit .353 in the 1907 World Series, and stole three bases.
Playing Career: *1901-1904, 1906-1915; Mil A, StL A, Chi N, Det A, Chi A, Pit F*

Doug Jones
Jones, Douglas Reid
B: Jun 24, 1957

Pos: P	ERA: 3.06
W-L: 41-50	Sos: 499
ShOs: 0	Saves: 190

A new style of reliever, Jones gets batters out by making good pitches and exhibiting good control. He signed with the Indians as a minor league free agent in 1985, and went to the bullpen to salvage his career. Jones has made the All-Star team four of the five years, 1988-1992.
Playing Career: *1982, 1986-; Mil A, Cle A, Hou N*

Fielder Jones
Jones, Fielder Allison
B: Aug 13, 1871 D: Mar 13, 1934

Pos: OF	BA: .284
Hits: 1,924	HRs: 20
RBI: 632	BBs: 818
Managerial Record	
Won: 683 Lost: 582 Pct: .540	

With a given name like Fielder, Jones was destined to play baseball. He was a top player – batted over .330 six times, scored 1,184 runs and stole 359 bases – but it was as manager that Jones truly excelled. He suspended players for drinking, being out of shape, or making bonehead plays, but he was also a champion of their rights. Jones would argue with umpires and was often ejected from games.

Jones is credited with inventing the "motion infield" and was one of the first to position outfielders according to the hitter. He managed the 1906 "Hitless Wonder" White Sox, who stunned the Cubs with a 4-2 World Series victory. Jones quit the White Sox in controversy, having lost the final game of the 1908 season and the pennant when he started a tired Doc White in place of a rested Frank Smith, whom he disliked.
Playing Career: *1896-1908, 1914-1915; Brk N, Chi A, StL F*
Managerial Career: *1904-1908, 1914-1918; Chi A, StL F, StL A*

Mack Jones
Jones, Mack (Mack the Knife)
B: Nov 6, 1938

Pos: OF	BA: .252
Hits: 778	HRs: 133
RBI: 415	BBs: 383

Jones ripped four hits in his debut, tying the 20th-century NL mark. He hit 31 homers in his first full season, contributing to the Braves' already powerful lineup of Hank Aaron, Eddie Mathews and Joel Torre. Jones hit the first NL home run in Canada.
Playing Career: *1961-1963, 1965-1971; Mil N, Atl N, Cin N, Mon N*

Randy Jones
Jones, Randall Leo
B: Jan 12, 1950

Pos: P	ERA: 3.42
W-L: 100-123	SOs: 735
ShOs: 19	Saves: 2

Jones had two tremendous seasons, winning 20 and 22 in 1975-1976. He pitched in the All-Star Game both years, and was runner-up, then winner of the Cy Young Award. The 315 innings he pitched in 1976 strained his arm; he was never the same.
Playing Career: *1973-1982; SD N, NY N*

Ruppert Jones
Jones, Ruppert Sanderson
B: Mar 12, 1955

Pos: OF	BA: .250
Hits: 1,103	HRs: 147
RBI: 579	BBs: 534

The first player selected in the 1976 expansion draft, Jones hit 24 homers in 1977 and 21 in 1979 for the Mariners. He still holds Seattle's record for runs scored in a season, with 109 in 1979. Jones appeared in the 1984 World Series for the champion Tigers.
Playing Career: *1976-1987; KC A, Sea A, NY A, SD N, Det A, Cal A*

Sad Sam Jones
Jones, Samuel (Toothpick, Red)
B: Dec 14, 1925 D: Nov 5, 1971

Pos: P	ERA: 3.59
W-L: 102-101	SOs: 1,376
ShOs: 17	No-hitters: 2

Known as Red in the Negro Leagues, Jones always chewed a toothpick as he tossed his curveball past hitters. He pitched the Cleveland Buckeyes to the Negro World Series in 1947. After spending almost five years in the minors, Jones became a star in his first full season of major league ball, tossing a no-hitter, leading the NL in strikeouts, and making the All-Star team. He led the NL in whiffs three times. Jones won 21 games in 1959, leading the league in ERA and shutouts, and made the All-Star team again.
Playing Career: *1951-1952, 1955-1964; Cle A, Chi N, StL N, SF N, Det A, Bal A*

Samuel Pond "Sad Sam" Jones.

Sad Sam Jones
Jones, Samuel Pond (Horsewhips)
B: Jul 26, 1892 D: Jul 6, 1966

Pos: P	ERA: 3.84
W-L: 229-217	SOs: 1,233
ShOs: 36	No-hitters: 1

Jones pitched 22 consecutive seasons in the AL, a record shared by Herb Pennock, Early Wynn and Red Ruffing. He was a workhorse, hurling 3,883 innings. Like most pitchers of his day, Jones relieved as well as started, and his eight saves in 1922 led the AL, and contributed to his 31 career total. Bill McGeehan of the *New York Herald-Tribune* called him "Sad Sam" because Jones looked downcast on the field.

Jones likened his sharp-breaking curve to a horsewhip. Once in the starting rotation he went 16-5, leading the AL with a .762 winning percentage. He won 23 games for the 1921 Red Sox, with a league-high five shutouts. As the Yankee ace in 1923, he was 21-8, hurling a September no-hitter against the Athletics and leading the Yankees to their first World Championship. His relief in the final game of the World Series clinched it.
Playing Career: *1914-1935; Cle A, Bos A, NY A, StL A, Was A, Chi A*

Sheldon Jones
Jones, Sheldon Leslie (Available)
B: Feb 2, 1922

Pos: P	ERA: 3.96
W-L: 54-57	SOs: 413
ShOs: 5	Saves: 12

Jones's nickname came from a character in the "Li'l Abner" comic strip. He was a starter and a reliever, winning 16 games in 1948 and averaging 200 innings, 1948-1950. He launched the Giants' stretch 1951 drive with a couple of relief wins in early September.
Playing Career: *1946-1953; NY N, Bos N, Chi N*

Tom Jones
Jones, Thomas
B: Jan 22, 1877   D: Jun 21, 1923

Pos: 1B, 2B	BA: .251
Hits: 964	HRs: 3
RBI: 336	BBs: 193

Jones hit only three homers in 3,847 at-bats, one of the 10 lowest home run ratios in baseball history. His fielding and clever baserunning kept him a regular for seven seasons. In 1906 he made 22 putouts at first in a nine-inning game to set the major league record.
Playing Career: *1902, 1904-1910; Bal A, StL A, Det A*

Willie Jones
Jones, Willie Edward (Puddin' Head)
B: Aug 16, 1925   D: Oct 18, 1983

Pos: 3B	BA: .258
Hits: 1,502	HRs: 190
RBI: 812	BBs: 755

A key member of the Phillies Whiz Kids who captured the 1950 pennant, Jones led NL third basemen in fielding six of seven years,

Willie Jones in 1950.

Eddie Joost leaps over Red Schoendienst in the 1949 All-Star Game.

including five in a row, 1951-1955. As a rookie, he tied a major league record with four consecutive doubles in a game. He hit 25 homers, scored 100 runs and drove in 88, all career-high marks in 1950. That year Jones batted .286 in the World Series, but his team lost to the veteran Yankees. He played 142 or more games eight years in a row, and made the NL All-Star squad in 1950 and 1951.
Playing Career: *1947-1961; Phi N, Cle A, Cin N*

Eddie Joost
Joost, Edwin David
B: Jun 5, 1916

Pos: SS, 2B, 3B	BA: .239
Hits: 1,339	HRs: 134
RBI: 601	BBs: 1,041
Managerial Record	
Won: 51 Lost: 103 Pct: .331	

Joost tasted glory as a reserve infielder with the Reds, playing in the 1940 World Series for the champion Cincinnati club. When he became their regular shortstop in 1941, he committed 45 errors. The next year, he again logged 45 miscues, leading the league. He was traded to the Braves, where he set an unofficial record of batting just .185 in more than 400 at-bats, the lowest ever for a regular player.

After World War II, Joost played shortstop for Connie Mack's A's. His hitting improved to .289 in 1951. He played in the All-Star Game twice, 1949 and 1952. From 1947 through 1952, he walked more than 100 times a season, twice having more walks than hits. Joost led shortstops in putouts four times to tie the league record. He was the A's manager in 1954.
Playing Career: *1936-1937, 1939-1943, 1945, 1947-1955; Cin N, Bos N, Phi A, Bos A*
Managerial Career: *1954; Phi A*

Buck Jordan
Jordan, Baxter Byerly
B: Jan 16, 1907   D: Mar 18, 1993

Pos: 1B, 3B	BA: .299
Hits: 890	HRs: 17
RBI: 281	BBs: 182

A contact hitter who compiled high averages in the minors, Jordan hit few home runs. He was a regular with the Braves for four years, batting more than .300 twice, reaching a high of .323 in 1936. Jordan twice had eight hits in a doubleheader.
Playing Career: *1927, 1929, 1931-1938; NY N, Was A, Bos N, Cin N, Phi N*

Tim Jordan
Jordan, Timothy Joseph
B: Sep 5, 1879   D: Sep 13, 1949

Pos: 1B	BA: .261
Hits: 474	HRs: 32
RBI: 232	BBs: 232

The most obscure of all 20th-century home run leaders, Jordan led the NL twice, with 12 in 1906 and 12 again in 1908. He was extremely popular with Brooklyn Superba fans, but ailing knees forced his early retirement from the national pastime.
Playing Career: *1901, 1903, 1906-1910; Was A, NY A, Brk N*

Mike Jorgensen
Jorgensen, Michael
B: Aug 16, 1948

Pos: 1B	BA: .243
Hits: 833	HRs: 95
RBI: 426	BBs: 532

The 1973 Gold Glove first baseman, Jorgensen was an asset to any club in a pennant race. The Cardinals picked him up for the 1985 season and he appeared in the World Series that year. They may have remembered Jorgensen's extra-inning grand slam that cost St. Louis the division title in 1973.
Playing Career: *1968, 1970-1985; NY N, Mon N, Oak A, Tex A, Atl N, StL N*

Von Joshua
Joshua, Von Everett
B: May 1, 1948

Pos: OF	BA: .273
Hits: 610	HRs: 30
RBI: 184	BBs: 108

After playing in the 1974 NLCS and World Series, Joshua had a great season in 1975. He led NL outfielders in fielding, and batted .318 with 25 doubles, 10 triples, 20 stolen bases and 75 runs scored, all career highs.
Playing Career: *1969-1971, 1973-1977, 1979-1980; LA N, SF N, Mil A, SD N*

Addie Joss
Joss, Adrian
B: Apr 12, 1880   D: Apr 14, 1911
Hall of Fame 1978

Pos: P	ERA: 1.88
W-L: 160-97	SOs: 926
ShOs: 46	No-hitters: 2

Joss was the hardest pitcher in baseball history to reach base against, allowing just 8.7 runners per nine innings, and only 1.4 of them were walked. Joss pitched with a pinwheel motion. He would pivot away from the hitter, then deliver sidearm with a "jump" ball that batters swore dipped, leveled off, and dipped again. It earned him the second lowest ERA in baseball history.

Joss was great in 1908, when the Indians made a run for the pennant against Ed Walsh's White Sox and Ty Cobb's Tigers. Joss won seven of his club's first 11 games. The three teams were neck and neck on October 2 when Joss faced Walsh, who was 40-14 at that point. Walsh pitched a four-hitter, fanning 15; Joss topped him 1-0 with a perfect game. Although the Indians lost to the Tigers by 1½ games, Joss was 24-11 with a 1.16 ERA. He tossed another no-hitter in 1910, but hurt his elbow and ended the season early with a 5-5 record. The next spring he died of tubercular meningitis.
Playing Career: *1902-1910; Cle A*

Bill Joyce
Joyce, William Michael (Scrappy Bill)
B: Sep 21, 1865   D: May 8, 1941

Pos: 3B, 1B	BA: .294
Hits: 970	HRs: 71
RBI: 607	BBs: 718
Managerial Record	
Won: 179 Lost: 122 Pct: .595	

In his debut, Joyce batted back-to-back bloop hits, which were dubbed "Texas League" hits in the Texan's honor. He is the only major league batter in baseball history to hit four triples in one game. Joyce sat out the 1893 season in a contract dispute and returned with the Nationals in 1894 to hit a career-high .355, the first of four consecutive .300-seasons. Joyce hit 17 home runs in both 1894 and 1895, including three in one game, August 20, 1894.
Playing Career: *1890-1892, 1894-1898; Brk P, Bos AA, Brk N, Was N, NY N*
Managerial Career: *1896-1898; NY N*

Wally Joyner
Joyner, Wally (Wally World)
B: Jun 16,1962

Pos: 1B	BA: .286
Hits: 1,224	HRs: 138
RBI: 649	BBs: 444

Joyner replaced Rod Carew as the Angels' first baseman in 1986 and became a celebrity almost instantly. He was the first rookie to start an All-Star Game since fan balloting was reinstated in 1970. He followed his rookie year with 34 homers and 117 RBI, plus 100 runs scored.
Playing Career: *1986-; Cal A, KC A*

Joe Judge
Judge, Joseph Ignatius
B: May 25, 1894   D: Mar 11, 1963

Pos: 1B	BA: .298
Hits: 2,352	HRs: 71
RBI: 1,037	BBs: 965

Judge set fielding standards for first basemen with graceful sure-handedness. He played from the dead-ball era to the rabbit-ball era of the 1920s and 1930s, leading or tying AL first

The Cleveland Indians' Hall of Fame pitcher Addie Joss.

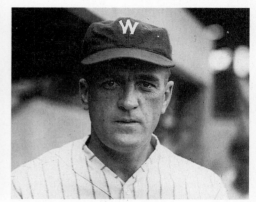

The Senators' Joe Judge, 1925.

basemen in fielding six times – still a league record. He anchored the Senators' infield that set the major league double play record two years in a row, with 168 in 1922 and 182 in 1923. Many feel that the Senators' 1924 infield quartet of Judge, Bucky Harris at second, Ossie Bluege at third, and MVP Roger Peckinpaugh at short, formed the finest defensive unit ever assembled.

Judge compiled a lifetime fielding average of .993, an AL record that stood for more than 30 years. At his retirement, he also held AL career first base marks for games, putouts, double plays and total chances. Judge batted .300 or more nine times. After retiring from active service, he became the baseball coach at Georgetown, 1937-1958, except for 1945-1946, when he coached for the Senators.
Playing Career: *1915-1934; Was A, Brk N, Bos A*

Wally Judnich
Judnich, Walter Franklin
B: Jan 24, 1917   D: Jul 12, 1971

Pos: OF	BA: .281
Hits: 782	HRs: 90
RBI: 420	BBs: 385

Judnich blazed through the Yankees' farm system, where he was tagged as the next "Joe DiMaggio." His only problem was that the Yanks still had DiMaggio in center. Judnich was traded to the Browns, where he led outfielders in fielding three times and averaged 18 homers a year.
Playing Career: *1940-1942, 1946-1949; StL A, Cle A, Pit N*

Billy Jurges
Jurges, William Frederick
B: May 9, 1908

Pos: SS, 3B	BA: .258
Hits: 1,613	HRs: 43
RBI: 656	BBs: 568
Managerial Record	
Won: 59 Lost: 63 Pct: .484	

It seemed that each NL pennant contender had a star at shortstop during the 1930s. Jurges was the Cubs' man. He was selected for three All-Star Games, but never played, yet he led NL shortstops in fielding four times in eight years, 1932-1939. As a rookie he displaced veteran Woody English and teamed with fellow rookie Billy Herman to become part of the NL's finest double play combination, as the Cubs won three pennants. Jurges once ripped nine straight hits.

In 1932 Violet Valli, a love-crazed fan, phoned Jurges, then entered his hotel room with a gun to attempt suicide. Jurges intervened and was shot in the hand and ribs. Jurges wound up missing only three weeks of action and the Cubs signed shortstop Mark Koenig to substitute. As a manager, Jurges was unexceptional in two seasons, but during his tenure, Pumpsie Green became the first black player for the Red Sox.
Playing Career: *1931-1947; Chi N, NY N*
Managerial Career: *1959-1960; Bos A*

Billy Jurges takes a cut in batting practice for the Chicago Cubs.

Jim Kaat
Kaat, James Lee
B: Nov 7, 1938

Pos: P	ERA: 3.45
W-L: 283-237	SOs: 2,461
ShOs: 31	Saves: 18

Perhaps the best-fielding pitcher ever, Kaat won 16 consecutive Gold Glove Awards. Kaat was also a fair batter and holds the pitchers' record for sacrifices, with 134. Warren Spahn, Eddie Plank and Steve Carlton are the only left-handers who won more games. Three times a 20-game winner, Kaat used a good fastball, guile and a brutal conditioning program to pitch for a record 25 seasons.

Kaat's best year was 1966 with Minnesota, when he led the league with 25 wins and was named Pitcher of the Year by *The Sporting News*. His other 20-win seasons came after the Twins sold him to the White Sox, where he was reunited with his former pitching coach Johnny Sain. Kaat won 20 and 21 in 1974 and 1975. He pitched more than 200 innings 14 times, more than 300 twice. Kaat is the Twins' all-time winningest pitcher with 189

Jim Kaat (c) after a 1965 WS win.

victories. After retiring as a player, he was the Reds' pitching coach, then went to the TV broadcasting booth for the Yankees.
Playing Career: *1959-1983; Was A, Min A, Chi A, Phi N, NY A, StL N*

Al Kaline
Kaline, Albert William
B: Dec 19, 1934
Hall of Fame 1980

Pos: OF	BA: .297
Hits: 3,007	HRs: 399
RBI: 1,583	BBs: 1,270

After signing with Detroit for a $35,000 bonus in 1953, Kaline went directly to the Tigers. Lacking minor league experience, he started slowly with the big club. Red Sox legend Ted Williams told the kid to build up his wrist strength by squeezing baseballs as hard as he could. Two years later, Kaline hit .340 to become the youngest batting champ ever.

Kaline and his powerful throwing arm won 11 Gold Glove Awards. In 1971 he played 133 games without an error. He spent his entire 22-year career with the Tigers, hitting more home runs and playing more games than anyone else in Tiger history. He scored 1,622 runs, hit 498 doubles, and was selected for 18 All-Star Games. Kaline appeared in only one World Series, batting .379 with 8 RBI to lead the Tigers to victory in seven games over the Cardinals in 1968. Kaline joined the Tigers' TV broadcasting crew after his retirement from the field.
Playing Career: *1953-1974; Det A*

Al Kaline.

Chicago's Willie Kamm, 1925.

Willie Kamm
Kamm, William Edward
B: Feb 2, 1900   D: Dec 21, 1988

Pos: 3B	BA: .281
Hits: 1,643	HRs: 29
RBI: 826	BBs: 824

The White Sox bought Kamm from the Pacific Coast League in 1923 for the sensational price of $100,000 to replace Buck Weaver. In Chicago, Kamm earned a reputation as one of the best-fielding third basemen ever. He led the AL in fielding average for his position eight times, and was consistently among the leaders in all fielding categories except errors.

Kamm was adept at the hidden-ball trick, claiming to have used it once or twice each season. Although he did not have home run power, he was a good contact hitter, and walked twice as often as he struck out. In 1936 and 1937 Kamm managed the San Francisco Missions in the Pacific Coast League. Although his highest baseball salary was $13,500, he retired as one of the wealthier players. Kamm survived the 1929 stock market crash to make substantial gains in the 1930s.
Playing Career: *1923-1935; Chi A, Cle A*

Alex Kampouris
Kampouris, Alexis William
B: Nov 13, 1912

Pos: 2B	BA: .243
Hits: 531	HRs: 45
RBI: 284	BBs: 244

The Chicago Hellenic Society assembled at Wrigley Field in 1937 to salute the Reds' second baseman. In an embarrassing sequence of events, Kampouris was heaped with praise and given a car before the game, then he proceeded to commit three errors in one inning.
Playing Career: *1934-1939, 1941-1943; Cin N, NY N, Brk N, Was A*

Eddie Kasko
Kasko, Edward Michael
B: Jun 27, 1932

Pos: SS, 3B, 2B	BA: .264
Hits: 935	HRs: 22
RBI: 261	BBs: 265

Managerial Record
Won: 345   Lost: 295   Pct: .539

When the Reds traded Roy McMillan to the Braves for Joey Jay, and moved Kasko to shortstop, the 1961 NL champs were built. He made the All-Star team that year despite hitting only .271, then batted .316 in the World Series. Kasko was known as a laid-back practical joker in the clubhouse. After managing for three years in the International League, he managed the Red Sox for four seasons, finishing second in the East twice.
Playing Career: *1957-1966; StL N, Cin N, Hou N, Bos A*
Managerial Career: *1970-1973; Bos A*

Benny Kauff
Kauff, Benjamin Michael
B: Jan 5, 1890   D: Nov 17, 1961

Pos: OF	BA: .311
Hits: 961	HRs: 49
RBI: 454	BBs: 367

The "Ty Cobb of the Federal League," Kauff led in batting and stolen bases in both FL seasons. When it disbanded, Kauff was tapped for the Giants by John McGraw. In 1917 he batted .308 and hit two home runs in the World Series.
Playing Career: *1912, 1914-1920; NY A, Ind F, Brk F, NY N*

Tony Kaufmann
Kaufmann, Anthony Charles
B: Dec 16, 1900   D: Jun 4, 1982

Pos: P	ERA: 4.18
W-L: 64-62	SOs: 345
ShOs: 9	Saves: 12

Tutored by Grover Cleveland Alexander, Kaufmann was 14-10 in 1923 and 16-11 the next year. He hit two home runs on the Fourth of July, 1925. From 1938 to 1961 Kaufmann worked for the Cardinals as a minor league manager, coach and scout.
Playing Career: *1921-1931, 1935; Chi N, Phi N, StL N, NY N*

Johnny Keane
Keane, John Joseph
B: Nov 3, 1911   D: Jan 6, 1967

Managerial Record
Won: 398   Lost: 350   Pct: .532

Keane spent 31 years in the Cardinals' organization as a player, manager, coach and scout. In 1964 he led the Red Birds to a World Championship, then, upset that Bing Devine had been fired, Keane resigned, and moved on to the Yankees.
Managerial Career: *1961-1966; StL N, NY A*

Tim Keefe.

Tim Keefe
Keefe, Timothy John
B: Jan 1, 1857   D: Apr 23, 1933
Hall of Fame 1964

Pos: P	ERA: 2.62
W-L: 342-225	SOs: 2,545
ShOs: 39	Saves: 2

One of the first great change-of-pace artists, Keefe combined that pitch with a fastball and curve to win 32 games or more for six straight years. In 1883 Keefe won both ends of a July 4 doubleheader – a one-hitter in the morning and a two-hitter in the afternoon. Five years later he won 19 consecutive starts. He and Mickey Welch pitched the Giants to the NL flag in 1888, and in the championship series against the St. Louis Browns that October, Keefe won all four of New York's victories. He led the league in wins, percentage, ERA, strikeouts and shutouts that year.

Actively concerned about ballplayers' welfare, Keefe helped his brother-in-law John Montgomery Ward establish the Players League. Keefe also served as secretary for the Brotherhood of Base Ball Players. He protested player salary ceilings and was among those who tested the reserve clause in court and won. Keefe even designed the Giants' famous "funeral uniforms" in 1889 – all black with "New York" in white letters across the shirt front.
Playing Career: *1880-1893; Tro N, NY AA, NY N, NY P, Phi N*

Willie Keeler
Keeler, William Henry (Wee Willie)
B: Mar 3, 1872   D: Jan 1, 1923
Hall of Fame 1939

Pos: OF	BA: .345
Hits: 2,962	HRs: 34
RBI: 810	BBs: 524

"I hit 'em where they ain't" was Keeler's oft-quoted explanation of his success with the bat. At 5'4½" and 140 pounds, Keeler looked like the batboy. He choked up on his 30-inch stick, the lightest in the league, and knocked the ball downward, resulting in the famous "Baltimore Chop." The ball bounced into the air; before it came down, Keeler was safe at first. He built a hitting streak of 44 games in 1897, setting NL and major league records.

Keeler hit .432 in 1897, leading the NL, and continued his lead the next year with a .379 mark. He had two other seasons over .390, stole 495 bases and scored 1,727 runs. A brilliant bunter, Keeler is one of the men responsible for the modern foul-strike rule. He could bunt innumerable fouls waiting for a pitch he liked. The rule was changed and umpires began calling outs on foul bunts after two strikes. Known as an outstanding right fielder, Keeler played his first major league games as a left-handed third baseman.
Playing Career: *1892-1910; NY N, Brk N, Bal N, NY A*

Wee Willie Keeler.

Bill Keister
Keister, William Hoffman (Wagon Tongue)
B: Aug 17, 1874   D: Aug 19, 1924

Pos: SS, 2B, OF, 3B	BA: .312
Hits: 758	HRs: 18
RBI: 400	BBs: 90

A tremendous slugger who played for seven teams in seven years, Keister led the AL in triples with 21 in 1901. That year he set the record for the lowest season fielding average for a shortstop in 100 or more games with a mark of .861 – 97 errors in 114 games.
Playing Career: *1896, 1898-1903; Bal N, Bos N, StL N, Bal A, Was A, Phi N*

George Kell played third base for the Detroit Tigers from 1947 to 1952.

George Kell
Kell, George Clyde
B: Aug 23, 1922
Hall of Fame 1983

Pos: 3B	BA: .306
Hits: 2,054	HRs: 78
RBI: 870	BBs: 620

Kell gave the Tigers and several other AL clubs steady fielding and .300 hitting after World War II. Nine times his batting average was over .300. He led the league in batting in 1949, edging out Ted Williams's .3428 average with a .3429 mark. Williams had led the batting race until the final week of the season, but Kell came back from an injury and had a hot streak. He batted .340 the following year, and led the AL with 218 hits and 56 doubles, but lost the batting title to Billy Goodman.

Never a power hitter, Kell drove in 101 runs with only 8 homers in 1950. He led the league in hits and doubles again in 1951. Possessing an excellent throwing arm and sure-handedness, Kell led AL third basemen in fielding average seven times, in assists four times, and in putouts and double plays twice. He made the AL All-Star team seven times. After concluding his career as the Orioles' third baseman, he was succeeded by Brooks Robinson. Kell became the Tigers' play-by-play announcer.
Playing Career: *1943-1957; Phi A, Det A, Bos A, Chi A, Bal A*

Charlie Keller
Keller, Charles Ernest (King Kong)
B: Sep 12, 1916   D: May 23, 1990

Pos: OF	BA: .286
Hits: 1,085	HRs: 189
RBI: 760	BBs: 784

Keller played in the Yankees' outfield alongside Joe DiMaggio and Tommy Henrich from 1939 to 1943. The Yankees won four pennants in those five years. Yankee fans claim it was their greatest outfield trio. In 1939 Keller hit .438 in the World Series; his two homers and four RBI won Game Three. He barreled into the Reds' Ernie Lombardi to score the deciding run in the 10th inning of the final game. In the 1941 Series, Keller hit .389. A bad back forced him to quit the game he loved.
Playing Career: *1939-1943, 1945-1952; NY A, Det A*

Joe Kelley
Kelley, Joseph James
B: Dec 9, 1871   D: Aug 14, 1943
Hall of Fame 1971

Pos: OF	BA: .317
Hits: 2,222	HRs: 65
RBI: 1,193	BBs: 910
Managerial Record	
Won: 338 Lost: 321	Pct: .513

The heavy-hitting left fielder for the famous Baltimore Orioles of the late 19th century, Kelley played on six pennant-winning teams in seven years, the final two with the Brooklyn Superbas, for whom he was captain. Kelley hit .300 or more for 11 consecutive seasons. He scored 1,424 runs and stole 443 bases during his career. In 1894, when he hit .393, he was 9-for-9 in a doubleheader, including four doubles in one game.

Kelley was a speedy outfielder with a powerful arm. He arrived at the ballpark by nine in the morning to practice his bunting and running. A handsome – and vain – man, reportedly he kept a mirror under his cap and liked to sneak looks at himself while playing outfield. As a manager, he figured in a bit of controversy at the end of the 1908 NL pennant race, when he fielded a team of young Boston players, allowing the Giants to sweep the Braves and tie with the Cubs.
Playing Career: *1891-1908; Bos N, Pit N, Bal N, Brk N, Bal A, Cin N*
Managerial Career: *1902-1905, 1908; Cin N, Bos N*

Alex Kellner
Kellner, Alexander Raymond
B: Aug 26, 1924

Pos: P	ERA: 4.41
W-L: 101-112	SOs: 816
ShOs: 9	Saves: 5

Kellner was an All-Star in 1949 when he went 20-12 as a rookie. Being forced to pitch for second-division teams, he never again won more than 12. He was the starting pitcher for the first game of the 1956 Athletic season in Kansas City. He batted .282 in 1958.
Playing Career: *1948-1959; Phi A, KC A, Cin N, StL N*

George Kelly
Kelly, George Lange (Highpockets)
B: Sep 10, 1895   D: Oct 13, 1984
Hall of Fame 1973

Pos: 1B, 2B	BA: .297
Hits: 1,778	HRs: 148
RBI: 1,020	BBs: 386

George Kelly was the slick-fielding, clutch-hitting first baseman for a Giants team that won four straight NL pennants, 1921-1924. Manager McGraw exclaimed that "Kelly made more important hits" for him than any other player he ever had. He led the NL in RBIs with 94 in 1920, then knocked home over 100 in each of the pennant-winning seasons. In 1924 he led the league again with 136 RBI. A

George "Highpockets" Kelly.

good home run hitter in a great home run park, he led the NL in 1921 with 23 and set a record in 1924 with seven homers in six games. The lanky "Highpockets" had one of the most powerful arms in the league. His rocket throw across the infield completed a brilliant double play to end the 1921 World Series. He consistently ranked high in assists and holds the NL records for most putouts and most chances in a season. He even played second base for most of 1925, when McGraw wanted Kelly's bat in the lineup while breaking in Bill Terry at first base. Kelly was a nephew of outfielder Bill Lange of the Chicago Colts (Cubs) in the 1890s, and the brother of Ren Kelly with the 1923 A's.
Playing Career: *1915-1917, 1919-1930, 1932; NY N, Pit N, Cin N, Chi N, Brk N*

King Kelly
Kelly, Michael Joseph (King Kel)
B: Dec 31, 1857   D: Nov 8, 1894
Hall of Fame 1945

Pos: C, OF, 1B, 3B, 2B   BA: .308
Hits: 1,813   HRs: 69
RBI: 793   BBs: 549
Managerial Record
Won: 173   Lost: 148   Pct: .539

The most popular and best dressed baseball player of the 19th century, Kelly rode to the park in a silk hat, ascot and patent leather

King Kelly.

shoes, in a carriage pulled by two white horses, or sometimes by his fans. He went on stage reciting "Casey at the Bat" and made $3,000 for the use of his picture on advertisements. He was a big gambler and was seen often at the races. Kelly was one of the first hitters to perfect the hit-and-run, one of the first catchers to give finger signals, and one of the first outfielders to play close to back up infield plays. He was one of the first runners to use the hook slide. His most famous slide knocked the ball out of George Wright's hand to clinch the 1882 flag. He also liked to cut from first base to third base without going near second, or from second base to home, there being only one umpire in those days. Kelly's dynamic play sparked the White Stockings to five flags in seven years, 1880-1886. He led the NL in hitting with .354 in 1884 and .388 in 1886. A noted run scorer, he crossed the plate 1,357 times and stole 315 bases in only the last seven years of his career. Researchers are still counting Kelly's pilfered sacks.
Playing Career: *1878-1893; Cin N, Chi N, Bos N, Bos P, Cin AA, Bos AA, NY N*
Managerial Career: *1887, 1890-1891; Bos N, Bos P, Cin AA*

Pat Kelly
Kelly, Harold Patrick
B: Jul 30, 1944

Pos: OF, DH   BA: .264
Hits: 1,147   HRs: 76
RBI: 418   BBs: 588

Kelly was picked up by the Royals in the expansion draft, then dealt to the White Sox, who saw him as their center fielder for the next decade. He played in the 1973 All-Star Game, and led outfielders with .991 in 1975. He hit .369 for the Orioles in the 1979 ALCS and .250 in World Series.
Playing Career: *1967-1981; Min A, KC A, Chi A, Bal A, Cle A*

Tom Kelly
Kelly, Jay Thomas
B: Aug 15, 1950

Pos: 1B   BA: .181
Hits: 23   HRs: 1
RBI: 11   BBs: 15
Managerial Record
Won: 598   Lost: 559   Pct: .517

Kelly was the surprise choice of General Manager Andy MacPhail for Twins manager in 1986. Beginning as a playing manager in the Twins' system in Tacoma in 1977, he is extremely popular wherever he manages. Being the youngest skipper in the AL did not prevent him from winning the 1987 World Series in the first ever all-home field winning Series. He won again in 1991 when the Twins triumphed over the talent-laden Braves. He let his seventh game starter Jack Morris go the 10-inning distance for a 1-0 championship victory.
Playing Career: *1975; Min A*
Managerial Career: *1986-; Min A*

Ken Keltner.

Ken Keltner
Keltner, Kenneth Frederick
B: Oct 31, 1916   D: Dec 12, 1991

Pos: 3B   BA: .276
Hits: 1,570   HRs: 163
RBI: 852   BBs: 514

Keltner made two fine stops on line drives that ended Joe DiMaggio's record hit streak at 56 on July 17, 1941, before a then-record night crowd of 67,468 in Cleveland. Before that night he was mainly known as an All-Star hitter. With media concentration on his fielding, Keltner led AL third sackers three times in fielding. He was recognized as Cleveland's all-time greatest third baseman for his 11 seasons there, making the All-Star team seven of those years. On October 4, 1948, in the first playoff in AL history, Keltner's single,

double and three-run homer defeated the Red Sox at Fenway Park to win the pennant for the Indians. That season Keltner hit 31 homers and drove in 119 runs, both career highs. In the Series he went into a slump and hit .095, but his Indians won, four games to two. When he left Cleveland, he was among the club's all-time leaders in games played, doubles, home runs, RBI and hits.
Playing Career: *1937-1944, 1946-1950; Cle A, Bos A*

Steve Kemp
Kemp, Steven F.
B: Aug 7, 1954

Pos: OF	BA: .278
Hits: 1,128	HRs: 130
RBI: 634	BBs: 576

A highly touted hitter from the University of Southern California, Kemp was the first player chosen in the January 1976 draft. The next year he was the Tigers' starting left fielder. Kemp made the All-Star team in 1979, when he batted .318 with 26 home runs and 105 RBI. In 1983 he was hit on the head during batting practice, and suffered blurry vision the rest of his career. Oddly, despite his .278 lifetime average, he wore out White Sox pitching for a .379 lifetime average.
Playing Career: *1977-1986, 1988; Det A, Chi A, NY A, Pit N, Tex A*

Fred Kendall
Kendall, Fred Lyn
B: Jan 31, 1949

Pos: C	BA: .234
Hits: 603	HRs: 31
RBI: 244	BBs: 189

Randy Jones credited Kendall with much of his success. Kendall caught all of Jones's league-leading 22 victories in 1976. He was the last of the original Padres when he was traded to the Indians in December 1976, and he returned to San Diego in 1979.
Playing Career: *1969-1980; SD N, Cle A, Bos A*

Bill Kennedy
Kennedy, William P. (Roaring Bill)
B: Oct 7, 1867 D: Sep 23, 1915

Pos: P	ERA: 3.96
W-L: 187-159	SOs: 797
ShOs: 13	Saves: 9

Conversing at the top of his lungs, Roaring Bill was a lovable, eccentric illiterate who dined in restaurants by ordering what he saw others eating. As a spot starter with the Pirates, Kennedy pitched in the 1903 World Series. Up 3 games to 1, Kennedy faced Cy Young. They matched zeros for five innings until the Pirates fell apart, making four errors, and losing 11-2. It was Kennedy's last game. Boston won the next three to become World Champions.
Playing Career: *1892-1903; Brk N, NY N, Pit N*

Bob Kennedy slides home to score as catcher Yogi Berra puts on the late tag, 1954.

Bob Kennedy
Kennedy, Robert Daniel
B: Aug 18, 1920

Pos: OF	BA: .254
Hits: 1,176	HRs: 63
RBI: 514	BBs: 364
Managerial Record	
Won: 264 Lost: 278 Pct: .487	

Kennedy went from popcorn vendor to professional player at Comiskey Park. He was one of the first players signed by the White Sox to stock their farm system in 1937. Two years later, he was one of the first prospects to come out of that system. Kennedy's best year was 1950, when he hit .291 with 9 homers and 27 doubles. He later managed the Cubs and A's, then was general manager of the Cubs and Astros. His son Terry became a starting major league catcher.
Playing Career: *1939-1942, 1946-1957; Chi A, Cle A, Bal A, Det A, Brk N*
Managerial Career: *1963-1965, 1968; Chi N, Oak A*

Terry Kennedy
Kennedy, Terrance Edward
B: Jun 4, 1956

Pos: C	BA: .264
Hits: 1,313	HRs: 113
RBI: 628	BBs: 365

At 6'4", 224 pounds, Kennedy was a big target for pitchers and had big potential, but was stuck behind Ted Simmons in St. Louis for too long. He was selected for four All-Star teams, and played in the World Series, making he and Bob Kennedy one of the few father-son duos to achieve the latter distinction.
Playing Career: *1978-1991; StL N, SD N, Bal A, SF N*

Vern Kennedy
Kennedy, Lloyd Vernon
B: Mar 20, 1907 D: Jan 28, 1993

Pos: P	ERA: 4.67
W-L: 104-132	SOs: 691
ShOs: 7	No-hitters: 1

During his playing days, Kennedy was the best athlete in baseball. At age 70, he became the nation's top senior pentathlon performer. He died at age 86 when a shed that he was rebuilding fell on him. Though he had a losing record, 104-132, Kennedy was a workhorse, pitching more than 190 innings seven times. He won a career-high 21 games for the White Sox in 1936, and made the All-Star team that year. He was selected for the 1938 All-Star squad as well. Kennedy played for six different teams during his last seven years.
Playing Career: *1934-1945; Chi A, Det A, StL A, Was A, Cle A, Phi N, Cin N*

Jim Kern
Kern, James Lester (Emu)
B: Mar 15, 1949

Pos: P	ERA: 3.32
W-L: 53-57	SOs: 651
ShOs: 0	Saves: 88

Nicknamed "Emu" because he looked and acted like a big bird, Kern was one of baseball's most fun-loving pranksters. His overpowering fastball and reputation for lunacy made him intimidating in short relief. Kern averaged 8.6 strikeouts per nine innings, 1976-1979, winning 41 games and saving 75. He was an All-Star three times, although the big right-hander also led the league in relief losses twice. After an elbow injury in 1980, Kern lost his effectiveness.
Playing Career: *1974-1986; Cle A, Tex A, Cin N, Chi A, Phi N, Mil A*

Buddy Kerr
Kerr, John Joseph
B: Nov 6, 1922

Pos: SS	BA: .249
Hits: 903	HRs: 31
RBI: 333	BBs: 324

Kerr was the shortstop for the struggling Giants during the 1940s. He led NL shortstops in assists, putouts and double plays in 1945, and made the All-Star team in 1948. When the Giants set the NL record of 221 home runs in 1947, Kerr batted a career-high .287.
Playing Career: *1943-1951; NY N, Bos N*

Dickie Kerr
Kerr, Richard Henry
B: July 3, 1893   D: May 4, 1963

Pos: P	ERA: 3.84
W-L: 53-34	SOs: 235
ShOs: 7	Saves: 6

There were some honest players on the 1919 White Sox team, and Kerr was one of them. He pitched and won two games in the tainted World Series. Denied a $500 raise in 1922, Kerr left to pitch for an independent team. He then had a long career as a minor league manager.
Playing Career: *1919-1921, 1925; Chi A*

Don Kessinger
Kessinger, Donald Eulon
B: Jul 17, 1942

Pos: SS	BA: .252
Hits: 1,931	HRs: 14
RBI: 527	BBs: 684
Managerial Record	
Won: 46 Lost: 60 Pct: .434	

Signing for a $25,000 bonus, Kessinger starred with the Cubs, making the NL All-Star team seven times. In the 1965 contest of stars, Kessinger and teammates Ernie Banks, Glenn Beckert and Ron Santo composed the starting infield.

Kessinger led NL shortstops in putouts three times, assists four times, double plays four times and fielding average once. He played 54 consecutive games without making an error in 1969, setting a record for shortstops. In 1970 Kessinger was 6-for-6 in a 10-inning game.
Playing Career: *1964-1979; Chi N, StL N, Chi A*
Managerial Career: *1979; Chi A*

Jimmy Key
Key, James Edward
B: Apr 22, 1961

Pos: P	ERA: 3.37
W-L: 134-87	SOs: 1,117
ShOs: 12	Saves: 10

Overcoming arm trouble in 1988, Key has become the best southpaw in the game today. He led the AL with a 2.76 ERA in 1987. Selected for the All-Star team in 1985, 1991 and 1993, he signed with the Yankees in 1993 and went 18-6.
Playing Career: *1984-; Tor A, NY A*

Harmon Killebrew
Killebrew, Harmon Clayton (Killer)
B: Jun 29, 1936
Hall of Fame 1984

Pos: 3B, 1B, DH	BA: .256
Hits: 2,086	HRs: 573
RBI: 1,584	BBs: 1,559

A home run hitter in a class with Jimmie Foxx and Ralph Kiner, Killebrew blasted one in every 16.9 appearances at the plate. He was the Senators' first "bonus baby," signing a week before his 18th birthday in 1954. Killebrew finally made the starting lineup in 1959 as a second baseman. He finished the season with an AL leading 42 round-trippers; it was the first of eight 40-homer seasons.

Killebrew played many positions, often shifting between two in a single game. In 1962 he hit a ball over the left field roof at Tiger Stadium. On June 3, 1967, he drilled a three-run shot six rows into Metropolitan Stadium's upper deck, shattering two seats. The ball was estimated to have gone 630 feet. The splintered seats were painted orange and remained empty ever after. Killebrew performed in 13 All-Star Games. In retirement, he became a broadcaster, first with the Royals, then with the Twins.
Playing Career: *1954-1975; Was A, Min A, KC A*

The Cubs' Don Kessinger, 1968.

The Minnesota Twins' big bat Harmon Killebrew.

Bill Killefer
Killefer, William Lavier (Reindeer Bill)
B: Oct 10, 1887   D: Jul 3, 1960

Pos: C	BA: .238
Hits: 751	HRs: 4
RBI: 240	BBs: 113

Managerial Record
Won: 524   Lost: 622   Pct: .457

Killefer was Grover Cleveland Alexander's favorite catcher, first with the Phillies and then with the Cubs, to whom they both were traded in 1917. As a good defensive receiver, Killefer led the NL in fielding three times. Managing, Killefer finished in the first division only once in nine years, but he developed young catchers, bringing Bob O'Farrell and Gabby Hartnett to stardom with the Cubs. Bill was the younger brother of utility player Red Killefer.
Playing Career: *1909-1921; StL A, Phi N, Chi N*
Managerial Career: *1921-1925, 1930-1933; Chi N, StL A*

Frank Killen
Killen, Frank Bissell
B: Nov 30, 1870   D: Dec 3, 1939

Pos: P	ERA: 3.78
W-L: 164-131	SOs: 725
ShOs: 13	No-hitters: 0

Unbelievably, Killen pitched more than 400 innings three times, and more than 300 innings two other times. He won 36 games in 1893, his first year with the Pirates. Connie Mack blamed the Bucs' loss of the 1895 NL pennant on a serious spiking injury Killen got while covering home plate. The hurler came back strong, leading the NL in games, starts, complete games and innings pitched, and winning 29 games in 1896. He was a lifetime .241 hitter, with 11 home runs in 998 at-bats.
Playing Career: *1891-1900; Cin-Mil AA, Was N, Pit N, Bos N, Chi N*

Ed Killian
Killian, Edwin Henry
B: Nov 12, 1876   D: Jul 18, 1928

Pos: P	ERA: 2.38
W-L: 102-78	SOs: 516
ShOs: 22	Saves: 6

When he won both games of a doubleheader against the Red Sox to clinch the 1907 AL pennant, Killian became a hero in Detroit. He was 25-13 with a 1.78 ERA that year, and batted .320. He pitched in both the 1907 and 1908 World Series. During his career he allowed only nine home runs in 1,598 innings of work.
Playing Career: *1903-1910; Cle A, Det A*

Matt Kilroy
Kilroy, Matthew Aloysius (Matches)
B: Jun 21, 1866   D: Mar 2, 1940

Pos: P, OF	ERA: 3.47
W-L: 142-133	SOs: 1,170
ShOs: 19	No-hitters: 2

NL home run champ Ralph Kiner in the Pirates' digout, 1950.

Incendiary on and off the mound – hence the nickname – Kilroy pitched 580 innings in each of his first two seasons, hurling 66 complete games both years. The southpaw fanned 513 batters in his rookie year for the last-place Orioles. Kilroy won 29 games in 1886 and 46 in 1887, 29 again in 1889. When his arm went dead he went back to the minors as an outfielder. In retirement Kilroy prospered as a bar owner.
Playing Career: *1886-1894, 1898; Bal AA, Bos P, Cin-Mil AA, Was N, Lou N, Chi N*

Ellie Kinder
Kinder, Ellis Raymond (Old Folks)
B: Jul 26, 1914   D: Oct 16, 1968

Pos: P	ERA: 3.43
W-L: 102-71	SOs: 749
ShOs: 10	Saves: 102

Kinder posted 23 victories and had league highs of six shutouts and a .793 winning percentage in 1949. With Boston and the Yankees tied for first place in the AL, Kinder pitched the season finale. He vowed to win if his teammates would provide three runs, but left the game after eight innings, trailing 1-0. The Yankees then won the game 5-4, and the pennant. Kinder switched to relief, and in 1951 he was 11-2 with an AL-high 14 saves.
Playing Career: *1946-1957; StL A, Bos A, StL N, Chi A*

Ralph Kiner
Kiner, Ralph McPherran
B: Oct 27, 1922
Hall of Fame 1975

Pos: OF	BA: .279
Hits: 1,451	HRs: 369
RBI: 1,015	BBs: 1,011

The second most prolific home run hitter of all time, Kiner has become one of baseball's most entertaining and beloved broadcasters. A bad back caused his premature departure from the field. Kiner was signed by the Pirates for an $8,000 bonus. He played two minor league seasons before serving in the military from 1943 to 1945, then returned in 1946 to blast 23 homers, tying for the NL lead in his rookie season.

Kiner was Pittsburgh's first home run champion since 1906. In 1947 the Pirates acquired Hank Greenberg and realigned Forbes Field to encourage home runs. Both sluggers benefited; but Kiner led the NL six more years in a row, 1947-1952, smashing 51, 40, 54, 47, 42 and 37 round-trippers. He averaged 101.5 RBI a year for his 10-year career, leading the NL with 127 in 1949. He led the league three times in slugging and three times in bases on balls. Kiner was an All-Star five times.
Playing Career: *1946-1955; Pit N, Chi N, Cle A*

Clyde King
King, Clyde Edward
B: May 23, 1925

Pos: P	ERA: 4.14
W-L: 32-25	SOs: 150
ShOs: 0	Saves: 11

Managerial Record
Won: 234   Lost: 229   Pct: .505

A relief pitcher who posted high ERAs, King was nonetheless the star of the Dodger bullpen in 1951, going 14-7 with six saves and leading the NL in relief wins. His managing career started off with a bang when his Giants finished in second place in 1969, King's first year at the helm. After his dismissal as Yankees manager in 1982, King stayed in New York as part of George Steinbrenner's brain trust.
Playing Career: *1944-1945, 1947-1948, 1951-1953; Brk N, Cin N*
Managerial Career: *1969-1970, 1974-1975, 1982; SF N, Atl N, NY A*

Jim King
King, James Hubert
B: Aug 27, 1932

Pos: OF	BA: .240
Hits: 699	HRs: 117
RBI: 401	BBs: 363

Unable to find a home in the NL, King joined the expansion Senators and stayed for six full seasons. He had a strong throwing arm. His best offensive year was 1963, when he hit 24 homers with 62 RBI.
Playing Career: *1955-1958, 1961-1967; Chi N, StL N, SF N, Was A, Chi A, Cle A*

Silver King
King, Charles Frederick
B: Jan 11, 1868   D: May 21, 1938

Pos: P	ERA: 3.18
W-L: 207-153	SOs: 1,229
ShOs: 20	No-hitters: 1

Before he was 21, King established his reign over the St.Louis Browns and pitched them to the AA pennant in 1887. Star Browns pitcher Bob Caruthers was then sold to archrival Brooklyn. Relying on King, the Browns won another pennant in 1888, their fourth in a row. He posted 45 victories, tossed 585 innings, 64 complete games and six shutouts, concluding the season with a 1.64 ERA. King topped the AA in each category.
A staunch supporter of the Players' Union movement, King starred with the pennant-winning Chicago team in the Players' League. Faced with a series of salary reductions, he jumped to the Giants, then quit altogether when the Reds tried to cut his salary another $1,000. King made a lackluster attempt to come back with the Nationals, but soon retired to join his father in the brick contracting business.
Playing Career: *1886-1893, 1896-1897; KC N, StL AA, Chi P, Pit N, NY N, Cin N, Was N*

Dave Kingman enters the Mets' dugout after homering at Wrigley Field, 1976.

Dave Kingman
Kingman, David Arthur (Kong)
B: Dec 21, 1948

Pos: OF, DH, 1B, 3B	BA: .236
Hits: 1,575	HRs: 442
RBI: 1,210	BBs: 608

One of the most dangerous sluggers of his time, Kingman generated tremendous power from his 6'6" frame. Once in Kansas City, he fell away from an inside pitch, poking feebly at it. The ball flew over the right field fence for a grand slam home run. Kingman was a pitcher at the University of Southern California when coach Rod Dedeaux converted him to an outfielder. Struggling to find a position in the major leagues, Kingman was called upon to pitch twice.
He retired 20th on the all-time home run list, but also holds down the fifth spot on the all-time strikeout roster, with 1,816. Shortening his stroke with the Cubs in 1979, Kingman batted .288 with 48 homers, leading the NL in round-trippers. He again led the NL with 37 homers for the 1982 Mets, but batted just .204. In 1984 Kingman overcame several poor seasons by whacking 35 dingers and driving in 118 runs while hitting .268. He won AL Comeback Player of the Year honors.
Playing Career: *1971-1986; SF N, NY N, SD N, Cal A, NY A, Chi N, Oak A*

Clay Kirby
Kirby, Clayton Laws
B: Jun 25, 1948

Pos: P	ERA: 3.83
W-L: 75-104	SOs: 1,061
ShOs: 8	No-hitters: 0

Pitching for the unfortunate Padres, Kirby lost 81 games in the first five years of his career, but became a winner with the Reds, posting records of 12-9 and 10-6 in 1974 and 1975. He was once removed for a pinch hitter in the eighth inning of a game in which he had not allowed a hit, but was losing 1-0.
Playing Career: *1969-1976; SD N, Cin N, Mon N*

Willie Kirkland
Kirkland, Willie Charles
B: Feb 17, 1934

Pos: OF	BA: .240
Hits: 837	HRs: 148
RBI: 509	BBs: 323

In July 1961, Kirkland hit home runs on three consecutive at-bats, then walked and sacrificed in two more plate appearances. Following the All-Star break, he homered in his first at-bat, tying the major league record with four consecutive home runs. Kirkland later played in Japan.
Playing Career: *1958-1966; SF N, Cle A, Bal A, Was A*

Ed Kirkpatrick
Kirkpatrick, Edgar Leon (Spanky)
B: Oct 8, 1944

Pos: OF, C	BA: .238
Hits: 824	HRs: 85
RBI: 424	BBs: 456

First appearing in the big leagues at age 17, Kirkpatrick struggled back and forth to the minors for seven years before finding his niche with the expansion Royals. He had 14 homers in 1969, then followed with 18 dingers and 62 RBI the next season. He played in two ALCS.
Playing Career: *1962-1977; LA A, Cal A, KC A, Pit N, Tex A, Mil A*

Bruce Kison
Kison, Bruce Eugene
B: Feb 18, 1950

Pos: P	ERA: 3.66
W-L: 115-88	SOs: 1,073
ShOs: 7	Saves: 12

Known for brush-back pitches and pressure performances, Kison was the 21-year-old rookie who relieved the Pirates' starter in Game Four of the 1971 World Series – the first night game in the history of the Fall Classic. Entering in the first inning with two out and three runs scored, he allowed the Orioles only one hit in the next six innings and won the game. He also hit three batters, a World Series record. Kison was 4-0 with a 1.21 ERA in five LCS. He was 1-1 in two World Series.
Playing Career: *1971-1985; Pit N, Cal A, Bos A*

Frank Kitson
Kitson, Frank L.
B: Apr 11, 1872   D: Apr 14, 1930

Pos: P	ERA: 3.17
W-L: 128-117	SOs: 729
ShOs: 20	Saves: 8

Kitson was one of the top right-handed pitchers at the turn of the century, winning 22 games for the Orioles in 1899, and 19 each for the Superbas in 1901-1902. He was 1-0 in 1900 postseason play. From 1899 to 1903 Kitson hurled 250 or more innings each season, topping 300 in 1899. Overwork in the NL limited his effectiveness after he jumped to the new AL in 1903. Kitson pitched for the most knowledgeable managers of his era – Frank Selee, John McGraw, Ed Barrow, Bobby Lowe and Clark Griffith.
Playing Career: *1898-1907; Bal N, Brk N, Det A, Was A, NY A*

Ron Kittle
Kittle, Ronald Dale
B: Jan 5, 1958

Pos: OF, DH	BA: .239
Hits: 648	HRs: 176
RBI: 460	BBs: 236

Kittle was an instant success with the White Sox in 1983, blasting 35 homers with 100 RBI and a .504 slugging percentage. He was named to the All-Star Game roster and picked as AL Rookie of the Year.
Playing Career: *1982-1991; Chi A, NY A, Cle A, Bal A*

Mal Kittridge
Kittridge, Malachi Jedediah
B: Oct 12, 1869   D: Jun 23, 1928

Pos: C	BA: .219
Hits: 882	HRs: 17
RBI: 390	BBs: 314
Managerial Record	
Won: 1 Lost: 16 Pct: .059	

Kittridge was a solid receiver for 16 years in the majors. The only year he played 100 games – 1901 – he led the NL in fielding. Baserunners did not try to steal on him because he had a strong arm.
Playing Career: *1890-1899, 1901-1906; Chi N, Lou N, Was N, Bos N, Was A, Cle A*
Managerial Career: *1904; Was A*

Billy Klaus
Klaus, William Joseph
B: Dec 9, 1928

Pos: SS, 3B, 2B, OF	BA: .249
Hits: 626	HRs: 40
RBI: 250	BBs: 331

Each of the five times Klaus played more than 100 games, he hit well. He rapped seven homers with a .283 average in his rookie season of 1955. Billy's brother Bobby played with the Reds and Giants.
Playing Career: *1952-1953, 1955-1963; Bos N, Mil N, Bos A, Bal A, Was A, Phi N*

Chuck Klein
Klein, Charles Herbert
B: Oct 7, 1904   D: Mar 28, 1958
Hall of Fame 1980

Pos: OF	BA: .320
Hits: 2,076	HRs: 300
RBI: 1,202	BBs: 601

The 280-foot right field fence at Baker Bowl made Klein one of baseball's most prodigious sluggers. A star from the day he joined the Phillies, Klein collected more than 200 hits for five straight seasons, leading the NL in 1932 and 1933. Klein had 250 hits in 1930, and batted .386 but still finished third behind Bill Terry and Babe Herman. Klein led the league in total bases for four consecutive years, 1930-1933, leading in doubles two seasons and in homers three seasons.

Klein also led in runs scored three straight years. He once hit six homers in a span of four games, and twice hit five in three games. He scored 1,168 runs and bashed 398 doubles, 59 of them in 1930. Klein was voted NL MVP in 1932 when he hit .348 with 38 homers and 137 RBI. He also led the league in stolen bases,

Chuck Klein receives the MVP trophy in 1932.

with 20, and whacked 15 triples. The next year Klein won the Triple Crown with a .368 average, 28 homers and 120 RBI, and finished second in MVP voting, behind Carl Hubbell of the Giants.
Playing Career: *1928-1944; Phi N, Chi N, Pit N*

Lou Klein
Klein, Louis Frank
B: Oct 22, 1918   D: Jun 20, 1976

Pos: 2B   BA: .259
Hits: 269   HRs: 16
RBI: 101   BBs: 105
Managerial Record
Won: 65   Lost: 83   Pct: .439

In 1943 Klein played every inning of every game for the Cardinals, including the World Series. Unable to start in 1946, he jumped to the outlaw Mexican League, but was reinstated. He was later a member of the Cubs' famous College of Coaches.
Playing Career: *1943, 1945-1946, 1949, 1951; StL N, Cle A, Phi A*
Managerial Career: *1961-1962, 1965; Chi N*

Umpire Bill Klem.

Bill Klem
Klem, William J. (The Old Arbitrator, Catfish)
B: Feb 22, 1874   D: Sep 1, 1951
Hall of Fame 1953

Though a colorful and flamboyant personality, Klem brought dignity and respect to his profession. He is generally regarded as the greatest umpire in the game's history. He officiated exclusively behind the plate his first 16 years because of his superior ability to call balls and strikes. Klem is credited with the origination of arm signals that coincide with his plate calls.
Testimony to his skill were his 18 World Series assignments. After his umpiring career, Klem served as chief of NL umpires. Early in Klem's career, Giants Manager John

McGraw threatened to get him fired. Klem replied, ''Mr. Manager, if it's possible for you to take my job away from me, I don't want it.'' He pioneered the use of the inside chest protector. Klem umpired at the 1933 All-Star Game. In 36 seasons, he was behind the plate for five no-hitters.
Umpiring Career: *1905-1940; NL (18 WS, 2 AS)*

Ron Kline
Kline, Ronald Lee
B: Mar 9, 1932

Pos: P   ERA: 3.75
W-L: 114-144   SOs: 989
ShOs: 8   Saves: 108

A starter the first half of his career, Kline converted to relief to become the AL's top stopper in 1965. He pitched on some dreadful teams – the 1950s Pirates and the 1960s Senators – leading the NL in losses with 18 in 1956 and 16 in 1958. In 1965 Kline led the AL with 29 saves and was second with 74 appearances, setting Senators single-season records for saves and games completed.
Playing Career: *1952, 1955-1970; Pit N, StL N, LA A, Det A, Was A, Min A, SF N, Bos A, Atl N*

John Kling
Kling, John
B: Feb 25, 1875   D: Jan 31, 1947

Pos: C   BA: .272
Hits: 1,152   HRs: 20
RBI: 513   BBs: 281
Managerial Record
Won: 52   Lost: 101   Pct: .340

Kling was the best catcher in baseball during the first decade of the 20th century; his team won four pennants in five years. With Kling behind the plate, the Cubs' pitching staff had ERAs of 1.75 in 1906 and 1.73 in 1907. From

John Kling.

1902 to 1908, Kling led the NL in fielding, putouts, assists and double plays numerous times. He once threw out four base stealers in one game. In the 1907 World Series, he nabbed seven Tigers in 13 tries – not even Ty Cobb could steal a base.
Faced with deteriorating relations with Cubs management, Kling sat out the 1909 season, and the Cubs lost the NL flag for the first time since 1905. Wooed back, Kling led his team to another pennant in 1910, but when the Athletics decimated the proud Cubs pitching staff in the World Series that fall, he was blamed. Christy Mathewson defended Kling in two chapters of his book *Pitching in a Pinch*, by showing that the A's had out-scouted the Cubs.
Playing Career: *1900-1908, 1910-1913; Chi N, Bos N, Cin N*
Managerial Career: *1912; Bos N*

Bob Klinger
Klinger, Robert Harold
B: Jun 4, 1908   D: Aug 19, 1977

Pos: P   ERA: 3.68
W-L: 66-61   SOs: 357
ShOs: 7   Saves: 23

When Enos Slaughter made his mad dash home to win Game Seven of the 1946 World Series, Klinger was on the mound. The hurler led the AL in saves that year. His best year as a starter was his rookie season, when he compiled a record of 12-5 with a 2.99 ERA.
Playing Career: *1938-1943, 1946-1947; Pit N, Bos A*

John Klippstein
Klippstein, John Calvin
B: Oct 17, 1927

Pos: P   ERA: 4.24
W-L: 101-118   SOs: 1,158
ShOs: 6   No-hitters: 1

After treading water as a spot starter, Klippstein was moved into the swim of relief pitching by Dodger manager Walt Alston in 1958. The hurler stayed in the bullpen for another 10 years, once leading the AL in saves with 14 in 1960. Klippstein became sought after to solidify relief staffs; he finished with 66 career saves. He never surrendered a run in two World Series. Klippstein is the son-in-law of pitcher Emil ''Dutch'' Leonard.
Playing Career: *1950-1967; Chi N, Cin N, LA N, Cle A, Was A, Phi N, Min A, Det A*

Ted Kluszewski
Kluszewski, Theodore Bernard (Big Klu)
B: Sep 10, 1924   D: Mar 29, 1988

Pos: 1B   BA: .298
Hits: 1,766   HRs: 279
RBI: 1,028   BBs: 492

Nobody who saw the Reds during the 1950s will forget the massive biceps extending from the cutout sleeves of the jersey of Ted Kluszewski. He had a rare combination of abilities – he was a contact hitter who hit for average

Ted Kluszewski is congratulated by teammates after belting a home run in 1955.

Phil Knell

Knell, Philip H.
B: Mar 2, 1865   D: Jun 5, 1944

Pos: P	ERA: 4.05
W-L: 79-90	SOs: 575
ShOs: 8	No-hitters: 0

Knell emerged as a top pitcher during baseball's most tumultuous season, 1890. He won 22 for the Players' club in Philadelphia, and followed that with 28 wins for Columbus in the AA's the next year.
Playing Career: *1888, 1890-1892, 1894-1895; Pit N, Phi P, Col AA, Was N, Phi N, Lou N, Cle N*

Bob Knepper, pitching in the 1986 NLCS.

Bob Knepper

Knepper, Robert Wesley
B: May 25, 1954

Pos: P	ERA: 3.68
W-L: 146-155	SOs: 1,473
ShOs: 30	Saves: 1

The winningest left-hander in Astros history, Knepper pitched them to two division titles, in 1981 and 1986. He twice racked up 17 wins, once with the Giants in 1978 and again with the Astros in 1986. He appeared in the 1981 and 1988 All-Star Games. Knepper led the NL in shutouts in 1978 and 1986. His career has been one of peaks and valleys; he won the Comeback Player of the Year Award in 1981, early in his career.
Playing Career: *1976-1990; SF N, Hou N*

Elmer Knetzer

Knetzer, Elmer Ellsworth (Baron)
B: Jul 22, 1885   D: Oct 3, 1975

Pos: P	ERA: 3.15
W-L: 69-69	SOs: 535
ShOs: 13	Saves: 6

A hard-headed, hard-throwing journeyman pitcher, Knetzer sat out the 1913 season in a salary dispute. He won 20 games with the Pittsburgh FL club in 1914. After his big league career, Knetzer played minor league ball until 1934, finishing in the Mid-Atlantic League at age 49.
Playing Career: *1909-1912, 1914-1917; Brk N, Pit F, Bos N, Cin N*

and with power. He led the NL with 49 homers and 141 RBI in 1954, while batting .326 and striking out only 35 times. The next year Kluszewski led the NL with 192 hits and slugged 47 homers, driving in 113 runs and scoring 116 runs while whiffing only 40 times.

For five consecutive years Big Klu's home run total exceeded his strikeout total. In 1955 he set a modern NL record by scoring runs in 17 straight games. He topped NL first basemen in fielding five straight years, as well as batting .300 or better for another five seasons in a row. An All-Star 1953-1956, Kluszewski was forced by injuries from a starting position, but he pinch-hit plenty. He even started every game of the 1959 World Series, bashing Dodgers pitching for three homers, 10 RBI and a .391 average for the losing White Sox.
Playing Career: *1947-1961; Cin N, Pit N, Chi A, LA A*

Otto Knabe

Knabe, Franz Otto
B: Jun 12, 1884   D: May 17, 1961

Pos: 2B	BA: .247
Hits: 1,103	HRs: 8
RBI: 364	BBs: 485

Managerial Record
Won: 131   Lost: 177   Pct: .425

A tough second sacker with wide range, Knabe gave the Phillies of the early teens formidable strength up the middle. Jumping to the Federal League in 1914, Knabe became manager of the famous Baltimore Terrapins, the only major league team to have a turtle on their uniforms.
Playing Career: *1905, 1907-1916; Pit N, Phi N, Bal F, Chi N*
Managerial Career: *1914-1915; Bal F*

Bill Knickerbocker
Knickerbocker, William Hart
B: Dec 29, 1911   D: Sep 8, 1963

Pos: SS	BA: .276
Hits: 943	HRs: 28
RBI: 368	BBs: 244

The Indians' starting shortstop, 1934-1936, Knickerbocker averaged over .300 and slugged 101 doubles in that time. Strangely, he was traded anyway – to the Browns for Lyn Lary. Knickerbocker hit .317 in 1934.
Playing Career: *1933-1942; Cle A, StL A, NY A, Chi A, Phi A*

John Knight
Knight, John Wesley
B: Oct 6, 1885   D: Dec 19, 1965

Pos: SS, 3B	BA: .239
Hits: 636	HRs: 14
RBI: 270	BBs: 211

Connie Mack claimed Knight was the only young player he ever regretted letting go. Knight had been the starting shortstop of the 1905 Athletics, but hit only .203. Mack traded him to the Red Sox for Jimmy Collins. Knight hit .312 for the 1910 Yankees.
Playing Career: *1905-1907, 1909-1913; Phi A, Bos A, NY A, Was A*

Lon Knight
Knight, Alonzo P.
B: Jun 16, 1853   D: Apr 23, 1932

Pos: OF, P	BA: .245
Hits: 549	HRs: 3
RBI: 129 (inc.)	BBs: 97
Managerial Record	
Won: 127 Lost: 78 Pct: .620	

A well-thought-of fixture in Philadelphia, Knight played for the old Athletics and managed the American Association A's. His players were known for taking advantage of his good humor, and the club had little discipline. Knight also pitched 38 games, going 10-23.
Playing Career: *1875-1876, 1880-1885; Phi Athletics n, Phi N, Wor N, Det N, Phi AA, Pro N*
Managerial Career: *1883-1884; Phi AA*
Umpiring Career: *1887, 1889-1890; AA, NL, PL*

Ray Knight
Knight, Charles Ray
B: Dec 28, 1952

Pos: 3B	BA: .271
Hits: 1,311	HRs: 84
RBI: 595	BBs: 343

Knight shook off the effects of platooning to hit .391 in the 1986 World Series, and win the Series MVP Award. He hit the decisive homer in Game Seven after having scored the Mets' winning run in Game Six on Mookie Wilson's ninth-inning grounder through Bill Buckner's legs.

WS MVP Ray Knight and his wife, 1986.

Knight kept illustrious company; in Cincinnati he had replaced Pete Rose at third, then three years later, was replaced by Johnny Bench. Knight later married professional golfer Nancy Lopez. He is now a popular ESPN broadcaster.
Playing Career: *1974, 1977-1988; Cin N, Hou N, NY N, Bal A, Det A*

Bobby Knoop
Knoop, Robert Frank
B: Oct 18, 1938

Pos: 2B	BA: .236
Hits: 856	HRs: 56
RBI: 331	BBs: 305

Knoop and his roommate Jim Fregosi turned an AL-record six double plays in a May 1, 1966 game. Knoop was a three-time Gold Glove winner who once made 12 putouts in a game at second, another AL record. He hit 17 homers in 1966, the year he made the All-Star squad.
Playing Career: *1964-1972; LA A, Cal A, Chi A, KC A*

Jack Knott
Knott, John Henry
B: Mar 2, 1907   D: Oct 13, 1981

Pos: P	ERA: 4.97
W-L: 82-103	SOs: 484
ShOs: 4	Saves: 19

A fourth starter laboring for second-division teams during the high-scoring 1930s and 1940s, Knott won only 44 percent of his decisions and never recorded an ERA under 4.15. His best years were 1934, when he was 10-3, and 1939, when he was 11-6. Knott won 13 games in 1941 for the Athletics.
Playing Career: *1933-1942, 1946; StL A, Chi A, Phi A*

Darold Knowles
Knowles, Darold Duane
B: Dec 9, 1941

Pos: P	ERA: 3.12
W-L: 66-74	SOs: 681
ShOs: 1	Saves: 143

Knowles appeared in all seven games of the 1973 World Series for the champion A's, saved two contests and did not allow an earned run. He made the All-Star team with the lowly Senators in 1969 when he was 9-2 with 13 saves. The next year Knowles tossed a career-high 27 saves, but finished with a 2-14 record. In 1972 he was nearly unbeatable, going 5-1 with a 1.37 ERA and saving 11 as the setup man for ace reliever Rollie Fingers.
Playing Career: *1965-1980; Bal A, Phi N, Was A, Oak A, Chi N, Tex A, Mon N, StL N*

Mark Koenig
Koenig, Mark Anthony
B: Jul 19, 1902   D: Apr 22, 1993

Pos: SS	BA: .279
Hits: 1,190	HRs: 28
RBI: 443	BBs: 222

Koenig and Tony Lazzeri were a rookie double play combination for the Yankees in 1926. Never before and never since has a team won the pennant with rookies at both key infield positions. In 1932 Koenig was the center of controversy during the World Series. He had been released to the minors by the Tigers that year, then was purchased by the Cubs in August. Koenig hit .353 in a 33-game drive to the pennant. The skinflint Cubs voted him only a one-half World Series share.

The Yankees – Koenig's former teammates, and the Cubs' opponents in the World

Mark Koenig (l) with Tony Lazzeri, 1926.

Series – reacted hotly to the news of Koenig's half share. When both clubs were awaiting introduction, Babe Ruth and some others went to the Cubs' dugout and said loudly, "Mark, who are those cheapskates with you?" The riding became ferocious. When Ruth hit his famous "Called Shot" home run, he circled the bases thumbing his nose at the Cubs, bellowing "Oigna, Oigna." The Cubs lost in four straight. Koenig played in five World Series with three different teams.
Playing Career: *1925-1936; NY A, Det A, Chi N, Cin N, NY N*

Don Kolloway
Kolloway, Donald Martin (Butch, Cab)
B: Aug 4, 1918

Pos: 2B, 1B, 3B	BA: .271
Hits: 1,081	HRs: 29
RBI: 393	BBs: 189

Kolloway stunned the opposing Indians pitching staff by stealing second, third and home on June 28, 1941. The rookie stole only 11 bases that year. The next season he led the AL in doubles with 40. A free swinger, Kolloway walked only nine times in both 1943 and 1944.
Playing Career: *1940-1943, 1946-1953; Chi A, Det A, Phi A*

Ray Kolp
Kolp, Raymond Carl (Jockey)
B: Oct 1, 1894   D: Jul 29, 1967

Pos: P	ERA: 4.08
W-L: 79-95	SOs: 439
ShOs: 11	Saves: 18

When Kolp was not pitching he was one of the best – or worst – bench jockeys in baseball. His loud mouth and salty language irritated opponents into making misplays. Kolp was an important part of the Browns' near-pennant miss in 1922, compiling a record of 14-4 that year. He won 13 for the Reds in 1928.
Playing Career: *1921-1924, 1927-1934; StL A, Cin N*

Ed Konetchy
Konetchy, Edward Joseph
B: Sep 3, 1885   D: May 27, 1947

Pos: 1B	BA: .281
Hits: 2,148	HRs: 74
RBI: 992	BBs: 689

Hal Chase was flashier, but Konetchy was the finest first baseman of his day. He led the league in fielding eight times in ten years. A prolific dead ball hitter, Konetchy had a 20-game hitting streak in 1910, and in 1911 led the NL with 38 doubles. He hit a fair ball out of old Robison Field in St. Louis. With the Dodgers in 1919, Konetchy collected a record 10 consecutive hits.

Konetchy also played the entire 26-inning contest between the Dodgers and Braves in 1920. Batting over .300 four times, Konetchy compiled 100 or more hits 11 consecutive seasons, and broke up four no-hitters. He stole

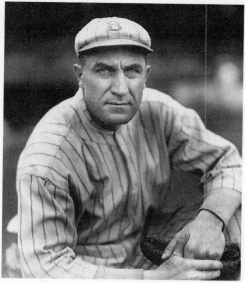
Dodger first baseman Ed Konetchy, 1920.

255 bases, and scored 971 runs and hit 344 doubles and 181 triples during his career. After his big league career, Konetchy played with the legendary Fort Worth Cats of the Texas League, winners of seven straight pennants. He batted .345 with 41 homers and 166 RBI in 1925.
Playing Career: *1907-1921; StL N, Pit N, Pit F, Bos N, Brk N, Phi N*

Jim Konstanty
Konstanty, Casimir James
B: Mar 2, 1917   D: Jun 11, 1976

Pos: P	ERA: 3.46
W-L: 66-48	SOs: 268
ShOs: 2	Saves: 74

An outstanding athlete at Syracuse University, Konstanty was neither a Kid nor a Whiz by the time he pitched the 1950 Phillies to the NL pennant. The first relief pitcher chosen as the NL MVP, Konstanty won 16 and saved 22 while making 74 appearances, all league highs in 1950. After relieving in 133 straight games for the Phillies, he finally started Game One of the World Series, losing to the Yankees 1-0.
Playing Career: *1944, 1946, 1948-1956; Cin N, Bos N, Phi N, NY A, StL N*

Cal Koonce
Koonce, Calvin Lee
B: Nov 18, 1940

Pos: P	ERA: 3.78
W-L: 47-49	SOs: 504
ShOs: 3	Saves: 24

Koonce started the 1962 season with a 9-1 record and looked like a future star. He ended the season 10-10, though, and arm problems reduced his effectiveness and eventually sent him to the bullpen. He saved 18 games for the Mets from 1968 to 1969.
Playing Career: *1962-1971; Chi N, NY N, Bos A*

Jerry Koosman
Koosman, Jerome Martin
B: Dec 23, 1942

Pos: P	ERA: 3.36
W-L: 222-209	SOs: 2,556
ShOs: 33	Saves: 17

Tom Seaver and Koosman formed the most potent lefty-righty combination in the NL for 11 years. In 1968 Koosman was NL Rookie Pitcher of the Year and runner-up to Johnny Bench for major league Rookie of the Year. The hurler set Mets club records with 19 wins, seven shutouts, and a 2.08 ERA, breaking those set by Tom Seaver the year before. Koosman also struck out 62 times in 91 at-bats, the most by an NL pitcher since 1900.

In 1969 Koosman posted 17 victories – six of them shutouts – and a 2.28 ERA as the Mets shocked the country by winning the NL pennant, then the World Series. He beat the Orioles twice in the Fall Classic, including a complete game, come-from-behind finale. Koosman also won a game in the 1973 NLCS and another in the World Series. Traded to the Twins following a 3-15 season in 1978, he rebounded with a 20-win season, followed by 16 wins in 1980. He made a brief appearance in the 1983 ALCS for the White Sox.
Playing Career: *1967-1985; NY N, Min A, Chi A, Phi N*

Jerry Koosman, 1968 rookie sensation.

Larry Kopf
Kopf, William Lorenz
B: Nov 3, 1890   D: Oct 15, 1986

Pos: SS	BA: .249
Hits: 749	HRs: 5
RBI: 266	BBs: 242

On May 2, 1917, Kopf rapped a 10th-inning single to break up a double no-hit duel between Hippo Vaughn and Fred Toney. Kopf then scored the game's only run on Jim Thorpe's scratch single. Kopf was the shortstop for the 1919 Reds and starred in the World Series.
Playing Career: *1913-1917, 1919-1923; Cle A, Phi A, Cin N, Bos N*

Dave Koslo
Koslo, George Bernard
B: Mar 31, 1920   D: Dec 1, 1975

Pos: P	ERA: 3.68
W-L: 92-107	SOs: 606
ShOs: 16	Saves: 22

Born George Bernard Koslowski, Dave Koslo was the only pitcher ever to lead the league in ERA without posting a shutout. He beat the Yankees in the 1951 World Series opener for the Giants, but lost the Game Six finale. He was 15-10 in 1947 with a 3.63 ERA.
Playing Career: *1941-1942, 1946-1955; NY N, Bal A, Mil N*

Pitching great Sandy Koufax.

Sandy Koufax
Koufax, Sanford
B: Dec 30, 1935
Hall of Fame 1972

Pos: P	ERA: 2.76
W-L: 165-87	SOs: 2,396
ShOs: 40	No-hitters: 4

For five years, 1962-1966, Koufax was the greatest left-hander in the history of baseball. He pitched four no-hitters, won five ERA titles, three Cy Young Awards, and one MVP Award, although he was in excruciating pain most of the time. Wild as a youngster, Koufax labored for six years to compile a 36-40 record. Then he found his groove and became a star. In 1965 he struck out 382, breaking Rube Waddell's season record of 349, and threw a perfect game.

In 1966 Koufax won more games, 27, and pitched more shutouts, 11, than any NL lefty in one year in the 20th century. Then his arm went bad, and he walked away from baseball at the age of 30, "while I could still comb my hair." As a fastball pitcher, Koufax ranked with Nolan Ryan, Walter Johnson, Bob Feller, Lefty Grove and Roger Clemens. Unlike Grove and Johnson, Koufax had a great curveball as well. Twice he whiffed 18 men in one game. Koufax compiled a World Series ERA of 0.95.
Playing Career: *1955-1966; Brk N, LA N*

Ernie Koy
Koy, Ernest Ányz (Chief)
B: Sep 17, 1909

Pos: OF	BA: .279
Hits: 515	HRs: 36
RBI: 260	BBs: 137

Koy, a University of Texas football star, homered in his first at-bat in the majors. He was half-American Indian and extremely fast, with a powerful swing, but he never came back to baseball after the war. His son played football with the New York Giants, 1965-1970.
Playing Career: *1938-1942; Brk N, StL N, Cin N, Phi N*

Jack Kralick
Kralick, John Francis
B: Jun 1, 1935

Pos: P	ERA: 3.56
W-L: 67-65	SOs: 668
ShOs: 12	No-hitters: 1

Kralick retired the first 25 batters to face him in his no-hitter versus the Athletics in 1962. The big left-hander won 14 while being traded by Minnesota for Jim Perry in May 1963. With a 12-7 record for the Indians in 1964, he was selected for the All-Star team. It was his last winning season.
Playing Career: *1959-1967; Was A, Min A, Cle A*

Jack Kramer
Kramer, John Henry
B: Jan 5, 1918

Pos: P	ERA: 4.24
W-L: 95-103	SOs: 613
ShOs: 14	Saves: 7

Kramer won Game Three in the 1944 World Series for the Browns versus the crosstown rival Cardinals. He was selected to the AL All-Star team three consecutive years, 1945-1947. He pitched for both pennant-winners in 1951, but did not make the World Series with either.
Playing Career: *1939-1941, 1943-1951; StL A, Bos A, NY N, NY A*

Ed Kranepool
Kranepool, Edward Emil
B: Nov 8, 1944

Pos: 1B	BA: .261
Hits: 1,418	HRs: 118
RBI: 614	BBs: 454

The brand-new Mets signed Kranepool right out of James Madison High School in the Bronx for $85,000 at the tender age of 17. He played for them for the next 18 years, and still holds club records for games, at-bats, hits, doubles and total bases. Kranepool ranks second on the Mets' all-time lists for RBI, and third for extra-base hits. He played in two World Series, in 1969 and 1973.

Ed Kranepool douses Tug McGraw with champagne after the Mets' 1969 WS victory.

Finally breaking into the Mets' regular lineup in 1964 with a .257 batting average, Kranepool was big and awkward, and became a target for the New York press and fans. He was persistent, if not a star; his best season was 1971, when he hit 14 homers, 20 doubles and slugged .447. Toward the end of his career, Kranepool became a top pinch hitter, compiling a pinch-hit batting average of .486 in 1974 – a major league record. After retiring from baseball, Kranepool made money as a stockbroker and restaurateur.
Playing Career: *1962-1979; NY N*

Lew Krausse
Krausse, Lewis Bernard, Jr.
B: Apr 25, 1943

Pos: P	ERA: 4.00
W-L: 68-91	SOs: 721
ShOs: 5	Saves: 21

Just days out of high school, Krausse shut out the Angels in his first start. He had been signed for $125,000 by his dad, an A's scout. Krausse led the culture war with owner Charles Finley that resulted in Ken Harrelson being released in 1967.
Playing Career: *1961, 1964-1974; KC A, Oak A, Mil A, Bos A, StL N, Atl N*

Mike Kreevich
Kreevich, Michael Andreas (Iron Mike)
B: Jun 10, 1908

Pos: OF	BA: .283
Hits: 1,321	HRs: 45
RBI: 514	BBs: 446

In his rookie season of 1936, Kreevich batted .307 and scored 99 runs while smashing 32 doubles and 11 triples, but hardly anyone noticed. Attention was focused on another rookie named Joe DiMaggio. The next year Kreevich continued his assault on AL pitching as he led the league in triples with 16. He was selected for the All-Star Game in 1938, the only year between 1936 and 1939 that he batted below .300. He led AL outfielders twice in fielding and in assists.
Playing Career: *1931, 1935-1945; Chi N, Chi A, Phi A, StL A, Was A*

Ray Kremer
Kremer, Remy Peter
B: Mar 23, 1893   D: Feb 8, 1965

Pos: P	ERA: 3.76
W-L: 142-85	SOs: 516
ShOs: 14	Saves: 10

The ace of the Pirates' staff during the 1920s, Kremer won the last two games of the 1925 World Series to give the Pirates a surprise win after being down three games to one. Kremer posted 20 victories twice, leading the league both times. He also led the NL in ERA in 1926 and 1927. A fun-loving heavy drinker, Kremer was known for pranks like throwing his teammates' shoes out of train windows en route to the next ballgame.
Playing Career: *1924-1933; Pit N*

The Giants' Red Kress, 1946.

Red Kress
Kress, Ralph
B: Jan 2, 1907   D: Nov 29, 1962

Pos: SS, 3B, 1B, OF, 2B	BA: .286
Hits: 1,454	HRs: 89
RBI: 799	BBs: 474

A strong-hitting, good-fielding shortstop, Kress was error-prone and always struggled to keep a job. Despite numerous miscues, he led AL shortstops in fielding twice. Kress was replaced by Jim Levey on the Browns and Luke Appling with the White Sox, and he competed with Joe Cronin at shortstop for the Senators. Kress could hit, stroking over .300 from 1929 to 1931 for the Browns. He later coached for the 1962 Mets.
Playing Career: *1927-1936, 1938-1940, 1946; StL A, Chi A, Was A, Det A, NY N*

Bill Krueger
Krueger, William Culp
B: Apr 24, 1958

Pos: P	ERA: 4.15
W-L: 63-61	SOs: 576
ShOs: 2	Saves: 4

A tremendous prospect, Krueger was injured in his first major league season and has endured a decade of seasons split between the big leagues and the minors. He threw two major league shutouts in 1992 and moved to the bullpen in the 1993 season with the Tigers.
Playing Career: *1983-; Oak A, LA N, Mil A, Sea A, Min A, Mon N, Det A*

John Kruk
Kruk, John Martin
B: Feb 9, 1961

Pos: 1B, OF	BA: .300
Hits: 1,044	HRs: 93
RBI: 531	BBs: 581

One of the collection of outcasts who ended up with the Phillies, Kruk has emerged as a powerful hitter and dependable first base-

man. He bashed 21 homers and drove in 92 in 1991, then batted .323 the next season, and .316 in 1993, all All-Star years for Kruk.
Playing Career: *1986-; SD N, Phi N*

Mike Krukow
Krukow, Michael Edward
B: Jan 21, 1952

Pos: P	ERA: 3.89
W-L: 124-117	SOs: 1,478
ShOs: 10	Saves: 1

After nine seasons of anonymity, Krukow became a star in 1986 when he posted career bests of 20 wins, a 2.94 ERA and 178 strikeouts. He finished third in the NL Cy Young Award voting and was selected for the All-Star team. The Giants were relying on him for their 1987 pennant drive, but due to arm injuries Krukow completed only three of 28 starts for a 5-6 record. His ERA jumped almost two full runs.
Playing Career: *1976-1989; Chi N, Phi N, SF N*

Tony Kubek
Kubek, Anthony Christopher
B: Oct 12, 1936

Pos: SS	BA: .266
Hits: 1,109	HRs: 57
RBI: 373	BBs: 217

In the 1960 World Series, Kubek was the Yankee shortstop who took the double play ball in the throat in Game Seven. The mishap allowed the Pirates to get back into the game and win it on Bill Mazeroski's dramatic home

Career Yankee Tony Kubek.

run. Kubek played in six World Series with the Yankees and was chosen for three All-Star Game squads. The AL Rookie of the Year in 1957, he batted .297 and showed versatility as he spent substantial time in the outfield, at shortstop, and at third base, with brief stints at second and first as well.

In the 1957 World Series against his hometown Milwaukee, Kubek hit two homers in Game Three. The next year, he displaced another former Rookie of the Year, Gil McDougald, and became the Yankees' regular shortstop. For eight seasons Kubek and Bobby Richardson formed one of baseball's best double play combinations. In 1961, Kubek cracked 38 doubles. In his first at-bat after returning from military duty late in 1962, he drilled a three-run homer. Kubek is now a popular broadcaster on national television.
Playing Career: *1957-1965; NY A*

Ted Kubiak
Kubiak, Theodore Roger
B: May 12, 1942

Pos: SS, 2B, 3B	BA: .231
Hits: 565	HRs: 13
RBI: 202	BBs: 271

Charlie Finley thought Kubiak was such a hot prospect that he moved star shortstop Bert Campaneris to the outfield to make room for the newcomer. Campaneris balked at the move, and Kubiak was traded, but reacquired in time for the A's championship seasons of 1972-1974.
Playing Career: *1967-1976; KC A, Oak A, Mil A, StL N, Tex A, SD N*

Bill Kuehne
Kuehne, William J.
B: Oct 24, 1858   D: Oct 27, 1921

Pos: 3B, SS	BA: .232
Hits: 996	HRs: 25
RBI: 313	BBs: 137

Born William J. Knelme in Leipzig, Germany, Kuehne played infield in an era when fielding was more important than hitting. He batted .299 in 1887, his first year in the NL.
Playing Career: *1883-1892; Col AA, Pit AA, Pit N, Pit P, Lou AA, Lou N, StL N, Cin N*

Harvey Kuenn
Kuenn, Harvey Edward
B: Dec 4, 1930   D: Feb 28, 1988

Pos: SS, OF, 3B	BA: .303
Hits: 2,092	HRs: 87
RBI: 671	BBs: 594
Managerial Record	
Won: 160 Lost: 118 Pct: .576	

A Milwaukee native, Kuenn was a coach for the Brewers from 1971 to 1982, during which time he endured heart and stomach surgeries and the amputation of his right leg below the knee. In June 1982 he became manager of the fifth-place Brewers. Under Kuenn the team exploded. Known as ''Harvey's Wallbangers,'' the Brewers batted themselves into the

Rookie of the Year Harvey Kuenn, 1953.

1982 World Series. They lost in seven games to the Cardinals, but Kuenn was named Manager of the Year.

As a player en route to the 1953 Rookie of the Year Award, Kuenn hit .308 with a league-leading 209 hits, setting a rookie record with 679 at-bats and an AL rookie record with 167 singles. Kuenn was the Tigers' shortstop from 1953 to 1957, then switched to the outfield. He led the AL in hits four times and won the AL batting title in 1959 with a .353 mark. Kuenn made the All-Star team eight straight years, 1953-1960. Scoring 951 career runs, he walloped 356 doubles.
Playing Career: *1952-1966; Det A, Cle A, SF N, Chi N, Phi N*
Managerial Career: *1975, 1982-1983; Mil A*

Joe Kuhel
Kuhel, Joseph Anthony
B: Jun 25, 1906   D: Feb 26, 1984

Pos: 1B	BA: .277
Hits: 2,212	HRs: 131
RBI: 1,049	BBs: 980
Managerial Record	
Won: 106 Lost: 201 Pct: .345	

In a July 20, 1941 doubleheader, Joe Kuhel recorded 17 putouts in the first game and 23 in the second, surpassing a 35-year-old record held by Hal Chase. In 1938 the Comiskeys took a lot of heat for trading colorful Zeke Bonura for Kuhel, but the deal brought the White Sox the AL's best-fielding first baseman. Kuhel rapped 412 doubles and 111 triples while scoring 1,236 runs and stealing 178 bases during his career.
Playing Career: *1930-1947; Was A, Chi A*
Managerial Career: *1948-1949; Was A*

The Senators' Joe Kuhel, 1931.

Commissioner Bowie Kuhn.

Bowie Kuhn
Kuhn, Bowie Kent
B: Oct 28, 1926

Kuhn was the commissioner of baseball from 1969 to 1984, during baseball's rise from ashes to the multibillion dollar industry that it is today. When he replaced Spike Eckert, baseball had fallen from its pedestal as the national pastime. Attendance was down. The AL and NL had been split into East and West divisions. Players had organized into a union and were demanding more money.

Kuhn made it clear that he believed his role to be representation of baseball team owners. Ironically many owners opposed him, and he was bypassed in negotiations with Marvin

Miller, the Executive Director of the Players' Union. A's owner Charlie Finley spearheaded a movement to remove Kuhn, but failed. Kuhn would later void Finley's sales of $3.5 million worth of stars, which helped to drive the cantankerous owner out of the game. One of Kuhn's better financial decisions was to sanction night games for the World Series, enlarging television contracts and increasing revenues.

Duane Kuiper
Kuiper, Duane Eugene
B: Jun 19, 1950

Pos: 2B	BA: .271
Hits: 917	HRs: 1
RBI: 263	BBs: 248

A tough man to face with a no-hitter on the line, Kuiper broke up bids by Nolan Ryan, Ron Guidry and Andy Hassler. On August 29, 1977, he hit his only home run. Kuiper led AL second basemen in fielding twice, in 1976 and 1979.
Playing Career: *1974-1985; Cle A, SF N*

Whitey Kurowski
Kurowski, George John
B: Apr 19, 1918

Pos: 3B	BA: .286
Hits: 925	HRs: 106
RBI: 529	BBs: 369

Kurowski was exempt from military duty during World War II because he had four inches of bone missing from his wrist due to childhood osteomyelitis. Amazingly, it did not interfere with his play – Kurowski become one of the finest fielding third basemen of the 1940s. He led the NL in putouts, fielding average, assists and double plays multiple times. He played in four World Series and was selected for the NL All-Star team three times.

Whitey, so-named for his blond hair, hit 20 or more home runs in three different seasons, including 27 in 1947. His ninth-inning home run off Red Ruffing in Game Five of the 1942 World Series broke a 2-2 tie to beat the Yankees and give the Cardinals the Championship. An arm injury in 1948 and an elbow injury in 1949 combined to end his playing career, so he became a coach and manager in the minors. At Tulsa during the early 1960s, Kurowski was assisted by coach Pepper Martin and Joe Medwick, the roving Cardinal instructor.
Playing Career: *1941-1949; StL N*

Bob Kuzava
Kuzava, Robert Leroy (Sarge)
B: May 28, 1923

Pos: P	ERA: 4.05
W-L: 49-44	SOs: 446
ShOs: 7	Saves: 13

Unable to break into the Indians' starting rotation, Kuzava reached his potential as a spot starter and long reliever with the Yanks. He pitched in three World Series for New York, going 0-0 with an ERA of 0.00 in the 1951 and 1952 Series, before continuing his journey around the majors.
Playing Career: *1946-1947, 1949-1955, 1957; Cle A, Chi A, Was A, NY A, Bal A, Phi N, Pit N, StL N*

George "Whitey" Kurowski, third baseman for the St. Louis Cardinals, in a 1946 publicity photograph.

Chet Laabs
Laabs, Chester Peter
B: Apr 30, 1912   D: Jan 26, 1983

Pos: OF   BA: .262
Hits: 813   HRs: 117
RBI: 509   BBs: 389

On the last day of the 1944 season, Laabs hit two homers against the rival Yankees to clinch the only pennant in Browns history. He hit 27 homers in 1942, and was selected for the 1943 All-Star Game. He also fanned five times in the game in which Bob Feller struck out 18 in 1938.
Playing Career: *1937-1947; Det A, StL A, Phi A*

Clem Labine
Labine, Clement Walter
B: Aug 6, 1926

Pos: P   ERA: 3.63
W-L: 77-56   SOs: 551
ShOs: 2   Saves: 96

Years after the Yankees' Don Larsen pitched a perfect game against the Dodgers in the 1956 World Series, Labine confessed that the Dodger bullpen had rooted for Larsen. One of the premier relievers in the 1950s NL, Labine helped the Dodgers win four pennants in Brooklyn and another in Los Angeles, and won again with the Pirates in 1960. He was 2-2 with two saves in five World Series. Labine's triumphs included a 10-0 victory in the second game of the 1951 NL playoff and a 1-0, 10-inning win in Game Six of the 1956 Series.
Playing Career: *1950-1962; Brk N, LA N, Det A, Pit N, NY N*

Candy LaChance
LaChance, George Joseph
B: Feb 15, 1870   D: Aug 18, 1932

Pos: 1B   BA: .280
Hits: 1,377   HRs: 39
RBI: 690   BBs: 219

A strapping big fellow for his day, LaChance stood 6'1" and weighed 183 pounds. He was prone to disagreements, and once wrestled Rube Waddell for an hour before a game. Waddell pinned him down, then went out and pitched a shutout. LaChance was whipped and did not appear in the game. He batted over .300 four times, and was a good baserunner, scoring 678 runs and stealing 192 bases. LaChance belted 197 doubles and 86 triples during his career.
Playing Career: *1893-1899, 1901-1905; Brk N, Bal N, Cle A, Bos A*

Pete LaCock
LaCock, Ralph Pierre
B: Jan 17, 1952

Pos: 1B   BA: .257
Hits: 444   HRs: 27
RBI: 224   BBs: 182

LaCock travelled between the minors and the majors before winning the American Association MVP Award in 1974 on the strength of a .327 batting average, 23 homers and 91 RBI. Player representative for the Cubs during the mid-1970s, LaCock made it to three ALCS with the Royals.
Playing Career: *1972-1980; Chi N, KC A*

Mike LaCoss
LaCoss, Michael James
B: May 30, 1956

Pos: P   ERA: 3.93
W-L: 98-103   SOs: 783
ShOs: 9   Saves: 12

Released on waivers in 1981, LaCoss fought his way back to appear in the 1987 and 1989 NLCS and 1989 World Series for the Giants. He was an All-Star in 1979, the year he compiled a record of 14-8. In 1985 LaCoss hit his only two home runs, in consecutive at-bats.
Playing Career: *1978-1991; Cin N, Hou N, KC A, SF N*

Lee Lacy hits a homer, 1986.

Lee Lacy
Lacy, Leondaus
B: Apr 10, 1948

Pos: OF, 2B   BA: .286
Hits: 1,303   HRs: 91
RBI: 458   BBs: 372

A useful fourth outfielder who could hit and field well, Lacy played in three LCS and four World Series. He batted .429 in the 1977 Fall Classic for the Dodgers. A dependable pinch hitter, Lacy belted five pinch-hit home runs in 1978, including a record-tying three in a row. He batted .335 in 1980, but his best season was 1984, when he hit .321 and led NL outfielders in fielding percentage.
Playing Career: *1972-1987; LA N, Atl N, Pit N, Bal A*

Clem Labine (c) is given a lift by Ray Campanella and Gil Hodges, 1956.

Pete Ladd
Ladd, Peter Linwood (Bigfoot)
B: Jul 17, 1956

Pos: P	ERA: 4.14
W-L: 17-23	SOs: 209
ShOs: 0	Saves: 39

After saving two games for the Brewers in the 1982 ALCS, Ladd was asked to fill in for injured Rollie Fingers in 1983. Ladd responded with 25 saves and a 2.55 ERA, but he was hit hard in 1984 and by the end of 1985 he was back in the minors. He had a one-year stint with Seattle the following season.
Playing Career: *1979, 1982-1986; Hou N, Mil A, Sea A*

Lerrin LaGrow
LaGrow, Lerrin Harris
B: Jul 8, 1948

Pos: P	ERA: 4.11
W-L: 34-55	SOs: 375
ShOs: 2	Saves: 54

A three-season Tiger rookie, LaGrow tossed a scoreless inning in the 1972 ALCS, but did not get a shot as a regular starter until 1974. In 1974 and 1975 he compiled records of 8-19 and 7-14. LaGrow finally found a niche in the bullpen, saving 41 games for the White Sox, 1977-1978.
Playing Career: *1970, 1972-1980; Det A, StL N, Chi A, LA N, Phi N*

Larry Lajoie
Lajoie, Napoleon (Nap)
B: Sep 5, 1874   D: Feb 7, 1959
Hall of Fame 1937

Pos: 2B	BA: .338
Hits: 3,242	HRs: 83
RBI: 1,599	BBs: 516

Managerial Record
Won: 377   Lost: 309   Pct: .550

On the final day of the 1910 season Lajoie was locked in a duel with Ty Cobb for the batting championship. Lajoie's team was playing the Browns, whose manager – like most of Cobb's contemporaries – disliked the Detroit star. He ordered the rookie third baseman to play deep to give Lajoie the advantage. Lajoie dropped seven bunts for an eight-hit doubleheader, yet lost the title by .0007.

Lajoie had always been popular. When he jumped contract from the NL Phillies to play ball in the new AL, his former league filed suit in federal court to prevent Lajoie from playing. The judge ruled that Lajoie had unique talent and could be enjoined from playing in Pennsylvania. The infielder was secretly traded to Cleveland, where he blossomed as a great star and carried the AL in its early, lean years. So beloved was Lajoie in Cleveland that the team was called the Naps. He hit over .300 in 16 of 21 seasons, scoring 1,503 runs and stealing 380 bases.
Playing Career: *1896-1916; Phi N, Phi A, Cle A*
Managerial Career: *1905-1909; Cle A*

Eddie Lake
Lake, Edward Erving
B: Mar 18, 1916

Pos: SS, 2B, 3B	BA: .231
Hits: 599	HRs: 39
RBI: 193	BBs: 546

Stuck behind Marty Marian in the Cardinals' farm system, it took a big year at Sacramento to get Lake to the major leagues. He became a regular with the Red Sox in 1943. Lake led the AL in on-base percentage in 1945, batting .279 while drawing 106 walks. In 1946, his first year with the Tigers, he scored 105 runs.
Playing Career: *1939-1941, 1943-1950; StL N, Bos A, Det A*

Bill Lamar
Lamar, William Harmong (Good Time Bill)
B: Mar 21, 1897   D: May 24, 1970

Pos: OF	BA: .310
Hits: 633	HRs: 19
RBI: 245	BBs: 86

A high-average, contact hitter, Lamar struck out less than he walked. Two years after he hit .356 for the A's they traded him to Washington. Lamar refused to report without a raise, and was suspended; he never played in the majors again.
Playing Career: *1917-1921, 1924-1927; NY A, Bos A, Brk N, Phi A*

Dennis Lamp
Lamp, Dennis Patrick
B: Sep 23, 1952

Pos: P	ERA: 3.93
W-L: 96-96	SOs: 857
ShOs: 7	Saves: 35

Switching to a bullpen job early in his career, Lamp was very effective in middle relief. In 1983 he saved 15 games for the White Sox, then compiled a record of 11-0 with a 3.32 ERA in relief for the division-winning Blue Jays in 1985. Lamp played on five division-winning teams.
Playing Career: *1977-1992; Chi N, Chi A, Tor A, Oak A, Bos A, Pit N*

Jim Landis
Landis, James Henry (Jungle Jim)
B: Mar 9, 1934

Pos: OF	BA: .247
Hits: 1,061	HRs: 93
RBI: 467	BBs: 588

Landis scored six runs in six World Series games for the 1959 "Go-Go" White Sox. Nicknamed for his wild nocturnal activities while in the minors, Landis had his best season in 1961, when he hit .283 with 22 homers and 85 RBI. He made the All-Star squad in 1962.
Playing Career: *1957-1967; Chi A, KC A, Cle A, Det A, Bos A, Hou N*

Larry "Nap" Lajoie.

Commissioner Kenesaw Mountain Landis.

Kenesaw M. Landis
Landis, Kenesaw Mountain
B: Nov 20, 1866   D: Nov 25, 1944
Hall of Fame 1944

Baseball's first commissioner, Kenesaw Mountain Landis, helped restore public confidence in the sport following the Black Sox World Series scandal of 1919. As a U.S. District Judge, Landis became well-known for fining John D. Rockefeller's Standard Oil Company $29 million and jailing 94 Socialist Labor Party leaders during World War I. Interestingly, Landis refused to rule in the Federal League's suit against the NL and AL, saying it "would be a blow against a national institution." The stance brought Landis the commissionership, which he held from 1920 to 1944.

Commissioner Landis banned eight White Sox players for life and subsequently issued other similarly arbitrary edicts to insure the game's integrity. Though hired by club owners to solve baseball's problems, Landis became the players' commissioner. He considered himself the game's number one fan, and later got into a scrap with J. G. Taylor Spink over who would be known as "Mr. Baseball." He has been called one of the five most influential people in baseball history.

Kenny Landreaux
Landreaux, Kenneth Francis
B: Dec 22, 1954

Pos: OF	BA: .268
Hits: 1,099	HRs: 91
RBI: 479	BBs: 299

In 1980 Landreaux hit safely in 31 straight games, the most in the AL since Dom DiMaggio had a streak of 34 in 1949. Landreaux also hit three triples in one game in 1980, to tie the AL record. He made the All-Star team that year, then was traded to the Dodgers.
Playing Career: *1977-1987; Cal A, Min A, LA N*

Bill Lange
Lange, William Alexander (Little Eva)
B: Jun 6, 1871   D: Jul 23, 1950

Pos: OF	BA: .330
Hits: 1,055	HRs: 40
RBI: 578	BBs: 350

Lange made a sensational catch that has become securely entrenched in baseball lore. Racing toward the outfield boundary, he reportedly crashed through a wooden fence, made the catch and held onto the ball for the out. Lange was the center of romantic speculation again when he quit baseball supposedly because he had fallen in love with the daughter of a San Francisco real estate magnate who forbade her to marry a ballplayer. Lange scored 689 runs and stole 399 bases in seven seasons.
Playing Career: *1893-1899; Chi N*

Rick Langford
Langford, James Rick
B: Mar 20, 1952

Pos: P	ERA: 4.01
W-L: 73-106	SOs: 671
ShOs: 10	No-hitters: 0

In 1980 Langford pitched 290 innings, completed 28 games, posted a 19-12 record, and fielded 230 consecutive chances flawlessly, setting the AL record for pitchers. Langford developed elbow trouble in 1983, and threw only 142 innings the last four years of his career.
Playing Career: *1976-1986; Pit N, Oak A*

Mark Langston
Langston, Mark Edward
B: Aug 20, 1960

Pos: P	ERA: 3.69
W-L: 144-126	SOs: 2,001
ShOs: 16	No-hitters: 1

Drafted in the 15th round while still in high school, Langston went to college instead, and was drafted in the 3rd round three years later. Langston spent three more years in the minors, but when he arrived, he was the Mariners' ace, leading the AL in strikeouts three times in his first four years. In 1985 Langston tore a flexor muscle in his elbow, but recovered and is one of the leading lefthanders in baseball. The big hurler went 19-8 for the Angels in 1991. He has been selected for the All-Star Game four times.
Playing Career: *1984-; Sea A, Mon N, Cal A*

Hal Lanier
Lanier, Harold Clifton
B: Jul 4, 1942

Pos: SS, 2B	BA: .228
Hits: 843	HRs: 8
RBI: 273	BBs: 136
Managerial Record	
Won: 254 Lost: 232 Pct: .523	

Chosen for the Topps All-Star Rookie team in 1964, Lanier was off to a great start, but a serious beaning in 1965 left him with epilepsy, and he never hit above .233 again. Nonetheless, Lanier spent seven seasons as a Giants regular. In 1968 he led all NL shortstops in putouts and fielding average. After his playing days, Lanier managed in the minors and coached in the majors, then managed the 1986 Astros to the NL West flag, and won Manager of the Year honors. Hal Lanier is the son of Max Lanier.
Playing Career: *1964-1973; SF N, NY A*
Managerial Career: *1986-1988; Hou N*

Max Lanier
Lanier, Hubert Max
B: Aug 18, 1915

Pos: P	ERA: 3.01
W-L: 108-82	SOs: 821
ShOs: 21	Saves: 17

Lanier had a 6-0 record in 1946 when he jumped to the outlaw Mexican League. He was suspended for five years, but was reinstated in 1949. Lanier pitched in three World Series, 1942-1944, compiling a record of 2-1. Major league player and manager Hal Lanier is his son.
Playing Career: *1938-1946, 1949-1953; StL N, NY N, StL A*

Johnny Lanning
Lanning, John Young
B: Sep 6, 1910   D: Nov 8, 1989

Pos: P	ERA: 3.58
W-L: 58-60	SOs: 295
ShOs: 4	Saves: 13

Mariners pitcher Mark Langston at spring training in 1986.

In September, 1936, Lanning made a stunning debut by defeating the Cardinals, Cubs and Giants in succession. All three were strong teams competing for the NL flag. He was a consistent .500 pitcher for 11 years. Lanning's brother Tom pitched for the Phillies in 1938.
Playing Career: *1936-1943, 1945-1947; Bos N, Pit N*

Carney Lansford.

Carney Lansford
Lansford, Carney Ray
B: Feb 7, 1957

Pos: 3B, DH, 1B	BA: .290
Hits: 2,074	HRs: 151
RBI: 874	BBs: 553

With his .336 average in 1981, Lansford won the AL batting title, and began a streak of four seasons of hitting .300 or more. He had been the Angels' Rookie of the Year in 1978, and finished third in the overall AL Rookie voting. Later traded by Boston to Oakland, Lansford appeared headed to first base until the emergence of Mark McGwire. When healthy, Lansford was a team leader, batting in the number two hole behind Rickey Henderson, where he protected him and frequently advanced or scored him.

Slowed by wrist and ankle injuries in 1983 and a broken right wrist in 1985, Lansford was healthy over the next four years and was usually the leadoff or number two hitter. When he retired he was Oakland's all-time career leading hitter, and among the club's all-time leaders in runs, hits, doubles and slugging percentage. During his 15-year career, Lansford scored 1,007 runs and stole 224 stolen bases.
Playing Career: *1978-1992; Cal A, Bos A, Oak A*

Dave LaPoint
LaPoint, David Jeffrey
B: Jul 29, 1959

Pos: P	ERA: 4.02
W-L: 80-86	SOs: 802
ShOs: 4	Saves: 1

The Cardinals dealt Ted Simmons and Rollie Fingers to Milwaukee, and got LaPoint. His spot starts and middle relief were instrumental in winning the pennant in 1982, when he compiled a record of 9-3. LaPoint also pitched in the World Series.
Playing Career: *1980-1991; Mil A, StL N, SF N, Det A, SD N, Chi A, Pit N, NY A*

Frank LaPorte
LaPorte, Frank Breyfogle
B: Feb 6, 1880   D: Sep 25, 1939

Pos: 2B, 3B, OF	BA: .281
Hits: 1,185	HRs: 14
RBI: 560	BBs: 288

As a strong line drive hitter, but lacking power, LaPorte nonetheless led the Federal League in RBI and batted .311 in 1914. When he played regularly he led second basemen in assists and double plays, but also in errors.
Playing Career: *1905-1915; NY A, Bos A, StL A, Was A, Ind F, Nwk F*

Jack Lapp
Lapp, John Walker
B: Sep 10, 1884   D: Feb 6, 1920

Pos: C	BA: .263
Hits: 416	HRs: 5
RBI: 166	BBs: 177

Lapp was Jack Coombs's favorite catcher; they were batterymates on four Athletics pennant-winning teams in five seasons. In 1911 Lapp batted .353 in 68 games. That year he threw out five Giants runners trying to steal in Game Three of the World Series, as the A's went on to become World Champions.
Playing Career: *1908-1916; Phi A, Chi A*

Ring Lardner
Lardner, Ring W.
B: Mar 6, 1885   D: Sep 25, 1933

Before Lardner became known as a writer of witty essays and short stories, he was a baseball beat writer for the *Chicago Tribune*. His collection of stories called *You Know Me Al: A Busher's Letters*, which were serialized in the *Saturday Evening Post*, were drawn from Lardner's experience covering the Cubs and the White Sox. Convinced that the White Sox were cheating in the 1919 World Series, Lardner walked through their train car singing "I'm Forever Blowing Ball Games" to the tune of the popular song "I'm Forever Blowing Bubbles."

Barry Larkin
Larkin, Barry Louis
B: Apr 28, 1964

Pos: SS	BA: .298
Hits: 1,045	HRs: 78
RBI: 419	BBs: 324

A high-average, power-hitting shortstop, Larkin hit .353 in the 1990 World Series to help the Reds sweep the heavily favored A's. A member of the 1984 Olympic baseball team, Larkin was also selected for the All-Star squad 1988-1991, 1993. He hit .342 in 1989, but injured his elbow, missing two months of the season.
Playing Career: *1986-; Cin N*

(R-l) Ring Lardner, Grantland Rice, Gene Tunney, Rube Goldberg, and Tex Rickard, 1928.

Gene Larkin
Larkin, Eugene Thomas
B: Oct 24, 1962

Pos: 1B, DH, OF	BA: .266
Hits: 618	HRs: 32
RBI: 266	BBs: 268

An integral part of two Twins World Series Championship teams, Larkin surpassed all of Lou Gehrig's college batting records at Columbia, and never hit below .302 in the minors. The line drive hitter was plunked by 15 pitches in 1988, leading the AL.
Playing Career: *1987-; Min A*

Henry Larkin
Larkin, Henry E. (Ted)
B: Jan 12, 1860   D: Jan 31, 1942

Pos: 1B	BA: .303
Hits: 1,430	HRs: 53
RBI: 549	BBs: 484
Managerial Record	
Won: 34 Lost: 45 Pct: .430	

When he was captain of the Athletics, Larkin led the team into frequent rows with umpires. Highly competitive, he once refused to leave the field after being ejected by the arbitrator. He continued to play – the other team protesting strenuously – and caused the A's to forfeit the game. Larkin averaged 100 runs or more per season from 1885 to 1891.
Playing Career: *1884-1893; Phi AA, Cle P, Was N*
Managerial Career: *1890; Cle P*

Dave LaRoche
LaRoche, David Eugene
B: May 14, 1948

Pos: P	ERA: 3.53
W-L: 65-58	SOs: 819
ShOs: 0	Saves: 126

In the 1981 World Series, LaRoche had an ERA of 0.00 for the Yankees. The foremost practitioner of the LaLob pitch, his blooper, LaRoche's best year was 1978, when he saved 25 while going 10-9 with a 2.81 ERA. He was the childhood inspiration for Goose Gossage, both being from Colorado Springs. In 1976 LaRoche was chosen for the All-Star team; he had 21 saves and a 2.24 ERA that year. He was the main stopper for the Indians for two years and for the Angels for three.
Playing Career: *1970-1983; Cal A, Min A, Chi N, Cle A, NY A*

Don Larsen
Larsen, Don James
B: Aug 7, 1929

Pos: P	ERA: 3.78
W-L: 81-91	SOs: 849
ShOs: 11	No-hitters: 1

Larsen had a losing record, a fairly high ERA, and not many strikeouts for a 14-year career, but he pitched a no-hitter, and it was a lulu.

Don Larsen.

After being knocked from the box in the second inning of Game Two of the 1956 World Series, Larsen started Game Five. He set down 27 Dodgers in a row, winning 2-0 for the first no-hitter in Series history. Dale Mitchell, the last batter, took a third strike called by plate umpire Babe Pinelli. Larsen had a perfect game. Catcher Yogi Berra jumped into Larsen's arms and pandemonium broke out. At the press conference a reporter asked Manager Casey Stengel, "Have you ever seen him pitch a better game?"

Larsen played in five World Series, four with the Yankees and another as a relief pitcher with the Giants against the Yankees in 1962. Larsen saved 11 games that year, 23 during his career. Larsen was a lifetime .242 hitter with 14 homers and 66 pinch-hit at-bats.
Playing Career: *1953-1965, 1967; StL A, Bal A, NY A, KC A, Chi A, SF N, Hou N, Chi N*

Tony LaRussa
LaRussa, Anthony
B: Oct 4, 1944

Pos: 2B	BA: .199
Hits: 35	HRs: 0
RBI: 7	BBs: 23
Managerial Record	
Won: 1,202 Lost: 1,043 Pct: .535	

Most baseball people consider LaRussa to be the best manager in the game today. It never hurts to have four potential Hall of Famers in your lineup – for a while LaRussa had Rickey Henderson, Dennis Eckersley, Jose Canseco and Mark McGwire – but the former attorney is a tough competitor and the supreme strategist. LaRussa won four AL West division titles in five years, including three pennants in a row and the 1989 World Championship

with the Athletics. In 1983 he had won a division title with the White Sox.
Playing Career: *1963, 1968-1971, 1973; KC A, Oak A, Atl N, Chi N*
Managerial Career: *1979-; Chi A, Oak A*

Frank Lary
Lary, Frank Strong (Yankee Killer)
B: Apr 10, 1930

Pos: P	ERA: 3.49
W-L: 128-116	SOs: 1,099
ShOs: 21	Saves: 11

Nicknamed "Yankee Killer" because he was especially tough on the Pinstripes, Lary was 5-1 against them in 1956 and 7-0 in 1958. It was the first time since 1916 that the Yankees had been beaten seven times in one season by the same pitcher. Lary defeated New York five times in a row in 1959, making 13 wins in 14 decisions. Lary played in three All-Star Games without allowing a run. He won 21 in 1956 and 23 in 1961. After pitching 220 or more innings for seven straight seasons, his arm wore out.
Playing Career: *1954-1965; Det A, NY N, Mil N, Chi A*

Lyn Lary
Lary, Lynford Hobart (Broadway)
B: Jan 28, 1906   D: Jan 9, 1973

Pos: SS	BA: .269
Hits: 1,239	HRs: 38
RBI: 526	BBs: 705

The Yankees paid $125,000 for Lyn Lary and Jimmy Reese, the double play combo of the Oakland Oaks in the Pacific Coast League. Lary stayed with the Yankees until 1934. In 1931 he accumulated 107 RBI, the most ever by a Yankee shortstop. One of six Yankees to score 100 runs that year, he cost Lou Gehrig the home run title when he allowed Gehrig to pass him on the basepaths. In 1936 Lary won the AL stolen base crown with 37 steals for the Browns.
Playing Career: *1929-1940; NY A, Bos A, Was A, StL A, Cle A, Brk N, StL N*

Tom Lasorda
Lasorda, Thomas Charles
B: Sep 22, 1927

Pos: P	ERA: 6.48
W-L: 0-4	SOs: 37
ShOs: 0	Saves: 1
Managerial Record	
Won: 1,422 Lost: 1,282 Pct: .526	

A perennial favorite with fans and the media, Lasorda personifies Dodger Blue. He was a top minor league pitcher, once fanning 25 in a Class C game, and holds most of the Montreal Royals' AAA left-handed pitching records. After three seasons in the big leagues, Lasorda managed in the minors, winning five pennants. Then he served as Dodgers Manager Walter Alston's understudy until September 29, 1976, when Alston retired.

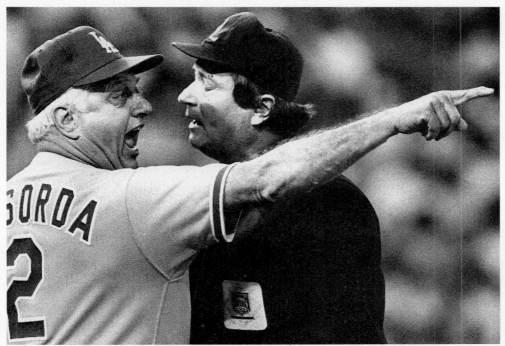

Dodgers Manager Tommy Lasorda gives Umpire Fred Brocklander a piece of his mind.

Lasorda inherited an infield of Steve Garvey, Davey Lopes, Bill Russell and Ron Cey. In 1977-1978, he became the first NL manager to win pennants his first two seasons. After the 1981 player strike, Lasorda's Dodgers defeated the Astros in the divisional playoff, beat the Expos in the NLCS, then crushed the Yankees in the World Series. Lasorda managed the Dodgers to division titles again in 1983 and 1985. In 1988 he shared NL Manager of the Year honors with Jim Leyland, taking the Dodgers to a win over the Mets in the NLCS and a surprising upset of the A's in the Fall Classic.

Playing Career: *1954-1956; LA N, KC A*
Managerial Career: *1976-; LA N*

Arlie Latham
Latham, Walter Arlington
(The Freshest Man on Earth)
B: Mar 15, 1860   D: Nov 29, 1952

Pos: 3B	BA: .269
Hits: 1,833	HRs: 27
RBI: 398	BBs: 589
Managerial Record	
Won: 0 Lost: 3 Pct: .000	

During the 1940s Latham was the attendant in the press box at the Polo Grounds. Only a few sportswriters knew that the octagenarian was once the best baserunner in baseball. He had been the first paid coach, hired by McGraw to teach the Giants how to steal bases. Under Latham's tutelage the Giants swiped 234 in 1909, then averaged 308 steals for the next three years.

A fine third baseman and leadoff hitter for the Browns when they won four straight AA pennants in the 1880s, he scored 100 or more runs nine times, leading the AA with 152 in 1886. Latham scored 1,478 runs during his career. In 1888 he led the AA with 109 stolen bases. Known as a humorist, Latham became famous for his comedy in the coach's box, taunting rivals while amusing the crowd with his antics. Latham became a regular attendee of Baseball Hall of Fame gatherings with Kid Nichols and Cy Young, representing the real old-timers.

Playing Career: *1880, 1883-1896, 1899, 1909; Buf N, StL AA, Chi P, Cin N, StL N, Was N, NY N*
Managerial Career: *1896; StL N*

Arlie Latham.

Barry Latman
Latman, Arnold Barry
B: May 21, 1936

Pos: P	ERA: 3.91
W-L: 59-68	SOs: 829
ShOs: 10	Saves: 16

The broad-shouldered, hard-throwing Latman won 13 games in 1961 and was selected for the All-Star team. Considered an outstanding prospect with the White Sox, in 1958 Latman was 3-0 with an ERA of 0.76, with a shutout in three starts. He did not fulfill his potential.

Playing Career: *1957-1967; Chi A, Cle A, Cal A, Hou N*

Charlie Lau in action, 1963.

Charlie Lau
Lau, Charles Richard
B: Apr 12, 1933   D: Mar 18, 1984

Pos: C	BA: .255
Hits: 298	HRs: 16
RBI: 140	BBs: 109

The premier batting coach in the majors at the time of his death, Lau was a lifetime .180 hitter until 1962, when he changed his batting style. He adopted a contact hitter's stance: feet wide apart, bat held almost parallel to the ground. His average jumped to .294 that year. After arm surgery in 1966, he was used solely as a pinch hitter. At a team party in August of that year, he saved Frank Robinson from drowning in a swimming pool accident.

Lau taught his hitting technique to the Orioles, A's, Royals, Yankees and White Sox. Most of the Royals adopted his spray-hitting style: Hal McRae, George Brett, Amos Otis and Willie Wilson all used his approach during their most successful seasons. In 1983 Lau voluntarily gave up his spot on the White Sox coaching staff to enable scout Loren Babe, who was dying of lung cancer, to qualify for his 10-year pension. Babe died in February 1984. Lau died from cancer of the colon a month later.

Playing Career: *1956, 1958-1967; Det A, Mil N, Bal A, KC A*

Cookie Lavagetto
Lavagetto, Harry Arthur
B: Dec 1, 1912   D: Aug 10, 1990

Pos: 3B, 2B	BA: .269
Hits: 945	HRs: 40
RBI: 486	BBs: 485

Managerial Record
Won: 271   Lost: 384   Pct: .414

In Game Four of the 1947 World Series, Lavagetto broke up Floyd Blevens's no-hit bid with a game-winning double off the right field wall. The third baseman made the All-Star team four years in a row, 1938-1941. As a manager Lavagetto did not fare so well, but he developed young sluggers Harmon Killebrew, Bob Allison, Earl Battey and Zoilo Versalles – the backbone of the Twins' 1965 pennant-winning team.
Playing Career: *1934-1941, 1946-1947; Pit N, Brk N*
Managerial Career: *1957-1961; Was A, Min A*

Doc Lavan
Lavan, John Leonard
B: Oct 28, 1890   D: May 29, 1952

Pos: SS	BA: .245
Hits: 954	HRs: 7
RBI: 377	BBs: 209

A light-hitting shortstop, Lavan had tremendous range but was prone to errors, making 75 with the Browns in 1915, and later leading NL shortstops in miscues twice. His best season was 1920, when he rapped .289 with 21 doubles and 10 triples.
Playing Career: *1913-1924; StL A, Phi A, Was A, StL N*

Gary Lavelle
Lavelle, Gary Robert
B: Jan 3, 1949

Pos: P	ERA: 2.93
W-L: 80-77	SOs: 769
ShOs: 0	Saves: 136

One of the top left-handed relievers of all time, Lavelle was the stopper for the Giants for 11 years, posting ERAs under 3.00 in eight of those seasons. In 1977 he set team records for game appearances with 73, and for saves with 20, and he holds the Giants' franchise record with 647 games and 127 saves. He was selected for two All-Star Game teams and appeared in the 1985 ALCS. Elbow problems put him on the shelf.
Playing Career: *1974-1985, 1987; SF N, Tor A, Oak A*

Rudy Law
Law, Rudy Karl
B: Oct 7, 1956

Pos: OF	BA: .271
Hits: 656	HRs: 18
RBI: 198	BBs: 184

As a Dodger rookie, Law stole 40 bases. The White Sox used him as a leadoff man in 1983

Pitcher Vernon Law on the mound for the Pittsburgh Pirates.

and he was a catalyst in their division championship that year. Law also led AL outfielders in fielding average while stealing a club record 77 bases that season.
Playing Career: *1978, 1980, 1982-1986; LA N, Chi A, KC A*

Vance Law
Law, Vance Aaron
B: Oct 1, 1956

Pos: 3B, 2B, SS, 1B, OF	BA: .256
Hits: 972	HRs: 71
RBI: 442	BBs: 408

The White Sox played by two Laws in 1983 – Rudy and Vance. The son of Vern Law, Vance was Chicago's third baseman in 1983. He played all 25 innings of the longest game in AL history. Law also hit 17 homers in 1984. He made the NL All-Star squad in 1988, then a bad back ended his career.
Playing Career: *1980-1989, 1991; Pit N, Chi A, Mon N, Chi N, Oak A*

Vern Law
Law, Vernon Sanders
B: Mar 12, 1930

Pos: P	ERA: 3.77
W-L: 162-147	SOs: 1,092
ShOs: 28	Saves: 13

Signed by Pirates owner Bing Crosby, Law became the heart and soul of the Pittsburgh team by the mid-1950s. Law won Games One and Four of the 1960 World Series, even though he was suffering from a late-season

sprained ankle. He was the starter for the famous Game Seven finale which was captured in dramatic fashion by Mazeroski's home run. In addition to the World Championship in 1960, Law won the Cy Young Award with a 20-9 record and a league-high 18 complete games. He also made an All-Star Game appearance.

After his outstanding 1960 season, Law missed most of 1961 with a torn rotator muscle. Pitching in pain during 1962, he rebounded to go 10-7, but more physical problems plagued him during his ineffective 1963 and 1964 seasons. He was back to form in 1965, at age 35, leading the Pirates with 17 wins and a 2.15 ERA. Law was honored with the Lou Gehrig Memorial Award as Comeback Player of the Year. Vern and his wife, VaNita, had six children: Veldon, Verl, Vaughn, Varlin, VaLynda and Vance.
Playing Career: *1950-1951, 1954-1967; Pit N*

Brooks Lawrence
Lawrence, Brooks Ulysses
B: Jan 30, 1925

Pos: P	ERA: 4.25
W-L: 69-62	SOs: 481
ShOs: 5	Saves: 22

Lawrence came out of the Negro Leagues to post a 15-6 record as a rookie starter and reliever for the 1954 Cardinals. Sent down to the minors for most of 1955, he returned with a vengeance when he opened with 13 straight victories in 1956. He was 19-10, then 16-13 in 1957.
Playing Career: *1954-1960; StL N, Cin N*

Tony Lazzeri
Lazzeri, Anthony Michael (Poosh 'em Up)
B: Dec 6, 1903   D: Aug 6, 1946
Hall of Fame 1992

Pos: 2B	BA: .292
Hits: 1,840	HRs: 178
RBI: 1,191	BBs: 870

As a 22-year-old rookie, Lazzeri struck out in the seventh game of the 1926 World Series, after he had hit a vicious line drive that landed two feet foul. But for those two feet Lazzeri would have been the hero and the pitcher – Grover Cleveland Alexander – the goat. The two shared another fate – they both suffered from epilepsy. Lazzeri struggled his entire career to keep the disease under control. Lazzeri holds the all-time minor league run record, having produced a monster 1925 season with Salt Lake City. He scored 202 times and drove in 222 runs in the 197-game season.

In the majors Lazzeri had seven 100-RBI seasons. He was the first player to hit two grand slam homers in one game, and still holds the AL record for RBI in one game with 11. Lazzeri played in the 1933 All-Star Game. In seven Fall Classics, he had 19 RBI and four homers, including a grand slam. His solid baseball instincts and leadership abilities made him a hero to many Italian-Americans.
Playing Career: *1926-1939; NY A, Chi N, Brk N, NY N*

Tony Lazzeri.

Charlie Lea
Lea, Charles William
B: Dec 25, 1956

Pos: P	ERA: 3.54
W-L: 62-48	SOs: 535
ShOs: 8	No-hitter: 1

After starting and winning the 1984 All-Star Game for the NL, Lea completed his season with a 15-10 record and a 2.89 ERA. A hiatus in the mid-1980s ended with Lea's 9-0 record with an ERA of 0.84 in the Southern League. He was called back up to Montreal.
Playing Career: *1980-1984, 1987-1988; Mon N, Min A*

Freddy Leach
Leach, Frederick
B: Nov 23, 1897   D: Dec 10, 1981

Pos: OF	BA: .307
Hits: 1,147	HRs: 72
RBI: 509	BBs: 163

Leach was a railroad telegrapher playing for local teams when he tried professional baseball. By 1923 he made it to the Phillies. After an up-and-down career as a .300-hitter, he was involved in McGraw's most controversial trade: Lefty O'Doul for Leach. Even though O'Doul outhit Leach by 100 points to win the 1929 batting race, McGraw said he was satisfied that Leach was more versatile and far better defensively. Leach averaged .319 for three years for the Giants.
Playing Career: *1923-1932; Phi N, NY N, Bos N*

Rick Leach
Leach, Richard Max
B: May 4, 1957

Pos: 1B, OF, DH	BA: .268
Hits: 460	HRs: 18
RBI: 183	BBs: 176

As a University of Michigan freshman, Leach quarterbacked his football team in the Orange Bowl. He went to a bowl game each year, but signed with the Tigers when it was time to choose a profession. Relegated to the status of role player, Leach was stuck at power positions, but had no power.
Playing Career: *1981-1990; Det A, Tor A, Tex A, SF N*

Tommy Leach
Leach, Thomas William
B: Nov 4, 1877   D: Sep 29, 1969

Pos: 3B, OF	BA: .270
Hits: 2,146	HRs: 62
RBI: 810	BBs: 820

An outstanding player during the deadball era, Leach's speed translated into 1,335 runs scored and 361 stolen bases. More importantly to teams of the time, he covered third base like a blanket. His play spearheaded the 1902-1904 Pirates which may have been the best team ever. They even took on the Boston

AL team in the 1903 World Series with only one pitcher. It still took the Pilgrims eight games to defeat Leach and his teammates.

That first World Series was played under peculiar circumstances. Ropes were used in the outfield to hold back the tremendous crowds. Balls hit into the roped-off areas were ground-rule triples instead of doubles. Leach ripped two three-baggers in Game One and had garnered four by the fifth game. Both those marks are standing Series records. Leach hit 62 major league home runs; 49 were inside the park. In 1902 he led the NL in homers with six, every one of them inside the park.
Playing Career: *1898-1915, 1918; Lou N, Pit N, Chi N, Cin N*

Tim Leary
Leary, Timothy James
B: Mar 21, 1958

Pos: P	ERA: 4.31
W-L: 77-104	SOs: 879
ShOs: 9	Saves: 1

An All-American in baseball at UCLA, Leary was the second overall major league draft pick in 1979. He pitched well out of the bullpen in the 1988 World Series. That year he won the NL Comeback Player of the Year Award based on his record of 17-11 with a 2.91 ERA.
Playing Career: *1981, 1983-; NY N, Mil A, LA N, Cin N, NY A, Sea A*

Bill Lee
Lee, William Crutcher (Big Bill, General)
B: Oct 21, 1909   D: Jun 15, 1977

Pos: P	ERA: 3.54
W-L: 169-157	SOs: 998
ShOs: 29	Saves: 13

A big right-hander who anchored the Cubs' staff during the 1930s, Lee had been buried in the Cardinals' farm system despite a 71-31 four-season minor league record. The Red Birds sold Lee to the Cubs in 1934, and he shut out the Phillies in his first start. In 1935 he led the NL with a .769 winning percentage, winning 20 games, five of them during the Cubs' historic 21-game winning streak. He was even better in 1938, winning 22, and posting a .710 winning percentage and a 2.66 ERA.
Playing Career: *1934-1947; Chi N, Phi N, Bos N*

Bill Lee
Lee, William Francis (Spaceman)
B: Dec 28, 1946

Pos: P	ERA: 3.62
W-L: 119-90	SOs: 713
ShOs: 10	Saves: 19

A colorful personality who could also pitch, Lee won 17 games each season, 1973-1975. He started two games in the 1975 World Series. Lee earned his nickname when, on his first view of the Green Monster – Fenway's left

field wall – he asked, "Do they leave it there during games?" Lee criticized domed stadiums, artificial turf, the designated hitter rule and Red Sox management, and he admitted to using marijuana, but only "sprinkled on his cereal."
Playing Career: *1969-1982; Bos A, Mon N*

Hal Lee
Lee, Harold Burnham (Sheriff)
B: Feb 15, 1905   D: Sep 4, 1989

Pos: OF	BA: .275
Hits: 755	HRs: 33
RBI: 323	BBs: 203

Lee had a fine if frustrating 1932 season for the "phutile Phillies" with a .303 average, 18 homers, 42 doubles and 10 triples. That season got him traded to the even worse bumbling Braves. Lee batted .303 again as Babe Ruth's teammate on the 1935 Braves.
Playing Career: *1930-1936; Brk N, Phi N, Bos N*

The Braves' Hal Lee, 1934.

Leron Lee
Lee, Leron
B: Mar 4, 1948

Pos: OF	BA: .250
Hits: 404	HRs: 31
RBI: 152	BBs: 133

After turning down football scholarships, Lee signed with the Cardinals for $50,000. His best year came with the Padres in 1972 when he batted .300, but he played 100 games or more only four times, 1970-1973. Lee became a big star in Japanese baseball during the 1980s.
Playing Career: *1969-1976; StL N, SD N, Cle A, LA N*

Manny Lee
Lee y Lora, Manuel
B: Jun 17, 1965

Pos: SS, 2B	BA: .251
Hits: 592	HRs: 17
RBI: 211	BBs: 180

Before he ever got to the majors, Lee was signed by the Mets, traded to the Astros, then drafted by the Blue Jays. Toronto kept the 19-year-old on the bench for two years, then played him at second. He is now back at his best position, shortstop, for the Rangers.
Playing Career: *1985-; Tor A, Tex A*

Thornton Lee
Lee, Thornton Starr
B: Sep 13, 1906

Pos: P	ERA: 3.56
W-L: 117-124	SOs: 937
ShOs: 14	Saves: 10

Ted Williams hit homers off Thornton Lee and his son Don Lee, the only such instance in the major leagues. Thornton was the top AL pitcher in 1941, winning 22, completing 30, tossing 300 innings and posting a 2.37 ERA. Only 29 percent of Lee's opposing batters reached base that year.
Playing Career: *1933-1948; Cle A, Chi A, NY N*

Cleveland's Thornton Lee, 1935.

Sam Leever
Leever, Samuel
(The Goshen Schoolmaster)
B: Dec 23, 1871   D: May 19, 1953

Pos: P	ERA: 2.47
W-L: 194-100	SOs: 847
ShOs: 39	Saves: 12

Sam Leever is a Hall of Fame candidate. He won 66 percent of his decisions, posting 20 victories or more four times, twice leading the NL in won-lost percentage and once with a 2.06 ERA. Leever was the mainstay of the Pirates' pitching staff during the team's glory days of three straight pennants, 1902-1904, under the leadership of Hall of Famers Fred Clarke and Honus Wagner.

Leever was born in Goshen, Ohio, and taught school before he became a major league pitcher. He was consistent, posting 11 consecutive winning seasons. In 1903 two of his 25 wins came in a string of six consecutive shutouts that the Pirates tossed, setting a major league record that still stands. Near the end of that season Leever injured his shoulder while trapshooting, another sport at which he excelled. As a result he had a sore arm during the 1903 World Series, losing twice to the Red Sox. He is 24th on the all-time career ERA list and 10th on the winning percentage list.
Playing Career: *1898-1910; Pit N*

Jim Lefebvre
Lefebvre, James Kenneth (Frenchy)
B: Jan 7, 1942

Pos: 2B, 3B, 1B	BA: .251
Hits: 756	HRs: 74
RBI: 404	BBs: 322
Managerial Record	
Won: 395 Lost: 415 Pct: .488	

Lefebvre played in two World Series in his first two years in the majors, hitting .400 in the 1965 Fall Classic versus the Twins, and homering in the 1966 opener for one of only two runs that the Dodgers would score in the Series. With Jim Gilliam, Maury Wills and Wes Parker, Lefebvre was a member of the Dodgers' switch-hitting infield of the mid-1960s. He played in Japan 1973-1976 and was named the manager of the Mariners in December 1988.
Playing Career: *1965-1972; LA N*
Managerial Career: *1989-; Sea A, Chi N*

Craig Lefferts
Lefferts, Craig Lindsay
B: Sep 29, 1957

Pos: P	ERA: 3.39
W-L: 57-71	SOs: 692
ShOs: 0	Saves: 100

An outstanding relief pitcher, Lefferts has moved into the starting role the last two years. He had been terrific in postseason play, compiling a record of 2-0 with a 1.29 ERA in three LCS, and one save and a 1.04 ERA in two World Series. In 1986 Lefferts led

the majors with 83 appearances, setting a Padres record for both single-season and career appearances. He has been a free agent twice, signing with the Padres in 1990, then the Rangers for 1993.
Playing Career: *1983-; Chi N, SD N, SF N, Bal A, Tex A*

Ron LeFlore
LeFlore, Ronald
B: Jun 16, 1948

Pos: OF, DH	BA: .288
Hits: 1,283	HRs: 59
RBI: 353	BBs: 363

Detroit native LeFlore was scouted by Tigers Manager Billy Martin at Jackson State Prison. LeFlore was serving a 5-to-15 year sentence for armed robbery, but was released to sign a contract with the Tigers at age 25 in July 1973. LeFlore might have been the fastest man in baseball during his prime. He stole 455 bases during his nine-year career, and was the only player to lead both the NL and AL in that category.

LeFlore batted .316 with 93 runs and 58 stolen bases in 1976, the year he made the All-Star team. He had a 30-game hitting streak that year. In 1977 he added power to his arsenal and pounded 16 homers, becoming the first Tiger since Al Kaline to get more than 200 hits in a season. The next year LeFlore led the AL with 126 runs and 68 stolen bases, he also had 62 RBI, a high total for a leadoff batter. He put together a second impressive hit-

Ron LeFlore.

ting streak of 27 consecutive games. LeFlore's autobiography, *Breakout*, was made into a movie called *One in a Million*.
Playing Career: *1974-1982; Det A, Mon N*

Hank Leiber
Leiber, Henry Edward
B: Jan 17, 1911

Pos: OF	BA: .288
Hits: 808	HRs: 101
RBI: 518	BBs: 274

A platoon outfielder on the Giants' back-to-back NL pennant-winners of 1936 and 1937, Leiber batted .367 in the 1937 Fall Classic. He hit .331 with 22 homers, 110 runs scored and 107 RBI in his only full season, 1935. Being a defensive liability did not prevent him from being an All-Star three times.
Playing Career: *1933-1942; NY N, Chi N*

Nemo Leibold
Leibold, Harry Loran
B: Feb 17, 1892   D: Feb 4, 1977

Pos: OF	BA: .266
Hits: 1,109	HRs: 4
RBI: 283	BBs: 571

Leibold played in four World Series, then had a long career managing in the minor leagues. In 1946 he was suspended for a season after a shoving match with an umpire. When Leibold was reinstated before the end of the season, several umpires quit in protest.
Playing Career: *1913-1925; Cle A, Chi A, Bos A, Was A*

Charlie Leibrandt
Leibrandt, Charles Louis, Jr.
B: Oct 4, 1956

Pos: P	ERA: 3.71
W-L: 140-119	SOs: 1,121
ShOs: 18	Saves: 2

One of the best deals in Royals history brought them Leibrandt from the Reds for Bob Tufts. Leibrandt won 76 games over six seasons, not counting Game Seven of the 1985 ALCS. After being a stalwart of the Royals' staff, he had to rebound from a rotator cuff injury. Following rehabilitation in the minors, Leibrandt won 15 games two years in a row as the Braves captured two straight pennants. He has pitched in three World Series.
Playing Career: *1979-1982, 1984-; Cin N, KC A, Atl N, Tex A*

Lefty Leifield
Leifield, Albert Peter
B: Sep 5, 1883   D: Oct 10, 1970

Pos: P	ERA: 2.47
W-L: 124-97	SOs: 616
ShOs: 32	No-hitters: 1

By age 28, Leifield had won 104 games, but a sore arm ended his effectiveness shortly thereafter. He won 20 games in 1907 and 19

for the 1909 pennant-winners. Leifield tossed three one-hitters. In one of them, he got his team's only hit, but lost to Mordecai Brown.
Playing Career: *1905-1913, 1918-1920; Pit N, Chi N, StL A*

Denny Lemaster
Lemaster, Denver Clayton
B: Feb 25, 1939

Pos: P	ERA: 3.58
W-L: 90-105	SOs: 1,305
ShOs: 14	Saves: 8

The Braves gave Lemaster a $60,000 signing bonus in 1958, and he showed early promise by fanning 11 batters in one game in the Texas League. His best big league season ended with a 17-11 record and 185 strikeouts. He was chosen for the All-Star team in 1967.
Playing Career: *1962-1972; Mil N, Atl N, Hou N, Mon N*

Johnnie LeMaster
LeMaster, Johnnie Lee
B: Jun 19, 1954

Pos: SS	BA: .222
Hits: 709	HRs: 22
RBI: 229	BBs: 241

LeMaster hit a home run in his first major league at-bat, then spent the rest of his career fighting low averages and lack of power. His best season was 1983, when he hit .240 and scored 81 runs on only 128 hits. LeMaster played shortstop for 10 years in the maelstrom known as Candlestick Park.
Playing Career: *1975-1985, 1987; SF N, Cle A, Pit N*

Bob Lemon
Lemon, Robert Granville
B: Sep 22, 1920
Hall of Fame 1976

Pos: P, 3B	ERA: 3.23
W-L: 207-128	SOs: 1,277
ShOs: 31	No-hitters: 1
Managerial Record	
Won: 430 Lost: 403 Pct: .516	

The Cleveland Indians of 1948-1956 had what was perhaps the finest pitching staff in AL history, and Lemon was their ace. Beginning as a third baseman, Lemon played 10 games before military service in World War II. In that short time, he demonstrated that he was not a good enough hitter to replace Ken Keltner at the hot corner. Moreover, Lemon's arm was erratic; he seemed unable to throw straight. When he returned in 1946, the Indians changed him into a pitcher.

By 1948 he was a star. As the Indians won their first pennant in 28 years, Lemon won 20 games, including a no-hitter and 10 shutouts. He added two more wins in the World Series. From 1948 to 1956, he had seven 20-win seasons and led the AL in victories three times. Frequently used as a pinch hitter, Lemon stroked 37 home runs. Managing under the duress of the first George Steinbrenner era in

Bob Lemon.

New York, Lemon nonetheless took the Yankees to a pennant and won the World Series in 1978.
Playing Career: *1941-1942, 1946-1958; Cle A*
Managerial Career: *1970-1972, 1977-1979, 1981-1982; KC A, Chi A, NY A*

Chet Lemon
Lemon, Chester Earl
B: Feb 12, 1955

Pos: OF	BA: .273
Hits: 1,875	HRs: 215
RBI: 884	BBs: 749

When the runaway Tigers won the World Championship in 1984, Lemon was in center field. He batted .287 with 34 doubles and 20 homers that year. Having been a third baseman in the minors, Lemon brought an infielder's instinct to the outfield. Getting a great jump on the ball, he broke two AL fielding records in 1977, most chances for an outfielder, 524, and most putouts, 512. He has scored 934 runs, hit 396 doubles, and appeared in three All-Star Games.
Playing Career: *1975-1990; Chi A, Det A*

Jim Lemon
Lemon, James Robert
B: Mar 23, 1928

Pos: OF	BA: .262
Hits: 901	HRs: 164
RBI: 529	BBs: 363
Managerial Record	
Won: 65 Lost: 96 Pct: .404	

The first Senator to hit three homers in one game, Lemon also tied two records by hitting two homers and driving in six runs in one

inning. He knocked in 100 runs in both 1959 and 1960, chasing Mickey Mantle for the AL home run crown in the latter year, but losing 40 to 38.
Playing Career: *1950, 1953-1963; Cle A, Was A, Min A, Phi N, Chi A*
Managerial Career: *1968; Was A*

Andy Leonard
Leonard, Andrew Jackson
B: Jun 1, 1846   D: Aug 21, 1903

Pos: OF	BA: .299
Hits: 717	HRs: 4
RBI: 218	BBs: 30

One of the original Cincinnati Red Stockings, Leonard batted fifth for the team that was undefeated through the 1869 season and well into the next. He had tremendous speed and batted .321 in the National Association. In 1873 he scored 81 runs in 58 games.
Playing Career: *1871-1878, 1880; Was Olympics n, Bos Red Stockings n, Bos N, Cin N*

Buck Leonard
Leonard, Walter
B: Sep 8, 1907
Hall of Fame 1972

Pos: 1B	BA: .328(inc.)
Hits: 525 (inc.)	HRs: 69 (inc.)
RBI: NA	BBs: NA

The black press called Leonard "the Black Gehrig." Like Larruping Lou, Buck was a durable, pull-hitting, first baseman with plenty of left-handed power. He teamed with Josh Gibson to give the Homestead Grays the mightiest one-two home run punch in Negro League history. After Leonard joined the

Grays in 1934, they captured nine straight Negro National League pennants. When Gibson left the club, 1940-1941, for Mexico, the Grays still won on Leonard's home run power.

In 1940 Leonard led all Negro League batters with a .383 average. He led the league again in batting in 1948 with a .395 mark. Leonard hit .382 in exhibitions against white major league players. He made a record 12 appearances in the annual Negro Leagues East-West all-star game, hitting .317 with a record three home runs. When the Grays disbanded, Leonard went south to play in Mexico from 1951 to 1955. In 1962 he helped organize the Rocky Mount, Carolina League, club, serving as vice-president.
Playing Career: *1933-1950; Brk Royal Giants, Hom Grays*

Dennis Leonard
Leonard, Dennis Patrick
B: May 18, 1951

Pos: P	ERA: 3.69
W-L: 144-106	SOs: 1,323
ShOs: 23	Saves: 1

Leonard won 20 games or more three of four years, 1977-1980, the Royals winning the division title each time. Leonard also hurled two no-hitters in the minors. After nearly three years on the disabled list, Leonard pitched a shutout in his return appearance. The result was one of the most emotional outbursts ever witnessed in sports. WOR-TV in New York interrupted the Mets broadcast to show the final inning. Fans who attended in Kansas City have never forgotten Leonard's performance.
Playing Career: *1974-1983, 1985-1986; KC A*

Negro Leagues batting powerhouse Buck Leonard.

Dutch Leonard.

Dutch Leonard
Leonard, Emil John
B: Mar 25, 1909   D: Apr 17, 1983

Pos: P	ERA: 3.25
W-L: 191-181	SOs: 1,170
ShOs: 30	Saves: 44

Eddie Cicotte and Eddie Rommel developed the knuckleball to augment their fading fastballs and not-so-sharp breaking curves, but Leonard was the first to rely exclusively on the pitch. He had the misfortune of pitching mostly for losing teams during his 20 years in the majors. Yet he posted a 191-181 record for a .513 winning percentage. His best season was 1945, when he compiled a 17-7 record with a 2.13 ERA in the Senators' unexpected entrance into the AL pennant race.

Washington owner Clark Griffith had been so confident that his club would not compete in 1945, that he had rented the stadium to the football Redskins, receiving permission from the league to end the baseball season early. Leonard and his teammates stood by helpless for a whole week, waiting to see if they would win the pennant on the strength of their shortened performance. The Senators lost by one and a half games.
Playing Career: *1933-1936, 1938-1953; Brk N, Was A, Phi N, Chi N*

Hub Leonard
Leonard, Hubert Benjamin (Dutch)
B: Apr 16, 1892   D: Jul 11, 1952

Pos: P	ERA: 2.76
W-L: 139-112	SOs: 1,160
ShOs: 33	No-hitters: 2

Pitching during the early Red Sox glory days, Leonard hurled a complete-game victory in both the 1915 and 1916 World Series. He holds the all-time record lowest ERA with a mark of 1.01 or 0.96 recorded in 1914. There is dispute over the figure, but either would be the record. Leonard was 19-5 that year, allowing only 18 percent of batters to hit safely. Though a starter, he was frequently rushed into games to clean up, and recorded 13 saves.
Playing Career: *1913-1921, 1924-1925; Bos A, Det A*

Jeff Leonard
Leonard, Jeffrey (Hac Man, One Flap Down)
B: Sep 22, 1955

Pos: OF, DH	BA: .266
Hits: 1,342	HRs: 144
RBI: 723	BBs: 342

In 1987 Leonard became only the third player in baseball history to win the LCS MVP Award when his team lost the series. He hit home runs in each of the first four games, taunting the Cardinals with his slow, deliberate "one-flap-down" trot – one arm held against his side and the other extended. When a foot injury reduced Leonard's effectiveness in the outfield, he became a DH and concentrated on home runs, banging 24 in 1989, driving in 93 runs and earning an All-Star spot.
Playing Career: *1977-1990; LA N, Hou N, SF N, Mil A, Sea A*

Phillies lefty Randy Lerch, 1977.

Randy Lerch
Lerch, Randy Louis
B: Oct 9, 1954

Pos: P	ERA: 4.54
W-L: 60-64	SOs: 507
ShOs: 2	Saves: 3

As a good fourth or fifth starter, Lerch helped his teams win five division titles, and come close a sixth time. Milwaukee lost in the 1981 split-season playoff despite having the best overall record. Lerch's best year was 1978; he was 11-8 with a 3.96 ERA in 184 innings pitched.
Playing Career: *1975-1984, 1986; Phi N, Mil A, Mon N, SF N*

Sam Leslie
Leslie, Samuel Andrew
B: Jul 26, 1905   D: Jan 21, 1979

Pos: 1B	BA: .304
Hits: 749	HRs: 36
RBI: 389	BBs: 216

Born and raised in Mississippi, Leslie spent his entire career in New York City, alternating between the Giants and Dodgers. In 1934 he hit .332 with 102 RBI for the Dodgers. The Giants got him back in time for the 1936-1937 World Series, where he pinch hit .500.
Playing Career: *1929-1938; NY N, Brk N*

Allan Lewis
Lewis, Allan Sydney (Panamanian Express)
B: Dec 12, 1941

Pos: PR, PH, OF	BA: .207
Hits: 6	HRs: 1
RBI: 3	BBs: 1

Once in awhile a team owner will have a significant idea – the farm system, designated hitters and night baseball, for example. Charlie Finley introduced the designated pinch runner. As such, Allan Lewis scored 47 runs and stole 44 bases in only 29 at-bats.
Playing Career: *1967-1970, 1972-1973; KC A, Oak A*

Buddy Lewis
Lewis, John Kelly
B: Aug 10, 1916

Pos: 3B, OF	BA: .297
Hits: 1,563	HRs: 71
RBI: 607	BBs: 573

Like his teammate Cecil Travis, Lewis lost nearly four years to World War II. Before the war, Lewis batted over .300 three times and scored 100 or more runs four times with a high of 122 in 1938. He led the AL in triples with 16 in 1939. In 1940 Lewis vacated the hot corner for right field, allowing veteran shortstop Travis, who was slowing down, to move to third. Lewis hit .333 in a short 1945 season, but struggled with injuries the remainder of his career.
Playing Career: *1935-1941, 1945-1947, 1949; Was A*

Duffy Lewis at bat, 1919.

Duffy Lewis
Lewis, George Edward
B: Apr 18, 1888   D: Jun 17, 1979

Pos: OF | BA: .284
Hits: 1,518 | HRs: 38
RBI: 793 | BBs: 352

Baseball's best defensive outfield ever was comprised of Duffy Lewis, Tris Speaker and Harry Hooper of the 1910-1915 Boston Red Sox. The steep incline from Fenway Park's left field fence toward the infield was known as "Duffy's Cliff," because Lewis played it so well. Other outfielders stumbled and fell, but Lewis swooped down on ground balls. Despite being one of the few players apparently liked by Ty Cobb, Lewis's fondest memories included throwing Cobb out as he attempted to stretch singles into doubles.

At the plate, Lewis was a dependable doubles hitter himself, averaging 31 per season for nine years. With line drive power he drove in 109 runs in 1912. He batted .284 in three World Series, playing each time for the champion Red Sox. In 1914 Lewis saw rookie Babe Ruth's first home run and, in 1935, when Lewis was traveling secretary for the Braves, he saw Ruth's last.
Playing Career: *1910-1917, 1919-1921; Bos A, NY A, Was A*

Ted Lewis
Lewis, Edward Morgan (Parson)
B: Dec 25, 1872   D: May 24, 1936

Pos: P | ERA: 3.53
W-L: 94-64 | SOs: 378
ShOs: 7 | Saves: 4

"Professor" seems like a better nickname for "Parson" Lewis, who won 21 games in 1896 and 26 in 1897 after graduating from Williams College. He matriculated at Harvard and coached their nine, then taught at Columbia. Lewis was later president of two colleges.
Playing Career: *1896-1901; Bos N, Bos A*

Jim Leyland
Leyland, James Richard
B: Dec 15, 1944

Managerial Record
Won: 667   Lost: 627   Pct: .515

Leyland has turned into a genius of a manager. Using patience and teaching skills, he took a low-budget franchise to the division title three years in a row, 1990-1992. He won Manager of the Year honors in 1988 for leading the Pirates to second place.
Managerial Career: *1986-; Pit N*

Sixto Lezcano
Lezcano y Curras, Sixto Joaquin
B: Nov 28, 1953

Pos: OF | BA: .271
Hits: 1,122 | HRs: 148
RBI: 591 | BBs: 576

As a power hitter for the Brewers, Lezcano figured prominently in the three-team trade that brought Ozzie Smith to St. Louis. Lezcano won a Gold Glove Award in 1979, the year he hit .321 with 101 RBI, and 28 homers, 10 of them in August.
Playing Career: *1974-1985; Mil A, StL N, SD N, Phi N, Pit N*

Fred Lieb
Lieb, Frederick
B: 1888   D: 1980

A longtime baseball enthusiast, Lieb began writing ballplayer biographies and submit-ting them to *Baseball Magazine* in 1909. Sub-sequently he wrote for several news bureaus and newspapers in Philadelphia and New York. Lieb was one of the original members of the Base Ball Writers Association of America, and held honorary card No. 1.

Lieb retired from baseball reporting in 1934 – at least, he thought he had. J.G. Taylor Spink soon persuaded him to write for *The Sporting News*. For the next 35 years, Lieb contributed a regular column and obituaries, sending them from his retirement home in St. Petersburg, Florida. Lieb is the author of several baseball books now considered classics, including: *Baseball As I Have Known It, Connie Mack – Grand Old Man of Baseball*, and team histories of the Tigers, Red Sox, Cardinals, Pirates, Orioles and Phillies in the highly regarded Putnam Series. Lieb received the J.G. Taylor Spink Award from the Hall of Fame in 1972.

Bob Lillis
Lillis, Robert Perry
B: Jun 2, 1930

Pos: SS | BA: .277
Hits: 549 | HRs: 3
RBI: 137 | BBs: 99
Managerial Record
Won: 276   Lost: 261   Pct: .514

Injuries delayed Lillis's debut at shortstop in 1957, then even though he batted .391 in 20 games in 1958, he lost the job to rookie Maury Wills. Drafted by the expansion Colt .45s in 1961, Lillis was their top player, and was honored as team MVP in 1962. A scout, instructor and coach in the Astros' system from 1968 to 1982, he became manager in August of that year. Leading the Astros to third place in 1983, Lillis finished second in NL Manager of the Year voting.
Playing Career: *1958-1967; LA N, StL N, Hou N*
Managerial Career: *1982-1985; Hou N*

Astros shortstop Bob Lillis goes for the double play in a 1965 game against the Giants.

Jose Lind
Lind, Jose Salgado
B: May 1, 1964

Pos: 2B	BA: .254
Hits: 824	HRs: 8
RBI: 286	BBs: 193

The 1992 Gold Glove winner for second base, Lind held the young Pirates' infield together through three straight division titles. He hit .322 during September 1987, causing the Bucs to trade Johnny Ray to make room for Lind, who hit .262 and scored 82 runs in 1988.
Playing Career: *1987-; Pit N, KC A*

Paul Lindblad
Lindblad, Paul Aaron
B: Aug 9, 1941

Pos: P	ERA: 3.29
W-L: 68-63	SOs: 671
ShOs: 1	Saves: 64

Two of the franchises Lindblad played for moved to new cities during his tenure. Although he never won nor saved more than nine games in any season, Lindblad pitched in four World Series games for the Athletics and Yankees.
Playing Career: *1965-1978; KC A, Oak A, Was A, Tex A, NY A*

Johnny Lindell
Lindell, John Harlan
B: Aug 30, 1916   D: Aug 27, 1985

Pos: OF, P	BA: .273
Hits: 762	HRs: 72
RBI: 404	BBs: 289

Lindell started as a pitcher, then switched to the outfield, playing in three World Series and leading the AL in triples, 1943-1944. He later developed a knuckleball, had a 24-9 AAA career, then returned to the majors, where he was 6-17 in 1953.
Playing Career: *1941-1950, 1953-1954; NY A, StL N, Pit N, Phi N*

Freddie Lindstrom
Lindstrom, Frederick Charles (Lindy)
B: Nov 21, 1905   D: Oct 4, 1981
Hall of Fame 1976

Pos: 3B, OF	BA: .311
Hits: 1,747	HRs: 103
RBI: 779	BBs: 334

Lindstrom became a regular at the tender age of 18, and figured in a few of baseball's interesting sidebars. Mrs. John McGraw, his manager's wife, attempted to catch his eye during a game to introduce the young bachelor to a female friend. She shouted, "Freddy, why don't you pay attention?" Misunderstanding, the astonished youngster called out, "Good grief, are you giving signs too?"

The Giants made it to the World Series in 1924, Lindstrom's rookie season. In the eighth inning of Game Seven, an infield grounder hit a pebble and the ball bounced

Freddie Lindstrom.

over Lindstrom's head, allowing the tying run to score. With astounding bad luck, the same thing occurred in the 12th inning, causing the Giants to lose the game. Ironically, Lindstrom developed into one of the NL's top fielding third basemen, a position he played until 1931, when a foot injury forced him into the outfield. A consistent .300 hitter, he led the NL with 231 hits and batted .358 in 1928, and hit .379 with 22 home runs in 1930.
Playing Career: *1924-1936; NY N, Pit N, Chi N, Brk N*

Frank Linzy
Linzy, Frank Alfred
B: Sep 15, 1940

Pos: P	ERA: 2.85
W-L: 62-57	SOs: 358
ShOs: 0	Saves: 111

The 1965 NL Rookie Pitcher of the Year, Linzy and his sinkerball won 9 games and saved 21 with a 1.43 ERA for the Giants. Two years later he was 7-7 with a 1.51 ERA. After appearing in a career-high 67 games in 1970, Linzy was injured in a collision with first baseman Bob Burda, and required facial surgery. He was one of the first big stars with the young Brewers, saving 25 games in 1972-1973. He was still a very effective hurler with a 3.28 ERA when he retired in 1974.
Playing Career: *1963, 1965-1974; NY N, StL N, Mil A, Phi N*

Johnny Lipon
Lipon, John Joseph
B: Nov 10, 1922

Pos: SS, 3B	BA: .259
Hits: 690	HRs: 10
RBI: 266	BBs: 347
Managerial Record	
Won: 18 Lost: 41 Pct: .305	

A long-time minor league manager, Lipon won eight pennants and division titles with the Tigers, Pirates and Indians farm clubs. Lipon was a starting shortstop for the Tigers. His best season was 1950, when he scored 104 runs with 27 doubles and hit .293.
Playing Career: *1942, 1946, 1948-1954; Det A, Bos A, StL A, Cin N*
Managerial Career: *1971; Cle A*

Mark Littell.

Mark Littell
Littell, Mark Alan
B: Jan 17, 1953

Pos: P	ERA: 3.32
W-L: 32-31	SOs: 466
ShOs: 0	Saves: 56

In pre-Quisenberry days, Littell was the bullpen ace for the Royals as they won division titles in 1976 and 1977. The Yankees' Chris Chambliss hit the famous pennant-winning home run in Game Five of the 1976 ALCS off Littell.
Playing Career: *1973, 1975-1982; KC A, StL N*

Dick Littlefield
Littlefield, Richard Bernard
B: Mar 18, 1926

Pos: P	ERA: 4.71
W-L: 33-54	SOs: 495
ShOs: 2	Saves: 9

One of the earliest bonus babies, Littlefield was an untried player who struggled with control all his career. His fastball was not quite fast enough for the big leagues. Littlefield's best performances came during a half season in 1952 with the Browns.
Playing Career: *1950-1958; Bos A, Chi A, Det A, StL A, Bal A, Pit N, StL N, NY N, Chi N, Mil N*

Danny Litwhiler
Litwhiler, Daniel Webster
B: Aug 31, 1916

Pos: OF	BA: .281
Hits: 982	HRs: 107
RBI: 451	BBs: 299

Classified 4-F during World War II due to severe knee injuries, Litwhiler played baseball instead. He made the All-Star Game roster and fielded 1.000 in 1942. In Game Five of the 1944 World Series, Litwhiler hit a home run. He once had a 21-game hitting streak.
Playing Career: *1940-1944, 1946-1951; Phi N, StL N, Bos N, Cin N*

John Henry Lloyd
Lloyd, John Henry (Pop)
B: Apr 25, 1884   D: Mar 19, 1965
Hall of Fame 1977

Pos: SS, 1B, 2B	BA: .363 (inc.)
Hits: 788 (inc.)	HRs: 27 (inc.)
RBI: NA	BBs: NA
Managerial Record (inc.)	
Won: 171 Lost: 158 Pct: .519	

John Henry "Pop" Lloyd.

Many of John Henry Lloyd's contemporaries, including Babe Ruth and Honus Wagner, considered him the greatest ballplayer they ever saw. Lloyd was a sensational fielder; admiring Cuban fans called him "el Cuchara," the scoop. In addition to his fielding prowess, Lloyd was an expert batsman who sprayed line drives all over the park. Although he was in his mid-thirties when the Negro National League was formed, Lloyd continued to play in organized Negro Leagues for 12 years and hit .564 in the 1928 Eastern Colored League at the age of 44.

Lloyd starred with the Chicago American Giants, 1914-1917, batting fourth in the lineup. They won two black World Championships during his tenure. A gentleman on and off the field, Lloyd's most emphatic curse was "Gosh bob it!"
Playing Career: *1905-1932; Macon Acmes, NY Cuban X-Giants, Phi Giants, Chi Leland Giants, NY Lincoln Giants, Chi Am Giants, NY Lincoln Stars, Chi Black Sox, Brk Royal Giants, Col Buckeyes, AC Bach Giants, Phi Hilldales, NY Harlem Stars*
Managerial Career: *1921-1931; Col Buckeyes, AC Bach Giants, Phi Hilldales, NY Lincoln Giants, NY Harlem Stars*

Hans Lobert
Lobert, John Bernard
B: Oct 18, 1881   D: Sep 14, 1968

Pos: 3B, SS, OF	BA: .274
Hits: 1,252	HRs: 32
RBI: 482	BBs: 395
Managerial Record	
Won: 42 Lost: 111 Pct: .275	

Lobert was exceptionally fast. He once raced a horse in Oxnard, California in 1914, Umpire Bill Klem officiating. The horse won by a nose. Lobert held the human record for circling the bases – 13.8 seconds – for 20 years. He stole home six times and once took second, third and home in succession. In 14 seasons, Lobert pilfered 316 sacks, including a career-high 47 for the Reds in 1908. He coached and managed at West Point and in the minors.
Playing Career: *1903, 1905-1917; Pit N, Chi N, Cin N, Phi N, NY N*
Managerial Career: *1938, 1942; Phi N*

Don Lock
Lock, Don Wilson
B: Jul 27, 1936

Pos: OF	BA: .238
Hits: 642	HRs: 122
RBI: 373	BBs: 373

Traded for Dale Long before he ever took a cut in the big leagues, Lock homered in his first at-bat. He was always a home run threat, and slammed 27 and 28 of them in 1963 and 1964, although his homer totals dropped off each year after that. Like many sluggers, Lock was susceptible to strikeouts; he whiffed 151 times in 1963.
Playing Career: *1962-1969; Was A, Phi N, Bos A*

Bob Locker
Locker, Robert Awtry (Foot)
B: Mar 15, 1938

Pos: P	ERA: 2.76
W-L: 57-39	SOs: 577
ShOs: 0	Saves: 95

As a 27-year-old rookie in 1965, Locker sat in the White Sox bullpen with knuckleball pitchers Hoyt Wilhelm and Eddie Fisher. He soon replaced them as the stopper, saving 20 in 1967 and leading AL pitchers with 77 appearances. Locker was 6-1 with 10 saves for the 1972 World Champion A's, and he appeared briefly in the World Series. When Rollie Fingers emerged as Oakland's ace reliever, Locker was traded to the Cubs, for whom he won 10 and saved 18 in 1973.
Playing Career: *1965-1973, 1975; Chi A, Sea A, Mil A, Oak A, Chi N*

The Giants' Whitey Lockman, 1952.

Whitey Lockman
Lockman, Carroll Walter
B: Jul 25, 1926

Pos: 1B, OF	BA: .279
Hits: 1,658	HRs: 114
RBI: 563	BBs: 552
Managerial Record	
Won: 157 Lost: 162 Pct: .492	

One of 66 batters who hit a homer in his first major league at-bat, Lockman also stroked the ninth-inning double in the 1951 NL playoff that set the stage for Bobby Thomson's pennant-winning home run. The Giants were trailing 4-1, and the Dodgers' ace had only to retire three more hitters to win the pennant. Al Dark scratched out a single, Don Mueller followed with another, then Monte Irvin popped out. Up came Lockman, who sliced an opposite-field double to left, driving in Dark and leaving runners on second and third. Thomson advanced to the plate. On deck was rookie Willie Mays. The 0-1 pitch looked good to Thomson and he whacked it into the lower left field stands to win the pennant for the Giants.

Lockman was a solid .280-.290 hitter with some home run power, topping 10 homers six times. He was one of the hardest men to double up in major league history, hitting into one double play in every 87 at-bats.

Playing Career: *1945, 1947-1960; NY N, StL N, Bal A, Cin N*
Managerial Career: *l972-1974; Chi N*

Skip Lockwood
Lockwood, Claude Edward (Jaws)
B: Aug 17, 1946

Pos: P	ERA: 3.55
W-L: 57-97	SOs: 829
ShOs: 5	Saves: 68

Signed for a $100,000 bonus, Lockwood played third base in 1965 before gravitating to the mound. Ten years later he hit his stride, saving 19 games in 1976 and 20 in 1977 for the Mets. He got his nickname from the movie *Jaws* – he "chewed up" batters.
Playing Career: *1965, 1969-1980; KC A, Oak A, Sea A, Mil A, Cal A, NY N, Bos A*

Billy Loes
Loes, William
B: Dec 13, 1929

Pos: P	ERA: 3.89
W-L: 80-63	SOs: 645
ShOs: 9	Saves: 32

After a miscue in the 1952 World Series, Loes claimed he lost the grounder because the sun got in his eyes. He once explained why he never won 20 games in a season with the statement, "If you win 20 games, they expect you to do it every year." Loes did go 50-25 over a four-year period, 1952-1955, the Dodgers winning the pennant in three of those seasons. He beat Whitey Ford in Game Four of the 1953 Fall Classic, and he made the AL All-Star team in 1957.
Playing Career: *1950, 1952-1961; Brk N, LA N, Bal A, SF N*

Tom Loftus
Loftus, Thomas Joseph
B: Nov 15, 1856   D: Apr 16, 1910

Pos: OF	BA: .182
Hits: 6	HRs: 0
RBI: 0 (inc.)	BBs: 2
Managerial Record	
Won: 454 Lost: 580 Pct: .439	

Loftus managed in the minor leagues for years, but was piloting a team in the NL during the Great Players' Rebellion of 1890. He was often accused of being too lax with his teams – he did not believe in changing pitchers, for example – but in his defense, the seasons following the failed Players' League were filled with resentful, disgusted men who spent as much time in the bars as on the playing fields. Loftus later served as president of the Three-I League.
Playing Career: *1877, 1883; StL N, StL AA*
Managerial Career: *l884, 1888-1891, 1900-1903; Mil U, Cle AA, Cle N, Cin N, Chi N, Was A*

Johnny Logan
Logan, John
B: Mar 23, 1927

Pos: SS	BA: .268
Hits: 1,407	HRs: 93
RBI: 547	BBs: 451

A favorite in Milwaukee, Logan made the All-Star squad four times, 1955, 1957-1959, as he helped the Braves take two NL pennants, tie for a third, and win the 1957 World Championship. He was a scrappy, pugnacious player who declared war on pitchers who used brushback and beanball pitches. Logan is reputed never to have backed down from a fight and never to have lost one. He led NL shortstops in fielding, 1952-1954.
Playing Career: *1951-1963; Bos N, Pit N*

Bill Lohrman
Lohrman, William Leroy
B: May 22, 1913

Pos: P	ERA: 3.69
W-L: 60-59	SOs: 330
ShOs: 9	Saves: 8

Some baseball historians credit Lohrman with the invention of the slider, though he did not use it as a strikeout pitch the way today's hurlers do. In 1942 Lohrman compiled a record of 14-5 with a 2.48 ERA, with the help of his slider.
Playing Career: *1934, 1937-1944; Phi N, NY N, StL N, Brk N, Cin N*

Mickey Lolich
Lolich, Michael Stephen
B: Sep 12, 1940

Pos: P	ERA: 3.44
W-L: 217-191	SOs: 2,832
ShOs: 41	Saves: 11

In 1971 Lolich won 25 games, completed 29, and struck out 308 batters in 376 innings – all AL leading totals – but the season was anti-climatic compared to his role in the 1968 World Series. Stealing the spotlight from teammate Denny McLain, who won 31 games in 1968, Lolich posted three complete game victories in the Fall Classic, and smacked his only major league home run. His triumphs included a 4-1 victory in Game Seven against Bob Gibson. In the sixth inning, Lolich picked speed demons Curt Flood and Lou Brock off first. The hurler gave up only five runs in all three games.

An All-Star selection in 1969, 1971 and 1972, Lolich was stupendous in postseason play, compiling a 1.42 ERA in the 1972 ALCS and a 1.67 mark in the 1968 Series. He pitched more than 200 innings a season for 12 straight years, four times exceeding 300 innings. Lolich finished second in Cy Young Award voting in both 1971 and 1972. Queried about his portly physique, the southpaw replied, "you don't pitch with your stomach."
Playing Career: *1963-1976, 1978-1979; Det A, NY N, SD N*

Southpaw Mickey Lolich displayed durability and talent on the mound.

Catcher Sherm Lollar shows his son Pete the tools of his trade in 1959.

Sherm Lollar
Lollar, John Sherman
B: Aug 23, 1924   D: Sep 24, 1977

Pos: C   BA: .264
Hits: 1,415   HRs: 155
RBI: 808   BBs: 671

An underrated backstop who anchored the Go-Go White Sox of the 1950s, Lollar was a crucial ingredient in their 1959 pennant-winning season. That year he socked 22 homers and drove in 84 runs. He even stole four bases. Lollar was always a dangerous hitter with power. In 1955 he collected two hits in one inning twice in the same game. He slugged a pair of homers with five RBI when the Sox massacred the Athletics 29-6. Lollar hit 244 doubles and struck out only 453 times in 5,351 at-bats.

A rock behind the plate and an excellent handler of pitchers, Lollar topped AL catchers four times in fielding, and his .992 career average ranks fifth on the all-time list. In 1954 Lollar played without permitting a single stolen base for five consecutive months. In 1962 he tied a major league backstop's record by catching six pop-ups in one game. Lollar played in the 1947 World Series, hitting .750, and he was chosen for the All-Star squad seven times.
Playing Career: *1946-1963; Cle A, NY A, StL A, Chi A*

Ernie Lombardi
Lombardi, Ernesto Natali (Schnozz)
B: Apr 6, 1908   D: Sep 26, 1977
Hall of Fame 1986

Pos: C   BA: .306
Hits: 1,792   HRs: 190
RBI: 990   BBs: 430

During the fourth and final game of the 1939 World Series, Lombardi was guarding home plate when a baserunner collided with him. He lay on the ground while his teammates scrambled to recover the ball, and another baserunner, Joe DiMaggio, circled the bags with the winning run. The press labelled the incident "Lombardi's Snooze," but the catcher had been kneed in the groin during the collision, and lay writhing in pain.

Lombardi was a slow runner; it was said he had to hit .400 to end up with a .300 average. Nonetheless, he was one of baseball's greatest catchers. Lombardi's home run totals were modest, the high being 20 in 1939, but he hit line drives with tremendous power. Only two receivers have led their leagues in hitting, and Lombardi was the only catcher to do it twice. The first time was in 1938, when he batted .342 and was voted league MVP. Five years later, he led the NL again with a .330 mark.
Playing Career: *1931-1947; Brk N, Cin N, Bos N, NY N*

Jim Lonborg
Lonborg, James Reynold
B: Apr 16, 1942

Pos: P   ERA: 3.86
W-L: 157-137   SOs: 1,475
ShOs: 15   Saves: 4

An off-season ski injury that Lonborg suffered following his Cy Young Award 1967 season resulted in the introduction of restrictive clauses in players' contracts. His great season culminated in his final game victory over the Twins to put the Red Sox into first place. In the World Series, he beat the Cardinals with a one-hit shutout to tie them at one game each. Lonborg tossed a 3-1 victory in Game Five to give Boston a 3-2 Series edge. He also pitched the seventh game on two days rest, but lost to Bob Gibson.
Playing Career: *1965-1979; Bos A, Mil A, Phi N*

Dale Long
Long, Richard Dale
B: Feb 6, 1926   D: Jan 27, 1991

Pos: 1B   BA: .267
Hits: 805   HRs: 132
RBI: 467   BBs: 353

Powerfully built, Long turned down a contract from the NFL Green Bay Packers, and made baseball his life's work. At the time of his death he was the roving ambassador of the National Association, the governing body of minor league baseball. Long smacked eight homers in eight days during May 1956.
Playing Career: *1951, 1955-1963; Pit N, StL A, Chi N, NY N, NY A, Was A*

Hall of Fame backstop Ernie Lombardi.

Herman C. "Germany" Long, 1900.

Herman Long
Long, Herman C. (Germany)
B: Apr 13, 1866   D: Sep 17, 1909

Pos: SS
Hits: 2,132
RBI: 1,052

BA: .278
HRs: 91
BBs: 612

A cartoonist depicted Long as an octopus snagging balls with each of his eight tentacles. He and his Boston Beaneater infield teammates must have appeared that way to their opponents in the 1890s. The Beaneaters had the finest infield quartet of the 19th century. Long had a powerful arm and a quick release, coupled with outstanding range speed, and agility. He made more errors than any other player – he was the only major leaguer to make 1,000 errors – yet he was the best shortstop of the 19th century.

Long's career chances per game percentage, 6.4, tops all shortstops. At the plate, Long twice knocked in over 100 runs and scored over 100 seven times. His 149 runs scored led the NL in 1893 and his 12 home runs led the league in 1900. Noisy on the field, he urged teammates to greater efforts, ragged opponents, and stirred up fans. He played with wild abandon, breaking Connie Mack's leg with a ferocious slide in 1893.
Playing Career: *1889-1904; KC AA, Bos N, NY A, Det A, Phi N*

Eddie Lopat
Lopat, Edmund Walter (Steady Eddie)
B: Jun 21, 1918   D: Jun 15, 1992

Pos: P
W-L: 166-112
ShOs: 28
Managerial Record
Won: 90   Lost: 124   Pct: .421

ERA: 3.21
SOs: 859
Saves: 3

Lopat won almost 60 percent of his decisions. He was 4-1 in World Series play with a 2.60 ERA. Yankees manager Casey Stengel pitched him between flamethrowers Allie Reynolds and Vic Raschi, and the contrast made Lopat's slow balls more unhittable. He averaged 16 wins a year in the World Championship seasons of 1949-1953. In 1953 Lopat led the AL with a 2.42 ERA and an .800 winning percentage. He stayed in baseball as a coach, manager, general manager and scout.
Playing Career: *1944-1955; Chi A, NY A, Bal A*
Managerial Career: *1963-1964; KC A*

Stan Lopata
Lopata, Stanley Edward
B: Sep 12, 1925

Pos: C
Hits: 661
RBI: 397

BA: .254
HRs: 116
BBs: 393

At the urging of Rogers Hornsby, Lopata assumed a deep crouch at the plate and significantly increased his power. The first NL catcher to wear eyeglasses, Lopata made the All-Star team in 1955 and 1956. He was also a highly decorated World War II veteran.
Playing Career: *1948-1960; Phi N, Mil N*

Davey Lopes
Lopes, David Earl
B: May 3, 1945

Pos: 2B
Hits: 1,671
RBI: 614

BA: .263
HRs: 155
BBs: 833

One of the best percentage base stealers of all time, Lopes was almost never caught; he once put together a streak of 38 stolen bases in a row. Lopes won a lot of games for his team without piling up big statistics. He was one fourth of the Dodger infield with Steve Garvey, Bill Russell and Ron Cey, who played together from 1973 to 1980. Lopes played in 23 World Series games for four pennant-winning teams. He also appeared in 22 NLCS games in six different years. Lopes was an All-Star four straight seasons, 1978-1981, and he won a Gold Glove Award in 1978.

Lopes was most effective on the basepaths; he stole five bases in a game on August 4, 1971, to tie a 70-year-old NL record. He led the NL in steals with 77 in 1975 and 63 in 1976, pilfering 557 sacks during his career. Lopes holds the NLCS career record for steals with nine. His 10 stolen bases in the World Series ranks third all-time.
Playing Career: *1972-1987; LA N, Oak A, Chi N, Hou N*

Al Lopez
Lopez, Alfonso Ramon
B: Aug 20, 1908
Hall of Fame 1977

Pos: C
Hits: 1,547
RBI: 652
Managerial Record
Won: 1,410   Lost: 1,004   Pct: .584

BA: .261
HRs: 52
BBs: 561

Lopez held the record for most games caught for four decades – it was finally broken by Bob Boone in 1987. Playing for 19 seasons with mostly second-division clubs taught him patience that bore fruit as he became one of baseball's greatest managers and most astute teachers. Taking the helm at Cleveland in 1951, he chased the Yankees with three straight second-place finishes. Lopez built his teams on strong catching, great pitching and home runs.

White Sox Manager Al Lopez (l) with Yankees Manager Casey Stengel in 1957.

Unfortunately for the Indians, the Yankees always seemed to have enough pitching and more home runs. But in 1954, Lopez put it all together, winning a record 111 games, more than any other AL skipper. Moving to Chicago in 1957, Lopez molded a team with little power and sketchy pitching into the Go-Go White Sox who won the pennant in 1959. He now serves on the Hall of Fame Veterans Committee.

Playing Career: *1928, 1930-1947; Brk N, Bos N, Pit N, Cle A*
Managerial Career: *1951-1965, 1968-1969; Cle A, Chi A*

Aurelio Lopez
Lopez y Rios, Aurelio Alejandro (Senor Smoke)
B: Sep 21, 1948   D: Sep 22, 1992

Pos: P	ERA: 3.56
W-L: 62-36	SOs: 635
ShOs: 0	Saves: 93

The reliever pitched in Mexico for nine years before joining the Royals for a cup of coffee in 1974. Returning home, Lopez was Mexican League MVP with a 19-8 record and a 2.01 ERA in 1977. The Cardinals bought his contract that fall.

Señor Smoke was coming off an All-Star year in 1983 with 18 saves and a 2.81 ERA when his Tigers launched an incredible 35-5 start in 1984. Lopez lost his bullpen stopper job to Willie Hernandez despite his 10-1 record with 14 saves.

Playing Career: *1974, 1978-1987; KC A, StL N, Det A, Hou N*

Hector Lopez
Lopez y Swainson, Hector Headley
B: Jul 8, 1929

Pos: OF, 3B, 2B	BA: .269
Hits: 1,251	HRs: 136
RBI: 591	BBs: 418

Lopez was used as a home run-hitting infielder and a good fielding outfielder. The versatile Panamanian was traded from the A's to the Yankees during the 1959 season, and he helped the New Yorkers win five straight pennants, 1960-1964. He hit .286 in five World Series. In the 1961 Series finale versus the Reds, Lopez drove home five runs in the 13-5 victory. Lopez would have been a regular player with star quality seasons had he played elsewhere.

Playing Career: *1955-1966; KC A, NY A*

Harry Lord
Lord, Harry Donald
B: Mar 8, 1882   D: Aug 9, 1948

Pos: 3B	BA: .278
Hits: 1,024	HRs: 14
RBI: 294	BBs: 226
Managerial Record	
Won: 60 Lost: 49 Pct: .550	

Something of an enigma, Lord was a very fast runner – 70 triples in seven full seasons and

206 career stolen bases – yet he set records for the fewest chances accepted and fewest assists by a third baseman in 150 or more games.

Playing Career: *1907-1915; Bos A, Chi A, Buf F*
Managerial Career: *1915; Buf F*

Grover Lowdermilk
Lowdermilk, Grover Cleveland
B: Jan 15, 1885   D: Mar 31, 1968

Pos: P	ERA: 3.58
W-L: 23-39	SOs: 296
ShOs: 2	No-hitters: 0

For many years a rookie pitcher who could not find the plate was called a "Lowdermilk." The original Wild Thing never fared well in the majors where he walked more batters than he struck out, but Lowdermilk is the all-time single-season minor league strikeout leader with 465 in 1907.

Playing Career: *1909, 1911-1912, 1915-1920; StL N, Chi N, StL A, Det A, Cle A, Chi A*

Bobby Lowe
Lowe, Robert Lincoln (Link)
B: Jul 10, 1868   D: Dec 8, 1951

Pos: 2B, 3B	BA: .273
Hits: 1,929	HRs: 70
RBI: 984	BBs: 473
Managerial Record	
Won: 30 Lost: 44 Pct: .405	

Lowe played second base in the Boston infield that has been called the best of the 19th century. He and teammates Kid Nichols and Henry Long played together on the five pennant-winning teams of 1891-1893, 1897 and 1898. The Beaneaters played at the South End

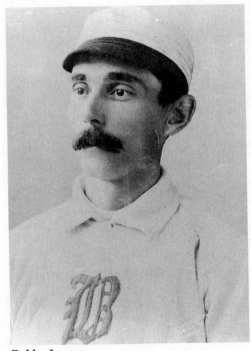
Bobby Lowe.

Grounds until an 1894 fire wiped out the right field bleachers and grandstand as well as 16 city blocks in Boston. They moved to the Congress Street Grounds, which had been abandoned by other teams because of small seating capacity and a short left field fence.

On Decoration Day, 1894, Lowe blasted a quartet of home runs – on consecutive at-bats – over that 250-foot fence, becoming the first major league player to hit four in one game. After the 20-11 Beaneater victory, the crowd showered Lowe with $160 in silver coins. The Tigers later acquired Lowe to give their young squad solidity in the infield and teach the rookies how to win. They won the 1907 AL pennant.

Playing Career: *1890-1907; Bos N, Chi N, Pit N, Det A*
Managerial Career: *1904; Det A*

John Lowenstein
Lowenstein, John Lee
B: Jan 27, 1947

Pos: OF	BA: .253
Hits: 881	HRs: 116
RBI: 441	BBs: 446

The platoon role suited Lowenstein. He reached career highs of a .320 average with 24 home runs, 66 RBI, 69 runs scored, 54 walks and a .602 slugging average in just 322 at-bats in 1982. Lowenstein was also a good fielder; he had five errorless seasons.

Playing Career: *1970-1985; Cle A, Tex A, Bal A*

Turk Lown
Lown, Omar Joseph
B: May 30, 1924

Pos: P	ERA: 4.12
W-L: 55-61	SOs: 574
ShOs: 1	Saves: 73

The top stopper in 1959, Lown, with reliever Gerry Staley, helped the White Sox win their first pennant since the infamous Black Sox won in 1919. The hard-throwing Turk was very wild as a starter. Switched to relief, he became a star, saving 25 games, 1956-1957, while leading the NL in appearances with 67 in 1957. In 1959 he was 9-2 with an AL-leading 15 saves, and a 2.89 ERA.

Playing Career: *1951-1954, 1956-1962; Chi N, Cin N, Chi A*

Peanuts Lowrey
Lowrey, Harry Lee
B: Aug 27, 1918   D: Jul 2, 1986

Pos: OF, 2B, 3B	BA: .273
Hits: 1,177	HRs: 37
RBI: 479	BBs: 403

Most of the 1950s baseball movies were filmed at Wrigley Field in Los Angeles. Lowrey lived nearby and frequently acted as the baseball consultant for the films. In 1945 he contributed a .283 average and 89 RBI to the last Cubs team to win a pennant. He batted .303 in 1951 and led the NL in pinch hits in

PCL alumnae (l-r) Red Lucas, Jim Edwards, Pid Purdy and Marty Callahan of the Reds.

both 1952 and 1953. Lowrey's nickname came from the days when he played child parts in silent movies and the actresses bribed him with peanuts to make him behave.
Playing Career: *1942-1943, 1945-1955; Chi N, Cin N, StL N, Phi N*

Red Lucas
Lucas, Charles Frederick
B: Apr 28, 1902   D: Jul 9, 1986

Pos: P, OF	ERA: 3.72
W-L: 157-135	SOs: 602
ShOs: 22	Saves: 7

Perhaps the best-hitting pitcher of all time, Lucas was tried in the outfield by the Giants, but his control as a pitcher was just too good to pass up. He walked only 18 in 218 innings in 1930. Lucas consistently hit for a higher average than NL batters hit off him. His career batting average was .281. Lucas pinch hit 437 times and made 114 hits in those at-bats. He once faced the minimum 27 batters, giving up one hit in a 3-0 victory.
Playing Career: *1923-1924, 1926-1938; NY N, Bos N, Cin N, Pit N*

Fred Luderus
Luderus, Frederick William
B: Sep 12, 1885   D: Jan 4, 1961

Pos: 1B	BA: .277
Hits: 1,344	HRs: 84
RBI: 647	BBs: 414

Playing during the early 20th-century glory days of the Phillies, Luderus was a strong hitter batting behind four-hole slugger Gavvy Cravath. The pair gave the Phillies a formidable lineup, especially in Baker Bowl, where Luderus became the first Phillie to hit two

home runs over the fence in a single game. He batted .438 in the 1915 World Series, then played 533 consecutive games, 1916-1919. Luderus was captain of the team, and claimed he was never removed for a pinch hitter.
Playing Career: *1909-1920; Chi N, Phi N*

Mike Lum
Lum, Michael Ken-Wai
B: Oct 27, 1945

Pos: OF, 1B	BA: .247
Hits: 877	HRs: 90
RBI: 431	BBs: 366

Lum was born in Hawaii, one of the few from that island who made the big leagues. In 1970 he hit three homers in one game. His most productive year was 1973, when he walloped 16 homers and 26 doubles while driving in 82 runs. Lum made 418 pinch-hit appearances, smacking 103 hits.
Playing Career: *1967-1981; Atl N, Cin N, Chi N*

Jerry Lumpe
Lumpe, Jerry Dean
B: Jun 2, 1933

Pos: 2B, 3B, SS	BA: .268
Hits: 1,314	HRs: 47
RBI: 454	BBs: 428

In 1962 Lumpe batted .301 with 10 homers and 83 RBI. He also put together a 20-game hitting streak. He was chosen for the All-Star team in 1964. Lumpe and two others had been traded to the A's in exchange for Hector Lopez and Ralph Terry.
Playing Career: *1956-1967; NY A, KC A, Det A*

Dick Lundy
Lundy, Richard
B: Jul 10, 1898   D: 1965

Pos: SS, 2B, 3B	BA: .324
Hits: 654 (inc.)	HRs: 47 (inc.)
RBI: NA	BBs: NA
Managerial Record (inc.)	
Won: 156 Lost: 90 Pct: .634	

One of the best shortstops in black baseball history, Lundy possessed a strong arm, sure hands and exceptional range. He hit .400 four times between 1921 and 1930 in the United States and Cuba. Big, graceful and a natural leader, Lundy played on several championship teams. In 1925, when he and Pop Lloyd, the nonpareil of black shortstops, were both members of the Atlantic City Bacharach Giants, Lloyd moved over to second base because of the younger man's superior range.

Lundy replaced Lloyd as manager of the Bacharachs and led them from fourth place to two straight pennants while hitting .347 and .307. In the 1926 Negro World Series, Lundy hit .325 with six RBI, scored four runs, and stole six bases. In 1933-1934 he was a starting shortstop in the first two Negro League East-West All-Star Games. In 33 games against white major leaguers, he hit .289. As a manager he won at least four pennants.
Playing Career: *1918-1937; AC Bach Giants, Phi Hilldales, Bal Black Sox, Phi Stars, Brk Eagles, NY Cubans, Nwk Dodgers, Nwk Eagles*
Managerial Career: *1926-1934, 1937; AC Bach Giants, Bal Black Sox, Phi Stars, Brk Eagles, Nwk Dodgers, NY Cubans, Nwk Eagles*

Dick Lundy with his wife.

Dolf Luque.

Dolf Luque
Luque, Adolfo Domingo de Guzman
(The Pride of Havana)
B: Aug 4, 1890   D: Jul 3, 1957

Pos: P	ERA: 3.24
W-L: 193-179	SOs: 1,130
ShOs: 26	Saves: 28

One of Cuba's first major league pitching stars, Luque relieved twice in the 1919 World Series without allowing a run. The next year he became a starter for the Reds. Luque was the leading pitcher in the NL in 1923. He was 27-8 for the second-place Reds, with a league-leading 1.93 ERA. Two years later, Luque led the NL in ERA again with a 2.63 mark.

In the 1930s Luque turned to relief pitching, earning 16 of his 28 total saves for the Giants. His 4⅓ shutout innings gave him the win in the 10th inning of the fifth and final game of the 1933 World Series. Always hot-tempered, he reportedly stomped into the opposing team's dugout one day in response to some unkind words, then popped Casey Stengel on the nose.
Playing Career: *1914-1915, 1918-1935; Bos N, Cin N, Brk N, NY N*

Greg Luzinski
Luzinski, Gregory Michael (The Baby Bull)
B: Nov 22, 1950

Pos: OF, DH, 1B	BA: .276
Hits: 1,795	HRs: 307
RBI: 1,128	BBs: 845

With bulging arms, a thick neck and a massive body, Luzinski earned the nickname "The Baby Bull." He teamed with Phillies third baseman Mike Schmidt to form the slugging combination that pushed Philadel-phia to four NL East championships in five years. In 1977 he logged career highs, batting .309 with 39 homers and 130 RBI. In the NLCS, Luzinski was just as dangerous, slugging home runs in Game Two in 1976, Game One in 1977, and Games Three and Four in 1978, but the Phillies lost all three series.

After the Phillies won the 1980 World Championship, Luzinski was sold to Chicago, where he became a full-time designated hitter. He played four seasons there, helping the White Sox to the AL West title in 1983 with 32 homers and 95 RBI. Luzinski hit several home runs over the left field roof at Comiskey Park. He is ranked fourth on the Phillies' all-time home run list behind Schmidt, Del Ennis and Chuck Klein. Luzinski was an All-Star 1975-1977.
Playing Career: *1970-1984; Phi N, Chi A*

Sparky Lyle
Lyle, Albert Walter
B: Jul 22, 1944

Pos: P	ERA: 2.88
W-L: 99-76	SOs: 873
ShOs: 0	Saves: 238

When the Yankees shelled out millions to acquire free agent Goose Gossage in 1978, Cy Young winner Lyle lost his job. Every one of Lyle's 899 lifetime pitching appearances was in relief. The durable left-hander, with 238 career saves, was a big factor in getting the Yankees into the 1976 and 1977 World Series; he posted 23 saves the first year and 26 the next.

In 1977 Lyle won 13 games in relief to earn the Cy Young Award. He was undefeated in postseason play, going 2-0 in the ALCS and 1-0 in the World Series. A clubhouse cutup, Lyle once leaped nude onto a birthday cake, only to learn later that it was intended for Yankees manager Ralph Houk. Lyle's books, *Bronx Zoo* and *The Year I Managed the Yankees*, are interesting insights into his world of the 1970s Yankees.
Playing Career: *1967-1982; Bos A, NY A, Tex A, Phi N, Chi A*

Jerry Lynch
Lynch, Gerald Thomas
B: Jul 17, 1930

Pos: OF, C	BA: .277
Hits: 798	HRs: 115
RBI: 470	BBs: 224

One of the top pinch hitters in his era, Lynch compiled a .404 pinch-hit batting average in 1961, and was a major factor in the Reds' pennant. Lynch is fifth on the all-time pinch hits list and second on the pinch-hit home runs list.
Playing Career: *1954-1966; Pit N, Cin N*

Tom Lynch
Lynch, Thomas J.
B: 1859   D: Feb 27, 1924

A New England native, Lynch was sometimes called the "King of the Umpires," and

Umpire and NL President Tom Lynch.

served adequately as NL president from 1909 to 1913. As an umpire in the rough-and-tumble NL in the days following the 1890 Players' Rebellion, Lynch struggled with the issues of crowd control, fan abuse and umpire prestige. He sometimes left the playing field when fans got out of hand. He also went on one-man strikes to raise the level of pay for umpires.

Lynch became National League president in 1909 as a compromise candidate. Two factions were deadlocked over the retention of emergency president John Heydler, who had been forced into the role when Harry Pulliam committed suicide in mid-summer. Lynch used his strong personality and brusque manner to provide solid leadership at this critical time in NL history. His personal traits and his consistent backing of umpires in disputes with club managers and owners led to his dismissal.
Umpiring Career: *1888-1899, 1902; NL*

Fred Lynn
Lynn, Frederic Michael
B: Feb 3, 1952

Pos: OF	BA: .283
Hits: 1,960	HRs: 306
RBI: 1,111	BBs: 857

Fred Lynn had a remarkable rookie year in 1975. He was the only player in history to win the MVP Award and Rookie of the Year in the same seasons. The Red Sox won the pennant as Lynn hit .331, leading the league with 47 doubles and 103 runs. He cracked 21 homers, and drove in 105 runs. Lynn continued to hit with good power, getting his home run total up to 39 in 1979, when he also won the batting title with a .333 mark.

In 1982 Lynn helped the Angels win the AL West division title, then batted .611 in the ALCS. He has won four Gold Gloves and was a perennial All-Star, making the team nine times in a row. He hit the only grand slam in All-Star Game history with a towering shot off Atlee Hammaker in the 1983 contest. It was his fourth All-Star home run. Lynn is one of the few players to hit 300 home runs.
Playing Career: *1974-1990; Bos A, Cal A, Bal A, Det A, SD N*

Denny Lyons
Lyons, Dennis Patrick Aloysius
B: Mar 12, 1866   D: Jan 3, 1929

Pos: 3B, 1B	BA: .310
Hits: 1,333	HRs: 62
RBI: 569	BBs: 621

Lyons started his professional career in the notorious Southern League as a 20-year-old, error-prone infielder. The league was filled with blacklisted veterans of the old International Association, who taught him how to drink and carouse. Lyons was a top hitter in the AA, hitting .367 in 1887 and .354 in 1890, when he led the league in slugging and on-base averages. He scored 100 or more runs four times, 135 in 1889.
Playing Career: *1885-1897; Pro N, Phi AA, StL AA, NY N, Pit N, StL N*

Ted Lyons
Lyons, Theodore Amar
B: Dec 28, 1900   D: Jul 25, 1986
Hall of Fame 1955

Pos: P	ERA: 3.67
W-L: 260-230	SOs: 1.073
ShOs: 27	No-hitters: 1

Managerial Record
Won: 185   Lost: 245   Pct: .430

For 21 years, Lyons pitched for the second-division White Sox. Fans in other cities celebrated pennants; in Chicago they celebrated Ted Lyons. Possibly the most popular player ever to take the mound in the Windy City, he earned fans' devotion with his upbeat personality, indomitable spirit, and by being one of the greatest pitchers of all time. He came straight out of Baylor University, skipped the minors, and relieved in the first major league game he ever saw.

By 1924 he was a regular starter. Using a fastball, curve and knuckler, he won 20 games or more three times. Always a good control pitcher, Lyons hurled 42 consecutive innings without issuing a base on balls in 1939. Near the end of his career he became a "Sunday" pitcher, always pitching on that day because the biggest crowds showed up then. He coached and scouted, retiring in 1966 to help his sister manage a Louisiana rice plantation.
Playing Career: *1923-1942, 1946; Chi A*
Managerial Career: *1946-1948; Chi A*

Chicago White Sox career pitcher Ted Lyons.

Biz Mackey, the brilliant Negro League catcher who mentored Roy Campanella.

Danny MacFayden
MacFayden, Daniel Knowles
B: Jun 10, 1905   D: Aug 26, 1972

Pos: P   ERA: 3.96
W-L: 132-159   SOs: 797
ShOs: 18   Saves: 9

Before his long career as baseball coach at Bowdoin College, MacFayden put in 17 years in the major leagues. He was a fine pitcher who toiled for the last-place Red Sox. In 1939 MacFayden pinch-hit in the Hall of Fame Game for another former Red Sox pitcher – Babe Ruth.
Playing Career: *1926-1941, 1943; Bos A, NY A, Cin N, Bos N, Pit N, Was A*

Connie Mack
Mack, Cornelius Alexander McGillicuddy
B: Dec 22, 1862   D: Feb 8, 1956
Hall of Fame 1937

Pos: C   BA: .245
Hits: 659   HRs: 5
RBI: 265   BBs: 169
Managerial Record
Won: 3,731   Lost: 3,948   Pct: .486

Always a shrewd businessman, and a top-drawer gentleman, Connie Mack had a long and varied baseball career. He caught for Buffalo in the Players' League, supported Ban Johnson in his upstart American League, introduced a designated hitter idea in 1905, led the AL response to the Federal League, built two of baseball's greatest dynasties – the 1910-1914 and 1928-1931 Philadelphia Athletics, was the first to scout Babe Ruth and Joe Jackson, and managed 15 Hall of Famers.

Mack was the first AL executive to realize the value of the college player, harvesting talents such as Eddie Plank and Eddie Collins from collegiate squads. He returned the favor by sending coaches to college teams. Always addressed as "Mr. Mack" out of respect, so beloved was he that Philadelphia fans demanded that Shibe Park be renamed Connie Mack Stadium.
Playing Career: *1886-1896; Was N, Buf P, Pit N*
Managerial Career: *1894-1896, 1901-1950; Pit N, Phi A*

Ray Mack
Mack, Raymond James Mickovsky
B: Aug 31, 1916   D: May 7, 1969

Pos: 2B   BA: .232
Hits: 629   HRs: 34
RBI: 278   BBs: 261

On Opening Day 1940, Mack made two spectacular plays, including the last play of the game, to save Bob Feller's no-hitter. A good all-around athlete, the acrobatic second baseman turned down professional football offers for a spot in the Indian infield.
Playing Career: *1938-1944, 1946-1947; Cle A, NY A, Chi N*

Biz Mackey
Mackey, Raleigh
B: Jul 27, 1897   D: 1959

Pos: C, SS   BA: .322 (inc.)
Hits: 942 (inc.)   HRs: 60 (inc.)
RBI: NA   BBs: NA
Managerial Record
Won: 112   Lost: 61   Pct: .647

One of the earliest practitioners of the catcher's "snap throw" to second base from the squatting crouch, Mackey was a Negro League star who taught Hall of Fame receiver Roy Campanella how to catch. Mackey played in the East-West All-Star Classic in 1933, 1935, 1936, 1938 – and in 1947 at the age of 50.

Philadelphia fans sign a scroll to be presented to Connie Mack at Opening Day, 1950.

The switch hitter's cherubic face and jolly nature never failed to delight fans and teammates. He completed his brilliant career as player-manager of the Newark Eagles, where he coached Larry Doby, Willie Wells, Don Newcombe and Monte Irvin. Mackey was one of the very best catchers; the absence of his name on the Hall of Fame roster is a glaring oversight.

Playing Career: *1920-1947; Ind ABCs,*
Phi Hilldales, Phi Stars, Bal Elite Giants,
Nwk Eagles
Managerial Career: *1940-1941, 1945-1946;*
Nwk Eagles

Andy MacPhail
MacPhail, Andrew Bowen
B: Apr 5, 1953

Continuing the baseball front office dynasty that started with his grandfather Larry Mac-Phail and his father Lee MacPhail, Andy is the general manager of the Minnesota Twins. He has transformed the franchise into a perennial AL West contender, largely by his flare for making the right deal – a skill that has endeared him to Twins fans. MacPhail was named 1987 General Manager of the Year by *The Sporting News*, after his club won the World Series. They were World Champions again in 1991.

Larry MacPhail
MacPhail, Leland Stanford, Sr.
B: Feb 3, 1890   D: Oct 1, 1975
Hall of Fame 1978

Larry MacPhail was a great promoter of the game of baseball. His legacy of innovations included press guides and night baseball, which he instituted for Columbus, Ohio, the Cincinnati Reds, the Brooklyn Dodgers and the New York Yankees. In Brooklyn, Mac-Phail ended the New York ban on the play-by-play radio broadcasts of baseball games,

and brought in Red Barber to announce Dodger contests.

MacPhail engineered a deal with two partners to buy the New York Yankees for $2.8 million. The Yankees achieved great success during MacPhail's tenure as general manager, finishing third in 1946, then winning the AL pennant and the World Series in 1947.

Lee MacPhail
MacPhail, Leland Stanford, Jr.
B: Oct 25, 1917

As greatly respected as his fiery, outspoken father, Lee MacPhail was director of personnel for the Yankees from 1948 to 1958, during which time the club won nine pennants. He was president of the Baltimore club from 1958 to 1964, then worked in the Commissioner's Office in 1965. MacPhail went back to the Yankees the next year and was named Executive of the Year. He served as AL President from 1974 to 1983, then became president of the Major League Player Relations Committee. He has always been known as a voice of reason and moderation serving the best interests of baseball.

Elliott Maddox
Maddox, Elliott
B: Dec 21, 1947

Pos: OF, 3B, SS	BA: .261
Hits: 742	HRs: 18
RBI: 234	BBs: 409

A switch-hitting utility player who made it to the World Series with the Yankees in 1976, Maddox had hit .300 the two previous seasons and made owner George Steinbrenner look like a genius for buying him from the Rangers.

Playing Career: *1970-1980; Det A, Was A,*
Tex A, NY A, Bal A, NY N

Garry Maddox
Maddox, Garry Lee
B: Sep 1, 1949

Pos: OF	BA: .285
Hits: 1,802	HRs: 117
RBI: 754	BBs: 323

A perennial Gold Glover in center field, Maddox played in five NLCS and two World Series for the Phillies during the 1970s and 1980s. His speed enabled him to play shallow in center yet cover the entire field, inspiring Hall of Famer and Mets broadcaster Ralph Kiner to proclaim, "Two-thirds of the earth is covered by water, the other one-third is covered by Garry Maddox."

Maddox broke in with the Giants in 1972, where he starred with Bobby Bonds and Gary Matthews in the outfield. He batted .319 in 1973, reached double figures in doubles, triples, home runs and steals, and had a career-high 76 RBI. Traded to the Phillies in 1975 for Willie Montanez, Maddox contributed significantly to one of baseball's better teams. He stole 248 bases and scored 777 runs during his 15-year career.

Playing Career: *1972-1986; SF N, Phi N*

Greg Maddux
Maddux, Gregory Alan
B: Apr 14, 1966

Pos: P	ERA: 3.19
W-L: 115-85	SOs: 1,134
ShOs: 14	No-hitters: 0

The first NL back-to-back Cy Young Award winner since Sandy Koufax, Maddux signed a five-year free-agent contract with the Braves following his first Cy Young season in 1992. He paid immediate dividends as he won 20 games, anchoring Atlanta's second-half drive that won the NL West title in 1993.

Playing Career: *1986-; Chi N, Atl N*

Bill Madlock
Madlock, Bill (Mad Dog)
B: Jan 2, 1951

Pos: 3B, 2B, DH, 1B	BA: .305
Hits: 2,008	HRs: 163
RBI: 860	BBs: 605

Traded from the languishing Pirates to the flourishing Dodgers in 1985, Madlock announced that he had been transformed from Mad Dog to Glad Dog. Either way, he was one of the finest hitters of the last 25 years. With four batting titles, Madlock has a good chance for the Baseball Hall of Fame.

After breaking in with the Rangers in 1973, Madlock was traded to the Cubs, where he made Wrigley Field fans forget popular third baseman Ron Santo. Chicago traded him to San Francisco, where he played second base. Madlock was rescued in 1979 by the Pirates, who returned him to third base, but their pervasive slump put a gridlock on his bat. The Dodgers traded for him and were rewarded with sparkling postseason play in 1985. Detroit picked him up for the 1987 division

Larry MacPhail, champion of night baseball and radio broadcasts of games.

race, taking Madlock to his third LCS. Mad Dog was selected for the All-Star team three times. He finished his career with one season in Japan in 1988.
Playing Career: *1973-1987; Tex A, Chi N, SF N, Pit N, LA N, Det A*

Lee Magee
Magee, Leo Christopher Hoernschemeyer
B: Jun 4, 1889   D: Mar 14, 1966

Pos: OF, 2B, 3B	BA: .275
Hits: 1,029	HRs: 12
RBI: 277	BBs: 265

Managerial Record
Won: 53   Lost: 64   Pct: .453

Peripatetic Lee Magee was a hard-hitting regular who changed positions and teams frequently. Admitting to throwing games for gamblers, Magee was banned from baseball even before the strict Judge Kenesaw Mountain Landis became commissioner in 1921.
Playing Career: *1911-1919; StL N, Brk F, NY A, StL A, Cin N, Brk N, Chi N*
Managerial Career: *1915; Brk F*

Sherry Magee
Magee, Sherwood Robert
B: Aug 6, 1884   D: Mar 13, 1929

Pos: OF	BA: .291
Hits: 2,169	HRs: 83
RBI: 1,182	BBs: 736

Some historians label Sherry Magee one of the very best deadball era players. It was his use of intentional fly-outs that fueled the campaign to establish a sacrifice fly rule. Magee led the league once in batting, and five times in RBI. He was an outstanding base stealer with a career total of 441; 23 of those were steals of home.

Intolerant of sloppy play on the field and managerial blunders, Magee possessed a terrible temper and an outspoken manner that shifted him around the NL. In 1911 he socked umpire Bill Finneran, who had ejected him for arguing a called third strike. Magee was suspended for the rest of the season. Aspiring to manage the Phillies, Magee demanded to be traded in 1915 when they chose someone else for the job. He went to Boston, where he played center field, and was later traded to the Reds, where he made his only World Series appearance, hitting .500 as a pinch hitter in the 1919 Series.
Playing Career: *1904-1919; Phi N, Bos N, Cin N*

Sal Maglie
Maglie, Salvatore Anthony (The Barber)
B: Apr 26, 1917

Pos: P	ERA: 3.15
W-L: 119-62	SOs: 862
ShOs: 25	No-hitters: 1

Maglie pitched in two of the most famous games in baseball history: the 1951 Bobby Thomson home run game, and Don Larsen's 1956 World Series perfect game. The Barber, who gave close shaves to plate-hugging batters, had been suspended by the commissioner for jumping to the Mexican League in 1946. The five-year ban and injuries cut short his career, yet he posted a .657 won-lost percentage, putting him in ninth place on the all-time list.
Playing Career: *1945, 1950-1958; NY N, Cle A, Brk N, NY A, StL N*

Art Mahaffey
Mahaffey, Arthur
B: Jun 4, 1942

Pos: P	ERA: 4.17
W-L: 59-64	SOs: 639
ShOs: 9	Saves: 1

The hard-throwing Phillies right-hander had plenty of smoke and an excellent pickoff move. As a rookie, Mahaffey fanned 17 in one game. He made two All-Star teams. Arm trouble ended his career prematurely.
Playing Career: *1960-1966; Phi N, StL N*

Roy Mahaffey
Mahaffey, Lee Roy
B: Feb 9, 1903   D: Jul 23, 1969

Pos: P	ERA: 5.01
W-L: 67-49	SOs: 365
ShOs: 0	Saves: 5

Mahaffey was a starter for the 1931 Athletics. He went 15-4 and appeared in the World Series that year against the Cardinals. Mahaffey pitched five years against the Yankees and never gave up a home run to Babe Ruth.
Playing Career: *1926-1927, 1930-1936; Pit N, Phi A, StL A*

Rick Mahler
Mahler, Richard Keith
B: Aug 5, 1953

Pos: P	ERA: 3.99
W-L: 96-111	SOs: 952
ShOs: 9	Saves: 6

Rick Mahler pitched Opening Day shutouts in 1982, 1986 and 1987. He was the ace of the Braves' staff during most of the 1980s, regularly starting 30 games. Mahler switched to relief work when he signed a contract with the Reds. He appeared in the 1982 and 1990 NLCS.
Playing Career: *1979-1991; Atl N, Cin N, Mon N*

Fritz Maisel
Maisel, Frederick Charles
B: Dec 23, 1889   D: Apr 22, 1967

Pos: OF	BA: .242
Hits: 510	HRs: 6
RBI: 148	BBs: 260

Fritz Maisel held the Yankees' stolen base record, with 74, until Rickey Henderson came along. Maisel pilfered 194 sacks and scored 295 runs in his big league career. A broken collarbone in 1916 hampered his swing, and he never hit well again.
Playing Career: *1913-1918; NY A, StL A*

Hank Majeski
Majeski, Henry
B: Dec 13, 1916   D: Aug 9, 1991

Pos: 3B	BA: .279
Hits: 956	HRs: 57
RBI: 501	BBs: 299

Majeski was one of the top third basemen in the late 1940s. He set a major league record for fielding percentage at the hot corner with a .988 mark in 1947. Majeski once hit six doubles in a doubleheader, and he hit a home run in the 1954 World Series.
Playing Career: *1939-1941; 1946-1955; Bos N, NY A, Phi A, Chi A, Cle A, Bal A*

Dave Malarcher
Malarcher, David Julius
B: Oct 18, 1894   D: May 11, 1982

Pos: 3B	BA: .267 (inc.)
Hits: 537 (inc.)	HRs: 5 (inc.)
RBI: NA	BBs: NA

Managerial Record (inc.)
Won: 138   Lost: 59   Pct: .700

Acclaimed as the Negro National League's premier third baseman throughout the 1920s, Malarcher helped the Chicago American Giants win five pennants and a pair of Black World Series Championships. Normally second in the batting order, he was constantly involved in decisive rallies, particularly in postseason play.

Succeeding Rube Foster as manager of the American Giants in 1926, Malarcher immediately piloted the club to successive

Reds outfielder Sherry Magee, 1919.

Playing Manager Dave Malarcher.

Series titles. He also guided the team into postseason league championship play in 1928 and again in 1934 as the American Giants came within one game of winning the hard-fought series. Malarcher's club claimed the 1933 Negro National League crown and then triumphed over the Negro Southern League and Black Dixie Series champion New Orleans Crescent Stars to lay claim to another Black World Title.

Playing Career: *1916-1934; Ind ABCs, Chi Am Giants*
Managerial Career: *1926-1928, 1931, 1933-1934; Chi Am Giants*

Candy Maldonado
Maldonado y Guadarrama, Candido
B: Sep 5, 1960

Pos: OF	BA: .259
Hits: 974	HRs: 132
RBI: 576	BBs: 340

Candy Maldonado was in postseason play six times in the first 12 years of his career. Three times Maldonado has hit 20 or more home runs. He seldom opens the season as a starter; in 1986 he did not play until August, but still hit 18 homers and drove in 85 runs.
Playing Career: *1981-; LA N, SF N, Cle A, Mil A, Tor A, Chi N*

Pat Malone
Malone, Perce Leigh
B: Sep 25, 1902   D: May 13, 1943

Pos: P	ERA: 3.74
W-L: 134-92	SOs: 1,024
ShOs: 16	Saves: 26

Malone was a hard throwing right-hander, leading the NL in strikeouts, shutouts and wins in 1929, and in wins and complete

games the following year. Pitching in Chicago during Prohibition, Malone is reputed to have imbibed too much, too often. He became a relief pitcher late in his career with the Yankees. Malone led the AL in saves in 1936, while losing one and saving one in that year's World Series.
Playing Career: *1928-1937; Chi N, NY A*

Billy Maloney
Maloney, William Alphonse
B: Jun 5, 1878   D: Sep 2, 1960

Pos: C	BA: .236
Hits: 585	HRs: 6
RBI: 177	BBs: 162

Maloney led the NL in stolen bases in 1905. His trade to the Dodgers for Jimmy Sheckard made the Cubs unbeatable and Maloney a forgotten man. He had come from Georgetown University to be the backstop for the 1901 Brewers in the newly formed AL.
Playing Career: *1901-1902, 1905-1908; Mil A, StL A, Cin N, Chi N, Brk N*

Jim Maloney
Maloney, James William
B: Jun 2, 1940

Pos: P	ERA: 3.19
W-L: 134-84	SOs: 1,605
ShOs: 30	No-hitters: 3

Before a sore arm ended his career at age 31, Maloney pitched three no-hitters and five one-hitters. Some say he was faster than Koufax. In 1963 Maloney struck out eight

Braves in a row. He was 23-7 that year for the fifth-place Reds. He also led the league in wild pitches.

In 1965 Maloney posted a 20-9 record, as Cincinnati finished fourth. Clocked at 99.5 mph that year, Maloney and his fastball were credited with two no-hitters. The first lasted 10 innings against the last-place Mets before two hits in the 11th beat him 1-0. Maloney fanned 18 in that game. He struck out more than 200 batters four years in a row, reaching a high of 265 in 1963 when NL batters hit just .202 off him. Maloney appeared in the 1961 World Series. After an All-Star appearance in 1965, he led the NL in shutouts with five in 1966.
Playing Career: *1960-1971; Cin N, Cal A*

Frank Malzone
Malzone, Frank James
B: Feb 28, 1930

Pos: 3B	BA: .274
Hits: 1,486	HRs: 133
RBI: 728	BBs: 337

Malzone was the best AL third baseman from 1957 to 1959. A dependable hitter, Malzone made the All-Star team six times and compiled double digit home run stats eight years in a row. He went 6-for-10 in his 1955 doubleheader debut, and drove in 103 runs in his rookie year, but fielding was his forte. Malzone led the league in double plays five straight years and in assists for three. He tied a since-broken AL single game record for third basemen with 10 assists.
Playing Career: *1955-1966; Bos A, Cal A*

Jim Maloney threw fastballs at lightning speed for the Reds in the 1960s.

Al Mamaux
Mamaux, Albert Leon
B: May 30, 1894   D: Jan 2, 1963

Pos: P	ERA: 2.90
W-L: 76-67	SOs: 625
ShOs: 15	Saves: 10

Mamaux led Pittsburgh's staff with 21 wins in both 1915 and 1916. Then he fell into a swoon and was traded to Brooklyn, where he helped the Dodgers take the 1920 NL flag. He managed Newark to International League pennants in 1930 and 1931.
Playing Career: *1913-1924; Pit N, Brk N, NY A*

Gus Mancuso
Mancuso, August Rodney
B: Dec 5, 1905   D: Oct 26, 1984

Pos: C	BA: .265
Hits: 1,194	HRs: 53
RBI: 543	BBs: 418

Mancuso was pennant insurance. He played on five pennant-winning teams in his first seven full seasons. Twice, teams who traded for him won the pennant the following year. Mancuso had been stuck in the St. Louis farm system until Commissioner Landis declared him a free agent.
Playing Career: *1928, 1930-1945; StL N, NY N, Chi N, Brk N, Phi N*

Les Mann
Mann, Leslie
B: Nov 18, 1893   D: Jan 14, 1962

Pos: OF	BA: .282
Hits: 1,332	HRs: 44
RBI: 503	BBs: 324

Mann's baseball career was eventful on and off the field. From the Miracle Braves of 1914, he jumped to the Federal League, leading it

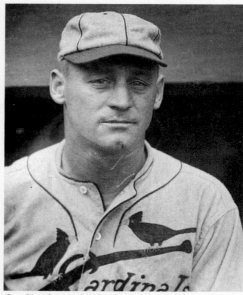
Cardinals outfielder Les Mann, 1922.

in triples. He joined Babe Ruth in a player revolt for more money before the fifth game of the 1918 World Series, turned in Phil Douglas for offering him a bribe in 1922, and formed the National Amateur Baseball Association. In 1936 Mann persuaded the World Olympic Committee to add baseball as an exhibition event.
Playing Career: *1913-1928; Bos N, Chi F, Chi N, StL N, Cin N, NY N*

Jack Manning
Manning, John E.
B: Dec 20, 1853   D: Aug 15, 1929

Pos: OF, 1B, 3B, SS, 2B	BA: .257
Hits: 725	HRs: 13
RBI: 101 (inc.)	BBs: 176
Managerial Record	
Won: 7 Lost: 12 Pct: .368	

After playing "scientific ball" under Harry Wright of the Red Stockings in 1873, Manning played all over the field, and even pitched, compiling a record of 38-27, including a 13-3 mark in 1875. He was later a manager and owner in the Western League.
Playing Career: *1873-1878, 1880-1881, 1883-1886; Bos Red Stockings n, Bal Lord Baltimores n, Har Dark Blues n, Bos N, Cin N, Buf N, Phi N, Bal AA*
Managerial Career: *1877; Cin N*

Max Manning
Manning, Max
B: Nov 18, 1919

Pos: P	ERA: NA
W-L: 68-33	SOs: 294
ShOs: 4 (inc.)	Saves: 2 (inc.)

Manning finished the 1946 season 10-0, the second Negro League pitcher to go undefeated, and led the Newark Eagles to the Negro National League pennant. He followed that season with a league-leading 15 wins and an appearance in the East-West All-Star Game. Manning retired from baseball to become a school teacher.
Playing Career: *1939-1942, 1946-1949; Nwk Eagles*

Rick Manning
Manning, Richard Eugene
B: Sep 2, 1954

Pos: OF, DH	BA: .257
Hits: 1,349	HRs: 56
RBI: 458	BBs: 471

When Manning hit .285 his first year in Cleveland, then followed with a .292 average the next year, he looked like the saviour of the franchise. He was fast, and could cover the cavernous center field at Municipal Stadium, winning a Gold Glove Award in 1976. It turned out that salvation was not in store for the Indians after all, and they traded Manning to the Brewers. In Milwaukee, he led major league outfielders with 478 chances in 1983.
Playing Career: *1975-1987; Cle A, Mil A*

Felix Mantilla
Mantilla y Lamela, Felix
B: Jul 29, 1934

Pos: 2B, 3B, SS, OF	BA: .261
Hits: 707	HRs: 89
RBI: 330	BBs: 256

Before he suffered a career-ending injury making the pivot at second base, Mantilla was a strong hitter. In 1964 he hit 30 home runs and had a slugging average of .553. Mantilla appeared in the 1957 and 1958 World Series with the Braves.
Playing Career: *1956-1966; Mil N, NY N, Bos A, Hou N*

Yankee slugger Mickey Mantle.

Mickey Mantle
Mantle, Mickey Charles
B: Oct 20, 1931
Hall of Fame 1974

Pos: OF	BA: .298
Hits: 2,415	HRs: 536
RBI: 1,509	BBs: 1,734

Mantle was the most powerful switch hitter ever, compiling terrific statistics despite a career marred with crippling injuries. In 1952 his awesome talent began to manifest itself as he hit .311. The following year, the Yankees' traveling secretary invented the "tape measure" home run when he marked Mantle's 565-foot blast off the Senators' Chuck Stobbs at Griffith Stadium. Mantle hit another, estimated at 600 feet, off the roof of the facade at old Yankee Stadium.

In 18 seasons Mantle hit more than 50

Mickey Mantle trots home with the winning HR in a 1959 extra-innings game.

homers twice, and led the AL in home runs four times. He won the Triple Crown in 1956, and earned MVP Awards in 1956, 1957 and 1962. In 1957 he hit .365 with an on-base mark of .515, but finished second in both categories. He played in 20 All-Star Games and in 12 World Series. Mantle holds World Series records for most home runs (18), most runs scored (42), and most runs batted in (40).
Playing Career: *1951-1968; NY A*

Heinie Manush
Manush, Henry Emmett
B: Jul 20, 1901   D: May 12, 1971
Hall of Fame 1964

Pos: OF	BA: .330
Hits: 2,524	HRs: 110
RBI: 1,173	BBs: 506

An outstanding hitter during the 1920s and 1930s, Manush played the first third of his career in Detroit, where he was overshadowed by Ty Cobb and Harry Heilmann. When Manush got away to St.Louis and Washington, he flourished. A line drive hitter, Manush hit 491 doubles, and 160 triples in a 17-year career. He led the AL twice in hits and doubles and once in triples. In 1926 Manush dueled Babe Ruth for the AL batting title. Manush went 6-for-9 in a doubleheader on the last day of the season to hit .378, beating Ruth by six points. In one of the Tigers' worst deals ever, Manush was traded with Lu Blue to the Browns for Elam Vanglider, Chick Galloway and Harry Rice. Free from the Tigers, Manush cracked 241 base hits to post a .378 average in 1928, losing the batting crown to Goose Goslin by one point. Two years later the two men were traded for each other. Manush played in the 1934 All-Star Game.
Playing Career: *1923-1939; Det A, StL A, Was A, Bos A, Bkn N, Pit N*

Rabbit Maranville
Maranville, Walter James Vincent
B: Nov 11, 1891   D: Jan 5, 1954
Hall of Fame 1954

Pos: SS	BA: .258
Hits: 2,605	HRs: 28
RBI: 884	BBs: 839
Managerial Record	
Won: 23 Lost: 30 Pct: .434	

The impetus behind the 1914 "Miracle Braves" was a hopping little infielder named

Cubs shortstop Rabbit Maranville.

Maranville. Rabbit hit only .246, but he put on an unparalleled show at shortstop. Sporting a "vest pocket catch," Maranville handled more chances than any shortstop ever had. He teamed with former Cub Johnny Evers to lead the league in double plays. Maranville had been ill and missed the first few weeks of the 1914 season. When he returned to the playing field he found the Braves in last place.

Led by hurlers Dick Rudolph, Bill James and Lefty Tyler, Maranville and the Braves stormed to the pennant. In the World Series he hit .308 as the Braves swept the mighty A's in four games. An irrepressible prankster, Maranville once bragged, "There's a lot less alcohol consumed since 1926, because that's when I stopped drinking." He distinguished himself as a manager by having only one rule – nobody could go to bed before he did.
Playing Career: *1912-1935; Bos N, Pit N, Chi N, Bkn N, StL N*
Managerial Career: *1925; Chi N*

Firpo Marberry
Marberry, Frederick
B: Nov 30, 1898   D: Jun 30, 1976

Pos: P	ERA: 3.63
W-L: 147-88	SOs: 822
ShOs: 8	Saves: 101

One of the earliest relief pitchers, Marberry was the forerunner of the great firemen of today. Nicknamed for the Argentine fighter Luis Firpo who fought Jack Dempsey, Marberry had a similar powerful physique. He worked as a starter and as a reliever, but his reputation was built on his prowess in the late innings. Marberry led the AL in saves five times and in appearances six times.

Instrumental in Washington's first two pennants, Marberry had 15 saves during the 1924 season and two more in the World Series. He posted 15 saves again in 1925, and 22 in 1926. Marberry had a 15-5 record with three saves for Detroit in 1934 to help them win their first flag in a quarter of a century. As a starter Marberry won 94 games for a .644 won-lost percentage. He also played for two more pennant-winners, the 1935 Tigers and 1936 Giants.
Playing Career: *1923-1936; Was A, Det A, NY N*

Ghost Marcelle
Marcelle, Oliver
B: Jun 24, 1897   D: Jun 12, 1949

Pos: 3B	BA: .304
Hits: 443	HRs: 12
RBI: NA	BBs: NA

The best-fielding third baseman in the Negro Leagues during the 1920s, Marcelle led the Negro National League in 1920 in games, at-bats and hits. In 17 exhibition games against white major leaguers, Marcelle hit .365. He played in two Negro World Series.
Playing Career: *1918-1930; Brk Royal Giants, AC Bach Giants, NY Lincoln Giants, Bal Black Sox*

Phil Marchildon
Marchildon, Philip Joseph
B: Oct 25, 1913

Pos: P	ERA: 3.93
W-L: 68-75	SOs: 481
ShOs: 6	Saves: 2

While serving in the Royal Canadian Air Force in World War II, Marchildon was captured in Germany and spent nine months in a POW camp. He never smiled again, even when he went 19-9 to pull the A's out of the cellar in 1947.
Playing Career: *1940-1942, 1945-1950; Phi A, Bos A*

Johnny Marcum
Marcum, John Alfred
B: Sep 9, 1909   D: Sep 10, 1984

Pos: P	ERA: 4.66
W-L: 65-63	SOs: 392
ShOs: 8	Saves: 7

Connie Mack discovered Marcum. He won 14 and 17 in his first two full years, but was traded to the Red Sox and had only one winning season in the next three. Marcum was a .265 lifetime hitter, and was used 99 times as a left-handed pinch hitter.
Playing Career: *1933-1939; Phi A, Bos A, StL A, Chi A*

Juan Marichal
Marichal y Sanchez, Juan Antonio
B: Oct 20, 1937
Hall of Fame 1983

Pos: P	ERA: 2.89
W-L: 243-142	SOs: 2,303
ShOs: 52	No-hitters: 1

Marichal's trademark was the high leg kick. It looked impractical, but once the leg came down, he delivered fastballs, curves and sliders from a sidearm, three-quarter or over-the-top position, yet always with marvelous control. The brilliant right-hander from the Dominican Republic was the major league's winningest pitcher from 1962 to 1969.

After winning 18 for the Giants in 1962, Marichal won 20 or more in six of the next seven seasons. He was 25-8 in 1963, the year he threw a no-hitter, and led the NL in wins. Marichal was 25-6 in 1966 and led the league in winning percentage. In 1968 he was back on top in wins with a 26-9 record. The next season he led in ERA. Marichal completed 244 of his 457 starts, and he issued only 707 walks in 3,509 innings. Manager Al Dark said, "Put your club a run ahead in the late innings, and Marichal is the greatest pitcher I ever saw."
Playing Career: *1960-1975; SF N, Bos A, LA N*

Marty Marion
Marion, Martin Whitford (Slats)
B: Dec 1, 1917

Pos: SS	BA: .263
Hits: 1,448	HRs: 36
RBI: 624	BBs: 470
Managerial Record	
Won: 356 Lost: 372 Pct: .489	

The mainstay of the 1940-1950 Cardinals' infield, Marion was one of the greatest fielding shortstops ever, yet he led NL shortstops in fielding only three times. His exceptional range caused him to make attempts at balls that less gifted infielders would simply watch go by. Marion's best seasons at the plate were during the war, when he hit .276, .280, .267 and .277. He also led the NL in doubles with 38 in 1942.

In 1944 Marion was chosen NL MVP and Player of the Year. He was chosen for the NL All-Star team six times on the strength of his fielding. Marion managed the Cardinals from the bench in 1951, then replaced Rogers Hornsby as player/manager for the Browns the next year before moving on to skipper the White Sox. A back injury shortened his playing career, but he later owned the Houston Buffs in the Texas League, and then managed the St. Louis Stadium Club.
Playing Career: *1940-1950, 1952-1953; StL N, StL A*
Managerial Career: *1951-1956; StL N, StL A, Chi A*

Roger Maris.

Roger Maris
Maris, Roger Eugene
B: Sep 10, 1934   D: Dec 14, 1985

Pos: OF	BA: .260
Hits: 1,325	HRs: 275
RBI: 851	BBs: 652

When Maris broke Babe Ruth's single-season home run record by hitting 61 in 1961, fans raised a ruckus. During the season Commissioner Ford Frick had decided that Maris's record should be marked by an asterisk denoting the longer 162-game schedule for his feat – though the asterisk was never used. Maris was an intelligent, likeable man, totally unprepared to deal with the media blitz that surrounded his 1961 season.

He was a talented player, surehanded in the outfield, with a fine arm. Maris was AL MVP in 1960, with 39 home runs and a league-leading 112 RBI. In 1961 he led the league in runs scored with 132, and in RBI with 142, in addition to the 61 home runs. This performance earned him a second MVP Award. He was the regular right fielder for five pennant-winning Yankees teams, 1960-1964. The last two seasons of his baseball career were with the 1967 and 1968 Cardinals, teams that won NL flags.
Playing Career: *1957-1968; Cle A, KC A, NY A, StL N*

Rube Marquard
Marquard, Richard William
B: Oct 9, 1889   D: Jun 1, 1980
Hall of Fame 1971

Pos: P	ERA: 3.08
W-L: 201-177	SOs: 1,593
ShOs: 30	No-hitters: 1

When Marquard won his first 19 games in 1912, he tied an NL record set in the 19th

The Cardinals' Marty Marion slides into home in a 1947 game.

century. Marquard had been bought by the Giants for a record $11,000 in 1908 and rushed into the pennant wars before he was ready. Sportswriters dubbed him "the $11,000 lemon." Under the tutelage of coach Wilbert Robinson, the lemon changed into lemonade.

In 1911 Marquard was 24-7 as he posted the first of three consecutive seasons of 20 or more wins. The Giants won pennants all three years. After a period of less success, Marquard had another good year in 1916 with Brooklyn, when he posted a record of 13-6, and the Dodgers won the NL flag. He upped that to 19-12 in 1917, and three years later, contributed to another Dodgers pennant. Marquard was sophisticated, a flashy dresser and a teetotaler. He married a Broadway actress, Blossom Seeley, with whom he collaborated on plays and musical shows.
Playing Career: *1908-1925; NY N, Bkn N, Cin N, Bos N*

Armando Marsans
Marsans, Armando
B: Oct 3, 1887   D: Sep 3, 1960

Pos: OF, 1B, 3B, SS, 2B   BA: .269
Hits: 612   HRs: 2
RBI: 221   BBs: 173

With one Cuban parent and one African-American parent, Marsans may have been the first 20th-century black player in the major leagues. A utility player, Marsans hit .317 in 1912. He struck out only 117 times in 2,273 at-bats.
Playing Career: *1911-1918; Cin N, StL F, StL A, NY A*

Mike Marshall
Marshall, Michael Allen
B: Jan 12, 1960

Pos: 1B, OF   BA: .270
Hits: 971   HRs: 148
RBI: 530   BBs: 247

An incomprehensible string of mishaps – appendicitis, back strain, foot surgery, food poisoning, a beaning, and others – prevented Marshall from achieving his potential. He won the Triple Crown in the Pacific Coast League in 1981; it had not been achieved for 25 years.
Playing Career: *1981-1991; LA N, NY N, Bos A, Cal A*

Mike Marshall
Marshall, Michael Grant
B: Jan 15, 1943

Pos: P   ERA: 3.14
W-L: 97-112   SOs: 880
ShOs: 1   Saves: 188

In 1974 Marshall won the Cy Young Award and became the first reliever honored with it. He set a record by appearing in 106 games that year, and compiled a record of 15-12 with 21 saves, all NL highs for relievers. The 106 appearances record is the all-time single-sea-

son high mark for pitchers, and likely will never be approached. Marshall holds both AL and NL season records for games pitched; he appeared in 90 games with the Twins in 1979.

Marshall, who earned a doctoral degree in physiology, designed his own conditioning program that included jogging four miles a day. He argued with coaches and managers, who generally found his education and manner intimidating, until he joined Montreal under Gene Mauch, who let him do what he wanted. Marshall's save totals shot up to 23 in 1971 and 31 in 1973. In Minnesota in 1979 he saved 32 games, his all-time high.
Playing Career: *1967, 1969-1981; Det A, Sea A, Hou N, Mon N, LA N, Atl N, Tex A, Min A, NY N*

Willard Marshall
Marshall, Willard Warren
B: Feb 8, 1921

Pos: OF   BA: .274
Hits: 1,160   HRs: 130
RBI: 604   BBs: 458

The shy, unknown Marshall so impressed Giants manager Mel Ott that Marshall made the starting team out of spring training in 1942. He batted .257 with 59 RBI in 116 games. After three years with the Marines, Marshall returned to hit 36 homers, driving in 107 runs in 1947.
Playing Career: *1942, 1946-1955; NY N, Bos N, Cin N, Chi A*

Billy Martin
Martin, Alfred Manuel
B: May 16, 1928   D: Dec 25, 1989

Pos: 2B   BA: .257
Hits: 877   HRs: 64
RBI: 333   BBs: 187
Managerial Record
Won: 1,253   Lost: 1,013   Pct: .553

Rickey Henderson is the player that Billy Martin wanted to be. As a manager Martin shaped teams and players to his likeness. Most also unraveled in his likeness, but Henderson remains a testament to Martin's skill and foresight. Scrappy and resilient, Martin won the 1952 World Series for the Yankees with a sensational diving catch off the bat of Jackie Robinson in Game Seven. He drove in the winning run in Game Seven of the 1953 Series.

Quick on the field, Martin was also quick with his fists. Of all the fights he started or finished, the most important one was the 1957 Copacabana night club brawl that led to his banishment from the Yankees and started a four-year odyssey. Martin's saddest and proudest moments came managing New York, where he was hired and fired five times. He won two pennants with the Yankees, and division titles for the Twins, Tigers and A's.
Playing Career: *1950-1961; NY A, KC A, Det A, Cle A, Cin N, Mil N, Min A*
Managerial Career: *1969, 1971-1983, 1988; Min A, Det A, Tex A, NY A, Oak A*

Third time lucky? Billy Martin returns as Yankees manager, 1983.

Jerry Martin
Martin, Jerry Lindsey
B: May 11, 1949

Pos: OF	BA: .251
Hits: 666	HRs: 85
RBI: 345	BBs: 207

A valuable fourth outfielder and pinch hitter, Martin played for three consecutive Phillies division-winning teams in the mid-1970s. His career was tarnished by his involvement in drugs; Martin and three Kansas City teammates served time in a Federal Correctional Institute in 1984.
Playing Career: *1974-1984; Phi N, Chi N, SF N, KC A, NY N*

Pepper Martin
Martin, John Leonard Roosevelt
(The Wild Horse of the Osage)
B: Feb 29, 1904   D: Mar 5, 1965

Pos: 3B, OF	BA: .298
Hits: 1,227	HRs: 59
RBI: 501	BBs: 369

Fans remember Martin in the 1931 World Series, running wild and stealing everything but the socks off A's catcher Mickey Cochrane. Martin batted .500 during that Series, despite being hitless in the last two games. His overall World Series batting average of .418 is the highest among players with more than 50 at-bats. The three-time All-Star was a leading prankster and Dizzy Dean's side kick. The two performed in their Mississippi Mudcat band in the off-season.

Martin epitomized the style of the Gashouse Gang, the Cardinals of the mid-1930s who played with wild abandon. He guarded the hot corner, letting grounders bounce off his chest, and throwing at runners who bunted on him. He stole bases with a belly-flop, head-first slide, leading the NL in steals three times in four years. He scored more than 120 runs three times, and led the NL in 1933. Martin returned to play for the Cardinals in 1944, then managed in the minors.
Playing Career: *1928, 1930-1940, 1944; StL N*

Stu Martin
Martin, Stuart McGuire
B: Nov 17, 1913

Pos: 2B, SS, 1B	BA: .268
Hits: 599	HRs: 16
RBI: 183	BBs: 190

The Cardinals used Martin to give Frankie Frisch an occasional rest and to nudge him toward retirement. Martin platooned with Frisch as a rookie, hit .268, and was chosen for the All-Star team in 1936.
Playing Career: *1936-1943; StL N, Pit N, Chi N*

Buck Martinez
Martinez, John Albert
B: Nov 7, 1948

Pos: C	BA: .225
Hits: 618	HRs: 58
RBI: 321	BBs: 230

One of the original Royals, Martinez played 17 years as a defensive catcher. Most successful in a platoon situation, Martinez batted .270 in 1979 and .253 in 1983. He suffered a compound leg fracture from a collision at the plate in 1985.
Playing Career: *1969-1971, 1973-1986; KC A, Mil A, Tor A*

Carmelo Martinez
Martinez y Salgado, Carmelo
B: Jul 28, 1960

Pos: OF	BA: .245
Hits: 713	HRs: 108
RBI: 424	BBs: 404

Martinez homered in his first at-bat in the major leagues. Becoming a power-hitting pinch hitter, he pounded a dramatic ninth-inning home run to tie a June 6, 1991 Nolan Ryan-Bret Saberhagen duel in Kansas City. The game went 18 innings and set several AL records.
Playing Career: *1983-1991; Chi N, SD N, Phi N, Pit N, KC A, Cin N*

Dave Martinez
Martinez, David
B: Sep 26, 1964

Pos: OF	BA: .267
Hits: 746	HRs: 44
RBI: 255	BBs: 241

When Martinez first played pro ball he pitched an 87-mph fastball. Switching to the outfield, he was a minor league batting champ and base stealer. The Expos traded him when rookies Moises Alou and Larry Walker came along.
Playing Career: *1986-; Chi N, Mon N, Cin N, SF N*

Expos hurler Dennis Martinez, 1992.

Dennis Martinez
Martinez y Emilia, Jose Dennis
B: May 14, 1955

Pos: P	ERA: 2.81
W-L: 208-165	SOs: 1,831
ShOs: 23	No-hitters: 1

The Nicaraguan pitched a perfect game on July 28, 1991, becoming one of only a handful of pitchers to accomplish that feat. After having won the International League Pitcher of the Year in 1976, Martinez arrived in the bigs with a big reputation. While an Oriole he was a hard-throwing starter and reliever. Martinez succeeded in winning 45 games in his first three years, then led the AL in games and innings pitched in 1979.

He came back from an injury to lead the AL in wins during the strike-shortened 1981 season. Injuries and inability to adapt to new pitching ideas led to his being out of a job in May 1987. A new country and a fresh begin-

"The Wild Horse of the Osage," Pepper Martin dives for third headfirst.

ning with Montreal turned Martinez into the dominating hurler that he always could have been. He has appeared in three consecutive All-Star Games, and led the NL in shutouts, complete games and ERA in 1991.
Playing Career: *1976-; Bal A, Mon N*

Edgar Martinez
Martinez, Edgar
B: Jan 2, 1963

Pos: 3B	BA: .306
Hits: 593	HRs: 49
RBI: 217	BBs: 242

One of the brightest young stars in baseball, Martinez led the AL in hitting with a .343 mark in 1992, the highest average by a right-handed batter since Harvey Kuenn hit .353 in 1959. Martinez is the second player to win the AL batting title while playing on a last-place club; the other was Dale Alexander with Boston in 1932. In 1992 Martinez also led the AL in doubles with 46, and set new Mariners club records for batting average, doubles and slugging average.

Seattle named Martinez Player of the Month for both July and August when he batted .388 and then .395. He was elected to the All-Star Game roster that year, and won his

Third baseman Edgar Martinez of the Seattle Mariners.

first Silver Slugger Award. High averages are not new to Martinez. He led the Pacific Coast League in batting with a .363 mark in 1988. He was voted Calgary MVP that season. Martinez later sat out most of the 1993 season with a pulled hamstring.
Playing Career: *1987-; Sea A*

Tippy Martinez
Martinez, Felix Anthony
B: Mar 31, 1950

Pos: P	ERA: 3.45
W-L: 55-42	SOs: 631
ShOs: 0	Saves: 115

Martinez once picked three runners off first base in one inning. The Orioles had put second baseman Lenn Sakata behind the plate, and their opponents were anxious to steal on him. Martinez trapped each one off the base. He was the constant in the Orioles' bullpen for 10 years, leading the staff in saves five times. He was the set-up man for Dan Stanhouse, then became the left-handed stopper. Martinez won one game in the 1983 ALCS, then saved two games in the World Series.
Playing Career: *1974-1986, 1988; NY A, Bal A, Min A*

Phil Masi
Masi, Philip Samuel
B: Jan 6, 1916   D: Mar 29, 1990

Pos: C	BA: .264
Hits: 917	HRs: 47
RBI: 417	BBs: 410

In the 1948 World Series opener, Masi was picked off second base, but the umpire did not call him out. He scored the only run in the game seconds later. Masi led NL catchers in fielding three times. He was selected to the NL All-Star squad four straight years.
Playing Career: *1939-1952; Bos N, Pit N, Chi A*

Walt Masterson
Masterson, Walter Edward
B: Jun 22, 1920

Pos: P	ERA: 4.15
W-L: 78-100	SOs: 815
ShOs: 15	Saves: 20

Mickey Mantle was sent back to the minor leagues in 1951 after Masterson struck him out in five consecutive at-bats. Working as a starter and reliever, Masterson once hurled 253 innings. He was selected for the AL All-Star team in 1947 and 1948.
Playing Career: *1939-1942, 1945-1953, 1956; Was A, Bos A, Det A*

Bobby Mathews
Mathews, Robert T.
B: Nov 21, 1851   D: Apr 17, 1898

Pos: P	ERA: 2.88 (inc.)
W-L: 297-248	SOs: 1,346
ShOs: 19	Saves: 3

Only Al Spalding and Dick McBride won more games in the National Association than Mathews, who posted 132 victories there. While playing for the Reds in 1877, Mathews participated in a curveball test monitored by professors from the University of Cincinnati. The academics declared that the pitched ball did not curve – it was an optical illusion. Thousands of batters know differently.
Playing Career: *1871-1877, 1879, 1881-1887; Keo Kekiongas n, Bal Lord Baltimores n, NY Mutuals n, NY N, Cin N, Pro N, Bos N, Phi AA*

Eddie Mathews
Mathews, Edwin Lee
B: Oct 13, 1931
Hall of Fame 1978

Pos: 3B	BA: .271
Hits: 2,315	HRs: 512
RBI: 1,453	BBs: 1,444
Managerial Record	
Won: 149 Lost: 161 Pct: .481	

A great home run hitting third baseman, Mathews batted in front of Hank Aaron, and the two of them formed one of the most potent three-hole and clean-up combinations of all time. Their total of 863 home runs while playing together is higher than the Mays-McCovey total of 800 and the Ruth-Gehrig sum of 772. Frequently driven in by Aaron, Mathews scored 1,509 runs.

His 512 home runs made him only the seventh man to reach 500. He had four seasons with more than 40 round-trippers, including NL-leading marks of 47 in 1953 and 46 in 1959. Mathews played 17 seasons in a Braves uniform. Beginning with the team's last season in Boston, moving with the team to Milwaukee, and ending with their first season in Atlanta, he was the only Brave to perform in all three franchise cities. Mathews was managing the Braves when Aaron hit his 715th home run.
Playing Career: *1952-1968; Bos N, Mil N, Atl N, Hou N, Det A*
Managerial Career: *1972-1974; Atl N*

Christy Mathewson
Mathewson, Christopher (Big Six, Matty)
B: Aug 12, 1878   D: Oct 7, 1925
Hall of Fame 1936

Pos: P	ERA: 2.13
W-L: 373-188	SOs: 2,502
ShOs: 80	No-hitters: 2
Managerial Record	
Won: 164 Lost: 176 Pct: .481	

Baseball idol Mathewson was handsome, intelligent, clean-living, and the best pitcher of his day. He was called "The Big Six" after New York's most famous fire engine.

Mathewson was a Bucknell graduate who sang in the glee club, belonged to the literary society, was president of his class, and could beat 12 foes at checkers at the same time. He refused to pitch on Sunday, yet he won 30 games three years in a row, 1903-1905. He won 37 in 1908 and had nine other seasons with 20 or more wins. He posted 27 saves in his 17-year career.

Much of his success is attributed to the "fadeaway," a screwball that Rube Foster taught him in 1902. With it, Mathewson brought the Giants five pennants. In the 1905 World Series, he tossed three shutouts in six days, giving up just 14 hits and one walk. Mathewson always had great control. In 1908 he posted 259 strikeouts, in 391 innings, with only 42 walks. In 1913 he went 68 straight innings without a walk. He once won a game throwing only 67 pitches.
Playing Career: *1900-1916; NY N, Cin N*
Managerial Career: *1916-1918; Cin N*

Jon Matlack
Matlack, Jonathan Trumpbour
B: Jan 19, 1950

Pos: P	ERA: 3.18
W-L: 125-126	SOs: 1,516
ShOs: 30	Saves: 3

Rookie of the Year in 1972, Matlack was a good, young left-hander. He won 75 games in his first five years with the Mets. In the 1973 NLCS Matlack tossed a two-hit shutout.

He led the NL in shutouts twice and was picked for three consecutive All-Star rosters. After an off-year the Mets traded him to the Rangers, where he rebounded with a 15-13 season. Beset by arm problems, Matlack had elbow surgery in 1979, but never regained his fastball.
Playing Career: *1971-1983; NY N, Tex A*

Gary Matthews
Matthews, Gary Nathaniel (Sarge)
B: Jul 5, 1950

Pos: OF	BA: .281
Hits: 2,011	HRs: 234
RBI: 978	BBs: 940

In 1981 the Braves traded Matthews to the Phillies where he was reunited with Garry Maddox, a former Giants teammate. The duo helped the Phillies to the NL pennant in 1983. Matthews was brilliant in the NLCS that year, batting .429 with three homers and eight RBI, and winning MVP honors. He slugged one round-tripper in each of the last three games.

Matthews came up with San Francisco. There, Bobby Bonds, Maddox and he formed the best outfield of the 1970s. Matthews won the NL Rookie of the Year Award in 1973 with a .300 average, 12 homers, 58 RBI and 74 runs scored. Aggressive in the field and on the basepaths, Matthews stole 183 bases during his career, but turned into a home run hitter as a Brave and a team leader for the Cubs. He led the NL in walks and on-base percentage in 1984 as the Cubs took the division title. Matthews played in one All-Star Game.
Playing Career: *1972-1987; SF N, Atl N, Phi N, Chi N, Sea A*

Don Mattingly
Mattingly, Donald Arthur
B: Apr 20, 1961

Pos: 1B	BA: .309
Hits: 1,908	HRs: 209
RBI: 999	BBs: 488

In 1984, his first full major league season, Mattingly won the AL batting title with a .343 mark, and has been one of the most consistent hitters in baseball ever since. Few other current players combine high average with home run power to the same extent. Mattingly topped 200 hits three times, 30 homers three times, and 100 RBI four times. His 145 RBI in 1985 led the AL. He led the league in doubles 1984-1986. Mattingly was MVP in 1985, and was voted the top baseball player in more than one poll.

A throwback to the past, Mattingly displays the work ethic and charisma reminiscent of the great Yankees tradition. He uses Yankee Stadium to his advantage, and holds the Yankees' club records for doubles with 53, and hits with 238, both set in 1986. His 53 doubles were the most in the AL since Hal McRae smashed 54 in 1977. Mattingly is the first left-handed Yankee to bat over .340 since Lou Gehrig hit .351 in 1937.
Playing Career: *1982-; NY A*

Legendary pitcher Christy Mathewson (r) with Giants Manager John McGraw.

Gene Mauch as Angels manager, 1982.

Gene Mauch
Mauch, Gene William
B: Nov 18, 1925

Pos: 2B, SS	BA: .239
Hits: 176	HRs: 5
RBI: 62	BBs: 104

Managerial Record
Won: 1,902   Lost: 2,037   Pct: .483

A marginally skilled infielder, Mauch none-theless worked his way through the Dodgers' farm system, learning baseball inside and out. He parlayed that knowledge into a managerial career surpassed by few. Only eight other managers have won more games than Mauch, whose teams, ironically, never won a pennant. In a close call, Mauch piloted a young Phillies team headed by Rookie of the Year Dick Allen. Only three years earlier the team had lost 23 consecutive games, but in 1964 it led the league most of the second half of the season, and had a 6½-game edge with two weeks left. Suddenly, the Phillies' pitching collapsed, and Philadelphia lost 10 games in a row as the Cardinals took the pennant.

Mauch won division titles in 1982 and 1986 with the Angels, taking the 1986 ALCS to the final strike when the Red Sox' Dave Henderson ripped a home run in the top of the ninth of Game Five to tie the score. Fired up, Boston went on to win three games and take the pennant.
Playing Career: *1944, 1947-1952, 1956-1957; Brk N, Pit N, Chi N, Bos N, StL N, Bos A*
Managerial Career: *1960-1982, 1985-1987; Phi N, Mon N, Min A, Cal A*

Al Maul
Maul, Albert Joseph
B: Oct 9, 1865   D: May 3, 1958

Pos: P	ERA: 4.43
W-L: 84-80	SOs: 346
ShOs: 4	Saves: 1

The Phillies purchased Maul from Nashville for $2,500 in 1887, reportedly the most ever paid for a minor leaguer at that time. The one year Maul played with a good team, the Orioles in 1898, he won 20 games. He led the NL with a 2.45 ERA in 1895.
Playing Career: *1884, 1887-1891, 1893-1901; Phi U, Phi N, Pit N, Pit P, Was N, Bal N, Brk N, NY N*

Dal Maxvill
Maxvill, Charles Dallan
B: Feb 18, 1939

Pos: SS	BA: .217
Hits: 748	HRs: 6
RBI: 252	BBs: 370

Coming from the Texas League with a .340 batting average, Maxvill shared shortstop duties with veteran Dick Groat. While Maxvill's bat never came alive in the majors, he proved to be so good at short that his bat was not a factor in his playing time. Maxvill anchored the infield for three Cardinal pennant-winners in the 1960s. He still excelled in the World Series, where he handled 87 chances without an error, turning 14 double plays in three Fall Classics.

The A's picked him up as infield insurance and he played on two more pennant-winning teams in the early 1970s. After his playing days were over, Maxvill coached for the A's, Mets, Braves and Cardinals before becoming general manager for St. Louis in 1985. His tenure has been marked with success on the field, and the ability to cope with change after the death of long-time owner Gussie Busch. Maxvill is also adept at dealing with the new generation of players.
Playing Career: *1962-1975; StL N, Oak A, Pit N*

Charlie Maxwell
Maxwell, Charles Richard
B: Apr 8, 1927

Pos: OF	BA: .264
Hits: 856	HRs: 148
RBI: 532	BBs: 484

Baby boomers remember Charlie Maxwell as the Sunday ballplayer. At a time when the Sunday doubleheader was a weekly staple, Maxwell frequently hit home runs or made important pinch hits for the church crowd. He had been a good everyday player with the Tigers from 1956 to 1960, averaging 24 homers and 82 RBI per year. Maxwell led AL outfielders in fielding percentage in 1957 and 1960. He was chosen for the All-Star teams in 1956 and 1957.
Playing Career: *1950-1952, 1954-1964; Bos A, Bal A, Det A, Chi A*

Carlos May
May, Carlos
B: May 17, 1948

Pos: OF, 1B, DH	BA: .274
Hits: 1,127	HRs: 90
RBI: 536	BBs: 512

Only one ballplayer has been able to wear his birthdate on his uniform back, "May 17." Headed for a spectacular rookie year, the Marine Corps reservist lost part of his thumb in a training accident. May continued to play despite painful skin graft operations. *The Sporting News* named him Rookie of the Year,

Dal Maxvill smacks a ball hurled by Jim Bouton at Busch Stadium in the 1964 WS.

but the BBWAA chose Lou Piniella. May played in the All-Star Game in 1969 and 1972. His brother Lee played 2,071 games in the majors.
Playing Career: *1968-1977; Chi A, NY A, Cal A*

Dave May
May, David LaFrance
B: Dec 23, 1943

Pos: OF	BA: .251
Hits: 920	HRs: 96
RBI: 422	BBs: 344

Involved in two notable trades, May was part of the deal that brought 1974 MVP Jeff Burroughs to the Braves, and was part of the package that returned Hank Aaron to Milwaukee. May was an All-Star in 1973 when he hit 25 homers and drove in 93 runs.
Playing Career: *1967-1978; Bal A, Mil A, Atl N, Tex A, Pit N*

Jakie May
May, Frank Spruiell
B: Nov 25, 1895   D: Jun 3, 1970

Pos: P	ERA: 3.88
W-L: 72-95	SOs: 765
ShOs: 7	Saves: 19

After winning 35 games in the Pacific Coast League in 1922, May finally got back to the big leagues in 1924, and stayed there. The left-hander was a regular starter with the Reds for two years, then was used as a spot starter and in long relief.
Playing Career: *1917-1921, 1924-1932; StL N, Cin N, Chi N*

Lee May
May, Lee Andrew
B: May 23, 1943

Pos: 1B	BA: .267
Hits: 2,031	HRs: 354
RBI: 1,244	BBs: 487

May averaged 100 RBI during the years 1969-1977, three times going over 100, and four

First baseman Lee May, 1993.

times posting 98 or 99. With just one or two more in those seasons, he would stand in line for the Hall of Fame. May hit 20 or more home runs for 11 consecutive years, three times topping 33. He was chosen for three All-Star Game squads, and played in two World Series.
Playing Career: *1965-1982; Cin N, Hou N, Bal A, KC A*

Milt May
May, Milton Scott
B: Aug 1, 1950

Pos: C	BA: .263
Hits: 971	HRs: 77
RBI: 443	BBs: 305

The son of major leaguer Pinky May, Milt hit .500 in both the 1971 World Series and 1972 NLCS, his only two postseason appearances. He was a regular with the Astros when he hit .289 in 1974. May drove in baseball's one millionth run in 1975.
Playing Career: *1970-1984; Pit N, Hou N, Det A, SF N*

Rudy May
May, Rudolph
B: Jul 18, 1944

Pos: P	ERA: 3.46
W-L: 152-156	SOs: 1,760
ShOs: 24	Saves: 12

The Angels brought May up in 1965 at age 20, but he was not ready. He returned four years later and gave the weak Angels team steady pitching until they relegated him to the bullpen after a 7-17 season. May starred with the Yankees and Orioles, winning 18 games in 1977 and posting a 15-5 record in 1980, the year he led the AL with a 2.46 ERA. He pitched in the ALCS for the Yankees in 1980 and 1981.
Playing Career: *1965, 1969-1983; Cal A, NY A, Bal A, Mon N*

John Mayberry
Mayberry, John Claiborn
B: Feb 18, 1949

Pos: 1B, DH	BA: .253
Hits: 1,379	HRs: 255
RBI: 879	BBs: 881

The mainstay of the Royals' offense during the early 1970s, Mayberry spent only six years with Kansas City, yet ranks in the franchise top 10 in home runs, RBI, runs scored and bases on balls. He averaged 24 homers, 92 RBI and 93 walks with the Royals, but was traded to the Blue Jays to make room for Pete LaCock to play first base.

   When Mayberry went to Toronto in 1978, he was the first big star for the Canadian city, and the first Blue Jay to have a $1 million contract. He slugged 30 homers in 1980. For a big man, Mayberry was remarkably agile with soft hands around first base. Two was a good number for Mayberry. He led the league's first sackers in fielding percentage

John Mayberry.

twice. Mayberry was selected for the AL All-Star squad two times, and he played in two ALCS, slugging two home runs. He hit three homers in a game twice, and he led the AL in bases on balls twice.
Playing Career: *1968-1982; Hou N, KC A, Tor A, NY A*

Lee Maye
Maye, Arthur Lee
B: Dec 11, 1934

Pos: OF	BA: .274
Hits: 1,109	HRs: 94
RBI: 419	BBs: 282

In 1971 there were six good-hitting position players whose last name was May, Maye, Mays or Mayberry in the major leagues. Lee Maye led the NL in doubles with 44 in 1964. He was also an accomplished singer who appeared with the Platters.
Playing Career: *1959-1971; Mil N, Hou N, Cle A, Was A, Chi A*

Erskine Mayer
Mayer, Erskine John
B: Jan 16, 1889   D: Mar 10, 1957

Pos: P	ERA: 2.96
W-L: 91-70	SOs: 482
ShOs: 12	Saves: 6

Mayer won 21 games for the Phillies in 1914 and again in 1915. The latter season he was instrumental in their winning the pennant. He pitched two games in the 1915 World Series, and played in the Fall Classic again in 1919, with the White Sox.
Playing Career: *1912-1919; Phi N, Pit N, Chi A*

Eddie Mayo
Mayo, Edward Joseph
B: Apr 15, 1910

Pos: 3B, 2B	BA: .252
Hits: 759	HRs: 26
RBI: 287	BBs: 258

A part-time player in the late 1930s, Mayo became a regular during the World War II years. He led AL third basemen in fielding in 1943, and AL second basemen in 1945. He played in two World Series and was chosen for the 1945 All-Star team.
Playing Career: *1936-1938, 1943-1948; NY N, Bos N, Phi A, Det A*

Carl Mays
Mays, Carl William (Sub)
B: Nov 12, 1891   D: Apr 4, 1971

Pos: P	ERA: 2.92
W-L: 208-126	SOs: 862
ShOs: 29	Saves: 31

Submarine pitcher Carl Mays threw the pitch that killed Ray Chapman, the Indians' shortstop, in 1920. That tragic incident has obscured the fact that Mays was one of the best pitchers of his day. While he had a reputation for throwing at batters, Mays did not purposefully throw at Chapman, who frequently crowded the plate, with his arms and head in the strike zone. Eyewitnesses claimed that the deadly pitch was actually a strike.

Mays was 26-11 that year, and 27-9 the next as the Yankees won the 1921 pennant. He played for six pennant-winning teams altogether, and had a record of 3-4 in four World Series. Mays's 1919 sale to New York had been voided by AL President Ban Johnson, and the pitcher had been suspended. Yankees owner Jake Ruppert sued the league, causing a rift that led to the eventual ousting of Johnson in 1927.
Playing Career: *1915-1929; Bos A, NY A, Cin N, NY N*

Submarine pitcher Carl Mays.

The Giants' legendary Willie Mays.

Willie Mays
Mays, Willie Howard (Say Hey)
B: May 6, 1931
Hall of Fame 1979

Pos: OF	BA: .302
Hits: 3,283	HRs: 660
RBI: 1,903	BBs: 1,463

Many old-timers say that Mays was the best player they ever saw. He was certainly the most exciting player of the 1950s and 1960s. Mays hit 660 home runs, stole 338 bases and made incredible catches in center field. His catch off Vic Wertz in the 1954 World Series is often cited as the best ever. Mays sprinted, with his back turned to home plate, making an over-the-shoulder catch in front of the 475-foot sign. Whirling, he fired the ball to second base to keep the runner on first.

Mays won 11 straight Gold Gloves. He set the record for career putouts by an outfielder and the NL record for total chances. Mays led the NL in homers four times, twice belting more than 50. He won the MVP Award and NL batting title in 1954. He slugged four homers in one game in 1961. In 1962 he hit 49 homers and accumulated 141 RBI to lead the Giants to a playoff victory over Los Angeles. In 1965 Mays slugged 52 homers, 17 of them in August, to pass 500 and win his second MVP Award.
Playing Career: *1951-1973; NYG N, SF N, NYM N*

Bill Mazeroski
Mazeroski, William Stanley
B: Sep 5, 1936

Pos: 2B	BA: .260
Hits: 2,016	HRs: 138
RBI: 853	BBs: 447

Leading off the bottom of the ninth in the seventh game of the 1960 World Series, Mazeroski hit Ralph Terry's second pitch over the left field wall at Forbes Field. The fans poured out of the stands to run the bases in celebration of the Pirates' first Series victory since 1925. The Yankees had set new World Series records for runs, hits, extra-base hits and batting average, all of which still stand, yet they lost to the scrappy Pirates.

Mazeroski turned double plays better than any second sacker before him. Accounting for 1,706 altogether, he set the all-time twin killing record. Around Pittsburgh he was called "no hands" because the ball seemed to ricochet from the shortstop to first without Mazeroski touching it. He led the league in assists nine times, double plays eight, putouts five, and fielding three. The seven-time All-Star was not bad at the plate either, batting over .270 five times.
Playing Career: *1956-1972; Pit N*

Lee Mazzilli
Mazzilli, Lee Louis
B: Mar 25, 1955

Pos: OF	BA: .259
Hits: 1,068	HRs: 93
RBI: 460	BBs: 642

A New York City kid, Mazzilli was traded to the Rangers and suffered horribly from culture shock in Texas. He had been an All-Star for the Mets in 1979. Reacquired by the Mets in time for 1986 post season play, Mazzilli hit .400 in the World Series.
Playing Career: *1976-1989; NY N, Tex A, NY A, Pit N, Tor A*

Jimmy McAleer
McAleer, James Robert
B: Jul 10, 1864   D: Apr 29, 1931

Pos: OF	BA: .253
Hits: 1,006	HRs: 13
RBI: 469	BBs: 365

Managerial Record
Won: 736   Lost: 889   Pct: .453

Admirers said there was no better outfielder than McAleer, who reportedly was the first to take his eyes off a fly ball, turn and run, then glance up and catch it. His early training included three years in the rough-and-tumble Southern League, which prepared him for the Cleveland Spiders. McAleer hit in the .290s for the Temple Cup-bound arachnids. After managing in the minors and majors, he became part owner of the 1912 Red Sox.
Playing Career: *1889-1898; 1901-1902, 1907; Cle N, Cle P, Cle A, StL A*
Managerial Career: *1901-1911; Cle A, StL A, Was A*

Dick McAuliffe
McAuliffe, Richard John
B: Nov 29, 1939

Pos: 3B, 2B, SS	BA: .247
Hits: 1,530	HRs: 197
RBI: 697	BBs: 882

Batting with the most wide-open stance of his day, McAuliffe was a middle infielder with power, topping 22 homers in three of four years. He was an All-Star three times. As a leadoff man he scored 888 runs, leading the AL with 95 in 1968. That year, he did not hit into any double plays. McAuliffe scored five runs in the 1968 World Series and three in the 1972 ALCS. Tough as nails, he once hit a home run just before going on the disabled list.
Playing Career: *1960-1975; Det A, Bos A*

Al McBean
McBean, Alvin O'Neal
B: May 15, 1938

Pos: P	ERA: 3.13
W-L: 67-50	SOs: 575
ShOs: 5	Saves: 63

Working as a photographer, McBean filmed a baseball tryout camp, then decided to try out himself, ending up with a 10-year major league career. McBean's best record as a starter was 15-10, followed by a 13-3 mark as a starter and reliever.
Playing Career: *1961-1970; Pit N, SD N, LA N*

Bake McBride
McBride, Arnold Ray
B: Feb 3, 1949

Pos: OF	BA: .299
Hits: 1,153	HRs: 63
RBI: 430	BBs: 248

The Cardinals seem to be able to clone .300-hitting, good-fielding, base stealing outfielders, and McBride was one of them. Rookie of the Year in 1974, he hit .309 with 81 runs and 30 steals. McBride's speed and solid center field play sparked the Phillies to four postseason appearances in five years. He batted .304 in the 1980 Fall Classic, winning the first two games with timely blows. McBride stole 183 bases.
Playing Career: *1973-1983; StL N, Phi N, Cle A*

Dick McBride
McBride, James Dickson
B: 1845   D: Oct 10, 1916

Pos: P	ERA: .273
W-L: 149-78	SOs: 84 (inc.)
ShOs: 7	Saves: 3

When the Athletics and White Stockings went to England in 1874 there was contention over which game – cricket or baseball – should be played. McBride was a world-class cricket bowler. He and the other colonists humbled the proud Marlebone Cricket club.
Playing Career: *1871-1876; Phi Athletics n, Bos N*

George McBride
McBride, George Florian
B: Nov 20, 1880   D: Jul 2, 1973

Pos: SS	BA: .218
Hits: 1,203	HRs: 7
RBI: 447	BBs: 419
Managerial Record	
Won: 80 Lost: 73 Pct: .523	

The premier shortstop in the AL during the early years of the 20th century, McBride led the league in fielding five times. Lucky to hit .230 in his heyday, his teammates nonetheless called him "pinch" for his ability in the clutch. While managing the Senators he was hit in the face with a ball during batting practice and suffered a nervous breakdown.
Playing Career: *1901, 1905-1906, 1908-1920; Mil A, Pit N, StL N, Was A*
Managerial Career: *1921; Was A*

Jack McCarthy
McCarthy, John Arthur
B: Mar 26, 1869   D: Sep 11, 1931

Pos: OF	BA: .287
Hits: 1,203	HRs: 7
RBI: 474	BBs: 268

The only NL outfielder ever to start three double plays in one game, McCarthy threw a trio of men out at the plate, April 26, 1905. A good, but inconsistent hitter, McCarthy batted over .300 three times, including a .321 mark in 1901.
Playing Career: *1893-1894, 1898-1907; Cin N, Pit N, Chi N, Cle A, Brk N*

Yankee Manager Joe McCarthy.

Joe McCarthy
McCarthy, Joseph Vincent
B: Apr 21, 1887   D: Jan 3, 1978
Hall of Fame 1957

Managerial Record
Won: 2,125   Lost: 1,333   Pct: .615

Joe McCarthy may have been the best manager of them all. McGraw, Mack, Stengel and the other great skippers all had losing records while they learned how to handle players and win games. But McCarthy and his Louisville (American Association) squad upset the heavily favored Baltimore Orioles 5

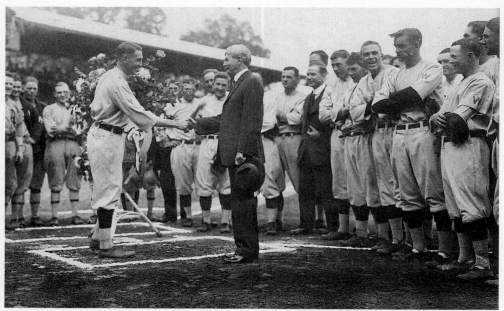

George McBride accepts a diamond watch from VP Thomas R. Marshall in 1913.

games to 4 in the 1925 Little World Series. At the major league level McCarthy was totally dominating; the winningest manager of all time. Over a 24-year period he guided his teams to nine pennants – one with the Chicago Cubs and the rest with the Yankees – and four World Championships in a row, 1936-1939. His teams wound up in second place seven times, and always finished in the first division. McCarthy was victorious in seven of the nine World Series his teams played in, with a record of 30 games won and 13 lost. McCarthy was a strict disciplinarian, but a warm, friendly man off the field.
Managerial Career: *1926-1946, 1948-1950; Chi N, NY A, Bos A*

Tommy McCarthy
McCarthy, Thomas Francis Michael
B: Jul 24, 1863   D: Aug 5, 1922
Hall of Fame 1946

Pos: OF	BA: .292
Hits: 1,496	HRs: 44
RBI: 666	BBs: 537

Managerial Record
Won: 11   Lost: 11   Pct: .500

Boston Beaneater fans named McCarthy and Hugh Duffy the "Heavenly Twins" for their defensive plays in the outfield, their hit-and-run techniques and their double steals. McCarthy scored 1,003 runs in nine full seasons, and stole 467 bases. Although he hit .346 in 1893, he was not nearly as good a hitter as fielder. His strengths were his speed, his powerful throwing arm, and his scientific approach. McCarthy was also an excellent bunter.

McCarthy popularized the practice of trapping fly balls and throwing runners out at second, starting double plays. He is the only member of the Baseball Hall of Fame who played in the Union Association, and the only member who performed significantly in the old American Association, excepting Charles Comiskey, who was inducted for other reasons.
Playing Career: *1884-1896; Bos U, Bos N, Phi N, StL AA, Brk N*
Managerial Career: *1890; StL AA*

Tim McCarver
McCarver, James Timothy
B: Oct 16, 1941

Pos: C	BA: .271
Hits: 1,501	HRs: 97
RBI: 645	BBs: 548

When McCarver broke in with the Cardinals, he was only 17 years old. He became their starting receiver in 1963 at age 21. The Cardinals won three pennants in the next five years, and McCarver was chosen for the All-Star team in 1966 and 1967. He hit .475 in the 1964 World Series, winning Game Five with a ninth-inning three-run homer. In 1966 McCarver led the NL in triples.

His best season was 1967, when he led the league in fielding and hit .350 in the first half before fading to .295 with 14 homers and 26

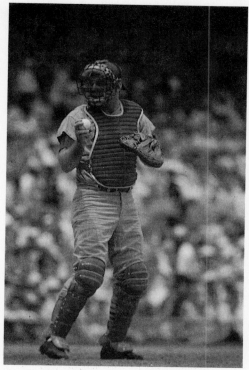

Cardinals catcher Tim McCarver, 1968.

doubles. McCarver finished second to teammate Orlando Cepeda in MVP Award voting that year. In 1965 McCarver and rookie pitcher Steve Carlton got into an argument over pitch selection. The debate lasted two decades and through two trades. When Carlton went to the Phillies, he asked them to acquire his favorite catcher, and they did. Today McCarver is a witty, urbane national baseball broadcaster.
Playing Career: *1959-1961, 1963-1980; StL N, Phi N, Mon N, Bos A*

Kirk McCaskill
McCaskill, Kirk Edward
B: Apr 9, 1961

Pos: P	ERA: 4.01
W-L: 94-95	SOs: 888
ShOs: 11	Saves: 2

An All-American in ice hockey at the University of Vermont and runner-up player of the year, McCaskill chose baseball as a career. Bone chips in his pitching elbow have limited his success, which looked likely when he went 17-10 with 202 strikeouts in 1986.
Playing Career: *1985-; Cal A, Chi A*

Steve McCatty
McCatty, Steven Earl
B: Mar 20, 1954

Pos: P	ERA: 3.99
W-L: 63-63	SOs: 541
ShOs: 7	Saves: 5

Cited as one of the victims of Billy Martin's pitcher burnout syndrome, McCatty participated in the A's record-setting 1980 season

when their staff completed 94 games. The next year McCatty won 14, completing 16 of 22 starts.
Playing Career: *1977-1985; Oak A*

Honest John McCloskey
McCloskey, John James
B: Apr 4, 1862   D: Nov 17, 1940

Managerial Record
Won: 190   Lost: 417   Pct: .313

The founder of the Texas League in 1888, McCloskey played some games there as a catcher. He is credited with founding four other minor leagues. In all McCloskey spent 36 seasons managing 30 different clubs.
Managerial Career: *1895-1896, 1906-1908; Lou N, StL N*

Bob McClure
McClure, Robert Craig
B: Apr 29, 1952

Pos: P	ERA: 3.81
W-L: 68-57	SOs: 701
ShOs: 1	Saves: 52

Baseball's best kept secret, McClure has spent 18 years at the major league level. The year he became a starter the Brewers won the AL pennant. He lost two but saved two in the 1982 World Series, and has an ERA of 0.00 in two ALCS. McClure was the stopper in the Brewers' bullpen until they acquired Rollie Fingers. He became a Marlin in the 1992 expansion draft.
Playing Career: *1975-; KC A, Mil A, Mon N, NY N, Cal A, StL N, Flo N*

Billy McCool
McCool, William John
B: Jul 14, 1944

Pos: P	ERA: 3.59
W-L: 32-42	SOs: 471
ShOs: 0	Saves: 58

The Reds' heir apparent to stoppers Jim Brosnan and Bill Henry, McCool was off to a strong beginning when he saved 39 games in two years. He was an All-Star in 1966. A wrist injury in 1968 reduced his effectiveness.
Playing Career: *1964-1970; Cin N, SD N, StL N*

Barry McCormick
McCormick, William J.
B: Dec 25, 1874   D: Jan 28, 1956

Pos: 3B, SS, 2B, OF	BA: .238
Hits: 867	HRs: 16
RBI: 418	BBs: 280

McCormick was a utility infielder who did not hit well, but played 100 or more games for eight straight years. He was 6-for-8 and scored five runs in the highest scoring game of all time, a 36-7 Chicago blowout over Louisville.
Playing Career: *1895-1904; Lou N, Chi N, StL A, Was A*

Harry McCormick
McCormick, Patrick Henry
B: Oct 25, 1855   D: Aug 8, 1889

Pos: P   ERA: 2.66
W-L: 41-58   SOs: 157
ShOs: 10   No hitters: 0

There were three hurlers who singlehandedly pitched their teams into the NL;
Indianapolis had "The Only Nolan," Buffalo
had Pud Galvin, and Syracuse had McCormick. He was the first NL pitcher to win a 1-0
shutout with his own home run.
Playing Career: *1879, 1881-1883; Syr N,
Wor N, Cin AA*

Jim McCormick
McCormick, James (Big Jim)
B: 1856   D: Mar 10, 1918

Pos: P   ERA: 2.43
W-L: 265-214   SOs: 1,704
ShOs: 33   Saves: 1
Managerial Record
Won: 106   Lost: 137   Pct: .436

Twenty-four-year-old Jim McCormick won
45 games, hurled 657 innings, posted a 1.85
ERA, and managed Cleveland to a third-
place finish in 1880. He first made a name for
himself as a member of the famous Buckeye
club of Ohio. For much of his career McCormick was saddled with losing clubs, but he
still won 40 or more twice and was ERA
champ twice, with a 1.84 in 1883 and a 1.54 in
1885. When he finally pitched for a pennant-
winning team, the 1885-1886 White Stockings, he was in a backup role, and posted
records of 21-7 and 31-11.
   White Stockings Manager Cap Anson said
of McCormick, "He was a great big fellow
with a florid complexion and blue eyes, and
was utterly devoid of fear, nothing that came
in his direction being too hot for him to
handle." McCormick, hailing from Scotland,
is one of five foreign born pitchers who won
250 or more games in the major leagues.
Playing Career: *1878-1887; Ind N, Cle N,
Cin U, Pro N, Chi N*
Managerial Career: *1879-1880; Cle N*

Mike McCormick
McCormick, Michael Francis
B: Sep 29, 1938

Pos: P   ERA: 3.73
W-L: 134-128   SOs: 1,321
ShOs: 23   No-hitters: 1

A game McCormick was pitching in 1959 was
called on account of rain. The score reverted
to the last full inning, wiping out a hit, and
giving him a no-hitter. McCormick had been
a highly sought-after 17-year-old, for whom
the Giants paid $60,000. By 1958 he was ready
to take his place in the starting rotation. He
was selected for the All-Star Game twice, and
blossomed in 1967 when he won 22 games
and the Cy Young Award.
Playing Career: *1956-1971; NY N, SF N,
Bal A, Was A, NY A, KC A*

Mike McCormick
McCormick, Myron Winthrop
B: May 6, 1917   D: Apr 14, 1976

Pos: OF   BA: .275
Hits: 640   HRs: 14
RBI: 215   BBs: 188

One of two McCormicks playing for the Reds
in the 1940 World Series, Mike set a Series
record with 24 outfield putouts. He lost three
years to military duty, and more time to a
broken leg, but he appeared in the 1948 and
1949 World Series.
Playing Career: *1940-1943, 1946-1951; Cin N,
Bos N, Brk N, NY N, Chi A, Was A*

Moose McCormick
McCormick, Frank Andrew (Buck)
B: Jun 9, 1911   D: Nov 21, 1982

Pos: 1B   BA: .299
Hits: 1,711   HRs: 128
RBI: 954   BBs: 399

McCormick led the NL in hits three consecutive years, 1938-1940, topping 40 doubles
and 100 RBI in each year. He was a strapping
lad of 6'4" who was turned away from a

Hall of Famer Willie McCovey.

Giants tryout because they wanted only left-
handed first basemen. McCormick vented
his disappointment by terrorizing NL
pitchers, winning the MVP Award in 1940,
and leading the NL in RBI in 1939 and doubles
in 1940.
   Deferred from the military by a back problem that seldom interfered with his ability to
play first base, McCormick played 652 consecutive games, averaging 149 per season
from 1938 through 1945. He led NL first basemen in fielding four times. A first-ball, fastball hitter, McCormick had a great eye at the
plate; he struck out only 189 times in 5,723 at-
bats. His final game was Game Six of the 1948
World Series with the Braves.
Playing Career: *1934, 1937-1948; Cin N,
Phi N, Bos N*

Barney McCoskey
McCosky, William Barney
B: Apr 11, 1917

Pos: OF   BA: .312
Hits: 1,301   HRs: 24
RBI: 397   BBs: 497

During his two first years in the majors,
McCoskey was the finest leadoff batter in the
AL. He batted .311 with 190 hits and 120 runs
in 1939, and .340 with 200 hits and 123 runs in
1940. The Tigers won the pennant and
McCoskey hit .304 in the World Series that
year. After losing three seasons to Uncle
Sam, McCoskey also suffered a back injury
that cost him the entire 1949 season and hastened his retirement.
Playing Career: *1939-1942, 1946-1948, 1950-
1953; Det A, Phi A, Cin N, Cle A*

Willie McCovey
McCovey, Willie Lee
B: Jan 10, 1938
Hall of Fame 1986

Pos: 1B, OF   BA: .270
Hits: 2,211   HRs: 521
RBI: 1,555   BBs: 1,345

McCovey slugged 18 grand slams, an NL
record, and led the league in homers three
times, but the ball he hit the hardest was an
out. The Giants were losing 1-0 in the ninth
inning of the seventh game of the 1962 World
Series, but they had the tying run on third
and the winning run at second. McCovey
lined a bullet at Yankees second baseman
Bobby Richardson for the final out. One foot
either way and the Giants would have been
champs.
   Although extremely shy in his first years,
McCovey became a friendly, even gregarious
team leader. He made four hits in his debut
and batted .354 that year to win the Rookie of
the Year Award. Ten years later he was NL
MVP with 45 homers and 126 RBI, both
league-leading totals, and a .320 batting average. McCovey played in four decades, returning to the Giants in the late 1970s. He
now serves as their ambassador of goodwill.
Playing Career: *1959-1980; SF N, SD N,
Oak A*

Tom McCraw
McCraw, Tommy Lee
B: Nov 21, 1940

Pos: 1B, OF
Hits: 972
RBI: 404

BA: .246
HRs: 75
BBs: 332

A much heralded rookie, McCraw won the American Association batting title, but hit closer to .230 in the majors until after Senators Manager Ted Williams worked with him. He hit a career-high .294 in 1974. McCraw once hit three home runs in a game, and narrowly missed hitting a fourth.
Playing Career: *1963-1975; Chi A, Was A, Cle A*

Tom McCreery
McCreery, Thomas Livingstone
B: Oct 19, 1874   D: Jul 3, 1941

Pos: OF, 1B, SS
Hits: 855
RBI: 387

BA: .290
HRs: 26
BBs: 308

On the 12th-place Louisville club in 1896 – his first full season – McCreery hit a career-high .351, slugged .546, and led the league in triples. He just missed championship seasons with the Pirates, who won after he left, and with the Dodgers, who had won the two years before he arrived.
Playing Career: *1895-1903; Lou N, NY N, Pit N, Brk N, Bos N*

Lance McCullers
McCullers, Lance Graye
B: Mar 8, 1964

Pos: P
W-L: 28-31
ShOs: 0

ERA: 3.25
SOs: 442
Saves: 39

When he filled in for an ailing Goose Gossage and saved three games in his first three appearances, McCullers was named the Padres' Rookie of the Year. By 1987 he was the Padres' stopper, recording 16 saves. McCullers was traded when Mark Davis emerged as a quality stopper.
Playing Career: *1985-1992; SD N, NY A, Det A, Tex A*

Clyde McCullough
McCullough, Clyde Edward
B: Mar 4, 1917   D: Sep 18, 1982

Pos: C
Hits: 785
RBI: 339

BA: .252
HRs: 52
BBs: 265

The rugged McCullough was platooned most of his playing career. He was selected for the NL All-Star Game twice but never got into either contest. He had one at-bat in the 1945 World Series after missing the regular season. A top defensive catcher, he later coached and managed for several different minor and major league teams.
Playing Career: *1940-1943, 1946-1956; Chi N, Pit N*

Brothers Lindy (l) and Von McDaniel show their combined victories, July 3, 1957.

Lindy McDaniel
McDaniel, Lyndall Dale
B: Dec 13, 1935

Pos: P
W-L: 141-119
ShOs: 2

ERA: 3.45
SOs: 1,361
Saves: 172

The premier relief pitcher of his day, McDaniel threw 1,694 innings in relief, winning 119 games and saving 172. He also started 74 games. His relief marks rank high on the all-time lists: second in relief appearances, second in relief wins, sixth in relief losses and second in relief innings.

McDaniel was a Cardinal teammate of his younger brother Von, who broke into the big leagues with a two-hit shutout over the Dodgers. Lindy led the NL in saves three times: 1959, 1960 and 1963. His All-Star year, 1960, was also spectacular; he posted a record of 12-4 with 26 saves, and a 2.09 ERA. His personal best came in 1970 with the Yankees, who acquired him in exchange for Bill Monboquette. McDaniel went 9-5 that year with 29 saves and a 2.01 ERA. None was an AL-leading mark, but he was one of the best relievers in the league at age 34.
Playing Career: *1955-1975; StL N, Chi N, SF N, NY A, KC A*

Mickey McDermott
McDermott, Maurice Joseph
B: Apr 29, 1928

Pos: P
W-L: 69-69
ShOs: 11

ERA: 3.91
SOs: 757
Saves: 14

Irish tenor and hurler McDermott pitched for the Red Sox and sang at Boston night clubs. McDermott worked as a starter and a reliever, winning 59 percent of his decisions with Boston. Sox fans were livid when he was traded following an 18-10 season.
Playing Career: *1948-1958, 1961; Bos A, Was A, NY A, KC A, Det A, StL N*

Gil McDougald
McDougald, Gilbert James
B: May 19, 1928

Pos: 3B, SS, 2B
Hits: 1,291
RBI: 576

BA: .276
HRs: 112
BBs: 559

The 1951 Rookie of the Year, McDougald came along the same year Mickey Mantle joined the Bronx Bombers. McDougald excelled at various infield positions. His versatility enabled the Yankees to shuffle regulars in and out of the lineup. Known for his peculiar open batting stance, McDougald was an outstanding hitter, once driving in six runs in one inning. McDougald was selected for the AL All-Star team five times and played in eight World Series.
Playing Career: *1951-1960; NY A*

Gil McDougald after a 1958 WS homer.

Jack McDowell
McDowell, Jack Burns (Black Jack)
B: Jan 16, 1966

Pos: P	ERA: 3.46
W-L: 71-49	SOs: 791
ShOs: 8	No-hitters: 0

The ace of the White Sox staff, McDowell led the AL in complete games, 1991-1992, and was named to the AL All-Star team three times. The big right-hander led the AL in wins and shutouts as he took Cy Young Award honors in 1993. McDowell also plays in a rock-and-roll band.
Playing Career: *1987-; Chi A*

Oddibe McDowell
McDowell, Oddibe
B: Aug 25, 1962

Pos: OF, DH	BA: .252
Hits: 667	HRs: 73
RBI: 251	BBs: 266

A two-time All-American at Arizona State and a member of the 1984 Olympic team, McDowell was an exalted rookie, expected to be an impact player. Instead he discovered that publicity would only go so far. He lacked major league level skills.
Playing Career: *1985-1990; Tex A, Cle A, Atl N*

Roger McDowell
McDowell, Roger Alan
B: Dec 21, 1960

Pos: P	ERA: 3.07
W-L: 62-62	SOs: 426
ShOs: 0	Saves: 151

After missing most of the 1984 season for elbow surgery, McDowell discovered that he could throw a sinking fastball. He became the stopper for the Mets as they won two division titles, and a World Championship in 1986. McDowell has a history of inconsistency, but has accumulated a large number of saves. His best season so far was 1986, when he compiled a record of 14-9 with 22 saves and a 3.02 ERA. In 1989 his ERA was 1.96.
Playing Career: *1985-; NY N, Phi N, LA N*

Sam McDowell
McDowell, Samuel Edward (Sudden Sam)
B: Sep 21, 1942

Pos: P	ERA: 3.17
W-L: 141-134	SOs: 2,453
ShOs: 23	Saves: 14

A little wild, and a little mean, McDowell had a 95-mph fastball and a problem with alcohol. At the top of his game, McDowell had a semblance of control and led the league five out of six years in strikeouts, 1965-1970, twice whiffing more than 300. A six-time All-Star, McDowell won 20 games once, and led the league in ERA with a 2.18 mark in 1965. He led in shutouts in 1966, then had an ERA of 1.81 in 1968. After his retirement, McDowell worked

Cleveland pitcher Sam McDowell, 1968.

in alcohol rehabilitation, and now serves as a counselor.
Playing Career: *1961-1975; Cle A, SF N, NY A, Pit N*

Will McEnaney
McEnaney, William Henry
B: Feb 14, 1952

Pos: P	ERA: 3.75
W-L: 12-17	SOs: 148
ShOs: 0	Saves: 29

Cincinnati's Big Red Machine had a bullpen stocked with stoppers, and McEnaney was one of them. He saved 22 games 1975-1976, and three more in World Series competition, where he compiled a 1.59 ERA. He retired after a good year with the Cardinals in 1979.
Playing Career: *1974-1979; Cin N, Mon N, Pit N, StL N*

Ed McFarland
McFarland, Edward William
B: Aug 3, 1874   D: Nov 28, 1959

Pos: C	BA: .275
Hits: 825	HRs: 12
RBI: 383	BBs: 254

A platoon catcher, McFarland batted .333 and .305 with the 1899 and 1900 Phillies. He jumped to the White Sox of the new AL in 1902, where he shared catching duties with Billy Sullivan. McFarland pinch-hit in the 1906 World Series.
Playing Career: *1893, 1896-1908; Cle N, StL N, Phi N, Chi A, Bos A*

Andy McGaffigan
McGaffigan, Andrew Joseph
B: Oct 25, 1956

Pos: P	ERA: 3.38
W-L: 38-33	SOs: 610
ShOs: 1	Saves: 24

When McGaffigan was good he was very good, but when he was bad, he was horrid. He was 10-5 with a 2.85 ERA in 1986, and saved 12 games in 1987, but once turned in a performance that resulted in a 17.36 ERA.
Playing Career: *1981-1991; NY A, SF N, Mon N, Cin N, KC A*

Dan McGann
McGann, Dennis Lawrence (Cap)
B: Jul 15, 1871   D: Dec 13, 1910

Pos: 1B	BA: .285
Hits: 1,511	HRs: 42
RBI: 736	BBs: 437

Genius John McGraw always claimed that his 1905 Giants team was the best one he ever managed. Dan McGann played first base on that championship squad, and for several other McGraw teams. McGann's fielding percentage was .991 in 1905; he led the league in fielding six times, finishing his career with a .989 mark. McGann batted .300 or more five times, drove in 106 runs in 1898 and scored 114 runs in 1899.
Playing Career: *1896, 1898-1908; Bos N, Bal N, Brk N, Was N, StL N, Bal A, NY N*

Chippy McGarr
McGarr, James B.
B: May 10, 1863   D: Jun 6, 1904

Pos: 3B, SS, 2B	BA: .268
Hits: 872	HRs: 9
RBI: 294	BBs: 183

An average performer on an exceptional nine, McGarr played for the Cleveland Spiders. Having started in the Union Association, he knew how to take advantage of a situation – a dominating trait of the Spiders. He hit .309 in 1893 and scored 94 runs the next year.
Playing Career: *1884, 1886-1890, 1893-1896; Chi-Pit U, Phi AA, StL AA, KC AA, Bal AA, Bos N, Cle N*

Willie McGee
McGee, Willie Dean
B: Nov 2, 1958

Pos: OF	BA: .298
Hits: 1,832	HRs: 61
RBI: 685	BBs: 353

As a quiet, serious rookie, McGee played for the Cardinals in their 1982 World Championship season. Altogether McGee has appeared in four World Series and played on four All-Star teams. He won three Gold Glove Awards for his center field coverage in spacious Busch Stadium, where his play was instrumental in the Cardinals capturing three pennants in the tough NL East Division during the 1980s.

A notorious bad-ball hitter, McGee racked up a .353 average in 1985 when he cut down his swing. That year he stole 56 bases and scored 114 runs, led the NL in hits and triples, and was chosen NL MVP. He won another NL batting title in 1990 when he was traded to

Willie McGee, with the Cards in 1989.

the Athletics late in the season, freezing his NL average at .335. McGee has stolen more than 300 bases. He helped fellow base thief Vince Coleman adapt to the majors when he broke in with a world of speed and talent, but lacking baseball skills.
Playing Career: *1982-; StL N, Oak A, SF N*

Willie McGill
McGill, William Vaness
B: Nov 10, 1873   D: Aug 29, 1944

Pos: P   ERA: 4.59
W-L: 72-74   SOs: 510
ShOs: 2   Saves: 1

One of the youngest players ever to appear in the majors, McGill was 16 years old when he pitched for Cleveland in 1890. At first his parents would not let him go on road trips, but they relented and McGill became a star, winning 21 games in 1891.
Playing Career: *1890-1896; Cle P, Cin AA, StL AA, Cin N, Chi N, Phi N*

Jumbo McGinnis
McGinnis, George Washington
B: Feb 22, 1864   D: May 18, 1934

Pos: P   ERA: 2.92
W-L: 102-79   SOs: 562
ShOs: 18   No-hitters: 0

Known as Jumbo because of his big belly, McGinnis had an off-season job as a glass blower. Although his career ended when he was 23, he won more than 100 games, pitched for two pennant-winners and led the AA in shutouts with six in 1883.
Playing Career: *1882-1887; StL AA, Bal AA, Cin AA*

Iron Man McGinnity
McGinnity, Joseph Jerome
B: Mar 19, 1871   D: Nov 14, 1929
Hall of Fame 1946

Pos: P   ERA: 2.64
W-L: 247-142   SOs: 1,068
ShOs: 32   Saves: 23

Iron Man was named for his off-season job as a smelter, but the moniker could be applied to his pitching stamina as well. He won three doubleheaders in August 1903. He led the league in innings pitched five times in his career. Counting major and minor league careers, McGinnity pitched 26 seasons, winning 471 games, and was still going at age 54. He posted a 29-2 record with Richmond in the Virginia League in 1919.

Throwing an underhand curveball, McGinnity had a motion so low his hand almost touched the ground. He called the pitch "Old Sal," and it must have put less strain on his arm than an overhand curve would have. He won 28 games as a rookie with Baltimore in 1899, but his greatest years were with the Giants, for whom he won 31 in 1903 and 35 in 1904. He had a reputation for throwing at batters, borne out by statistics – he hit one batsman for every 19 he faced, a major league record.
Playing Career: *1899-1908; Bal N, Brk N, Bal A, NY N*

Lynn McGlothen
McGlothen, Lynn Everett
B: Mar 27, 1950   D: Aug 14, 1984

Pos: P   ERA: 3.98
W-L: 86-93   SOs: 939
ShOs: 13   Saves: 2

A three-time Louisiana State tennis champ, McGlothen was a good starting pitcher until the strain of throwing baseballs put too much pressure on his joints. He was 16-12 with a 2.69 ERA for the Cardinals in 1974 and was chosen for the All-Star squad that year.
Playing Career: *1972-1982; Bos A, StL N, SF N, Chi N, Chi A, NY A*

NY Giants curveballer "Iron Man" Joe McGinnity.

Jim McGlothlin
McGlothlin, James Milton
B: Oct 6, 1943   D: Dec 23, 1975

Pos: P   ERA: 3.61
W-L: 67-77   SOs: 709
ShOs: 11   Saves: 3

McGlothlin was another of the pitchers who fueled the Big Red Machine during the 1970s. He helped the Reds win pennants in 1970 and 1972. Formerly a starter for the Angels, McGlothlin was an All-Star in 1967, compiling a record of 12-8 with a 2.96 ERA.
Playing Career: *1965-1973; Cal A, Cin N, Chi A*

Bill McGowan
McGowan, William
B: Jan 18, 1896   D: Dec 9, 1954
Hall of Fame 1992

If there was an exception to the old adage "Fans don't pay to see the umpire," McGowan was it. He introduced a colorful style with vigorous, aggressive gestures bordering on the pugnacious; yet he ejected very few players. McGowan's hustle and skill commanded respect from ballplayers. His enthusiasm never waned over 30 AL seasons. The most durable umpire in the history of the national pastime, McGowan did not miss an inning for more than 16 years, working 2,541 consecutive games.

One of McGowan's decisions cost Lou Gehrig the 1931 home run title. Gehrig had smashed a ball into the Senators' center field bleachers, but it bounced back on to the playing field. The right fielder went after the ball, confusing the baserunner, who stopped before reaching second base. Barreling around first with his head down, Gehrig plowed past the runner and was called out to end the inning. Gehrig and Ruth tied for the AL home run crown with 46.
Umpiring Career: *1925-1954; AL (4 AS, 8 WS)*

John McGraw
McGraw, John Joseph (Little Napoleon)
B: Apr 7, 1873   D: Feb 25, 1934
Hall of Fame 1937

Pos: 3B   BA: .333
Hits: 1,308   HRs: 13
RBI: 462   BBs: 836
Managerial Record
Won: 2,784   Lost: 1,959   Pct: .587

Ensconced in the nation's biggest city, McGraw was bread and butter for sportswriters from the area's 22 daily papers, and the dominant force in baseball for 35 years. He had managed the NL Baltimore club, and had a reputation for being a rowdy umpire baiter. It was a surprise when Ban Johnson, president of the new AL, hired McGraw to manage in the "reform league" where rowdyism was not allowed and gentlemanly behavior was encouraged. Johnson and McGraw quickly came to cross-purposes, and the fiery-tempered manager went to

John McGraw.

New York, taking the best Baltimore players with him.

One of the first to grasp the concepts of relief pitching and platooning, McGraw nonetheless drove his players hard, called pitches from the bench and argued relentlessly. His Giants won 10 pennants and three World Championships. McGraw had played third base for the legendary Orioles, who won three straight pennants. His career batting average is the highest of all third basemen in the Hall of Fame.
Playing Career: *1891-1906; Bal AA, Bal N, StL N, Bal A, NY N*
Managerial Career: *1899, 1901-1932; Bal N, Bal A, NY N*

Tug McGraw
McGraw, Frank Edwin
B: Aug 30, 1944

Pos: P   ERA: 3.13
W-L: 96-92   SOs: 1,109
ShOs: 1   Saves: 180

One of the premier relief pitchers in baseball, McGraw was 9-3 with 12 saves for the 1969 Miracle Mets, pitching three scoreless innings in the NLCS. In 1973 McGraw coined the phrase, "You gotta believe," and rallied the unheralded Mets to the division title and then the pennant. Fifteen times in September, McGraw charged off the mound slapping his glove on his leg and yelling to the sky. In those outings, he saved 11 games and won 4. He won one and saved one in the World Series.

McGraw's best season was 1972, when he was 8-6 with 27 saves and a 1.70 ERA – his second consecutive 1.70 mark. It won him a trip to the All-Star Game, where he picked the victory. He was also chosen for the 1975 All-Star team. McGraw led the former "Phutile Phillies" to division pay dirt six of eight seasons, 1976-1983. He won a game and saved two in the 1980 World Series for the champion Philadelphia team.
Playing Career: *1965-1967, 1969-1984; NY N, Phi N*

Scott McGregor
McGregor, Scott Houston
B: Jan 18, 1954

Pos: P   ERA: 3.99
W-L: 138-108   SOs: 904
ShOs: 23   Saves: 5

Reliever Tug McGraw lent his talents to the NY Mets and then to the Phillies.

For nine years, McGregor was the mainstay of the pitching staff for one of the best teams in baseball – Earl Weaver's Baltimore Orioles. Two of McGregor's teammates, Jim Palmer and Brooks Robinson, are already in the Hall of Fame. McGregor had an overall winning percentage of .561. Three times he won more than 70 percent of his games in a season. McGregor was an All-Star in 1981, and he tossed a shutout in the finale of the 1983 World Series.

Playing Career: *1976-1988; Bal A*

Fred McGriff
McGriff, Frederick Stanley
B: Oct 31, 1963

Pos: 1B	BA: .281
Hits: 1,001	HRs: 228
RBI: 616	BBs: 629

The Yankees made a big mistake when they dealt McGriff out of their farm system to Toronto – he has become the left-handed slugger the Bronx Bombers have been looking for since Reggie Jackson left. McGriff has hit 30 home runs or more for six consecutive seasons, and has led both the AL and NL in homers. He was elected to the All-Star Game roster in 1992.

Playing Career: *1986-; Tor A, SD N*

Deacon McGuire
McGuire, James Thomas
B: Nov 18, 1863   D: Oct 31, 1936

Pos: C	BA: .278
Hits: 1,749	HRs: 45
RBI: 787 (inc.)	BBs: 515
Managerial Record	
Won: 210 Lost: 287 Pct: .423	

A man of temperate habits, Deacon McGuire played parts of 26 years, and was 20 when he made the major leagues. McGuire's best

Deacon McGuire.

years were spent with the lowly Washington Nationals, sometimes called the Senators, from 1894 to 1897. Although the team finished in ninth place or below, McGuire hit .306, .336, .321 and .343. In the 1895 season, he caught every game for the Senators, a feat never before achieved. He also scored 89 runs and batted in 97 that year, both career highs.

McGuire became an assistant for Hugh Jennings in 1911. Appearing for the last time at age 48 for the Tigers in the 1912 Ty Cobb strike game, McGuire singled and scored a run, handling eight chances with two errors behind the plate. He later coached at Albion College.

Playing Career: *1884-1888, 1890-1908, 1910, 1912; Tol AA, Det N, Phi N, Cle AA, Roc AA, Was AA, Was N, Brk N, Det A, NY A, Bos A, Cle A*

Managerial Career: *1898, 1907-1911; Was N, Bos A, Cle A*

Bill McGunnigle
McGunnigle, William Henry (Gunner)
B: Jan 1, 1855   D: May 7, 1979

Pos: P, OF	BA: .173
Hits: 35	HRs: 0
RBI: 6	BBs: 5
Managerial Record	
Won: 210 Lost: 287 Pct: .423	

McGunnigle was the only manager to win back-to-back pennants in different leagues with the same team. Taking advantage of the confusion in baseball in 1889 and 1890, McGunnigle removed his Brooklyn club from the American Association and jumped to the NL, which had openings because most of its good players had jumped to the Players' League. Earlier, McGunnigle won 11 games as a pitcher with a 2.81 ERA.

Playing Career: *1879-1880, 1882; Buf N, Wor N, Cle N*

Managerial Career: *1888-1891, 1896; Brk AA, Brk N, Pit N, Lou N*

Mark McGwire
McGwire, Mark David
B: Oct 1, 1963

Pos: 1B	BA: .249
Hits: 800	HRs: 229
RBI: 632	BBs: 548

The greatest offensive threat in the major leagues, McGwire is capable of hitting a home run in any ballpark, on any at-bat, against any pitcher. From 1988 through 1992 McGwire batted between Rickey Henderson and Jose Canseco in Oakland's lineup – it would take monumental statistics for anyone in that position to be recognized. Yet McGwire has never lacked recognition. He swatted 49 homers in his rookie season, shattering the old Wally Berger rookie mark of 35.

Named AL Rookie of the Year in 1987, McGwire has hit consistently ever since, except for the 1991 season, when the entire A's squad was in the doldrums. Oakland has won division titles in 1988, 1989, 1990 and 1992. McGwire slugged .618 in 1987 and .585

in 1992, both league-leading figures. An All-Star six times, McGwire has played in four ALCS and three World Series.

Playing Career: *1986-; Oak A*

Austin McHenry
McHenry, Austin Bush
B: Sep 22, 1895   D: Nov 27, 1922

Pos: OF	BA: .302
Hits: 592	HRs: 34
RBI: 286	BBs: 117

Branch Rickey rated McHenry one of the best left fielders ever. He batted .350 with 201 hits – 37 doubles, 17 homers – in 1921. The next year he faded to .303 and was diagnosed as having a brain tumor. He died that fall.

Playing Career: *1918-1922; StL N*

Stuffy McInnis
McInnis, John Phalen
B: Sep 19, 1890   D: Feb 16, 1960

Pos: 1B	BA: .308
Hits: 2,406	HRs: 20
RBI: 1,060	BBs: 380
Managerial Record	
Won: 51 Lost: 103 Pct: .331	

Observers on the sandlots of Boston frequently complimented McInnis with "That's the stuff, kid," and "Stuffy" became his nickname. In the big leagues, McInnis once sauntered toward the plate as the pitcher lobbed warmup tosses. He suddenly reached over and knocked the ball into the outfield, then circled the bases while fielders stood looking at each other. The umpire called it a home run, but officials quickly instituted a new rule

Stuffy McInnis.

allowing pitchers a specific number of warm-up tosses.

One of the best-fielding first basemen ever, McInnis set a major league record with a .9993 fielding average in 1921, making only one error all season. He played for six pennant-winning teams, but did not fare as well managing. When his 1927 Phillies finished in last place, McInnis retired to coach the Harvard nine.

Playing Career: *1909-1927; Phi A, Bos A, Cle A, Bos N, Pit N, Phi N*
Managerial Career: *1927; Phi N*

Harry McIntire
McIntire, John Reid
B: Jan 11, 1879   D: Jan 9, 1949

Pos: P	ERA: 3.22
W-L: 71-117	SOs: 626
ShOs: 17	No-hitters: 1

While the Dodgers sunk to 40–60 games out of first place, McIntire lost an average 19 games a year from 1905 to 1909. He pitched a no-hitter on August 1, 1906, but lost. He was 13-9 for the 1910 Cubs, and played in the World Series that year.

Playing Career: *1905-1913; Brk N, Chi N, Cin N*

Matty McIntyre
McIntyre, Matthew W.
B: Jun 12, 1880   D: Apr 2, 1920

Pos: OF	BA: .269
Hits: 1,066	HRs: 4
RBI: 319	BBs: 439

A minor league batting champion, McIntyre played three seasons with Ty Cobb and Sam Crawford in the Tigers' outfield. He led off, scoring a league-high 105 runs in 1908, 562 in his career. McIntyre played in the 1908-1909 World Series for the Tigers.

Playing Career: *1901, 1904-1912; Phi A, Det A, Chi A*

Doc McJames
McJames, James McCutchen
B: Aug 27, 1873   D: Sep 23, 1901

Pos: P	ERA: 3.43
W-L: 79-80	SOs: 593
ShOs: 6	Saves: 4

After leading the NL in shutouts and strikeouts pitching for the lowly Senators, McJames won 27 games for the Orioles in 1897. Malaria struck him in the latter part of the 1899 season, causing him to miss 1900. He died during the 1901 season.

Playing Career: *1895-1899, 1901; Was N, Bal N, Brk N*

Ed McKean
McKean, Edwin John
B: Jun 6, 1864   D: Aug 16, 1919

Pos: SS	BA: .302
Hits: 2,083	HRs: 66
RBI: 1,070	BBs: 635

Ed McKean.

One of the original Cleveland Spiders, McKean was their only shortstop; he stayed with the team when it entered the NL, and remained with them when many NL players jumped to the Players' League in 1890. When the Robison brothers – who owned both the Cleveland and St. Louis NL clubs – sent all their good players to St. Louis and dumped all the second-rate players in Cleveland, McKean went to St. Louis.

From 1893 to 1896, McKean averaged 112 runs, 123 RBI and a .337 batting average. In three Temple Cup playoffs, he hit .444, .300, and .313. When the new AL team in Cleveland called him in 1901, McKean came out of retirement and began practicing, but never got closer to the big leagues than player-manager in Rochester in the Eastern League. He also piloted Springfield and Dayton in the Central League.

Playing Career: *1887-1899; Cle AA, Cle N, StL N*

Bill McKechnie
McKechnie, William Boyd (Deacon)
B: Aug 7, 1886   D: Oct 29, 1965
Hall of Fame 1962

Pos: 3B	BA: .251
Hits: 713	HRs: 8
RBI: 240	BBs: 188
Managerial Record	
Won: 1,899 Lost: 1,724 Pct: .524	

The Federal League was the beneficiary of McKechnie's best year (1914), when he batted .304 with 24 doubles and scored 107 runs. With the New York Highlanders, McKechnie played for manager Frank Chance, who said the infielder "knew more baseball than all the rest of my team put together." McKechnie became a manager himself, and won pennants with three different NL clubs.

In 1922 he took over the Pirates and brought them from the second division to the World Championship in 1925. He went to St. Louis and piloted the Cardinals to a pennant in 1928. During an eight-year sojourn with the Braves, McKechnie was credited with Wally Berger's rise to stardom. In Cincinnati he earned two more pennants, 1939 and 1940, and developed Bucky Walters and Paul Derringer into fine starting pitchers.

Playing Career: *1907, 1910-1918, 1920; Pit N, Bos N, NY A, Ind F, Nwk F, NY N, Cin N*
Managerial Career: *1915, 1922-1926, 1928-1946; Nwk F, Pit N, StL N, Bos N, Cin N*

Jack McKeon
McKeon, John Aloysius (Trader Jack)
B: Nov 23, 1930

Managerial Record
Won: 442   Lost: 431   Pct: .506

Between managing stints, McKeon worked in the front office for the Padres and the A's, acquiring his nickname by wheeling and dealing in baseball players. McKeon's Padres captured the NL flag in 1984.

Managerial Career: *1973-1975, 1977-1978, 1988-1990; KC A, Oak A, SD N*

Bill McKechnie with his son, 1925.

LEFT: First baseman Willie McCovey began his lengthy Hall of Fame career in San Francisco as the 1959 NL Rookie of the Year. (Photo by Malcolm Emmons)
ABOVE: Author of six 20-win seasons and a no-hitter, Hall of Famer Juan Marichal hurled his magic for the Giants from 1960 to 1973. (National Baseball Library, Cooperstown, NY)
BELOW: Yankee baseball legend Mickey Mantle – winner of three MVP Awards – played in 20 All-Star Games and 12 World Series. (Brompton Photo Library)

FAR LEFT: Winner of 11 Gold Gloves, Willie Mays made sparkling plays in center field, including his famous ''circus catch'' in the World Series in 1954, the year he won the MVP Award and batting title (Photo by Malcolm Emmons)

LEFT: In 1956 the Dodgers' Don Newcombe won the first Cy Young Award, with a 27-7 record. He was equally skilled at the plate, batting .359 in 1955 while leading the NL in winning percentage. (TV Sports Mailbag, Elmsford, NY)

BELOW: Oakland's Mark McGwire was named AL Rookie of the Year in 1987, when he set a rookie record with 49 home runs. (Photo by Robert Beck/Allsport)

OPPOSITE ABOVE: Nine-time All-Star Joe Morgan helped the Reds win consecutive World Championships, 1975-1976. (Photo by Malcolm Emmons)

OPPOSITE BELOW: Yankee team leader and Gold Glove catcher Thurman Munson. (Photo by Malcolm Emmons)

OPPOSITE: Hall of Fame hurler Jim Palmer posted pennant-clinching wins for the Orioles in 1966, 1969, 1970 and 1971. In 1975, when he won his second of three Cy Young Awards, Palmer's 23 wins, 2.09 ERA and 10 shutouts led the AL. (Photo by Malcolm Emmons)

ABOVE: Gold Glove third baseman Terry Pendleton is a terror in the postseason, batting .429 for St. Louis in the 1987 World Series, and .367 with two homers for the Braves in the 1991 Fall Classic. (Photo by Mike Powell/Allsport)

RIGHT: A vital cog in the wheel of Cincinnati's Big Red Machine for 10 years, Tony Perez ended the longest All-Star Game in history with a home run in the 15th inning of the 1967 contest. (Photo by Malcolm Emmons)

FAR RIGHT: Charismatic Hall of Fame pitcher Satchel Paige hurled his magic for two decades in the Negro Leagues before becoming a 42-year-old rookie with Cleveland in the 1948 American League. (Photo by UPI/Bettmann Newsphotos)

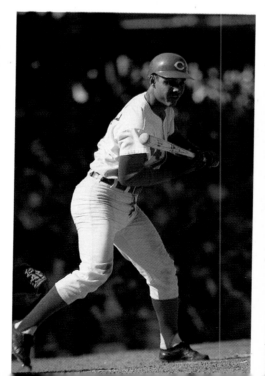

OPPOSITE: In his first big league game, in 1984, Kirby Puckett collected four hits, then went on to lead AL outfielders that season in assists, with 16. His .357 mark in the 1987 World Series and game-winning, 11th-inning homer in Game Six of the 1991 World Series helped the Twins become World Champs twice over. (Photo by Stephen Dunn/Allsport)

LEFT: Jim Rice continued Fenway's tradition of great left fielders – following in the footsteps of Ted Williams and Carl Yastrzemski – when he slugged .600 with 213 hits, 46 homers, 15 triples and 139 RBI in 1978 – all league-leading marks. The eight-time All-Star batted .333 for the Red Sox in the 1986 World Series. (Photo by Janis Rettaliata/Allsport)

BELOW LEFT: During his stellar 20-year career Frank Robinson collected many honors, including the NL Rookie of the Year Award, 11 All-Star Game selections, AL and NL MVP Awards, and an AL Triple Crown in 1966 for Baltimore. He was elected to the Hall of Fame in 1982. (Photo by Chance Brockway)

BELOW: Hall of Famer Brooks Robinson holds almost every defensive lifetime record for third basemen. (Photo by Malcolm Emmons)

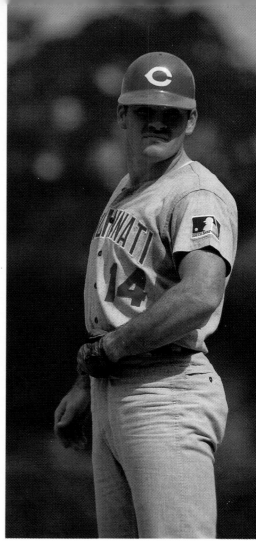

ABOVE LEFT: Dodger great Jackie Robinson. (TV Sports Mailbag, Elmsford, NY)
ABOVE: All-time hits leader Pete Rose. (Photo by Malcolm Emmons)
LEFT: Nolan Ryan pitched seven no-hitters. (Photo by Nancy Hogue)
BELOW: A legend in his own time, Babe Ruth is baseball's all-time best slugger. (Brompton Photo Library)

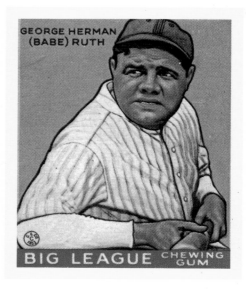

GEORGE HERMAN (BABE) RUTH

BIG LEAGUE CHEWING GUM

Alex McKinnon
McKinnon, Alexander J.
B: Aug 14, 1856   D: Jul 24, 1887

Pos: 1B
Hits: 465   BA: .296
RBI: 219   HRs: 14
                    BBs: 45
Managerial Record
Won: 6   Lost: 32   Pct: .158

McKinnon was the power hitter for the legendary Syracuse Stars before they entered the NL. He recovered from an undiagnosed malady that paralyzed one side, and returned to baseball, but eventually died from typhoid fever. McKinnon was on a road trip to Philadelphia and was batting .340 at the time of his death.
Playing Career: *1884-1887; NY N, StL N, Pit N*
Managerial Career: *1885; StL N*

Denny McLain
McLain, Dennis Dale
B: Mar 29, 1944

Pos: P
W-L: 131-91   ERA: 3.39
ShOs: 29   SOs: 1,282
                    Saves: 2

One of baseball's tragic figures, McLain had bountiful talent, but held the law in disdain and paid the price. McLain was incarcerated for bookmaking and extortion; he served time in a Federal penitentiary. On the mound McLain used a fastball and sharp breaking curve to lead the AL in wins and innings pitched in 1968 and 1969. He captured the AL Cy Young Award in 1968, the year he won 31 games.
Playing Career: *1963-1972; Det A, Was A, Oak A, Atl N*

Joey McLaughlin
McLaughlin, Joey Richard
B: Jul 11, 1956

Pos: P
W-L: 29-28   ERA: 3.85
ShOs: 0   SOs: 268
                    Saves: 36

Inspired by watching his older brother play ball in Tulsa, Oklahoma, McLaughlin made it to the big leagues. His best season was 1982, when he was 8-6 with 10 saves and posted an ERA of 2.85. McLaughlin was the Blue Jays' saves leader before Tom Henke.
Playing Career: *1977, 1979-1984; Atl N, Tor A, Tex A*

Larry McLean
McLean, John Bannerman
B: Jul 18, 1881   D: Mar 24, 1921

Pos: C
Hits: 694   BA: .262
RBI: 298   HRs: 6
                    BBs: 136

At 6'5" tall, 230 pounds, and often drunk, McLean batted .500 and went on a 6-for-12 hitting rampage in the 1913 World Series for the Giants. But he tried to pick a fight with manager John McGraw outside a St. Louis hotel, and was cut from the squad.
Playing Career: *1901, 1903-1904, 1906-1915; Bos A, Chi N, StL N, Cin N, NY N*

Cal McLish
McLish, Calvin Coolidge Julius Caesar Tuskahoma
B: Dec 1, 1925

Pos: P
W-L: 92-92   ERA: 4.01
ShOs: 5   SOs: 713
                    Saves: 6

Oklahoma Indian McLish is ambidextrous, though he pitched only right-handed in the majors. He moved directly from American Legion ball to the NL with the Dodgers in 1944. A long-time friend of Gene Mauch, McLish served as his pitching coach.
Playing Career: *1944, 1946-1949, 1951, 1956-1964; Brk N, Pit N, Chi N, Cle A, Cin N, Chi A, Phi N*

Don McMahon
McMahon, Donald John
B: Jan 4, 1930   D: Jul 22, 1987

Pos: P
W-L: 90-68   ERA: 2.96
ShOs: 0   SOs: 1,003
                    Saves: 153

When McMahon retired he was fourth on the all-time appearances list. Pitching before bullpen stoppers were common, he never saved more than 19 games in a season. Even so, McMahon led the NL in saves with 15 in 1959, and was selected for the All-Star Game that season. McMahon had ERAs under 2.00 five times, his best being 1.48 with a 4-0 record in 1973 with the Giants. He pitched in one NCLS and three World Series.
Playing Career: *1957-1974; Mil N, Hou N, Cle A, Bos A, Chi A, Det A, SF N*

Sadie McMahon
McMahon, John Joseph
B: Sep 19, 1867   D: Feb 20, 1954

Pos: P
W-L: 175-127   ERA: 3.49
ShOs: 14   SOs: 967
                    Saves: 4

The Athletics traded McMahon, Wilbert Robinson and Curt Welch to the Orioles in 1890. McMahon became the ace of their staff and, with Robinson, comprised the "Dumpling Battery," so named for their plumpness. In 1890 and 1891 McMahon led the league in wins with 36 and 35, and in complete games and innings pitched.
Playing Career: *1889-1897; Phi AA, Bal AA, Bal N, Brk N*

Marty McManus
McManus, Martin Joseph
B: Mar 14, 1900   D: Feb 18, 1966

Pos: 2B, SS, 3B, 1B
Hits: 1,926   BA: .289
RBI: 996   HRs: 120
                    BBs: 674
Managerial Record
Won: 95   Lost: 153   Pct: .383

A great utility infielder, McManus batted over .300 on four occasions. He led the AL in doubles with 44 in 1925, and in stolen bases with 23 in 1930. That year McManus led third basemen in fielding. Twice scoring more than 100 runs, in 1925 and 1926, he tallied 1,008 in his career. McManus was the player-manager of the Red Sox in the dark days before Thomas Yawkey purchased them.
Playing Career: *1920-1934; StL A, Det A, Bos A, Bos N*
Managerial Career: *1932-1933; Bos A*

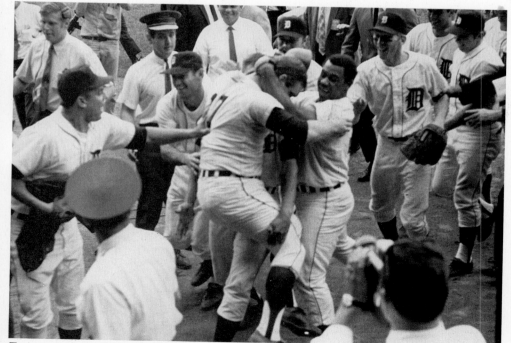
Teammates mob Denny McLain after he won his 30th game of the 1968 season.

Reds shortstop Roy McMillan puts Duke Snider out and fires to first in 1956.

Roy McMillan
McMillan, Roy David
B: Jul 17, 1930

Pos: SS	BA: .243
Hits: 1,639	HRs: 68
RBI: 594	BBs: 665

Managerial Record
Won: 27   Lost: 28   Pct: .491

After 10 years of brilliant play for the Reds, McMillan was traded to the Braves in 1961, and missed Cincinnati's pennant victory. McMillan was a three-time Gold Glove Award winner, 1957-1959, in an era when only one was given for each position in all the major leagues. He was also elected to the NL All-Star squad in 1956 and 1957. McMillan played a streak of 584 consecutive games.
Playing Career: *1951-1966; Cin N, Mil N, NY N*
Managerial Career: *1972, 1975; Mil A, NY N*

Ken McMullen
McMullen, Kenneth Lee
B: Jun 1, 1942

Pos: 3B	BA: .248
Hits: 1,273	HRs: 156
RBI: 606	BBs: 510

Batting guru Ted Williams improved many players' hitting, including McMullen's. His best season was 1972, when he hit .272 and slugged .425, scoring 83 runs and driving in 87. McMullen led AL third sackers in total chances three times, 1967-1969.
Playing Career: *1962-1977; LA N, Was A, Cal A, Oak A, Mil A*

Eric McNair
McNair, Donald Eric
B: Apr 12, 1909   D: Mar 11, 1949

Pos: SS, 3B, 2B, 1B, OF	BA: .274
Hits: 1,240	HRs: 82
RBI: 633	BBs: 261

Discovered by Connie Mack, McNair was heralded as a future star, but struggled to find a position, and never fulfilled the predic-

tion. He played in the 1930 and 1931 World Series as a pinch hitter and runner. In 1932 McNair led the AL in doubles with 47. His best season was 1939 for the White Sox in spacious Comiskey Park, where he hit .324 and slugged .426.
Playing Career: *1929-1942; Phi A, Bos A, Chi A, Det A*

Dave McNally
McNally, David Arthur
B: Oct 31, 1942

Pos: P	ERA: 3.24
W-L: 184-119	SOs: 1,512
ShOs: 33	Saves: 2

McNally successfully sued Major League Baseball to end the reserve clause. After play-ing the 1975 season without a contract, McNally was declared a free agent by arbitrator Peter Seitz. The decision, rejected by the owners for three months, affected the baseball salary structure more than any other single instance since professional baseball began.

McNally was a top AL pitcher. He outdueled Don Drysdale 1-0 in the 1966 World Series to give the Orioles a four-game sweep of the Dodgers, who were loaded with good pitching. McNally won 20 or more games four straight years, including a league-leading 24 in 1970. His winning percentage for the years 1968 to 1971 was .737 on a record of 87-31. In five ALCS McNally was 3-2, and in four World Series, he was 4-2 with a 2.34 ERA. In Game Three of the 1970 Series he became the only hurler ever to hit a grand slam in the Fall Classic.
Playing Career: *1962-1975; Bal A, Mon N*

John McNamara
McNamara, John Francis
B: Jun 4, 1932

Managerial Record
Won: 1,150   Lost: 1,215   Pct: .486

Fired by Charlie Finley in 1970 for being too nice, McNamara had molded the A's into a team that became three-time World Champions, 1972-1974. He later managed in Cincinnati, and won a division title with the Reds in 1979. After bringing the Angels to a second-place finish, he moved on to the Red Sox, where he captured the 1986 AL flag and won honors as Manager of the Year.
Managerial Career: *1969-1970, 1974-1991; Oak A, SD N, Cin N, Cal A, Bos A, Cle A*

Baltimore Orioles pitcher Dave McNally.

Earl McNeely
McNeely, George Earl
B: May 12, 1898   D: Jul 16, 1971

Pos: OF	BA: .272
Hits: 614	HRs: 4
RBI: 213	BBs: 183

Senators owner Clark Griffith paid $40,000 and three players for McNeely, who proved his value in Game Seven of the 1924 World Series. He hit a ground ball that hopped over the third baseman's head, giving the Senators the World Championship.
Playing Career: *1924-1931; Was A, StL A*

Bid McPhee
McPhee, John Alexander
B: Nov 1, 1859   D: Jan 3, 1943

Pos: 2B	BA: .272
Hits: 2,260	HRs: 52
RBI: 727	BBs: 981
Managerial Record	
Won: 79 Lost: 124 Pct: .389	

Some scholars of 19th-century baseball consider McPhee the best player of that era who is not in the Hall of Fame. Although he disdained the use of a glove until late in his career, McPhee compiled fielding statistics that are remarkable, even by the standards of today's game. He led the NL in double plays 11 times, and in fielding average nine times. In 1886 McPhee became the only second baseman to record more than 500 putouts in a season. Only Eddie Collins had more career putouts and total chances, and only Frank Frisch had more total chances in a single season.

When McPhee put on a glove to protect a sore finger in 1896, he compiled a .982 fielding mark, setting a record that stood for 30 years. Though he batted over .300 only twice, he scored more than 100 runs 10 times, 1,684 altogether. He also stole 528 bases, with a high of 95 in 1887. He once smote three triples off Amos Rusie in one game.
Playing Career: *1882-1899; Cin AA, Cin N*
Managerial Career: *1901-1902; Cin N*

George McQuillan
McQuillan, George Watt
B: May 1, 1885   D: May 30, 1940

Pos: P	ERA: 2.38
W-L: 85-89	SOs: 590
ShOs: 17	Saves: 14

McQuillan was a former Phillie standout whom the club called back as pennant insurance in 1915. He won 23 games in 1908, posting ERAs of 1.53, 2.14 and 1.60 from 1908 to 1910. His effectiveness decreased after illness and injuries.
Playing Career: *1907-1911, 1913-1916, 1918; Phi N, Cin N, Pit N, Cle A*

Hugh McQuillan
McQuillan, Hugh A.
B: Sep 15, 1897   D: Aug 26, 1947

Pos: P	ERA: 3.83
W-L: 88-94	SOs: 446
ShOs: 10	Saves: 16

In 1922 the Giants acquired McQuillan late in the season, and like the Yankees, were accused of trying to "buy the pennant." The situation led to the adoption of the June 15 trading deadline. McQuillan appeared in three straight World Series.
Playing Career: *1918-1927; Bos N, NY N*

George McQuinn
McQuinn, George Hartley
B: May 29, 1910   D: Dec 24, 1978

Pos: 1B	BA: .276
Hits: 1,588	HRs: 135
RBI: 794	BBs: 712

For six years, McQuinn was stuck in the Yankees' farm system behind Lou Gehrig. When McQuinn got his chance he hit .324 and .316, scoring 100 and 101 runs in 1938 and 1939. He led the league in fielding three times. McQuinn led the Browns into their only World Series in 1944, batting .438 and slugging .750 in the Fall Classic. The six-time All-Star set All-Star Game records with 14 putouts and 14 total chances in the 1948 contest.
Playing Career: *1936, 1938-1948; Cin N, StL A, Phi A, NY A*

The Royals' Hal McRae, 1981.

Hal McRae
McRae, Harold Abraham
B: Jul 10, 1945

Pos: DH, OF, 3B, 2B	BA: .290
Hits: 2,091	HRs: 191
RBI: 1,097	BBs: 648
Managerial Record	
Won: 222 Lost: 226 Pct: .496	

The term "designated hitter" could have been invented for Hal McRae. Once a promising second baseman whose career was in jeopardy after an accident during a double play, McRae found a home and new career with the Royals. Called "Mr. Ribbie" by his teammates, McRae was named the top designated hitter in the AL five times. A disciple of the Charley Lau school of batting, McRae combined power and average in what the Royals Stadium scoreboard frequently termed a "Big Mac Attack."

McRae played on eight division-winning teams and in four World Series, hitting .400 in 17 Fall Classic games. He was named to three All-Star squads. He led the AL in doubles twice, with 54 in 1977 and 46 in 1982 when he also had 133 RBI. McRae has been a major league coach and manager since his retirement as an active player. His son Brian is the Royals' center fielder.
Playing Career: *1968, 1970-1987; Cin N, KC A*
Managerial Career: *1991-; KC A*

Kevin McReynolds
McReynolds, Walter Kevin
B: Oct 16, 1959

Pos: OF	BA: .266
Hits: 1,393	HRs: 207
RBI: 786	BBs: 502

Quiet and steady, McReynolds was once considered the NL's best left fielder. On the offensive side, he averaged 21 homers and

John Alexander "Bid" McPhee.

81 RBI for the nine years, 1984-1992. He has a good batting eye and has more walks than strikeouts in three of his last four seasons. McReynolds is a streak hitter, prone to long slumps. He hit .300 in the 1984 NLCS to lead the Padres past the Cubs, but missed the World Series with an injury.
Playing Career: *1983-; SD N, NY N, KC A*

Cal McVey
McVey, Calvin Alexander
B: Aug 30, 1850   D: Aug 20, 1926

Pos: OF, C, 1B, 3B, P   BA: .345
Hits: 866   HRs: 13
RBI: 289   BBs: 28
Managerial Record
Won: 90   Lost: 64   Pct: .584

One of the original Red Stockings, McVey played on their undefeated 1869 team that changed America's attitude toward professional baseball. With a strong arm, steady batting eye and sharp reflexes, the versatile McVey was one of baseball's most popular players in the early days. He played on four pennant-winning teams before going to California, where he organized baseball teams and leagues.
Playing Career: *1871-1879; Bos Red Stockings n, Bal Lord Baltimores n, Chi N, Cin N*
Managerial Career: *1873, 1878-1879; Bal Lord Baltimores n, Cin N*

Larry McWilliams
McWilliams, Larry Dean
B: Feb 10, 1954

Pos: P   ERA: 3.99
W-L: 78-90   SOs: 940
ShOs: 13   Saves: 3

McWilliams made the surprising catch that helped end Pete Rose's 44-game hitting streak. McWilliams began his major league career with seven straight victories, but was plagued by arm trouble ever after. He was 15-8 with four shutouts, 199 whiffs and a 3.25 ERA in 1983.
Playing Career: *1978-1990; Atl N, Pit N, StL N, Phi N, KC A*

Lee Meadows
Meadows, Henry Lee (Spec)
B: Jul 12, 1894   D: Jan 29, 1963

Pos: P   ERA: 3.38
W-L: 188-180   SOs: 1,063
ShOs: 25   Saves: 7

Struggling early in his career playing for second-division teams, Meadows lost 20 or more games twice, though he won in double figures every year but 1918. He excelled in Pittsburgh, leading the NL in wins with 20 in 1926. He pitched in the 1925 and 1927 World Series, and led the NL in complete games with 25 in 1927. Meadows was the first major league player to wear eyeglasses since Will White in the 1870s.
Playing Career: *1915-1929; StL N, Phi N, Pit N*

Doc Medich
Medich, George Francis (Doc)
B: Dec 9, 1948

Pos: P   ERA: 3.78
W-L: 124-105   SOs: 955
ShOs: 16   Saves: 2

The day after his major league pitching debut, Medich began medical school at the University of Pittsburgh. He was knocked out of that first game in the first inning, but he went on to a successful baseball career as well as finishing medical school. Medich won 49 games for the Yankees 1973-1975. He led the AL in shutouts during the strike-shortened 1981 season. Medich appeared in the 1982 World Series.
Playing Career: *1972-1982: NY A, Pit N, Oak A, Sea A, NY N, Tex A, Mil A*

Joe Medwick
Medwick, Joseph Michael (Muscles, Ducky Wucky)
B: Nov 24, 1911   D: Mar 21, 1975
Hall of Fame 1968

Pos: OF   BA: .324
Hits: 2,471   HRs: 205
RBI: 1,383   BBs: 437

The last NL batter to win the Triple Crown, Medwick led the league with his .374 average, 31 home runs, and 154 RBI in 1937. He also was named MVP that year. His lifetime statistics include 1,198 runs and 540 doubles. Medwick hit .326 in two World Series. In the 1934 Series, he slid hard into Tigers third baseman Marv Owen, cutting him. The fans were enraged; when Medwick took up his position in left field they pelted him with fruit and trash, stopping Game Seven for more than 20 minutes. Commissioner Landis

Joe "Ducky" Medwick.

ordered Medwick out of the game so that it could continue.

When Medwick was traded to the Dodgers in mid-1941, he badmouthed the Cardinals in the press. The next time the Cardinals played the Dodgers, Medwick suffered a near fatal beaning by his former teammate Bob Bowman. The resulting beanball war escalated until the Dodgers took to wearing helmet-like cap inserts for protection – the first NL team to do so.
Playing Career: *1932-1948; StL N, Brk N, NY N, Bos N*

Jouett Meekin
Meekin, Jouett
B: Feb 21, 1867   D: Dec 14, 1944

Pos: P   ERA: 4.07
W-L: 153-133   SOs: 900
ShOs: 9   Saves: 2

A successful NL hurler known for one extraordinary season, Meekin endured dismal records in his first three years. He was traded to the Giants and exploded in 1894, compiling a 33-9 record with a 3.70 ERA, yet finishing second in the league to teammate Amos Rusie, who won 36 games. The Giants finished in second place and wiped out the Orioles in four straight contests for the Temple Cup Championship.
Playing Career: *1891-1900; Lou AA, Lou N, Was N, NY N, Bos N, Pit N*

Heinie Meine
Meine, Henry William
B: May 1, 1896   D: Mar 8, 1968

Pos: P   ERA: 3.95
W-L: 66-50   SOs: 199
ShOs: 7   Saves: 3

The spitball was his best pitch, but Meine made it to the majors after the wet one was outlawed in 1920. He returned to the minors where the pitch was still allowed. He left baseball altogether in 1927, and operated a tavern in St. Louis. Convinced by his bar patrons to try his hand at baseball again, Meine went to the NL as a junkball pitcher. In 1931 he led the league in wins with 19, and innings pitched with 284.
Playing Career: *1922, 1929-1934; StL A, Pit N*

Sam Mele
Mele, Sabath Anthony
B: Jan 23, 1923

Pos: OF, 1B   BA: .267
Hits: 916   HRs: 80
RBI: 544   BBs: 311
Managerial Record
Won: 524   Lost: 436   Pct: .546

A New York University basketball star in the 1940s, Mele chose baseball for a career. He managed the new Minnesota Twins to the AL pennant in 1965. They lost the World Series to the veteran Dodgers, but getting to the Series was a milestone achievement. Mele had

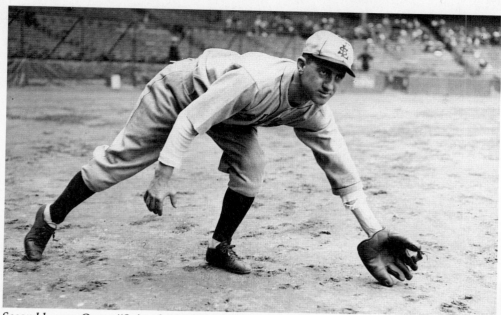

Second bagger Oscar "Spinach" Melillo of the St. Louis Browns.

some home run power during his playing career, and he led the AL doubles with 36 in 1951.
Playing Career: *1947-1956; Bos A, Was A, Chi A, Bal A, Cin N, Cle A*
Managerial Career: *1961-1967; Min A*

Oscar Melillo
Melillo, Oscar Donald (Spinach)
B: Aug 4, 1899   D: Nov 14, 1963

Pos: 2B	BA: .260
Hits: 1,316	HRs: 22
RBI: 548	BBs: 327

Managerial Record
Won: 2   Lost: 7   Pct: .222

Suffering from Bright's disease, Melillo was under doctor's orders to eat spinach every day, and the infielder assumed the name of his constant vegetable companion. One of the better fielding second sackers in the AL, Melillo played more than 98 games a season for 10 of 12 years. At his best in 1931, he batted .306 with 34 doubles, scored 88 runs, and had a .407 slugging average.
Playing Career: *1926-1937; StL A, Bos A*
Managerial Career: *1938; StL A*

Bill Melton
Melton, William Edwin
B: Jul 7, 1945

Pos: 3B	BA: .253
Hits: 1,004	HRs: 160
RBI: 591	BBs: 479

Once a feared home run slugger, Melton was the White Sox career leader when he retired. A herniated disc caused him to miss most of the 1972 season, disrupting his string of five 20-homer seasons in six years. Melton was an All-Star in 1971.
Playing Career: *1968-1977; Chi A, Cal A, Cle A*

Cliff Melton
Melton, Clifford George (Mountain Music, Mickey Mouse)
B: Jan 3, 1912   D: Jul 28, 1986

Pos: P	ERA: 3.42
W-L: 86-80	SOs: 660
ShOs: 13	Saves: 16

Melton won 20 games and led the NL in shutouts in his rookie year, helping the Giants to the World Series in 1937. He had been in the Yankees' system, but could not handle razzing about his country heritage and big ears.
Playing Career: *1937-1944; NY N*

Mario Mendoza
Mendoza y Aizpuru, Mario
B: Dec 26, 1950

Pos: SS	BA: .215
Hits: 287	HRs: 4
RBI: 101	BBs: 52

In regard to a hitting slump, Johnny Bench said he checked regularly to be sure he was above Mendoza in the batting averages. The mythical line is .200. In five of nine seasons, Mendoza himself fell below it. But he made it to the 1974 NLCS.
Playing Career: *1974-1982; Pit N, Sea A, Tex A*

Jock Menefee
Menefee, John
B: Jan 15, 1868   D: Mar 11, 1953

Pos: P	ERA: 3.81
W-L: 58-70	SOs: 293
ShOs: 8	No-hitters: 0

Menefee played the outfield and pitched for the turn-of-the-century NL Chicagos under Frank Selee. He became a solid starter for what would become a blue ribbon staff.

Menefee's best year was 1902, when he was 12-10 with a 2.42 ERA.
Playing Career: *1892-1895, 1898, 1900-1903; Pit N, Lou N, NY N, Chi N*

Denis Menke
Menke, Denis John
B: Jul 21, 1940

Pos: SS, 2B, 3B, 1B, OF	BA: .250
Hits: 1,270	HRs: 101
RBI: 606	BBs: 698

In the 1972 World Series, Menke walloped a home run off Catfish Hunter. It was a fitting climax to a 13-year career that included two trips to the All-Star Game. Menke played a vital role on the 1969 Astros team that competed for the NL pennant.
Playing Career: *1962-1974; Mil N, Atl N, Hou N, Cin N*

Denis Menke (sliding).

Mike Menosky
Menosky, Michael William
B: Oct 16, 1894   D: Apr 11, 1983

Pos: OF	BA: .278
Hits: 685	HRs: 18
RBI: 250	BBs: 295

Menosky was a gung-ho player who frequently crashed against outfield fences. Acquired by Boston just 17 days after they sold Babe Ruth to the Yankees, Menosky was supposed to fill the void left by Ruth. He batted .297, .300 and .283, but had no power.
Playing Career: *1914-1917, 1919-1923; Pit F, Was A, Bos A*

Win Mercer
Mercer, George Barclay
B: Jun 20, 1874   D: Jan 12, 1903

Pos: P	ERA: 3.98
W-L: 131-164	SOs: 525
ShOs: 11	Saves: 9

The peak of Mercer's career came in 1896 and 1897 when he won 25, then 20 games. Mercer was appointed manager of the Tigers after the 1902 season. He checked himself into a San Francisco hotel and committed suicide by inhaling poison gas, leaving a note about evil women and gambling.
Playing Career: *1894-1902; Was N, NY N, Was A, Det A*

First baseman Fred Merkle.

Fred Merkle
Merkle, Frederick Charles
B: Dec 20, 1888   D: Mar 2, 1956

Pos: 1B   BA: .273
Hits: 1,580   HRs: 61
RBI: 733   BBs: 454

As a rookie, Merkle became the focus of one of the most controversial rulings ever to come out of the NL office. On what appeared to be the last play of a 2-1 Giants victory, Merkle, the runner on first base, followed the practice of the day and headed for the dugout rather than touching second base. Cubs second baseman Johnny Evers called for the ball, tagged second, and appealed to umpire Hank O'Day, who called Merkle out. The decision was protested but NL President Harry Pulliam upheld O'Day's call. The rookie was unfairly labelled a bonehead by the press, and in fact, the incident is still known as the Merkle Boner. To his credit, Merkle settled into a respectable career after such an infamous beginning. He hit 290 doubles and stole 272 bases during his career. Merkle played in five World Series for three different teams, the Giants, Dodgers and Cubs.
Playing Career: *1907-1920, 1925-1926; NY N, Brk N, Chi N, NY A*

Jim Merritt
Merritt, James Joseph
B: Dec 9, 1943

Pos: P   ERA: 3.65
W-L: 81-86   SOs: 932
ShOs: 9   Saves: 7

Backed by Cincinnati's offensive power and supported by the bullpen, Merritt led the staff in 1969 and 1970 with 17-9 and 20-12 records. The following year, he plummeted to 1-11, and ended his career before the age of 30 due to arm trouble.
Playing Career: *1965-1975; Min A, Cin N, Tex A*

Sam Mertes
Mertes, Samuel Blair (Sandow)
B: Aug 6, 1872   D: Mar 11, 1945

Pos: OF   BA: .279
Hits: 1,227   HRs: 40
RBI: 721   BBs: 422

Mertes was the slugger for John McGraw's Giants in the early years of the 20th century. He led the league with 32 doubles and 104 RBI in 1903. Mertes drove in 108 runs for the 1905 Giants, and three more in the World Series.
Playing Career: *1896, 1898-1906; Phi N, Chi N, Chi A, NY N, StL N*

Andy Messersmith
Messersmith, John Alexander
B: Aug 6, 1945

Pos: P   ERA: 2.86
W-L: 130-99   SOs: 1,625
ShOs: 27   Saves: 15

In a monumental struggle between labor and management, Messersmith sued Major League Baseball and set the scene for free agency. Messersmith and Dave McNally had played the 1975 season without contracts in their so-called option years. The two men

Andy Messersmith in action, 1970.

and the Players' Union contended that the reserve clause bound them to their contracts plus one additional year, but no more. Owners insisted that the reserve clause was automatic and perpetual. Arbitrator Peter Seitz ruled in favor of the players, and a new era was inaugurated.

When Messersmith challenged the reserve clause he was coming off a strong 1974 season. He was 20-6 with a 2.59 ERA, leading the NL in winning percentage and tying in wins. He won Gold Glove Awards in 1974 and 1975, and was selected for the All-Star team three times.
Playing Career: *1968-1979; Cal A, LA N, Atl N, NY A*

Catfish Metkovich
Metkovich, George Michael
B: Oct 8, 1921

Pos: 1B, OF   BA: .261
Hits: 934   HRs: 47
RBI: 373   BBs: 307

After a fishing accident involving a hook, Casey Stengel nicknamed Metkovich "Catfish." He batted .277 with a 25-game hitting streak in 1944, while replacing Ted Williams in left field. Metkovich hit .500 in the 1946 World Series.
Playing Career: *1943-1947, 1949, 1951-1954; Bos A, Cle A, Chi A, Pit N, Chi N, Mil N*

Roger Metzger
Metzger, Roger Henry
B: Oct 10, 1947

Pos: SS   BA: .231
Hits: 972   HRs: 5
RBI: 254   BBs: 355

A Gold Glove honoree in 1973, Metzger was at home in the Astrodome, leading the NL twice in triples and twice in fielding. His fielding percentage went down following a trade to windswept, rocky Candlestick Park in 1978.
Playing Career: *1970-1980; Chi N, Hou N, SF N*

Bob Meusel
Meusel, Robert William (Long Bob, the Rifle)
B: Jul 19, 1896   D: Nov 28, 1977

Pos: OF   BA: .309
Hits: 1,693   HRs: 156
RBI: 1,067   BBs: 375

Commissioner Landis wanted to stop major leaguers from barnstorming with amateurs in the off-season, so he singled out Meusel and Babe Ruth for punishment. Their 1921 World Series checks were withheld and both players were suspended for the first 39 days of the 1922 season. Meusel, the 1925 AL home run and RBI champ, led the Yankees in stolen bases five times. Meusel had an excellent arm; he tied a record with four outfield assists in one game.
Playing Career: *1920-1930; NY A, Cin N*

Bob and Irish Meusel and Tony Lazzeri on the set of **Slide, Kelly, Slide** *(1927).*

Irish Meusel
Meusel, Emil Frederick
B: Jun 9, 1893   D: Mar 1, 1963

Pos: OF	BA: .310
Hits: 1,521	HRs: 106
RBI: 819	BBs: 269

The older brother of Bob Meusel, Irish batted cleanup for the 1921-1924 Giants, who won four pennants in a row. The siblings went head to head in the 1921-1923 World Series. Irish outhit Bob, but not by much. Nicknamed for his Celtic features, Irish spent the best years of his career with John McGraw and the Giants. He had more than 100 RBI every year from 1922 to 1925, with a career-high 132 in 1922, and a league-high 125 in 1923.
Playing Career: *1914, 1918-1927; Was A, Phi N, NY N, Brk N*

Billy Meyer
Meyer, William Adam
B: Jan 14, 1892   D: Mar 31, 1957

Pos: C	BA: .236
Hits: 71	HRs: 1
RBI: 21	BBs: 15
Managerial Record	
Won: 317 Lost: 452 Pct: .412	

Meyer began his big league career with brief stints as a White Sox and A's backstop. A very successful minor league manager, Meyer spent 16 years in the Yankees' organization, winning 1,605 games – and nine pennants – and losing 1,325 contests. Branch Rickey brought Meyer in to teach the young Pirates in the early 1950s.
Playing Career: *1913, 1916-1917; Chi A, Phi A*
Managerial Career: *1948-1952; Pit N*

Dan Meyer
Meyer, Daniel Thomas
B: Aug 3, 1952

Pos: 1B, 3B, OF	BA: .253
Hits: 944	HRs: 86
RBI: 459	BBs: 220

One of the Mariners' first hitting stars was Meyer, who belted 22 home runs in 1977 and 20 in 1979. He had been a minor league batting champ in the Tigers' system, but never hit for average at the major league level.
Playing Career: *1974-1985; Det A, Sea A, Oak A*

Russ Meyer
Meyer, Russell Charles (Mad Monk)
B: Oct 25, 1923

Pos: P	ERA: 3.99
W-L: 94-73	SOs: 672
ShOs: 13	Saves: 5

Meyer had an explosive temper; he once took off his spikes and stuck them on the shower ceiling. He won 17 games with the 1949 Phillies and was 15-5 for the NL champion Dodgers in 1953. Meyer also played for the 1955 World Champion Dodgers.
Playing Career: *1946-1957, 1959; Chi N, Phi N, Brk N, Cin N, Bos A, KC A*

Levi Meyerle
Meyerle, Levi Samuel (Long Levi)
B: Jul 1845   D: Nov 4, 1921

Pos: 3B, OF, SS, 2B	BA: .358
Hits: 516	HRs: 10
RBI: 176	BBs: 10

Known as the first Jewish major leaguer, and as the tallest player of his day, Meyerle was neither. Long Levi was not Jewish, and there were several contemporary ballplayers taller than he, including Al Spalding, Nat Hicks and Ev Mills. Meyerle was an extraordinary hitter, but a poor fielder. He led the Athletics in the decisive game of the year for the 1871 pennant, in what was – for Meyerle – a typical performance of three hits and one error.

That year he won the National Association batting title with the highest average ever, .496, slugged .700 and had an on-base average of .500, but fielded at the rate of .654. Despite winning the batting title Meyerle lost his job at the hot corner. Playing for the Chicago White Stockings on May 16, 1874, Meyerle made six errors at third base. He won the batting title that year with a .403 average.
Playing Career: *1871-1877, 1884; Phi Athletics n, Phi White Stockings n, Chi White Stockings n, Phi N, Cin N, Phi U*

Chief Meyers
Meyers, John Tortes
B: Jul 29, 1880   D: Jul 25, 1971

Pos: C	BA: .291
Hits: 826	HRs: 14
RBI: 363	BBs: 274

A Cahuilla Indian from California, educated at Dartmouth, Meyers did not play in the major leagues until he was 29 years old. He batted .290 in four World Series for the Giants and Dodgers. Meyers was batterymate to three Hall of Fame pitchers: Christy Mathewson, Rube Marquard and Jack Coombs. The Giants won three straight pennants, 1911-1913, with Meyers behind the plate. He batted well over .300 in those years, peaking at .358 in 1912.

Meyers was involved in the controversial finish to the 1912 World Series when Tris Speaker raised a pop foul toward the Giants' first baseman Fred Merkle, but pitcher Mathewson called, "Meyers, Meyers," for the play. He raced for it in vain. Given a re-

Chief Meyers (r) with Rube Marquard.

prieve, Speaker lined a single to right, tying the game at 2-2 in the 10th inning. The Giants lost the game and the World Series on a sacrifice fly later in the inning. After six straight seasons catching more than 100 games, Meyers retired at age 37.
Playing Career: *1909-1917; NY N, Brk N, Bos N*

Gene Michael
Michael, Eugene Richard (Stick)
B: June 2, 1938

Pos: SS   BA: .229
Hits: 642   HRs: 15
RBI: 226   BBs: 234
Managerial Record
Won: 206   Lost: 200   Pct: .507

A basketball star at Kent State University, Michael was dubbed "Stick" because of his linear appearance. Rejecting the hoops in favor of baseball, Michael found a home at Yankee Stadium, where he started at shortstop from 1969 to 1973. He had extraordinary range and a steady glove. He worked his way through the Yankee system as manager, coach and finally general manager under George Steinbrenner.
Playing Career: *1966-1975; Pit N, LA N, NY A, Det A*
Managerial Career: *1981-1982, 1986-1987; NY A, Chi N*

Cass Michaels
Michaels, Casimir Eugene
B: Mar 4, 1926   D: Nov 12, 1982

Pos: 2B, 3B, SS   BA: .262
Hits: 1,142   HRs: 53
RBI: 501   BBs: 566

At age 17, Michaels began his major league career under his original name, Casimir Eugene Kwietniewski. From shortstop he moved to second to make room for Luke Appling. Michaels made the All-Star squad in 1949 and 1950.
Playing Career: *1943-1954; Chi A, Was A, StL A, Phi A*

Pete Mikkelsen
Mikkelsen, Peter James
B: Oct 25, 1939

Pos: P   ERA: 3.38
W-L: 45-40   SOs: 436
ShOs: 0   Saves: 49

As a rookie sinkerball pitcher, Mikkelsen served up Tim McCarver's 10th-inning three-run homer in Game Five of the 1964 World Series. Mikkelsen's best year came two seasons later, when the Pirate reliever won nine games and saved 14.
Playing Career: *1964-1972; NY A, Pit N, Chi N, StL N, LA N*

Eddie Miksis
Miksis, Edward Thomas
B: Sep 11, 1926

Pos: 3B, SS, 2B, OF   BA: .236
Hits: 722   HRs: 44
RBI: 228   BBs: 215

Running for Pete Reiser in Game Four of the 1947 World Series, Miksis scored the Dodgers' winning run. Cookie Lavagetto ripped the two-out ninth-inning double that ended Bill Bevens's bid for the first World Series no-hitter, and drove in Miksis.
Playing Career: *1944, 1946-1958; Brk N, Chi N, StL N, Bal A, Cin N*

Clyde Milan
Milan, Jesse Clyde (Deerfoot)
B: Mar 25, 1887   D: Mar 3, 1953

Pos: OF   BA: .285
Hits: 2,100   HRs: 17
RBI: 617   BBs: 685
Managerial Record
Won: 69   Lost: 85   Pct: .448

The AL stolen base record that Ty Cobb broke in 1915 had been set by Milan. He stole 495 bases altogether. Senators owner Clark Griffith claimed that Milan was the best center fielder in Washington baseball history. He played shallow, using his speed to go back for fly balls hit deep. Griffith found Milan on the same scouting trip to the Northwest that netted Walter Johnson. The two players were roommates for 15 years.

Milan was the Senators' player-manager in 1922 but was considered too easygoing. He managed in the minors until 1937, when he returned to Washington as a coach. While hitting fungoes in spring training, Milan suffered a fatal heart attack. His brother Horace played outfield for the Senators in 1915 and 1917.
Playing Career: *1907-1922; Was A*
Managerial Career: *1922; Was A*

Larry Milbourne
Milbourne, Lawrence William
B: Feb 14, 1951

Pos: 2B, 3B, SS, DH   BA: .254
Hits: 623   HRs: 11
RBI: 184   BBs: 133

A part-time utility player, Milbourne hit .462 in the 1981 ALCS as a substitute for the Yankees' injured shortstop Bucky Dent. He had starred in the divisional playoff versus the Brewers. Milbourne also played in the World Series.
Playing Career: *1974-1984; Hou N, Sea A, NY A, Min A, Cle A, Phi N*

Felix Millan
Millan y Martinez, Felix Bernardo
B: Aug 21, 1943

Pos: 2B   BA: .279
Hits: 1,617   HRs: 22
RBI: 403   BBs: 318

Clyde Milan, outfielder for the Washington Senators, in 1916.

Signed by the Athletics in Puerto Rico in 1964, Millan was drafted by the Braves before he ever wore an A's uniform. He filled the void at second base in Atlanta in 1968. In 1970 Millan hit a career-high .310 and had a 6-for-6 game. He was an All-Star selection for three years, 1969-1971. Millan was the toughest batter in the NL to strike out from 1973 to 1975, the year he compiled a 19-game hitting streak. He hit .323 in two NLCS.

Playing Career: *1966-1977; Atl N, NY N*

Bing Miller
Miller, Edmund John
B: Aug 30, 1894   D: May 7, 1966

Pos: OF	BA: .312
Hits: 1,936	HRs: 116
RBI: 990	BBs: 383

There was always a bit of confusion about where Miller should be playing ball. Both the Senators and Pirates signed him as a 16-year-old; Commissioner Landis had to decide which team Miller should play with. He was later involved in the famed Jumping Joe Dugan three-way trade. Later still, Miller was swapped even-up for Baby Doll Jacobson, but Manager Connie Mack realized his mistake and reacquired the outfielder 18 months later.

Miller hit .368 in the 1929 World Series, driving in the winning run in the dramatic 10-run seventh inning of Game Four. He led the AL in pinch hits in 1934 and 1935. He scored 946 runs and whacked 389 doubles. A contact hitter, Miller struck out only 340 times in 6,212 at-bats. After retiring from active play, Miller coached for the Red Sox and Tigers, then for the White Sox and Athletics with his good friend Jimmy Dykes.

Playing Career: *1921-1936; Was A, Phi A, StL A, Bos A*

Bob Miller
Miller, Robert John
B: Jun 16, 1926

Pos: P	ERA: 3.96
W-L: 42-42	SOs: 263
ShOs: 6	Saves: 15

In 1950, his rookie year with the Phillies, Miller injured his back when he stumbled while carrying a suitcase. His promising year finished at 11-6. He pitched in the World Series for the Whiz Kids, then went to the bullpen in 1955.

Playing Career: *1949-1958; Phi N*

Bob Miller
Miller, Robert Lane (R.B.)
B: Feb 18, 1939

Pos: P	ERA: 3.37
W-L: 69-81	SOs: 895
ShOs: 0	Saves: 52

Among 17 years and 12 trades Miller was best known for the 1962 season that he spent with the original Mets. He was 1-12 for the worst team in the 20th century. Fans confused him with another pitcher named Robert (Bob) Miller; they even roomed together.

Playing Career: *1957, 1959-1974; StL N, NY N, LA N, Min A, Cle A, Chi A, Chi N, SD N, Pit N, Det A*

Doc Miller
Miller, Roy Oscar
B: 1883   D: Jul 31, 1938

Pos: OF	BA: .295
Hits: 507	HRs: 12
RBI: 235	BBs: 121

Canadian-born Miller hit .333 with 36 doubles and an NL-leading 192 hits in 1911, losing the batting title to Honus Wagner by only one percentage point. Miller lost his regular position due to poor fielding. He stole 32 bases in 1911.

Playing Career: *1910-1914; Chi N, Bos N, Phi N, Cin N*

Doggie Miller
Miller, George Frederick (Foghorn, Calliope)
B: Aug 15, 1864   D: Apr 6, 1909

Pos: C, OF, 3B, 2B	BA: .267
Hits: 1,380	HRs: 33
RBI: 518	BBs: 467
Managerial Record	
Won: 56 Lost: 76 Pct: .424	

One of the leading proponents of "foghorn" coaching, Miller would stand near the on-deck circle and harass opposing catchers and umpires into making mistakes. Miller's best season was 1894, when the NL league batting average jumped 29 points and the batting champ's average shot up 60 points. Miller's average was .339 with 11 triples that year. He scored 839 runs and stole 225 bases in his career.

Playing Career: *1884-1896; Pit AA, Pit N, StL N, Lou N*
Managerial Career: *1894; StL N*

Dots Miller.

Dots Miller
Miller, John Barney
B: Sep 9, 1886   D: Sep 5, 1923

Pos: 2B, 1B, SS	BA: .263
Hits: 1,526	HRs: 32
RBI: 715	BBs: 391

A rookie surprise, Miller pushed the Pirates over the top to win the 1909 pennant – the only flag not won by the Cubs from 1906 to 1910. He went to the Cardinals in a five-players-for-three trade, one of the biggest deals in the NL up to that time. The Pirates dropped out of sight, but the Cardinals fought the Giants for the 1914 pennant until both fell to the charging Braves. Miller managed San Francisco to the 1922 Pacific Coast League championship.

Playing Career: *1909-1917, 1919-1921; Pit N, StL N, Phi N*

A's outfielder Bing Miller, 1929.

Dusty Miller
Miller, Charles Bradley
B: Sep 10, 1868   D: Sep 3, 1945

Pos: OF	BA: .301
Hits: 769	HRs: 22
RBI: 411 (inc.)	BBs: 174

Born in the Pennsylvania boom town, Oil City, Miller played semipro, minor league and part-time major league ball until 1895, when the Reds put him in their outfield, where he hit everything in sight. He hit over .300 each of his first three seasons in Cincinnati. In his seven-year career, Miller stole 206 bases and scored 444 runs, but had trouble catching the ball.
Playing Career: *1889-1890, 1895-1899; Bal AA, StL AA, Cin N, StL N*

Eddie Miller
Miller, Edward Robert (Eppie)
B: Nov 26, 1916

Pos: SS, 2B	BA: .238
Hits: 1,270	HRs: 97
RBI: 640	BBs: 351

A contemporary of Marty Marion, Miller was a slick-fielding shortstop who made the NL All-Star team seven times, 1940-1947. There was no All-Star Game in 1945. Miller led the NL in fielding five of six years. He led the NL with 38 doubles in 1947.
Playing Career: *1936-1937, 1939-1950; Cin N, Bos N, Phi N, StL N*

Frank Miller
Miller, Frank Lee (Bullet)
B: Mar 13, 1886   D: Aug 20, 1975

Pos: P	ERA: 3.01
W-L: 52-66	SOs: 359
ShOs: 14	Saves: 4

After striking out 265 batters in the 1909 Western League and 279 in the Pacific Coast League in 1912, Miller was nicknamed "Bullet." He pitched an average of 190 innings a year for the Pirates and Braves. He was the ace of Boston's hapless 1922 staff with an 11-13 record.
Playing Career: *1913, 1916-1919, 1922-1923; Chi A, Pit N, Bos N*

Jake Miller
Miller, Jacob Walter
B: Feb 28, 1898   D: Aug 20, 1975

Pos: P	ERA: 4.09
W-L: 60-58	SOs: 305
ShOs: 8	Saves: 3

Fourth or fifth in the Indians' starting rotation, Miller led their 1927 staff with a 3.21 ERA. He was frequently injured, and had an odd record of winning 10 or more games every other season, 1925, 1927 and 1929. His best season was 1927, when he was 10-8 with a 3.21 ERA.
Playing Career: *1924-1931, 1933; Cle A, Chi A*

Players' union director Marvin Miller.

Marvin Miller
Miller, Marvin Julian
B: Apr 14, 1917

Trained as an economist, Miller became a labor leader, and had as much influence on baseball as Babe Ruth in his heyday. Hired by the players in 1966, Miller was faced with a union that was controlled by management, yet represented the product by which management achieved wealth. Coming from the tough steelworkers' union, Miller's knowledge, organizational ability, and resolve completely overmatched baseball team owners and their representatives, particularly Commissioners Spike Eckert and Bowie Kuhn.

Miller's tough tactics finally got the players not only a "bigger piece of the pie," but also greater respect. Miller found himself in charge of a union whose rank-and-file understood little about labor/management conflicts. His most difficult task was to prevent players from signing away hard-earned Basic Agreement rights in private contractual arrangements. He came to be revered by ballplayers. By his retirement in 1984, Miller had built the strongest, most successful union in the history of labor/management bargaining.

Otto Miller
Miller, Lowell Otto (Moonie)
B: Jun 1, 1889   D: Mar 29, 1962

Pos: C	BA: .245
Hits: 695	HRs: 5
RBI: 231	BBs: 104

Miller was the Dodgers' starting catcher for a decade. He peaked in 1920 with a .289 batting average and a league-leading .986 fielding

Dodgers catcher Otto Miller.

average. In the World Series, Miller blundered into Wambsganss for the third out of an unassisted triple play.
Playing Career: *1910-1922; Brk N*

Rick Miller
Miller, Richard Alan
B: Apr 19, 1948

Pos: OF	BA: .269
Hits: 1,046	HRs: 28
RBI: 369	BBs: 454

Mostly a part-time player in Boston, Miller signed with California for the 1978 season, and played regularly, winning a Gold Glove Award. The next year, he batted .293 as leadoff man for the 1979 AL West Champion Angels.
Playing Career: *1971-1985; Bos A, Cal A*

Stu Miller
Miller, Stuart Leonard
B: Dec 26, 1927

Pos: P	ERA: 3.24
W-L: 105-103	SOs: 1,164
ShOs: 5	Saves: 154

Little Stu Miller was the pitcher who was blown off the mound during the 1961 All-Star Game at windswept Candlestick Park. Miller was NL Fireman of the Year that season, leading the league in relief wins and saves. He posted a 0.00 ERA in the 1962 World Series for the Giants, then led the AL in saves the following year with Baltimore. Miller also pitched a combination no-hitter with Steve Barber in 1967.
Playing Career: *1952-1954, 1956-1968; StL N, Phi N, NY N, SF N, Bal A, Atl N*

Ward Miller
Miller, Ward Taylor (Grump, Windy)
B: Jul 5, 1884   D: Sep 4, 1958

Pos: OF	BA: .278
Hits: 623	HRs: 8
RBI: 221	BBs: 318

A good hitter, but a poor fielder, Miller had a .327 lifetime batting average as a left-handed pinch hitter. He stole 128 bases. Miller's best seasons were as the starting left fielder for the St. Louis Federal League franchise.
Playing Career: *1909-1910, 1912-1917; Pit N, Cin N, Chi N, StL F, StL A*

Jocko Milligan
Milligan, John
B: Aug 8, 1861   D: Aug 29, 1923

Pos: C	BA: .286
Hits: 848	HRs: 50
RBI: 363 (inc.)	BBs: 210

As a rookie in 1884, Milligan led AA receivers in fielding. He batted .303 in 1891 and led the league in doubles with 35. Milligan once socked four doubles in a Sunday game in Brooklyn. He hit .400 in the 1888 postseason championship series.
Playing Career: *1884-1893; Phi AA, StL AA, Phi P, Was N, Bal N, NY N*

Giants pitcher Stu Miller.

Randy Milligan
Milligan, Randy Andre
B: Nov 27, 1961

Pos: 1B	BA: .262
Hits: 534	HRs: 68
RBI: 272	BBs: 433

Acquired by the Reds in 1993 as a backup, Milligan was thrust into a starting role when Hal Morris went down. Milligan was traded to Cleveland midseason, where he hit .426. He is known for a good eye at the plate, walking more than he strikes out.
Playing Career: *1987-; NY N, Pit N, Bal A, Cin N, Cle A*

Cleveland pitcher Al Milnar, 1938.

Al Milnar
Milnar, Albert Joseph
B: Dec 26, 1913

Pos: P	ERA: 4.22
W-L: 57-58	SOs: 350
ShOs: 10	Saves: 7

As second banana to Bob Feller, Milnar pitched more than 200 innings a year, 1939-1942. He won 18 games in 1940, and led the AL in shutouts. Milnar suffered control problems, however, walking more batters than he struck out almost every year.
Playing Career: *1936, 1938-1943, 1946; Cle A, StL A, Phi N*

Eddie Milner
Milner, Edward James
B: May 21, 1955

Pos: OF	BA: .253
Hits: 607	HRs: 42
RBI: 195	BBs: 286

The only year Milner left the Reds' system, he played in the NLCS with the Giants in 1987. Surehanded and speedy, he stole 145 bases, 41 in 1983 alone. Milner hit 15 homers and put together a 20-game hitting streak in 1986.
Playing Career: *1980-1988; Cin N, SF N*

John Milner
Milner, John David (The Hammer)
B: Dec 28, 1949

Pos: 1B, OF	BA: .249
Hits: 855	HRs: 131
RBI: 498	BBs: 504

The ultimate pinch-hitting achievement is a grand slam home run, and Milner accomplished it twice, in 1979 and 1982. He belted 10 grand slams altogether, including three for the Mets in 1976. In two World Series Milner batted .306. Eddie Milner is John's cousin.
Playing Career: *1971-1982; NY N, Pit N, Mon N*

Don Mincher
Mincher, Donald Ray
B: Jun 24, 1938

Pos: 1B	BA: .249
Hits: 1,003	HRs: 200
RBI: 643	BBs: 606

A two-time All-Star, Minch was a power hitter for the pennant-winning 1965 Twins. In the 1972 World Series for the A's, Mincher slashed a single in the ninth inning of Game Four, driving in the tying run for his last big league at-bat.
Playing Career: *1960-1972; Was A, Min A, Cal A, Sea A, Oak A, Tex A*

Steve Mingori
Mingori, Stephen Bernard
B: Feb 29, 1944

Pos: P	ERA: 3.04
W-L: 18-33	SOs: 329
ShOs: 0	Saves: 42

Popular Mingori pitched in three ALCS for the Royals, recording one save and posting a 4.32 ERA. Using a tough screwball, he once retired 16 Red Sox batters in a row. In 1971 Mingori recorded a 1.43 ERA in 54 appearances for the Indians.
Playing Career: *1970-1979; Cle A, KC A*

Paul Minner
Minner, Paul Edison (Tall Paul, Lefty)
B: Jul 30, 1923

Pos: P	ERA: 3.94
W-L: 69-84	SOs: 481
ShOs: 9	Saves: 10

In the late innings of Game Five of the 1949 World Series, the stadium lights were turned on at Ebbets Field, and Minner became the first to pitch under lights in the Fall Classic. A severe back injury in 1956 ended his career.
Playing Career: *1946, 1948-1956; Brk N, Chi N*

Minnie Minoso (c), 1951.

Minnie Minoso
Minoso y Arrieta, Saturnino Orestes Armas
B: Nov 29, 1922

Pos: OF, 3B	BA: .298
Hits: 1,963	HRs: 186
RBI: 1,023	BBs: 814

After playing with the New York Cubans in the Negro Leagues, Minoso graced the major leagues for 16 years. He batted .326 as a rookie, leading the AL in triples and stolen bases, the first of three times he would lead in both categories. Minoso was chosen for the All-Star Game squad six times and he was honored with three Gold Glove Awards. He scored 1,136 runs and stole 205 bases. In 16 AL seasons, Minoso was hit by a pitch 189 times. He led the AL in Hit by Pitch six consecutive seasons – still a league record.

The White Sox' first African-American player, Minoso was traded to Cleveland for Early Wynn and Al Smith in 1958. In 1964 Minoso retired from baseball. Or did he? There were eight at-bats in 1976, and two pinch-hit at-bats in 1980. Minoso had an appearance planned for 1990, at age 67, but Commissioner Francis Vincent, Jr. prevented it. He batted in the independent Northern League in 1993.
Playing Career: *1949, 1951-1964, 1976, 1980; Cle A, Chi A, StL N, Was A*

Greg Minton
Minton, Gregory Brian
B: Jul 29, 1951

Pos: P	ERA: 3.10
W-L: 59-65	SOs: 479
ShOs: 0	Saves: 150

A sinkerball-throwing reliever, Minton made the NL All-Star team in 1982, the year he won 10 games and saved 30 with a 1.83 ERA. In 1983 he and Gary Lavelle became the first NL teammates to save 20 games apiece in a season. After undergoing elbow surgery before the 1987 season, Minton was released by the Giants in May. He signed with the Angels five days later, saved 10 games and remained a star reliever throughout the 1980s.
Playing Career: *1975-1990; SF N, Cal A*

Clarence Mitchell
Mitchell, Clarence Elmer
B: Feb 22, 1891   D: Nov 6, 1963

Pos: P	ERA: 4.12
W-L: 125-139	SOs: 543
ShOs: 12	Saves: 9

It was Mitchell who lined into Bill Wambsganss's famous unassisted triple play in the 1920 World Series. To top off the day, in his next at-bat Mitchell hit into a double play, accounting for five outs in two at-bats. He was 0-0 with a 0.00 ERA for that World Series. Mitchell was otherwise a fine pitcher with an 18-year major league career. At the age of 40 in 1931, he posted 13 victories for the Giants.
Playing Career: *1911, 1916-1932; Det A, Cin N, Brk N, Phi N, StL N, NY N*

Dale Mitchell
Mitchell, Loren Dale
B: Aug 23, 1921   D: Jan 5, 1987

Pos: OF	BA: .312
Hits: 1,244	HRs: 41
RBI: 403	BBs: 346

Called out on strikes to end Don Larsen's perfect game in the 1956 World Series, Mitchell retired after the Series, and so did plate umpire Babe Pinelli. Mitchell played in the 1948 and 1954 World Series for the Indians as well as in the 1949 and 1952 All-Star Games. He whacked more than 200 hits in a season twice, and led the AL in hits (203) and triples (23) in 1949. Mitchell was also a league-leading fielder.
Playing Career: *1946-1956; Cle A, Brk N*

Fred Mitchell
Mitchell, Frederick Francis
B: Jun 5, 1878   D: Oct 13, 1970

Pos: P, C, 1B	ERA: 4.10
W-L: 31-49	SOs: 216
ShOs: 2	Saves: 1
Managerial Record	
Won: 494 Lost: 543 Pct: .476	

Mitchell started his career as pitcher, relieving Cy Young in the first Red Sox game of 1901. He tried to come back as a catcher in 1910, but his success came as manager of the Cubs, who won the 1918 pennant. They lost the World Series to the Red Sox that year. Mitchell coached at Harvard for 30 years.
Playing Career: *1901-1905, 1910, 1913; Bos A, Phi A, Phi N, Brk N, NY A, Bos N*
Managerial Career: *1917-1923; Chi N, Bos N*

Kevin Mitchell
Mitchell, Kevin Darnell
B: Jan 13, 1962

Pos: OF, 3B, DH, SS	BA: .282
Hits: 969	HRs: 190
RBI: 612	BBs: 377

During the first 1986 telecast of a Mets spring training game, Mitchell hit a game-tying home run in the ninth inning, then smashed another four-bagger in extra innings to win the game. Mitchell made that team, and played six different positions that season. In 1989 he was named NL MVP after compiling a slugging average of .635 with 47 homers and 125 RBI. If Mitchell ever finds a home, he has a tremendous future in baseball.
Playing Career: *1984-; NY N, SD N, SF N, Sea A, Cin N*

Mike Mitchell
Mitchell, Michael Francis
B: Dec 12, 1879   D: Jul 16, 1961

Pos: OF	BA: .278
Hits: 1,138	HRs: 27
RBI: 514	BBs: 368

Dale Mitchell brings in a homer for the Indians in the 1948 WS.

Johnny Mize after his 2000th hit, 1952.

Using his speed to turn doubles into triples, Mitchell led the NL in three-baggers twice. He hit 22 triples in a year that he did not lead the league! Mitchell was also a good base stealer, and pilfered 202 bases, three times more than 35 in a season.
Playing Career: *1907-1914; Cin N, Chi N, Pit N, Was A*

Willie Mitchell
Mitchell, William
B: Dec 1, 1889   D: Nov 23, 1973

Pos: P	ERA: 2.86
W-L: 84-92	SOs: 921
ShOs: 16	Saves: 4

At age 20, Mitchell was one of the top left-handers in the AL, compiling a record of 12-8 with a 2.60 ERA in 1910. He was 14-8 with a 1.91 ERA in 1913, while limiting opposing hitters to a .190 batting average.
Playing Career: *1909-1919; Cle A, Det A*

George Mitterwald
Mitterwald, George Eugene
B: Jun 7, 1945

Pos: C	BA: .236
Hits: 623	HRs: 76
RBI: 301	BBs: 222

A part-time catcher, Mitterwald never appeared in more than 125 games, but he hit .333 in two ALCS for the Twins. His best season was 1973, when he batted .259 with 16 homers and 64 RBI. He was playing for the Cubs the next year when he hit for the cycle.
Playing Career: *1966, 1968-1977; Min A, Chi N*

Johnny Mize
Mize, John Robert (The Big Cat)
B: Jan 7, 1913   D: Jun 2, 1993
Hall of Fame 1981

Pos: 1B	BA: .312
Hits: 2,011	HRs: 359
RBI: 1,337	BBs: 856

You could always recognize Mize by his size. Eighth on the all-time slugging list with a .562 mark, the burly first baseman led the league in slugging four times. Mize is the only man to hit three home runs in a game six times. He had 36 multi-homer games, and seven pinch-hit home runs. Mize homered in all of the major league parks in use during his career. A contact hitter as well as a slugger, he struck out only 524 times in 15 years.

A perennial All-Star, Mize became a World Series fixture, playing in the Fall Classic five times. He batted .286 in World Series play, adding three World Series pinch hits to his lexicon of records. Named World Series MVP in 1952, Mize batted .400 with three home runs in the seven-game series. After three years in the Navy during World War II, he tied Ralph Kiner for the NL home run title with 51 in 1947, when the Giants set a record with 221 team homers. Mize won or tied for four NL home run crowns.
Playing Career: *1936-1942, 1946-1953; StL N, NY N, NY A*

Vinegar Bend Mizell
Mizell, Wilmer David
B: Aug 13, 1930

Pos: P	ERA: 3.85
W-L: 90-88	SOs: 918
ShOs: 15	No-hitters: 0

Nicknamed for his hometown, Mizell currently serves in the U.S. House of Representatives. After a solid beginning with the Car-dinals, he was traded to the Pirates in 1960, posting a 13-5 record to help them win the pennant.
Playing Career: *1952-1953, 1956-1962; StL N, Pit N, NY N*

Danny Moeller
Moeller, Daniel Edward
B: Mar 23, 1885   D: Apr 14, 1951

Pos: OF	BA: .243
Hits: 618	HRs: 15
RBI: 192	BBs: 302

On July 19, 1915, Moeller stole second, third and home in the first inning of a game against the Indians. The Senators stole a major league record eight bases that inning. Moeller hit 10 triples a year, 1912-1915. The speedy outfielder stole 171 bases and scored 379 runs.
Playing Career: *1907-1908, 1912-1916; Pit N, Was A, Cle A*

Randy Moffitt
Moffitt, Randall James
B: Oct 13, 1948

Pos: P	ERA: 3.65
W-L: 43-52	SOs: 455
ShOs: 0	Saves: 96

A consistent performer out of the Giants' bullpen, Moffitt averaged 58 appearances and 11 saves a year from 1972 to 1978. The 6' 3" right-hander missed most of 1980 and 1981 with a mysterious stomach ailment. The problem was found to be a fungus so rare that his case was only the third identified. Moffitt recovered to appear in 75 games and save 13 over the next two years for the Astros and Blue Jays. Tennis great Billie Jean King is his sister.
Playing Career: *1972-1983; SF N, Hou N, Tor A*

Randy Moffitt (in jacket) chats with his sister, Billie Jean King, in 1973.

George Mogridge
Mogridge, George Anthony
B: Feb 18, 1889   D: Mar 4, 1962

Pos: P	ERA: 3.20
W-L: 132-131	SOs: 678
ShOs: 20	No-hitters: 1

When Dave Righetti pitched a no-hitter on July 4, 1983, it was the first one thrown by a Yankee in regular season play since Mogridge pitched one against the Red Sox in 1917. He was a tough left-hander with good control, issuing only 565 bases on balls in 2,265 innings. He was traded just before New York's golden years, 1921-1924, but pitched in the 1924 Series for the Senators, winning 1 with 2.25 ERA. Mogridge saved 20 games in relief.
Playing Career: *1911-1912, 1915-1927; Chi A, NY A, Was A, StL A, Bos N*

Paul Molitor
Molitor, Paul Leo
B: Aug 22, 1956

Pos: 3B, 2B, OF, DH	BA: .306
Hits: 2,492	HRs: 182
RBI: 901	BBs: 832

After he batted successfully in 39 consecutive games as a designated hitter in 1987, Molitor changed the way baseball management looks at the DH. He proved that the role can be filled by a fast, lithe leadoff hitter as well as by the heavy-footed slugger of the past. The Brewers had a record of 76-41 with Molitor in the DH role in 1987; 22-23 without him.

Molitor was named 1978 AL Rookie of the Year by *The Sporting News*. Voted into the

Paul Molitor, 1978 Rookie of the Year.

Rick Monday played with the Dodgers from 1977 to 1984.

1980 All-Star Game at the keystone sack, Molitor moved to center field in 1981, then to right field after surgery repaired torn left ankle ligaments. He moved to third base in 1982, leading the AL with a club-record 136 runs scored. In Game One of the 1982 World Series he slashed five hits; he batted .355 for the Series. A six-time All-Star, Molitor has scored 1,396 runs, leading the AL three times.
Playing Career: *1978-; Mil A, Tor A*

Bill Monboquette
Monboquette, William Charles (Monbo)
B: Aug 11, 1936

Pos: P	ERA: 3.68
W-L: 114-112	SOs: 1,122
ShOs: 18	No-hitters: 1

Using a change-of-pace and good control, Monboquette became the ace of the Red Sox staff. In 1961 he fanned 17 Senators in a nine-inning game. He no-hit the White Sox on August 1, 1962, defeating Early Wynn 1-0; a second no-hit bid was foiled in September 1964 when Zoilo Versalles hit a home run. Monboquette won 20 games in 1963. The three-time All-Star has recently been active in the movement to start baseball programs overseas.
Playing Career: *1958-1968; Bos A, Det A, NY A, SF N*

Rick Monday
Monday, Robert James
B: Nov 20, 1945

Pos: OF	BA: .264
Hits: 1,619	HRs: 241
RBI: 775	BBs: 924

The first player chosen in the newly reconstituted baseball draft of 1965, Monday was a very good major league player, but chronic back problems prevented him from achieving the greatness predicted for him. Monday appeared in 112 or more games for 12 straight years, and scored 950 runs. Selected for the All-Star Game twice, Monday played in five LCS, including three winning efforts with the Dodgers.

After the 1971 season he was traded by Oakland for Cubs pitcher Ken Holtzman. Monday benefited from the move to cozy Wrigley Field. His home run and doubles totals shot up. In 1972 he homered in three consecutive at-bats. When he batted leadoff in 1976 – his last year in Chicago before being traded to the Dodgers – he scored 107 runs with 32 homers while slugging .507. Monday made headlines when he took away the American flag from a protester who was going to burn it on a televised game.
Playing Career: *1966-1984; KC A, Oak A, Chi N, LA N*

Don Money
Money, Donald Wayne
B: Jun 7, 1947

Pos: 3B, 2B, DH, SS	BA: .261
Hits: 1,623	HRs: 176
RBI: 729	BBs: 600

Originally signed by the Pirates' Syd Thrift, Money was traded to the Phillies with Woody Fryman and two others in return for Jim Bunning. In 1969, his rookie season, Money was the Phillies' regular shortstop. When Larry Bowa came up in 1970, Money moved to third base, and hit .295 with 14 home runs and 66 RBI. As a regular in 1972, he led NL third basemen in putouts, double plays and fielding.

Money was sent to the Brewers in a seven-player deal after the season to make room for future superstar Mike Schmidt. In Milwaukee, Money led off, batted in the .280s, and stole bases – 22 in 1973 and 19 in 1974. He led AL third basemen in fielding in 1973 and 1974. Moved to second base in 1977 after the Brewers got Sal Bando, Money had his best year, reaching career highs with 25 homers, 83 RBI and 86 runs scored. He made the All-Star squad four times, and saw postseason action for the Brewers in 1981 and 1982.
Playing Career: *1968-1983; Phi N, Mil A*

Sid Monge
Monge, Isidro Pedroza
B: Apr 11, 1951

Pos: P	ERA: 3.53
W-L: 49-40	SOs: 471
ShOs: 0	Saves: 56

Third on the Indians' all-time saves list, Monge had excellent control, a fastball, slider and a screwball. He also had one great year, 1979, when he was selected for the All-Star team and finished the year with 12 wins, 19 saves and a 2.40 ERA.
Playing Career: *1975-1984; Cal A, Cle A, Phi N, SD N, Det A*

Willie Montanez
Montanez y Naranjo, Guillermo
B: Apr 1, 1948

Pos: 1B, OF	BA: .275
Hits: 1,604	HRs: 139
RBI: 802	BBs: 465

When Curt Flood refused to report to the Phillies in 1970, Montanez was sent as a replacement. Used in center field in lieu of Flood, Montanez hit a career-high 30 homers and drove in 99 runs as a rookie in 1971. The flashy fielder led the NL with 39 doubles and 22 outfield assists the following year. Elected to the All-Star squad in 1977, he finished the season with 20 homers and 31 doubles. Counting five seasons with the Phillies, he played for eight different teams in as many seasons, ending up back with the Phillies.
Playing Career: *1966, 1970-1982; Cal A, Phi N, SF N, Atl N, NY N, Tex A, SD N, Mon N, Pit N*

John Montefusco
Montefusco, John Joseph (The Count)
B: May 25, 1950

Pos: P	ERA: 3.54
W-L: 90-83	SOs: 1,081
ShOs: 11	No-hitters: 1

The 1975 NL Rookie of the Year, Montefusco made predictions and backed them with sensational performances. He once predicted a shutout and whipped the Dodgers 1-0. He made the All-Star team in 1976, the year he had 16 wins, a 2.84 ERA, and an NL-leading six shutouts.
Playing Career: *1974-1986; SF N, Atl N, SD N, NY A*

Jeff Montgomery
Montgomery, Jeffrey Thomas (Monty)
B: Jan 7, 1962

Pos: P	ERA: 2.52
W-L: 34-27	SOs: 460
ShOs: 0	Saves: 160

In a Horatio Alger-like scene, the Royals were planning to send Montgomery down to the minors when they decided to give him one last chance in spring training in 1989. A coach suggested that he rear back and throw it over the middle of the plate – and so he did. Montgomery had enough natural stuff to become one of the AL's best relievers. He posted a 1.37 ERA in 1989, and saved 117 games in three years, 1991-1993. Montgomery made the 1992-1993 All-Star teams.
Playing Career: *1987-; Cin N, KC A*

Wally Moon
Moon, Wallace Wade
B: Apr 3, 1930

Pos: OF	BA: .289
Hits: 1,399	HRs: 142
RBI: 661	BBs: 644

When Moon arrived in Los Angeles he found a 250-foot foul line with a 42-foot-high wire screen in left field. He developed an "inside-out" swing to bat the ball onto the screen. He would sometimes golf the ball over the wire screen, calling those hits "moon shots." Rookie of the Year in 1954, Moon homered in his first major league at-bat, and batted .295 or more his first four NL seasons. He made the All-Star team when he whacked 24 homers and 28 doubles in 1957, both personal highs.

The Cardinals traded him after one sub-par season in 1958. In his new life as a Dodger, Moon led the NL in triples with 11 in 1959. His .302 led his new team into the World Series versus the Go-Go White Sox. He launched a homer in the Game Six finale to spark the Dodger victory. Moon won the Gold Glove Award in 1960 and led the NL in on-base percentage in 1961. He played for the 1963 and 1965 pennant-winning Dodgers.
Playing Career: *1954-1965; StL N, LA N*

Charlie Moore
Moore, Charles William
B: Jun 21, 1953

Pos: C, OF, DH	BA: .261
Hits: 1,052	HRs: 36
RBI: 408	BBs: 346

A crowd favorite in Milwaukee, Moore was the Brewers' catcher who played right field and terrorized Angels and Cardinals pitchers during 1982 postseason play. He batted .462 in the ALCS and .346 in the World Series.
Playing Career: *1973-1987; Mil A, Tor A*

Donnie Moore
Moore, Donnie Ray
B: Feb 13, 1954   D: Jul 18, 1989

Pos: P	ERA: 3.66
W-L: 43-40	SOs: 416
ShOs: 0	Saves: 89

Moore made one bad pitch that haunted him the rest of his life. One strike away from the World Series, he gave up a home run to Dave Henderson in Game Five of the 1986 ALCS. Henderson then won the extra-inning contest on a sacrifice fly, also hit off Moore.

Wally Moon crosses the plate with a two-run homer in the 1959 WS.

Boston won the next two games and the pennant. Moore brooded over his mistake, and beset by injuries, took his own life in 1989.
Playing Career: *1975, 1977-1988; Chi N, StL N, Mil A, Atl N, Cal A*

Earl Moore
Moore, Earl Alonzo (Crossfire)
B: Jul 29, 1879   D: Nov 28, 1961

Pos: P	ERA: 2.78
W-L: 161-154	SOs: 1,397
ShOs: 34	No-hitters: 1

A strong-willed, intimidating pitcher, Moore was the first star on Cleveland's new AL club, and he pitched the new league's first no-hitter. His sweeping sidearm motion accounted for 79 victories and 1,288 innings during the AL's first five years. He led the league in ERA with a 1.74 mark in 1903. After fading somewhat, Moore regained his stuff in the NL, winning 22 games for the 1910 Phillies, and leading the league in strikeouts and shutouts.
Playing Career: *1901-1914; Cle A, NY A, Phi N, Chi N, Buf F*

Eddie Moore
Moore, Graham Edward
B: Jan 18, 1899   D: Feb 10, 1976

Pos: SS, OF, 3B, 2B	BA: .285
Hits: 706	HRs: 13
RBI: 257	BBs: 272

When Moore replaced Rabbit Maranville at second base in 1925, he hit .298 in the leadoff spot, and led the Pirates to the NL pennant and World Championship. Moore's trade the next year began a series of blunders that would undo the Pirates.
Playing Career: *1923-1930, 1932, 1934; Pit N, Bos N, Brk N, NY N, Cle A*

Pirates infielder Eddie Moore.

Gene Moore
Moore, Eugene, Jr. (Rowdy)
B: Aug 26, 1909   D: Mar 12, 1978

Pos: OF	BA: .270
Hits: 958	HRs: 58
RBI: 436	BBs: 317

The St. Louis Browns tallied precious few runs in their only World Series appearance (1944), and Moore scored the first one. With the Braves in 1936, he led NL outfielders with 32 assists, and batted .290 with 13 homers, 38 doubles, 91 runs scored and 67 RBI.
Playing Career: *1931, 1933-1945; Cin N, StL N, Bos N, Brk N, Was A, StL A*

Johnny Moore
Moore, John Francis
B: Mar 23, 1902   D: Apr 4, 1991

Pos: OF	BA: .307
Hits: 926	HRs: 73
RBI: 452	BBs: 195

Another player who opted for the Pacific Coast League over the majors, Moore batted over .300 in five of six NL seasons and even played in the 1932 World Series. But he left the big leagues in 1938 to play for Los Angeles in the PCL.
Playing Career: *1928-1929, 1931-1937, 1945; Chi N, Cin N, Phi N*

Jo-Jo Moore
Moore, Joseph Gregg
B: Dec 25, 1908

Pos: OF	BA: .298
Hits: 1,615	HRs: 79
RBI: 513	BBs: 348

Scoring 809 runs, Moore set the table for the slugging Giants of the 1930s. He batted leadoff, with various hitters in the second spot, then Bill Terry and Mel Ott in the three and four holes. This combination won three pennants for the Giants and made Moore a six-time All-Star. He tied records with two hits in one inning in the 1933 World Series, and with nine hits in the 1937 Series.

Moore was a notorious first-pitch hitter, and managers fined their hurlers for throwing him a strike on the first pitch.
Playing Career: *1930-1941; NY N*

Mike Moore
Moore, Michael Wayne
B: Nov 26, 1959

Pos: P	ERA: 4.16
W-L: 145-151	SOs: 1,541
ShOs: 16	Saves: 2

The first overall draft choice by the Mariners in 1981, Moore had a world of talent, and has compiled a solid starting record. His control, once good, slipped in Oakland's pitchers' ballpark and has been regained in Detroit's hitters' paradise. Moore averaged 228 innings and 13 wins from 1984 to 1993. He is 2-2 in three ALCS and 2-1 in two World Series. He

Mike Moore with the A's in 1989.

won three postseason games in 1989, including two in the earthquake-disrupted 1989 Series win over the Giants.
Playing Career: *1982-; Sea A, Oak A, Det A*

Randy Moore
Moore, Randolph Edward
B: Jun 21, 1906   D: Jun 12, 1992

Pos: OF, 1B, 3B, C	BA: .278
Hits: 627	HRs: 27
RBI: 308	BBs: 158

A Texan who made a fortune in the oil business, Moore acted as an investment advisor, helping his Boston teammates after retiring from the playing field. He was a regular for four years with the Braves, hitting .293 and .302 in 1932 and 1933, but with little power.
Playing Career: *1927-1928, 1930-1937; Chi A, Bos N, Brk N, StL N*

Ray Moore
Moore, Raymond Leroy (Farmer)
B: Jun 1, 1926

Pos: P	ERA: 4.06
W-L: 63-59	SOs: 612
ShOs: 5	Saves: 46

A right-handed fastball pitcher with control problems, Moore played for three pennant-winning teams, but only got into the 1959 World Series for the White Sox. As a starter he won 42 games in four years, 1955-1958. Moore hit six career home runs.
Playing Career: *1952-1953, 1955-1963; Brk N, Bal A, Chi A, Was A, Min A*

Terry Moore
Moore, Terry Bluford
B: May 27, 1912

Pos: OF   BA: .280
Hits: 1,318   HRs: 80
RBI: 513   BBs: 406
Managerial Record
Won: 35   Lost: 42   Pct: .455

Moore was captain of two World Championship teams, the 1942 and 1946 Cardinals. As a rookie in 1935, he hit two doubles and two homers in one game. He went 6-for-6 later that year. An All-Star 1939-1942, Moore was popular with both fans and his teammates.
Playing Career: *1935-1942, 1946-1948; StL N*
Managerial Career: *1954; Phi N*

Wilcy Moore.

Wilcy Moore
Moore, William Wilcy
B: May 20, 1897   D: Mar 29, 1963

Pos: P   ERA: 3.69
W-L: 51-44   SOs: 204
ShOs: 2   Saves: 49

Babe Ruth wagered that Moore would not get more than three hits in 1927. Moore collected six hits and used the payoff to buy two oxen whom he named ''Babe'' and ''Ruth.'' As a 30-year-old rookie Moore won 19 games and saved 13 with an AL-leading 2.28 ERA. He played in two World Series.
Playing Career: *1927-1929, 1931-1933; NY A, Bos A*

Bob Moose
Moose, Robert Ralph
B: Oct 9, 1947   D: Oct 9, 1976

Pos: P   ERA: 3.50
W-L: 76-71   SOs: 827
ShOs: 13   No-hitters: 1

A starter for the three-time division-winning Pirates, Moose underwent surgery for a blood clot in his shoulder in 1974. A rib was removed to solve the problem, and Moose recovered. In 1976 he saved 10 games as a reliever.
Playing Career: *1967-1976; Pit N*

Jerry Morales
Morales y Torres, Julio Ruben
B: Feb 18, 1949

Pos: OF   BA: .259
Hits: 1,173   HRs: 95
RBI: 570   BBs: 366

The Padres picked Morales during the 1969 expansion draft. His best years were 1974-1977 with the Cubs. He had a very good year in 1977 when he made the All-Star squad, hit .290 with 34 doubles and compiled .447 slugging and .350 on-base averages.
Playing Career: *1969-1983; SD N, Chi N, StL N, Det A, NY N*

Jose Morales
Morales, Jose Manuel
B: Dec 30, 1944

Pos: DH, PH   BA: .287
Hits: 375   HRs: 26
RBI: 207   BBs: 89

Morales holds the season record of 25 pinch-hits in 78 pinch hit at-bats in 1976. He ranks third all-time with 123 career pinch hits and fifth with 445 career pinch-hit at-bats. Morales led the league three times in both categories, and he batted .300 five times.
Playing Career: *1973-1984; Oak A, Mon N, Min A, Bal A, LA N*

Pat Moran
Moran, Patrick Joseph
B: Feb 7, 1876   D: Mar 7, 1924

Pos: C   BA: .235
Hits: 618   HRs: 18
RBI: 262   BBs: 142
Managerial Record
Won: 748   Lost: 586   Pct: .561

The first 20th-century manager to win pennants with two different teams, Moran piloted the 1915 Phillies and 1919 Reds. Throughout the scandal following the 1919 World Series, Moran and his Reds maintained that the White Sox did not fix the games, that they whipped the Sox fair and square. As evidence, the Reds pointed out their own left-handed pitching, four great catches in clutch situations by center fielder Edd Roush, and sterling batting performances by unsung players.
Playing Career: *1901-1914; Bos N, Chi N, Phi N*
Managerial Career: *1915-1923; Phi N, Cin N*

Keith Moreland
Moreland, Bobby Keith
B: May 2, 1954

Pos: OF, C, 3B   BA: .279
Hits: 1,279   HRs: 121
RBI: 674   BBs: 405

A Wrigley Field favorite, Moreland could be counted on to provide defensive and offensive excitement during hot afternoon games. His batting peaked in 1985 with a .307 mark, 14 homers and 106 RBI. Two years later, he belted 27 homers.
Playing Career: *1978-1989; Phi N, Chi N, SD N, Det A, Bal A*

Jose Morales set a major league record with his 25th pinch hit of the 1976 season.

Omar Moreno gets back to first as Kent Hrbek stares him down, 1984.

Omar Moreno
Moreno y Quintero, Omar Renan
B: Oct 24, 1952

Pos: OF	BA: .252
Hits: 1,257	HRs: 37
RBI: 386	BBs: 387

From 1978 to 1980 Moreno was the most potent leadoff batter in the NL. He stole 243 bases and scored 292 runs in the three-year period. His Pirates won the 1979 pennant, then became World Champions in a thrilling seven-game series with Moreno batting .333, including three singles in Game Six.
Playing Career: *1975-1986; Pit N, Hou N, NY A, KC A, Atl N*

Roger Moret
Moret y Torres, Rogelio
B: Sep 16, 1949

Pos: P	ERA: 3.67
W-L: 47-27	SOs: 408
ShOs: 5	Saves: 12

In 1975 Moret compiled a 14-3 record for the Red Sox, then was 1-0 in the ALCS. He did not give up a run in postseason play that year. Moret quit the big leagues when he was 30, and worked as a carpenter in Canada, frequently pitching for independent teams in the minors.
Playing Career: *1970-1978; Bos A, Atl N, Tex A*

Bobby Morgan
Morgan, Robert Morris
B: Jun 29, 1926

Pos: 2B, SS	BA: .233
Hits: 487	HRs: 53
RBI: 217	BBs: 327

Following an MVP year in the International League, Morgan was slated to replace Pee-wee Reese at shortstop. Reese, however, continued to play well for the Dodgers, so they traded Morgan. He played in the 1952-1953 World Series.
Playing Career: *1950, 1952-1958; Brk N, Phi N, StL N, Chi N*

Cy Morgan
Morgan, Harry Richard
B: Nov 10, 1878   D: Jun 28, 1962

Pos: P	ERA: 2.51
W-L: 78-78	SOs: 667
ShOs: 15	Saves: 3

Wild but effective, Morgan and his spitball gave Connie Mack and the Athletics a formidable starting rotation that included Jack Coombs, Eddie Plank and Chief Bender. Morgan won 18 games in 1910 and 15 the next year, and the A's won pennants both years.
Playing Career: *1903-1905, 1907-1913; StL A, Bos A, Phi A, Cin N*

Joe Morgan
Morgan, Joe Leonard (Little Joe)
B: Sep 19, 1943
Hall of Fame 1990

Pos: 2B	BA: .271
Hits: 2,517	HRs: 268
RBI: 1,133	BBs: 1,865

Probably the best all-around, all-time second baseman, Morgan had a stellar career. He scored 1,650 runs and stole 689 bases, both high on the all-time lists. He won back-to-back MVP Awards, 1975-1976, won five straight Gold Gloves, 1973-1977, and made nine NL All-Star teams, including eight in a row, 1972-1979. His lifetime on-base percentage is .395.

Morgan was the fuel of the Big Red Machine, the first NL team to win consecutive World Championships since John McGraw's Giants in 1921-1922. Morgan played more years in Houston than in Cincinnati, but came to prominence with the Reds. Playing for the Giants near the end of his career, Morgan hit a homer on the final day of the season to beat the Dodgers. It cost them the division title. Today he is a top network broadcaster.
Playing Career: *1963-1984; Hou N, Cin N, SF N, Phi N, Oak A*

Joe Morgan
Morgan, Joe Michael
B: Nov 19, 1930

Pos: 2B, 3B	BA: .193
Hits: 36	HRs: 2
RBI: 10	BBs: 18
Managerial Record	
Won: 301 Lost: 262 Pct: .535	

Three future managers played on the 1959 Athletics: Morgan, Dick Williams and Whitey Herzog. Morgan won the 1988 division title after taking over the Red Sox from John McNamara during the All-Star break. He spent 31 seasons in the minors as player and manager.
Playing Career: *1959-1961, 1964; Mil N, KC A, Phi N, Cle A, StL N*
Managerial Career: *1988-1991; Bos A*

Mike Morgan
Morgan, Michael Thomas
B: Oct 8, 1959

Pos: P	ERA: 3.89
W-L: 93-127	SOs: 894
ShOs: 10	Saves: 3

Talented, but frequently traded, Morgan has found a home with the Cubs. After strug-

gling to gain control of his 95-mph fastball and wicked slider, Morgan won 41 games in three years, 1990-1992. Morgan was a high school phenom who was rushed to the majors.
Playing Career: *1978-; Oak A, NY A, Sea A, Bal A, LA N, Chi N*

Ray Morgan
Morgan, Raymond Caryll
B: Jun 14, 1889   D: Feb 15, 1940

Pos: 2B	BA: .254
Hits: 630	HRs: 4
RBI: 254	BBs: 320

A catalyst for the early Senators, Morgan batted against Babe Ruth when he pitched with the Red Sox. Once he led off against Ruth with a walk. The big guy protested so much he was booted from the game. Ernie Shore entered the game in relief, caught Morgan stealing, then retired the next 26 batters to pitch a perfect game.
Playing Career: *1911-1918; Was A*

Tom Morgan
Morgan, Tom Stephen (Plowboy)
B: May 20, 1930   D: Jan 13, 1987

Pos: P	ERA: 3.61
W-L: 67-47	SOs: 364
ShOs: 7	Saves: 64

Morgan surprised the Yankees by jumping from Class A to the big club in one year. Used as a spot starter and a reliever – he was the bullpen stopper before Ryne Duren – Morgan helped the Yankees win four pennants. He pitched in three World Series.
Playing Career: *1951-1952, 1954-1963; NY A, KC A, Det A, Was A, LA A*

George Moriarty
Moriarty, George Joseph
B: Jun 7, 1884   D: Apr 8, 1964

Pos: 3B	BA: .251
Hits: 920	HRs: 5
RBI: 376	BBs: 234
Managerial Record	
Won: 150 Lost: 157 Pct: .489	

During 50 years in baseball, Moriarty was a player, manager, umpire – and a chaperone! Commissioner Landis appointed Moriarty to accompany the major league baseball players' tour of Japan in 1922. As a player, Moriarty hit .273 in the 1909 World Series. He had stolen 34 bases that year, on his way to a career total of 248, including 11 steals of home. After managing the Tigers to a sixth-place finish, Moriarty turned to umpiring.

One of his first encounters with an angry player was with Jimmy Dykes. He called a third strike on Dykes, who demanded, "How do you spell your name?" Moriarty spelled it out. Dykes retorted, "That's what I thought. Only one i!" The White Sox once disputed his decisions, so Moriarty, a former boxer, challenged the entire team to a fight under the stands. He decked the one player who dared

Umpire George Moriarty.

step forward, breaking his hand on the player's jaw.
Playing Career: *1903-1904, 1906-1915; Chi N, NY A, Det A, Chi A*
Managerial Career: *1927-1928; Det A*
Umpiring Career: *1917-1926, 1929-1940; AL (5 WS, 1 AS)*

Honest John Morrill
Morrill, John Francis
B: Feb 19, 1855   D: Apr 2, 1932

Pos: 1B	BA: .260
Hits: 1,275	HRs: 43
RBI: 582	BBs: 358
Managerial Record	
Won: 348 Lost: 334 Pct: .510	

Honest John got his nickname when he responded frankly to the Red Stockings' 1883 pennant victory. "Good pitching, and catching, and lucky hitting won for us. When the season started I thought we would finish fourth or fifth," he said. Morrill came from Boston, and served the Red Stockings as captain and manager before moving on to Washington.
Playing Career: *1876-1890; Bos N, Was N, Bos P*
Managerial Career: *1882-1889; Bos N, Was N*

Cannonball Morris
Morris, Edward
B: Sep 29, 1862   D: Apr 12, 1937

Pos: P	ERA: 2.82
W-L: 171-122	SOs: 1,217
ShOs: 28	No-hitters: 1

One of the earliest West Coast players, Morris helped prove that the brand of baseball out west was of a sufficiently high grade that its stars could play in the NL. He was a hard-throwing left-hander who won 30 games twice and 40 once. He pitched more than 500

innings in 1885 and 1886. Morris led the league twice in complete games and twice in shutouts, but he was often his own worst enemy. He was suspended frequently for excessive drinking.
Playing Career: *1884-1890; Col AA, Pit AA, Pit N, Pit P*

Jack Morris
Morris, John Scott
B: May 16, 1955

Pos: P	ERA: 3.83
W-L: 244-180	SOs: 2,378
ShOs: 28	No-hitters: 1

Morris was never greater than he was in Game Seven of the 1991 World Series for his hometown Twins against the talented Braves. He tossed a 10-inning shutout over the NL champs to win the World Series. Morris started three games, won the first and last, and posted a 1.17 ERA. The next two years Morris and the Blue Jays were World Champions, but the hurler's postseason magic was stifled. He lost a game in the ALCS and two more in the 1992 World Series.

Morris was the top winner of the 1980s, winning 162 games despite having an off year in 1989. He posted 20 victories or more three times, twice leading the AL in wins. In 1983 he was 20-13 with league-leading totals for innings pitched and strikeouts. The most consistent pitcher in baseball over the past 14 years, he averaged 241 innings per season, 1979-1992.
Playing Career: *1977-; Det A, Min A, Tor A*

Jack Morris with the Tigers in 1983.

Jim Morrison
Morrison, James Forrest
B: Sep 23, 1952

Pos: 3B, 2B, SS, 1B	BA: .260
Hits: 876	HRs: 112
RBI: 435	BBs: 213

A valuable multi-position player, Morrison's best performance was in the 1986 season, when he batted .274 with 23 homers and 88 RBI. He batted .333 in three LCS games with the Phillies and Tigers. In 1986 he claimed the dubious honor of fewest chances accepted by a third baseman.
Playing Career: *1977-1988; Phi N, Chi A, Pit N, Det A, Atl N*

Johnny Morrison
Morrison, John Dewey (Jughandle Johnny)
B: Oct 22, 1895   D: Mar 20, 1966

Pos: P	ERA: 3.65
W-L: 103-80	SOs: 546
ShOs: 13	Saves: 23

Throwing a sweeping curveball, Morrison accounted for 25 Pirates victories in 1923. His curve is considered among the best ever. Morrison led the NL in games pitched, 1924-1925, and he helped the Pirates to the 1925 World Championship with a 17-14 record.
Playing Career: *1920-1927, 1929-1930; Pit N, Brk N*

Carl Morton
Morton, Carl Wendle
B: Jan 18, 1944   D: Apr 12, 1983

Pos: P	ERA: 3.73
W-L: 87-92	SOs: 650
ShOs: 13	Saves: 1

Morton won NL Rookie of the Year honors in 1970 when he compiled an 18-11 record.

Carl Morton, 1970 Rookie of the Year.

Starting as an outfielder, then converting to a pitcher, he was reacquired by the Braves, who had signed him but then let him go in the expansion draft. Morton won 48 games in three years for them.
Playing Career: *1969-1976; Mon N, Atl N*

Guy Morton
Morton, Guy, Sr.
B: Jun 1, 1893   D: Oct 18, 1934

Pos: P	ERA: 3.13
W-L: 98-88	SOs: 830
ShOs: 19	Saves: 6

Tenacity paid off for Morton, who lost his first 13 major league games, setting a record that stood until 1982, when it was broken by Terry Felton. Morton posted 16 victories in 1915. On June 11, 1916, he struck out four A's batters in one inning.
Playing Career: *1914-1924; Cle A*

Walt Moryn
Moryn, Walter Joseph (Moose)
B: Apr 12, 1926

Pos: OF	BA: .266
Hits: 667	HRs: 101
RBI: 354	BBs: 251

On May 30, 1958, Moryn hit three home runs in one game. He belted 26 dingers and made the All-Star team that year. Not a Willie Mays in the outfield, Moryn's surprising shoe-string catch in the ninth inning saved Don Cardwell's no-hitter in 1960.
Playing Career: *1954-1961; Brk N, Chi N, StL N, Pit N*

Lloyd Moseby
Moseby, Lloyd Anthony
B: Nov 5, 1959

Pos: OF	BA: .257
Hits: 1,494	HRs: 169
RBI: 737	BBs: 616

The early success of the Toronto franchise owes a great deal to Moseby. Coming along in the 1978 free agent draft, the youngster was rushed into the big leagues. He holds the Blue Jays' club record for games, at-bats, runs, hits, doubles, stolen bases, bases on balls, strikeouts and hit-by-pitcher.
Playing Career: *1980-1991; Tor A, Det A*

Wally Moses
Moses, Wallace
B: Oct 8, 1910   D: Oct 10, 1990

Pos: OF	BA: .291
Hits: 2,138	HRs: 89
RBI: 679	BBs: 821

A star batter who hit .417 in the 1946 World Series, Moses had been turned down by a Giants scout who was under orders to find a Jewish player. Moses went to Philadelphia, where he batted over .300 his first seven years in the majors. Chosen for the 1937 All-Star squad, Moses belted 25 homers, 13

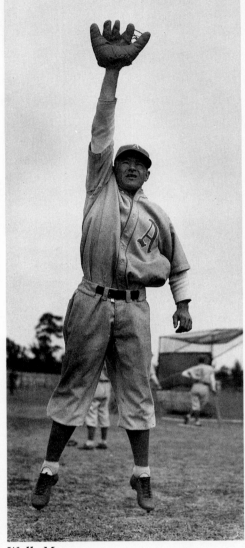

Wally Moses.

triples and 48 doubles, scored 113 runs, and batted .320. In 1943 he stole 56 bases and led the AL in triples with 12.
Playing Career: *1935-1951; Phi A, Chi A, Bos A*

Les Moss
Moss, John Lester
B: May 14, 1925

Pos: OF	BA: .247
Hits: 552	HRs: 63
RBI: 276	BBs: 282
Managerial Record	
Won: 39 Lost: 50 Pct: .438	

For nearly 30 years, Moss scouted, coached and managed in the White Sox' and Tigers' systems. He was interim manager of the White Sox while Al Lopez was hospitalized, and piloted the Tigers before being replaced by Sparky Anderson.
Playing Career: *1946-1958; StL A, Bal A, Bos A, Chi A*
Managerial Career: *1968, 1979; Chi A, Det A*

Don Mossi
Mossi, Donald Louis
B: Jan 11, 1929

Pos: P	ERA: 3.43
W-L: 101-80	SOs: 932
ShOs: 8	Saves: 50

As a rookie Mossi watched from the 1954 Indians bullpen the best pitching staff of the 1950s. Mossi pitched four scoreless innings in three World Series games that year. Traded to the Tigers, he became a starter in Detroit, and was 17-9 in 1959. Two years later, Mossi fashioned a 15-7 record with a 2.96 ERA for the second-place Tigers, who won 101 games. He retired with one of the best-ever fielding averages for a pitcher, charged with only three errors in 12 years of play.
Playing Career: *1954-1965; Cle A, Det A, Chi A, KC A*

Johnny Mostil
Mostil, John Anthony
B: Jun 1, 1896   D: Dec 10, 1970

Pos: OF	BA: .301
Hits: 1,054	HRs: 23
RBI: 376	BBs: 415

In a 1925 spring training game, Mostil snared a foul fly on the left field line while playing center field. He also used his speed to top the AL in stolen bases in 1925 and 1926. Mostil later managed in the minors.
Playing Career: *1918, 1920-1929; Chi A*

Manny Mota
Mota y Geronimo, Manuel Rafael
B: Feb 18, 1938

Pos: OF, PH	BA: .304
Hits: 1,149	HRs: 31
RBI: 438	BBs: 289

Probably the best pinch hitter of all time, Mota could get on base any time the Dodgers needed him to score. He is first on the all-time list with 150 pinch hits in 505 at-bats. He batted .600 in three NLCS, and played in two World Series, wearing Dodger blue. While serving as the Pirates' fourth outfielder, Moto studied hitting under Manager Harry Walker, a former NL batting champion.

Under Walker's tutelage Mota hit .332 in 1966, the first of seven .300 seasons in eight years. As a Dodger, he emerged as a valuable pinch hitter. In the ninth inning of Game Three of the 1977 NLCS, Mota doubled home a run to lead the Dodgers to a three-run rally and a 6-5 victory. Near the end of his career, he often started the season as a coach, then was activated for the stretch drive. He retired with a .297 pinch-hitting batting average.
Playing Career: *1962-1980, 1982; SF N, Pit N, Mon N, LA N*

Manny Mota pinch-hits for the Dodgers in 1973.

Frank Mountain
Mountain, Frank Henry
B: May 17, 1860   D: Nov 19, 1939

Pos: P	ERA: 3.47
W-L: 58-83	SOs: 383
ShOs: 9	No-hitters: 1

Mountain was a big star for the American Association's original Columbus team. He had his best years there, winning 26 and 23 games in 1883 and 1884. His 2.45 ERA in 1884 caught the eye of the new owner, who moved the squad and Mountain to Pittsburgh, leaving most of the players behind.
Playing Career: *1880-1886; Tro N, Det N, Wor N, Phi AA, Col AA, Pit AA*

Mike Mowrey
Mowrey, Harry Harlan
B: Apr 20, 1884   D: Mar 20, 1947

Pos: 3B	BA: .256
Hits: 1,098	HRs: 7
RBI: 461	BBs: 469

A solid-fielding, average-hitting third sacker in the dead ball era. Mowrey walked more than he struck out. He pounded out 20 or more doubles four times. He led the league's third basemen in fielding twice, then jumped to the Federal League for more money.
Playing Career: *1905-1917; Cin N, StL N, Pit N, Pit F, Brk N*

Don Mueller
**Mueller, Donald Frederick
(Mandrake the Magician)**
B: Apr 14, 1927

Pos: OF	BA: .296
Hits: 1,292	HRs: 65
RBI: 520	BBs: 167

A second-generation major league ballplayer – his father, Don, played in the 1920s – Mueller had a spectacular season in 1954. He batted .342, led the NL in hits with 212, smoked 35 doubles and scored 90 runs. Then he hit .389 in the 1954 World Series. He was selected for the All-Star team in both 1954 and 1955. He broke his ankle the ninth inning of the Bobby Thomson home run playoff game, and missed the 1951 World Series.
Playing Career: *1948-1959; NY N, Chi A*

Heinie Mueller
Mueller, Clarence Francis
B: Sep 16, 1899   D: Jan 23, 1975

Pos: OF	BA: .282
Hits: 597	HRs: 22
RBI: 272	BBs: 168

Entering both games of a 1927 doubleheader as a pinch hitter, Mueller drove in eight runs in three at-bats. One of the early farm system graduates, Mueller could not break into the Cardinal lineup despite hitting .343 in 1923 and .313 in 1925.
Playing Career: *1920-1929, 1935; StL N, NY N, Bos N, StL A*

Ray Mueller
Mueller, Ray Coleman (Iron Man)
B: Mar 8, 1912

Pos: C	BA: .252
Hits: 733	HRs: 56
RBI: 373	BBs: 250

Mueller caught 155 games for the Reds in 1943, making the All-Star team that year. His first major league hit was a home run off Carl Hubbell in 1935. Mueller responded to the World War II baseball manpower shortage by catching 233 consecutive games.
Playing Career: *1935-1940, 1943-1944, 1946-1951; Bos N, Pit N, Cin N, NY N*

Hugh Mulcahy
Mulcahy, Hugh Noyes (Losing Pitcher)
B: Sep 9, 1913

Pos: P	ERA: 4.49
W-L: 45-89	SOs: 314
ShOs: 5	Saves: 9

Toiling for the dismally bad Phillies, Mulcahy was mentioned over the wire services as the pitcher of record for the losing team so frequently that announcers began referring to him as "Losing Pitcher Mulcahy." Despite a 13-22 record, he was an All-Star Game selection in 1940.
Playing Career: *1935-1940, 1945-1947; Phi N, Pit N*

Tony Mullane
Mullane, Anthony John
(Count, the Apollo of the Box)
B: Jan 30, 1859   D: Apr 25, 1944

Pos: P	ERA: 3.05
W-L: 285-220	SOs: 1,812
ShOs: 31	No-hitters: 1

Extremely talented – he could pitch left- or right-handed – and stubborn, Mullane sat out the entire 1885 season in a contract dispute. Born in County Cork, Ireland, Mullane

Tony Mullane.

Early Tigers hurler George Mullin was a good hitter, batting over .300 twice.

began his major league career by winning 30 or more games each of his first five seasons. He led the American Association twice in shutouts, and would have led the league five times in saves if those statistics had been kept.

Mullane was one of baseball's first great showmen. His handsome features and waxed mustachio gave him a noble appearance and attracted female fans to the games that he pitched. Mullane pitched more than 400 innings six times and never experienced serious arm trouble. He was a fastball pitcher, but also threw an effective dropball and was adept at making batters chase bad pitches. Mullane is one of a handful of pitchers with 280 wins who is not in the Hall of Fame.
Playing Career: *1881-1884, 1886-1894; Det N, Lou AA, StL AA, Tol AA, Cin AA, Cin N, Bal N, Cle N*

George Mullin
Mullin, George Joseph (Wabash George)
B: Jul 4, 1880   D: Jan 7, 1944

Pos: P	ERA: 2.82
W-L: 228-196	SOs: 1,482
ShOs: 35	No-hitters: 1

Born on the Fourth of July, Mullin once pitched a no-hitter and garnered three hits on his birthday, July 4, 1912. Less than three weeks earlier the Tigers had asked waivers on the 32-year-old hurler. On Independence Day he was just wild enough to prevent the Browns from digging in on him. Ty Cobb made four outstanding catches in the last two innings to preserve the no-hitter. Mullin was a star performer, winning more than 20 games five times, including an AL-leading 29 in 1909. He hurled 300 innings or more five years in a row and 200 or more innings in 12 of his 14 seasons.

Mullin possessed a sharp breaking curveball that set up his fastball. A good hitter, his career average is .262, and he batted over .300 twice. He was used as a pinch hitter 101 times. Mullin had 45 hits in 1904, including 10 doubles. Mullin played semipro ball in Wabash, Indiana, then signed contracts with both the Dodgers and Tigers. He went with the Tigers because they were closer to Wabash.
Playing Career: *1902-1915; Det A, Was A, Ind F, Nwk F*

Pat Mullin
Mullin, Patrick Joseph
B: Nov 1, 1917

Pos: OF	BA: .271
Hits: 676	HRs: 87
RBI: 385	BBs: 330

Jerry Mumphrey (r), at 1981 pennant win.

As a rookie Mullin batted .341, then missed four years due to military service. He was chosen for the All-Star Game in 1947 and again in 1948, his best year. Mullin batted .288 with 23 homers and 80 RBI that season.
Playing Career: *1940-1941, 1946-1953; Det A*

Rance Mulliniks
Mulliniks, Steven Rance
B: Jan 15, 1956

Pos: 3B, SS, DH, 2B	BA: .272
Hits: 972	HRs: 73
RBI: 435	BBs: 460

Platooned at the hot corner with Garth Iorg, Mulliniks set several Blue Jays single-season records with a .324 batting average, 34 doubles, and eight consecutive hits. Mulliniks led AL third basemen in fielding percentage three years in a row, 1984-1986.
Playing Career: *1977-1992; Cal A, KC A, Tor A*

Joe Mulvey
Mulvey, Joseph H.
B: Oct 27, 1858   D: Aug 21, 1928

Pos: 3B	BA: .261
Hits: 1,059	HRs: 29
RBI: 431 (inc.)	BBs: 134

Mulvey learned baseball playing for Harry Wright with the 1880s NL Phillies. His best year was 1890 with the Players' League, when he scored 96 runs with 26 doubles and 15 triples. A good baserunner, he stole 174 bases between 1886 and 1895.
Playing Career: *1883-1893, 1895; Pro N, Phi N, Phi P, Phi AA, Was N, Brk N*

Jerry Mumphrey
Mumphrey, Jerry Wayne
B: Sep 9, 1952

Pos: OF	BA: .289
Hits: 1,442	HRs: 70
RBI: 575	BBs: 478

Improving steadily as he got older, Mumphrey finished his career with five .300 seasons in seven years. He hit .500 as the Yankees destroyed the A's in the 1981 ALCS. Mumphrey hit 13 homers in 1987, his next to last year. A speedster, he twice legged out 10 triples in a season, and stole 174 bases. In 1980 he was traded to the Yankees and shared the World Series gold. Mumphrey made the NL All-Star team in 1984.
Playing Career: *1974-1988; StL N, SD N, NY A, Hou N, Chi N*

Bob Muncrief
Muncrief, Robert Cleveland
B: Jan 28, 1916

Pos: P	ERA: 3.80
W-L: 80-82	SOs: 525
ShOs: 11	Saves: 9

Contributing to the Browns only pennant in the franchise history, Muncrief won 13 games four times in five years. After pitching in the 1944 World Series, he moved on to the Indians, where he made another World Series appearance in 1948.
Playing Career: *1937, 1939, 1941-1949, 1951; StL A, Cle A, Pit N, Chi N, NY A*

George Munger
Munger, George David (Red)
B: Oct 4, 1918

Pos: P	ERA: 3.83
W-L: 77-56	SOs: 564
ShOs: 13	Saves: 12

A wartime hurler for the 1944 Cardinals, Munger was 11-3 with a 1.34 ERA before going into the military in midseason. When he returned, Munger pitched in the 1946 World Series, winning one game. He was an All-Star selection three times, 1944, 1947 and 1949.
Playing Career: *1943-1944, 1946-1952, 1956; StL N, Pit N*

Van Lingle Mungo
Mungo, Van Lingle
B: Jun 8, 1911   D: Feb 12, 1985

Pos: P	ERA: 3.47
W-L: 120-115	SOs: 1,242
ShOs: 20	Saves: 16

A ballplayer could not have a better name than Van Lingle Mungo. One of the fastest pitchers ever, Mungo's fastball was measured by draftsmen at West Point, and rated at 100 mph. Delivering with a high kick, Mungo was wild and mean and had a ferocious temper. He was a heavy drinker, and was involved in bizarre off-the-field inci-

dents. He was once smuggled out of Cuba to escape the machete-wielding husband of a nightclub dancer with whom he had an affair.

Mungo's career went downhill following an arm injury in the 1937 All-Star Game, the same one in which Dizzy Dean broke his toe. In his glory days, Mungo was great despite being saddled with sorry Dodgers teams. He wore himself out trying to strike out every batter. An All-Star pitcher three times, Mungo was the toughest NL hurler to hit against in 1936 and 1937.
Playing Career: *1931-1943, 1945; Brk N, NY N*

Thurman Munson
Munson, Thurman Lee
B: Jun 7, 1947   D: Aug 2, 1979

Pos: C, DH	BA: .292
Hits: 1,558	HRs: 113
RBI: 701	BBs: 438

In the midst of a tremendous career, Munson hit .529 during the 1976 World Series in a losing effort. Munson was the AL MVP that year. He led AL catchers twice in assists and twice in double plays during his career. Under his leadership the Yankees went from a mediocre team to win their own back-to-back World Championships in 1977 and 1978. After a slow start Munson had hit .302 and captured the AL Rookie of the Year Award in 1970.

Munson's honors were many: three Gold Gloves, seven All-Star selections, three division titles, three pennants and three World Series. He hit .339 in the ALCS and .373 in the

Yankee catcher Thurman Munson, 1978.

Fall Classics. Off the field, he was a leader in the Yankees' clubhouse, no mean feat considering that Billy Martin, Sparky Lyle, Goose Gossage, Reggie Jackson and George Steinbrenner were also there. Munson died tragically on August 2, 1979, when the private plane he was piloting crashed near Canton, Ohio.

Playing Career: *1969-1979; NY A*

Bobby Murcer
Murcer, Bobby Ray
B: May 20, 1946

Pos: OF	BA: .277
Hits: 1,862	HRs: 252
RBI: 1,043	BBs: 862

Heralded as the next Mickey Mantle, Murcer was from Oklahoma and hit home runs, but failed to lead the Bronx Bombers to pennants like Mantle did. After two brief stints with the Yankees in 1965 and 1966, Murcer spent the next two years maturing in the Army. When he returned he did not recognize the famous Yankees. Gone were Mantle, Maris, Ford, Richardson, Boyer and Howard. He was given Mantle's locker and expected to fill Mantle's shoes. He tried.

In 1970 Murcer hit home runs on four consecutive at-bats, the only Yankee other than Lou Gehrig to accomplish that. During the 1971 season, he began to hit to left field and reduce his strikeouts, boosting his average by 80 points to .331. Murcer finished second in the batting race that year, and it marked his arrival as a star. He hit at least 22 homers in each of his first five full seasons, bashing a career-high 33 in 1972. He drove in a league- and career-high 102 runs that year and won a Gold Glove.

Playing Career: *1965-1966, 1969-1983; NY A, SF N, Chi N*

Tim Murnane
Murnane, Timothy Hayes
B: Jun 4, 1852   D: Feb 7, 1917

Pos: 1B, OF, 2B	BA: .261
Hits: 425	HRs: 3
RBI: 86 (inc.)	BBs: 44

Managerial Record
Won: 58   Lost: 51   Pct: .532

A beloved figure, Murnane became a sportswriter and Connecticut State League president after his playing days. He defended players' rights, deplored high salaries, and criticized umpires. When he died in 1917, leaving a widow and four young children, his colleagues organized a fund-raising game. The Red Sox donated the use of Fenway Park, and pitcher Babe Ruth shut out an all-star team, raising $10,000.

Playing Career: *1872-1878, 1884; Mid Mansfields n, Phi Athletics n, Phi White Stockings n, Bos N, Pro N, Bos U*
Managerial Career: *1884; Bos U*

Dale Murphy
Murphy, Dale Bryan
B: Mar 12, 1956

Pos: OF, 1B, C	BA: .265
Hits: 2,111	HRs: 398
RBI: 1,266	BBs: 986

A real-life Chip Hilton, Murphy looked and acted like a hero, both on the field and off. Winner of back-to-back MVP Awards, 1982 and 1983, he led the NL in home runs the following two years, with 36 and 37. He also won Gold Glove Awards five straight years, 1982-1986, as a Braves outfielder. At one time Murphy looked like a sure bet for the Hall of Fame, but he had five tough years at the end of his career.

Before switching to the outfield, Murphy struggled to become a catcher, but he had trouble throwing the ball back to the pitcher. He also led the NL in strikeouts, with 145 in 1978 and 133 in 1980, before his metamorphosis. Murphy was the top vote-getter for the

Atlanta's heavy-hitting outfielder Dale Murphy at the plate in 1989.

Yankee outfielder Bobby Murcer, 1980.

1985 All-Star Game, one of seven times he was elected. He played more games than any other Atlanta Brave, including 740 consecutive games. The streak should have ended when Murphy cut the palm of his right hand – requiring nine stitches – but the next day he blasted a pinch-hit home run.

Playing Career: *1976-1993; Atl N, Phi N, Col N*

Danny Murphy
Murphy, Daniel Francis
B: Aug 11, 1876   D: Nov 22, 1955

Pos: 2B, OF	BA: .288
Hits: 1,577	HRs: 44
RBI: 708	BBs: 338

Captain of the A's and one of Connie Mack's favorites, Murphy was an expert sign stealer. He pilfered 161 bags and batted .300 seven times, including five in a row after the introduction of the lively baseball with a cork center.

Playing Career: *1900-1915; NY N, Phi A, Brk F*

Dwayne Murphy
Murphy, Dwayne Keith
B: Mar 18, 1955

Pos: OF	BA: .246
Hits: 1,089	HRs: 166
RBI: 609	BBs: 747

One of the most underrated outfielders, Murphy won six straight Gold Gloves, 1980-1985. A defensive star with surprising power, he hit 33 homers in 1984 and drove in 94 runs in 1982. Back and foot injuries ended his career.

Playing Career: *1978-1989; Oak A, Det A, Phi N*

Eddie Murphy
Murphy, John Edward (Honest Eddie)
B: Oct 2, 1891   D: Feb 21, 1969

Pos: OF	BA: .287
Hits: 680	HRs: 4
RBI: 195	BBs: 294

Labelled "Honest Eddie" because he did not participate in the 1919 World Series fix, Murphy played in three Fall Classics altogether. He led the AL with eight pinch hits, hitting .486, as a member of the 1919 White Sox.

Playing Career: *1912-1921, 1926; Phi A, Chi A, Pit N*

Johnny Murphy
Murphy, John Joseph (Grandma, Fireman)
B: Jul 14, 1908   D: Jan 14, 1970

Pos: P	ERA: 3.50
W-L: 93-53	SOs: 378
ShOs: 0	Saves: 107

When New York was reeling from the success of the 1969 Mets, they applauded Murphy, who as farm director, was the

Johnny Murphy, ace reliever for the Yankees from 1932 to 1946.

genius behind the team. Many had forgotten that he had also been the great reliever on the powerful Bronx Bombers, winners of four World Championships in a row. When Lefty Gomez was asked to predict how many games he would win, he replied "Go ask Murphy." Murphy led the AL in saves four times, and was 2-0 with four saves in six World Series.

Playing Career: *1932, 1934-1947; NY A, Bos A*

Tom Murphy
Murphy, Thomas Andrew
B: Dec 30, 1945

Pos: P	ERA: 3.78
W-L: 68-101	SOs: 621
ShOs: 3	Saves: 59

As a starter in the early 1970s, Murphy led the Angels to their winningest season in their first 18 years with his 16-13 record. The Brewers switched him to relief; he won 10 and saved 20 with a 1.90 ERA in 1974. The Blue Jays later used him in middle relief.

Playing Career: *1968-1979; Cal A, KC A, StL N, Mil A, Bos A, Tor A*

Dale Murray
Murray, Dale Albert
B: Feb 2, 1950

Pos: P	ERA: 3.85
W-L: 53-50	SOs: 400
ShOs: 0	Saves: 60

As a rookie Murray recorded a 1.03 ERA with 10 saves in 1974. He seldom gave up home runs. The Yankees traded Dave Collins, Fred McGriff, Mike Morgan and $400,000 for him in December 1982, but the deal backfired when Murray developed a medical condition that ended his career.

Playing Career: *1974-1985; Mon N, Cin N, NY N, Tor A, NY A, Tex A*

Eddie Murray
Murray, Eddie Clarence
B: Feb 24, 1956

Pos: 1B, DH	BA: .290
Hits: 2,820	HRs: 441
RBI: 1,662	BBs: 1,187

Murray is a potent Hall of Fame candidate. The only non-Hall of Famer with more RBI is

Baltimore's Eddie Murray, 1982.

Manager Danny Murtaugh (c) awaits a shower after winning the 1960 NL pennant.

Tony Perez. Elected to the All-Star roster eight times, Murray led the league in various categories seven times, three times in fielding average. He was honored with the Gold Glove Award three times, 1982-1984. Rookie of the Year in 1977, Murray batted .283 with 27 homers and 88 RBI. The RBI figure turned out to be low for the switch hitter; he exceeded that mark every year but two.

In the strike-shortened 1981 season, Murray led the AL in RBI with 78. He has 17 career grand slams, ranking him third on the all-time list. He is 17th on the career RBI chart, and 20th on the home run list. Faring poorly in the 1979 World Series surprise loss to the Pirates, Murray fared better in the 1983 Fall Classic, hitting two homers in the fifth game Series victory over the Phillies. Murray has been put on the disabled list only once, in 1986.
Playing Career: 1977- Bal A, LA N, NY N

Red Murray
Murray, John Joseph
B: Mar 4, 1884   D: Dec 4, 1958

Pos: OF	BA: .270
Hits: 1,170	HRs: 37
RBI: 579	BBs: 298

Murray stole 321 bases, and played in three World Series for the black-shirted Giants. He led the NL with seven home runs in 1909, and he finished second each year in stolen bases, 1908-1910. A strong-armed right fielder, he led the NL with 30 assists in 1909 and 26 in 1910. Two years later, Murray made the greatest catch in Forbes Field history. Fans recalled that heavy thunderclouds threatened throughout the game. At the moment of his leaping, fingertip catch, a blinding lightning bolt lit up the sky.
Playing Career: 1906-1915, 1917; StL N, NY N, Chi N

Danny Murtaugh
Murtaugh, Daniel Edward
B: Oct 8, 1917   D: Dec 2, 1976

Pos: 2B	BA: .254
Hits: 661	HRs: 8
RBI: 219	BBs: 287
Managerial Record	
Won: 1,115 Lost: 950 Pct: .540	

One of the most successful major league managers, Murtaugh won two World Series, both of them the most exciting of their era. He captured four division titles in five years. As a player, Murtaugh was inconsistent; he led the NL in stolen bases with 18 in 1941, but batted only .219. He hit over .290 twice but under .220 four times. He began managing in the Pirates' system in 1952 during Branch Rickey's youth experiment.

Murtaugh's *coup de grâce* was the 1960 World Series when he upset Casey Stengel and the Yankees in a seven-game Series in which the Bronx Bombers set records for runs, hits and batting average, and still lost. Suffering ill health, Murtaugh retired several times, but always returned when the Pirates needed him. He rebuilt the Pittsburgh club, taking them to four division titles and another World Championship in 1971.
Playing Career: 1941-1943, 1946-1951; Phi N, Bos N, Pit N
Managerial Career: 1957-1964, 1970-1971, 1973-1976; Pit N

Stan "The Man" Musial is greeted by teammates as he returns to the dugout in 1962.

Stan Musial
Musial, Stanley Frank (Stan the Man)
B: Nov 21, 1920
Hall of Fame 1969

Pos: OF, 1B	BA: .331
Hits: 3,630	HRs: 475
RBI: 1,951	BBs 1,599

One of baseball's most beloved and greatest players, Musial batted from a peek-a-boo stance in which he curled himself like a question mark, looking at the pitcher from over his right shoulder. He won the NL batting title in his second full year. Musial led the NL in hits six times, doubles eight times, triples five times, runs five times, and won five more batting titles. Preacher Roe claimed he knew the best way to pitch Musial: ''I throw him four wide ones and then I try to pick him off first base.''

Musial was so consistent that he seldom experienced a slump. He scored 1,949 runs, swatted 725 doubles and 177 triples while slugging .559. He played 3,026 games. When he retired, Musial owned or shared 29 NL records, 17 major league records, nine All-Star records, including most All-Star home runs, and almost every Cardinals career offensive record.
Playing Career: *1941-1944, 1945-1963; StL N*

Jim Mutrie
Mutrie, James J.
B: Jun 13, 1851   D: Jan 24, 1938

Managerial Record
Won: 658   Lost: 419   Pct: .611

Ranked second on the all-time won-lost percentage list with a .611 mark, Mutrie never appeared in a major league game. His teams won three pennants, two back-to-back in the NL and one in the American Association. He managed the original New York Mets and gave the Giants their nickname. Mutrie's Giants finished second to the White Stockings with a .795 percentage in 1885, the highest second-place mark in history.
Managerial Career: *1883-1891; NY AA, NY N*

Glenn Myatt
Myatt, Glenn Calvin
B: Jul 9, 1897   D: Aug 9, 1969

Pos: C	BA: .270
Hits: 722	HRs: 38
RBI: 387	BBs: 249

A platoon catcher with the Indians during the 1920s, Myatt was another find of Connie Mack. Myatt joined the A's after spending 1919 in the Navy, then was shipped to Cleveland. He batted .342 as the Indians' starting catcher in 1924, but played backup to Luke Sewell.
Playing Career: *1920-1921, 1923-1936; Phi A, Cle A, NY N, Det A*

Buddy Myer
Myer, Charles Solomon
B: Mar 16, 1904   D: Oct 31, 1974

Pos: 2B	BA: .303
Hits: 2,131	HRs: 38
RBI: 850	BBs: 965

Author Bill James did an interesting study comparing Hall of Famer Billy Herman with Buddy Myer. The conclusion was that everything Herman did, Myer did better, but in a different league. Myer won a batting title in 1935 on several last-minute hits when the Indians' Joe Vosmik attempted to win by sitting out the last game. Myer led the league with 30 stolen bases and batted .313 in 1928. He led AL second basemen in fielding, 1931-1938.

Myer played for two Senators pennant-winning teams, batting .250 in 1925 and .300 in 1933. He was also selected for the AL All-Star squad twice. He scored 1,174 runs, four times going over 100. He also drove in 100 runs in 1935. Washington owner Clark Griffith had to give up five players to get Myer back after the 1928 season after trading him to the Red Sox for Topper Rigney in 1927. Griffith always acknowledged it as the dumbest thing he ever did.
Playing Career: *1925-1941; Was A, Bos A*

Al Myers
Myers, James Albert
B: Oct 22, 1863   D: Dec 24, 1927

Pos: 2B	BA: .245
Hits: 788	HRs: 13
RBI: 331	BBs: 294

The stress-filled 1890 season was Myers's best. With three major leagues competing for fans and players, Myers hit .277 with 29 doubles, scored 95 runs, and stole 44 bases. The latter was astounding considering he stole only 111 altogether.
Playing Career: *1884-1891; Mil U, Phi N, KC N, Was N*

Billy Myers
Myers, William Harrison
B: Aug 14, 1910

Pos: SS	BA: .257
Hits: 616	HRs: 45
RBI: 243	BBs: 250

Myers was glue that held together the 1939 Reds infield. He batted .281 and scored 79 runs that year. He was adept at picking up hit-and-run and steal signs. He batted .333 in the 1939 World Series, and his sacrifice fly drove in the winning run in the seventh game of the 1940 World Series.
Playing Career: *1935-1941; Cin N, Chi N*

Buddy Myer at Red Sox training camp after being traded by the Senators, 1928.

Elmer Myers
Myers, Elmer Glenn
B: Mar 2, 1894   D: Jul 29, 1976

Pos: P	ERA: 4.06
W-L: 55-72	SOs: 428
ShOs: 8	Saves: 7

Myers arrived in Philadelphia when Connie Mack was dismantling his first dynasty. The right-hander shut out the Senators 4-0 in his first game. As a rookie in 1916, the youngster tossed 315 innings, losing 23, but winning 14 for the last-place A's.
Playing Career: *1915-1922; Phi A, Cle A, Bos A*

Hy Myers
Myers, Henry Harrison
B: Apr 27, 1889   D: May 1, 1965

Pos: OF, 2B, 3B	BA: .281
Hits: 1,380	HRs: 32
RBI: 559	BBs: 195

One of the best unknown players in baseball history, Myers played 11 years with the Dodgers, 1909-1922, encompassing the Nap Rucker to Zack Wheat eras. When Myers first came to Brooklyn he was a hayseed out of East Liverpool, Ohio, the stomping grounds of Cy Young. By the time he left the borough he was one of the most popular Dodgers ever, yet few outside New York knew him.

Myers led the NL twice in triples, garnering a total of 100. In 1919 he led the league in three offensive categories and one defensive category, but was lost in the shadows of illuminaries Zack Wheat, Ivy Olson, Ed Konetchy and Otto Miller, and a pitching staff that included Burleigh Grimes and Sherry Smith. Myers hit a home run off Babe Ruth in the first inning of Game Two of the 1916 World Series. The Dodgers then went the next 13 innings without a run, starting Ruth's Series pitching record of consecutive scoreless innings.
Playing Career: *1909, 1911, 1914-1925; Brk N, StL N, Cin N*

Randy Myers
Myers, Randall Kirk
B: Sep 19, 1962

Pos: P	ERA: 3.07
W-L: 32-42	SOs: 622
ShOs: 0	Saves: 184

The possessor of a 98-mph fastball, Myers set the NL single-season saves record with 53 in 1993. Now one of the most feared closers in baseball, he had frequently been used as a setup man, first for Roger McDowell of the Mets, then for Rob Dibble of the Reds. Myers is at his best in postseason play. He was 2-0 with a 0.00 ERA for the Mets in the 1988 NLCS, saved three for the Reds in the 1990 NLCS, and saved one with another 0.00 ERA in the World Series that year. He was chosen for the 1990 NL All-Star team.
Playing Career: *1985-; NY N, Cin N, SD N, Chi N*

Brooklyn Dodgers favorite Henry Harrison "Hy" Myers.

Ray Narleski
Narleski, Raymond Edmond
B: Nov 25, 1928

Pos: P	ERA: 3.60
W-L: 43-33	SOs: 454
ShOs: 1	Saves: 58

A bullpen ace early in his career, Narleski served in the Indians' relief corps that included Don Mossi and Hal Newhouser. Narleski pitched four innings with a 2.25 ERA in the 1954 World Series. In 1955 he led the AL in appearances and saves. He was an All-Star twice.
Playing Career: *1954-1959; Cle A, Det A*

Billy Nash
Nash, William Mitchell
B: Jun 24, 1865   D: Nov 15, 1929

Pos: OF	BA: .275
Hits: 1,606	HRs: 61
RBI: 977	BBs: 803
Managerial Record	
Won: 62 Lost: 68 Pct: .477	

As the Phillies' manager in 1896, Nash went to Fall River, Massachusetts, to scout a player and returned with Nap Lajoie. Nash was a very popular, top-fielding third baseman in Boston for 11 seasons, counting his stint in the Players' League. He scored 1,072 runs and stole 249 bases, with 43 in 1887 alone. He led NL third basemen in fielding four times, and played on three pennant-winning teams.
Playing Career: *1884-1898; Ric AA, Bos N, Bos P, Phi N*
Managerial Career: *1896; Phi N*

Jim Nash
Nash, James Edwin
B: Feb 9, 1945

Pos: P	ERA: 3.59
W-L: 68-64	SOs: 771
ShOs: 11	Saves: 4

In 1966 Nash looked like the second coming of Cy Young. Breaking in with a 12-1 record and a 2.02 ERA, Nash was easily the AL Rookie Pitcher of the Year. Later he became easy to hit, and yielded hits to more than 30 percent of the batters he faced during his last four years.
Playing Career: *1966-1972; KC A, Oak A, Atl N, Phi N*

Frank Navin
Navin, Frank (Lucky Frank)
B: Mar 7, 1871   D: Nov 13, 1935

While working for Tigers owner Sam Angus as an accountant, Navin persuaded William Yawkey to purchase the team from his boss. Navin was allowed to buy a $5,000 share in the club – he reputedly won the money in a poker game. In 1905 Navin forced Ed Barrow out, and took over as general manager of the Tigers. Acting on the advice of manager Bill Armour, Navin signed a tenacious teenager from Georgia named Ty Cobb. The youngster was a troublemaker, but Navin was shrewd enough to resist trading him. The Cobb deal and other astute acquisitions made the Tigers into three-time AL champions, 1907-1909. In gratitude, Yawkey gave Navin half ownership of the club, which Navin served as president from 1908 until his death. Navin became a wealthy civic leader, but was nearly ruined by the Depression in 1931. To save himself from financial disaster he sold most of his Tigers stock to William O. Briggs. The baseball park known as Tiger Stadium was called Navin Field from 1912 to 1937, when it became known as Briggs Stadium.

Charlie Neal
Neal, Charles Leonard
B: Jan 30, 1931

Pos: 2B, SS	BA: .259
Hits: 858	HRs: 87
RBI: 391	BBs: 337

A consistent fielder, Neal won a Gold Glove Award in 1958. When the Dodgers moved to the Coliseum in Los Angeles, his bat came alive. He hit 22 homers in 1958, and batted .370 with a .667 slugging average in the 1959 World Series. Neal was chosen for the All-Star Game twice.
Playing Career: *1956-1963; Brk N, LA N, NY N, Cin N*

Greasy Neale
Neale, Alfred Earle
B: Nov 5, 1891   D: Nov 2, 1973

Pos: OF	BA: .259
Hits: 688	HRs: 8
RBI: 200	BBs: 201

A celebrated football coach and a member of the Pro Football Hall of Fame, Neale batted .357 in the Reds' stunning 1919 World Series victory. Cincinnati fans acclaimed Neale as the surprise great performer of the Series.
Playing Career: *1916-1922, 1924; Cin N, Phi N*

Art Nehf
Nehf, Arthur Neukom
B: Jul 31, 1892   D: Dec 18, 1960

Pos: P	ERA: 3.20
W-L: 184-120	SOs: 844
ShOs: 30	Saves: 13

John McGraw paid $55,000 for Nehf in 1919. McGraw was impressed with the hurler's 15-15 record the year before, when he started 31 games and completed 28. Nehf won a career-high 21 games in 1920, but the Giants came up short against the Dodgers. Over the next four years Nehf was 66-37, and the Giants won four straight pennants.

He was a terror in postseason play. In the 1921 Subway Series, Nehf lost the first two games as the Giants scored only one unearned run, but he whipped the Yankees 1-0 in the finale to give the Giants a prestige championship. In the 1922 World Series, Nehf again won the decisive contest. He pitched another 1-0 shutout against the Yankees in Game Three of the 1923 Series. In

Tigers President Frank Navin.

Giants hurler Art Nehf.

the 1924 Series opener, Nehf beat the Senators' Walter Johnson in 12 innings, but he lost Game Six 2-1. Washington took the title the following day. Nehf was 4-4 with a 2.16 ERA in five World Series.
Playing Career: *1915-1929; Bos N, NY N, Cin N, Chi N*

Candy Nelson
Nelson, John W.
B: Mar 12, 1854   D: Sep 4, 1910

Pos: SS	BA: .253
Hits: 831	HRs: 3
RBI: 63 (inc.)	BBs: 353

Nelson played baseball for more than 30 years, starting with the amateur Eckfords. The little shortstop did not smoke or drink and never missed a game due to illness. In 1890 the Brooklyn AA team refused to pay him, so he sued them.
Playing Career: *1872-1875, 1878-1879, 1881, 1883-1887, 1890; Tro Haymakers n, Brk Eckfords n, NY Mutuals n, Ind N, Tro N, Wor N, NY AA, Brk AA*

Dave Nelson
Nelson, David Earl
B: Jun 20, 1944

Pos: 2B	BA: .244
Hits: 630	HRs: 20
RBI: 211	BBs: 220

Playing with the Senators for Ted Williams, Nelson stole a career-high 51 bases in 1972. His best season came the next year when he hit .286 with 7 home runs, 24 doubles and 71 runs scored. Nelson was selected for the All-Star squad that year.
Playing Career: *1968-1977; Cle A, Was A, Tex A, KC A*

Gene Nelson
Nelson, Wayland Eugene
B: Dec 3, 1960

Pos: P	ERA: 4.13
W-L: 53-64	SOs: 655
ShOs: 1	Saves: 28

Former White Sox manager Tony LaRussa spotted Nelson in the minor leagues and took him along when he went to manage Oakland. Nelson is a valuable man out of the bullpen and was an integral part of the A's four division titles in five years.
Playing Career: *1981-; NY A, Sea A, Chi A, Oak A, Cal A, Tex A*

Rocky Nelson
Nelson, Glenn Richard
B: Nov 18, 1924

Pos: 1B	BA: .249
Hits: 347	HRs: 31
RBI: 173	BBs: 130

Between cups of coffee in the major leagues, Nelson won the Triple Crown in the International League in 1955 and 1958. He shared first base duties with Dick Stuart of the Pirates in 1960, and batted .333 in the World Series that year.
Playing Career: *1949-1952, 1954, 1956, 1959-1961; StL N, Pit N, Chi A, Brk N, Cle A*

Graig Nettles
Nettles, Graig
B: Aug 20, 1944

Pos: 3B	BA: .248
Hits: 2,225	HRs: 390
RBI: 1,314	BBs: 1,088

One of the slickest infielders of the 1970s, Nettles burst into the headlines following his trade to the Indians. In 1971 he set AL records with 412 assists and 54 double plays. He led the league in assists again in 1972. Like others who have exceptional range, Nettles took risks and made lots of errors. He won only two Gold Glove Awards, but he made some thrilling plays. In Game Three of the 1978 World Series, Nettles made four dazzling stops, enabling the Yankees – who lost the first two games to the Dodgers – to win that contest. They went on to win the next three as well, and became World Champions.

Nettles also made significant offensive contributions. He scored 1,193 runs. On September 14, 1974, he and his brother Jim homered in the same game. Graig led the AL in homers in 1976, and holds the record for AL third basemen with 319 home runs. In the 1981 Fall Classic, he batted .400. Nettles played in seven ALCS, and was voted onto the All-Star team six times.
Playing Career: *1967-1988; Min A, Cle A, NY A, SD N, Atl N, Mon N*

Johnny Neun
Neun, John Henry
B: Oct 28, 1900

Pos: 1B	BA: .289
Hits: 273	HRs: 2
RBI: 85	BBs: 110
Managerial Record	
Won: 125 Lost: 143 Pct: .466	

On May 31, 1927, Neun, a part-time player, turned an unassisted triple play – the only first baseman to do so in the majors. Neun snagged Homer Summa's line drive, tagged Charlie Jamieson off first, then dashed toward second and tagged the base before Glenn Myatt could get back.
Playing Career: *1925-1928, 1930-1931; Det A, Bos N*
Managerial Career: *1946-1948; NY A, Cin N*

Don Newcombe
Newcombe, Donald (Newk, Big Newk)
B: Jun 14, 1926

Pos: P	ERA: 3.56
W-L: 149-90	SOs: 1,129
ShOs: 24	Saves: 7

When the Baseball Writers Association of America chose the first Cy Young Award winner in 1956, they honored Don New-

Dodgers ace Don Newcombe.

combe. He had a record of 27-7, leading the NL with a .794 winning percentage, but he did not make the All-Star team that year. Newcombe was the only player to be the Rookie of the Year, the MVP, and the Cy Young Award winner during his career. At 6'4" and 220 pounds, he was physically imposing, and had an exploding fastball that AL hitters ranked with those of Bob Feller and Virgil Trucks.

Newcombe was the mainstay on the pitching staff of the "Boys of Summer" – the Dodgers of 1949 to 1956. Newcombe could also hit. He batted .271 for 10 years; his best season was 1955 when he batted .359, hit 7 homers and drove in 23 runs. He also hit .361 for the Reds in 1959. Newcombe made the All-Star team four times, and won 20 games or more three times. Before inking a Dodger contract, Newcombe pitched with the Newark Eagles in the Negro Leagues.
Playing Career: *1949-1951, 1954-1960; Brk N, Cin N, Cle A*

Hal Newhouser
Newhouser, Harold (Prince Hal)
B: May 20, 1921
Hall of Fame 1992

Pos: P	ERA: 3.06
W-L: 207-150	SOs: 1,796
ShOs: 33	Saves: 26

A fierce competitor, Newhouser had to learn to control both his temper and his fastball. Once he accomplished that, he was nearly unbeatable, with records of 29-9, 25-9, and 26-9 from 1944 to 1946. Leading the AL in multiple pitching categories in 1944 and 1945, he became the only pitcher to win two consecutive MVP Awards. Newhouser led the league in ERA again in 1946.

Newhouser was an All-Star choice from 1942 through 1948, and won two games in the 1945 World Series, including the finale. On two days rest, he defeated Bob Feller on the last day of the 1948 season, forcing a playoff in the AL pennant race. Averaging 21.5 wins per season, 1944-1950, Newhouser succumbed to shoulder trouble that landed him in the bullpen. He was successful in that role

Hal Newhouser, the only pitcher ever to win consecutive MVPs (1944 and 1945).

Doc Newton
Newton, Eustace James
B: Oct 26, 1877   D: May 14, 1931

Pos: P	ERA: 3.22
W-L: 53-72	SOs: 502
ShOs: 9	Saves: 3

A major league caliber pitcher, Newton preferred the laid-back conditions of the Pacific Coast League to the intensity of the AL and NL pennant races. He set a record for errors by NL pitchers in 1901. Newton had back-to-back 30-win seasons in the PCL.
Playing Career: *1900-1902, 1905-1909; Cin N, Brk N, NY A*

Kid Nichols
Nichols, Charles Augustus
B: Sep 14, 1869   D: Apr 11, 1953
Hall of Fame 1949

Pos: P	ERA: 2.94
W-L: 361-208	SOs: 1,877
ShOs: 48	Saves: 17
Managerial Record	
Won: 80 Lost: 88 Pct: .476	

The Kid may have been the best pitcher in baseball history. He started the same year as Cy Young, and after 10 years had more wins than the master. Nichols was a contemporary of Amos Rusie, but outpointed him in the statistics while Rusie got the headlines. A star from the moment he made his major league debut at age 20 in 1890, Nichols topped the

as well, saving 26 games and winning 20 in relief during his career. Newhouser rose, Phoenix-like, with the 1954 Indians, who won an all-time AL high 111 games. He was 7-2 with 7 saves for the Tribe that year and pitched in the World Series.
Playing Career: *1939-1955; Det A, Cle A*

Bobo Newsom
Newsom, Louis Norman (Bobo, Buck)
B: Aug 11, 1907   D: Dec 7, 1962

Pos: P	ERA: 3.98
W-L: 211-222	SOs: 2,082
ShOs: 31	No-hitters: 1

Newsom pitched 20 seasons of major league baseball. He had three consecutive 20-game seasons, 1938-1940, but he was dogged by bad luck. Newsom lost 222 games and issued 1,732 bases on balls, ranking him sixth on the all-time list. He played for the hapless Senators five different times. On September 18, 1934, Newsom pitched nine no-hit innings, only to lose 2-1 on a 10th-inning hit. He was suspended by his own manager for throwing a spitball. He once had his kneecap broken by a line drive, yet hobbled on to a complete-game victory.

In 1940 Newsom compiled a record of 21-5 and pitched the opening game of the World Series. His father died suddenly after watching his son's victory. Newsom dedicated his next game to his father, and won that one as well. But he lost Game Seven to the Reds, 2-1. He appeared in the 1947 World Series for the Yankees, and was selected to three All-Star squads.
Playing Career: *1929-1930, 1932, 1934-1948, 1952-1953; Brk N, Chi N, StL A, Was A, Bos A, Det A, Phi A, NY A, NY N*

Skeeter Newsome
Newsome, Lamar Ashby
B: Oct 18, 1910   D: Aug 31, 1989

Pos: SS, 3B, 2B	BA: .245
Hits: 910	HRs: 9
RBI: 292	BBs: 246

A middle infielder who played regularly for five years, Newsome stroked over 100 hits each full-time season. He became a minor league manager extraordinaire, winning three pennants in three different leagues during the 1950s.
Playing Career: *1935-1939, 1941-1947; Phi A, Bos A, Phi N*

Boston Beaneaters pitcher Kid Nichols.

25-victory mark in each of his first nine seasons, leading the Beaneater staff to five NL pennants.

He was an overhand pitcher with a smooth delivery, control and a dangerous fastball. Nichols was 27-19 as a rookie, then won 30 games or more for seven seasons in a row – a feat never equaled in baseball history. He led the league in wins, 1896-1898. As the staff ace, he threw more than 400 innings five years in a row, then 300 innings in six of the next seven years. Nichols had posted 300 victories by age 30. Returning to the majors after three years in business, he managed the Cardinals, for whom he won 21 games in 1904.
Playing Career: *1890-1901, 1904-1906; Bos N, StL N, Phi N*
Managerial Career: *1904-1905; StL N*

Bill Nicholson
Nicholson, William Beck (Swish)
B: Dec 11, 1914

Pos: OF   BA: .268
Hits: 1,484   HRs: 235
RBI: 948   BBs: 800

It was the seventh inning of a 1944 doubleheader at the Polo Grounds – New York 12, Chicago 9, bases loaded with Cubs, Nicholson at the plate. He had already hit four consecutive home runs that day, so he was intentionally walked. The Giants won 12-10. Swish was the sound fans made when they wanted Nicholson to hit a home run, which he did frequently. He led the NL with 29 homers and 128 RBI in 1943, and again in 1944 with 33 homers and 122 RBI.
Playing Career: *1936, 1939-1953; Phi A, Chi N, Phi N*

Hugh Nicol
Nicol, Hugh N.
B: Jan 1, 1858   D: Jun 27, 1921

Pos: OF   BA: .235
Hits: 813   HRs: 5
RBI: 631   BBs: 337
Managerial Record
Won: 8   Lost: 32   Pct: .200

Nicol stole a whopping 138 bases in 1887, the all-time record. He was mad at the Browns for having let him go at the end of 1886 and was determined to show them up. Nicol scored 122 runs that year with only 102 hits. In 1888 he stole 103 bases and scored 112 runs.
Playing Career: *1881-1890; Chi N, StL AA, Cin AA, Cin N*
Managerial Career: *1897; StL N*

Tom Niedenfuer
Niedenfuer, Thomas Edward
B: Aug 13, 1959

Pos: P   ERA: 3.29
W-L: 36-46   SOs: 474
ShOs: 0   Saves: 97

Cardinal fans remember Neidenfuer as the man who served up homers to Ozzie Smith and Jack Clark in the 1985 NLCS; Clark's blow won the pennant for the Red Birds. In the 1981 World Series, Niedenfuer had not given up a run in 5⅔ pressure-filled innings.
Playing Career: *1981-1990; LA N, Bal A, Sea A, StL N*

Joe Niekro, with Houston in 1980.

Joe Niekro
Niekro, Joseph Franklin
B: Nov 7, 1944

Pos: P   ERA: 3.59
W-L: 221-204   SOs: 1,747
ShOs: 29   Saves: 16

When Joe Niekro reached 21 wins in 1979, he tied another pitcher for the NL lead – his brother Phil. The pair is baseball's winningest duo of brothers, with 539 victories. Joe Niekro struggled early in his career, his fastball faded and his curveball flattened. He developed a knuckleball, and with it, reached his peak in 1979. He was chosen for the All-Star team that year, and led the NL in shutouts with five. Niekro won NL Pitcher of the Year and was runner-up in Cy Young Award voting.

Niekro won a single-game playoff for the Astros over the Dodgers in 1980, another 20-game season. He then tossed 10 shutout innings in Game Three of the NLCS. He won more games than any other pitcher in Astros history, and ranks in the top three for every Astros pitching category except ERA and saves. Caught with a nail file in his pocket while pitching, Niekro was suspended during the 1987 season, but he finally made it to the World Series that year.
Playing Career: *1967-1988; Chi N, SD N, Det A, Atl N, Hou N, NY A, Min A*

The Cubs' home run king Bill "Swish" Nicholson.

Phil Niekro
Niekro, Philip Henry (Knucksie)
B: Apr 1, 1939

Pos: P	ERA: 3.35
W-L: 318-274	SOs: 3,342
ShOs: 45	No-hitters: 1

Phil Niekro tossed his flutterball until he was 48 years old, the oldest man to play regularly in the major leagues. He had great endurance, pitching more than 300 innings four times, a stunning 5,403 innings altogether. Once he led the NL in strikeouts, another time in ERA, with a 1.87 mark. Niekro completed 20 or more games, 1977-1979, leading the NL each season. He won 32 games for the Yankees, 1984-1985, at age 45-46.

Niekro was selected for five All-Star teams and appeared in two NLCS. A good-fielding pitcher, he won five Gold Glove Awards. During his time in Atlanta, Niekro became extremely popular, and was active with charitable organizations and community groups. Sadly, he was playing for the Braves when they were poor-fielding, bad-hitting teams that provided little support. But he did not complain. Niekro won the 1979 Lou Gehrig Award for exemplary character.
Playing Career: *1965-1987; Mil N, Atl N, NY A, Cle A, Tor A*

Atlanta stalwart Phil Niekro.

Bob Nieman
Nieman, Robert Charles
B: Jan 26, 1927   D: Mar 10, 1985

Pos: OF	BA: .295
Hits: 1,018	HRs: 125
RBI: 544	BBs: 435

A two-time minor league batting champion, Nieman is the only player in history to homer in his first two major league at-bats. Nieman combined high averages with double-figure home run power. He appeared in the 1962 World Series in his last major league year.
Playing Career: *1951-1962; StL A, Det A, Chi A, Bal A, StL N, Cle A, SF N*

Johnny Niggeling
Niggeling, John Arnold
B: Jul 10, 1903   D: Sep 16, 1963

Pos: P	ERA: 3.22
W-L: 64-69	SOs: 620
ShOs: 13	No-hitters: 0

Although he did not make the major leagues until age 35, Niggeling flourished during the war years, winning 15 for the Browns in 1942. He was one of the four knuckleball pitchers on the Senators' wartime staff. Niggeling had a low hits-to-innings-pitched ratio.
Playing Career: *1938-1946; Bos N, Cin N, StL A, Was A*

Otis Nixon
Nixon, Otis Junior
B: Jan 9, 1959

Pos: OF	BA: .259
Hits: 637	HRs: 7
RBI: 197	BBs: 269

The center fielder and leadoff batter for the two-time NL champion Braves, Nixon is extremely fast and a good baserunner. He has stolen 352 bases and scored 458 runs. Finally getting 400 at-bats in 1991-1993, he became a .295 hitter. Former major leaguer Donnell Nixon is his brother.
Playing Career: *1983-; NY A, Cle A, Mon N, Atl N*

Russ Nixon
Nixon, Russell Eugene
B: Feb 19, 1935

Pos: C	BA: .268
Hits: 670	HRs: 27
RBI: 266	BBs: 154
Managerial Record	
Won: 231 Lost: 347 Pct: .400	

As the Indians' catcher in 1958, Nixon batted .301, his career best. He worked in the Reds' farm system for many years, and has coached and managed at the big league level. As skipper of the Braves, he helped prepare the teams that won pennants in 1991 and 1992.
Playing Career: *1957-1968; Cle A, Bos A, Min A*
Managerial Career: *1982-1983, 1988-1990; Cin N, Atl N*

Willard Nixon
Nixon, Willard Lee
B: Jun 17, 1928

Pos: P	ERA: 4.39
W-L: 69-72	SOs: 616
ShOs: 9	Saves: 3

In 1955 Nixon beat the mighty New York Yankees four times, allowing only five runs in the quartet of games. He was considered an excellent hitter for a pitcher, and was best of all AL hurlers with a .293 average in 1957. He won 12 games twice, in 1955 and 1957.
Playing Career: *1950-1958; Bos A*

Gary Nolan
Nolan, Gary Lynn
B: May 27, 1948

Pos: P	ERA: 3.08
W-L: 110-70	SOs: 1,039
ShOs: 14	No-hitters: 0

Nolan arrived in the big leagues with a blazing fastball, and was 14-8 with 206 strikeouts and a 2.58 record in 1967. He had good control, several times leading the NL in fewest walks per nine innings. One of the aces of the Big Red Machine's staff, Nolan won 61 percent of his decisions, pitching the Reds to four pennants during the 1970s. He played in four NLCS, compiling a 1.35 ERA. Nolan was selected for the All-Star squad in 1972, the year he led the league in winning percentage with a 15-5 record.
Playing Career: *1967-1973, 1975-1977; Cin N, Cal A*

Jerry Nops
Nops, Jeremiah H.
B: Jun 23, 1875   D: Mar 26, 1937

Pos: P	ERA: 3.70
W-L: 71-41	SOs: 294
ShOs: 7	Saves: 1

Nops was one of the few left-handed pitchers in the majors in his era. The 22-year-old won 20 games with a 2.81 ERA for the Orioles in 1897. That year Nops pitched the opener of the Temple Cup Series, losing 13-12, but won Game Four 12-11.
Playing Career: *1896-1901; Phi N, Bal N, Brk N, Bal A*

Irv Noren
Noren, Irving Arnold
B: Nov 29, 1924

Pos: OF	BA: .275
Hits: 857	HRs: 65
RBI: 453	BBs: 335

Signed by the Dodgers, Noren got to the big leagues with the Senators, who traded him to New York. There Noren played for the Yankees in the 1952, 1953 and 1955 World Series against the Dodgers. He also appeared in the 1954 All-Star Game.
Playing Career: *1950-1960; Was A, NY A, KC A, StL N, Chi N, LA N*

Fred Norman
Norman, Fredie Hubert
B: Aug, 20 1942

Pos: P	ERA: 3.64
W-L: 104-103	SOs: 1,303
ShOs: 15	Saves: 8

After a mediocre beginning, Norman found himself in the starting rotation for the Big Red Machine. He won 11 or more games seven years in a row as the Reds captured four division titles, and back-to-back World Championships in 1975-1976.
Playing Career: *1962-1964, 1966-1967, 1970-1980; KC A, Chi N, LA N, StL N, SD N, Cin N, Mon N*

Mike Norris
Norris, Michael Kelvin
B: Mar 19, 1955

Pos: P	ERA: 3.86
W-L: 58-59	SOs: 636
ShOs: 7	No-hitters: 0

Norris was a one-year sensation in 1980. He was 22-9 as the A's surprisingly finished second under new manager Billy Martin. Norris led the AL in the hits-per-nine-innings category, and batters hit only .209 off him. He made the All-Star team in 1981.
Playing Career: *1975-1983, 1990; Oak A*

Billy North
North, William Alex
B: May 15, 1948

Pos: OF	BA: .261
Hits: 1,016	HRs: 20
RBI: 230	BBs: 627

Injuries cut short North's promising career. He was a catalyst for the A's in the golden years of 1973-1976. He turned an unassisted double play in 1974. North also led AL outfielders three times in total chances per game. He stole 395 bases, including a league-high 75 in 1976.
Playing Career: *1971-1981; Chi N, Oak A, LA N, SF N*

Ron Northey
Northey, Ronald James
B: Apr 26, 1920   D: Apr 16, 1971

Pos: OF	BA: .276
Hits: 874	HRs: 108
RBI: 513	BBs: 361

A batter who hit the famous Abe Stark sign in Ebbets Field was supposed to win a free suit of clothes – Northey was one of the few reputed to do that. He had nine career pinch-hit home runs, three of them grand slams, which tied a major league record. Northey hit eight grand slam homers in his career. In 1944 he belted 22 homers, drove in 104 runs, and made 24 outfield assists. His son, Scott Northey, played briefly for Kansas City.
Playing Career: *1942-1944, 1946-1950, 1952, 1955-1957; Phi N, StL N, Cin N, Chi N, Chi A*

Jim Northrup
Northrup, James Thomas
B: Nov 24, 1939

Pos: OF	BA: .267
Hits: 1,254	HRs: 153
RBI: 610	BBs: 449

The Cardinals lost the 1968 World Series chiefly due to the heroics of Northrup. He hit a triple off Bob Gibson that went over the head of Curt Flood, and knocked in the first two runs of Game Seven. Northrup slugged .536 in the Series. In 1968 – the Year of the Pitcher – he led the Tigers with 153 hits and 90 RBI, breaking up three no-hitters in April and May. Northrup hit four grand slams that year. Two came in consecutive at-bats on June 24; he added another on June 29, making three in one week, a major league record. He belted a fourth off Larry Jaster in Game Six of the World Series. In 1969 he had a 6-for-6 game, the first Tiger since Ty Cobb to do so. Northrup finished that game with a 13th-inning home run over the Tiger Stadium roof. He batted .357 in the 1972 ALCS. In 1973 Northrup had a second eight-RBI game, and hit a career-high .307. Traded twice in 1974, he retired a year later. He is now a very good, very popular broadcaster with the Tigers.
Playing Career: *1964-1975; Det A, Mon N, Bal A*

Don Nottebart
Nottebart, Donald Edward
B: Jan 23, 1936

Pos: P	ERA: 3.65
W-L: 36-51	SOs: 525
ShOs: 2	No-hitters: 1

A top prospect, Nottebart showed flashes of brilliance as in 1963 when he was 11-8 with a 3.17 ERA, pitching a no-hitter and walking only one batter to every three strikeouts. Nottebart turned to the bullpen when he was traded to the Reds in 1966. He had 21 career saves.
Playing Career: *1960-1967, 1969; Mil N, Hou N, Cin N, NY A, Chi N*

In 1968 Jim Northrup's three grand slam HRs in a week set a major league record.

Edwin Nunez
Nunez y Martinez, Edwin
B: May 27, 1963

Pos: P   ERA: 4.04
W-L: 28-36   SOs: 493
ShOs: 0   Saves: 54

Another Puerto Rican gem, Nunez signed with the Mariners as a 16-year-old. He spent two years as a stopper, in 1985 and 1987, and holds the franchise record for most consecutive scoreless innings in relief, with 24. Nunez is used in middle relief now.
Playing Career: *1982-; Sea A, NY N, Det A, Mil A, Tex A, Oak A*

Joe Nuxhall as a 15-year-old rookie.

Joe Nuxhall
Nuxhall, Joseph Henry
B: Jul 30, 1928

Pos: P   ERA: 3.90
W-L: 135-117   SOs: 1,372
ShOs: 20   Saves: 19

The Reds put 15-year-old Nuxhall on the mound against the 1944 NL Champion Cardinals. He got the first two batters out, but reality set in when he faced Stan Musial. Rattled, Nuxhall gave up five runs on two hits and five walks. It took him seven years to get over it, but he returned to the Reds and won 17 games for them in 1955, leading the league in shutouts, and pitching 3.1 scoreless innings in the All-Star Game. Nuxhall is now a top broadcaster.
Playing Career: *1944, 1952-1966; Cin N, KC A, LA A*

Ken Oberkfell
Oberkfell, Kenneth Ray (Obie)
B: May 4, 1956

Pos: 3B   BA: .278
Hits: 1,354   HRs: 29
RBI: 446   BBs: 546

Wearing a Cardinals uniform, Oberkfell led the NL in fielding three times and batted over .289, 1979-1983. He was durable, averaging 130 games per season, 1979-1989, despite knee surgery, a broken thumb, and an elbow injury. Traded to the Braves in 1984, Oberkfell said he would always be a Cardinal fan; nonetheless he performed well for Atlanta and San Francisco, where he helped the 1989 Giants to the NL pennant with a .319 second half, slugging .431.
Playing Career: *1977-1990; StL N, Atl N, Pit N, SF N, Hou N, Cal A*

Darby O'Brien
O'Brien, William D.
B: Sep 1, 1863   D: Jun 15, 1893

Pos: OF   BA: .282
Hits: 805   HRs: 20
RBI: 321 (inc.)   BBs: 231

O'Brien played for the Brooklyn Bridegrooms, who became the Trolley Dodgers, then the Dodgers. They won back-to-back pennants 1889 in the AA and 1890 in the NL. O'Brien scored 146 runs and stole 91 bases in 1889. He scored 577 runs and stole 321 bases altogether.
Playing Career: *1887-1892; NY AA, Brk AA, Brk N*

Pete O'Brien
O'Brien, Peter Michael
B: Feb 9, 1958

Pos: 1B, OF, DH   BA: .261
Hits: 1,421   HRs: 169
RBI: 736   BBs: 641

A left-handed pull hitter, O'Brien averaged 20 homers for five straight years, 1984-1988. One of the best fielders in the league, O'Brien led AL first basemen in assists in 1983 and 1987, and in fielding average in 1991. He started three double plays in one game in 1984, tying a record for first basemen. He lives in Texas and is known for his charity work in the Dallas-Ft. Worth area.
Playing Career: *1982-; Tex A, Cle A, Sea A*

Danny O'Connell
O'Connell, Daniel Francis
B: Jan 21, 1927   D: Oct 2, 1969

Pos: 2B, SS, 3B   BA: .260
Hits: 1,049   HRs: 39
RBI: 320   BBs: 431

Part of the Pirates' baby Buc brigade of the early 1950s, O'Connell hit .290 in 1950 and 1953. He was a favorite in Pittsburgh, and fans were riled when he was traded to the Braves. In 1956 he tied a 20th-century major league record with three triples in a game.
Playing Career: *1950, 1953-1959, 1961-1962; Pit N, Mil N, NY N, SF N, Was A*

Jack O'Connor
O'Connor, John Joseph (Peach Pie, Rowdy Jack)
B: Jun 2, 1869   D: Nov 14, 1937

Pos: C   BA: .263
Hits: 1,417   HRs: 18
RBI: 671 (inc.)   BBs: 301
Managerial Record
Won: 47   Lost: 107   Pct: .305

Known as a two-fisted drinker, O'Connor somehow played parts of 21 seasons, but appeared in 100 games or more only five times. He was expelled from the AA in 1891 for "drunkenness, rowdy conduct, and insubordination." O'Connor led AA catchers in fielding 1889-1890. He joined the infamous Cleveland Spiders for their glory years.
Playing Career: *1887-1904, 1906-1907, 1910; Cin AA, Col AA, Cle N, StL N, Pit N, NY A, StL A*
Managerial Career: *1910; StL A*

Hank O'Day
O'Day, Henry Francis
B: Jul 8, 1862   D: Jul 2, 1935

Pos: P   ERA: 3.79
W-L: 70-110   SOs: 654
ShOs: 4   Saves: 4
Managerial Record
Won: 153   Lost: 154   Pct: .498

An NL pitcher and batterymate of Connie Mack, O'Day made his name as an umpire. His best year pitching was 1890 in the Players' League, with a 22-13 record. He managed the Reds and Cubs to fourth-place finishes. O'Day toiled for five decades in baseball. As an umpire, he presided over the Merkle Boner game and was working at second base when Bill Wambsganss turned an unassisted triple play in the 1920 World Series.
Playing Career: *1884-1890; Tol AA, Pit AA, Was N, NY N, NY P*
Managerial Career: *1912, 1914; Cin N, Chi N*
Umpiring Career: *1895, 1897-1911, 1913, 1915-1927; NL (10 WS)*

Ken O'Dea
O'Dea, James Kenneth
B: Mar 16, 1913   D: Dec 17, 1985

Pos: C	BA: .255
Hits: 560	HRs: 40
RBI: 323	BBs: 273

O'Dea played in five World Series, but spent his entire career as a backup catcher for All-Stars Gabby Hartnett and Walker Cooper. He batted .462 in 13 World Series games, including a record three pinch hits in eight at-bats.
Playing Career: *1935-1946; Chi N, NY N, StL N, Bos N*

Billy O'Dell
O'Dell, William Oliver (Digger)
B: Feb 10, 1933

Pos: P	ERA: 3.29
W-L: 105-100	SOs: 1,133
ShOs: 13	Saves: 48

Nicknamed "Digger" for the radio character in "The Life of Riley," O'Dell was a character himself. A gentleman farmer from South Carolina, he was sometimes more interested in quail hunting and chicken fighting than pitching. O'Dell kept sign-stealing opponents off balance by disregarding catcher's signals, much to the chagrin of his battery-mates. O'Dell was a top left-hander, going 19-14 for the 1962 NL champion Giants.
Playing Career: *1954, 1956-1967; Bal A, NY N, SF N, Mil N, Atl N, Pit N*

Blue Moon Odom
Odom, Johnny Lee
B: May 29, 1945

Pos: P	ERA: 3.70
W-L: 84-85	SOs: 857
ShOs: 15	No-hitters: 1

Nineteen-year-old Odom pitched a shutout three months after graduating from high school, but was not quite ready for the big leagues. Blossoming after the A's move to Oakland, Odom made the All-Star team in 1968 and 1969. He pitched in three ALCS and three World Series.
Playing Career: *1964-1976; KC A, Oak A, Cle A, Atl N, Chi A*

Lefty O'Doul
O'Doul, Francis Joseph
B: Mar 4, 1897   D: Dec 7, 1969

Pos: OF, P	BA: .349
Hits: 1,140	HRs: 113
RBI: 542	BBs: 333

After trying to make it as a pitcher, O'Doul returned to the majors as a hitter. As a sore-armed pitcher, O'Doul saw little action with the Yankees in 1919, 1920 and 1922, but went 25-9 in the PCL during 1921. He pitched for the Red Sox as a reliever in 1923. Then his arm went dead. He returned to the PCL to begin a second career as an outfielder. In four years with the Phillies and Dodgers, 1929-1932, he

Lefty O'Doul.

averaged .373 with 212 hits, 34 doubles, 120 runs, 20 homers and 96 RBI, leading the NL in batting in 1929 and 1932.

In 1929 O'Doul batted .398 with 32 home runs, and set an NL record with 254 hits. He had a lifetime .413 on-base average. At age 37 he returned to the PCL to manage the San Francisco Seals. There he became known for developing players, including Joe DiMaggio. O'Doul made several visits to Japan in the 1930s as a baseball ambassador of goodwill.
Playing Career: *1919-1920, 1922-1923, 1928-1934; NY A, Bos A, NY N, Phi N, Brk N*

Joe Oeschger
Oeschger, Joseph Carl
B: May 24, 1891   D: Jul 28, 1986

Pos: P	ERA: 3.81
W-L: 83-116	SOs: 535
ShOs: 18	Saves: 7

Sturdy Joe Oeschger pitched 26 innings to a 1-1 tie on May 1, 1920. He gave up nine hits, walked four, and set a major league record by tossing 21 consecutive scoreless innings. Oeschger was tired, but said he wanted to go 27 innings – three complete games.
Playing Career: *1914-1925; Phi N, NY N, Bos N, Brk N*

Ron Oester
Oester, Ronald John
B: May 5, 1956

Pos: 2B, SS	BA: .265
Hits: 1,118	HRs: 42
RBI: 344	BBs: 369

The huge gap left by Joe Morgan's departure from Cincinnati was filled by Ron Oester. He

played 150 or more games, for five consecutive years, until he broke his leg in a collision with Mookie Wilson in July 1987. Oester's best years were 1981-1986. In 1990, his farewell year, he hit .333 in the NLCS, then went 1-for-1 for the Champion Reds in the World Series.
Playing Career: *1978-1990; Cin N*

Bob O'Farrell
O'Farrell, Robert Arthur
B: Oct 19, 1896   D: Feb 20, 1988

Pos: C	BA: .273
Hits: 1,120	HRs: 51
RBI: 549	BBs: 547
Managerial Record	
Won: 122 Lost: 121 Pct: .502	

Babe Ruth made a surprise attempt to steal second base at the end of the 1926 World Series, but O'Farrell gunned the ball to Rogers Hornsby. The Babe was out, and the Cardinals were World Champions. O'Farrell batted .304 in the Fall Classic, after turning in a .293 performance during the regular season. He was named NL MVP. Playing for the Cubs earlier in his career, O'Farrell caught Grover Cleveland Alexander, and appeared in the 1918 World Series.
Playing Career: *1915-1935; Chi N, StL N, NY N, Cin N*
Managerial Career: *1927, 1934; StL N, Cin N*

Rowland Office
Office, Rowland Johnie
B: Oct 25, 1952

Pos: OF	BA: .259
Hits: 626	HRs: 32
RBI: 242	BBs: 189

In 1976, with the Braves, Office hit safely in 29 consecutive games, batting .397 during the streak. He also made the greatest defensive play in Fulton County Stadium history. Office leapt onto the seven-foot center field fence, then fell over it, but robbed Mike Ivie of a home run.
Playing Career: *1972, 1974-1983; Atl N, Mon N, NY A*

Ben Oglivie
Oglivie, Benjamin Ambrosio
B: Feb 11, 1949

Pos: OF	BA: .273
Hits: 1,615	HRs: 235
RBI: 901	BBs: 560

When given a chance to start with the Brewers, Oglivie flourished, making the All-Star team three times, and twice driving in more than 100 runs. He still holds the Brewers' record for most single-season home runs by a left-handed hitter. Oglivie became a power hitter late in his career, socking an AL-leading 41 homers at the age of 31, in 1980. More of a contact hitter than slugger, he batted over .300 twice, and belted 277 doubles.
Playing Career: *1971-1986; Bos A, Det A, Mil A*

Bob Ojeda gets a "high five" from Gary Carter after a win in the 1986 NLCS.

Bob Ojeda
Ojeda, Robert Michael
B: Dec 17, 1957

Pos: P	ERA: 3.62
W-L: 115-98	SOs: 1,125
ShOs: 16	Saves: 1

Victimized by injuries throughout his career, Ojeda was seriously injured in a spring training boating mishap that killed Indians teammates Tim Crews and Steve Olin in 1993. Ojeda was 18-5 for the World Champion Mets in 1986.
Playing Career: *1980-; Bos A, NY N, LA N, Cle A*

Rube Oldring
Oldring, Reuben Henry
B: May 30, 1884   D: Sep 9, 1961

Pos: OF	BA: .270
Hits: 1,268	HRs: 27
RBI: 471	BBs: 206

Hailing from the Bronx as an infielder, Oldring was converted to a center fielder by Connie Mack. Oldring led his position in fielding twice as the A's won four pennants in five years from 1910 to 1914. A broken leg late in

The Twins' batting champ, Tony Oliva.

the season kept Oldring out of the 1910 World Series, but he played in the other three, hitting a three-run homer in the 1911 Series. Oldring seldom walked, but scored 616 runs and stole 197 bases in a 13-year career.
Playing Career: *1905-1916, 1918; NY A, Phi A*

Charley O'Leary
O'Leary, Charles Timothy
B: Oct 15, 1882   D: Jan 6, 1941

Pos: SS	BA: .226
Hits: 731	HRs: 4
RBI: 213	BBs: 164

Shortstop and leadoff batter for the Tigers, O'Leary helped them win three pennants. In the off season, he and Germany Schaefer played the vaudeville circuit. O'Leary was 51 years old in 1934 when he asked the Browns for one last at-bat. He singled.
Playing Career: *1904-1913, 1934; Det A, StL N, StL A*

John Olerud
Olerud, John Garrett
B: Aug 5, 1968

Pos: 1B, DH	BA: .297
Hits: 544	HRs: 74
RBI: 289	BBs: 309

When the Blue Jays first signed Olerud, they did not know where to play him. Setting both pitching and hitting records at Washington State University, Olerud went directly to the major leagues. He batted .308 in the 1992 World Series, and was an All-Star in 1993, when he won the AL batting crown.
Playing Career: *1989-; Tor A*

Tony Oliva
Oliva y Lopez, Pedro
B: Jul 20, 1940

Pos: OF, DH	BA: .304
Hits: 1,917	HRs: 220
RBI: 947	BBs: 448

Entering the U.S. on his brother's passport, Pedro Oliva became Tony Oliva, and AL pitchers suffered for it through more than a dozen seasons. He won three batting titles, in 1964, 1965 and 1971, and led the AL in hits five times. Oliva batted .323 in 1964 – his rookie season – and pounded 217 hits to lead the AL in hits, runs, doubles and batting average. He was named Rookie of the Year. Oliva also hit 32 home runs and made the All-Star squad. He was an All-Star in each of his first eight years in the majors.

In 1966 Oliva hit .307, and captured the Gold Glove Award for right field. He led the AL in doubles four times. Winning his third batting title in 1971, he also endured a serious knee injury chasing a fly ball in Oakland. He played only 10 games the next year and spent the rest of his career hampered by his knee. Forced into a pinch hitter and designated hitter role, Oliva belted the first DH home run in major league history on April 6, 1973.
Playing Career: *1962-1976; Min A*

Al Oliver, with Texas in 1981.

Al Oliver
Oliver, Albert (Scoops)
B: Oct 14, 1946

Pos: 1B, OF, DH	BA: .303
Hits: 2,743	HRs: 219
RBI: 1,326	BBs: 535

Quiet and unassuming, Oliver left the headlines to more flamboyant players. He began his career as the 1969 NL Rookie of the Year. When the seven-time All-Star retired he was among baseball's all-time top 50 in games played, hits, total bases, RBI and extra-base hits. Oliver's batting average reached .300 nine straight seasons, and he hit .375 in the 1985 ALCS, his last performance in the majors.

Oliver played on five Pirates division-winning teams and ranks among the all-time Pirates leaders in doubles, home runs, RBI and extra-base hits. In 1982 Oliver batted a career-high .331 to capture the NL batting title. He also led the NL in hits, doubles and RBI that year. *The Sporting News* named Oliver to their Silver Slugger team for three straight years, at three different positions – left field in 1980, DH in 1981, and first base in 1982.
Playing Career: *1968-1985; Pit N, Tex A, Mon N, SF N, Phi N, LA N, Tor A*

Bob Oliver
Oliver, Robert Lee
B: Feb 8, 1943

Pos: 1B, OF, 3B	BA: .256
Hits: 745	HRs: 94
RBI: 419	BBs: 156

A jack-of-all-trades, Oliver played more than 110 games six seasons in a row, 1969-1974. He was 6-for-6 in a game for the expansion Royals in 1969, his rookie season. Oliver's best season was 1970, when he hit .260 with 27 homers, 99 RBI and 83 runs.
Playing Career: *1965, 1969-1975; Pit N, KC A, Cal A, Bal A, NY A*

Gene Oliver
Oliver, Eugene George
B: Mar 22, 1935

Pos: C, 1B	BA: .246
Hits: 546	HRs: 93
RBI: 320	BBs: 215

The Braves set a major league record by fielding six players who hit 20 or more home runs in 1965. Oliver was a backup catcher, but he belted 21 round-trippers that year. He once hit three homers in one game. Oliver was traded for Bob Uecker in 1967.
Playing Career: *1959, 1961-1969; StL N, Mil N, Phi N, Bos A, Chi N*

Gregg Olson
Olson, Greggory William
B: Oct 11, 1966

Pos: P	ERA: 2.26
W-L: 17-21	SOs: 347
ShOs: 0	Saves: 160

The 1989 AL Rookie of the Year Gregg Olson saved 27 games with a 1.69 ERA, which kept the surprising Orioles in the AL pennant race until the last month of the season. Signed for a $200,000 bonus, Olson pitched only 24 innings in the minors before joining the big club.
Playing Career: *1988-; Bal A*

Ivy Olson
Olson, Ivan Massie
B: Oct 14, 1885   D: Sep 1, 1965

Pos: SS	BA: .258
Hits: 1,575	HRs: 13
RBI: 446	BBs: 285

Adept at the hidden-ball trick, Olson was the steady shortstop of the NL champion Dodgers of 1916 and 1920. He batted .293 in the two World Series. Olson and Casey Stengel were Dodger teammates, and went to grade school together in Kansas City. Stengel said of Olson, who was five years his senior, "They let him be the boss. He was the strongest boy in school." After his playing career, Olson managed in the minors and coached for the Dodgers and Giants.
Playing Career: *1911-1924; Cle A, Cin N, Brk N*

Walter O'Malley
O'Malley, Walter J.
B: Oct 9, 1903   D: Aug 9, 1979

Baseball has to be conducted as business, or so they say, but no businessman has broken so many hearts as O'Malley did when he relocated his Brooklyn Dodgers franchise to Los Angeles. Brooklyn's Ebbets Field was small, seating under 35,000, did not have adequate parking, and was in a deteriorating neighborhood. While O'Malley lobbied local politicians for a new stadium in downtown Brooklyn, he opened discussions with Los Angeles city officials about a stadium site.

He struck a deal for an area called Chavez Ravine, agreeing to use his own money to build the stadium and move the team to the West Coast. O'Malley then convinced Horace Stoneham to move his New York Giants to San Francisco. In 1962 O'Malley opened showcase Dodger Stadium. The team has won pennants – four on the backs of a dominating pitching staff, and four with home run power – and it has developed a new following. But Brooklyn still mourns.

Walter O'Malley fumed when tax assessors valued Dodger Stadium at $32.3 million.

Buck O'Neil
O'Neil, John Jordan
B: Nov 13, 1911

Pos: 1B	BA: .292
Hits: 397	HRs: 12
RBI: NA	BBs: NA

Managerial Record
Won: 70   Lost: 27   Pct: .722

Trained by legendary baseball coach Ox Clemons at Edward G. Waters College in Jacksonville, Florida, O'Neil entered professional baseball in 1937 and is still employed as a scout for the Royals. O'Neil has been a player, coach and manager along the way. He led the Kansas City Monarchs into two Negro League World Series. He also coached and scouted for the Chicago Cubs, signing several future Hall of Famers.
Playing Career: *1937-1943, 1946-1953; Mem Red Sox, KC Monarchs*
Managerial Career: *1948-1953; KC Monarchs*

Steve O'Neill
O'Neill, Stephen Francis
B: Jul 6, 1891   D: Jan 26, 1962

Pos: C	BA: .263
Hits: 1,259	HRs: 13
RBI: 537	BBs: 592

Managerial Record
Won: 1,040   Lost: 821   Pct: .559

The best of four baseball-playing O'Neill brothers, Steve batted .333 in the 1920 World Series for the Indians, and managed the 1945 Tigers to the World Championship. A star catcher for the Indians, he caught more than 100 games nine consecutive seasons, 1915-1923. As a manager, he never had a losing season and earned a reputation for developing young players, notably Lou Boudreau and Bob Feller.
Playing Career: *1911-1925, 1927-1928; Cle A, Bos A, NY A, StL A*
Managerial Career: *1935-1937, 1943-1948, 1950-1954; Cle A, Det A, Bos A, Phi N*

Tip O'Neill
O'Neill, James Edward
B: May 25, 1858   D: Dec 31, 1915

Pos: OF	BA: .326
Hits: 1,386	HRs: 52
RBI: 430 (inc.)	BBs: 421

The best batsman from Canada to date, O'Neill had an adjusted average of .435 in 1887, the year walks counted as hits and batters were allowed four strikes and seven balls. He was the first person inducted into the Canadian Baseball Hall of Fame. He would have won the Triple Crown in 1887 if RBI had been counted. Even so, he led the AA in eight offensive categories: runs, hits, doubles, triples, home runs, and batting, slugging and on-base averages. O'Neill led the league in hits and batting average the next year.
To a great degree responsible for the Browns' four AA pennants in a row, O'Neill

James "Tip" O'Neill.

was a big star and a hero to Irish-American fans, who frequently named their sons after him. His nickname was a result of his practice of tipping pitches foul while waiting for one he could drive. In his time, foul balls did not count as strikes. O'Neill batted .400 with two home runs and two triples in the 1886 "winner take all" Championship Series victory over the NL White Stockings.
Playing Career: *1883-1892; NY N, StL AA, Chi P, Cin N*

Steve Ontiveros
Ontiveros, Steven Robert
B: Oct 26, 1951

Pos: 3B	BA: .274
Hits: 600	HRs: 24
RBI: 224	BBs: 309

A part-time switch hitter, Ontiveros is best remembered in Chicago for doing commercials for a scalp treatment clinic that specialized in resodding bald heads. He hit .299 with 32 doubles and .285 with 28 doubles in 1977 and 1979, his only seasons as a regular.
Playing Career: *1973-1980; SF N, Chi N*

Jose Oquendo
Oquendo y Contreras, Jose Manuel
B: Jul 4, 1963

Pos: SS, 2B, OF, 3B	BA: .260
Hits: 741	HRs: 12
RBI: 228	BBs: 392

At age 19, Oquendo was the starting shortstop for the Mets. Traded to the Cardinals in 1986, the versatile Oquendo was a valuable substitute – he played every position in 1988 – but became a regular second baseman in 1989, leading the NL in fielding in 1989 and 1990.
Playing Career: *1983-1984, 1986-; NY N, StL N*

Jesse Orosco
Orosco, Jesse Russell
B: Apr 21, 1957

Pos: P	ERA: 2.86
W-L: 66-63	SOs: 826
ShOs: 0	Saves: 130

The Mets could hardly have won the World Championship in 1986 without Orosco. He was the hero of the NLCS, setting a playoff record with three wins. His courage was apparent in the series-clinching sixth game, when he struck out the Astros' Kevin Bass with the tying and winning runs on base in the bottom of the 16th inning. In the 13th Orosco had given up a game-tying home run to Billy Hatcher. Exhausted from three previous outings, the hurler lacked his good, moving fastball and was having trouble getting right-handed batters out.
He did the job with his "backdoor slider," which starts outside to right-handers and breaks late to catch the corner of the plate. Orosco also won Games Three and Five with scoreless relief, and until Game Six had given up only one hit in five innings. He saved Games Four and Seven of the World Series and even had an RBI single in the clincher.
Playing Career: *1979, 1981-; NY N, LA N, Cle A, Mil A*

Frank O'Rourke
O'Rourke, James Francis (Blackie)
B: Nov 28, 1894   D: May 14, 1986

Pos: 3B, SS, 1B	BA: .254
Hits: 1,032	HRs: 15
RBI: 430	BBs: 314

O'Rourke had a 70-year career in baseball – playing, coaching, managing and scouting. In 1925 he batted .293 with 40 doubles and led AL second basemen in fielding. After managing in the minors, O'Rourke was a scout for the Reds and Yankees, 1941-1983.
Playing Career: *1912, 1917-1918, 1920-1922, 1924-1931; Bos N, Brk N, Was A, Bos A, Det A, StL A*

Jim O'Rourke
O'Rourke, James Henry (Orator)
B: Sep 1, 1850   D: Jan 8, 1919
Hall of Fame 1945

Pos: OF, 1B, C	BA: .311
Hits: 2,646	HRs: 62
RBI: 1,071 (inc.)	BBs: 509

Managerial Record
Won: 246   Lost: 258   Pct: .488

"Words of great length and thunderous sound simply flowed out of his mouth," states O'Rourke's obituary. The Yale Law School graduate liked to talk about his base-

Jim O'Rourke (r) with his father.

ball career, and with good reason. He scored 1,732 runs, clubbed 467 doubles and 149 triples. He stole at least 196 bases (statistics on his career steals are incomplete). O'Rourke played for 22 seasons, then appeared in a 1904 contest with the Giants, stroking a single and scoring a run at age 54.

O'Rourke was a very good player who frequently found himself surrounded by stars; he played for eight pennant-winning teams. He made the first hit in NL history, on April 2, 1876. O'Rourke later managed in the minors, and served as president of the Connecticut League and the Eastern Association.
Playing Career: *1872-1893, 1904; Mid Mansfields n, Bos Red Stockings n, Bos N, Pro N, Buf N, NY N, NY P, Was N*
Managerial Career: *1881-1884, 1893; Buf N, Was N*
Umpiring Career: *1895; NL*

Dave Orr
Orr, David L.
B: Sep 29, 1859   D: Jun 3, 1915

Pos: 1B	BA: .342
Hits: 1,126	HRs: 37
RBI: 270 (inc.)	BBs: 98

Managerial Record
Won: 3   Lost: 5   Pct: .375

One of the top sluggers in the 19th century, Orr slashed 31 triples in 1886, and became the first major leaguer to total 300 bases as he led the AA in hits, triples and homers while batting .354. Altogether, Orr pounded 198 doubles and 108 triples for a .502 slugging average, making him one of four 19th-century players with a lifetime slugging average over .500. The others – Dan Brouthers, Ed

Delahanty and Sam Thompson – are in the Hall of Fame.

Orr was a huge man, weighing more than 250 pounds. He was said to have "the frame of a giant and the face of a boy." In 1884 he became the hero of New York by using his immense strength to extricate passengers from a train wreck. Another time he saved a woman from attack by tossing her assailant down a flight of stairs. Orr was injury-prone, but he could hit, and twice led the AA in slugging. In 1890 he batted .373 with 124 RBI before suffering a paralyzing, career-ending stroke.
Playing Career: *1883-1890; NY AA, NY N, Brk AA, Col AA, Brk P*
Managerial Career: *1887; NY AA*

Ernie Orsatti
Orsatti, Ernest Ralph
B: Sep 8, 1902   D: Sep 4, 1968

Pos: OF	BA: .306
Hits: 663	HRs: 10
RBI: 237	BBs: 176

As a youngster, Orsatti hung around Buster Keaton's movie lot, working as an extra. He was a football player, boxer and auto racer in addition to baseball player. Orsatti hit .273 in four World Series for the Cardinals, and posted a .318 mark in the 1934 Series.
Playing Career: *1927-1935; StL N*

Joe Orsulak
Orsulak, Joseph Michael
B: May 31, 1962

Pos: OF, DH	BA: .279
Hits: 933	HRs: 45
RBI: 300	BBs: 249

Orsulak's exceptional arm allowed him to post 22 assists in 1991, setting an Oriole record. A part-time player, he hit safely in 21 straight games that year. A singles hitter early in his career, Orsulak batted .300 in 1985, and has developed power recently.
Playing Career: *1983-1986, 1988-; Pit N, Bal A, NY N*

Jorge Orta
Orta y Nunez, Jorge
B: Nov 26, 1950

Pos: 2B, OF, DH	BA: .278
Hits: 1,619	HRs: 130
RBI: 745	BBs: 500

In Cuba, Orta's father, Pedro, was known as the Babe Ruth of the Cuban Leagues. Orta the younger hit .333 in the 1985 World Series for the champion Royals. He was soft-spoken, and struggled with English and fielding before becoming a hitting star in 1974. That year he finished second to Rod Carew in the AL batting race, stroking .316, and three times collecting five hits in a game. In 1976 Orta was inducted into the Mexican Baseball Hall of Fame.
Playing Career: *1972-1987; Chi A, Cle A, LA N, Tor A, KC A*

Al Orth
Orth, Albert Lewis
(The Curveless Wonder)
B: Sep 5, 1872   D: Oct 8, 1948

Pos: P	ERA: 3.37
W-L: 202-189	SOs: 948
ShOs: 31	Saves: 5

Orth hated curveballs. He thought throwing them would hurt his arm. Instead, he developed a change-of-pace and a spitball. He broke in with the 1895 Phillies, going 8-1 and batting .356. That year they had four starters and one substitute who batted over .380 – the team average was .330. Orth's ERA and batting average kept going down, but his wins went up to 20 in 1899, and he led the NL with a 2.49 ERA.

Orth had excellent control, walking just 19 in 145 innings that season. Altogether he walked 661 in 3,354 innings pitched, averaging 1.7 walks per nine innings. He jumped leagues in 1902 to play with the Senators in the new AL. After losing 22 games, he was traded to the New York Highlanders, where he picked up the spitball from Jack Chesbro and almost took his team to the AL pennant. When Chesbro's great arm went lame, Orth took to the mound, pitching more than 300 innings in 1905 and 1906, and winning 27 games in 1906. Orth averaged .273 for 15 years as a hitter.
Playing Career: *1895-1909; Phi N, Was A, NY A*

Al Orth.

Pitcher Claude Osteen in action with the Dodgers in 1969.

Claude Osteen
Osteen, Claude Wilson (Gomer, Wimpy)
B: Aug 9, 1939

Pos: P	ERA: 3.30
W-L: 196-195	SOs: 1,612
ShOs: 40	Saves: 1

A dead ringer for TV character Gomer Pyle, Osteen was the third starter behind Sandy Koufax and Don Drysdale on powerful Dodgers teams. He spun an ERA of 0.86 in World Series play. After Drysdale and Koufax lost Games One and Two of the 1965 World Series, Osteen shut out the Twins and put the Dodgers back on track in Game Three. Don Sutton arrived in 1966, giving the Dodgers one of the greatest four-man starting rotations ever. They pitched only one year together, but the quartet's career wins totaled 894.

Bouncing back from 18 losses in 1968, Osteen worked on his slow stuff, going 20-15 in 1969 despite allowing the most hits in the NL. His best year was 1972, when he was 20-11 with a 2.64 ERA, finishing with seven complete-game victories in his last nine starts. He pitched three shutout innings to win the 1970 All-Star Game, then threw two more scoreless innings in the 1973 contest. Osteen became a pitching coach for the Cardinals and Phillies.

Playing Career: *1957, 1959-1975; Cin N, Was A, LA N, Hou N, StL N, Chi A*

Fritz Ostermueller
Ostermueller, Frederick Raymond
B: Sep 15, 1907   D: Dec 17, 1957

Pos: P	ERA: 3.99
W-L: 114-115	SOs: 774
ShOs: 11	Saves: 15

A starter for Tom Yawkey's Red Sox, Ostermueller compiled a 13-5 record in 1938 and was 11-7 in 1939. The Red Sox were regular contenders, but somehow could not win. Ostermueller's career revived in Pittsburgh, where he won 13 games three times.

Playing Career: *1934-1948; Bos A, StL A, Brk N, Pit N*

Amos Otis
Otis, Amos Joseph (A.O.)
B: Apr 26, 1947

Pos: OF	BA: .277
Hits: 2,020	HRs: 193
RBI: 1,007	BBs: 757

Royals fans remember Otis as one of the most exciting players in franchise history. He starred on four Kansas City division championship teams and batted .478 in the 1980 World Series. Mets fans think of Otis as the one that got away. The Royals acquired him and Bob Johnson for Joe Foy. Otis made center field his home for 14 years – and he made playing there look easy. Positioning himself deep, he could come in on a ball better than anyone since Tris Speaker.

Otis was criticized at times for lacking aggressiveness and for making one-handed catches, but he won three Gold Glove Awards. He was named the Royals' Player of the Year three times. His 36 doubles led the AL in 1970 and his 40 two-baggers led again in 1976. He stole five bases in a September 7, 1971 game, and led the AL with 52 that year. In 1975 he tied an AL record by stealing seven bases in two consecutive games. He batted .300 twice, hitting 26 homers in 1973, He scored 1,092 runs, hit 374 doubles and stole 341 bases altogether.

Playing Career: *1967, 1969-1984; NY N, KC A, Pit N*

Jim O'Toole
O'Toole, James Jerome
B: Jan 10, 1937

Pos: P	ERA: 3.57
W-L: 98-84	SOs: 1,039
ShOs: 18	Saves: 4

The ace of the Reds' staff in the early 1960s, O'Toole was 19-9 in 1961 as the Reds captured the NL pennant, but lost Games One and Four of the World Series to the powerful Yankees. O'Toole won 81 games in the five seasons from 1960 to 1964; a shoulder injury ended his career in 1967.

Playing Career: *1958-1967; Cin N, Chi A*

Mel Ott
Ott, Melvin Thomas (Master Melvin)
B: Mar 2, 1909   D: Nov 21, 1958
Hall of Fame 1951

Pos: OF	BA: .304
Hits: 2,876	HRs: 511
RBI: 1,860	BBs: 1,708
Managerial Record	
Won: 464 Lost: 530 Pct: .467	

Giants Manager John McGraw watched 17-year-old Mel Ott, found by a friend in New Orleans, work out at the Polo Grounds and decided that the heavy-legged kid should stay in the big leagues, right beside him on the bench. Ott had such an unusual, yet natural batting style that McGraw did not want to take a chance on a minor league manager changing his stance and swing. Ott kicked his right leg up, whipping the bat through the hitting zone in an upward motion toward the inviting 257-foot right field fence at the Polo Grounds.

He scored 1,859 runs and swatted 488 doubles, while posting a lifetime .533 slugging percentage. Ott was the first NL player to hit 500 home runs, and was the NL home run leader until Willie Mays passed him in 1967. He scared pitchers, holding the NL record for walks until 1982, when it was broken by Joe Morgan. Ott walked five times in a game on four occasions. He scored six times in one game twice. Ott is ninth on the career RBI and career runs scored lists.

Playing Career: *1926-1947; NY N*
Managerial Career: *1942-1948; NY N*

Jimmy Outlaw
Outlaw, James Paulus
B: Jan 20, 1913

Pos: OF, 3B	BA: .268
Hits: 529	HRs: 6
RBI: 184	BBs: 188

One of the major leaguers who played admirably during the World War II years, Outlaw appeared in the 1945 World Series for the Tigers. He began his career at the hot corner for the Reds, but his best years were in Detroit. In 1944 he hit .273 with 57 RBI.
Playing Career: *1937-1939, 1943-1949; Cin N, Bos N, Det A*

Orval Overall
Overall, Orval
B: Feb 2, 1881   D: Jul 14, 1947

Pos: P	ERA: 2.23
W-L: 108-71	SOs: 935
ShOs: 30	Saves: 12

Though he pitched only seven years in the majors leagues, Overall appeared in four World Series, compiling a postseason record of 3-1 with a 1.58 ERA. He struck out four men in one inning, the only pitcher to do so in World Series play. Overall is the only major leaguer to pitch and win two shutouts in a doubleheader. He posted ERAs under 2.00 three years in a row, and won 60 percent of his games. His career ERA is the eighth best in baseball history.
Playing Career: *1905-1910, 1913; Cin N, Chi N*

Stubby Overmire
Overmire, Frank
B: May 16, 1919   D: Mar 3, 1977

Pos: P	ERA: 3.96
W-L: 58-67	SOs: 301
ShOs: 11	Saves: 10

An important part of the 1945 World Champion Tigers team, Overmire lost Game Three of the World Series when Claude Passeau pitched a one-hitter against Detroit. Overmire was 9-9 with nine complete games and four saves that year. He won 11 games two other seasons.
Playing Career: *1943-1952; Det A, StL A, NY A*

Frank Owen
Owen, Frank Malcolm (Yip)
B: Dec 23, 1879   D: Nov 24, 1942

Pos: P	ERA: 2.55
W-L: 82-67	SOs: 443
ShOs: 16	Saves: 2

Owen was the first AL pitcher to win two complete games in one day, and the first AL pitcher to steal home. A top AL hurler, Owen won 64 games, 1904-1906, and pitched for the White Sox in the 1906 World Series. He was a fine fielder and possessed pinpoint control. Owen later became a physician.
Playing Career: *1901, 1903-1909; Det A, Chi A*

Marv Owen
Owen, Marvin James
B: Mar 22, 1906   D: Jun 22, 1991

Pos: 3B	BA: .275
Hits: 1,040	HRs: 31
RBI: 497	BBs: 338

When Joe Medwick slid hard into Owen, cutting him, it started the 1934 World Series ruckus that led to Medwick being showered with fruit and having to be removed from the game. Owen hit .317 with 96 RBI in 1934, when four Tiger teammates each topped 100 RBI.
Playing Career: *1931, 1933-1940; Det A, Chi A, Bos A*

Mickey Owen
Owen, Arnold Malcolm
B: Apr 4, 1916

Pos: C	BA: .255
Hits: 929	HRs: 14
RBI: 378	BBs: 326

Owen dropped the infamous third strike in Game Four of the 1941 World Series that enabled the Yankees to come back, winning the game, then the Series on the next day. Owen now runs a successful baseball training camp in the Missouri Ozark Mountains.
Playing Career: *1937-1945, 1949-1951, 1954; StL N, Brk N, Chi N, Bos A*

Spike Owen
Owen, Spike Dee
B: Apr 19, 1961

Pos: SS	BA: .243
Hits: 1,078	HRs: 42
RBI: 374	BBs: 502

Named captain of the Mariners in 1986, slick-fielding Owen was surprisingly traded in August of that year. He batted .429 in two ALCS and .300 for the Red Sox in the 1986 World Series. He scored six runs in a Red Sox game that year.
Playing Career: *1983-; Sea A, Bos A, Mon N, NY A*

Jim Owens
Owens, James Philip (Bear)
B: Jan 16, 1934

Pos: P	ERA: 4.31
W-L: 42-68	SOs: 516
ShOs: 1	Saves: 21

A minor league leader in both strikeouts and walks, Owens developed control after his military stint in 1957-1958, but spent his early career as a starter for the dreadful Phillies. He became a reliever with the Astros, winning 16 and saving 16 in his last four years, and later served them as a coach, 1967-1972.
Playing Career: *1955-1956, 1958-1967; Phi N, Cin N, Hou N*

Danny Ozark
Ozark, Daniel Leonard (Ozark Ike)
B: Nov 24, 1923

Managerial Record
Won: 618   Lost: 542   Pct: .533

A minor league player-manager, Ozark toiled in the Dodger chain for many years, then coached under Walter Alston until he was named Phillies manager in 1973. He won three division titles, 1976-1978, but was never victorious in the NLCS.
Managerial Career: *1973-1979, 1984; Phi N, SF N*

Spike Owen scores in Game Six of the 1986 WS. Bill Buckner is there to greet him.

Tom Paciorek
Paciorek, Thomas Marian
B: Nov 2, 1946

Pos: OF, 1B, DH, 3B   BA: .282
Hits: 1,162   HRs: 86
RBI: 503   BB: 245

A trio of Paciorek brothers played major league baseball, but Tom was the only one with staying power. Tom batted .294 in two LCS and .500 in the 1974 World Series. He was an All-Star in 1981, when he hit .326 and slugged .509 for the Mariners.
Playing Career: *1970-1987; LA N, Atl N, Sea A, Chi A, NY N, Tex A*

Tom Paciorek.

Gene Packard
Packard, Eugene Milo
B: Jul 13, 1887   D: May 19, 1959

Pos: P   ERA: 3.01
W-L: 85-69   SOs: 488
ShOs: 15   Saves: 17

In the two-year history of the Federal League, there was only one pitcher who had back-to-back 20-game seasons – Packard. He was also a fine hitter, and batted .288 in 1917 with the Cardinals.
Playing Career: *1912-1919; Cin N, KC F, Chi N, StL N, Phi N*

Dick Padden
Padden, Richard Joseph (Brains)
B: Sep 17, 1870   D: Oct 31, 1922

Pos: 2B   BA: .258
Hits: 814   HRs: 11
RBI: 334   BB: 224

Padden was a slick-fielding second baseman who played in the AL in 1900, when it was a minor league. Padden played with the Cardinals in 1901 while recruiting teammates to the new league. In 1902 an AL franchise started in St. Louis, and Padden went back to his former league.
Playing Career: *1896-1899, 1901-1905; Pit N, Was N, StL N, StL A*

Andy Pafko
Pafko, Andrew (Handy Andy, Pruschka)
B: Feb 25, 1921

Pos: OF, 3B   BA: .285
Hits: 1,796   HRs: 213
RBI: 976   BB: 561

Following Pafko's 1951 trade to the Dodgers, he combined with Duke Snider in center field and Carl Furillo in right to give Brooklyn its best outfield ever. Pafko's 19 homers and 85 RBI helped the powerful Dodgers team to the 1952 pennant. Traded to the Braves, Pafko joined Hank Aaron and Billy Bruton in the potent Milwaukee outfield that competed with the Dodgers for pennants the rest of the decade. Pafko played a platoon role on the Braves' back-to-back pennant-winners of 1957-1958.

Earlier in his career, Pafko was an All-Star at two positions for the Cubs. Leading NL outfielders with a .995 fielding average in 1945, Pafko catapulted the Cubs into the World Series with 110 RBI. He was 3-for-4 with three runs scored in Game One, but fell into a slump as the Cubs lost in seven games. He played in four consecutive All-Star Games, 1947-1950. Pafko was immensely popular; fans were dismayed when he was traded to Brooklyn.
Playing Career: *1943-1959; Chi N, Brk N, Mil N*

Jose Pagan
Pagan y Rodriguez, Jose Antonio
B: May 5, 1935

Pos: SS   BA: .250
Hits: 922   HRs: 52
RBI: 372   BB: 244

In the 1971 World Series, Pagan drove in the deciding run in the Pirates' 2-1, Game Seven victory over the Orioles. In another Fall Classic, he hit .368 to lead the Giants in hitting during their seven-game loss to the Yankees in 1962.
Playing Career: *1959-1973; SF N, Pit N*

Joe Page
Page, Joseph Francis (Fireman, The Gay Reliever)
B: Oct 28, 1917   D: Apr 21, 1980

Pos: P   ERA: 3.53
W-L: 57-49   SOs: 519
ShOs: 1   Saves: 76

Page made Casey Stengel look like a genius when he saved 27 games in 1949, setting a record that stood until Luis Arroyo broke it in 1961. Page's 14 relief wins in 1947 also stood as an AL record until Arroyo broke that one too, in 1961. Leading the AL twice in saves, relief wins, and appearances, Page was 2-1 with

Andy Pafko brings in a 12th-inning HR for Brooklyn at Ebbets Field in 1952.

two saves in two World Series for the Yankees. He was one of the first relievers to be used daily in crucial situations as an integral member of the team.
Playing Career: *1944-1950, 1954; NY A, Pit N*

Mitchell Page
Page, Michell Otis
B: Oct 15, 1951

Pos: OF, DH	BA: .266
Hits: 560	HRs: 72
RBI: 259	BB: 245

Named the 1977 AL Rookie of the Year by *The Sporting News*, Page hit 21 homers, stole 42 bases, scored 85 runs, and batted .307. He never matched those figures again, and played regularly only two more years.
Playing Career: *1977-1984; Oak A, Pit N*

Jim Pagliaroni
Pagliaroni, James Vincent (Pags)
B: Dec 8, 1937

Pos: C	BA: .252
Hits: 622	HRs: 90
RBI: 326	BB: 330

A $70,000 bonus baby, Pagliaroni set a Pirates record for homers by a catcher with 17 in 1965, while leading NL catchers with 14 double plays. The next year he led NL receivers with a .997 fielding average.
Playing Career: *1955, 1960-1969; Bos A, Pit N, KC A, Sea A*

Mike Pagliarulo
Pagliarulo, Michael Timothy (Pags)
B: Mar 15, 1960

Pos: 3B	BA: .242
Hits: 886	HRs: 130
RBI: 478	BB: 328

Considered a budding superstar early in his career, Pagliarulo swatted 28 home runs in 1986 and 32 in 1987 for the Yankees. Visions of left-handed power danced in their heads, but Pagliarulo surprisingly has become better known for his glove work.
Playing Career: *1984-; NY A, SD N, Min A, Bal A*

Satchel Paige
Paige, Leroy Robert
B: Jul 7, 1906   D: Jun 8, 1982
Hall of Fame 1971

Pos: P	ERA: 3.29
W-L: 28-31	SOs: 290
ShOs: 4	Saves: 32

After two decades of prominence in the Negro Leagues, Paige became a 42-year-old rookie in the 1948 AL. He played on two of the greatest Negro League teams: the Pittsburgh Crawfords and Kansas City Monarchs. At age 59 Paige tossed three innings for the A's when they faced the Red Sox on September 25, 1965. He allowed one hit, but issued no walks and struck out one.

Hall of Famer Satchel Paige.

Lanky, charismatic Paige made more than $30,000 per year during the 1930s, a lofty sum for the Depression era. He named his pitches the "two-hump blooper," a moving change-up; "Little Tom," a medium fastball; "Long Tom," his hard fastball; and the "hesitation," in which he stopped in mid-delivery. In 1939 Paige used rest and a home snake oil remedy to recover from a sore arm. His greatest triumph came in the 1942 Negro World Series. Paige won all four games for the Kansas City Monarchs over the favored Homestead Grays.
Playing Career: *1948-1949, 1951-1953, 1965; Cle A, StL A, KC A*

Rafael Palmeiro
Palmeiro y Corrales, Rafael
B: Sep 24, 1964

Pos: 1B	BA: .296
Hits: 1,144	HRs: 132
RBI: 526	BB: 378

A college teammate of Will Clark and Bobby Thigpen at Mississippi State, Palmeiro led the AL with 191 hits in 1990 and 49 doubles in 1991. Traded by the Cubs after he made the NL All-Star team in 1988, Palmeiro is now one of the rising stars in the AL.
Playing Career: *1986-; Chi N, Tex A*

Dave Palmer
Palmer, David William
B: Aug 19, 1957

Pos: P	ERA: 3.78
W-L: 64-59	SOs: 748
ShOs: 4	No-hitters: 1

Palmer tossed a five-inning, rain-shortened perfect game against the Cardinals in 1984 in just his second start after elbow surgery. Repeated injuries prevented Palmer from achieving the potential shown when he was 10-2 with a 2.64 ERA as a rookie in 1979.
Playing Career: *1978-1980, 1982, 1984-1989; Mon N, Atl N, Phi N, Det A*

Jim Palmer
Palmer, James Alvin
B: Oct 15, 1945
Hall of Fame 1990

Pos: P	ERA: 2.86
W-L: 268-152	SOs: 2,212
ShOs: 53	No-hitters: 1

As a 20-year-old, Palmer pitched a four-hit shutout victory over Sandy Koufax in Game Two of the 1966 World Series. Following that great performance the right-hander suffered from arm, shoulder and back injuries, and spent the majority of the next two years on the disabled list and in the minors. Twice, Palmer posted 20 victories or more four years in a row, 1970-1973, and 1975-1978. Only Walter Johnson had more 20-win seasons in the AL.

Palmer won his first ERA title with a 2.40 in 1973, going 22-9, and his second in 1975 with a 2.09 mark. That year he tossed an AL-high 10 shutouts and won 23 games. His three Cy Young Awards have been matched only by Sandy Koufax and Tom Seaver, and exceeded only by Steve Carlton. Palmer won four Gold Glove Awards. His clutch wins included the Orioles' pennant-clinchers in 1966, 1969, 1970 and 1971. He holds ALCS records with 46 strikeouts and five complete games, going 4-1 in six pennant series. Palmer was 4-2 in World Series play.
Playing Career: *1965-1967, 1969-1984; Bal A*

Jim Palmer in action in 1974.

Milt Pappas.

Milt Pappas
Pappas, Milton Stephen (Gimpy)
B: May 11, 1939

Pos: P	ERA: 3.40
W-L: 209-164	SOs: 1,728
ShOs: 43	No-hitters: 1

On September 2, 1972, Pappas was one out away from a perfect game against the Padres when he walked Larry Stahl, and had to settle for a no-hitter. The unwitting victim of one of the worst trades in Reds history – Pappas and two journeymen for Frank Robinson – he won more than 10 games 14 of 15 seasons, totaling 110 in the AL and 99 in the NL. He averaged nearly 15 wins a season from 1960 to 1964.

Pappas pitched only three games in the minors before coming up as a 19-year-old rookie in 1958, and he compiled a record of 15-9 the next year. He developed a reputation as a five-inning pitcher and a hypochondriac. The cantankerous hurler would show up the umpires with his griping and posturing on the mound, and once called the press box during a game to complain about an official scorer's decision that had cost him four earned runs. Pappas tossed seven shutouts, including a one-hitter against the Twins, for a 16-7 record in 1964. He started the 1965 All-Star Game for the AL.
Playing Career: *1957-1973; Bal A, Cin N, Atl N, Chi N*

Freddie Parent
Parent, Frederick Alfred
B: Nov 25, 1875   D: Nov 2, 1972

Pos: SS	BA: .262
Hits: 1,306	HRs: 20
RBI: 471	BB: 333

Parent was the longest surviving player of the 1903 World Series. He was also the batter when Yankee Jack Chesbro threw his famous wild pitch on the last day of the 1904 season. Parent's defensive plays saved four no-hit-ters – including Cy Young's perfect game – and Parent spoiled three no-hitters for opponents by getting hits. In teammate Frank Smith's 1908 no-hitter, Parent drove in the only run by hitting an attempted intentional walk in the bottom of the ninth inning.
Playing Career: *1899, 1901-1911; StL N, Bos A, Chi A*

Dave Parker
Parker, David Gene (Cobra)
B: Jun 9, 1951

Pos: OF, DH	BA: .290
Hits: 2,712	HRs: 339
RBI: 1,493	BB: 683

Parker looked like a sure bet for the Hall of Fame until his drug use diminished his career. At 6'5", 230 pounds, he was one of the most imposing hitters in baseball and a worthy successor to Roberto Clemente in the Pirates' outfield. He won batting titles in 1977 and 1978, led the NL in hits and doubles in 1977, and led in slugging average with 30 homers, 12 triples and 117 RBI in 1978. Parker won Gold Gloves three years in a row, and was honored with the 1978 NL MVP Award. He was an All-Star seven times.

At his best in postseason play, he batted .345 in the Bucs' 1979 World Series comeback over the Orioles. He was a fixture in Pittsburgh, but as his power and average dwindled, the Pirates regretted his multi-year contract and swapped him to the Reds. In 1985 Parker had a .312 average, 42 doubles, 34 homers and 125 RBI. In Oakland, he provided leadership and a big bat to help the A's win pennants in 1988 and 1989.
Playing Career: *1973-1991; Pit N, Cin N, Oak A, Mil A, Cal A, Tor A*

Wes Parker
Parker, Maurice Wesley
B: Nov 13, 1939

Pos: 1B	BA: .267
Hits: 1,110	HRs: 64
RBI: 470	BB: 532

Lithe and graceful, Parker was one of the best glovemen ever to play first base, earning six Gold Gloves. He combined with Maury Wills, Jim Lefebvre and Jim Gilliam on the 1965-1966 Dodgers to comprise the only switch-hitting infield. Parker retired to a broadcasting and acting career.
Playing Career: *1964-1972; LA N*

Dave Parker on deck for the Pirates.

Roy Parmelee
Parmelee, Leroy Earl (Tarzan, Bud)
B: Apr 25, 1907   D: Aug 31, 1981

Pos: P	ERA: 4.27
W-L: 59-55	SOs: 514
ShOs: 6	Saves: 3

Named "Tarzan" by the press because his pitching was out on a limb, Parmelee was wild as the jungle, and led the NL four times in hit batsmen and once in bases on balls. In 1933, his best year, he beat Dizzy Dean and the Cardinals 1-0, striking out 13 and walking none.
Playing Career: *1929-1937, 1939; NY N, StL N, Chi N, Phi A*

Mel Parnell
Parnell, Melvin Lloyd
B: Jun 13, 1922

Pos: P	ERA: 3.50
W-L: 123-75	SOs: 732
ShOs: 20	No-hitters: 1

No one believed that lefties could win at Fenway Park until Parnell proved they could. He was 70-30 in the face of the Green Monster. In 1949 he led the the AL with 25 wins, posting a 2.77 ERA. In each of the next two years, Parnell won 18 games, and made the All-Star team for the second time in 1951. He put up a 21-8 mark in 1953. A bad elbow caused his early retirement in 1956, but in his final season, he tossed the Red Sox' first no-hitter in 33 years.
Playing Career: *1947-1956; Bos A*

Jeff Parrett
Parrett, Jeffrey Dale
B: Aug 26, 1961

Pos: P	ERA: 3.87
W-L: 49-33	SOs: 481
ShOs: 0	Saves: 22

Used as the A's set-up man for closer Dennis Eckersley in 1992, Parrett was 9-1 with a 3.02 ERA, and appeared in the ALCS. He won 12 games in 1988 and again in 1989, saving six games in each season. He was the bullpen hope for the Rockies – but struggled in Mile High Stadium – in their initial season.
Playing Career: *1986-; Mon N, Phi N, Atl N, Oak A, Col N*

Lance Parrish
Parrish, Lance Michael
B: Jun 15, 1956

Pos: C, DH	BA: .253
Hits: 1,712	HRs: 316
RBI: 1,031	BB: 579

An early advocate of weight training for baseball players, Parrish rapped 32 homers in 1982, and Tigers Manager Sparky Anderson considered putting the whole team on the program. A former third baseman turned eight-time All-Star catcher, Parrish once served as a bodyguard for Tina Turner. After committing 21 passed balls in 1979, he worked hard to improve his catching skills, and was the recipient of the Gold Glove Award 1983-1985.

Parrish hit home runs in the 1984 ALCS and World Series. His seventh-inning blast in Game Five was the Series-winning run for the Tigers. In 1982 he broke Yogi Berra's AL record for home runs by a catcher with 32, but Carlton Fisk broke Parrish's record the following year. With recurring back problems he became a backup receiver, first with the Phillies, then with the Angels, where he replaced the aging Bob Boone.
Playing Career: *1977-; Det A, Phi N, Cal A, Sea A, Cle A*

Larry Parrish
Parrish, Larry Alton
B: Nov 10, 1953

Pos: 3B, OF, DH	BA: .263
Hits: 1,789	HRs: 256
RBI: 992	BB: 529

A star third-sacker during the Gary Carter era with the Expos, Parrish still holds club records for total bases in a single game with 14 – and he did it twice. Parrish belted three home runs in one game on four occasions. After being a major contributor in Montreal, he was traded to the Rangers for Al Oliver. In Texas he became an RBI man. Moving to the outfield, Parrish was the Rangers' Player of the Year in 1984.

Suffering a severe knee injury in 1985, he moved to a designated hitter role, becoming the AL's top DH, 1985-1987. In 1986 he was the Rangers' Player of the Year for the second time. Parrish pounded 32 homers in 1987, setting a club record, and becoming the 13th player to have 30-homer seasons in both the AL and NL. Phenom Juan Gonzalez broke his single-season club record in 1992, but Parrish is number two on the Rangers' all-time home run list, and third on their extra-base hits and RBI lists.
Playing Career: *1974-1988; Mon N, Tex A, Bos A*

Larry Parrish, with Montreal in 1979.

Camilo Pascual
Pascual y Lus, Camilo Alberto
(Little Potato)
B: Jan 20, 1934

Pos: P	ERA: 3.63
W-L: 174-170	SOs: 2,167
ShOs: 36	Saves: 10

Little Potato was recommended to the Senators by his older brother Carlos "Big Potato" Pascual, who played in Cuba before entering the major leagues in the U.S. The younger Pascual was a dominant right-hander in the late 1950s and early 1960s. He won 20 games in 1962 and 21 the next year, making the All-Star squad 1959-1962, and again in 1964.

Pascual led the league in strikeouts three years in a row, 1961-1963, and was tops in complete games three times. He had absolutely overpowering stuff on a wicked sidearm curve and a blazing fastball. Combined with good control, his skills produced a 17-10 record for the eighth-place Senators in 1959. Later in his career Pascual had chronic arm problems that reduced the number of pitching starts, but he was 9-3 for the 1965 pennant-winning Twins. He started Game Three in the World Series that year.
Playing Career: *1954-1971; Was A, Min A, Cin N, LA N, Cle A*

Tigers catcher Lance Parrish, 1980.

Dode Paskert
Paskert, George Henry
B: Aug 28, 1881   D: Feb 12, 1959

Pos: OF	BA: .268
Hits: 1,613	HRs: 42
RBI: 577	BB: 715

A top defensive outfielder, Paskert was a regular for 13 years on NL pennant contending teams. A good leadoff hitter, he set personal highs with 102 runs in 1912 and 51 stolen bases in 1910. Paskert scored 868 runs and stole 293 bases during his career. In World Series play his teams lost to the Red Sox in 1915 and 1918. The Phillies acquired Paskert from Cincinnati for a quartet of unknown players in 1911; the Cubs traded slugger Cy Williams for him; and he returned to Cincinnati for the 1921 season.
Playing Career: *1907-1921; Cin N, Phi N, Chi N*

Dan Pasqua
Pasqua, Daniel Anthony
B: Oct 17, 1961

Pos: OF, 1B, DH	BA: .244
Hits: 633	HRs: 115
RBI: 386	BB: 335

A minor league home run champion, Pasqua is a left-handed pull hitter, but has yet to become a home run slugger in the mold of Babe Ruth and Lou Gehrig. In his first year with the White Sox he hit 20 home runs and led AL outfielders in fielding.
Playing Career: *1985-; NY A, Chi A*

Claude Passeau
Passeau, Claude William
B: Apr 9, 1909

Pos: P	ERA: 3.32
W-L: 162-150	SOs: 1,104
ShOs: 27	Saves: 21

Passeau wore uniform number 13. His license plate was number 13; the serial number on his rifle was number 13; his life insurance policy number ended in 13; and his address was 113 London Street. Passeau spent 13 years in the majors, and his name has 13 letters. Despite that, he was pretty lucky. He pitched a one-hitter in the 1945 World Series. For 10 years, Passeau tossed 217 or more innings, averaging 15 victories per year, and making the All-Star team five times.
Playing Career: *1935-1947; Pit N, Phi N, Chi N*

Freddie Patek
Patek, Frederick Joseph
B: Oct 9, 1944

Pos: SS	BA: .242
Hits: 1,340	HRs: 41
RBI: 490	BB: 523

A 5'5" David who hit like Goliath, Patek once smashed three home runs in one game. He liked to hit, and led the AL in triples with 11 in 1971. Patek batted .389 in both the 1976 and 1977 ALCS, and hit a home run in the Royals' only victory in the 1978 ALCS. He was even better on the basepaths; he stole 51 bases in 1976 and a league-leading 53 in 1977.

Freddie Patek at bat in 1975.

Patek's early training came from the Pirates' superlative second baseman Bill Mazeroski. The shortstop learned how to turn the double play like nobody else. He led AL shortstops in double plays for four consecutive seasons, 1971-1974. Patek is in the Royals' top 10 leaders in every offensive category, and ranks third in stolen bases. He stole 385 bases during his big league career. Beloved by Kansas City fans, Patek retained his home there after retiring from baseball.
Playing Career: *1968-1981; Pit N, KC A, Cal A*

Casey Patten
Patten, Case Lyman
B: May 7, 1876   D: May 31, 1935

Pos: P	ERA: 3.36
W-L: 105-128	SOs: 757
ShOs: 16	Saves: 5

Before the Senators had Walter Johnson, Patten was the ace of their pitching staff. He won 105 games for teams that never finished higher than sixth place, and finished last three times. Patten averaged more than 300 innings for six years, and completed 206 of 238 starts.
Playing Career: *1901-1908; Was A, Bos A*

Roy Patterson
Patterson, Roy Lewis (The St. Croix Boy Wonder)
B: Dec 17, 1876   D: Apr 14, 1953

Pos: P	ERA: 2.75
W-L: 81-73	SOs: 442
ShOs: 16	Saves: 2

Tagged the "St. Croix Boy Wonder" when he pitched for a local team and beat Comiskey's St. Paul team, Patterson later won the very first AL game, beating the Cleveland Blues 8-2. He was 20-16 in 1901 and 19-14 the next year.
Playing Career: *1901-1907; Chi A*

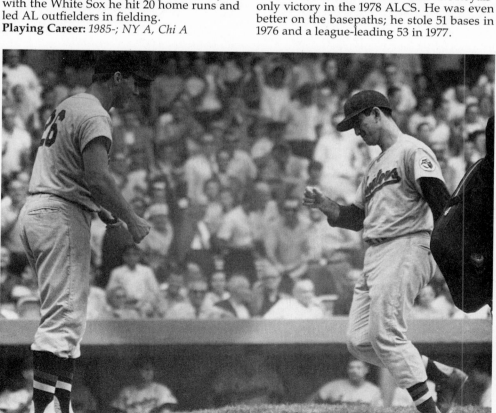

Senators pitcher Camilo Pascual brings in his first home run – a grand slam – in 1960.

Marty Pattin
Pattin, Martin William (Duck, Bulldog)
B: Apr 6, 1943

Pos: P	ERA: 3.62
W-L: 114-109	SOs: 1,179
ShOs: 14	Saves: 25

Currently the popular baseball coach at the University of Kansas, Pattin earned a master's degree at Eastern Illinois University and is in the NAIA Hall of Fame. He spent the majority of his major league career in the Royals' bullpen – perfecting his imitation of Donald Duck between relief stints – but had considerable success as a starter, winning 32 games in two years with the Red Sox, and 28 in two seasons in Milwaukee. Pattin was selected for the 1971 All-Star Game.
Playing Career: *1968-1980; Cal A, Sea A, Mil A, Bos A, KC A*

Dickie Pearce.

Dickie Pearce
Pearce, Richard J.
B: Feb 29, 1836   D: Oct 12, 1908

Pos: SS	BA: .252
Hits: 334	HRs: 2
RBI: 83 (inc.)	BB: 34
Managerial Record	
Won: 49 Lost: 35 Pct: .583	

Performing at a top level from 1855 to 1877, Pearce spanned the era from the game's beginnings to the formation of the National League. He and pitcher James Creighton were probably the two first professional baseball players. Pearce sometimes caught Creighton during the famous Brooklyn versus New York all-star games in the 1850s. Pearce was on the field in 1870 when the Atlantics defeated the Cincinnati Red Stockings, breaking their 88-game winning streak.

At the time the Atlantics placed him at shortstop it was the least important position; there was no base to guard and no field to protect. Pearce developed his role, roaming into the outfield, taking relay throws, backing up bases and shifting positions according to each batter's strengths. Pearce invented the bunt or "baby hit," and was also a master of the fair-foul hit. He was considered the best shortstop in baseball during his entire career, except for George Wright during his very best years.
Playing Career: *1871-1877; NY Mutuals n, Brk Atlantics n, StL Brown Stockings n, StL N*
Managerial Career: *1872, 1875; NY Mutuals n, StL Brown Stockings n*
Umpiring Career: *1878, 1882; NL*

Albie Pearson
Pearson, Albert Gregory (Little Albie)
B: Sep 12, 1934

Pos: OF	BA: .270
Hits: 831	HRs: 28
RBI: 214	BB: 477

At 5'5,"140 pounds, Pearson was the smallest man in the majors throughout most of his career. He batted .275 and doubled 25 times in 1958, and was named Rookie of the Year. With the 1962 Angels Pearson used his size to draw walks; he scored 115 runs that year.
Playing Career: *1958-1966; Was A, Bal A, Cal A*

Monte Pearson
Pearson, Montgomery Marcellus
B: Sep 2, 1909   D: Jan 27, 1978

Pos: P	ERA: 4.00
W-L: 100-61	SOs: 703
ShOs: 5	No-hitters: 1

A graduate of the University of California–Berkeley with a degree in physics, Pearson led the AL with a 2.33 ERA as a rookie in 1933. He pitched four outstanding World Series games, compiling a record of 4-0 with a 1.01 ERA for the Yankees, 1936-1939.
Playing Career: *1932-1941; Cle A, NY A, Cin N*

Roger Peckinpaugh
Peckinpaugh, Roger Thorpe
B: Feb 5, 1891   D: Nov 17, 1977

Pos: SS	BA: .259
Hits: 1,876	HRs: 48
RBI: 739	BB: 814
Managerial Record	
Won: 500 Lost: 491 Pct: .505	

Broad-shouldered and bow-legged, Peckinpaugh was the widest ranging shortstop of his day. A good hitter, he had a 29-game hitting streak in 1919, batting a career-high .305 that season. After nine years with the Yankees, including the franchise's first pennant-winning season, 1921, he was traded to the Senators with Jack Quinn for Everett Scott, Sad Sam Jones and Joe Bush in a swap that helped both clubs. With the Senators he teamed with young second baseman Bucky Harris to turn a record 168 double plays in 1922. Peckinpaugh batted .417 in the 1924 World Series, doubling home the winning

Roger Peckinpaugh in 1924.

run in Game Two and saving Game Six with a key fielding play. After an AL MVP season the following year, his 1925 Series was dreadful; he made eight errors as the Senators lost. During his career, he scored 1,006 with 207 stolen bases. His 1914 managerial stint made him the youngest manager in baseball history.
Playing Career: *1910, 1912-1927; Cle A, NY A, Was A, Chi A*
Managerial Career: *1914, 1928-1933, 1941; NY A, Cle A*

Heinie Peitz
Peitz, Henry Clement
B: Nov 28, 1870   D: Oct 23, 1943

Pos: C	BA: .271
Hits: 1,117	HRs: 16
RBI: 560	BB: 409

The German duo of Peitz and left-handed pitcher Ted Breitenstein formed the Pretzel Battery, known for their mutual fondness for post-game beer and pretzels at a Cincinnati saloon. Pietz hit over .300 twice and led NL receivers in fielding in 1897.
Playing Career: *1892-1906, 1913; StL N, Cin N, Pit N*

Barney Pelty
Pelty, Barney
B: Sep 10, 1880   D: May 24, 1939

Pos: P	ERA: 2.63
W-L: 92-117	SOs: 693
ShOs: 23	Saves: 4

Stuck with the Browns for 10 years in the second division, the Yiddish Curver did his best to bring them up, going 16-11 with a 1.59 ERA in 1906. He hurled 301 innings in 1904. Pelty was washed up by the time the second-place Senators acquired him in 1912.
Playing Career: *1903-1912; StL A, Was A*

Alejandro Pena
Pena y Vasquez, Alejandro
B: Jun 25, 1959

Pos: P	ERA: 2.95
W-L: 50-48	SOs: 743
ShOs: 7	Saves: 67

As a starter Alejandro Pena led the NL in shutouts and ERA in 1984. Shoulder surgery the next year turned him into a reliever. With control and a 95-mph fastball, Pena developed into a closer after 1987. He contributed to the Braves' pennants of 1991 and 1992.
Playing Career: *1981-1992; LA N, NY N, Atl N*

Orlando Pena
Pena y Quevara, Orlando Gregorio
B: Nov 17, 1933

Pos: P	ERA: 3.70
W-L: 56-77	SOs: 818
ShOs: 4	Saves: 40

In the minor leagues Pena posted a record of 146-85 as a starter, but he was a reliever for all of his major league teams except the Athletics. In three years Pena went 30-38 for the awful A's. He later scouted for the Tigers.
Playing Career: *1958-1960, 1962-1967, 1970-1971, 1973-1975; Cin N, KC A, Det A, Cle A, Pit N, Bal A, StL N, Cal A*

Tony Pena
Pena y Padilla, Antonio Francesco
B: Jun 4, 1957

Pos: C	BA: .262
Hits: 1,536	HRs: 99
RBI: 633	BB: 407

You can always recognize Pena from his distinctive catching style. With no runners on, he squats with one leg splayed out, almost sitting on the ground. Using a more conventional catcher's crouch with runners on, he snaps throws, picking runners off first or gunning them down at second. He owns four Gold Glove Awards. With the Pirates he batted over .285 in five of six years, twice going over .300. Since his trade in 1987, Pena has not hit over .265 in the regular season, but led Cardinals regulars with a .381 average in the 1987 NLCS and posted a .409 mark in the World Series.

While not approaching his earlier doubles or home runs totals, Pena has worked on his catching in Fenway Park. His fielding averages have improved 10 percentage points from his Gold Glove years at Pittsburgh. Fans and Pena are still adjusting to his shocking trade from the Pirates, even though the Bucs won three straight division titles with players from that deal, which included Andy Van Slyke.
Playing Career: *1980-; Pit N, StL N, Bos A*

Terry Pendleton
Pendleton, Terry Lee
B: Jul 16, 1960

Pos: 3B	BA: .273
Hits: 1,446	HRs: 104
RBI: 717	BB: 368

A tremendous gloveman who takes risks at third, Pendleton hit .324 during a late season call up in 1984, causing the Cardinals to trade Ken Oberkfell. The switch-hitting Pendleton has always been a good contact batter. He did not have the speed of many of his teammates, but good judgment and good jumps enabled him to steal 24 bases in 1986.

From the beginning, Pendleton showed great range, lightning reflexes, and a rifle arm. In 1986 he led NL third basemen in chances, putouts and assists. He won Gold Gloves in 1987, 1989 and 1992, leading the league in fielding percentage in 1989. Pendle-

Terry Pendleton, with St. Louis in 1989.

ton's bat suddenly came to life, and he won the NL batting title with a .319 mark for Atlanta in 1991; he led the NL in hits in 1991 and 1992. A terror in the World Series, he batted .429 in the 1987 Fall Classic, and .367 with two home runs in the 1991 Series.
Playing Career: *1984-; StL N, Atl N*

Herb Pennock
Pennock, Herbert Jefferis
(The Squire of Kennett Square)
B: Feb 10, 1894   D: Jan 30, 1948
Hall of Fame 1948

Pos: P	ERA: 3.61
W-L: 240-162	SOs: 1,227
ShOs: 35	Saves: 33

A graceful southpaw, Pennock was unbeatable in the World Series, going 5-0 with a 1.95 ERA and three saves in five Fall Classics for the Athletics and Yankees. In the 1927 Series, he retired the first 22 Pirates in Game Three. Pennock was one of the few players whom Connie Mack misjudged. Mack thought that Pennock was too wealthy to work hard enough to be a top ballplayer.

The Pennocks came from historic Kennett Square, Pennsylvania, where they raised horses and participated in fox hunts. Pennock was an expert rider and a master of hounds. As a profitable hobby, he raised silver foxes for their pelts. On the pitching mound he was a master of batters. For 22 seasons, he allowed more than a hit an inning, yet gave up only 3.61 earned runs a game. He yielded many lazy flies to the outfield. Even-tempered, Pennock never got rattled under pressure. His contemporaries said Pennock memorized the weaknesses of each batter.
Playing Career: *1912-1917, 1919-1934; Phi A, Bos A, NY A*

Catcher Tony Pena, while with the St. Louis Cardinals, in 1989.

Joe Pepitone
Pepitone, Joseph Anthony (Pepi)
B: Oct 9, 1940

Pos: 1B, OF	BA: .258
Hits: 1,315	HRs: 219
RBI: 721	BB: 302

Pepitone spent his $20,000 signing bonus on a fancy car and a motorboat. He spent his career on another planet. The talented three-time All-Star led AL first basemen in fielding three times, and won two Gold Gloves. He played in two World Series for the Yankees. But Pepitone had a reputation for being eccentric. When he started going bald, he wore wigs; a short one on the playing field, and a longer, more fashionably cut wig after the game.
Playing Career: *1962-1973; NY A, Hou N, Chi N, Atl N*

Hub Perdue
**Perdue, Herbert Rodney
(The Gallatin Squash)**
B: Jun 7, 1882   D: Oct 31, 1968

Pos: P	ERA: 3.85
W-L: 51-64	SOs: 317
ShOs: 5	Saves: 7

Writer Grantland Rice called Perdue "the Gallatin Squash" because his hometown was Gallatin, Tennessee, and his nickname "Hub" reminded Rice of the vegetable called a Hubbard squash. Perdue had his best season in 1913, when he compiled a 16-13 record for the Braves.
Playing Career: *1911-1915; Bos N, StL N*

Marty Perez
Perez, Martin Roman
B: Feb 28, 1947

Pos: SS, 2B, 3B	BA: .246
Hits: 771	HRs: 22
RBI: 241	BB: 245

A gloveman in a lineup of sluggers, Perez solidified the Braves' infield from 1971 to 1975. He even hit eight home runs, scoring 66 runs and driving in 57, in 1973. Perez struck out only 369 times in 3,131 at-bats, but he walked even fewer times.
Playing Career: *1969-1978; Cal A, Atl N, SF N, NY A, Oak A*

Melido Perez
Perez, Melido Turpen
B: Feb 15, 1966

Pos: P	ERA: 4.09
W-L: 64-76	SOs: 939
ShOs: 5	No-hitters: 1

Once known only as Pascual Perez's little brother, Melido Perez is now one of the star pitchers in the AL, despite an off-year in 1993. He fanned 218 batters in 1992. A starter since age 22, Perez has begun to harness his fastball and slider with the Yankees.
Playing Career: *1987-; KC A, Chi A, NY A*

Pascual Perez
Perez, Pascual Gross
B: May 17, 1957

Pos: P	ERA: 3.44
W-L: 67-68	SOs: 822
ShOs: 4	No-hitters: 1

In 1982, having just passed the driver's test, Perez got on the freeway in Atlanta to drive to the ballpark, but could not determine where to exit. He circled the city for hours and missed his first start with the Braves. The next two years he won 29 games, and was an All-Star in 1983.
Playing Career: *1980-1985, 1987-1992; Pit N, Atl N, Mon N, NY A*

Tony Perez
Perez y Rigal, Atanasio (Doggie)
B: May 14, 1942

Pos: 1B, 3B	BA: .279
Hits: 2,732	HRs: 379
RBI: 1,652	BB: 925
Managerial Record	
Won: 20 Lost: 24 Pct: .455	

The Cincinnati Reds' organization embarrassed itself in June 1993 by firing Manager Perez in an ungraceful manner after just 44 games. For 10 years Perez had been one of the vital members of Cincinnati's Big Red Machine. The Reds won four pennants with him in the infield. In 1970 Perez hit .317 with 40 homers and 134 RBI. He belted three home runs in the 1975 World Series against the Red Sox. One of baseball's best run producers, Perez batted in the five-hole behind Johnny Bench, and drove in 90 or more runs for 11 consecutive years.

Perez scored 1,272 runs and belted 505 doubles. Although striking out 1,867 times, he compiled a slugging average of .463 in a 23-year career. He played in six NLCS and

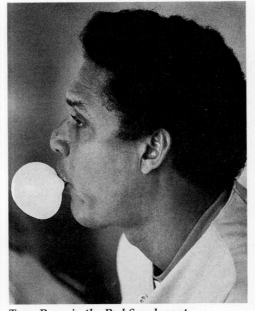
Tony Perez in the Red Sox dugout.

five World Series, and made the All-Star squad seven times. After platooning at first base for two years, Perez switched to third so the Reds could get slugger Lee May into the lineup. At the hot corner, Perez built a Hall of Fame caliber career in Cincinnati. Some other lucky city will be his proving ground as a manager.
Playing Career: *1964-1986; Cin N, Mon N, Bos A, Phi N*
Managerial Career: *1993; Cin N*

Cy Perkins
Perkins, Ralph Foster
B: Feb 27, 1896   D: Oct 2, 1963

Pos: C	BA: .259
Hits: 933	HRs: 30
RBI: 409	BB: 301

Perkins caught for the Athletics during seven straight last-place finishes. He taught catching techniques to future Hall of Famer Mickey Cochrane. As a Phillies coach, Perkins developed pitchers Robin Roberts and Curt Simmons.
Playing Career: *1915, 1917-1931, 1934; Phi A, NY A, Det A*

Bill Perkins
Perkins, William George
B: Unknown   D: Deceased

Pos: C	BA: .287 (inc.)
Hits: 315 (inc.)	HRs: 19 (inc.)
RBI: NA	BB: NA
Managerial Record	
Won: 25 Lost: 17 Pct: .595	

"Thou Shalt Not Steal" was the warning emblazoned on Perkins's chest protector. The receiver accompanied Satchel Paige, Josh Gibson and Cool Papa Bell to the Dominican Republic, where the quartet played for the dictator Rafael Trujillo.
Playing Career: *1928-1947; Bir Black Barons, Cle Cubs, Pit Crawfords, Phi Stars, Bal Elite Giants, NY Black Yankees*
Managerial Career: *1945; Bal Elite Giants*

Ron Perranoski
Perranoski, Ronald Peter
B: Apr 1, 1936

Pos: P	ERA: 2.79
W-L: 79-74	SOs: 687
ShOs: 0	Saves: 179

Somehow the name Perzanowski got changed to Perranoski, and that is the name that became a household word in the early 1960s. The Michigan State University graduate came to the Dodgers from the Cubs' organization, where he had been a starter. The Dodger brain trust turned him into a relief pitcher and won three pennants in four years. In 1962 he led the majors with 70 appearances. The next year Perranoski was brilliant, going 16-3 with a 1.67 ERA, and leading the NL in won-lost percentage and appearances.

Using a fastball, curve and sinker, Perra-

Gaylord Perry in action in 1974.

Ron Perranoski made frequent trips from the bullpen to the mound in the 1960s.

noski remained the mainstay of the Dodger bullpen through 1967, leading the NL in appearances. Traded to the Twins, he led the AL with 31 saves in 1969, then 34 saves in 1970, and was the AL Fireman of the Year both seasons. He appeared in three World Series for the Dodgers, and two ALCS with the Twins. Perranoski later served 12 years as the Dodgers' pitching coach under manager Tommy Lasorda.
Playing Career: *1961-1973; LA N, Min A, Det A, Cal A*

Pol Perritt
Perritt, William Dayton
B: Aug 30, 1892   D: Oct 15, 1947

Pos: P	ERA: 2.89
W-L: 92-78	SOs: 543
ShOs: 23	Saves: 8

After Perritt signed a Federal League contract in 1915, he got traded to the Giants. Since he

was a promising pitcher, Giants manager John McGraw talked him into staying in the NL. Perritt was 17-7 while leading the Giants to the NL pennant in 1917, then won 18 games the next year.
Playing Career: *1912-1921; StL N, NY N, Det A*

Gaylord Perry
Perry, Gaylord Jackson
B: Sep 15, 1938
Hall of Fame 1991

Pos: P	ERA: 3.10
W-L: 314-265	SOs: 3,534
ShOs: 53	No-hitters: 1

Perry signed a $90,000 contract with the Giants, and earned a regular spot in their starting rotation in 1963 after four years in the farm system. He emerged as a star in August 1966 when he had an incredible 20-2 record; he finished the season 21-8. Late in 1968, he

beat Bob Gibson and the Cardinals with a 1-0 no-hitter. In 1970 Perry led the NL in victories with 23. His best season was 1972, when he was 24-16 with a 1.92 ERA for the fifth-place Indians. Jim Perry is Gaylord's brother.

The first and only pitcher to win the Cy Young Award in both leagues, Perry was honored by the AL in 1972 and the NL in 1978. During a 22-year career, he posted a 314-265 record and 5,351 innings pitched. In Seattle – where he was called "the Ancient Mariner" – Perry won his 300th game. He won 20 or more games five times, totaling 139 in the AL and 175 in the NL. He led the league in wins three times – 1970, 1972 and 1978. Perry was selected for the All-Star team five times.
Playing Career: *1962-1983; SF N, Cle A, Tex A, SD N, NY A, Atl N, Sea A, KC A*

Gerald Perry
Perry, Gerald June
B: Oct 30, 1960

Pos: 1B, DH, OF	BA: .266
Hits: 794	HRs: 56
RBI: 373	BB: 307

A minor league batting champ, Perry is a speedy line drive hitter in a power position. He stole 42 bases in 1987. An All-Star in 1988, Perry hit .300 with 29 doubles and 74 RBI that year, but has been plagued by recurring shoulder problems since.
Playing Career: *1983-; Atl N, KC A, StL N*

Jim Perry
Perry, James Evan
B: Oct 30, 1936

Pos: P	ERA: 3.45
W-L: 215-174	SOs: 1,576
ShOs: 32	Saves: 10

In 1974 the Perry brothers won 38 games – the most wins by siblings on the same team since Dizzy and Paul Dean won 47 in 1935. Jim Perry led the AL in wins twice, with 18 in 1960 and 24 in 1970. Perry was selected for the AL All-Star team three times. Coming up when he was 22 years old, he posted 12 victories with a 2.65 ERA and batted .300 for Cleveland. In Minnesota, he landed in Manager Sam Mele's doghouse for being too nice, and was shuttled between the bullpen and starting rotation for six seasons.

In 1965 Minnesota placed Perry on waivers, but he went unclaimed. He then won seven straight games to help the Twins get to the World Series. Billy Martin became the Twins' manager in 1969, and Perry immediately took over as the number-one starter, going 20-12 with a 2.82 ERA as the Twins won the AL West championship. The following year, he won the AL Cy Young Award with his 24-12 record and 3.03 ERA as the Twins won a second straight division title.
Playing Career: *1959-1975; Cle A, Min A, Det A, Oak A*

Shortstop Johnny Pesky led the AL in hits his first three years with Boston.

Jim Perry, 1970 Cy Young Award winner.

Johnny Pesky
Pesky, John Michael
B: Sep 27, 1919

Pos: SS	BA: .307
Hits: 1,455	HRs: 17
RBI: 404	BB: 663
Managerial Record	
Won: 147 Lost: 179 Pct: .451	

Born John Michael Paveskovich, Pesky led the AL in base hits with 205 in 1942, but did not see another major league pitch for three years. When he returned from military duty, Pesky led the AL in hits the next two years, with 208 in 1946, and 207 in 1947. He is remembered for the play that he did not make in the 1946 World Series against the St. Louis Cardinals.

The Cardinals and the Red Sox were tied 3-3 in the ninth inning of Game Seven. With two out and Enos Slaughter on first, Harry Walker blooped a double into center field. Slaughter was running with the pitch. Pesky took the cutoff throw with his back to the plate, checked Walker at first, then saw too late that Slaughter was racing home. Pesky's throw was late. The Cardinals won the game and became World Champions.
Playing Career: *1942, 1946-1954; Bos A, Det A, Was A*
Managerial Career: *1963-1964, 1980; Bos A*

Gary Peters
Peters, Gary Charles
B: Apr 21, 1937

Pos: P	ERA: 3.25
W-L: 124-103	SOs: 1,420
ShOs: 23	Saves: 5

The 1963 AL Rookie of the Year, Peters could hit as well as pitch. He made 16 hits in 66 at-bats as a pinch hitter, including four home runs, one in extra innings. On May 26, 1968, Manager Eddie Stanky batted Peters sixth in the order, ahead of Luis Aparicio, Duane Josephson and Tim Cullen. The two-time All-Star won 20 games in 1964 and 16 in 1967. He led the AL twice in ERA, posting a 2.33 mark in 1963 and a 1.98 mark in 1966.
Playing Career: *1959-1972; Chi A, Bos A*

Johnny Peters
Peters, John Paul
B: Apr 8, 1850   D: Jan 4, 1924

Pos: SS, 2B	BA: .276
Hits: 749	HRs: 3
RBI: 190 (inc.)	BB: 24

Staying with the Chicago White Stockings through their move from the National Association to the National League, Peters hit a career-high .351 in the first NL season as the White Stockings captured the flag. Peters was the National League's top fielding shortstop in 1876 and 1880.
Playing Career: *1874-1884; Chi White Stockings n, Chi N, Mil N, Pro N, Buf N, Pit AA*

Fritz Peterson
Peterson, Fred Ingles
B: Feb 8, 1942

Pos: P	ERA: 3.30
W-L: 133-131	SOs: 1,015
ShOs: 20	Saves: 1

Peterson won 20 games, posted a 2.91 ERA and was selected for the All-Star team in 1970. He was cunning and sharp on the mound, but an incident in 1973 overshadowed his career. Peterson and teammate Mike Kekich traded wives, kids and station wagons early in 1973. The press had a field day. The Yankees responded by immediately shipping Kekich to Cleveland. Ironically, Peterson was traded to the Indians a year later.
Playing Career: *1966-1976; NY A, Cle A, Tex A*

Rico Petrocelli
Petrocelli, Americo Peter
B: Jun 27, 1943

Pos: SS, 3B	BA: .251
Hits: 1,352	HRs: 210
RBI: 773	BB: 661

Five Italian-Americans have hit 40 or more home runs in one season – Petrocelli, Roy Campanella, Yogi Berra, Rocky Colavito and Jim Gentile. Petrocelli played in two World Series with the Red Sox. In Game Six of the 1967 Series, Petrocelli, Carl Yastrzemski and Reggie Smith set a record by hitting three homers in one inning. In 1969 Petrocelli set an AL record for home runs by a shortstop with 40, and tied a record for fewest errors by a shortstop, with 14.
Playing Career: *1963, 1965-1976; Bos A*

Dan Petry
Petry, Daniel Joseph
B: Nov 13, 1958

Pos: P	ERA: 3.95
W-L: 125-104	SOs: 1,063
ShOs: 11	Saves: 1

Coming up as a 20-year-old, Petry helped pitch the Tigers to two ALCS and the 1984 World Championship. He went 0-0 with a 1.74 ERA in ALCS play. Petry was 19-11 in 1983, leading AL pitchers with 38 starts, and compiled an 18-8 record, with a 3.24 ERA, in 1984. He was traded to the Angels for Gary Pettis in November 1987.
Playing Career: *1979-1991; Det A, Cal A, Atl N, Bos A*

Gary Pettis
Pettis, Gary George
B: Apr 3, 1958

Pos: OF	BA: .236
Hits: 855	HRs: 21
RBI: 259	BB: 521

With a sprinter's speed and a fly-paper glove Pettis had 354 stolen bases, 568 runs scored and five Gold Glove Awards. He hit .346 in the 1986 ALCS, scoring four times and driving in four runs.
Playing Career: *1982-1992; Cal A, Det A, Tex A, SD N*

Jesse Petty
Petty, Jesse Lee (The Silver Fox)
B: Nov 23, 1894   D: Oct 23, 1971

Pos: P	ERA: 3.68
W-L: 67-78	SOs: 407
ShOs: 6	Saves: 4

Petty was "tried and found wanting" in a famous mock trial by the Dodgers' Daffiness Boys because he did not know the meaning of the word "ignominy." In 1926 he compiled a record of 17-17; two years later he cut down his losses and was 15-15.
Playing Career: *1921, 1925-1930; Cle A, Brk N, Pit N, Chi N*

Bruce Petway
Petway, Bruce
B: 1883   D: Jul 14, 1941

Pos: C, OF	BA: .254 (inc.)
Hits: 221 (inc.)	HRs: 6 (inc.)
RBI: NA	BB: NA
Managerial Record	
Won: 173 Lost: 126 Pct: .579	

A student at Meharry Medical College, Petway quit school to become a pro baseball player in 1906. In 1910 he batted .390 against the Detroit Tigers and threw Ty Cobb out at second. Petway may have been the first catcher to throw from a squat.
Playing Career: *1906-1925; NY Cuban X-Giants, Phi Giants, Chi Leland Giants, Chi Am Giants, Det Stars*
Managerial Career: *1922-1925; Det Stars*

Fred Pfeffer
Pfeffer, Nathaniel Frederick (Fritz, Dandelion)
B: Mar 17, 1860   D: Apr 10, 1932

Pos: 2B	BA: .255
Hits: 1,671	HRs: 95
RBI: 859 (inc.)	BB: 527
Managerial Record	
Won: 40 Lost: 54 Pct: .426	

A top player and a member of Chicago's "Stonewall Infield" that won the 1885-1886 NL pennants, Pfeffer stole 382 bases and scored 1,094 runs in 1,670 games. He also compiled a 2-1 record with a 2.62 ERA as a pitcher. Pfeffer hit 25 homers in 1884, the year

Fred Pfeffer.

his team hit 142 altogether. He was the first infielder to cut off a catcher's throw to second on a double-steal attempt and get the runner at the plate.

Travelling with the baseball world tour in 1888-1889, Pfeffer and other ballplayers boarded a German freighter going from Australia to Ceylon. The Teutonic-looking Pfeffer convinced the captain that he was a count and dined with the officers every night, while the others ate with the crew. Privilege aside, when the first players' union developed – the Brotherhood of Professional Base Ball Players – Pfeffer served as its vice-president.
Playing Career: *1882-1897; Tro N, Chi N, Chi P, Lou N, NY N*
Managerial Career: *1892; Lou N*

Jeff Pfeffer
Pfeffer, Edward Joseph
B: Mar 4, 1888   D: Aug 15, 1972

Pos: P	ERA: 2.77
W-L: 158-112	SOs: 836
ShOs: 28	Saves: 10

Nicknamed "Jeff" after Big Jeff Pfeffer, his elder brother, Ed Pfeffer was the ace of a pitching staff that included Sherry Smith, Larry Cheney, Rube Marquard, Nap Rucker and Burleigh Grimes. Pfeffer won 25 games and led the Dodgers into the 1916 World Series, but was stifled by an excellent Red Sox team. After almost a season of military duty, Pfeffer returned to help Grimes win the 1920 flag for the Dodgers.
Playing Career: *1911, 1913-1924; StL A, Brk N, StL N, Pit N*

Jack Pfiester
Pfiester, John Albert (Jack the Giant Killer)
B: May 24, 1878   D: Sep 3, 1953

Pos: P	ERA: 2.02
W-L: 71-44	SOs: 503
ShOs: 17	No-hitters: 0

In a career lasting only eight seasons, Pfiester pitched in four World Series. He compiled a 15-5 lifetime record against the Giants. With three seasons of ERAs under 2.00 – he led the NL with a 1.17 mark in 1907 – Pfiester compiled the third lowest ERA in history.
Playing Career: *1903-1904, 1906-1911; Pit N, Chi N*

Babe Phelps
Phelps, Ernest Gordon (Blimp)
B: Apr 16, 1908

Pos: C	BA: .310
Hits: 657	HRs: 54
RBI: 345	BB: 160

Platooned at catcher, as was the practice of his day, Phelps could not get his big bat in the lineup enough times to be a big star. His .367 average in 1936 is a record for receivers. He battled hypochondria and fear of heights during his career.
Playing Career: *1931, 1933-1942; Was A, Chi N, Brk N, Pit N*

Ken Phelps
Phelps, Kenneth Allen
B: Aug 6, 1954

Pos: DH, 1B   BA: .239
Hits: 443   HRs: 123
RBI: 313   BB: 390

A Seattle native, Phelps had one of the AL's best ratios of home runs to at-bats. He played more than 100 games only three times, but hit 24 homers one year and 27 another. Phelps was used in a platoon designated hitter role for the majority of his career.
Playing Career: *1980-1990; KC A, Mon N, Sea A, NY A, Oak A, Cle A*

Dave Philley
Philley, David Earl
B: May 16, 1920

Pos: OF   BA: .270
Hits: 1,700   HRs: 84
RBI: 729   BB: 596

Fans remember Philley as a top pinch hitter who slashed 93 hits in 311 attempts, but many have forgotton that he was also a good outfielder with the White Sox and Indians. Philley led AL outfielders in assists three different years, but he lacked power at the plate, and managers looked elsewhere for regular players. Philley hit 14 homers in 1950 and 30 doubles in 1953.

In 1958 the switch hitter had a league-high 18 hits off the Phillies' bench, including eight consecutive pinch hits at the end of the season. On Opening Day 1959, he poked a pinch double, establishing a record of nine straight successful pinch-hit appearances. In 1961 Philley collected an AL record of 24 pinch hits with Baltimore. So respected was his hitting ability that Philley was traded for cash four times in his career.
Playing Career: *1941, 1946-1962; Chi A, Phi A, Cle A, Bal A, Det A, Phi N, SF N, Bos A*

Deacon Phillippe
Phillippe, Charles Louis
B: May 23, 1872   D: Mar 30, 1952

Pos: P   ERA: 2.59
W-L: 189-109   SOs: 929
ShOs: 27   No-hitters: 1

Injuries had incapacitated the Pirates' pitching staff by the end of the 1903 season, yet they were slated to play in the first modern World Series. Phillippe was called on to pitch five complete games in the best-of-nine Series. He defeated Cy Young in Game One, then threw a four-hitter to win Game Three. Following a rain-out, he won Game Four. After two straight Pirate losses, Phillippe pitched his fourth complete game but lost to Young. Three days later, he tossed a fifth complete game, allowing only three runs but losing to Boston's Bill Dinneen.

Phillippe averaged just 1.25 walks per nine innings thoughout his career. He won 21 games as a rookie with the NL Louisville team in 1899, then went to Pittsburgh when Barney Dreyfuss purchased the Pirates. The tall right-hander won 22, 10, then 24 games for Pirates' pennant-winning teams of 1901-1903. After a slump in 1904, Phillippe came back to post 22 victories in 1905.
Playing Career: *1899-1911; Lou N, Pit N*

Charles "Deacon" Phillippe.

Bill Phillips
Phillips, William B.
B: 1857   D: Oct 7, 1900

Pos: 1B   BA: .266
Hits: 1,130   HRs: 17
RBI: 298 (inc.)   BB: 178

One of the least known of the better 19th-century players, Phillips led AA first basemen in fielding twice. When the Cleveland team began to break up, he went to Brooklyn, where he batted .302 in 1885.
Playing Career: *1879-1888; Cle N, Brk AA, KC AA*

Bill Phillips
Phillips, William Corcoran (Whoa Bill, Silver Bill)
B: Nov 9, 1868   D: Oct 25, 1941

Pos: P   ERA: 4.10
W-L: 71-76   SOs: 374
ShOs: 6   Saves: 3
Managerial Record
Won: 114   Lost: 92   Pct: .553

Up for a cup of coffee in 1890 and again in 1895, Phillips finally got to the major leagues to stay in 1899 when he won 17 games for the Reds. He pitched more than 200 innings a year for four consecutive seasons, 1899-1902.
Playing Career: *1890, 1895, 1899-1903; Pit N, Cin N*
Managerial Career: *1914-1915; Ind F, Nwk F*

Bubba Phillips
Phillips, John Melvin
B: Feb 24, 1930   D: Jun 22, 1993

Pos: 3B, OF   BA: .255
Hits: 835   HRs: 62
RBI: 356   BB: 182

A prototype of today's multi-position players, Phillips started as an outfielder but suffered a power shortage and moved to

Dave Philley holds up a jersey showing teammate Bobby Shantz's 24 wins in 1952.

third base. Ironically, there he started hitting home runs, 18 of them in 1961. He played in the 1959 World Series for the Sox.
Playing Career: *1955-1964; Det A, Chi A, Cle A*

Horace Phillips
Phillips, Horace B.
B: May 14, 1853   D: Deceased

Managerial Record
Won: 338   Lost: 395   Pct: .461

Phillips played baseball professionally in upstate New York in the late 1870s. He was the Phillies' manager in 1882, the year before they entered the NL. Phillips started the Columbus club without much money, but put together a competitive squad.
Managerial Career: *1879, 1883-1889; Tro N, Col AA, Pit AA, Pit N*

The Tigers' Tony Phillips.

Tony Phillips
Phillips, Keith Anthony
B: Apr 25, 1959

Pos: 2B, 3B, OF, DH	BA: .265
Hits: 1,297	HRs: 75
RBI: 507	BB: 766

Long considered the secret weapon of the powerful Athletics, Tony Phillips emerged as one of the best players in the AL when given a chance to play regularly. He led the A's in games played in 1983 and 1984, but then had a series of freak injuries that made him a part-time player. In 1989 Phillips set a World Series record by playing three positions (2B, 3B, OF) in Game Three. He led the AL in runs scored with 114 in 1992.
Playing Career: *1982-; Oak A, Det A*

Tom Phoebus
Phoebus, Thomas Harold
B: Apr 7, 1942

Pos: P	ERA: 3.33
W-L: 56-52	SOs: 725
ShOs: 11	Saves: 6

After pitching shutouts in his first two major league starts, Phoebus went on to be AL Rookie Pitcher of the Year in 1967. During a three-season span, 1967-1969, Phoebus compiled a record of 43-32 with nine shutouts. He won Game Two in the 1970 World Series.
Playing Career: *1966-1972; Bal A, SD N, Chi N*

Wiley Piatt
Piatt, Wiley Harold (Iron Man)
B: Jul 13, 1874   D: Sep 20, 1946

Pos: P	ERA: 3.60
W-L: 85-79	SOs: 517
ShOs: 12	Saves: 1

Piatt began his major league career by winning 24 games in 1898 and 23 in 1899, hurling more than 300 innings both seasons. On June 25th of his final year the Iron Man tossed two complete games for the Braves.
Playing Career: *1898-1903; Phi N, Phi A, Chi A, Bos N*

Val Picinich
Picinich, Valentine John
B: Sep 8, 1896   D: Dec 5, 1942

Pos: C	BA: .258
Hits: 741	HRs: 27
RBI: 298	BB: 313

During an 18-year career Picinich caught three no-hitters. As a rookie in 1916, he caught Joe Bush's gem. Four years later with the Senators, he handled Walter Johnson's only nine-inning no-hitter. With Boston in 1923, he caught Howard Ehmke's no-hitter.
Playing Career: *1916-1933; Phi A, Was A, Bos A, Cin N, Brk N, Pit N*

Ollie Pickering
Pickering, Oliver Daniel
B: Apr 9, 1870   D: Jan 20, 1952

Pos: OF	BA: .272
Hits: 910	HRs: 9
RBI: 287	BB: 286

The speedy Pickering was the first batter in AL history. Even though he hit .309 in the premier 1901 season, the Cleveland Blues traded him to the Senators for Case Patten and John Farrell. Patten vetoed the trade and Pickering stayed with Cleveland awhile longer. He stole 194 bases.
Playing Career: *1896-1897, 1901-1904, 1907-1908; Lou N, Cle N, Cle A, Phi A, StL A, Was A*

Billy Pierce
Pierce, Walter William
B: Apr 2, 1927

Pos: P	ERA: 3.27
W-L: 211-169	SOs: 1,999
ShOs: 38	Saves: 32

Narrowly missing a chance at immortality in a 1958 game, Pierce had retired 26 consecutive batters when backup catcher Ed Fitz Gerald got a pinch hit down the right field line, ending the perfect game. Pierce was a left-hander with a great deal of style and poise. He became a mainstay of the White Sox pitching staff, where he toiled for 13 years, leading the league three times in complete games. He tossed four one-hitters, and in 1953 he had seven shutouts, and pitched 51 consecutive innings without yielding an earned run. His 186 strikeouts that year led the league. In 1955 Pierce's 1.97 ERA also led the league. He posted 20 victories in both 1956 and 1957. A seven-time All-Star, Pierce ended his career with the Giants, going 16-6 for the 1962 NL pennant winners. He was 1-1 in the World Series against the Yankees, including a three-hit 2-0 victory in Game Six.
Playing Career: *1945, 1948-1964; Det A, Chi A, SF N*

Billy Pierce winds up in a practice session with Manager Al Lopez in 1960.

Jimmy Piersall, as a Red Sox rookie.

Jimmy Piersall
Piersall, James Anthony
B: Nov 14, 1929

Pos: OF	BA: .272
Hits: 1,604	HRs: 104
RBI: 591	BB: 523

Combat was a way of life for Piersall, who fought with his father, teammates, fans — even himself. Anthony Perkins starred in a movie entitled "Fear Strikes Out" about Piersall's life and nervous breakdown in 1952. The outfielder recovered and played another 15 seasons of big league baseball. Positioning himself more shallow than any centerfielder in the majors, Piersall won two Gold Glove Awards. He was voted onto the All-Star team twice.

Piersall's best years at the plate included 1956, when he led the AL with 40 doubles. That year he scored 91 runs, drove in 87 runs, and batted .293. Waived to the Mets in 1963, Piersall celebrated his 100th home run by running backwards around the bases. Such antics and a .194 average irked manager Casey Stengel, and Piersall was released. He hit .314 for the Angels in 1964 as a part-timer before retiring in 1967. He became an outspoken and controversial broadcaster with the White Sox.
Playing Career: *1950, 1952-1967; Bos A, Cle A, Was A, NY N, LA A, Cal A*

Tony Piet
Piet, Anthony Francis
B: Dec 7, 1906   D: Dec 1, 1981

Pos: 2B, 3B	BA: .277
Hits: 717	HRs: 23
RBI: 312	BB: 247

Piet batted .323, driving the Pirates to second place in 1933, but his all-around best season was 1932 when he batted .285 with 85 RBI, 25 doubles, 7 home runs and 8 triples. Piet started his career at shortstop, but lacked range and switched to second base.
Playing Career: *1931-1938; Pit N, Cin N, Chi A, Det A*

Lip Pike
Pike, Lipman Emanuel
B: May 25, 1845   D: Oct 10, 1893

Pos: OF	BA: .319
Hits: 634	HRs: 20
RBI: 237 (inc.)	BB: 43
Managerial Record	
Won: 21 Lost: 51 Pct: .292	

One of the earliest ballplayers to become known for hitting home runs, in 1874 Pike became the first batter to hit a homer to win a 1-0 game. He led the league in round-trippers four times, the National Association 1871-1873, and the NL in 1877. Pike's slugging average was .654 in 1871 and he led the NA in slugging average in 1874.
Playing Career: *1871-1878, 1881, 1887; Tro Haymakers n, Bal Lord Baltimores n, Har Dark Blues n, StL Brown Stockings n, StL N, Cin N, Pro N, Wor N, NY AA*
Managerial Career: *1871, 1874, 1877; Tro Haymakers n, Har Dark Blues n, Cin N*
Umpiring Career: *1889; AA*

Horacio Pina
Pina y Garcia, Horacio
B: Mar 12, 1945

Pos: P	ERA: 3.25
W-L: 23-23	SOs: 278
ShOs: 0	Saves: 38

Traded to the A's for Mike Epstein after the 1972 season, Pina was 6-3 with eight saves in helping them to a World Championship the following year. He went home to Mexico after being released in 1975, and pitched a 3-0 perfect game in the Mexican League in 1978.
Playing Career: *1968-1974, 1978; Cle A, Was A, Tex A, KC A, Chi N, Cal A, Phi N*

George Pinckney
Pinckney, George Burton
B: Jan 11, 1862   D: Nov 10, 1926

Pos: 3B, 2B, SS	BA: .263
Hits: 1,212	HRs: 21
RBI: 391	BB: 525

Pinckney played on the back-to-back Brooklyn AA and NL champs, the only team to win two consecutive pennants in different leagues. He scored 874 runs and stole 296 bases. Pinckney led the AA in runs scored with 134 in 1888, and topped AA third basemen in fielding in 1887 and 1889.
Playing Career: *1884-1893; Cle N, Brk AA, Brk N, StL N, Lou N*

Lou Piniella
Piniella, Louis Victor (Sweet Lou)
B: Aug 28, 1943

Pos: OF, DH	BA: .291
Hits: 1,705	HRs: 102
RBI: 766	BB: 368
Managerial Record	
Won: 561 Lost: 504 Pct: .527	

Best known in Yankee pinstripes, Piniella first had tryouts with the Orioles and Indians, then was drafted by the expansion Seattle Pilots but was traded to the Royals. He was named AL Rookie of the Year in 1969, when he batted .282 with 21 doubles, 11 homers and 68 RBI. Traded to New York in 1974, Piniella's consistent play and clutch hitting made him extremely popular with the fans. He hit .305 in five ALCS and .319 in four World Series, all with the Yankees.

After his playing career Piniella served the Yankees as hitting coach, scout and manager. Happy to escape the Bronx madhouse after

Lou Piniella (c) brings in a run for the Yankees in 1980.

two second-place finishes, he went to Cincinnati and won a pennant in his first season with the Reds. His game-winning strategy relied on the "Nasty Boys" trio of closers – Rob Dibble, Randy Myers and Norm Charlton – whom he alternated for the last three innings of every game. Piniella and the Reds blew away Tony LaRussa and the highly favored Athletics in a four-game sweep of the 1990 World Series.

Playing Career: *1964, 1968-1984; Bal A, Cle A, KC A, NY A*
Managerial Career: *l986-1988, 1990-; NY A, Cin N, Sea A*

Vada Pinson
Pinson, Vada Edward
B: Aug 11, 1936

Pos: OF	BA: .286
Hits: 2,757	HRs: 256
RBI: 1,170	BB: 574

A star from the moment he first walked onto the playing field, Pinson quickly convinced the Reds he was ready for the majors by assaulting California League and PCL pitching for a .357 average in 1957-1958. Called up briefly in 1958, he hit a grand slam in his second game. The next year he led the NL with 131 runs scored and 47 doubles and was fourth in batting with a .316 mark. He also belted 20 home runs.

Pinson was only the fourth NL rookie to collect 200 hits. He lost Rookie of the Year honors to Willie McCovey, who played only 52 games. Pinson proved his sensational start was no fluke. In his first five full seasons with the Reds he averaged 197 hits, 108 runs scored, 37 doubles, 20 home runs, 88 RBI, 26 stolen bases, and a .310 batting average. Three times he led NL outfielders in putouts.

Vada Pinson at bat for the Reds, 1966.

Altogether Pinson scored 1,366 runs, hit 485 doubles and stole 305 bases. He made the All-Star team twice, 1959-1960, and won the Gold Glove Award in 1961.
Playing Career: *1958-1975; Cin N, StL N, Cle A, Cal A, KC A*

George Pipgras
Pipgras, George William
B: Dec 20, 1899   D: Oct 19, 1986

Pos: P	ERA: 4.09
W-L: 102-73	SOs: 714
ShOs: 15	Saves: 12

In 1928 Pipgras won 24 games, pitched more than 300 innings, and compiled a 3.38 ERA. He was 3-0 in three World Series; his wins included the game in which Babe Ruth hit his famous "called shot" home run. While umpiring, Pipgras once ejected 17 players in a Browns-White Sox game.
Playing Career: *1923-1924, 1927-1935; NY A, Bos A*
Umpiring Career: *1938-1946; AL (1 AS, 1 WS)*

Wally Pipp
Pipp, Walter Clement
B: Feb 17, 1893   D: Jan 11, 1965

Pos: 1B	BA: .281
Hits: 1,941	HRs: 90
RBI: 996	BB: 596

After Pipp suffered a beanball, his manager advised, "Take some aspirin, go home and take a few days off. We'll let the new kid Gehrig play." Pipp later joked about the Yankees sending him home for a 14-year vacation, but inside he was deeply hurt. He was a two-time AL home run champ and a .300 hitter as well as the league's smoothest fielding first baseman. He had led AL first basemen in fielding average three times.

Pipp played in three World Series for the Yankees, knocking in seven runs. Altogether he scored 974 runs, and slashed 148 triples, leading the AL with 19 in 1924. He also hit 311 doubles. Pipp batted over .300 three times and drove in 90 or more runs six times. Pipp's story was a familiar one: the Yankees bought him for the waiver price, got 11 years of top-notch play and a couple of home run titles, then sold him to the Reds for $7,500.
Playing Career: *1913, 1915-1928; Det A, NY A, Cin N*

Togie Pittinger
Pittinger, Charles Reno
B: Jan 12, 1871   D: Jan 14, 1909

Pos: P	ERA: 3.10
W-L: 116-113	SOs: 832
ShOs: 22	Saves: 2

At the turn of the century, Pittinger was the ace of the Braves' pitching staff. He won 27 games in 1902. Pittinger tossed more than 335 innings four straight years. His 23 wins in 1905 fueled the Phillies' drive from eighth place to the first division.
Playing Career: *1900-1907; Bos N, Phi N*

Juan Pizarro
Pizarro y Cordova, Juan Roman
B: Feb 7, 1937

Pos: P	ERA: 3.43
W-L: 131-105	SOs: 1,522
ShOs: 17	Saves: 28

Pizarro participated in two sets of postseason play 17 years apart. He pitched for the Braves in the World Series in 1957 and 1958, and in the 1974 NLCS for the Pirates he posted a 0.00 ERA. In 1962 Pizarro threw a pair of two-hitters. In 1964 he was 19-9, and was selected for the All-Star team for the second year in a row. He once outdueled Mets ace Tom Seaver 1-0, hitting a home run for the Cubs' only score.
Playing Career: *1957-1974; Mil N, Chi A, Pit N, Bos A, Cle A, Oak A, Chi N, Hou N*

Eddie Plank
Plank, Edward Stewart (Gettysburg Eddie)
B: Aug 31, 1875   D: Feb 24, 1926
Hall of Fame 1946

Pos: P	ERA: 2.34
W-L: 327-194	SOs: 2,246
ShOs: 69	Saves: 23

Graduating from Gettysburg College at age 25 in 1901, Plank went directly to the major leagues. He became the top left-hander for the first great Athletics teams. Rube Waddell was the top attraction and capable of high strikeout games, but Plank was consistent. Until Warren Spahn came along, he was the winningest left-hander in baseball history. Plank was responsible for 23 percent of the Athletics' victories from 1901 through 1914, 285 games.

Like many early 1900s pitchers, Plank had

Hall of Fame hurler Eddie Plank.

control and threw with finesse. He mixed a fastball with a sidearm curve, called a "crossfire," that cut the plate at an angle disconcerting to batters. He issued less than two walks per nine innings, posting only one ERA over 2.60 in his last 15 years. Plank's ERA was 1.79 in his final season. He completed 410 of 529 starts. He pitched 69 shutouts, ranking him fifth on the all-time list. On the mound, Plank was a serious, self-contained man who deliberately annoyed batters by talking to himself and to the ball before each pitch.
Playing Career: *1901-1917; Phi A, StL F, StL A*

Dan Plesac
Plesac, Daniel Thomas
B: Feb 4, 1962

Pos: P	ERA: 3.30
W-L: 31-38	SOs: 495
ShOs: 0	Saves: 133

In addition to a 95-mph fastball and a devastating slider, Plesac has remarkable control. He was 10-7 with a 2.97 ERA and 14 saves as a rookie. Making the All-Star team three straight years, he has posted ERAs under 3.00 in five of eight years in the majors.
Playing Career: *1986-; Mil A, Chi N*

Johnny Podres
Podres, John Joseph
B: Sep 30, 1932

Pos: P	ERA: 3.67
W-L: 148-116	SOs: 1,435
ShOs: 24	Saves: 11

Twenty-three-year-old Johnny Podres pitched the most important game in the history of the Brooklyn Dodgers. Beating the Yankees 2-0 in Game Seven of the 1955 World Series, Podres secured the only World Championship Brooklyn ever won. He was 4-1 with a 2.11 ERA in four World Series for the Dodgers. He possessed one of the best change-ups of all time, and has taught the pitch, as a coach, to hurlers for the Padres, Red Sox, Twins and Phillies.

After spending 1956 in the Navy, Podres was a consistent winner on strong Dodger staffs, 1957-1963. In 1957 he led the NL with a 2.66 ERA and six shutouts. In 1961 he won a career-high 18 games and led the NL with a .783 winning percentage. On July 2, 1962, he retired the first 20 Phillies before Ted Savage singled. He fanned eight batters in a row in that game. He made the NL All-Star team three times, 1958, 1960 and 1962.
Playing Career: *1953-1955, 1957-1967, 1969; Brk N, LA N, Det A, SD N*

Spottsford Poles
Poles, Spottsford (Spot, The Black Ty Cobb)
B: Nov 7, 1886   D: Sep 12, 1962

Pos: OF	BA: .292 (inc.)
Hits: 79 (inc.)	HRs: 2 (inc.)
RBI: NA	BB: NA

Cool Papa Bell was said to be so fast that he could turn off the bedroom light, and be in bed before the room got dark. Poles may have been even faster. The bowlegged, switch-hitting outfielder was nicknamed "The Black Ty Cobb." He broke in as the center fielder and leadoff hitter for the powerful 1909 Philadelphia Giants. With the Lincoln Giants in 1911, he batted .440 and stole 41 bases in only 60 games. He hit .398 in 1912, and .487 in 1914.

Poles scored 11 runs in the 1915 Negro Championship Series. He averaged a .319 batting mark in four winters in Cuba. In 10 exhibition games against major leaguers, he collected 25 hits in 41 at-bats for an amazing .610 average. Poles enlisted in the 369th Infantry in 1917 at the age of 30, earning five battle stars and a Purple Heart fighting in France. He resumed his baseball career after World War I, but tired of the constant travel and left the game in 1923. He is buried in Arlington National Cemetery.
Playing Career: *1909-1917, 1919-1922; Phi Giants, NY Lincoln Giants, Brk Royal Giants, NY Lincoln Stars, Phi Hilldales*

Howie Pollet
Pollet, Howard Joseph
B: Jun 26, 1921   D: Aug 8, 1974

Pos: P	ERA: 3.51
W-L: 131-116	SOs: 934
ShOs: 25	Saves: 20

Coming up through the Cardinals' farm system, Pollett broke in with a 1.93 ERA and led the NL with a 1.75 mark in 1943. After more than two years in the U.S. military, he returned with a vengeance, leading the NL with 21 wins, 266 innings and a 2.10 ERA. In the World Series that year he lost Game One in the tenth inning. Pollet won 20 games with a 2.77 ERA in 1949 and pitched an NL-leading five shutouts, earning his third All-Star selection.
Playing Career: *1941-1943, 1946-1956; StL N, Pit N, Chi N, Chi A*

Luis Polonia
Polonia y Almonte, Luis Andrew
B: Dec 10, 1964

Pos: OF	BA: .294
Hits: 974	HRs: 14
RBI: 274	BB: 248

A dynamic leadoff man, Polonia stole 48 bases and scored 92 runs in 1991, then stole 51 bases and scored 83 runs in 1992. He is the catalyst for Whitey Herzog's revamped Angels in the 1990s, and the Angels will be difficult to stop if Polonia begins drawing more walks.
Playing Career: *1987-; Oak A, NY A, Cal A*

Tom Poorman
Poorman, Thomas Iverson
B: Oct 14, 1857   D: Feb 18, 1905

Pos: OF, P	BA: .244
Hits: 498	HRs: 12
RBI: 111 (inc.)	BB: 102

Starting his baseball career as a pitcher, Poorman featured a swift curve and fast headwork. He was 3-9 with a 4.02 ERA for his career as an NL hurler, going 2-0 for the 1880 pennant-winning White Stockings. At the plate he scored 140 runs and 19 triples in 1887 for the Philadelphia Athletics.
Playing Career: *1880, 1884-1888; Buf N, Chi N, Tol AA, Bos N, Phi AA*

Johnny Podres with Manager Walter Alston at Dodger training camp.

Darrell Porter after 1980 division win.

Darrell Porter
Porter, Darrell Ray
B: Jan 17, 1952

Pos: C	BA: .247
Hits: 1,369	HRs: 188
RBI: 826	BB: 905

Porter was the MVP of both the NLCS and World Series in 1982. He batted .556 in the NLCS and .286 in the Fall Classic that year. In postseason play Porter batted .317 in five LCS for the Royals and Cardinals, and played in three World Series. Coming up with the Brewers when he was only 19, Porter learned catching on the job. Traded to the Royals, he made the All-Star team three straight years, driving in 112 runs with 20 homers and 101 runs in 1979.
Playing Career: *1971-1987; Mil A, KC A, StL N, Tex A*

Dick Porter
Porter, Richard Twilley (Twitchy)
B: Dec 30, 1901   D: Sep 24, 1974

Pos: OF	BA: .308
Hits: 774	HRs: 11
RBI: 284	BB: 268

Constantly wiggling and gyrating at the plate, Porter played on the famous Baltimore Orioles team that won seven minor league pennants. He came up with the Indians and batted in the upper .300s four straight years, 1929-1932. Porter scored 426 runs in 675 games.
Playing Career: *1929-1934; Cle A, Bos A*

Henry Porter
Porter, Henry
B: Jun 1858   D: Dec 30, 1906

Pos: P	ERA: 3.70
W-L: 96-107	SOs: 659
ShOs: 9	No-hitters: 0

Beginning his career with Milwaukee in the Union Association, Porter played for the team that had replaced the Chicago-Pittsburgh franchise. When the UA disbanded, Porter went to Brooklyn, where he won 60 games in 1885 and 1886.
Playing Career: *1884-1889; Mil U, Brk AA, KC AA*

Bob Porterfield
Porterfield, Erwin Cooledge
B: Aug 10, 1923   D: Apr 28, 1980

Pos: P	ERA: 3.79
W-L: 87-97	SOs: 572
ShOs: 23	Saves: 8

Porterfield was outstanding in 1953, leading the AL with 22 wins and nine shutouts for the fifth-place Senators. He also batted .255 with three home runs, including a grand slam. The next year Porterfield was an All-Star.
Playing Career: *1948-1959; NY A, Was A, Bos A, Pit N, Chi N*

Cum Posey
Posey, Cumberland Willis Jr.
B: Jun 20, 1890   D: Mar 28, 1946

Owner and founder of the Homestead Grays, Cum Posey discovered Josh Gibson sitting in the stands, tried him out and started him on the same day. Posey had been an outfielder with the team when they were called the Murdock Grays in 1910. In 1916 he was named their manager. He fielded talented teams – some of them integrated – throughout the 1920s. Posey joined the Negro National League in 1929 when it was on the verge of breaking up.

He started the East-West League in 1932, the depths of the Depression era. When this league broke up, Posey and his Grays returned to barnstorming. He possessed a great baseball mind and a keen sense of business. By the early 1920s, he had gained ownership of the Grays, and had turned the team into a profitable venture. After taking leadership roles in the organized black baseball leagues, he returned to run the Grays, eventually turning them into the most dominant team ever in baseball.

Wally Post
Post, Walter Charles
B: Jul 9, 1929   D: Jan 6, 1982

Pos: OF	BA: .266
Hits: 1,064	HRs: 210
RBI: 699	BB: 331

Post took out years of baseball frustration on the Yankees' pitching staff when he hit .333 in the 1961 World Series for the Reds. In his best year, 1955, Post batted .309 with 40 homers, 109 RBI, 116 runs scored and a .574 slugging percentage. He hit 36 home runs the next year. These performances provoked Reds fans into stuffing the ballot box for the 1957 All-Star team. Post and Gus Bell were elected, but later removed from the roster by order of Commissioner Ford Frick.
Playing Career: *1949, 1951-1964; Cin N, Phi N, Min A, Cle A*

Wally Post slides past the Giants' Ray Katt to score as Bobby Adams waves him on.

Nelson Potter
Potter, Nelson Thomas
B: Aug 23, 1911   D: Sep 30, 1990

Pos: P	ERA: 3.99
W-L: 92-97	SOs: 747
ShOs: 6	Saves: 22

After compiling a 19-7 record for the pennant-winning Browns in 1944, Potter gave up only one earned run in two World Series starts, but six Browns errors left him with an 0-1 record. He had been suspended for throwing a spitball earlier in that season.
Playing Career: *1936, 1938-1941, 1943-1949; StL N, Phi A, Bos A, StL A, Bos N*

Abner Powell
Powell, Charles Abner
B: Dec 15, 1860   D: Aug 7, 1953

Pos: OF, P	BA: .257
Hits: 78	HRs: 0
RBI: 0 (inc.)	BB: 8

The 19th-century Bill Veeck, Powell influenced baseball profoundly with his Ladies Day and Rain Check promotions. Both of these baseball staples can trace their origin to New Orleans in the late 1880s. Though he played other positions as well, as a pitcher he was 8-18 over two seasons. Powell went from the big leagues in 1886 to "the Big Easy" in 1887 as manager and club owner in the three-year-old Southern League. When the league folded in 1888, Powell took his team to the Texas League.
Playing Career: *1884, 1886; Was U, Bal AA, Cin AA*

Boog Powell
Powell, John Wesley
B: Aug 17, 1941

Pos: 1B, OF	BA: .266
Hits: 1,776	HRs: 339
RBI: 1,187	BB: 1,001

When Powell stepped to the plate in Baltimore's Memorial Stadium, 35,000 fans would call in unison, "Boooooo-g, Booooo-g." He

John Wesley "Boog" Powell.

batted cleanup for the Orioles for over a decade and helped them to four World Series in six years. Powell hit .306 in five ALCS for the Orioles. After three seasons as a slow-footed left fielder, he moved to first base in 1965. Replacing Jim Gentile, Powell was an immediate success, hitting 25 homers in 1963, then leading the AL with a .606 slugging percentage the next year.

Powell won the AL Comeback Player of the Year Award in 1966 with a .287 batting average, 34 home runs and 109 RBI. Then came his heyday. A four-time All-Star, 1968-1971, he won the AL MVP Award in 1970 when he batted .297 with 35 homers and 114 RBI. He was a pure home run hitter, totaling only 270 doubles and 11 triples. Powell hit three home runs in a game three times, and is second only to Eddie Murray on the Orioles' all-time home run list.
Playing Career: *1961-1977; Bal A, Cle A, LA N*

Jack Powell.

Jack Powell
Powell, John Joseph
B: Jul 9, 1874   D: Oct 17, 1944

Pos: P	ERA: 2.97
W-L: 245-254	SOs: 1,621
ShOs: 46	Saves: 15

Despite a lifetime ERA under 3.00, Powell lost 254 games. Built like his contemporary Cy Young, he threw with the same loose sidearm delivery. A workhorse, like many hurlers of the period, Powell tossed 300 or more innings six times and topped the 200 mark in 15 of 16 years. He won 23 games three times, going 23-15 in 1898, 23-19 in 1899, and 23-19 in 1904. In retirement, Powell ran a saloon with his former batterymate Jack "Peach Pie" O'Connor, in St. Louis.
Playing Career: *1897-1912; Cle N, StL N, StL A, NY A*

Jake Powell
Powell, Alvin Jacob
B: Jul 15, 1908   D: Nov 4, 1948

Pos: OF	BA: .271
Hits: 689	HRs: 22
RBI: 327	BB: 174

Yankee skipper Joe McCarthy handled the difficult Powell well enough to play him in three World Series, in which the outfielder averaged .435. He reached a peak in the 1936 Fall Classic when he batted .455. Powell was reckless, and once broke Hank Greenberg's wrist.
Playing Career: *1930, 1934-1940, 1943-1945; Was A, NY A, Phi N*

Ray Powell
Powell, Raymond Raeth (Rabbit)
B: Nov 20, 1888   D: Oct 16, 1962

Pos: OF	BA: .268
Hits: 890	HRs: 35
RBI: 276	BB: 321

Stealing only 51 bases in his career, Powell was not named "Rabbit" for his ability to get a jump on the pitch. A minor league manager for decades, he hit over .300 during the early 1920s, leading the NL in triples with 18 for the Boston Braves in 1921. He scored 114 runs that year.
Playing Career: *1913, 1917-1924; Det A, Bos N*

Ted Power
Power, Ted Henry
B: Jan 31, 1955

Pos: P	ERA: 4.00
W-L: 68-70	SOs: 701
ShOs: 3	Saves: 70

A Kansas State University graduate, Power has worked both as a starter and in relief. He led the NL with 78 appearances in 1984, saving 11 games. The next year Power saved 27 as the prime stopper for the Reds. Forced into a starting role, he was 10-13 in 1986.
Playing Career: *1981-; LA N, Cin N, KC A, Det A, StL N, Pit N, Cle A, Sea A*

Vic Power
Power, Victor Pellot
B: Nov 1, 1931

Pos: 1B	BA: .284
Hits: 1,716	HRs: 126
RBI: 658	BB: 279

Today one-handed plays are considered normal, but when Power made them during the 1950s it was considered showing off. He won seven Gold Gloves, leading the AL in fielding three times on the way to a lifetime .994 average. An All-Star in 1955, 1956, 1959 and 1960, Power batted .319 in 1955 and .309 in 1956. An aggressive baserunner, he led the AL in triples with 10 in 1958 and stole home twice in one game against the Tigers that year.
Playing Career: *1954-1965; KC A, Min A, LA N, Phi N, Cal A*

Doc Powers
Powers, Michael Riley
B: Sep 22, 1870   D: Apr 26, 1909

Pos: C   BA: .216
Hits: 451   HRs: 4
RBI: 199   BB: 72

Collapsing in the 7th inning of Shibe Park's inaugural game, April 12, 1909, Powers died two weeks later from internal injuries resulting from his squatting catching position. His death was even more shocking considering that Powers was a practicing physician.
Playing Career: *1898-1899, 1901-1909; Lou N, Was N, Phi A, NY A*

Del Pratt
Pratt, Derrill Burnham
B: Jan 10, 1888   D: Sep 30, 1977

Pos: 2B, 1B   BA: .292
Hits: 1,996   HRs: 43
RBI: 966   BB: 513

A former All-American running back at Alabama, Pratt chose professional baseball as a career since pro football was not yet viable. Miller Huggins was blasted by the New York press when he traded Urban Shocker to the Browns for Pratt in 1918. But Huggins, a former second baseman himself, knew a good keystone sack man when he saw one. The hard-nosed Pratt was a top AL infielder for 10 years. He hit 392 doubles and 117 triples as well as stealing 246 bases during his career.

More than 25 percent of Pratt's hits were for extra bases. He scored 856 runs, reaching a high of 85 in 1914. Twice he knocked home more than 100 runs, leading the AL in 1916 with 103. Considered to have good range, he led the league five times in total chances per game. He argued with his managers and even sued Browns owner Phil Ball for slander when Ball charged his team with easing up on an opponent. The matter was settled out of court to Pratt's advantage.
Playing Career: *1912-1924; StL A, NY A, Bos A, Det A*

Joe Price
Price, Joseph Walter
B: Nov 29, 1956

Pos: P   ERA: 3.65
W-L: 45-49   SOs: 657
ShOs: 1   Saves: 13

Price once struck out six consecutive batters in relief, tying the NL record. As a starter he compiled a record of 10-6 for the Reds in 1983, and won Game Five of the 1987 NLCS. But Price was plagued by injuries and spent much time on the disabled list.
Playing Career: *1980-1990; Cin N, SF N, Bos A*

Gerry Priddy
Priddy, Gerald Edward
B: Nov 9, 1919   D: Mar 3, 1980

Pos: 2B, 3B, 1B, SS   BA: .265
Hits: 1,252   HRs: 61
RBI: 541   BB: 624

Coming up through the minor leagues together, Priddy and Phil Rizzuto ended up in the 1942 World Series for the Yankees. They made a great double play combination that was broken up after that season when Priddy was traded to the Senators. He later played professional golf.
Playing Career: *1941-1943, 1946-1953; NY A, Was A, StL A, Det A*

Hub Pruett
Pruett, Hubert Shelby (Shucks)
B: Sep 1, 1900   D: Jan 28, 1982

Pos: P   ERA: 4.63
W-L: 29-48   SOs: 357
ShOs: 1   Saves: 13

Babe Ruth fanned in 10 of his first 13 at-bats against Pruett. The left-handed screwball that troubled the Bambino also injured Pruett's arm. In the off-season he studied to become a dentist, and left baseball to set up a practice in St.Louis.
Playing Career: *1922-1924, 1927-1928, 1930, 1932; StL A, Phi N, NY N, Bos N*

The Twin's heavy-hitting Kirby Puckett.

Kirby Puckett
Puckett, Kirby
B: Mar 14, 1961

Pos: OF   BA: .318
Hits: 1,996   HRs: 164
RBI: 874   BB: 366

Defying stereotypes, Puckett is the first player with 500 at-bats to hit no home runs in one season and 30 in another. His emergence as a power hitter has astounded player development gurus. Puckett was *Baseball America*'s Appalachian League Player of the Year in 1982, the California League Rookie of the Year in 1983, and the Twins' Rookie of the Year in 1984. In his big league debut, Puckett collected four hits. He led AL outfielders with 16 assists in 1984, and went almost a year before hitting his first big league homer on April 22, 1985.

Puckett has been elected to the All-Star

Del Pratt swings during the opening game between the Yanks and Red Sox in 1919.

team eight times, and has been awarded six Gold Gloves. He has led the AL in hits four times, and he won the AL batting title in 1989 with a .339 average, becoming only the second right-handed batter to lead in the last 20 years. He hit .357 in the 1987 World Series and played in the Fall Classic again in 1991, helping the Twins win two World Championships. Puckett destroyed the Blue Jays in the 1991 ALCS with a .429 average, two homers and six RBI.
Playing Career: *1984-; Min A*

Terry Puhl
Puhl, Terry Stephen
B: Jul 8, 1956

Pos: OF	BA: .280
Hits: 1,361	HRs: 62
RBI: 435	BB: 505

In the 1980 NLCS, Puhl terrorized Phillies pitching for a .526 batting average. The mark remains a record for a five-game LCS. Rarely striking out, the Canadian batted .301 as a rookie in 1977. He made the All-Star team in 1978, hitting .289 with 32 stolen bases as Houston's left fielder. Puhl is in the top five on the Astros' all-time lists for games, at-bats, hits, runs, doubles, triples, stolen bases and total bases.
Playing Career: *1977-1991; Hou N, KC A*

Harry Pulliam
Pulliam, Harry Clay
B: Feb 8, 1869   D: Jul 29, 1909

Described as "an idealist, a dreamer, a lover of solitude and nature," Pulliam was city editor of the *Louisville Commercial* when Barney Dreyfuss convinced him to become club secretary for his newly purchased NL Louisville team. In 1900 Pulliam moved with Dreyfuss to Pittsburgh. His reputation for honesty and his businesslike approach to baseball got him elected NL president in 1903. He helped forge a peace between the AL and NL that resulted in the National Agreement, the document that governed baseball.

Fearless and honest in enforcing league rules, Pulliam was strongly criticized by John McGraw over the 1908 Merkle Boner incident and also came into conflict with Charles W. Murphy, the Chicago owner, over a ticket-scalping controversy. Pulliam had a nervous temperament and did not cope with criticism well. In February 1909 he showed signs of mental illness and was given a leave of absence. On July 29, he took his own life.

Blondie Purcell
Purcell, William Aloysius
B: Mar 16, 1854   D: Feb 20, 1912

Pos: OF, P, 3B	BA: .267
Hits: 1,217	HRs: 13
RBI: 310 (inc.)	BB: 284
Managerial Record	
Won: 13 Lost: 68 Pct: .160	

Purcell, who used peroxide on his hair, was the first pitcher to be fined for cutting the ball.

Harry Pulliam, NL president from 1903 to 1909.

The presiding umpire assessed him the value of the ball, $5. He was a good hitter but only a marginal pitcher, going 15-43 with a 3.73 ERA. Purcell scored at least 767 runs, and stole 197 bases, but most of his statistics are incompletely recorded.
Playing Career: *1879-1890; Syr N, Cin N, Cle N, Buf N, Phi N, Phi AA, Bos N, Bal AA*
Managerial Career: *1883; Phi N*

Bob Purkey
Purkey, Robert Thomas
B: Jul 14, 1929

Pos: P	ERA: 3.79
W-L: 129-115	SOs: 793
ShOs: 13	Saves: 9

A knuckleball pitcher with control, Purkey once pitched an 11-hit shutout. He was a three-time All-Star and a top starter for the Reds from 1958 to 1962. Leading the NL with a winning percentage of .821 in 1962, Purkey posted a 23-5 record with a 2.81 ERA. He had been severely disappointed in 1961 when the Reds faced the mighty Yankees in the World Series. Roger Maris homered off Purkey in the ninth, causing him to lose Game Three 3-2. He also pitched two innings in Game Five, as the Reds used eight pitchers in a futile attempt to stop the Yankee onslaught.
Playing Career: *1954-1966; Pit N, Cin N, StL N*

Pat Putnam
Putnam, Patrick Edward
B: Dec 3, 1953

Pos: 1B	BA: .255
Hits: 508	HRs: 63
RBI: 255	BB: 144

In his rookie year, Putnam swatted 18 homers and slugged .458, finishing fourth in the AL Rookie of the Year balloting. Moving to the Kingdome in 1983, Putnam whacked 19 homers and 23 doubles. Always a contact hitter, he never struck out more than 57 times in any season.
Playing Career: *1977-1984; Tex A, Sea A, Min A*

Frankie Pytlak
Pytlak, Frank Anthony
B: Jul 30, 1908   D: May 8, 1977

Pos: C	BA: .282
Hits: 677	HRs: 7
RBI: 272	BB: 247

A backup catcher, Pytlak batted more than .300 four times in the 1930s, topping out at .321 in 1936. His biggest thrill in baseball was throwing out Ty Cobb in an exhibition game when he was a teenage backstop.
Playing Career: *1932-1941, 1945-1946; Cle A, Bos A*

Jack Quinn
Quinn, John Picus
B: Jul 5, 1883   D: Apr 17, 1946

Pos: P	ERA: 3.27
W-L: 247-218	SOs: 1,329
ShOs: 28	Saves: 57

Many of his other old-age records were broken by Tommy John and Charley Hough, but Quinn retains the record of being the oldest man ever to pitch in the World Series. He started Game Four of the 1929 World Series at age 46, and relieved in Game Three of the Series the following year. Quinn hurled for eight teams in three major leagues during four decades, making his final appearance at age 50. Granted permission to continue throwing the spitball after it was made illegal in 1920, Quinn started and relieved with equal skill.

The Yankees won their first pennant in 1921 with Quinn's assistance. But he was traded to the Red Sox that winter with Roger Peckinpaugh for Everett Scott, Joe Bush and Sad Sam Jones. Quinn later aided the powerhouse Athletics to two successive flags in 1929-1930. He was 18-7 with a 2.90 ERA in 1928 at age 45. In his last years, Quinn was exclusively a relief pitcher, leading the NL with 15 saves in 1931 and 8 in 1932 for the Dodgers, and ending his 23-year career in Cincinnati.
Playing Career: *1909-1915, 1918-1933; NY A, Bos N, Bal F, Chi A, Bos A, Phi A, Brk N, Cin N*

Joe Quinn
Quinn, Joseph J.
B: Dec 25, 1864   D: Nov 12, 1940

Pos: 2B, SS, OF, 1B, 3B	BA: .261
Hits: 1,797	HRs: 30
RBI: 796	BB: 364
Managerial Record	
Won: 23 Lost: 132 Pct: .148	

Starting his career as an "onion," the name for the Union Association players, Quinn played for three pennant-winning Boston teams and one Baltimore flag bearer. He was the luckless manager of the Cleveland Spiders, the worst team of all time. Not even being married to a mortician's daughter prepared him for the death knell of the 1899 season, when the team's owner shipped all of the good players to St. Louis, leaving Quinn the leftovers.
Playing Career: *1884-1886, 1888-1901; StL U, StL N, Bos N, Bos P, Bal N, Cle N, Cin N, Was N*
Managerial Career: *1895, 1899; StL N, Cle N*

Jamie Quirk
Quirk, James Patrick
B: Oct 22, 1954

Pos: C, DH, 1B, 3B	BA: .240
Hits: 544	HRs: 43
RBI: 247	BB: 177

In order to stay in the majors with his buddy George Brett, Quirk, a left-handed hitter, learned how to catch in 1983. Nine years later, both were still in the majors, although Quirk had constantly struggled to find a team. Hard work and a good attitude served him well.
Playing Career: *1975-1992; KC A, Mil A, StL N, Chi A, Cle A, NY A, Oak A, Bal A*

Dan Quisenberry.

Dan Quisenberry
Quisenberry, Daniel Raymond (The Quiz)
B: Feb 7, 1953

Pos: P	ERA: 2.76
W-L: 56-46	SOs: 379
ShOs: 0	Saves: 244

Quisenberry can recite "Casey at the Bat" by heart and frequently does so in the Kansas City area. The Quiz used a submarine delivery and pinpoint control on low strikes to pile up a massive number of saves in a short time, averaging 35 saves for six years, 1980-1985. The Royals won a World Championship, two pennants, three division titles and a playoff appearance in the strike-shortened season of 1981 during the Quisenberry era.

A three-time All-Star, Quisenberry's control of his sharp-breaking slider was legendary. Only three times in 10 years did he issue more than 15 walks in a season, despite pitching over 125 innings five times. In his first full season Quiz won 12 and saved 33 while appearing in 75 games. He led the AL in saves five times, including a record-setting 45 in 1983 and 44 the following year. He was AL Fireman of the Year five times. Quiz signed a lifetime contract with the Royals worth over $30 million.
Playing Career: *1979-1990; KC A, StL N, SF N*

Spitballer Jack Quinn, at age 47 the oldest player to pitch in a WS (1930).

Dick Radatz
Radatz, Richard Raymond (The Monster)
B: Apr 2, 1937

Pos: P   ERA: 3.13
W-L: 52-43   SOs: 745
ShOs: 0   Saves: 122

At 6'6", Radatz was fearsome to behold on the pitcher's mound, and he simply blew the ball by hitters. His ability to enter the game in the ninth and retire the opposition on strikes influenced a whole generation of managers. Radatz single-handedly changed the stopper role from the Elroy Face model – make them hit into a double play – to the Goose Gossage method – blow them away. Radatz saved 100 games and won 49 in four years, 1962-1965.

As a rookie in 1962, he led the AL with 62 appearances, posting nine relief wins and 24 saves to earn Fireman of the Year honors. The next year Radatz compiled a 15-6 record with a 1.97 ERA and 25 saves. Named to the 1963 All-Star squad, he struck out Willie Mays,

Dick Groat, Duke Snider, Willie McCovey and Julian Javier. In 1964 he took another Fireman of the Year Award, leading the AL with 29 saves and 16 relief wins. In fact, he recorded a win or a save in 45 of Boston's 72 wins, striking out 181 batters in 157 innings.
Playing Career: *1962-1967, 1969; Bos A, Cle A, Chi N, Det A, Mon N*

Old Hoss Radbourn
Radbourn, Charles Gardner
B: Dec 11, 1854   D: Feb 5, 1897
Hall of Fame 1939

Pos: P   ERA: 2.67
W-L: 309-195   SOs: 1,830
ShOs: 35   No-hitters: 1

Baseball commentator Tim McCarver once said, "Old Hoss? At 5'9" and 168 pounds, he's more like a little pony." Radbourn worked like a draft horse, completing 489 of 503 starts over 11 years. His reputation was built on one great season. In 1884 Radbourn was forced to pitch every game in the last half of the season because Charley Sweeney had jumped his contract and gone to the rival Union Association. Radbourn completed all 73 of his starts, winning 60 games (some revisionist sources say 59), striking out 441 batters in 678 innings, and posting a 1.38 ERA.

He won 18 consecutive games that year, and pitched 11 shutouts. In postseason play Radbourn pitched every inning as the Grays swept three games from the Metropolitans and became champions. Radbourn pitched from the corner of the pitcher's box and threw "crossfire" to right-handed hitters. He was so successful in 1884 that the width of the box was reduced from six feet to four the following season.
Playing Career: *1880-1891; Buf N, Pro N, Bos N, Bos P, Cin N*

Alec Radcliff
Radcliff, Alexander
B: Jul 26, 1905   D: Jul 18, 1983

Pos: 3B   BA: .291 (inc.)
Hits: 450 (inc.)   HRs: 24 (inc.)
RBI: NA   BB: NA

Dave Malarcher once said, "Radcliff became one of the truly great third basemen in baseball history: a fast man, a powerful hitter and one who possessed the mind which enabled him to fit into our system." Radcliff led the league in home runs in 1944 and 1945.
Playing Career: *1926-1949; Day Marcos, Chi Am Giants, NY Cubans, Bir Black Barons, Mem Red Sox*

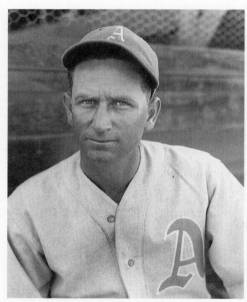

Raymond "Rip" Radcliff.

Rip Radcliff
Radcliff, Raymond Allen
B: Jan 19, 1906   D: May 23, 1962

Pos: OF, 1B, PH   BA: .311
Hits: 1,267   HRs: 42
RBI: 532   BB: 310

A member of the all-time Oklahoma team, Radcliff did not reach the majors until age 28. He quickly made up for lost time by being selected for the 1936 All-Star roster on the strength of his .335 average. He made an outstanding defensive play in the contest.

The next day, Radcliff went 6-for-7, including two doubles. His career was typical of the plight of Depression-era ballplayers attempting to fill the limited number of spots on a major league roster. Radcliff had won the Southeastern League Triple Crown in 1930 with Selma. After a trade to the Browns, he led the AL with 200 hits in 1940, and batted .342. In his last season he led the league with 44 appearances as a pinch hitter. Traded to the A's in 1943, he went into the military and never played for Mr. Mack.
Playing Career: *1934-1943; Chi A, StL A, Det A*

Unstoppable stopper Dick "The Monster" Radatz in 1963.

Ted Radcliffe
Radcliffe, Ted (Double Duty)
B: Jul 7, 1902

Pos: C, P

Hits: 303 (inc.)	BA: .280 (inc.)
RBI: NA	HRs: 20 (inc.)
	BB: NA

Pos: P

W-L: 49-33 (inc.)	ERA: NA
ShOs: 1 (inc.)	SOs: 150 (inc.)
	Saves: 9 (inc.)

Managerial Record (inc.)
Won: 57   Lost: 35   Pct: .620

Damon Runyon tagged the label "Double Duty" on Radcliffe after watching him catch Satchel Paige in a 5-0 victory in the first game of a doubleheader, then pitch a shutout in the nightcap. Radcliffe was the master of the emery ball and other questionable pitches.
Playing Career: *1928-1946; Det Stars, StL Stars, Det Wolves, Hom Grays, Pit Crawfords, Cle Giants, Col Blue Birds, Chi Am Giants, Brk Eagles, Cin Tigers, Mem Red Sox, Cle Red Sox, Bir Black Barons*
Managerial Career: *1937-1938, 1943; Cin Tigers, Mem Red Sox, Chi Am Giants*

Dave Rader
Rader, David Martin
B: Dec 26, 1948

Pos: C

Hits: 619	BA: .257
RBI: 235	HRs: 30
	BB: 245

The Giants' number-one draft choice, Rader was named 1972 NL Rookie of the Year by *The Sporting News*, after he batted .259. With little power and barely adequate fielding aver-ages, it is mysterious that Rader was the Giants' regular catcher, 1972-1975.
Playing Career: *1971-1980; SF N, StL N, Chi N, Phi N, Bos A*

Doug Rader
Rader, Douglas Lee (Rojo, Rooster)
B: Jul 30, 1944

Pos: 3B

Hits: 1,302	BA: .251
RBI: 722	HRs: 155
	BB: 528

Managerial Record
Won: 388   Lost: 417   Pct: .482

Rader once boxed for money on a dare while in the minors. Perhaps he thought it was the Golden Gloves tournament; he later won five consecutive Gold Glove Awards in baseball. Three times he hit more than 20 home runs. Wild and eccentric, Rader was hardly the first man one would think of as a manager, but the Rangers named him skipper in 1983. He guided his club to a third-place finish that year.
Playing Career: *1967-1977; Hou N, SD N, Tor A*
Managerial Career: *1983-1986, 1989-1991; Tex A, Chi A, Cal A*

Paul Radford
Radford, Paul Revere (Shorty)
B: Oct 14, 1861   D: Feb 21, 1945

Pos: OF, SS, 3B, 2B, P

Hits: 1,206	BA: .242
RBI: 417 (inc.)	HRs: 13
	BB: 791

Playing for the famous Providence Grays in 1884, Radford was used as the change pitcher for Old Hoss Radbourn the year he won 60 games. Radford spent most of the season in the outfield, and had a record of 0-2 that year. He was very fast, and batted leadoff for the Kansas City Cowboys in their only NL season. Radford led the AA in walks in 1887, the year that walks counted as base hits. He scored 945 runs and stole 346 bases during his career.
Playing Career: *1883-1894; Bos N, Pro N, KC N, NY AA, Brk AA, Cle N, Cle P, Bos AA, Was N*

Ken Raffensberger
Raffensberger, Kenneth David
B: Aug 8, 1917

Pos: P

W-L: 119-154	ERA: 3.60
ShOs: 31	SOs: 806
	Saves: 16

After he pitched and won the 1944 All-Star Game for the National League, Raffensberger ended the season with a record of 13-20 for the Phillies. The big left-hander led the NL in shutouts in 1949 and 1952, going 18-17 and 17-13 for Cincinnati those years. Raffensberger threw four one-hitters, two against the Cardinals in 1948.
Playing Career: *1939-1941, 1943-1954; StL N, Chi N, Phi N, Cin N*

Pat Ragan
Ragan, Don Carlos Patrick
B: Nov 15, 1888   D: Sep 4, 1956

Pos: P

W-L: 77-104	ERA: 2.99
ShOs: 12	SOs: 680
	Saves: 6

Just before Brooklyn's old Washington Park was replaced by Ebbets Field, Ragan pitched the last game there. His best year was 1915, when he had a combined record of 17-12 with the Dodgers and Braves. Ragan once struck out the side on nine pitches.
Playing Career: *1909, 1911-1919, 1923; Cin N, Chi N, Brk N, Bos N, NY N, Chi A, Phi N*

Tim Raines
Raines, Timothy (Rock)
B: Sep 16, 1959

Pos: OF, 2B, DH

Hits: 2,050	BA: .298
RBI: 710	HRs: 124
	BB: 1,003

Hard-hitting at the plate, fast on the base-paths, and surehanded in the outfield, Raines is a manager's dream player. Converted from a second baseman to an outfielder in 1981, Raines led the NL in stolen bases with 71 in the strike-shortened season, and led the NL in steals the next three years as well. Having been caught stealing only 134 times, Raines has an 85 percent success rate. He was selected for the All-Star Game roster seven years in a row, and won the 1987 contest with a two-run triple in the 13th inning. After winning the 1986 NL batting championship, Raines declared free agency. The team owners acted in unison in not signing free

Tim Raines signs autographs for Expos fans during his years in Montreal.

agents, prompting lawsuits and leaving players like Raines without an offer.

According to baseball rules, Raines had to sit out until May 1. Without the benefit of spring training, he homered in his first game of the 1987 season. He led the NL with 123 runs scored despite missing the first month of the season. He also hit 18 home runs that year.

Playing Career: *1979-; Mon N, Chi A*

Rafael Ramirez
Ramirez y Peguero, Rafael Emilio
B: Feb 18, 1958

Pos: SS, 3B, 2B	BA: .261
Hits: 1,432	HRs: 53
RBI: 484	BB: 264

Another slick-fielding infielder from San Pedro de Macoris, Ramirez led NL shortstops in double plays four straight years. He made the NL All-Star team in 1984 with a .304 average at midseason. After torn knee ligaments limited him to 56 games in 1987, he went to the Astros, where he plugged the shortstop hole in the Astrodome. In 1988 Ramirez posted his best batting average since 1983 and drove in a career-high 59 runs.

Playing Career: *1980-1992; Atl N, Hou N*

Pedro Ramos
Ramos y Guerra, Pedro
B: Apr 28, 1935

Pos: P	ERA: 4.08
W-L: 117-160	SOs: 1,305
ShOs: 13	Saves: 55

Claiming – tongue-in-cheek – to be the fastest runner in the majors, Ramos challenged Mickey Mantle to a footrace, but the event never materialized. Despite losing 160 games and leading the AL in losses four straight years, 1958-1961, Ramos was a good pitcher with bad teams – Washington and Minnesota. He was selected for the All-Star team in 1959. Traded by the Indians to New York in September of 1964, he went 1-0 with a 1.25 ERA for the Yankees, saving eight games that month. Ramos saved 32 games in the next two years. He also hit 15 home runs.

Playing Career: *1955-1967, 1969-1970; Was A, Min A, Cle A, NY A, Phi N, Pit N, Was A*

Toad Ramsey
Ramsey, Thomas A.
B: Aug 8, 1864   D: Mar 27, 1906

Pos: P	ERA: 3.29
W-L: 114-124	SOs: 1,515
ShOs: 5	No-hitters: 0

During back-to-back seasons of 38 then 37 wins, Ramsey tossed 1,149 innings, 1886-1887. He fanned 499 batters in 1886, the second highest total ever, and pitched three of his five career shutouts. His invention of the "Ramsey Cocktail," whiskey in beer, may have contributed to Chris Von der Ahe's offer to sell him for a nickle.

Playing Career: *1885-1890; Lou AA, StL AA*

Lenny Randle
Randle, Leonard Shenoff
B: Feb 12, 1949

Pos: 3B, 2B, OF, DH	BA: .257
Hits: 1,016	HRs: 27
RBI: 322	BB: 372

While with the Mariners, Randle got down on all fours and tried to blow a rolling bunt foul at the Kingdome. These and other antics failing to ensure his job, Randle went to Italy to play ball, and became a big star there.

Playing Career: *1971-1982; Was A, Tex A, NY N, NY A, Chi N, Sea A*

Willie Randolph
Randolph, Willie Larry
B: Jul 6, 1954

Pos: 2B	BA: .276
Hits: 2,210	HRs: 54
RBI: 687	BB: 1,243

Selected for the All-Star squad six times, Randolph is compared favorably to the Royals' Frank White. After a 30-game stint with the Pirates in 1975, Randolph was traded to the Yankees for Doc Medich. He immediately started at second, lasting 13 seasons and wearing out 32 shortstops. During Randolph's first six Yankee seasons, they won five division championships, four AL pennants, and two World Series. In 1980 Randolph led the AL with 119 walks.

Playing Career: *1975-1992; Pit N, NY A, LA N, Oak A, Mil A, NY N*

Bill Rariden
Rariden, William Angel (Bedford Bill)
B: Feb 4, 1888   D: Aug 28, 1942

Pos: C	BA: .237
Hits: 682	HRs: 7
RBI: 272	BB: 340

Flourishing in the Federal League, Rariden set the record for asists by a catcher with 215 in 1914, then broke it the next year with 238. Rariden caught the Giants' 26-game winning streak in 1916, and batted .385 in the 1917 World Series.

Playing Career: *1909-1920; Bos N, Ind F, Nwk F, NY N, Cin N*

Vic Raschi
Raschi, Victor John Angelo (The Springfield Rifle)
B: Mar 28, 1919   D: Oct 14, 1988

Pos: P	ERA: 3.72
W-L: 132-66	SOs: 944
ShOs: 26	Saves: 3

Fifth on the all-time list for won-lost percentage, Raschi lost only 66 games for a .667 mark. He beat the Red Sox on the final day of the 1949 season to break the Yankees' first-place tie with them. At the plate, Raschi drove in the winning run of the 1948 All-Star Game. In 1953 he drove in seven runs to set an AL single-game record for pitchers. Raschi was 5-3 in six World Series for the Yankees.

Playing Career: *1946-1955; NY A, StL N, KC A*

Second bagger Willie Randolph played 13 seasons with the Yankees.

Dennis Rasmussen
Rasmussen, Dennis Lee
B: Apr 18, 1959

Pos: P	ERA: 4.05
W-L: 91-76	SOs: 829
ShOs: 5	No-hitters: 0

Rasmussen was the Yankees' top hurler in 1986, winning 18 games and posting a 3.88 ERA. In 1988 he won 10 of his last 13 decisions. Rasmussen once pinch-hit a three-run double. He has relieved in only 12 games in 11 years of pitching.
Playing Career: *1983-; SD N, NY A, Cin N, Chi N, KC A*

Eric Rasmussen with St. Louis in 1980.

Eric Rasmussen
Rasmussen, Eric Ralph (Harold)
B: Mar 22, 1952

Pos: P	ERA: 3.85
W-L: 50-77	SOs: 12
ShOs: 12	Saves: 5

In his first major league start, Rasmussen pitched a shutout against the Padres, but he never had a winning season. He tossed more than 200 innings in 1977 and 1978. Rasmussen's ERA zoomed up over 4.00 and landed him in the bullpen.
Playing Career: *1975-1980, 1982-1983; StL N, SD N, KC A*

Morrie Rath
Rath, Morris Charles
B: Dec 25, 1886   D: Nov 18, 1945

Pos: 2B, 3B, SS	BA: .254
Hits: 521	HRs: 4
RBI: 92	BB: 258

A part-time infielder, Rath was unknowingly used as an indicator in the 1919 Black Sox scandal. He was the first batter in the Series, and pitcher Eddie Cicotte hit him with a pitch as a signal to gamblers that the fix was on.
Playing Career: *1909-1910, 1912-1913, 1919-1920; Phi A, Cle A, Chi A, Cin N*

Doug Rau
Rau, Douglas James
B: Dec 15, 1948

Pos: P	ERA: 3.35
W-L: 81-60	SOs: 697
ShOs: 11	Saves: 3

A solid third or fourth starter, Rau appeared in three NLCS and two World Series for the Dodgers. He shut out the Cardinals in his debut. Rau won a career-high 16 games in 1976, and 57 percent of his decisions overall. Unfortunately, he did not recover from a 1979 rotator cuff injury.
Playing Career: *1972-1979, 1981; LA N, Cal A*

Shane Rawley
Rawley, Shane William
B: Jul 27, 1955

Pos: P	ERA: 4.02
W-L: 111-118	SOs: 991
ShOs: 7	Saves: 40

After a trade to the Yankees, who moved him into the starting role, Rawley flourished, winning 14 games in 1983. As a Phillie in 1986, he was leading the NL in wins, innings pitched and complete games when he suffered a broken shoulder.
Playing Career: *1978-1989; Sea A, NY A, Phi N, Min A*

Pittsburgh's Johnny Rawlings in 1925.

Johnny Rawlings
Rawlings, John William
B: Aug 17, 1892   D: Oct 16, 1972

Pos: 2B, SS	BA: .250
Hits: 928	HRs: 14
RBI: 303	BB: 257

A singles hitter who had only 164 extra-base hits, Rawlings batted .333 in the 1921 World Series for the Giants, then lost his job to Frank Frisch. Rawlings played for two more World Champion teams, the Giants in 1922 and the 1925 Pirates, but did not play in the World Series with either team.
Playing Career: *1914-1915, 1917-1926; Cin N, KC F, Bos N, Phi N, NY N, Pit N*

Jim Ray
Ray, James Francis (Sting)
B: Dec 1, 1944

Pos: P	ERA: 3.61
W-L: 43-30	SOs: 407
ShOs: 0	Saves: 25

In the 24-inning Astros-Mets game of April 15, 1968, Ray pitched seven scoreless innings, striking out 11, and allowing only two hits. Ray was 8-2 as a starter and middle reliever in 1969. His best season was 10-4 with 2.12 ERA in 1971.
Playing Career: *1965-1966, 1968-1974; Hou N, Det A*

Johnny Ray
Ray, John Cornelius
B: Mar 1, 1957

Pos: 2B, OF, DH	BA: .291
Hits: 1,390	HRs: 48
RBI: 551	BB: 334

A Rookie of the Year candidate in 1982, Ray batted .281 with 30 doubles, 79 runs scored and 16 stolen bases. He also led NL second basemen in putouts, assists and total chances as well as errors, playing 162 games. The next two years Ray led the NL in doubles, and swatted 30 or more seven seasons in a row, 1982-1988. He made the All-Star team in 1988 and ended the season batting .306 with 42 doubles, 75 runs and 83 RBI for the Angels. He struck out only 329 times in 5,188 at-bats.
Playing Career: *1981-1990; Pit N, Cal A*

Claude Raymond
Raymond, Jean Claude Marc (Frenchy)
B: May 7, 1937

Pos: P	ERA: 3.66
W-L: 46-53	SOs: 497
ShOs: 0	Saves: 83

A genuine French-Canadian, Raymond came to the Expos toward the end of a lengthy career as a reliever. He saved 23 games for Montreal in 1970, then became their French-language broadcaster. Raymond played on the 1966 NL All-Star team.
Playing Career: *1959, 1961-1971; Chi A, Mil N, Hou N, Mon N*

Al Reach
Reach, Alfred James
B: May 25, 1840   D: Jan 14, 1928

Pos: 2B, OF	BA: .247
Hits: 97	HRs: 0
RBI: 54 (inc.)	BB: 9

Managerial Record
Won: 4   Lost: 7   Pct: .364

The earliest known professional baseball player, and the founder of a sporting goods empire, Al Reach was an English emigrant who learned America's national pastime and made a fortune from it. In 1865 the left-handed second baseman was earning $25 a week. By 1887 he was the wealthiest ex-player, but he made most of his money from the Reach Sporting Goods company he founded in the early 1870s. Considered an excellent batter, Reach hit .353 in 1871 when the Athletics won the first National Association championship.

Reach was one of the founders of the Phillies, and served as team president from 1883 to 1902. *The Reach Guide*, an annual compilation of baseball statistics with team and league records, began publication in 1883. The guide featured the American Association and minor leagues in greater detail than the rival *Spalding Guide*. The two publications were the basis for the depth of recorded baseball history that fans enjoy today.
Playing Career: *1871-1875; Phi Athletics n*
Managerial Career: *1890; Phi N*

Randy Ready
Ready, Randy Max
B: Jan 8, 1960

Pos: OF, 3B, 2B	BA: .258
Hits: 527	HRs: 39
RBI: 236	BB: 315

A two-time minor league batting champ, Ready became a successful platoon outfielder. He batted .309 in 1987, slugged .520 and had a .420 on-base percentage. Ready's career minor league batting average was .343.
Playing Career: *1983-; Mil A, SD N, Phi N, Oak A, Mon N*

Jeff Reardon
Reardon, Jeffrey James (The Terminator)
B: Oct 1, 1955

Pos: P	ERA: 3.07
W-L: 72-77	SOs: 873
ShOs: 0	Saves: 365

The bearded Terminator entered the 1993 season as the all-time saves leader, passing Rollie Fingers in 1992. Reardon has been instrumental in resurgences in both Montreal and Minnesota. He played for four division-winning teams, two pennant winners, and the 1987 World Champion Twins. He saved at least 20 games a year for 11 seasons, 1982-1992, the only reliever to do so. Reardon led the majors with 41 saves in 1985.

In Minnesota, Reardon's relief work earned him the Twins' MVP Award in 1987. He saved two games and won one in the ALCS. During the World Series, Reardon saved a game and did not give up an earned run in four appearances. An All-Star reliever 1985-1986, he has never started in the majors and rarely works more than one inning in any game. Relegated to the setup position with the Reds in 1993, Reardon stepped into the closer's role admirably when Rob Dibble broke his arm early in the season.
Playing Career: *1979-; NY N, Mon A, Min A, Bos A, Atl N, Cin N*

Dick Redding (r) with Smokey Joe Williams.

Dick Redding
Redding, Dick (Cannonball)
B: 1891   D: 1940

Pos: P	ERA: NA
W-L: 69-44 (inc.)	SOs: 271 (inc.)
ShOs: 13 (inc.)	No-hitters: 1

Managerial Record (inc.)
W: 69   L: 114   Pct: .377

A large, intimidating man at 6' 4" and 210 pounds, Redding was reputed to be the hardest-throwing pitcher in black baseball history. Eyewitnesses say that Redding had a better fastball than Satchel Paige, and that he used the hesitation pitch before Paige made it famous. In Redding's first season he posted 17 consecutive wins. He teamed with Smokey Joe Williams, 1911-1914, to give the New York Lincoln Giants one of the greatest one-two pitching lineups ever.

Redding was 43-12 in 1912 against all opposition, and tossed a 17-strikeout perfect game. He won 20 consecutive games in 1915, including several games against major league all-star squads.
Playing Career: *1911-1931; NY Lincoln Giants, NY Lincoln Stars, Chi Am Giants, Brk Royal Giants, AC Bach Giants*
Managerial Career: *1923-1931; Brk Royal Giants*

"The Terminator," Jeff Reardon, with the Red Sox in 1991.

Gary Redus
Redus, Gary Eugene
B: Nov 1, 1956

Pos: OF
Hits: 877
RBI: 350

BA: .252
HRs: 90
BB: 477

The highest minor league batting average ever recorded belongs to Redus. He hit .462 with Billings in 1978. He has blazing speed, and has stolen 322 bases, reaching a high of 52 in 1987. Redus now works as a platoon player with the Rangers.
Playing Career: *1982-; Cin N, Phi N, Chi A, Pit N, Tex A*

Jody Reed
Reed, Jody Eric
B: Jul 26, 1962

Pos: SS
Hits: 866
RBI: 258

BA: .279
HRs: 19
BB: 357

In 1988 new Red Sox Manager Joe Morgan put Reed in as the everyday shortstop. Reed responded with a .293 batting average and 23 doubles in 109 games, leading the Sox to the division title. He hit more than 40 doubles in each of the next three seasons.
Playing Career: *1987-; Bos A, LA N*

Ron Reed
Reed, Ronald Lee
B: Nov 2, 1942

Pos: P
W-L: 146-140
ShOs: 8

ERA: 3.46
SOs: 1,481
Saves: 103

Reed had two careers, one as a starter with the Braves and another as a reliever with the Phillies. He fueled five division titles for Philadelphia, plus another with the 1969 Braves. A basketball star at Notre Dame University, Reed played in the NBA for three years as a forward for Dave DeBusschere's Pistons, but the Braves asked him to give up roundball. In two World Series Reed went 0-0 with one save and a 1.69 ERA. He made the All-Star team in 1968.
Playing Career: *1966-1984; Atl N, StL N, Phi N, Chi A*

Pee Wee Reese
Reese, Harold Henry
(The Louisville Colonel)
B: Jul 23, 1918
Hall of Fame 1984

Pos: SS
Hits: 2,170
RBI: 885

BA: .269
HRs: 126
BB: 1,210

One of the finest gentlemen of the game, Reese exudes charm and style. Growing up in Louisville, Reese was a champion of the game of marbles, and was nicknamed for the pee wee marble. He later starred in baseball for the Louisville Colonels. Arriving in Brooklyn, he was named captain of the

Harold "Pee Wee" Reese.

Dodgers and led the team to seven pennants in the 1940s and 1950s.

When Jackie Robinson arrived amid enormous pressure and player resentment, it was Reese who set the example of acceptance by putting his arm around Robinson's shoulder on the playing field to show the world he was Robinson's teammate and friend. A 10-time All-Star, Reese stole 232 bases and scored 1,338 runs while knocking out 330 doubles. He led the NL with 132 runs in 1949 and 104 walks in 1947. He batted .309 in 1954.
Playing Career: *1940-1942, 1947-1958; Brk N, LA N*

Rich Reese
Reese, Richard Benjamin
B: Sep 29, 1941

Pos: 1B, OF
Hits: 512
RBI: 245

BA: .253
HRs: 52
BB: 158

One of the co-holders for the record number of pinch-hit grand slam home runs, Reese belted three of them. He had an occasional burst of power, especially in 1969 when he batted .322 and hit 16 homers, helping the Twins to the first of two straight division titles.
Playing Career: *1964-1973; Min A, Det A*

Bill Regan
Regan, William Wright
B: Jan 23, 1899   D: Jun 11, 1968

Pos: 2B
Hits: 632
RBI: 292

BA: .267
HRs: 18
BB: 122

In 1928 Regan hit only three home runs, but two of them came in the same inning on June 16th. Playing for the Red Sox when they were down in the standings, Regan batted over .260 every year but the last. His highest mark was .288 in 1929.
Playing Career: *1926-1931; Bos A, Pit N*

Phil Regan
Regan, Philip Raymond (The Vulture)
B: Apr 6, 1937

Pos: P
W-L: 96-81
ShOs: 1

ERA: 3.84
SOs: 743
Saves: 92

Regan had a monster season in 1966. He was 14-1 with an NL-leading 21 saves. He followed with a 0.00 ERA in the Series that year. Sandy Koufax called Regan "the Vulture" because he was always picking up wins by throwing a couple of innings in short relief.
Playing Career: *1960-1972; Det A, LA N, Chi N, Chi A*

Rick Reichardt
Reichardt, Frederic Carl
B: Mar 16, 1943

Pos: OF
Hits: 864
RBI: 445

BA: .261
HRs: 116
BB: 263

Teams vying for Reichardt touched off the 1964 bidding war that led to the initiation of the draft to prevent such competition. He reportedly signed for $200,000. Reichardt could never have lived up to the expectations. His best season was 1968, with 21 homers and 73 RBI for California.
Playing Career: *1964-1974; LA A, Cal A, Was A, Chi A, KC A*

Charlie Reilly
Reilly, Charles Thomas
B: Jun 24, 1855   D: Dec 16, 1937

Pos: 3B
Hits: 595
RBI: 234

BA: .250
HRs: 17
BB: 180

Mischievous and ornery, Reilly was the ringleader of the Columbus club who brought umpire baiting to new lows – after a bad call, players would kneel on the infield, arms stretched toward heaven, "praying" for the umpire.
Playing Career: *1889-1895, 1897; Col AA, Pit N, Phi N, Was N*

Long John Reilly
Reilly, John Good
B: Oct 5, 1858   D: May 31, 1937

Pos: 1B
Hits: 1,352
RBI: 335

BA: .289
HRs: 67
BB: 157

A fan survey in 1886 resulted in Reilly being named the "longest" player, hence his nickname. When the Reds adopted red and white striped uniforms Reilly was said to look like a candy cane. He was an AA star, slugging .551 in 1884 and .501 in 1888, both league-leading marks. He led the AA in home runs twice, in triples once – with 26, and in RBI with 103 in 1888, the first year that statistic was tracked in the AA. Reilly stole 245 bases.
Playing Career: *1880, 1883-1891; Cin N, Cin AA*

Pete Reiser
Reiser, Harold Patrick (Pistol Pete)
B: Mar 17, 1919   D: Oct 25, 1981

Pos: OF	BA: .295
Hits: 786	HRs: 58
RBI: 368	BB: 343

No second-year player ever looked as good as Reiser did in 1941. He won the batting title with a .343 mark, led the NL in runs, doubles, triples and slugging average, and stole home seven times. Reiser was the youngest NL batting champion ever. He was hitting .383 on July 2, 1942, when he smashed into the center field wall chasing a ball in St. Louis. It was one of 11 times that Reiser was carried off the field with severe injuries.
Playing Career: *1940-1942, 1946-1952; Brk N, Bos N, Pit N, Cle A*

Heinie Reitz
Reitz, Henry P.
B: Jun 29, 1867   D: Nov 10, 1914

Pos: 2B	BA: .292
Hits: 800	HRs: 11
RBI: 462	BB: 266

Reitz had one of the best jobs in baseball: he was the second baseman for the legendary NL Orioles. Surrounded by Hall of Famers John McGraw, Hughie Jennings and Dan Brouthers in the infield, Reitz hit 31 triples and led the league in fielding average in 1894.
Playing Career: *1893-1899; Bal N, Was N, Pit N*

Kenny Reitz
Reitz, Kenneth John
B: Jun 24, 1951

Pos: 3B	BA: .260
Hits: 1,243	HRs: 68
RBI: 548	BB: 184

Termed a "can't miss" prospect, Reitz fell short of expectations and was traded, but the Cardinals got him back the next year. Returning as a slugger, Reitz hit a career-high 17 homers in 1977. He won six fielding titles, but only one Gold Glove (in 1975).
Playing Career: *1972-1982; StL N, SF N, Chi N, Pit N*

Jack Remsen
Remsen, John J.
B: Apr 1851   D: Deceased

Pos: OF, 1B	BA: .244
Hits: 574	HRs: 8
RBI: 128 (inc.)	BB: 71

Sporting a full-grown beard, Remsen was an outfielder when the position required good fielding rather than heavy hitting. A well-known substitute umpire, he was asked to arbitrate the 1884 tournament that was the 19th-century World Series.
Playing Career: *1872-1879, 1881, 1884; Brk Atlantics n, NY Mutuals n, Har Dark Blues n, Har N, StL N, Chi N, Cle N, Phi N, Brk AA*

Jerry Remy
Remy, Gerald Peter
B: Nov 8, 1952

Pos: 2B	BA: .275
Hits: 1,226	HRs: 7
RBI: 329	BB: 356

Only one balk has been issued to a player who was not a pitcher or catcher. While positioned in a deep shift for a pull hitter, second baseman Remy stepped over the foul line. Baseball rules say all players except the catcher must be in fair territory, so Remy's misstep was called a balk. An All-Star in 1978 when he hit .278 with 24 doubles, Remy had been on the Topps All-Rookie team in 1975.
Playing Career: *1975-1984; Cal A, Bos A*

Steve Renko
Renko, Steven
B: Dec 10, 1944

Pos: P	ERA: 4.00
W-L: 134-146	SOs: 1,455
ShOs: 8	Saves: 6

A popular Kansas City native, Renko ended his 15-year career in his hometown. Renko won 15 games twice for the Expos, in 1971 and 1973. He was once charged with three wild pitches in one inning. In 1972 the big right-hander struck out seven Mets in a row. In retirement he is active in baseball camps and youth leagues.
Playing Career: *1969-1983; Mon N, Chi N, Oak A, Bos A, Cal A, KC A*

Rip Repulski
Repulski, Eldon John
B: Oct 4, 1927   D: Feb 10, 1993

Pos: OF	BA: .269
Hits: 830	HRs: 106
RBI: 416	BB: 207

The 1953 Cardinals had two hot young prospects in the outfield; one was Ray Jablonski and the other Rip Repulski. After four good years in St. Louis, he was traded to the Phillies for Del Ennis. Repulski played in the 1959 World Series for the Dodgers.
Playing Career: *1953-1961; StL N, Phi N, LA N, Bos A*

Merv Rettenmund
Rettenmund, Mervin Weldon
B: Jun 6, 1943

Pos: OF, DH	BA: .271
Hits: 693	HRs: 66
RBI: 329	BB: 445

A football player at Ball State University, Rettenmund was drafted by the Dallas Cowboys, but chose to play baseball. He played in six LCS and four World Series with three different teams. A career platoon player, he was a regular for only one year, batting .318 that year – 1971.
Playing Career: *1968-1980; Bal A, Cin N, SD N, Cal A*

Ed Reulbach.

Ed Reulbach
Reulbach, Edward Marvin (Big Ed)
B: Dec 1, 1882   D: Jul 17, 1961

Pos: P	ERA: 2.28
W-L: 181-106	SOs: 1,137
ShOs: 40	Saves: 11

For three consecutive seasons, Reulbach led NL pitchers in won-lost percentage, a league record that still stands. He was 60-15 for those years. Reulbach was 2-0 with a 3.03 ERA in four World Series for the Cubs. He is the only major league pitcher to throw a doubleheader shutout – and he allowed just eight hits! The twin victories came on September 26 in the midst of the 1908 pennant race, and helped the weary Cubs staff keep up with the Giants, then make it to the momentous playoff game.

Reulbach's eyesight was so poor that his catcher used a glove with white paint on it. His career was overshadowed by his teammates, Three Finger Brown and infielders Tinker, Evers and Chance, as well as crosstown rival Big Ed Walsh. Reulbach stole the limelight, however, with the first one-hitter in World Series play in 1906. His ratio of 5.33 hits per nine innings that year is the third best in history. Only 10 other pitchers have better lifetime ERAs.
Playing Career: *1905-1917; Chi N, Brk N, Nwk F, Bos N*

Rick Reuschel
Reuschel, Rickey Eugene (Big Daddy)
B: May 16, 1949

Pos: P   ERA: 3.37
W-L: 214-191   SOs: 2,015
ShOs: 26   Saves: 5

Rick and his brother Paul once combined for a major league shutout, the first brothers ever to do so. Rick won 20 games in 1977, making the All-Star team in 1977, then rotator cuff surgery caused him to miss the 1982 season. Coming back with a 14-8, 2.27 performance for the Pirates, he earned the Comeback Player of the Year Award in 1985. Going to the Giants and Roger Craig revived his career, as he won 36 games 1988-1989, pitching the Giants into the 1989 division title.
Playing Career: *1972-1981, 1983-1991; Chi N, NY A, Pit N, SF N*

Jerry Reuss
Reuss, Jerry
B: Jun 19, 1949

Pos: P   ERA: 3.64
W-L: 220-191   SOs: 1,907
ShOs: 39   No-hitters: 1

A big, broad-shouldered kid who looked like he could throw the ball through a barn door, Reuss was actually a finesse pitcher. Combining skill with great control, Reuss pitched for major league teams for 22 years. Three times he posted 18 victories, twice more 16. He won 53.5 percent of his decisions and he pitched for five division-winning teams and one World Championship team. Reuss was the Comeback Player of the Year in 1980, when he was 18-6, finishing second in the Cy Young Award voting.

His no-hit game, also in 1980, was marred only by an error at shortstop. Reuss struck out all three batters he faced in that year's All-Star Game. In 1981 he outdueled Ron Guidry

Pitcher Jerry Reuss in 1969.

Allie Reynolds was both a starter and a reliever for the Yankees, 1947-1954.

in the pivotal fifth game of the World Series, beating the Yankee star 2-1, and giving the Dodgers a lead of three games to two on their way to the championship. Reuss returned to the minor leagues after his big league career.
Playing Career: *1969-1990; StL N, Hou N, Pit N, LA N, Cin N, Cal A, Chi A, Mil A*

Dave Revering
Revering, David Allen
B: Feb 12, 1953

Pos: 1B   BA: .265
Hits: 486   HRs: 62
RBI: 234   BB: 148

The Reds agreed to deal minor leaguer Revering and $1.7 million to the A's for Vida Blue in 1977, but after deliberating for two months, Commissioner Bowie Kuhn nixed the deal. It exceeded the $400,000 limit on cash transactions. One month later Revering was again traded to the A's.
Playing Career: *1978-1982; Oak A, NY A, Tor A, Sea A*

Allie Reynolds
Reynolds, Allie Pierce (Superchief)
B: Feb 10, 1915

Pos: P   ERA: 3.30
W-L: 182-107   SOs: 1,423
ShOs: 36   No-hitters: 2

Reynolds was a throwback to the old days when starters relieved in between outings; he posted 49 saves during his career. Reynolds was 7-2 with four saves in six World Series for the Yankees. In six World Series relief appearances, he recorded either a win or a save each time. As a starter, Reynolds beat the Dodgers 1-0 on a two-hitter in the 1949 Fall Classic.

Traded by Cleveland to the Yankees in exchange for Joe Gordon and Eddie Bockman in October 1946, Reynolds led AL pitchers in winning percentage his first season in New York. He was chosen for the All-Star team five of his last six years. Despite painful bone chips in his elbow, Reynolds won 16 games in 1950. In 1951 he became the first AL pitcher to toss two no-hitters in one season. That year Reynolds was awarded the Hickock Belt, signifying that he was the top professional athlete of the year. In 1952 he recorded 20 wins and six saves, and led the AL in ERA and shutouts.
Playing Career: *1942-1954; Cle A, NY A*

Carl Reynolds
Reynolds, Carl Nettles
B: Feb 1, 1903   D: May 29, 1978

Pos: OF   BA: .302
Hits: 1,357   HRs: 80
RBI: 695   BB: 262

Inconsistency, thy name is Reynolds. Although he batted over .300 six times, Reynolds was sent down to the minors after 10 years. He proceeded to bat .355 in the minor league American Association, and returned to the Cubs, with whom he played in the 1938 World Series.
Playing Career: *1927-1939; Chi A, Was A, StL A, Bos A, Chi N*

Craig Reynolds
Reynolds, Gordon Craig
B: Dec 27, 1952

Pos: SS, 2B, 3B, 1B	BA: .256
Hits: 1,142	HRs: 42
RBI: 377	BB: 227

Having lost his job to Dickie Thon, Reynolds in turn replaced Thon after he was beaned. Reynolds played in three NLCS with the Pirates and Astros, batting .333 in the 1986 contest. He led the NL in triples with 12 in 1981, including three in one game. He made the All-Star team twice.
Playing Career: *1975-1989; Pit N, Sea A, Hou N*

Harold Reynolds
Reynolds, Harold Craig
B: Nov 26, 1960

Pos: 2B	BA: .259
Hits: 1,185	HRs: 21
RBI: 342	BB: 457

Slick-fielding Reynolds won the 1988 Gold Glove Award over the gazelle-like Frank White, prompting Bill James to comment that anyone being acclaimed from Seattle is probably twice as good as advertised because of the lack of publicity in the Northwest. Reynolds has earned three Gold Gloves and two All-Star Game berths. A contact hitter, he has struck out only 399 times in 4,575 at-bats, and has stolen 240 bases.

Reynolds set a club record with the Mariners with 60 steals in 1987, a mark that also led the AL. He has participated in five triple plays. Reynolds established the Harold Reynolds Youth Foundation and Role Models Unlimited. He once hosted a Super Bowl party for 1,000 underprivileged youth. He received President George Bush's 195th Daily Point of Light, and the Martin Luther King Humanitarian Award in 1990. The next year he was honored with the Roberto Clemente Award, given to the player who best exemplifies the spirit of baseball, on and off the field.
Playing Career: *1983-; Sea A, Bal A*

R. J. Reynolds
Reynolds, Robert James (Shoes)
B: Apr 19, 1959

Pos: OF	BA: .267
Hits: 605	HRs: 35
RBI: 294	BB: 190

Dubbed "Shoes" by Dodger teammates for his vast assortment of footwear, Reynolds seldom played regularly, only once getting more than 100 hits. He played in the 1990 NLCS for the Pirates. Reynolds had a career average of more than .300 against the Dodgers and Mets.
Playing Career: *1983-1992; LA N, Pit N*

Flint Rhem
Rhem, Charles Flint (Shad)
B: Jan 24, 1901   D: Jul 30, 1969

Pos: P	ERA: 4.20
W-L: 105-97	SOs: 536
ShOs: 8	Saves: 10

Reportedly kidnapped in 1930, Rhem said a gang of Dodgers supporters forced whiskey down his throat for three days, hoping to keep him from pitching. Rhem survived the experience to pitch in World Series that year. He posted a record of 20-7 in 1926.
Playing Career: *1924-1928, 1930-1936; StL N, Phi N, Bos N*

Billy Rhines
Rhines, William Pearl (Bunker)
B: Mar 14, 1869   D: Jan 30, 1922

Pos: P	ERA: 3.47
W-L: 114-103	SOs: 555
ShOs: 13	Saves: 1

Notoriously stingy with hits, Rhines led the NL in ERA with a 1.95 mark in 1890, and 2.45 in 1896. In those two years he was also the most difficult pitcher to reach base against. Rhines was thrifty with his money, too, once saving $1,700 of his $2,100 salary.
Playing Career: *1890-1893, 1895-1899; Cin N, Lou N, Pit N*

Bob Rhoads
Rhoads, Robert Barton (Dusty)
B: Oct 4, 1879   D: Feb 12, 1967

Pos: P	ERA: 2.61
W-L: 97-82	SOs: 522
ShOs: 21	No-hitters: 1

During spring training in 1905, Rhoads's team was stuck in San Antonio with no money because their exhibition games had been rained out. He went to the notorious Crystal Palace and won $1,800 shooting craps – enough to settle accounts and get the team out of town.
Playing Career: *1902-1909; Chi N, StL N, Cle A*

Rick Rhoden
Rhoden, Richard Alan
B: May 16, 1953

Pos: P	ERA: 3.59
W-L: 151-125	SOs: 1,419
ShOs: 17	Saves: 1

Overcoming childhood osteomyelitis, Rhoden became a star major league pitcher. He won 16 games in 1977 and again in 1987. An All-Star in his rookie season with a 12-3 record and a 2.98 ERA, Rhoden made the squad one other time. He led the Pirates in wins three times and the Yankees once. Rhoden committed only six errors in his first 14 seasons. He compiled a .239 batting average, winning three Silver Slugger Awards.
Playing Career: *1974-1992; LA N, Pit N, NY A, Hou N*

The Mariners' Harold Reynolds goes for the double play in a 1990 game.

All-Star slugger Jim Rice.

Yankees pitcher Rick Rhoden licks his fingers during a 1988 game.

Del Rice
Rice, Delbert W.
B: Oct 27, 1922   D: Jan 26, 1983

Pos: C	BA: .237
Hits: 908	HRs: 79
RBI: 441	BB: 382

Managerial Record
Won: 75   Lost: 80   Pct: .484

Playing in two World Series, Rice batted .500 in the 1946 Fall Classic. He became Bob Buhl's "personal catcher" on the Braves in the late 1950s. Buhl was particularly effective against the Dodgers, the Braves' bitterest foes. Rice won Minor League Manager of the Year after leading Salt Lake City to the 1970 PCL pennant. But he could not do the same for the 1972 Angels, who finished in fifth place.
Playing Career: *1945-1961; StL N, Bos N, Chi N, Bal A, LA A*
Managerial Career: *1972; Cal A*

Harry Rice
Rice, Harry Francis
B: Nov 22, 1901   D: Jan 1, 1971

Pos: OF	BA: .299
Hits: 1,118	HRs: 48
RBI: 506	BB: 376

A member of the powerhouse Browns, Rice batted .359 in 1925. His worst average was .287. Rice pounded more than 20 doubles for six years in a row, and scored 97 runs in 1929. He led NL outfielders in fielding average in 1933.
Playing Career: *1923-1931, 1933; StL A, Det A, NY A, Was A, Cin N*

Jim Rice
Rice, James Edward
B: Mar 8, 1953

Pos: OF, DH	BA: .298
Hits: 2,452	HRs: 382
RBI: 1,451	BB: 670

In 1978 Rice wrote his name beside Yastrzemski and Williams when he belted 213 hits, 46 homers, 15 triples, 139 RBI, and ended the season with a .600 slugging percentage, all league-leading marks. He also scored 126 runs and batted .315 that year as the Red Sox fought the Yankees down to the wire. It was Bucky Dent's short home run that kept Boston out of the World Series.

An eight-time All-Star, Rice broke in with teammate Fred Lynn in the Red Sox' outfield in 1975. The duo formed baseball's most powerful rookie tandem. Rice hit .309 with 22 homers and 102 RBI. Lynn was AL Rookie of the Year and MVP as the Sox reached the World Series. Rice missed the entire postseason after Tigers pitcher Vern Ruhle broke his left hand with a pitch during the last week of the regular season. He came back to hit .282 with 25 homers in 1976. He led the AL in home runs in 1977 with 39, while batting .320. Rice batted .333 in the 1986 Fall Classic.
Playing Career: *1974-1989; Bos A*

Sam Rice
Rice, Edgar Charles
B: Feb 20, 1890   D: Oct 13, 1974
Hall of Fame 1963

Pos: OF	BA: .322
Hits: 2,987	HRs: 34
RBI: 1,078	BB: 709

In Game Three of the 1925 World Series, Rice leapt and backhanded a drive off Earl Smith's bat. Falling into the stands, he and the ball disappeared from sight. When Rice emerged with the ball in his glove, the umpire called Smith out. Rice left a sealed letter to be opened at the time of his death. In it he wrote, "At no time did I lose possession of the ball."

Rice had overcome an incredible childhood. When he was four, a tornado destroyed his home and killed several family members. Young Edgar wandered for years, suffering from amnesia. He joined the Coast Guard, but jumped ship in Mexico, and began his baseball career as a pitcher under the name Sam Rice. Clark Griffith heard of him and offered him a contract. Switching to the outfield, Rice became one of the greatest singles hitters of all time. He scored 1,515 runs, stole 351 bases, and smashed 497 doubles.
Playing Career: *1915-1934; Was A, Cle A*

J. R. Richard
Richard, James Rodney
B: Mar 7, 1950

Pos: P	ERA: 3.15
W-L: 107-71	SOs: 1,493
ShOs: 19	No-hitters: 0

A 6'8" Goliath with a 100-mph fastball, Richard posted back-to-back seasons of more than 300 strikeouts in 1978 and 1979. At the

height of his success he suffered a paralyzing stroke in 1980. Richard had complained about a dead arm, but nobody took him seriously; he had a 10-4 record with 1.90 ERA, and pitched in the All-Star Game that season. Doctors found a blood clot that restricted blood flow to his brain. Richard recovered, but his career was ended.
Playing Career: *1971-1980; Hou N*

Gene Richards
Richards, Eugene
B: Sep 29, 1953

Pos: OF	BA: .290
Hits: 1,028	HRs: 26
RBI: 255	BB: 356

The Padres' first big star, Richards stole 56 bases as a rookie in 1977. In 1980 Richards, Ozzie Smith and Jerry Mumphrey each stole over 50 bases, the first trio from one team in NL history to do so. Richards led the majors in outfield assists with 21 in 1980.
Playing Career: *1977-1984; SD N, SF N*

Paul Richards.

Paul Richards
Richards, Paul Rapier
B: Nov 21, 1908   D: May 4, 1986

Pos: C	BA: .227
Hits: 321	HRs: 15
RBI: 155	BB: 157
Managerial Record	
Won: 923 Lost: 901 Pct: .506	

In the minor leagues, Richards once pitched left-handed and right-handed in the same game. An innovative and creative force in baseball, he invented an oversized catcher's mitt to help beleaguered receivers handle Hoyt Wilhelm's knuckleball. Richards credited Bill Terry with his success as a minor league manager.

When World War II manpower shortages called Richards back to the big leagues, he caught for the Tigers, and played in the 1945 World Series. After the war, he returned to managing in the minor leagues, but in 1951 he took over the White Sox. Dubbed the "Go-Go" Sox, they achieved four winning seasons under his management. Richards then used his talents to revive failing teams. Serving as general manager and manager of the Orioles, he introduced the Kiddie Corps pitching staff that revitalized the whole franchise. He also worked for the Astros.
Playing Career: *1932-1935, 1943-1946; Brk N, NY N, Phi A, Det A*
Managerial Career: *1951-1961, 1976; Chi A, Bal A*

Bobby Richardson
Richardson, Robert Clinton
B: Aug 19, 1935

Pos: 2B	BA: .266
Hits: 1,432	HRs: 34
RBI: 390	BB: 262

In one thrilling inning of the 1960 World Series, Richardson smacked a two-run single and belted a grand slam home run, setting a World Series RBI record. He also won the 1962 World Series by snaring Willie McCovey's rocket line drive with the bases loaded in the ninth inning of the Game Seven. Yankee manager Casey Stengel platooned Richardson with Jerry Lumpe in 1957 and 1958, never giving Richardson more than 469 at-bats a year. Stengel once said of the young second baseman, "He don't smoke, he don't drink, and he still can't hit .250."

Ralph Houk, who took over the Yankees in 1961, liked a set lineup. He played Richardson every day and placed him at the top of the order. The combination of leading off for the best offense in the league and rarely walking resulted in Richardson leading the AL in at-bats each year from 1962 through 1964, setting an AL record with 692 in 1962. That year his 209 hits were the AL high. He batted .302 and finished second to Mickey Mantle in MVP voting.
Playing Career: *1955-1966; NY A*

Danny Richardson
Richardson, Daniel
B: Jan 25, 1863   D: Sep 12, 1926

Pos: OF	BA: .254
Hits: 1,129	HRs: 32
RBI: 558	BB: 283
Managerial Record	
Won: 12 Lost: 31 Pct: .279	

In the 1889 postseason championship series with Jim Mutrie's "We, the People" Giants,

Bobby Richardson engages in some infield acrobatics in this publicity photo.

Richardson stole the show with a .314 average and three home runs. He scored 102 runs and stole 37 bases in the Players' League the next year; he pilfered 213 sacks altogether.
Playing Career: *1884-1894; NY N, NY P, Was N, Brk N, Lou N*
Managerial Career: *1892; Was N*

Hardy Richardson
Richardson, Abram Harding (Old True Blue)
B: Apr 21, 1855   D: Jan 14, 1931

Pos: 2B, 3B, SS, 1B, OF   BA: .299
Hits: 1,688   HRs: 73
RBI: 645 (inc.)   BB: 377

The Buffalo Bison stars, called the "Big Four," were Hardy Richardson, Dan Brouthers, Jack Rowe and Deacon White. When Buffalo dropped out of the NL after the 1885 season, Detroit paid $7,000 for the entire Buffalo team in order to acquire the Big Four. Richardson alone was worth the price; he hit .351, leading the NL in hits and home runs in 1886. The next season the Big Four led Detroit to the NL pennant, with Richardson hitting 11 home runs.
Playing Career: *1879-1892; Buf N, Det N, Bos N, Bos P, Bos AA, Was N, NY N*

Lance Richbourg
Richbourg, Lance Clayton
B: Dec 18, 1897   D: Sep 10, 1975

Pos: OF   BA: .308
Hits: 806   HRs: 13
RBI: 247   BB: 174

Richbourg batted over .300 four years in a row, 1927-1930, for the Braves. In 1927 he set an NL record by playing an 18-inning game in right field without a fielding chance. Richbourg later managed four years at Nashville in the minors.
Playing Career: *1921, 1924, 1927-1932; Phi N, Was A, Bos N, Chi N*

Pete Richert
Richert, Peter Gerard
B: Oct 29, 1939

Pos: P   ERA: 3.19
W-L: 80-73   SOs: 925
ShOs: 3   Saves: 51

In his major league debut, Richert struck out the first six batters he faced, including four in one inning. As a starter he made the All-Star team twice with the new Senators. Going to the bullpen for the Orioles, he became a stopper, appearing in the 1969 World Series.
Playing Career: *1962-1974; LA N, Was A, Bal A, StL N, Phi N*

Lew Richie
Richie, Lewis A.
B: Aug 23, 1883   D: Aug 15, 1936

Pos: P   ERA: 2.54
W-L: 74-65   SOs: 438
ShOs: 20   Saves: 8

The comic inspiration for many of Ring Lardner's baseball characters, Richie was a gifted pantomime artist as well as a ballplayer. He won 44 games in a stretch of two seasons and parts of two others. Richie pitched a scoreless inning in the 1910 World Series.
Playing Career: *1906-1913; Phi N, Bos N, Chi N*

Lee Richmond
Richmond, J. Lee
B: May 5, 1857   D: Oct 1, 1929

Pos: P   ERA: 3.06
W-L: 75-100   SOs: 552
ShOs: 8   No-hitters: 1

While a student at Brown University, Richmond pitched the school nine to the Big Five Championship, then three days later tossed a four-hitter against the NL champion Boston Red Stockings. He pitched a perfect game in 1880, and posted 79 percent of Worcester's victories, 1880-1882.
Playing Career: *1879-1883, 1886; Bos N, Wor N, Pro N, Cin AA*

Francis Richter
Richter, Francis C.
B: Jan 26, 1854   D: Feb 12, 1926

Richter was the editor and genius behind the *Reach Baseball Guide*, a publication that reported in depth on major and minor league seasons. He died after completing the 1926 edition. Richter began his baseball writing career with the *Philadelphia Day* in 1872. He was the first to set up a sports department at a newspaper. After stints at the *Sunday World* and *Public Ledger*, he helped form the original American Association in 1882, securing a place in it for the Philadelphia Athletics.

The next year he helped organize the Phillies in the NL. In 1883 he started *Sporting Life*, a weekly newspaper which competed successfully with *The Sporting News* until its demise in 1917. In 1907, Richter was offered the presidency of the NL, but turned it down, a real tragedy for the old league in light of subsequent events. Harry Pulliam was hired and the 1908 Merkle Boner incident ensued which led to Pulliam's suicide in 1909. Richter was a World Series official for many years and wrote a history of baseball.

Branch Rickey
Rickey, Wesley Branch (The Mahatma)
B: Dec 20, 1881   D: Dec 9, 1965
Hall of Fame 1967

Pos: C   BA: .239
Hits: 82   HRs: 3
RBI: 39   BB: 27
Managerial Record
Won: 597   Lost: 664   Pct: .473

Few people have influenced the sport of baseball as Branch Rickey did. He was re-

The Braves' Lance Richbourg in 1929.

"The Mahatma," Branch Rickey (r), shares a word with ex-Dodgers boss Larry MacPhail.

sponsible for the formation of the farm system of minor league teams; he brought about racial integration in baseball; and he paved the way for expansion of the major leagues. Trained as a lawyer, Rickey had an extraordinarily logical and flexible mind. These traits, combined with his keen ability to assess talent and his strong sense of morality, made him one of the most creative and respected baseball figures.

After gaining experience on the playing field as a catcher, Rickey worked as a manager, general manager and president of major league baseball clubs. He served the St. Louis Cardinals, the Brooklyn Dodgers and the Pittsburgh Pirates, in a career that spanned five and a half decades. His legacy to baseball included his son, Branch Rickey, Jr., who was a scout and player development executive, and grandson Branch Rickey III, who headed player development for the Cincinnati Reds before becoming president of the American Association in 1992.
Playing Career: *1905-1907, 1914; StL A, NY A*
Managerial Career: *l913-1915, 1919-1925; StL A, StL N*

Elmer Riddle
Riddle, Elmer Ray
B: Jul 31, 1914   D: May 14, 1984

Pos: P	ERA: 3.40
W-L: 65-52	SOs: 342
ShOs: 13	Saves: 8

Riddle pitched one scoreless inning in the 1940 World Series. The next year he was 19-4, leading the NL with a 2.24 ERA and a won-lost percentage of .826. He posted a league-leading 21 victories in 1943, but faded the next year, and won only two games. His brother Johnny was a major league catcher.
Playing Career: *1939-1945, 1947-1949; Cin N, Pit N*

Lew Riggs
Riggs, Lewis Sidney
B: Apr 22, 1910   D: Aug 12, 1975

Pos: 3B	BA: .262
Hits: 650	HRs: 28
RBI: 271	BB: 181

An All-Star early in his career, Riggs lost his job to Billy Werber in 1939 when the Reds won the NL flag. Riggs played on three straight NL pennant-winning teams, 1939-1941. His best season was 1941, when he hit .305 for the Dodgers.
Playing Career: *1934-1942, 1946; StL N, Cin N, Brk N*

Dave Righetti
Righetti, David Allan (Rags)
B: Nov 28, 1958

Pos: P	ERA: 3.33
W-L: 79-76	SOs: 1,069
ShOs: 2	No-hitters: 1

The Yankees' all-time saves leader, Righetti set the major league single-season mark of 46

Yankee saves leader Dave Righetti.

in 1986, since bested. He began his career as a starter, tossing a no-hitter on the Fourth of July at Yankee Stadium in 1983. He also set the Texas League single-game strikeout record with 21, including seven in a row, in 1978. Three years later, he earned the AL Rookie of the Year Award with a record of 8-4 and a 2.06 ERA; opposing batters hit only .196 off him that year.

Righetti was effective in postseason play. In 1981 he won two games against the Brewers in division playoffs, then another against Oakland in the ALCS. He began a new career as a reliever in the late 1980s, and has racked up 252 saves. Righetti made the All-Star squad in 1986 and 1987. In his record-setting 1986 season, he converted 29 of his final 30 save opportunities, including both ends of a season-ending doubleheader against the Red Sox.
Playing Career: *1979, 1981-; NY A, SF N*

Bill Rigney
Rigney, William Joseph (Specs, The Cricket)
B: Jan 29, 1918

Pos: 2B, SS, 3B	BA: .259
Hits: 510	HRs: 41
RBI: 212	BB: 208
Managerial Record	
Won: 1,239 Lost: 1,321 Pct: .484	

The Giants hit 221 home runs in 1947, and 17 of them were Rigney's. He was elected to the All-Star team the next year, but dropped 30 points on his slugging average and began to look for another career. Studying Leo Durocher, Rigney eventually replaced him. Like Durocher, Rigney was often ejected from games for his caustic comments to umpires. He managed the Giants in New York and San Francisco, then won a division title with the Twins in 1970.
Playing Career: *1946-1953; NY N*
Managerial Career: *1956-1972, 1976; NY N, SF N, Cal A, Min A*

Johnny Rigney
Rigney, John Dungan
B: Oct 28, 1914   D: Oct 21, 1984

Pos: P	ERA: 3.59
W-L: 63-64	SOs: 605
ShOs: 10	Saves: 5

A top pitcher with the White Sox, Rigney pitched the first night game at Comiskey Park in 1939, and married into the Comiskey family. After military service, he returned with a sore arm and moved into team administration, eventually becoming a vice-president.
Playing Career: *1937-1942, 1946-1947; Chi A*

Topper Rigney
Rigney, Emory Elmo
B: Jan 7, 1897   D: Jun 6, 1972

Pos: SS	BA: .288
Hits: 669	HRs: 13
RBI: 314	BB: 377

Playing for Ty Cobb, Rigney flourished under his tutelage, and batted over .300 in his first two years. He had a good eye, and drew over 100 bases on balls in 1924 and 1926. Rigney drove in 94 runs in 1924. He led AL shortstops in fielding twice.
Playing Career: *1922-1927; Det A, Bos A, Was A*

The Reds' Jose Rijo in 1991.

Jose Rijo
Rijo, Jose
B: May 13, 1965

Pos: P	ERA: 3.13
W-L: 97-77	SOs: 1,323
ShOs: 4	Saves: 3

The Yankees rushed 18-year-old Jose Rijo to the majors in 1984 to counter the popularity of Dwight Gooden of the Mets. Rijo had been named the Florida State League MVP with a 15-5 record and a 1.68 ERA in 1983. The Yankees lost the battle for New York during the mid-1980s as Rijo proved to be too young and too raw to compete with AL batters. He was sent back to the minors and later traded to the A's as part of the Rickey Henderson deal.

Rijo fanned 16 Mariners in early April 1986, the same month that Roger Clemens struck out 20 Mariners. After three uneventful years in Oakland, Rijo was traded to the Reds. He was only 22 when the 1988 season began, but it was his fifth year in the majors. With the Reds he began to achieve the success that had been forecast. Winning more than 60 percent of his games in Cincinnati, Rijo has never had an ERA over 2.84 in a Reds uniform. He was the MVP of the 1990 World Series sweep over the favored A's. Rijo won two games, surrendering only one run in 15 innings.
Playing Career: *1984-; NY A, Oak A, Cin N*

Ernest Riles
Riles, Ernest
B: Oct 2, 1960

Pos: SS, 3B, 2B	BA: .254
Hits: 637	HRs: 48
RBI: 284	BB: 244

A Texas League batting champ, Riles riled up opposing pitchers to the tune of a .349 average in 1983. He then batted .286 in his major league rookie season, and was a contender for the 1985 AL Rookie of the Year Award, finishing fourth in the voting.
Playing Career: *1985-; Mil A, SF N, Oak A, Hou N, Bos A*

Jimmy Ring
Ring, James Joseph
B: Feb 15, 1895 D: Jul 6, 1965

Pos: P	ERA: 4.06
W-L: 118-149	SOs: 835
ShOs: 9	Saves: 11

In the most famous trade of the 1920s, the Giants sent Frank Frisch and Ring to the Cardinals for Rogers Hornsby. Ring beat Ed Cicotte in the 1919 World Series, but lost Game Six to Dickey Kerr. Ring won 18 games in 1923 with the Phillies.
Playing Career: *1917-1928; Cin N, Phi N, NY N, StL N*

Cal Ripken
Ripken, Calvin Edwin, Jr.
B: Aug 24, 1960

Pos: 3B, SS	BA: .275
Hits: 2,087	HRs: 297
RBI: 1,104	BB: 817

In 1993 Ripken completed his 11th consecutive season without missing a game, for a total of 1,897 appearances. He started as a third baseman, but was moved to shortstop by manager Earl Weaver on July 1, 1982, and finished the campaign as AL Rookie of the Year. Ripken batted .264 with 28 home runs

Shortstop Cal Ripken, Jr., does his job for the Orioles in 1987.

and 93 RBI. He also began a streak of consecutive innings played that did not end until September 14, 1987. Defying the sophomore jinx in 1983, Ripken was honored with the MVP Award when he hit .318 with 27 home runs and 102 RBI, and led the AL in hits, doubles and runs scored. He made the final putout in the 1983 World Series as the Orioles defeated the Phillies. Ripken's great range accounted for an AL-record 583 assists in 906 total chances in 1984. That year he led the AL in putouts and double plays as well. Perennially at or near the top in defensive categories, Ripken led the league in assists in 1983, 1986 and 1987, putouts in 1985, and double plays in 1983 and 1985. He has been elected to the All-Star team for 11 years in a row, and won another MVP Award in 1991.
Playing Career: *1981-; Bal A*

Jimmy Ripple
Ripple, James Albert
B: Oct 14, 1909 D: Jul 16, 1959

Pos: OF	BA: .282
Hits: 510	HRs: 28
RBI: 257	BB: 156

When the Dodgers did not use the waiver system properly in 1940, Judge Landis made Ripple a free agent. He signed with the Reds and hit .307 that year. In the World Series, he hit a home run to win Game Two, then scored the winning run in the finale.
Playing Career: *1936-1941, 1943; NY N, Brk N, Cin N, Phi N*

Swede Risberg
Risberg, Charles August
B: Oct 13, 1894 D: Oct 13, 1975

Pos: SS	BA: .243
Hits: 394	HRs: 6
RBI: 175	BB: 148

A strong-armed shortstop, Risberg was identified as the instigator of the 1919 World Series fix with gamblers. He batted .080 in that Series. Banned from organized baseball, Risberg played semipro ball in the upper Midwest and the Arizona Copper League.
Playing Career: *1917-1920; Chi A*

Claude Ritchey
Ritchey, Claude Cassius (Little All Right)
B: Oct 5, 1873 D: Nov 8, 1951

Pos: 2B	BA: .273
Hits: 1,618	HRs: 18
RBI: 673	BB: 607

Ritchey was a flashy fielder who led NL second basemen in fielding percentage five times and in double plays three times. With him, the Pirates won three straight pennants, including the 1902 flag by a record 27.5 games. Ritchey had a poor Series in 1903, hitting only .111, but the mighty Honus Wagner batted only .222. In the Chronicle-Telegraph Cup Series of 1900 – featuring the first- and second-place NL teams – Ritchey batted .333.
Playing Career: *1897-1909; Cin N, Lou N, Pit N, Bos N*

Jim Rivera
Rivera, Manuel Joseph (Jungle Jim)
B: Jul 22, 1922

Pos: OF	BA: .256
Hits: 911	HRs: 83
RBI: 422	BB: 365

Rivera enthused White Sox fans with his belly-slides and basepath antics. In 1955 he led the AL with 25 steals. In Game Five of the 1959 World Series, Rivera's catch of Charley Neal's long fly ball preserved a 1-0 Sox victory in front of more than 90,000 Dodger fans.
Playing Career: *1952-1961; StL A, Chi A, KC A*

Mickey Rivers
Rivers, John Milton (Mick the Quick)
B: Oct 31, 1948

Pos: OF	BA: .295
Hits: 1,660	HRs: 61
RBI: 499	BB: 266

An intimidating leadoff man who batted left-handed, Rivers was a line drive hitter who led the AL in triples in 1974 and 1975. He stole a league-high 70 bases in 1975, 267 altogether. Traded to the Yankees, Rivers was their sparkplug for three straight pennants, 1976-1978. He hit .385 in three ALCS. Owner George Steinbrenner traded him to the Rangers in August 1979, saying, "We had to get him out of the New York environment. He's just a sweet, sweet kid."
Playing Career: *1970-1984; Cal A, NY A, Tex A*

Eppa Rixey
Rixey, Eppa
B: May 3, 1891 D: Feb 28, 1963
Hall of Fame 1963

Pos: P	ERA: 3.15
W-L: 266-251	SOs: 1,350
ShOs: 36	Saves: 14

Warren Spahn is the winningest NL left-hander, and Rixey is second. A man of contrasts, Rixey was a Virginia gentleman of easy charm and boyish humor, but was a fierce competitor. He was crafty on the mound, but hot-tempered, and after a loss, destructive to clubhouse furniture. He starred in basketball and baseball at the University of Virginia. There he was encouraged to become a professional baseball player by Cy Rigler, an umpire in the NL who also coached the University of Virginia team.

Signed by the Phillies in 1912 on Rigler's recommendation, Rixey never played in a minor league game. He blossomed under the patient handling of Manager Pat Moran. Rixey pitched in the 1915 World Series for Philadelphia. After a stint with the military during World War I, Rixey was traded to the contending Reds. Posting 25 victories in 1922, he led the NL in wins and innings pitched, but his team finished second.
Playing Career: *1912-1917, 1919-1933; Phi N, Cin N*

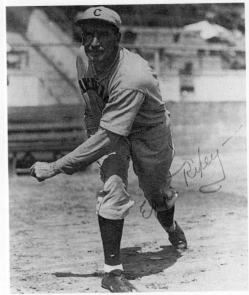
Hall of Famer Eppa Rixey.

Phil Rizzuto
Rizzuto, Philip Francis (Scooter)
B: Sep 25, 1917

Pos: SS	BA: .273
Hits: 1,588	HRs: 38
RBI: 562	BB: 651

In 1950 a poll of sportswriters and baseball historians chose the team of the half century. Interviewed at the time, Ty Cobb said that only one player currently performing could make the team in his day. That one player was Rizzuto. He could bunt, steal bases and turn the double play. He had a winner's attitude, and brought it to bear in 52 World Series games as the Yankees went to the Fall Classic nine times in 13 years. Rizzuto drew 30 walks, stole 10 bases and scored 21 runs in those games.

Yankee shortstop Phil Rizzuto.

One of the outstanding shortstops in the AL in his era, Rizzuto led three times in double plays and total chances per game, twice in fielding and putouts, and once in assists. In 1949 he moved into the leadoff spot and scored 110 runs, batted .275, and finished second in MVP voting. Rizzuto's 1950 season earned him the MVP Award by over 100 points; he had career highs of a .324 batting average, 125 runs scored, 92 walks, 36 doubles and a .439 slugging average. Retiring to the broadcast booth, Rizzuto became famous for expressions like "Holy Cow," and "He's a huckleberry."
Playing Career: *1941-1942, 1946-1956; NY A*

Dave Roberts
Roberts, David Arthur
B: Sep 11, 1944

Pos: P	ERA: 3.78
W-L: 103-125	SOs: 957
ShOs: 20	Saves: 15

Roberts was traded 10 times. "The way I look at it," he said, "either I'm a bum or everybody wants me." He had a 0.00 ERA in the 1971 NLCS. In his best year, Roberts was 17-11 with six shutouts and a 2.85 ERA for the 1973 Astros.
Playing Career: *1969-1981; SD N, Hou N, Det A, Chi N, SF N, Pit N, Sea A, NY N*

Leon Roberts
Roberts, Leon Kauffman
B: Jan 22, 1951

Pos: OF, DH	BA: .267
Hits: 731	HRs: 78
RBI: 328	BB: 256

The Mariners' MVP in 1978, Leon Roberts led the club in batting average, runs scored, home runs, RBI and triples, with career high marks. He also slugged .515 that year. His very first hit in a Seattle uniform was a grand slam home run.
Playing Career: *1974-1984; Det A, Hou N, Sea A, Tex A, Tor A, KC A*

Robin Roberts
Roberts, Robin Evan
B: Sep 30, 1926
Hall of Fame 1976

Pos: P	ERA: 3.41
W-L: 286-245	SOs: 2,357
ShOs: 45	Saves: 25

The winningest right-hander in Phillies history, Roberts won 28 games in 1952 in a career that featured six consecutive seasons of more than 20 wins. In 1949, his first full season, Roberts won 15 games. The next year he pitched the Phillies to their first pennant in 35 years, going 20-11. He posted number 20 on the final day of the season at Brooklyn, in a pennant-deciding 10-inning game.

Though he pitched over 300 innings in six straight seasons, he never walked more than 77. All those innings may have taken their toll – shoulder problems began in 1956. Roberts

Phillies hurler Robin Roberts.

became involved with the Players' Union, working on the pension plan. Largely due to efforts of Roberts and Bob Feller, ballplayers began to realize that they had the power to plan their financial future. Roberts was later the baseball coach at the University of South Florida.
Playing Career: *1948-1966; Phi N, Bal A, Hou N, Chi N*

Bob Robertson
Robertson, Robert Eugene
B: Oct 2, 1946

Pos: 1B, DH, OF, 3B	BA: .242
Hits: 578	HRs: 115
RBI: 368	BB: 317

A one-man postseason wrecking crew, Robertson hit a record three homers and drove in five runs for the Pirates in Game Two of the 1971 NLCS. He homered again in Game Three, then homered twice in the World Series to help Pittsburgh win it all. He has a lifetime slugging average of .821 and .321 batting average in five NLCS.
Playing Career: *1967, 1969-1979; Pit N, Sea A, Tor A*

Charlie Robertson
Robertson, Charles Culbertson
B: Jan 31, 1896   D: Aug 23, 1984

Pos: P	ERA: 4.44
W-L: 49-80	SOs: 310
ShOs: 6	No-hitters: 1

Robertson tossed a perfect game in just his third major league start, beating the Tigers 2-0 in 1922. A diving foul-line catch by left fielder Johnny Mostil preserved the gem. Plagued with arm trouble the rest of his career, Robertson lost 80 games, never turning in a winning season.
Playing Career: *1919, 1922-1928; Chi A, StL A, Bos N*

Dave Robertson
Robertson, Davis Aydelotte
B: Sep 25, 1889   D: Nov 5, 1970

Pos: OF	BA: .287
Hits: 812	HRs: 47
RBI: 364	BB: 113

In the 1917 World Series, Robertson tapped 11 hits and batted .500, setting the benchmark for a six-game Series that would stand until broken by Billy Martin in 1953. Robertson led the NL in homers twice. His best batting average was .308 in 1921.
Playing Career: *1912, 1914-1917, 1919-1922; NY N, Chi N, Pit N*

Gene Robertson.

Gene Robertson
Robertson, Eugene Edward
B: Dec 25, 1898   D: Oct 21, 1981

Pos: 3B	BA: .280
Hits: 615	HRs: 20
RBI: 249	BB: 203

A college football player, Robertson played the hot corner like a gridiron denizen, but he could hit. Batting .319 in 1924, he followed with a 14 home run season with 97 runs scored. A St. Louis native, Robertson faced the Cardinals in the 1928 World Series.
Playing Career: *1919, 1922-1926, 1928-1930; StL A, NY A, Bos N*

Aaron Robinson
Robinson, Aaron Andrew
B: Jun 23, 1915   .D: Mar 9, 1966

Pos: C	BA: .260
Hits: 478	HRs: 61
RBI: 272	BB: 337

Robinson hit 16 home runs and batted .297 in 1946, but lost his job to Yogi Berra. Ironically,

he made the All-Star team in 1947 – the year Yogi took over. Robinson swatted 13 round-trippers for the Tigers in 1949.
Playing Career: *1943, 1945-1951; NY A, Chi A, Det A, Bos A*

Bill Robinson
Robinson, William Henry
B: Jun 26, 1943

Pos: OF, 1B, 3B	BA: .258
Hits: 1,127	HRs: 166
RBI: 641	BB: 263

Another poor soul touted as the next Mickey Mantle, Robinson had career highs of a .304 batting average, 26 homers and 104 RBI in 1977. He hit 24 homers in 1979 as he and the Pirates won World Championship rings. He collected another as batting coach for the 1986 Mets.
Playing Career: *1966-1969, 1972-1983; Atl N, NY A, Phi N, Pit N*

Brooks Robinson
Robinson, Brooks Calbert
B: May 18, 1937
Hall of Fame 1983

Pos: 3B	BA: .267
Hits: 2,848	HRs: 268
RBI: 1,357	BB: 860

One of the most popular players ever, Brooks Robinson inspired his fans to set an attendance record in Cooperstown when he was inducted into the Baseball Hall of Fame. Robinson had some great days. In front of 100 million television fans, he hit .348 in five ALCS and .429 in the 1970 World Series. He batted .318 in the 1971 Fall Classic and made fantastic plays in the field, shown again and again on TV. Robinson led AL third basemen in assists eight times and in fielding 11 times.

He holds almost every lifetime record for

The Orioles' Brooks Robinson in 1964.

third basemen: games, fielding percentage, putouts, assists, chances and double plays. In his only .300 season Robinson won the 1964 MVP Award on the strength of a .317 average, 28 homers and 118 RBI. A 15-time All-Star, he was named MVP of the 1966 contest, getting three hits and scoring the AL's lone run. In the 1966 World Series, Robinson's presence discouraged the heavily favored Dodgers from bunting. The Orioles won four straight close games. In the 1970 World Series he was the MVP.
Playing Career: *1955-1977; Bal A*

Don Robinson
Robinson, Don Allen
B: Jun 8, 1957

Pos: P	ERA: 3.79
W-L: 109-106	SOs: 1,251
ShOs: 6	Saves: 57

Robinson had a world of talent, but was hampered by elbow and shoulder injuries. He was the best hitting pitcher of the 1980s, and won the Giants' 1987 division-clinching game with a home run. His lifetime batting average is .231. Robinson won NL Rookie Pitcher of the Year honors with a 14-6 record. He won 15 games in 1982, but left the starting role for the bullpen. He was 3-2 in postseason play with the Pirates and Giants.
Playing Career: *1978-1992; Pit N, SF N, Cal A, Phi N*

Eddie Robinson
Robinson, William Edward
B: Dec 15, 1920

Pos: 1B	BA: .268
Hits: 1,146	HRs: 172
RBI: 723	BB: 521

An unsung hero of the 1948 Indians, Robinson contributed 16 home runs and 83 RBI, and batted .300 in the World Series. A four-time All-Star, in 1951 Robinson hit 29 homers – the White Sox record until 1970 – and drove in 117 runs.
Playing Career: *1942, 1946-1957; Cle A, Was A, Chi A, Phi A, NY A, Det A, Bal A*

Floyd Robinson
Robinson, Floyd Andrew
B: May 9, 1936

Pos: OF	BA: .283
Hits: 929	HRs: 67
RBI: 426	BB: 408

In his rookie season, 1961, Robinson hit .310, then followed with a .312 average, 109 RBI and a league-leading 45 doubles the next year. On July 22, Robinson was 6-for-6 against Boston. After a salary holdout in 1964 he slumped badly, never quite recovering.
Playing Career: *1960-1968; Chi A, Cin N, Oak A, Bos A*

Frank Robinson
Robinson, Frank
B: Aug 31, 1935
Hall of Fame 1982

Pos: OF	BA: .294
Hits: 2,943	HRs: 586
RBI: 1,812	BB: 1,420
Managerial Record	
Won: 591 Lost: 642 Pct: .479	

One of the finest ballplayers in baseball history, Robinson compiled impressive numbers, including 1,829 runs scored, 528 doubles and 204 stolen bases. Collecting many honors during his career, Robinson was Rookie of the Year, an All-Star 11 times, and MVP in both the AL and NL. He was the AL Triple Crown winner in 1966, following his controversial trade to Baltimore for Milt Pappas when Reds General Manager Bill DeWitt said that Robinson was an old 30. DeWitt must have choked on those words

many times, for Robinson had his greatest years after the trade.

As a manager, Robinson once put himself into a game at a crucial moment and hit a home run to win it. Saddled with poor teams in Cleveland and San Francisco, he started at rock bottom with the Orioles – in the midst of their record 21-game losing streak. Robinson remodeled the team, and it was in contention for the 1989 AL flag until the last week of the season.
Playing Career: *1956-1976; Cin N, Bal A, LA N, Cal A, Cle A*
Managerial Career: *1975-1977, 1981-1984, 1988-1991; Cle A, SF N, Bal A*

Jackie Robinson at his big league debut.

Jackie Robinson
Robinson, Jack Roosevelt
B: Jan 31, 1919   D: Oct 24, 1972
Hall of Fame 1962

Pos: 1B, 2B, 3B	BA: .311
Hits: 1,518	HRs: 137
RBI: 734	BB: 740

Robinson played the 1947 season under more pressure than any other player had ever experienced. Not only was he the first black man in the majors in the 20th century, but he was the symbol of racial integration in American society. The NAACP got busy and started legal proceedings against graduate schools in 1949, but for 18 months Jackie Robinson carried the brunt of societal reformation on his proud and determined shoulders. Branch Rickey hand-picked Robinson for the job, and he could not have chosen better. Robinson controlled his emotions and disciplined himself to turn the other cheek like no one else has done.

Robinson was an outstanding baseball

Frank Robinson in his first year with the Orioles, 1966, when he won the Triple Crown.

Jackie Robinson brings in a homer in April 1947, his rookie year.

player and a great all-around athlete. The first four-letter man at UCLA, he excelled at football, basketball and track as well as baseball. He would have followed in his brother Mack's Olympic footsteps if the 1940 Games had not been cancelled due to World War II. Robinson worked his way into the Dodgers' lineup and contributed to six pennants. He was Rookie of the Year, MVP, a six-time All-Star, NL batting champion, and one of the best baserunners ever.
Playing Career: *1947-1956; Brk N*

Jeff Robinson
Robinson, Jeffrey Daniel
B: Dec 13, 1960

Pos: P	ERA: 3.79
W-L: 46-57	SOs: 629
ShOs: 1	Saves: 39

There was a pattern to Robinson's pitching. When he worked as a starter his ERA shot up. Conversely when he came out of the bullpen it went down. Robinson's best season was 1987, when he compiled a record of 6-8 with a 2.79 ERA.
Playing Career: *1984-1992; SF N, Pit N, NY A, Cal A, Chi N*

Ron Robinson
Robinson, Ronald Dean
B: Mar 24, 1962

Pos: P	ERA: 3.63
W-L: 48-39	SOs: 473
ShOs: 2	Saves: 19

A first-round draft choice, Robinson took four years to reach the majors and five to stick. In 1986 he was 10-3 with 14 saves and a 3.24 ERA. In 1988 he came within one pitch of a perfect game when pinch hitter Wallace Johnson singled for the Expos.
Playing Career: *1984-1992; Cin N, Mil A*

Wilbert Robinson
Robinson, Wilbert (Uncle Robby)
B: Jun 29, 1863   D: Aug 8, 1934
Hall of Fame 1945

Pos: C	BA: .273
Hits: 1,388	HRs: 18
RBI: 622	BB: 286
Managerial Record	
Won: 1,399 Lost: 1,398 Pct: .500	

Relatively unknown among Hall of Fame members, Robinson was the catcher for the legendary NL Orioles, who won three consecutive pennants. He was later the skipper of the Brooklyn Dodgers, and led them to two pennants. Robinson was so beloved in Brooklyn that the team name was changed to "Robins" in his honor.
Robinson once got seven hits in a game. He caught a rare tripleheader in 1896 and a doubleheader the next day. John McGraw's partner on and off the field, the two jumped teams and signed contracts together. After he went to the Giants, McGraw hired Robinson to coach pitchers. Then came a bitter break. The two never spoke to each other again, and Robinson took the Brooklyn job so that he could compete against McGraw.
Playing Career: *1886-1902; Phi AA, Bal AA, Bal N, StL N, Bal A*
Managerial Career: *1902, 1914-1931; Bal A, Brk N*

Yank Robinson
Robinson, William H.
B: Sep 19, 1859   D: Aug 25, 1894

Pos: 2B, 3B, SS	BA: .241
Hits: 825	HRs: 15
RBI: 219 (inc.)	BB: 664

A pesky, patient hitter, Robinson led the league in walks three times, going over 100 each time – and he played in the era when it took seven balls to get a walk! Robinson scored 697 runs on 825 hits and stole 272 bases.
Playing Career: *1882, 1884-1892; Det N, StL U, StL AA, Pit P, Cin AA, Was N*

Andre Rodgers
Rodgers, Kenneth Andre Ian
B: Dec 2, 1934

Pos: SS	BA: .249
Hits: 628	HRs: 45
RBI: 245	BB: 290

A talented cricket player from the Bahamas, Rodgers paid his way to a baseball tryout in Florida. A graceful 6'3", Rodgers became the Cubs' shortstop in 1962 when Ernie Banks moved to first.
Playing Career: *1957-1967; NY N, SF N, Chi N, Pit N*

Dodgers Manager Wilbert Robinson with Chief Meyers (l) and Rube Marquard (r) in 1916.

Buck Rodgers
Rodgers, Robert Leroy (Bob)
B: Aug 16, 1938

Pos: C	BA: .232
Hits: 704	HRs: 31
RBI: 288	BB: 234

Managerial Record
Won: 768   Lost: 750   Pct: .506

Breaking Mickey Cochrane's rookie record of 133 games, Rodgers barely lost the AL Rookie of the Year Award to Tom Thresh. He caught regularly for six years until injuries halted his career. While coaching the Brewers, Rodgers replaced George Bamberger as manager in 1980, and led the team to a second-half title in strike-torn 1981.
Playing Career: *1961-1969; LA A, Cal A*
Managerial Career: *1980-1982, 1985-; Mil A, Mon N, Cal A*

Aurelio Rodriguez
Rodriguez y Ituarte, Aurelio
B: Dec 28, 1947

Pos: 3B	BA: .237
Hits: 1,570	HRs: 124
RBI: 648	BB: 324

In a 17-season career, Rodriguez batted over .300 only once, and it was a doozy. In 1981 he hit .346 for the Yankees, then annihilated the Dodgers at a .417 clip in the World Series. Rodriguez played in four ALCS. He won a Gold Glove Award in 1976.
Playing Career: *1967-1983; Cal A, Det A, SD N, NY A, Chi A, Bal A*

Ellie Rodriguez
Rodriguez y Delgado, Eliseo
B: May 24, 1946

Pos: C	BA: .245
Hits: 533	HRs: 16
RBI: 203	BB: 332

Twice an All-Star, Rodriguez grew up idolizing Yogi Berra. He tied an AL record with 19 putouts in a nine-inning game, and set another with 21 in an extra-inning game as Nolan Ryan struck out 19 each time in 1974. Rodriguez caught Ryan's fourth no-hitter.
Playing Career: *1968-1976; NY A, KC A, Mil A, Cal A, LA N*

Preacher Roe
Roe, Elwin Charles
B: Feb 26, 1915

Pos: P	ERA: 3.43
W-L: 127-84	SOs: 956
ShOs: 17	Saves: 10

Preacher Roe made disciples of the NL when he compiled a record of 22-3 in 1951. He had been successful during the war years, leading the league in strikeouts in 1945, and going 14-13 with a 2.87 ERA. Then he fractured his skull in a game fight while coaching basketball during the off-season. His effectiveness suffered and his records the next two seasons

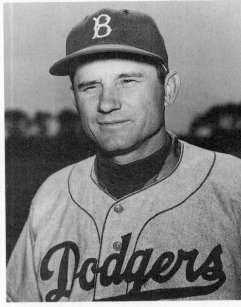
Preacher Roe.

plummeted to 3-8 and 4-15. He was traded to the Dodgers in December 1947.

Roe explained his dismal situation, "I got three pitches: my change, my change off my change, and my change off my change off my change." After he retired, fans discovered a fourth pitch. In a 1955 *Sports Illustrated* article by Dick Young, the Preacher confessed to throwing spitballs. A five-time All-Star, Roe pitched in three World Series.
Playing Career: *1938, 1944-1954; StL N, Pit N, Brk N*

Ed Roebuck
Roebuck, Edward Jack
B: Jul 3, 1931

Pos: P	ERA: 3.35
W-L: 52-31	SOs: 477
ShOs: 0	Saves: 62

Roebuck was in the bullpen when the Dodgers finally won the World Series in 1955. In two Fall Classics he posted a 1.42 ERA as a relief specialist. Roebuck was 8-3 and 10-2 with eight and nine saves in 1960 and 1962.
Playing Career: *1955-1958, 1960-1966; Brk N, LA N, Was A, Phi N*

Gary Roenicke
Roenicke, Gary Steven
B: Dec 5, 1954

Pos: OF	BA: .247
Hits: 670	HRs: 121
RBI: 410	BB: 406

A secret weapon, Roenicke batted .444 and slugged .889 in two ALCS for the Orioles, batting a phenomenal .750 in the 1983 World Series. In platoon with John Lowenstein, the left field duo hit 45 homers and 140 RBI in 1982, 34 homers with 124 RBI the next year.
Playing Career: *1976, 1978-1988; Mon N, Bal A, NY A, Atl N*

Wally Roettger
Roettger, Walter Henry
B: Aug 28, 1902   D: Sep 14, 1951

Pos: OF	BA: .285
Hits: 556	HRs: 19
RBI: 245	BB: 99

A part-time player, Roettger batted .341 for the 1928 pennant-winning Cardinals. Traded to the Giants, he led NL outfielders with a .992 fielding average in 1930. He later coached at the University of Illinois.
Playing Career: *1927-1934; StL N, NY N, Cin N, Pit N*

Bullet Joe Rogan
Rogan, Wilbur
B: Jul 28, 1889   D: Mar 4, 1967

Pos: OF	BA: .343 (inc.)
Hits: 599 (inc.)	HRs: 52 (inc.)
RBI: NA	BBs: NA

Pos: P	ERA: NA
W-L: 113-45 (inc.)	SOs: 677 (inc.)
ShOs: 18 (inc.)	Saves: 15 (inc.)

Rogan was a star both on the pitcher's mound and at the plate. In 11 seasons with the Monarchs, he compiled a .343 batting average, 10th highest among all Negro Leaguers. On the pitcher's mound Rogan used a no-windup delivery with a fastball, curveball, forkball, palmball and a legal spitball. Satchel Paige once said Rogan "was the onliest pitcher I ever saw, I ever heard of pitching and hitting in the clean-up place."

The finest-fielding pitcher in the Negro Leagues, Rogan began as a catcher, but

Wilbur "Bullet Joe" Rogan.

eventually played every position. In 1911 he began his pitching career with the 25th Infantry Wreckers army team. After nine years of army ball, he was discovered at age 30 by Casey Stengel, then referred to Monarchs owner J. L. Wilkinson. As a Monarch in 1922, Rogan hit 16 home runs in 74 games. He led the league with 16 victories and batted .412 in 1924. He is ranked third on the Negro Leagues' all-time winning percentage list, with a .715 mark.
Playing Career: *1920-1938; KC Monarchs*

Billy Rogell
Rogell, William George
B: Nov 24, 1904

Pos: SS	BA: .267
Hits: 1,375	HRs: 42
RBI: 609	BB: 649

The switch-hitting Rogell was one of the top shortstops during the 1930s, a time when pennant contenders had dynamic double play combinations. The Tigers' keystone combo of Rogell and Charlie Gehringer was a key factor in the team's 1934 and 1935 pennants. Rogell drove in four runs in Game Four of the 1934 Series as the Tigers won 10-4. He led AL shortstops in fielding for three years, 1935-1937, and in assists for two, 1934-1935.
Playing Career: *1925, 1927-1928, 1930-1940; Bos A, Det A, Chi N*

Steve Rogers
Rogers, Stephen Douglas
B: Oct 26, 1949

Pos: P	ERA: 3.17
W-L: 158-152	SOs: 1,621
ShOs: 37	Saves: 2

In postseason play for the Expos, Rogers went 3-1 in 1981, beating the Phillies twice and Dodgers once. A five-time All-Star, Rogers led the NL in shutouts twice, 1979 and 1983, and in ERA with 2.40 in 1982. The winningest pitcher in Expos history, Rogers started with a flash: 10-5, with a 1.54 ERA in the second half of 1973. For nine straight years he posted ERAs under 3.50, three times under 2.99. Arm troubles in 1984 ended his career one year later.
Playing Career: *1973-1985; Mon N*

Saul Rogovin
Rogovin, Saul Walter
B: Oct 10, 1923

Pos: P	ERA: 4.06
W-L: 48-48	SOs: 388
ShOs: 9	Saves: 2

In 1952, 14 Red Sox fell victim to Rogovin, who struck them out in 16 innings before a relief pitcher took over. The year before, he had led the AL with a 2.78 ERA. Retiring from baseball, Rogovin became an English teacher in his hometown of Brooklyn.
Playing Career: *1949-1953, 1955-1957; Det A, Chi A, Bal A, Phi N*

Cookie Rojas
Rojas y Rivas, Octavio Victor
B: Mar 6, 1939

Pos: 2B, OF	BA: .263
Hits: 1,660	HRs: 54
RBI: 593	BB: 396
Managerial Record	
Won: 75 Lost: 79 Pct: .487	

Selected in a 1969 poll as the Phillies' greatest second baseman ever, Rojas was an All-Star five times and played 10 different positions during his career. He was the expansion Royals' first proven quality player, teaming with Freddie Patek to give Kansas City instant credibility in the AL West division races. Always considered a glove man, Rojas led NL second basemen with a .987 fielding average in 1968 and topped AL keystone sackers twice.

At the plate, Rojas reached the coveted .300 mark twice, in 1965 and 1971. The extremely popular infielder was a reserve by the time the Royals hit divisional pay dirt, but he still hit .308 in two ALCS against the Yankees. After coaching the Cubs in 1978-1981, Rojas replaced Gene Mauch as manager of the Angels in 1988.
Playing Career: *1962-1977; Cin N, Phi N, StL N, KC A*
Managerial Career: *1988; Cal A*

Red Rolfe
Rolfe, Robert Abial
B: Oct 17, 1908 D: Jul 8, 1969

Pos: 3B	BA: .289
Hits: 1,394	HRs: 69
RBI: 497	BB: 526
Managerial Record	
Won: 278 Lost: 256 Pct: .521	

The leadoff man for the best Yankees team ever, Rolfe batted first for the Bronx Bombers from 1936 to 1939. In nine years, he scored 942 runs, and hit 257 doubles and 67 triples. He stole only 44 bases, but who needed to steal with sluggers Lou Gehrig, Bill Dickey, Joe DiMaggio and Tony Lazzeri batting behind him? The Yankees won six pennants in seven years with Rolfe at the hot corner. He hit .284 in six World Series.

A four-time All-Star, his best year was 1939, when he took up the slack from Gehrig stepping down to lead the AL in hits, runs and doubles as he batted .329 and knocked in 80 runs. Stomach ulcers and World War II shortened Rolfe's career. He coached the Yankees in 1946, then served as Yale baseball coach. For three and a half seasons he managed the Tigers, bringing them home in second place in 1950.
Playing Career: *1931, 1934-1942; NY A*
Managerial Career: *1949-1952; Det A*

The Yankees' Red Rolfe reaches for a high throw to third in 1937.

Rich Rollins
Rollins, Richard John
B: Apr 16, 1938

Pos: 3B   BA: .269
Hits: 887   HRs: 77
RBI: 399   BB: 266

A rookie sensation, Rich Rollins received the most All-Star votes and started both All-Star Games in 1962. That year he hit .298 with 16 homers and 96 RBI. Never a solid fielder, when his home runs fell off Rollins quickly lost his starting job.
Playing Career: *1961-1970; Min A, Sea A, Mil A, Cle A*

Johnny Romano
Romano, John Anthony (Honey)
B: Aug 23, 1934

Pos: C   BA: .255
Hits: 706   HRs: 129
RBI: 417   BB: 414

Power-hitting Johnny Romano was one sweet catcher. He was an All-Star in 1961 and 1962 when he hit 21 then 25 homers. He and Earl Battey backed up Sherman Lollar on the 1959 White Sox pennant-winning team. A broken hand hampered him after 1963.
Playing Career: *1958-1967; Chi A, Cle A, StL N*

Ed Rommel
Rommel, Edwin Americus
B: Sep 13, 1897   D: Aug 26, 1970

Pos: P   ERA: 3.54
W-L: 171-119   SOs: 599
ShOs: 18   Saves: 29

In Rommel's final season, he pitched 17 innings in relief to win an 18-inning, 18-17 thriller for the Athletics over the Indians. He earned the win despite giving up 29 hits, 14 runs and eight walks! An early knuckleballer, Rommel

A's pitcher Ed Rommel.

was a workhorse who exhibited fine control, walking only 724 in 2,556 innings. He won 27 games in 1922 and 21 in 1925, leading the league both times. Three times Rommel appeared in more than 50 games. He became a relief pitcher for the 1929-1931 pennant-winning A's.

Rommel won Game Four of the 1929 World Series when the A's rallied for ten runs in the seventh inning. After his playing career, Rommel umpired for 22 years in the AL. In one game, the Red Sox had Dick Gernert on third with one out and Gene Mauch at bat. Mauch grounded to the first baseman who stepped on first and threw home to catch Gernert. Mauch threw up his hands to deflect the ball. Rommel declared both runners out for Mauch's interference.
Playing Career: *1920-1932; Phi A*
Umpiring Career: *1938-1959; AL (6 AS, 2 WS)*

Enrique Romo
Romo y Rivera, Enrique
B: Jul 15, 1947

Pos: P   ERA: 3.45
W-L: 44-33   SOs: 436
ShOs: 0   Saves: 52

Using a large repertoire of pitches, Romo was a Mexican League star before he ever signed with the Mariners. As a reliever he steadied the young franchise with experience and savvy, going 8-10 with 16 saves and a 2.83 ERA in 1977. He pitched in the 1979 World Series.
Playing Career: *1977-1982; Sea A, Pit N*

Vicente Romo
Romo y Navarro, Vicente
B: Apr 12, 1943

Pos: P   ERA: 3.36
W-L: 32-33   SOs: 416
ShOs: 1   Saves: 52

Vicente is the brother of Enrique Romo, both stars in Mexico during the 1970s. Up with the Indians in 1968, Romo saved 12 with a 1.60 ERA. Being Cleveland, they traded him to Boston the following year, where he saved 11 more.
Playing Career: *1968-1974, 1982; LA N, Cle A, Bos A, Chi A, SD N*

Jim Rooker
Rooker, James Phillip
B: Sep 23, 1941

Pos: P   ERA: 3.46
W-L: 103-109   SOs: 976
ShOs: 15   Saves: 7

The Pirates' radio broadcaster who promised to walk to Philadelphia if he lost a bet, Rooker did lose, but remains busy in Pittsburgh. A star with the Pirates, Rooker won 15 and 13 for the division-winning Bucs in 1974 and 1975. He pitched in the 1979 World Series.
Playing Career: *1968-1980; Det A, KC A, Pit N*

Cubs ace Charley Root.

Charley Root
Root, Charles Henry (Chinski)
B: Mar 17, 1899   D: Nov 5, 1970

Pos: P   ERA: 3.58
W-L: 201-160   SOs: 1,459
ShOs: 21   Saves: 40

The leathery, tobacco-squirting Root will forever be associated with Babe Ruth's "called shot" home run in the 1932 World Series. Root himself is the best argument against the called shot, claiming he would have knocked the bum down if he had tried it. Root says the Babe was really saying, "there's one more," and gesturing to the pitcher to emphasize his point.

The ace of the Cubs' staff, Root took them to four World Series. He led the NL in wins with 26 in 1927, tossing a career-high 309 innings that year. He also led the league twice in relief wins. In a period of high ERAs, Root's best marks were 2.60 in 1933 and 2.86 in 1938. Considered a below-average hitter, he swatted .262 in 1930; another year he had 27 hits for a .221 average. Altogether Root pitched 632 games and 3,197 innings.
Playing Career: *1923, 1926-1941; StL A, Chi N*

Buddy Rosar
Rosar, Warren Vincent
B: Jul 3, 1914

Pos: C	BA: .261
Hits: 836	HRs: 18
RBI: 367	BB: 315

A five-time All-Star catcher, Rosar nonetheless had difficulty making the team. Backup to Bill Dickey in New York and Jim Hegan in Cleveland, he finally found a home with the A's, where he set a record by fielding 1.000 in 1946. His streak of errorless games extended to 147.
Playing Career: *1939-1951; NY A, Cle A, Phi A, Bos A*

Pete Rose
Rose, Peter Edward (Charlie Hustle)
B: Apr, 14 1941

Pos: 2B, 3B, OF, 1B	BA: .303
Hits: 4,256	HRs: 160
RBI: 1,314	BB: 1,566
Managerial Record	
Won: 414 Lost: 373 Pct: .526	

Derisively nicknamed "Charlie Hustle" by the haughty Yankees because he ran out walks to first base, Rose showed them – he made an entire career of hustling. Reds skipper Sparky Anderson declared that he had never seen a more competitive player than Rose, who once portrayed Ty Cobb in a movie. The two became entwined in baseball lore. Named 1963 Rookie of the Year, Rose went on to break Cobb's formidable record and became the career leader in hits with 4,256. He also leads in singles (3,215), at-bats (14,053) and games played (3,562).

Rose is second all-time in doubles (746) and fourth in runs (2,165). He also stole 198 bases. In seven NLCS for the Reds and Phillies, he batted .381. He played in six World Series.

During his playing career, the NL swamped the AL 21 games to two in the annual All-Star Classic, in which Rose played 16 times. He became an effective and extremely popular manager. Then, controversy – the dreaded and despised combination of gambling and baseball. Rose was banned for life. But the Hall of Fame is not complete without him.
Playing Career: *1963-1986; Cin N, Phi N, Mon N*
Managerial Career: *1984-1989; Cin N*

John Roseboro
Roseboro, John Junior
B: May 13, 1933

Pos: C	BA: .249
Hits: 1,206	HRs: 104
RBI: 548	BB: 547

In 1965 Roseboro was the top NL catcher. He had been an All-Star three times, won a Gold Glove and called signals for the best pitching staff since Mathewson and McGinnity. Then in the hot summer of 1965 – the Watts riots had just erupted – Juan Marichal hit Roseboro over the head three times with a bat. With graphic violence just making its way onto the TV screen, viewers of the national pastime saw Roseboro, blood streaming down his face, being led away in daze. The outcry from fans caused baseball to take stock of itself. When the answers were not forthcoming, baseball zoomed downward in popularity, reaching a nadir in January 1969 when nationwide polls showed football to be more popular than its bigger and more intelligent brother.

Roseboro set records for putouts in 1959 and 1961, leading NL catchers six times in total chances, four times in putouts, and twice in double plays as the Dodgers won four pennants with him behind the plate.
Playing Career: *1957-1970; Brk N, LA N, Min A, Was A*

Chief Roseman
Roseman, James John
B: Jul 4, 1856   D: Jul 4, 1938

Pos: OF, P, 1B	BA: .263
Hits: 726	HRs: 17
RBI: 43 (inc.)	BB: 133
Managerial Record	
Won: 7 Lost: 8 Pct: .467	

The 1885 New York Mets went bonkers over Native American culture, and the fans took to calling the players by tribal names. Chief Roseman was the only one with Indian blood, and was the ringleader despite his .227 batting average that year.
Playing Career: *1882-1887, 1890; Tro N, NY AA, Phi AA, Brk AA, StL AA, Lou AA*
Managerial Career: *1890; StL AA*

Al Rosen.

Al Rosen
Rosen, Albert Leonard (Flip)
B: Feb 29, 1924

Pos: 3B	BA: .285
Hits: 1,063	HRs: 192
RBI: 717	BB: 587

"Flip" was a sandlot nickname that accompanied Al Rosen throughout his baseball career. An amateur boxer who sometimes found himself involved in fisticuffs on the diamond, Rosen's nose was broken 11 times. He hit 37 homers as a rookie in 1950, then won the AL MVP Award in 1953. Losing the batting title on the last day of the 1953 season, he hit 43 homers, had 145 RBI and scored 115 runs.

Whiplash injuries suffered in an auto accident caused Rosen to quit at age 32 to become a stockbroker. Returning to baseball 20 years later, he served as president of the Yankees, then the Astros, and then he took a rebuild-

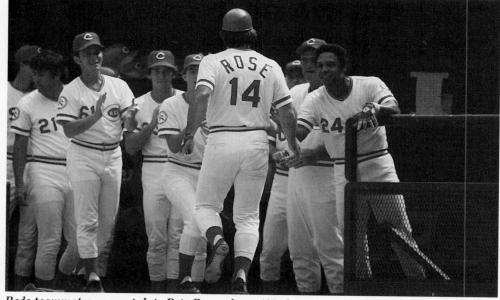

Reds teammates congratulate Pete Rose after a 1974 homer.

ing job with the Giants. As president and general manager in San Francisco, his leadership brought the last-place 1985 Giants to the division title two years later. The Giants won the 1989 NL pennant, but suffered a four-game sweep by their neighbors across the bay.
Playing Career: *1947-1956; Cle A*

Goody Rosen
Rosen, Goodwin George
B: Aug 28, 1912

Pos: OF	BA: .291
Hits: 557	HRs: 22
RBI: 197	BB: 218

A member of the Canadian Baseball Hall of Fame, Rosen was selected for the 1945 All-Star Game – the year it was cancelled – on the strength of a .325 average, 126 runs, 24 doubles, 11 triples and 12 homers for the Dodgers. His career ended with a busted clavicle.
Playing Career: *1937-1939, 1944-1946; Brk N, NY N*

Braggo Roth
Roth, Robert Frank
B: Aug 28, 1892   D: Sep 11, 1936

Pos: OF	BA: .284
Hits: 804	HRs: 30
RBI: 422	BB: 335

Roth led the AL with seven homers in 1915, a year which he split between the White Sox and Indians in the Joe Jackson trade. Struggling to reach his potential, Roth was traded for Amos Strunk and Jack Barry, and again for Duffy Lewis and George Mogridge.
Playing Career: *1914-1921; Chi A, Cle A, Phi A, Bos A, Was A, NY A*

Jack Rothrock
Rothrock, John Houston
B: Mar 14, 1905   D: Feb 2, 1980

Pos: OF	BA: .276
Hits: 924	HRs: 28
RBI: 327	BB: 299

California-bred Rothrock fit in fine with the hillbillies of the Gas House Gang in the mid-1930s. As the right fielder, he led the victorious Cardinals with six RBI in the 1934 World Series.
Playing Career: *1925-1932, 1934-1937; Bos A, Chi A, StL N, Phi N*

Edd Roush
Roush, Edd J.
B: May 8, 1893   D: Mar 21, 1988
Hall of Fame 1962

Pos: OF	BA: .323
Hits: 2,376	HRs: 68
RBI: 981	BB: 484

In the 1919 World Series, Roush made four outstanding catches, each one with runners on base, each one being the turning point in a

Edd Roush lays down a bunt.

Reds victory. He maintained to his dying day that the Reds beat the Black Sox fair and square. Despite batting only .214, Roush scored six runs and drove in seven on only six hits. He walked three times, was hit twice by pitches and stole two bases, leading all World Series participants.

Never losing sight of the fact that professional athletes play for money, Roush was tough at contract time, and held out much of the 1922 season and the entire 1930 season. A high-demand player, Roush batted over .322 for 10 straight seasons. Twice fashioning 27-game hitting streaks, he barely missed three batting titles in a row due to sloppy scorekeeping. Roush lost to Zack Wheat in 1918 by an eyelash – some at-bats were not counted. Roush accrued 1,099 runs, 182 triples and 268 stolen bases.
Playing Career: *1913-1929, 1931; Chi A, Ind F, Nwk F, NY N, Cin N*

Jack Rowe
Rowe, John Charles
B: Dec 8, 1857   D: Apr 26, 1911

Pos: SS, C, OF	BA: .286
Hits: 1,256	HRs: 28
RBI: 644	BB: 224
Managerial Record	
Won: 27 Lost: 72 Pct: .270	

One of baseball's original Big Four, Rowe went to Detroit for the wonderful 1887 season when the Wolverines ran roughshod over the NL. He batted an adjusted .318 with 135 runs scored and 22 stolen bases as he became part of the second Big Four who soundly defeated the AA Browns, conquerors of Spaldings' White Stockings the previous year. Disgusted with the game after the 1890 Players' League experience, Rowe retired.
Playing Career: *1879-1890; Buf N, Det N, Pit N, Buf P*
Managerial Career: *1890; Buf P*

Schoolboy Rowe
Rowe, Lynwood Thomas
B: Jan 11, 1910   D: Jan 8, 1961

Pos: P	ERA: 3.87
W-L: 158-101	SOs: 913
ShOs: 22	Saves: 12

"How'm I doin', Edna?" asked Rowe of his wife during a pre-World Series radio interview. That phrase was all he heard during the 1934 Fall Classic between his Tigers and the Gas House Gang Cardinals. A three-time All-Star, Rowe was an ace for three Tigers pennant winners, going 24-8 in 1934, 19-13 in 1935 and 16-3 in 1940.

His World Series record was only 2-5, but he tossed four complete games in the first two encounters. One was a 12-inning seven-hit win in Game Two of the 1934 Series. Suffering arm trouble, Rowe won only one game in 1937 and 1938 combined. After World War II, he revived his career with the Phillies, making the All-Star team in 1947. A career .263 hitter, he was often used as a pinch hitter, once banging out a pinch-hit grand slam. He led the NL in pinch hits and appearances in 1943, going 15-for-49.
Playing Career: *1933-1943, 1946-1949; Det A, Brk N, Phi N*

Lynwood "Schoolboy" Rowe.

Bama Rowell
Rowell, Carvel William
B: Jan 13, 1916

Pos: 2B, OF	BA: .275
Hits: 523	HRs: 19
RBI: 217	BB: 113

The line-drive that broke the clock in the film *The Natural* was inspired by Rowell, who busted the clock with a line-drive at Ebbets Field. The Alabaman hit .305 as a rookie.
Playing Career: *1939-1941, 1946-1948; Bos N, Phi N*

Pants Rowland
Rowland, Clarence Henry
B: Feb 12, 1879   D: May 17, 1969

Managerial Record
Won: 339   Lost: 247   Pct: .578

Called a "Bush League" manager by John McGraw, Rowland whipped the knickers off McGraw and the Giants in the 1917 World Series, four games to two. It was the nastiest

World Series ever played. Rowland later umpired in the AL and served as the president of the PCL. He became the executive vice-president of the Cubs in 1954.
Managerial Career: *1915-1918; Chi A*
Umpiring Career: *1923-1927; AL*

Jerry Royster
Royster, Jeron Kennis
B: Oct 18, 1952

Pos: 3B, 2B, SS, OF	BA: .249
Hits: 1,049	HRs: 40
RBI: 352	BB: 411

Royster was named Pacific Coast League Player of the Year in 1975, earning him a regular big league spot. Royster played five years as a Braves regular within a 16-year career, including a 1982 appearance in the NLCS. He stole 189 career bases.
Playing Career: *1973-1988; LA N, Atl N, SD N, Chi A, NY A*

Dave Rozema
Rozema, David Scott
B: Aug 5, 1956

Pos: P	ERA: 3.47
W-L: 60-53	SOs: 448
ShOs: 7	Saves: 17

After leading the Southern Association with a 1.57 ERA in 1976, Rozema was the AL Rookie Pitcher of the Year with the Tigers in 1977, going 15-7 with a 3.10 ERA. He never again topped nine victories in a season.
Playing Career: *1977-1986; Det A, Tex A*

Johnny Rucker
Rucker, John Joel (The Crabapple Comet)
B: Jan 15, 1917   D: Aug 7, 1985

Pos: OF	BA: .272
Hits: 711	HRs: 21
RBI: 214	BB: 109

The nephew of Dodger great Nap Rucker, Johnny was the *Life* magazine coverboy for the spring training prospects issue in his rookie season. His best full season was 1941, when he led the NL in at-bats, scoring 95 runs and whacking 38 doubles.
Playing Career: *1940-1941, 1943-1946; NY N*

Nap Rucker
Rucker, George Napoleon
B: Sep 30, 1884   D: Dec 19, 1970

Pos: P	ERA: 2.42
W-L: 134-134	SOs: 1,217
ShOs: 38	No-hitters: 1

With little to cheer about in the early days, Brooklyn fans packed the park when red-haired Rucker took the mound. Averaging more than 300 innings for eight years, 1907-1913, Rucker was 116-123, winning 22 in 1911. He basked in the Dodgers' glory in 1916, going 2-1 with a 1.69 ERA for the NL pennant winners.
Playing Career: *1907-1916; Brk N*

Joe Rudi played in three World Series for the champion Oakland A's (1972-74).

Joe Rudi
Rudi, Joseph Oden
B: Sep 7, 1946

Pos: OF	BA: .264
Hits: 1,468	HRs: 179
RBI: 810	BB: 369

Rudi hit .310 in three World Series for the A's but is remembered for one spectacular play. In Game Two of the 1972 World Series against the Reds, Rudi homered, then saved the win with a spectacular ninth-inning catch – the image is still used in highlights films and network promotions. Rudi was an underrated superstar, overshadowed by the more dynamic personalities of his colorful teammates. With him, Oakland won three consecutive World Series, 1972-1974, the last team to do so.

The power-packed A's featured a lineup of Reggie Jackson, Sal Bando, Catfish Hunter, Vida Blue and Rollie Fingers, but nobody was more important to their success than Rudi. He was an excellent defensive player, a smart hitter and a good baserunner. His arm was strong and accurate, and he was outstanding in the clutch. He made three All-Star trips and won three Gold Gloves. His best year was 1972, when he hit .305 with 94 runs, leading the AL in hits and triples.
Playing Career: *1967-1982; Oak A, Cal A, Bos A*

Dick Rudolph
Rudolph, Richard (Baldy)
B: Aug 25, 1887   D: Oct 20, 1949

Pos: P	ERA: 2.66
W-L: 122-108	SOs: 786
ShOs: 27	Saves: 8
Managerial Record	
Won: 11 Lost: 27 Pct: .289	

The trio of Rudolph, Bill James and Lefty Tyler pulled off one of the greatest pennant wins in baseball history. Pitching every third start, they took the Braves from last place on July 4 to the 1914 pennant. Then the amazing Braves – with Rudolph going 2-0 with a 0.50 ERA – defeated the heavily-favored Athletics in a four-game sweep. Rudolph paced the staff with 27 wins.
Playing Career: *1910-1911, 1913-1920, 1922-1923, 1927; NY N, Bos N*
Managerial Career: *1924; Bos N*

Herold "Muddy" Ruel.

Muddy Ruel
Ruel, Herold Dominic
B: Feb 20, 1896   D: Nov 13, 1963

Pos: C	BA: .275
Hits: 1,242	HRs: 4
RBI: 532	BB: 606

Managerial Record
Won: 59   Lost: 95   Pct: .383

Given a second chance when Hank Gowdy stumbled over his catcher's mask in the 12th inning of Game Seven in the 1924 World Series, Ruel doubled to left, then scored the Senators' winning run on Earl McNeely's bad hop single over Fred Lindstrom's head. Baseball legend was built in that game. Walter Johnson, bombed in previous appearances, sparkled in the last showdown for all the chips, despite not having his best stuff. Ruel's easy pop foul was missed, yet he came through on the second chance. McNeely hit an easy double play ball, but it hit a rock and shot over the third sacker's head to give the Senators an improbable World Series victory.

Ruel had a law degree and was admitted to practice before the Supreme Court. He was the Tigers' general manager and special assistant to Commissioner Happy Chandler. He caught more than 1,400 games and batted over .300 three times.
Playing Career: *1915, 1917-1934; StL A, NY A, Bos A, Was A, Det A, Chi A*
Managerial Career: *1947; StL A*

Dutch Ruether
Ruether, Walter Henry
B: Sep 13, 1893   D: May 16, 1970

Pos: P	ERA: 3.50
W-L: 137-95	SOs: 708
ShOs: 18	Saves: 8

Ruether was the hitting star of the 1919 World Series, whacking two game-winning triples and a double in six at-bats. He hit .667 and slugged 1.500 for the Series, and pitched a Game One victory. Following his 19-6 1919 season with a 16-12 record in 1920, Ruether moved on to Brooklyn, where he won 21 games in 1922. He won 18 for the 1925 AL champion Senators and 13 for the 1927 Yankees. He played on AL pennant-winning teams his last three years in the majors.
Playing Career: *1917-1927; Chi N, Cin N, Brk N, Was A, NY A*

Red Ruffing
Ruffing, Charles Herbert
B: May 3, 1904   D: Feb 17, 1986
Hall of Fame 1967

Pos: P	ERA: 3.80
W-L: 273-225	SOs: 1,987
ShOs: 45	Saves: 16

Below average with the Red Sox, Ruffing won 39 games and lost 96 in six years. In 1930 the Boston owners, badly in need of money, sold Ruffing to New York for backup outfielder Cedric Durst and $50,000. Ruffing was 15-5 for the Yankees with a 4.14 ERA. The high ERA would gradually come down as Ruffing learned to guide the hitters toward the huge center field of Yankee Stadium. The Hall of Fame great won 231 games in the next 14 years. Ruffing was also a good hitter, batting .269 with 36 homers and numerous pinch hits. He batted over .300 eight times, including .364 in 1930. He was 7-2 in World Series play, second to Whitey Ford on the all-time wins list. Ruffing won 20 or more games four straight years. His Yankees captured seven AL flags, including six in seven years. Ruffing accomplished all that he did despite the handicap of missing four toes on his left foot. It did not keep him off the mound or out of World War II.
Playing Career: *1924-1942, 1945-1947; Bos A, NY A*

Red Ruffing.

Vern Ruhle
Ruhle, Vernon Gerald
B: Jan 25, 1951

Pos: P	ERA: 3.73
W-L: 67-88	SOs: 582
ShOs: 12	Saves: 11

Currently the pitching coach at the University of Oklahoma, Ruhle speared a soft liner in Game Four of the 1981 NLCS that the Astros claimed led to a triple play. The Phillies protested that he had trapped the ball, and the umpires let stand a double play.
Playing Career: *1974-1986; Det A, Hou N, Cle A, Cal A*

Pete Runnels with Boston in 1962.

Pete Runnels
Runnels, James Edward
B: Jan 28, 1928   D: May 20, 1991

Pos: 1B, 2B, SS	BA: .291
Hits: 1,854	HRs: 49
RBI: 630	BB: 844

Managerial Record
Won: 8   Lost: 8   Pct: .500

Runnels won two batting titles, but remembered the season he lost as his most enjoyable. In 1958 Ted Williams had a chance to become the oldest man ever to win a batting title. His late season, neck-and-neck battle with teammate Runnels is one of Runnels's fondest memories, "I enjoyed Williams's 1958 catching me on the final day more than the later titles of 1960 and 1962 because of the great competition. Wasn't he capable!"

Runnels was not too shabby himself. An All-Star in 1960 and 1962, he won the 1960 batting title with .320 and the 1962 title with a .326 average. A minor league second baseman, Runnels came up as a shortstop, but

played 644 games at first, 642 at second and 463 at shortstop. He led the AL in fielding at second base in 1960, then at first base the following year. At the plate Runnels was consistent; his averages varied by only 12 points from 1958 to 1962.
Playing Career: *1951-1964; Was A, Bos A, Hou N*
Managerial Career: *1966; Bos A*

Jake Ruppert
Ruppert, Jacob (Colonel)
B: Aug 5, 1867   D: Jan 13, 1939

The pinstriped, patrician image of the New York Yankees came from Colonel Ruppert. He was on the New York social register and a lifelong bachelor. Working in the family brewery from age 19, he became president of it in 1915. Heavily involved in Republican politics, Ruppert was elected to four terms in Congress, beginning in 1898. At the suggestion of John McGraw, Ruppert and Colonel Tillinghast Huston, an engineer who had made a fortune in Cuba, bought the Yankees in 1914 for $450,000.

A rift developed between the partners over the hiring of Miller Huggins. That, the arrival of Babe Ruth, and the selection of Ed Barrow as general manager, were actions that led to Yankee dynasties, and they set a benchmark by which all baseball success has been measured. Ruppert answered to those who wanted to disband the team, "I found out a long time ago there is no charity in baseball. Every club owner must make his own fight for existence. I went into baseball purely for the fun of it. I had no idea I would spend so much money."

Bob Rush
Rush, Robert Ransom
B: Dec 21, 1925

Pos: P	ERA: 3.65
W-L: 127-152	SOs: 1,244
ShOs: 16	Saves: 8

A two-time All-Star, Rush gave the second-division Cubs solid starting pitching for 10 years, winning 17 games in 1952 and three times finishing above .500, though the Cubs did not. Granted a reprieve from second-division purgatory when he was traded to the World Champion Braves, Rush went 10-6, losing Game Three of the 1958 World Series to hero Don Larsen and his perfect game.
Playing Career: *1948-1960; Chi N, Mil N, Chi A*

Amos Rusie
Rusie, Amos Wilson
(The Hoosier Thunderbolt)
B: May 30, 1871   D: Dec 6, 1942
Hall of Fame 1977

Pos: P	ERA: 3.07
W-L: 246-174	SOs: 1,934
ShOs: 30	No-hitters: 1

Pitching from 50 feet Rusie was horrible to behold. Nicknamed "The Hoosier Thunder-

Hall of Fame hurler Amos Rusie.

bolt" because he threw lightning, Rusie led the NL in both strikeouts and shutouts for five of six years, 1890-1895. Moving the mound back to 60' 6" in 1893 hardly stopped the Indiana lad. He came to the Giants from his hometown Indianapolis team after being signed by John T. Brush, who would buy the Giants in 1902 after Rusie had passed from the baseball scene.

Rusie starred in the 1890 season when most of the NL stars had jumped to the Players' League, winning 36 games. In 1985 Andrew Freedman bought the Giants and set off a series of events, centering on Rusie, that would drive him from the league. Fined excessively, Rusie held out in 1896 for remittance of fines. Freedman used fines as a way to pay less money to his players. When Rusie sat out the entire year, the other owners banded together to pay his salary; he was the biggest gate attraction in the game.
Playing Career: *1889-1895, 1897-1898, 1901; Ind N, NY N, Cin N*

Allen Russell
Russell, Allen E.
B: Jul 31, 1893   D: Oct 20, 1972

Pos: P	ERA: 3.52
W-L: 71-76	SOs: 603
ShOs: 5	Saves: 42

A spitball pitcher and a reliever, Russell led the AL with five saves for the Yankees and Red Sox in 1919 and with nine for the Senators

in 1923. He appeared in the 1924 World Series for the Senators, going 0-0 with a 3.00 ERA in three innings.
Playing Career: *1915-1925; NY A, Bos A, Was A*

Bill Russell
Russell, William Ellis
B: Oct 21, 1948

Pos: SS	BA: .263
Hits: 1,926	HRs: 46
RBI: 627	BB: 483

Russell came out Cherokee County, Kansas, in the same coal belt that produced Carl Hubbell, Mickey Mantle, Jerry Adair, Darrell Porter and Ralph Terry – from a high school that was too small to field a baseball nine. He stayed in the big leagues 18 years through five division winners, four NL flag bearers and a 1981 World Championship.

Russell teamed with Steve Garvey, Davey Lopes and Ron Cey for over eight years, the longest-lived infield quartet in baseball history. Only Zack Wheat played more games and seasons in Dodger Blue – though in Wheat's time some of it was Dodger check. A three-time All-Star, Russell retired when a finger injury led to erratic throwing. He had a .337 mark in five NLCS, including .412 in 1978. He also played in four World Series, and hit .423 in the 1978 Classic. He was a Dodger coach from 1987 to 1991.
Playing Career: *1969-1986; LA N*

Jack Russell
Russell, Jack Erwin
B: Oct 24, 1905   D: Nov 3, 1990

Pos: P	ERA: 4.47
W-L: 85-141	SOs: 418
ShOs: 3	Saves: 38

With a new lease on life as a reliever for the pennant-winning Senators and Cubs, Russell led the AL in saves, 1933-1934. He posted a 0.87 ERA in the 1933 World Series and 0.00 in the 1938 Fall Classic. After retiring, he settled in Clearwater, Florida, becoming the city commissioner. The Phillies' spring-training stadium is named for him.
Playing Career: *1926-1940; Bos A, Cle A, Was A, Det A, Chi N, StL N*

Jeff Russell
Russell, Jeffrey Lee
B: Sep 2, 1961

Pos: P	ERA: 3.74
W-L: 51-64	SOs: 621
ShOs: 2	Saves: 146

A free-agent pickup in 1993, Jeff Russell has filled the gap in the Red Sox bullpen left when closer Jeff Reardon departed. He blossomed as a stopper in 1988 when he led the AL with 38 saves. Russell was an All-Star in 1988 and 1989.
Playing Career: *1983-; Cin N, Tex A, Oak A, Bos A*

Jim Russell
Russell, James William
B: Oct 1, 1918   D: Nov 24, 1987

Pos: OF   BA: .267
Hits: 959   HRs: 67
RBI: 428   BB: 503

A speedy outfielder, Russell once had a home run voided when a teammate on the bases called time to tie his shoelace, and the pitcher, not hearing, delivered the pitch. A regular with the Pirates, 1943-1947, he played for the NL champion Braves.
Playing Career: *1942-1951; Pit N, Bos N, Brk N*

Reb Russell
Russell, Ewell Albert
B: Apr 12, 1889   D: Sep 30, 1973

Pos: P, OF   ERA: 2.34
W-L: 81-59   SOs: 495
ShOs: 24   Saves: 13

A top pitcher with the White Sox, Russell revived his career, threatened by arm troubles, to hit .368 in 1922 for the Pirates. He was released to make room for Kiki Cuyler. As a hurler, Russell won 22 games his rookie year, posting a 1.90 ERA.
Playing Career: *1913-1919, 1922-1923; Chi A, Pit N*

Marius Russo
Russo, Marius Ugo (Lefty)
B: Jul 19, 1914

Pos: P   ERA: 3.13
W-L: 45-34   SOs: 311
ShOs: 6   Saves: 5

A spot starter, Russo won 14 games in both the 1940 and 1941 seasons. He went 2-0 in two World Series. In Game Three of the 1941 Series, Russo whipped the Dodgers 2-1. In 1943 he held the Cardinals to one unearned run, then doubled and scored the winning run.
Playing Career: *1939-1943, 1946; NY A*

Babe Ruth
Ruth, George Herman (Jidge, The Sultan of Swat, Bambino)
B: Feb 6, 1895   D: Aug 16, 1948
Hall of Fame 1936

Pos: P, OF   BA: .342
Hits: 2,873   HRs: 714
RBI: 2,211   BB: 2,056

Pos: P   ERA: 2.28
W-L: 94-46   SOs: 488
ShOs: 17   Saves: 4

Yankee Stadium was called "the House that Ruth Built" with good reason. Ruth changed the way owners looked at their clubs. He proved that one could make a lot of money off spectators. It was claimed that Ruth created a new fan, one who did not know the teams and who did not keep score. They came to see "Baby Root." When he hit a home run, they

The Babe bundles up during a 1933 exhibition game at Ebbets Field

The greatest: Babe Ruth (l) and Lou Gehrig converse during spring training, 1928.

came back the next day and brought their friends.

Ruth was the greatest player in baseball history. He is the all-time slugger and he was a top pitcher, once tossing 29⅔ consecutive scoreless innings in the World Series. His incredible statistics include 2,174 runs, 506 doubles, 136 triples, and a .690 slugging average. Ruth was 3-0 with a 0.87 ERA in two World Series for the Red Sox. He was the first player to hit 30, 40, 50, then 60 home runs in a season. He slugged .847 and .846 in back-to-back seasons, and scored 177 runs in 1921. It seemed he could hit home runs on cue.
Playing Career: *1914-1935; Bos A, NY A, Bos N*

Dick Ruthven
Ruthven, Richard David
B: Mar 27, 1951

Pos: P	ERA: 4.14
W-L: 123-127	SOs: 1,145
ShOs: 17	Saves: 1

A two-time All-Star, Ruthven won the deciding game of the 1980 NLCS in relief, throwing the final two innings of a 10-inning, 8-7 win over the Astros. A 6-1 start earned him a spot on the 1981 NL All-Star team, but his ERA ballooned to 5.14, and he finished the season at 12-7. Early on he was known for temper tantrums and high ERAs. He even got into a dispute with Braves owner Ted Turner, which got him traded back to the Phillies.
Playing Career: *1973-1986; Phi N, Atl N, Chi N*

Connie Ryan
Ryan, Cornelius Joseph
B: Feb 27, 1920

Pos: 2B	BA: .248
Hits: 988	HRs: 56
RBI: 381	BB: 518
Managerial Record	
Won: 11 Lost: 22 Pct: .333	

A 1944 All-Star at second base while batting .295, Ryan appeared in the 1948 World Series for the Braves. Known as a good team player, he coached at the big league level with the Braves and Rangers, even briefly taking over each squad as manager.
Playing Career: *1942-1944, 1946-1954; NY N, Bos N, Cin N, Phi N, Chi A*
Managerial Career: *1975, 1977; Atl N, Tex A*

Jimmy Ryan
Ryan, James Edward
B: Feb 11, 1863   D: Oct 26, 1923

Pos: OF	BA: .307
Hits: 2,506	HRs: 118
RBI: 1,093	BB: 803

Many historians feel Ryan is the best 19th-century player who is not in the Baseball Hall of Fame. His hit totals include 451 doubles, 157 triples, 1,643 runs, 408 stolen bases, and a 6-1 record as a pitcher. He was the catalyst for the pennant-winning Chicago White Stock-

Jimmy Ryan in 1889.

ings and Players clubs. Ryan was a power hitter, leading the NL with 16 homers, 33 doubles, 182 hits, and a .515 slugging average in 1888.

A free spirit and engaging personality, he was one of the leaders of the Players' revolt in 1890. That the Chicago club won the only pennant of that league is a testament to his persuasive powers. Seldom striking out, he was almost a sure bet to score once he got on base, scoring 100 or more runs eight times despite playing schedules of less than 140 games throughout most of his career.
Playing Career: *1885-1900, 1902-1903; Chi N, Chi P, Was A*

Nolan Ryan
Ryan, Lynn Nolan (The Ryan Express)
B: Jan 31, 1947

Pos: P	ERA: 3.25
W-L: 324-292	SOs: 5,714
ShOs: 61	No-hitters: 7

Perhaps the best pitcher of all time, Ryan still threw 95-mph fastballs at age 46. The author of the all-time strikeout record and no-hit mark, Ryan starred as a second year hurler in the 1969 World Series victory by the Mets over the highly favored Orioles. He had won the deciding game of the NLCS with seven innings of relief, then saved Game Three of the Series that featured two spectacular catches by Tommy Agee.

In California, Ryan studied pitching under coach Tom Morgan and veteran catcher Jeff Torborg, then the Ryan Express arrived. He fanned 329 batters, winning 19 with a 2.28 ERA. The next year, 1973, Ryan tossed two no-hitters, fanning 17 Tigers in the second one. In his last start of the season he fanned

Nolan Ryan sets SO record, 1973.

16 Twins in 10 innings to eclipse Sandy Koufax's 382-strikeout record by one. In 39 starts that year, Ryan whiffed 10 or more batters 23 times. Ryan posted three seasons in a row of more than 300 strikeouts.
Playing Career: *1966, 1968-1993; NY N, Cal A, Hou N, Tex A*

Rosy Ryan
Ryan, Wilfred Patrick Dolan
B: Mar 15, 1898   D: Dec 10, 1980

Pos: P	ERA: 4.14
W-L: 52-47	SOs: 315
ShOs: 1	Saves: 19

The long man out of the Giants' bullpen, Ryan's 3.01 ERA in 1922 led the NL. He holds the record with three World Series relief wins, with one in each Series, 1922-1924. In 1924 he became the second pitcher to hit a homer in the Fall Classic.
Playing Career: *1919-1926, 1928, 1933; NY N, Bos N, NY A, Brk N*

Mike Ryba
Ryba, Dominic Joseph
B: Jun 9, 1903   D: Dec 13, 1971

Pos: P	ERA: 3.66
W-L: 52-34	SOs: 307
ShOs: 2	Saves: 16

Ryba was one of Branch Rickey's secret weapons. He managed, coached and scouted for the Red Birds' farm system in addition to pitching in the majors. His top year was 1944, when he was 12-7 with two saves. In 1945 he posted a 2.49 ERA.
Playing Career: *1935-1938, 1941-1946; StL N, Bos A*

Bret Saberhagen
Saberhagen, Bret William (Sabes)
B: Apr 11, 1964

Pos: P	ERA: 3.24
W-L: 120-90	SOs: 1,267
ShOs: 16	No-hitters: 1

Not many fans can forget 21-year-old Saberhagen mowing down the Cardinals 11-0 in Game Seven of the 1985 World Series. Jeanine Saberhagen had just given birth to the couple's first child two days earlier, and five days earlier Sabes had won Game Three. In high school, Saberhagen tossed a no-hitter in the Los Angeles city championship game. A 19th-round draft pick – as a shortstop – he got back to the mound and posted a 16-7 record in his first minor league season, winning a job with the big club the very next year.

He became the jewel of a young Royals

Bret Saberhagen.

Teammates congratulate Johnny Sain on winning Game One of the 1948 WS.

pitching staff that included Mark Gubicza and Danny Jackson. Saberhagen was 20-6 in 1985, and 23-6 with a 2.16 ERA in 1989, winning the Cy Young Award both years. In 1987 he had a 15-1 record by the All-Star Game, in which he hurled three scoreless innings, but developed arm trouble that nagged him the rest of the season. Saberhagen pitched 1,329 innings before the age of 26. He won a Gold Glove in 1989.
Playing Career: *1984-; KC A, NY N*

Chris Sabo
Sabo, Christopher Andrew (Spuds)
B: Jan 19, 1962

Pos: 3B	BA: .270
Hits: 790	HRs: 101
RBI: 357	BB: 232

The Reds' injured Buddy Bell was replaced by Sabo and never got the position back. Sabo was named NL Rookie of the Year, batting .271 with 74 runs and 40 doubles, plus leading NL third sackers in fielding. He was an All-Star in three of his first five years.
Playing Career: *1988-; Cin N*

Ray Sadecki
Sadecki, Raymond Michael
B: Dec 26, 1940

Pos: P	ERA: 3.79
W-L: 135-131	SOs: 1,614
ShOs: 20	Saves: 7

The Cardinals were the surprise winners of the NL pennant in 1964, partly due to Sadecki winning 20 games. He beat Whitey Ford and the Yankees in the World Series opener. Joining the Cardinals at age 19, Sadecki was 9-9 in 26 starts, and earned the 1960 St. Louis Rookie of the Year Award. Traded to the Mets later in his career, Sadecki both started and relieved, and appeared in four 1973 World Series games.
Playing Career: *1960-1977; StL N, SF N, NY N, Atl N, KC A, Mil A*

Vic Saier
Saier, Victor Sylvester
B: May 4, 1891   D: May 14, 1967

Pos: 1B	BA: .263
Hits: 774	HRs: 55
RBI: 395	BB: 378

A minor league hitting star, Saier replaced "The Peerless Leader" Frank Chance at first base with the Cubs. In 1913 he batted .288 with a league-leading 21 triples, and drove in a career-high 92 runs. A back injury effectively ended his career in 1917.
Playing Career: *1911-1917, 1919; Chi N, Pit N*

Johnny Sain
Sain, John Franklin
B: Sep 25, 1917

Pos: P	ERA: 3.49
W-L: 139-116	SOs: 910
ShOs: 16	Saves: 51

"Spahn and Sain and two days of rain" was the Braves' pitching strategy in 1948, and somehow it won Boston a pennant. Sain led the NL with 24 wins, 39 starts, 28 complete games and 314 innings that year. The three-time All-Star had spent 1943-1945 in the military, then put together four 20-win seasons in five years, 1946-1950. Swapped to the Yankees for Lew Burdette and $50,000 in 1951, Sain was 11-6 and 14-7 in 1952 and 1953; the Yankees won pennants both years. As a reliever he led the AL with 22 saves in 1954.

A good-hitting pitcher, Sain compiled a .245 batting average, and he had a couple of outstanding years at the plate. He hit .346 in 1947 and .353 in 1954. As a pitching coach after his playing career, Sain counseled young hurlers to "Go up those Golden Stairs" – to demand the amount of money their pitching was worth. He was well-liked by his students, but was often in conflict with club officials.
Playing Career: *1942, 1946-1955; Bos N, NY A, KC A*

Luis Salazar
Salazar y Garcia, Luis Ernesto
B: May 19, 1956

Pos: 3B, OF, SS	BA: .267
Hits: 827	HRs: 63
RBI: 345	BB: 134

Salazar had good seasons in the early 1980s with the Padres, culminating in the 1984 World Series, when he turned in a .333 performance at the plate. He batted .368 for the Cubs in the 1989 NLCS, and revived with them in the early 1990s.
Playing Career: *1980-1992; SD N, Chi A, Det A, Chi N*

Slim Sallee.

Slim Sallee
Sallee, Harry Franklin
B: Feb 3, 1885   D: Mar 22, 1950

Pos: P	ERA: 2.56
W-L: 174-143	SOs: 836
ShOs: 25	Saves: 36

The Higginsport, Ohio sheriff in the off-season, Sallee was the Cardinals' top hurler for eight years. The front office staff contended that he would have been even better if he had gone to bed at night instead of staying up to greet the sunrise. Sallee won 19 games in 1913 and 18 in 1914 and 1917. He led the NL in saves three times. Sold to the Giants in July 1916, he won several games in their sensational 26-game winning streak.

From 1909 to 1919 Sallee never posted an ERA higher than 2.97. He helped the Giants to the 1917 NL pennant with an 18-7 record, but lost World Series Games One and Five to the White Sox. Released by the Giants, he was picked up on waivers in March 1919 by the Reds. He won 21 games for the World Champion Reds, then defeated Ed Cicotte in Game One of the 1919 World Series. Sallee walked only 20 batters in 227 innings that season. He went back to the Giants in 1920.
Playing Career: *1908-1921; StL N, NY N, Cin N*

Joe Sambito
Sambito, Joseph Charles
B: Jun 28, 1952

Pos: P	ERA: 3.04
W-L: 37-38	SOs: 489
ShOs: 1	Saves: 84

Sambito threw left-handed smoke, posting ERAs of 1.77 in 1979 – an All-Star year – 1.84 in 1981, and 0.71 in 1982 before bone chips damaged ligaments in his elbow. Coming back, he lasted long enough to appear in the 1986 World Series with the Red Sox.
Playing Career: *1976-1982, 1984-1987; Hou N, NY N, Bos A*

Billy Sample
Sample, William Amos
B: May 2, 1955

Pos: OF	BA: .272
Hits: 684	HRs: 46
RBI: 230	BB: 195

Now a savvy baseball commentator, Sample was called up to the Rangers in 1978 after a monster PCL season at Tucson – a .352 average and 141 runs scored. As a rookie in Texas the next year he hit .292, which turned out to be his best.
Playing Career: *1978-1986; Tex A, NY A, Atl N*

Juan Samuel
Samuel, Juan Milton
B: Dec 9, 1960

Pos: 2B, OF, 3B	BA: .259
Hits: 1,398	HRs: 132
RBI: 600	BB: 369

Setting a rookie stolen base record with 72 in 1984, Samuel leapt onto the big league scene with a .272 average, 36 doubles, a league-leading 19 triples, 105 runs scored, and an NL-record 701 at-bats in his rookie season. He was named NL Rookie Player of the Year by *The Sporting News*. Tremendously fast and aggressive at the plate, Samuel scored more than 100 runs in three of his first four full seasons. He has been chosen for the All-Star squad three times.
Playing Career: *1983-; Phi N, NY N, LA N, KC A, Cin N*

Luis Sanchez
Sanchez, Luis Mercedes
B: Aug 24, 1953

Pos: P	ERA: 3.75
W-L: 28-21	SOs: 216
ShOs: 0	Saves: 27

Starring in the 1974 Midwest League, Sanchez parlayed a stint in the 1980 Mexican League into a job in the majors. Working exclusively in relief for the Angels, he won 10 games with seven saves in 1983, and saved 11 more the following year. He pitched in the 1982 ALCS.
Playing Career: *1981-1985; Cal A*

Heinie Sand
Sand, John Henry
B: Jul 3, 1897   D: Nov 3, 1958

Pos: SS	BA: .258
Hits: 781	HRs: 18
RBI: 251	BB: 382

Giants outfielder Jimmy O'Connell offered Sand a bribe in 1924, saying certain players would make it worth $500 if he did not "bear down too hard." Sand reported the offer. O'Connell and Giants coach Cozy Dolan were banned for life.
Playing Career: *1923-1928; Phi N*

Ryne Sandberg
Sandberg, Ryne Dee (Ryno)
B: Sep 18, 1959

Pos: 2B	BA: .290
Hits: 2,080	HRs: 240
RBI: 881	BB: 656

New Cubs General Manager Dallas Green had just been fired by the Phillies and he exacted the ultimate revenge – he took a future Hall of Fame player out of their system. Sandberg, who has a chance to be the best second baseman ever, was a steal as a last minute throw-in when Philadelphia dealt Larry Bowa for Ivan DeJesus in January 1982. Sandberg was the 1984 NL MVP on the strength of a .314 batting average, 114 runs scored, 36 doubles, 19 triples and 19 homers.

He has accumulated nine Gold Gloves and made ten straight All-Star Game appearances. He has already scored 1,143 runs, and stolen 323 bases. Sandberg emerged as a superstar on the nationally televised "Game of the Week," Memorial Day weekend, 1984. He pounded two clutch home runs, with men on base, off Cardinals ace reliever Bruce Sutter. The first one, in the bottom of the ninth, tied the score. The second won the game in extra innings.
Playing Career: *1981-; Phi N, Chi N*

Ryne Sandberg.

Ben Sanders
Sanders, Alexander Bennett
B: Feb 16, 1865   D: Aug 29, 1930

Pos: P	ERA: 2.98
W-L: 81-70	SOs: 486
ShOs: 10	Saves: 2

Southern-born in the waning days of the Civil War, Sanders went north to make his living playing baseball. He won 19 games in each of his first two years in Philadelphia, and won 20 in 1890. He became a Quaker City favorite as the team moved through three different leagues.
Playing Career: *1888-1892; Phi N, Phi P, Phi AA, Lou N*

Ken Sanders
Sanders, Kenneth George (Daffy)
B: Jul 8, 1941

Pos: P	ERA: 2.98
W-L: 29-45	SOs: 360
ShOs: 0	Saves: 86

A well-travelled reliever, Sanders reached his peak as a stopper with the Brewers, going 5-2 with 13 saves and a 1.75 ERA in 1970, then won seven with an AL-leading 83 games and 31 saves in 1971, the year he also led the league in losses, with 12. He posted a 1.92 ERA that season.
Playing Career: *1964, 1966, 1968, 1970-1976; KCA A, Bos A, Oak A, Mil A, Min A, Cle A, Cal A, NY N, KCR A*

Ray Sanders
Sanders, Raymond Floyd
B: Dec 4, 1916   D: Oct 28, 1983

Pos: 1B	BA: .274
Hits: 597	HRs: 42
RBI: 329	BB: 328

Sanders is the player who caused the Cardinals to trade first baseman Johnny Mize. Playing for the 1942-1944 NL pennant winners, Sanders hit .275 with two homers in 14 World Series games. Then when St. Louis had to make room for Stan Musial at first base, Sanders was traded.
Playing Career: *1942-1946, 1948-1949; StL N, Bos N*

Scott Sanderson
Sanderson, Scott Douglas
B: Jul 22, 1956

Pos: P	ERA: 3.74
W-L: 154-134	SOs: 1,506
ShOs: 14	Saves: 5

A control artist, Sanderson has been accused of throwing too many strikes, allowing batters to dig in on him. His teams have won three division titles and one pennant. Moribund with the Cubs, the big right-hander revived his career with Oakland, New York and California.
Playing Career: *1978-; Mon N, Chi N, Oak A, NY A, Cal A*

Jack Sanford
Sanford, John Stanley
B: May 18, 1929

Pos: P	ERA: 3.69
W-L: 137-101	SOs: 1,182
ShOs: 14	Saves: 11

After seven years in the minor leagues and a stint in the military, Sanford became the NL Rookie of the Year in 1957 at age 28. Chosen for the All-Star team that year, Sanford led the NL in strikeouts while going 19-8 with a 3.08 ERA and 15 complete games. He led the NL in shutouts in 1960, then produced a monster year in 1962. Sanford posted 24 victories, tossing 265 innings and shutting out the Yankees in Game Two of the 1962 World Series.
Playing Career: *1956-1967; Phi N, SF N, Cal A, KC A*

Manny Sanguillen
Sanguillen y Magan, Manuel de Jesus
B: Mar 21, 1944

Pos: C, OF, DH, 1B	BA: .296
Hits: 1,500	HRs: 65
RBI: 585	BB: 223

Sanguillen had no strike zone, putting the ball in play 95 percent of his at-bats in the major leagues. He walked only 223 times and struck out only 331 times. Using Sanguillen's big bat, the Pirates captured six division titles and two pennants. Overshadowed by the Reds' ace receiver Johnny Bench, Sanguillen nonetheless made the NL All-Star team three times, 1971, 1972 and 1975. Batting over .300 in his first three seasons, he peaked at .328 in 1975 when his walk total ballooned to 48,

The Pirates' Manny Sanguillen, 1972.

more than double any previous mark. In an odd deal, Sanguillen went to Oakland for Chuck Tanner and $100,000 in late 1976. Tanner became the Pirates' manager, and reacquired Sanguillen in April 1978. He stroked a two-out, ninth-inning pinch-hit single to win Game Two of the 1979 World Series. In two World Series, Sanguillen batted .375.
Playing Career: *1967, 1969-1980; Pit N, Oak A*

Rafael Santana
Santana y del la Cruz, Rafael Francisco
B: Jan 31, 1958

Pos: SS, 2B	BA: .246
Hits: 497	HRs: 13
RBI: 156	BB: 138

A strong-armed Dominican infielder, Santana was slated to be the Mets' shortstop of the future, but arm injuries slowed his career. He drove in a run and scored another in a dramatic seventh-inning rally that won the 1986 World Championship for the Mets.
Playing Career: *1983-1988, 1990; StL N, NY N, NY A, Cle A*

Benito Santiago
Santiago y Rivera, Benito
B: Mar 9, 1965

Pos: C	BA: .259
Hits: 866	HRs: 98
RBI: 425	BB: 176

The 1987 NL Rookie of the Year, Santiago put together a 34-game hitting streak, the longest in the NL since Pete Rose's 44-gamer. A four-time All-Star, Santiago has a rocket arm – he nailed 33 percent of base stealers in 1987 – and three Gold Glove Awards.
Playing Career: *1986-; SD N, Flo N*

Ron Santo
Santo, Ronald Edward
B: Feb 25, 1940

Pos: 3B	BA: .277
Hits: 2,254	HRs: 342
RBI: 1,331	BB: 1,108

An immensely popular Chicago area player, Santo gave Cubs fans nine All-Star seasons, scoring 1,138 runs on 365 doubles and 342 home runs. His RBI total is one of the highest for players who are not in the Hall of Fame. Santo's best overall season was 1964, when he hit .313 with 30 homers, 114 RBI, and a league-leading 13 triples. He followed with three more seasons of more than 30 home runs. Santo topped 100 RBI four times, and led the NL in walks four times. His on-base percentage was the best in the league twice.

Santo batted .312 in 1966, hitting in 28 consecutive games. The next year he set a record with 393 assists at the hot corner. An excellent fielder, he won five Gold Glove Awards, 1964-1968. Santo led NL third basemen in putouts and assist seven times, and double plays four times. An emotional player, Santo was the cheerleader for the 1969

Ron Santo.

Cubs during their run at the pennant. His post-game heel-clicking victory dance became a symbol in Chicago.
Playing Career: *1960-1974; Chi N, Chi A*

Louis Santop
Santop, Louis Loftin (Top)
B: Jan 17, 1890   D: Jan 6, 1942

Pos: C, OF	BA: .321
Hits: 236	HRs: 14
RBI: NA	BB: NA

A fearsome and confident slugger, Santop sometimes called his home runs before he hit them. At 6'4", 240 pounds, the left-handed-hitting catcher was one of black baseball's earliest superstars. He walloped tape-measure home runs in places where fences did not exist. In the early 1920s, Santop was paid $500 a month – an astonishing salary for black baseball – by the Hilldale club of the Eastern Colored League. He caught two of the all-time greats, Smokey Joe Williams and Cannonball Dick Redding. Santop is credited with batting as high as .470 against all levels of competition in 1911. After serving in the Navy during World War I, he finished his career with the Hilldales. In 1924 Santop hit .389, leading the Hilldales to another pennant. In 14 exhibition games against white major leaguers, he batted .296.
Playing Career: *1910-1926; Phi Giants, NY Lincoln Giants, NY Lincoln Stars, Brk Royal Giants, Phi Hilldales*

Hank Sauer
Sauer, Henry John
B: Mar 17, 1917

Pos: OF	BA: .266
Hits: 1,278	HRs: 288
RBI: 876	BB: 561

After several skirmishes, Sauer won a major league position on the strength of a 50-home run season for Syracuse in the 1947 International League. The onslaught continued in the majors, and Sauer was named NL MVP in 1952. That year he bashed 37 homers and drove in 121 runs, leading the NL in both categories. The two-time All-Star hit three home runs off Curt Simmons on two different occasions. Sauer belted 30 or more taters five straight years, 1948-1952, and hit 41 two years later.
Playing Career: *1941-1942, 1945, 1948-1959; Cin N, Chi N, StL N, NY N, SF N*

Carl Sawatski
Sawatski, Carl Ernest (Sweet Swats)
B: Nov 4, 1927   D: Nov 24, 1991

Pos: C	BA: .242
Hits: 351	HRs: 58
RBI: 213	BB: 191

Sawatski belted 132 home runs in his final four minor league seasons, then worked in the major leagues as a reserve catcher. His best year was 1961, when he hit .299 with 10 home runs and 10 pinch hits. Sawatski was president of the Texas League when he died suddenly, and it was discovered that he had no health insurance. The situation became a rallying point for better pay and benefits for minor league officials.
Playing Career: *1948, 1950, 1953-1954, 1957-1963; Chi N, Mil N, Phi N, StL N*

Eddie Sawyer
Sawyer, Edwin Milby
B: Sep 10, 1910

Managerial Record
Won: 390   Lost: 423   Pct: .480

An injury in the minors kept Sawyer from playing big league ball, but he made up for it as a manager. He piloted the Phillies to a tremendous extra-inning victory on the last day of the 1950 season, winning the NL pennant.
Managerial Career: *1948-1952, 1958-1960; Phi N*

Steve Sax
Sax, Stephen Louis
B: Jan 29, 1960

Pos: 2B, OF	BA: .282
Hits: 1,915	HRs: 53
RBI: 541	BB: 548

Unbelievably good some years, but inconsistent, Sax arrived in the big leagues with expectations that he would soon replace Ryne Sandberg as the best active second baseman. An All-Star appearance and Rookie of the Year honors in 1982 led fans to believe he was on track for the Superstar Express when an odd problem developed: inability to throw to first base on routine plays. This situation led to an exchange between Manager Tom Lasorda and third baseman Pedro Guerrero: "Pedro, what do you think about when the ball is hit?" Guerrero returned, "First I think, I hope they don't hit it to me. Then I think, I hope they don't hit it to Sax." Sax used a 25-game hitting streak in September 1986 to come within two points of the batting title. Becoming a free agent after the Dodgers' 1988 World Championship, he signed with New York, where he made the AL All-Star team. Steve and older brother Dave played four minor league seasons together.
Playing Career: *1981-1992; LA N, NY A, Chi A*

Steve Sax in 1988, his last year with the LA Dodgers.

George Scales
Scales, George (Tubby)
B: Aug 16, 1900   D: Apr 1976

Pos: 2B, 3B, OF, SS	BA: .309 (inc.)
Hits: 627 (inc.)	HRs: 66
RBI: NA	BB: NA

An intelligent clutch hitter, Scales batted fifth for the 1931 Homestead Grays, the team that compiled a record of 136-17. Scales hit .389, leading the league that year. He played in the Dominican Republic in 1937, and was an All-Star in 1943. A versatile player, he was credited with teaching Junior Gilliam major league infield skills.
Playing Career: *1921-1946; StL Giants, StL Stars, NY Lincoln Giants, Hom Grays, NY Black Yankees, Bal Elite Giants*

Doc Scanlan
Scanlan, William Dennis
B: Mar 7, 1881   D: May 29, 1949

Pos: P	ERA: 3.00
W-L: 66-71	SOs: 584
ShOs: 15	Saves: 5

Scanlan paid for his medical education by pitching in the NL. After coming up with the 1903 NL champion Pirates team, he was sold to the Dodgers, where he was 18-13 in 1906. In 1910 he posted a 2.61 ERA with a 9-11 record with Brooklyn. His younger brother, Frank Scanlan, pitched briefly for the Phillies.
Playing Career: *1903-1907, 1909-1911; Pit N, Brk N*

Ray Scarborough
Scarborough, Rae Wilson
B: July 23, 1917   D: Jul 1, 1982

Pos: P	ERA: 4.13
W-L: 80-85	SOs: 564
ShOs: 9	Saves: 12

A hot prospect with the Senators after World War II, Scarborough had to settle for spot starting with the Yankees, but it earned him a World Series ring in 1952. He batted .281 that year. His best record was 15-8 with a 2.82 ERA with Washington in 1948, and his best year at the plate was 1943, when he hit .333.
Playing Career: *1942-1943, 1946-1953; Was A, Chi A, Bos A, NY A, Det A*

Paul Schaal
Schaal, Paul
B: Mar 3, 1943

Pos: 3B, 2B, SS	BA: .244
Hits: 869	HRs: 57
RBI: 323	BB: 516

The third baseman for the 1965 Topps Rookie Team, Schaal studied medicine while holding down the hot corner until George Brett came along. Schaal's best season was 1971, when he played 161 games, batting .274 with 11 homers, 31 doubles and 103 walks.
Playing Career: *1964-1974; LA A, Cal A, KC A*

Germany Schaefer
Schaefer, Herman A.
B: Feb 4, 1877   D: May 16, 1919

Pos: 2B, 1B, 3B, SS, OF	BA: .257
Hits: 972	HRs: 9
RBI: 308	BB: 333

In a 1908 game, Schaefer stole second base. Failing to draw a throw, he returned to first and restole second. The next day, AL rule-makers made such plays illegal. He spent many years with the Senators, where he taught Nick Altrock how to clown.
Playing Career: *1901-1902, 1905-1916, 1918; Chi N, Det A, Was A, Nwk F, NY A, Cle A*

Ray Schalk
Schalk, Raymond William (Cracker)
B: Aug 12, 1892   D: May 19, 1970
Hall of Fame 1955

Pos: C	BA: .253
Hits: 1,345	HRs: 12
RBI: 594	BB: 638
Managerial Record	
Won: 102 Lost: 125 Pct: .449	

Schalk played for the 1919 White Sox, but was not a party to the World Series fix that got eight players banned for life. In fact, Schalk needled and cursed Chicago hurlers Eddie Cicotte and Lefty Williams as they delivered fat pitches to the Reds' batters. Schalk batted .304 in the Series. Catching a major league record four no-hitters, he received a great

White Sox catcher Ray Schalk.

deal of credit for the development of the White Sox pitching staff. In 1920 he caught four 20-game winners.

The 165-pound workhorse caught 100 or more games for 12 seasons. For eight consecutive years, Schalk led AL catchers in fielding and in putouts; he led four times in double plays, and twice in assists. His .989 fielding average in 1922 tied an AL record. Schalk set catching records for career games and putouts, and retains the career record for double plays as well as the AL mark for assists. An important innovator, he is credited with being the first catcher to back up plays at first and third base.
Playing Career: *1912-1929; Chi A, NY N*
Managerial Career: *1927-1928; Chi A*

Wally Schang in 1922.

Wally Schang
Schang, Walter Henry
B: Aug 22, 1889   D: Mar 6, 1965

Pos: C, OF, 3B	BA: .284
Hits: 1,506	HRs: 59
RBI: 710	BB: 849

His contemporaries believed Schang to be even a better catcher and hitter than Ray Schalk. Schang was traded three times to teams that immediately won pennants. He was a strong hitter who batted over .300 six times, and a good baserunner who stole 122 bases. His defensive skills were outstanding; Schang once threw out six Browns baserunners in one game. In another game he had eight assists for the Red Sox against the Indians. Both feats are AL records.

Playing on seven pennant-winning teams, Schang caught the leading AL pitchers of his day, including Herb Pennock, Joe Bush, Eddie Plank, Chief Bender, Babe Ruth, Waite Hoyt and Lefty Grove. In six World Series Schang batted .287, including a .357 mark in 1913, .444 in the Red Sox's six-game victory over the Cubs in 1918, and .318 in 1923. He was the first man to play for three different World Championship teams.
Playing Career: *1913-1931; Phi A, Bos A, NY A, StL A, Det A*

ABOVE: The powerful, switch-hitting outfielder, Ruben Sierra. (Photo by Louis Deluca/Allsport)

LEFT: The Phillies' 12-time All-Star third baseman Mike Schmidt. (Photo by Nancy Hogue)

BELOW: Hall of Famer Tom Seaver won 25 percent of the Mets' games from 1967 to 1976. (Photo by Chance Brockway)

LEFT: Flame-throwing Lee Smith is the all-time saves leader. (Photo by Stephen Dunn/Allsport)

ABOVE: Ted Simmons was a top catcher and slugging switch hitter for 21 years, 1968-1988. (Photo by Nancy Hogue)

BELOW: Willie Stargell set World Series records in 1979 with 25 total bases and seven extra-base hits. (Photo by Nancy Hogue)

OPPOSITE: Dodger favorite and Hall of Famer Duke Snider is the only man to hit four homers in two Fall Classics. (TV Sports Mailbag, Elmsford, NY)

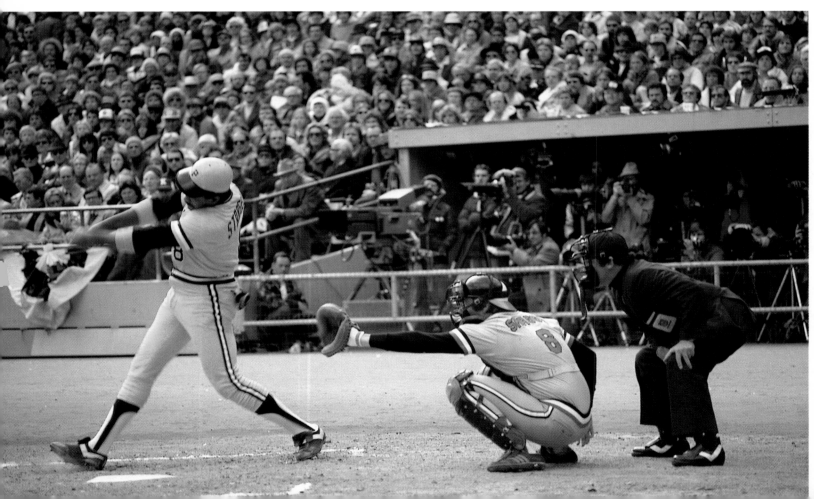

ABOVE: The winningest left-handed pitcher in baseball history and fifth overall, Hall of Famer Warren Spahn won 363 games during his 21-year career, 1942-1965. He recorded 20 or more victories for the Braves 13 times – eight of them league-leading marks. His 63 career shutouts is sixth of the all-time list. (Brompton Photo Library)

LEFT: In 1979, his first season as a regular, the Dodgers' Rick Sutcliffe earned NL Rookie of the Year honors. Five years later, in a season split between the Indians and Cubs, Sutcliffe went 20-6 to win the Cy Young Award. Joining Baltimore in 1992, the big right-hander won 16 games, including an Opening Day shutout at the new Camden Yards. (Photo by Nancy Hogue)

OPPOSITE: Don Sutton fanned 209 batters in his rookie 1966 season, the most by an NL rookie since 1911. With consistency and hard work, during his 23-year career the durable pitcher won 324 games – 58 of them shutouts. (Photo by Chance Brockway)

OPPOSITE: Danny Tartabull belted 25 or more homers for five of seven years from 1968 to 1992. He joined the Yankees in 1992. (Photo by Otto Greule, Jr./Allsport)

RIGHT: Eccentric and colorful Rube Waddell led the AL in 1905 with 26 wins, 287 strikeouts and a 1.48 ERA for the pennant-winning A's. (Brompton Photo Library)

MIDDLE RIGHT: Hall of Fame shortstop Honus Wagner batted .300 or better for 15 straight years, 1899-1913. (Brompton Photo Library)

FAR RIGHT: Talented Ted Williams earned six AL batting titles, two Triple Crowns and two MVP Awards during his Red Sox career. (Brompton Photo Library)

BELOW: Succeeding Ted Williams, Carl Yastrzemski also shaped a lengthy Hall of Fame career in Boston. He won the Triple Crown in 1967, then batted .400 in the World Series. (Photo by Malcolm Emmons).

TED WILLIAMS

LEFT: A consistent, dependable star for 14 seasons with the Cubs, Billy Williams began his Hall of Fame career as NL Rookie of the Year in 1961. (Photo by Malcolm Emmons) BELOW: In his 1982 AL MVP year, the Brewers' stalwart Robin Yount pounded two homers to clinch the pennant for Milwaukee on the final day of the season. He went on to hit .414 with two four-hit games in the World Series. (Photo by Malcolm Emmons)

Dan Schatzeder
Schatzeder, Daniel Ernest
B: Dec 1, 1954

Pos: P	ERA: 3.74
W-L: 69-68	SOs: 748
ShOs: 4	Saves: 10

A left-hander who could start or relieve, Schatzeder showed glimpses of greatness, as in 1990 when he posted a 2.20 ERA. He was an excellent hitter, compiling a .240 average. Schatzeder's five pinch hits in 1986 were the most by a pitcher since Don Newcombe in 1959.
Playing Career: *1977-1991; Mon N, Det A, SF N, Phi N, Min A, Cle A, Hou N, KC A*

Bob Scheffing
Scheffing, Robert Boden
B: Aug 11, 1913   D: Oct 26, 1985

Pos: C	BA: .263
Hits: 357	HRs: 20
RBI: 187	BB: 103
Managerial Record	
Won: 418 Lost: 427 Pct: .495	

As a catcher with the Cubs, Scheffing batted .300 in 293 at-bats, never batting more than 363 times in any season.

In the 1961 AL pennant race, Scheffing's Tigers finished second with 101 wins; Ralph Houk and the Yankees bested them by eight games. That season held valuable lessons for Norm Cash and Al Kaline, who remembered how to win. Seven seasons later the Tigers took the 1968 pennant.
Playing Career: *1941-1942, 1946-1951; Chi N, Cin N, StL N*
Managerial Career: *1957-1959, 1961-1963; Chi N, Det A*

Carl Scheib
Scheib, Carl Alvin
B: Jan 1, 1927

Pos: P	ERA: 4.88
W-L: 45-65	SOs: 290
ShOs: 6	Saves: 17

The youngest player in AL history, 16-year-old Scheib made his pro debut in the second game of a doubleheader on September 6, 1943. Returning from World War II, he was 14-8 with a 3.94 ERA. Scheib went to the bullpen in 1951, saving 10 games.
Playing Career: *1943-1945, 1947-1954; Phi A, StL N*

Fred Scherman
Scherman, Frederick John
B: Jul 25, 1944

Pos: P	ERA: 3.66
W-L: 33-26	SOs: 297
ShOs: 0	Saves: 39

A workhorse out of the Detroit bullpen in the early 1970s, Scherman relieved 170 times in three years, saving 33 contests. In 1973 Manager Billy Martin ordered him to throw spitballs in retaliation for Gaylord Perry's spitters. The resulting uproar led to Martin's dismissal.
Playing Career: *1969-1976; Det A, Hou N, Mon N*

Calvin Schiraldi
Schiraldi, Calvin Drew
B: Jun 16, 1962

Pos: P	ERA: 4.28
W-L: 21-39	SOs: 471
ShOs: 1	Saves: 21

A teammate of Roger Clemens, Greg Swindell and Bruce Ruffin on the 1983 Texas Longhorn NCAA baseball championship team, Schiraldi struggled to live up to his potential. His best year was 1986, when he was 4-2 with nine saves and a 1.41 ERA, but he lost three games in postseason play.
Playing Career: *1984-1991; NY N, Bos A, Chi N*

Calvin Schiraldi in the 1986 ALCS.

Gus Schmelz
Schmelz, Gustavus Heinrich
B: Sep 26, 1850   D: Oct 14, 1925

Managerial Record	
Won: 624 Lost: 703 Pct: .470	

Schmelz was a highly respected manager who believed the most important factor in success was the players' confidence in themselves and their leader. He had a big, thick beard and gave signals by pointing with it.
Managerial Career: *1884, 1886-1891, 1894-1897; Col AA, StL N, Cin AA, Cle N, Was N*

Boss Schmidt
Schmidt, Charles
B: Sep 12, 1880   D: Nov 14, 1932

Pos: C	BA: .243
Hits: 360	HRs: 3
RBI: 124	BB: 36

Strongman Schmidt once boxed against heavyweight champ Jack Johnson and administered several beatings to fiesty Ty Cobb. As the Tigers' spiritual leader, Schmidt helped them to three AL pennants.
Playing Career: *1906-1911; Det A*

Dave Schmidt
Schmidt, David Joseph
B: Apr 22, 1957

Pos: P	ERA: 3.88
W-L: 54-55	SOs: 479
ShOs: 3	Saves: 50

A career reliever, Schmidt found himself starting against the Blue Jays in the last week of the 1989 season with the division title on the line. He pitched well but was beaten, ending the Orioles' bid to go from last place to first in consecutive seasons.
Playing Career: *1981-1992; Tex A, Chi A, Bal A, Mon N, Sea A*

Mike Schmidt
Schmidt, Michael Jack
B: Sep 27, 1949

Pos: 3B, 1B, SS	BA: .267
Hits: 2,234	HRs: 548
RBI: 1,595	BB: 1,507

At bat and in the field, Schmidt was baseball's all-time best third baseman. Twelve times an All-Star, Schmidt led the NL in homers eight times, in slugging five times and in RBI four times. He is seventh on the all-time home run list. Schmidt led the league in walks and also in strikeouts four times; he is third on the all-time strikeout list. Strikeouts were troublesome early in his career, but he learned to be more selective, and became the consummate ballplayer.

One thinks of Schmidt as a hitter, but he was an outstanding fielder as well, and won 11 Gold Glove Awards. On July 17, 1976, he

Phillie Mike Schmidt on deck.

hit four dingers in one game at Wrigley Field, beating the Cubs 18-16 in 10 innings. His first homer came off Rick Reuschel, the fourth off Rick's brother, Paul. Banging 48 homers in 1980, he was the runaway selection for MVP, also taking the World Series MVP honors with a .381 average and two more homers in the Phillies' six-game victory. In the 1981 strike-shortened season, Schmidt won a second MVP Award.
Playing Career: *1972-1989; Phi N*

Walter Schmidt
Schmidt, Walter Joseph
B: Mar 20, 1887   D: Jul 4, 1973

Pos: C	BA: .257
Hits: 619	HRs: 3
RBI: 234	BB: 137

The younger brother of Boss Schmidt, Walter replaced George Gibson in the Pirates' platoon system. He did his job for nine years, hitting .282 in 114 games in 1921, and leading NL catchers in fielding. The next year Schmidt batted .329 in 40 games.
Playing Career: *1916-1925; Pit N, StL N*

Johnny Schmitz
Schmitz, John Albert (Bear Tracks)
B: Nov 27, 1920

Pos: P	ERA: 3.55
W-L: 93-114	SOs: 746
ShOs: 17	Saves: 19

Schmitz won almost 20 percent of the Cubs' victories against the Dodgers from 1941 through 1950. A two-time All-Star, he had an 11-11 record in 1946 and led the NL with 135 strikeouts. Schmitz won 18 games in 1948. Both years, he was the toughest NL hurler to bat against.
Playing Career: *1941-1942, 1946-1956; Chi N, Brk N, NY A, Cin N, Was A, Bos A, Bal A*

Pete Schneider
Schneider, Peter Joseph
B: Aug 29, 1895   D: Jun 1, 1957

Pos: P	ERA: 2.62
W-L: 58-86	SOs: 491
ShOs: 11	Saves: 4

Schneider won 20 games in 1917, but faltered the next year, going 10-15, walking 117 and striking out only 51. In 1923 Schneider hit five home runs in one Pacific Coast League game, knocking in 14 and claiming the pitching victory.
Playing Career: *1914-1919; Cin N, NY A*

Red Schoendienst
Schoendienst, Albert Fred
B: Feb 2, 1923
Hall of Fame 1989

Pos: 2B, OF, SS, 3B	BA: .289
Hits: 2,449	HRs: 84
RBI: 773	BB: 606
Managerial Record	
Won: 1,028 Lost: 944	Pct: .521

Red Schoendienst in the 1946 WS.

Since signing his first contract with St. Louis for $75 a month in 1942, Schoendienst has been in uniform for more than 50 years. He has worked for the Cardinals as a player, coach and manager, piloting them to pennants in 1967-1968. Schoendienst led the NL in stolen bases with 26 in 1945. The next year he led the league in fielding at the keystone sack for the first of six times. He handled 320 consecutive chances without an error in 1950. Schoendienst set a league fielding record in 1956 with a .9934 mark.

In the 1950 All-Star Game, the Redhead hit a dramatic 14th-inning home run to win it for the NL. He batted .342, finishing second to Carl Furillo, in the 1953 batting race. In 1957 Schoendienst led the NL with 200 hits, helping Milwaukee to the World Championship. The next year he played 106 games despite bruised ribs, a broken finger, and pleurisy. Tuberculosis cost him part of a lung in 1959, causing him to miss all but five games of the season.
Playing Career: *1945-1963; StL N, NY N, Mil N*
Managerial Career: *1965-1976, 1980; StL N*

Dick Schofield
Schofield, John Richard (Ducky)
B: Jan 7, 1935

Pos: SS, 3B, 2B	BA: .227
Hits: 699	HRs: 21
RBI: 211	BB: 390

Playing in the big leagues from age 18, Schofield was a weak hitter, though he batted .333 in two World Series. He played more than 100 games in only three seasons, but in one of them, 1965, he led NL shortstops in fielding. Richard Craig Schofield is his son.
Playing Career: *1953-1971; StL N, Pit N, SF N, NY A, LA N, Bos A, Mil A*

Dick Schofield
Schofield, Richard Craig
B: Nov 21, 1962

Pos: SS	BA: .228
Hits: 896	HRs: 52
RBI: 319	BB: 506

Like his father, Schofield was a weak hitter, but hit well in the big games, averaging .300 with one home run in the 1986 ALCS. He once hit a two-out grand slam in the bottom of the ninth to win 13-12 over Detroit, capping an eight-run rally that inning.
Playing Career: *1983-; Cal A, NY N, Tor A*

Ossee Schreckengost
Schreckengost, Ossee Freeman
(aka Ossee Schreck)
B: Apr 11, 1875   D: Jul 9, 1914

Pos: C	BA: .271
Hits: 828	HRs: 9
RBI: 338	BB: 102

Schreckengost was known for three things: he disdained shinguards, he discovered Rube Waddell, and he once demonstrated his opinion of a tough steak by nailing it to the dining room wall. Waddell and Schreckengost started their careers together with the Louisville Colonels.
Playing Career: *1897-1899, 1901-1908; Lou N, Cle N, StL N, Bos A, Cle A, Phi A, Chi A*

Pop Schriver
Schriver, William Frederick
B: Jul 11, 1865   D: Dec 27, 1932

Pos: C	BA: .264
Hits: 720	HRs: 16
RBI: 375	BB: 223

At Cap Anson's insistence, Schriver caught a ball dropped from the Washington Monument, and was the first to be successful, though the feat had been tried before. Schriver batted only 200 or 300 times per year, but hit over .300 on three occasions, in 1891, 1895 and 1897.
Playing Career: *1886, 1888-1895, 1897-1901; Brk AA, Phi N, Chi N, NY N, Cin N, Pit N, StL N*

Fred Schulte
Schulte, Fred William (Fritz)
B: Jan 13, 1901   D: May 20, 1983

Pos: OF	BA: .292
Hits: 1,241	HRs: 47
RBI: 593	BB: 462

Coming to the Senators with Goose Goslin in 1933, Fred Schulte had a solid .295 year as they won the AL pennant. Schulte led AL outfielders in putouts that year and capped the season by whacking .333 in the five-game World Series loss to the Giants. He managed and scouted in the minors for 18 years, from 1947 to 1964.
Playing Career: *1927-1937; StL A, Was A, Pit N*

Wildfire Schulte
Schulte, Frank M.
B: Sep 17, 1882   D: Oct 2, 1949

Pos: OF   BA: .270
Hits: 1,766   HRs: 93
RBI: 823   BB: 545

One of the first players to shave his bat handles thin and grip the stick at the very end, Wildfire Schulte was a slugger in the deadball era. He socked 21 homers – four of them grand slams – for the 1911 Cubs, and compiled a .534 slugging average with 105 runs scored, 107 RBI, 21 triples and 30 doubles. Schulte won the 1911 NL MVP Award, which was a Chalmers automobile. Playing in four World Series, he averaged .309, including .389 in 1908 and .353 in 1910.
Playing Career: *1904-1918; Chi N, Pit N, Phi N, Was A*

Barney Schultz
Schultz, George Warren
B: Aug 15, 1926

Pos: P   ERA: 3.63
W-L: 20-20   SOs: 264
ShOs: 0   Saves: 35

The star relief pitcher for the 1964 Cardinals, Schultz was as responsible as any starter for the Red Birds' surprise pennant that year. He saved 14 games and had a 1.64 ERA. It was his career year, marred only by losing Game Three of the World Series.
Playing Career: *1955, 1959, 1961-1965; StL N, Det A, Chi N*

Joe Schultz
Schultz, Joseph Charles, Jr.
B: Aug 29, 1918

Pos: C   BA: .259
Hits: 85   HRs: 18
RBI: 46   BB: 37
Managerial Record
Won: 78   Lost: 112   Pct: .411

The manager of the legendary Seattle Pilots, Schultz was made famous by Jim Bouton in his book, *Ball Four*, which chronicles the daily exploits of Schultz's bedraggled but hilarious club. Schultz once pinch-hit in the Texas League at age 13 while he was the batboy for the Houston club. Playing briefly on the 1944 Browns World Champions, he spent 50 years in baseball as player, coach and manager.
Playing Career: *1939-1941, 1943-1948; Pit N, StL A*
Managerial Career: *1969, 1973; Sea A, Det A*

Hal Schumacher
Schumacher, Harold Henry (Prince Hal)
B: Nov 23, 1910   D: Apr 21, 1993

Pos: P   ERA: 3.36
W-L: 158-121   SOs: 906
ShOs: 29   Saves: 7

The number two starter behind Carl Hubbell, Schumacher and he pitched the Giants to three pennants and one World Championship. He won 19 games in 1933, 23 in 1934 and 19 again in 1935. After a shoulder injury, Schumacher developed a palmball, notching 13 victories four years in a row. He almost died from heat exhaustion on the mound in St. Louis. After collapsing in the sixth inning, Schumacher had no heartbeat, but he was packed in ice and revived.
Playing Career: *1931-1942, 1946; NY N*

Ferdie Schupp
Schupp, Ferdinand Maurice
B: Jan 16, 1891   D: Dec 16, 1971

Pos: P   ERA: 3.32
W-L: 61-39   SOs: 553
ShOs: 11   Saves: 6

Schupp's arrival in New York coincided with the Giants' 26-game winning streak. He was 9-3 with an ERA of 0.90 that year, the lowest mark in NL history. Schupp posted 21 victories in 1917, and tossed a winning shutout in the 1917 World Series.
Playing Career: *1913-1922; NY N, StL N, Brk N, Chi A*

Don Schwall
Schwall, Donald Bernard
B: Mar 2, 1936

Pos: P   ERA: 3.72
W-L: 49-48   SOs: 408
ShOs: 5   Saves: 4

With a record of 15-7 and a 3.22 ERA, Schwall was the 1961 AL Rookie of the Year. Two years later he was in the bullpen. A 6'6" All-Big Eight basketball star at the University of Oklahoma, Schwall regained some of his lost glory with the Pirates, posting ERAs of 2.92 and 2.16.
Playing Career: *1961-1967; Bos A, Pit N, Atl N*

Mike Scioscia
Scioscia, Michael Lorri
B: Nov 27, 1958

Pos: C   BA: .259
Hits: 1,131   HRs: 68
RBI: 446   BB: 567

Signed as a free agent by the Padres in 1993, Mike Scioscia spent the entire year on the disabled list. Widely regarded as the best NL fielding catcher and a superb plate blocker, Scioscia was knocked unconscious by the Cardinals' Jack Clark, but still held the ball for the out. The two-time All-Star led the Dodgers to three division titles, two NL pennants, and two World Championships – one over the haughty Yankees and the other over the invincible A's. A good clutch hitter, Scioscia rapped a game-tying, ninth-inning homer off Dwight Gooden in Game Four of the 1988 NLCS, as the Dodgers went on to win in the 12th. He batted .364 with eight hits and three runs for the entire NLCS. He came back from a torn rotator cuff injury in 1983. He used good footwork and a quick release to make up for a weaker arm.
Playing Career: *1980-1992; LA N*

Herb Score
Score, Herbert Jude
B: Jun 7, 1933

Pos: P   ERA: 3.36
W-L: 55-46   SOs: 837
ShOs: 11   Saves: 3

In his first two AL seasons, Score struck out 508 batters, leading the league both years. Then a line drive from Gil McDougald bounced off his face. During his struggle to recover, Score set a minor league AA record with 330 strikeouts. He is now the Indians' radio announcer.
Playing Career: *1955-1962; Cle A, Chi A*

Mike Scioscia in the crouch for the Dodgers in 1989.

Everett Scott
Scott, Lewis Everett (Deacon)
B: Nov 19, 1892   D: Nov 2, 1960

Pos: SS	BA: .249
Hits: 1,455	HRs: 20
RBI: 549	BB: 243

Everett Scott played in 1,307 consecutive games, the major league record until Lou Gehrig came along. Although the streak overshadowed his entire career, Scott was an outstanding infielder, leading AL shortstops in fielding average for eight straight seasons, 1916-1923. He played on six pennant winners and appeared in five World Series for the Red Sox and Yankees, on the winning side four times, 1915-1916, 1918, 1923, batting .318 in the latter Series. In all, he played 27 World Series games, handling an even 150 chances with only three errors. His .980 Series fielding average included 17 double plays. Scott's best year was 1920, when he batted .269 with 21 doubles, 12 triples and four homers for the Red Sox. He slugged a career-high .369 that season. Sore knees ended his consecutive game streak in June 1925; ironically Lou Gehrig's 2,130-game streak began the same month. Scott played less than 100 games after his streak ended.
Playing Career: *1914-1926; Bos A, NY A, Was A, Chi A, Cin N*

George Scott
Scott, George Charles
B: Mar 23, 1944

Pos: 1B, 3B	BA: .268
Hits: 1,992	HRs: 271
RBI: 1,051	BB: 699

Despite his bulging waistline, Scott was an extremely good fielder, winning eight Gold

George Scott and son, 1970.

The Astros' Mike Scott gets wet after his no-hitter won the 1986 NL West title.

Gloves at first base. After winning the Eastern League Triple Crown in 1965, he was the AL's starting first sacker in the 1966 All-Star Game, his first of three appearances. Scott batted .303 as a key member of the Red Sox "Impossible Dream" 1967 pennant-winning team. He led the AL with 36 homers and 109 RBI in 1975 with the Brewers.
Playing Career: *1966-1979; Bos A, Mil A, KC A, NY A*

Jack Scott
Scott, John William
B: Apr 18, 1892   D: Nov 30, 1959

Pos: P	ERA: 3.85
W-L: 103-109	SOs: 657
ShOs: 11	Saves: 19

In two World Series, Scott compiled a record of 1-1 with a 3.00 ERA. In Game Three of the 1922 Series, he tossed a complete game shutout to defeat Waite Hoyt. Three times Scott led the NL in appearances. He had a .275 career batting average.
Playing Career: *1916-1917, 1919-1929; Pit N, Bos N, Cin N, NY N, Phi N*

Jim Scott
Scott, James (Death Valley)
B: Apr 23, 1888   D: Apr 7, 1957

Pos: P	ERA: 2.32
W-L: 107-113	SOs: 945
ShOs: 26	No-hitters: 1

Born in Deadwood, South Dakota, Scott later lived near Death Valley, California. In 1913 he was 20-20 with a 1.90 ERA, then compiled a 24-11 record with a 2.03 ERA in 1915. Scott once tossed a shutout in 68 minutes. He later umpired in the minors.
Playing Career: *1909-1917; Chi A*

Mike Scott
Scott, Michael Warren
B: Apr 26, 1955

Pos: P	ERA: 3.54
W-L: 124-108	SOs: 1,469
ShOs: 22	No-hitters: 1

In 1986 Scott was 31 years old, and had never struck out more than 137 batters in a season, when suddenly he caught fire. Scott captured the Cy Young Award after leading the NL in shutouts, innings pitched, ERA and whiffs – an amazing 306 of them. He also tossed a no-hitter in the Astros' division-clinching game. Unbeatable in the NLCS, Scott was 2-0 with a 0.50 ERA. He did it with a split-finger pitch, the type taught by Roger Craig.
Playing Career: *1979-1991; NY N, Hou N*

Tony Scott
Scott, Anthony
B: Sep 18, 1951

Pos: OF	BA: .249
Hits: 699	HRs: 17
RBI: 253	BB: 186

Traded by the Cardinals for future back-to-back 20-game winner Joaquin Andujar, Scott went to the Astros in a deal that helped win two pennants for the Red Birds and a division title for Houston. Scott's best year was 1979, when he batted .259 with 68 RBI.
Playing Career: *1973-1975, 1977-1984; Mon N, StL N, Hou N*

Rod Scurry
Scurry, Rodney Grant
B: Mar 17, 1956   D: Nov 5, 1992

Pos: P
W-L: 19-32
ShOs: 0

ERA: 3.24
SOs: 431
Saves: 39

Scurry had hot stuff, but he could not stay away from cocaine, and his career suffered. In 1982 he saved 14 games, going 4-5 with a 1.74 ERA. In 460 innings of work, Scurry struck out 431 batters.
Playing Career: *1980-1986, 1988; Pit N, NY A, Sea A*

Tom Seaton
Seaton, Thomas Gordon
B: Aug 30, 1887   D: Apr 10, 1940

Pos: P
W-L: 94-65
ShOs: 16

ERA: 3.14
SOs: 644
Saves: 11

Fellow Cornhuskers Grover Cleveland Alexander and Seaton provided the 1913 Phillies with a formidable 1-2 punch. Seaton was 27-12 and Alexander 22-8. Tainted by the Black Sox scandal, Seaton was blacklisted, but was cleared in Federal Court.
Playing Career: *1912-1917; Phi N, Brk F, Nwk F, Chi N*

Tom Seaver
Seaver, George Thomas (Tom Terrific, The Franchise)
B: Nov 17, 1944
Hall of Fame 1992

Pos: P
W-L: 311-205
ShOs: 61

ERA: 2.86
SOs: 3,640
No-hitters: 1

A champion on and off the field, Seaver is a beloved and much decorated hero. An All-

Tom Seaver.

Star 11 times, he won 20 or more games five times and 16 or more 12 times. Seaver led the NL in ERA three times. Starting out as Rookie of the Year in 1967, Seaver won Cy Young Awards in 1969, 1973 and 1975, and barely lost a fourth to rookie sensation Fernando Valenzuela in a controversial 1981 vote. Seaver posted a 14-2 record in the strike-shortened year.

Dubbed "The Franchise" because of his value to the Mets' organization, Seaver won crucial Game Four of the 1969 World Series, 2-1 in 10 innings, leading to their improbable World Championship. In 10 years, Seaver won 25 percent of the Mets' games. New Yorkers were wild with disbelief when he was left unprotected in the compensation draft and ended up with Cincinnati. The 17th 300-game winner in major league history, Seaver set a record by striking out 200 or more hitters in 10 seasons. On July 9, 1969, he lost a perfect game when Cubs rookie Jimmy Qualls singled with one out in the ninth. It was not perfect, but it was Terrific.
Playing Career: *1967-1986; NY N, Cin N, Chi A, Bos A*

Bob Seeds
Seeds, Robert Ira (Suitcase Bob)
B: Feb 24, 1907

Pos: OF
Hits: 537
RBI: 233

BA: .277
HRs: 28
BB: 160

"Have bat, will travel" was Seeds's motto. He once bought a Class D franchise in Texas, put his wife in charge and went to play baseball at a higher classification. Seeds once hit seven homers in two days, going 9-for-10 with 17 RBI in the 1938 International League.
Playing Career: *1930-1934, 1936, 1938-1940; Cle A, Chi A, Bos A, NY A, NY N*

Emmett Seery
Seery, John Emmett
B: Feb 13, 1861   D: Deceased

Pos: OF
Hits: 893
RBI: 300

BA: .252
HRs: 27
BB: 471

Seery played one game for the only UA team to make money, Kansas City. He also toiled for Kelly's Killers, a notorious club managed by King Kelly and familiar with every saloon and jail on the circuit. Seery hit .314 in 1889. He stole at least 240 bases – the statistics are incomplete.
Playing Career: *1884-1892; Bal U, KC U, StL N, Ind N, Brk P, Cin AA, Lou N*

Diego Segui
Segui y Gonzalez, Diego Pablo
B: Aug 17, 1937

Pos: P
W-L: 92-111
ShOs: 7

ERA: 3.81
SOs: 1,298
Saves: 71

A lukewarm starter with the early sixties Athletics, Segui got hotter with each passing

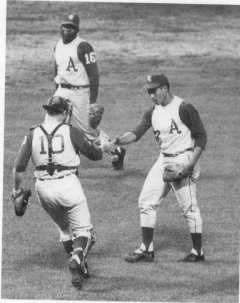

Diego Segui (right) in 1964.

year, and led the AL with a 2.56 ERA in 1970. In relief, Segui saved 12 games for the Seattle Pilots and 17 for the Cardinals. He pitched in the 1975 World Series.
Playing Career: *1962-1977; KC A, Was A, Sea P A, StL N, Bos A, Sea M A*

Socks Seibold
Seibold, Harry
B: Apr 3, 1896   D: Sep 21, 1965

Pos: P
W-L: 48-86
ShOs: 8

ERA: 4.43
SOs: 296
Saves: 5

Washing out as an infielder, Seibold was changed to a pitcher by Connie Mack. Relegated to second-division – often last-place – teams, Seibold struggled, retiring twice during the 1920s before gaining a starting role with the Braves. He won 15 games in 1930.
Playing Career: *1916-1917, 1919, 1929-1933; Phi A, Bos N*

Kip Selbach
Selbach, Albert Karl
B: Mar 24, 1872   D: Feb 17, 1956

Pos: OF
Hits: 1,803
RBI: 779

BA: .293
HRs: 44
BB: 783

At 5'7", 190 pounds, Selbach was pudgy and frequently the target of dissatisfied fans, especially in New York. His 1,064 runs and 334 stolen bases failed to stimulate the teams he played for, all but one finishing in the second division. With the Red Sox in 1904, Selbach made a sensational catch to end the game that won the pennant. He was a great bowler, winning the national doubles title in 1903 and captaining the Columbus national squad.
Playing Career: *1894-1906; Was N, Cin N, NY N, Bal A, Was A, Bos A*

Manager Frank Selee.

Frank Selee
Selee, Frank Gibson
B: Oct 26, 1859   D: Jul 5, 1909

Managerial Record
Won: 1,284   Lost: 862   Pct: .598

One of the best team builders in baseball history, Selee won five pennants for the Boston Beaneaters in the 1890s. He was a brilliant talent evaluator; he discovered Dummy Hoy and Kid Nichols. Selee won with his talent at all levels, capturing minor league flags at Oshkosh and Omaha before molding the Beaneaters into the finest 19th-century team. The nasty boys in Baltimore and Cleveland got the headlines, but Selee took the victories with the best fielding infield of the 1890s.

Boston's Jimmy Collins, Herman Long, Bobby Lowe and Fred Tenney pioneered defensive shifts and signals, and were expert at the 3-6-3 double play. In a 16-year career Selee never finished lower than fifth place. When he went to the Cubs, they had not had a winning record since the mid-1880s. He moved Frank Chance to first and traded Jack Taylor for Mordecai Brown. Tuberculosis forced Selee to turn the team over to Chance, but they won four flags in five years on Selee's groundwork. Twelve of his players are in the Hall of Fame, and a good case can be made for Selee himself.
Managerial Career: *1890-1905; Bos N, Chi N*

George Selkirk
Selkirk, George Alexander (Twinkle Toes)
B: Jan 4, 1908   D: Jan 19, 1987

Pos: 1B	BA: .290
Hits: 810	HRs: 108
RBI: 576	BB: 486

Replacing Babe Ruth in 1935, Selkirk was even given Ruth's uniform number – three. Selkirk batted over .300 in five of his first six seasons. A two-time All-Star, he played on six pennant-winning teams and five World Champion teams, batting .333 in the 1936 Series.
Playing Career: *1934-1942; NY A*

Dick Selma
Selma, Richard Jay
B: Nov 4, 1943

Pos: P	ERA: 3.62
W-L: 42-54	SOs: 681
ShOs: 6	Saves: 31

Selma tossed a 1-0 shutout with 13 K's in his second start in the majors. He won the 1969 expansion Padres' first game. Traded to Chicago, where he became the bleacher bums' cheerleader, he was rewarded with showers of coins from Wrigley Field fans.
Playing Career: *1965-1974; NY N, SD N, Chi N, Phi N, Cal A, Mil A*

Andy Seminick
Seminick, Andrew Wasil
B: Sep 12, 1920

Pos: C	BA: .243
Hits: 953	HRs: 164
RBI: 556	BB: 582

The Whiz Kid catcher, Seminick was a 1949 All-Star when he hit three homers in one game and contributed to the Phillies' five homers in one inning. He was involved in the celebrated fracas with opposing second baseman Eddie Stanky who waved his arms from the infield while Seminick batted in 1950.
Playing Career: *1943-1957; Phi N, Cin N*

Hank Severeid
Severeid, Henry Levai
B: Jun 1, 1891   D: Dec 17, 1968

Pos: C	BA: .289
Hits: 1,245	HRs: 17
RBI: 539	BB: 329

As a backup for the 1925 Senators and the 1926 Yankees, Severeid played in the World Series both years. Swinging a 48-ounce bat, he hit over .300 five times. After leaving the majors, Severeid batted over .300 for five seasons in the Pacific Coast League.
Playing Career: *1911-1913, 1915-1926; Cin N, StL A, Was A, NY A*

Ed Seward
Seward, Edward William
B: Jun 29, 1867   D: Jul 30, 1947

Pos: P	ERA: 3.40
W-L: 89-72	SOs: 589
ShOs: 13	No-hitters: 0

Seward won 35 games, leading the AA in shutouts and strikeouts in 1888. He was very popular in Philadelphia before injuries ended his career prematurely.
Playing Career: *1885, 1887-1891; Pro N, Phi AA, Cle N*
Umpiring Career: *1893; NL*

Joe Sewell
Sewell, Joseph Wheeler
B: Oct 9, 1898   D: Mar 6, 1990
Hall of Fame 1977

Pos: SS, 3B, 2B	BA: .312
Hits: 2,226	HRs: 49
RBI: 1,051	BB: 844

Few rookies have faced a more emotional debut than Sewell. Signed off the University of Alabama campus, Sewell stepped into the Indians' lineup in 1920, taking Ray Chapman's place following his death from being struck by a Carl Mays pitch. It was August and the Indians were in a hot pennant race with the White Sox and Yankees. Sewell came through, batting .329 in the remaining 22 games as the Indians held off challengers.

Sewell was the most difficult man to strike out in the history of the game, fanning only

Brothers Joe (l) and Luke Sewell played together with the Indians from 1920 to 1930.

114 times in 7,132 at-bats, and most of those early in his career. Twice he struck out only three times all year! In three other seasons, he whiffed only four times. A terrific hitter, Sewell socked 436 doubles, five times hitting more than 40 in one season, and leading the AL in 1924 with 45 two-baggers. An able fielder as well, he led AL shortstops in fielding three of four years, 1925-1928. He joined the Yankees in 1931, and hit .333 for them in the 1932 World Series.

Playing Career: *1920-1933; Cle A, NY A*

Luke Sewell
Sewell, James Luther
B: Jan 5, 1901   D: May 14, 1987

Pos: C	BA: .259
Hits: 1,393	HRs: 20
RBI: 696	BB: 486

Managerial Record
Won: 606   Lost: 644   Pct: .485

The younger brother of Hall of Famer Joe Sewell, Luke spent 40 years in baseball as a player, manager and coach. He played on one pennant-winning team, the 1933 Senators, and managed one, the 1944 Browns. Taught by the Indians' Steve O'Neill, Sewell brought defense and leadership to the catcher position. Appearing in a career-high 141 games in 1933, he led the Senators to the AL pennant.

As manager of the Browns, Sewell skillfully wove 4Fs and career minor leaguers into a championship blend that captured the 1944 AL pennant on the last day of the season. The next year, he became resentful of the ownership, who sent him the one-armed outfielder Pete Gray. Sewell felt that the defending AL champs were no team to be using gimmicks to draw crowds. He coached in 1939-1941 and 1949, then managed in the minors during the 1950s.

Playing Career: *1921-1939, 1942; Cle A, Was A, Chi A, StL A*
Managerial Career: *1941-1946, 1949-1952; StL A, Cin N*

Rip Sewell
Sewell, Truett Banks
B: May 11, 1907   D: Sep 3, 1989

Pos: P	ERA: 3.48
W-L: 143-97	SOs: 636
ShOs: 20	Saves: 15

The hoopla surrounding Sewell's famous blooper pitch, or "eephus" ball as he called it, overshadowed his significant career as a top NL starter. Playing all but his first year in Pittsburgh, Sewell won 21 games in back-to-back seasons, 1943-1944, and was selected for the All-Star team both years. He set NL pitchers' records for chances accepted in a game with 12, including 11 assists in a game in 1941. He also had three assists in one inning. Sewell became an outspoken critic of the new players' union organized by Robert Murphy after World War II.

Playing Career: *1932, 1938-1949; Det A, Pit N*

Socks Seybold
Seybold, Ralph Orlando
B: Nov 23, 1870   D: Dec 22, 1921

Pos: OF, 1B	BA: .294
Hits: 1,084	HRs: 51
RBI: 556	BB: 293

Seybold held the AL home run record that Babe Ruth shattered in 1919. When Connie Mack went from the Western League to the newly formed AL in 1901, he took Seybold with him. That year, the outfielder compiled a 27-game hitting streak. A victim of the new foul strike rule, Seybold's slugging average dropped 100 points when umpires began to call foul balls strikes. He had two unassisted double plays from the outfield in 1907.

Playing Career: *1899, 1901-1908; Cin N, Phi A*

Cy Seymour
Seymour, James Bentley
B: Dec 9, 1872   D: Sep 20, 1919

Pos: OF, P	BA: .304
Hits: 1,722	HRs: 52
RBI: 799	BB: 354

Pos: P	ERA: 3.70
W-L: 63	SOs: 584
ShOs: 6	Saves: 1

A good pitcher and a heavy hitter, Seymour played outfield and pitched until his control deserted him. He led the NL in bases on balls two straight seasons, 1897-1898. In the latter year, Seymour compiled a record of 25-19, leading the league with 239 strikeouts and 219 walks. He posted a 3.19 ERA – a good mark for the heavy-hitting period in which he worked. John McGraw turned Seymour into a full-time outfielder. He batted .303 with 84 runs scored for the AL Orioles in 1901.

The next time McGraw saw Seymour, he was a slugger for the Reds, leading the 1905

Cy Seymour.

NL in hits, doubles, triples, RBI and batting and slugging averages. McGraw got him back the next year. Seymour figured in the Giants' exciting 1908 pennant drive when, playing shallow as was his custom, he allowed Joe Tinker's fly ball to go over his head for a triple in the playoff game. Reportedly he took refuge in the clubhouse and wept about the mistake.

Playing Career: *1896-1910, 1913; NY N, Bal A, Cin N, Bos N*

Orator Shaffer
Shaffer, George
B: 1852   D: Deceased

Pos: OF, 2B, 1B	BA: .282
Hits: 1,000	HRs: 11
RBI: 241 (inc.)	BB: 227

Shaffer played for three famous teams: the 1877 Louisville club that was caught throwing games and had four players who were banned for life; the 1878 Indianapolis team that had The Only Nolan, who pitched his club into the NL; and the UA St. Louis squad that won 83 percent of their games, an all-time record. With the latter he led the league in doubles with 40 in 1884.

Playing Career: *1874-1875, 1877-1886, 1890; Har Dark Blues n, NY Mutuals n, Phi White Stockings n, Lou N, Ind N, Chi N, Cle N, Buf N, StL U , StL N, Phi AA*

Art Shamsky
Shamsky, Arthur Louis
B: Oct 14, 1941

Pos: OF, 1B	BA: .253
Hits: 426	HRs: 68
RBI: 233	BB: 188

A Mets hero, Shamsky hit a career-high .300 in the regular season, then hit .538 in the 1969 NLCS to drive his team into the World Series. Shamsky had homered in four consecutive at-bats in 1966, hitting 21 round-trippers in 96 games that year.

Playing Career: *1965-1972; Cin N, NY N, Chi N, Oak A*

Howie Shanks
Shanks, Howard Samuel (Hank)
B: Jul 21, 1890   D: Jul 30, 1941

Pos: OF, 3B, SS, 2B, 1B	BA: .253
Hits: 1,440	HRs: 25
RBI: 619	BB: 414

Despite having little power, Shanks performed in 1,665 games over a span of 14 years, an unusually high number of appearances for a utility player. A true jack-of-all-trades, he led AL third basemen in fielding and the league in triples when he got to play the entire 1921 season at one postion. Shanks also hit .302 that year. During his career he stole 185 bases, but was thrown out more than 100 times. Shanks belted 96 triples and 211 doubles.

Playing Career: *1912-1925; Was A, Bos A, NY A*

Mike Shannon
Shannon, Thomas Michael (Moonman)
B: Jul 15, 1939

Pos: 3B, OF	BA: .255
Hits: 710	HRs: 68
RBI: 367	BB: 224

Now a popular Cardinals broadcaster, Shannon hit three home runs, driving in eight runs in three World Series for the Red Birds, 1964, 1967 and 1968. When Roger Maris came along to play right field in 1967, Shannon moved to third base.
Playing Career: *1962-1970; StL N*

Spike Shannon
Shannon, William Porter
B: Feb 7, 1878   D: Apr 12, 1970

Pos: OF	BA: .259
Hits: 677	HRs: 3
RBI: 183	BB: 286

Shannon's fielding and batting ability accounted for the Cardinals' rise from last place to fifth in 1904. In 1907 John McGraw purchased him for $10,000 to bat leadoff for the Giants. Shannon led the NL in runs scored with 104 that year.
Playing Career: *1904-1908; StL N, NY N, Pit N*
Umpiring Career: *1914-1915; FL*

Bobby Shantz in 1952, his MVP year.

Bobby Shantz
Shantz, Robert Clayton
B: Sep 26, 1925

Pos: P	ERA: 3.38
W-L: 119-99	SOs: 1,072
ShOs: 16	Saves: 48

A slick-fielding left-hander, Shantz won 24 games for the fifth-place Athletics in 1952. He was honored with the AL MVP Award. The winner of eight Gold Gloves, Shantz was put on the All-Star roster three times. He tossed nine hitless innings in his major league debut, winning the 13-inning contest in relief. Coming to the Yankees in a 12-player deal, Shantz revived his career by winning the 1957 ERA title. He pitched for four pennant winners and in two World Series.
Playing Career: *1949-1964; Phi A, NY A, Pit N, Hou N, StL N, Chi N, Phi N*

Bill Sharsig
Sharsig, William A.
B: 1855   D: Feb 1, 1902

Managerial Record
Won: 271   Lost: 239   Pct: .531

Highly respected by his contemporaries, Sharsig was considered an able teacher. Both Harry Stovey and Wilbert Robinson benefited from his tutorial sessions. Sharsig came to the Athletics during the tumultuous Players' League war.
Managerial Career: *1886, 1888-1891; Phi AA*

Joe Shaute
Shaute, Joseph Benjamin (Lefty)
B: Aug 1, 1899   D: Feb 21, 1970

Pos: P	ERA: 4.15
W-L: 99-109	SOs: 512
ShOs: 5	Saves: 18

In his major league debut, and on at least 29 other occasions, Shaute struck out Babe Ruth. Ruth tried to even the score in 1927, socking three homers off him. Shaute won 20 in 1924 and posted a 3.75 ERA.
Playing Career: *1922-1934; Cle A, Brk N, Cin N*

Bob Shaw
Shaw, Robert John
B: Jun 29, 1933

Pos: P	ERA: 3.52
W-L: 108-98	SOs: 880
ShOs: 14	Saves: 32

One of the men who gave pitchers the reputation of being flaky, Shaw nonetheless turned in solid performances. He won 18 games with a 2.69 ERA for the Go-Go White Sox in 1959, and notched another in the World Series. His *How to Pitch* book was a top-selling instructional aid and is still in use. An All-Star in 1962, Shaw was 15-9 with a 2.80 ERA for the Braves, replacing Bob Buhl in the pitching rotation.
Playing Career: *1957-1967; Det A, Chi A, KC A, Mil N, SF N, NY N, Chi N*

Dupee Shaw
Shaw, Frederick Lander
B: May 31, 1859   D: Jun 11, 1938

Pos: P	ERA: 3.10
W-L: 83-121	SOs: 950
ShOs: 13	No-hitters: 1

In 1884, overhand pitching was allowed in all of the major leagues for the first time. Since batters had never seen an overhand curve, they whiffed at record rates. Shaw fanned 142 in the NL and 309 in the UA, totaling 451 K's in 1884, the fourth highest total ever.
Playing Career: *1883-1888; Det N, Bos U, Pro N, Was N*

Jim Shaw
Shaw, James Aloysius (Grunting Jim)
B: Aug 19, 1893   D: Jan 27, 1962

Pos: P	ERA: 3.07
W-L: 84-98	SOs: 767
ShOs: 17	Saves: 17

A workhorse who was tortured by a bad hip, Shaw started and relieved, leading the AL in saves twice and in games and innings pitched once. When he pitched, Shaw exerted so much effort that he grunted loudly – like Nolan Ryan – with each throw.
Playing Career: *1913-1921; Was A*

White Sox pitcher Bob Shaw clowns around on a police motorcycle in 1959.

Yankee ace Bob Shawkey.

Bob Shawkey
Shawkey, James Robert (Sailor Bob, Bob the Gob)
B: Dec 4, 1890   D: Dec 31, 1980

Pos: P	ERA: 3.09
W-L: 196-150	SOs: 1,360
ShOs: 33	Saves: 27
Managerial Record	
Won: 86 Lost: 68 Pct: .558	

The Yankees' ace for eight years, Shawkey pitched for seven pennant-winning teams, including the 1913-1914 Athletics. After his playing career, Shawkey got the job that Babe Ruth wanted, when he replaced Miller Huggins as Yankee manager. As a pitcher, Shawkey was another of Connie Mack's finds, going 16-8 in 1914. Moving to the Yanks in 1915, he won 24 in 1916 and saved eight. Most of 1918 was spent in the Navy as a petty officer aboard the battleship *Arkansas*, hence the nautical nicknames. Three more times he won exactly 20 games, 1919-1920, 1922, and led the AL with a 2.45 ERA in 1920. He tossed seven 1-0 wins, a Yankee record. In 1923 he pitched the first game played at Yankee Stadium, beating the Red Sox 3-1; appropriately, Ruth walloped the first Stadium homer, but Shawkey got the second. He had a long career in the minors, managing and coaching in the Pirate and Tiger farm systems. He was later the baseball coach at Dartmouth. As an old man, he threw out the first ball at refurbished Yankee Stadium in 1976.
Playing Career: *1913-1927; Phi A, NY A*
Managerial Career: *1930; NY A*

Spec Shea
Shea, Francis Joseph (The Naugatuck Nugget)
B: Oct 2, 1920

Pos: P	ERA: 3.80
W-L: 56-46	SOs: 361
ShOs: 12	Saves: 5

Breaking in with a 14-5 record, Shea made the All-Star team and won two more games in the 1947 World Series. Batters hit only .200 off him that year. A neck injury limited his effectiveness and forced him to visit chiropractors in each AL city.
Playing Career: *1947-1949, 1951-1955; NY A, Was A*

Jimmy Sheckard
Sheckard, Samuel James Tilden
B: Nov 23, 1878   D: Jan 15, 1947

Pos: OF	BA: .274
Hits: 2,085	HRs: 56
RBI: 813	BB: 1,135

The catalyst for the great Cubs teams of 1906-1910, Sheckard was an extraordinary baserunner, stealing 465, with a high of 77 in 1899. In 1911 Sheckard announced that anyone could draw walks, and that he would prove it by trying for a walk each time at bat. He drew a record 147 bases on balls. The record stood as the NL mark until Eddie Stanky broke it in 1949. Sheckard also scored 121 runs and posted a .434 on-base percentage, easily tops in the NL in 1911.

Sheckard had his best years with Brooklyn, batting .353 while leading the league with 19 triples and a .536 slugging percentage for the 1901 Superbas. His 11 homers and 104 RBI were career highs. In 1903 his nine home runs captured the NL title. He also tied for the league lead with 67 stolen bases. Sheckard played on five pennant-winning teams, batting .286 in the 1910 World Series.
Playing Career: *1897-1913; Brk N, Bal N, Bal A, Chi N, StL N, Cin N*

Jimmy Sheckard.

Earl Sheely
Sheely, Earl Homer (Whitey)
B: Feb 12, 1893   D: Sep 16, 1952

Pos: 1B	BA: .300
Hits: 1,340	HRs: 48
RBI: 747	BB: 563

Sheely replaced banned Black Sox player Chick Gandil at first base. More of a slugger and less of a fancy fielder than Gandil, Sheely nonetheless led the league in fielding average twice. He drove in more than 100 runs twice and hit more than 25 doubles six times.
Playing Career: *1921-1927, 1929, 1931; Chi A, Pit N, Bos N*

John Shelby
Shelby, John T.
B: Feb 23, 1958

Pos: OF	BA: .239
Hits: 739	HRs: 70
RBI: 313	BB: 182

Highlights of Shelby's 11-year career included batting .444 in the 1983 World Series and belting a career-high 22 homers in 1987. He made a shoestring catch that was the last out of Game Four of the 1988 NLCS, saving the Dodgers' 12-inning victory.
Playing Career: *1981-1991; Bal A, LA N, Det A*

Willie Sherdel
Sherdel, William Henry (Wee Willie)
B: Aug 15, 1896   D: Nov 14, 1968

Pos: P	ERA: 3.72
W-L: 165-146	SOs: 839
ShOs: 12	Saves: 26

Happy-go-lucky Sherdel fired a quick pitch over the plate for strike three against Babe Ruth in the 1928 World Series, but the Cardinals and Yankees had agreed before the Series that no quick pitches would be used. Given a reprieve, the Babe homered seconds later. Sherdel won 21 games with a 2.86 ERA in 1928. He led the NL in saves three times. Sherdel once entered a game with the bases loaded and no outs, and tossed one pitch, getting a triple play.
Playing Career: *1918-1932; StL N, Bos N*

Pat Sheridan
Sheridan, Patrick Arthur
B: Dec 4, 1957

Pos: OF	BA: .253
Hits: 611	HRs: 51
RBI: 257	BB: 236

Sheridan hit three ALCS homers. In 1985 his ninth-inning pinch homer tied Game Two; in Game Seven his shot in the fourth inning was a catalyst in the Royals' 6-2 victory; and in the 1987 ALCS, Sheridan's two-run, eighth-inning home run won Game Three for the Tigers.
Playing Career: *1981, 1983-1989, 1991; KC A, Det A, SF N*

Dodgers swarm around reliever Larry Sherry (center left, smiling), 1959 WS.

Larry Sherry
Sherry, Lawrence
B: Jul 25, 1935

Pos: P	ERA: 3.67
W-L: 53-44	SOs: 606
ShOs: 1	Saves: 82

A genuine World Series hero, Sherry won two, saved two and posted an ERA of 0.50 in the 1959 Fall Classic for the Dodgers. He later relieved with the Tigers, saving 20 games in 1966. His brother Norm was a reserve catcher and Dodger teammate from 1959 to 1962.
Playing Career: *1958-1968; LA N, Det A, Hou N, Cal A*

Bill Shettsline
Shettsline, William Joseph
B: Oct 25, 1863   D: Feb 22, 1933

Managerial Record
Won: 367   Lost: 303   Pct: .548

For more than 44 years, Shettsline worked in Philadelphia as a ticket seller, manager, president and business manager. Shettsline even managed the 1902 Phillies' pro football team that starred Rube Waddell.
Managerial Career: *1898-1902; Phi N*

Ben Shibe
Shibe, Benjamin Franklin
B: Jan 23, 1838   D: Jan 14, 1922

An injury required Shibe to wear a leg brace, and aroused his interest in the development of sports equipment. Joining Al Reach's sporting goods firm, Shibe developed the two-piece "figure-eight" baseball cover, which replaced the "lemon peel" style cover in use at the time. In 1910 he introduced the cork-center ball, bringing on the lively ball era. The rubber centers previously used were "dead" and could be manipulated by heating or cooling them – Connie Mack used a freezer in the Pirates' office to chill game balls.

Shibe became a team owner when Ban Johnson, founder of the AL, approached him about sponsoring a club in Philadelphia. Shibe and Connie Mack – his partner on the field – gave Philadelphia fans six pennants and three World Championships. Shibe's decision to build a concrete and reinforced steel stadium touched off a wave of ballpark building. The choice of stairways became a negative example, and ramps became *de rigueur* for ballpark construction. Shibe also instituted the use of a big scoreboard to help all the fans follow the game.

Browns pitcher Urban Shocker.

Bill Shindle
Shindle, William
B: Dec 5, 1863   D: Jun 3, 1936

Pos: 3B, SS	BA: .269
Hits: 1,560	HRs: 30
RBI: 758	BB: 388

Scoring 993 runs and stealing 316 bases, Shindle was considered a reliable veteran player. He had broken in with the Detroit Wolverines in 1887, the squad that decimated the defending World Champion Browns in a 15-game World Series. In the 1890 Players' League, Shindle ripped 21 doubles, 21 triples and batted .322. His leaving the Orioles made room for a kid named John McGraw. Shindle stayed with the Dodgers until they got good in 1899.
Playing Career: *1886-1898; Det N, Bal AA, Phi P, Phi N, Bal N, Brk N*

Bob Shirley
Shirley, Robert Charles
B: Jun 25, 1954

Pos: P	ERA: 3.82
W-L: 67-94	SOs: 790
ShOs: 2	Saves: 18

Seattle Seahawks wide receiver Steve Largent was Shirley's high school catcher. Shirley fanned 11 Reds in his 1977 debut. He once retired the first 25 Astros he faced before settling for a 4-2 win. After a good rookie season, Shirley's career faded.
Playing Career: *1977-1987; SD N, StL N, Cin N, NY A, KC A*

George Shoch
Shoch, George Quintus
B: Jan 6, 1859   D: Sep 30, 1937

Pos: OF, SS, 2B, 3B	BA: .265
Hits: 671	HRs: 10
RBI: 323	BB: 298

A teammate of Connie Mack on the 1886 Senators, Shoch was a utility fielder throughout his NL career. He played on the AA Milwaukee nine that replaced Kelly's Killers in the league. Shoch's best year was 1894 when he hit .322. He stole 138 career bases.
Playing Career: *1886-1889, 1891-1897; Was N, Mil AA, Bal N, Brk N*

Urban Shocker
Shocker, Urban James
B: Aug 22, 1890   D: Sep 9, 1928

Pos: P	ERA: 3.17
W-L: 187-117	SOs: 979
ShOs: 28	Saves: 25

One of the great names in baseball, Urban Shocker was born with an even more entertaining moniker – Urbain Jacques Shockcor. He was one of the top pitchers of the 1920s, winning 61 percent of his games. In a 13-year career Shocker never had a losing season. Originally a catcher, he showed such accuracy in his throws that he was switched to the

Phillies Manager Burt Shotton.

Chris Short
Short, Christopher Joseph
B: Sep 19, 1937   D: Aug 1, 1991

Pos: P	ERA: 3.43
W-L: 135-132	SOs: 1,629
ShOs: 24	Saves: 18

A 20-game winner in 1966, Short was the first Phillies left-hander since Eppa Rixey to reach that mark. A two-time All-Star, Short fanned 18 hitters in 15 innings of an 18-inning 0-0 game in 1965. Severe back trouble ended his career.
Playing Career: *1959-1973; Phi N, Mil A*

Burt Shotton
Shotton, Burton Edwin (Barney)
B: Oct 18, 1884   D: Jul 29, 1962

Pos: OF, 1B	BA: .270
Hits: 1,338	HRs: 9
RBI: 290	BB: 714
Managerial Record	
Won: 697 Lost: 764 Pct: .477	

The dapper Shotton was the last manager to wear street clothes on the bench. As a surprise substitute for Dodgers manager Leo Durocher – who had been suspended for one year by Commissioner Happy Chandler – Shotton won the 1947 NL pennant. Branch Rickey's Sunday manager, Shotton apprenticed with the dreadful Phillies, then won two pennants with the Dodgers.
Playing Career: *1909, 1911-1923; StL A, Was A, StL N*
Managerial Career: *1928-1934, 1947-1950; Phi N, Cin N, Brk N*

Clyde Shoun
Shoun, Clyde Mitchell (Hardrock)
B: Mar 20, 1912   D: Mar 20, 1968

Pos: P	ERA: 3.91
W-L: 73-59	SOs: 483
ShOs: 3	No-hitters: 1

Swapped for Dizzy Dean in 1938, Shoun starred as a reliever for the Cardinals. He appeared in 147 games over the next three years. Starting only 85 times in his career, Shoun tossed a no-hitter in May 1944 over Jim Tobin, who had tossed one 18 days earlier.
Playing Career: *1935-1944, 1946-1949; Chi N, StL N, Cin N, Bos N, Chi A*

Eric Show
Show, Eric Vaughn
B: May 19, 1956

Pos: P	ERA: 3.66
W-L: 101-69	SOs: 971
ShOs: 11	Saves: 7

Pete Rose got hit number 4,192 off Show. In 1988 Show posted 16 victories. The Padres' all-time win and strikeout leader, Show is second in games, shutouts and complete games. He pitched in the 1984 NLCS and World Series.
Playing Career: *1981-1991; SD N, Oak A*

Frank Shugart
Shugart, Frank Harry
B: Dec 10, 1866   D: Sep 9, 1944

Pos: SS, OF	BA: .267
Hits: 804	HRs: 22
RBI: 384	BB: 218

Starting his career in the Players' League for the champion Chicagos, Shugart hit three home runs in one game for St. Louis in 1894. A year later, he bashed three triples in a game. He hit 110 doubles and 101 triples and home runs combined.
Playing Career: *1890-1895, 1897, 1901; Chi P, Pit N, StL N, Lou N, Phi N, Chi A*

Norm Siebern
Siebern, Norman Leroy
B: Jul 26, 1933

Pos: 1B	BA: .272
Hits: 1,217	HRs: 132
RBI: 636	BB: 708

Named the Minor League Player of the Year in 1957, Siebern hit .300 as a rookie in the majors. The three-time All-Star first baseman reached career highs with 25 homers, 114 runs, 117 RBI, 110 walks, and a .308 batting average in 1962. Sieburn played in three World Series.
Playing Career: *1956, 1958-1968; NY A, KC A, Bal A, Cal A, SF N, Bos A*

Dick Siebert
Siebert, Richard Walther
B: Feb 19, 1912   D: Dec 9, 1978

Pos: 1B	BA: .282
Hits: 1,104	HRs: 32
RBI: 482	BB: 276

An All-Star in 1943, Siebert had batted .334 two years earlier, and led the AL in assists two years later. After his playing career, Siebert became baseball coach at the University of Minnesota, where his teams won the College World Series six times.
Playing Career: *1932, 1936-1945; Brk N, StL N, Phi A*

Sonny Siebert
Siebert, Wilfred Charles
B: Jan 14, 1937

Pos: P	ERA: 3.21
W-L: 140-114	SOs: 1,512
ShOs: 21	No-hitters: 1

Twenty-eight years old before he was a regular starter, Siebert got busy and had an eventful career. He won 16 games three times, and posted four straight ERAs under 2.98. Siebert led the AL with a .667 winning percentage in 1966. In the All-Star Game that year, he pitched two scoreless innings. With the Red Sox Siebert won 57 games in four years and even hit six home runs in 1971. He saved 16 games.
Playing Career: *1964-1975; Cle A, Bos A, Tex A, StL N, SD N, Oak A*

mound. Throwing a spitball and a slow breaking curve, his delivery was helped by a permanent crook in the end joint of his ring finger. He always said the crooked finger improved his grip and effectiveness.

Turned down by the Yankees early in his career, Shocker flourished with the Browns, posting more than 20 victories four straight years. He was particularly tough on the Yankees, who reacquired him in self-defense in 1924. Shocker then had his worst season in 1925, the year of the great Yankee slump. He won 37 games over the next two years, both pennant-winning seasons. Retiring early in 1928, Shocker had brief success with his radio show until his death later that year.
Playing Career: *1916-1928; NY A, StL A*

Ernie Shore
Shore, Ernest Grady
B: Mar 24, 1891   D: Sep 24, 1980

Pos: P	ERA: 2.45
W-L: 65-43	SOs: 311
ShOs: 9	No-hitters: 1

Starting pitcher Babe Ruth was ejected from a 1917 game for protesting a walk to the first batter he faced. Shore relieved Ruth, caught the runner stealing, and retired the next 26 batters for a perfect game.
Playing Career: *1912, 1914-1917, 1919-1920; NY N, Bos A, NY A*

Ruben Sierra.

Ruben Sierra
Sierra y Garcia, Ruben Angel
B: Oct 6, 1965

Pos: OF	BA: .274
Hits: 1,307	HRs: 178
RBI: 774	BB: 350

As a budding superstar, Sierra was the youngest batter to hit 30 homers since Tony Conigliaro in 1965. Sierra averaged 103 RBI in the six-year span, 1987-1992, and was chosen for his first of three All-Star squads in 1989 when he batted .306. That year he led the AL in slugging percentage, RBI and triples, and posted 35 doubles, 29 homers and 101 runs scored. In 1991 Sierra had 201 hits and scored 110 runs to join two teammates in becoming the first 200-hit, 100-run trio since the Brewers in 1982.

After playing only seven years, Sierra is the Rangers' all-time leader in home runs, RBI, doubles, triples, total bases and extra-base hits. The powerful switch hitter started the La Sierra Foundation to help needy Latinos in the Dallas-Ft. Worth area.
Playing Career: *1986-; Tex A, Oak A*

Ed Siever
Siever, Edward T.
B: Apr 2, 1877 D: Feb 5, 1920

Pos: P	ERA: 2.60
W-L: 83-83	SOs: 470
ShOs: 14	Saves: 2

Siever broke in with 18 wins as a rookie, then led the AL with a 1.91 ERA in 1902, but posted an 8-11 record for Detroit that year. Winning 18 for the Tigers again in 1907, he

went to the World Series. With great endurance, Siever averaged 241 innings for six years.
Playing Career: *1901-1904, 1906-1908; Det A, StL A*

Roy Sievers
Sievers, Roy Edward
B: Nov 18, 1926

Pos: 1B, OF, 3B	BA: .267
Hits: 1,703	HRs: 318
RBI: 1,147	BB: 841

The AL Rookie of the Year in 1949, Sievers batted .306 with 16 homers, 91 RBI and 84 runs that year. Following a series of injuries, the Browns traded him to the Senators, where he became a favorite of Vice-President Richard Nixon. Driving in more than 100 runs a year 1954-1958, Sievers led the AL with 42 home runs in 1957, becoming the first Senator to win the RBI crown since Goose Goslin in 1924. Sievers pinch-hit grand slams in both the AL and NL.
Playing Career: *1949-1965; StL A, Was A, Chi A, Phi N*

Al Simmons
Simmons, Aloysius Harry (Bucketfoot Al)
B: May 22, 1902 D: May 26, 1956
Hall of Fame 1953

Pos: OF	BA: .334
Hits: 2,927	HRs: 307
RBI: 1,827	BB: 615

Connie Mack's favorite player, and the only one whose photograph graced his office, was Al Simmons. He is underrated by the modern fan. Just missing 3,000 hits, he later regretted the times he had sat out of games to nurse a

Hall of Famer Al Simmons.

hangover, or left a one-sided game early for a quick shower and a head start out the door. Proud of his Polish ancestry – he was born Aloys Szymanski – Simmons advised another Polish player, "Never relax on anytime at bat; never miss a game you can play." It was the young Stan Musial he counseled.

Hitting in an unorthodox stance, with one foot in the bucket, Simmons won two batting titles, leading the AL in hits on two different occasions. He batted over .380 four times. In 1925 he belted 253 hits for a .387 average. He slugged over .600 four times and led the AL with a .599 mark in 1925. Driving in more than 100 runs for 11 years in a row helped place his RBI total at 12th on the all-time list. Simmons's season of 253 hits ranks the fourth best in baseball history.
Playing Career: *1924-1941, 1943-1944; Phi A, Chi A, Det A, Was A, Bos N, Cin N*

The Phillies' Curt Simmons in 1948.

Curt Simmons
Simmons, Curtis Thomas
B: May 19, 1929

Pos: P	ERA: 3.54
W-L: 193-183	SOs: 1,697
ShOs: 36	Saves: 5

A $65,000 bonus baby, Simmons mastered his control by 1950, and led the Phillie Whiz Kids to the NL pennant. He was 17-8 despite missing more than a month of the season when his National Guard unit was activated. Returning in 1952, he compiled a record of 14-8 with a league-high six shutouts. Released by the Phillies in 1960 after suffering arm trouble, the three-time All-Star signed with the Cardinals, making a successful adjustment from hard thrower to breaking-ball pitcher.

Simmons won a career-high 18 games for the 1964 Cardinals, helping them to the pennant. In Game Three of the World Series, he held the mighty Yankees to one run in eight innings, but was not involved in the decision.

He lost Game Six, surrendering homers to Roger Maris and Mickey Mantle, but the Cardinals persevered and won the World Championship. Simmons's best year was 1963, when he was 15-9 with a 2.48 ERA and six shutouts.

Playing Career: *1947-1950, 1952-1967; Phi N, StL N, Chi N, Cal A*

Ted Simmons
Simmons, Ted Lyle (Simba)
B: Aug 9, 1949

Pos: C, DH, 1B	BA: .285
Hits: 2,472	HRs: 248
RBI: 1,389	BB: 855

Joining the Cardinals at age 19, Simmons was groomed to succeed Tim McCarver behind the plate. He became a slugger as well, batting over .300 seven times, belting 20 or more home runs six times, and driving in 90 or more runs eight times. Simmons was a rare commodity – a switch hitter with power. Three times he swatted switch-hit home runs in a game. He set the NL career record for a switch hitter with 182 homers. Simmons also walloped 483 doubles, peaking at 40 in 1978.

Voted onto the All-Star team eight times, Simmons played in only one World Series,

with the 1982 Brewers against his former Cardinals teammates. Altogether Simmons scored 1,074 runs while posting a .437 slugging average. Retiring from the playing field, he was named director of player development for St. Louis in October 1988. Simmons later became general manager of the Pirates, but suffered a heart attack, and stepped down in 1993. His Pittsburgh clubs won three straight NL division titles.

Playing Career: *1968-1988; StL N, Mil A, Atl N*

Harry Simpson
Simpson, Harry Leon (Suitcase)
B: Dec 3, 1925   D: Apr 3, 1979

Pos: OF, 1B	BA: .266
Hits: 752	HRs: 73
RBI: 381	BB: 271

Called "Suitcase" because he was always available, Simpson played for five teams in eight years. He made the 1956 All-Star team, and led the AL in triples that year, as well as driving in 105 runs for the Royals. Simpson played first base for the Yankees in the 1957 World Series.

Playing Career: *1951-1953, 1955-1959; Cle A, KC A, NY A, Chi A, Pit N*

Duke Sims
Sims, Duane B.
B: Jun 5, 1941

Pos: C, 1B, OF	BA: .239
Hits: 580	HRs: 100
RBI: 310	BB: 338

Normally a low-average hitter, Sims batted .316 down the stretch in 1972, helping the Tigers to the division crown. As a platoon hitter, he belted 23 homers in 1970. A statistical anomaly, Sims hit more homers than doubles, and was caught stealing more often than not.

Playing Career: *1964-1974; Cle A, LA N, Det A, NY A, Tex A*

Bill Singer
Singer, William Robert
(The Singer Throwing Machine)
B: Apr 24, 1944

Pos: P	ERA: 3.39
W-L: 118-127	SOs: 1,515
ShOs: 24	No-hitters: 1

Brief stints with LA the three previous years led to Singer's emergence in 1967 as a starter for World Champion Dodgers team in place of retired Sandy Koufax. Singer's injury-plagued career included two great seasons: 1969 when he was 20-12, and 1973 when he was 20-14. He made the All-Star team and tossed 315 innings both years. Singer teamed with Nolan Ryan on the 1973 Angels' staff for 624 strikeouts, more than any other pair of teammates. Singer's no-hitter was against the Phillies in 1970.

Playing Career: *1964-1977; LA N, Cal A, Tex A, Min A, Tor A*

Ken Singleton
Singleton, Kenneth Wayne
B: Jun 10, 1947

Pos: OF, DH	BA: .282
Hits: 2,029	HRs: 246
RBI: 1,065	BB: 1,263

Singleton did not get a chance to play regularly until 1972. Always a good eye at the plate, he emerged in 1973, hitting 23 homers with 103 RBI, 100 runs scored, 123 walks and a .302 batting average. The next year he slumped and was traded to Baltimore.

With the Orioles he became a star, setting a club record in 1977 with a .438 on-base percentage and a .328 batting average. Switch-hitting Singleton was the power successor to Boog Powell and Frank Robinson; he batted .375 in the 1979 World Series. The three-time All-Star also holds Oriole season records with 118 walks in 1975 and 35 switch-hit homers in 1979. He ranks fifth on the Orioles' all-time list in hits, doubles, home runs, total bases, RBI and extra-base hits. In major league history, only Singleton, Mickey Mantle and Howard Johnson have switch-hit 35 or more home runs in one season.

Playing Career: *1970-1984; NY N, Mon N, Bal A*

Switch hitter Ted Simmons played for the Cardinals from 1968 to 1980.

Doug Sisk
Sisk, Douglas Randall
B: Sep 26, 1957

Pos: P	ERA: 3.22
W-L: 20-20	SOs: 189
ShOs: 0	Saves: 33

An unsung Mets hero, Sisk did not give up an earned run in 1986 postseason play. He even went that entire season without surrendering a home run. Sisk's best years were 1983-1984, when he saved 11 and 15 games with 2.24 and 2.09 ERAs.
Playing Career: *1982-1988; NY N, Bal A*

Dave Sisler
Sisler, David Michael
B: Oct 16, 1931

Pos: P	ERA: 4.33
W-L: 38-44	SOs: 355
ShOs: 1	Saves: 29

Sisler's father was a Hall of Fame player and his brother was a major leaguer who helped win the Whiz Kids' pennant of 1950. Dave was a Princeton grad who pitched middle relief. His best season was 1960, when he posted seven wins, six saves and a 2.48 ERA.
Playing Career: *1956-1962; Bos A, Det A, Was A, Cin N*

Dick Sisler
Sisler, Richard Allan
B: Nov 2, 1920

Pos: 1B, OF	BA: .276
Hits: 720	HRs: 55
RBI: 360	BB: 226
Managerial Record	
Won: 121 Lost: 94 Pct: .563	

All-Star Sisler hit a dramatic 10th-inning, game-winning home run at Ebbets Field on the final day of the 1950 season to clinch the pennant for the Phillies. Returning to the minors in 1953, he managed Nashville in the Southern Association, and other minor league teams. Sisler was coach for the Reds, then succeeded Fred Hutchinson as their manager. He later coached for the Cardinals, Padres, Mets and Yankees.
Playing Career: *1946-1953; StL N, Phi N, Cin N*
Managerial Career: *1964-1965; Cin N*

George Sisler
Sisler, George Harold (Gorgeous George)
B: Mar 24, 1893   D: Mar 26, 1973
Hall of Fame 1939

Pos: 1B	BA: .340
Hits: 2,812	HRs: 100
RBI: 1,175	BB: 472
Managerial Record	
Won: 218 Lost: 241 Pct: .475	

Many eye witnesses claim that Sisler was the best player they ever saw. Starting his career as a pitcher, he once beat his idol Walter Johnson, 2-1. Coached at Michigan by Branch

Hall of Famer George Sisler.

Rickey, Sisler's maneuvering to void a contract he signed as a minor almost broke up the National Commission. Sisler led the AL in assists seven times, and his career total of 1,528 is the third best of all time for first basemen. In double plays he topped the league three times, starting 13 of the difficult 3-6-3 double plays in 1920.

Sisler's 257 hits in 1920 is the best single-season mark ever. That year he hit .407 with 399 total bases, including 49 doubles, 18 triples and 19 home runs. In 1922, his MVP season, when the Browns missed the pennant by one game, Sisler hit safely in 41 consecutive games, posting a .420 average. In 1923 severe sinusitis caused an optic nerve infection and he missed the entire season.
Playing Career: *1915-1922, 1924-1930; StL A, Was A, Bos N*
Managerial Career: *1924-1926; StL A*

Sibby Sisti
Sisti, Sebastian Daniel
B: Jul 26, 1920

Pos: 2B, 3B, SS, OF	BA: .244
Hits: 732	HRs: 27
RBI: 260	BB: 283

Appearing as a coach in the film *The Natural*, Sisti showed the same versatility off the field as he did on the field during his playing days. He returned from World War II to spell Alvin Dark and Eddie Stanky with the 1948 NL pennant-winning Braves.
Playing Career: *1939-1942, 1946-1954; Bos N*

Ted Sizemore
Sizemore, Theodore Crawford
B: Apr 15, 1945

Pos: 2B, SS	BA: .262
Hits: 1,311	HRs: 23
RBI: 430	BB: 469

Now a vice-president of Rawlings Sporting Goods, Sizemore started his baseball career

as the 1969 NL Rookie of the Year with the Dodgers. He hit three bases-loaded triples that year. Traded to St. Louis for Richie Allen, Sizemore batted second in the lineup behind Lou Brock, taking pitches to allow Brock to steal. Sizemore was the second baseman for the 1977 and 1978 division-winning Phillies teams. He batted .308 in those two NLCS.
Playing Career: *1969-1980; LA N, StL N, Phi N, Chi N, Bos A*

Bob Skinner
Skinner, Robert Ralph
B: Oct 3, 1931

Pos: OF, 1B	BA: .277
Hits: 1,198	HRs: 103
RBI: 531	BB: 485
Managerial Record	
Won: 93 Lost: 123 Pct: .431	

A three-time .300 hitter with Pittsburgh, Skinner batted a career-high .321 in 1958, making the NL's All-Star team. As a rookie in 1954, Skinner set a first base record with eight assists in a game. Two years later he led the NL with 54 pinch-hitting appearances. During a torrid three-game stretch against Cincinnati in 1959, he hit five homers, including a grand slam and a three-run shot. He was selected for the All-Star Game a second time in 1960. As a pinch hitter for the Cardinals in the 1964 World Series, Skinner went 2-for-3; he led the NL with 15 pinch hits in 1965.

From 1970 through 1988 – with time out for one season as interim manager – Skinner coached the Padres, Pirates, Angels and Braves. Bob's son, Joel, was a catcher with the White Sox and Yankees.
Playing Career: *1954, 1956-1966; Pit N, Cin N, StL N*
Managerial Career: *1968-1969, 1977; Phi N, SD N*

Bob Skinner.

Bill Skowron.

Bill Skowron
Skowron, William Joseph (Moose)
B: Dec 18, 1930

Pos: 1B	BA: .282
Hits: 1,566	HRs: 211
RBI: 888	BB: 383

As a joke, Skowron's grandfather called him Mussolini as a baby. The family shortened it to Moose. A place kicker for Purdue, Skowron signed with the Yankees in 1951, coming up in 1954. An opposite-field hitter with power, he topped the .300-mark five times, batting .340 his first year. A six-time All-Star, 1957-1961 and 1965, he played in eight World Series in nine years.

Skowron was the hero of the 1958 World Series against the Braves, driving in the winning run in Game Six, and hitting a three-run homer in the final game. When he homered in the 14th inning of a Yankees-Senators game on April 22, 1959, the teams set an AL record for the longest 1-0 game to end on a home run. After helping New York win seven pennants, Skowron was traded to the Dodgers for Stan Williams. Facing his former team in the 1963 World Series, Skowron hit .385 as the Dodgers swept the Yankees.
Playing Career: *1954-1967; NY A, LA N, Was A, Chi A, Cal A*

Jimmy Slagle
Slagle, James Franklin (Rabbit, Shorty)
B: Jul 11, 1873   D: May 10, 1956

Pos: OF	BA: .268
Hits: 1,340	HRs: 2
RBI: 344	BB: 619

Fast as lightning, Slagle scored 779 runs, twice as many as he drove in. He scored 115 times for the Phillies in 1900, and 104 times for the 1903 Cubs. Slagle played in the 1907 World Series, batting .273 and leading the Cubs in RBI. His six steals were the Series

record until Lou Brock stole seven 60 years later. In 1902 Slagle hit .315 with 40 stolen bases.
Playing Career: *1899-1908; Was N, Phi N, Bos N, Chi N*

Jim Slaton
Slaton, James Michael
B: Jun 19, 1950

Pos: P	ERA: 4.03
W-L: 151-158	SOs: 1,191
ShOs: 22	Saves: 14

The Brewers' all-time leader in wins, shutouts and innings pitched, Slaton was with the Tigers, however, when he posted a career-high 17 victories. The Brewers reacquired him after just one season. Slaton turned in a career performance in 1979 with a record of 15-9, but tore a rotator cuff. In a 1983 comeback, Slaton was 14-6 with five saves as a reliever, a record that returned him to the starting role. Slaton won Game Four of the 1982 World Series.
Playing Career: *1971-1986; Mil A, Det A, Cal A*

Don Slaught
Slaught, Donald Martin (Sluggo)
B: Sep 11, 1958

Pos: C, DH	BA: .282
Hits: 972	HRs: 69
RBI: 406	BB: 248

Acquired by the Pirates late in his career, Slaught played in the NLCS three seasons in a row, 1990-1992, and batted .333 with five RBI and six walks in the 1992 contest. Slaught hit .345 that season, a career best. As a student at UCLA, he set the school's batting record with a .428 average.
Playing Career: *1982-; KC A, Tex A, NY A, Pit N*

Enos Slaughter
Slaughter, Enos Bradsher (Country)
B: Apr 27, 1916
Hall of Fame 1985

Pos: OF	BA: .300
Hits: 2,383	HRs: 169
RBI: 1,304	BB: 1,018

Chastised by minor league manager Clay Hopper for failing to run out a ground ball, Slaughter never again walked on the baseball field. He ran himself right into the Hall of Fame. Along the way he scored 1,247 runs, and belted 148 triples and 413 doubles. He batted .291 for 27 games in five World Series. Slaughter led the NL with doubles in 1939, hits in 1942, and triples in 1942 and 1949. He captured the NL RBI title with 130 in 1946.

Slaughter drove in 10 runs in a doubleheader in 1947. Elected to the NL All-Star team for 10 consecutive years, Slaughter's NL days are epitomized by an event in the 1946 World Series finale. He scored the game-winning run from first base on a short double to left field. Slaughter crossed home plate while the Red Sox shortstop, with his back to the infield, held the ball.
Playing Career: *1938-1942, 1946-1959; StL N, NY A, KC A, Mil N*

Enos "Country" Slaughter in a 1946 publicity shot.

Roy Smalley
Smalley, Roy Frederick, Jr.
B: Jun 9, 1926

Pos: SS	BA: .227
Hits: 601	HRs: 61
RBI: 305	BB: 257

Due to his wide range at shortstop, Smalley led the NL in erors three straight years, 1948-1950, and led in total chances per game in 1949 and 1950. He hit 21 homers, driving in 85 in 1950, his last season as a regular. Smalley married teammate Gene Mauch's sister.
Playing Career: *1948-1958; Chi N, Mil N, Phi N*

Roy Smalley
Smalley, Roy Frederick III
B: Oct 25, 1952

Pos: SS, DH, 3B	BA: .257
Hits: 1,454	HRs: 163
RBI: 694	BB: 771

The number one draft choice in 1974, Smalley's success as a power-hitting middle infielder diminished after he contracted spondylitis, but he still produced three years of 20 or more home runs. An All-Star in 1979, Smalley socked 24 round-trippers with 95 RBI and 94 runs as well as covering more ground at shortstop than anyone else in the AL. He batted .500 for the Twins in the 1987 World Series. The son of Roy Smalley, Jr., Smalley played five years for his uncle Gene Mauch.
Playing Career: *1975-1987; Tex A, Min A, NY A, Chi A*

John Smiley
Smiley, John Patrick
B: Mar 17, 1965

Pos: P	ERA: 3.68
W-L: 79-60	SOs: 757
ShOs: 5	Saves: 4

With the Pirates Smiley won an NL-best 20 games in 1991 and was the number two starter for the pennant winners, 1990-1991. He was tagged with two losses and a 13.50 ERA in two NLCs. In 1992 he was 16-9 for the Twins. The left-hander averaged 200 innings and 30 starts over the five-year span, 1988-1992. A high-priced free agent in 1993, Smiley signed with the Reds, then endured an embarrassing season.
Playing Career: *1986-; Pit N, Min A, Cin N*

Al Smith
Smith, Alfred John
B: Oct 12, 1907   D: Apr 28, 1977

Pos: P	ERA: 3.72
W-L: 99-101	SOs: 587
ShOs: 16	Saves: 17

Smith was one of the two pitchers who stopped Joe DiMaggio's historic 56-game hitting streak in 1941. Smith led the NL in shutouts in 1936, and played in two World Series, 1936-1937 with the Giants. He was selected for the All-Star team in 1943, the year he was 17-7 for the Indians. He retired after posting losing records the next two seasons.
Playing Career: *1934-1945; NY N, Phi N, Cle A*

Al Smith
Smith, Alphonse Eugene (Fuzzy)
B: Feb 7, 1928

Pos: OF, 3B	BA: .272
Hits: 1,458	HRs: 164
RBI: 676	BB: 674

With Cleveland in 1955, Smith led the AL in runs with 123, and made the All-Star team. Traded to the White Sox in 1958 for the popular Minnie Minoso, Smith had to deal with booing fans. Owner Bill Veeck held Al Smith Night on August 26, 1959. Any fan named Smith, Smythe, Schmidt or Smithe was admitted free and given a button that said, "I'm a Smith and I'm for Al." On his big night, Smith hit into two double plays and dropped a fly ball. Luckily, the 1959 White Sox were pennant winners.
Playing Career: *1953-1964; Cle A, Chi A, Bal A, Bos A*

Bob Smith
Smith, Robert Eldridge
B: Apr 22, 1895   D: Jul 19, 1987

Pos: P, SS	ERA: 3.95
W-L: 106-139	SOs: 618
ShOs: 16	Saves: 40

Toiling in obscurity, Smith began his big league career as a shortstop before turning to pitching. He hurled a complete-game, 22-inning loss in 1927. Traded to the Cubs in 1931, Smith was 15-12 and pitched one inning in the World Series the following year.
Playing Career: *1923-1937; Bos N, Chi N, Cin N*

Bryn Smith
Smith, Bryn Nelson
B: Aug 11, 1955

Pos: P	ERA: 3.53
W-L: 108-94	SOs: 1,028
ShOs: 8	Saves: 6

The top starter available in the 1993 expansion draft, Smith was picked by the Rockies, but spent most of the season on the disabled list. He was 18-5 with a 2.91 ERA for the Expos in 1985. Four years later he went to the Cardinals as a free agent.
Playing Career: *1981-; Mon N, StL N, Col N*

Charley Smith
Smith, Charles William
B: Sep 15, 1937

Pos: 3B, SS, OF	BA: .239
Hits: 594	HRs: 69
RBI: 281	BB: 130

St. Louis traded Smith for Roger Maris in 1966; the deal made the Cardinals pennant winners in 1967 and 1968. Smith had been one of the multitude who toiled at third base for the Mets. He hit a career-high 20 home runs for them in 1964.
Playing Career: *1960-1969; LA N, Phi N, Chi A, NY N, StL N, NY A, Chi N*

Al "Fuzzy" Smith dives for second under Gil McDougald in 1957 action.

Charlie Smith
Smith, Charles Edwin
B: Apr 20, 1880 D: Jan 3, 1929

Pos: P	ERA: 2.81
W-L: 66-87	SOs: 570
ShOs: 10	Saves: 3

A Cleveland native, Smith burst on the big league scene in his hometown, beating Rube Waddell, then pitching and winning a shutout for a record of 2-1 with a 4.05 ERA. But his other start was a bomb, and he went back to the minors for three years.
Playing Career: *1902, 1906-1914; Cle A, Was A, Bos A, Chi N*

Chino Smith
Smith, Chino
B: 1903 D: Jan 16, 1932

Pos: OF, 2B	BA: .428
Hits: 261	HRs: 37
RBI: NA	BB: NA

Satchel Paige called Smith one of the two greatest hitters in Negro Leagues history, and available statistics support Paige's opinion. Smith led the league twice in hitting, with a .454 average in 1929 and a .492 mark in 1930. He crushed 20 homers in 60 games, leading the American Negro League in 1929. He hit .335 in the Cuban Winter League and .405 in exhibitions against white major leaguers. He died tragically from yellow fever before he was 30 years old.
Playing Career: *1925-1930; Brk Royal Giants, NY Lincoln Giants*

Dave Smith
Smith, David Stanley
B: Jan 21, 1955

Pos: P	ERA: 2.67
W-L: 53-53	SOs: 548
ShOs: 0	Saves: 216

The Astros' all-time saves and games pitched leader, Smith used control and savvy instead of the 100-mph hummer. His 1986 season was

Dave Smith with the Astros in 1982.

beautiful to behold – 54 games, 56 innings, 33 saves, and only 39 hits surrendered for a 2.73 ERA. The following year he did not allow a home run all season, and in the next two years he allowed only two. In his only major league start, in 1982, Smith committed three balks. Becoming the Astro closer in 1985, he saved 27 in 31 opportunities.
Playing Career: *1980-1992; Hou N, Chi N*

Earl Smith
Smith, Earl Sutton (Oil)
B: Feb 14, 1897 D: Jun 8, 1963

Pos: C	BA: .303
Hits: 686	HRs: 46
RBI: 355	BB: 247

Playing in five World Series for three different teams, Smith developed a reputation as a money player, but with a difficult personality. Ignoring John McGraw's signs and his bed checks, Smith was suspended a month for punching Braves manager Davy Bancroft.
Playing Career: *1919-1930; NY N, Pit N, StL N*

A's hurler Eddie Smith in 1938.

Eddie Smith
Smith, Edgar
B: Dec 14, 1913

Pos: P	ERA: 3.82
W-L: 73-113	SOs: 694
ShOs: 8	Saves: 12

The losing pitcher in Bob Feller's Opening Day no-hitter in 1940, Smith spent his career with second-division clubs. He was selected for the 1941 All-Star team and was 13-17 that year. In 1942 he won only seven games and lost 20, but made the All-Star team again.
Playing Career: *1936-1943, 1946-1947; Phi A, Chi A, Bos A*

Elmer Smith
Smith, Elmer Ellsworth
B: Mar 23, 1868 D: Nov 5, 1945

Pos: OF	BA: .310
Hits: 1,455	HRs: 37
RBI: 638	BB: 636

Pos: P	ERA: 3.35
W-L: 75-58	SOs: 526
ShOs: 9	No-hitters: 0

A 30-game winner at age 19, Smith was released with a dead arm at age 21. He went back to the minors, learned to play the outfield and returned for 10 more years in the majors. Although he swung a 54-ounce bat and knocked in 103 runs in 1893, he frequently hit leadoff. Smith scored 914 runs and stole 233 bases. His top averages were .346 in 1893 and .356 in 1894. His .342 average in 1898 fueled the Reds' pennant drive.
Playing Career: *1886-1889, 1892-1901; Cin AA, Pit N, Cin N, NY N, Bos N*

Elmer Smith
Smith, Elmer John
B: Sep 21, 1892 D: Aug 3, 1984

Pos: OF	BA: .276
Hits: 881	HRs: 70
RBI: 540	BB: 319

In 1920 Smith had his best season, batting .316 with 12 homers and 103 RBI to help the Indians to the pennant. Smith then batted .308 in the World Series, and hit the first grand slam in Series history. He later played for the 1922-1923 pennant-winning Yankees.
Playing Career: *1914-1917, 1919-1923, 1925; Cle A, Was A, Bos A, NY A*

Frank Smith
Smith, Frank Elmer (Piano Mover)
B: Oct 28, 1879 D: Nov 3, 1952

Pos: P	ERA: 2.59
W-L: 139-111	SOs: 1,051
ShOs: 27	No-hitters: 2

Headstrong Smith pitched two no-hitters and won more than 20 games twice for the White Sox, but infuriated equally headstrong owner Charles Comiskey by drinking habitually. Upset with his contract and fines, Smith frequently threatened to return to his off-season occupation of piano moving. In 1909 he recorded 25 wins, 37 complete games and 177 strikeouts, all AL-leading totals.
Playing Career: *1904-1915; Chi A, Bos A, Cin N, Bal F, Brk F*

Frank Smith
Smith, Frank Thomas
B: Apr 4, 1928

Pos: P	ERA: 3.81
W-L: 35-33	SOs: 277
ShOs: 0	Saves: 44

Known as a knockdown artist, Smith made 50 relief appearances three times for the Reds

as they struggled with losing records. Smith's best year was 1954, when he was 5-8 with 20 saves and a 2.67 ERA. He won 12 games with seven saves in 1952, starting two and completing one.
Playing Career: *1950-1956; Cin N, StL N*

Germany Smith
Smith, George J.
B: Apr 21, 1863   D: Dec 1, 1927

Pos: SS	BA: .243
Hits: 1,592	HRs: 45
RBI: 618	BB: 408

The Brooklyn Bridegroom team won the AA pennant in 1889 and the NL flag in 1890 with Smith at shortstop. They lost the championship series in 1889 but won it in 1890, largely on the strength of Smith's seven RBI and .276 batting average. A shortstop with wide range, he led his position in fielding in the AA in 1887 and in the NL in 1893. He also led the NL in assists, 1891-1894. Smith scored 907 runs, hit 251 doubles and stole 235 bases.
Playing Career: *1884-1898; Alt U, Cle N, Brk AA, Brk N, Cin N, StL N*

Hal Smith
Smith, Harold Wayne
B: Dec 7, 1930

Pos: C	BA: .267
Hits: 715	HRs: 58
RBI: 323	BB: 196

In Game Seven of the 1960 World Series, Smith hit a home run that set the stage for an even more dramatic one by Bill Mazeroski. Trailing 7-6 in the eighth inning, Smith's three-run blast restored the Pirates' lead, 9-7, only to see the Yankees tie it in the top of the ninth.
Playing Career: *1955-1964; Bal A, KC A, Pit N, Hou N, Cin N*

Hilton Smith.

Harry Smith
Smith, Harry Thomas
B: Oct 31, 1874   D: Feb 17, 1933

Pos: C	BA: .213
Hits: 214	HRs: 2
RBI: 89	BB: 55
Managerial Record	
Won: 22 Lost: 54 Pct: .289	

In a 10-year career, Smith never appeared in more than 75 games during a season. As a backup catcher, he started one game in the 1903 World Series. Taking over a last-place team in 1909, he managed the Braves but could not get them out of the cellar.
Playing Career: *1901-1910; Phi A, Pit N, Bos N*
Managerial Career: *1909; Bos N*

Hilton Smith
Smith, Hilton
B: Feb 27, 1912   D: Nov 18, 1983

Pos: P	ERA: NA
W-L: 69-32 (inc.)	SOs: 338 (inc.)
ShOs: 5 (inc.)	No-hitters: 1

The story goes that Satchel Paige would pitch the first three innings and Smith would come in to put away the last six. Picked for the Negro East-West All-Star Game six straight years, 1937-1942, Smith tossed a no-hitter in 1937 and lost only one game the following year. Smith was more feared than Paige because he had a good curveball that broke sharply. He was 6-1 in exhibition games against major leaguers and 10-5 over two Cuban Winter League stints.

Smith was the top pitcher for the 1946-1947 Venezuelan Winter League champion Vargas. Early in 1947, the Vargas whipped the New York Yankees 4-3 with Smith starting. He did not allow a run, and gave up only one hit in five innings. Smith captured two Negro World Series wins, one over the favored Homestead Grays, and the other to the fabulous Newark Eagles. Smith made his home in Kansas City, where he was active in the city's youth baseball programs.
Playing Career: *1933-1948; New Orleans, KC Monarchs*

Jack Smith
Smith, Jack
B: Jun 23, 1895   D: May 2, 1972

Pos: OF	BA: .287
Hits: 1,301	HRs: 40
RBI: 382	BB: 334

As a leadoff hitter for the Cardinals and Braves, Smith scored 783 runs, more than twice as many as he knocked in. He stole 228 bases, reaching a high of 32 in 1923. Smith exceeded the .300 mark six times, including four consecutive seasons, 1920-1923, with a high of .332 in 1920. In 1917 he made five pinch hits in a row for the Cardinals. Smith led the NL with nine pinch hits for the 1928 Braves, batting .360 as pinch hitter.
Playing Career: *1915-1929; StL N, Bos N*

Flamethrowing reliever Lee Smith.

Lee Smith
Smith, Lee Arthur
B: Dec 4, 1957

Pos: P	ERA: 2.91
W-L: 67-78	SOs: 1,110
ShOs: 0	Saves: 401

The intimidating 6'6", 245-pound Lee Smith is the all-time saves leader. He also holds the Cubs' and Cardinals' all-time saves records. Smith has used a menacing glare and a 95-mph fastball to lead the NL in saves three times; 29 in 1983, 47 in 1991, and 43 in 1992. He has saved more than 27 games for 11 years in a row, going over 30 seven times. A five-time All-Star, Smith won the 1987 event by tossing three shutout innings.

In 1983 Smith was 4-10 with a 1.65 ERA. The NL batted only .194 against him that year, but the fireman had trouble keeping his weight down. The Cubs feared that it would affect his knees and traded him for Calvin Schiraldi and Al Nipper. Struggling in Boston, Smith nonetheless pitched the Red Sox into the 1988 ALCS with 29 saves and a 2.80 ERA. With the Cardinals in 1991 he set the NL record with 47 saves and posted a 2.34 ERA. Smith set a major league record by saving 14 games in the month of June 1993.
Playing Career: *1980-; Chi N, Bos A, StL N, NY A*

Lonnie Smith
Smith, Lonnie (Skates)
B: Dec 22, 1955

Pos: OF, DH	BA: .289
Hits: 1,471	HRs: 96
RBI: 528	BB: 604

Called a catalyst or instant offense, Smith has played in five World Series. He was named Rookie of the Year by *The Sporting News* in 1980, and was selected for the All-Star Game roster once. When drugs forced Smith to reconsider his career, he went to the Winter Leagues as a free agent. The Braves signed him in 1988 after he batted over .400 in winter ball. Smith hit .315 with 21 homers, 34 doubles and a league-leading .420 on-base percentage in 1989.
Playing Career: *1978-; Phi N, StL N, KC A, Atl N, Pit N*

Mayo Smith
Smith, Edward Mayo
B: Jan 17, 1915   D: Nov 24, 1977

Pos: OF	BA: .212
Hits: 43	HRs: 0
RBI: 11	BB: 36
Managerial Record	
Won: 662 Lost: 612 Pct: .520	

A 20-year veteran minor league outfielder, Smith was once ejected from a game before the teams ever took the field. He asked Umpire Frank Dascoli if they were going to play that day's game according to the rules. As Detroit manager in the 1968 World Series, Smith moved outfielder Mickey Stanley to shortstop and benched the weak-hitting Ray Oyler to keep Al Kaline, Jim Northrup and Willie Horton in the lineup. The Tigers beat the Cardinals in seven games.
Playing Career: *1945; Phi A*
Managerial Career: *1955-1959, 1967-1970; Phi N, Cin N, Det A*

Ozzie Smith
Smith, Osborne Earl (The Wizard of Oz)
B: Dec 26, 1954

Pos: SS	BA: .262
Hits: 2,265	HRs: 23
RBI: 734	BB: 992

Ozzie Smith was the greatest shortstop of the 1980s, and perhaps the greatest ever. He sealed his reputation as a star with the Padres in a spectacular play his rookie year. He broke to the left for a ground ball that struck a pebble and shot to his right. Smith lunged right, grabbed the ball barehanded, dragged his foot across second and threw to first in one motion for a double play. He was traded to the Cardinals in 1982 for shortstop Garry Templeton.

An All-Star for 13 consecutive years, Smith needs a vault for storing his 13 Gold Glove Awards. As a fielder, he is in a league of his own. He set the major league shortstop record in 1980 with 621 assists in a season, and has led the league in assists eight times and in chances accepted eight times – more than any other shortstop. Smith also holds the record for the most double plays in an extra-inning game. He tied the NL record by leading the league in fielding average for seven years. Smith has played in three World Series – 1982, 1985 and 1987.
Playing Career: *1978-; SD N, StL N*

Phenomenal Smith
Smith, John Francis
B: Dec 12, 1864   D: Apr 3, 1952

Pos: P	ERA: 3.90
W-L: 57-78	SOs: 534
ShOs: 2	No-hitters: 0

A washout in two previous years, Smith picked up a "rough" pitch in 1886 that brought him success and controversy. Similar to an emery ball, the pitch was subjected to lawsuits and injunctions. Smith was 25-30 with the Orioles in 1887.
Playing Career: *1884-1891; Bal U, Phi AA, Pit AA, Brk AA, Det N, Bal AA, Phi N, Pit N*

Pop Smith
Smith, Charles Marvin
B: Oct 12, 1856   D: Apr 18, 1927

Pos: 2B, SS, 3B	BA: .224
Hits: 935	HRs: 24
RBI: 264 (inc.)	BB: 313

Peripatetic Smith holds the major league record of appearing for 11 different clubs in his 12-year career. A good baserunner and stable fielder, he was known to use "California tactics" against opponents and umpires, needling them and making snide remarks.
Playing Career: *1880-1891; Cin N, Cle N, Wor N, Buf N, Bal AA, Lou AA, Col AA, Pit AA, Pit N, Bos N, Was AA*

Red Smith
Smith, James Carlisle
B: Apr 6, 1890   D: Oct 11, 1966

Pos: 3B, OF	BA: .278
Hits: 1,087	HRs: 27
RBI: 514	BB: 420

Traded to the Braves in August of 1914, Smith was one of the keys to the Miracle Braves' pennant. A top third baseman, he led his peers in putouts, assists, double plays, and total chances per games in 1914. Smith's .314 average in 60 games was the team high.
Playing Career: *1911-1919; Brk N, Bos N*

Reggie Smith
Smith, Carl Reginald
B: Apr 2, 1945

Pos: OF	BA: .287
Hits: 2,020	HRs: 314
RBI: 1,092	BB: 890

An all-state football and baseball player from California, Smith had a tryout with the Astros at Dodger Stadium his senior year in high school, but signed with the Twins as a shortstop in 1963. He was acquired by the Red Sox, who played him in the outfield at the minor league level. As a rookie, Smith helped Boston to the 1967 pennant and homered twice in the World Series. Elected to the All-Star team seven times, he batted .300 or more seven times and won a Gold Glove Award in 1968 when he led AL outfielders in

The Cardinals' All-Star shortstop Ozzie Smith.

Reggie Smith with LA in 1980.

putouts. In 1968 and 1971, Smith led the AL in doubles. He hit three home runs in a game in 1976 for the Cards. With the 1977 Dodgers, Smith, Steve Garvey, Dusty Baker and Ron Cey became the first four teammates in baseball history to each hit 30 or more homers. Smith was a major factor in the Dodgers' 1978 league title, with 29 homers plus three more in the World Series. Injuries plagued Smith in his final playing years.
Playing Career: *1966-1982; Bos A, StL N, LA N, SF N*

Sherry Smith
Smith, Sherrod Malone
B: Feb 18, 1891   D: Sep 12, 1949

Pos: P	ERA: 3.32
W-L: 114-118	SOs: 428
ShOs: 16	Saves: 21

"Strong as a horse and tireless as a Missouri Mule," Smith also had the best pickoff move in the majors. Those who saw him universally claim his move to first was the best ever. Never a big winner – 14 was his high mark – Smith did what Brooklyn manager Wilbert Robinson wanted him to do. After two brief stints with the Pirates, he was acquired by Robinson, who molded him into a winning pitcher.

Very tough with runners on base, Smith was 14-10 with a 2.34 ERA in 1916 and 11-9 with a 1.85 ERA in 1920, both pennant-winning years. Smith pitched three strong World Series games, but lost two of them. In 1916 he lost a 14-inning Game Two duel with Babe Ruth, 2-1. In 1920 Smith won Game Three, a

three-hitter, 2-1, but lost 1-0 in Game Six. Smith frequently helped himself with his excellent fielding, going through both the 1923 and 1926 seasons without committing an error.
Playing Career: *1911-1912, 1915-1917,1919-1927; Pit N, Brk N, Cle A*

Zane Smith
Smith, Zane William
B: Dec 28, 1960

Pos: P	ERA: 3.59
W-L: 78-93	SOs: 860
ShOs: 14	Saves: 3

Picked up off the scrap heap by the Pirates, Smith used the opportunity to renovate his career. Before injuries, he had been a dependable starter with the Braves, and was selected for the NL All-Star Game in 1987, the year he was 15-10 with a 4.09 ERA.
Playing Career: *1984-; Atl N, Mon N, Pit N*

Mike Smithson
Smithson, Billy Mike
B: Jan 21, 1955

Pos: P	ERA: 4.58
W-L: 76-86	SOs: 731
ShOs: 6	Saves: 2

A 6'8" sinkerball hurler, Smithson led the AL in games started in 1984 and 1985, winning 15 contests each year for the Twins, but was released after a 4-7, 5.94 ERA season in 1987. Acquired by the Boston Red Sox, he contributed nine victories to their 1988 division-winning season.
Playing Career: *1982-1989; Tex A, Min A, Bos A*

Homer Smoot
Smoot, Homer Vernon
B: Mar 23, 1878   D: Mar 25, 1928

Pos: OF	BA: .290
Hits: 763	HRs: 15
RBI: 269	BB: 149

One of the earliest ballplayers to wear eyeglasses, Smoot was a fleet center fielder in the major leagues until his eyesight began to fail. He had been a hitting star in the minor leagues, where he won the Eastern League batting title in 1901.
Playing Career: *1902-1906; StL N, Cin N*

Duke Snider
Snider, Edwin Donald
B: Sep 19, 1926
Hall of Fame 1980

Pos: OF	BA: .295
Hits: 2,116	HRs: 407
RBI: 1,333	BB: 971

Dodgers fans pronounced Snider the best center fielder in New York during the 1950s. He hit more home runs and drove in more runs during that decade than the Yankees' Mickey Mantle or the Giants' Willie Mays. Snider joined Babe Ruth and Ralph Kiner as the only players who ever had five straight seasons of 40 or more homers. Snider's slugging average topped .600 for three consecutive years. He was elected to the All-Star squad eight times, the last being 1963 while with the Mets.

Snider, Pee Wee Reese, Jackie Robinson, Gil Hodges, Roy Campanella and Carl Furillo teamed up for five World Series in the eight-year span of 1949-1956. Snider hit four

Duke Snider brings in another home run for the Dodgers.

homers in two Fall Classics, the only man to do so. He made his sixth World Series appearance with the 1959 Dodgers in Los Angeles, wrapping up NL World Series home run and RBI records of 11 and 26. After a career that included 358 doubles, 1,259 runs scored, and countless honors, Snider became an announcer for the Expos. His autobiography became a bestseller in 1988.
Playing Career: *1947-1964; Brk N, LA N, NY N, SF N*

Fred Snodgrass
Snodgrass, Frederick Charles
B: Oct 19, 1887   D: Apr 5, 1974

Pos: OF	BA: .275
Hits: 852	HRs: 11
RBI: 351	BB: 386

Made famous by the muff of a routine fly ball in the last inning of Game Eight in the 1912 World Series, Snodgrass made a stunning catch off the very next batter. Manager John McGraw gave Snodgrass, a top base stealer, a generous raise for the next season.
Playing Career: *1909-1916; NY N, Bos N*

Cory Snyder
Snyder, James Cory
B: Nov 11, 1962

Pos: OF, SS, 1B	BA: .247
Hits: 866	HRs: 143
RBI: 470	BB: 312

A member of the 1984 Olympic baseball team, Snyder was the first of them to play regularly in the majors. An instant success as a home run hitter, he was a key player as a right fielder in the Dodgers' 1993 resurgence.
Playing Career: *1986-; Cle A, Chi A, Tor A, SF N, LA N*

Pancho Snyder
Snyder, Frank Elton
B: May 27, 1893   D: Jan 5, 1962

Pos: C	BA: .265
Hits: 1,122	HRs: 47
RBI: 525	BB: 281

During the Giants' streak of four consecutive pennants, 1921-1924, Snyder pounded out three seasons of .300 averages and led the NL in fielding three times. Snyder batted .364 and .333 in the 1921 and 1922 World Series.
Playing Career: *1912-1927; StL N, NY N*

Pop Snyder
Snyder, Charles N.
B: Oct 6, 1854   D: Oct 29, 1924

Pos: C	BA: .235
Hits: 855	HRs: 9
RBI: 145 (inc.)	BB: 84
Managerial Record	
Won: 163 Lost: 122 Pct: .572	

Playing 18 years of major league ball, Snyder witnessed the game's evolution from gentleman's club sport to the acrimonious Players'

League rebellion. He played on the Red Stockings' 1878 NL pennant-winning team and managed them to a pennant in the first AA season.
Playing Career: *1873-1879, 1881-1891; Was Washingtons n, Bal Lord Baltimores n, Phi White Stockings n, Lou N, Bos N, Cin AA, Cle AA, Cle N, Cle P, Was AA*
Managerial Career: *1882-1884, 1891; Cin AA, Was AA*

Russ Snyder in 1966 WS action.

Russ Snyder
Snyder, Russell Henry
B: Jun 22, 1934

Pos: OF	BA: .271
Hits: 984	HRs: 42
RBI: 319	BB: 294

Breaking in with a .313 batting average in 73 games in 1959, Snyder hit over .300 three times in 11 full seasons. During the expanded strike zone era, 1962-1968, his average dropped to the .250 range four times. He once pinch-hit safely twice in one inning.
Playing Career: *1959-1970; KC A, Bal A, Chi A, Cle A, Mil A*

Arthur Soden
Soden, Arthur
B: Apr 23, 1843   D: 1915

Known as the originator of the reserve clause, Soden was a member of the War Committee during the 1890 Players' League battle, and one of the triumvirate who ruled Boston baseball in the 19th century. Soden and Al Spalding are the two people most responsible for turning baseball into a thriving business, ensuring its continuation as a professional sport. Soden developed a reserve clause in September 1879 to prevent team owners from feuding over players.

Eric Soderholm
Soderholm, Eric Thane
B: Sep 24, 1948

Pos: 3B, DH	BA: .264
Hits: 764	HRs: 102
RBI: 383	BB: 295

A number one draft choice by the Twins, Soderholm hit a homer in his second big league at-bat. After two knee operations,

Soderholm delivered 25 home runs, 67 RBI, a .280 average and an AL-leading fielding average for third basemen in 1977 to become the AL Comeback Player of the Year.
Playing Career: *1971-1975, 1977-1980; Min A, Chi A, Tex A, NY A*

Moose Solters
Solters, Julius Joseph
B: Mar 22, 1906   D: Sep 28, 1975

Pos: OF	BA: .289
Hits: 990	HRs: 83
RBI: 599	BB: 221

Solters was a minor league slugger who went on to hit three homers in one 1935 game for the St. Louis Browns. When he played regularly he could hit. Solters posted three consecutive 100-RBI seasons, 1935-1937. He was a member of the Cleveland "cry babies" who tried to depose their manager during their pennant run.
Playing Career: *1934-1941, 1943; Bos A, StL A, Cle A, Chi A*

Moose Solters.

Charley Somers
Somers, Charles W.
B: Oct 13, 1868   D: Jun 29, 1934

Ban Johnson's new American League needed a financial angel, and found one in Somers. Johnson had the western cities, Chicago, Detroit, Milwaukee and St. Louis, firmly on his side because he had a network of key people in those cities, but he lacked contacts and money in the East. Young, idealistic Somers came along with a healthy bankroll to firmly establish the AL as a reform league.

Not only did Ban Johnson want to rid the league of rowdyism and make the ballparks fit places to take women and children, but he also wanted to give ballplayers fair deals. Salaries had been on the downslide ever since the Players' Rebellion in 1890 and the formation of the monopolistic National League of 1892. Johnson appealed to Somers' sense of fair play, and Somers responded with his checkbook. He invested heavily in the Cleveland franchise, and loaned money to the Boston and Philadelphia clubs.

Joe Sommer
Sommer, Joseph John
B: Nov 20, 1858   D: Jan 16, 1938

Pos: OF, 3B, 2B   BA: .248
Hits: 911   HRs: 11
RBI: 77 (inc.)   BB: 238

A member of the Reds team that was kicked out of the NL for selling beer on Sunday, Sommer continued to play for the Reds when officials founded the American Association. Sommer led AA outfielders with a .925 fielding percentage in 1882.
Playing Career: *1880, 1882-1890; Cin N, Cin AA, Bal AA, Cle N*

Lary Sorenson
Sorensen, Lary Alan
B: Oct 4, 1955

Pos: P   ERA: 4.15
W-L: 93-103   SOs: 569
ShOs: 10   Saves: 6

In 1978 Sorensen was 18-12, and pitched three shutout innings in the All-Star Game. He was a key player in the 1981 deal that sent Ozzie Smith to St. Louis and Rollie Fingers to Milwaukee. Sorenson worked in radio and TV during the off-season.
Playing Career: *1977-1985, 1987-1988; Mil A, StL N, Cle A, Oak A, Chi N, Mon N, SF N*

Vic Sorrell
Sorrell, Victor Garland
B: Apr 9, 1901   D: May 4, 1972

Pos: P   ERA: 4.43
W-L: 92-101   SOs: 619
ShOs: 8   Saves: 10

One of the Tigers' starters during the "Five Dreary Years Under Bucky," 1929-1933, Sorrell compiled a record of 16-11 with a 3.86 ERA in 1930, his best season. The right-hander hung on for the 1934-1935 back-to-back Tigers' pennants, contributing 10 wins and 2 saves.
Playing Career: *1928-1937; Det A*

Elias Sosa
Sosa y Martinez, Elias
B: Jun 10, 1950

Pos: P   ERA: 3.32
W-L: 59-51   SOs: 538
ShOs: 0   Saves: 83

Sosa appeared in the 1977 World Series with the Dodgers, the year he posted a 1.98 ERA. The Expos picked him up in 1979. He was 8-7 with 18 saves and a 1.95 ERA for them. Sosa appeared in the 1977 and 1981 NLCS and in the 1977 World Series.
Playing Career: *1972-1983; SF N, StL N, Atl N, LA N, Oak A, Mon N, Det A, SD N*

Allen Sothoron
Sothoron, Allen Sutton (Dixie)
B: Apr 27, 1893   D: Jun 17, 1939

Pos: P   ERA: 3.31
W-L: 91-100   SOs: 576
ShOs: 17   Saves: 9
Managerial Record
Won: 2   Lost: 6   Pct: .250

One of the veteran spitball pitchers allowed to continue the pitch after 1920, Sothoron won 20 games in 1919 and spun ERAs of 1.94 in 1918 and 2.20 in 1919 for the Browns. He was a lifelong baseball man, working as a player, manager and coach.
Playing Career: *1914-1915, 1917-1922, 1924-1926; StL A, Bos A, Cle A, StL N*
Managerial Career: *1933; StL A*

Mario Soto
Soto, Mario Melvin
B: Jul 12, 1956

Pos: P   ERA: 3.47
W-L: 100-92   SOs: 1,449
ShOs: 13   Saves: 4

Shoulder problems sidetracked Soto's career, but before that he looked like a sure-fire Hall of Famer. Number two on the Reds' all-time strikeout list, he set their single-season mark of 274 in 1982. A three-time All-Star, Soto started the 1983 contest. He tossed two scoreless innings in the 1979 NLCS. Soto was the Reds' Opening Day hurler five straight years. In 1983 he won the Buck Canel Award for the outstanding Latin ballplayer in the majors.
Playing Career: *1977-1988; Cin N*

Warren Spahn collected 100 or more strikeouts in each of his 17 seasons.

Elias Sosa.

Billy Southworth
Southworth, William Harrison
B: Mar 9, 1893   D: Nov 15, 1969

Pos: OF   BA: .297
Hits: 1,296   HRs: 52
RBI: 561   BB: 402
Managerial Record
Won: 1,044   Lost: 704   Pct: .597

The manager of four pennant-winning teams, Southworth had played in two World Series, with the Giants in 1924, and for the Cardinals in their 1926 victory over the Yankees. In 13 years as a major league manager, Southworth finished in the second division only once. *The Sporting News* named him Manager of the Year in 1941 and 1942. His .597 won-lost percentage ranks him sixth on the all-time list.
Playing Career: *1913, 1915, 1918-1927, 1929; Cle A, Pit N, Bos N, NY N, StL N*
Managerial Career: *1929, 1940-1951; StL N, Bos N*

Warren Spahn
Spahn, Warren Edward
B: Apr 23, 1921
Hall of Fame 1973

Pos: P   ERA: 3.09
W-L: 363-245   SOs: 2,583
ShOs: 63   No-hitters: 2

The winningest left-handed pitcher in baseball history, Spahn won 20 or more games in a season 13 times. A strikeout leader early in his career, Spahn made the crucial adjustment from thrower to pitcher by picking up a screwball and slider midway through his career. He was the master of changing speeds. The 14-time All-Star did not win a major league game until he was 25. His career was interrupted by World War II, during which he earned a Purple Heart for service at the Battle of the Bulge.

Spahn is number 15 on the all-time complete games list; the first 14 all started their careers before 1910. He is sixth in shutouts, eighth in innings pitched and fifth on the wins list, only 10 games shy of the marks of Grover Alexander and Christy Mathewson as the NL leaders. Spahn once fanned 18 batters in 15 innings, hit a solo home run, but lost, 2-1. Johnny Sain said, "Spahn was one of the smartest men ever to play the game."
Playing Career: *1942, 1946-1965; Bos N, Mil N, NY N, SF N*

Al Spalding
Spalding, Albert
B: Sep 2, 1850   D: Sep 9, 1915
Hall of Fame 1939

Pos: P, 1B   ERA: 2.14 (inc.)
W-L: 253-65   SOs: 122 (inc.)
ShOs: 24   Saves: 11
Managerial Record
Won: 78   Lost: 47   Pct: .624

The best player of the 1870s, Spalding teamed with George Wright to take Boston to four

Al Spalding.

consecutive NA pennants, 1872-1875. Spalding led the league in victories each year, going 55-5 in 1875 with a 1.52 ERA. He was one of the NL founders and played with the White Stockings in 1876, combining with Cap Anson to drive the club to the league's first pennant. Still in the pitcher's box, he compiled a record of 47-12 that year.

In 1877 Spalding pitched only four games, but played regularly at first base so that he could show off his new fielder's glove. He retired at age 28 to devote himself to the sporting goods business, which he ran with his brother Walter, but later served as the president of the White Stockings from 1882 to 1891. Spalding's sporting goods became known worldwide, especially after the firm sponsored a trip around the world for the White Stockings and a selected All-American team. Spalding was the most prominent figure in baseball until Babe Ruth came along.
Playing Career: *1871-1877; Bos Red Stockings n, Chi N*
Managerial Career: *1876-1877; Chi N*

Al Spangler
Spangler, Albert Donal
B: Jul 8, 1933

Pos: OF   BA: .262
Hits: 594   HRs: 21
RBI: 175   BB: 295

A slap hitter with little range, Spangler could not break into the powerful Braves' lineup. Drafted by the Colt 45s, he had back-to-back .280 seasons, hitting 25 doubles in 1963 and nine triples in 1962. He played with Leo Durocher's 1969 Cubs.
Playing Career: *1959-1971; Mil N, Hou N, Cal A, Chi N*

Tully Sparks
Sparks, Thomas Frank
B: Dec 12, 1874   D: Jul 15, 1937

Pos: P   ERA: 2.79
W-L: 121-136   SOs: 778
ShOs: 19   Saves: 8

When foul balls were counted as strikes beginning in 1903, Sparks became an effective pitcher. His ERAs plummeted to less than 3.00 for seven straight years, and he pitched more than 200 innings each year. He was 22-8 with a 2.00 ERA in 1907. The Phillies finished in the first division four of six years that he was a top starter – no mean feat since the Giants, Pirates or Cubs had a virtual lock on first, second and third places.
Playing Career: *1897, 1899, 1901-1910; Phi N, Pit N, Mil A, NY N, Bos A*

Joe Sparma
Sparma, Joseph Blase
B: Feb 4, 1942   D: May 14, 1986

Pos: P   ERA: 3.95
W-L: 52-52   SOs: 586
ShOs: 10   No-hitters: 0

After pitching the 1968 pennant clincher for the Tigers, Sparma emerged from Manager Mayo Smith's doghouse as the hero of the hour. Smith allowed him one-third of an inning, in a mop-up role in Game Four of the World Series. Sparma was 16-9 in 1967, his best mark.
Playing Career: *1964-1970; Det A, Mon N*

Tris Speaker
Speaker, Tristram E. (The Gray Eagle, Spoke)
B: Apr 4, 1888   D: Dec 8, 1958
Hall of Fame 1937

Pos: OF   BA: .344
Hits: 3,515   HRs: 117
RBI: 1,559   BB: 1,381
Managerial Record
Won: 617   Lost: 520   Pct: .543

The seventh player elected to the Hall of Fame, Speaker's plaque reads, "the greatest center fielder of his day," but in retrospect that seems like a modest understatement. Speaker positioned himself in shallow center

Tris Speaker.

field so that he could pick up grounders, tossing the runner out at second on a force play as an infielder would do. He is the all-time leader in outfield assists and double plays.

At the plate, Speaker was a hitting machine. He won the AL batting title in 1916, the only year Ty Cobb did not win it from 1907 to 1919. Speaker hit more doubles than any other major league ballplayer, 792. He also belted 223 triples and stole 443 bases. He played for the 1912 World Champion Red Sox and was named AL MVP, receiving a $1,950 Chalmers automobile as a prize. Speaker and the Sox were victorious in the 1915 World Series as well. Under his management, the Indians won the 1920 World Series over the Dodgers.

Playing Career: *1907-1928; Bos A, Cle A, Was A, Phi A*
Managerial Career: *1919-1926; Cle A*

Chris Speier
Speier, Chris Edward
B: Jun 28, 1950

Pos: SS, 3B, 2B	BA: .246
Hits: 1,759	HRs: 112
RBI: 720	BB: 847

The Giants' starting shortstop in the 1971 NLCS, Speier batted .357 in four games. Toward the end of his career, he returned to the Giants, and was a defensive replacement in their campaign during the 1987 NLCS. A three-time All-Star, Speier hit well enough to stay in the majors for 19 seasons. He hit for the cycle twice, belted 302 doubles and scored 770 runs. Originally a shortstop, Speier changed positions when his range began to diminish.

Playing Career: *1971-1989; SF N, Mon N, StL N, Min A, Chi N*

Stan Spence
Spence, Stanley Orville
B: Mar 20, 1915   D: Jan 9, 1983

Pos: OF	BA: .282
Hits: 1,090	HRs: 95
RBI: 575	BB: 520

A star outfielder during World War II, Spence batted .323 in 1942 and led the AL in triples with 15. He hit .316 in 1944, then walloped 50 doubles and drove in 100 runs in 1946, but did not lead the AL. The four-time All-Star was a far-ranging, solid glove man.
Playing Career: *1940-1944, 1946-1949; Bos A, Was A, StL A*

Daryl Spencer
Spencer, Daryl Dean (Big Dee)
B: Jul 13, 1929

Pos: SS, 2B, 3B	BA: .244
Hits: 901	HRs: 105
RBI: 428	BB: 449

A prized rookie, Spencer hit 20 home runs in 1953, his first full season, but lost his job after spending two years in the military. He came back as a utility player. One of the best Gaijin hitters in Japan in the late 1960s and early 1970s, he hit 152 home runs there.
Playing Career: *1952-1953, 1956-1963; NY N, StL N, LA N, Cin N*

Jim Spencer
Spencer, James Lloyd
B: Jul 30, 1946

Pos: 1B	BA: .250
Hits: 1,227	HRs: 146
RBI: 599	BB: 407

Following in the footsteps of his grandfather Ben Spencer, Spencer became a major league ballplayer. He won two Gold Gloves as he led AL first basemen in fielding four times. The Yankees used him as a platoon player; he belted 23 homers in only 295 at-bats in 1979.
Playing Career: *1968-1982; Cal A, Tex A, Chi A, NY A, Oak A*

Dan Spillner
Spillner, Daniel Ray
B: Nov 27, 1951

Pos: P	ERA: 4.21
W-L: 73-89	SOs: 878
ShOs: 3	Saves: 50

As a starter, Spillner grew tired of watching the Padres' bullpen blow leads, so he joined them. Spillner, Rollie Fingers and Dave Tomlin appeared in 76, 78 and 76 games, respectively, in 1977. In 1982 with Cleveland, Spillner posted a 12-10 record with 21 saves and a 2.49 ERA in relief.
Playing Career: *1974-1985; SD N, Cle A, Chi A*

J. G. Taylor Spink
Spink, J. G. Taylor
B: Nov 6, 1888   D: Dec 8, 1962

Becoming editor of *The Sporting News* in 1914, Spink worked seven days a week, and would call anybody at any time of the day or night to get a story. Under his direction, the paper became "the Bible of Baseball," using a core of permanent staff and 250 correspondents. Spink took the paper's guardianship of the game seriously, furnishing officials with information about players involved in gambling, and helping to uncover the 1919 Black Sox scandal. The J. G. Taylor Spink Award, granted by the BBWAA, recognizes journalists who have made outstanding contributions to baseball.

Paul Splittorff
Splittorff, Paul William
B: Oct 8, 1946

Pos: P	ERA: 3.81
W-L: 166-143	SOs: 1,057
ShOs: 17	Saves: 1

A popular TV announcer today, Splittorff was the first player originally signed by the Royals to make it in the majors. He led the AL with a .727 winning percentage in 1977, and compiled a record of 16-6 despite a 1-4 start.

J.G. Taylor Spink (c) with (l-r) Hodges, Maris, Ford and Mantle.

The heart and soul of the early Royals' pitching staff, Splittorff is their all-time leader in games, starts, innings pitched, wins and losses. In a 1976 game he retired the last 26 A's in order.
Playing Career: *1970-1984; KC A*

Al Spohrer
Spohrer, Alfred Ray
B: Dec 3, 1902   D: Jul 17, 1972

Pos: C	BA: .259
Hits: 575	HRs: 6
RBI: 199	BB: 124

Spohrer once set up a boxing match with teammate Art "the Great" Shires. Commissioner Landis threatened to ban both of them for making a mockery of their baseball careers. Spohrer batted .317 for the Boston Braves in 1930, with 22 doubles and 8 triples, slugging .441.
Playing Career: *1928-1935; NY N, Bos N*

Mike Squires
Squires, Michael Lynn (Spanky)
B: Mar 5, 1952

Pos: 1B	BA: .260
Hits: 411	HRs: 6
RBI: 141	BB: 143

A Gold Glove first baseman in 1981, Squires played 14 games at third and two behind the plate even though he was left-handed. Chosen by the White Sox to hoist their division flag in 1983, the popular Squires batted .283 in 1980 on 97 hits, his personal best.
Playing Career: *1975, 1977-1985; Chi A*

Bill Stafford
Stafford, William Charles
B: Aug 13, 1939

Pos: P	ERA: 3.52
W-L: 43-40	SOs: 449
ShOs: 6	Saves: 9

Another of those young Yankee hurlers who posted fine beginnings but faded due to injuries and overwork, Stafford was 14-9 with a 2.68 ERA in 1961. He pitched in three World Series, winning Game Three of the 1962 Series despite being nailed by a line drive.
Playing Career: *1960-1967; NY A, KC A*

General Stafford
Stafford, James Joseph (Jamsey)
B: Jul 9, 1868   D: Sep 18, 1923

Pos: OF, 2B, SS, 3B	BA: .274
Hits: 583	HRs: 21
RBI: 290	BB: 164

Breaking into the big leagues with the Buffalo Players' League franchise – the one that went bankrupt – Stafford was a true utility man. He played on the 1894 Giants team that shocked the Orioles with a four-game Temple Cup sweep.
Playing Career: *1890, 1893-1899; Buf P, NY N, Lou N, Bos N, Was N*

Chick Stahl
Stahl, Charles Sylvester
B: Jan 10, 1873   D: Mar 28, 1907

Pos: OF	BA: .305
Hits: 1,546	HRs: 36
RBI: 622	BB: 470
Managerial Record	
Won: 14 Lost: 26 Pct: .350	

After a bad day in spring training in 1907, Stahl drank carbolic acid, and died. The story goes that he saw no hope for the Red Sox that year and committed suicide. Investigation showed, however, that he had been served with a paternity suit. Stahl batted .358 as an 1897 rookie, and topped .300 five of his first six seasons. He had six hits in one game in 1899. In the 1903 World Series Stahl hit three triples for the Red Sox, then led the AL with 19 triples in 1904.
Playing Career: *1897-1906; Bos N, Bos A*
Managerial Career: *1906; Bos A*

Jake Stahl
Stahl, Jacob Garland
B: Apr 13, 1879   D: Sep 18, 1922

Pos: 1B, OF	BA: .260
Hits: 891	HRs: 31
RBI: 437	BB: 221
Managerial Record	
Won: 263 Lost: 270 Pct: .493	

College-educated and also independently wealthy, Stahl worked for clubs at both extremes in baseball – the 1904 Senators, who had no spring training because the team had no money, and the 1912 Red Sox, who polished off the Giants in an eight-game World Series. Stahl led the AL in home runs in 1910.
Playing Career: *1903-1906, 1908-1910, 1912-1913; Bos A, Was A, NY A*
Managerial Record: *1905-1906, 1912-1913; Was A, Bos A*

Tuck Stainback
Stainback, George Tucker
B: Aug 4, 1911

Pos: OF	BA: .259
Hits: 585	HRs: 17
RBI: 204	BB: 64

Though he played for four pennant-winning teams, Stainback got into only two World Series, in 1942 and 1943 with the Yankees. But his ejection from a game in the 1935 Series – in which he was a Cubs reserve – for riding Umpire George Moriarty led to the entire bench being thrown out.
Playing Career: *1934-1946; Chi N, StL N, Phi N, Brk N, Det A, NY A, Phi A*

Gerry Staley
Staley, Gerald Lee
B: Aug 21, 1920

Pos: P	ERA: 3.70
W-L: 134-111	SOs: 727
ShOs: 9	Saves: 61

Yankees pitcher Gerry Staley in 1956.

In Chicago Staley was reunited with his former Cardinals manager, Marty Marion, who converted him to a reliever. In late September 1959, Staley entered a game and made only one pitch, resulting in a game-ending double play with the bases loaded, to capture the AL pennant for the White Sox. He was 0-1 with one save in the 1959 Fall Classic. Elected to the All-Star Game three times, Staley won 77 games in five years, 1949-1953.
Playing Career: *1947-1961; StL N, Cin N, NY A, Chi A, KC A, Det A*

Harry Staley
Staley, Henry E.
B: Nov 3, 1866   D: Jan 12, 1910

Pos: P	ERA: 3.80
W-L: 136-119	SOs: 746
ShOs: 10	Saves: 1

Staley and Pud Galvin whitewashed Boston in an 1888 doubleheader, the first time it was achieved in the NL. A four-time 20-game winner, Staley later won 65 percent of his decisions for the contending Beaneater teams of early 1890s. In an 1893 game that he pitched, Staley also slugged two homers. Known for his pickoff move, he once nailed Hall of Famer John Montgomery Ward off first.
Playing Career: *1888-1895; Pit N, Pit P, Bos N, StL N*

George Stallings
Stallings, George Tweedy
(The Miracle Man)
B: Nov 17, 1867   D: May 13, 1929

Pos: C	BA: .100
Hits: 2	HRs: 0
RBI: 0	BB: 1
Managerial Record	
Won: 879 Lost: 898 Pct: .495	

As a player Stallings appeared in only seven major league games. But as a manager Stallings stunned the baseball world in the last

half of the 1914 season. With the Braves in last place on July 4, he went to a three-man pitching rotation, sweeping the pennant and World Series. Superstitious and obsessive about bits of scrap paper, he was constantly picking them up from the field. The New York and Philadelphia clubs assigned fans to tear up and throw paper in Stallings's path, to distract him from the game.
Playing Career: *1890, 1897-1898; Brk N, Phi N*
Managerial Career: *1897-1898, 1901, 1909-1910, 1913-1920; Phi N, Det A, NY A, Bos N*

Oscar Stanage
Stanage, Oscar Harland
B: Mar 17, 1883   D: Nov 11, 1964

Pos: C	BA: .234
Hits: 819	HRs: 8
RBI: 321	BB: 219

A strong defensive catcher, Stanage was a platoon player for 12 years with the Tigers, catching more than 1,000 games. Stanage raised his batting average to the .260 level when the cork center ball was introduced in 1911.
Playing Career: *1906, 1909-1920, 1925; Cin N, Det A*

Lee Stange
Stange, Albert Lee (Stinger)
B: Oct 27, 1936

Pos: P	ERA: 3.56
W-L: 62-61	SOs: 718
ShOs: 8	Saves: 21

Stange had a 10-year major league pitching career, working as a starter and a reliever. He struggled with high ERAs, but put together a 12-5 record in 1963, and had an ERA of 2.77 in 1967, the year he tossed two scoreless innings for the Red Sox in the World Series.
Playing Career: *1961-1970; Min A, Cle A, Bos A, Chi A*

Bob Stanley in 1977 action.

Don Stanhouse
Stanhouse, Donald Joseph (Stan the Man Unusual)
B: Feb 12, 1951

Pos: P	ERA: 3.84
W-L: 38-54	SOs: 408
ShOs: 2	Saves: 64

Denizens of the Orioles' bullpen in 1978 and 1979 had Stanhouse to entertain them. He also did some work, saving 24 games with a 2.89 ERA in 1978. Stanhouse was selected for the All-Star Game roster in 1979, the year he saved 21 games with a 2.85 ERA.
Playing Career: *1972-1980, 1982; Tex A, Mon N, Bal A, LA N*

Eddie Stanky
Stanky, Edward Raymond (The Brat)
B: Sep 3, 1916

Pos: 2B, SS	BA: .268
Hits: 1,154	HRs: 29
RBI: 364	BB: 996
Managerial Record	
Won: 467 Lost: 435 Pct: .518	

Playing in three World Series with three different teams, Stanky was the topic for one of Dodger Manager Leo Durocher's colorful speeches. "Look at Mel Ott over there," Durocher said. "He's a nice guy, and he finishes second. Now look at The Brat [Stanky]. He can't hit, can't run, can't field. He's no nice guy, but all the little SOB can do is win." In Stanky's first full year with Brooklyn, 1945, he batted only .258 but led the NL in runs, with 128, and walks, with 148.
Playing Career: *1943-1953; Chi N, Brk N, NY N, StL N*
Managerial Career: *1952-1955, 1966-1968, 1977; StL N, Chi A, Tex A*

Bob Stanley
Stanley, Robert William (Bigfoot, The Steamer)
B: Nov 10, 1954

Pos: P	ERA: 3.64
W-L: 115-97	SOs: 693
ShOs: 7	Saves: 132

Stanley was the ultimate fireman, setting an AL record with 168⅓ relief innings in 1982. Compiling a record of 15-2 with 10 saves and a 2.60 ERA in 1978, he was moved into the starting rotation. There he tossed four shutouts, winning 16 games and an All-Star berth in 1979. He was an All-Star again in 1983. Stanley pitched six scoreless innings in the 1986 World Series, but gave up the tying run in the infamous 10th inning of Game Six on a two-out wild pitch.
Playing Career: *1977-1989; Bos A*

Oscar Stanage (third row, left) with the 1927 Pittsburgh Pirates, for whom he coached from 1927 to 1931.

Mickey Stanley
Stanley, Mitchell Jack
B: Jul 20, 1942

Pos: OF
Hits: 1,243
RBI: 500

BA: .248
HRs: 117
BB: 371

A four-time Gold Glove center fielder, Stanley moved to shortstop for the 1968 World Series in order to get Al Kaline's bat into the lineup. Although Stanley committed two errors, the Tigers won the Series. Four times in his career he had a 1.000 fielding average.
Playing Career: *1964-1978; Det A*

Leroy Stanton
Stanton, Leroy Bobby
B: Apr 10, 1946

Pos: OF
Hits: 628
RBI: 358

BA: .244
HRs: 77
BB: 236

Breaking into the majors with the Mets, Stanton became a platoon player, yet played in more than 100 games four years in a row. Part of the Jim Fregosi for Nolan Ryan trade, he was a saviour to the expansion Mariners, belting 27 homers and driving in 90 runs for them in 1977.
Playing Career: *1970-1978; NY N, Cal A, Sea A*

Dave Stapleton
Stapleton, David Leslie
B: Jan 16, 1954

Pos: 1B, 2B, SS
Hits: 550
RBI: 234

BA: .271
HRs: 41
BB: 114

Despite his short career, Stapleton was a Red Sox hero, batting .667 in the 1986 ALCS win over the Angels. After hitting .321 his rookie season, his average went down each year until he was, ironically, a defensive replacement for injured Bill Buckner.
Playing Career: *1980-1986; Bos A*

Willie Stargell
Stargell, Wilver Dornel (Pops, Sarge)
B: Mar 6, 1940
Hall of Fame 1988

Pos: 1B, OF
Hits: 2,232
RBI: 1,540

BA: .282
HRs: 475
BB: 937

On July 22, 1964, Stargell hit for the cycle. That year, the left-handed slugger began a string of 13 consecutive 20-homer seasons, and set out on the path to the Hall of Fame. A seven-time All-Star, he whacked five extra-base hits in one 1970 game, tying the major league record. When Roberto Clemente died, Stargell stepped in to lead the Pirates. As baseball mourned Clemente, Stargell's spectacular 1973 season was overshadowed. That year he batted .299, hit 44 home runs, and had 119 RBI.

As captain of the 1979 "We are Family"

Willie Stargell.

Bucs, Stargell drove the team to a pennant with his bat, hitting .281 with 32 home runs and 82 RBI. He awarded Stargell Stars to deserving teammates. In the World Series win, he set records with 25 total bases and seven extra-base hits, three homers and four doubles. Stargell was named NL co-MVP, NLCS and World Series MVP, *The Sporting News* Man of the Year, and *Sports Illustrated* co-Man of the Year. Stargell retired as the Pirates' career leader in 10 categories, including home runs and RBI.
Playing Career: *1962-1982; Pit N*

Joe Start
Start, Joseph (Old Reliable)
B: Oct 14, 1842   D: Mar 27, 1927

Pos: 1B
Hits: 1,411
RBI: 468 (inc.)
Managerial Record
Won: 18   Lost: 7   Pct: .720

BA: .298
HRs: 15
BB: 164

Called "Old Reliable" at an early age, Start was one of the top stars of the 19th century. His career began with the Brooklyn Atlantics, the team that stopped the Cincinnati Red Stockings' 88-game winning streak in 1870, largely due to Start's 11th-inning triple. He won two national titles with the Atlantics, who were undefeated in 1864 and 1865.

Moving to the New York Mutuals when the Atlantic club voted to go back to amateur status in 1871, Start put in five years in the old National Association before joining the new NL in 1876. He led NL first basemen in fielding for three of the league's first four years. Start is credited with being the first player to position himself away from first base; his chances per game and putouts per game surpassed all other first basemen of his time. He led the Providence Grays to NL pennants in 1879 and 1884.
Playing Career: *1871-1886; NY Mutuals n, Har N, Chi N, Pro N, Was N*
Managerial Career: *1873; NY Mutuals n*

Jigger Statz
Statz, Arnold John
B: Oct 20, 1897   D: Mar 16, 1988

Pos: OF
Hits: 737
RBI: 215

BA: .285
HRs: 17
BB: 194

One of the brightest stars in the minor leagues, Statz played 3,473 professional baseball games. His best major league year was 1923 with the Cubs, when he hit .319 with 209 hits, 110 runs scored and 29 stolen bases. Statz played 18 years with the Los Angeles PCL team.
Playing Career: *1919-1920, 1922-1928; NY N, Bos A, Chi N, Brk N*

Rusty Staub.

Rusty Staub
Staub, Daniel Joseph (Le Grand Orange)
B: Apr 1, 1944

Pos: OF, DH
Hits: 2,716
RBI: 1,466

BA: .279
HRs: 292
BB: 1,255

Staub is the answer to the trivia question: "What player had 500 or more hits for four different major league clubs?" Staub signed a $100,000 bonus with Houston in 1961 to begin a career in which he would score 1,189 runs, hit 499 doubles and pinch-hit 358 times with 100 hits. A star and a popular player everywhere he went, the redhead joined two expansion franchises. He provided instant excitement and credibility for the Colt .45s and the Expos, whose fans dubbed him "Le Grand Orange."

Staub played a dramatic role in the Mets' 1973 postseason. He hurt his shoulder in Game Four of the NLCS when he caught Dan Driessen's 11th-inning drive at the right field wall in Shea Stadium. He took cortisone shots and threw underhand in the World Series against the A's. Though unable to pull the ball, Staub hit an opposite field homer off Ken Holtzman to win Game Four.
Playing Career: *1963-1985; Hou N, Mon N, NY N, Det A, Tex A*

Turkey Stearnes
Stearnes, Norman Thomas
B: May 8, 1901   D: Sep 4, 1979

Pos: OF	BA: .352
Hits: 1,183	HRs: 181
RBI: NA	BB: NA

"One of the greatest hitters we ever had. He was as good as anybody who ever played ball," said Satchel Paige of Stearnes. The all-time Negro League home run champion, Stearnes played in four of the first five East-West All-Star Games. Batting in the three hole, he holds most of the Detroit Stars' career batting records, winning the league home run title five times. Although a good portion of his career statistics are yet to be compiled, he already is credited with more than 200 doubles, 100 triples, 100 home runs and 100 stolen bases.

In 1931 Stearnes was enjoying another excellent season when the Detroit owners failed to pay his salary on time. He jumped to the Monarchs, who never missed a payday. The following year he joined the American Giants, whose manager Dave Malarcher batted him in the leadoff position, taking full advantage of his talents. Stearnes led Chicago to another championship.
Playing Career: *1923-1940; Det Stars, NY Lincoln Giants, KC Monarchs, Chi Am Giants, Phi Stars*

John Stearns
Stearns, John Hardin (Bad Dude)
B: Aug 21, 1951

Pos: C, 1B, 3B	BA: .260
Hits: 696	HRs: 46
RBI: 312	BB: 323

An all-Big Eight conference football player at the University of Colorado, Stearns once batted in 12 runs in a losing effort at Oklahoma State. An All-Star four times, Stearns's best year was 1978, when he hit 15 homers with 73 RBI and a .413 slugging average with the New York Mets.
Playing Career: *1974-1984; Phi N, NY N*

Bill Stein
Stein, William Allen
B: Jan 21, 1947

Pos: 3B, 2B, 1B, OF	BA: .267
Hits: 751	HRs: 44
RBI: 311	BB: 186

Socking a homer for his first hit in the majors, Stein played regularly only one year, with the Mariners in 1977. He hit .259 with 13 homers and 67 RBI. With the Rangers, Stein set an AL record with seven straight pinch hits, and led the league with nine.
Playing Career: *1972-1985; StL N, Chi A, Sea A, Tex A*

Ed Stein
Stein, Edward F.
B: Sep 5, 1869   D: May 10, 1928

Pos: P	ERA: 3.96
W-L: 110-78	SOs: 535
ShOs: 12	No-hitters: 1

Winning 58 percent of his decisions, Stein was the main starter for the Trolley Dodgers from Brooklyn. Averaging more than 300 innings, 1892-1895, he succumbed to arm trouble, possibly from overuse. Stein won 27 games – six of them shutouts – in 1892, and 26 two years later.
Playing Career: *1890-1896, 1898; Chi N, Brk N*

Terry Steinbach
Steinbach, Terry Lee
B: Mar 2, 1962

Pos: C	BA: .274
Hits: 786	HRs: 71
RBI: 373	BB: 207

One of the best young catchers in the game, Steinbach's rise mirrored Oakland's four division titles in five years. His selection as the starting AL catcher for the 1988 All-Star Game was ridiculed as he was hitting only .216 at the All-Star break while platooning with Ron Hassey as the A's catcher. But he silenced critics with a home run in his first All-Star at-bat, and a sacrifice fly that just missed being a grand slam in his second at-bat, to win All-Star Game MVP honors.

Steinbach also homered in his first major league at-bat. He completed his rookie season of 1987 with 16 dingers and a .284 average. In postseason play in 1989, Steinbach hit a home run and drove in five runs in the ALCS, as Oakland wiped out the Blue Jays in five games. In the earthquake-disrupted World Series, he hit another homer and led the A's with seven RBI.
Playing Career: *1986-; Oak A*

George Steinbrenner
Steinbrenner, George (The Boss)
B: Jul 4, 1930

"Don't blame George, he's from Cleveland," begged a headline in the *New York Times*. The article went on to elucidate the miscalculations that Steinbrenner, the owner of the Yankees, made in assuming what New Yorkers want. Steinbrenner may not be able to forget his football background, but he brought winning back to the Yankees. To a franchise that had not seen a pennant race since 1964, Steinbrenner brought high-priced Reggie Jackson and street fighter Billy Martin to lead the Yankees back to glory.

They won AL pennants in 1976, 1977 and 1978, and back-to-back World Series victories over the Dodgers in 1977 and 1978. Known for frequent managerial changes – the rule against managerial changes during the World Series is known as the Steinbrenner rule – and a direct, hands-on approach, Steinbrenner understands baseball as a business. He knows that baseball in New York is competing for the entertainment dollar against Madison Square Garden and Broadway.

A's catcher Terry Steinbach.

George Steinbrenner toasts Manager Billy Martin after NY won the 1977 AL pennant.

Harry Steinfeldt
Steinfeldt, Harry M.
B: Sep 29, 1877   D: Aug 17, 1914

Pos: 3B	BA: .268
Hits: 1,578	HRs: 27
RBI: 762	BB: 471

The potent Cubs did not break the Pirates' and Giants' grip on the NL pennant until Steinfeldt joined their famous infield. Steinfeldt played third base in the Tinker-to-Evers-to-Chance infield. He could hit; he led the 1906 deadball era NL with 176 hits and 83 RBI while batting .327. Left out of Franklin P. Adams's poem, Steinfeldt nevertheless dominated third basemen of his era, winning the fielding title three times in five years as the Cubs won four NL flags in the same span. Playing in four World Series, Steinfeldt batted .471 in the 1907 blitz of the Tigers.

A St. Louis native, he had originally hoped for a career in the theatre, but played ball so well in games put on by his touring troupe that he switched from the stage to the diamond. After eight years with the Reds, leading the NL in doubles with 32 in 1903, Steinfeldt was traded to the Cubs, and became part of baseball history.
Playing Career: *1898-1911; Cin N, Chi N, Bos N*

Casey Stengel
Stengel, Charles Dillon
(The Old Professor)
B: Jul 30, 1890   D: Sep 29, 1975
Hall of Fame 1966

Pos: OF	BA: .284
Hits: 1,219	HRs: 60
RBI: 535	BB: 437
Managerial Record	
Won: 1,905 Lost: 1,842 Pct: .508	

As manager of the Yankees, Stengel explained to rookie phenom Mickey Mantle how to play the tricky right field corner in Ebbets Field. Mantle looked at him with wide, disbelieving eyes, prompting Stengel to quip, "he thinks I was born at 60 and began managing immediately." Actually, Stengel learned to manage while cooking breakfast for Mr. and Mrs. John McGraw during spring training. The two ballplayers would pore over statistics and theories, arguing all morning, then continuing the discussion at night after the day's rigors.

On the playing field Stengel had his best season as a platoon outfielder for McGraw; he hit .368 in 1922 and .339 in 1923, both pennant-winning years. He batted .393 in 12 games for three World Series with the Dodgers and Giants. Stengel socked an inside-the-park homer in Game Three of the 1923 Series – pumping his old legs, and losing a shoe – and barely beat the throw to the plate to win 1-0 over the Yankees. As the Yankees' manager he won 10 pennants in 12 years, taking seven World Series in 10 attempts.
Playing Career: *1912-1925; Brk N, Pit N, Phi N, NY N, Bos N*
Managerial Career: *1934-1936, 1938-1943, 1949-1960, 1962-1965; Brk N, Bos N, NY A, NY N*

Rennie Stennett
Stennett y Porte, Renaldo Antonio
B: Apr 5, 1951

Pos: 2B, SS	BA: .274
Hits: 1,239	HRs: 41
RBI: 432	BB: 207

Going 7-for-7 in a nine-inning game, Stennett tied Wilbert Robinson's 19th-century NL record. A budding superstar, Stennett beat out Dave Cash and Willie Randolph for the second base job with the Pirates. He led NL second sackers in putouts and total chances per game in 1974 and 1976. He fell eight games short of Ken Hubbs's record 418 consecutive errorless chances. Hitting .336 in 1977, Stennett seemed headed for the Hall of Fame when he broke his ankle the next year and never regained his snap.
Playing Career: *1971-1981; Pit N, SF N*

Jake Stenzel
Stenzel, Jacob Charles
B: Jun 24, 1867   D: Jan 6, 1919

Pos: OF	BA: .339
Hits: 1,024	HRs: 33
RBI: 533	BB: 299

Stenzel produced a high batting average while hitting at the top of the lineup. He scored 662 runs, mainly in the four-year span of 1894-1897. Leading the NL in doubles with 43 in 1897, Stenzel helped the old Orioles to a Temple Cup championship over the NL pennant-winning Beaneaters, with seven runs scored and a .381 average on eight hits in five games. Stenzel stole 292 bases, reaching a high of 69 in 1897.
Playing Career: *1890, 1892-1899; Chi N, Pit N, Bal N, StL N, Cin N*

Vern Stephens.

Vern Stephens
Stephens, Vernon Decatur (Junior, Buster)
B: Oct 23, 1920   D: Nov 3, 1968

Pos: SS	BA: .286
Hits: 1,859	HRs: 247
RBI: 1,174	BB: 692

The best power-hitting shortstop in the major leagues until Ernie Banks came along, Stephens was signed by the Browns at age 17 and was a regular in their infield by age 21. He was a steady fielder, but it was his bat that brought him glory. After the Browns' pennant-winning season of 1944, Stephens led the league in home runs in 1945. The next year, he was lured to the outlawed Mexican League by a lucrative $175,000 contract. Stephens had been south of the border only a

Casey Stengel led the Yankees in 10 pennants and 7 WS victories in 12 seasons.

few days when his father, who was a minor league umpire, and Browns scout Jack Fournier drove to Mexico and brought him back. The players who stayed to play in Mexico were suspended by Commissioner Chandler, and few regained their pre-suspension career status.

Selected for the All-Star Game seven times, Stephens batted behind Ted Williams for five years, forming one of the best three-four hole hitting combinations in the AL. Stephens led the AL in RBI in 1944 and in 1949-1950. He scored 1,001 runs.

Playing Career: *1941-1955; StL A, Bos A, Chi A, Bal A*

Riggs Stephenson
Stephenson, Jackson Riggs
B: Jan 5, 1898   D: Nov 15, 1985

Pos: OF	BA: .336
Hits: 1,515	HRs: 63
RBI: 773	BB: 494

A hot bat and a stone-cold glove kept Stephenson in the major leagues but out of the limelight. A football injury at the University of Alabama damaged his shoulder and kept him from being a top-notch fielder. He was signed as a second baseman, but could not make pivot throws, so learned to play the outfield during a stint in the minor leagues. Stephenson's weak arm hampered his career in the outfield as well. During one season with the Cubs, he had only one assist.

Luckily, Stephenson could really hit. He batted .319 or better for 12 of his 14 major league seasons. In 1927 he led the NL in doubles with 46. Stephenson combined with Kiki Cuyler and Hack Wilson on the 1929

Riggs Stephenson.

Cubs, to make the last outfield trio in baseball history in which all three players had more than 100 RBI. In two World Series for Chicago, Stephenson batted .378. He managed in the minors from 1934 to 1939.

Playing Career: *1921-1934; Cle A, Chi N*

Bud Stewart
Stewart, Edward Perry
B: Jun 15, 1916

Pos: OF	BA: .268
Hits: 547	HRs: 32
RBI: 260	BB: 252

A promising rookie who became a leading pinch hitter in both the AL and NL, Stewart worked his way back to the major leagues after his stint with Uncle Sam. He developed some doubles and triples power, socking 13 triples in 1948 and 23 two-baggers in 1949.

Playing Career: *1941-1942, 1948-1954; Pit N, NY A, Was A, Chi A*

Dave Stewart, with Oakland in 1992.

Dave Stewart
Stewart, David Keith (Smoke)
B: Feb 19, 1957

Pos: P	ERA: 3.75
W-L: 158-114	SOs: 1,572
ShOs: 9	No-hitters: 1

A perennial Cy Young Award candidate, Stewart won 20 or more games four straight years, the first pitcher to do so since Hall of Famer Jim Palmer. Stewart had won 30 games by age 29 when the Athletics acquired him from the Phillies. Learning the forkball, Stewart became the most potent mound force in the AL, winning 116 games in the next seven years for a team that won four division titles in five years. Strangely, he was chosen only once for the All-Star team.

Stewart's lack of media coverage is difficult to understand. He does his job extremely well and was the leader of the power-laden Athletics, yet Jose Canseco, Mark McGwire, Rickey Henderson and Dennis Eckersley got the accolades. In ALCS play for the A's and

Blue Jays, Stewart was 8-0 in 10 starts. In the World Series, he was 2-3 in six starts, winning two, and tossing a shutout in Game One in the A's sweep of the 1989 Giants. Stewart signed a free-agent contract with the Blue Jays in 1993, reaching the Series once again.

Playing Career: *1978, 1981-; LA N, Tex A, Phi N, Oak A, Tor A*

Lefty Stewart
Stewart, Walter Cleveland
B: Sep 23, 1900   D: Sep 26, 1974

Pos: P	ERA: 4.19
W-L: 101-98	SOs: 503
ShOs: 8	Saves: 8

A former minor league manager gave Stewart a job with the Browns in 1927, but Stewart's appendix burst that winter, and he nearly died. He recovered, however, and won 20 games in 1930. He was 15-6 for the 1933 AL champion Senators.

Playing Career: *1921, 1927-1935; Det A, StL A, Was A, Cle A*

Sammy Stewart
Stewart, Samuel Lee
B: Oct 28, 1954

Pos: P	ERA: 3.59
W-L: 59-48	SOs: 586
ShOs: 1	Saves: 45

The Orioles' postseason secret weapon, Stewart was unscored upon in four games in one ALCS and two World Series. He fanned seven straight Indians in his major league debut, September 1, 1978. Stewart had career highs of 10 wins in 1982 and 13 saves in 1984.

Playing Career: *1978-1987; Bal A, Bos A, Cle A*

Dave Stieb
Stieb, David Andrew
B: Jul 22, 1957

Pos: P	ERA: 3.41
W-L: 175-135	SOs: 1,642
ShOs: 30	No-hitters: 1

The Blue Jays' all-time pitching leader, Stieb was originally signed as a third baseman. His fielding ability has kept him in some games. Displaying a bad temper, Stieb glowered at umpires and teammates who made errors. The seven-time All-Star won a career-high 18 games in 1990 and posted 17 victories on three other occasions.

In 1988 Stieb went 16-8 with a 3.04 ERA. He pitched a one-hitter against the Brewers that year, allowing only one single to B. J. Surhoff, then in his last two starts of the season Stieb pitched to within one strike of no-hitters. Julio Franco spoiled the first bid with a bad-bounce grounder past the second baseman, and Jim Traber ruined the second with a clean single to right. In his second start of 1989, Stieb one-hit the Yankees, giving him three one-hitters in four starts. The following year he finally pitched his no-hitter.

Playing Career: *1979-; Tor A, Chi A*

Blue Jays ace Dave Stieb.

Jack Stivetts.

Dick Stigman
Stigman, Richard Lewis
B: Jan 24, 1936

Pos: P	ERA: 4.03
W-L: 46-54	SOs: 755
ShOs: 5	Saves: 16

An aloof hurler with lots of stuff, Stigman made the 1960 All-Star team as a rookie, but never made it again, despite going 12-5 in 1962 and winning 15 for the Twins in 1963. He had high ERAs. Stigman tossed 241 innings in 1963.
Playing Career: 1960-1966; Cle A, Min A, Bos A

Snuffy Stirnweiss
Stirnweiss, George Henry
B: Oct 26, 1918   D: Sep 15, 1958

Pos: 2B, 3B	BA: .268
Hits: 989	HRs: 29
RBI: 281	BB: 541

Winning the 1945 AL batting title, Stirnweiss led the league in batting, slugging, at-bats, hits, triples, runs and stolen bases. Playing in three World Series for the Yankees, he could not make the team four years later, and was traded to the Browns.
Playing Career: 1943-1952; NY A, StL A, Cle A

Jack Stivetts
Stivetts, John Elmer (Happy Jack)
B: Mar 31, 1868   D: Apr 18, 1930

Pos: P	ERA: 3.74
W-L: 204-132	SOs: 1,223
ShOs: 14	No-hitters: 2

From the anthracite coal fields of Pennsylvania, Stivetts came to the big leagues with a big bat and a strong pitching arm. When he re-tired he left a legacy of big game performances, tossing two no-hitters, one the day after he broke up a scoreless pitching duel with a 12th-inning home run. The same year, 1892, Stivetts pitched both the morning and afternoon games of the Labor Day doubleheader. On the final day of the season, he tossed his second no-hitter as Boston won their 102nd game.

In the opening game of the 1892 Championship Series, Stivetts battled Cy Young to a 0-0, 11-inning tie. He won his next two decisions as the Beaneaters beat the second-place Spiders in five straight contests. Stivetts pitched and batted Boston to four pennants. He had a .297 career batting average with 35 home runs. In 1894 he knocked in 64 runs in 68 games, slugging .533. On the mound he won more than 60 percent of his games, posting 20 or more victories in six of his 11 seasons. Stivetts and Kid Nichols gave the Beaneaters the most powerful one-two rotation in the 1890s.
Playing Career: 1889-1899; StL AA, Bos N, Cle N

Chuck Stobbs
Stobbs, Charles Klein
B: Jul 2, 1929

Pos: P	ERA: 4.29
W-L: 107-130	SOs: 897
ShOs: 7	Saves: 19

Surrendering Mickey Mantle's 565-foot home run in 1953 brought Stobbs recognition – if not quite the kind he wanted. In 1957 with Washington, Stobbs endured a losing streak of 11 games. The left-hander changed his uniform number to 13, and fans brought him rabbits' feet and other lucky charms, but he had only one more winning season – 1960, when he went 12-7.
Playing Career: 1947-1961; Bos A, Chi A, Was A, StL N, Min A

Milt Stock
Stock, Milton Joseph
B: Jul 11, 1893   D: Jul 16, 1977

Pos: 3B, 2B, SS	BA: .289
Hits: 1,806	HRs: 22
RBI: 696	BB: 455

Guarding the hot corner for 11 years, Stock played in the 1915 World Series as a 22-year-old. He batted over .300 five times, twice topping the .318 mark. Stock stole 155 bases and scored 839 runs. After his playing career, he coached in the majors. Stock was the Dodgers' third base coach who waved Cal Abrams home, only to be nailed by the Phillies' Richie Ashburn, costing Brooklyn the 1950 pennant. Stock was fired several days later.
Playing Career: 1913-1926; NY N, Phi N, StL N, Brk N

Tim Stoddard
Stoddard, Timothy Paul
B: Jan 24, 1953

Pos: P	ERA: 3.95
W-L: 41-35	SOs: 582
ShOs: 0	Saves: 76

A starter for the 1974 NCAA basketball champs at North Carolina State, Stoddard anchored the bullpen for the Orioles, who won two pennants in 1979 and 1983. He was 1-0 in the 1979 World Series, driving in a run in his very first major league at-bat. Stoddard saved 26 games in 1980.
Playing Career: 1975, 1978-1989; Chi A, Bal A, Chi N, SD N, NY A, Cle A

George Stone
Stone, George Heard
B: Jul 9, 1946

Pos: P	ERA: 3.89
W-L: 60-57	SOs: 590
ShOs: 5	Saves: 5

An essential ingredient in the Mets' surprise 1973 pennant, Stone was 12-3 with a 2.80 ERA and put together a string of eight victories at the end of the season. The big left-hander pitched in two NLCS and in the 1973 World Series.
Playing Career: 1967-1975; Atl N, NY N

George Stone
Stone, George Robert
B: Sep 3, 1877   D: Jan 3, 1945

Pos: OF	BA: .301
Hits: 984	HRs: 23
RBI: 268	BB: 282

Peaking in 1905, Stone led the AL in hits with 187, then won the batting crown the next year with a .358 average. After his major league playing career, Stone became owner of a minor league team in Lincoln, Nebraska, and was later a minor league president.
Playing Career: 1903, 1905-1910; Bos A, StL A

The Senators' John Stone in 1935.

John Stone
Stone, John Thomas (Rocky)
B: Oct 10, 1905   D: Nov 30, 1955

Pos: OF	BA: .310
Hits: 1,391	HRs: 77
RBI: 707	BB: 463

Highly sought-after in the early 1930s, Stone was acquired by the Senators in 1933 in exchange for Hall of Famer Goose Goslin. In Stone's best year, 1932, he batted .297 with 17 home runs and 35 doubles, driving in 108 and scoring 106 runs. He hit in the .300 range seven times during his 11-season career. In 1936 Stone pounded the ball at the rate of .341 with 15 home runs and 90 RBI. He scored 95 times that year.

Some of Stone's batting exploits included a 34-game hitting streak in 1930, his first year as a regular. He became the first player to have six extra-base hits in a doubleheader without extra innings when he hit two home runs and four doubles during a twin-bill on May 30, 1933. An illness in 1938 ended Stone's major league playing career.
Playing Career: *1928-1938; Det A, Was A*

Steve Stone
Stone, Steven Michael
B: Jul 14, 1947

Pos: P	ERA: 3.96
W-L: 107-93	SOs: 1,065
ShOs: 7	Saves: 1

After snoozing in the majors for 10 years, Stone suddenly came alive in 1980, posted a 25-7 record with a 3.23 ERA, and won the Cy Young Award. He led the AL in wins and in winning percentage that year. Selected for the All-Star Game, Stone pitched three perfect innings. He had relied on throwing heat until arm trouble made him concentrate on control. After his playing career, Stone became a broadcaster with the Cubs.
Playing Career: *1971-1981; SF N, Chi A, Chi N, Bal A*

Charles Stoneham
Stoneham, Charles A.
B: Jul 5, 1876   D: Jan 6, 1936

As the owner of the New York Giants, Charles Stoneham was able to endure tough times and bad publicity to pass his shares on to his son, Horace, who only recently sold the club to real estate magnate Robert Lurie. Stoneham made his money as a runner on Wall Street, and as an independent stockbroker on the New York Curb Exchange. His operations have been characterized as lucrative "Bucket Shops."

In 1919 the Giants called a press conference to announce that Charles A. Stoneham, Francis McQuade and John J. McGraw had purchased the club from the estate of John T. Brush. The three new owners also purchased Cuban properties including a racetrack, casino and newspaper in Havana. When the three-man syndicate dissolved in 1921, Stoneham was indicted on charges of mail fraud and perjury. The New York press began a three-year campaign, possibly instigated by one of the other two partners, to force Stoneham to relinquish his shares in the Giants. He hung on and passed the ownership of the Giants to his family.

Horace Stoneham
Stoneham, Horace
B: Apr 27, 1903

A graduate of Fordham University, where he played baseball and hockey, Horace Stoneham began his interest in the Giants in 1929 when he took a job with the club. Stoneham had already performed his father's duties for a year when the elder Stoneham died in 1936 and passed on the club ownership to his son. At age 32 Horace Stoneham became the youngest NL owner in baseball history. In contrast to his father, he was sentimental, business-oriented and conservative.

Working with Bill Terry, he built up the Giants' farm system, turned down offers of

Giants owner Horace Stoneham (c).

$1 million for Willie Mays, and convinced other owners to bring black and Latin talent to the big leagues. Faced with deteriorating conditions in New York, Stoneham wanted to move the team to Minneapolis, but was persuaded to go to the West Coast instead. Stoneham did not fare well with the move to San Francisco; despite a wealth of talent, he lost millions of dollars. Refusing to sell the Giants to Labatts Brewery, he eventually sold to Robert Lurie and retired from public life.

Bill Stoneman
Stoneman, William Hambly (Stoney)
B: Apr 7, 1944

Pos: P	ERA: 4.08
W-L: 54-85	SOs: 934
ShOs: 15	No-hitters: 2

Now vice-president of baseball operations for the Expos, Stoneman tossed two no-hitters for Montreal. The first was just 10 days after the franchise opened, and the second was the only major league no-hitter at Jarry Park. Twice Stoneman struck out 14 batters in a game. He retains the Expos' single-season strikeout, complete game and shutout records, all set in 1971 when he was 17-16, completed 20 games, and compiled 251 strikeouts for a 3.15 ERA.
Playing Career: *1967-1974; Chi N, Mon N, Cal A*

Lil Stoner
Stoner, Ulysses Simpson Grant
B: Feb 28, 1899   D: Jun 26, 1966

Pos: P	ERA: 4.76
W-L: 50-58	SOs: 299
ShOs: 1	Saves: 14

The winner of 27 games in the 1923 Texas League, Stoner won 11 for Ty Cobb and the Tigers in 1924. He posted 10 victories in 1925 and again in 1927 working both as a starter and reliever. He tended to walk too many and give up too many home runs.
Playing Career: *1922, 1924-1931; Det A, Pit N, Phi N*

Mel Stottlemyre
Stottlemyre, Melvin Leon
B: Nov 13, 1941

Pos: P	ERA: 2.97
W-L: 164-139	SOs: 1,257
ShOs: 40	Saves: 1

Stottlemyre whacked an inside-the-park grand slam home run in 1965, the last pitcher to do so. Called up in 1964, he contributed nine victories to the Yankees' campaign for their fifth straight pennant. Stottlemyre won Game Two of the World Series and gave up only two runs in Game Five, but lost the finale, being forced to hurl three games in the Fall Classic as a rookie. He won 20 or more games three times, and was chosen for the All-Star team five times. Pitcher Todd Stottlemyre is his son.
Playing Career: *1964-1974; NY A*

Todd Stottlemyre
Stottlemyre, Todd Vernon
B: May 20, 1965

Pos: P	ERA: 4.41
W-L: 62-63	SOs: 557
ShOs: 3	No-hitters: 0

A solid starter in the Blue Jays' rotation, Stottlemyre helped them win three division titles in four years. In the 1992 World Series, when the Jays used the Reds' method of shortening the game with three relievers, he had a 0.00 ERA in 3.2 innings in four games.
Playing Career: *1988-; Tor A*

George Stovall
Stovall, George Thomas
B: Nov 23, 1878   D: Nov 5, 1951

Pos: 1B, 2B, 3B	BA: .265
Hits: 1,381	HRs: 15
RBI: 174	BB: 174
Managerial Record	
Won: 313 Lost: 376 Pct: .454	

Addie Joss had a perfect game in 1908 thanks to Stovall's stunning scoop of a throw in the dirt to make the last out. He later engineered a "strike" so that players could attend Joss's funeral in 1911. Barely into that season Stovall was named playing manager for the Indians. He was one of the first stars to defect to the Federal League, and recruited others.
Playing Career: *1904-1915; Cle A, StL A, KC F*
Managerial Career: *1911-1915; Cle A, StL A, KC F*

Harry Stovey
Stovey, Harry Duffield
B: Dec 20, 1856   D: Sep 20, 1937

Pos: OF	BA: .288
Hits: 1,769	HRs: 121
RBI: 547 (inc.)	BB: 661
Managerial Record	
Won: 63 Lost: 75 Pct: .457	

Stovey was a baserunning fool. One of only four players who scored more runs than games played, he chalked up 1,492 runs in 1,486 games. Stovey pilfered 509 sacks with a high of 97 to lead the Players' League in 1890. He was the original power and speed man, hammering 174 triples to lead the league four times.

Stovey led the league twice in stolen bases and five times in home runs. In 1891 he signed a contract with the Boston Nationals, in violation of the 1890 Players' Rebellion settlement which stated that players were to return to their 1889 clubs. The 1889 AA Athletics, however, left Stovey off the reserve list by mistake. The Board of Arbitration decided to let him play with the NL team, causing a new war to break out that destroyed the AA one year later.
Playing Career: *1880-1893; Wor N, Phi AA, Bos P, Bos N, Bal N, Brk N*
Managerial Career: *1881, 1885; Wor N, Phi AA*

Sammy Strang
Strang, Samuel Nicklin (The Dixie Thrush)
B: Dec 16, 1876   D: Mar 13, 1932

Pos: 3B, 2B, OF, SS	BA: .269
Hits: 790	HRs: 16
RBI: 253	BB: 464

Southerner Strang was the 1905 Giants' main utility player, leading the NL with eight pinch hits that season. The New York press tagged him a "pinch" hitter because he came through in a "pinch." Strang scored 101 and 109 runs in back-to-back seasons.
Playing Career: *1896, 1900-1908; Lou N, Chi N, NY N, Chi A, Brk N*

Scott Stratton
Stratton, C. Scott
B: Oct 2, 1869   D: Mar 8, 1939

Pos: P	ERA: 3.88
W-L: 97-114	SOs: 570
ShOs: 10	Saves: 1

The main reason for the Louisville AA club's last-to-first turnaround in 1890 was Stratton's pitching. He went from a 3-13 record to 34-14 with 207 strikeouts and an AA-leading 2.36 ERA. An outstanding hitter, Stratton batted .323 or more three times.
Playing Career: *1888-1895; Lou AA, Pit N, Lou N, Chi N*

Darryl Strawberry
Strawberry, Darryl Eugene
B: Mar 12, 1962

Pos: OF	BA: .259
Hits: 1,210	HRs: 290
RBI: 869	BB: 690

Back trouble and surgery have derailed the Strawberry express. An eight-time All-Star, he hit 26 or more homers in each of his first nine years in the majors, leading the NL with 39 in 1988. He was a crucial participant in the

Harry Stovey.

Darryl Strawberry at bat in 1984.

Mets' 1986 World Championship, with key hits in postseason play. In the NLCS he hit a three-run homer in Game Three, and a game-tying solo shot in Game Five. His leadoff double in the 16th inning of Game Six started the Mets' pennant-winning rally. Strawberry belted a long home run in the World Series.

The 1983 NL Rookie of the Year, Strawberry is known for streaks and slumps. His hot streaks carried the Mets for months at a time; his slumps left them writhing. Usually batting cleanup, he aimed for the apple that rises out of a top hat beyond deep center field in Shea Stadium. One of his shots went into the hat, jamming the apple. In an October series against the first-place Cardinals in 1985, Strawberry hit a blast off Ken Dayley that hit the scoreboard and broke its clock.
Playing Career: *1983-; NY N, LA N*

Gabby Street
Street, Charles Evard (Sarge)
B: Sep 30, 1882   D: Feb 6, 1951

Pos: C	BA: .208
Hits: 312	HRs: 2
RBI: 105	BB: 119
Managerial Record	
Won: 367 Lost: 339 Pct: .520	

One of baseball's lively characters, Street caught a ball dropped from the Washington Monument, managed the Cardinals' Gas House Gang to a World Championship with the Wild Horse of the Osage – Pepper Martin – and invented Walter Johnson's phantom pitch. During a Senators' game at dusk, Street pounded his mitt as Johnson faked a pitch. The umpire called strike three, and the batter argued that it was a foot outside!
Playing Career: *1904-1905, 1908-1912, 1931; Cin N, Bos N, Was A, NY A, StL N*
Managerial Career: *1929-1933, 1938; StL N, StL A*

Cub Stricker
Stricker, John A.
B: Jun 8, 1859   D: Nov 19, 1937

Pos: 2B, SS, OF, P	BA: .239
Hits: 1,107	HRs: 12
RBI: 259 (inc.)	BB: 414

Managerial Record
Won: 6   Lost: 17   Pct: .261

A flashy second baseman, Stricker starred in the old AA. He was 2-0 with one save as a pitcher. In 1887 he scored 122 runs and stole 86 bases for Cleveland. Stricker was a leader in the Players' Brotherhood and the 1890 rebellion.
Playing Career: *1882-1885, 1887-1893; Phi AA, Cle AA, Cle N, Cle P, Bos AA, StL N, Bal N, Was N*
Managerial Career: *1892; StL N*

George Strickland
Strickland, George Bevan (Bo, Clown)
B: Jan 10, 1926

Pos: SS, 2B, 3B, 1B	BA: .224
Hits: 633	HRs: 36
RBI: 284	BB: 362

Managerial Record
Won: 48   Lost: 63   Pct: .432

Smooth-fielding Strickland played shortstop for the 1954 Indians, who set the AL record for victories, then played in the World Series. He started five double plays in a single 1952 game, then led AL shortstops in double plays in 1953 and in fielding in 1955.
Playing Career: *1950-1957, 1959-1960; Pit N, Cle A*
Managerial Career: *1964, 1966; Cle A*

Joe Stripp
Stripp, Joseph Valentine (Jersey Joe)
B: Feb 3, 1903   D: Jun 10, 1989

Pos: 3B, 1B, OF	BA: .294
Hits: 1,238	HRs: 24
RBI: 464	BB: 280

While still playing in the major leagues, Stripp opened Jersey Joe Stripp's Baseball School in Orlando, Florida, for Depression-era boys who wanted to make a living playing baseball. Batting over .300 three times, Stripp frequently held out for a better contract.
Playing Career: *1928-1938; Cin N, Brk N, StL N, Bos N*

Amos Strunk
Strunk, Amos Aaron
B: Jan 22, 1889   D: Jul 22, 1979

Pos: OF, 1B	BA: .283
Hits: 1,415	HRs: 15
RBI: 528	BB: 573

One of Connie Mack's favorites, Strunk led AL outfielders in fielding five times. After three partial years, including time in the minors for more seasoning, Strunk replaced Rube Oldring in center field, becoming an A's regular in 1914. In a nine-year span, the speedster played in five World Series for the Athletics and the Red Sox. He hit two World Series home runs. At the plate, Strunk rarely struck out. He led the 1923 AL with 12 pinch hits in 39 at-bats.
Playing Career: *1908-1924; Phi A, Bos A, Chi A*

Dick Stuart
Stuart, Richard Lee (Dr. Strangeglove)
B: Nov 7, 1932

Pos: 1B	BA: .264
Hits: 1,055	HRs: 228
RBI: 743	BB: 301

Stuart crushed 66 homers in the Western League in 1956, marking him as a slugger. Unfortunately, his fielding was not on the same level. An official scorer once gave a batter a hit when the ball went between Stuart's legs, explaining by pointing out that the rule book says "able to make the play with reasonable effort." Stuart drove in more than 114 runs three times, and hit 35 homers for the Pirates and 42 for the Red Sox. He appeared in the 1960 and 1966 World Series.
Playing Career: *1958-1966, 1969; Pit N, Bos A, Phi N, NY N, LA N, Cal A*

Franklin Stubbs
Stubbs, Franklin Lee
B: Oct 21, 1960

Pos: 1B, OF, DH	BA: .232
Hits: 573	HRs: 102
RBI: 329	BB: 241

The Dodgers' home run leader in 1986, Stubbs took 23 pitches downtown that year. He played first base and left field for Los Angeles, and was used as a designated hitter in Milwaukee.
Playing Career: *1984-1992; LA N, Mil A*

Tom Sturdivant (c) with Hank Bauer (l) and Mickey Mantle during the 1956 WS.

Tom Sturdivant
Sturdivant, Thomas Virgil
B: Apr 28, 1930

Pos: P	ERA: 3.74
W-L: 59-51	SOs: 704
ShOs: 7	Saves: 17

A good-hitting knuckleball pitcher, Sturdivant pitched in three World Series, including a six-hit, complete game victory in Game Four of the 1956 Fall Classic. Sturdivant won 16 games in 1956 and again in 1957, then a sore arm turned him into a middle reliever.
Playing Career: *1955-1964; NY A, KC A, Bos A, Was A, Pit N, Det A, NY N*

Pete Suder
Suder, Peter
B: Apr 16, 1916

Pos: 2B, 3B, SS	BA: .249
Hits: 1,268	HRs: 49
RBI: 541	BB: 288

The pivot man for the Athletics' infield that turned a franchise-record 217 double plays in 1949, Suder was the regular second baseman and went to Kansas City when the team moved. He surpassed the .280 mark twice and hit 10 home runs with 75 RBI in 1949.
Playing Career: *1941-1943, 1946-1955; Phi A, KC A*

Willie Sudhoff
Sudhoff, John William (Wee Willie)
B: Sep 17, 1874   D: May 25, 1917

Pos: P	ERA: 3.56
W-L: 103-135	SOs: 520
ShOs: 11	Saves: 3

One of the victims of syndicate baseball at its worst, Sudhoff began the 1899 season in

Cleveland as a St. Louis castoff, but won three games and was returned to St. Louis in order to punish the Cleveland team. He was 21-15 with a 2.27 ERA in 1903.
Playing Career: *1897-1906; StL N, Cle N, StL A, Was A*

Joe Sugden
Sugden, Joseph
B: Jul 31, 1870   D: Jun 28, 1959

Pos: C, 1B	BA: .255
Hits: 695	HRs: 3
RBI: 283	BB: 220

When Connie Mack was playing injured in the 1890s with Pittsburgh, Sugden was his designated pinch runner. He hit .331 in 1894 when the Pirates made a dash for the NL pennant. Sugden led AL receivers in fielding in 1904. He was a longtime scout for the St. Louis Cardinals.
Playing Career: *1893-1899, 1901-1905, 1912; Pit N, StL N, Cle N, Chi A, StL A, Det A*

George Suggs
Suggs, George Franklin
B: Jul 7, 1882   D: Apr 4, 1949

Pos: P	ERA: 3.11
W-L: 99-91	SOs: 588
ShOs: 16	Saves: 17

Pitching for Clark Griffith, Suggs was the ace of the Reds' staff from 1910 to 1913. His defection to the Federal League hurt – despite his 8-15 record in 1913 – because he influenced three teammates to jump as well. Suggs won 20 in 1910 and 24 in 1914.
Playing Career: *1908-1915; Det A, Cin N, Bal F*

Gus Suhr warms up in 1938.

Gus Suhr
Suhr, August Richard
B: Jan 3, 1906

Pos: 1B	BA: .279
Hits: 1,446	HRs: 84
RBI: 818	BB: 718

Suhr annihilated PCL pitching in 1929 with a .381 average, 51 home runs and 177 RBI. He was a good fielder, and led NL first basemen

in fielding once. Suhr drove in more than 100 runs three times, peaking at 118 in 1936, the year he made the All-Star team.
Playing Career: *1930-1940; Pit N, Phi N*

Clyde Sukeforth
Sukeforth, Clyde Leroy (Sukey)
B: Nov 30, 1901

Pos: C	BA: .264
Hits: 326	HRs: 2
RBI: 96	BB: 95
Managerial Record	
Won: 2 Lost: 0 Pct: 1.000	

A backup catcher for 10 years, Sukeforth coached the Dodgers, 1943-1951, and the Pirates, 1952-1957. He was Branch Rickey's right-hand man on the field. Sukeforth was instrumental in easing the players' concerns with integration in Jackie Robinson's first year.
Playing Career: *1926-1935; Cin N, Brk N*
Managerial Career: *1947; Brk N*

Big Mike Sullivan
Sullivan, Michael Joseph
B: Oct 23, 1866   D: Jun 14, 1906

Pos: P	ERA: 5.11
W-L: 54-66	SOs: 286
ShOs: 1	Saves: 4

A victim of control problems, Sullivan once allowed nine triples in one game, a record that still stands. Enduring losing seasons in eight of 11 years, Sullivan turned it around with a 12-4 year for the Reds in 1892. He walked 577 and fanned 286 in his career.
Playing Career: *1889-1899; Was N, Chi N, Phi AA, NY N, Cin N, Cle N, Bos N*

Billy Sullivan
Sullivan, William Joseph, Jr.
B: Oct 23, 1910

Pos: C, 1B, 3B, OF	BA: .289
Hits: 820	HRs: 29
RBI: 388	BB: 240

Emulating their batterymate fathers, Sullivan, Jr. and Ed Walsh, Jr. appeared as catcher and pitcher for a publicity stunt in a 1932 game. A top left-handed pinch hitter, Sullivan was difficult to strike out. He played in the 1940 World Series.
Playing Career: *1931-1933, 1935-1942, 1947; Chi A, Cin N, Cle A, StL A, Det A, Brk N, Pit N*

Frank Sullivan
Sullivan, Franklin Leal
B: Jan 23, 1930

Pos: P	ERA: 3.60
W-L: 97-100	SOs: 959
ShOs: 15	Saves: 18

A two-time All-Star, Sullivan led the AL in wins, starts and innings pitched in 1955. Averaging 221 innings and 30 starts a year in a six-year span, Sullivan was 83-63 from 1954 to

1959. The 6'6½" Sullivan was traded for 6'8" Gene Conley in a "giant" deal.
Playing Career: *1953-1963; Bos A, Phi N, Min A*

Haywood Sullivan
Sullivan, Haywood Cooper
B: Dec 15, 1930

Pos: C	BA: .226
Hits: 192	HRs: 13
RBI: 87	BB: 109
Managerial Record	
Won: 54 Lost: 82 Pct: .397	

A highly sought-after receiver, Sullivan signed for $50,000 with the Red Sox, who dealt him to the A's when they found he could not hit. Sullivan jumped from managing the A's to vice-president in charge of Red Sox personnel at age 35. He later became the Sox' general manager and was part of the group that bought the team when Tom Yawkey died, becoming a general partner. His son Marc caught for the Red Sox in the 1980s.
Playing Career: *1955, 1957, 1959-1963; Bos A, KC A*
Managerial Career: *1965; KC A*

Red Sox catcher Haywood Sullivan.

Joe Sullivan
Sullivan, Joseph Daniel
B: Jan 6, 1870   D: Nov 2, 1897

Pos: SS, OF, 2B	BA: .299
Hits: 493	HRs: 11
RBI: 227	BB: 116

A part-time player, Sullivan could not break into the 1894-1895 Phillies' lineup, despite hitting .335 and .338. The team sported a .349 average in 1894 and batted .330 the following year. Sold to St. Louis, Sullivan hit .292 but did not stick due to poor fielding.
Playing Career: *1893-1896; Was N, Phi N, StL N*

Ted Sullivan
Sullivan, Theodore Paul (T.P.)
B: 1851   D: Jul 5, 1929

Pos: OF   BA: .333
Hits: 4   HRs: 0
RBI: NA   BB: 1
Managerial Record
Won: 132   Lost: 132   Pct: .500

The founder of several minor leagues, including the first one in organized ball, the Northwestern League, Sullivan's Dubuque team featured Hall of Famers Charles Comiskey at first and Old Hoss Radbourn in the box. Baseball lore has it that Sullivan coined the term "fan" when he, Comiskey and others were relaxing in the off-season and a baseball enthusiast appeared and began spouting statistics at them. Asked what he thought of such a man, Sullivan replied that he must be a fanatic.
Playing Career: *1884; KC U*
Managerial Career: *1883-1884, 1888; StL AA, StL U, KC U, Was N*

Homer Summa
Summa, Homer Wayne
B: Nov 3, 1898   D: Jan 29, 1966

Pos: OF   BA: .302
Hits: 905   HRs: 18
RBI: 361   BB: 166

A two-time minor league batting champion, Summa hit .328 in his 1923 rookie year. Despite having a great baseball name and a .300 lifetime average, Summa was a full-time player for only five seasons. He lined into Johnny Neun's unassisted triple play.
Playing Career: *1920, 1922-1930; Pit N, Cle A, Phi A*

Ed Summers
Summers, Oron Edgar (Kickapoo Chief)
B: Dec 5, 1884   D: May 12, 1953

Pos: P   ERA: 2.42
W-L: 68-45   SOs: 362
ShOs: 9   Saves: 2

Going 24-12 as a rookie, Summers provided the push that put the Tigers into the 1908 World Series. On September 25, he tossed a doubleheader victory over the rival Athletics. The next year he pitched an 18-inning scoreless tie and also won 19 games.
Playing Career: *1908-1912; Det A*

Billy Sunday
Sunday, William Ashley (The Evangelist)
B: Nov 9, 1862   D: Nov 6, 1935

Pos: OF   BA: .248
Hits: 498   HRs: 12
RBI: 137   BB: 134

While recovering from a drunken binge as a member of the White Stockings, Sunday attended a tent revival held by the Moody Bible Institute. He began attending church meetings at the local YMCA, and became Moody's most famous recruit and a leading evangelist. An outstanding ballplayer, Sunday was fast but weak-hitting. His Chicago teammates would bet on his footraces. When Sunday beat Arlie Latham in a footrace the Browns were broke until payday.
Playing Career: *1883-1890; Chi N, Pit N, Phi N*

The Rangers' Jim Sundberg, 1981.

Jim Sundberg
Sundberg, James Howard
B: May 18, 1951

Pos: C   BA: .248
Hits: 1,493   HRs: 95
RBI: 624   BB: 699

Arriving in Kansas City in 1985, Sundberg helped make the Royals World Champions. Ironically, it was one of the few years that he did not lead the AL in fielding, putouts or assists. With six Gold Gloves and three All-Star selections, Sundberg was a star receiver, spending only one season in Double A ball before being called up in 1974. For many seasons, Sundberg's percentage of throwing out base stealers hovered near 50. He tied the AL record with 155 games caught in 1975.
Playing Career: *1974-1989; Tex A, Mil A, KC A, Chi N*

Steve Sundra
Sundra, Stephen Richard (Smokey)
B: Mar 27, 1910   D: Mar 23, 1952

Pos: P   ERA: 4.17
W-L: 56-41   SOs: 214
ShOs: 4   Saves: 2

Another of the role players who helped the Yankees win their string of pennants in the late 1930s, Sundra won his first 11 games in 1939, going 11-1 with a 2.76 ERA. He tossed three scoreless innings in the World Series that year. He also pitched for the 1944 pennant-winning Browns.
Playing Career: *1936, 1938-1944, 1946; NY A, Was A, StL A*

B.J. Surhoff
Surhoff, William James
B: Aug 4, 1964

Pos: C, 3B, DH   BA: .269
Hits: 896   HRs: 39
RBI: 429   BB: 241

After playing on the 1984 Olympic baseball team, Surhoff was the first player selected in the 1985 free-agent draft. He batted .299 in his rookie year. Having too much speed for a catcher – with 95 steals already – Surhoff has been shuttled about in search of a position.
Playing Career: *1987-; Mil A*

Max Surkont
Surkont, Matthew Constantine
B: Jun 16, 1922   D: Oct 8, 1986

Pos: P   ERA: 4.38
W-L: 61-76   SOs: 571
ShOs: 7   Saves: 8

Surkont once fanned eight Reds in a row, the last one after a 35-minute rain delay. Signed at age 15, he starred in the minors for 12 years before coming up with the White Sox. His only winning season in the majors was 1953, when he was 11-5.
Playing Career: *1949-1957; Chi A, Bos N, Mil N, Pit N, StL N, NY N*

Rick Sutcliffe
Sutcliffe, Richard Lee
B: Jun 21, 1956

Pos: P   ERA: 4.01
W-L: 165-135   SOs: 1,653
ShOs: 18   Saves: 6

Dodger pitcher Rick Sutcliffe.

A three-time All-Star, Sutcliffe sometimes tosses a hesitation pitch as he cocks his arm swing behind his back. The pitch was good enough to earn 1979 NL Rookie of the Year honors and the 1984 NL Cy Young Award. The latter year he was 4-5 for the Indians and 16-1 for the Cubs, leading the Cubs to a division title. He was the first pitcher since the Federal League era to win 20 games split between two clubs. When Sutcliffe is pitching well he is unstoppable.

His career revived in Baltimore after chronic back problems kept him out of the starting rotation for most of 1990 and 1991. Changes of scenery have always done him good. Arriving in Cleveland in 1982, he had led the AL with a 2.96 ERA. Going to the Cubs, he had won the Cy Young Award. In Baltimore he won 16 games and tossed 237 innings in 1992 after hurling just 117 in the two previous years combined. He tossed a shutout on Opening Day at the new Camden Yards.

Playing Career: *1976, 1978-; LA N, Cle A, Chi N, Bal A*

Gary Sutherland
Sutherland, Gary Lynn
B: Sep 27, 1944

Pos: 2B, SS, 3B	BA: .243
Hits: 754	HRs: 24
RBI: 239	BB: 207

Playing with four expansion franchises, Sutherland displayed a high degree of adaptability, but little power and a mediocre batting average, yet he appeared in more than 100 games seven times. He was a backup guard on three UCLA national champion basketball teams.

Playing Career: *1966-1978; Phi N, Mon N, Hou N, Det A, Mil A, SD N, StL N*

Bruce Sutter
Sutter, Howard Bruce
B: Jan 8, 1953

Pos: P	ERA: 2.84
W-L: 68-71	SOs: 861
ShOs: 0	Saves: 300

The best reliever of his day, Sutter almost ended his career in 1973 with arm surgery. His friend and former catcher, Mike Roarke, taught him the split-finger fastball. In Sutter's long, supple fingers the pitch dropped like a rock when it reached the plate, and it made him an instant success in the Cubs' bullpen. He saved 31 games with a 1.35 ERA in 1977. Two years later, his 37 saves earned him the NL Cy Young Award.

Sutter peaked with a record 45 saves in 1984. The Cardinals hired Roarke, who was teaching high school at the time, to watch Sutter's mechanics. He needed little help though, winning two games and saving two for the NL in All-Star Game competition. Sutter held the NL record for career saves and was voted NL Fireman of the Year four times. In 1982 he was 2-0 with three saves in the NLCS and World Series. After signing a

Ace reliever Bruce Sutter in 1981.

multi-year, multi-million dollar contract with the Braves, shoulder problems ended his career.

Playing Career: *1976-1986, 1988; Chi N, StL N, Atl N*

Mule Suttles
Suttles, George
B: Mar 2, 1901   D: 1968

Pos: 1B, OF	BA: .329
Hits: 1,001	HRs: 190
RBI: NA	BB: NA
Managerial Record	
Won: 19 Lost: 22 Pct: .463	

"Kick Mule, Kick," the fans would roar when Mule Suttles advanced to the plate. He played professional baseball for 25 years. With the St. Louis Stars, Suttles led the Negro Leagues in homers twice and in doubles, triples and batting average once. In five East-West All-Star Games he batted .412 with two home runs and six RBI. His average in 26 documented games against white major leaguers was .374, with five home runs.

Playing Career: *1923-1944; Bir Black Barons, StL Stars, Bal Black Sox, Det Wolves, Was Pilots, Chi Am Giants, Nwk Eagles, Ind ABCs, NY Black Yankees*
Managerial Career: *1944; Nwk Eagles*

Don Sutton
Sutton, Donald Howard
B: Apr 2, 1945

Pos: P	ERA: 3.26
W-L: 324-256	SOs: 3,574
ShOs: 58	Saves: 5

In 1986 Sutton pitched against Phil Niekro in the first meeting of 300-game winners since

Tim Keefe and Pud Galvin opposed one another in 1892. With a strong work ethic and consistency Sutton won more than 300 games, but posted 20 victories in a season only once. He achieved the 3,000-strikeout mark by posting a record 21 consecutive seasons of more than 100 strikeouts. Sutton's high mark was 217 whiffs in 1969; he hit the 200-strikeout mark five times.

Named Rookie Pitcher of the Year by *The Sporting News*, Sutton fanned 209 batters in his debut season, the most by an NL rookie since Grover Cleveland Alexander in 1911. In a career in which he beat every major league team, Sutton ranks fifth in strikeouts, fourth in home runs allowed, seventh in innings, tenth in shutouts, third in starts, twelfth in wins and seventh in losses. He never appeared on the disabled list. A polished speaker, Sutton is the TV announcer for the Braves.

Playing Career: *1966-1988; LA N, Hou N, Mil A, Oak A, Cal A*

Ezra Sutton
Sutton, Ezra Ballou (Uncle Ezra)
B: Sep 17, 1850   D: Jun 20, 1907

Pos: 3B, SS	BA: .294
Hits: 1,575	HRs: 26
RBI: 583 (inc.)	BB: 169

A solid contributor to Boston's 1877, 1878 and 1883 championships, Sutton was an early slugger, bashing 229 doubles and 97 triples, and scoring 992 runs in his career. He twice scored 100 runs. Orignally a cross-handed batter, he was a star in the National Association, and was the league's first player to hit a home run, the first to homer twice in the same game, and the first to commit an error. He once whacked three consecutive triples in an 1876 NL game.

Playing Career: *1871-1888; Cle Forest Citys n, Phi Athletics n, Phi N, Bos N*

Craig Swan
Swan, Craig Steven
B: Nov 30, 1950

Pos: P	ERA: 3.74
W-L: 59-72	SOs: 673
ShOs: 7	Saves: 2

Signing the most lucrative contract in Mets history in 1979, Swan suffered a rotator cuff injury in 1980 that cost him his fastball. He had led the NL with a 2.43 ERA in 1978 and won 14 games in 1979. An arm injury in 1983 ended his career.

Playing Career: *1973-1984; NY N, Cal A*

Ed Swartwood
Swartwood, Cyrus Edward
B: Jan 12, 1859   D: May 15, 1924

Pos: OF, 1B	BA: .299
Hits: 861	HRs: 15
RBI: 4 (inc.)	BB: 324

One of the old AA's earliest sluggers, Swartwood led the league in runs and doubles in

1882, and in hits, batting average and on-base average the next season. A creditable runner, he stole 119 bases in three years, and hit 63 triples during his career.
Playing Career: *1881-1887, 1890, 1892; Buf N, Pit AA, Brk AA, Tol AA, Pit N*

Bill Sweeney
Sweeney, William John
B: Mar 6, 1886   D: May 26, 1948

Pos: 2B, 3B, SS	BA: .272
Hits: 1,004	HRs: 11
RBI: 389	BB: 423

Using the heaviest stick in the majors, Sweeney hit in 31 straight games in 1911. He batted .344, driving in 100 runs and posting a .416 on-base average. The Cubs swapped Hall of Famer Johnny Evers to reacquire him before the 1914 season.
Playing Career: *1907-1914; Chi N, Bos N*

Charlie Sweeney
Sweeney, Charles J.
B: Apr 13, 1863   D: Apr 4, 1902

Pos: P	ERA: 2.87
W-L: 64-52	SOs: 505
ShOs: 8	No-hitters: 1

Well-known for jumping from the Providence team, abandoning former teammate Old Hoss Radbourn to win 60 games, Sweeney sought a better contract in the 1884 Union Association. He won 41 games that year, and set a record with 19 strikeouts that was finally broken by Roger Clemens in 1986.
Playing Career: *1882-1887; Pro N, StL U, StL N, Cle AA*

The Pirates' Bill Swift in 1938.

The Tigers' Bob Swift slides safely into third against the Yankees in 1949.

Bill Swift
Swift, William Charles
B: Oct 27, 1961

Pos: P	ERA: 3.52
W-L: 61-52	SOs: 526
ShOs: 4	Saves: 25

A reliever for the 1984 Olympic team, Swift was 1-2 with 17 saves and a 1.99 ERA in 1991 before he made a successful change to become an ace starter for the Giants, going 10-4 with a league-leading 2.08 ERA the following season. He has 14 siblings and is a member of the State of Maine Hall of Fame.
Playing Career: *1985-1986, 1988-; Sea A, SF N*

Bill Swift
Swift, William Vincent
B: Jan 10, 1908   D: Feb 23, 1969

Pos: P	ERA: 3.58
W-L: 95-82	SOs: 636
ShOs: 7	Saves: 20

A late-season acquisition for the Dodgers in 1941, Swift contributed three victories and a save to help Brooklyn to the NL pennant. He had been a starter for the Pirates, winning 70 games and averaging 222 innnings from 1932 to 1936.
Playing Career: *1932-1941, 1943; Pit N, Bos N, Brk N, Chi A*

Bob Swift
Swift, Robert Virgil
B: Mar 6, 1915   D: Oct 17, 1966

Pos: C	BA: .231
Hits: 635	HRs: 14
RBI: 238	BB: 323
Managerial Record	
Won: 56 Lost: 43 Pct: .566	

The catcher when midget Eddie Gaedel batted in a promotional gimmick in 1951, Swift practically laid on the ground to give the pitcher a target low enough. A skilled instructor, he was a winning minor league manager, coach and interim manager for Chuck Dressen.
Playing Career: *1940-1953; StL A, Phi A, Det A*
Managerial Career: *1965-1966; Det A*

Greg Swindell
Swindell, Forrest Gregory
B: Jan 2, 1965

Pos: P	ERA: 3.68
W-L: 84-76	SOs: 1,018
ShOs: 11	No-hitters: 0

As the youngest member of the 1984 Olympic Team, Swindell was the Indians' number one draft pick and was rushed to the majors. A solid starter, he won 18 games in 1988 and made the All-Star team in 1989. His career has been slowed by arm trouble.
Playing Career: *1986-; Cle A, Cin N, Hou N*

Ron Swoboda
Swoboda, Ronald Alan (Rocky)
B: Jun 30, 1944

Pos: OF	BA: .242
Hits: 624	HRs: 73
RBI: 344	BB: 299

Swoboda made one of the greatest catches in baseball history when he speared a liner by Brooks Robinson in Game Four of the 1969 World Series, fueling the Mets' amazing upset win. In a September 15 game that year he hit two home runs off Steve Carlton to beat him 4-3 although Carlton fanned 19 batters.
Playing Career: *1965-1973; NY N, Mon N, NY A*

Pat Tabler
Tabler, Patrick Sean
B: Feb 2, 1958

Pos: 1B, OF, DH, 3B	BA: .282
Hits: 1,101	HRs: 47
RBI: 512	BB: 375

Before his retirement, Tabler was the best active hitter with the bases loaded, according to Elias Sports Bureau. He made the All-Star team in 1987, the only year he played more than 150 games. His 1987 batting average of .307 followed a .326 mark in 1986.
Playing Career: *1981-1992; Chi N, Cle A, KC A, NY N, Tor A*

Jim Tabor
Tabor, James Reubin (Rawhide)
B: Nov 5, 1916   D: Aug 22, 1953

Pos: 3B	BA: .270
Hits: 1,021	HRs: 104
RBI: 598	BB: 286

A tough Southerner, Tabor broke in with the Red Sox in 1939, the same year as Ted Williams. Tabor socked 33 doubles and drove in 95 runs that season. In a 1940 game, he was one of four Red Sox players to hit home runs in the same inning. Tabor drove in 101 runs in 1941.
Playing Career: *1938-1944, 1946-1947; Bos A, Phi N*

Frank Tanana
Tanana, Frank Daryl
B: Jul 3, 1953

Pos: P	ERA: 3.66
W-L: 240-236	SOs: 2,773
ShOs: 34	Saves: 1

Teaming with Nolan Ryan, Tanana gave the 1974-1979 Angels the best 1-2 strikeout punch in AL history. The duo led the AL in K's for eight straight years, Tanana fanning an AL-high 269 in 1975. The three-time All-Star was *The Sporting News* AL Rookie Pitcher of the Year in 1974, and notched three 200-strikeout seasons in a row, 1975-1977. He led the league in ERA and shutouts in 1977.

Throwing his arm out by age 25, Tanana

The Angels' Frank Tanana, 1978.

was forced to make the transition from fast-ball thrower to crafty pitcher. On the Angels' all-time list he was second to Nolan Ryan in wins, starts, complete games, strikeouts, innings and shutouts when he left the team for greener pastures. Seemingly washed up in 1985, Tanana caught fire after being traded to the Tigers. Becoming the staff ace, he beat the Blue Jays on the final day of the 1987 season to win the AL West division for Detroit.
Playing Career: *1973-; Cal A, Bos A, Tex A, Det A, NY N, NY A*

Jesse Tannehill
Tannehill, Jesse Niles
B: Jul 14, 1874   D: Sep 22, 1956

Pos: P, OF	ERA: 2.77
W-L: 197-116	SOs: 943
ShOs: 34	No-hitters: 1

Pitching at the turn of the century, Tannehill was also a switch-hitting outfielder whose .256 batting average was better than the .220 mark his infielder brother Lee compiled. Jesse won more than 20 games six times, peaking at 25 in 1898 and posting 24 wins the next year. He led the NL with a 2.18 ERA in 1901. Tannehill was 20-6, with a .769 winning percentage and a 1.95 ERA for the 1902 Pirates, the team that won the NL flag by a record 27½ games.

When the AL invaded New York in 1903, Tannehill and Jack Chesbro were lured away from the Pirates for big bucks to join the fledging Highlanders. That pair plus Willie Keeler gave the upstart AL instant credibility in New York. Not happy there, however, Tannehill went to the archrival Pilgrims in Boston. In 1904 the two clubs battled down to the last day of the season, with the Pilgrims beating the Highlanders on a wild pitch.
Playing Career: *1894, 1897-1909, 1911; Cin N, Pit N, NY A, Bos A, Was A*

Jesse Tannehill with the Senators.

Lee Tannehill
Tannehill, Lee Ford
B: Oct 26, 1880   D: Feb 16, 1938

Pos: 3B, SS, 1B, 2B	BA: .220
Hits: 833	HRs: 3
RBI: 346	BB: 229

The third baseman for the "Hitless Wonders" pennant-winning White Sox of 1906, Tannehill was a poor hitter, but an outstanding fielder with exceptional range. Ironically, he hit the first home run in Comiskey Park. He once made two unassisted double plays in one game as a shortstop.
Playing Career: *1903-1912; Chi A*

Chuck Tanner
Tanner, Charles William
B: Jul 4, 1929

Pos: OF	BA: .261
Hits: 231	HRs: 21
RBI: 105	BB: 82
Managerial Record	
Won: 1,352 Lost: 1,381	Pct: .495

From his debut with a pinch-hit home run, Tanner has spent most of his life as a baseball player, coach or manager. He was one of the fabulous Milwaukee Braves whose ranks included Eddie Mathews, Hank Aaron, Joe Adcock, Warren Spahn, Lou Burdette and Bob Buhl. With the Cubs in 1958, he stole a league-high 53 bases. As the A's skipper in 1976, Tanner was dealt to the Pirates for Manny Sanguillen and $100,000, becoming one of the few managers to be traded. Under his direction, the Bucs won the World Series in 1979.
Playing Career: *1955-1962; Mil N, Chi N, Cle A, LA A*
Managerial Career: *1970-1988; Chi A, Oak A, Pit N, Atl N*

Danny Tartabull.

Danny Tartabull
Tartabull, Danilo (Bull)
B: Oct 30, 1962

Pos: OF, DH, 2B, SS	BA: .280
Hits: 1,078	HRs: 208
RBI: 722	BB: 591

In the minor leagues, Tartabull was an infielder, and was twice named his league's Player of the Year. He made it to the big leagues with a big bat that strafed 1985 Pacific Coast League pitching for 43 home runs and 109 RBI. Switching to the outfield in the majors, Tartabull learned his position in Seattle's Kingdome, then went to Kansas City where his father, Jose Tartabull, had his best years.

In 1991, with 121 strikeouts, Tartabull still hit .316 with 31 home runs and 35 doubles in spacious Royals Stadium. He belted more than 25 homers for six of eight years from 1986 to 1993. During that period Tartabull drove in 708 runs, four times reaching 100. In a late 1992 game, he went 5-for-5 with a double and two homers, knocking in nine runs. Only five AL batters ever drove in more runs in a single game.
Playing Career: *1984-; Sea A, KC A, NY A*

Ken Tatum
Tatum, Kenneth Ray
B: Apr 25, 1944

Pos: P	ERA: 2.92
W-L: 16-12	SOs: 156
ShOs: 0	Saves: 52

A surprisingly good hitter – he belted four home runs in 44 career at-bats – Tatum broke

in with a 7-2 record with 22 saves and a 1.36 ERA. When he produced nearly identical stats the following season, the Angels traded him to Boston in a multi-player deal. Tatum was bothered by arm trouble the rest of his short career.
Playing Career: *1969-1974; Cal A, Bos A, Chi A*

Jackie Tavener
Tavener, John Adam
B: Dec 27, 1897   D: Sep 14, 1969

Pos: SS	BA: .255
Hits: 543	HRs: 13
RBI: 243	BB: 186

Dismissed at a glance in 1921 by Tigers Manager Ty Cobb as being too small, 5'5" Tavener went back to the minors, finally emerging in 1925. He was a regular for four straight years, displaying consistent hitting, good range and a great arm.
Playing Career: *1921, 1925-1929; Det A, Cle A*

Frank Taveras
Taveras y Fabian, Franklin Crisostomo
B: Dec 24, 1949

Pos: SS	BA: .255
Hits: 1,029	HRs: 2
RBI: 214	BB: 249

Taveras scored 503 runs and stole 300 bases. He set the then Pirates' single-season base swiping record with 70 in 1977 – a career-high mark that led the league that year. Somewhat deficient in fielding, Taveras's trade to the Mets for steady Tim Foli was a key to the 1979 Pirates' pennant.
Playing Career: *1971-1972, 1974-1982; Pit N, NY N, Mon N*

Ben Taylor
Taylor, Ben
B: Jul 1, 1888   D: Jan 24, 1953

Pos: 1B, P	BA: .324
Hits: 695	HRs: 25
RBI: NA	BB: NA
Managerial Record	
Won: 123 Lost: 122 Pct: .502	

The youngest of four baseball playing Taylor brothers – C.I., Candy Jim, and Steel Arm Johnny – Ben was probably the best. He was the premier Negro League first baseman during the first quarter of the 20th century. His fielding was graceful, his hitting demonic, and his demeanor gentlemanly. He hit a career-high .407 with the Indianapolis ABCs in 1921. Though research is not complete, Taylor likely played in excess of 20 years. Hall of Famer Buck Leonard credits Ben Taylor with teaching him fundamental baseball skills.
Playing Career: *1909-1922, 1924-1929; Bir Giants, WB Sprudels, Chi Am Giants, Ind ABC's, Ind Jewells, Was Potomacs, Hbg Giants, Bal Black Sox*
Managerial Career: *1924, 1926-1929; Was Potomacs, Bal Black Sox*

Chuck Taylor
Taylor, Charles Gilbert
B: Apr 18, 1942

Pos: P	ERA: 3.07
W-L: 28-20	SOs: 282
ShOs: 2	Saves: 31

Hurling for three expansion franchises, Taylor won 58 percent of his decisions and posted a low ERA, but could never break through. The Cardinals' starting staff and Mike Marshall in the Expos' bullpen held him back.
Playing Career: *1969-1976; StL N, NY N, Mil A, Mon N*

Danny Taylor
Taylor, Daniel Turney
B: Dec 23, 1900   D: Oct 11, 1972

Pos: OF	BA: .297
Hits: 650	HRs: 44
RBI: 305	BB: 267

A Southern Association triples leader and International League batting champion, Taylor put together five seasons of .285 batting averages or better for the rowdy Dodgers of the 1930s. His best year was 1932, when he hit .319 with 11 home runs in a season split between Chicago and Brooklyn.
Playing Career: *1926, 1929-1936; Was A, Chi N, Brk N*

Dummy Taylor
Taylor, Luther Haden
B: Feb 21, 1875   D: Aug 22, 1958

Pos: P	ERA: 2.75
W-L: 115-106	SOs: 767
ShOs: 21	Saves: 3

Taylor was a starting pitcher for John McGraw's greatest teams, the 1904-1905 Giants. His best season was 1904, when he went 21-15 with a 2.34 ERA. When his teammates learned American Sign Language to communicate with Taylor, they developed the basis for coaching signs in use today. After retirement he headed the Kansas School for the Deaf.
Playing Career: *1900-1908; NY N, Cle A*

Jack Taylor
Taylor, John Budd (Brewery Jack)
B: May 23, 1873   D: Feb 7, 1900

Pos: P	ERA: 4.23
W-L: 120-117	SOs: 528
ShOs: 7	Saves: 9

Called Brewery Jack for good reason, Taylor pitched and won 85 games for one of the hardest-hitting teams ever assembled, the 1894-1897 Phillies. Only one year later he lost 29 games with a 3.90 ERA for the 1898 Cardinals, giving up 465 hits. After going 9-10 with Cincinnati the following year, Taylor died of Bright's disease at age 26.
Playing Career: *1891-1899; NY N, Phi N, StL N, Cin N*

Jack Taylor
Taylor, John W.
B: Jan 14, 1874   D: Mar 4, 1938

Pos: P	ERA: 2.66
W-L: 151-139	SOs: 657
ShOs: 20	Saves: 5

Among the 278 completed games of 287 games started, Taylor compiled a streak of 187 completed games in a row, and it is doubtful that record will ever be approached. His string lasted from June 20, 1901 to August 9, 1906, stretching over a period of five years. Included in the streak were 19-inning and 18-inning games. Taylor relieved in 15 other contests. Even being traded – to St. Louis for Mordecai Brown – failed to break the streak.

Returning to Chicago with the 1906 Cubs, the winningest team of all time, Taylor finally required a relief pitcher. Nonetheless, he finished the season with a 12-3 record. Posting three ERAs under 2.00, Taylor won the 1902 NL ERA crown with a 1.33 mark for 324 innings pitched. A sometimes difficult person to deal with because of his heavy drinking, Taylor tossed 2,453 innings in eight years. Not reaching the majors until he was 24 years old, he burned himself out by age 33, yet left behind a legacy of a man who finished what he started.
Playing Career: *1898-1907; Chi N, StL N*

Ron Taylor
Taylor, Ronald Wesley
B: Dec 13, 1937

Pos: P	RA: 3.93
W-L: 45-43	SOs: 464
ShOs: 0	Saves: 72

Compiling a 0.00 ERA and saving three games out of six in two World Series for the Cardinals and Mets, Taylor made a baseball

Jack Taylor.

career out of the bullpen, starting only 17 games. He graduated from medical school in 1977 and became the Blue Jays' team physician.
Playing Career: *1962-1972; Cle A, StL N, Hou N, NY N, SD N*

Tony Taylor.

Tony Taylor
Taylor y Sanchez, Antonio Nemesio
B: Dec 19, 1935

Pos: 2B, 3B	BA: .261
Hits: 2,007	HRs: 75
RBI: 598	BB: 613

Traded to Philadelphia in a deal for Don Cardwell and Ed Bouchee, Taylor paid Phillies dividends for 15 years. He had an off-year, batting .251, in 1964, the year the Phillies almost won the pennant. He scored 1,005 runs and belted 298 doubles in his career. A savvy base stealer, Taylor's six steals of home ranks him in a second-place tie on the Phillies' all-time list. He stole 234 bases altogether.
Playing Career: *1958-1976; Chi N, Phi N, Det A*

Zack Taylor
Taylor, James Wren
B: Jul 27, 1898   D: Sep 19, 1974

Pos: C	BA: .261
Hits: 748	HRs: 9
RBI: 311	BB: 161
Managerial Record	
Won: 235 Lost: 410 Pct: .364	

A 50-year veteran of baseball as a player, manager, coach and scout, Taylor was the manager who sent pint-sized Eddie Gaedel to the plate in a 1951 publicity stunt. Taylor caught for 16 years, leading NL receivers in fielding in 1924. The next year he batted .310.
Playing Career: *1920-1935; Brk N, Bos N, NY N, Chi N, NY A*
Managerial Career: *1946, 1948-1951; StL A*

Birdie Tebbetts
Tebbetts, George Robert
B: Nov 10, 1912

Pos: C	BA: .270
Hits: 1,000	HRs: 38
RBI: 469	BB: 389
Managerial Record	
Won: 748 Lost: 705 Pct: .515	

Providence College classmates nicknamed Tebbetts "Birdie" because he was talkative and had a high-pitched voice. In the major leagues, he was a platoon catcher who was elected to four All-Star teams and played in the 1940 World Series with the Tigers. After batting a career-high .310 in 1950 for the Red Sox, he was sold to Cleveland.

As a manager Tebbetts guided the Reds through integration, encouraging fans to focus on home run power, not skin color. Tebbetts is a member of the Veterans Committee of the Baseball Hall of Fame.
Playing Career: *1936-1942, 1946-1952; Det A, Bos A, Cle A*
Managerial Career: *1954-1958, 1961-1966; Cin N, Mil N, Cle A*

Patsy Tebeau
Tebeau, Oliver Wendell
B: Dec 5, 1864   D: May 15, 1918

Pos: 1B, 2B, 3B	BA: .280
Hits: 1,291	HRs: 27
RBI: 735	BB: 319
Managerial Record	
Won: 729 Lost: 583 Pct: .556	

Working for the infamous Cleveland Spiders, one of the dirtiest teams ever, Tebeau was an average player, but an exceptional manager. He had losing years only in his first and last NL seasons. His quote, "Show me a team of fighters, and I'll show you a team that has a chance," was indicative of how the Spiders played ball. Tebeau's minions lost the championship playoff in 1892 to the Beaneaters, but they won the 1895 Temple Cub from the Orioles.
Playing Career: *1887, 1889-1900; Chi N, Cle N, Cle P, StL N*
Managerial Career: *1890-1900; Cle P, Cle N, StL N*

White Wings Tebeau
Tebeau, George E. (Hard Call)
B: Dec 26, 1861   D: Feb 4, 1923

Pos: OF, 1B	BA: .269
Hits: 622	HRs: 15
RBI: 242	BB: 324

The brother of Patsy, George Tebeau had a good 1889 season with the Reds, batting .252, scoring 110 runs and stealing 61 bases. Tebeau ended his career after batting .326 – his personal best – in 1895 for Cleveland. He owned the Kansas City Blues in the AA before selling out in the mid-1910s and buying the Denver franchise in the Western League.
Playing Career: *1887-1890, 1894-1895; Cin AA, Tol AA, Was N, Cle N*

assists and double plays. A great all-around player, he struck out only 338 times in 5,218 at-bats and stole 140 bases in 188 tries.
Playing Career: *1952-1964; Cin N, Cle A, Bal A, Hou N*

Garry Templeton.

Garry Templeton
Templeton, Garry Lewis
B: Mar 24, 1956

Pos: SS   BA: .271
Hits: 2,096   HRs: 70
RBI: 728   BB: 375

In 1979 switch-hitter Templeton became the first batter ever to get 100 hits from each side of the plate in a single season. The youngest shortstop to reach the 200-hit plateau since 1900, he also led the league in triples in 1979. It was his third consecutive year to lead in triples – another NL first. Then in August 1981, Templeton made a series of obscene gestures to Busch Stadium fans, who booed him for not running out a ground ball. He was suspended and fined, and agreed to psychiatric examination.

In the off-season Templeton was traded to the Padres for defensive whiz Ozzie Smith. Though Templeton set a club record for shortstops with 64 RBI in 1982, earned the Silver Slugger Award in 1984, and was voted Padres MVP in 1985, he never lived up to the Padres' expectations. Chronic knee and other leg problems ended his career. He stole more than 240 bases and hit 106 triples and 329 doubles.
Playing Career: *1976-1991; StL N, SD N, NY N*

Reliever Kent Tekulve displays his sidearm delivery in 1979.

Kent Tekulve
Tekulve, Kenton Charles
B: Mar 5, 1947

Pos: P   ERA: 2.85
W-L: 94-90   SOs: 779
ShOs: 0   Saves: 184

Tekulve appeared in more games in relief than any other player in major league history, 1,050. He led the Pirates to a tremendous World Series upset over the Orioles in 1979 with three saves. All the "We Are Family" spirit would have gone for naught if Tekulve had not been there to protect the come-from-behind victories. With a sidearm delivery, Tekulve established himself as one of baseball's most successful relievers, ranking high among the all-time leaders in games, saves, and relief wins.

In 1978 Tekulve set a Pirates record with 31 saves, then matched it the following year. He led the NL in appearances four times, posting back-to-back seasons of more than 90 games in 1978 and 1979, and setting a club record with 94 in 1979. He is the Pirates' all-time leader in saves. Traded to the Phillies, he became the set-up man for Steve Bedrosian, who won the NL Cy Young Award in 1987.
Playing Career: *1974-1989; Pit N, Phi N, Cin N*

Johnny Temple
Temple, John Ellis
B: Aug 8, 1928

Pos: 2B   BA: .284
Hits: 1,484   HRs: 22
RBI: 395   BB: 648

A four-time All-Star second baseman, Temple was a doubles hitting infielder who batted leadoff for the 1956 Reds, the club who set the NL single-season home run record with 221 round-trippers. Temple batted .300 or more three times and tied for the NL lead in walks in 1957 with 94. He led NL second basemen three times in putouts and once each in

Gene Tenace
Tenace, Fury Gene
B: Oct 10, 1946

Pos: C, 1B   BA: .241
Hits: 1,060   HRs: 201
RBI: 674   BB: 984

The Italian Stallion of baseball, Tenace was born Fiore Gino Tennaci. He hit home runs for Oakland in his first two at-bats in the 1972

World Series, batting .348 and slugging at the phenomenal rate of .913 in the Fall Classic. Tenace was named Series MVP. One of the best on-base percentage players, he walked more than 100 times in six of seven years and posted on-base marks in excess of .400 six times. He played in five LCS and four World Series.
Playing Career: *1969-1983; Oak A, SD N, StL N, Pit N*

John Tener.

John Tener
Tener, John Kinley
B: Jul 23, 1863   D: May 19, 1946

Pos: P	ERA: 4.30
W-L: 25-31	SOs: 174
ShOs: 2	No-hitters: 0

Somehow Tener got a lot of mileage out of an average fastball and lack of control. He was a pitcher for the White Stockings when they toured around the world playing exhibition baseball games in the off-season of 1888-1889. The players asked Tener, who was trained as an accountant, to be treasurer for the trip. When they returned to discover that major league owners had imposed salary restrictions in their absence, Tener became secretary of the Brotherhood of Professional Players, and jumped to Pittsburgh in the new Players' League.

When that league folded in 1890, Tener entered banking and politics, and was elected to Congress in 1908. He served as governor of Pennsylvania for four years, then was asked to take the NL presidency. He was president from 1914 to 1918, a period of intense conflict in baseball, especially in the National Commission, which was set up to settle disputes. Tener resigned due to turmoil among the leagues and the three National Commission members.
Playing Career: *1885, 1888-1890; Bal AA, Chi N, Pit P*

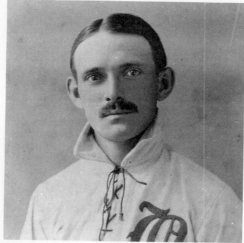

Fred Tenney.

Fred Tenney
Tenney, Frederick
B: Nov 26, 1871   D: Jul 3, 1952

Pos: 1B, OF	BA: .294
Hits: 2,231	HRs: 22
RBI: 688	BB: 874
Managerial Record	
Won: 202 Lost: 402 Pct: .334	

Joining Jimmy Collins, Herman Long and Bobby Lowe, Tenney completed the Boston Beaneaters' infield, which quickly became the best of the 19th century. He ranged farther from the bag than any previous first baseman, specializing in the 3-6-3 double play. He batted .325 and .334 as Boston cruised to NL titles in 1897 and 1898. Staying with the sinking ship as the franchise declined, Tenney had an opportunity to purchase majority ownership in 1906, but he did not, and subsequently found himself fired by the new owners.

Traded to New York, he scored 101 runs for the Giants in 1908, leading the NL. Tenney missed only one game at first base that year, but it was a lulu – the Merkle Boner game. During his career Tenney scored 1,278 runs and stole 285 bases. A graduate of Brown University, he wrote a World Series column for the *New York Times* before retiring from baseball completely.
Playing Career: *1894-1909, 1911; Bos N, NY N*
Managerial Career: *1905-1907, 1911; Bos N*

Jerry Terrell
Terrell, Jerry Wayne
B: Jul 13, 1946

Pos: 3B, SS, 2B, DH	BA: .253
Hits: 412	HRs: 4
RBI: 125	BB: 76

Terrell was the only player who voted against the 1981 baseball strike. He did so because of religious convictions. A versatile player, he posted a 0.00 ERA in two innings of work as a pitcher. In his best year, 1975, he batted .286 with 16 doubles.
Playing Career: *1973-1980; Min A, KC A*

Walt Terrell
Terrell, Charles Walter
B: May 11, 1958

Pos: P	ERA: 4.22
W-L: 111-124	SOs: 929
ShOs: 14	No-hitters: 0

Once hitting two homers off Fergie Jenkins in one game, Terrell was a consistent, durable starter, pitching over 200 innings in seven of eight years, 1984-1991. He won 15 or more games three times. Originally signed by the Rangers, Terrell was traded to the Mets with Ron Darling for Lee Mazzilli.
Playing Career: *1982-1992; NY N, Det A, SD N, NY A*

Adonis Terry
Terry, William H.
B: Aug 7, 1864   D: Feb 24, 1915

Pos: P	ERA: 3.72
W-L: 197-196	SOs: 1,555
ShOs: 18	No-hitters: 2

Pos: OF	BA: .249
Hits: 595	HRs: 15
RBI: 163 (inc.)	BB: 146

Greek god look-alike Terry brought more women to the ballpark than Count Tony Mullane and Ladies' Day promotions. He usually pitched, but also played 216 games in the outfield, sometimes batting high in the lineup. Terry won 20 games or more three times, and no-hit St. Louis in 1886 and Louisville in 1888, while pitching for the AA Brooklyn club. Terry and the Brooklyn club won back-to-back pennants, in the AA in 1889, then in the NL in 1890.
Playing Career: *1884-1897; Brk AA, Brk N, Bal N, Pit N, Chi N*

Bill Terry
Terry, William Harold (Memphis Bill)
B: Oct 30, 1896   D: Jan 9, 1989
Hall of Fame 1954

Pos: 1B, OF	BA: .341
Hits: 2,193	HRs: 154
RBI: 1,078	BB: 537
Managerial Record	
Won: 823 Lost: 661 Pct: .555	

A superstar first baseman for the Giants, Terry once told John McGraw that he could make more money being an electrician back home in Memphis. His independence impressed the Giants' brass so much that in 1932 they selected Terry to be McGraw's successor instead of Fred Lindstrom, who had been groomed for the job for the previous seven years. Terry, who scored 1,120 runs on 2,193 hits, including 373 doubles and 112 triples, led the Giants to three pennants during the 1930s. As a player, his .401 batting average in 1930 is the last NL .400 mark.

Terry hit .429 in the 1924 World Series, but the Giants lost to the Senators after a string of improbable events. Despite his accomplishments with the bat and glove, Terry was

never popular with the New York writers. As a manager, he was blunt and unwilling to cater to them. Most of all, they resented his refusal to give out his private telephone number. He was available for 16-18 hours a day at the Polo Grounds, and that was enough, as far as he was concerned.
Playing Career: *1923-1936; NY N*
Managerial Career: *1932-1941; NY N*

Ralph Terry
Terry, Ralph Willard
B: Jan 9, 1936

Pos: P   ERA: 3.62
W-L: 107-99   SOs: 1,000
ShOs: 20   Saves: 11

After serving up the famous Mazeroski home run pitch in the 1960 World Series, Terry went on to become the Yankees' ace by 1962. He led the AL in wins and innings that year, and was victorious in Game Seven of the World Series. He later became a successful golf pro.
Playing Career: *1956-1967; NY A, KC A, Cle A, NY N*

Zeb Terry
Terry, Zebulon Alexander
B: Jun 17, 1891   D: Mar 14, 1988

Pos: SS, 2B   BA: .260
Hits: 605   HRs: 2
RBI: 216   BB: 179

A four-year starter in the early 1920s, Terry's major league career ended abruptly when the Cubs acquired George Grantham to play the keystone sack. Terry had been purchased from the Pirates as one of new president William Veeck's first acquisitions.
Playing Career: *1916-1922; Chi A, Bos N, Pit N, Chi N*

Wayne Terwilliger
Terwilliger, Willard Wayne (Twig)
B: Jun 27, 1925

Pos: 2B   BA: .240
Hits: 501   HRs: 22
RBI: 162   BB: 247

A star shortstop at Western Michigan University and a Marine, Terwilliger collected eight consecutive hits for the Cubs in 1949. The next year he was traded to the Dodgers. After his playing career, he became a coach for the Senators, Rangers and Twins.
Playing Career: *1949-1951, 1953-1956, 1959-1960; Chi N, Brk N, Was A, NY N, KC A*

Jeff Tesreau
Tesreau, Charles Monroe
B: Mar 5, 1889   D: Sep 24, 1946

Pos: P   ERA: 2.43
W-L: 115-72   SOs: 880
ShOs: 27   No-hitters: 1

With a .615 lifetime won-lost percentage, Tesreau was the number three starter in the Giants' rotation from 1912 to 1917. The spit-baller led the 1912 NL with a 1.96 ERA and a 17-7 record. He was Manager John McGraw's choice to pitch the World Series opener against Boston's 34-game winner, Smoky Joe Wood. Tesreau lost Games One and Four to Wood, but whipped him in Game Seven, forcing another contest. He was later a popular baseball coach at Dartmouth.
Playing Career: *1912-1918; NY N*

Mickey Tettleton.

Mickey Tettleton
Tettleton, Mickey Lee
B: Sep 16, 1960

Pos: C, DH, 1B, OF   BA: .242
Hits: 821   HRs: 169
RBI: 516   BB: 647

The more Tettleton plays, the better he becomes. After four years as a part-time catcher for the A's and another year platooning with Terry Kennedy in Baltimore, the switch hitter blossomed as an everyday catcher in 1989, pounding 26 homers. Attributing his prowess to eating Fruit Loops, Tettleton flourished in Tiger Stadium, belting 95 homers in three years, 1991-1993. He has become an AL offensive leader.
Playing Career: *1984-; Oak A, Bal A, Det A*

Tim Teufel
Teufel, Timothy Shawn
B: Jul 7, 1958

Pos: 2B   BA: .254
Hits: 789   HRs: 86
RBI: 379   BB: 387

Struggling with the Twins, Teufel was traded to the Mets, where Manager Davey Johnson remembered him from International League days. In New York, Teufel platooned with Wally Backman, helping the Mets win the 1986 World Series. The next year he batted .308 and slugged .545.
Playing Career: *1983-; Min A, NY N, SD N*

Bob Tewksbury
Tewksbury, Robert Alan
B: Nov 30, 1960

Pos: P   ERA: 3.35
W-L: 65-49   SOs: 402
ShOs: 3   Saves: 1

After trying, and failing, to fit the Yankees' concept of a fastball pitcher, Tewksbury went to the Cardinals – by way of the Cubs – as a control pitcher. He was 16-5 with a 2.16 ERA in 1992, walking only 20 in 233 innings pitched. By the All-Star break in 1993, he was the ace of the staff.
Playing Career: *1986-; NY A, Chi N, StL N*

Tommy Thevenow
Thevenow, Thomas Joseph
B: Sep 6, 1903   D: Jul 29, 1957

Pos: SS, 2B, 3B   BA: .247
Hits: 1,030   HRs: 2
RBI: 456   BB: 210

The Cardinals pasted the Yankees in seven games of the 1926 World Series with Thevenow hitting .417. He led NL shortstops in putouts and assists that year, and hit the only two homers of his career in the World Series, though he was credited with a third when Babe Ruth dropped his long fly ball.
Playing Career: *1924-1938; StL N, Phi N, Pit N, Chi N, Bos N*

Bobby Thigpen
Thigpen, Robert T.
B: Jul 17, 1963

Pos: P   ERA: 3.35
W-L: 28-33   SOs: 362
ShOs: 0   Saves: 201

A college teammate of Rafael Palmiero and Will Clark, Thigpen set a single-season record of 57 saves in 1990. He appeared in an

Ace reliever Bobby Thigpen.

AL-high 77 games with a 1.83 ERA. Thigpen once published his salary demands in doggerel verse in the *Wall Street Journal*. The club responded in kind and grudgingly upped his wages. He saved 22 games in 1992 but ended with a 4.75 ERA and lost his closing job.
Playing Career: *1986-; Chi A, Phi N*

Clint Thomas
Thomas, Clinton C. (Hawk, Buckeye)
B: Nov 25, 1896   D: Dec 12, 1990

Pos: OF, 2B	BA: .305 (inc.)
Hits: 729 (inc.)	HRs: 51 (inc.)
RBI: NA	BB: NA

Though he started out at second base, Thomas was moved to the outfield by Detroit Stars Manager Bruce Petway, and became an instant success. He was nicknamed "Hawk" for his defensive abilities. Thomas was a key player in the Hilldales' 1923-1925 Eastern Colored League championships.

The Negro Hall of History in Ashland, Kentucky, was founded as the result of a gathering to celebrate Thomas's birthday. The group got corporate sponsorship from Marathon Oil and returned each year for a player reunion.
Playing Career: *1920-1938; Brk Royal Giants, Col Buckeyes, Det Stars, Phi Hilldales, AC Bach Giants, NY Lincoln Giants, NY Harlem Stars, Ind ABCs, NY Black Yankees, NY Cubans, Nwk Eagles*

Derrel Thomas
Thomas, Derrel Osborn
B: Jan 14, 1951

Pos: 2B, OF, SS, 3B, OF	BA: .249
Hits: 1,163	HRs: 43
RBI: 370	BB: 456

A speedster and jack-of-all-trades, Thomas played in two NLCS with the Dodgers, batting .545. He was considered one of the NL's better defensive outfielders, but played regularly in the Padres' and Giants' infields during his first five seasons.
Playing Career: *1971-1985; Hou N, SD N, SF N, LA N, Mon N, Cal A, Phi N*

Frank Thomas
Thomas, Frank Edward
B: May 27, 1968

Pos: 1B	BA: .321
Hits: 600	HRs: 104
RBI: 383	BB: 416

A scholarship football player at Auburn, Thomas signed with the White Sox in 1989. Today he is the best young slugger in the game. He led the AL in walks and on-base percentage in 1991 and 1992. He also hit 56 homers in those two years. Breaking in on August 2, 1990, Thomas hit in 45 of his first 60 games, including a 13-game hitting streak for a .330 average. He hit .317 with 106 runs, 128 RBI, 41 homers and 112 walks in 1993.

The key to Thomas's success is a good eye at the plate; he has drawn 416 walks and struck out only 308 times in more than three years. Thomas makes just as big an impact off the field as on it. He participates in the United Way Crusade of Mercy Home Run Night program and is a spokesperson for Major League Baseball/National Education Association "Give School a Major League Effort" program. As an amateur, he played on the U.S. National Team and was a member of the Pan-Am Team.
Playing Career: *1990-; Chi A*

Frank Joseph Thomas.

Frank Thomas
Thomas, Frank Joseph
B: Jun 11, 1929

Pos: OF, 3B, 1B	BA: .266
Hits: 1,671	HRs: 286
RBI: 962	BB: 484

As a rookie Thomas hit 30 home runs in 1953. Many thought of him as a successor to Ralph Kiner. For the next 12 years, Thomas hit more than 20 homers a season, three times belting more than 30. In 1959 he hit three dingers in one game. An All-Star outfielder in 1954-1955, he was the NL starting third baseman in the 1958 contest. Thomas changed teams eight times between 1959 and 1966. He led the 1962 expansion Mets with 34 round-trippers and 94 RBI.
Playing Career: *1951-1966; Pit N, Cin N, Chi N, Mil N, NY N, Phi N, Hou N*

Gorman Thomas
**Thomas, James Gorman
(Stormin' Gorman)**
B: Dec 12, 1950

Pos: OF, DH	BA: .225
Hits: 1,051	HRs: 268
RBI: 782	BB: 697

A minor league home run champion, Thomas led the AL in homers twice, with 45 in 1979 and 39 in 1982. Frequent strikeouts – 1,339 in his 13-year career – and low batting averages kept him from being a regular until 1978, the first of six years that he averaged 33 home runs a season. Acquired in the original first-round draft for the Seattle Pilots, Thomas put together a 32-homer and 87-RBI season in 1985 after sitting out much of the 1984 season.
Playing Career: *1973-1976, 1978-1986; Mil A, Cle A, Sea A*

Lee Thomas
Thomas, James Leroy
B: Feb 5, 1936

Pos: OF, 1B	BA: .255
Hits: 847	HRs: 106
RBI: 428	BBs: 332

Thomas hit 50 home runs in his first two big league seasons. Playing in both 1962 All-Star Games the next year, he earned the spot with a 26-homer, 104-RBI record. He is now the general manager of the wacky Phillies, who won the 1993 NL pennant.
Playing Career: *1961-1968; NY A, LA A, Bos A, Atl N, Chi N, Hou N*

Roy Thomas
Thomas, Roy Allen
B: Mar 24, 1874   D: Nov 20, 1959

Pos: OF	BA: .290
Hits: 1,537	HRs: 7
RBI: 299	BB: 1,042

One of the best leadoff hitters of his decade, Thomas topped the NL in walks seven times, going over 100 seven times. His 1,011 runs scored include 137 in 1899 and 132 in 1900. Thomas has a lifetime on-base average of .413, ranking 22nd on the all-time list. His ability to foul off pitches endlessly in pursuit of a free pass led to the rule that fouls must be

Roy Thomas in 1900.

counted as strikes. He was a fast singles hitter who batted as high as .327, surpassing the .300 mark five times.

Thomas had an on-base average above .400 each of his first seven seasons, and led the NL with a .415 mark in 1902 and a .453 average in 1903. When he scored 132 runs in 1900, Thomas had only 33 RBI. His speed enabled him to steal 244 bases. He ranged widely in center field, leading the NL three times in putouts, twice in total chances per game, and once each in fielding and assists. His .986 fielding average in 1906 tied the contemporary NL record. Thomas played all but two of his 13 seasons with the Phillies.
Playing Career: *1899-1911; Phi N, Pit N, Bos N*

Tommy Thomas
Thomas, Alphonse
B: Dec 23, 1899　D: Apr 27, 1988

Pos: P	ERA: 4.12
W-L: 117-128	SOs: 735
ShOs: 15	Saves: 12

A mainstay of the fabulous minor league Baltimore Orioles, winners of seven straight International League pennants in the 1920s, in the majors Thomas averaged 32 starts and 13 wins a season for the White Sox, 1926-1931. He surrendered the first upper deck homer in Comiskey Park, hit by Babe Ruth. Thomas pitched in the 1933 World Series with the Washington Senators.
Playing Career: *1926-1937; Chi A, Was A, Phi N, StL A, Bos A*

Gary Thomasson
Thomasson, Gary Leah
B: Jul 29, 1951

Pos: OF, 1B	BA: .249
Hits: 591	HRs: 61
RBI: 294	BB: 291

The ball Thomasson hit for a home run on Opening Day at Dodger Stadium in 1977 went into the Baseball Hall of Fame as the first major league home run with a Rawlings baseball. He made the Topps Rookie All-Star squad in 1973 by hitting .285. He played in the 1978 World Series with the Yankees.
Playing Career: *1972-1988; SF N, Oak A, NY A, LA N*

Danny Thompson
Thompson, Danny Leon
B: Feb 1, 1947　D: Dec 10, 1976

Pos: SS, 3B, 2B	BA: .248
Hits: 550	HRs: 15
RBI: 194	BB: 120

A contact hitter with alley power, Thompson led all regular shortstops in 1972 with a .276 batting average. Diagnosed with leukemia before the 1973 season, he courageously played four more years, hitting .270 in 1975. He appeared in 98 games in 1976 and died that winter.
Playing Career: *1970-1976; Min A, Tex A*

Hank Thompson with Monte Irvin (bottom) in 1949.

Fresco Thompson
Thompson, Lafayette Fresco (Tommy)
B: Jun 6, 1902　D: Nov 20, 1968

Pos: 2B	BA: .298
Hits: 762	HRs: 13
RBI: 215	BB: 215

Quick-witted and entertaining, Thompson was frequently used as an after-dinner speaker, and later became a successful baseball executive. He batted .303 in 1927, and .324, with 115 runs scored, in 1929. He worked for the Dodgers after retiring in 1934.
Playing Career: *1925-1932, 1934; Pit N, NY N, Phi N, Brk N*

Hank Thompson
Thompson, Henry Curtis
B: Dec 8, 1925　D: Sep 30, 1969

Pos: 3B, OF	BA: .267
Hits: 801	HRs: 129
RBI: 482	BB: 493

A Negro League star with the Kansas City Monarchs for six years, Thompson was the first black player for both the Browns and the Giants. When he batted against Don Newcombe in 1949, it was the first time in major league history a black batter faced a black pitcher. Thompson hit .302 with 24 homers in 1953. He belted three homers in a game in 1954. Playing in two World Series for the Giants, he drew 12 walks in nine games. In the 1954 Series he hit .364 with a record seven walks.
Playing Career: *1947, 1949-1956; StL A, NY N*

Jason Thompson
Thompson, Jason Dolph
B: Jul 6, 1954

Pos: 1B	BA: .261
Hits: 1,253	HRs: 208
RBI: 782	BB: 816

Thompson ripped 31 homers in both leagues, in 1977 with Detroit and in 1982 with Pittsburgh. He also led each league in total chances at first base those same years . The left-handed hitter was well-suited to Tiger Stadium, belting two home runs over the right field roof in 1977. Altogether he hit 98 homers in just over four seasons. The three-time All-Star was the third Pirate ever to draw 100 walks and drive in 100 runs in a season.
Playing Career: *1976-1986; Det A, Cal A, Pit N, Mon N*

Junior Thompson
Thompson, Eugene Earl
B: Jun 7, 1917

Pos: P	ERA: 3.26
W-L: 47-35	SOs: 315
ShOs: 6	Saves: 7

A rookie with the 1939 Reds, Thompson was 13-5, earning a World Series start against the Yankees. He lost, allowing seven runs on only five hits, a testament to the Yankees' power. The next year the Tigers knocked him out in Game Five of the Fall Classic, scoring six runs. He posted a 1.29 ERA in 1946.
Playing Career: *1939-1942, 1946-1947; Cin N, NY N*

Milt Thompson
Thompson, Milton Bernard
B: Jan 5, 1959

Pos: OF	BA: .279
Hits: 927	HRs: 41
RBI: 302	BB: 291

A speedy spray hitter, Thompson has all of the tools to play pro ball. He has stolen 200 bases, but seldom gets regular starting jobs. As a rookie he led the NL with a .433 pinch-hitting average. He starred for the pennant-winning Phillies in 1993.
Playing Career: *1984-; Atl N, Phi N, StL N*

Robby Thompson
Thompson, Robert Randall
B: May 10, 1962

Pos: 2B	BA: .253
Hits: 992	HRs: 104
RBI: 323	BB: 358

Banging two homers on two consecutive days in 1993, Thompson appears headed for the superstardom which was predicted when he jumped from Double A to the majors in 1986. That year he set a record by being thrown out stealing four times in one game.
Playing Career: *1986-; SF N*

Sam Thompson
Thompson, Samuel Luther (Big Sam)
B: Mar 5, 1860   D: Nov 7, 1922
Hall of Fame 1974

Pos: OF	BA: .331
Hits: 1,986	HRs: 128
RBI: 1,299	BB: 450

In 1894 with Philadelphia Thompson was a member of the only .400-hitting outfield in major league history. He batted .404, left fielder Ed Delahanty hit .400, backup out-fielder Tuck Turner hit .416, and center field-er Billy Hamilton hit .399. Thompson's .670 slugging percentage that season was the third best of the century. He hit for the cycle in a 6-for-7 game against Louisville that year. Trained as a carpenter, Thompson began playing pro ball in 1884, and was acquired by the Detroit NL club the following year.

Thompson batted .300 in his first three years, eight times in all. With his powerful throwing arm, he won the right field job. In 1887 Thompson led the NL with 545 at-bats, 203 hits, 23 triples, 166 RBI – the highest RBI total in the 19th century – a .372 batting aver-age, and a .571 slugging percentage. He hit two bases-loaded triples that year. Thomp-son's last great season was 1895, when his 18 homers, 165 RBI, and .654 slugging percent-age were NL highs. He batted .392.
Playing Career: *1885-1898, 1906; Det N, Phi N, Det A*

Bobby Thomson
Thomson, Robert Brown (The Flying Scot, The Staten Island Scot)
B: Oct 25, 1923

Pos: OF, 3B	BA: .270
Hits: 1,705	HRs: 264
RBI: 1,026	BB: 559

The batsman responsible for the most famous home run in baseball history, Thomson's name is indelibly etched on the soul of base-ball. His dramatic "shot heard 'round the world" on October 3, 1951, was a three-run, ninth-inning homer off Dodgers pitcher Ralph Branca. The dinger capped the Giants' amazing comeback to win the NL pennant. Thomson had also hit a sixth-inning homer off Branca in Game One of the playoffs, a shot that erased the 1-0 Dodger lead.

The key to the 1951 Giants' pennant was Thomson's switch to third base, allowing phenom Willie Mays to move into the lineup. After the 1953 season, Thomson was traded to the Braves for young Johnny Antonelli. Thomson broke his ankle in spring training with the Braves in 1954. That injury kept Hank Aaron from being sent to the minors. Known as a good low-ball hitter, Thomson

Bobby Thomson takes a ride after hitting the "shot heard 'round the world," 1951.

was named to the Giants' all-time outfield along with Mel Ott and Willie Mays.
Playing Career: *1946-1960; NY N, Mil N, Chi N, Bos A, Bal A*

Dickie Thon
Thon, Richard William
B: Jun 20, 1958

Pos: SS, 2B	BA: .264
Hits: 1,176	HRs: 71
RBI: 435	BB: 348

The grandson of one of Puerto Rico's greatest players, Thon found his career changed with one pitch from Mike Torrez in 1984. Before the beanball, Thon was the NL's best offen-sive shortstop. The injury caused double vision, and lots of time on the disabled list.
Playing Career: *1979-; Cal A, Hou N, SD N, Phi N, Tex A, Mil A*

Andre Thornton
Thornton, Andre
B: Aug 13, 1949

Pos: DH, 1B	BA: .254
Hits: 1,342	HRs: 253
RBI: 895	BB: 876

The most visible Cleveland player during the late 1970s and 1980s, Thornton might have become the Tribe's all-time home run leader if not for injuries. He hit 214 homers, only 14 fewer than Hal Trosky, despite missing all of the 1980 season and much of 1981. First base-man on the *Baseball Digest* 1974 All-Rookie team, Thorton led the club in homers seven times. He came to the Indians in exchange for pitcher Jackie Brown.
Playing Career: *1973-1979, 1981-1987; Chi N, Mon N, Cle A*

Marv Throneberry
Throneberry, Marvin Eugene (Marvelous Marv)
B: Sep 2, 1933

Pos: 1B, OF	BA: .237
Hits: 281	HRs: 53
RBI: 170	BB: 130

A minor league home run champ, Throne-berry became a pitiable crowd favorite of the 1962-1963 Mets. He was the living symbol of Mets futility with his untimely hitting, inept fielding, and atrocious baserunning.
Playing Career: *1955, 1958-1963; NY A, Oak A, Bal A, NY N*

Mark Thurmond
Thurmond, Mark Anthony
B: Sep 12, 1956

Pos: P	ERA: 3.69
W-L: 40-46	SOs: 320
ShOs: 3	Saves: 21

Thurmond's one good year, 1984, led to a pennant for San Diego and new owner Joan Kroc. Thurmond was 14-8 with a 2.97 ERA that season, then 0-1 in the World Series.
Playing Career: *1983-1992; SD N, Det A, Bal A, SF N*

Sloppy Thurston
Thurston, Hollis John
B: Jun 2, 1899   D: Sep 14, 1973

Pos: P	ERA: 4.26
W-L: 89-86	SOs: 306
ShOs: 8	Saves: 13

Named for his propensity to spill soup in his father's restaurant, Thurston was a dandy

Jazz Age dresser. He once fanned the side on nine pitches. He won 20 games for the last-place 1924 White Sox. As a scout he recruited Ralph Kiner for the Pirates.
Playing Career: *1923-1927, 1930-1933; StL A, Chi A, Was A, Brk N*

Luis Tiant
Tiant y Vega, Luis Clemente
B: Nov 23, 1940

Pos: P	ERA: 3.30
W-L: 229-172	SOs: 2,416
ShOs: 49	Saves: 15

The son of Cuba's greatest pitcher, Tiant was signed to his first contract by ex-major league star Bobby Avila for the 1959 Mexican League season. In 1964 Tiant set a PCL record with a .938 winning percentage before joining the Indians in midseason. He pitched a four-hit shutout against the Yankees in his first start. Tiant was 10-4 with a 2.83 ERA as a rookie in 1964. In 1966 he pitched four consecutive shutouts.

Tiant was practically unbeatable after he altered his delivery so that he turned away from the plate during his motion, in effect creating a hesitation pitch. He led the AL in 1968 with a 1.60 ERA, nine shutouts, and 5.3 hits per nine innings while striking out more than a batter per inning on his way to a 21-9 record. In the same year he struck out 19 Twins in a 10-inning game, setting an AL record for games of that length. In his previous start he fanned 13 Red Sox, giving him a major league record 32 strikeouts in two starts.
Playing Career: *1964-1982; Cle A, Min A, Bos A, NY A, Pit N, Cal A*

Dick Tidrow
Tidrow, Richard William
B: May 14, 1947

Pos: P	ERA: 3.68
W-L: 100-94	SOs: 975
ShOs: 5	Saves: 55

The Sporting News AL Rookie Pitcher of the Year in 1972, Tidrow pitched in three ALCS and World Series with the Yankees, 1976-1978. His best season was 1977, when he was 11-4 with five saves. Tidrow was a valuable set-up man for Cy Young Award winner Sparky Lyle in 1976.
Playing Career: *1972-1984; Cle A, NY A, Chi N, Chi A, NY N*

Mike Tiernan
Tiernan, Michael Joseph (Silent Mike)
B: Jan 21, 1867   D: Nov 9, 1918

Pos: OF	BA: .311
Hits: 1,834	HRs: 108
RBI: 851	BB: 747

With a booming home run, Tiernan broke up a 13-inning, 0-0 tie in 1890. Three years earlier, he scored six runs in a game at the Polo Grounds, an NL feat that has been equaled but never surpassed. Tiernan

Mike Tiernan.

whacked two triples, three singles and a walk in that 29-1 rout of the Phillies. Starting his pro career as a pitcher, he gained recognition by fanning 15 Providence Grays in an 1884 exhibition game. Later that season he beat the NL Phillies, but refused to sign a baseball contract to pitch.

The Giants finally allowed him to play outfield, where he batted .287 and hit doubles, triples and homers in double digits. With a lifetime .463 slugging percentage, Tiernan slugged under .400 only once. He stole 428 bases in 13 seasons, and scored more than 100 runs seven times, leading the NL with 147 in 1889. He survived the lean days under Andrew Freedman to retire and open a popular cafe in the Bronx.
Playing Career: *1887-1899; NY N*

Bob Tillman
Tillman, John Robert
B: Mar 24, 1937

Pos: C	BA: .232
Hits: 540	HRs: 79
RBI: 282	BB: 228

As a Boston receiver, Tillman caught two no-hitters, one by Earl Wilson and another by Dave Morehead. In 1964 he batted .278 with 17 home runs and 61 RBI, all career highs. Tillman hit three home runs in one game on July 30, 1969.
Playing Career: *1962-1970; Bos A, NY A, Atl N*

Tom Timmerman
Timmerman, Thomas Henry
B: May 12, 1940

Pos: P	ERA: 3.78
W-L: 35-35	SOs: 315
ShOs: 2	Saves: 35

Voted "Tiger of the Year" in 1970, the bespectacled Timmerman went 6-7 with a club record 27 saves and 61 appearances. He had spent nine plus years in the Tiger farm system before coming up in 1969. Manager Billy Martin made Timmerman an 8-10 starter in 1972 with 2.89 ERA.
Playing Career: *1969-1974; Det A, Cle A*

Cubs shortstop Joe Tinker.

Joe Tinker
Tinker, Joseph Bert
B: Jul 27, 1880   D: Jul 27, 1948
Hall of Fame 1946

Pos: SS, 3B	BA: .263
Hits: 1,695	HRs: 31
RBI: 782	BB: 416
Managerial Record	
Won: 304 Lost: 308 Pct: .497	

An intelligent, smooth-fielding, but light-hitting shortstop, Tinker combined with second baseman Johnny Evers, first baseman Frank Chance, and third baseman Harry Steinfeldt to form the best defensive infield of their era. Under Chance's leadership the Cubs devised defensive strategies to defeat the bunt, the hit-and-run, and the stolen base, and implemented the first known version of the rotation play. They brought Chicago to four NL pennants and two World Series titles, 1906-1910.

Tinker led NL shortstops four times in

fielding percentage, three times in total chances, twice each in putouts and assists, and once in double plays. He also led Federal League shortstops in total chances in 1914. He had superior speed, and stole an average of 28 bases a season for Chicago. In 1910 Tinker stole home twice in one game. He and his colleagues were immortalized in Franklin P. Adams's poem with the refrain "Tinker to Evers to Chance."
Playing Career: *1902-1916; Chi N, Cin N, Chi F*
Managerial Career: *1913-1916; Cin N, Chi F, Chi N*

John Titus
Titus, John Franklin (Silent John)
B: Feb 21, 1876   D: Jan 8, 1943

Pos: OF	BA: .282
Hits: 1,401	HRs: 38
RBI: 561	BB: 620

Reaching the majors at age 27, Titus was a steady player for nine years with the Phillies. He batted a career-high .309 in 1912, when he was traded to the Braves. Titus chewed toothpicks while batting, and also wore a handlebar mustache – out of fashion since the 1880s. Titus was a steady and reliable player, starting regularly for eight years, and appearing in 143 games or more for seven years in a row. He scored 738 runs and stole 140 bases.
Playing Career: *1903-1913; Phi N, Bos N*

Jack Tobin
Tobin, John Thomas
B: May 4, 1892   D: Dec 10, 1969

Pos: OF	BA: .309
Hits: 1,906	HRs: 64
RBI: 581	BB: 498

A leadoff man who smacked 200 hits four years in a row, Tobin was a St. Louis native who starred in his hometown with the Browns. An expert at drag bunting, Tobin had a career-high .352 batting average in 1921, when he led the AL with 671 at-bats. In 1922 and 1923, he joined Ken Williams and Baby Doll Jacobson in an all-.300-hitting outfield. Tobin hit two grand slams off Hall of Famer Walter Johnson. He later coached and scouted for the Browns.
Playing Career: *1914-1916, 1918-1927; StL F, StL A, Was A, Bos A*

Jim Tobin
Tobin, James Anthony (Abba Dabba)
B: Dec 27, 1912   D: May 19, 1969

Pos: P	ERA: 3.44
W-L: 105-112	SOs: 498
ShOs: 12	No-hitters: 2

A good-hitting pitcher, Tobin socked three homers in one 1942 game. Toiling for the Braves before they got good, he completed 100 games and 1,045 innings in four years, 1941-1944. Tobin was an All-Star in 1944, and he pitched in the 1945 World Series.
Playing Career: *1937-1945; Pit N, Bos N, Det A*

Al Todd
Todd, Alfred Chester
B: Jan 7, 1902   D: Mar 8, 1985

Pos: C	BA: .276
Hits: 768	HRs: 35
RBI: 366	BB: 104

In 1937 Todd hit .307 with 86 RBI, eight homers and 10 triples while catching 128 games without allowing a single passed ball – the latter a record that still stands. He once punched Dizzy Dean in a Texas League beanball incident.
Playing Career: *1932-1941, 1943; Phi N, Pit N, Brk N, Chi N*

Phil Todt
Todt, Philip Julius
B: Aug 9, 1901   D: Nov 15, 1973

Pos: 1B	BA: .258
Hits: 880	HRs: 57
RBI: 453	BB: 207

While Todt played first base for the Red Sox, they finished last six straight years. A fine fielder, he led the AL with a .997 average in 1928. Todt socked 58 triples and 183 doubles in seven years at Fenway Park. He played in the 1931 World Series.
Playing Career: *1924-1931; Bos A, Phi A*

Bobby Tolan
Tolan, Robert
B: Nov 19, 1945

Pos: OF, 1B	BA: .265
Hits: 1,121	HRs: 86
RBI: 497	BB: 258

One of the best looking prospects in baseball history, Tolan hit .417 in the 1970 NLCS. He stole 193 bases in a career that included three NLCS and four World Series, two with the Cardinals and two more with the Reds. A torn Achilles tendon curtailed his career.
Playing Career: *1965-1970, 1972-1977, 1979; StL N, Cin N, SD N, Phi N, Pit N*

Wayne Tolleson
Tolleson, Jimmy Wayne
B: Nov 22, 1955

Pos: SS, 2B, 3B, DH	BA: .244
Hits: 548	HRs: 9
RBI: 129	BB: 213

An All-American wide receiver at Western Carolina University, Tolleson led the nation in pass receptions his senior year. He looked like a budding baseball star in 1985 when he hit .313 for the Rangers, but two years with an average under .200 finished his career five years later.
Playing Career: *1981-1990; Tex A, Chi A, NY A*

Fred Toney
Toney Fred Alexandra
B: Dec 11, 1888   D: Mar 11, 1953

Pos: P	ERA: 2.69
W-L: 137-102	SOs: 718
ShOs: 28	No-hitters: 1

Stubborn as a bull, Toney won the famed double-no-hit game on May 2, 1917, in 10 innings. He once tossed a 17-inning no-hitter, striking out 17 and walking none, in the 1909 Blue Grass League. He made 42 starts for the Reds in 1917, tossing 339 innings, and going 24-16 with a 2.20 ERA. That year he pitched both ends of a doubleheader, defeating the Pirates 4-1 and 5-1. The big right-hander later pitched on two NL pennant winners, the 1921 and 1922 Giants.
Playing Career: *1911-1913, 1915-1923; Chi N, Cin N, NY N, StL N*

Jack Tobin, outfielder for the St. Louis Browns, 1921.

Specs Toporcer
Toporcer, George
B: Feb 9, 1899   D: May 17, 1989

Pos: SS   BA: .279
Hits: 437   HRs: 9
RBI: 151   BB: 150

Toporcer is remembered as the first infielder to wear glasses in the majors. Primarily a Cardinals utility player, he batted .324 in 1922. Twenty-two years later he wrote *Baseball, from Backyards to the Big Leagues*, one of the best instruction manuals for coaches.
Playing Career: *1921-1928; StL N*

Jeff Torborg
Torborg, Jeffrey Allen
B: Nov 26, 1941

Pos: C   BA: .214
Hits: 297   HRs: 8
RBI: 101   BB: 103
Managerial Record
Won: 491   Lost: 551   Pct: .471

A $100,000 bonus baby, Torborg hit .537 his senior year at Rutgers, an NCAA record. A backup catcher in the big leagues, he caught three no-hitters, including Sandy Koufax's perfect game, and no-hit gems by Bill Singer and Nolan Ryan, plus the fifth and sixth shutouts in Don Drysdale's streak. He had accepted the Princeton coaching job when the White Sox lured him back into pro ball.
Playing Career: *1964-1973; LA N, Cal A*
Managerial Career: *1977-1979, 1989-1993; Cle A, Chi A, NY N*

Earl Torgeson
Torgeson, Clifford Earl
(The Earl of Snohomish)
B: Jan 1, 1924   D: Nov 8, 1990

Pos: 1B   BA: .265
Hits: 1,318   HRs: 149
RBI: 740   BB: 980

A graceful left-handed first baseman, Torgeson batted .281 with 16 homers in his rookie year. In the 1948 World Series, he led all hitters with a .389 batting average. Injuring his left shoulder trying to break up a double play, Torgeson missed most of the 1949 season, but came back to lead the NL with 120 runs in 1950. He was like a bull when enraged. Opponents seldom crossed him.
Playing Career: *1947-1961; Bos N, Phi N, Det A, Chi A, NY A*

Joe Torre
Torre, Joseph Paul (The Godfather)
B: Jul 18, 1940

Pos: 3B, C, 1B   BA: .297
Hits: 2,342   HRs: 252
RBI: 1,185   BB: 779
Managerial Record
Won: 821   Lost: 915   Pct: .473

A nine-time All-Star, Torre started his career as a catcher but excelled at the hot corner as

Joe Torre as Braves manager, 1982.

well. In 1965 he hit 27 homers and won a Gold Glove Award. His two-run home run in the 1965 All-Star Game secured the NL's victory. When the Braves moved to Atlanta in 1966, Torre hit a career-high 36 round-trippers while batting .315 with 101 RBI. The Braves traded Torre to the Cardinals straight-up for former MVP Orlando Cepeda, whom Torre replaced at first base. He reached 100 RBI each of the next three seasons.

Torre had a great year in 1971; he socked 230 hits for a .363 batting average, driving in 137 runs, all league-leading marks. He also walloped 24 homers and 34 doubles to score 97 runs. Torre was the NL MVP that year. As a manager he won in Atlanta by jumping off to a 13-0 start and coasting to the 1982 division title with an 89-73 record. The Braves were swept 3-0 by the Cardinals, whom Torre took over in 1990. Between managing jobs he was a popular Angels broadcaster.
Playing Career: *1960-1977; Mil N, Atl N, StL N, NY N*
Managerial Career: *1977-1984, 1990-; NY N, Atl N, StL N*

Mike Torrez
Torrez, Michael Augustine
B: Aug 28, 1946

Pos: P   ERA: 3.97
W-L: 185-160   SOs: 1,404
ShOs: 15   No-hitters: 0

Surrendering the Bucky Dent home run in the 1978 playoff made Red Sox fans forget that Mike Torrez was a pitcher who won more than 15 games five seasons in a row, 1974-1978, for five different teams. He would win 16 for the BoSox again the next season.

He had helped the Yankees to the 1977 pennant with seven straight wins in July and August. Tossing two complete-game victories in the Series against the Dodgers, he was the beneficiary of Reggie Jackson's three home runs in the sixth and final game. His wife wrote a best-selling book about their life in Montreal.
Playing Career: *1967-1984; StL N, Mon N, Bal A, Oak A, NY A, Bos A, NY N*

Cristobal Torriente
Torriente, Cristobal
B: 1895   D: 1938 (?)

Pos: OF, P   BA: .335
Hits: 774   HRs: 53
RBI: NA   BB: NA

C. I. Taylor, longtime manager and Negro League executive, said, "If I should see Torriente walking up the other side of the street, I would say, 'there walks a ballclub.'" In the 12 documented years that Torriente played in the Cuban League, he batted .352. He led that league in doubles twice, in hits and in stolen bases three times, in triples and in homers four times. Against major leaguers in exhibition play, he hit .281 with three home runs.
Playing Career: *1913-1928, 1932; NY Cubans, Chi Am Giants, All Nations, KC Monarchs, Det Stars, Cle Cubs*

Cesar Tovar
Tovar, Cesar Leonardo
B: Jul 3, 1940

Pos: OF, 3B, 2B, DH   BA: .278
Hits: 1,546   HRs: 46
RBI: 435   BB: 413

The hustling Tovar played all nine positions in a game against the A's. He pitched one scoreless inning in which he struck out Reggie Jackson. The first batter he faced was Bert Campaneris, the only other man to perform in nine positions in a game. In 1969 Tovar stole a career-high 45 bases. On May 18, he and teammate Rod Carew each stole home in the second inning against a Detroit battery of Mickey Lolich and Bill Freehan.
Playing Career: *1965-1976; Min A, Phi N, Tex A, Oak A, NY A*

Alan Trammell
Trammell, Alan Stuart
B: Feb 21, 1958

Pos: SS, 3B   BA: .288
Hits: 2,182   HRs: 174
RBI: 936   BB: 797

Trammell and Lou Whitaker formed the Tiger keystone combination for 14 years, 1978-1991. Ironically, Trammell, the acknowledged leader of the Tigers, was the first to slow. A 1992 injury allowed the Tigers to bring up Travis Fryman. When the four-time Gold Glove winner returned he had lost his shortstop job, but regained it late in 1993.

His .319 batting average in 1983 was the AL high for right-handed batters. Driving in all of Detroit's runs in Game Four of the 1984 World Series and tying a five-game Series record with nine hits, he was named Series MVP. After a subpar 1985, a more muscular Trammell was part of the Tigers' all-20-home run infield in 1986. Surprisingly, Sparky Anderson moved him to the cleanup spot in Detroit's 1987 offense. The once-scrawny infielder rose to the occasion with a career season, hitting .343 with 28 homers, 105 RBI, 205 hits and 109 runs, narrowly missing the AL

MVP Award. He is among Detroit's all-time leaders in doubles, runs scored, hits and stolen bases.
Playing Career: *1977-; Det A*

George Trautman
Trautman, George McNeal
B: Jan 11, 1890   D: Jun 24, 1963

Serving professional baseball for more than 40 years, Trautman came to be the protector of the minor leagues and supporter of the National Baseball Library in Cooperstown, New York. He made the statement, "the professional game must remain out of the hands of the opportunist, the fly-by-night operator who knows no history, has no feeling of responsibility and whose sole concern is the making of a fast dollar. Baseball is a public trust. The franchise owner in any league must assume responsibility of preservation of baseball's good name in his community."

Trautman served as president of the American Association, 1935-1945, a period of rebirth from the depths of the Depression to a holding pattern during the war. He was elected as a compromise candidate to the presidency of the National Association of Professional Baseball Clubs in 1947. His era began amid tremendous prosperity; there were 52 leagues with more than 350 clubs operating, and there were 59 leagues by 1949. When Trautman left office, the minors were better run and better prepared to take on the challenges of the 1960s.

Bill Travers
Travers, William Edward (Stork)
B: Oct 27, 1952

Pos: P	ERA: 4.10
W-L: 65-71	SOs: 488
ShOs: 10	Saves: 1

A 1976 All-Star, Travers was 15-16 with 240 innings and a 2.81 ERA despite suffering from Legionnaires' disease in midseason. He missed most of 1977 with a sore arm, but came back to win 38 games over the next three years.
Playing Career: *1974-1981, 1983; Mil A, Cal A*

Cecil Travis
Travis, Cecil Howell
B: Aug 8, 1913

Pos: SS, 3B	BA: .314
Hits: 1,544	HRs: 27
RBI: 657	BB: 402

The player whose career was most damaged by military duty in World War II was Travis. The modest, southern-born infielder was a great hitter for the Senators before the war, batting over .300 eight of nine years. Breaking in with five hits in his first major league game, Travis set an AL record and tied Fred Clarke's long-standing NL record for solid beginnings.

Early in his career, Travis slapped most of his hits to left field. Later he learned to pull the ball, cracking 19 triples in 1941. That season he led the AL with 218 hits and also had 101 RBI with a .359 average. *The Sporting News* named him the top shortstop in the majors. When he returned from military service in 1945 at age 41, his skills had eroded. After hitting .252 and .216, the three-time All-Star retired from major league play.
Playing Career: *1933-1941, 1945-1947; Was A*

The Senators' Cecil Travis.

Pie Traynor
Traynor, Harold Joseph
B: Nov 11, 1899   D: Mar 16, 1972
Hall of Fame 1948

Pos: 3B, SS	BA: .320
Hits: 2,416	HRs: 58
RBI: 1,273	BB: 472
Managerial Record	
Won: 457 Lost: 406 Pct: .530	

Named for his childhood taste for pies, Traynor gave the Pirates and their fans 14 years of greatness at third base. Until Mike Schmidt came along, he was generally considered the best all-around third sacker in baseball history. Traynor scored 1,183 runs while slashing 164 triples and 371 doubles. In two World Series he batted .293 for 11 games, including a .346 mark in the seven-game 1925 World Series victory over Washington. He handled 24 Series chances without an error.

Traynor came up as a shortstop but was moved to third base by Manager Bill McKechnie in 1922. He topped the .300 mark 10 times. Playing on teams that featured the Waner brothers, he led the Pirates in hitting just once, with a .356 mark in 1929. When he hit .366 in 1930, teammate Paul Waner hit .368. Traynor struck out only 278 times in 7,559 at-bats, including only seven K's in 540 at-bats in 1930. Selected for the first two All-Star Games, he is among the Pirates' all-time leaders in every offensive category but home runs.
Playing Career: *1920-1935, 1937; Pit N*
Managerial Career: *1934-1939; Pit N*

George Trautman (r) with Commissioner Ford Frick.

Tom Tresh belts a three-run homer for the Yankees in Game Five of the 1962 WS.

Tom Trebelhorn
Trebelhorn Thomas Lynn
B: Jan 27, 1948

Managerial Record
Won: 422   Lost: 397   Pct: .515

A school teacher in the off-season, Trebelhorn took over as Brewers manager when George Bamberger retired. The career minor league catcher led the team to third-place finishes in his first two full seasons.
Managerial Career: *1986-1991, 1994-; Mil A, Chi N*

Ted Trent
Trent, Theodore
B: Dec 17, 1903   D: Jan 10, 1944

Pos: P
W-L: 93-49
ShOs: 16
ERA: NA
SOs: 505 (inc.)
Saves: 3

A four-time All-Star in the annual East-West Negro League Classic, Trent ranks high in lifetime wins in the Negro Leagues. He was 21-2 in 1928, and he led the Negro National League in complete games three straight years. His teams won five pennants.
Playing Career: *1927-1939; StL Stars, Det Wolves, Was Pilots, NY Black Yankees, Chi Am Giants*

Mike Tresh
Tresh, Michael
B: Feb 23, 1914   D: Oct 4, 1966

Pos: C
Hits: 788
RBI: 297
BA: .249
HRs: 2
BB: 402

A top-notch defensive catcher, Tresh was durable enough to catch all 150 White Sox games in 1945, and was selected for the All-Star Game even though it was called off due to the war. He batted .281 with 15 doubles in 1940, both career high marks.
Playing Career: *1938-1949; Chi A, Cle A*

Tom Tresh
Tresh, Thomas Michael
B: Sep 20, 1937

Pos: OF, SS
Hits: 1,041
RBI: 530
BA: .245
HRs: 153
BB: 550

The son of Mike Tresh, Tom was AL Rookie of the Year in 1962 when he hit .286 with 20 home runs and 93 RBI. The switch-hitting Gold Glove shortstop was the heir-apparent to Mickey Mantle when the Yanks moved him to the outfield. The two-time All-Star continued to hit homers, but his batting average declined steadily.
Playing Career: *1961-1969; NY A, Det A*

Alex Trevino
Trevino y Castro, Alejandro
B: Aug 26, 1957

Pos: C, 3B, 2B
Hits: 604
RBI: 244
BA: .249
HRs: 23
BB: 205

Discovered in the Mexican Central League by the Mets, Trevino socked a career-high .271 in 1979. Then the Mets swapped him for George Foster in 1982 and he became the Reds' regular catcher, hitting .251 in 120 games that year.
Playing Career: *1978-1990; NY N, Cin N, Atl N, SF N, LA N, Hou N*

Gus Triandos
Triandos, Gus Constantine
B: Jul 30, 1930

Pos: C
Hits: 954
RBI: 608
BA: .244
HRs: 167
BB: 440

Big, powerful, strong-armed and slow-footed, Triandos came to the Orioles as part of a 17-player trade in 1954 and was their regular catcher for seven seasons. He hit more than 20 home runs three times, tying an AL record for catchers with 30 in 1958. With the Phillies on June 21, 1964, Triandos caught Jim Bunning's perfect game, the first in the NL in 84 years. Oddly, he owns the major league record with 1,206 consecutive games without being caught stealing.
Playing Career: *1953-1965; NY A, Bal A, Det A, Phi N, Hou N*

Manny Trillo
Trillo, Jesus Manuel Marcano
B: Dec 25, 1950

Pos: 2B
Hits: 1,562
RBI: 571
BA: .263
HRs: 61
BB: 452

Winning his third Gold Glove in 1982 with the Phillies, Trillo set major league second baseman records for 89 consecutive errorless games and 479 consecutive errorless chances accepted. The streak inexplicably gripped the nation. He also set a record with a .993 fielding percentage. Sent to Cleveland in a deal for Von Hayes that December, in 1983 he became the first player to be chosen to the starting All-Star squad in successive years in different leagues.
Playing Career: *1973-1987; Oak A, Chi N, Phi N, Cle A, Mon N, SF N, Cin N*

Hal Trosky
Trosky, Harold Arthur, Sr.
B: Nov 11, 1912   D: Jun 18, 1979

Pos: 1B
Hits: 1,561
RBI: 1,012
BA: .302
HRs: 228
BB: 545

Cleveland's all-time best slugger and one of the AL's best during the 1930s, Trosky swung a bat in an unparalleled era of power hitting. Tarnished by a leadership role in the Cleve-

Heavy-hitting Hal Trosky.

land "Crybaby" incident, Trosky built his reputation by averaging 29 homers, 122 RBI, 101 runs and a .314 batting average over a seven-year period, 1934-1940. Hitting .330 as a rookie in 1934, he showed his left-handed power with 35 homers, 45 doubles and 142 RBI, second to Lou Gehrig.

In 1936 Trosky put together a 28-game hitting streak, leading the AL with an Indians-record 162 RBI, reaching career highs of .343 and 42 homers. He drove in 100 or more runs six straight years. Twice Trosky hit three homers in a game. Retiring after the 1941 season, Trosky went home to Iowa, but came back to play with the 1944 White Sox after being declared 4F by the military. Hitting just 10 homers in 1944, he sat out a season, then played in 1946.

Playing Career: *1933-1941, 1944, 1946; Cle A, Chi A*

Dizzy Trout
Trout, Paul Howard
B: Jun 29, 1915   D: Feb 28, 1972

Pos: P	ERA: 3.23
W-L: 170-161	SOs: 1,256
ShOs: 28	Saves: 35

A colorful, fun-loving right-hander, Trout led the AL in wins in 1943, and formed a fearsome duo with Hal Newhouser. In 1944 the pair won 56 games – Newhouser 29 and Trout 27 – as the Bengals missed the AL flag by one game. The remainder of the pitching staff could manage only 32 additional victories. In that year, Trout led the AL with a 2.12 ERA and seven shutouts. He also hit five home runs while batting .271. He had 20 career homers.

The two-time All-Star was the Tigers' workhorse in the 1945 pennant drive, pitching six games and winning four over a nine-game late-season stretch. In Game Four of the 1945 World Series, Trout beat the Cubs 4-1 on a five-hitter. He remained a Tiger mainstay into the 1950s. Five years after Dizzy "retired," he signed with the desperate Orioles after an impressive showing in an Old-Timers' Game. He pitched twice and "re-retired." Dizzy is the father of pitcher Steve Trout.

Playing Career: *1939-1952, 1957; Det A, Bos A, Bal A*

Steve Trout
Trout, Steven Russell (Rainbow)
B: Jul 30, 1957

Pos: P	ERA: 4.18
W-L: 88-92	SOs: 656
ShOs: 9	Saves: 4

Recommended to the White Sox by his father, Dizzy Trout, Steve was Chicago's first pick in the 1976 June draft. The 6'4" left-hander went 11-8 in 1979. Moving to the Cubs, he was 13-7 in the 1984 season, then 1-0 in the NLCS.

Playing Career: *1978-1989; Chi A, Chi N, NY A, Sea A*

Virgil Trucks
Trucks, Virgil Oliver (Fire)
B: Apr 26, 1919

Pos: P	ERA: 3.39
W-L: 177-135	SOs: 1,534
ShOs: 35	No-hitters: 2

Burning everything in his path like General Sherman, Trucks ravaged the Alabama-Florida League with 418 strikeouts in 1938. In 1952 he tossed a pair of no-hitters against the Senators and Yankees, joining Johnny Vander Meer, Allie Reynolds and Nolan Ryan as the only pitchers to hurl two no-nos in a single season. Trucks also pitched four no-hitters in the minors, and had a near major league miss in 1954.

The fireballer had returned to Detroit from the military in 1945, appearing in the World Series against the Cubs. He had been in only one game during the regular season, but was given special clearance to play in the Series. He is likely to be the only 20th-century pitcher to win more games in the Series than during the season. Trucks was an All-Star in 1949 when he led the AL in shutouts and strikeouts, and in 1954 when he won 19 and again led the AL in shutouts. He also saved 30 games and made nearly 150 relief appearances.

Playing Career: *1941-1943, 1945-1958; Det A, StL A, Chi A, KC A, NY A*

Thurman Tucker
Tucker, Thurman Lowell (Joe E.)
B: Sep 26, 1917   D: May 7, 1993

Pos: OF	BA: .255
Hits: 570	HRs: 9
RBI: 191	BB: 291

A dead ringer for the comedian Joe E. Brown, Thurman was called "Joe E. Tucker" by the Chicago press. Leading the AL in hitting during the first half of 1944, Tucker batted leadoff in the All-Star Game. Very fast, he ran races for promotional stunts.

Playing Career: *1942-1944, 1946-1951; Chi A, Cle A*

Tommy Tucker
Tucker, Thomas Joseph (Foghorn)
B: Oct 28, 1863   D: Oct 22, 1935

Pos: 1B	BA: .290
Hits: 1,882	HRs: 42
RBI: 848	BB: 479

One of the earliest and flashiest players, Tucker scored 1,084 runs in a relatively short career, five times surpassing the 100 mark. He led the AA in batting with a .372 average in 1889, and led in hits and on-base percentage as well. Nicknamed for his loudmouthed style as a base coach, he was once assaulted by Philadelphia fans after leading Boston's stalling tactics in hope of a rainout.

Playing Career: *1887-1899; Bal AA, Bos N, Was N, Brk N, StL N, Cle N*

John Tudor
Tudor, John Thomas
B: Feb 2, 1954

Pos: P	ERA: 3.12
W-L: 117-72	SOs: 988
ShOs: 16	Saves: 1

The hope of the Cardinals in the 1985 World Series, overworked Tudor came out of Game Seven and put his fist through a rotating fan, a frustrating end to an improbable season. He tossed 10 shutouts that year, including two 1-0 wins over the Mets. Honing his accuracy by pitching five years in Fenway Park, a field

Paul Howard "Dizzy" Trout.   *Virgil "Fire" Trucks.*

that eats lefties alive, Tudor arrived in the NL with pinpoint control. His ERA had never been below 3.00 in the AL, it was above 3.00 only once in five full NL seasons.
Playing Career: *1979-1990; Bos A, Pit N, StL N, LA N*

Bob Turley
Turley, Robert Lee (Bullet Bob)
B: Sep 19, 1930

Pos: P	ERA: 3.64
W-L: 101-85	SOs: 1,265
ShOs: 24	Saves: 12

The greatest sign stealer in the last half century, Turley was one of the reasons the Yankees and Casey Stengel won 10 pennants in 12 years. He was 4-3 in five World Series with the Yankees. His big year was 1958 when he went 21-7, leading the AL in wins, won-lost percentage, complete games and opponents' batting average. A real fastballer, he led the AL in strikeouts with 185 in 1954, and fanned 210 the next year.
Playing Career: *1951, 1953-1963; StL A, Bal A, NY A, LA A, Bos A*

Jim Turner
Turner, James Riley (Milkman)
B: Aug 6, 1903

Pos: P	ERA: 3.22
W-L: 69-60	SOs: 329
ShOs: 8	Saves: 20

Called the "Milkman" because he always delivered the goods, Turner won 20 games as a 33-year-old Braves rookie in 1937. He led the NL that season in complete games, shutouts and ERA. He played in the World Series with the Reds and Yankees.
Playing Career: *1937-1945; Bos N, Cin N, NY A*

Ted Turner
Turner, Robert Edward
B: Nov 19, 1938

Managerial Record
Won: 0   Lost: 1   Pct: .000

The multimillionaire owner of CNN, TBS and the Atlanta Braves, Turner managed his own club from the bench for one game. He purchased the Braves in 1976 to keep them in Atlanta, then he put them on his nationwide cable-TV station, making the Braves "America's Team."
Managerial Career: *1977; Atl N*

Terry Turner
Turner, Terrance Lamont (Cotton)
B: Feb 28, 1881   D: Jul 18, 1960

Pos: SS, 3B, 2B, OF	BA: .253
Hits: 1,499	HRs: 8
RBI: 528	BB: 435

A 15-year Indians veteran, Turner holds Tribe records with 1,619 games and 254 stolen bases. He retains the AL record for most assists in a 154-game season, with 570 in 1906. He hit a career-high .308 in 1912, breaking up no-hitters three times. He pioneered the use of the head-first slide because of tender ankles. Turner had failed in his first try with the Pirates because he was used to playing on a dirt infield, not grass – a common problem with young players in that era. He played his last season with the A's.
Playing Career: *1901, 1904-1919; Pit N, Cle A, Phi A*

Tuck Turner
Turner, George A.
B: Feb 13, 1873   D: Jul 16, 1945

Pos: OF	BA: .320
Hits: 478	HRs: 7
RBI: 213	BB: 128

A switch-hitting second-string outfielder with the powerful Phillies of the 1890s, Turner was unable to break into the Hall of Fame outfield lineup of Sam Thompson, Ed Delahanty and Billy Hamilton. Turner batted .416 behind Hugh Duffy in 1894.
Playing Career: *1893-1898; Phi N, StL N*

The Tigers' Bill Tuttle in 1956.

Bill Tuttle
Tuttle, William Robert
B: Jul 4, 1929

Pos: OF	BA: .259
Hits: 1,105	HRs: 67
RBI: 443	BB: 480

A star athlete from Bradley University, Tuttle, who always wore number 13, played seven years as a regular for the Tigers and A's. He walloped 14 homers with 23 doubles and 102 runs scored in 1955. Tuttle led AL outfielders in putouts and assists in 1960.
Playing Career: *1952, 1954-1963; Det A, KC A, Min A*

"Bullet Bob" Turley threw a mean fastball for the Yankees in the 1950s.

Larry Twitchell
Twitchell, Lawrence Grant
B: Feb 18, 1864   D: Apr 23, 1930

Pos: OF, P	BA: .263
Hits: 676	HRs: 18
RBI: 384	BB: 168

Going 11-1 as a pitcher and batting .333 for the 1887 Detroit Wolverines, Twitchell did not pitch in the exhausting 15-game championship series won by Detroit. That season he set the major league record for most long hits in a game with a double, three triples and a home run.
Playing Career: *1886-1894; Det N, Cle N, Cle P, Buf P, Col AA, Was N, Lou N*

Wayne Twitchell
Twitchell, Wayne Lee
B: Mar 10, 1948

Pos: P	ERA: 3.98
W-L: 48-65	SOs: 789
ShOs: 6	Saves: 2

An All-Star in 1973, Twitchell went 13-9 with a 2.50 ERA and five shutouts for the Phillies. He also pitched a scoreless inning in the All-Star Game. Suffering a knee injury playing basketball, he seldom displayed his winning stuff again. The big right-hander was 3-1 with a 1.75 ERA in 1976.
Playing Career: *1970-1979; Mil A, Phi N, Mon N, NY N, Sea A*

Lefty Tyler
Tyler, George Albert
B: Dec 14, 1889   D: Sep 29, 1953

Pos: P	ERA: 2.95
W-L: 127-116	SOs: 1,003
ShOs: 33	Saves: 7

One of the Big Three who carried the Miracle Braves to their pennant in 1914, Tyler was 16-13. For seven straight years he posted ERAs under 2.87, being halted by the lively ball in 1920. He once won a 21-inning, 2-1 game, scattering 13 hits and walking one in a complete game performance. Tyler started three games in the 1918 World Series, going 1-1 with a 1.17 ERA. He had 10 complete-game 1-0 victories in his career.
Playing Career: *1910-1921; Bos N, Chi N*

Mike Tyson
Tyson, Michael Ray (Rocky)
B: Jan 13, 1950

Pos: 2B, SS	BA: .241
Hits: 714	HRs: 27
RBI: 269	BB: 175

Fiercely competitive, Tyson was a top Cardinals prospect, and was their Rookie of the Year in 1973. He was flourishing, hitting .286 in 1976, when he broke his finger making a tag. Tyson lost the second base job to Ken Oberkfell and was traded to the Cubs.
Playing Career: *1972-1981; StL N, Chi N*

Peter Ueberroth
Ueberroth, Peter
B: Sep 2, 1937

A millionaire California travel agent who became commissioner of baseball, Ueberroth held the national pastime's highest position for six years, 1984-1989. The organizer of the 1984 Olympics, he sought to put baseball on better financial footing and to deal with its drug problem.

Bob Uecker
Uecker, Robert George
B: Jan 26, 1935

Pos: C	BA: .200
Hits: 146	HR: 14
RBI: 74	BBs: 96

Baseball's best jokester, Ueker was also a good defensive catcher, starting the 1965 season for the Cardinals. Besides his beer commercials and his TV sitcom, "Mr. Belvedere," Uecker is a long-time Brewers broadcaster and played himself in the movie, *Major League.*
Playing Career: *1962-1967; Mil N, StL N, Phi N*

George Uhle
Uhle, George Ernest (The Bull)
B: Sep 18, 1898   D: Feb 26, 1985

Pos: P	ERA: 3.99
W-L: 200-166	SOs: 1,135
ShOs: 21	Saves: 25

The best-hitting pitcher of all time, next to Babe Ruth, Uhle batted .288 with six full seasons over .300, reaching the .361 level in 1923 with Cleveland. He also led the AL in wins twice, with 26 in 1923 and 27 in 1926. Uhle tossed 3,119 innings altogether, including a 20-inning shutout in 1919. He was a workhorse and paid the price for overwork with a chronic sore arm that plagued him after the 1926 season, hampering his effectiveness. Uhle experimented with the slider, naming it after the motion it made.
Playing Career: *1919-1934, 1936; Cle A, Det A, NY N, NY A*

Wayne Twitchell on the mound for the NY Mets in 1979.

Tom Underwood
Underwood, Thomas Gerald
B: Dec 22, 1953

Pos: P   ERA: 3.89
W-L: 86-87   SOs: 948
ShOs: 6   Saves: 18

In 1979 Underwood started a game for the Blue Jays against his brother Pat with the Tigers. Pat won. Tom played for three division winners in six years, giving up only two runs in four different series, yet never seeing a pennant. He won 14 games in 1975.
Playing Career: *1974-1984; Phi N, StL N, Tor A, NY A, Oak A, Bal A*

Bob Unglaub
Unglaub, Robert Alexander
B: Jul 31, 1881 Nov 29, 1916

Pos: 1B, 3B, 2B   BA: .258
Hits: 554   HRs: 5
RBI: 216   BB: 88
Managerial Record
Won: 9   Lost: 20   Pct: .310

A minor league hitting star, Unglaub came to the majors with high hopes. His trade to the Red Sox for Patsy Dougherty during the 1904 season was perceived as an AL plot to stock the New York franchise with better players at the expense of other AL teams.
Playing Career: *1904-1905, 1907-1910; NY A, Bos A, Was A*
Managerial Career: *1907; Bos A*

Del Unser
Unser, Delbert Bernard
B: Dec 9, 1944

Pos: OF   BA: .258
Hits: 1,344   HRs: 87
RBI: 481   BB: 481

The Sporting News Rookie of the Year in 1968, 13 years later Unser pinch-hit .316 in the Phillies' 1980 World Championship season. In Game Five of the 1980 NLCS, he went 2-for-2, driving in a run and scoring the game-winning tally in the 10th inning as the Phillies beat the Astros 8-7 to take the series. Unser socked two more game-winning pinch hits off the Royals in the 1980 Series. He once walloped three pinch-hit homers in three straight appearances, a major league record.
Playing Career: *1968-1982; Was A, Cle A, Phi N, NY N, Mon N*

Cecil Upshaw
Upshaw, Cecil Lee
B: Oct 22, 1942

Pos: P   ERA: 3.13
W-L: 34-36   SOs: 323
ShOs: 0   Saves: 86

Nearly severing a finger demonstrating how to dunk a basketball, Upshaw ended his effectiveness as a stopper. Using a sidearm delivery, he had saved 27 for the Braves in 1969. He appeared in every game of the NLCS that year, posting a 2.84 ERA in a losing effort.
Playing Career: *1966-1969, 1971-1975; Atl N, Hou N, Cle A, NY A, Chi A*

Willie Upshaw
Upshaw, Willie Clay
B: Apr 27, 1957

Pos: 1B, OF, DH   BA: .262
Hits: 1,103   HRs: 123
RBI: 528   BB: 452

The cousin of NFL great Gene Upshaw, Willie took over the Blue Jays' first base duty from John Mayberry, who had been the franchise's premier power hitter. In 1982 Upshaw set a team record for extra-base hits which he broke the following year, hitting a career-high .306 with 27 homers, 99 runs and 104 RBI in 1983. He had at least one RBI in a team-record eight straight games in 1983. He played in the 1985 World Series. The emergence of Fred McGriff led to Upshaw's 1988 trade to the Indians.
Playing Career: *1978, 1980-1988; Tor A, Cle A*

Billy Urbanski
Urbanski, William Michael
B: Jun 5, 1903   D: Jul 12, 1973

Pos: SS, 3B   BA: .260
Hits: 791   HRs: 19
RBI: 207   BB: 198

Urbanski was a surehanded but unspectacular shortstop who held his own for five seasons in the Braves' infield at a time when the team was glued down in the second division. He batted over .300 for four seasons in the International League.
Playing Career: *1931-1937; Bos N*

Jose Uribe
Uribe, Jose Altagracia
B: Jan 21, 1952

Pos: SS   BA: .241
Hits: 738   HRs: 19
RBI: 219   BB: 256

Born Jose Gonzalez, Uribe changed his name because there were too many Gonzalezes in the majors. Coming to the Giants in the Jack Clark deal, he played in the 1987 NLCS, the 1989 NLCS and the 1989 World Series. His batting improved after his brother pitched peanuts at him one winter.
Playing Career: *1984-; StL N, SF N, Hou N*

Willie Upshaw steals second as Tony Bernarzard tries to intercept him, 1982.

Bobby Valentine
Valentine, Robert John
B: May 13, 1950

Pos: SS, OF, 2B, 3B	BA: .260
Hits: 441	HRs: 12
RBI: 157	BB: 140

Managerial Record
Won: 581   Lost: 605   Pct: .490

Groomed to be the Dodgers' manager, Valentine would go through brick walls to be in a baseball uniform. After two seasons as a jack-of-all-trades with Los Angeles, he was traded in a multi-player deal to the Angels in late 1972. Early the next season Valentine crashed into the wall at Anaheim Stadium, catching his spikes as he fell, and suffered a serious fracture, seriously hampering his big league playing career.
Playing Career: *1969, 1971-1979; LA N, Cal A, SD N, NY N, Sea A*
Managerial Career: *1985-1992; Tex A*

Dodgers ace Fernando Valenzuela, 1985.

Ellis Valentine
Valentine, Ellis Clarence
B: Jul 30, 1954

Pos: OF	BA: .278
Hits: 881	HRs: 123
RBI: 474	BB: 180

Predicted to be a star with the Expos, Valentine was hit in the face by a Roy Thomas pitch in 1980 , fracturing the cheekbone. Valentine had been an All-Star in 1977 and a Gold Glove Award winner the next year. He averaged 22 homers, 30 doubles and 80 RBI before the beaning.
Playing Career: *1975-1983, 1985; Mon N, NY N, Cal A, Tex A*

Fernando Valenzuela
Valenzuela y Anguamea, Fernando
B: Nov 1, 1960

Pos: P	ERA: 3.45
W-L: 149-128	SOs: 1,842
ShOs: 31	No-hitters: 1

Fernando is back! Tossing a shutout over the White Sox in 1993, Valenzuela turned the corner on his comeback journey. In his heyday, the 1981 Rookie of the Year and Cy Young Award winner packed the house. Every start at Dodger Stadium was a fiesta as he broke in with five shutouts in his first seven appearances. Valenzuela is 5-1 in postseason play for the Dodgers. The six-time All-Star won Game Three of the 1981 World Series on 187 pitches.
Playing Career: *1980-1991, 1993-; LA N, Cal A, Bal A*

Dave Valle
Valle, David
B: Oct 30, 1960

Pos: C	BA: .235
Hits: 588	HRs: 72
RBI: 318	BB: 225

After seven years in the minors and three years in the majors, Valle earned his starting position in 1987. He led AL receivers in fielding in 1990. Known as a defensive catcher, Valle emerged in the 1993 season as an offensive threat.
Playing Career: *1984-; Sea A*

Elmer Valo
Valo, Elmer William
B: Mar 5, 1921

Pos: OF	BA: .282
Hits: 1,420	HRs: 58
RBI: 601	BB: 943

The only Czech born player in major league history, Valo played 20 years, striking out only 284 times. He hit .300 five times, reaching a high of .364 for the Athletics in 1956. Valo smashed 228 doubles and 73 triples in his career. Strangely, he played for three franchises that relocated: the Athletics, Dodgers and Senators/Twins. Each time, he faithfully accompanied the team to its new location. He became an outstanding pinch hitter.
Playing Career: *1940-1943, 1946-1961; Phi A, KC A, Phi N, Brk N, LA N, Cle A, NY A, Was A, Min A*

Dazzy Vance.

Dazzy Vance
Vance, Clarence Arthur
B: Mar 4, 1891   D: Feb 16, 1961
Hall of Fame 1955

Pos: P	ERA: 3.24
W-L: 197-140	SOs: 2,045
ShOs: 29	No-hitters: 1

Bursting on to the NL scene to stay in 1922 with a high-kicking fastball delivery, the late blooming Vance did not win a major league game until he was 31 years old. After that he led the NL seven straight years in strikeouts, 1922-1928. In 1924 Vance wore a red long-sleeved undershirt slit into tassels which flopped in the wind as he pitched. The fastball coming out of the flayed shirtsleeves was so devastating that officials banned frayed sleeves.

That year Vance topped the NL with a 2.16 ERA, 28 wins, 262 strikeouts and 30 complete games. He had only six losses as the Dodgers fell one win short of the first-place Giants. He was named NL MVP over Rogers Hornsby, who batted .424. Vance led the league in wins a second time in 1925, with 22. He won 22 again in 1928 with a league-best 2.09 ERA. Earning a final ERA title in 1930 with a 2.61 mark, he led the NL in shutouts for the fourth time.
Playing Career: *1915, 1918, 1922-1935; Pit N, NY A, Brk N, StL N, Cin N*

Johnny Vander Meer
Vander Meer, John Samuel
(The Dutch Master)
B: Nov 2, 1914

Pos: P	ERA: 3.44
W-L: 119-121	SOs: 1,294
ShOs: 30	No-hitters: 2

Double no-hit Vander Meer was the NL strikeout champ three consecutive years, 1941-1943. The four-time All-Star will always be remembered as the only pitcher ever to throw back-to-back no-hit games. The Reds' hurler no-hit the Boston Bees 3-0 on June 11, 1938, then on three days' rest he no-hit the Dodgers 6-0 on June 15 in the first night game ever played at Ebbets Field. In his next start, Vander Meer did not allow a hit until Boston's Deb Garms singled in the fourth, ending the hitless string at a National League record 21 innings.

On the last out of the second no-hitter, Umpire Bill Stewart recalled missing a 1-2 pitch, ''If Leo (Durocher) got a hit, I was to blame as I missed the pitch and the batter should have been struck out on the previous pitch.'' Vander Meer, who was Minor League Player of the Year in 1936 and the Major League Player of the Year in 1938, always struggled with control. He walked more than 100 batters five times.
Playing Career: *1937-1943, 1946-1951; Cin N, Chi N, Cle A*

Elam Vangilder
Vangilder, Elam Russell
B: Apr 23, 1896   D: Apr 30, 1977

Pos: P	ERA: 4.29
W-L: 99-102	SOs: 474
ShOs: 13	Saves: 19

Vangilder set the Browns' record for games pitched with 323. He was involved in stopping two lengthy minor league hitting streaks. He nailed Joe Wilhoit after a string of 69 games in 1919, then stopped Joe Quellich's string of 15 consecutive hits in 1929.
Playing Career: *1919-1929; StL A, Det A*

George Van Haltren
Van Haltren, George Edward Martin (Rip)
B: Mar 30, 1866   D: Sep 29, 1945

Pos: OF, P, SS	BA: .316
Hits: 2,532	HRs: 69
RBI: 1,014	BB: 868

Pos: P	ERA: 4.05
W-L: 40-31	SOs: 281
ShOs: 5	No-hitters: 1
Managerial Record	
Won: 5 Lost: 16 Pct: .238	

Growing up in California, Van Haltren was reluctant to leave the state for his baseball career. Starting as a pitcher for the White Stockings, he walked 16 batters in an 1887 game, a major league record, in his debut losing effort. He was 11-7, that year, however, and hit three home runs in 45 games. Pitch-

ing in the Players' League in 1890, Van Haltren was 15-10 for the Brooklyn team, while batting .335. As his batting prowess increased his mound appearances decreased, and both took on the aura of a celebrity stunt, especially after he joined the Giants in 1894.

Truly an exceptional baserunner, Van Haltren scored 1,639 runs, going over 100 11 times, including 10 seasons in a row. He stole 583 bases, reaching 75 in 1891 in the old AA, and leading the NL with 45 in 1900. He led the NL in triples with 21 in 1896. A broken ankle in 1902 slowed Van Haltren's career. Going to the Pacific Coast League as player/manager, he put in six more years, garnering 1,012 hits, making a total of 3,595 hits in his professional career.
Playing Career: *1887-1903; Chi N, Brk P, Bal AA, Bal N, Pit N, NY N*
Managerial Career: *1891-1892; Bal AA, Bal N*

Andy Van Slyke
Van Slyke, Andrew James
B: Dec 21, 1960

Pos: OF	BA: .278
Hits: 1,408	HRs: 152
RBI: 738	BB: 582

An upstate New York basketball scoring champ, Van Slyke helped take the Cardinals to the 1985 NL pennant and the Pirates to three straight division titles, 1990-1992. Swapped for Tony Pena, Van Slyke has become a superstar, winning five straight Gold Gloves, 1988-1992. Making the All-Star squad for the second time in 1992, that season he belted 199 hits and 45 doubles, both NL-leading figures, with a .324 batting average.
Playing Career: *1983-; StL N, Pit N*

Arky Vaughan
Vaughan, Joseph Floyd
B: Mar 9, 1912   D: Aug 30, 1952
Hall of Fame 1985

Pos: SS	BA: .318
Hits: 2,103	HRs: 96
RBI: 926	BB: 937

A heavy-hitting shortstop, Vaughan was a perennial on the NL All-Star squad, making the ''dream team'' nine successive years. In the 1941 contest he hit two home runs. Rooming with Pirates coach Honus Wagner in 1935, Vaughan batted .385, with a .491 on-base percentage, setting all-time Pirate marks for both these categories. His 19 homers, 99 RBI and 108 runs only magnified his 18 strikeouts in 499 at-bats. In 1936, leading the NL in walks, Vaughan set a club record by reaching base 313 times. He scored 122 runs that year and 1,173 in his career, going over 100 five times.

Vaughan was not one to mess with. Dick Bartell once threatened revenge for a close play at second. Vaughan walked over to his dugout, suggesting they settle it that night under the grandstand. Bartell wisely backed off. When Dodger Manager Leo Durocher raised the ire of the shortstop, Vaughan turned in his uniform. Sitting at home for three years, he refused to explain the nature

Hall of Famer Arky Vaughan.

of his disagreement with Durocher, but in 1947 when Durocher was under suspension, Vaughan returned to hit .325.
Playing Career: *1932-1943, 1947-1948; Pit N, Brk N*

Farmer Vaughn
Vaughn, Henry Francis
B: Mar 1, 1864   D: Feb 21, 1914

Pos: C, 1B, OF, 3B	BA: .274
Hits: 946	HRs: 19
RBI: 525	BB: 151

Purchased from Memphis in the Southern League for $1,800 in 1888, Vaughn appeared sober and solvent in a turbulent time. He honored an 1891 AA contract even when the manager, King Kelly, jumped his. Vaughn led NL catchers in fielding in 1893.
Playing Career: *1886, 1888-1899; Cin AA, Lou AA, NY P, Mil AA, Cin N*

Hippo Vaughn
Vaughn, James Leslie
B: Apr 9, 1888   D: May 29, 1966

Pos: P	ERA: 2.49
W-L: 178-137	SOs: 1,416
ShOs: 41	No-hitters: 1

Nicknamed Hippo for his running gait, not his large frame, Vaughn pitched in the famous double no-hit game, losing in 10 innings to Fred Toney of the Reds. He never liked to talk about the 1917 double no-hit loss when big Jim Thorpe rolled a swinging bunt toward third to drive in the winning run. A veritable workhorse, Vaughn won more than 20 games five times in six years, 1914-1919. Tossing more than 260 innings seven years in a row, his work during the World War I years is today largely forgotten. Twice he led the NL in innings pitched and strikeouts. He led the NL with a 1.74 ERA in 1918 and won 22 games in a war-shortened year.

Four times Vaughn posted ERAs under 2.00, dropping to 1.45 in 1913. He was the toughest and best left-hander of the 1910 decade, showing more longevity and durability than Rube Marquard and Babe Ruth. Fated to go against Babe Ruth in the 1918 World Series, Vaughn was 1-2 with a 1.00 ERA for three complete games.

Playing Career: *1908, 1910-1921; NY A, Was A, Chi N*

James "Hippo" Vaughn.

Bobby Veach
Veach, Robert Hayes
B: Jun 29, 1888   D: Aug 7, 1945

Pos: OF
Hits: 2,064
RBI: 1,166

BA: .310
HRs: 64
BB: 571

Surrounded by hitting talent, Veach found himself overshadowed in the outfield and at the plate by Hall of Fame teammates Sam Crawford, Ty Cobb and Harry Heilmann. Nonetheless, Veach was the Tigers' left fielder for more than 11 years, batting .306 or better in eight of them. He drove in more than 100 runs six times, tying Crawford for the AL lead with 112 RBI in 1915, and leading with 103 RBI in 1917 and 78 in the war-shortened 1918 season.

During the 1919 campaign, Veach topped the league in hits, doubles and triples but finished second to Cobb in the AL batting race, hitting .355 to Cobb's .384. With the Yankees in 1925, Veach joined the list of those who pinch-hit for Babe Ruth. He went to the pennant-winning Senators that August. In the closing weeks of that season he broke up Ted Lyons's no-hit bid with a screaming, two-out, ninth-inning single. His major league career ended with his only World Series appearance.

Playing Career: *1912-1925; Det A, Bos A, NY A, Was A*

Bill Veeck, St. Louis Browns president, accepts a trophy from his team in 1952.

Bob Veale
Veale, Robert Andrew
B: Oct 28, 1935

Pos: P
W-L: 120-95
ShOs: 20

ERA: 3.08
SOs: 1,703
Saves: 21

Big and a little wild, left-hander Veale was picked by players as the one pitcher they did not want to face. Veale led the NL in strikeouts in 1964. He fanned 16 Phillies in a nine-inning game in 1965 and 16 Reds in 12 innings in 1964. His lifetime ratio of 7.96 strikeouts per nine innings ranks fifth all-time. A two-time All-Star, Veale posted 18 victories in 1964 and 17 the next year. He was 6-0 as a reliever during the Pirates' 1971 World Championship year.

Playing Career: *1962-1974; Pit N, Bos A*

Bill Veeck
Veeck, William Jr.
B: Feb 9, 1914   D: Jan 2, 1987
Hall of Fame 1991

Veeck lived in Wrigley Field when he was a kid. His father, who planted the now famous ivy, was president of the Cubs, and part of his compensation package was an apartment at the ballpark. A man of the people, the younger Veeck frequently sat in the center field bleachers at Comiskey Park, drinking beer and talking baseball. Perhaps best remembered for sending midget Eddie Gaedel to bat for the Browns in a game against the Tigers in 1951, Veeck was baseball's most imaginative promoter.

During the war he promoted a bankrupt Milwaukee team with early morning games for night shift workers. The ushers wore nightgowns and served orange juice and biscuits. For a Mother's Day promotion, Veeck once flew in thousands of orchids from Hawaii. He might have upset some of the other owners with his publicity-seeking shenanigans, but they paid attention when Veeck conquered Cleveland. In 1947 the Indians doubled attendance to 1.5 million; a year later they drew an AL-record 2,620,627 while winning the pennant. He signed Larry Doby, the first black player in the AL, and Satchel Paige.

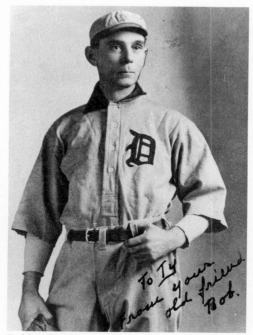

Bobby Veach.

Otto Velez
Velez y Franceschi, Otoniel
B: Nov 29, 1950

Pos: OF   BA: .251
Hits: 452   HRs: 78
RBI: 272   BB: 336

A hero with the early Blue Jays, Velez batted .442 and slugged .865 in April, 1977, and was one of Toronto's first Player of the Month honorees. The marks are still club records. Velez pounded three home runs in a 1980 game.
Playing Career: *1973-1983; NY A, Tor A, Cle A*

Emil Verban
Verban, Emil Matthew (Dutch, The Antelope)
B: Aug 27, 1915   D: Jun 8, 1989

Pos: 2B   BA: .272
Hits: 793   HRs: 1
RBI: 241   BB: 108

As a 29-year-old rookie with the Cardinals, Verban batted .412 in the 1944 World Series, going 3-for-3 in the final game, and driving in the winning run. Many years after he retired, a group of diehard Cubs fans in Washington D.C. put together the Emil Verban Society, mystifying Verban.
Playing Career: *1944-1950; StL N, Phi N, Chi N, Bos N*

Johnny Vergez
Vergez, John Louis
B: Jul 9, 1906

Pos: 3B   BA: .255
Hits: 593   HRs: 52
RBI: 292   BB: 171

The Giants gave Vergez third base so they could move aging Hall of Famer Freddie Lindstrom to the outfield. In 1933 Vergez was having his best year – he batted .271 with 16 home runs, 21 doubles and 72 RBI – when he developed appendicitis. He never quite regained his form.
Playing Career: *1931-1936; NY N, Phi N, StL N*

Mickey Vernon
Vernon, James Barton
B: Apr 22, 1918

Pos: 1B   BA: .286
Hits: 2,495   HRs: 172
RBI: 1,311   BB: 934
Managerial Record
Won: 135   Lost: 227   Pct: .373

A seven-time All-Star, Vernon played in four decades, starting with Senators in 1939 and lasting until 1960. He set a number of AL records, including most games played at first base, 2,237, and most assists, 1,444. In one 1943 game, Vernon made two unassisted double plays. During his career, he scored 1,196 runs and pounded 490 doubles.

Vernon led the AL in batting with a .353 average in 1946, and again with a .337 mark in 1953 at age 35. He won the 1953 title on the last day of the season in a game against the Athletics. Late in the contest, Vernon hit a caught line drive that brought his average down to .337. Word arrived that Al Rosen, vying for the Triple Crown, was through for the day. If Vernon did not bat again, he would win the batting title by a margin of .0011. Vernon's teammates protected his title by bunting and being thrown out on the basepaths.
Playing Career: *1939-1943, 1946-1960; Was A, Cle A, Bos A, Mil N, Pit N*
Managerial Career: *1961-1963; Was A*

Zoilo Versalles
Versalles y Rodriguez, Zoilo Casanova (Zorro)
B: Dec 18, 1939

Pos: SS   BA: .242
Hits: 1,246   HRs: 95
RBI: 471   BB: 318

Another of the talented Latin infielders, Versalles was the recipient of two Gold Glove Awards, and was elected to the All-Star Game team two times, both honors occurring in 1963 and 1965. The latter year Versalles had his best season. He was the catalyst of the postseason-bound Twins' offense, leading the league with 45 doubles, 12 triples and 126 runs scored in more than 660 at-bats, as well as stealing 27 bases.

In the 1965 World Series, Versalles blasted a three-run home run in the opening game – it was the key hit in Minnesota's 8-2 victory. He went on to bat .286 for the Series, and afterwards, was named the 1965 AL MVP. In 1967 – the Year of Yastrzemski – Yaz was elected AL MVP almost unanimously, but one baseball writer cast a vote for Versalles. Plagued by back problems late in his career, Versalles played ball in the Mexican League in 1970 before his final major league season.
Playing Career: *1959-1969, 1971; Was A, Min A, LA N, Cle A, Atl N*

Zoilo Versalles steals second in 1965 WS.

Tom Veryzer
Veryzer, Thomas Martin
B: Feb 11, 1953

Pos: SS   BA: .241
Hits: 687   HRs: 14
RBI: 231   BB: 143

Named to the Topp's Rookie All-Star team, Veryzer was the starting shortstop for the Tigers from 1975 to 1977, when Alan Trammell came along. Traded to Cleveland, Veryzer played regularly for the next four years, but injuries limited his effectiveness.
Playing Career: *1973-1984; Det A, Cle A, NY N, Chi N*

Lee Viau
Viau, Leon A.
B: Jul 5, 1866   D: Dec 17, 1947

Pos: P   ERA: 3.33
W-L: 83-77   SOs: 554
ShOs: 5   Saves: 1

Teenager Ty Cobb had a point to prove to his father when he got a chance to hit against major leaguer Viau in an exhibition game. Cobb got four hits off Viau, and gained grudging parental consent to pursue baseball as a career. Viau won 27 games in 1888, then 22 in 1889.
Playing Career: *1888-1892; Cin AA, Cin N, Cle N, Lou N, Bos N*

Frank Viola.

Frank Viola
Viola, Frank John
B: Apr 19, 1960

Pos: P   ERA: 3.67
W-L: 174-145   SOs: 1,813
ShOs: 16   No-hitters: 0

The 1988 AL Cy Young Award winner, Viola grew up on Long Island and went to St. John's University, where he beat future major leaguer Ron Darling and the Yale squad in a famous NCAA playoff game.

Darling no-hit St. John's for 11 innings, but Viola won 1-0 in the 12th.

Viola helped Minnesota win a World Championship in 1987, posting victories in Games One and Seven. The next year he compiled a record of 24-7. Viola pitched 210 innings or more for nine years in a row, 1983-1992. Following his Cy Young season in 1988, he got into a contract dispute with the Twins. The issues divided the team and city. Local hero Kent Hrbek attacked Viola in the press, and even Gary Gaetti, a man of deep religious convictions, made acerbic comments regarding Viola's contract. Viola was traded to the Mets in mid-1989.
Playing Career: *1982-; Min A, NY N, Bos A*

Bill Virdon
Virdon, William Charles
B: Jun 9, 1931

Pos: OF	BA: .267
Hits: 1,596	HRs: 91
RBI: 502	BB: 442
Managerial Record	
Won: 995 Lost: 921 Pct: .519	

The center fielder for the World Champion Pirates in 1960, Bill Virdon hit .241 in that World Series victory over the Yankees. All of his awards – 1955 Rookie of the Year, 1962 Gold Glove – paled in comparison to the World Series experience. He led the NL in triples with 10 in 1962. Virdon later returned to manage the hated Yankees to a surprising second-place finish in 1974. Virdon won three division titles as leader of the Bucs and Astros.
Playing Career: *1955-1965, 1968; StL N, Pit N*
Managerial Career: *1972-1984; Pit N, NY A, Hou N, Mon N*

Ozzie Virgil
Virgil y Lopez, Osvaldo Jose
B: Dec 7, 1956

Pos: C, DH	BA: .243
Hits: 549	HRs: 98
RBI: 307	BB: 248

A former Carolina League MVP, All-Star and home run champion, Virgil followed his father, Ozzie Sr., into a major league baseball career. In 1985 Virgil led all catchers with a .994 fielding average and fewest errors. He made the NL All-Star team that year and again in 1987.
Playing Career: *1980-1990; Phi N, Atl N, Tor A*

Ossie Vitt
Vitt, Oscar Joseph
B: Jan 4, 1890 D: Jan 31, 1963

Pos: 2B, 3B, OF	BA: .238
Hits: 894	HRs: 4
RBI: 294	BB: 455
Managerial Record	
Won: 262 Lost: 198 Pct: .570	

A manager at both the minor and major league levels, Vitt built a reputation for fielding aggressive teams, always in contention for the pennant. Hired by Cleveland to instill life into the Indians in 1938, Vitt finished third in 1938 and 1939 because his tactics were resisted by the players. They petitioned for his removal in 1940, and became known as the "Cleveland Crybabies." When they lost the 1940 AL flag by one game, Vitt was replaced.
Playing Career: *1912-1921; Det A, Bos A*
Managerial Career: *1938-1940; Cle A*

Bill Voiselle
Voiselle, William Symmes (Big Bill, Ninety-Six)
B: Jan 29, 1919

Pos: P	ERA: 3.83
W-L: 74-84	SOs: 637
ShOs: 13	Saves: 3

Hailing from Ninety-six, South Carolina, Voiselle wore number 96, the highest uniform number ever in the major leagues until Mitch Williams. As a rookie in 1944 he won 21 games, pitched an NL-high 312 innings and struck out on NL-high 161 batters. He played in the 1948 World Series.
Playing Career: *1942-1950; NY N, Bos N, Chi N*

Clyde Vollmer
Vollmer, Clyde Frederick (Big 'Un)
B: Sep 24, 1921

Pos: OF	BA: .251
Hits: 508	HRs: 69
RBI: 339	BB: 243

Vollmer homered on the first big league pitch he saw, the third player to do so. Playing with sporadic success, he had a torrid July in 1951 for the Red Sox, smashing 13 homers and driving in 30 runs. He had one three-homer game and once hit a 16th-inning grand slam.
Playing Career: *1942, 1946-1954; Cin N, Was A, Bos A*

Joe Vosmik.

Chris Von der Ahe
Von der Ahe, Christopher Frederick Wilhelm (Der Poss Bresident)
B: Nov 7, 1851 D: Jun 7, 1913

Managerial Record
Won: 3 Lost: 14 Pct: .176

Beer guzzling, convivial Chris Von der Ahe bought a baseball club in 1882 because he thought it might be a good way to advertise his brewery. He became a baseball fanatic and was certainly the most colorful team owner of the 19th century. When he hired Charles Comiskey as Browns manager, the club won four straight AA pennants. With Chris riding in beer wagons emblazoned "World Champions," St. Louis celebrated the only winner-take-all World Series, in 1886.
Managerial Career: *1895-1897; StL N*

Joe Vosmik
Vosmik, Joseph Franklin
B: Apr 4, 1910 D: Jan 27, 1962

Pos: OF	BA: .307
Hits: 1,682	HRs: 65
RBI: 874	BB: 514

At a tryout camp, handsome, blond Vosmik caught the eye of the wife of Indians' General Manager Billy Evans. Needing to sign one more local boy, Evans asked his wife's opinion. She advised choosing "the good-looking blond boy." Vosmik spent two seasons in the minors, batting .381 the first year and winning the batting title with a .397 mark the next year. He hit .320 in his rookie year for Cleveland in 1931.

Vosmik topped the .300 mark in six of his 10 seasons as a regular. A solid RBI man, he drove in 117 in 1931 and 110 in 1935. He scored 106 runs in 1932 and six years later he hit the 121 mark. In 1935 Vosmik led the AL with 216 hits, 47 doubles and 20 triples. He batted .348, one percentage point behind Buddy Myer in the 1935 AL batting race, and made the All-Star team. Vosmik was traded to the Browns in 1947. The following year he banged out a league-high 201 hits for the Red Sox.
Playing Career: *1930-1941, 1944; Cle A, StL A, Bos A, Brk N, Was A*

Pete Vuckovich
Vuckovich, Peter Dennis
B: Oct 27, 1952

Pos: P	ERA: 3.66
W-L: 93-69	SOs: 882
ShOs: 8	Saves: 10

Vuckovich starred in the movie *Major League* as a hitter. Becoming a Blue Jay in the expansion draft, he tossed the first shutout in franchise history. A principle in the Ozzie Smith trade, Vuckovich won the AL Cy Young Award in 1982, going 18-6 with a 3.34 ERA.
Playing Career: *1975-1983, 1985-1986; Chi A, Tor A, StL N, Mil A*

Rube Waddell
Waddell, George Edward
B: Oct 13, 1876   D: Apr 1, 1914
Hall of Fame 1946

Pos: P	ERA: 2.16
W-L: 193-143	SOs: 2,316
ShOs: 50	No-hitters: 1

Flaky and eccentric, but talented, Waddell pitched like no one anybody had ever seen – he was a left-hander with control. Throughout his career Waddell kept a ratio of nearly 3-to-1 in strikeouts over walks. He joined Connie Mack's Athletics in 1902 and was 24-7, leading the AL in strikeouts for the first of six straight seasons. In 1904 Waddell struck out 349 batters and walked only 91. The whiff record stood as the major league mark for over 60 years until Sandy Koufax surpassed it.

Waddell led the AL with 26 wins, eight of them in relief, 287 strikeouts, and a 1.48 ERA in 1905. Injuring his left arm during horseplay, Waddell missed the World Series against the Giants. Though he pitched four more seasons, he never again threw with the

Rube Waddell.

Hall of Fame shortstop Honus Wagner (r) with John McGraw.

same snap. Waddell wrestled alligators in Florida, hung around firehouses, was married twice to women who left him, and tended bar when he was not engaged in being the bar's best customer. He pitched a 20-inning win over Cy Young, then turned cartwheels off the mound to celebrate.
Playing Career: *1897, 1899-1910; Lou N, Pit N, Chi N, Phi A, StL A*

Heinie Wagner
Wagner, Charles F.
B: Sep 23, 1880   D: Mar 20, 1943

Pos: SS	BA: .250
Hits: 834	HRs: 10
RBI: 343	BB: 310

Managerial Record
Won: 52   Lost: 102   Pct: .338

Since rules against blocking baserunners were rarely enforced in Wagner's era, he used his exceptionally large feet to good advantage. Wagner played in the 1912 World Series with the Champion Red Sox, and later became their coach, then manager.
Playing Career: *1902, 1906-1913, 1915-1916, 1918; NY N, Bos A*
Managerial Career: *1930; Bos A*

Honus Wagner
Wagner, John Peter (The Flying Dutchman)
B: Feb 24, 1874   D: Dec 6, 1955
Hall of Fame 1936

Pos: SS, OF, 1B, 3B, 2B	BA: .327
Hits: 3,415	HRs: 101
RBI: 1,732	BB: 963

Managerial Record
Won: 1   Lost: 4   Pct: .200

Wagner retired in 1908, but his Pirates teammates talked him into playing again. He responded with his greatest season, batting .354 with 201 hits, 39 doubles, 19 triples, 109 RBI, a .415 on-base average, and a .542 slugging – all 1908 league-leading marks. He kept the Pirates in the three-way pennant race until the last day, the famous playoff game with the Merkle Boner incident. Both Branch Rickey and John McGraw declared that Wagner was the greatest player they had ever seen.

Ed Barrow discovered Wagner while scouting Honus's older brother Al, who also played in the majors. The younger Wagner led the NL eight times in hitting, five times in steals, and six times in slugging average. His batting average was over .300 for 17 straight years. Ranked high on the all-time lists, Wagner had 643 doubles, 252 triples, 722 stolen bases and 1,736 runs scored. The Pirates won the 1909 World Series over the Tigers in seven games with NL and AL batting champs Wagner and Ty Cobb going head-to-head.
Playing Career: *1897-1917; Lou N, Pit N*
Managerial Career: *1917; Pit N*

Leon Wagner
Wagner, Leon Lamar (Daddy Wags)
B: May 13, 1934

Pos: OF	BA: .272
Hits: 1,202	HRs: 211
RBI: 669	BB: 656

''Buy Your Rags at Daddy Wags''' was the slogan Wagner used for the clothing store he owned. The slick dresser was also a good ballplayer. An outfielder on *The Sporting News* Rookie All-Star team in 1958, Wagner hit .317 that year with 13 home runs. A left-handed pull hitter, Wagner belted 37 home runs in 1962 and hit 97 more for Cleveland from 1964 to 1967. Later he became a respected pinch hitter, leading the AL with 46 appearances in 1968.
Playing Career: *1958-1969; SF N, StL N, LA A, Cle A, Chi A*

Eddie Waitkus
Waitkus, Edward Stephen
B: Sep 4, 1919   D: Sep 15, 1972

Pos: 1B	BA: .285
Hits: 1,214	HRs: 24
RBI: 373	BB: 372

One of Philadelphia's Whiz Kids in 1950, Waitkus had worked hard to come back from a gunshot wound in the chest suffered in June 1949. As the Phillies' leadoff batter in 1950, Waitkus batted .284 and scored 102 runs in 154 games.
Playing Career: *1941, 1946-1955; Chi N, Phi N, Bal A*

Rick Waits
Waits, Michael Richard
B: May 15, 1952

Pos: P	ERA: 4.25
W-L: 79-92	SOs: 659
ShOs: 10	Saves: 8

The ace of Cleveland's pitching rotation in the late 1970s, Waits posted a complete-game victory on the last day of the 1978 season, forcing the Yankees-Red Sox playoff. He led the Indians' staff with 16 wins in 1979, and won Opening Day games in 1979 and 1980.
Playing Career: *1973, 1975-1985; Tex A, Cle A, Mil A*

Dick Wakefield
Wakefield, Richard Cummings
B: May 6, 1921   D: Aug 26, 1985

Pos: OF	BA: .293
Hits: 625	HRs: 56
RBI: 315	BB: 360

Signed from the University of Michigan, Wakefield pounded a league-leading 200 hits as a rookie in 1943, also topping the AL with 38 doubles and 633 at-bats. After duty in World War II, his play lacked sparkle. His father, Howard, was also a pro ballplayer.
Playing Career: *1941, 1943-1944, 1946-1950, 1952; Det A, NY A, NY N*

Rube Walberg
Walberg, George Elvin
B: Jul 27, 1896   D: Oct 27, 1978

Pos: P	ERA: 4.17
W-L: 155-141	SOs: 1,085
ShOs: 15	Saves: 32

Hardworking but a tad wild, Walberg walked more batters than he struck out. He pitched in the major leagues for 15 seasons, his best being 1931 when he compiled a record of 20-12, and led the AL with 291 innings pitched. The Athletics were AL Champions that year, one of three World Series they reached with the help of Walberg. Switching to relief work during the last four years of his career with the Red Sox, Walberg pitched his last game at age 41.
Playing Career: *1923-1937; NY N, Phi A, Bos A*

Bob Walk
Walk, Robert Vernon
B: Nov 26, 1956

Pos: P	ERA: 4.03
W-L: 79-81	SOs: 648
ShOs: 5	Saves: 2

Taking a cue from his surname, Walk made lots of trips back to the minor leagues during his major league career. As a rookie, he pitched in the NLCS and the World Series. Two years later, he was selected for the All-Star Game squad.
Playing Career: *1980-; Phi N, Atl N, Pit N*

Bill Walker
Walker, William Henry
B: Oct 7, 1903   D: Jun 14, 1966

Pos: P	ERA: 3.59
W-L: 97-77	SOs: 626
ShOs: 15	Saves: 8

In his second full season, 1929, Walker led the NL in ERA with a 3.09 mark, and topped the league again in 1931 with a 2.26 ERA. That year he was 17-9. Walker missed nearly two months of the 1934 season, but still won 12 games, and pitched in the World Series.
Playing Career: *1927-1936; NY N, StL N*

Curt Walker
Walker, William Curtis (Honey, Judge)
B: Jul 3, 1896   D: Dec 9, 1955

Pos: OF	BA: .304
Hits: 1,475	HRs: 64
RBI: 688	BB: 535

A good hitter and a fast runner, Walker batted .300 or more in six of ten major league seasons, and hit 117 triples. He even hit two triples in one inning in a July 22, 1926 game. The left-handed hitter led the Phillies in six offensive categories in 1922, including batting average. His mark that year was .337. Hailing from Beeville, Texas, Walker picked up the nickname "Honey," and was later called "Judge" because he had been elected a justice of the peace.
Playing Career: *1919-1930; NY A, NY N, Phi N, Cin N*

Dixie Walker
Walker, Fred (The People's Choice)
B: Sep 24, 1910   D: May 17, 1982

Pos: OF	BA: .306
Hits: 2,064	HRs: 105
RBI: 1,023	BB: 817

An Ebbets Field favorite, Walker spent eight seasons in the AL before coming to Brooklyn. Starting with the Yankees in 1933, he was unable to break into the lineup. He hit .300 for the White Sox and Tigers, even leading the AL with 16 triples in 1938 before being traded to the Dodgers, where he proved himself by hitting .436 against the hated Giants. Inexplicably, Manager Leo Durocher opened the 1941 campaign with the newly acquired

Dixie Walker.

Paul Waner in Walker's outfield spot. Brooklyn fans were outraged.

Waner had won the job in spring training but faded fast and was traded. Walker joined Pete Reiser and Joe Medwick in an all-.300-hitting outfield that led Brooklyn to the 1941 NL pennant. In 1944 he led the NL with a .357 batting average, and he won the 1945 RBI title with 124. Walker was traded to the Pirates for Preacher Roe and Billy Cox. In the 1948 season in Pittsburgh, Walker topped the .300 mark for the 10th time.
Playing Career: *1931, 1933-1949; NY A, Chi A, Det A, Brk N, Pit N*

Fleet Walker
Walker, Moses Fleetwood
B: Oct 7, 1856   D: May 11, 1924

Pos: C, OF	BA: .263
Hits: 40	HRs: 0
RBI: NA	BB: 8

The first black major league player, Walker was joined on the 1884 Toledo AA club by his brother Welday later in the season. Walker was generally well received. In 1887 he teamed with George Stovey in Newark of the International League to form the first black battery in organized baseball, with Stovey winning 35 games – still the IL record. That year White Stockings Manager Cap Anson prevented the two stars from playing against his team in an exhibition game.

Anson had tried the same maneuver in 1883 with Toledo. That time Walker had gotten out of a sickbed to play right field, and got two hits. Syracuse, ignoring the informal color ban, signed Walker for the 1888-1889 seasons. There he met another black pitcher, Robert Higgins. The Syracuse Stars won the IL flag in 1888. Every player except Higgins had playing time in the major leagues. Well-educated, handsome, gentlemanly and a good all-around athlete, Walker attended Oberlin College in Ohio and the University of Michigan.
Playing Career: *1884; Tol AA*

The Tigers' Gee Walker, 1934.

Gee Walker
Walker, Gerald Holmes
B: Mar 19, 1908   D: Mar 20, 1981

Pos: OF   BA: .294
Hits: 1,991   HRs: 124
RBI: 997   BB: 330

One of Detroit's "G-Men" during the 1930s – Gehringer, Greenberg, Goslin and Gee – Walker batted .300 or better in five of his first seven seasons. Though he stole 223 bases, Walker frequently was caught off base due to inattention. Sometimes overzealous, he would try to steal a base while the batter was being given an intentional walk. In one game he was caught off base twice in the same inning.

During the 1934 World Series, Walker was picked off first while arguing with the Cardinals' benchjockeys. The situation became ludicrous. Tigers Manager Mickey Cochrane held a team vote to determine whether they should get rid of the Gee-man, but the players voted almost unanimously in Walker's favor. Chosen for the 1937 AL All-Star team, he posted career highs with 213 hits, 105 runs, 18 homers and 113 RBI that year. Walker hit 399 doubles and scored 954 runs in his career.
Playing Career: *1931-1945; Det A, Chi A, Was A, Cle A, Cin N*

Greg Walker
Walker, Gregory Lee
B: Oct 6, 1959

Pos: 1B   BA: .260
Hits: 746   HRs: 113
RBI: 444   BB: 268

In praise of Walker, Tony LaRussa said, "Everybody sees his swing and knows it's great. But his toughness – that's something you don't appreciate until you're around him." Walker batted .333 with the White Sox in the 1983 ALCS, then became their regular first baseman in 1984.
Playing Career: *1982-1990; Chi A, Bal A*

Harry Walker
Walker, Harry William (The Hat)
B: Oct 22, 1916

Pos: OF   BA: .296
Hits: 786   HRs: 10
RBI: 214   BB: 245
Managerial Record
Won: 630   Lost: 604   Pct: .511

Called "Harry The Hat" because while batting he would adjust his cap after each pitch, Walker wore out 20 hats a season. He was the son of pitcher Dixie Walker, and the brother of 1944 NL batting champ Fred "Dixie" Walker. Harry the Hat won the NL batting title himself in 1947, becoming the only player to do so after splitting a season with two teams. Walker was elected to the All-Star squad that year. He played in three World Series.
Playing Career: *1940-1943, 1946-1951, 1955; StL N, Phi N, Chi N, Cin N*
Managerial Career: *1955, 1965-1972; StL N, Pit N, Hou N*

Tilly Walker
Walker, Clarence William
B: Sep 4, 1887   D: Sep 21, 1959

Pos: OF   BA: .281
Hits: 1,423   HRs: 118
RBI: 679   BB: 416

One of the best outfielders of the dead ball era, Walker led the AL in assists four times. He was also a potent home run hitter, and tied Babe Ruth for the league lead in 1918. Walker continued to belt homers until 1923, when Connie Mack said he wanted speed and defense rather than long-ball offense, which he considered a fad. Walker was benched. He returned to the minors, and later umpired and managed there. Walker played in the 1916 World Series.
Playing Career: *1911-1923; Was A, StL A, Bos A, Phi A*

Bobby Wallace
Wallace, Rhoderick John (Rhoddy)
B: Nov 4, 1873   D: Nov 3, 1960
Hall of Fame 1953

Pos: SS, 3B, P, 2B, OF   BA: .268
Hits: 2,309   HRs: 34
RBI: 1,121   BB: 774
Managerial Record
Won: 62   Lost: 154   Pct: .287

Playing 25 years and drawing a baseball paycheck for more than 60, Wallace did everything in the sport except play for a consistent winner. Breaking in with the Cleveland Spiders as a pitcher, he won 10 games and hurled two shutouts in 1896. Wallace played in the 1895 and 1896 Temple Cup championship series. Moving to short in 1899, there he stayed. Known primarily for fielding skills, Wallace batted .335 in 1897 and hit .324 in 1901.

He hammered 21 triples in 1897, then finished second in home runs in the NL in

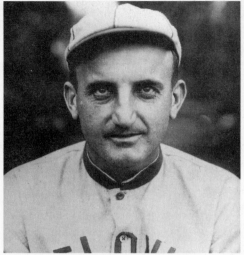

Hall of Famer Bobby Wallace.

1899. Twice he drove in more than 100 runs. He became a highly coveted player. In 1902 the Browns lured him away from the Cardinals with a five-year, no-trade contract worth more than $32,000, a fortune at the time. That June 10, he set the AL record with 17 chances accepted at shortstop in a nine-inning game. Among shortstops he is seventh in chances per game and ninth in putouts.
Playing Career: *1894-1918; Cle N, StL N, StL A*
Managerial Career: *1911-1912, 1937; StL A, Cin N*
Umpiring Career: *1914-1915; AL*

Tim Wallach
Wallach, Timothy Charles
B: Sep 14, 1957

Pos: 3B   BA: .257
Hits: 1,800   HRs: 216
RBI: 967   BB: 546

Traded to his hometown Los Angeles Dodgers in December 1992, Wallach looked forward to revitalizing a career that had fallen into a weird platoon situation in Montreal. After Expos Manager Felipe Alou took over May 23, he had Wallach playing first base against right-handed pitchers and third against lefties. The result was his lowest output ever, a .223 average with nine homers. Steady and durable, Wallach played more than 150 games for 11 years in a row, 1982-1992.

A terrific hitter, Wallach has hit 379 doubles with league-highs of 42 in both 1987 and 1989. Walloping 12 or more homers for 10 straight years, 1982-1991, he reached 20 four times. His best season was 1987, when he took over the cleanup spot from injured Hubie Brooks, and set a club record with 123 RBI. Wallach is among Montreal's all-time leaders in homers, doubles and RBI. The five-time All-Star won Gold Glove Awards in 1985 and 1988, and led NL third basemen in putouts three times, and in assists, total chances and double plays twice.
Playing Career: *1980-; Mon N, LA N*

Denny Walling
Walling, Dennis Martin
B: Apr 17, 1954

Pos: OF, 1B, 3B   BA: .271
Hits: 799   HRs: 49
RBI: 380   BB: 308

Signed off the Clemson campus, Walling spent the bulk of of his career as a platoon player in Houston. He is on the Astros' all-time lists for games played, batting average and slugging average, and is their all-time leader in pinch hits.
Playing Career: *1975-1992; Oak A, Hou N, StL N, Tex A*

Lee Walls
Walls, Ray Lee
B: Jan 6, 1933

Pos: OF   BA: .262
Hits: 670   HRs: 66
RBI: 284   BB: 245

Starting as a batboy in the PCL during the mid-1940s, Lee Walls made it to the majors, and played regularly after 1956. His best season was 1958, when he batted .304 with 24 home runs and 72 RBI. That year he hit three homers in one game.
Playing Career: *1952, 1956-1964; Pit N, Chi N, Cin N, Phi N, LA N*

Ed Walsh
Walsh, Edward Augustine (Big Ed)
B: May 14, 1881   D: May 26, 1959
Hall of Fame 1946

Pos: P   ERA: 1.82
W-L: 195-126   SOs: 1,736
ShOs: 57   No-hitters: 2
Managerial Record
Won: 1   Lost: 2   Pct: .333

In 1908 Walsh pitched 464 innings – the AL record. He won 40 games in the White Sox' futile attempt to catch the Tigers that year. In October he lost 1-0 to the Indians and Addie Joss, although he gave up only four hits and one unearned run while fanning 15. The problem was that Joss pitched a perfect game. Walsh has the best career ERA in baseball history. He walked only 617 batters in 2,964 innings.

Walsh claimed that his main pitch, the spitball, was easy on his arm. He learned the pitch from Elmer Stricklett in 1904, and by 1906 was an expert with it. He compiled a record of 17-13 with a 1.88 ERA and 10 shutouts for the World Champion White Sox that year. Walsh led the AL with a 1.60 ERA in 1907, going 24-18, and tossing more than 400 innings that year and the next.
Playing Career: *1904-1917; Chi A, Bos N*
Managerial Career: *1924; Chi A*
Umpiring Career: *1922; AL*

Bucky Walters
Walters, William Henry
B: Apr 19, 1909   D: Apr 20, 1991

Pos: P, 3B, 2B   ERA: 3.30
W-L: 198-160   SOs: 1,107
ShOs: 42   Saves: 4
Managerial Record
Won: 81   Lost: 123   Pct: .397

Signed as a third baseman, Walters earned a solid shot at the majors by hitting .376 in the Pacific Coast League in 1933. At the suggestion of Phillies Manager Jimmie Wilson, Walters tried pitching. Under Wilson's guidance Walters lost a lot of games, but made the All-Star team in 1937. Traded to Cincinnati, he blossomed with 27 wins in 1939 and 22 in 1940, leading the NL in wins both seasons.

The sidearming flamethrower with a sinking fastball pitched the Reds to two straight pennants, 1939-1940. In both seasons he led the NL in wins, ERA, complete games and innings pitched. Walters was the NL's MVP Award winner in 1939. Losing two games in the World Series that year, he entered the 1940 season looking for revenge. In the 1940 Fall Classic, he defeated the Tigers twice, throwing a three-hitter in Game Two and a five-hit shutout in Game Six. Walters won 23 games with a 2.40 ERA in 1944, leading the NL for the third time in wins. He coached the Braves and Giants during the 1950s.
Playing Career: *1931-1948, 1950; Bos N, Bos A, Phi N, Cin N*
Managerial Career: *1948-1949; Cin N*

Bill Wambsganss in 1920.

Bill Wambsganss
Wambsganss, William Adolph (Wamby)
B: Mar 19, 1894   D: Dec 8, 1985

Pos: 2B   BA: .259
Hits: 1,359   HRs: 7
RBI: 520   BB: 356

The name Wambsganss will always be associated with the unassisted triple play in the 1920 World Series. In the fifth inning of Game Five , with Pete Kilduff on second base and Otto Miller on first, Dodger hurler Clarence Miller hit a low line drive toward second. Thinking the ball was through the infield, the runners took off. Wambsganss stabbed the liner, touched second in one motion, then turned to see Otto Miller frozen on the basepath. He walked over and tagged him out. The feat has never been duplicated.

In the same World Series contest, Elmer Smith walloped the first Series grand slam home run in the first inning, then in the fourth, Indians pitcher Jim Bagby hit a home run into the center field bleachers, the first pitcher to hit a homer in the World Series. A fine second baseman when healthy, Wambsganss had little power but walloped 41 doubles and scored 93 runs in 1924. He coached and managed in the minors after his playing career ended.
Playing Career: *1914-1926; Cle A, Bos A, Phi A*

Big Ed Walsh.

Bucky Walters.

Little brother Lloyd (l) and big brother Paul Waner of the Pittsburgh Pirates.

Lloyd Waner
Waner, Lloyd James (Little Poison)
B: Mar 16, 1906   D: Jul 22, 1982
Hall of Fame 1967

Pos: OF	BA: .316
Hits: 2,459	HRs: 28
RBI: 598	BB: 420

As a pitcher in high school, Waner regularly beat Carl Hubbell, and gained a reputation as a hot pitching prospect. The younger brother of the Pirates' hard-hitting, hard-drinking Paul Waner, Lloyd Waner had the best rookie season that any batter ever had. He hit .355 with 223 hits and 133 runs scored, the latter two still major league standards for rookies. Waner's hits included 198 singles, the all-time single-season record. The Pirates won the 1927 pennant.

Brother Paul was known as "Big Poison," which was Brooklynese for "Big Person." Naturally Lloyd Waner became "Little Poison." A left-handed line drive hitter, Waner collected 214 or more hits in four of his first five seasons. He led the NL with 20 triples in 1929, amassing 118 three-baggers altogether. One of the greatest singles hitters of all time, Waner scored 1,201 runs. An All-Star in 1938, he scouted for both the Pirates and Orioles after his playing days.
Playing Career: *1927-1942, 1944-1945; Pit N, Bos N, Cin N, Phi N, Brk N*

Paul Waner
Waner, Paul Glee (Big Poison)
B: Apr 16, 1903   D: Aug 29, 1965
Hall of Fame 1952

Pos: OF	BA: .333
Hits: 3,152	HRs: 112
RBI: 1,309	BB: 1,091

In 1942 the Braves visited Forbes Field with Waner at 2,999 hits. He launched a drive that the shortstop knocked down, but Waner beat it out. It might have been a hit, but Waner quickly and openly signaled that he did not want a tainted 3,000th hit. The scorer obliged

by charging the shortstop with an error. In his next at-bat he lined the ball off the right field wall, becoming the sixth player to attain 3,000 hits.

A four-time All-Star, Waner marched to his own drumbeat. He left college to play in the PCL. His batting averages there were .369, .356, and .401 for the years 1923-1925. Waner broke into the NL with a .336 batting average, leading the league in triples and batting. He never stopped hitting, winning four batting titles, and winning an MVP Award in 1927. He got 200 hits eight times, whacked 603 doubles and 190 triples and scored 1,626 runs. Needless to say, Waner found steady employment as a hitting coach after his retirement, but his distaste for enforcing discipline cost him managerial jobs.
Playing Career: *1926-1945; Pit N, Brk N, Bos N, NY A*

Aaron Ward
Ward, Aaron Lee
B: Aug 28, 1896   D: Jan 30, 1961

Pos: 2B, 3B, SS	BA: .268
Hits: 966	HRs: 50
RBI: 446	BB: 339

Playing mostly second base, Ward was a reliable fielder for the Yankees during their string of pennant-winning years in the early 1920s. He hit .286 in 19 games in three World Series for New York, but was traded in 1927 and missed the later series of pennants.
Playing Career: *1917-1928; NY A, Chi A, Cle A*

Duane Ward
Ward, Roy Duane
B: May 28, 1964

Pos: P	ERA: 3.19
W-L: 32-36	SOs: 676
ShOs: 0	Saves: 121

Now that the Blue Jays have installed Ward as their number one closer, his career should flourish. A flamethrower who is also wild,

Ward split fireman duties with Tom Henke in 1988 and 1989, and acted as a setup man in 1992, Toronto's first World Championship season. Ward was a postseason hero, going 1-0 in the ALCS and 2-0 with a 0.00 ERA in the World Series. In regular season play that year, Ward posted a 1.95 ERA. He saved 45 games in 1993.
Playing Career: *1986-; Tor A*

Gary Ward
Ward, Gary Lamell
B: Dec 6, 1953

Pos: OF	BA: .276
Hits: 1,236	HRs: 130
RBI: 597	BB: 351

Ward had a tough time getting to the majors, but after eight years in the minors, was *Baseball Digest*'s AL Rookie of the Year in 1981. He led all outfielders with 24 assists in 1983, and had good years offensively in the mid-1980s.
Playing Career: *1979-1990; Min A, Tex A, NY A, Det A*

Monte Ward.

Monte Ward
Ward, John Montgomery
B: Mar 3, 1860   D: Mar 4, 1925
Hall of Fame 1964

Pos: 2B, SS	BA: .275
Hits: 2,105	HRs: 26
RBI: 867	BB: 420

Pos: P	ERA: 2.10
W-L: 164-102	SOs: 920
ShOs: 24	No-hitters: 1
Managerial Record	
Won: 412 Lost: 320 Pct: .563	

One of the most talented players in baseball history, Ward was a Columbia University-trained lawyer. He formed the first player's union, leading to the great Player Rebellion of 1890. Ward is likely the instigator of the pitcher's mound, having requested that the Giants' groundskeepers build up the pitching box in the mid-1880s. As a pitcher for the Providence Grays, he won 47 games in 1879, leading them to the pennant.

In 1880 his 40 wins included the second perfect game in major league history. When his arm gave out – he pitched 2,401 innings in six years – Ward switched to shortstop and helped the New York Giants win pennants in 1888-1889. He also organized the Players' League and put on all-star games to benefit widows. He was involved in the Federal League, and was a serious candidate for the NL presidency in 1909 until the Pirates owner Barney Dreyfus and his clique threatened to join the new AL if Ward was elected.
Playing Career: *1878-1894; Pro N, NY N, Brk P, Brk N*
Managerial Career: *1880, 1884, 1890-1894; Pro N, NY N, Brk P, Brk N*

Pete Ward
Ward, Peter Thomas
B: Jul 26, 1939

Pos: 3B	BA: .254
Hits: 776	HRs: 98
RBI: 427	BB: 371

The Sporting News named Ward AL Rookie of the Year in 1962, based on his .295 batting average, 22 home runs, 84 RBI and 80 runs scored. Developing into a tough clutch hitter, Ward had a bizarre batting stance that resembled a fencing position.
Playing Career: *1962-1970; Bal A, Chi A, NY A*

Preston Ward
Ward, Preston Meyer
B: Jul 24, 1927

Pos: 1B	BA: .253
Hits: 522	HRs: 50
RBI: 262	BB: 231

The Baseball Hall of Fame has the bat and ball from the home run Ward hit on the last day of the 1953 season. It was homer number 1,197 in the major leagues that year – a record. Ward had been a batting leader in the 1947 Western League.
Playing Career: *1948, 1950, 1953-1959; Brk N, Chi N, Pit N, Cle A, KC A*

Jack Warhop
Warhop, John Milton (Crab, Chief)
B: Jul 4, 1884   D: Oct 4, 1960

Pos: P	ERA: 3.09
W-L: 69-93	SOs: 463
ShOs: 4	Saves: 7

Warhop holds the Yankees' season record for hit batsmen with 26. Called "Crab" because it described his disposition, Warhop gave up Babe Ruth's first home run. Warhop led the AL in relief wins in 1909, with four.
Playing Career: *1908-1915; NY A*

Cubs hurler Lon Warneke.

Lon Warneke
Warneke, Lonnie (The Arkansas Hummingbird)
B: Mar 28, 1909   D: Jun 23, 1976

Pos: P	ERA: 3.18
W-L: 193-121	SOs: 1,140
ShOs: 31	No-hitters: 1

Sold to the Cubs as a minor leaguer for $100, Warneke posted 100 victories for them between 1930 and 1936, making the All-Star team three times during that period. His 22 wins, four shutouts and 2.37 ERA – all league-leading marks – led the 1932 Cubs into the World Series against the Yankees. Warneke lost Game Two, but three years later won two games in the 1935 Fall Classic. He tossed a four-hit shutout in Game One.

Traded to the Cardinals for Rip Collins and Roy Parmelee, Warneke joined the Red Birds' hillbillies in the Mississippi Mudcat Band, a clubhouse combo starring Dizzy Dean that actually performed in semi-respectable places. Still a top-notch pitcher, Warneke won 61 percent of his games as a Cardinal, including a no-hitter over the Reds in 1941. The next year, the Cubs paid $75,000 to get him back but lost him to military service. After World War II, Warneke returned to the NL as an umpire.
Playing Career: *1930-1943, 1945; Chi N, StL N*
Umpiring Career: *1949-1955; NL (1 WS, 1 AS)*

Jack Warner
Warner, John Joseph
B: Aug 15, 1872   D: Dec 21, 1943

Pos: C	BA: .249
Hits: 870	HRs: 6
RBI: 303	BB: 181

A long-time catcher with the Giants, Warner was finally replaced behind the plate by future Hall of Famer Roger Bresnahan. While with the Senators, Warner was the batterymate of young Walter Johnson, and is credited with helping develop Johnson's expertise.
Playing Career: *1895-1908; Bos N, Lou N, NY N, Bos A, StL N, Det A, Was A*

Rabbit Warstler
Warstler, Harold Burton
B: Sep 13, 1903   D: May 31, 1964

Pos: SS, 2B, 3B	BA: .229
Hits: 935	HRs: 11
RBI: 332	BB: 405

A light hitter but a fine shortstop, Warstler was "the best defensive infielder in the American League," according to Connie Mack. Babe Ruth complained that Warstler stole hits from him because he played so deep and threw with such strength.
Playing Career: *1930-1940; Bos A, Phi A, Bos N, Chi N*

Jimmy Wasdell
Wasdell, James Charles
B: May 15, 1914   D: Aug 6, 1983

Pos: OF, 1B	BA: .273
Hits: 782	HRs: 29
RBI: 341	BB: 243

An all-around good player and dependable left-handed pinch hitter, Wasdell was a valued backup player in Brooklyn until they traded him for Arky Vaughan in 1941. He was the starting left fielder for the Pirates in 1942, and played regularly until the end of World War II.
Playing Career: *1937-1947; Was A, Brk N, Pit N, Phi N, Cle A*

Ray Washburn
Washburn, Ray Clark
B: May 31, 1938

Pos: P	ERA: 3.54
W-L: 72-64	SOs: 700
ShOs: 10	No-hitters: 1

Part of the Cardinals' pitching rotation during their 1967 and 1968 pennant-winning seasons, Washburn was 10-7 and 14-8 in those years. He won Game Three of the 1968 World Series. Washburn had come back from a serious injury in his second full season. His 1968 no-hitter versus the Giants came on the heels of Gaylord Perry's no-hit win over the Cards, producing back-to-back no-hit scores for the first time in major league history.
Playing Career: *1961-1970; StL N, Cin N*

Claudell Washington steals home against the Twins as Joe Rudi looks on, 1976.

Claudell Washington
Washington, Claudell
B: Aug 31, 1954

Pos: OF	BA: .278
Hits: 1,884	HRs: 164
RBI: 824	BB: 468

Washington burst upon the major league scene by playing each outfield position in the 1974 World Series as a rookie. His second year was his best statistically; he batted .308 with 77 RBI and stole 40 bases. Traded frequently the next few years, Washington seemed to find a niche eventually with the Braves. He was the team's Player of the Month for September, 1982, as he drove Atlanta to the playoffs. Altogether he played in three LCS, one World Series and one All-Star Game.
Playing Career: *1974-1990; Oak A, Tex A, Chi A, NY N, Atl N, NY A, Cal A*

U. L. Washington
Washington, U. L.
B: Oct 27, 1953

Pos: SS, 2B	BA: .251
Hits: 703	HRs: 27
RBI: 255	BB: 261

The nonchalance with which Washington constantly carried a toothpick in his mouth belied his strength and agility always waiting to spring into action. In Washington and Frank White, the Royals had a graceful and wide-ranging middle infield into the early 1980s.
Playing Career: *1977-1987; KC A, Mon N, Pit N*

John Wathan
Wathan, John David (Duke)
B: Oct 4, 1949

Pos: C	BA: .262
Hits: 656	HRs: 21
RBI: 261	BB: 199
Managerial Record	
Won: 326 Lost: 320 Pct: .505	

Nicknamed for his propensity to imitate John Wayne, as a catcher Wathan was dependable and quick on his feet. He stole 36 bases in 1982 – despite missing six weeks of the season with a broken ankle – setting a record for receivers. Wathan played in five ALCS and two World Series with the Royals. Managing in the minor and major leagues, Wathan has done a fine job as radio talk show host and color commentator.
Playing Career: *1976-1985; KC A*
Managerial Career: *1987-1992; KC A, Cal A*

Bill Watkins
Watkins, William Henry
B: May 5, 1858   D: Jun 9, 1937

Managerial Record	
Won: 452 Lost: 444 Pct: .504	

A well-known manager in the majors and minors, Will or Bill Watkins spent 20-plus years in baseball. He skippered the hardest-hitting team of the 1880s, the Detroit Wolverines, which was made by combining the Buffalo and Detroit teams. His great squad defeated the AA Browns in the 15-game 1887 championship series, played in 10 cities.
Managerial Career: *1884-1889, 1893, 1898-1899; Ind AA, Det N, KC AA, StL N, Pit N*

George Watkins
Watkins, George Archibald
B: Jun 4, 1900   D: Jun 1, 1970

Pos: OF	BA: .288
Hits: 925	HRs: 73
RBI: 420	BB: 246

Held captive in the well-stocked St. Louis farm system, Watkins was 28 years old before he got to the big leagues. He hit .373 – still a rookie record – with 17 home runs in 1930, helping the Red Birds to pennants in his first and second years. Watkins played in two World Series.
Playing Career: *1930-1936; StL N, NY N, Phi N, Brk N*

The Astros' Bob Watson, May 1979.

Bob Watson
Watson, Robert Jose (Bull)
B: Apr 10, 1946

Pos: 1B, OF, DH, C	BA: .295
Hits: 1,826	HRs: 184
RBI: 989	BB: 653

Scoring major league baseball's millionth run in 1976 brought Watson more publicity than his entire career. Signed as a catcher, he caught only 10 major league games, playing mostly outfield and first base, which he took over when the Astros traded Lee May in late 1971. Watson batted a career-high .324 that year and topped the .300 mark in six of his 11 seasons as a regular. He drove in more than 100 runs in both 1976 and 1977, and was the Astros' all-time leader in hits and RBI when traded to Boston in June 1979.

Helped by the introduction of the designated hitter role, Watson had a late-career renaissance in the AL. On September 15, 1979, he became the first major leaguer to hit for the cycle in both leagues. He signed as a free agent with the Yankees for 1980. In 1981 Watson tied a record by homering in his first World Series plate appearance; the three-run shot boosted the Yankees to a 5-3 Game One victory over the Dodgers. He became the Astros' general manager in October 1993.
Playing Career: *1966-1984; Hou N, Bos A, NY A, Atl N*

Eddie Watt
Watt, Edward Dean
B: Apr 4, 1941

Pos: P	ERA: 2.91
W-L: 38-36	SOs: 462
ShOs: 0	Saves: 80

Pitching in three ALCS and three World Series for the Orioles, Watt was an integral part of Manager Earl Weaver's bullpen. In Watt's rookie season, the Orioles won the first pennant in franchise history. He was 7-2 with four saves. His best season was 1969 (5-2 with 16 saves). Watt never had a losing season in eight years with Baltimore. He played on four Oriole pennant winners.
Playing Career: *1966-1975; Bal A, Phi N, Chi A*

Roy Weatherly
Weatherly, Cyril Roy (Stormy)
B: Feb 25, 1915 D: Jan 19, 1991

Pos: OF	BA: .286
Hits: 794	HRs: 43
RBI: 290	BB: 180

After military duty in World War II, Weatherly returned to a big league career that had begun with two triples and a single in his Cleveland debut. He was used almost exclusively as a platoon outfielder. Weatherly had played in the 1943 World Series with New York.
Playing Career: *1936-1943, 1946, 1950; Cle A, NY A, NY N*

Buck Weaver
Weaver, George Daniel
B: Aug 18, 1890 D: Jan 31, 1956

Pos: SS, 3B	BA: .272
Hits: 1,310	HRs: 21
RBI: 421	BB: 183

Banned from baseball for life after the 1919 World Series scandal, Weaver was not in on the fix, but knew about it, and failed to tell the authorities. Weaver's postseason play was excellent; he batted .327 in two World Series with the White Sox, and had 11 hits in the 1919 Series. He batted .333 in the 1920 season. But Judge Landis did not appreciate Weaver's no-snitch attitude, and he became the eighth man out.
Playing Career: *1912-1920; Chi A*

Earl Weaver
Weaver, Earl Sidney
B: Aug 14, 1930

Managerial Record
Won: 1,480   Lost: 1,060   Pct: .583

Winning pennants by shunning the sacrifice bunt, Weaver lived by and for the three-run homer. His teams won six division titles, four pennants and the 1970 World Championship. Weaver used skills and philosophy learned from two decades of minor league playing and managing in the Cardinals',

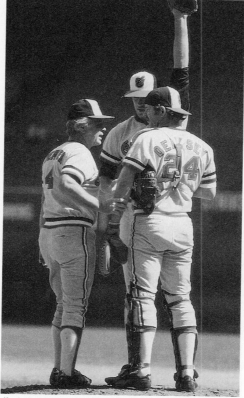

(l-r) Earl Waver, J. Palmer, R. Dempsey.

Pirates' and Orioles' systems. He began managing the big club midway through the 1968 season. The next season he led the Orioles to 109 victories and their first pennant since moving from St. Louis 14 years previously.

Weaver's heavily favored team fell to the Miracle Mets in the World Series. The Orioles won 108 games in 1970, and won the Series over the Reds, thanks to Brooks Robinson's glove work at third. The next year Weaver won his third straight pennant, but lost to Pittsburgh in seven games in the World Series. Weaver was an umpire-baiter, being thrown out of almost 100 games and suspended four times. In 1985 he was ejected from both ends of a doubleheader before the second game even started.
Managerial Career: *1968-1982, 1985-1986; Bal A*

Jim Weaver
Weaver, James Dement (Big Jim)
B: Nov 25, 1903 D: Dec 12, 1983

Pos: P	ERA: 3.88
W-L: 57-36	SOs: 449
ShOs: 7	Saves: 3

One of the first major league pitchers to throw a forkball, Weaver added the pitch to his repertoire when he needed something besides heat. He led the NL in shutouts in 1935. Weaver never had a losing season, yet never pitched in postseason play.
Playing Career: *1928, 1931, 1934-1938; Was A, NY A, StL A, Chi N, Pit N, Cin N*

Monte Weaver
Weaver, Montie Morton (Prof)
B: Jun 15, 1906

Pos: P	ERA: 4.36
W-L: 71-50	SOs: 297
ShOs: 2	Saves: 4

As a rookie phenom, Weaver compiled a record of 22-10 for the 1932 Senators. He then became a vegetarian and lost a considerable amount of weight, not to mention speed off his fastball. Weaver pitched in the 1933 World Series, but was back in the minors for most of the 1935 season. Over his next four major league seasons he won only 26 games, 8 of them in relief. After he retired from baseball he earned a master's degree in mathematics and taught at Emory and Henry College in Virginia.
Playing Career: *1931-1939; Was A, Bos A*

Earl Webb
Webb, William Earl
B: Sep 17, 1898 D: May 23, 1965

Pos: OF	BA: .306
Hits: 661	HRs: 56
RBI: 333	BB: 260

Webb holds the major league record for doubles in a season with 67. He achieved the milestone in 1931 with the Red Sox. Although Webb never hit even half as many two-baggers in one season again, his record is all the more notable because he was a slow runner.
Playing Career: *1925, 1927-1928, 1930-1933; NY N, Chi N, Bos A, Det A, Chi A*

Skeeter Webb
Webb, James Laverne
B: Nov 4, 1909 D: Jul 8, 1986

Pos: SS, 2B	BA: .219
Hits: 498	HRs: 3
RBI: 166	BB: 132

In spite of World War II and an uncooperative bat, Webb compiled a 12-season major league career. He was a fine glove man and was the starting shortstop for the 1945 World Champion Tigers. Webb married his Detroit manager's daughter.
Playing Career: *1932, 1938-1948; StL N, Cle A, Chi A, Det A, Phi A*

Mitch Webster
Webster, Mitchell Dean
B: May 16, 1959

Pos: OF	BA: .264
Hits: 867	HRs: 65
RBI: 327	BB: 313

When Herm Winningham, Montreal's starting center fielder, was injured in midseason 1985, the Expos traded for Webster to fill the position, and he kept it for the next three years. Traded to the Cubs, Webster batted .333 in their 1989 NLCS campaign.
Playing Career: *1983-; Tor A, Mon N, Chi N, Cle A, Pit N, LA N*

Bill Wegman
Wegman, William Edward
B: Dec 19, 1962

Pos: P	ERA: 4.06
W-L: 68-79	SOs: 587
ShOs: 4	No-hitters: 0

A 6'6" flamethrower, Wegman was the Brewers' Minor League Player of the Year in 1982 when he led the California League in wins and ERA. He made it to the big club in 1985 and was in the starting rotation by 1986, where he has won in double digits four times.
Playing Career: *1985-; Mil A*

Herm Wehmeier
Wehmeier, Herman Ralph
B: Feb 18, 1927   D: May 21, 1973

Pos: P	ERA: 4.80
W-L: 92-108	SOs: 794
ShOs: 9	Saves: 9

Turning down several college football scholarships to play major league baseball, Wehmeier signed with Cincinnati. Reds General Manager Gabe Paul said the pitcher was "one of the finest natural athletes we ever had in Cincinnati."
Playing Career: *1945, 1947-1958; Cin N, Phi N, StL N, Det A*

Stump Weidman
Weidman, George Edward
B: Feb 17, 1861   D: Mar 3, 1905

Pos: P	ERA: 3.61
W-L: 100-156	SOs: 910
ShOs: 13	Saves: 2

Weidman led the NL in ERA with a 1.80 mark in 1881. Three times he pitched over 400 innings in a season. He became an umpire after

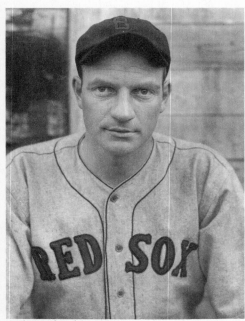

Bob Weiland in 1934.

Yankees GM George Weiss (l) with asst. GM Roy Hamey and Mickey Mantle, 1959.

his pitching career, and was involved in one of the biggest fiascos in baseball – a three-day series between Cleveland and Louisville resulting in fights and arrests each day.
Playing Career: *1880-1888; Buf N, Det N, KC N, NY AA, NY N*
Umpiring Career: *1896; NL*

Bob Weiland
Weiland, Robert George
B: Dec 14, 1905   D: Nov 9, 1988

Pos: P	ERA: 4.24
W-L: 62-94	SOs: 614
ShOs: 7	Saves: 7

After a shutout debut with the White Sox in 1928, Weiland struggled for several years with four clubs until he was traded to the Cardinals in 1937. In St. Louis he became a regular starter and posted 15 victories in 1937 and 16 in 1938. Weiland's brother Ed also played pro ball.
Playing Career: *1928-1935, 1937-1940; Chi A, Bos A, Cle A, StL A, StL N*

Carl Weilman
Weilman, Carl Woolworth
B: Nov 29, 1889   D: May 25, 1924

Pos: P	ERA: 2.67
W-L: 85-95	SOs: 536
ShOs: 15	Saves: 10

Playing for the pitiful last-place Browns, Weilman tied the league lead with 20 losses in 1913, but he won 18 games in 1914 and again in 1915. Constantly battling illness and injury, Weilman died just four years after he left baseball.
Playing Career: *1912-1920; StL A*

Jake Weimer
Weimer, Jacob (Tornado Jake)
B: Nov 29, 1873   D: Jun 19, 1928

Pos: P	ERA: 2.23
W-L: 98-69	SOs: 657
ShOs: 22	No-hitters: 1

A hot young prospect with Chicago, Weimer did a good job for three years before the Cubs traded him to Cincinnati for Harry Steinfeldt. Weimer posted 20 victories with the Reds in 1906, then faded. The Cubs won three consecutive pennants without him.
Playing Career: *1903-1909; Chi N, Cin N, NY N*

Al Weis
Weis, Albert John
B: Apr 2, 1938

Pos: 2B, SS, 3B, OF	BA: .219
Hits: 346	HRs: 7
RBI: 115	BB: 117

Those amazing Mets had some unlikely heroes in 1969, and Weis was one of them. New York had acquired the light-hitting infielder because he was 29 – too old to be drafted for military duty in Vietnam. Weis surprised everyone by batting .455 in the 1969 World Series.
Playing Career: *1962-1971; Chi A, NY N*

George Weiss
Weiss, George
B: Jun 23, 1894   D: Aug 13, 1972
Hall of Fame 1971

George Weiss bought the New Haven club in the Eastern League in 1919 at the age of 24, and went on to become one of baseball's most successful executives. He moved to Baltimore in the International Loop in 1929. Joining the Yankees in 1932, Weiss built a farm system which at one point boasted more than 20 teams. At Newark in the International League, such standouts as Joe Gordon and Charlie Keller were developed.

At one point the Junior World Series, between the top Triple A teams, had two Yankee farm clubs facing each other. Graduating from farm director to general manager in 1948, he ran the club, like Ed Barrow, along conservative lines. However, when the Yankees finished third that year, Weiss fired Manager Bucky Harris and hired Casey Stengel. Many felt that Weiss had blundered, that he had hired a clown to manage the Yankees, but Weiss knew the real Stengel, having hired him at Toledo during the mid-1920s. Stengel's Yankee teams won 10 pennants and seven World Series.

Walt Weiss
Weiss, Walter William
B: Nov 28, 1963

Pos: SS	BA: .250
Hits: 528	HRs: 9
RBI: 169	BB: 238

As soon as Weiss showed the A's he could handle the job, Oakland traded Alfredo Griffin and installed the rookie at shortstop. Weiss had a great season in 1988, and became the third Oakland player in three years to be named AL Rookie of the Year. Weiss was involved in postseason play four times in his first six years in the major leagues.
Playing Career: *1987-; Oak A, Flo N*

Bob Welch
Welch, Robert Lynn
B: Nov 3, 1956

Pos: P	ERA: 3.39
W-L: 208-140	SOs: 1,925
ShOs: 2	Saves: 8

A Cy Young Award winner in 1990, Welch was 27-6 with a 2.95 ERA. As a Dodger rookie he was victorious in a celebrated battle in which the Yankees' Reggie Jackson fouled off four full-count pitches before fanning to end Game Two of the 1978 World Series.

Welch wrote of his experiences with alcoholism and its treatment in *Five O'Clock Comes Early: A Young Man's Battle With Alcoholism*, and has since been active in alcohol abuse prevention programs.

A mainstay on one of baseball's top pitching staffs with the Dodgers, Welch also once played left and right field in a 21-inning game. Traded to the A's after the 1987 season in a three-way deal that also involved the Mets, Welch helped the A's win the 1988 AL pennant, with his 17-9 record. Subsequently he became an important part of the A's staff, helping them capture four division titles in five years. Welch was 3-2 in six starts in eight LCS. In four World Series he has yet to win.
Playing Career: *1978-; LA N, Oak A*

Curt Welch
Welch, Curtis Benton
B: Feb 11, 1862   D: Aug 29, 1896

Pos: OF	BA: .263
Hits: 1,152	HRs: 15
RBI: 186	BB: 381

Welch made the famed $15,000 slide that won the 1886 World Championship for the St. Louis Browns over the Chicago White Stockings. It was the only winner-take-all championship series ever played, and Welch made a lot of people happy with that slide. He was fast, and stole 453 bases, reaching 95 in 1888. As Welch moved from team to team, he bartered baseballs and memorabilia for drinks in saloons.
Playing Career: *1884-1893; Tol AA, StL AA, Phi AA, Bal AA, Bal N, Cin N, Lou N*

Frank Welch
Welch, Frank Tiguer (Bugger)
B: Aug 10, 1897   D: Jul 25, 1957

Pos: OF	BA: .274
Hits: 634	HRs: 41
RBI: 295	BB: 250

A utility outfielder for the Athletics during the 1920s, Welch helped build the team up to their 1929-1931 juggernaut. Following his playing days, Welch managed in the minor leagues for a few years. His brother pitched in the minors before an arm injury ended his career.
Playing Career: *1919-1927; Phi A, Bos A*

Mickey Welch
Welch, Michael Francis (Smiling Mickey)
B: Jul 4, 1859   D: Jul 30, 1941
Hall of Fame 1973

Pos: P	ERA: 2.71
W-L: 307-210	SOs: 1,850
ShOs: 41	Saves: 4

Although his playing weight was listed as 160 pounds, estimates from eyewitnesses put Welch closer to 220. An Irishman who liked his beer, he enjoyed celebrating victories – and he had many to celebrate. Baseball's third 300-game winner, Welch learned the fundamentals of the game in Brooklyn, the hotbed of post-Civil War baseball. During his 13 big league seasons, he won more than 20 games nine times.

After two minor league seasons with Auburn and Holyoke, Welch joined the NL's Troy Haymakers in 1880, going 34-30 and throwing 574 innings. He pitched two complete-game victories over Buffalo on July 4, 1881, and completed his first 105 major league starts. The Troy franchise moved to New York in 1883, and Welch hurled the first game at the original Polo Grounds. In 1884 he completed 62 of 65 starts, winning 39, and had a career-high 345 strikeouts. Welch won 17 consecutive games in 1885, threw seven shutouts, and teamed with Tim Keefe to win 76 games.
Playing Career: *1880-1892; Tro N, NY N*

Ed Wells
Wells, Edwin Lee
B: Jun 7, 1900   D: May 1, 1986

Pos: P	ERA: 4.65
W-L: 68-69	SOs: 403
ShOs: 7	Saves: 13

Bouncing back and forth between the minor leagues and the majors, Wells was sent down to the Southern Association repeatedly, but kept working his way back. With Detroit in 1926, he compiled a 12-10 record, and led the league in shutouts.
Playing Career: *1923-1927, 1929-1934; Det A, NY A, StL A*

Willie Wells.

Willie Wells
Wells, Willie James (El Diablo)
B: Aug 10, 1908   D: Jan 22, 1989

Pos: SS	BA: .328 (inc.)
Hits: 1,133 (inc.)	HRs: 126 (inc.)
RBI: NA	BB: NA
Managerial Record: NA	

A superior batsman, Wells hit for average and with power, and was a skilled bunter and an expert hit-and-run man when the situation called for it. Playing with the St. Louis Stars, he hit .378, .382, .353, .368 and .403 in the five years 1926-1930, taking a batting title in 1930 and a home run title in 1929 with 27 home runs in 88 games. In 1933 he played in the first East-West All-Star Game, appearing in eight such series altogether.

Wells played in the Newark Eagles' "million-dollar infield" in the late 1930s, batting .404 in 1938. He spent seven winters in Cuba, hitting .328 for the pennant-winning Almendares club and was named league

MVP in 1939-1940. After jumping to Mexico, Wells returned to the Eagles in 1942 to top the league with a .342 mark. He finished his career with lifetime marks of .328 in the Negro Leagues, .320 in Cuba, .378 in Puerto Rico and .392 against major leaguers in exhibition games.
Playing Career: *1924-1939, 1942-1948; StL Stars, KC Monarchs, Det Wolves, Hom Grays, Chi Am Giants, Nwk Eagles, NY Black Yankees, Bal Elite Giants, Mem Red Sox*
Managerial Career: *1946; NY Black Yankees*

Bill Werber
Werber, William Murray
B: Jun 20, 1908

Pos: 3B	BA: .271
Hits: 1,363	HRs: 78
RBI: 539	BB: 701

Scout Paul Krichell signed Bill Werber off the campus of Duke University, reporting that the youngster had "the best baseball legs I ever saw, including Cobb." Werber was an excellent baserunner. He once made it to second after a walk while the catcher was talking to the umpire. He led the AL in stolen bases in 1934 and 1935 and tied the leader in 1937. He played in 11 World Series games for the Reds, batting .326.
Playing Career: *1930, 1933-1942; NY A, Bos A, Phi A, Cin N, NY N*

Perry Werden
Werden, Percival Wheritt (Moose)
B: Jul 21, 1865   D: Jan 9, 1934

Pos: 1B, P, OF	BA: .282
Hits: 773	HRs: 26
RBI: 367	BB: 281

Before an arm injury shifted Werden to first base, he was a rookie phenom pitcher, compiling a record of 12-1 in the 1884 UA. He led both the AA and NL in triples once. In the minors Werden smashed 42 home runs and batted .417 in 1894, then hit 45 homers and batted .428 in 1895.
Playing Career: *1884, 1888, 1890-1893, 1897; StL U, Was N, Tol AA, Bal AA, StL N, Lou N*

Don Wert
Wert, Donald Ralph
B: Jul 29, 1938

Pos: 3B	BA: .242
Hits: 929	HRs: 77
RBI: 366	BB: 389

The Tigers had Wert at the hot corner in 1968 when they won the World Series. It was his ninth-inning, game-winning single that clinched the pennant for Detroit that year. Wert had led AL third basemen in fielding in 1965, playing in all 162 Tigers games.
Playing Career: *1963-1971; Det A, Was A*

Vic Wertz
Wertz, Victor Woodrow
B: Feb 9, 1925   D: Jul 7, 1983

Pos: OF, 1B	BA: .277
Hits: 1,692	HRs: 266
RBI: 1,178	BB: 828

A left-handed power hitter, Wertz was immortalized by the fly ball that Willie Mays caught over his shoulder in the 1954 World Series. Chosen for the All-Star Game four times, Wertz drove in 133 runs with the Tigers in 1949, and had 123 RBI in 1950. Overcoming a bout with polio in 1955 and a serious leg injury in 1958, Wertz led the AL with 17 pinch hits in 1962.
Playing Career: *1947-1963; Det A, StL A, Bal A, Cle A, Bos A, Min A*

Max West
West, Max Edward
B: Nov 28, 1916

Pos: OF	BA: .254
Hits: 681	HRs: 77
RBI: 380	BB: 353

A good outfielder with a strong and accurate throwing arm, West had potential for a great career, but was stymied by three years of military duty in World War II. He was a left-handed hitter with line drive power.
Playing Career: *1938-1942, 1946, 1948; Bos N, Bos A, Pit N*

Sammy West
West, Samuel Filmore
B: Oct 5, 1904   D: Nov 23, 1985

Pos: OF	BA: .299
Hits: 1,838	HRs: 75
RBI: 838	BB: 696

Hall of Famer Tris Speaker taught rookie West defensive fundamentals with the Senators in 1927. Speaker was a good teacher – West became a far-ranging outfielder who set an AL record with a .996 fielding percentage in 1928. For eight of his 12 seasons as a regular player, West batted .300 or better. In 1933 he put together a streak of eight consecutive hits that included a 6-for-6 game.
Playing Career: *1927-1942; Was A, StL A, Chi A*

Wally Westlake
Westlake, Waldon Thomas
B: Nov 8, 1920

Pos: OF	BA: .272
Hits: 848	HRs: 127
RBI: 539	BB: 317

Popular in Pittsburgh, Westlake hit with power, was fast and had a strong throwing arm in the outfield. He hit 23 home runs with 104 RBI in 1949, and 24 home runs with 95 RBI the next year. Westlake was an All-Star in 1951, and played in the 1954 World Series with Cleveland.
Playing Career: *1947-1956; Pit N, StL N, Cin N, Cle A, Bal A, Phi N*

Wes Westrum
Westrum, Wesley Noreen
B: Nov 28, 1922

Pos: C	BA: .217
Hits: 503	HRs: 96
RBI: 315	BB: 489
Managerial Record	
Won: 260 Lost: 366 Pct: .415	

In the 1949 International League, Westrum hit five grand slam home runs in just 51 games. The Giants' regular catcher in 1950, he hit 23 home runs, set the fielding record for catchers with a .999 average, and led the league in double plays and assists. The two-time All-Star played in the 1951 and 1954 World Series. While coaching for the Mets, Westrum filled in as manager for the injured Casey Stengel, and kept the job for two years.
Playing Career: *1947-1957; NY N*
Managerial Career: *1965-1967, 1974-1975; NY N, SF N*

Gus Weyhing
Weyhing, August (Cannonball)
B: Sep 29, 1866   D: Sep 4, 1955

Pos: P	ERA: 3.89
W-L: 264-132	SOs: 1,665
ShOs: 28	No-hitters: 1

Weyhing walked 1,566 men, the fourth most in baseball history, in his 4,324-inning career.

Cleveland's Vic Wertz is safe at third with a triple in Game One of the 1954 WS.

Gus Weyhing.

Dodger favorite Zack Wheat.

Performing in four major leagues, he was the epitome of the workhorse concept, and pitched 448 complete games, winning 264 and losing 232 of the games in which he appeared. He pitched more than 400 innings five of six years. One of the outstanding pitchers of the 19th century, Weyhing had his best years before the mound was moved back to 60'6" from home plate in 1893.

Weyhing won more than 30 games four straight seasons and more than 20 games seven times between 1887 and 1894. He was also a seven-time 20-game loser. Weyhing holds the career record for hit batsmen, with 286. After leaving the big leagues he spent a couple of years playing for Grand Rapids, Memphis, Atlanta and Little Rock. He managed the Tulsa club, and later opened a tavern in Louisville.
Playing Career: *1887-1896, 1898, 1901; Phi AA, Brk P, Phi N, Pit N, Lou N, Was N, StL N, Brk N, Cle A, Cin N*

Zack Wheat
Wheat, Zachary Davis
B: May 23, 1888   D: Mar 11, 1972
Hall of Fame 1959

Pos: OF	BA: .317
Hits: 2,884	HRs: 132
RBI: 1,261	BB: 650

One of the nicest guys in baseball, Wheat played 18 years for the Dodgers, helping them win pennants in 1916 and 1920. He was the club's star performer, and a team leader who was never thrown out of a game in his career. He batted over .300 13 times, and remains the franchise all-time leader in games played, at-bats, hits, doubles, triples and total bases. He could handle a curveball so well that Giants Manager John McGraw forbade his pitchers to throw him one.

Wheat topped the .320 mark only once during the dead-ball era, in 1918 when he had a 26-game hitting streak and won the batting title with a .335 average. He was 32 years old by the time the ball was made livelier. Wheat batted .320 or better each year from 1920 through 1925, with .375 marks in both 1923 and 1924, and a .359 average in 1925. Playing his last year with Connie Mack in Philadelphia, Wheat had Ty Cobb for a teammate.
Playing Career: *1909-1927; Brk N, Phi A*

Lou Whitaker
Whitaker, Louis Rodman (Sweet Lou)
B: May 12, 1957

Pos: 2B, DH	BA: .275
Hits: 2,199	HRs: 218
RBI: 997	BB: 1,125

Named Rookie of the Year in 1978, Whitaker is greeted by friendly fans calling "Looouuuu" every time he come to the plate in Tiger Stadium. His career has been entwined with that of shortstop Alan Trammell; the two formed the longest-lived double play combination in baseball history. Starting as a third sacker, Whitaker moved to second at Montgomery in the Southern League in 1977, where he roomed with Trammell.

Whitaker had the flashier debut in 1978, but took longer to develop power at the plate. In 1982 he batted .286 with 15 homers. Honored as Tiger of the Year in 1983, Whitaker was Detroit's first left-handed hitter with 200 hits since 1943, and he was a contender for the batting title with a .320 mark. Whitaker's power improved with maturity; he set a record for Tigers second basemen with 21 home runs in 1985. A three-time Gold Glove Award winner, he was part of Detroit's all-20-homer infield in 1986. Whitaker has been an All-Star five times and is among the Tigers' all-time leaders in doubles, runs scored and hits.
Playing Career: *1977-; Det A*

Bill White
White, William DeKova
B: Jan 28, 1934

Pos: 1B	BA: .286
Hits: 1,706	HRs: 202
RBI: 870	BB: 596

A seven-time Gold Glove infielder, White homered for the Giants in his first major league at-bat. He subsequently topped the 20-home run level eight times, but he was more of a line drive hitter than a slugger, slashing 278 doubles and 65 triples. With the Cardinals in 1961, White tied Ty Cobb's record with 14 hits in consecutive doubleheaders on July 17 and 18. He had more than 100 RBI four times, reaching 109 in 1963.

The five-time All-Star hit only .111 in his only World Series appearance, with the World Champion Cardinals in 1964. Moving to his hometown Philadelphia in 1966, he hit 22 home runs. White retired as a player after the 1969 season, and in 1971 began a long, successful career as a Yankees broadcaster. In 1989 White became the NL president, replacing Bart Giamatti, who moved to the commissionership. With the resignation of Faye Vincent as commissioner, White became a leading candidate to replace him.
Playing Career: *1956, 1958-1969; NY N, SF N, StL N, Phi N*

Bill White had 14 hits in two twin-bills.

Deacon White with Detroit in 1888.

Deacon White
White, James Laurie
B: Dec 7, 1847   D: Jul 7, 1939

Pos: 3B, C, 1B, OF   BA: .303
Hits: 1,619   HRs: 18
RBI: 602   BB: 292
Managerial Record
Won: 9   Lost: 11   Pct: .450

Abstemious, non-smoking, Bible-toting and church-going, White was part of baseball's original Big Four with Al Spalding, Ross Barnes and Cal McVey in Boston. White helped win five straight pennants for three different teams, 1873-1877. He and brother Will White made up the Reds' battery for three years in Cincinnati. In 1881 he and Will went to Buffalo where, with Dan Brouthers, Hardy Richardson and Jack Rowe, Jim made up a second powerful hitting quartet. The owners sold the franchise to Detroit in 1886.

The lads found Ned Hanlon, Sam Thompson and Charley Bennett already there, and added their two cents worth to a Wolverines pennant in 1887. Then they thrashed the Browns in a grueling 15-game "World Series." White and Rowe bought the Buffalo minor league franchise in 1889, but they were prohibited from playing there by Pittsburgh, who held reserve rights on the two players. After a bitter legal fight they were forced to play for the Pittsburgh Alleghenys, a situation that led to the formation of the Players' League. When the Brotherhood collapsed, the Deacon retired, honored and respected by all who knew him.
Playing Career: *1871-1890; Cle Forest Citys n, Bos Red Stockings n, Chi N, Bos N, Cin N, Buf N, Det N, Pit N, Buf P*
Managerial Career: *1872, 1879; Cle Forest Citys n, Cin N*

Devon White
White, Devon Markes
B: Dec 29, 1962

Pos: OF   BA: .256
Hits: 1,054   HRs: 108
RBI: 413   BB: 303

White won the Angels' right field job after hitting .291 with 14 home runs and 60 RBI, and stealing a league-leading 42 bases in the PCL in 1986. He played brief stints with the Angels in 1985 and 1986, then was named to the Topps All-Rookie Team in 1987 when he hit 24 home runs and stole 32 bases. White moved to center field in 1988, and won his first of four Gold Glove Awards for what was often spectacular defensive play. An All-Star in 1989 and 1993, White has appeared in three ALCS and two World Series.
Playing Career: *1985-; Cal A, Tor A*

Doc White
White, Guy Harris
B: Apr 9, 1879   D: Feb 19, 1969

Pos: P   ERA: 2.38
W-L: 190-156   SOs: 1,384
ShOs: 46   Saves: 5

The toughest pitcher whom Ty Cobb faced, White held the mighty Georgian to a .197 lifetime average against him. The side-winding lefty was graduated in dental surgery from

White Sox hurler Doc White.

Georgetown University, but continued to operate on White Sox opponents for 11 years. In September 1904 he threw five consecutive shutouts. The string ended when he was called upon to pitch both ends of a doubleheader.

During his career White pitched 24 games that ended 1-0, winning 13 of them. One was an 11-inning win over Walter Johnson. Five days later the two battled to a 17-inning, 1-1 tie. White was a control pitcher, walking only 670 in 3,041 innings. He set an early AL record by pitching 65 consecutive innings without a walk. A violinist and songwriter, White combined with Ring Lardner in 1910 to produce "A Little Puff of Smoke, Goodnight," a bestseller in sheet music. He was also a college coach, and later owned a Texas League franchise.
Playing Career: *1901-1913; Phi N, Chi A*

Frank White
White, Frank Jr.
B: Sep 4, 1950

Pos: 2B   BA: .255
Hits: 2,006   HRs: 160
RBI: 886   BB: 412

The most successful graduate from the Baseball Academy run by the Royals during the 1970s, White was one of the best fielding second basemen ever. In 1987 he made no fielding errors, only four throwing miscues. By 1989, White and George Brett had been Royals for 18 seasons, playing together longer than anyone else in baseball history. The trio of White, Brett and Willie Wilson played together 15 years. The quartet of White, Brett, Wilson and Dan Quisenberry were together 10 years.

In 1977 White played 62 consecutive games without an error. He has eight Gold Glove Awards, and captured six in a row. Three times he led the league in fielding percentage. A dead pull hitter, White slapped 407 doubles, most of them down the third base line. He swatted 45 doubles in 1982. Bulking up, he belted 22 homers in back-to-back seasons, 1985-1986. In the 1985 "I-70" World Series, White was the first second baseman to bat in the four hole since Rogers Hornsby. *The Sporting News* awarded the five-time All-Star a Silver Slugger Bat in 1986.
Playing Career: *1973-1990; KC A*

Hal White
White, Harold George
B: Mar 18, 1919

Pos: P   ERA: 3.78
W-L: 46-54   SOs: 349
ShOs: 7   Saves: 25

A rookie in the 1942 season, White had a good beginning, compiling a record of 12-12 with a 2.91 ERA for the Tigers. The next year he was 7-12 with a 3.39 mark, then spent two years working for Uncle Sam. When White returned, he was used almost entirely in relief.
Playing Career: *1941-1943, 1946-1954; Det A, StL A, StL N*

Jo-Jo White
White, Joyner Clifford
B: Jun 1, 1909   D: Oct 9, 1986

Pos: OF   BA: .256
Hits: 678   HRs: 8
RBI: 229   BB: 384
Managerial Record
Won: 1   Lost: 0   Pct: 1.000

Center fielder and catalyst for the 1934 and 1935 AL champion Tigers, White walked 13 times in 12 World Series games. He spent most of his baseball career in the minors. He was a Texas League base-stealing champion and pennant-winning manager and coach.
Playing Career: *1932-1938, 1943-1944; Det A, Phi A, Cin N*
Managerial Career: *1960; Cle A*

Roy White
White, Roy Hilton
B: Dec 27, 1943

Pos: OF   BA: .271
Hits: 1,803   HRs: 160
RBI: 758   BB: 934

The first Yankee regular with an errorless season, White compiled a 1.000 fielding average in 1975. His performance was consistently outstanding, but he was stuck on the abysmal Yankees teams of the late 1960s and early 1970s. An excellent switch hitter, White belted home runs from both sides of the plate in the same game five times, and switch-hit a pair of triples once. He led the AL in walks twice, and stole 233 bases. He played in three ALCS and three World Series.
Playing Career: *1965-1979; NY A*

Sammy White
White, Samuel Charles
B: Jul 7, 1928   D: Aug 5, 1991

Pos: C   BA: .262
Hits: 916   HRs: 66
RBI: 421   BB: 218

Boston's top-notch defensive catcher from 1952 through 1959, White became the only 20th-century player to score three runs in one inning. His best offensive marks were compiled in 1954, when he hit .282 with 14 home runs and 75 RBI.
Playing Career: *1951-1959, 1961-1962; Bos A, Mil N, Phi N*

Sol White
White, Sol
B: Jun 12, 1868   D: 1948

Playing and Managerial Records: NA

A black baseball pioneer, White played for several minor league teams in the 1880s before the insidious color line was drawn in organized baseball. He batted .381 for Wheeling in the Ohio State League in 1887, and .358 for the 1891 York Monarchs. With H. Walter Schlichter, White established and captained the Philadelphia Giants, who won the Black

Roy White jogs around the bases with a Yankee HR in Game 3 of the 1978 WS.

World Championship three years in a row, 1905-1907. *Sol White's Official Base Ball Guide* is the only known surviving record of the early years of black baseball.
Playing Career: *1887-1912; Pit Keystones, Was Capital Citys, NY Gothams, York Monarchs, NY Cuban Giants, NY Genuine Cuban Giants, Page Fence Giants, NY Cuban X-Giants, Chi Columbia Giants, Phi Giants, NY Lincoln Giants, Phi Quaker Giants, Cle Browns, NY New Stars*
Managerial Career: *1902-1907, 1911-1912, 1924: Phi Giants, NY Lincoln Giants, Bos Giants, Cle Browns*

Will White
White, William Henry (Whoop-La)
B: Oct 11, 1854   D: Aug 31, 1911

Pos: P   ERA: 2.28
W-L: 229-166   SOs: 1,041
ShOs: 36   No-hitters: 0
Managerial Record
Won: 44   Lost: 27   Pct: .620

The first ballplayer to wear glasses, White started and finished 75 games in 1878. He started 401 games and finished 394 during his career. In the words of baseball historian Lee Allen, White was "one of the game's greats who never received his due." His brother Deacon was already a star player when Will arrived in Boston in 1877. For a few games they formed a brother battery there.

All but two of White's 229 career victories came in a Cincinnati uniform. In 1878 he won 30 games for the NL Reds and followed with 43 the next year. In both seasons his ERA was under 2.00. When it rose to 2.14 in 1880, he led the NL in losses with 42. In eight of the losses the weak-hitting Reds were shut out. White returned with Cincinnati's team in the new American Association in 1882. He was

the biggest star in the early AA, having consecutive seasons of 40, 43, 34 and 18 wins. Upon his retirement, he became a successful businessman in upstate New York in the field of optics.
Playing Career: *1877-1886; Bos N, Cin N, Det N, Cin AA*
Managerial Career: *1884; Cin AA*

Burgess Whitehead
Whitehead, Burgess Urquhart (Whitey)
B: Jun 29, 1910

Pos: 2B   BA: .266
Hits: 883   HRs: 17
RBI: 245   BB: 150

General Manager Bill Terry was criticized in 1935 when he acquired Whitehead, who had been sickly. But he played every game in the Giants' 1936 and 1937 pennant-winning seasons, and led NL second basemen in several defensive categories. Whitehead was in three World Series.
Playing Career: *1933-1937, 1939-1941, 1946; StL N, NY N, Pit N*

Earl Whitehill
Whitehill, Earl Oliver
B: Feb 7, 1900   D: Oct 22, 1954

Pos: P   ERA: 4.36
W-L: 218-185   SOs: 1,350
ShOs: 16   Saves: 11

An outstanding AL hurler during the 1930s, Whitehill married Miss California Raisin, a model and friend of Claire Hodgsen, who became Mrs. Babe Ruth. The flashy, temperamental left-hander often told off teammates, umpires and Manager Ty Cobb if he thought they were impeding his progress toward victory. A hard worker, he achieved

Earl Whitehill pitching in 1934.

11 winning seasons despite allowing 3,917 hits and 1,431 walks.

Whitehill gave up home runs, but he was a battler. His lifetime ERA of 4.36 is higher than any other 200-game winner. Traded to Washington for pitchers Firpo Marberry and Carl Fischer, he won a career-high 22 games in 1933. Whitehill went to the Indians in a three-way trade in 1936. After several seasons as a coach for the Indians, Phillies, and Buffalo in the International League, he became a sales representative for A.G. Spalding Sporting Goods.
Playing Career: *1923-1939; Det A, Was A, Cle A, Chi N*

Fred Whitfield
Whitfield, Fred Dwight (Wingy)
B: Jan 7, 1938

Pos: 1B	BA: .253
Hits: 578	HRs: 108
RBI: 356	BB: 139

Dubbed "Wingy" because of the way he threw, Whitfield was valued more for his bat than his glove. In the five-season span of 1963 to 1967, he belted 93 home runs for Cleveland. In Cincinnati, Whitfield played first base and specialized in pinch hitting.
Playing Career: *1962-1970; StL N, Cle A, Cin N, Mon N*

Terry Whitfield
Whitfield, Terry Bertland
B: Jan 12, 1953

Pos: OF	BA: .281
Hits: 537	HRs: 33
RBI: 179	BB: 138

After Whitfield toted a suitcase back and forth between New York and Syracuse a number of times, the Yankees finally traded him to San Francisco, where he played from 1977 to 1980, and hit in the .290 range. In 1981 he became a home run hitter in Japan.
Playing Career: *1974-1980, 1984-1986; NY A, SF N, LA N*

Art Whitney
Whitney, Arthur Wilson
B: Jan 16, 1858   D: Aug 15, 1943

Pos: 3B, SS, P, 2B	BA: .223
Hits: 820	HRs: 6
RBI: 266 (inc.)	BB: 302

As a fitting end to his playing career, Whitney held down third for Kelly's Killers, the Cincinnati AA team. His quitting guaranteed when the New York papers published an article saying that his salary would be cut 33 percent, he played three games for St Louis before hanging up his spikes. He led the league four times in fielding at shortstop and third base.
Playing Career: *1880-1882, 1884-1891; Wor N, Det N, Pro N, Pit AA, Pit N, NY N, NY P, Cin AA, StL AA*

Jim Whitney
Whitney, James Evans (Grasshopper)
B: Nov 10, 1857   D: May 21, 1891

Pos: P, OF, 1B	ERA: 2.97
W-L: 191-204	SOs: 1,571
ShOs: 26	Saves: 2

A perennial 20-game winner early in his career, Whitney led the NL in both wins and losses in his rookie season. In 1883 he compiled a record of 37-21 with a league-leading 345 strikeouts, and helped Boston to the pennant. Valued for his bat as well, Whitney was often the cleanup hitter in the batting order. When he was not on the mound, he played center field. He suffered a serious pitching slump for more than two seasons, but rallied for the 1887 campaign, putting together a record of 24-21.
Playing Career: *1881-1890; Bos N, KC N, Was N, Ind N, Phi AA*

Pinky Whitney
Whitney, Arthur Carter
B: Jan 2, 1905   D: Sep 1, 1987

Pos: 3B	BA: .295
Hits: 1,701	HRs: 93
RBI: 927	BB: 400

Whitney was a member of the only team in NL history to have four batters get 200 or more hits in a season – the 1929 Phillies. He batted .327 and had 200 hits that year. Teammates Lefty O'Doul with 254 hits, Chuck Klein with 219, and Fresco Thompson with 202, rounded out the historic quartet. Continuing his onslaught at the plate, Whitney batted .342 in 1930 with 207 hits. In 1937 his batting average soared again, to .341. Outstanding with the glove as well, he led NL third baseman in fielding three times.
Playing Career: *1928-1939; Phi N, Bos N*

Ed Whitson
Whitson, Eddie Lee
B: May 19, 1955

Pos: P	ERA: 3.79
W-L: 126-123	SOs: 1,266
ShOs: 12	Saves: 8

Between trades and injuries, Whitson did some good pitching for San Diego. He became the first Padres hurler to win a game in postseason play when he defeated the Cubs in Game Three of the 1984 NLCS. Whitson's record in the regular season that year was 14-8 with a 3.24 ERA. He appeared in the World Series, then signed a free-agent contract with the Yankees, but was dealt back to the Padres. Whitson led their staff in wins in 1987 and 1989.
Playing Career: *1977-1991; Pit N, SF N, Cle A, SD N, NY A*

Ernie Whitt
Whitt, Leo Ernest
B: Jun 13, 1952

Pos: C	BA: .253
Hits: 892	HRs: 132
RBI: 521	BB: 405

As the Toronto Blue Jays' franchise developed from an expansion team to perennial pennant contenders, Whitt emerged as an All-Star defensive catcher. Platooned for most of his career, he was nonetheless extremely popular. He played in two ALCS.
Playing Career: *1976-1978, 1980-1991; Bos A, Tor A, Atl N, Bal A*

Pinky Whitney.

Possum Whitted
Whitted, George Bostic
B: Feb 4, 1890   D: Oct 16, 1962

Pos: OF	BA: .270
Hits: 978	HRs: 23
RBI: 451	BB: 215

With a knack for being in the right place at the right time, Whitted lucked into the last half of the Miracle Braves' 1914 World Championship season. He was dealt to Philadelphia the next year, and played in the 1915 World Series for the Phillies.
Playing Career: *1912-1922; StL N, Bos N, Phi N, Pit N, Brk N*

Bob Wicker
Wicker, Robert Kitridge
B: May 24, 1878   D: Jan 22, 1955

Pos: P, OF	ERA: 2.73
W-L: 63-52	SOs: 472
ShOs: 10	No-hitters: 1

Pitching for the Cubs, Wicker won 49 games in a three-year span from 1903 to 1905. He also played 26 games in the outfield. A career highlight was a 1904 game against New York. After nine innings without a hit, Wicker gave up a hit in the 10th, then won 1-0 in the 12th.
Playing Career: *1902-1906; StL N, Chi N, Cin N*

Dave Wickersham
Wickersham, David Clifford
B: Sep 27, 1935

Pos: P	ERA: 3.66
W-L: 68-57	SOs: 638
ShOs: 5	Saves: 18

Never ejected from a major league game until his fifth season, Wickersham got the thumb in a 1964 game that likely cost him a 20-win season. His record was 19-12 with a 3.44 ERA that year, and he tied for third place for wins in the AL.
Playing Career: *1960-1969; KCA A, Det A, Pit N, KCR A*

Alan Wiggins
Wiggins, Alan Anthony
B: Feb 17, 1958   D: Jan 6, 1991

Pos: 2B, OF	BA: .259
Hits: 581	HRs: 5
RBI: 118	BB: 235

The catalyst for the 1984 Padres, Wiggins walked 75 times, stole 70 bases (242 overall), and scored 106 runs. He batted .316 in the NLCS that year and .364 in the World Series. The promise of Wiggins's potential disappeared in the shadows of drug abuse. He died of AIDS.
Playing Career: *1981-1987; SD N, Bal A*

Bill Wight
Wight, William Robert
B: Apr 12, 1922

Pos: P	ERA: 3.95
W-L: 77-99	SOs: 574
ShOs: 15	Saves: 8

Capturing the title of most frustrated at the plate, Wight was 0-for-61 in 1950. As a rookie he became the number one starter for Chicago in 1948, but had a record of 9-20 for the last-place team. His best season was 1949, when he compiled a record of 15-13.
Playing Career: *1946-1953, 1955-1958; NY A, Chi A, Bos A, Det A, Cle A, Bal A, Cin N, StL N*

Milt Wilcox
Wilcox, Milton Edward
B: Apr 20, 1950

Pos: P	ERA: 4.08
W-L: 119-113	SOs: 1,137
ShOs: 10	Saves: 6

The thrill of victory and the agony of defeat were depicted in Wilcox's career. He pitched in two LCS and two World Series, winning the deciding contest in the 1970 NLCS. In 1983 Wilcox was one out from a perfect game when a pinch hitter singled. His best years were with Detroit, where he posted 97 vic-

tories, with a high of 17 in 1984. Wilcox never recovered from shoulder surgery in 1985.
Playing Career: *1970-1975, 1977-1986; Cin N, Bos A, Cle A, Chi N, Det A, Sea A*

Rob Wilfong
Wilfong, Robert Daniel
B: Sep 1, 1953

Pos: 2B	BA: .248
Hits: 668	HRs: 39
RBI: 261	BB: 205

In his first season as a regular, Wilfong batted .313 with nine home runs and 59 RBI. Those turned out to be career-high marks, but Wilfong developed into a reliable bunter and contact hitter. He set an AL fielding record for second basemen in 1980.
Playing Career: *1977-1987; Min A, Cal A, SF N*

Hoyt Wilhelm (r) with Leo Durocher.

Hoyt Wilhelm
Wilhelm, James Hoyt
B: Jul 26, 1923
Hall of Fame 1985

Pos: P	ERA: 2.52
W-L: 143-122	SOs: 1,610
ShOs: 5	No-hitters: 1

The wizard of the knuckleball, Wilhelm was not a typical hurler. His trademark pitch was a fluttering masterpiece that deceived and frustrated the best hitters of his time. In a rare starting performance, Wilhelm pitched a no-hitter against the Yankees. Mickey Mantle was so frustrated during the game that he batted right-handed against the right-handed knuckleballer.

In his first season with the Giants Wilhelm was 15-3, and led the NL with 71 games, compiling an .833 winning percentage and a 2.43 ERA. One of the few pitchers of his time to specialize in relief, he saved 227 games altogether. During a 21-year career he appeared in 1,070 contests, more than any other pitcher in major league history. Wilhelm set records for relief wins and innings pitched in relief, and he was the first relief pitcher elected to the Hall of Fame.
Playing Career: *1952-1972; NY N, StL N, Cle A, Bal A, Chi A, Cal A, Atl N, Chi N, LA N*

Milt Wilcox shows off his good luck charm, 1975.

Kaiser Wilhelm
Wilhelm, Irvin Key
B: Jan 26, 1874   D: May 21, 1936

Pos: P   ERA: 3.44
W-L: 57-105   SOs: 444
ShOs: 12   Saves: 5
Managerial Record
Won: 83   Lost: 137   Pct: .377

Nicknamed "Kaiser" long before World War I, Wilhelm was a ballplayer, coach, manager and umpire. He made his debut with the 1903 pennant-winning Pirates, and later played in the Federal League. He coached the Cubs and Phillies.
Playing Career: *1903-1905, 1908-1910, 1914-1915, 1921; Pit N, Bos N, Brk N, Bal F, Phi N*
Managerial Career: *1921-1922; Phi N*
Umpiring Career: *1915; FL*

Curtis Wilkerson
Wilkerson, Curtis Vernon
B: Apr 26, 1961

Pos: 2B, SS, 3B   BA: .245
Hits: 600   HRs: 8
RBI: 179   BB: 138

A shortstop in the American Association for most of 1983, when he batted .312, Wilkerson played the position for the Rangers for two years, but has been a utility infielder since. He batted .293 in 1988. He played for the division champion Cubs of 1989 and Pirates of 1991.
Playing Career: *1983-; Tex A, Chi N, Pit N, KC A*

J. L. Wilkinson
Wilkinson, James Leslie (Wilkie)
B: 1874   D: Aug 21, 1964

More than anyone except Rube Foster, the Negro Leagues owed its prosperity to J. L. Wilkinson, the founder and owner of the

Billy Williams (r) and Catfish Hunter are inducted into the Hall of Fame in 1987.

Kansas City Monarchs. Foster shunned Wilkinson at first because he was white, but came to rely upon him more than any of the other owners. Wilkinson was the only non-family member to sign the incorporation papers for the Negro National League.

The Monarchs began as the All-Nations team, a multi-racial club based in Des Moines, then Kansas City, Missouri. Wilkinson gave up his dry goods business in Iowa for the life of a baseball promoter. His portable lighting system enabled thousands in the Midwest to see baseball players like Satchel Paige, Bullet Joe Rogan, Joe Greene, Willard Brown, Cristobal Torriente, Martin Dihigo, Newt Allen and Cool Papa Bell. Wilkinson put lights on portable vehicles instead of building them into a stadium. The innovation revolutionized baseball – games lit up the midwestern night. The Monarchs team was the best paid, best organized operation in the Negro Leagues.

Ted Wilks
Wilks, Theodore
B: Nov 13, 1915   D: Aug 21, 1989

Pos: P   ERA: 3.26
W-L: 59-30   SOs: 403
ShOs: 5   Saves: 46

During World War II, when the Cardinals' pitching staff was depleted, Wilks came up from the minors and had a great rookie season in 1944. He was 17-4 with a league-leading .810 winning percentage. From 1946 to 1950, Wilks went 30-9, undefeated in 1946 and 1947.
Playing Career: *1944-1953; StL N, Pit N, Cle A*

Ed Willett
Willett, Robert Edgar
B: Mar 7, 1884   D: May 10, 1934

Pos: P   ERA: 3.08
W-L: 102-99   SOs: 600
ShOs: 12   Saves: 5

In a four-year span from 1910 to 1913, Willett won 59 games for the Tigers. This effort followed a career year in 1909, when he was 21-10 with a 2.34 ERA and pitched in the World Series for Detroit. Willett was the second AL pitcher to hit two home runs in a game.
Playing Career: *1906-1915; Det A, StL F*

Billy Williams
Williams, Billy Leo (Sweet)
B: Jun 15, 1938
Hall of Fame 1987

Pos: OF, DH, 1B   BA: .290
Hits: 2,711   HRs: 426
RBI: 1,475   BB: 1,045

The 1961 NL Rookie of the Year, Williams quietly carved out a Hall of Fame career. Overshadowed by flashier players, he was a consistent, dependable star for 14 full seasons

J.L. Wilkinson (2nd from l) with his team, the Kansas City Monarchs.

with the Cubs. He played 1,117 consecutive games – an NL record that stood until Steve Garvey broke it in 1983. Williams also set NL marks for games played by an outfielder in one season, 164 in 1965, and for nine consecutive years with 600 or more at-bats, 1962-1970.

Williams tied major league records with five homers in two consecutive games in 1968, and four consecutive doubles in a 1969 contest. June 29, 1969 was Billy Williams Day at Wrigley Field; he broke Stan Musial's NL record of 896 consecutive games played, and went 8-for-9 as the Cubs took two from the Cardinals. The six-time All-Star led the 1970 NL in hits and in runs scored, and finished second to Johnny Bench with 42 home runs and 129 RBI. In 1972 he hit .333 to win the NL batting crown. That July 11, he went 8-for-8 in a doubleheader.
Playing Career: *1959-1976; Chi N, Oak A*

Cy Williams
Williams, Fred
B: Dec 21, 1887   D: Apr 23, 1974

Pos: OF   BA: .292
Hits: 1,981   HRs: 251
RBI: 1,005   BB: 690

One of the deadball era's top sluggers, Williams became a home run hitter in the lively ball era, beginning in 1920. An architecture student at Notre Dame, Williams was a fine collegiate sprinter and hurdler and played football with Knute Rockne. On the baseball diamond he was a strong-hitting center fielder, and attracted the attention of the Cubs, who brought him directly to the majors after his graduation. They traded him to Philadelphia, where he became a star.

The original "Williams shift" was created to limit the effects of his bat in Baker Bowl. Managers would load up the right side of the field with players. A four-time NL home run champ, Williams hit 41 taters in 1923, tying Babe Ruth for the major league lead. Williams hit 12 inside-the-park homers and seven grand slams in his career; his 11 pinch homers were a record until 1960. After Williams retired from baseball, he became a prominent architect in Wisconsin.
Playing Career: *1912-1930; Chi N, Phi N*

Dick Williams
Williams, Richard Hirschfeld
B: May 7, 1928

Pos: OF, 3B, 1B   BA: .260
Hits: 768   HRs: 70
RBI: 331   BB: 227
Managerial Record
Won: 1,571   Lost: 1,451   Pct: .520

A versatile player and bench jockey extraordinaire – he was taught by Leo Durocher – Williams is one of two managers to win league titles with three different teams. In 1967 he took over a Red Sox team that had finished in ninth place the year before, and guided them to victory in an incredible four-club pennant race. Owner Tom Yawkey grew

A's Manager Dick Williams (r), 1972.

impatient when the Red Sox did not repeat in the following two years. After a year as Expos coach, Williams was hired by Charlie Finley to manage the A's, a team loaded with burgeoning stars.

Williams, Finley's 11th manager in as many years, led the A's to a division title in 1971, then to their first pennant in 41 years in 1972. He repeated in 1973. After a chaotic World Series during which players revolted against Finley's suspension of Mike Andrews, Williams resigned. He took the Padres to their only World Series in 1984, where they lost to the much stronger Tigers. A lively and opinionated personality, Williams was one of the best managers in baseball.
Playing Career: *1951-1964; Brk N, Bal A, Cle A, KC A, Bos A*
Managerial Career: *1967-1969, 1971-1988; Bos A, Oak A, Cal A, Mon N, SD N, Sea A*

Earl Williams
Williams, Earl Craig, Jr.
B: Jul 14, 1948

Pos: C, 1B, DH, 3B   BA: .247
Hits: 756   HRs: 138
RBI: 457   BB: 298

An All-Star in 1971 as a rookie, Williams walked away with Rookie of the Year honors based on his 33 home runs and 87 RBI. Adding first base and designated hitter roles to his duties as catcher, he played in two ALCS with the Orioles, hitting .278 in the 1973 ALCS with four RBI in five games.
Playing Career: *1970-1977; Atl N, Bal A, Mon N, Oak A*

Jimmy Williams
Williams, James Thomas (Home Run)
B: Dec 20, 1876   D: Jan 16, 1965

Pos: 2B, 3B   BA: .275
Hits: 1,507   HRs: 49
RBI: 796   BB: 474

Dubbed "Home Run" when he broke in with nine round-trippers in 1899, Williams should

rightfully have been called "Three-bagger" – he banged out 138 of those in his career. Williams led the NL in triples in 1899 with 27, and later topped the AL with 21 in both 1901 and 1902. He was a good fielder, and edged out Nap Lajoie for fielding titles twice. Williams played for good teams, one of which almost won the 1904 AL pennant.
Playing Career: *1899-1909; Pit N, Bal A, NY A, StL A*

Ken Williams
Williams, Kenneth Roy
B: Jun 28, 1890   D: Jan 22, 1959

Pos: OF   BA: .319
Hits: 1,552   HRs: 196
RBI: 913   BB: 566

Born and raised in Grants Pass, Oregon, Williams was a small-town boy whose mother was a logging-camp cook, and later operated an all-night restaurant serving the railroad crews. After spending 1917 and most of 1918 in the military, Williams joined the Browns in 1919. The following year the club put together its celebrated outfield of Williams, Baby Doll Jacobson, and Jack Tobin.

Finishing one game behind the Yankees for the 1922 pennant, Williams and the Browns had their best year together. He led the AL with 39 home runs and 155 RBI, while batting .337 and stealing 37 bases that year. The performance made him the first player ever to hit .300 with 30 home runs and 30 steals. In one game Williams swatted three homers, in another, two in one inning. He once had six homers in six consecutive games. Popular with teammates and fans, Williams missed some games in 1925 after being skulled by a pitch, but led the AL with a .613 slugging percentage that year.
Playing Career: *1915-1916, 1918-1929; Cin N, StL A, Bos A*

Browns outfielder Ken Williams, 1921.

Lefty Williams
Williams, Claude Preston
B: Mar 9, 1893   D: Nov 4, 1959

Pos: P	ERA: 3.13
W-L: 82-48	SOs: 515
ShOs: 10	Saves: 5

Banned from baseball for life because he threw three games in the 1919 World Series, Lefty Williams roomed with an equally moody and inarticulate Joe Jackson. Williams was in his prime with 22 wins in 1919 and 23 in 1920, when faced with suspension.
Playing Career: *1913-1914, 1916-1920; Det A, Chi A*

Mitch Williams
Williams, Mitchell Steven (Wild Thing)
B: Nov 17, 1964

Pos: P	ERA: 3.39
W-L: 43-51	SOs: 620
ShOs: 0	Saves: 186

Cubs fans would sing the rock song "Wild Thing" from the movie *Major League* when Mitch Williams emerged from the Chicago bullpen in 1989. He obliged in 1990 by fanning the flames of opponents' rallies as he went 1-8 with a 3.93 ERA, following his best season of 36 saves and 2.76 ERA. He has now found a home in Phillie land. Saving games for a team with a young pitching staff and colorful veterans, he is no longer the weird kid on the block. Loaded with rejects, the 1993 Phillies surprised the NL by winning the pennant.
Playing Career: *1986-; Tex A, Chi N, Phi N*

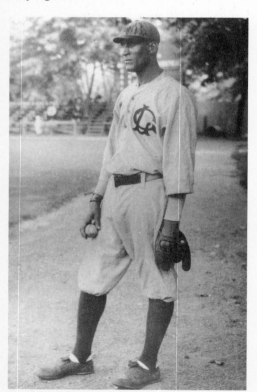

Smokey Joe Williams.

Smokey Joe Williams
Williams, Joe (Cyclone Joe)
B: Apr 6, 1885   D: Mar 12, 1946

Pos: P	ERA: NA
W-L: 78-47 (inc.)	SOs: 341 (inc.)
ShOs: 10 (inc.)	Saves: 2 (inc.)

In 1952 the *Pittsburgh Courier* voted Williams the greatest black pitcher of the 20th century. He was a 6'5" man of African-American and Native American ancestry, and weighed 215 pounds. His best seasons came before the Negro National League was established in 1920. In 1914 he was 12-2 against top black teams and 41-3 overall. Williams's best-documented season was 1930. He was 44 years old and compiled a record of 5-1 in Negro League play.

Williams's strikeout ability was legendary. In 1924 he struck out 24 batters in a 12-inning game against the Bushwicks, a powerful semipro team. In 1930 he struck out 27 batters while constructing a 12-inning one-hitter against the Kansas City Monarchs. In games against major leaguers, Williams was 22-7-1 with 12 shutouts. In 1915 the big right-hander struck out 10 while hurling a 1-0, three-hit shutout against Grover Cleveland Alexander of the Phillies. In a 1917 exhibition, he no-hit the Giants and struck out 20, but lost 1-0 on an error.
Playing Career: *1910-1924, 1927-1932; Chi Leland Giants, NY Lincoln Giants, Chi Am Giants, Brk Royal Giants, AC Bach Giants, Hom Grays, Det Wolves*

Stan Williams
Williams, Stanley Wilson (Big Daddy)
B: Sep 14, 1936

Pos: P	ERA: 3.48
W-L: 109-94	SOs: 1,305
ShOs: 11	Saves: 43

Williams was a hulking 6'4" right-hander with blistering speed who loved to throw inside. An All-Star in 1960, he never gave up a run in postseason play, appearing in the World Series with the 1959 Dodgers and 1963 Yankees, and in the 1970 ALCS with the Twins.
Playing Career: *1958-1965, 1967-1972; LA N, NY A, Cle A, Min A, StL N, Bos A*

Ted Williams
Williams, Theodore Samuel (The Splendid Splinter, The Thumper, Teddy Ballgame)
B: Aug 30, 1918
Hall of Fame 1966

Pos: OF	BA: .344
Hits: 2,654	HRs: 521
RBI: 1,839	BB: 2,019
Managerial Record	
Won: 273 Lost: 364 Pct: .429	

No one loved hitting more, nor worked harder at his craft than Williams. With exceptional eyesight – he was said to be able to read the label on a spinning record album – and constant attention to improving his per-

Hall of Famer Ted Williams in 1950.

formance, Williams excelled in baseball and was one of its greatest hitters ever. Outspoken, patriotic and immensely talented, Williams earned six AL batting titles, two Triple Crowns, four home run titles and two MVP Awards.

Ironically, he did not win the MVP Award in his best year – 1941 when he hit .406 – nor in his Triple Crown years – 1942 and 1947. Serving in the military in both World War II and Korea, Williams's career was shortened by nearly five seasons, but he still put up some incredible numbers. He hit 525 doubles, scored 1,798 runs, and batted .316 or higher every season but one. After his playing career, Williams became a good-teaching manager who coaxed career years from marginal players.
Playing Career: *1939-1942, 1946-1960; Bos A*
Managerial Career: *1969-1972; Was A, Tex A*

Walt Williams
Williams, Walter Allen (No Neck)
B: Dec 19, 1943

Pos: OF	BA: .270
Hits: 640	HRs: 33
RBI: 173	BB: 126

A two-time minor league batting champ, Williams batted with an open stance because his head did not turn very far. He batted .304 in 1969 and .294 in 1971. He even hit .281 in his last year with the Yankees before becoming a coach in the major leagues.
Playing Career: *1964, 1967-1975; Hou N, Chi A, Cle A, NY A*

Ned Williamson
Williamson, Edward Nagle
B: Oct 24, 1857   D: Mar 3, 1894

Pos: 3B, SS, C	BA: .255
Hits: 1,159	HRs: 63
RBI: 523	BB: 506

In 1884 Williamson set the major league single-season home run record that Babe Ruth broke in 1919. Williamson lifted 27

homers over the 180-foot left field fence at Chicago's Lake Front Park. The previous season, hits over that wall had been counted as doubles, and Williamson had topped the NL with 49. An exceptional third baseman, leading the NL in fielding five of seven years, Williamson moved to shortstop and led the White Stockings to another pennant in 1886.
Playing Career: *1878-1890; Ind N, Chi N, Chi P*

Vic Willis
Willis, Victor Gazaway
B: Apr 12, 1876   D: Aug 3, 1947

Pos: P	ERA: 2.63
W-L: 249-205	SOs: 1,651
ShOs: 50	No-hitters: 1

An eight-time 20-game winner, Willis received the requisite number of votes to be elected to the Baseball Hall of Fame, but a problem came up. The Veterans Committee was allowed to elect only two players at a time. Enos Slaughter and Arky Vaughan both received more votes than Willis, so he was left out. Winning 25 games in 1898 as a Beaneater rookie, Willis became the anchor of the club's pitching staff for eight years.

The durable Willis hurled more than 300 innings eight times, leading the NL once, and set the modern NL record with 45 complete games. He completed 388 of his 471 career starts. During the baseball war at the turn of the century, both the AL and NL laid claim to Willis's contract, but he stayed with the NL Boston club. After setting a major league record with 29 losses in 1905 for the only team in history to have four 20-game losers, Willis posted four consecutive 20-win seasons with the Pirates, 1906-1909.
Playing Career: *1898-1910; Bos N, Pit N, StL N*

Jim Willoughby
Willoughby, James Arthur
B: Jan 31, 1949

Pos: P	ERA: 3.79
W-L: 26-36	SOs: 250
ShOs: 1	Saves: 34

A starter early in his career, Willoughby was a relief pitcher by the time he appeared in the 1975 World Series with the Red Sox. He pitched more than six innings without surrendering an earned run, but lost Game Three in the 10th inning, in a questionable play at home plate.
Playing Career: *1971-1978; SF N, Bos A, Chi A*

Bump Wills
Wills, Elliott Taylor
B: Jul 27, 1952

Pos: 2B	BA: .266
Hits: 807	HRs: 36
RBI: 302	BB: 310

Like his father, Maury, Bump Wills could really move. He stole 196 bases in six years,

with a high of 52 in 1978. He was a star ballplayer at Arizona State University when their squad won the national title. In 1980 Wills scored 102 runs for the Rangers.
Playing Career: *1977-1982; Tex A, Chi N*

Maury Wills
Wills, Maurice Morning
B: Oct 2, 1932

Pos: SS	BA: .281
Hits: 2,134	HRs: 20
RBI: 458	BB: 552
Managerial Record	
Won: 26 Lost: 56 Pct: .317	

Wills changed baseball by re-introducing the stolen base as an offensive weapon. He scored 1,067 runs and stole 586 bases despite spending 10 years in the minors. Even the Topps Baseball Card Company would not sign him to a photo contract! Wills became the first player Topps ever rejected to become a major league star. In 1960, his first full season in the majors, Wills hit .295 and led the NL with 50 steals – the highest total in the NL since Max Carey stole 51 in 1923.

In 1961 Wills scored 104 runs with 35 steals. The three-time All-Star won Gold Glove Awards in 1961 and 1962. The latter year he set a new major league record of 104 stolen bases, shattering Ty Cobb's mark of 96. Wills also led the NL with 10 triples and reached career highs with 130 runs, 48 RBI, six homers and 208 hits. His 695 at-bats missed the major league record by one. Wills was named NL MVP.
Playing Career: *1959-1972; LA N, Pit N, Mon N*
Managerial Career: *1980-1981; Sea A*

Maury Wills.

Walt Wilmot
Wilmot, Walter Robert
B: Oct 18, 1863   D: Feb 1, 1929

Pos: OF	BA: .276
Hits: 1,100	HRs: 59
RBI: 594	BB: 349

Missing the great White Stocking clubs of the 1880s, Walt Wilmot held down center field for Chicago Manager Cap Anson from 1890 to 1895. He hit .330 in 1894 with 45 doubles, 134 runs and 130 RBI. In the Go-Go Sox tradition he stole 381 bases in his career, twice going over 70. He had started out with Connie Mack in Washington.
Playing Career: *1888-1895, 1897-1898; Was N, Chi N, NY N*

Art Wilson
Wilson, Arthur Earl (Dutch)
B: Dec 11, 1885   D: Jun 12, 1960

Pos: C	BA: .261
Hits: 536	HRs: 24
RBI: 226	BB: 292

A reserve catcher for the Giants, Wilson played for their 1911-1913 pennant-winning teams. In the 1912 World Series, he was doubled off second base by Tris Speaker for the only outfielder unassisted double play in Series history. Wilson later caught the double no-hit game for the Cubs.
Playing Career: *1908-1921; NY N, Chi F, Pit N, Chi N, Bos N, Cle A*

Don Wilson
Wilson, Donald Edward
B: Feb 12, 1945   D: Jan 5, 1975

Pos: P	ERA: 3.15
W-L: 104-92	SOs: 1,283
ShOs: 20	No-hitters: 2

With two no-hitters and an 18-strikeout game notched early in his career, Wilson was already a big star when he died accidentally at age 29. The previous September he had pitched eight innings of no-hit ball, but trailed in the game 2-1. In a highly controversial move, Manager Preston Gomez pulled Wilson out of the game before he could achieve his third no-hitter.
Playing Career: *1966-1974; Hou N*

Earl Wilson
Wilson, Robert Earl
B: Oct 2, 1934

Pos: P	ERA: 3.69
W-L: 171-109	SOs: 1,452
ShOs: 13	No-hitters: 1

The first black player signed by the Red Sox, Wilson served in the military in 1956 and 1957, delaying his major league debut. Originally signed as a catcher and switched to the mound in the minors, he was one of baseball's greatest power-hitting pitchers. Wilson smashed 35 homers in only 740 at-bats, including two in one game, and seven

in a season twice. He also posted 22 victories in 1967 for the Tigers, tying Jim Lonborg for the AL lead in wins.
Playing Career: *1959-1960, 1962-1970; Bos A, Det A, SD N*

Glenn Wilson
Wilson, Glenn Dwight
B: Dec 22, 1958

Pos: OF, 1B	BA: .265
Hits: 1,096	HRs: 98
RBI: 521	BB: 253

A first-round draft choice, Wilson batted .292 his rookie season. Building a reputation for defense with a strong, accurate throwing arm, he led NL outfielders in assists with 18 in 1985 and 20 in 1986. Wilson was chosen for the All-Star team in 1985.
Playing Career: *1982-1990; Det A, Phi N, Sea A, Pit N, Hou N*

Hack Wilson
Wilson, Lewis Robert
B: Apr 26, 1900   D: Nov 23, 1948
Hall of Fame 1979

Pos: OF	BA: .307
Hits: 1,461	HRs: 244
RBI: 1,062	BB: 674

Built like a fireplug, Wilson was 5'6" and weighed close to 200 pounds – all muscle. He wore an 18-inch collar and a size six shoe. Though he played well for the Giants, they were loaded with talent in 1925, and tried to hide him temporarily in the minors. The Cubs found Wilson and drafted him for only $5,000. New York protested but Commissioner Landis upheld the deal. Batting cleanup in the Cubs' awesome lineup, he became one of the NL's top power hitters.

Wilson tomahawked many a high fastball into the Wrigley Field stands. He had 25- and

Cubs slugger Hack Wilson.

Cubs Manager Jimmie Wilson (l) with Tom Taggert (c), Jason Dykes, and mascots.

27-game hitting streaks, hit for the cycle, and slugged .723 in 1930. Wilson set two NL records that year, most home runs in a season with 56, and most RBI in a season with 190. The latter is also a major league record that has not been approached in 65 years. Wilson's problem was alcohol. Joe McCarthy knew how to handle him, but subsequent Cubs skippers did not. After his brilliant 1930 season Wilson slumped badly, and by 1934 his career had ended.
Playing Career: *1923-1934; NY N, Chi N, Brk N, Phi N*

Jack Wilson
Wilson, John Francis (Black Jack)
B: Apr 12, 1912

Pos: P	ERA: 4.59
W-L: 68-72	SOs: 590
ShOs: 5	Saves: 20

A weak-hitting third baseman in the minors, Wilson took up pitching. In his initial Red Sox outing he relieved Wes Ferrell and hit an 11th-inning homer, claiming his first major league hit and first victory. He was 16-10 in 1937, starting and relieving.
Playing Career: *1934-1942; Phi A, Bos A, Was A, Det A*

Jim Wilson
Wilson, James Alger
B: Feb 20, 1922   D: Sep 2, 1986

Pos: P	ERA: 4.01
W-L: 86-89	SOs: 692
ShOs: 19	No-hitters: 1

Beaned by a line drive as a rookie, Wilson lay on the mound unconscious, but recovered. The three-time All-Star pitched a no-hitter against the Phillies in 1954. He was 15-8 for the 1957 White Sox, leading the AL in shutouts with five that season.
Playing Career: *1945-1946, 1948-1949, 1951-1958; Bos A, StL A, Phi A, Bos N, Mil N, Bal A, Chi A*

Jimmie Wilson
Wilson, James
B: Jul 23, 1900   D: May 31, 1947

Pos: C	BA: .284
Hits: 1,358	HRs: 32
RBI: 621	BB: 356
Managerial Record	
Won: 493 Lost: 735 Pct: .401	

One of the top catchers of the 1920s and early 1930s, Wilson was coaching for the Reds when he was called on to play in the 1940 World Series. Ernie Lombardi's injury and Willard Hershberger's suicide had left the Reds without proven catchers. Wilson filled in, catching six of the seven World Series games against the Tigers. He batted .353 and had the only stolen base of the Series.
Playing Career: *1923-1940; Phi N, StL N, Cin N*
Managerial Career: *1934-1938, 1941-1944; Phi N, Chi N*

Jud Wilson
Wilson, Judson Ernest (Boojum)
B: Feb 28, 1899   D: Jun 26, 1963

Pos: 3B, 1B	BA: .347
Hits: 960	HRs: 63
RBI: NA	BB: NA

A Negro League All-Star 1933-1935, Wilson was an intense, intimidating competitor. He was built like a wrestler, and his fights with umpires and players were legendary as his will to win. Wilson led the league in doubles in 1930 while batting .372.
Playing Career: *1922-1945; Bal Black Sox, Hom Grays, Pit Crawfords, Phi Stars*

Mookie Wilson
Wilson, William Hayward
B: Feb 9, 1956

Pos: OF	HRs: .274
Hits: 1,397	HRs: 67
RBI: 438	BBs: 282

Desperately fouling off each offering, the Mets' Wilson fought off 10 pitches in the bottom of the 10th inning of Game Six of the 1986 World Series. With a 2-2 count, reliever Bob Stanley was one strike away from the first Red Sox World Championship since 1918. He threw a pitch in the dirt, allowing the Mets' Kevin Mitchell to score, tying the game, and moving Ray Knight to second base. After several more fouls, Wilson slapped a slow roller to first baseman Bill Buckner. The ball went between his legs, and Knight scored the winning run.
Playing Career: *1980-1991; NY N, Tor A*

Owen Wilson
Wilson, John Owen (Chief)
B: Aug 21, 1883   D: Feb 22, 1954

Pos: OF	BA: .269
Hits: 1,246	HRs: 59
RBI: 571	BB: 241

Renowned for hitting 36 triples in 1912, Wilson retains that all-time organized ball record. He was a speedy left-handed line drive hitter. Most of the triples were hit in Forbes Field, the site of his 31 career inside-the-park home runs.
Playing Career: *1908-1916; Pit N, StL N*

Willie Wilson
Wilson, Willie James
B: Jul 9, 1955

Pos: OF	BA: .286
Hits: 2,202	HRs: 41
RBI: 585	BB: 424

Fleet-footed Wilson was the Royals' first-round draft choice in 1974 after he turned down a football scholarship to the University of Maryland. His great speed and Gold Glove ability to come in on the ball made him one of the best and most exciting outfielders in the

Willie Wilson.

AL. Batting leadoff, he drove the Royals to four division titles, and played in another ALCS with the A's in 1992. Wilson has scored 1,165 runs in his career, including an AL-high 133 in 1980 when he swatted 230 hits, at least 100 from each side of the plate.

Two years later Wilson took the AL batting crown with a .332 average. Extremely fast, he topped the league in triples five times. The two-time All-Star has swiped 667 bases, leading the league once, with 83 in 1979. He played 148 straight errorless games in 1987, accepting 325 chances. Wilson's 12 strikeouts in the 1980 World Series set a record, but he batted .367 in the 1985 "I-70 Series" against the Cardinals. In October 1983 Wilson was one of four Royals to plead guilty to cocaine charges; he served three months in prison.
Playing Career: *1976-; KC A, Oak A, Chi N*

Zeke Wilson
Wilson, Frank Ealton
B: Dec 24, 1869   D: Apr 26, 1928

Pos: P	ERA: 4.03
W-L: 52-44	SOs: 194
ShOs: 3	Saves: 1

Good enough to be promoted from the 1899 Spiders, Wilson moved with his teammates to St. Louis in the worst abuse of syndicate baseball ever, the 1899 Spiders-Perfectos swap. A starter for the 1896 Temple Cup defending champs, he was ill and did not pitch in the series.
Playing Career: *1895-1899; Bos N, Cle N, StL N*

Hooks Wiltse
Wiltse, George Leroy
B: Sep 7, 1880   D: Jan 21, 1959

Pos: P	ERA: 2.47
W-L: 139-90	SOs: 965
ShOs: 27	No-hitters: 1

When Wiltse won his first 13 games in 1904, Manager John McGraw overcame his prejudice against left-handed pitchers. It was a bias that was prevalent throughout major league baseball, and Wiltse accomplished a good deal toward removing it. With a distinctive hawk-like nose and swooping eagle-like arms, Wiltse was quite a figure and a good enough fielder to play first base in the 1913 World Series. He made several sensational plays to save Christy Mathewson's Game Two shutout.
Playing Career: *1904-1915; NY N, Brk N*

Bobby Wine
Wine, Robert Paul, Sr.
B: Sep 17, 1938

Pos: SS, 3B	BA: .215
Hits: 682	HRs: 30
RBI: 268	BB: 214
Managerial Record	
Won: 16 Lost: 25 Pct: .390	

Known for his strong arm and bad back, Wine earned a Gold Glove Award in 1963,

then lost his shortstop job to Ruben Amaro, who won a Gold Glove the next year. Wine set a major league record with 137 double plays in 1970, the only year he played 150 games.
Playing Career: *1960, 1962-1972; Phi N, Mon N*
Managerial Career: *1985; Atl N*

Dave Winfield
Winfield, David Mark
B: Oct 3, 1951

Pos: OF	BA: .285
Hits: 3,014	HRs: 453
RBI: 1,786	BB: 1,171

Likely the best athlete ever to play baseball, Winfield made a miraculous comeback from back surgery. In 1992 he hit 26 home runs and drove in his customary 100 runs, leading the Blue Jays to their first World Series triumph. Winfield went home to Minnesota to play for the Twins in 1993. A star pitcher and basketball player at the University of Minnesota, he had been named MVP of the College World Series in 1973. He batted over .400 while compiling a 13-1 pitching record that year.

Drafted by four teams in three sports after his senior year, Winfield signed with the Padres, bypassing the minor leagues to join them immediately. Tall and stately in appearance, Winfield was established as a star by his fourth season; he was selected for the All-Star squad 12 seasons in a row. He won seven Gold Glove Awards, but earned his paycheck with his bat, knocking in more than 100 runs eight times and more than 90 three other times. He hit 520 doubles and scored 1,623. He even stole 220 bases.
Playing Career: *1973-1988, 1990-; SD N, NY A, Cal A, Tor A, Min A*

Dave Winfield with the Yanks in 1982.

Ivey Wingo
Wingo, Ivey Brown
B: Jul 8, 1890   D: Mar 1, 1941

Pos: C   BA: .260
Hits: 1,039   HRs: 25
RBI: 455   BB: 264
Managerial Record
Won: 1   Lost: 1   Pct: .500

Another of the bit players who came through for the 1919 World Champion Reds, Wingo hit .571 in the World Series as his team whipped the favored White Sox. He retired in 1929 with the then NL record of 1,231 games caught, a record which has since been surpassed.
Playing Career: *1911-1926, 1929; StL N, Cin N*
Managerial Career: *1916; Cin N*

Herm Winningham
Winningham, Herman Son
B: Dec 1, 1961

Pos: OF, DH   BA: .239
Hits: 452   HRs: 19
RBI: 147   BB: 157

Breaking in with a .407 average, Winningham looked like a budding star when the Mets shipped him to the Expos in the Gary Carter deal. Since suffering a knee injury in 1985, he has been a reserve outfielder. In 1993 he filed for free agency, but there were no takers.
Playing Career: *1984-1992; NY N, Mon N, Cin N, Bos A*

George Winter
Winter, George Lovington (Sassafras)
B: Apr 27, 1878   D: May 26, 1951

Pos: P   ERA: 2.87
W-L: 83-102   SOs: 568
ShOs: 9   Saves: 4

A Gettysburg College teammate of Eddie Plank, Winter twice won 16 games for the Red Sox, then called the Pilgrims. He pitched for Boston's 1903-1904 AL pennant winners, and tossed a scoreless inning for the Tigers in the 1908 World Series. He also served as an early player rep.
Playing Career: *1901-1908; Bos A, Det A*

Nip Winters
Winters, Jesse
B: 1899   D: Dec 1971

Pos: P   ERA: NA
W-L: 95-54 (inc.)   SOs: 345 (inc.)
ShOs: 9 (inc.)   Saves: 3 (inc.)

The ace of the Hilldales, Winters starred in the 1924 Negro League World Series, going 3-1 against the Kansas City Monarchs. He led the Eastern Colored League in the 1920s with marks of 19-5 in 1924, 21-10 in 1925, and 15-5 in 1926.
Playing Career: *1921-1932; AC Bach Giants, Phi Hilldales, NY Lincoln Giants, Nwk Browns*

Rick Wise brings in a homer, 1973.

Rick Wise
Wise, Richard Charles
B: Sep 13, 1945

Pos: P   ERA: 3.69
W-L: 188-181   SOs: 1,647
ShOs: 30   No-hitters: 1

A member of the 1964 near-miss Phillies, Wise was traded even up for Cardinals star left-hander Steve Carlton at the 1971 winter meetings. This was the last unencumbered owner deal – "I'll swap my complaining pitcher for your complaining pitcher." Wise won 16 games in each of the next two years, and made the All-Star team for the second time in 1973.
Playing Career: *1964, 1966-1982; Phi N, StL N, Bos A, Cle A, SD N*

Sam Wise
Wise, Samuel Washington (Modoc)
B: Aug 18, 1857   D: Jan 22, 1910

Pos: SS, 2B, 1B   BA: .272
Hits: 1,281   HRs: 49
RBI: 631   BB: 389

As the new shortstop in Boston, Wise helped the Red Stockings to a surprising pennant in 1883. Boston had to defend him twice in federal court for jumping his contract with the newly formed AA club in Cincinnati. He loved to sing "Modoc, the Big Indian."
Playing Career: *1881-1891, 1893; Det N, Bos N, Was N, Buf P, Bal AA*

Mickey Witek
Witek, Nicholas Joseph
B: Dec 19, 1915

Pos: 2B, SS, 3B   BA: .277
Hits: 595   HRs: 22
RBI: 196   BB: 148

Originally signed by the Yankees, Witek debuted with the Giants after being named MVP in the 1939 International League. In 1943 he hit a league-high 172 singles while batting .314, and led NL second basemen in putouts, assists and errors.
Playing Career: *1940-1943, 1946-1947, 1949; NY N, NY A*

Bobby Witt
Witt, Robert Andrew
B: May 11, 1964

Pos: P   ERA: 4.52
W-L: 83-86   SOs: 1,207
ShOs: 6   No-hitters: 0

A member of the 1984 U.S. Olympic baseball team, Witt has been wild ever since leaving the University of Oklahoma. In his first two seasons, the flamethrower led the AL in both strikeouts per nine innings, 9.93 then 10.07, and walks, 143 then 140. As a rookie he uncorked an AL-high 22 wild pitches.
Playing Career: *1986-; Tex A, Oak A*

Mike Witt
Witt, Michael Atwater
B: Jul 20, 1960

Pos: P   ERA: 3.83
W-L: 117-116   SOs: 1,373
ShOs: 11   No-hitters: 2

Tossing the majors' 13th perfect game, a 1-0 win over Texas on the last day of the 1984 season, Witt has been plagued by arm trouble, missing the entire 1992 season after arm surgery. Selected to the 1986-1987 All-Star squads, Witt is second on the all-time Angels' list in wins, starts, innings pitched and strikeouts, while ranking number one in games.
Playing Career: *1981-1991, 1993-; Cal A, NY A*

Whitey Witt
Witt, Lawton Walter
B: Sep 28, 1895   D: Jul 14, 1988

Pos: OF   BA: .287
Hits: 1,195   HRs: 18
RBI: 302   BB: 489

The leadoff man for the 1922-1923 AL champion Yankees, Witt's propensity to party with Babe Ruth kept his number of games played and statistics down. Witt badgered Connie Mack into trading him to New York. In the heat of the 1922 pennant race, Witt was injured when he stepped on a bottle thrown from the St. Louis crowd. The incident led to the banning of glass bottles.
Playing Career: *1916-1917, 1919-1926; Phi A, NY A, Brk N*

Lawton Walter "Whitey" Witt played in two World Series (1922-23) for the Yankees.

John Wockenfuss
Wockenfuss, Johnny Bilton
B: Feb 27, 1949

Pos: C, 1B, DH, OF	BA: .262
Hits: 543	HRs: 86
RBI: 310	BB: 277

After perservering through eight seasons in the minor leagues, Wockenfuss made it to the big leagues and stayed for 12 years. Used as a backup catcher, he played more than 100 games only once, in 1980, when he hit .274 with 16 home runs and 65 RBI.
Playing Career: *1974-1985; Det A, Phi N*

Jim Wohlford
Wohlford, James Eugene
B: Feb 28, 1951

Pos: OF	BA: .260
Hits: 793	HRs: 21
RBI: 305	BB: 241

Named to the Topps junior college All-American team in 1970, Wohlford was the American Association rookie of the year two years later. A line drive hitter, Wohlford displayed good speed in the outfield and on the basepaths. He played in the 1976 ALCS.
Playing Career: *1972-1986; KC A, Mil A, SF N, Mon N*

Chicken Wolf
Wolf, William Van Winkle
B: May 12, 1862   D: May 16, 1903

Pos: OF	BA: .290
Hits: 1,440	HRs: 17
RBI: 207 (inc.)	BB: 229
Managerial Record	
Won: 14 Lost: 51 Pct: .215	

During the 10 years that the American Association was a major league, Wolf was considered one of the best outfielders in the league. Normally a solid but unspectacular batsman, he erupted in 1890 to lead the AA with a .363 batting average, 197 hits and 260 total bases. Some explain Wolf's outburst by pointing out that the AA had been weakened by numerous defections to the new Players' League.
Playing Career: *1882-1892; Lou AA, StL N*
Managerial Career: *1889; Lou AA*

Miles Wolff
Wolff, Miles
B: Dec 30, 1943

Founder of *Baseball America*, the leading publication on minor league baseball, Wolff is also the co-editor of the *Encyclopedia of Minor League Baseball*. He is the former owner of the Durham Bulls, and founder and president of the revived Northern League, an independent minor league.

Roger Wolff
Wolff, Roger Francis
B: Apr 10, 1911

Pos: P	ERA: 3.41
W-L: 52-69	SOs: 430
ShOs: 8	Saves: 13

A knuckleball pitcher used both as a starter and in relief, Wolff was part of the Senators' pitching rotation that cornered the market on junk pitches during World War II. Washington had four knuckleballers – more than any other major league team.
Playing Career: *1941-1947; Phi A, Was A, Cle A, Pit N*

Harry Wolter
Wolter, Harry Meigs
B: Jul 11, 1884   D: Jul 7, 1970

Pos: OF, 1B, P	BA: .270
Hits: 514	HRs: 12
RBI: 167	BB: 268

Going 5-6 as a pitcher, Wolter became a full-time outfielder in 1910. He led the Pacific Coast League in batting twice. A native Californian, Wolter coached at Stanford University for 26 years.
Playing Career: *1907, 1909-1913, 1917; Cin N, Pit N, StL N, Bos A, NY A, Chi N*

Harry Wolverton
Wolverton, Harry Sterling
B: Dec 6, 1873   D: Feb 4, 1937

Pos: 3B	BA: .278
Hits: 833	HRs: 7
RBI: 352	BB: 166
Managerial Record	
Won: 50 Lost: 102 Pct: .329	

Wolverton was a solidly-built third baseman who batted more than .300 for the Phillies in 1901 and 1903. He rapped out three triples in a 1900 game. While managing the New York Highlanders in 1912, Wolverton frequently put himself in the lineup as a pinch hitter.
Playing Career: *1898-1905, 1912; Chi N, Phi N, Was A, Bos N, NY A*
Managerial Career: *1912; NY A*

George Wood
Wood, George A.
B: Nov 9, 1858   D: Apr 4, 1924

Pos: OF	BA: .273
Hits: 1,467	HRs: 68
RBI: 489	BB: 418
Managerial Record	
Won: 67 Lost: 55 Pct: .549	

A very fast left-handed leadoff man, Wood threw out George Wright on an apparent home run in the 15th inning of the famous 1-0, 18-inning game won by Old Hoss Radbourn's homer. In the 1890 Player's League, Wood drove in 102 runs and scored 115. The next year he hit .309 in the AA's last season as a major league. Wood was a players' rep in the Brotherhood, the 1880s players' union, and was present when the baseball peace of 1891 was negotiated.
Playing Career: *1880-1892; Wor N, Det N, Phi N, Bal AA, Phi P, Phi AA, Bal N, Cin N*
Managerial Career: *1891; Phi AA*
Umpiring Career: *1898; NL*

Roger Wolff (l) and Al Evans, 1945.

Smoky Joe Wood
Wood, Joe
B: Oct 25, 1889   D: Jul 27, 1985

Pos: P	ERA: 2.03
W-L: 116-57	SOs: 989
ShOs: 28	No-hitters: 1

Pos: OF, P	BA: .283
Hits: 553	HRs: 24
RBI: 325	BB: 208

While no reports of actual smoke were filed, Walter Johnson declared that no man threw as hard as Smoky Joe Wood. Shifted in the pitching rotation so he could stop Wood's winning streak in 1912, Johnson went down in flames. The AL record had been 16 consecutive victories, set by Johnson earlier in the season, and Wood had 13 straight. Smoky Joe beat Sir Walter 1-0 and eventually tied the AL record, but did not break it.

Wood played on two World Series Championship teams with his friend Tris Speaker, once as a Red Sox pitcher and a second time as an Indians outfielder. Winning three games in the 1912 World Series was a fitting cap on Wood's greatest season – he was 34-5 with a 1.91 ERA and 10 shutouts. After slipping on wet grass in spring training, 1913, Wood never regained his fire. His problems sounded suspiciously like a torn rotator cuff. Wood came back as an outfielder. He later coached at Yale University; his team members included future U.S. President George Bush.
Playing Career: *1908-1915, 1917-1922; Bos A, Cle A*

Wilbur Wood
Wood, Wilbur Forrester
B: Oct 22, 1941

Pos: P	ERA: 3.24
W-L: 164-156	SOs: 1,411
ShOs: 24	Saves: 57

Taught the knuckleball by his father and perfecting it with Chicago teammate and flutterball master Hoyt Wilhelm, Wood used the pitch to become the AL's leading workhorse, 1968-1975. At first a reliever, he led the AL in appearances three straight years, 1968-1970, reaching a high of 88 in 1968. Then Wood became a tough endurance starter, tossing 300 innings or more four straight years, and exceeding 350 in 1972 and 1973. He won 20 or more games four straight years, leading the AL with 24 in both 1972 and 1973.

It was in 1971 that White Sox Manager Chuck Tanner and pitching coach Johnny Sain moved Wood into the starting rotation. He was so successful that he was soon pitching regularly on two days' rest. An All-Star from 1971 to 1974, Wood started both ends of a doubleheader against the Yankees in 1973, but was hit hard and failed to finish the nightcap. His ERA as a starter continued to expand from 1.91 in 1971 to 4.11 in 1975. A line drive hit by Ron LeFlore shattered his kneecap and ended his effectiveness in 1976.
Playing Career: *1961-1965, 1967-1978; Bos A, Pit N, Chi A*

Hal Woodeshick
Woodeshick, Harold Joseph
B: Aug 24, 1932

Pos: P	ERA: 3.56
W-L: 44-62	SOs: 484
ShOs: 1	Saves: 61

An All-Star in 1963, Woodeshick led the NL in saves with 23 the following year. Rarely starting, he spent his career toiling in relief. In Game Six of the 1967 World Series, he was the eighth Cardinals pitcher in the game, tying a record.
Playing Career: *1956, 1958-1967; Det A, Cle A, Was A, Hou N, StL N*

Gene Woodling
Woodling, Eugene Richard (Old Faithful)
B: Aug 16, 1922

Pos: OF	BA: .284
Hits: 1,585	HRs: 147
RBI: 830	BB: 921

A four-time minor league batting champ, Woodling was a left-handed batter for the Giants in the 1920s, and had his best years as a platoon outfielder. He struck paydirt with Yankee Skipper Casey Stengel, who turned

Knuckleballer Wilbur Wood winds up for the White Sox in 1972.

Gene Woodling.

Woodling's weakness against left-handers into a club strength as he platooned Woodling with Hank Bauer except in the World Series when the ol' Perfessor played both of them. An exceptional postseason hitter, Woodling batted .318 in 26 World Series games for five straight years, including a .400 mark in 1949 and .429 in 1950.

Woodling ranks 10th on the World Series record list with 21 runs and 19 bases on balls. Following the 1954 season, he was traded to the Orioles as part of a record 17-player deal. He moved on to the Indians, with whom he reached career highs in 1957 with 19 homers, 78 RBI and a .321 batting average. A few months before his 40th birthday, Woodling was purchased by the futile 1962 Mets, managed by Stengel. "He gave me hell all those years about wanting to play," said Stengel. "Now he can play all he wants."
Playing Career: *1943, 1946-1947, 1949-1962; Cle A, Pit N, NY A, Bal A, Was A, NY N*

Al Woods
Woods, Alvis
B: Aug 8, 1953

Pos: OF	BA: .271
Hits: 538	HRs: 35
RBI: 196	BB: 167

In the Blue Jays' first game, Woods became the 11th player to hit a pinch home run in his first major league at-bat. An instant hero, he later went 6-for-6 in a 1980 game, a year he batted .300. Substandard defensive skills limited his playing time.
Playing Career: *1977-1982, 1986; Tor A, Min A*

Woody Woodward
Woodward, William Frederick
B: Sep 23, 1942

Pos: SS, 2B, 3B	BA: .236
Hits: 517	HRs: 1
RBI: 148	BB: 169

A cousin of actress Joannne Woodward, Woody played in the 1970 World Series for the Reds. He began his front office career with the Reds in 1978 and advanced to the Yankees as general manager, then to his current job as general manager with the Mariners.
Playing Career: *1963-1971; Mil N, Atl N, Cin N*

Todd Worrell
Worrell, Todd Roland
B: Sep 28, 1959

Pos: P	ERA: 2.85
W-L: 34-34	SOs: 396
ShOs: 0	Saves: 130

A cinch Rookie of the Year in 1986, Worrell pitched the Cardinals to the 1985 pennant with second-half heroics that included five saves and three wins. He tied a World Series record by fanning six straight Royals in Game Five. He even played right field for Manager Whitey Herzog in the White Rat's sometimes bizarre pitching changes. Worrell saved 30 or more games in each of his first three full seasons. Arm trouble caused him to miss 1990 and 1991.
Playing Career: *1985-1989, 1992-; StL N, LA N*

Al Worthington
Worthington, Allan Fulton (Red)
B: Feb 5, 1929

Pos: P	ERA: 3.39
W-L: 75-82	SOs: 834
ShOs: 3	Saves: 110

Worthington actually had three careers – hot prospect, starter and revitalized reliever. He pitched shutouts in his first two starts, but had limited success in six seasons with the Giants. Becoming a relief specialist in 1960 with the Twins, he blossomed into one of the AL's best firemen, saving 21 games in 1965 and a league-high 18 in 1968. He pitched in the 1965 World Series and the 1969 ALCS.
Playing Career: *1953-1954, 1956-1960, 1963-1969; NY N, SF N, Bos A, Chi A, Cin N, Min A*

Clyde Wright
Wright, Clyde (Skeeter)
B: Feb 20, 1941

Pos: P	ERA: 3.50
W-L: 100-111	SOs: 667
ShOs: 9	No-hitters: 2

Beginning his career with a tidy four-hitter, Wright pitched 25 consecutive innings without allowing a walk in 1968, and he combined with Ricky Clark to no-hit the Orioles. In 1970 he was AL Comeback Player of the Year with a 22-12 mark, another no-hit gem and a trip to the All-Star Game.
Playing Career: *1966-1975; Cal A, Mil A, Tex A*

George Wright
Wright, George
B: Jan 28, 1847   D: Aug 21, 1937
Hall of Fame 1937

Pos: SS	BA: .302
Hits: 870	HRs: 10
RBI: 224 (inc.)	BB: 69
Managerial Record	
Won: 59 Lost: 25 Pct: .702	

Baseball's first franchise player, the fun-loving, egotistical George Wright anchored the Cincinnati Red Stockings, baseball's first professional team, and easily the most successful with 88 straight wins spanning two seasons. Unlike his older brother Harry, George was born in the United States. He played both professional cricket, like his father, and amateur baseball during the Civil War years before turning full-time to baseball with the Union Baseball Club of Morrisania in 1866.

Wright convinced the 1867 Washington Nationals to take the first road trip west, where they lost to Rockford and their young

Hall of Famer George Wright.

pitcher, Al Spalding. When Cincinnati hired Harry Wright as a full-time manager, the first player he hired was brother George. When the National Association was formed in 1871, Wright joined the Boston Red Stockings. As a shortstop, Wright was the first to move off the baseline when fielding. His dropping of pop flies to turn them into double plays led to the infield fly rule. In his one attempt at managing, Wright won the 1879 pennant over his brother's Boston club.
Playing Career: *1871-1882; Bos Red Stockings n, Bos N, Pro N*
Managerial Career: *1879; Pro N*

George Wright
Wright, George DeWitt
B: Dec 22, 1958

Pos: OF	BA: .245
Hits: 529	HRs: 42
RBI: 208	BB: 126

The left-handed-hitting Wright was the Rangers' center fielder from 1982 to 1984, and in 1983 played in all 162 Texas games, hitting .276 with 18 homers and 82 RBI. His average plummeted to .190 by 1985.
Playing Career: *1982-1986; Tex A, Mon N*

Glenn Wright
Wright, Forest Glenn (Buckshot)
B: Feb 6, 1901   D: Apr 6, 1984

Pos: SS	BA: .294
Hits: 1,219	HRs: 93
RBI: 723	BB: 209

An outstanding shortstop who led the NL in assists and double plays his first two seasons, Wright also led the NL with 616 at-bats as a rookie in 1924. In 1925 he made an unassisted triple play on a line drive hit by the Cardinals' Jim Bottomley. Wright batted more than .300 three times and played in the 1925 and 1927 World Series. Called "Buckshot" because of his strong arm, Wright lost some of his effectiveness after a handball injury in 1929.
Playing Career: *1924-1933, 1935; Pit N, Brk N, Chi A*

Baseball pioneer Harry Wright.

Harry Wright
Wright, William Henry
B: Jan 10, 1835   D: Oct 3, 1895
Hall of Fame 1953

Pos: OF	BA: .272
Hits: 222	HRs: 4
RBI: 81 (inc.)	BB: 36

Managerial Record
Won: 1,225   Lost: 885   Pct: .581

One of the true geniuses in baseball history, Wright devised practice drills, enabling players to improve. His Cincinnati and Boston Red Stocking teams consistently outclassed the opposition by a better grasp of the fundamentals of the game, because Wright invented those fundamentals. His teams took batting practice, infield and outfield practice, and worked on cutoff plays from the outfield. They dominated baseball. The Cincinnatis captured 88 straight victories, and the Bostons took four pennants in five years in the old National Association, the first professional league.

In fact, Boston's dominance was said to be the cause of the breakup of the National Association. One of Wright's better assets was his brother George, who was the best player of the 1860s. Harry Wright, the son of a professional cricketeer at the fashionable St. George's Cricket Club in England, moved on to the Phillies, where he managed until blindness overcame him. A benefit game for his widow turned out to be a tremendous gathering of baseball old-timers to pay their respect to baseball's pioneering innovator.
Playing Career: *1871-1877; Bos Red Stockings n, Bos N*
Managerial Career: *1871-1893; Bos Red Stockings n, Bos N, Pro N, Phi N*

Taffy Wright
Wright, Taft Shedron
B: Aug 10, 1911   D: Oct 22, 1981

Pos: OF	BA: .311
Hits: 1,115	HRs: 38
RBI: 553	BB: 347

Wide-shouldered Wright was a left-handed hitting machine with adequate fielding skills. He was switched from pitcher to outfielder in the minors, and as a Senators rookie in 1938, led the AL with 13 pinch hits in 39 attempts. Wright had a career .328 batting average when he was drafted for military duty in 1942. After three years out of baseball, he batted .275 in 1946 .324 in 1947, but faded to .235 in 1949.
Playing Career: *1938-1942, 1946-1949; Was A, Chi A, Phi A*

Russ Wrightstone
Wrightstone, Russell Guy
B: Mar 18, 1893   D: Feb 25, 1969

Pos: 3B, 1B, OF, SS, 2B	BA: .297
Hits: 889	HRs: 60
RBI: 425	BB: 215

During the 1920s, Wrightstone could play any position on the field, and the Phillies used him to great advantage. He batted .300

or higher five times, and was often used as a left-handed pinch hitter.
Playing Career: *1920-1928; Phi N, NY N*

P. K. Wrigley
Wrigley, Philip Knight
B: Dec 5, 1894   D: Apr 12, 1977

Known as P.K. to his close associates, Wrigley succeeded his father as president of the Cubs in 1932. He was generous with money and financial advice to both players and former players. His favorite was Charlie Grimm, whom he kept on the payroll all his life. Wrigley was known for being straightforward with the press, but never gave radio or TV interviews. He insisted on maintaining his privacy. With meticulous integrity, he would dock his salary as president of the Wrigley Chewing Gum Company for time spent with the Cubs.

John Wyatt
Wyatt, John Thomas
B: Apr 19, 1935

Pos: P	ERA: 3.47
W-L: 42-44	SOs: 540
ShOs: 0	Saves: 103

A Kansas City native, Wyatt set a short-lived major league record for his home team with

Cubs President Philip K. Wrigley (l) with Manager Charlie Grimm in 1934.

81 appearances in 1964. An All-Star that year, he was 9-8 with a 3.59 ERA. An important reliever for the Red Sox during their ''Impossible Dream'' pennant, he was 10-7 with 20 saves. Then he won Game Six in the 1967 World Series to extend the contest to a seventh game. His is one of the toughest autographs for collectors to get.
Playing Career: *1961-1969; KC A, Bos A, NY A, Det A*

Whitlow Wyatt
Wyatt, John Whitlow
B: Sep 27, 1907

Pos: P	ERA: 3.79
W-L: 106-95	SOs: 872
ShOs: 17	Saves: 13

A four-time All-Star, Wyatt had struggled to make the big leagues despite outstanding minor league seasons. Becoming a beanball Dodger starter in 1939, he won a league-high 22 games in 1941 as they won their first pennant in 21 years. He was 1-1 in the World Series.
Playing Career: *1929-1937, 1939-1945; Det A, Chi A, Cle A, Brk N, Phi N*

Butch Wynegar
Wynegar, Harold Delano
B: Mar 14, 1956

Pos: C	BA: .255
Hits: 1,102	HRs: 65
RBI: 506	BB: 625

Named *The Sporting News* AL Rookie of the Year in 1976, Butch Wynegar made the AL All-Star team in 1976-1977, becoming the youngest player to appear. As a Yankee catcher, he was criticized by the New York media when it was discovered that batterymate Gossage had a large ERA when pitching to him.
Playing Career: *1976-1988; Min A, NY A, Cal A*

Early Wynn
Wynn, Early (Gus)
B: Jan 6, 1920
Hall of Fame 1972

Pos: P	ERA: 3.54
W-L: 300-244	SOs: 2,334
ShOs: 49	Saves: 15

''Early Wynn,'' said a young sportswriter, ''isn't the name of a ballplayer, he's gotta be a race horse.''

Wynn was certainly a stud. Pitching 4,664 innings, starting 612 games, he won 300 and lost 244, striking out 2,334 batters and walking 1,775. Nearly a third of the batters he faced reached base on him and he gave up 3½ runs per game, but he pitched effectively for 22 years. The story that he would knock down his own grandmother was not true. ''Granny knew better than to crowd the plate on me,'' Wynn growled.

Winning 18 and 17 games for the Senators, he came into his own when he was traded to the Indians in 1949. During the 1950s decade Wynn would capture 188 games, leading the AL twice – 23 in 1954 and 22 in 1959 – as he won 20 or more five times. The six-time All-Star won the Cy Young Award in 1959 as he led the White Sox to their first pennant since 1919. Wynn is remembered for his gallant attempts to win number 300, when he fought back after being cut from the team in spring training, then losing two close games before winning the coveted one.
Playing Career: *1939, 1941-1944, 1946-1963; Was A, Cle A, Chi A*

Jimmy Wynn
Wynn, James Sherman (The Toy Cannon)
B: Mar 12, 1942

Pos: OF	BA: .250
Hits: 1,665	HRs: 291
RBI: 964	BB: 1,224

A small man but a big hitter, Wynn was the Astros' first slugging star. Combining speed and power, he stole 225 bases and scored 1,105 runs while socking 285 doubles. He ranks high on the Astros' lists, leading in all-time walks, strikeouts and home runs, and in single-season runs, home runs, extra-base hits and walks. The three-time All-Star slugged 32 homers while driving the Dodgers into the 1974 World Series.
Playing Career: *1963-1977; Hou N, LA N, Atl N, NY A, Mil A*

Marvell Wynne
Wynne, Marvell
B: Dec 17, 1959

Pos: OF	BA: .247
Hits: 664	HRs: 40
RBI: 244	BB: 191

Playing regularly in 1984, Wynne batted .266 with 24 doubles, 11 triples, 77 runs and 24 stolen bases. When the Pirates realized that Wynne was not another Omar Moreno they traded him to the Padres. He later played in four 1989 NLCS games for the Cubs.
Playing Career: *1983-1989; Pit N, SD N, Chi N*

Johnny Wyrostek
Wyrostek, John Barney
B: Jul 12, 1919   D: Dec 12, 1986

Pos: OF	BA: .271
Hits: 1,149	HRs: 58
RBI: 481	BB: 482

As a Cardinals farm hand, Wryostek led the minor league American Association in batting in 1944, then went off to war. Upon returning he made the NL All-Star team twice when he hit .285 in 1950 and .311 in 1951. He hit 20 or more doubles a season, 1946-1951.
Playing Career: *1942-1943, 1946-1954; Pit N, Phi N, Cin N*

Hank Wyse
Wyse, Henry Washington (Hooks)
B: Mar 1, 1918

Pos: P	ERA: 3.52
W-L: 79-70	SOs: 362
ShOs: 11	No-hitters: 1

Wyse suffered a spinal injury that ranked him 4F during the war, and required him to wear a corset while pitching. He won 22 games as the ace of the 1945 pennant-winning Cubs, including an eight-inning no-hit gem. He pitched in the 1945 World Series.
Playing Career: *1942-1947, 1950-1951; Chi N, Phi A, Was A*

Hall of Fame hurler Early Wynn pitched for the Indians from 1949 to 1957.

Carl Yastrzemski
Yastrzemski, Carl Michael (Yaz)
B: Aug 22, 1939
Hall of Fame 1989

Pos: OF	BA: .285
Hits: 3,419	HRs: 452
RBI: 1,844	BBs: 1,845

Replacing Ted Williams in the Red Sox outfield, Yastrzemski patrolled left field, playing caroms off the Green Monster in Fenway Park for 23 years. Boston fans did not forget the Splendid Splinter, but they grew to love Yaz. For one unforgettable month, Yastrzem-

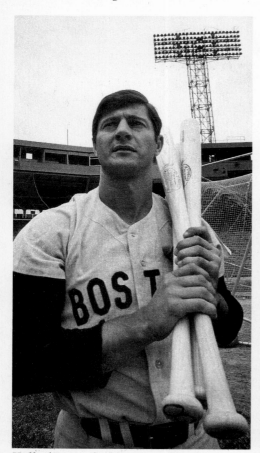

ski was the greatest ballplayer who ever lived. He had almost singlehandedly lifted the Red Sox from ninth place in 1966 to the pennant race in 1967.

In September Yastrzemski was awesome, making fielding plays and throws that are still described in reverent tones whenever Red Sox faithful gather. He went 7-for-8 in a final doubleheader victory over Minnesota, securing the flag for Boston. That year Yastrzemski won the Triple Crown and the MVP Award. During his career, he won three batting titles and was selected for the AL All-Star Game 18 times. His statistics rank high on the all-time charts: second in games, 3,308; third in at-bats, 11,988; sixth in doubles, 646; fourth in walks, 1,845; and ninth in RBI, 1,844.
Playing Career: *1961-1983; Bos A*

Tom Yawkey
Yawkey, Thomas
B: Feb 21, 1903   D: Jul 9, 1976
Hall of Fame 1980

For more than four decades, modest, philanthropic Tom Yawkey was owner of the Boston Red Sox. He poured millions of dollars into the club in an unceasing effort to win a World Series Championship. Three times his teams captured AL pennants – 1946, 1967 and 1975 – only to lose the World Series each time in seven games.

The son of one-time Detroit Tigers owner William Yawkey, Tom purchased the Red Sox in 1933 and began acquiring star players. Joe Cronin, Lefty Grove, Jimmie Foxx and Wes Ferrell were among the luminaries Yawkey brought in to light up Fenway. The owner was close to his players and often worked out with them before the ballpark gates opened. Dizzy Dean once said that "All ballplayers want to end their careers with the Cubs, Yankees or Red Sox." Yawkey's generosity provided New England fans opportunities to see first-class players while operating out of the smallest park in the majors. In addition to owning the Red Sox from 1933 to 1976, Yawkey served as AL vice-president, 1956-1957.

Emil Yde
Yde, Emil Ogden
B: Jan 28, 1900   D: Dec 4, 1968

Pos: P	ERA: 4.02
W-L: 49-25	SOs: 160
ShOs: 6	No-hitters: 0

Submariner Yde was a Pirates rookie sensation in 1924, going 16-3 to lead the NL with an .842 winning percentage. His 17-9 record the next year helped Pittsburgh win the pennant. Yde was a good switch hitter and was used 34 times as a pinch hitter.
Playing Career: *1924-1927, 1929; Pit N, Det A*

Steve Yeager
Yeager, Stephen Wayne
B: Nov 24, 1948

Pos: C	BA: .228
Hits: 816	HRs: 102
RBI: 410	BBs: 342

Yeager invented the throat protector that hangs from the catcher's mask. As a Dodger stalwart, he played on six division-winning teams, hitting .298 in four World Series. On August 8, 1972, Yeager tied an NL record for catchers with 22 putouts, and set another with 24 chances.
Playing Career: *1972-1986; LA N, Sea A*

Rudy York
York, Rudolph Preston
B: Aug 17, 1913   D: Feb 5, 1970

Pos: 1B, C	BA: .275
Hits: 1,621	HRs: 277
RBI: 1,152	BBs: 791
Managerial Record	
Won: 0 Lost: 1 Pct: .000	

In August 1937, York slugged 18 home runs for a one-month record that has never been equaled. He hit 35 homers in only 375 at-bats that year. When York joined the Tigers, he had a difficult time breaking into their lineup; crafty Birdie Tebbetts handled Detroit

Hall of Famer Carl Yastrzemski, 1968.   *Red Sox owner Tom Yawkey (r) with Manager Joe Cronin (c) and farm team head, 1943.*

Heavy-hitting Rudy York.

pitchers, and future Hall of Famer Hank Greenberg was on first. The Tigers, needing York's bat, confronted controversy by installing him at first base and moving Greenberg to left field. Sportswriters quipped, "York is part Cherokee and part first baseman."

Detroit had the last laugh, though, as they captured the pennant in 1940. York picked up the slack when Greenberg went to the army by leading the AL in home runs and RBI during the 1943 campaign. He helped the Tigers win another flag in 1945. Traded to the Red Sox in 1946, he found himself on another pennant winner. York was selected for the All-Star team six times.
Playing Career: *1934, 1937-1947; Det A, Bos A, Chi A, Phi A*
Managerial Career: *1959; Bos A*

Tom York
York, Thomas J.
B: Jul 13, 1851   D: Feb 17, 1936

Pos: OF	BA: .274
Hits: 1,096	HRs: 15
RBI: 417 (inc.)	BBs: 199
Managerial Record	
Won: 56 Lost: 37 Pct: .602	

One of the early stars of the National Association, York was sold to Baltimore and considered retiring, but was wooed with the scorecard concession as his signing bonus. He tried umpiring after his playing days, but quit, declaring, "I'd rather live on a dollar a day than withstand the blackguarding which every umpire is subject to."
Playing Career: *1871-1885; Tro Haymakers n, Bal Lord Baltimores n, Phi Philadelphias n, Har Dark Blues n, Har N, Pro N, Cle N, Bal AA*
Managerial Career: *1878, 1881; Pro N*
Umpiring Career: *1886; NL, AA*

Eddie Yost
**Yost, Edward Frederick
(The Walking Man)**
B: Oct 13, 1926

Pos: 3B	BA: .254
Hits: 1,863	HRs: 139
RBI: 683	BBs: 1,614
Managerial Record	
Won: 0 Lost: 1 Pct: .000	

The Walking Man never played a day in the minors, going directly from the campus of New York University to Griffith Stadium.

After serving a hitch with Uncle Sam, Yost returned to the ballpark with his eagle eye, leading the AL in bases on balls six times, despite competition from Ted Williams and Mickey Mantle. Yost also collected 1,614 walks, placing him in seventh place on the all-time list.

When Yost retired in 1962 he had played a major league record 2,008 games at third base, and he held the AL record for putouts, assists and chances at third. He had hit 28 leadoff home runs, and scored 1,215 times. Yost led the AL in doubles in 1951 and in runs scored in 1959. He was chosen for the All-Star Game in 1952.
Playing Career: *1944, 1946-1962; Was A, Det A, LA A*
Managerial Career: *1963; Was A*

Babe Young
Young, Norman Robert
B: Jul 1, 1915   D: Dec 25, 1983

Pos: 1B	BA: .273
Hits: 656	HRs: 79
RBI: 415	BBs: 274

Young was working out at Yankee Stadium when he got a phone call from the Giants, inviting him to travel with them. They placed Young in their farm system and after his MVP 1939 season in the Southern Association, made him their first baseman. After a stint with the Coast Guard in World War II, Young was relegated to pinch-hitting when the Giants acquired Johnny Mize.
Playing Career: *1936, 1939-1942, 1946-1948; NY N, Cin N, StL N*

Eddie Yost creates a cloud of dust as he heads for third for the Senators in a 1951 game vs. the Yankees.

Bobby Young
Young, Robert George
B: Jan 22, 1925   D: Jan 28, 1985

Pos: 2B	BA: .249
Hits: 609	HRs: 15
RBI: 137	BBs: 208

A smooth second baseman who rose through the Cardinals' farm system, Young was bought by the Browns in 1951. When the franchise shifted to Baltimore in 1954, Young was the first player signed to a contract.
Playing Career: *1948, 1951-1956, 1958; StL N, StL A, Bal A, Cle A, Phi N*

Curt Young
Young, Curtis Allen
B: Apr 16, 1960

Pos: P	ERA: 4.31
W-L: 69-53	SOs: 536
ShOs: 3	No-hitters: 0

A left-hander with two one-hitters to his credit, Curt Young is trying to rebound to the starting form he exhibited with Oakland when he won 37 games in three years. Young has yet to yield an earned run in postseason play in three appearances.
Playing Career: *1983-; Oak A, KC A, NY A*

Cy Young
Young, Denton True
B: Mar 29, 1867   D: Nov 4, 1955
Hall of Fame 1937

Pos: P	ERA: 2.63
W-L: 511-316	SOs: 2,800
ShOs: 76	No-hitters: 3

Managerial Record
Won: 3   Lost: 3   Pct: .500

Cy Young once told a neophyte sportswriter, "Sonny, I've won more major league games than you've seen." By the time sportswriters had seen the end of Young's career, his records included most innings pitched, 7,356; most complete games, 751; most wins, 511; and most losses, 316. Seven times he led the league in shutouts; five times he won more than 30 games. He posted 20 victories or more in 15 other seasons. Young pitched 400 or more innings four times and 300 or more innings in 15 consecutive seasons.

His longevity and durability were attributed to an off-season regime of chopping wood, plowing fields and doing farm chores. A strapping farm lad with a steaming fastball, Young was the ace pitcher for the Cleveland Spiders from the moment he joined the team in 1890. In his last game, he was beaten 1-0 by another rookie phenom, the Phillies' Grover Cleveland Alexander. In retirement Young was a regular at Hall of Fame induction ceremony weekends.
Playing Career: *1890-1911; Cle N, StL N, Bos A, Cle A, Bos N*
Managerial Career: *1907; Bos A*

Irving Young
Young, Irving Melrose (Young Cy, Cy the Second)
B: Jul 21, 1877   D: Jan 14, 1935

Pos: P	ERA: 3.11
W-L: 63-95	SOs: 560
ShOs: 21	Saves: 4

In 1905 another rookie pitcher named Young got off to such a great start that he was called "Cy the Second." Irving Young posted 20 wins, pitched 378 innings and completed 41 games. Those are still post-1900 high marks for rookies.
Playing Career: *1905-1908, 1910-1911; Bos N, Pit N, Chi A*

Matt Young
Young, Matthew John
B: Aug 9, 1958

Pos: P	ERA: 4.40
W-L: 55-95	SOs: 857
ShOs: 5	No-hitters: 1

A rookie record of 11-15 with a 3.27 ERA for the last-place Mariners led to a 1983 All-Star berth for Young. Subsequent arm trouble and injuries led to the bullpen, where he posted 25 saves. He made it to the World Series with Oakland in 1989.
Playing Career: *1983-1987, 1989-; Sea A, LA N, Oak A, Bos A, Cle A*

Legendary pitcher Cy Young holds several all-time records, including most wins (511).

Innovator and NL President Nick Young.

Nick Young
Young, Nicholas Emanuel
B: Sep 12, 1840   D: Oct 31, 1916

Managerial Record
Won: 25   Lost: 53   Pct: .321

Baseball pioneer Nick Young is pictured in what may be the first photograph of the game ever taken, an 1862 shot of the New York Regiment playing ball during the Civil War. He was instrumental in the formation of the Olympic club of Washington, and later, the National professional club which he served as secretary and business manager, arranging baseball's first western road trip.

Young organized the National Association, the first professional league of baseball teams. In 1876 he became the secretary-treasurer of the new National League. Young served as NL president during its most eventful times, leading it through the postseason Temple Cup series, the 4-strike-7-ball season of 1887, the player strike of 1890, the demise of the American Association, the economic panic of 1893, and the emergence of the American League. The success and endurance of the NL is a tribute to Young's vision and leadership.
Managerial Career: *1871-1873; Was Olympics n, Was Nationals n*

Pep Young
Young, Lemuel Floyd
B: Aug 29, 1907   D: Jan 14, 1962

Pos: 2B   BA: .262
Hits: 645   HRs: 32
RBI: 347   BBs: 152

In his debut against Carl Hubbell at Forbes Field, Young went 4-for-4. He hit .300 for that partial season. A regular for four years, Young anchored the infield of the Pirates who competed with the Cardinals and Cubs for the NL flag in the late 1930s.
Playing Career: *1933-1941, 1945; Pit N, Cin N, StL N*

Ralph Young
Young, Ralph Stuart
B: Sep 19, 1889   D: Jan 24, 1965

Pos: 2B   BA: .247
Hits: 898   HRs: 4
RBI: 254   BBs: 495

An ideal leadoff man, Young had the ability to draw walks and score runs. For reasons unknown, however, he batted second, between Donie Bush and Ty Cobb. He played regularly for six years before retiring to coach at Temple and St. Joseph's universities.
Playing Career: *1913, 1915-1922; NY A, Det A, Phi A*

Joel Youngblood
Youngblood, Joel Randolph
B: Aug 28, 1951

Pos: OF   BA: .265
Hits: 969   HRs: 80
RBI: 422   BBs: 332

The first major league player to collect hits for two different teams on the same day, Youngblood singled for the Mets in a day game, was traded to the Expos, and singled again that night. He hit .350 in 1981 and was chosen for the All-Star Game.
Playing Career: *1976-1989; Cin N, StL N, NY N, Mon N, SF N*

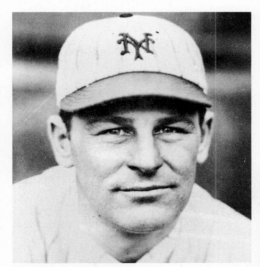

The Giants' Ross Youngs.

Ross Youngs
Youngs, Royce Middlebrook
B: Apr 10, 1897   D: Oct 22, 1927
Hall of Fame 1972

Pos: OF   BA: .322
Hits: 1,491   HRs: 42
RBI: 592   BBs: 550

One of John McGraw's favorite ballplayers, Youngs scored 812 runs during his career, and batted .286 in four World Series with the Giants, including .368 in 1923. He died prematurely at age 30, but before he went, Youngs taught Mel Ott how to play the outfield. Youngs hit .300 or more for nine of his ten seasons. The stocky outfielder led the NL in doubles with 31 in 1919, and in runs with 121 in 1923.

He led the league in outfield assists and also in errors in 1920 and 1922. Youngs stole 153 bases and was the Giants' best baserunner next to Frankie Frisch. In the midst of an excellent career, tragedy struck. Youngs struggled at the plate for a .264 mark in 1925. During the off-season he was diagnosed with Bright's disease. He then played the 1926 season on sheer guts. Manager McGraw kept a picture of Youngs on the wall behind his desk, next to Christy Mathewson's.
Playing Career: *1917-1926; NY N*

Robin Yount
Yount, Robin R.
B: Sep 16, 1955

Pos: SS, OF   BA: .285
Hits: 3,142   HRs: 251
RBI: 1,406   BBs: 966

As a teenager, Yount became the Brewers' regular shortstop in 1974. By 1982 he was the best hitter in the AL, pounding two home runs off Jim Palmer to clinch the pennant for Milwaukee on the final day of the season. Yount ended the year with 29 homers, a .331 average and the best slugging average in the league. He won the MVP Award by a landslide. Staying hot in the World Series, Yount hit .414 with a record-setting two four-hit games.

After 1,479 games at shortstop, a shoulder injury in 1984 sent him to the outfield, where he is still a fixture at Brewers games. Fans watched him rip his 3,000th hit in 1992 – at age 36 – one of the youngest ever to achieve that Hall of Fame goal. Among active players, Yount ranks first in runs scored with 1,632, third in triples with 126, and first in doubles, with 583 (11th all-time).
Playing Career: *1974-; Mil A*

Robin Yount.

Tom Zachary
Zachary, Jonathan Thompson Walton
B: May 7, 1896   D: Jan 24, 1969

Pos: P	ERA: 3.72
W-L: 186-191	SOs: 720
ShOs: 24	Saves: 22

Zachary gave up Babe Ruth's historic 60th home run in the last game of the 1927 season. When he broke in with the Athletics, who were desperate – being in the middle of seven straight last-place finishes – he used the name Zach Walton to protect his college eligibility. Pitching for 19 years, Zachary won two games in the 1924 World Series when the Senators won their only Championship. Altogether he was 3-0 with a 2.86 ERA in three World Series.
Playing Career: *1918-1936; Phi A, Was A, StL A, NY A, Bos N, Brk N, Phi N*

Pat Zachry
Zachry, Patrick Paul
B: Apr 24, 1952

Pos: P	ERA: 3.52
W-L: 69-67	SOs: 669
ShOs: 8	Saves: 3

Capturing Rookie of the Year honors in 1976, Zachry's first big league season ended at 14-7 with a 2.74 ERA. He compiled records of 1-0 in the NLCS, and 1-0 in the 1976 World Series for the Big Red Machine. He made the All-Star team in 1978, and pitched for the Dodgers in the 1983 NLCS.
Playing Career: *1976-1985; Cin N, NY N, LA N, Phi N*

Geoff Zahn
Zahn, Geoffrey Clayton
B: Dec 19, 1945

Pos: P	ERA: 3.74
W-L: 111-109	SOs: 705
ShOs: 20	Saves: 1

Zahn was a good fourth or fifth starter who strung together seven seasons of double-digit victories. He led the AL in shutouts with five in 1984 after enduring several injuries. Zahn appeared in the 1982 ALCS for the Angels.
Playing Career: *1973-1985; LA N, Chi N, Min A, Cal A*

Al Zarilla
Zarilla, Allen Lee (Babe, Zeke)
B: May 1, 1919

Pos: OF	BA: .276
Hits: 975	HRs: 61
RBI: 456	BBs: 415

In Game Three of the 1944 World Series, Zarilla was a batting star for the St. Louis Browns. He was chosen for the All-Star team in 1948. On June 8, 1950, Zarilla tied a major league record by whacking four doubles in one game.
Playing Career: *1943-1944, 1946-1953; StL A, Bos A, Chi A*

Rollie Zeider
Zeider, Rollie Hubert
B: Nov 16, 1883   D: Sep 12, 1967

Pos: 2B, SS, 3B, 1B, OF	BA: .240
Hits: 769	HRs: 5
RBI: 253	BBs: 334

Called "Hook" by his teammates, Zeider's nickname changed to "Bunions" after he developed blood poisoning from being spiked in the foot by Ty Cobb. Zeider was a utility man who walked twice in two pinch-hit appearances in the 1918 World Series for the Cubs.
Playing Career: *1910-1918; Chi A, NY A, Chi F, Chi N*

Tom Zachary.

The Angels' left-hander Geoff Zahn in 1982, when he went 18-8.